2/94

# THE WORLD ALMANAC®
# Biographical
# Dictionary

# THE WORLD ALMANAC.

# Biographical
# Dictionary

### The Editors of
### The World Almanac

WORLD ALMANAC
AN IMPRINT OF PHAROS BOOKS • A SCRIPPS HOWARD COMPANY
NEW YORK

First published in 1990.

Library of Congress Cataloging-in-Publication Data
The World almanac biographical dictionary / the editors of the World almanac.
   p.    cm.
   Includes index.
   ISBN 0-88687-564-1 : $19.95
   1. Biography—Dictionaries.  I. World almanac.
CT103.W66  1990
920.02—dc20                90-45309
                                 CIP

Printed in the United States of America

Cover design by Nancy Carey
Text design by Bea Jackson

World Almanac
An Imprint of Pharos Books
A Scripps Howard Company
New York, New York 10166

10  9  8  7  6  5  4  3  2  1

# Contents

# Acknowledgments

This book is the culmination of the work of many talented, resourceful individuals who put their best efforts into the many aspects of compiling such a book. They all deserve to be recognized individually.

First, the editors of *The World Almanac®* verified all entries that had originally appeared in *The World Almanac Book of Who*, the genesis of this volume. Their work covered all bases, but Associate Editor June Foley must be especially cited for her work on American writers, Senior Assistant Editor Thomas McGuire for his work on sports figures and entertainers, and Editor Mark Hoffman for his work on scientists. Administrative Assistant Aris Georgiadis was of great help in tracking down experts to review material for inclusion in the final volume. Additional verification of entries was ably done by Elizabeth Miles Montgomery.

Second, dozens of experts reviewed the entries and made recommendations on who should be included, certainly one of the most difficult parts of compiling a book of this kind. These experts included: Janet Baldwin of the Explorers Club; The Carriage House recording studio, especially Matthew Lane and John Montagnese; Claus Clüver, Department of Comparative Literature, Indiana University; Sid Goldberg, vice president and director, international syndication, United Media; Dr. Joel Herskowitz, assistant clinical professor, Boston University Medical School; Richard Kleiner, columnist on the arts and entertainment nationally syndicated by Newspaper Enterprise Association; Les Krantz, editor, *The New York Art Review*; Robert Levy, assistant managing editor, United Feature Syndicate; Larry H. Peer, professor of comparative literature, Brigham Young University; Priscilla Ridgeway, Mystery Writers of America; Bettie Sprigg and others at the Office of the Assistant Secretary of Defense for Public Affairs, Robert J. Wagman, political columnist nationally syndicated by Newspaper Enterprise Association; Dr. Roland J. Wiley, University of Michigan; and at Pharos Books Theodore Hill, James R. Keenley, Kevin McDonough, and Eileen Schlesinger.

Then there were the able researchers: Thomas G. Aylesworth (who also wrote many entries); Jill Bortner, and Beth Fulgum. And a special thanks to Donald C. Wilson whose hard work during the last weeks before the editorial deadline and photographic memory brought all the last bits and pieces together.

And, last but not least, there are those at United Media who readily and enthusiastically answered all queries in their fields of expertise: Lynn Hoogenboom, Chris Hull, and Wendy Wallace. And special thanks go to Diana Loevy, editor of TV Update, for her time, patience, and expertise in aiding in the editing the entertainment section. And, finally, thanks to Shari Jee, assistant editor at Pharos Books, for her assistance in tracking down last bits of pieces on information on American writers.

H.U.L.

# Editor's Note

The entries in THE WORLD ALMANAC® BIOGRAPHICAL DIC-TIONARY are designed to give the reader the necessary information in as few words as possible.

Individuals are listed according to the names by which they are best known, including any titles. Names enclosed in parentheses alone signify parts of the individual's given name, i.e., ELIOT, T(homas) S(tearns). Names enclosed in parentheses and quotes signify nicknames, i.e., GOOD-MAN, BENNY ("The King of Swing"). Also appearing in parentheses in some cases is the name at birth if considerably different from name by which that person is best known. When a pseudonym is used for the individual listing, the real name is enclosed in parentheses following "pseud. of", i.e., TEY, JOSEPHINE (pseud. of Elizabeth MacKintosh.) Chinese names are given in the form most commonly understood; the pinyin version follows in parentheses if it is not the same.

The individual's birth date, the exact date whenever possible, follows the name. The birthplace appears in parentheses following the birth date. The death date, if applicable, follows the place of birth.

In many cases, major works of the individual, e.g. books, compositions, films, etc., are listed following the main body of the entry. In no case are the works given intended to be a complete listing of that individual's accomplishments, but are merely a representative selection made at the discretion of the editor.

Names which appear in capital letters within an entry signify cross-references to other entries in the book.

Most of the abbreviations used in this book require no explanation. The following is a selected list of abbreviations and acronyms which may be unclear to the reader.

AA, Academy Award
ABA, American Basketball Association
ABT, American Ballet Theatre
ACLU, American Civil Liberties Union
AEC, Atomic Energy Commission
AFL-CIO, American Federation of Labor and Congress of Industrial Organizations
A.-H., Austria-Hungary
AL, American League
Alta., Alberta
AP, Associated Press
ASCAP, American Society of Composers, Authors, and Publishers
B.C., British Columbia
bd., board

C., College
c., circa
CEO, chief executive officer
CIA, Central Intelligence Agency
chmn., chairman
cm., committee
cmsr., commissioner
Co., County, Company
Ct., Court
D (in parentheses only), Democrat
del., delegate
dep., deputy
D.R., Dominican Republic
ERA, Earned Run Average
FAA, Federal Aviation Agency
FBI, Federal Bureau of Investigation

Fed (in parentheses only), Federalist
FDA, Food and Drug Administration
fl., flourished
Fndn., Foundation
F.R.S., Fellow of the Royal Society
Ft., Fort
FTC, Federal Trade Commission
HEW, Department of Health, Education, and Welfare
HUD, Department of Housing and Urban Development
I., Island
Ind (in parentheses only), Independent
leg., legislature
K.G., Knight of (order of) the Garter
m, meter
MVP, Most Valuable Player
NAACP, National Association for Advancement of Colored People
NASCAR, National Association of Stock Car Auto Racing
NATO, North Atlantic Treaty Organization
N.B., New Brunswick
NBA, National Basketball Association
NFL, National Football League
Nfld., Newfoundland

NHL, National Hockey League
NL, National League
N.S., Nova Scotia
NYCB, New York City Ballet
NYSE, New York Stock Exchange
OAS, Organization of American States
Ont., Ontario
O.M., Order of Merit
Par., Parish
PBA, Professional Bowlers Association
Pen., Peninsula
Phil., Philharmonic
P.R., Puerto Rico
Prog (in parentheses only), Progressive
Que., Quebec
R (in parentheses only), Republican
R., River
RBIs, Runs Batted In
RR, Railroad
S.A., South Africa
Ter., Territory
Twp., Township
UN, United Nations
USAC, United Nations Auto Club
USIA, United States Information Agency
V.I., Virgin Islands

# Writers

ADAMS, ALICE, Aug. 14, 1926 (Fredericksburg, Va.). U.S. novelist. *Careless Love*, 1966; *Listening to Billie*, 1978; *Second Chances*, 1988.

ADE, GEORGE, Feb. 9, 1866 (Kentland, Ind.)–May 16, 1944. U.S. humorist, playwright. Author of a humorous column for the *Chicago Record*. *Fables in Slang*, 1899; *The College Widow* (play), 1904; *The Sultan of Sulu* (musical), 1903.

AIKEN, CONRAD, Aug. 5, 1889 (Savannah, Ga.) –Aug. 17, 1973. U.S. poet, novelist, critic. Volumes of poetry include *The Charnel Rose* (1918), *Selected Poems* (1929; Pulitzer Prize in poetry, 1930). *Blue Voyage* (novel), 1927; *Ushant* (autobiography), 1952.

AKINS, ZOË, Oct. 30, 1886 (Humansville, Mo.) –Oct. 29, 1958. U.S. dramatist, screenwriter. Wrote urbane comedies for the stage. *A Royal Fandango*, 1923; *The Greeks Had a Word for It*, 1930; *The Old Maid* (1935 Pulitzer Prize in drama), 1935.

ALBEE, EDWARD, Mar. 12, 1928 (Washington, D.C.). U.S. dramatist. Initially wrote one-act plays, including *The Zoo Story and Other Plays* (1960); his first full-length play, *Who's Afraid of Virginia Woolf?* (1962) was his greatest critical and popular success. *Tiny Alice*, 1965, *A Delicate Balance* (1967 Pulitzer Prize in drama), 1967, *Seascape* (1975 Pulitzer Prize in drama), 1975.

ALCOTT, LOUISA MAY, Nov. 29, 1832 (Germantown, Pa.)–Mar. 6, 1888. U.S. novelist. Her most famous book, *Little Women* (1868), sold millions of copies, and continues to be popular. *Little Men*, 1871; *Eight Cousins*, 1875; *Jo's Boys*, 1886. (Daughter of A. B. ALCOTT.)

ALGER, HORATIO, JR., Jan. 13, 1832 (Revere, Mass.)–July 18, 1899. U.S. writer. His 100 best-selling books for boys told the stories of poor bootblacks and newsboys whose honesty and industry gained them economic success. *Ragged Dick*, 1867; *Luck and Pluck*, 1869; *Tattered Tom*, 1871.

ALGREN, NELSON, Mar. 28, 1909 (Detroit, Mich.) –May 9, 1981. U.S. novelist. Wrote realistic novels, most set in slums of Chicago's West Side. *The Man with the Golden Arm*, 1949; *A Walk on the Wild Side*, 1956.

ANDERSON, MAXWELL, Dec. 15, 1888 (Atlantic, Pa.)–Feb. 28, 1959. U.S. dramatist. *What Price Glory?* (with LAURENCE STALLINGS), 1924; *Both Your Houses* (1933 Pulitzer Prize in drama), 1933; *Winterset*, 1935; *Knickerbocker Holiday* (with KURT WEILL), 1938; *Anne of a Thousand Days*, 1948; *The Bad Seed*, 1955.

ANDERSON, SHERWOOD, Sept. 13, 1876 (Camden, Ohio)–Mar. 8, 1941. U.S. short-story writer, novelist, journalist, poet. His major work, *Winesburg, Ohio* (1919), is a collection of short stories about American small-town life. *The Triumph of the Egg*, 1921; *Horses and Men*, 1923, *Tar, A Midwest Childhood*, 1926.

ARMOUR, RICHARD, July 15, 1906 (San Pedro, Calif.)–Feb. 28, 1989. U.S. humorist noted for his satires of historical and literary scholarship. *It All Started with Columbus*, 1953; *Twisted Tales from Shakespeare*, 1957.

ASCH, SHOLEM, Nov. 1, 1880 (Kutno, Pol.)–July 10, 1957. U.S. novelist. Wrote tales of Jewish life and Biblical novels, chiefly in Yiddish. *The Nazarene*, 1939; *The Apostle*, 1943; *Mary*, 1949; *Moses*, 1951.

AUCHINCLOSS, LOUIS, Sept. 27, 1917 (Lawrence. N.Y.). U.S. novelist, short-story writer. Chronicler of upper-class American life. *The Great World and Timothy Colt*, 1956; *The Rector of Justin*, 1964; *The Winthrop Covenant*, 1976, *Diary of a Yuppie*, 1986.

AUEL, JEAN M., Feb. 18, 1936 (Chicago, Ill.). U.S. novelist. Originally an employee of a technology company, she wrote technical works before becoming a novelist. *The Clan of the Cave Bear*, 1980; *The Valley of Horses*, 1982; *The Mammoth Hunters*, 1985.

BALDWIN, JAMES, Aug. 2, 1924 (New York, N.Y.)–Dec. 1, 1987. U.S. novelist, essayist. Spokesman for American blacks in the late 1950s and early 1960s. *Go Tell It on the Mountain*, 1953;

*Notes of a Native Son*, 1955; *Nobody Knows My Name*, 1961; *Another Country*, 1962.
**BARAKA, IMANU AMIRI** (born LeRoi Jones), Oct. 7, 1934 (Newark, N.J.). U.S. playwright, poet, essayist, novelist. Author of plays, poems, and polemics about interracial hostility. *Dutchman*, 1964; *The Toilet*, 1964; *The Slave*, 1966.
**BARNES, DJUNA**, June 12, 1892 (Cornwall-On-Hudson, N.Y.)–June 18, 1982. U.S. novelist and short-story writer. *Ryder*, 1928; *Nightwood*, 1936; *Selected Works*, 1962.
**BARRY, PHILIP**, June 18, 1896 (Rochester, N.Y.)–Dec. 3, 1949. U.S. playwright. Wrote sophisticated comedies of manners. *Holiday*, 1928; *The Philadelphia Story*, 1939.
**BARTH, JOHN**, May 27, 1930 (Cambridge, Md.). U.S. novelist. Author of experimental, often comic novels and novellas. *The Sot-Weed Factor*, 1962; *Giles Goat-Boy*, 1966; *Chimera*, 1972; *Letters*, 1979; *The Friday Book*, 1984.
**BARTHELME, DONALD**, Apr. 7, 1931 (Philadelphia, Pa.)–July 23, 1989. U.S. novelist, short-story writer. Author of experimental fiction, using parody and black humor. *Unspeakable Practices, Unnatural Acts*, 1968; *Sadness*, 1972; *Great Acts*, 1979; *Paradise*, 1986.
**BAUM, L(yman) FRANK**, May 15, 1856 (Chittenango, N.Y.)–May 6, 1919. U.S. writer of children's books about the land of "Oz," made into the classic movie. *The Wonderful Wizard of Oz*, 1900.
**BEATTIE, ANN**, Sept. 8, 1947 (Washington, D.C.). U.S. author. *Chilly Scenes of Winter*, 1976; *The Burning House*, 1982; *Where You'll Find Me*, 1986.
**BELLAMY, EDWARD**, Mar. 26, 1850 (Chicopee Falls, Mass.)–May 22, 1898. U.S. author. Achieved fame with his Utopian romance, *Looking Backward, 2000–1887* (1888), which depicted a socialist world in 2000 A.D.
**BELLOW, SAUL**, June 10, 1915 (Lachine, Quebec, Can.). U.S. novelist, short-story writer. Author of rich, complex, often comic works; won Nobel Prize in literature, 1976. *The Adventures of Augie March*, 1953; *Henderson the Rain King*, 1959; *Herzog*, 1964; *Mr. Sammler's Planet*, 1970; *Humboldt's Gift* (1976 Pulitzer Prize in fiction), 1975; *Him With His Foot in His Mouth*, 1984.
**BENCHLEY, ROBERT**, Sept. 15, 1889 (Worcester, Mass.)–Nov. 21, 1945. U.S. humorist. Noted for his understated comic essays, drama critic (1929–40), columnist for *New Yorker* magazine; Algonquin Round Table wit. *From Bed to Worse*, 1934; *My Ten Years in a Quandry*, 1936; *Benchley Beside Himself*, 1943; *Chips off the Old Benchley*, 1949.
**BENÉT, STEPHEN VINCENT**, July 22, 1898 (Bethlehem, Pa.)–Mar. 13, 1943. U.S. poet, short-story writer, novelist. Awarded two Pulitzer Prizes in poetry, for *John Brown's Body* (1928) and *Western Star* (1943). *The Devil and Daniel Webster* (short stories), 1937. (Brother of W. R. BENÉT.)
**BENÉT, WILLIAM ROSE**, Feb. 2, 1886 (Brooklyn, N.Y.)–May 4, 1950. U.S. poet, editor. Edited several magazines, including the *Saturday Review of Literature* which he helped found (1924); edited *The Reader's Encyclopedia* and *The Oxford Anthology of American Literature*; awarded 1942 Pulitzer Prize in poetry for *The Dust Which Is God* (1941). (Brother of S. V. BENÉT.)
**BERRYMAN, JOHN**, Oct. 25, 1914 (McAlester, Okla.)–Jan. 7, 1972. U.S. poet. His best-known poem "Homage to Mistress Bradstreet" (1956) addressed the spirit of the colonial poet ANNE BRADSTREET; awarded 1965 Pulitzer Prize in poetry for *77 Dream Songs* (1964); committed suicide, 1972.
**BIERCE, AMBROSE**, July 24, 1842 (Meigs County, Ohio)–1914? U.S. journalist, short-story writer. Noted for his cynical, sardonic, grotesque stories and his Civil War stories, the most famous of which is "Occurrence at Owl Creek Bridge." *Cobwebs from an Empty Skull*, 1874; *The Devil's Dictionary*, 1906.
**BLUME, JUDY**, Feb. 12, 1938 (Elizabeth, N.J.). U.S. novelist. Author of realistic novels, especially for preteens and teenagers. *Deenie*, 1973; *Blubber*, 1974; *Forever*, 1976; *Wifey*, 1978; *Superfudge*, 1980; *Tiger Eyes*, 1981.
**BLY, ROBERT**, Dec. 23, 1926 (Madison, Minn.). U.S. poet. Leading figure in the revolt against rhetoric in poetry; prominent among anti-Vietnam War intellectuals as organizer of the American Writers Against the Vietnam War, 1966. *Silence in the Snowy Fields*, 1962; *The Light around the Body*, 1967; *Point Reyes Poems*, 1974; *Loving a Woman in Two Worlds*, 1985.
**BRADFORD, BARBARA TAYLOR**, May 10, 1933 (Leeds, England). U.S. novelist. *A Woman of Substance*, 1979; *Voice of the Heart*, 1982; *To Be the Best*, 1987.
**BRADSTREET, ANNE**, c.1612 (Northampton, Eng.)–Sept. 16, 1672. U.S. poet. The first important woman writer in America. *The Tenth Muse Lately Sprung Up in America*, 1650.
**BRAND, MAX** (pseud. of Frederick Faust), Mar. 20, 1892 (Seattle, Wash.)–May 16, 1944. U.S. novelist, screenwriter. "King of the pulp writers"; wrote some 100 books about the West, including *Destry Rides Again* (1930); wrote a series of books and screenplays about "Dr. Kildare."
**BRODSKY, JOSEPH**, May 24, 1940 (Leningrad, U.S.S.R.). Soviet-born U.S. lyric poet. *Stikhotvoreniya i poemy* (*Short and Long Poems*), 1965; *Ostanovka v pustyne* (*A Halt in the Wilderness*), 1970; *Konets prekrasnoy epokhi* (*The End of a Lovely Era*), 1977.
**BROMFIELD, LOUIS**, Dec. 27, 1896 (Mansfield, Ohio)–Mar. 18, 1956. U.S. writer. His books *The Green Bay Tree* (1924), *Possession* (1925), *Early Autumn* (1926; awarded 1927 Pulitzer Prize in fiction), and *A Good Woman* (1927) comprise a tetralogy called *Escape*.
**BROOKS, GWENDOLYN**, June 7, 1917 (Topeka, Kan.). U.S. poet. The first black woman poet to win a Pulitzer Prize (1950; for *Annie Allen*, 1949) and to be elected to the National Inst. of Arts

(1960); poet laureate of Illinois, 1969. *The World of Gwendolyn Brooks,* 1970.

**BRYANT, WILLIAM CULLEN,** Nov. 3, 1794 (Cummington, Mass.)–June 12, 1878. U.S. poet, critic, newspaper editor. Editor of the New York *Evening Post,* 1829–78; first effective U.S. theorist of poetry; in 1830's, regarded as the leading American poet. *To A Waterfowl,* 1815; *Thanatopsis,* 1817.

**BUCK, PEARL,** July 26, 1892 (Hillsboro, W.Va.)– Mar. 6, 1973. U.S. novelist raised in China, where her parents were missionaries. *The Good Earth,* 1931 (1932 Pulitzer Prize in fiction); awarded Nobel Prize in literature, 1938. *A House Divided,* 1935; *Fighting Angel,* 1936; *The Exile,* 1936; *Dragon Seed,* 1942.

**BUNTLINE, NED** (pseud. of Edward Zane Carroll Judson), Mar. 20, 1823 (Stamford, N.Y.) –July 16, 1886. U.S. novelist, adventurer. Founded sensationalist magazine, *Ned Buntline's Own,* 1845; dismissed from the army for drunkenness and lynched (but secretly cut down) for murder, 1846; wrote some 400 sensationalist books, originating the so-called dime novel in the U.S., e.g., *Magdalena, the Beautiful Mexican Maid* (1847), *The Black Avenger* (1847); led Astor Place riot in New York City, 1849; organized and said to have named the Know-Nothing Party, 1850s.

**BURNETT, FRANCES ELIZA HODGSON,** Nov. 24, 1849 (Manchester, Eng.)–Oct. 29, 1924. U.S. novelist. Noted for writing children's books, especially *Little Lord Fauntleroy* (1886), which she also dramatized (1886). *Sara Crewe,* 1888; *The Secret Garden,* 1911.

**BURROUGHS, EDGAR RICE, Sept. 1, 1875** (Chicago, Ill.)–Mar. 19, 1950. U.S. novelist. Best known for the series of Tarzan books, beginning with *Tarzan of the Apes* (1914), which inspired comic strips, movies, radio and TV series, and the cities of Tarzana, Calif. and Tex.

**BURROWS, ABE,** Dec. 18, 1910 (New York, N.Y.)– May 17, 1985. U.S. playwright, writer for radio, TV, and nightclubs. Coauthored several plays, including *Guys and Dolls* (1950), *How To Succeed in Business Without Really Trying* (1961; Pulitzer Prize in drama, 1961). Author, director, *Cactus Flower,* 1965.

**CAIN, JAMES M.,** July 1, 1892 (Annapolis, Md.)– Oct. 27, 1977. U.S. novelist. Writer of "hardboiled" fiction, which flourished in the U.S. in the 1930s and '40s. *The Postman Always Rings Twice,* 1934; *Double Indemnity,* 1936; *Mildred Pierce,* 1941.

**CALDWELL, ERSKINE, P.** Dec. 17, 1903 (White Oak, Ga.). U.S. novelist. Author of tragicomic stories about poverty and degeneracy in the rural South. *Tobacco Road,* 1932 (dramatized on Broadway, for more than 3,000 performances, 1933–1941); *God's Little Acre,* 1933; *You Have Seen Their Faces* (with M. BOURKE-WHITE, his first wife), 1937.

**CALISHER, HORTENSE,** Dec. 20, 1911 (New York, N.Y.). U.S. novelist and short-story writer.

*In the Absence of Angels,* 1951; *Eagle Eye,* 1972; *The Bobby-Soxer,* 1986.

**CAPOTE, TRUMAN,** Sept. 30, 1924 (New Orleans, La.)–Aug. 25, 1984. U.S. novelist, short-story writer. *Other Voices, Other Rooms,* 1948; *Breakfast at Tiffany's,* 1958; *In Cold Blood* (a "nonfiction novel"), 1966.

**CARNEGIE, DALE,** Nov. 24, 1888 (Maryville, Mo.)–Nov. 1, 1955. U.S. author, teacher of public speaking. Noted as the author of the hugely popular *How to Win Friends and Influence People* (1936), a guide to achieving success through poise, concentration, and self-confidence. *How to Stop Worrying and Start Living,* 1948.

**CARVER, RAYMOND,** May 25, 1938 (Clatskanie, Ore.)–August 2, 1988. U.S. poet and short story writer. *Near Klamath,* 1968; *Ultramarine,* 1986; *Where I'm Calling From: New and Selected Stories,* 1988.

**CATHER, WILLA,** Dec. 7, 1873 (near Winchester, Va.) Apr. 24, 1947. U.S. novelist, short-story writer. Awarded 1923 Pulitzer Prize in fiction for *One of Ours* (1922), *O Pioneers!,* 1913; *My Ántonia,* 1918; *Death Comes for the Archbishop,* 1927.

**CHASE, MARY,** Feb. 25, 1907 (Denver, Col.)–Oct. 20, 1981. U.S. playwright. Best known for *Harvey,* about an invisible six-foot rabbit, which won the 1945 Pulitzer Prize in drama.

**CHAYEFSKY, PADDY,** Jan. 29, 1923 (New York, N.Y.)– Aug. 1, 1981. U.S. playwright, TV and film screenwriter. Best known for his 1950s TV screenplays about urban working-class life, especially *Marty* (1953). He won Academy Awards for his screenplay for the film version of *Marty* in 1955, and for his original screenplay for *Network* in 1976.

**CHEEVER, JOHN,** May 27, 1912 (Quincy, Mass.) –June 18, 1982. U.S. novelist, short-story writer. Noted for his subtle, ironic, comic writing about suburbia; awarded 1979 Pulitzer Prize in fiction for *The Stories of John Cheever* (1978). *The Wapshot Chronicle,* 1957, *The Wapshot Scandal,* 1964; *Bullet Park,* 1969; *Falconer,* 1977; *Oh What a Paradise It Seems,* 1982.

**CHESNUTT, CHARLES W.** June 20, 1858 (Cleveland, Ohio)–Nov. 15, 1932. U.S. novelist. One of the first black writers to gain recognition in the U.S. *Conjure Woman,* 1899; *The Wife of His Youth and Other Stories of the Color Line,* 1899; *The House behind the Cedars,* 1900.

**CHOPIN, KATE** Feb. 8, 1851 (St. Louis, Mo.)– Aug. 22, 1904. U.S. novelist, short-story writer. Wrote stories of Creole and Cajun life in Louisiana, including *Bayou Folk* (1894) and *A Night in Acadie* (1897); her novel, *The Awakening* (1899), dealing with female sexuality, aroused great criticism and was ignored for 60 years before being rediscovered.

**CIARDI, JOHN,** June 24, 1916 (Boston, Mass.)– Mar 30, 1986. U.S. poet, critic, editor. Poetry editor of *The Saturday Review,* 1956–73; author of verse translations of DANTE's *Inferno* (1954), *Purgatorio* (1961) and *Paradiso* (1970). *Homeward to America,* 1940; *As If,* 1955; *I Marry You,*

1958; *How Does a Poem Mean?*, 1959; *I Met a Man*, 1961; *The Wish Tree*, 1962; *Manner of Speaking*, 1972.

**CLARK, WALTER VAN TILBURG,** Aug. 3, 1909 (E. Orland, Me.)–Nov. 10, 1971. U.S. novelist, short-story writer. Wrote books about the West. *The Ox-Bow Incident*, 1940.

**CLANCY, TOM** (Thomas L. Clancy, Jr.), 1947 (Baltimore, Md.). U.S. novelist. Formerly an insurance broker, he is now master of what have been called "technico-military thrillers." *The Hunt for Red October*, 1984; *Red Storm Rising*, 1986; *Clear and Present Danger*, 1989.

**CLAVELL, JAMES,** Oct. 10, 1924 (Sydney, Austral.) U.S. novelist, screenwriter, director. *King Rat*, 1962; *Taipan*, 1966; *Shogun*, 1975; *Whirlwind*, 1986.

**CLEARY, BEVERLY,** 1916 (McMinnville, Ore.). U.S. author of children's novels, best known for her series of books about two children named Henry Huggins and Ramona Quimby; she is noted for her humor and realism. *Henry Huggins*, 1950; *Dear Mr. Henshaw* (1983 Newbery Medal); *A Girl from Yamhill*, 1988.

**CONNELLY, MARC,** Dec. 13, 1890 (McKeesport, Pa.)–Dec. 21, 1980. U.S. dramatist. Best known for his Pulitzer Prize-winning play, *The Green Pastures* (1930); with GEORGE S. KAUFMAN, wrote comedies *Dulcy* (1921), *Merton of the Movies* (1922), *To the Ladies* (1923), *Beggar on Horseback* (1923).

**CONROY, PAT**(rick), Oct. 26, 1955 (Atlanta, Ga.). U.S. novelist. *The Boo*, 1970; *The Great Santini*, 1976; *The Lords of Discipline*, 1980.

**COOK, ROBIN,** May 4, 1940 (New York, N.Y.). U.S. novelist. A physician with a specialty in ophthalmology, he taught at the Harvard Medical School before writing his suspense novels. *The Year of the Intern*, 1972; *Coma*, 1977, *Harmful Intent*, 1989.

**COOPER, JAMES FENIMORE,** Sept. 15, 1789 (Burlington, N.J.)–Sept. 14, 1851. U.S. novelist. The first important native American novelist; wrote about the conflict between frontier life and encroaching civilization; best known for the Leatherstocking Tales: *The Pioneers* (1823), *The Last of the Mohicans* (1826), *The Prairie* (1827), *The Pathfinder* (1840), *The Deerslayer* (1841).

**COZZENS, JAMES GOULD,** Aug. 19, 1903 (Chicago, Ill.)–Aug. 9, 1978. U.S. novelist. *SS San Pedro*, 1931; *Guard of Honor* (1949 Pulitzer Prize in fiction), 1948; *By Love Possessed*, 1957.

**CRANE,** (Harold) **HART,** July 21, 1899 (Garrettsville, Ohio)–Apr. 27, 1932. U.S. poet. In his best-known work, *The Bridge* (1930), used the Brooklyn Bridge as a symbol of America. *White Buildings*, 1926; *Collected Verse*, 1933.

**CRANE, STEPHEN,** Nov. 1, 1871 (Newark, N.J.)–June 5, 1900. U.S. novelist, short-story writer, poet. A pioneer of naturalism in American literature. Died of tuberculosis at age 28. *Maggie: A Girl of the Streets*, 1893; *The Red Badge of Courage*, 1895; *The Open Boat and Other Tales of Adventure*, 1898.

**CREWS, HARRY,** June 6, 1935 (Alma, Ga.). U.S. novelist. *The Gospel Singer*, 1968; *Blood and Grits*, 1979; *All We Need of Hell*, 1987.

**CRICHTON, MICHAEL,** Oct. 23, 1942 (Chicago, Ill.). U.S. novelist, filmmaker. *The Andromeda Strain* (1969), *The Terminal Man* (1972), and *The Great Train Robbery* (1975) were made into films.

**CROUSE, RUSSEL,** Feb. 20, 1893 (Findlay, Ohio)–Apr. 3, 1966. U.S. playwright. Collaborated with HOWARD LINDSAY on long-running *Life with Father* (1939). Also, *State of the Union* (1946; Pulitzer Prize in drama, 1946), *Call Me Madam* (1950), and (with RICHARD RODGERS and OSCAR HAMMERSTEIN II) *The Sound of Music*, 1959.

**cummings, e**(dward) **e**(stlin), Oct. 14, 1894 (Cambridge, Mass.)–Sept. 3, 1962. U.S. poet noted for eccentric language and typography. *The Enormous Room* (autobiographial novel), 1922; *Tulips Are Chimneys*, 1923; *Is 5*, 1926; *50 Poems*, 1940; *95 Poems*, 1958.

**DANA, RICHARD HENRY, JR.,** Aug. 1, 1815 (Cambridge, Mass.)–Jan. 6, 1882. U.S. novelist, lawyer. Based his classic sea novel, *Two Years Before the Mast* (1840), on a diary he kept on a voyage around Cape Horn.

**DAY, CLARENCE,** Nov. 18, 1874 (New York, N.Y.)–Dec. 28, 1935. U.S. essayist whose sketches about his parents were adapted for the stage as *Life with Father* (1935) and *Life with Mother* (1937), by HOWARD LINDSAY and RUSSEL CROUSE.

**DE VRIES, PETER,** Feb. 27, 1910 (Chicago, Ill.). U.S. novelist and humorist. *The Tunnel of Love*, 1954; *Reuben, Reuben*, 1964, *Peckham's Marbles*, 1986.

**DICKEY, JAMES,** Feb. 2, 1923 (Atlanta, Ga.). U.S. poet, novelist. *Into the Stone*, 1960; *Buckdancer's Choice*, 1965; *Deliverance*, 1969.

**DICKINSON, EMILY,** Dec. 10, 1830 (Amherst, Mass.)–May 15, 1866. U.S. poet. A unique stylist, she typically wrote short pieces combining spare lyricism and metaphysical speculation with highly unorthodox diction and meter. She withdrew from society before age 30; published virtually nothing during her lifetime, over 1,000 poems were found in her bureau after her death. *Collected Poems*, 1924.

**DIDION, JOAN,** Dec. 5, 1934 (Sacramento, Calif.) U.S. novelist, journalist. *Run River*, 1963; *Slouching Towards Bethlehem*, 1969; *Play It as It Lays*, 1971; *A Book of Common Prayer*, 1977; *The White Album*, 1979; *Democracy*, 1984; *Miami*, 1987. (Wife of J. G. DUNNE.)

**DOCTOROW, E**(dgar) **L**(awrence), Jan. 6, 1931 (New York, N.Y.). U.S. novelist. *Welcome to Hard Times*, 1960; *The Book of Daniel*, 1971; *Ragtime*, 1975; *Lives of the Poets*, 1984.

**DODGE, MARY MAPES,** Jan. 26, 1831 (New York, N.Y.)–Aug. 21, 1905. U.S. editor, writer. Edited *St. Nicholas* (1873–1905), a leading children's magazine; wrote the classic children's novel, *Hans Brinker; or, The Silver Skates* (1865).

DONLEAVY, J(ames) P(atrick), Apr. 23, 1926 (Brooklyn, N.Y.). U.S. Irish novelist. Best known for his lusty, picaresque first novel, *The Ginger Man* (1955).

DOOLITTLE, HILDA ("H.D."), Sept. 10, 1886 (Bethlehem, Pa.)–Sept. 27, 1961. U.S. poet. A prominent member of the imagist movement. *Sea Garden*, 1916; *Hymen*, 1921; *Red Shores for Bronze*, 1931; *Helen in Egypt*, 1961.

DOS PASSOS, JOHN, Jan 14, 1896 (Chicago, Ill.)–Sept. 18, 1970. U.S. novelist. In his novel *Manhattan Transfer* (1925) and the trilogy *U.S.A.* (1930–36), created an impressionistic picture of the first three decades of the 20th century.

DREISER, THEODORE, Aug. 27, 1871 (Terre Haute, Ind.)–Dec. 28, 1945. U.S. novelist. Pioneer of naturalism in American literature. *Sister Carrie*, 1900; *The Financier*, 1912; *The Titan*, 1914; *An American Tragedy*, 1925.

DUNBAR, PAUL LAWRENCE, June 27, 1872 (Dayton, Ohio)–Feb. 9, 1906. U.S. poet, short-story writer, novelist. The son of escaped slaves; best known for dialect verse and stories. *Lyrics of Lowly Life*, 1896; *Folks from Dixie*, 1898.

DUNNE, JOHN GREGORY, May 25, 1932 (Hartford, Conn.). U.S. writer. *The Studio*, 1969; *Vegas*, 1974; *True Confessions*, 1977; *Dutch Shea, Jr.*, 1982. (Husband of J. DIDION.)

EBERHART, RICHARD, Apr. 5, 1904 (Austin, Minn.). U.S. poet. One of the major lyric voices of the 20th century; won 1966 Pulitzer Prize in poetry for *Selected Poems, 1930–1965* (1966). *Collected Poems, 1930– 1976*, 1977.

ELKIN, STANLEY, May 11, 1930 (New York, N.Y.) U.S. novelist. *Criers and Kibitzers, Kibitzers and Criers*, 1966; *The Sixties*, 1971; *The Coffee Room*, 1988.

ELLISON, RALPH, Mar. 1, 1914 (Oklahoma City, Okla.). U.S. novelist, essayist. His highly-praised *The Invisible Man* (1952) tells of a young black man's search for his own identity and place in society. Essays: *Shadow and Act*, 1964.

EMERSON, RALPH WALDO, May 25, 1803 (Boston, Mass.)–Apr. 27, 1882. U.S. philosopher, poet, essayist. The main spokesman for American transcendentalism; his philosophy was marked by moral optimism and belief in the individual, intuition, mystical unity of nature; his poems include "Brahma," "The Problem," "The Concord Hymn"; his essays, "Nature," (1836), "The American Scholar" (1837), and "Divinity School Address" (1838).

EPHRON, NORA, May 19, 1941 (New York, N.Y.). U.S. novelist. *Wallflower at the Orgy*, 1970; *Scribble Scribble*, 1978; *Heartburn*, 1983.

ERDMAN, PAUL, May 19, 1932 (Stratford, Ont., Canada). U.S. novelist. Specializes in books set in high financial circles. *The Billion Dollar Sure Thing*, 1973; *The Crash of '79*, 1976; *The Panic of '89*, 1987.

FARRELL, JAMES T., Feb. 27, 1904 (Chicago, Ill.)–Aug. 22, 1979. U.S. novelist. Best known for his Studs Lonigan trilogy: *Young Lonigan* (1932), *The*

*Young Manhood of Studs Lonigan* (1934), and *Judgment Day* (1935).

FAST, HOWARD (sometime pseud.: E. V. Cunningham), Nov. 11, 1914 (New York, N.Y.). U.S. novelist, screenwriter. Noted for historical novels and best-selling family sagas; under his pseudonym, writes suspense novels, screenplays, science fiction. *Citizen Tom Paine*, 1943; *Spartacus*, 1951; *The Immigrants*, 1977; *The Immigrant's Daughter*, 1985.

FAULKNER, WILLIAM, Sept. 25, 1897 (New Albany, Miss.)–July 6, 1962. U.S. novelist. One of the most important figures in 20th-cent. literature, he created Yoknapatawpha County, Miss. as a microcosm of the post-Civil War deep South; won Nobel Prize in literature, 1949; awarded Pulitzer Prizes in fiction in 1955 (for *A Fable*, 1954) and 1963 (for *The Reivers*, 1962). *The Sound and the Fury*, 1929; *As I Lay Dying*, 1930; *Sanctuary*, 1931; *Light in August*, 1932; *Absalom, Absalom!*, 1936; *The Hamlet*, 1940; *Intruder in the Dust*, 1948.

FEARING, KENNETH, July 28, 1902 (Oak Park, Ill.)–June 26, 1961. U.S. poet, novelist. In his poetry, such as *The Afternoon of a Pawnbroker and Other Poems* (1943), satirized the U.S. as a mechanized society.

FERBER, EDNA, Aug. 15, 1887 (Kalamazoo, Mich.)–Apr. 16, 1968. U.S. novelist, playwright. *So Big* (1925 Pulitzer Prize in fiction), 1924; *Show Boat*, 1926; *The Royal Family* (with GEORGE S. KAUFMAN), 1927. *Cimarron*, 1930; *Stage Door*, 1936; *Giant*, 1952, were made into classic films.

FERLINGHETTI, LAWRENCE, Mar. 24, 1919 (Yonkers, N.Y.). U.S. poet, publisher. A leader of the mid-1950s Beat movement in San Francisco; owned City Lights bookshop, the first all-paperback store; published City Lights Books. *A Coney Island of the Mind*, 1958.

FIELD, EUGENE, Sept. 2, 1850 (St. Louis, Mo.)–Nov. 4, 1895. U.S. poet, journalist; wrote column "Sharps and Flats" for *Chicago Morning News* (renamed the *Record*); known for children's poems "Little Boy Blue" and "Wynken, Blynken, and Nod." *A Little Book of Western Verse*, 1889.

FIELD, RACHEL, Sept. 19, 1894 (New York, N.Y.)–Mar. 15, 1942. U.S. novelist. Wrote popular New England novels and children's books. *Hitty, Her First Hundred Years*, 1929; *All This, and Heaven Too*, 1938.

FINLEY, MARTHA, Apr. 26, 1828 (Chillicothe, Ohio) –Jan, 30, 1909. U.S. novelist. Wrote stories for little girls, including 28 volumes of Elsie Dinsmore tales (1868–1905), the most popular such books of the day.

FINNEY, JACK, ? (Milwaukee, Wisc.). U.S. novelist. Best known as author of the cult classic *Time and Again* (1970). *The Invasion of the Body Snatchers*, 1954.

FITZGERALD, F(rancis) SCOTT, Sept. 24, 1896 (St. Paul, Minn.)–Dec. 21, 1940. U.S. novelist, short-story writer. The success of his first novel, *This Side of Paradise* (1920), made him at age 24 the spokesman for the "lost generation" of the Jazz Age. *The Beautiful and the Damned*, 1921; *The Great Gatsby*, 1925; *Tender Is the Night*, 1934; *The Last Tycoon* (unfinished), 1940.

**FORBES, KATHRYN,** Mar. 20, 1909 (San Francisco, Cal.)–May 15, 1966. U.S. short-story writer. Her 1943 collection of short stories, *Mama's Bank Account*, was dramatized by John Van Druten as *I Remember Mama* (1944), later made into a TV series (1949–57), and a Broadway musical (1979).

**FROST, ROBERT,** Mar. 26, 1874 (San Francisco, Calif.)–Jan. 29, 1963. U.S. poet. America's unofficial poet laureate. Wrote poetry about rural New England, traditional in form and colloquial in style; awarded Pulitzer Prizes in poetry in 1924 (for *New Hampshire*, 1923), 1931 (for *Collected Poems*, 1931), 1937 (for *A Further Range*, 1937), and 1943 (for *A Witness Tree*, 1943).

**FULLER, CHARLES,** March 5, 1939 (Philadelphia, Pa.). U.S. dramatist. *Perfect Party*, 1968; *The Brownsville Raid*, 1976; *A Soldier's Play*, 1982 (1982 Pulitzer Prize in drama).

**GADDIS, WILLIAM,** 1922 (New York, N.Y.). U.S. novelist. Known for black comedy. *The Recognitions*, 1955; *JR*, 1975; *Carpenter's Gothic*, 1985.

**GALLICO, PAUL WILLIAM,** July 26, 1897 (New York, N.Y.)–July 15, 1976. U.S. novelist. *The Snow Goose*, 1941; *Mrs. 'Arris Goes to Paris*, 1958; *The Poseidon Adventure*, 1969.

**GARDNER, JOHN,** Oct. 8, 1933 (Batavia, N.Y.)–Sept. 14, 1982. U.S. novelist and medievalist. *Grendel*, 1971; *The Sunlight Dialogues*, 1972; *Jason and Medeia*, 1973.

**GARLAND, (Hannibal) HAMLIN,** Sept. 14, 1860 (W. Salem, Wisc.)–Mar. 4, 1940. U.S. short-story writer, novelist, essayist. Wrote about the difficult lives of Midwest farmers; awarded 1922 Pulitzer Prize for his autobiographical volume, *A Daughter of the Middle Border* (1921). *Main-Travelled Roads*, 1891; *A Little Norsk*, 1892.

**GEISEL, THEODOR SEUSS** ("Dr. Seuss"), Mar. 2, 1904 (Springfield, Mass.). U.S. author/illustrator of children's books. Launched the "beginner book" industry. *Horton Hears a Who*, 1954; *How the Grinch Stole Christmas*, 1957; *The Cat in the Hat*, 1957; *Hop on Pop*, 1963; *The Butter Battle Book* (1984).

**GIBSON, WILLIAM,** Nov. 13, 1914 (New York, N.Y.). U.S. dramatist. *Two for the Seesaw*, 1958; *The Miracle Worker*, 1960; *Handy Dandy*, 1987.

**GILROY, FRANK,** Oct. 13, 1925 (New York, N.Y.). U.S. dramatist. *Who'll Save the Plowboy?*, 1957; *The Subject Was Roses* (1962 Pulitzer Prize in drama); *Last Licks*, 1979.

**GINSBERG ALLEN,** June 3, 1926 (Newark) U.S. poet. Prominent Beat Generation figure. "Howl," 1955; "Home," 1956; "Kaddish," 1960, *Planet News, 1961–1967*, 1968.

**GLASGOW, ELLEN,** Apr. 22, 1873 (Richmond, Va.)–Nov. 21, 1945. U.S. novelist. Dealt with Virginia social history and manners. *The Descendant*, 1897; *Barren Ground*, 1925; *In This Our Life*, (1942 Pulitzer Prize in fiction), 1941.

**GODWIN, GAIL,** June 18, 1937 (Birmingham, Ala.). U.S. novelist. *The Perfectionists*, 1970; *The Odd Woman*, 1974; *A Southern Family*, 1987.

**GOLDEN, HARRY,** May 6, 1902 (New York, N.Y.)–Oct. 2, 1981. U.S. nonfiction writer. *Only in America*, 1958; *For 2 Cents Plain*, 1959; *Mr. Kennedy and the Negroes*, 1964; *The Greatest Jewish City in the World*, 1972.

**GOLDMAN, WILLIAM,** Aug. 12, 1931 (Chicago, Ill.). U.S. screenwriter. *Butch Cassidy and the Sundance Kid* (1970 Academy Award for best screenplay); *Marathon Man*, 1976; *All the President's Men* (1977 Academy Award for best screenplay adaptation).

**GORDON, MARY,** Dec. 8, 1949 (Long Island, N.Y.). U.S. novelist. *Final Payments*, 1978; *The Company of Women*, 1981; *Men and Angels*, 1985.

**GRAU, SHIRLEY ANN,** July 8, 1929 (New Orleans, La.). U.S. short-story writer, novelist. *The Black Prince and Other Stories*, 1955; *The Hard Blue Sky*, 1958; *The Keepers of the House* (1965 Pulitzer Prize in fiction), 1964, *Nine Women*, 1986.

**GREELEY, ANDREW M.,** Feb. 5, 1928 (Oak Park, Ill.). U.S. sociologist and novelist. *The Church and the Suburbs*, 1959; *The Cardinal Sins*, 1981; *Angel Fire*, 1988.

**GREY, ZANE,** Jan. 31, 1875 (Zanesville, Ohio) –Oct. 23, 1939. U.S. novelist. Author of 54 bestselling Western romances that helped define the genre; his depiction of the hero as a lone wolf gunfighter greatly influenced movies and TV. *The Last of the Plainsmen*, 1908; *Riders of the Purple Sage*, 1912.

**GUARE, JOHN,** Feb. 5, 1938 (New York, N.Y.). U.S. dramatist. *Muzeeka* (1968 Obie Award for best play); *House of Blue Leaves* (1972 Tony Awards for best musical and best libretto); *Women and Water*, 1985.

**GUEST, EDGAR A(lbert),** Aug. 20, 1881 (Birmingham, Eng.)–Aug. 5, 1959. U.S. poet. His sentimental verses on such subjects as home, mother, and hard work were widely syndicated in newspapers, and collections were very successful. *A Heap o' Livin'*, 1916; *Just Folks*, 1917; *Life's Highway*, 1933.

**HAILEY, ARTHUR,** Apr. 5, 1920 (Luton, Eng.). U.S. novelist. *Hotel*, 1965; *Airport*, 1968; *Wheels*, 1971; *The Moneychangers*, 1975; *Strong Medicine*, 1984.

**HALEY, ALEX,** Aug. 11, 1921 (Ithaca, N.Y.). U.S. author. His acclaimed fictionalized account of his black heritage, *Roots* (1976; a special citation Pulitzer Prize, 1977), was adapted into a highly successful TV series. *The Autobiography of Malcolm X*, 1965.

**HALL, JAMES,** Apr. 22, 1887 (Colfax, Ia.)–July 5, 1951. U.S. novelist, short-story writer. Collaborated with CHARLES NORDHOFF on seafaring trilogy: *Mutiny on the Bounty* (1932), *Men against the Sea* (1933), and *Pitcairn Island* (1934).

**HALLECK, FITZ-GREENE,** July 8, 1790 (Guilford, Conn.)–Nov. 19, 1867. U.S. poet, known for both satirical and romantic verse. *Croaker Papers* (with Joseph Rodman Drake), *Marco Bozzaris*, 1825.

HANSBERRY, LORRAINE, May 19, 1930 (Chicago, Ill.)–Jan. 12, 1965. U.S. playwright. Her *Raisin in the Sun* (1959) was the first Broadway play written by a black woman. *The Sign in Sidney Brustein's Window*, 1964; *To Be Young, Gifted, and Black*, 1969.

HARRIS, JOEL CHANDLER, Dec. 9, 1848 (Eatonton, Ga.)–July 3, 1908. U.S. journalist, short-story writer, novelist. Author of the Uncle Remus stories, humorous tales in Southern black dialect, that featured animal characters. *Uncle Remus, His Songs and His Sayings*, 1880; *The Tar Baby*, 1904; *Uncle Remus and Br'er Rabbit*, 1906.

HART, MOSS, Oct. 24, 1904 (New York, N.Y.)–Dec. 20, 1961. U.S. playwright, director. With GEORGE S. KAUFMAN, wrote the comedies *You Can't Take It With You* (1936; Pulitzer Prize in drama, 1937) and *The Man Who Came to Dinner* (1939); with KURT WEILL and IRA GERSHWIN, wrote the musical *Lady in the Dark*, 1941. *Act One* (autobiography), 1959.

HARTE, BRET, Aug. 25, 1836 (Albany, N.Y.)–May 5, 1902. U.S. short-story and verse writer; in his time, the most influential writer of fiction about the American West. *The Luck of Roaring Camp*, 1868; *The Outcasts of Poker Flat*, 1869; *Plain Language from Truthful James*, 1870.

HAWKES, JOHN, Aug. 17, 1925 (Stamford, Conn.). U.S. novelist. *The Cannibal*, 1949; *Travesty*, 1976; *Innocence in Extremis*, 1985.

HAWTHORNE, NATHANIEL, July 4, 1804 (Salem, Mass.)–May 19, 1864. U.S. novelist, short-story writer; the leading American native fiction-writer of the 19th cent.; through his influence on HERMAN MELVILLE and HENRY JAMES, has continued to affect the development of American fiction. *Twice-Told Tales*, 1837 and 1842; *The Scarlet Letter*, 1850; *The House of the Seven Gables*, 1851; *The Marble Faun*, 1860.

HECHT, BEN, Feb. 28, 1894 (New York, N.Y.)–Apr. 18, 1964. U.S. journalist, playwright, novelist, film writer. With CHARLES MACARTHUR, wrote the stage comedies *The Front Page* (1928), about brash newspapermen, and *Twentieth Century* (1933).

HELLER, JOSEPH, May 1, 1923 (Brooklyn, N.Y.). U.S. novelist. Best known for his comic novel *Catch-22* (1961), about the absurdities of war. *Something Happened*, 1974; *Good as Gold*, 1979; *God Knows*, 1984.

HELLMAN, LILLIAN, June 20, 1905 (New Orleans, La.)–June 30, 1984. U.S. dramatist. Wrote the plays *The Children's Hour* (1934), *Watch on the Rhine* (1941), *Another Part of the Forest* (1946), and *The Little Foxes* (1959); also wrote memoirs: *An Unfinished Woman* (1969), *Pentimento* (1973).

HEMINGWAY, ERNEST, July 21, 1899 (Oak Park, Ill.)–July 2, 1961. U.S. novelist, short-story writer. His terse, understated journalistic style influenced a generation of American writers; awarded Nobel Prize in literature, 1954. *In Our Time*, 1924; *The Sun Also Rises*, 1926; *A Farewell to Arms*, 1929; *For Whom the Bell Tolls*, 1940; *The Old Man and the Sea* (1953 Pulitzer Prize in fiction), 1952.

HENRY, O. (pen name of William Sidney Porter), Sept. 11, 1862 (Greensboro, N.C.)–June 5, 1910. U.S. short-story writer. Prolific writer of short stories with a surprising twist at the end, including "The Gift of the Magi" and "The Ransom of Red Chief"; convicted of embezzling, served three years in prison, where he wrote extensively. *Cabbages and Kings*, 1904; *The Four Million*, 1906.

HERSEY, JOHN, June 17, 1914 (Tientsin, China). U.S. novelist, journalist. War correspondent during WW II. *A Bell for Adano* (1945 Pulitzer Prize in fiction), 1944; *Hiroshima*, 1946; *The Wall*, 1950; *The War Lover*, 1959; *The Child Buyer*, 1960; *The Algiers Motel Incident*, 1968.

HIGGINS, GEORGE V., Nov. 13, 1939 (Brockton, Mass.). U.S. novelist. Best known as author of realistic novels about small-time Boston criminals. *The Friends of Eddie Coyle*, 1972; *The Digger's Game*, 1973; *City on the Hill*, 1975; *Penance for Jerry Kennedy*, 1985.

HINTON, S(usan) E(loise), 1950 (Tulsa, Okla.). U.S. novelist. Writes for teenagers. *That Was Then, This Is Now*, 1971; *Tex*, 1979; *Rumble Fish*, 1983.

HOLMES, OLIVER WENDELL, Aug. 29, 1809 (Cambridge, Mass.)–Oct. 7, 1894. U.S. poet, essayist. The preeminent American man of letters of his day; named the *Atlantic Monthly* and contributed to it witty and warmly humane sketches; his poems include "Old Ironsides" (1830), "The Moral Bully" (1836), "The Chambered Nautilus" (1858), and "The Deacon's Masterpiece; or, the Wonderful 'One Hoss Shay'" (1858). (Father of jurist O. W. HOLMES.)

HOWE, JULIA WARD, May 27, 1819 (New York, N.Y.)–Oct. 17, 1910. U.S. poet, writer, social reformer. Wrote the words for "The Battle Hymn of the Republic," 1862, also wrote poetry, biographies, and books on social themes; the first woman elected to the National Institute of Arts and Letters (1907), and the American Academy of Arts and Letters (1908). *On Sex and Education*, 1874; *Modern Society*, 1881; *Reminiscences*, 1899.

HOWELLS, WILLIAM DEAN, Mar. 1, 1837 (Martin's Ferry, Ohio)–May 11, 1920. U.S. novelist, editor, critic. An editor at *Atlantic Monthly* (1872–81) and *Harper's* (1886–91); a champion of realism and mentor of MARK TWAIN, H. GARLAND, STEPHEN CRANE, and others. *A Modern Instance*, 1882; *The Rise of Silas Lapham*, 1885; *Criticism and Fiction*, 1891.

HUGHES, LANGSTON, Feb. 1, 1902 (Joplin, Mo.)–May 22, 1967. U.S. poet, writer, editor. An important figure in the Harlem Renaissance; wrote in dialect, using blues and jazz rhythms, about black Americans. *The Weary Blues*, 1926; *Shakespeare in Harlem*, 1942; *One-way Ticket*, 1949; *Simple Speaks His Mind*, 1950.

HUNTER, EVAN (pseud.: Ed McBain), Oct. 15, 1926 (New York, N.Y.). U.S. novelist. His novels *Blackboard Jungle* (1954) and *Strangers When We Meet* (1958) were made into films; under his pseudonym, writes "police procedural" crime novels.

HURST, FANNIE, Oct. 18, 1889 (Hamilton, Ohio)–

Feb. 23, 1968. U.S. novelist, short-story writer. Author of popular, sentimental novels and stories. *Humoresque*, 1919; *Back Street*, 1931; *Imitation of Life*, 1933.

**INGE, WILLIAM,** May 3, 1913 (Independence, Kan.)–June 10, 1973. U.S. playwright. Wrote dramas about small-town Midwestern life. *Come Back, Little Sheba*, 1950; *Picnic* (1953 Pulitzer Prize in drama), 1953; *The Dark at the Top of the Stairs*, 1957.

**IRVING, JOHN,** Mar. 2, 1942 (Exeter, N.H.). U.S. novelist. *The World According to Garp*, 1978; *The Hotel New Hampshire*, 1981; *Cider House Rules*, 1985.

**IRVING, WASHINGTON** (pseud.: Diedrich Knickerbocker), Apr. 3, 1783 (New York, N.Y.)–Nov. 28, 1859. U.S. essayist. The first American man of letters to be admired abroad; best-known sketches include "Rip Van Winkle" and "The Legend of Sleepy Hollow" (both 1820). *Salmagundi* (with Wm. Irving and J. K. Paulding), 1807–8; *A History of New York* (as Knickerbocker), 1809; *The Sketchbook of Geoffrey Crayon, Gent.*, 1820.

**JACKSON, HELEN HUNT,** Oct. 15, 1830 (Amherst, Mass.)–Aug. 12, 1885. U.S. novelist, poet, essayist. Her novel *Ramona* (1884), a historical romance sympathetic to the American Indians, helped change white attitudes.

**JACKSON, SHIRLEY,** Dec. 14, 1919 (San Francisco, Calif.)–Aug. 8, 1965. U.S. short-story writer, novelist. Noted for tales dealing with the supernatural and for humorous stories about family life. *The Lottery*, 1949; *We Have Always Lived in the Castle*, 1953; *Life Among the Savages*, 1953.

**JAFFE, RONA,** June 12, 1932 (New York, N.Y.). U.S. novelist. Although her novels often do not receive critical praise, she is an effective story teller. *The Best of Everything*, 1958; *Family Secrets*, 1974; *After the Reunion: A Novel*, 1985.

**JAMES, HENRY,** Apr. 15, 1843 (New York, N.Y.) –Feb. 28, 1916. U.S. novelist (later a British citizen). A major figure in American literature, his principal motif was the innocent American versus experienced Europeans. *The American*, 1877; *Daisy Miller*, 1878; *The Portrait of a Lady*, 1881; *Washington Square*, 1881; *The Spoils of Poynton*, 1897; *The Turn of the Screw*, 1898; *The Ambassadors*, 1903; *The Golden Bowl*, 1904. (Son of H. JAMES; brother of W. JAMES.)

**JARRELL, RANDALL,** May 6, 1914 (Nashville, Tenn.)–Oct. 14, 1965. U.S. poet, critic, novelist. *Blood for a Stranger*, 1942; *Little Friend, Little Friend*, 1945; *Losses*, 1948; *Pictures from an Institution*, 1954; *The Lost World*, 1965.

**JEFFERS,** (John) **ROBINSON,** Jan. 10, 1887 (Pittsburgh, Pa.)–Jan. 20, 1962. U.S. poet. Based much of his original, powerful poetry on Greek myths. "Tamar," 1925; "The Woman at Point Sur," 1927; "Medea," 1946; *Hungerfield and Other Poems*, 1954 (1954 Pulitzer Prize in poetry).

**JEWETT, SARAH ORNE,** Sept. 3, 1849 (So. Berwick, Me.)–June 24, 1909. U.S. novelist, short-story writer. Author of realistic regional fiction

centered in New England. *The Country of the Painted Firs*, 1896; *A Country Doctor*, 1884.

**JONES, JAMES,** Nov. 6, 1921 (Robinson, Ill.)–May 9, 1977. U.S. novelist best known for *From Here to Eternity*, 1951; *Some Came Running*, 1957; *The Thin Red Line*, 1962.

**JONG, ERICA,** Mar. 26, 1942 (New York, N.Y.). U.S. novelist, poet. Noted for her best-selling bawdy, quasi-autobiographical novel, *Fear of Flying*, 1973. *Fruits and Vegetables* (poems), 1973; *Loveroot* (poems), 1975; *How to Save Your Own Life*, 1977; *Parachutes and Kisses*, 1984.

**KANTOR, MCKINLAY,** Feb. 4, 1904 (Webster City, Ia.).–Oct. 11, 1977. U.S. novelist. *Long Remember*, 1934; *The Voice of Bugle Ann*, 1935; *Andersonville* (1956 Pulitzer Prize in fiction), 1955.

**KAUFMAN, GEORGE S.** Nov. 16, 1889 (Pittsburgh, Pa.)–June 2, 1961. U.S. dramatist, drama critic, director. Best known for plays with MOSS HART, including the Pulitzer Prize-winner *You Can't Take It With You* (1936) and *The Man Who Came to Dinner* (1939), and *Of Thee I Sing* (with Morrie Ryskind; 1932 Pulitzer Prize in drama), 1931.

**KEILLOR, GARRISON,** Aug. 7, 1942 (Anoka, Minn.). U.S. writer and radio announcer. *Happy to be Here*, 1982; *Lake Wobegon Days*, 1985; *Leaving Home*, 1987.

**KENNEDY, WILLIAM,** Jan. 16, 1928 (Albany, N.Y.). U.S. novelist. *The Ink Truck*, 1969; *Ironweed* (1984 Pulitzer Prize in fiction); *Quinn's Book*, 1988.

**KEROUAC, JACK** (born Jean-Louis Kerouac), Mar. 12, 1922 (Lowell, Mass.)–Oct. 21, 1969. U.S. novelist, poet. A leading representative of the Beat Generation of the 1950s, which was defined by his book *On the Road* (1957). *The Subterraneans*, 1958; *The Dharma Bums*, 1958.

**KERR, JEAN,** July 1923 (Scranton, Pa.). U.S. humorist, playwright. *Please Don't Eat the Daisies*, 1957; *The Snake Has All the Lines*, 1960; *Mary, Mary* (play), 1961; *How I Got to Be Perfect*, 1978. (Wife of W. KERR.)

**KESEY, KEN,** Sept. 17, 1935 (La Hunta, Col.). U.S. novelist, editor. *One Flew Over the Cuckoo's Nest* (also a successful play and film), 1962; *Sometimes a Great Notion*, 1964.

**KEY, FRANCIS SCOTT,** Aug. 1, 1779 (now Carroll Co., Md.)–Jan. 11, 1843. U.S. poet, attorney. After watching the bombardment of Ft. McHenry during the War of 1812, wrote "The Star-spangled Banner," which became the official U.S. national anthem in 1931.

**KILMER,** (Alfred) **JOYCE,** Dec. 6, 1886 (New Brunswick, N.J.)–July 30, 1918. U.S. poet. Best known for his poem "Trees" (1914).

**KNOWLES, JOHN,** Sept. 16, 1926 (Fairmont, W. Va.). U.S. novelist. *A Separate Peace*, 1960; *Phineas*, 1968; *Peace Breaks Out*, 1981.

**KRANTZ, JUDITH,** Jan. 9, 1928 (New York, N.Y.). U.S. novelist. *Scruples*, 1978; *Princess Daisy*, 1980; *I'll Take Manhattan*, 1986.

**KUMIN, MAXINE,** June 6, 1925 (Philadelphia,

Pa.). U.S. poet, novelist, children's-book writer. *Nightmare Factory*, 1970; *Up Country* (1973 Pulitzer Prize in poetry), 1972; *The Long Approach*, 1985.

KUNITZ, STANLEY, July 29, 1905 (Worcester, Mass.). U.S. poet, editor, teacher. Metaphysical poet. *Intellectual Things*, 1930; *Selected Poems, 1928–1958* (1959 Pulitzer Prize in poetry), 1958; *Next-to-Last Things*, 1985.

LA FARGE, OLIVER, Dec. 19, 1901 (New York, N.Y.)–Aug. 2, 1963. U.S. novelist, anthropologist. Wrote fiction based on his anthropological field work in Arizona, Guatemala, and Mexico. *Laughing Boy* (1930 Pulitzer Prize in fiction), 1929; *Sparks Fly Upward*, 1931.

L'AMOUR, LOUIS, 1908 (Jamestown, N.D.)–June 10, 1988. U.S. novelist. Prolific writer of western novels. *Hondo*, 1953; *Shalako*, 1980; *The Haunted Mesa*, 1987.

LANIER, SIDNEY, Feb. 3, 1842 (Macon, Ga.)–Sept. 7, 1881. U.S. poet. The most important Southern poet of his time. *Corn*, 1874; *The Symphony*, 1875; *Song of a Chattahoochee*, 1877; *The Marshes of Glynn*, 1878.

LARDNER, RING(old), Mar. 6, 1885 (Niles, Mich.)–Sept. 25, 1933. U.S. humorist, short-story writer. Known for social satire using American vernacular speech, including "Haircut," "Love Nest," and "Alibi Ike." *You Know Me, Al* (1916); *Gullible's Travels* (1917); coauthored (with GEORGE S. KAUFMAN) plays, notably *June Moon* (1929).

LAZARUS, EMMA, July 22, 1849 (New York, N.Y.)–Nov. 19, 1887. U.S. poet, essayist. Best known for her sonnet "The New Colossus," engraved on the pedestal of the Statue of Liberty; spokesperson for Judaism. *Admetus and Other Poems*, 1871; *Songs of a Semite*, 1882.

LEE, HARPER, Apr. 28, 1926 (Monroeville, Ala.). U.S. novelist. Her only novel was a sensational success: *To Kill a Mockingbird* (1960).

L'ENGLE, MADELEINE, Nov. 29, 1918 (New York, N.Y.). U.S. novelist. *The Small Rain*, 1945; *A Wrinkle in Time* (1963 Newbery Award); *A Cry Like a Bell*, 1987.

LEONARD, ELMORE, Oct. 11, 1925 (New Orleans, La.). U.S. novelist. *Hombre*, 1961; *City Primeval*, 1980; *Bandits*, 1987.

LEVERTOV, DENISE, Oct. 24, 1923 (Ilford, Essex, Eng.). U.S. poet. *Here and Now*, 1957; *The Jacob's Ladder*, 1962; *The Sorrow Dance*, 1967; *Oblique Prayers*, 1984.

LEVIN, IRA, Aug. 27, 1929. U.S. novelist, playwright. *No Time for Sergeants* (play), 1956; *Rosemary's Baby*, 1967; *The Stepford Wives*, 1972; *Deathtrap* (play), 1978.

LEWIS, SINCLAIR, Feb. 7, 1885 (Sauk Centre, Minn.)–Jan. 10, 1951. U.S. novelist. The first American to receive the Nobel Prize in literature, 1930; his major novels portrayed the provincialism of small-town middle-class America. *Main Street*, 1920; *Babbitt*, 1922; *Arrowsmith*, 1925; *Elmer Gantry*, 1927; *Dodsworth*, 1929.

LINDBERGH, ANN MORROW, 1906 (Englewood, N.J.). U.S. writer, poet. *Gift From the Sea*, 1955; *The Unicorn and Other Poems*, 1956; *Bring Me a Unicorn*, 1972; *War Within and Without*, 1980. (Wife of C. A. LINDBERGH.)

LINDSAY, HOWARD, Mar. 29, 1889 (Waterford, N.Y.)–Feb. 11, 1968. U.S. playwright. With RUSSEL CROUSE, adapted for the stage *Life with Father* (1939), played the leading role for 3,000+ performances; also with Crouse, wrote *Anything Goes* (1934), *State of the Union* (1945; Pulitzer Prize in drama, 1946), and *Call Me Madam* (1950).

LINDSAY, (Nicholas) VACHEL, Nov. 10, 1879 (Springfield, Ill.)–Dec. 5, 1931. U.S. poet. Chanted his rhythmic and onomatopoeic poems from lecture platforms. *General William Booth Enters into Heaven and Other Poems*, 1913; *The Congo*, 1914; *The Chinese Nightingale*, 1917.

LOFTING, HUGH, Jan. 14, 1886 (Maidenhead, Eng.)–Sept. 26, 1947. Eng.-U.S. author/illustrator of children's stories. *The Story of Dr. Dolittle*, 1920; *The Voyages of Dr. Dolittle*, 1922; *Dr. Dolittle and the Secret Lake*, 1948.

LONDON, JACK, Jan. 12, 1876 (San Francisco, Calif.)–Nov. 22, 1916. U.S. novelist, short-story writer, essayist. Best known writer of his time; noted for stories of adventure in the Yukon, esp. the classic *The Call of the Wild* (1903), *The Sea-Wolf*, 1904; *White Fang*, 1906; *Martin Eden*, 1909; *John Barleycorn; or, Alcoholic Memoirs*, 1913.

LONGFELLOW, HENRY WADSWORTH, Feb. 27, 1807 (Portland, Me.)–Mar. 24, 1882. U.S. poet. The most popular U.S. poet of the 19th century. *Ballads and Other Poems* (including "The Wreck of the Hesperus," "The Village Blacksmith," "Excelsior"), 1842; *Evangeline*, 1847; *The Song of Hiawatha*, 1855; *The Courtship of Miles Standish*, 1858; *Paul Revere's Ride*, 1860.

LOOS, ANITA, Apr. 26, 1893 (Sisson, Calif.)–Aug. 18, 1981. U.S. screenwriter, novelist. Her satirical novel, *Gentlemen Prefer Blondes* (1925), was adapted into a play (1926), musical comedy (1949), and film (1953).

LOTHROP, HARRIET (pseud.: Margaret Sidney), June 22, 1844 (New Haven, Conn.)–Aug. 2, 1924. U.S. children's-book writer. *Five Little Peppers and How They Grew*, 1881.

LOWELL, AMY LAWRENCE, Feb. 9, 1874 (Brookline, Mass.)–May 12, 1925. U.S. poet, critic. Championed new poetry, publishing a three-volume anthology *Some Imagist Poets* (1915, 1916, 1917); awarded posthumous Pulitzer Prize in poetry for *What's O'Clock*, 1925. *Dome of Many-Colored Glass*, 1912. (Sister of P. LOWELL.)

LOWELL, JAMES RUSSELL, Feb. 22, 1819 (Cambridge, Mass.)–Aug. 12, 1891. U.S. poet, critic, editor. In his time, a highly-regarded man of letters. Editor of the *Atlantic Monthly*, (1857–61) and the *North American Review* (1864–72). *A Fable for Critics*, 1848; *The Vison of Sir Launfal*, 1848; *Fireside Travels*, 1864.

LOWELL, ROBERT, Mar. 1, 1917 (Boston, Mass.)–Sept. 12, 1977. U.S. poet. Influential, expressing major tensions of 1950s and 1960s. *Lord Weary's Castle* (1947 Pulitzer Prize in poetry), 1946; *The*

*Mills of the Kavanaughs,* 1951; *Life Studies,* 1959; *For the Union Dead,* 1964; *The Dolphin* (1974 Pulitzer Prize in poetry), 1973.

**LURIE, ALISON,** Sept. 3, 1926 (Chicago, Ill.). U.S. novelist. *Love and Friendship,* 1962; *The War Between the Tates,* 1974; *Foreign Affairs* (1985 Pulitzer Prize for literature).

**MACARTHUR, CHARLES,** Nov. 5, 1895 (Scranton, Pa.)–Apr. 21, 1956. U.S. journalist, playwright. Collaborated with BEN HECHT on the plays *The Front Page* (1928) and *Twentieth Century* (1932). (Husband of H. HAYES.)

**MACLEISH, ARCHIBALD,** May 7, 1892 (Glencoe, Ill.)–Apr. 20, 1982. U.S. poet, playwright, public official. Poet laureate of the New Deal; librarian of Congress, 1939–44; asst. secy. of state, 1944–45; won 1959 Pulitzer Prize in drama for *J.B.* (1958), and two Pulitzer Prizes in poetry: 1933 (for *Conquistador,* 1932) and 1953 (for *Collected Poems: 1917–1952,* 1952).

**MAILER, NORMAN,** Jan. 31, 1923 (Long Branch, N.J.). U.S. novelist, journalist. Prominent U.S. postwar writer, known for his iconoclastic writing on American life; ran for mayor of New York City on platform of statehood for the city, 1969. *The Naked and the Dead,* 1948; *The White Negro* (essay), 1957; *Armies of the Night* (Pulitzer Prize in general nonfiction, 1969), 1968; *The Executioner's Song,* 1979.

**MALAMUD, BERNARD,** Apr. 26, 1914 (Brooklyn, N.Y.)–Mar. 18, 1986. U.S. novelist, short-story writer. Noted for creating a fictional world related to Jewish folklore. *The Natural,* 1952; *The Assistant,* 1957; *The Magic Barrel,* 1958; *The Fixer* (1966 Pulitzer Prize in fiction), 1966; *Pictures of Fidelman* (1969); *The Tenants,* 1971; *Dubin's Lives,* 1979.

**MAMET, DAVID,** Nov. 30, 1947 (Chicago, Ill.). U.S. dramatist. *Sexual Perversity in Chicago,* 1973; *Glengarry Glen Ross* (1984 Pulitzer Prize for drama); *Speed-the-Plow,* 1987. (Husband of LINDSAY CROUSE.)

**MANCHESTER, WILLIAM,** Apr. 1, 1922 (Attleboro, Mass.). U.S. novelist, biographer. Best known for *The Death of a President* (1967). *The Arms of Krupp,* 1968; *American Caesar,* 1978; *The Last Lion,* 1983.

**MARKHAM, EDWIN,** Apr. 23, 1852 (Oregon City, Ore.)–Mar. 7, 1940. U.S. poet, lecturer. Best known for his poem of social protest, "The Man with the Hoe" (1899). *Lincoln and Other Poems,* 1901.

**MARQUAND, J(ohn) P(hillips),** Nov. 10, 1893 (Wilmington, Del.)–July 16, 1960. U.S. novelist. Wrote satires about New England middle- and upper-class society. *The Late George Apley,* (1938 Pulitzer Prize in fiction), 1937; *Wickford Point,* 1939; *H. M. Pulham, Esquire,* 1941.

**MARSHALL, CATHERINE,** Sept. 27, 1914 (Johnson City, Tenn.). U.S. writer. Noted for *A Man Called Peter,* a best-selling biography of her husband, PETER MARSHALL, chaplain of the U.S. Senate.

**MASTERS, EDGAR LEE,** Aug. 23, 1869 (Garnett, Kan.)–Mar. 5, 1950. U.S. poet, novelist. Best known

for *Spoon River Anthology* (1915), free-verse monologues spoken from the grave by the former inhabitants of a small town. *Across Spoon River* (autobiography), 1936.

**MCCARTHY, MARY,** June 21, 1912 (Seattle, Wash.)–Oct. 25, 1989. U.S. novelist, critic. In addition to witty, acerbic novels, writes about politics, art, and travel. *The Company She Keeps,* 1942; *Venice Observed,* 1956; *Memories of a Catholic Girlhood,* 1957; *The Group,* 1963; *Birds of America,* 1971; *How I Grew,* 1987. (Once married to E. WILSON; sister of actor K. MCCARTHY.)

**MCCULLERS, CARSON,** Feb. 19, 1917 (Columbus, Ga.)–Sept. 29, 1967. U.S. novelist. Wrote about outcasts and misfits. *The Heart Is a Lonely Hunter,* 1940; *A Member of the Wedding* (later dramatized and filmed), 1946; *The Ballad of the Sad Café* (later dramatized by EDWARD ALBEE), 1951.

**MCGINLEY, PHYLLIS,** Mar. 21, 1905 (Ontario, Ore.)–Feb. 22, 1978. U.S. poet. Wrote witty light verse. *Love Letters of Phyllis McGinley,* 1954; *Times Three: Selected Verse From Three Decades* (1961 Pulitzer Prize in poetry), 1960; *Sixpence in Her Shoe,* 1964.

**MCINERNEY, JAY,** Jan. 13, 1955 (Hartford, Conn.). U.S. novelist. Formerly a reporter and editor. *Bright Lights, Big City,* 1984; *Ransom,* 1985.

**MCKUEN, ROD,** April 29, 1933 (Oakland, Calif.). U.S. poet. Wrote best-selling poetry in the late 1960s, early 1970s. *Stanyan Street and Other Sorrows,* 1966; *Listen to the Warm,* 1967; *Come to Me in Silence,* 1973.

**MCMURTRY, LARRY,** June 3, 1936 (Wichita Falls, Tex.). U.S. realistic novelist. *Horseman, Pass By,* 1961; *The Last Picture Show,* 1966; *Terms of Endearment,* 1975; *Lonesome Dove* (1986 Pulitzer Prize for fiction).

**MELVILLE, HERMAN,** Aug. 1, 1819 (New York, N.Y.)–Sept. 28, 1891. U.S. novelist. Initially wrote novels reflecting his experiences as a cabin boy and seaman; after early success, sank into obscurity as a writer, but rediscovered and celebrated in the 1920s. *Moby Dick* (1851) is considered a masterpiece of world literature. *Typee,* 1846; *Omoo,* 1847; *White-Jacket,* 1850; *Pierre,* 1852; *Billy Budd,* 1924.

**MICHENER, JAMES,** Feb. 3, 1907 (New York, N.Y.). U.S. novelist. Noted for best-selling books about specific locales. *Tales of the South Pacific* (1948 Pulitzer Prize in fiction, adapted into a musical by RICHARD RODGERS and OSCAR HAMMERSTEIN), 1947; *The Bridges at Toko-Ri,* 1953; *Sayonara,* 1954; *Hawaii,* 1959; *The Source,* 1965; *Space,* 1982; *Alaska,* 1988; *Caribbean,* 1989.

**MILLAY, EDNA ST. VINCENT,** Feb. 22, 1892 (Rockland, Me.)–Oct. 19, 1950. U.S. poet, dramatist. Best known for her early poem "Renascence" (1917) and the sonnets in *A Few Figs from Thistles* (1920). *The Harp Weaver* (1923 Pulitzer Prize in poetry), 1923.

**MILLER, ARTHUR,** Oct. 17, 1915 (New York, N.Y.). U.S. dramatist. Deals with social and political problems. Best known for *Death of a Salesman* (Pulitzer Prize in drama, 1950), 1949; *All My Sons*, 1947; *The Crucible*, 1953; *After the Fall*, (about his marriage to MARILYN MONROE), 1964; *The Price*, 1968; *The American Clock*, 1981.

**MILLER, HENRY,** Dec. 26, 1891 (New York, N.Y.)–June 7, 1980. U.S. novelist. His sexually candid novels were banned in the U.S. and Great Britain until the 1960s. *Tropic of Cancer*, 1934 (France) and 1961 (U.S.); *Tropic of Capricorn*, 1939 (France) and 1961 (U.S.); *Rosy Crucifixion* trilogy, 1949–1959 (France), 1965 (U.S.).

**MILLER, JOAQUIN,** Sept. 8, 1837 (nr. Liberty, Ind.)–Feb. 17, 1913. U.S. poet, journalist. "The Byron of Oregon," best known for his romantic poems about the Old West. *Pacific Poems*, 1871; *Songs of the Sierras*, 1871; *Songs of the Sunlands*, 1873.

**MITCHELL, MARGARET,** 1900 (Atlanta, Ga.)–Aug. 16, 1949. U.S. novelist. Her only novel, *Gone with the Wind* (1936), about the Civil War and Reconstruction, was the biggest seller in the U.S. up to its time and won the 1937 Pulitzer Prize in fiction; the film based on the novel won an Academy Award for best picture (1940) and is among the most popular movies ever made.

**MOORE, CLEMENT,** July 15, 1779 (New York, N.Y.)–July 10, 1863. U.S. writer, poet, educator. Best known as the author of "A Visit from St. Nicholas" (1823).

**MOORE, MARIANNE,** Nov. 15, 1887 (St. Louis, Mo.)–Feb. 5, 1972. U.S. poet. Wrote witty, intellectual poems, notably "The Pangolin," "To a Steam Roller," "When I Buy Pictures," and "Poetry." *Poems*, 1921; *Observations*, 1924; *What Are Years?*, 1941; *Collected Poems* (1952 Pulitzer Prize in poetry), 1951.

**MORRIS, WILLIE,** Nov. 29, 1934 (Jackson, Miss.). U.S. editor, novelist, nonfiction writer. Editor (1963–67) and editor in chief (1967–71) of *Harper's*, *North toward Home*, 1967; *Yazoo*, 1971; *The Last of the Southern Girls*, 1973.

**MORRIS, WRIGHT,** Jan. 6, 1910 (Central City, Neb.). U.S. novelist and photographer. *The Inhabitants*, 1946; *Plains Song*, 1980; *A Cloak of Light*, 1985.

**MORRISON, TONI,** Feb. 18, 1931 (Lorain, Oh.). U.S. novelist. *The Bluest Eye*, 1970; *Tar Baby*, 1985; *Beloved* (1988 Pulitzer Prize in fiction).

**NABOKOV, VLADIMIR,** Apr. 22, 1899 (St. Petersburg, Rus. [now Leningrad, USSR])–July 2, 1977. Russian-U.S. novelist, short-story writer. A brilliant stylist, he gained international renown for *Lolita* (1955), a satirical novel about a middle-aged man's obsession for a 12-year-old nymphet; also a distinguished lepidopterist. *The Defense*, 1930; *The Real Life of Sebastien Knight*, 1941; *Bend Sinister*, 1947; *Pale Fire*, 1962; *Ada*, 1969.

**NASH, (Frederic) OGDEN,** Aug. 19, 1902 (Rye, N.Y.)–May 19, 1971. U.S. poet. Wrote witty verses with improbable rhymes; wrote lyrics for *One Touch of Venus* (with S. J. PERELMAN, 1943). *I'm a*

*Stranger Here Myself*, 1938; *Everyone but Thee and Me*, 1938.

**NEMEROV, HOWARD,** Mar. 1, 1920 (New York, N.Y.). U.S. poet, critic, novelist, teacher; named third U.S. poet laureate, 1988. *The Image and the Law*, 1947; *The Salt Garden*, 1955; *Mirrors and Windows*, 1958; *Blue Swallows*, 1967.

**NORDHOFF, CHARLES BERNARD,** Feb. 1, 1887 (London, England)–Apr. 11, 1947. U.S. novelist. With JAMES NORMAN HALL, wrote the trilogy: *Mutiny on the Bounty* (1932), *Men against the Sea* (1933), and *Pitcairn's Island* (1934).

**NORRIS, (Benjamin) FRANK(lin),** Mar. 5, 1870 (Chicago, Ill.)–Oct. 25, 1902. U.S. novelist. An influential muckraker best known for his unfinished trilogy *The Epic of the Wheat*, which included *The Octopus* (1901) and *The Pit* (1903). *McTeague*, 1899; *Vandover and the Brute*, 1914.

**OATES, JOYCE CAROL,** June 16, 1938 (Lockport, N.Y.). U.S. novelist, short-story writer, poet, critic, teacher. *A Garden of Earthly Delights*, 1967; *Them*, 1969; *Wonderland*, 1971; *Do with Me What You Will*, 1973; *Childwold*, 1976; *A Bloodsmoor Romance*, 1982; *Solstice*, 1985.

**O'CONNOR, EDWIN,** July 29, 1918 (Providence, R.I.)–Mar. 23, 1968. U.S. novelist. Wrote about the Irish-American middle class. *The Last Hurrah*, 1956; *The Edge of Sadness* (1962 Pulitzer Prize in fiction), 1961.

**O'CONNOR, FLANNERY,** Mar. 25, 1925 (Savannah, Ga.)–Aug. 3, 1964. U.S. short-story writer, novelist. Wrote fierce, funny stories grounded in her Southern and Roman Catholic background. *A Good Man Is Hard to Find and Other Stories*, 1955; *Wise Blood*, 1952; *Everything That Rises Must Converge*, 1965.

**ODETS, CLIFFORD,** July 18, 1906 (Philadelphia, Pa.)–Aug. 14, 1963. U.S. dramatist. Leading dramatist of the Depression, wrote plays of social protest for the Group Theatre in New York City. *Waiting for Lefty*, 1935; *Awake and Sing*, 1935; *Paradise Lost*, 1935; *Golden Boy*, 1937; *The Big Knife*, 1949; *The Country Girl*, 1950.

**O'HARA, JOHN,** Jan. 31, 1905 (Pottsville, Pa.)–Apr. 11, 1970. U.S. short-story writer, novelist. His short-story collection *Pal Joey* (1940) was made into a Broadway musical and later a film. *Appointment in Samarra*, 1934; *Butterfield 8*, 1935; *The Doctor's Son and Other Stories*, 1935.

**O'NEILL, EUGENE,** Oct. 16, 1888 (New York, N.Y.)–Nov. 27, 1953. U.S. dramatist. Set a new standard for American drama. First U.S. playwright to be awarded Nobel Prize in literature, 1936; received Pulitzer Prizes in drama in 1920 for *Beyond the Horizon* (1920), 1922 for *Anna Christie* (1922), 1928 for *Strange Interlude* (1928), 1957 for *A Long Day's Journey into Night* (1956). *The Emperor Jones*, 1921; *Desire Under the Elms*, 1921; *Mourning Becomes Electra*, 1931; *Ah, Wilderness!* 1933; *The Iceman Cometh*, 1946.

**OZICK, CYNTHIA,** April 17, 1928 (New York, N.Y.). U.S. author. *Trust*, 1966; *Levitation: Five Fictions*, 1982; *The Messiah of Stockholm*, 1987.

**PALEY, GRACE,** Dec. 11, 1922 (New York, N.Y.). U.S. short-story writer. *The Little Disturbances of Man,* 1959; *Enormous Changes at the Last Minute,* 1975; *Later the Same Day,* 1985.

**PARKER, DOROTHY,** Aug. 22, 1893 (West End, N.J.)–June 7, 1967. U.S. humorist, short-story writer. Celebrated wit of the 1920s; member of the Algonquin Round Table group. *Enough Rope,* 1926; "The Big Blonde," 1929.

**PERCY, WALKER,** May 28, 1916 (Birmingham, Ala.)–May 10, 1990. U.S. novelist, essayist. *The Moviegoer,* 1961; *The Last Gentleman,* 1966; *Love in the Ruins; Lost in the Cosmos,* 1983.

**PERELMAN, S**(idney) J(oseph), Feb. 1, 1904 (New York, N.Y.)–Oct. 17, 1979. U.S. humorist. Noted for the wild word play of his *New Yorker* pieces; coauthored MARX BROTHERS movies, including *Monkey Business* (1931) and *Horsefeathers* (1932). *One Touch of Venus* (with OGDEN NASH), 1943; *The Best of S. J. Perelman,* 1947.

**PIERCY, MARGE,** March 31, 1936 (Detroit, Mich.). U.S. poet and novelist. *Breaking Camp,* 1968; *Dance the Eagle to Sleep,* 1970; *Gone to Soldiers,* 1987.

**PLATH, SYLVIA,** Oct. 27, 1932 (Boston, Mass.)–Feb. 11, 1963. U.S. poet. Best known for her posthumously published volume of poetry, *Ariel* (1965), written shortly before her suicide, and her novel *The Bell Jar* (1962), a fictionalized account of her nervous breakdown; won 1982 Pulitzer for *The Collected Poems,* 1981. (Wife of T. HUGHES.)

**PORTER, KATHERINE ANNE,** May 15, 1890 (Indian Creek, Tex.). U.S. short-story writer, novelist. Master of the short story, especially "Noon Wine" (1919), "Old Morality" (1919), "Theft" (1935), and "Hacienda" (1935); won wide readership with the novel *Ship of Fools* (1962), the 1966 Pulitzer Prize in fiction for *Collected Short Stories* (1965). *Flowering Judas,* 1930; *Pale Horse, Pale Rider,* 1939.

**POTOK, CHAIM,** Feb. 17, 1929 (New York, N.Y.). U.S. novelist. Noted for his novels about Jewish life. *The Chosen,* 1967; *The Promise,* 1969; *My Name Is Asher Lev,* 1972; *Davita's Harp,* 1985.

**POUND, EZRA,** Oct. 30, 1885 (Hailey, Ida.)–Nov. 1, 1972. U.S. poet, critic, translator. Exerted a profound influence on 20th-cent. lit.; during WW II, broadcast fascist propaganda to the U.S.; indicted for treason, confined to hospital as insane, 1946–58; his most famous work is *Cantos,* a cycle of poetry written from 1925 to 1960.

**PRICE, REYNOLDS,** Feb. 1, 1933 (Macon, N.C.). U.S. novelist and poet. *A Long and Happy Life,* 1962; *The Surface of Earth,* 1975; *Good Hearts,* 1988.

**PUZO, MARIO,** Oct. 15, 1920 (New York, N.Y.). U.S. novelist. *The Fortunate Pilgrim,* 1965; *The Godfather,* 1969; *The Sicilian,* 1984.

**PYNCHON, THOMAS,** May 8, 1937 (Glen Cove, N.Y.) U.S. novelist. Noted for the erudition and black humor of his experimental fiction. *V,* 1963; *The Crying of Lot 49,* 1966; *Gravity's Rainbow,* 1973; *Vineland,* 1990.

**RABE, DAVID,** March 10, 1940 (Dubuque, Iowa),

U.S. dramatist. *The Basic Training of Pavlo Hummel,* 1971; *Streamers,* 1976; *Hurlyburly,* 1984. (Husband of JILL CLAYBURGH.)

**RAND, AYN,** Feb. 2, 1905 (St. Petersburg [now Leningrad], Rus.). U.S. novelist, nonfiction writer. In her novels, created superior, self-made individuals to illustrate objectivism, her philosophy of "rational self-interest." *The Fountainhead,* 1943; *Atlas Shrugged,* 1957; *For the New Intellectual,* 1961.

**RANSOM, JOHN CROWE,** Apr. 30, 1888 (Pulaski, Tenn.)–July 3, 1974. U.S. poet, critic. The foremost theorist of the post-WW I Southern literary renaissance; founded, edited the *Kenyon Review,* 1939–59; his *The New Criticism* (1941) began an influential school of criticism that focused on the text itself. *Chills and Fever,* 1924.

**RAWLINGS, MARGARET KINNAN,** Aug. 8, 1896 (Washington, D.C.)–Dec. 14, 1953. U.S. novelist. Wrote books set in rural Florida; best known for the juvenile classic *The Yearling* (1938), (1939 Pulitzer Prize in fiction). *The Sojourner,* 1953.

**REED, ISHMAEL,** Feb. 22, 1938 (Chattanooga, Tenn.). U.S. novelist and poet. *The Free-Lance Pallbearers,* 1967, *The Last Days of Louisiana Red,* 1974; *Cab Calloway Stands in for the Moon,* 1986.

**RICE, ELMER,** Sept. 28, 1892 (New York, N.Y.)–May 8, 1967. U.S. dramatist. Noted for plays that dramatized liberal social and political views. *The Adding Machine,* 1922; *Street Scene,* 1928 (1929 Pulitzer Prize in drama; later made into opera by KURT WEILL); 1929; *Counsellor-at-Law,* 1931; *We, the People,* 1933.

**RILEY, JAMES WHITCOMB,** Oct. 7, 1849 (Greenfield, Ind.)–July 22, 1916. U.S. poet. "The poet of the common people"; early poems in Hoosier dialect earned him the name "The Hoosier Poet." *The Old Swimmin' Hole and 'Leven More Poems,* 1883; *Home Folks,* 1900.

**ROBBINS, HAROLD,** May 21, 1916 (New York, N.Y.). U.S. novelist. *Never Love a Stranger,* 1948; *The Dream Merchants,* 1949; *A Stone for Danny Fisher,* 1952; *The Carpetbaggers,* 1961; *The Adventurers,* 1966; *The Betsy,* 1971; *The Lonely Lady,* 1976; *The Storyteller,* 1985.

**ROBERTS, KENNETH,** Dec. 8, 1885 (Kennebunk, Me.)–July 21, 1957. U.S. novelist. Awarded 1957 Pulitzer Special Citation for his historical novels. *Arundel,* 1930; *Rabble in Arms,* 1933; *Northwest Passage,* 1937.

**ROBINSON, EDWARD ARLINGTON,** Dec. 22, 1869 (Head Tide, Me.)–Apr. 6, 1935. U.S. poet. Introduced naturalism to American poetry; best-known poems include "Richard Cory" and "Miniver Cheevy." *Collected Poems* (Pulitzer Prize in poetry, 1922), 1921; *The Man Who Died Twice* (Pulitzer Prize in poetry, 1925), 1924; *Tristram* (1928 Pulitzer Prize in poetry), 1927.

**ROETHKE, THEODORE,** May 25, 1908 (Saginaw, Mich.)–Aug. 1, 1963. U.S. poet noted for evocations of childhood, old age, and images of horticulture. *Open House,* 1941; *The Lost Son and*

*Other Poems*, 1948; *The Waking* (1954 Pulitzer Prize in poetry), 1953; *Words for the Wind*, 1957.
ROGERS, ROSEMARY, Dec. 7, 1932 (Ceylon). U.S. novelist. Author of best-selling historical and contemporary romances. *Sweet Savage Love*, 1974; *Lost Love, Last Love*, 1980; *The Wanton*, 1984.
RÖLVAAG, O(le) E(dvart), Apr. 22, 1876 (Dönna I., Nor.)–Nov. 5, 1931. Norwegian-U.S. novelist, educator. Noted for his portrayal of the Norwegian immigrants on the Dakota prairie. *Giants in the Earth*, 1927; *Peder Victorious*, 1929; *Their Father's God*, 1931.
ROTH, HENRY, Feb. 8, 1906 (Austria-Hungary). U.S. proletarian novelist. His only novel, *Call It Sleep*, was written in 1934, but was not critically praised until it was reissued in 1964.
ROTH, PHILIP, Mar. 19, 1933 (Newark, N.J.). U.S. novelist, short-story writer. His themes include Jewish identity, the life of the artist, and sexual desire versus renunciation. *Goodbye Columbus*, 1959; *Letting Go*, 1962; *Portnoy's Complaint*, 1969; *The Professor of Desire*, 1978; *The Ghost Writer*, 1979; *The Zuckerman Trilogy* (1979, 1981, 1983); *The Facts*, 1990.
RUKEYSER, MURIEL, Dec. 15, 1913 (New York, N.Y.)–Feb. 12, 1980. U.S. poet, translator. Writes on social and political themes, including feminism; translated poetry of OCTAVIO PAZ. *Theory of Flight*, 1935; *Beast in View*, 1944; *The Speed of Darkness*, 1968; *Breaking Open*, 1973.
RUNYON, (Alfred) DAMON, Oct. 4, 1884 (Manhattan, Kan.)–Dec. 10, 1946. U.S. short-story writer, journalist. Wrote humorous stories about colorful Broadway and underworld characters. *Guys and Dolls* (made into a hit Broadway musical, 1950, and later a movie), 1931; *Blue Plate Special*, 1934; *Money from Home*, 1935; *Runyon à la Carte*, 1944.
SALINGER, J(erome) D(avid), Jan. 1, 1919 (New York, N.Y.). U.S. novelist, short-story writer. Best known for his critically acclaimed and immensely popular novel *The Catcher in the Rye* (1951), about a sensitive adolescent's flight from the "phony" adult world; ceased publishing and became a recluse, 1963. *Nine Stories*, 1953; *Franny and Zooey*, 1961; *Raise High the Roof Beam, Carpenters*, 1963; *Seymour: An Introduction*, 1963.
SANDBURG, CARL, Jan. 6, 1878 (Galesburg, Ill.)–July 22, 1967. U.S. poet, biographer. Influential in the pre-WW I Chicago Renaissance movement; noted for vigorous free verse celebrating America and its common people; won 1940 Pulitzer Prize in history for the second section of his biography of ABRAHAM LINCOLN, *The War Years* (4 vols., 1939). *Chicago Poems*, 1916; *Good Morning, America*, 1928; *The People, Yes*, 1936.
SAROYAN, WILLIAM, Aug. 31, 1908 (Fresno, Calif.). U.S. short-story writer, playwright. Noted for his optimism, sentimentality, and mastery of the vernacular. *The Daring Young Man on the Flying Trapeze*, 1934; *My Name Is Aram*, 1940; *The Human Comedy*, 1943; *The Time of Your Life*

(awarded, but refused, 1940 Pulitzer Prize in drama), 1939.
SCHULBERG, BUDD, March 27, 1914 (New York, N.Y.). U.S. novelist and screenwriter. *What Makes Sammy Run?*, 1941; *On the Waterfront* (1954 Acad. Award for best story and screenplay); *Everything That Moves*, 1980. (Former husband of G. BROOKS.)
SCHWARTZ, DELMORE, Dec. 8, 1913 (Brooklyn, N.Y.)–July 11, 1966. U.S. poet, short-story writer, critic. *In Dreams Begin Responsibilities*, 1938; *The World Is a Wedding*, 1948.
SENDAK, MAURICE, June 10, 1928 (New York, N.Y.). U.S. author, illustrator. Author and illustrator of children's books, many of which have become modern classics. *The Nutshell Library*, 1963; *Where the Wild Things Are*, 1963; *In the Night Kitchen*, 1970.
SERLING, ROD, Dec. 25, 1924 (Syracuse, N.Y.)–June 28, 1975. U.S. writer. Best known as the writer/creator/narrator of TV series *Twilight Zone*, 1959–64; Peabody Award, 1957. Screenplays: *Requiem for a Heavyweight* (TV), 1963; *Seven Days in May*, 1964; *Planet of the Apes*, 1967.
SEXTON, ANNE, Nov. 9, 1928 (Newton, Mass.)–Oct. 4, 1974. U.S. poet. Noted for revelations about her troubled personal life. *To Bedlam and Part Way Back*, 1960; *All My Pretty Ones*, 1962; *Live or Die* (1966 Pulitzer Prize in poetry), 1966; *Love Poems*, 1969; *Transformations*, 1971.
SHAPIRO, KARL, Nov. 10, 1913 (Baltimore, Md.). U.S. poet, critic. Noted for his bold verse and controversial criticism. *Poem, Place and Thing*, 1942; *V-Letter and Other Poems* (1945 Pulitzer Prize in poetry), 1944; *Beyond Criticism*, 1953; *Poems of a Jew*, 1958; *In Defense of Ignorance*, 1960; *White Haired Lover*, 1968.
SHAW, IRWIN, Feb. 27, 1913 (New York, N.Y.)–May 16, 1984. U.S. novelist, short-story writer. Noted for works that explore contemporary social issues. *The Young Lions*, 1948; *Two Weeks in Another Town*, 1959; *Rich Man, Poor Man*, 1970; *Evening in Byzantium*, 1973; *Beggarman, Thief*, 1977; *Bread Upon The Waters*, 1981.
SHELDON, SIDNEY, Feb. 11, 1917 (Chicago, Ill.). U.S. novelist. *The Other Side of Midnight*, 1973; *Bloodline*, 1977; *Rage of Angels*, 1980; *If Tomorrow Comes*, 1985.
SHEPARD, SAM(uel), Nov. 5, 1943 (Ft. Sheridan, Ill.). U.S. dramatist and actor. Author: *Chicago*, 1966; *Buried Child* (1979 Pulitzer Prize for drama); *A Lie of the Mind*, 1985. Actor: *Raggedy Man*, 1981; *The Right Stuff*, 1983; *Crimes of the Heart*, 1986.
SHERWOOD, ROBERT, Apr. 4, 1896 (New Rochelle, N.Y.)–Nov. 14, 1955. U.S. dramatist. Noted for social and political dramas, including *The Petrified Forest* (1935); won Pulitzer Prizes in 1936 for *Idiot's Delight* (1936), 1939 for *Abe Lincoln in Illinois* (1938), 1941 for *There Shall Be No Night* (1940), and 1949 for the biography *Roosevelt and Hopkins: An Intimate History* (1948).
SIMON, NEIL, July 4, 1927 (New York, N.Y.)

U.S. playwright, screenwriter. Had four comedies running simultaneously during the 1966–67 Broadway season, three during the 1969–70 season; perhaps best known for *The Odd Couple* (1965), which became a movie and a long-running TV series. *Come Blow Your Horn*, 1961; *Barefoot in the Park*, 1963; *Sweet Charity*, 1966; *Promises, Promises* (1969); *The Sunshine Boys*, 1972; *Chapter Two*, 1978; *Brighton Beach Memoirs*, 1983; *Biloxi Blues*, 1984; *Broadway Bound*, 1987.

**SIMPSON, LOUIS**, Mar. 27, 1923 (Jamaica). U.S. poet, teacher. *The Arrivistes: Poems 1940–48*, 1949; *At the End of the Open Road* (1964 Pulitzer Prize in poetry), 1963; *North of Jamaica*, 1972; *Caviare at the Funeral*, 1980.

**SINCLAIR, UPTON**, Sept. 20, 1878 (Baltimore, Md.).–Nov. 25, 1968. U.S. novelist. Noted for his muckraking novels, including *The Jungle* (1906), which led to reform of federal food inspection laws. *King Coal*, 1917; *Oil!*, 1927; *Dragon's Teeth* (1943 Pulitzer Prize in fiction), 1942.

**SINGER, ISAAC BASHEVIS**, July 14, 1904 (Radzymin, Pol.) Polish-U.S. novelist, short-story writer. Yiddish writer noted for his imagination, irony, and wit; awarded Nobel Prize in literature, 1978. *Satan in Goray*, 1935; *The Family Moskat*, 1950; *Gimpel the Fool and Other Stories*, 1957; *The Magician of Lublin*, 1960; *In My Father's Court*, 1966; *Old Love*, 1979; *Yentl, the Yeshiva Boy*, 1983.

**SMITH, BETTY**, Dec. 15, 1906 (Brooklyn, N.Y.). U.S. novelist. Best known for *A Tree Grows in Brooklyn* (1943), a partly autobiographical novel. *Maggie—Now* (1958); *Joy in the Morning*, 1963.

**SNODGRASS, W(illiam) D(ewitt)**, Jan. 5, 1926 (Wilkinsburg, Pa.) U.S. poet. *Heart's Needle* (1960 Pulitzer Prize in poetry), 1959. *After Experience*, 1968.

**STAFFORD, JEAN**, July 1, 1915 (Covina, Calif.) –Mar. 26, 1979. U.S. short-story writer, novelist. *Boston Adventure*, 1944; *Childen Are Bored on Sundays*, 1953; *A Mother in History*, 1966; *Collected Stories* (1970 Pulitzer Prize in fiction), 1969.

**STALLINGS, LAURENCE**, Nov. 25, 1894 (Macon, Ga.). U.S. playwright. *What Price Glory?* (with MAXWELL ANDERSON), 1924; *First Flight* (with Anderson), 1925; *The Buccaneer* (with Anderson), 1925; *The First World War* (book), 1933.

**STEEL, DANIELLE**, Aug. 14, 1947 (New York, N.Y.) Novelist. *Passion's Promise*, 1977; *Remembrance*, 1981; *Changes*, 1983; *Kaleidoscope*, 1987.

**STEFFENS, LINCOLN**, Apr. 6, 1866 (San Francisco, Calif.)–Aug. 9, 1936. U.S. journalist. A leading muckraker, best known for uncovering political corruption in *The Shame of the Cities*, 1904. *The Struggle for Self-Government*, 1906.

**STEGNER, WALLACE**, Feb. 18, 1909 (Lake Mills, Iowa). U.S. novelist. *The Woman on the Wall*, 1950; *Angle of Repose* (1972 Pulitzer Prize for fiction); *Crossing to Safety*, 1987.

**STEIN, GERTRUDE**, Feb. 3, 1874 (Allegheny, Pa.)–July 27, 1946. U.S. writer. In the 1920s conducted a celebrated salon for writers in her Paris home; the friend, patron, and mentor of many post-WW I American expatriates, whom she collectively named the Lost Generation; with her brother Leo, was one of the first collectors of avant-garde paintings. *Three Lives*, 1933; *The Autobiography of Alice B. Toklas*, 1933; *Four Saints in Three Acts* (opera libretto), 1934.

**STEINBECK, JOHN**, Feb. 27, 1902 (Salinas, Calif.)– Dec. 20, 1968. U.S. novelist. Noted for his novels about the disinherited; awarded Nobel Prize in literature, 1962. *Tortilla Flat*, 1935; *In Dubious Battle*, 1936; *Of Mice and Men*, 1937; *The Grapes of Wrath* (1940 Pulitzer Prize in fiction), 1939; *Cannery Row*, 1945; *The Pearl*, 1947; *East of Eden*, 1952; *The Winter of Our Discontent*, 1961.

**STEVENS, WALLACE**, Oct. 2, 1879 (Reading, Pa.)–Aug. 2, 1955. U.S. poet. Noted for his subtle verse on the theme of the interaction of reality and imagination; best-known poems include "Sunday Morning," "Le Monocle de Mon Oncle," "Peter Quince at the Clavier," "The Comedian as the Letter C." *Harmonium*, 1923; *Ideas of Order*, 1935; *The Man With the Blue Guitar*, 1937; *Collected Poems* (1955 Pulitzer Prize in poetry), 1954.

**STONE, IRVING**, July 14, 1903 (San Francisco, Cal.)–Aug. 26, 1989. U.S. author. Noted for writing popular fictional biographies. *Lust for Life*, 1934; *Sailor on Horseback*, 1938; *The President's Lady*, 1951; *The Agony and the Ectasy*, 1961; *I Michelangelo, Sculptor*, 1962; *Passions of the Mind*, 1971.

**STOWE, HARRIET BEECHER**, June 14, 1811 (Litchfield, Conn.)–July 1, 1896. U.S. novelist. Best known as the author of *Uncle Tom's Cabin* (1852), which prior to the Civil War aroused considerable anti-slavery feeling. *The Key to Uncle Tom's Cabin*, 1853. (Daughter of L. BEECHER; sister of H. W. BEECHER and C. E. BEECHER.)

**STYRON, WILLIAM**, June 11, 1925 (Newport News, Va.). U.S. novelist. Best known as author of the controversial (1968) Pulitzer Prize-winning novel, *The Confessions of Nat Turner* (1967), about the leader of the 1831 slave rebellion. *Lie Down in Darkness*, 1951; *Set This House on Fire*, 1960; *Sophie's Choice*, 1979.

**TARKINGTON, BOOTH**, July 29, 1869 (Indianapolis, Ind.)–May 19, 1946. U.S. novelist. Noted for his novels about Midwestern life. *Penrod*, 1914; *Seventeen*, 1917; *The Magnificent Ambersons* (1919 Pulitzer Prize in fiction, later filmed by ORSON WELLES), 1918; *Alice Adams* (1922 Pulitzer Prize in fiction), 1921.

**TATE, ALLEN**, Nov. 11, 1899 (Winchester, Ky.)– Feb. 9, 1979. U.S. poet and critic. Wrote of the yearning for the rural Southern way of life. *Stonewall Jackson: The Good Soldier*, 1928; *Memoirs and Opinions*, 1975; *Collected Poems: 1919–1976*, 1977.

**TAYLOR, PETER**, Jan. 8, 1917 (Trenton, Tenn.). U.S. novelist and short-story writer. *A Woman of Means*, 1950; *The Widows of Thornton*, 1954; *A*

*Summons to Memphis* (1987 Pulitzer Prize for literature).

**TEASDALE, SARA,** Aug. 8, 1884 (St. Louis, Mo.) –Jan. 29, 1933. U.S. poet. Member of the *Poetry* magazine circle. *Rivers to the Sea,* 1915; *Love Songs* (1918 Pulitzer Prize in poetry), 1917; *Flame and Shadow,* 1920; *Strange Victory,* 1933.

**TERHUNE, ALBERT PAYSON,** Dec. 21, 1872 (Newark, N.J.)–Feb. 18, 1942. U.S. novelist. Prolific author of popular books about dogs. *Lad, A Dog,* 1919; *Bruce,* 1920; *The Heart of a Dog,* 1924.

**TERKEL, STUDS,** May 16, 1912 (New York, N.Y.). U.S. writer. Noted for books based on tape-recorded interviews. *Giants of Jazz,* 1956; *Division Street America,* 1966; *Hard Times,* 1970; *Working,* 1974; *The Good War,* 1985 (1985 Pulitzer Prize in fiction).

**THEROUX, PAUL,** Apr. 10, 1941 (Medford, Mass.). U.S. novelist, nonfiction writer. *Saint Jack,* 1973; *The Great Railway Bazaar,* 1975; *The Family Arsenal,* 1976; *The Consul's File,* 1977; *The Old Patagonian Express,* 1979; *The Mosquito Coast,* 1981; *The Kingdom by the Sea,* 1983; *Riding the Iron Rooster,* 1988.

**THOMPSON, KAY,** ? (St. Louis, Mo.). U.S. author, entertainer. Wrote books about Eloise, the over-privileged six-year-old who terrorized New York City's Plaza Hotel. *Eloise,* 1955; *Eloise in Paris,* 1977.

**THURBER, JAMES,** Dec. 8, 1894 (Columbus, Ohio) –Nov. 2, 1961. U.S. humorist, cartoonist. A leading contributor to *The New Yorker,* his drawings first appeared in *Is Sex Necessary?* (1929), written with E. B. WHITE. *My Life and Hard Times,* 1933; *Fables for Our Time,* 1940; *The Male Animal* (play; with Elliot Nugent), 1941; "The Secret Life of Walter Mitty," 1942; *The Thurber Album,* 1952.

**TOOLE, JOHN KENNEDY,** 1937 (New Orleans, La.)–March 26, 1969. U.S. novelist. A college teacher in New York and Louisiana, he committed suicide in 1969; twelve years later his only novel, *A Confederacy of Dunces,* was finally published and it won the Pulitzer Prize for literature in 1981.

**TRILLIN, CALVIN,** Dec. 5, 1935 (Kansas City, Mo.). U.S. humorous author. *An Education in Georgia,* 1964; *American Fried,* 1974; *If You can't Say Something Nice,* 1987.

**TWAIN, MARK** (pseud. of Samuel Langhorne Clemens), Nov. 30, 1835 (Florida, Mo.)–Apr. 21, 1910. U.S. writer. Great American humorist; a self-made man, worked as a printer as age 12, an itinerant typesetter at 17, later a river pilot; married an heiress; became internationally famous as a "people's author." *The Innocents Abroad,* 1869; *The Gilded Age* (with Charles Dudley Warner), 1873; *The Adventures of Tom Sawyer,* 1876; *The Prince and the Pauper,* 1882; *Life on the Mississippi,* 1883; *The Adventures of Huckleberry Finn,* 1885; *A Connecticut Yankee in King Arthur's Court,* 1889; *Pudd'n head Wilson,* 1894.

**TYLER, ANNE,** Oct. 25, 1931 (Minneapolis, Minn.).

U.S. novelist. *If Morning Ever Comes,* 1964; *Earthly Possessions,* 1977; *The Accidental Tourist,* 1985.

**UPDIKE, JOHN,** Mar. 18, 1932 (Shillington, Pa.). U.S. novelist, short-story writer, poet. Writes about contemporary American small-town and suburban life. *Rabbit, Run,* 1960; *Pigeon Feathers, and Other Stories,* 1962; *The Centaur,* 1963; *The Music School,* 1967; *Couples,* 1968; *Rabbit Redux,* 1971; *The Coup,* 1978; *Too Far To Go,* 1979; *The Witches of Eastwick,* 1984.

**URIS, LEON,** Aug. 3, 1924 (Baltimore, Md.). U.S. novelist. *Battle Cry,* 1953; *Exodus,* 1958; *Mila 18,* 1961; *Ireland: A Terrible Beauty* (with Jill Uris), 1975; *Trinity,* 1976; *The Haj,* 1984.

**VIDAL, GORE,** Oct. 3, 1925 (West Point, N.Y.). U.S. novelist, playwright, critic. *Williwaw,* 1946; *The City and the Pillar,* 1948; *Julian,* 1964; *Washington, D.C.,* 1967; *Myra Breckinridge,* 1968; *Burr,* 1973; *1876,* 1976; *Matters of Fact and Fiction,* 1977; *Lincoln,* 1984; *Empire,* 1987.

**VONNEGUT, KURT, JR.,** Nov. 11, 1922 (Indianapolis, Ind.). U.S. novelist. Black-humor novels about the horrors of the 20th cent. *Piano Player,* 1951; *Cat's Cradle,* 1963; *Slaughterhouse Five,* 1969; *Breakfast of Champions,* 1973; *Deadeye Dick,* 1982; *Galápagos,* 1985.

**WALLACE, IRVING,** Mar. 19, 1916 (Chicago, Ill.)–June 29, 1990. U.S. novelist. *The Chapman Report,* 1960; *The Prize,* 1962; *The Man,* 1964; *Seven Minutes,* 1964; *The Fan Club,* 1974; *The Miracle,* 1984. With his son, David Wallechinsky, has created "entertainment reference books," including *The People's Almanac* (1975), *The Book of Lists* (1977), and *The Intimate Sex Lives of Famous People,* 1981.

**WALKER, ALICE,** Feb. 9, 1944 (Eatonton, Ga.). U.S. novelist. *Once,* 1968; *The Color Purple,* 1982 (1983 Pulitzer Prize in literature); *Horses Make a Landscape More Beautiful,* 1984

**WAMBAUGH, JOSEPH,** Jan. 22, 1937 (East Pittsburgh, Pa.). U.S. novelist. Formerly a Los Angeles Police Department detective; writes realistic novels about police work. *The New Centurions,* 1971; *The Blue Knight,* 1972; *The Onion Field,* 1973; *The Choirboys,* 1975; *The Glitter Dome,* 1981; *The Secrets of Harry Bright,* 1985.

**WARREN, MERCY OTIS,** Sept. 25, 1728 (Barnstable, Mass.)–Oct. 19, 1814. U.S. playwright, historian. Wrote a three-volume history of the American Revolution, *History of the Rise, Progress and Termination of the American Revolution* (1805), and two anti-Tory satirical plays, *The Adulateur* (1773) and *The Group* (1775).

**WARREN, ROBERT PENN,** Apr. 24, 1905 (Guthrie, Ky.)–Sept. 15, 1989. U.S. novelist, poet, critic. Noted for novels with Southern themes and characters; expanded the New Criticism; won 1947 Pulitzer Prize in fiction for his novel *All the King's Men* (1946); won Pulitzers in poetry in 1958 for *Promises* (1957) and in 1979 for *Now and Then* (1978). Named first U.S. poet laureate (1986).

**WELTY, EUDORA,** Apr. 13, 1909 (Jackson, Miss.). U.S. short-story writer, novelist. Noted for use of monologue and dialogue, and focus on small-town Mississippi. *A Curtain of Green,* 1941; *The Golden Apples,* 1949; *The Ponder Heart,* 1954; *The Optimist's Daughter* (1973 Pulitzer Prize in fiction), 1972.

**WEST, NATHANAEL,** Oct. 17, 1903 (New York, N.Y.)–Dec. 22, 1940. U.S. novelist. Noted for his surrealistic satires that anticipated black humor. *The Dream Life of Balso Snell, Miss Lonelyhearts,* 1933; *A Cool Million,* 1934; *The Day of the Locust,* 1939.

**WHARTON, EDITH,** Jan. 24, 1862 (New York, N.Y.)–Aug. 11, 1937. U.S. novelist, short-story writer. Wrote about upper-class New York society. *The House of Mirth,* 1905; *Ethan Frome,* 1911; *The Age of Innocence* (1921 Pulitzer Prize in fiction), 1920.

**WHEATLEY, PHILLIS,** 1753? (Africa)–Dec. 5, 1784. American colonial poet. First important black poet in America; in childhood, brought to Boston as a slave in the Wheatley household, where she was educated; began writing poetry at age 13, published at age 20. *Poems on Various Subjects, Religious and Moral, by Phillis Wheatley, Negro Servant to Mr. John Wheatley of Boston, in New England,* 1773; *Memoir and Poems of Phillis Wheatley,* 1834; *The Letters of Phillis Wheatley, the Negro Slave-Poet of Boston,* 1864.

**WHITE, E(lwyn) B(rooks),** July 11, 1899 (Mt. Vernon, N.Y.)–Oct. 1, 1985. U.S. humorist, essayist, novelist. Staff member and contributor to *The New Yorker,* from 1927, and *Harper's,* 1938–1943; his children's books, *Stuart Little* (1945), *Charlotte's Web* (1952), and *The Trumpet of the Swan* (1970), have become classics. *Is Sex Necessary?* (with JAMES THURBER), 1929; *One Man's Meat,* 1942; *Here Is New York,* 1949; *The Elements of Style* (with William Strunk, Jr.), 1959.

**WHITMAN, WALT(er),** May 31, 1819 (West Hills, N.Y.)–Mar. 26, 1892. U.S. poet. His *Leaves of Grass* (1855), revolutionary in its use of free verse, made him a major poetic figure. "Song of Myself," 1856; "Out of the Cradle, Endlessly Rocking," 1857; "When Lilacs Last in the Dooryard Bloom'd," 1866; "O Captain! My Captain," 1866.

**WHITTIER, JOHN GREENLEAF,** Dec. 17, 1807 (Haverhill, Mass.)–Sept. 7, 1892. U.S. poet, social reformer. Popular poet of rural New England; a crusading abolitionist; founder of the Liberal party. "Snow-Bound," (1866); "Barbara Frietchie"; "The Barefoot Boy."

**WIESEL, ELIE,** Sept. 30, 1928 (Sighet, Rum.). U.S. novelist, nonfiction writer. Writes about the plight of the Jew. *Night,* 1960; *Dawn,* 1961; *The Accident,* 1962; *The Jews of Silence: A Personal Report of Soviet Jewry,* 1966; *Souls on Fire,* 1972; *The Golem,* 1983.

**WIGGLESWORTH, MICHAEL,** Oct. 18, 1631 (Yorkshire, Eng.)–May 27, 1705. American colonial poet, clergyman. His poem "The Day of Doom: or, a Poetical Description of the Great and Last Judgment" (1662), was the first American best-

seller. *God's Controversy with New England,* written c.1662, pub. 1873.

**WILBUR, RICHARD,** Mar. 1, 1921 (New York, N.Y.) U.S. poet. Named second U.S. poet laureate (1987). *The Beautiful Changes,* 1947; *Things of This World* (1956 Pulitzer Prize in poetry), 1956; *The Poems of Richard Wilbur,* 1963; *Waking to Sleep,* 1969; *The Whale,* 1982.

**WILDER, LAURA INGALLS,** Feb. 7, 1867 (Lake Pepin, Wisc.)–Jan. 10, 1957. U.S. juvenile novelist. Created the Little House series, classic books about frontier family life, which was adapted into a popular TV series. *Little House in the Big Woods,* 1932; *Farmer Boy,* 1933; *Little House on the Prairie,* 1935; *On the Banks of Plum Creek,* 1937.

**WILDER, THORNTON,** Apr. 17, 1897 (Madison, Wis.)–Dec. 7, 1975. U.S. playwright, novelist. His play *The Merchant of Yonkers* (1938), revised into *The Matchmaker* (1954), was later made into the musical *Hello Dolly! The Bridge of San Luis Rey* (1928 Pulitzer Prize in fiction), 1927; *Our Town* (1938 Pulitzer Prize in drama), 1938; *The Skin of Our Teeth* (1943 Pulitzer Prize in drama), 1942.

**WILLIAMS, TENNESSEE** (born Thomas Lanier Williams) Mar. 26, 1911 (Columbus, Miss.).–Feb. 25, 1983. U.S. dramatist. Major playwright, often dealt with controversial themes such as homosexuality. *The Glass Menagerie,* 1944; *A Streetcar Named Desire* (1947 Pulitzer Prize in drama), 1947; *Cat on a Hot Tin Roof* (1955 Pulitzer Prize in drama), 1955; *The Night of the Iguana,* 1962; *Suddenly Last Summer,* 1958; *Sweet Bird of Youth,* 1959.

**WILLIAMS, WILLIAM CARLOS,** Sept. 17, 1883 (Rutherford, N.J.)–Mar. 4, 1963. U.S. poet. Influential in his use of idiomatic speech patterns and details of commonplace experience; best-known work is the epic poem *Paterson* (5 vols., 1946–58); practiced medicine for 40 years in Rutherford. *Al Que Quiere?,* 1917; *Sour Grapes,* 1921; *Journey to Love,* 1955; *Pictures from Brueghel, and Other Poems* (1963 Pulitzer Prize in poetry), 1962.

**WILSON, AUGUST,** 1945 (Pittsburgh, Pa.). U.S. dramatist and theater director. *Ma Rainey's Black Bottom,* 1984; *Fences* (Pulitzer Prize for drama and Tony Award for best play, 1987), 1985; *Joe Turner's Come and Gone,* 1986.

**WILSON, LANFORD,** April 13, 1937 (Lebanon, Mo.). U.S. dramatist. *So Long at the Fair,* 1963; *The Hot L Baltimore,* 1972; *Talley's Folly* (1980 Pulitzer Prize for drama).

**WISTER, OWEN,** July 14, 1860 (Philadelphia, Pa.)–July 21, 1938. U.S. novelist. His prototypal Western novel, *The Virginian* (1902), helped establish the cowboy as a U.S. folk hero.

**WOLFE, THOMAS,** Oct. 3, 1900 (Asheville, N.C.) –Sept. 15, 1938. U.S. novelist, best known for his first novel, *Look Homeward, Angel,* 1929; *Of Time and the River,* 1935; *The Web and the Rock,* 1939; *You Can't Go Home Again,* 1940.

**WOUK, HERMAN,** May 27, 1915 (New York, N.Y.) U.S. novelist. *The Caine Mutiny* (1952 Pulitzer Prize in fiction), 1951; *Marjorie Morningstar,* 1955;

*The Winds of War*, 1971; *War and Remembrance*, 1978; *Inside, Outside*, 1985.
**WRIGHT, RICHARD**, Sept. 4, 1908 (nr. Natchez, Miss.)–Nov. 28, 1960. U.S. novelist, short-story writer. Author of the first influential protest novel by a black writer, *Native Son* (1940), later staged on Broadway by ORSON WELLES. *Black Boy*, 1945;

*The Outsider*, 1953; *White Man, Listen!*, 1957.
**ZINDEL, PAUL**, May 15, 1936 (New York, N.Y.) U.S. playwright, novelist. *The Effect of Gamma Rays on Man-in-the-Moon Marigolds* (1971 Pulitzer Prize in drama), 1970; *The Pigman*, 1968; *My Darling, My Hamburger*, 1969; *The Girl Who Wanted a Boy*, 1981.

## BRITISH AND IRISH WRITERS

**ADAMS, DOUGLAS**, March 11, 1952 (Cambridge, England). British writer. He began as a script writer for radio and televison for the BBC, writing episodes for *Dr. Who* and *Hitchhiker's Guide to the Galaxy*. His novels inclued *Hitchhiker's Guide to the Galaxy* (1979), *The Restaurant at the End of the Universe* (1980), and *Life, the Universe and Everything* (1982).
**ADDISON, JOSEPH**, May 1, 1672 (Milston, Eng.)–June 17, 1719. English poet, essayist, critic, playwright. Contributor to *The Tatler* (1709–11) and *The Spectator* (1711–12, 1714); poetry includes *The Campaign* (1704) and *The Spacious Firmament on High* (1712); plays include *Rosamund* (1705) and *Cato* (1713).
**ARCHER, JEFFREY**, April 15, 1940 (England). British novelist. A writer with a taste for the unusual subject, he has been a minister of Parliament (1969–1974) and the chairman of the British Conservative Party (1985–1986). *Not a Penny More, Not a Penny Less*, 1976; *Kane & Abel*, 1980; *A Matter of Honor*, 1986.
**ARNOLD, MATTHEW**, Dec. 24, 1822 (Laleham, Eng.)–Apr. 15, 1888. English poet, critic. Crusaded for classicism, critical traditionalism, and the idea that literature should ennoble. *Empedocles on Etna and Other Poems*, 1852; *Poems* (inc. "The Scholar Gypsy"), 1853; *New Poems* (inc. "Dover Beach"), 1867; *Culture and Anarchy*, 1869; *Literature and Dogma*, 1873.
**AUDEN, W(ystan) H(ugh)**, Feb. 21, 1907 (York, Eng.)–Sept. 28, 1973. English-U.S. poet, dramatist, editor. Wrote about post-WW I England, which he termed the "age of anxiety." *Poems*, 1928; *The Dance of Death*, 1933; *The Dog beneath the Skin* (with CHRISTOPHER ISHERWOOD), 1935; *The Age of Anxiety* (1948 Pulitzer Prize in poetry), 1947; *Homage to Clio*, 1960; *Epistle to a Godson and Other Poems*, 1972.
**AUSTEN, JANE**, Dec. 16, 1775 (Hampshire, Eng.)–July 18, 1817. English novelist. A "masterful miniaturist" who wrote comedies of manners about provincial middle-class life in a spare, witty style. *Sense and Sensibility*, 1811; *Pride and Prejudice*, 1813; *Mansfield Park*, 1814; *Emma*, 1816; *Northanger Abbey*, 1818; *Persuasion*, 1818.
**AYCKBOURN, ALAN**, Apr. 12, 1939 (London, Eng.) English dramatist. A prolific playwright, he had four plays running simultaneously in London's West End in 1975. *The Norman Conquests*, 1975.
**BAGNOLD, ENID** (Lady Roderick Jones), Oct. 27, 1889 (Rochester, Eng.)–Mar. 31, 1981. English novelist, playwright. *Serena Blandish*, 1925; *Na-*

*tional Velvet*, 1935; *The Chalk Garden*, 1956; *The Chinese Prime Minister*, 1961.
**BARRIE, SIR J(ames) M(atthew)**, May 9, 1860 (Kirriemuir, Scot.)–June 19, 1937. Scottish dramatist, novelist. Best known for *Peter Pan* (1904). *The Little Minister*, 1897; *Quality Street*, 1901; *The Admirable Crichton*, 1902; *What Every Woman Knows*, 1908; *Dear Brutus* (1917).
**BEAUMONT, FRANCIS**, 1584 (Grace-Dieu, Eng.)–Mar. 6, 1616. English dramatist. Best known for collaboration with JOHN FLETCHER on several tragicomedies, including *Philaster* (1609), *A King and No King* (1611), and *The Maid's Tragedy* (c.1611), which influenced Restoration drama. *The Woman Hater*, c.1606; *The Knight of the Burning Pestle*, c.1607.
**BECKETT, SAMUEL**, Apr. 13, 1906 (Dublin, Ire.)–Dec. 22, 1989. French playwright, novelist. A major writer in the literature of the absurd; awarded Nobel Prize in literature, 1969; author of a trilogy composed of *Molloy* (1951), *Malone Dies* (1951), *The Unnameable* (1953). *Waiting for Godot*, 1952; *Endgame*, 1957; *Krapp's Last Tape*, 1958.
**BEERBOHM, SIR MAX**, Aug. 24, 1872 (London, Eng.)–May 20, 1956. English essayist, caricaturist, parodist. Noted for his polished, elegant essays and brilliant parodies; succeeded G. B. SHAW as drama critic of *Saturday Review*, 1878. *The Poet's Corner*, 1904; *Zuleika Dobson*, 1911; *A Christmas Garland*, 1912; *And Even Now*, 1920; *Rossetti and His Circle*, 1922.
**BEHAN, BRENDAN**, Feb. 9, 1923 (Dublin, Ire.)–Mar. 20, 1964. Irish playwright. Noted for the "gallows humor" of his plays; an Irish Republican Army member imprisoned for his political offenses. *The Quare Fellow*, 1956; *The Hostage*, 1958; *Borstal Boy*, 1958.
**BEHN, APHRA**, July 1640 (Kent, Eng.)–Apr. 16, 1689. English novelist, dramatist. The first Englishwoman to earn her living by writing. Plays noted for broad, bawdy humor; her novel *Oroonoko* (c.1688) was the first English philosophical novel.
**BENNETT, ARNOLD**, May 27, 1867 (Staffordshire, Eng.)–Mar. 27, 1931. English novelist noted for his realistic works about "Five Towns," a fictional English manufacturing district. *The Old Wives' Tale*, 1908; *Clayhanger*, 1910.
**BETJEMAN, SIR JOHN**, Apr. 6, 1906 (London, Eng.)–May 19, 1984. English poet. Wrote of nostalgia for near past, alternating between comic satire and polished lyricism; named poet laureate of England, 1972. *Mount Zion*, 1933; *Slick but Not Streamlined* (1947). *A Few Late Chrysanthemums*, 1954; *High and Low*, 1966.

**BLAKE, WILLIAM,** Nov. 28, 1757 (London, Eng.) –Aug. 12, 1827. English poet, artist. A visionary, he created his own elaborate mythology with poetry and art; illustrated, engraved, and published all but the first of his many books. *Songs of Innocence* (inc. "The Lamb"), 1789; *Songs of Experience,* (inc. "The Tyger"), 1794; *The Marriage of Heaven and Hell,* c.1790; *Milton,* 1804–08, *Jerusalem,* 1804–20.

**BOSWELL, JAMES,** Oct. 29, 1740 (Edinburgh, Scot.)–May 19, 1795. Scottish biographer, diarist. Best known for his masterwork, *The Life of Samuel Johnson, L.L.D. (1791). An Account of Corsica,* 1768; *The Journal of a Tour to the Hebrides with Samuel Johnson, L.L.D.,* 1785.

**BOWEN, ELIZABETH,** June 7, 1899 (Dublin, Ire.)– Feb. 22, 1973. English-Irish novelist, short-story writer. Author of stories and novels that explored psychological relationships within the upper middle class. *The House in Paris,* 1935; *The Death of the Heart,* 1938; *Look at All Those Roses,* 1941; *The Heat of the Day,* 1949.

**BRONTË, ANNE,** Jan. 17, 1820 (Thornton, Yorkshire, Eng.)–May 28, 1849. English novelist, poet. Her first and best-known work, *Agnes Grey* (1847), was published as a set with her sister EMILY BRONTË's *Wuthering Heights. The Tenant of Wildfell Hall,* 1848.

**BRONTË, CHARLOTTE,** Apr. 21, 1816 (Thornton, Yorkshire, Eng.)–Mar. 31, 1855. English novelist, poet. Wrote of modern woman's paradoxical drive for independence and need for love. *Jane Eyre,* 1847; *Shirley,* 1849; *Villette,* 1853; *The Professor,* 1857; *Poems of Currer, Ellis and Acton Bell,* 1846.

**BRONTË, EMILY,** July 30, 1818 (Thornton, Yorkshire, Eng.)–Dec. 19, 1848. English novelist, poet. Her reputation rests on a single great novel, *Wuthering Heights* (1847); noted poems include "The Prisoner," "Remembrance," "The Old Stoic," "The Visionary."

**BROWNING, ELIZABETH BARRETT,** Mar. 6, 1806 (Durham, Eng.)–June 29, 1861. English poet. Best known for her *Sonnets From the Portuguese* (1850), love poems addressed to her husband, the poet ROBERT BROWNING. *The Seraphim and Other Poems,* 1838; *Poems,* 1844; *Aurora Leigh,* 1856.

**BROWNING, ROBERT,** May 7, 1812 (Camberwell, Eng.)–Dec. 12, 1889. English poet. Master of dramatic monologue. "My Last Duchess," 1842; "Soliloquy in a Spanish Cloister," 1842; "Fra Lippo Lippi," 1855; *Bells and Pomegranates,* 1846; *Dramatis Personae,* 1864; *The Ring and the Book,* 4 vols. 1868–69; *Dramatic Idyls,* 2 vols., 1879–80.

**BUNYAN, JOHN,** Nov. 30, 1628 (Bedfordshire, Eng.)–Aug. 31, 1688. English author. Best known for *Pilgrim's Progress* (1678), an allegory that describes the journey of Christian and his wife, Christiana, from the City of Destruction to the Celestial City; while imprisoned for 12 years for unlicensed preaching, wrote nine books, including *Grace Abounding to the Chief of Sinners* (1666).

**BURGESS, ANTHONY,** Feb. 25, 1917 (Manchester, Eng.). English novelist, critic. Noted for his comic imagination and use of language; best known for *A Clockwork Orange* (1962), a thriller set in a classless futuristic society. *Inside Mr. Enderby,* 1961; *MF,* 1971; *Napoleon Symphony: A Novel in Four Movements,* 1974.

**BURNEY, FANNY,** June 13, 1752 (King's Lynn, Norfolk, Eng.)–Jan. 6, 1840. English novelist, diarist. Author of novels of manners. *Diaries and Letters, 1778–1840,* 1842–48; *Evelina, or the History of a Young Lady's Entrance Into the World,* 1778; *Cecilia,* 5 vols., 1782.

**BURNS, ROBERT,** Jan. 25, 1759 (Alloway, Ayrshire, Scot.)–July 21, 1796. Scottish poet. Best known for his descriptive, humorous, playful poems in conversational rhythms about rural Scotland, including "Auld Lang Syne," "Comin' Thru the Rye," "Flow Gently, Sweet Afton." *Poems, Chiefly in the Scottish Dialect,* 1786.

**BUTLER, SAMUEL,** Dec. 4, 1835 (Langar, Nottinghamshire, Eng.)–June 18, 1902. English novelist, satirist, scholar. Best known for his ironic, witty, semiautobiographical novel, *The Way of All Flesh* (1903); and for his utopian novel satirizing English society, *Erewhon,* 1872. *Erewhon Revisited,* 1901.

**BYRON, GEORGE GORDON, 6TH BARON BYRON,** Jan. 22, 1788 (London, Eng.)–Apr. 19, 1824. English poet. Embodied in his poetry and his profligate life-style the essence of Romanticism. *Hours of Idleness,* 1807; *English Bards and Scotch Reviewers,* 1809; *Childe Harold's Pilgrimage,* 1812, 1816, 1818; *The Siege of Corinth,* 1816; *Beppo,* 1818; *Don Juan,* 1819–24.

**CARROLL, LEWIS** (pseud. of Charles Lutwidge Dodgson), Jan. 27, 1832 (Daresbury, Cheshire, Eng. )–Jan. 14, 1898. English children's-book author, mathematician, photographer. Best known for the classic fantasies *Alice in Wonderland* (1865) and *Through the Looking Glass* (1872); a lecturer in mathematics, Oxford U., 1855–81; wrote several books on mathematical subjects. *The Hunting of the Snark, An Agony in Eight Fits,* 1876.

**CARTLAND, BARBARA,** July 9, 1904 (England). English novelist. Author of over 250 books, including over 170 romantic novels; her books have sold over 100 million copies.

**CARY,** (Arthur) **JOYCE,** Dec. 7, 1888 (Londonderry, Ire.)–Mar. 29, 1957. Anglo-Irish novelist. Wrote humorous English social history; the best known of his eccentric characters is Gully Jimson, a painter and likable scoundrel in *The Horse's Mouth* (1944). *Except the Lord,* 1953.

**CHAUCER, GEOFFREY,** c.1340 (London, Eng.)– Oct. 25, 1400. English poet. The greatest literary figure of medieval England; best known for *Canterbury Tales* (c.1387–1400), a 1700-line unfinished collection of stories, mostly in verse, told by pilgrims. *The Book of the Duchess,* 1369; *The House of Fame,* c.1380; *Troilus and Criseyde,* c.1385.

**CLELAND, JOHN,** 1709 (London, Eng.)–Jan. 23, 1789. English novelist. Author of *Fanny Hill; or,*

*Memoirs of a Woman of Pleasure* (1748–49), a classic of erotic literature that was suppressed many times.

**COLERIDGE, SAMUEL TAYLOR,** Oct. 21, 1772 (Devonshire, Eng.)–July 25, 1834. English poet, critic, essayist. Written jointly with WILLIAM WORDSWORTH in 1798, *Lyrical Ballads* (inc. Coleridge's "Rime of the Ancient Mariner") was a landmark of the Romantic movement; the philosophy of criticism expressed in his *Biographia Literia* (1817) had a profound impact on modern critical theory. "Kubla Khan," 1797–1816; "Christabel," 1797–1800.

**COLLINS, JACKIE,** (England). British novelist. Her risqué novels are generally best sellers. *The World Is Full of Married Men,* 1968; *The Bitch,* 1979; *Hollywood Husbands,* 1986. (Sister of JOAN COLLINS.)

**CONGREVE, WILLIAM,** Jan. 24, 1670 (Yorkshire, Eng.)–Jan. 19, 1729. English dramatist. A master of Restoration comedy. *The Old Bachelor,* 1693; *The Double Dealer,* 1694; *Love for Love,* 1695; *The Way of the World,* 1700.

**CONRAD, JOSEPH** (born Jozef Konrad Korzeniowski), Dec. 3, 1857 (Berdichev, Pol., now in Ukrainian SSR.) Aug. 3, 1924. British novelist, short story writer. A master of English prose. Served as seaman in French (1874–78) and British (1878–94) merchant marine. *The Nigger of the 'Narcissus',* 1897; *Lord Jim,* 1900; *Nostromo,* 1904; *The Secret Agent,* 1907.

**COWARD, SIR NOEL,** Dec. 16, 1899 (Teddington, Eng.)–Mar. 26, 1973. English playwright, actor, composer, director. Noted for sophisticated, witty comedies about the spoiled, snobbish rich. *Fallen Angels,* 1925; *Hay Fever,* 1925; *Private Lives,* 1930; *Design for Living,* 1932; *Blithe Spirit,* 1941.

**COWPER, WILLIAM,** Nov. 15, 1731 (Hertfordshire, Eng.)–Apr. 25, 1800. English poet. Foreshadowed Romanticism; best known for the poems that begin "O for a closer walk with God" and "God moves in a mysterious way" in *Olney Hymns* (1779), and for *The Task,* a long poem in blank verse extolling rural living.

**DAHL, ROALD,** Sept. 13, 1916 (Llandaff, Wales). British short-story and children's-book writer. Noted for macabre stories; children's books include *James and the Giant Peach* (1961) and *Charlie and the Chocolate Factory* (1964); *Matilda,* 1988.

**DEFOE** (or De Foe), **DANIEL,** (born Daniel Foe), c.1660 (London, Eng.)–Apr. 24, 1731. English journalist, novelist, pamphleteer. The father of modern journalism and, with Samuel Richardson, of the English novel; single-handedly wrote and published a journal of European affairs, 1704–13; at age 59 wrote his first novel, *Life and Strange Adventures of Robinson Crusoe* (1719). *Moll Flanders,* 1722; *A Journal of the Plague Year,* 1722.

**DE LA MARE, WALTER,** Apr. 25, 1873 (Kent, Eng.)–June, 22, 1956. English poet. The "poet of childhood," often wrote about nature, dreams, the supernatural. *Songs of Childhood,* 1902; *Peacock Pie,* 1913; *Memoirs of a Midget,* 1921; *Poems for Children,* 1930.

**DE QUINCY, THOMAS,** Aug. 15, 1785 (Manchester, Eng.)–Dec. 8, 1859. English essayist, critic. Established his reputation with *Confessions of An English Opium-Eater* (1822), a vivid account of the progress of the drug habit he had acquired at Oxford; his essays include "On Murder Considered as One of the Fine Arts" and "On the Knocking at the Gate in *Macbeth*."

**DICKENS, CHARLES,** Feb. 7, 1812 (Portsmouth, Eng.)–June 9, 1870. English novelist. Among the greatest, most prolific, and most popular English novelists; his works combine humor, pathos, and humanitarian purpose, have often been translated, dramatized, filmed and made into musicals. *Sketches by Boz,* 1836; *The Posthumous Papers of the Pickwick Club,* 1836–37; *Oliver Twist,* 1838; *Nicholas Nickleby,* 1838–39; *A Christmas Carol,* 1843; *David Copperfield,* 1850; *Bleak House,* 1853; *Little Dorritt,* 1857; *A Tale of Two Cities,* 1859; *Great Expectations,* 1861.

**DONNE, JOHN,** 1572 (London, Eng.) Mar. 31, 1631. English poet. The chief exponent of the "metaphysical" style in 17th-cent. English poetry; neglected until the 20th cent., when his works influenced W. B. YEATS, T. S. ELIOT, and W. H. AUDEN; best-known poems include "A Valediction," "Go and Catch a Falling Star," "Hymn to God the Father," and "Death Be Not Proud."

**DOWSON, ERNEST,** Aug. 2, 1867 (Lee, Kent, Eng.)–Feb. 23, 1900. English poet. One of the English decadents; his best-known poem is "Non Sum Qualis Eram Bonae sub Regno Cynarae" (in *Verses,* 1896), which has the refrain "I have been faithful to thee, Cynara! in my fashion." *Verses,* 1896; *The Pierrot of the Minute,* 1897.

**DRABBLE, MARGARET,** June 5, 1939 (Sheffield, Eng.). English novelist, critic. Noted for her novels about intelligent women. *The Garrick Year,* 1964; *The Millstone,* 1965; *The Needle's Eye,* 1972; *The Radiant Way,* 1987.

**DRYDEN, JOHN,** Aug. 9, 1613 (Northampton shire, Eng.)–May 1, 1700. English poet, dramatist, critic. The complete man of letters, noted particularly for his satiric verse; poet laureate of England, 1668–1700; based his blank-verse masterpiece, *All for Love* (1677), on SHAKESPEARE's *Antony and Cleopatra. The Conquest of Granada* (2-part drama), 1670–71; *Marriage a la Mode* (comedy), 1672; *Absalom and Achitophel* (2-part verse satire), 1681–82; *MacFlecknoe* (verse satire), 1682.

**DU MAURIER, DAPHNE,** May 13, 1907 (London, Eng.)–Apr. 19, 1989. English novelist. Known for best-selling suspense novels *Rebecca,* 1933; *My Cousin Rachel,* 1952; *The Birds,* 1963.

**DURRELL, LAWRENCE,** Feb. 27, 1912 (Darjeeling, India). Anglo-Irish novelist, poet, playwright, travel writer. Best known for *The Alexandria Quartet: Justine* (1957), *Balthazar* (1958), *Mountolive* (1958), *Clea* (1960).

**ELIOT, GEORGE** (pseud. of Mary Ann or Marian Evans), Nov. 22, 1819 (Warwickshire, Eng.) –Dec.

22, 1880. English novelist. The foremost woman novelist of her day who was to influence Thomas Hardy, Henry James, and D. H. Lawrence; wrote with humor and compassion about life in rural towns, stressing concern for moral development; her masterpiece was *Middlemarch* (1871–72). *Adam Bede*, 1859; *The Mill on the Floss*, 1860; *Silas Marner*, 1861.

**ELIOT,** T(homas) S(tearns), Sept. 26, 1888 (St. Louis, Mo.)–Jan. 4, 1965. U.S.-English poet, critic, playwright. A major figure in 20th-cent. literature; dwelled on the theme of emptiness of modern life, especially in *Prufrock and Other Observations* (1917), "Gerontion" (1919), *The Waste-Land* (1922), and *Ash Wednesday* (1930), *The Four Quartets* (1943); his plays, such as *Murder in the Cathedral* (1935) and *The Cocktail Party* (1950), were intended to revive verse drama; awarded Nobel Prize in literature, 1948.

**FARQUHAR, GEORGE,** 1678 (Londonderry, Ire.) –Apr. 29, 1707. English dramatist. His plays marked the transition between Restoration and 18th-cent. comedy. *The Recruiting Officer*, 1706; *The Beaux' Strategem*, 1707.

**FIELDING, HENRY,** Apr. 22, 1707 (nr. Glastonbury, Eng.)–Oct. 8, 1754. English novelist, playwright. One of the founders of the English novel, best known for *Tom Jones* (1749) and *Joseph Andrews* (1742), "comic epic-poems in prose" that depart radically from the sober works of Defoe and Richardson; a leading playwright of his day. *Tom Thumb*, (play) 1730.

**FLETCHER, JOHN,** Dec. 1579 (Sussex, Eng.)– Aug. 1625. English playwright who collaborated with FRANCIS BEAUMONT on a series of plays, including *Philaster, The Maid's Tragedy, A King and No King* (all 1607–13).

**FORD, FORD MADOX** (born Ford Madox Hueffer), Dec. 17, 1873 (Surrey, Eng.)–July 26, 1939. English novelist, essayist, critic. Best known for *The Good Soldier*, (1915) and a series of novels published as *Parade's End* (1950).

**FORD, JOHN,** Apr. 1586 (Devonshire, Eng.)–c. 1640. English dramatist. Considered by many the last of the Jacobeans; his passionate plays have noble characters, melodramatic plots. *'Tis Pity She's a Whore*, c.1627; *The Broken Heart*, c.1629; *Perkin Warbeck*, c.1633.

**FORESTER,** C(ecil) S(cott), Aug. 27, 1899 (Cairo, Egypt)–Apr. 2, 1966. English novelist. His 12-novel series about swashbuckling Captain Horatio Hornblower includes *The Happy Return* (1937) and *A Ship of the Line* (1939). *The African Queen*, 1935.

**FORSTER,** E(dward) M(organ), Jan. 1, 1879 (London, Eng.)–June 7, 1970. English novelist, critic. Best known for *A Passage to India* (1924), a novel about conflicts between British colonists and native Indians; also wrote novels of manners about the British middle class. *Where Angels Fear to Tread*, 1905; *A Room with a View*, 1908; *Maurice*, 1923; *Aspects of the Novel* (criticism), 1927.

**FOWLES, JOHN,** Mar. 31, 1926 (Essex, Eng.). English novelist. *The Collector*, 1963; *The Magus*,

1966 (revised edition, 1978); *The French Lieutenant's Woman*, 1969; *The Ebony Tower*, 1974; *Daniel Martin*, 1977; *Mantissa*, 1982.

**FRY, CHRISTOPHER** (born Christopher Harris), Dec. 18, 1907 (Bristol, Eng.). English dramatist. Author of witty verse plays and religious dramas. *The Lady's Not for Burning*, 1948; *Venus Observed*, 1950; *A Sleep of Prisoners*, 1951. Translated JEAN GIRAUDOUX's *Tiger at the Gates* (1955) and JEAN ANOUILH's *Ring Round the Moon* (1950).

**GALSWORTHY, JOHN,** Aug. 14, 1867 (Surrey, Eng.)– Jan. 31, 1933. English novelist, dramatist. Best known for three trilogies about a late Victorian man of property, Soames Forsyte: *The Forsyte Saga* (1922), *A Modern Comedy* (1928), and *End of the Chapter* (1934); wrote dramas about social problems; awarded Nobel Prize in literature, 1932. *Silver Box*, 1909; *Strife*, 1909; *Justice*, 1910.

**GASKELL, ELIZABETH,** Sept. 29, 1810 (London, Eng.)–Nov. 12, 1865. English novelist. Wrote about English country life and the problems of the working class; first biographer of CHARLOTTE BRONTË (1857). *Mary Barton*, 1848; *Cranford*, 1853; *Ruth*, 1853; *North and South*, 1855.

**GAY, JOHN,** c. Sept. 16, 1685 (Barnstable, Eng.)– Dec. 4, 1732. English playwright, poet. His play *The Beggar's Opera* (1728), a satire on SIR ROBERT WALPOLE and the court of George II, provided the basis for BERTOLT BRECHT and KURT WEILL's *Threepenny Opera*.

**GILBERT, SIR WILLIAM S.,** Nov. 18, 1836 (London, Eng.)–May 29, 1911. English dramatist. Collaborated with composer SIR ARTHUR SULLIVAN on 14 comic operas; wrote satirical lyrics that poked fun at English society. *Trial by Jury*, 1875; *H.M.S. Pinafore*, 1878; *The Pirates of Penzance*, 1880; *The Mikado*, 1885; *Yeoman of the Guard*, 1888; *The Gondoliers*, 1889.

**GOLDING, WILLIAM,** Sept. 19, 1911 (Cornwall, Eng.). English novelist. Best known for his allegorical novel *Lord of the Flies* (1954); awarded Nobel Prize in literature, 1983. *Pincher Martin*, 1956; *The Spire*, 1964; *Rites of Passage*, 1980.

**GOLDSMITH, OLIVER,** Nov. 10, 1730? (Ireland) –Apr. 4, 1774. Anglo-Irish essayist, poet, novelist, dramatist. His realistic works are characterized by a lively, humorous style. *The Vicar of Wakefield* (novel), 1766; *The Deserted Village* (poem), 1770; *She Stoops to Conquer* (play), 1773.

**GRAHAME, KENNETH,** Mar. 8, 1859 (Edinburgh, Scot.)–July 6, 1932. English writer of children's books. Best known for the classic *The Wind in the Willows* (1908), about the adventures of Toad, Ratty, Badger, and Mole.

**GRAVES, ROBERT,** July 26, 1895 (London, Eng.) –Dec. 7, 1985. English poet, novelist, critic. *Goodbye to All That* (autobiographical novel), 1929; *I, Claudius* (historical novel), 1934; *The White Goddess* (criticism), 1947; *Poems About Love*, 1968.

**GRAY, THOMAS,** Dec. 26, 1716 (London, Eng.)– July 30, 1771. English poet. Best known poet of his time, for his charming neoclassical light verse and melancholy lyrics and odes; refused position of poet laureate in favor of a life of scholarship at Cambridge; "Elegy Written in a Country Churchyard" (1751) is his most famous poem.

GREENE, GRAHAM, Oct. 2, 1904 (Hertfordshire, Eng.). English novelist, short-story writer, playwright. Noted both for "entertainments' and serious novels, which often are set in exotic locations and usually hinge on profound moral crises. *The Power and the Glory*, 1940; *The Heart of the Matter*, 1948; *The Third Man*, 1949; *The Quiet American*, 1955; *Our Man in Havana*, 1958; *The Comedians*, 1966; *The Human Factor*, 1978.

GREGORY, LADY ISABELLA AUGUSTA, Mar. 15, 1852 (Roxborough, Ire.)–May 22, 1932. Irish playwright. A major figure in the Irish literary renaissance; dir. of the Irish National Theatre (later the Abbey Theatre), for which she wrote one-act plays; collected and translated Celtic folk tales. *The Rising of the Moon*, (play), 1907; *Our Irish Theatre*, (nonfiction), 1914.

HARDY, THOMAS, June 2, 1840 (Dorset, Eng.)–Jan. 11, 1928. English novelist, poet. Influential lyric poet (seven vols. 1898–1928). Best known for his pessimistic, powerful novels portraying rural life in fictional "Wessex." *Far From the Madding Crowd*, 1874; *The Return of the Native*, 1878; *Tess of the D'Urbervilles*, 1891; *Jude the Obscure*, 1896.

HARRIS, FRANK, Feb. 14, 1856 (Galway, Ire.)–Aug. 26, 1931. British U.S. editor, journalist, biographer, novelist; noted for his scandalous autobiography, *My Life and Loves* (3 vols., 1923–27), banned in England and the U.S.; also wrote biographies, including *The Man Shakespeare* (1908), and *Oscar Wilde, His Life and Confessions* (1916).

HERBERT, GEORGE, April 3, 1539 (North Wales)–March 3, 1633. British metaphysical poet. "Easter Wings," 1633; *A Priest to the Temple*, 1652.

HERRICK, ROBERT, 1591 (London, Eng.)–Oct. 1674. English poet. Major Cavalier poet noted for his simple, sensuous, graceful poems, including "Gather Ye Rosebuds While Ye May," and "Delight in Disorder." *Hesperides*, 1648.

HERRIOT, JAMES, Mar. 10, 1916 (Glasgow, Scot.). Scottish veterinarian, author. Author of best-selling books about the life of a rural Scottish veterinarian. *All Creatures Great and Small*, 1972; *All Things Wise and Wonderful*, 1977; *The Lord God Made Them All*, 1981.

HILTON, JAMES, Sept. 9, 1900 (Leigh, Eng.)–Dec. 20, 1954. English novelist. *Lost Horizon*, 1933; *Goodbye, Mr. Chips*, 1934; *Random Harvest*, 1941.

HOPKINS, GERARD MANLEY, July 28, 1844 (Stratford, Eng.)–June 8, 1889. English lyric poet. The highly original poetry of this Jesuit priest is characterized by alliteration, puns, internal rhymes, "sprung rhythm"; first published 30 years after his death; noted poems include "The Windhover," "Pied Beauty," "Carrion Comfort," and "God's Grandeur."

HOUSMAN, A(lfred) E(dward), March 26, 1859 (Fockbury, Worcestershire, Eng.)–Apr. 30, 1936. English poet. His volume of poetry *A Shropshire Lad* (1896) was an influential reaction against Victorianism; an outstanding classical scholar. *Last Poems*, 1922; *More Poems*, 1936; *Collected Poems*, 1939.

HUGHES, TED, Aug. 16, 1930 (Mytholmroyd, Yorkshire, Eng.). English poet. His verse is characterized by violent images, controlled diction and style; poet laureate, 1984– . *The Hawk in the Rain*, 1957; *Lupercal*, 1960; *Crow. From the Life and Songs of the Crow*, 1971. (Husband of S. PLATH.)

HUGHES, THOMAS, Oct. 18, 1822 (Berkshire, Eng.)–Mar. 22, 1896. English reformer, author. Best known as the author of *Tom Brown's School Days* (1857) and *Tom Brown at Oxford* (1861).

HUXLEY, ALDOUS, July 26, 1894 (Godalming, Surrey, Eng.)–Nov. 22, 1963. English novelist, essayist. His early novels were witty satires on contemporary life; later novels reflected his interest in drugs, mysticism, and the occult. *Antic Hay*, 1923; *Point Counter Point*, 1928; *Brave New World*, 1932; *Eyeless in Gaza*, 1936; *The Doors of Perception*, 1954.

ISHERWOOD, CHRISTOPHER, Aug. 26, 1904 (High Lane, Cheshire, Eng.)–Jan. 4, 1986. English novelist, playwright. In early novels, wrote about the social disintegration in Berlin during the rise of Nazism; *Good-bye to Berlin* (1939) was dramatized by John Van Druten as *I Am a Camera* (1951) and as the musical *Cabaret* (1966); coauthored verse dramas with W. H. AUDEN. *A Meeting by the River*, 1967; *Kathleen and Frank* (memoir), 1971.

JOHNSON, SAMUEL, Sept. 18, 1709 (Lichfield, Staffordshire, Eng.)–Dec. 13, 1784. English poet, critic, essayist, journalist, lexicographer. An outstanding literary figure of his time, best-known works include his pioneering *Dictionary of the English Language* (1755), his edition of Shakespeare's works, and his 10 volume *Lives of the Poets* (1779–81). "The Vanity of Human Wishes" (satirical poem), 1749; *The Rambler*, 1750–52; *The Idler*, 1758–60; *Rasselas, Prince of Abyssinia*, 1759.

JONSON, BEN, probably June 11, 1572 (London, Eng.)–Aug. 6, 1637. English dramatist, poet, critic. Best known for his four masterpieces of dramatic satire; *Volpone* (1606), *Epicoene* (1609), *The Alchemist* (1610), and *Bartholomew Fair* (1614); his most famous poems include "Drink to me only with thine eyes" and "Come, my Celia, let us prove" (both in *The Forrest*, 1616).

JOYCE, JAMES, Feb. 2, 1882 (Dublin, Ire.)–Jan. 13, 1941. Irish novelist, lyric poet, playwright. One of the foremost writers of the 20th cent.; his novels are characterized by subtle, frank portraits of human nature and the original and varied style; his masterpiece, *Ulysses* (1922), notable for its complex design and combination of realism and stream of consciousness, was banned as obscene in the U.S. until 1933. *Dubliners* (short stories), 1914; *A Portrait of the Artist As a Young Man*, (1914); *Finnegans Wake*, 1939.

KEATS, JOHN, Oct. 31, 1795 (London, Eng.)–Feb.

23, 1821. English poet. One of the foremost English Romantic poets; although he died of tuberculosis at age 25, left a large and mature body of work; most famous poems include the odes "To Psyche," "On Melancholy," "To a Nightingale," "Ode On a Grecian Urn," and "To Autumn"; the ballad "La Belle Dame Sans Merci"; and the narrative poems "Lamia," and "The Eve of St. Agnes," virtually all written 1816–1819.

KIPLING, RUDYARD, Dec. 30, 1865 (Bombay, India)–Jan. 18, 1936. English poet, novelist, short-story and children's-book writer. Wrote many works about India; later accused of imperialism and racism; besk-known poems include "The White Man's Burden," "Mandalay," "Gunga Din," and "If"; won England's first Nobel Prize in literature, 1907; refused laureateship. *The Jungle Book*, 1894; *Captains Courageous*, 1897; *Kim*, 1901; *Just So Stories*, 1902.

KYD, THOMAS, Nov. 5, 1558 (London, Eng.)–Dec. 1594. English dramatist. With Christopher Marlowe, the father of English tragedy. *The Spanish Tragedy* (c.1592) was the first "revenge tragedy," and perhaps the most popular play of its time.

LAMB, CHARLES, Feb. 10, 1775 (London, Eng.)–Dec. 27, 1834. English essayist. One of the masters of the essay, best known for *Essays of Elia* (1823), including "A Dissertation on Roast Pig"; his critical essays helped revive Elizabethan drama; with his sister Mary Ann Lamb, wrote a popular children's book, *Tales from Shakespeare* (1807).

LANGLAND, WILLIAM, c.1330 (probably Ledbury, Shropshire, Eng.)–c.1400. English poet. According to conjecture, wrote at least two of the three versions of *The Vision of William Concerning Piers Plowman*, one of the greatest pre-Chaucerian English verse narratives.

LARKIN, PHILIP, Aug. 9, 1922 (Coventry, Eng.). English poet, novelist, editor. Led the post-WW II antiromantic movement. *The Less Deceived*, 1955; *The Whitsun Weddings*, 1964; *High Window*, 1974.

LAWRENCE, D(avid) H(erbert), Sept. 11, 1885 (Eastwood, Nottinghamshire, Eng.)–Mar. 2, 1930. English novelist, short-story writer, poet. His works reflected his radical individualism and interest in the natural, primitive, and mystical; his controversial novel *Lady Chatterley's Lover* (1928, unexpurgated ed. 1959) was banned in England and the U.S. *Sons and Lovers*, 1913; *The Rainbow*, 1915; *Women in Love*, 1920.

LESSING, DORIS, Oct. 22, 1919 (Kermanshah, Iran). British novelist, short-story writer. Raised in Southern Rhodesia [now Zimbabwe], about which she wrote her first novel; her works are marked by strong interest in social issues; best known for *The Golden Notebook* (1962), a complex examination of the lives of "free women." *The Grass is Singing*, 1950; *Briefing for a Descent into Hell*, 1971; *The Summer before the Dark*, 1973.

LEWIS, C(live) S(taples), Nov. 29, 1898 (Belfast, Ire.)–Nov. 22, 1963. English novelist, critic, scholar. Wrote Christian apologetics (*The Screwtape Letters*, 1942), a series of fantasies for children (*The Chronicles of Narnia*, 1954–1962), science fiction novels (*Out of the Silent Planet*, 1983), and scholarly works (*The Discarded Image: An Introduction to Medieval and Renaissance Literature*, 1964).

LEWIS, MATTHEW GREGORY ("MONK"), July 9, 1775 (London, England)–May 14, 1818. British novelist and dramatist and collaborator with SIR WALTER SCOTT and Robert Southey. *Ambrosio, or The Monk*, 1795; *Tales of Wonder*, 1891.

LEWIS, (Percy) WYNDHAM, Nov. 18, 1882 (at sea in the Bay of Fundy, off Maine)–Mar. 7, 1957. English novelist, essayist, artist. Chiefly known for his satiric novels (esp. *The Apes of God*, 1930) and political and literary essays (*The Art of Being Ruled*, 1926; *Men Without Art*, 1934); a leader in the vorticist movement; edited *Blast*, 1914–15, the vorticist magazine, with EZRA POUND.

LLEWELLYN, RICHARD (pseud. of Richard Lloyd), Dec. 8, 1906 (St. David's, Pembrokeshire, Wales)–Nov. 30, 1983. Welsh novelist. *How Green Was My Valley*, 1939; *None But the Lonely Heart*, 1943.

LOVELACE, RICHARD, 1618? (Woolwich, Kent, Eng.)–1656 or 1657. English poet. A Cavalier poet noted chiefly for two poems, "To Althea, from Prison" ("Stone walls do not a prison make/ Nor iron bars a cage..."; 1642) and "To Lucasta, Going to the Wars" ("I could not love thee dear, so much/ Loved I not honor more..."; 1649).

LOWRY, (Clarence) MALCOLM, July 28, 1909 (Merseyside, Cheshire, Eng.)–June 27, 1957. English novelist. Noted for one book, the autobiographical novel *Under the Volcano* (1947); his other works, published posthumously, include *Selected Poems* (1963) and a collection of stories, *Hear Us O Lord in Heaven thy Dwelling Place* (1961).

MACDIARMID, HUGH (pseud. of Christopher Murray Grieve), Aug. 11, 1892 (Langholm, Dumfriershire, Scot.)–Sept. 9, 1978. Scottish poet, critic. The most important Scottish poet of the 20th century, and a leader of the Scottish literary renaissance; founded the Scottish Nationalist Party. *A Drunk Man Looks at the Thistle*, 1926; *To Circumjack Cencrastus*, 1930; *A Kist of Whistles*, 1947.

MALORY, SIR THOMAS, d.1470 or 1471. English writer. Identity uncertain, widely believed to be the Sir Thomas Malory of Newbold Revell, Warwickshire, who represented Warwickshire in Parliament (1445), then pleaded not guilty but was jailed eight times for assault, church plundering, extortion, and other crimes; wrote *Morte Darthur* (1485), the first English prose collection of Arthurian fables, and one of the great works of English literature.

MANSFIELD, KATHERINE (pseud. of Kathleen Mansfield Beauchamp), Oct. 14, 1888 (Wellington, N.Z.)–Jan. 12, 1923. British short-story writer. A master of the short story, whose works strongly influenced modern fiction. *In a German Pension*, 1911; *Bliss and Other Stories*, 1920; *The Garden Party*, 1922; *The Dove's Nest*, 1923.

MARLOW, CHRISTOPHER, Feb. 26, 1564 (Canterbury, Kent, Eng.)–May 30, 1593. English dramatist, poet. First great English dramatist; introduced into drama the probing of a hero's inner conflicts; established blank verse in drama. *Tamburlaine the Great*, 1587; *The Tragical History of Dr. Faustus*, 1604; *The Famous Tragedy of the Rich Jew of Malta*, 1633; *The Troublesome Raigne and Lamentable Death of Edward the Second, King of England*, 1594.

MARVELL, ANDREW, Mar. 31, 1621 (Winstead, Yorkshire, Eng.)–Aug. 18, 1678. English poet, pamphleteer, politician. Metaphysical poet best known for his brilliant early lyric verse, notably "The Garden" (1681), "The Definition of Love" (1681), "To His Coy Mistress" (1650), and "An Horatian Ode upon Cromwell's Return from Ireland" (1650).

MASEFIELD, JOHN, June 1, 1878 (Ledbury, Herefordshire, Eng.)–May 12, 1967. English poet. Best known for his poems about the sea (e.g., *Salt Water Ballads*, 1902) and his long narrative poems (*The Everlasting Mercy*, 1911); poet laureate of England, 1930–67. *Dauber*, 1913; *Reynard the Fox*, 1919.

MAUGHAM W(illiam) SOMERSET, Jan. 25, 1874 (Paris, Fr.)–Dec. 16, 1965. English novelist, short-story writer, playwright. An expert storyteller whose works, many of them set in exotic locales, were immensely popular. *Of Human Bondage*, 1915; *The Moon and Sixpence*, 1919; *The Constant Wife*, 1927; *Cakes and Ale*, 1930; *The Razor's Edge*, 1944.

MEREDITH, GEORGE, Feb. 12, 1828 (Hampshire, Eng.)–May 18, 1909. English novelist, poet. Best known for his first novel, *The Ordeal of Richard Feverel*, 1859; *The Egoist*, 1879; *Diana of the Crossways*, 1885.

MILNE, A(lan) A(lexander), Jan. 18, 1882 (London, Eng.)–Jan. 31, 1956. English humorist, children's-book author. Created Christopher Robin, Winnie-the-Pooh, Piglet, Kanga, Roo, and Eeyore, whose adventures have become classics. *When We Were Very Young*, 1924; *Winnie-the-Pooh*, 1926; *Now We Are Six*, 1927; *The House at Pooh Corner*, 1928.

MILTON, JOHN, Dec. 9, 1608 (London, Eng.)–Nov. 8, 1674. English poet, essayist. Among the greatest figures in English literature; his masterpiece, *Paradise Lost* (1667, 1674), is considered by some to be the greatest English-language epic poem; also wrote English and Italian sonnets, political pamphlets; on becoming totally blind, worked through secretaries, including ANDREW MARVELL. "On the Morning of Christ's Nativity," 1629; *Comus*, 1634; *Areopagitica*, 1644; *Paradise Regained*, 1671; *Samson Agonistes*, 1671.

MITFORD, NANCY, Nov. 28, 1904 (London, Eng.)–June 30, 1973. English novelist, biographer, editor. Noted for witty novels about upper-class British life; biographies of VOLTAIRE, MME. DE POMPADOUR, and LOUIS XIV; coedited *Noblesse Oblige* (1956), essays contrasting the language and behavior of the upper ("U") and non-upper ("non-U") classes. *Love in a Cold Climate*, 1949.

MORE, BRIAN, Aug. 25, 1921 (Belfast, Ire.). Irish-U.S.-Canadian novelist. Best known for his first novel, *The Lonely Passion of Judith Hearne* (1955). *The Luck of Ginger Coffey*, 1960; *The Emperor of Ice Cream*, 1965.

MOORE, GEORGE, Feb. 24, 1852 (Ballyglass, County Mayo, Ire.)–Jan. 21, 1933. Irish novelist. A figure in the Irish literary revival. *Esther Waters*, 1894; *Hail and Farewell* (3-vol. novel, purportedly autobiography), 1911, 1912, 1914.

MURDOCH, (Jean) IRIS, July 15, 1919 (Dublin, Ire.). British novelist, university lecturer. Noted for her intelligent, witty novels; 1948–1963, fellow and tutor in philosophy at Oxford U. *Under the Net*, 1954; *The Flight from the Enchanter*, 1956; *A Severed Head*, 1961; *The Nice and the Good*, 1968; *The Black Prince*, 1973; *Henry and Cato*, 1976.

O'BRIEN, EDNA, Dec. 15, 1930 (County Clare, Ire.). Irish novelist and short-story writer. Known for a trilogy of novels about the lives of two Irish women: *The Country Girls* (1960), *The Lonely Girl* (1962), and *Girls in Their Married Bliss* (1964), and for short stories, collected in *A Rose in the Heart*.

O'CASEY, SEAN (born John Casey), Mar. 30, 1880 (Dublin, Ire.)–Sept. 18, 1964. Irish dramatist, a major figure in the modern theater. Best known for plays he wrote for Dublin's Abbey Theatre, including *Juno and the Paycock* (1924) and *The Plough and the Stars* (1926)—realistic, tragicomic works set in Dublin's slums.

O'CONNOR, FRANK (pseud. for Michael O'Donovan), 1903 (Cork, Ire.)–Mar. 10, 1966. A master of the modern short story, for realistic vignettes of everyday Irish life. *Guests of the Nation* (1931), *Crab Apple Jelly* (1944), *Domestic Relations* (1957); autobiographies: *An Only Child*, 1961; *My Father's Son*, 1969.

O'FAOLÁIN, SEAN (born Sean Whelan), Feb. 22, 1900 (Cork, Ire.). Irish short-story writer, novelist, essayist, biographer. A short-story master. *Midsummer Night Madness and Other Stories*, 1932; *A Nest of Simple Folk* (novel), 1933; *A Life of Daniel O'Connell*, 1938; *Vive moi!* (autobiography), 1964.

O'FLAHERTY, LIAM, 1896 (Aran Is., Ire.). Irish novelist, short-story writer. Best known for his realistic novel *The Informer* (1925), adapted by JOHN FORD into an Academy Award-winning film (1935); and for poetic short stories, inc. *The Wild Swan and Other Stories* (1932).

ORTON, JOE (born John Kingsley Orton), Jan. 1, 1933 (Leicester, Eng.)–Aug. 9, 1967. English playwright. Wrote black comedies, combining murder, sexual perversion, and blackmail with genteel, epigrammatic dialogue. *Entertaining Mr. Sloane*, 1964; *Loot*, 1966; *What the Butler Saw*, 1969.

ORWELL, GEORGE (pseud. of Eric Arthur Blair), June 23, 1903 (Motihari, India)–Jan. 21, 1950. English novelist, essayist, critic. Best known for his satrical novels *Animal Farm* (1945) and *Nineteen Eighty-Four* (1949), about the dangers of totalitarianism. *Down and Out in Paris and London*, 1933; *The Road to Wigan Pier*, 1937; *Homage to Catalonia*, 1938.

**OSBORNE, JOHN,** Dec. 12, 1929 (London, Eng.). British playwright, screenwriter. Leader of the "Angry Young Men" of the British theater in the 1950s and 1960s. Plays: *Look Back in Anger*, 1956; *The Entertainer*, 1957; *Luther*, 1961 (Tony Award, 1963); *Inadmissable Evidence*, 1964. Films: *Tom Jones*, 1964.

**OWEN, WILFRED,** Mar. 18, 1893 (Owestry, Shropshire, Eng.)–Nov. 4, 1918. English poet. An antiwar poet, killed in action a week before the end of WW I; *Poems* (1920) was published posthumously by his friend SIEGFRIED SASSOON.

**PEPYS, SAMUEL,** Feb. 23, 1633 (London, Eng.)–May 26, 1703. English dramatist. A secy. to the admiralty, he kept the most famous diary in the English language; first published in 1825, the diary gives a brilliant description of early Restoration life.

**PINERO, SIR ARTHUR WING,** May 24, 1855 (London, Eng.)–Nov. 23, 1934. English playwright. Noted for "well-made" problem plays, inc. *The Second Mrs. Tanqueray*, 1889; farces; and light comedies, inc. *Trelawny of the Wells*, 1898.

**PINTER, HAROLD,** Oct. 10, 1930 (London, Eng.). English playwright, screenwriter. His "comedies of menace" feature ordinary characters in an atmosphere of mystery and horror, along with understated and ambiguous dialogue, and long silences; wrote screenplays for the films *The Servant* (1962), *Accident* (1967), and *The Go-Between* (1971). *The Caretaker*, 1960; *The Homecoming*, 1965.

**POPE, ALEXANDER,** May 21, 1688 (London, Eng.)–May 30, 1744. English poet. With Jonathan Swift, one of the major satirists of the Augustan age. *Essay on Criticism*, 1711; *The Rape of the Lock*, 1714; *The Dunciad*, 1728–43; *An Essay on Man*, 1743.

**POTTER, (Helen) BEATRIX,** July 6, 1866 (So. Kensington, Middlesex, Eng.)–Dec. 22, 1943. English children's book author/illustrator. Her animal stories, illustrated with watercolors based on realistic nature studies, have become children's classics. Best known for *The Tale of Peter Rabbit*, 1902. *The Tailor of Gloucester*, 1903; *The Tale of Squirrel Nutkin*, 1903; *The Tale of Mrs. Tiggy-Winkle*, 1905.

**PRIESTLEY, J(ohn) B(oynton),** Sept. 13, 1894 (Bradford, Yorkshire, Eng.). English novelist, dramatist, essayist. A versatile and prolific author, also known for patriotic radio broadcasts during WW II. *The Good Companions*, (comic novel), 1929; plays: *Dangerous Corner*, 1932, *When We Are Married*, 1938.

**RATTIGAN, SIR TERENCE MERVYN,** June 10, 1911 (London, Eng.). English playwright. Best known for dramas with social or psychological themes. Knighted, 1971. *O Mistress Mine*, 1945; *The Winslow Boy*, 1947; *Separate Tables*, 1954.

**READE, CHARLES,** June 8, 1814 (Oxfordshire, Eng.)–Apr. 11, 1884. English novelist. Noted for historical romance esp. *The Cloister and the Hearth* (1861); and for novels that exposed social injustice e.g., *It Is Never Too Late to Mend*, 1856.

**RENAULT, MARY** (pseud. of Mary Challans), Sept. 4, 1905 (London, Eng.)–Dec. 13, 1983. English novelist. Author of popular historical novels of the ancient world. *The Last of the Wine*, 1956; *The King Must Die*, 1958; *The Mask of Apollo*, 1966; *The Persian Boy*, 1977.

**RHYS, JEAN,** 1894 (Dominica, W. Indies)–May 15, 1979. English novelist. Her early works about bohemian life in Europe in the 1920s and 1930s were rediscovered by feminists in the 1970s. *After Leaving Mr. MacKenzie*, 1931; *Good Morning, Midnight*, 1939; *Tigers Are Better Looking*, 1965; *Wide Sargasso Sea*, 1966.

**RICHARDSON, SAMUEL,** July 31, 1689 (Mackworth, Derbyshire, Eng.)–July 4, 1761. English novelist. Author of *Pamela: or, Virtue Unrewarded* (1740–41), often called the first modern English novel. *Clarissa; or, The History of a Young Lady*, 1747–48; *The History of Sir Charles Grandison*, 1753–54.

**ROSSETTI, DANTE GABRIEL,** May 12, 1828 (London, Eng.)–Apr. 9, 1882. English poet, painter. A leader of the Pre-Raphaelite Brotherhood, which romanticized the Middle Ages. "The Blessed Damzel," 1850; "Sister Helen," 1870; "The House of Life," 1881.

**RUSHDIE, SALMAN,** June 19, 1947 (Bombay, India). British novelist. His novel, *Satanic Verses* (1989) so enraged the Ayatollah Ruhollah Khomeini of Iran, because of its alleged anti-Moslem sentiments, that he urged Moslems around the world to kill the author; Rushdie was forced to go into hiding. *Grimus*, 1975; *Midnight's Children*, 1981.

**RUSKIN, JOHN,** Feb. 8, 1819 (London, Eng.)–Jan. 20, 1900. English writer. Influential art critic of Victorian England, who championed the landscape painter J.M.W. Turner; also wrote about social problems. *Modern Painters*, 5 vols., 1843–60; *The Seven Lamps of Architecture*, 1849; *The Stones of Venice*, 3 vols., 1851–53; *Fors Clavigera: Letters to the Workmen and Laborers of Great Britain*, 1871–84.

**SACKVILLE, THOMAS, 1ST EARL OF DORSET, BARON BUCKHURST,** 1536 (Sussex, Eng.)–Apr. 19, 1608. English statesman, poet, dramatist. With others, wrote *Gorboduc* (1561), a blank-verse drama generally considered the first English tragedy; his "Induction" has been called the greatest English poem between "Canterbury Tales" and "Faerie Queen."

**SAKI** (pseud. of H(ector) H(ugh) Munro), Dec. 18, 1870 (Akyab, Burma)–Nov. 14, 1916. British short-story writer, journalist. Noted for his fantastic, witty stories about the Edwardian social scene. *Not So Stories*, 1902; *Reginald*, 1904; *Reginald in Russia*, 1910; *The Chronicles of Clovis*, 1911; *Beasts and Super-Beasts*, 1914.

**SASSOON, SIEGFRIED,** Sept. 8, 1886 (Brenchley,

Kent, Eng.)–Sept. 1, 1967. English poet, novelist. Wrote grim, realistic antiwar poetry (*The Old Huntsman*, 1917; *Counterattack*, 1918); and fictionalized autobiographies (*The Complete Memoris of George Sherston*, 1937).

**SCOTT, SIR WALTER,** Aug. 15, 1771 (Edinburgh, Scot.)–Sept. 21, 1832. Scottish novelist, poet. Popular and influential, as the father of the historical novel; also wrote romances of Scottish life; in his narrative poems, introduced the popular form of the verse tale; made baronet, 1820. *Waverly, 1814; The Heart of Midlothian, 1818; The Bride of Lammermoor, 1819; Ivanhoe, 1820; The Fortunes of Nigel, 1822.*

**SHAFFER, PETER,** May 15, 1926 (London, Eng.). English playwright. Noted for his wide range. *Five-Finger Exercise, 1958; The Private Ear and the Public Eye, 1962; The Royal Hunt of the Sun, 1964; Black Comedy, 1965; Equus, 1973; Amadeus, 1979.*

**SHAKESPEARE, WILLIAM,** baptized Apr. 26, 1564 (Stratford on Avon, Eng.)–Apr. 23, 1616. English dramatist, poet. Widely considered the greatest writer in any language, of any time; has had a profound influence on English speech; his plays have been performed almost continuously to this day; wrote comedies, histories, tragedies, as well as 154 sonnets and two heroic narratives. Comedies include; *The Comedy of Errors, 1592/93; The Taming of the Shrew, 1593/94; The Two Gentlemen of Verona, 1594/95; Midsummer Night's Dream, 1595/96; The Merchant of Venice, 1596/97; Twelfth Night, 1601/02; The Tempest, 1611/12.* Tragedies include: *Romeo and Juliet, 1594/95; Julius Caesar, 1599/1600; Hamlet, 1600/01; Othello, 1604/05; King Lear, 1605/06; Macbeth, 1605/06; Antony and Cleopatra, 1606/07; Coriolanus, 1607/08.* Histories include 1 and 2 *Henry IV, 1597–98; Richard II, 1595; Richard III, 1592–93; Henry VI 1590–92.*

**SHAW, GEORGE BERNARD,** July 26, 1856 (Dublin, Ire.)–Nov. 2, 1950. British playwright, critic. Major British dramatist; wrote "dramas of ideas" that reflected his passion for social reform; his plays are noted for their memorable characters, brilliant language and wit; journalist; political pamphleteer; a leader in the socialist Fabian Soc.; a music and drama critic, refused Nobel Prize in literature, 1925. *Candida, 1894; Caesar and Cleopatra, 1898; Man and Superman, 1905; Major Barbara, 1905; Androcles and the Lion, 1912; Pygmalion, 1913; Saint Joan, 1923.*

**SHELLEY, PERCY BYSSHE,** Aug. 4, 1792 (Field Place, Sussex, Eng.)–July 8, 1822. English poet. The archetype of the Romantic idealist; his best verse is noted for grandeur, beauty, mastery of language, and influence on social and political thought; led a tempestuous, highly unconventional life. *Queen Mab, 1813; Hymn to Intellectual Beauty, 1816; Prometheus Unbound, 1820; Epipsychidion, 1821; Adonais, 1821.* (Husband of M. W. SHELLEY.)

**SHERIDAN, RICHARD BRINSLEY,** baptized Nov. 4, 1751 (Dublin, Ire.)–July 7, 1816. Irish playwright, politician. Noted for his comedies of manners, which combined Restoration wit with 18th cent. sensibility; *The Rivals* (1775) is notable for the character Mrs. Malaprop. *The School for Scandal, 1777; The Critic, 1779.*

**SIDNEY, SIR PHILIP,** Nov. 30, 1554 (Penshurst, Kent, Eng.)–Oct. 17, 1586. English poet, statesman, soldier. A model of the Renaissance gentleman; an influential patron, critic and poet; *Arcadia* (1590) is the earliest known pastoral in English; *Astrophel and Stella* (1591) began the vogue for the sonnet sequence; knighted, 1583. *The Defense of Poesie, 1595; An Apology for Poetry, 1595.*

**SILLITOE, ALAN,** Mar. 4, 1928 (Nottingham, Eng.). English fiction writer, poet. Noted for his angry accounts of working-class life in the novel *Saturday Night and Sunday Morning*, 1958, and the short-story collection, *The Loneliness of the Long Distance Runner*, 1959.

**SITWELL, DAME EDITH,** Sept. 7, 1887 (Scarborough, Yorkshire, Eng.)–Dec. 9, 1964. English poet, prose writer. With her brothers, Osbert and Sacheverell, a member of a celebrated literary family; turned from early frivolous verse to religious poetry; known for her eccentricity and wit. *Clowns' Houses, 1918; Facade, 1923; A Poet's Notebook, 1943; Gardeners and Astronomers, 1953.*

**SMOLLETT, TOBIAS,** baptized Mar. 19, 1721 (Cardross, Dumbarton, Scot.)–Sept. 17, 1771. Scottish novelist. The father of the satirical novel. Rich in comic characters, his works give a panoramic view of his times. *Roderick Random, 1748; Peregrine Pickle, 1751; Sir Lancelot Greaves, 1760–62; Humphey Clinker, 1771.*

**SNOW, C(harles) P(ercy), BARON,** Oct. 15, 1905 (Leicester, Eng.)–July 1, 1980. English novelist, scientist, government administrator. Best known for his controversial *The Two Cultures and the Scientific Revolution* (1959), about the breach between the scientific and literary communities, and for his 11-volume novel series, *Strangers and Brothers* (1940–70); knighted, 1957; made a life peer, 1964.

**SPARK, MURIEL,** 1918 (Edinburgh, Scot.). Scottish novelist, critic, poet. Best known for her novel *The Prime of Miss Jean Brodie* (1961). *Memento Mori, 1959; Collected Poems I, 1967.*

**SPENDER, STEPHEN,** Feb. 28, 1909 (London, Eng.). English poet, critic. In 1930s wrote poetry of social protest; his poetry became increasingly autobiographical; since 1940s, he had concentrated on criticism and editing influential reviews, including *Horizon* (1939–41) and *Encounter* (1953–67). *Twenty Poems, 1930; The Destructive Element, 1935; The Creative Element, 1953; The Making of a Poem, 1955; The Struggle of the Modern, 1963.*

**SPENSER, EDMUND,** 1552/53 (London, Eng.)–Jan. 13, 1599. English poet. Best known for his unfinished masterpiece, *The Faerie Queene* (6 books; 1596), an allegory for which he invented the Spenserian stanza, a form later revived by the Romantic poets.

**STEELE, SIR RICHARD,** 1672 (Dublin, Ire.)–Sept. 1, 1729. English journalist, essayist, dramatist, politician. With JOSEPH ADDISON, coauthored several periodicals, including the brilliant *Tatler* and *Spectator*; was a founder of the *Guardian*, and of sentimental comedy; knighted, 1715. *The Funeral*, 1701; *The Lying Lover*, 1703; *The Conscious Lovers*, 1722.

STERNE, LAURENCE, Nov. 24, 1713 (Clonmel, County Tipperary, Ire.)–Mar. 18, 1768. English novelist. His masterpiece, *Tristram Shandy* (9 vols., 1759–67), anticipated the interior-monologue device of 20th-cent. fiction.

STEVENSON, ROBERT LOUIS, Nov. 13, 1850 (Edinburgh, Scot.).–Dec. 3, 1894. Scottish novelist, essayist, critic, poet. Best known for his children's classics, *Treasure Island* (1883), *A Child's Garden of Verses* (1885), and *Kidnapped* (1886); and for his horror story, *The Strange Case of Dr. Jekyll and Mr. Hyde* (1886).

STOPPARD, TOM, July 3, 1937 (Czech.). English playwright. Author of plays noted for their verbal brilliance. *Rosencrantz and Guildenstern Are Dead*, 1967; *The Real Inspector Hound*, 1968; *Travesties*, 1975; *The Real Thing*, 1983.

SWIFT, JONATHAN, Nov. 30, 1667 (Dublin, Ire.)–Oct. 19, 1745. Anglo-Irish satirist, poet, political pamphleteer, clergyman. A foremost satirist whose masterpiece was *Gulliver's Travels* (4 parts, 1726); also, a leading Tory writer, and an Irish national hero for *Drapier Letters* (1724) and *A Modest Proposal* (1729). "The Battle of the Books," 1704; "A Tale of a Tub," 1704; *Argument against Abolishing Christianity*, 1708; *Journal to Stella*, 1710–13.

SWINBURNE, ALGERNON CHARLES, Apr. 5, 1837 (London, Eng.)–Apr. 10, 1909. English poet, critic. Wrote poetry noted for its vigor, music, and prosodic innovations; a symbol of the mid-Victorian poetic revolt. *Atalanta in Calydon*, 1865; *Poems and Ballads*, 1866; *Songs before Sunrise*, 1871; *Essays and Studies*, 1871; *Erechtheus*, 1876.

SYNGE, JOHN MILLINGTON, Apr. 16, 1871 (nr. Dublin, Ire.)–Mar. 24, 1909. Irish dramatist, poet. A major figure of the Irish literary renaissance; wrote poetic dramas about the lives of peasants and fishers of the Aran Is. and western Ireland. Non-fiction: *The Aran Islands*, 1907. Plays: *Riders to the Sea*, 1904; *The Playboy of the Western World*, 1907; *Deirdre of the Sorrows*, 1910.

TENNYSON, ALFRED, 1ST BARON (known popularly as Alfred, Lord Tennyson), Aug. 6, 1809 (Somersby, Lincolnshire, Eng.)–Oct. 6, 1892. English poet. Spokesman for the Victorian age; poet laureate, 1850–92; best-known poems include "The Lotus-Eaters," "The Lady of Shalott," "Crossing the Bar," "Morte d' Arthur," and "The Charge of the Light Brigade"; created a peer, 1884. *In Memoriam*, 1850; *Idylls of the King*, 1859.

THACKERAY, WILLIAM MAKEPEACE, July 18, 1811 (Calcutta, India)–Dec. 24, 1863. English novelist. Noted for his satirical novels about upper- and middle-class life in 19th-cent. London; best known for *Vanity Fair* (1848), in which he created the unscrupulous yet appealing Becky Sharp. *Book*

*of Snobs*, 1848; *The History of Henry Esmond Esq.*, 1852.

THOMAS, DYLAN, Oct. 27, 1914 (Swansea, Wales)–Nov. 9, 1953. Welsh poet, prose writer. Created an individualistic poetic style, based on sound and rhythm; gained fame through readings on radio, records, and lecture tours. *Portrait of the Artist as a Young Dog*, 1940; *Deaths and Entrances*, 1946; *A Child's Christmas in Wales*, 1954; *Under Milk Wood*, 1954; *Adventures in the Skin Trade*, 1955.

TOLKIEN, J(ohn) R(onald) R(euel), Jan. 3, 1892 (Bloemfontein, S.A.)–Sept. 2, 1973. English author, scholar. Created fanciful tales that gained great popularity during the 1960s; a prominent philologist, taught at Oxford U., 1925–59. *The Hobbit*, 1938; *The Lord of the Rings*, (trilogy), 1954–56; *The Silmarillion*, 1977.

TROLLOPE, ANTHONY, Apr. 24, 1815 (London, Eng.)–Dec. 6, 1882. English novelist. Best known for his Barsetchire (or Barchester) novels, chronicles of Victorian life in a cathedral town. *The Warden*, 1855; *Barchester Towers*, 1857; *Doctor Thorne*, 1858; *Phineas Finn*, 1869; *The Way We Live Now*, 1875; *Autobiography*, 2 vols., 1883.

WALPOLE, HORACE (or Horatio) 4TH EARL OF ORFORD, Sept. 24, 1717 (London, Eng.)–Mar. 2, 1797. English novelist, letter-writer. Wrote over 3,000 witty, charming letters (1626–96), giving a picture of Georgian England; his medieval horror tale, *The Castle of Otranto* (1765), began the fashion for Gothic romances. (Son of Sir ROBERT WALPOLE.)

WALTON, IZAAK, Aug. 9, 1593 (Stafford, Eng.)–Dec. 15, 1683. English writer. Best known for *The Compleat Angler* (1676), a discourse on the pleasures of fishing that was revised and reissued several times; also wrote intimate biographies of friends, including JOHN DONNE (1640), and George Herbert.

WAUGH, ALEC, July 8, 1898 (London, Eng.). English novelist, travel writer. Author of popular novels, many about tropical countries. *Island in the Sun*, 1956; *The Mule on the Minaret*, 1965. (Brother of EVELYN WAUGH.)

WAUGH, EVELYN, Oct 28, 1903 (London, Eng.)–Apr. 10, 1966. English novelist. Wrote sophisticated satires on 20th-cent. modern life. *Decline and Fall*, 1928; *Vile Bodies*, 1930; *Black Mischief*, 1932; *Brideshead Revisited*, 1945; *The Loved One*, 1948. (Brother of A. WAUGH.)

WEBSTER, JOHN, c.1575 (London, Eng.)–c.1634. English dramatist. His two masterpieces of poetic drama are the revenge tragedies, *The White Devil* (c.1612) and *The Duchess of Malfi* (c.1613), notable for their graphic language, portrayal of evil and human suffering, and strong satiric element.

WEST, DAME REBECCA (born Cicily Isabel Fairfield), Dec. 25, 1892 (County Kerry, Ire.)–Mar. 15, 1983. English novelist, critic, journalist. Noted for social and cultural criticism—especially her reports on the Nuremberg trials, collected in *A Train of Powder* (1955), and her examination of

Balkan politics, culture, and history in *Black Lamb and Grey Falcon* (2 vols., 1942).

**WHITE, T(erence) H(anbury),** May 29, 1906 (Bombay, Ind.)–Jan. 17, 1964. English novelist, social historian. Best known for his adaptation of Sir THOMAS MALORY's *Morte D'Arthur* as *The Once and Future King* (4 vols., 1938–58), which became the musical *Camelot* (1960). Autobiography: *England Have My Bones*, 1936.

**WILDE, OSCAR,** Oct. 16, 1854 (Dublin, Ire.)–Nov. 30, 1900. Anglo-Irish playwright, novelist. Wrote witty, sophisticated plays, with *The Importance of Being Earnest* (1895) his masterpiece; renowned for wit and eccentricity; at the height of his career, sentenced to two years' hard labor for homosexuality, during which time he wrote the confessional "De Profundis" (1905). *Lady Windermere's Fan*, 1892; *A Woman of No Importance*, 1893; *An Ideal Husband*, 1895; "The Ballad of Reading Gaol," 1898.

**WODEHOUSE, SIR P(elham) G(renville),** Oct. 15, 1881 (Guildford, Surrey, Eng.)–Feb. 14, 1975. English novelist, humorist. Best known for his farces about English gentry in the late Edwardian era; knighted, 1975. *The Man with Two Left Feet*, 1917; *The Inimitable Jeeves*, 1924; *Bertie Wooster Sees It Through*, 1955.

**WOOLF, (Adeline) VIRGINIA,** Jan. 25, 1882 (London, Eng.)–Mar. 28, 1941. English novelist, critic. Wrote experimental novels noted for a poetic, symbolic style and stream-of-consciousness technique; her criticism includes the classic feminist essay, "A Room of One's Own" (1929); with her husband, Leonard Woolf, was at the center of the "Bloomsbury group" of intellectuals, founded and ran the Hogarth Press, 1917. Novels: *Jacob's Room*, 1922; *Mrs. Dalloway*, 1925; *To the Lighthouse*, 1927; *Orlando*, 1928; *The Waves*, 1931. Essays: *The Common Reader*, 1925 and 1932. *A Writer's Diary*, 1953. (Daughter of Sir L. STEPHEN.)

**WORDSWORTH, WILLIAM,** Apr. 7, 1770 (Cockermouth, Cumberland, Eng.)–Apr. 23, 1850. English poet. A leader of the English Romantic movement; known for his worship of nature and humanitarianism; with his friend S. T. COLERIDGE, wrote *Lyrical Ballads* (1798); poet laureate of England, 1843–50. Best-known poems include "Tintern Abbey," "Ode to Duty," "Ode: Intimations of Immortality," "Lucy," "Dafffodils," and "The World Is Too Much with Us." *The Prelude*, 1850.

**YEATS, WILLIAM BUTLER,** June 13, 1865 (Dublin, Ire.)–Jan. 28, 1939. Irish poet, playwright. Leader of the Irish literary renaissance; in his early, lyrical poetry, was influenced by the Pre-Raphaelites and Irish mythology; later turned to more realistic and profound themes; a founder of the Abbey Theatre in Dublin, for which he wrote and produced plays; awarded Nobel Prize in literature, 1923. Play: *The Countess Cathleen* (1899). Poetry: *The Wanderings of Oisin*, 1889; *The Wild Swans at Coole*, 1917; *The Tower*, 1928; *Last Poems*, 1940.

## FRENCH WRITERS

**ANOUILH, JEAN,** June 23, 1910 (Bordeaux, Fr.). French dramatist, screenwriter. *Antigone*, 1942; *Ring Round the Moon*, 1947; *The Waltz of the Toreadors*, 1952; *The Lark*, 1953; *Becket*, 1959.

**APOLLINAIRE, GUILLAUME,** Aug. 26, 1880 (Rome, Italy)–Nov, 1918. French poet and critic. A friend of PABLO PICASSO, GEORGES BRAQUE, and other avant-garde artists, he first established cubism as a school of painting, and named the surrealist movement. *Les Peintres cubistes (The Cubist Painters)*, 1913; *Le Poète assassiné (The Poet Assassinated)*, 1916; *Couleur du temps*, 1918.

**ARAGON, LOUIS,** Oct. 3, 1897 (Paris, Fr.). French poet, novelist, critic. A leader of the Dadaists and later of the surrealists; spokesman for the French Resistance during WW II; intellectual leader of the French Communist Party. *The Peasant of Paris*, 1926; *A Poet of Resurgent France*, 1946; *Background for Death*, 1965.

**BALZAC, HONORÉ DE,** May 16, 1799 (Tours, Fr.)– Aug. 18, 1850. French novelist. A founder of the realistic school; his masterpiece, *Le comédie humaine* (inc. *Eugénie Grandet*, 1833; and *Le Pere Goriot*, 1835), composed mostly in the 1830s, consists of nearly 100 novels and short stories, and 50 unfinished works. *Les chouans*, 1829; *La peau de chagrin*, 1831.

**BAUDELAIRE, CHARLES,** Apr. 9, 1821 (Paris, Fr.)– Aug. 31, 1867. French poet, critic, translator. Author of powerful, expressionistic poetry, much of which was banned during his lifetime, later highly influential; credited with inventing symbolism; translated EDGAR ALLEN POE; led an eccentric, decadent, tragic life. *Les fleurs du mal*, 1857; *Curiosités esthétiques*, 1868; *Petits poemes en proses*, 1869.

**BEAUMARCHAIS, PIERRE AUGUSTIN DE,** Jan. 24, 1732 (Paris, Fr.)–May 18, 1799. French dramatist. Two of his comic masterpieces satirizing upper-class behavior were adapted into famous operas: *The Barber of Seville* (1775), by G. A. ROSSINI; and *The Marriage of Figaro* (1784), by W. A. MOZART.

**BEAUVOIR, SIMONE DE,** Jan 9, 1908 (Paris, Fr.) –Apr. 14, 1986. French novelist, essayist. Part of the existentialist movement; an influential feminist. *The Blood of Others*, 1948; *The Second Sex*, 1949–50; *The Mandarins*, 1955; *Memoirs of a Dutiful Daughter*, 1959; *The Coming of Age*, 1970.

**BÉRANGER, PIERRE-JEAN DE,** August 19, 1780 (Paris, France)–July 16, 1857. French poet and songwriter. Even though he was a protégé of Lucien Bonaparte, his work lampooned the French Second Empire. *Chansons morales et autres*, 1815; *Chansons nouvelles*, 1825; *Chansons nouvelles et dernières*, 1833.

**BOILEAU-DESPREAUX, NICOLAS,** 1636? (Paris, France)–1711. French poet and critic. Became King Louis XIV's royal historian; he advocated lively and emotional writing. *The Art of Poetry*, 1674; *Satires*, 1666–1711; *Espistles*, 1668–1698.

BRETON, ANDRÉ, Feb. 19, 1896 (France)–Sept. 28, 1966. French poet, novelist, essayist. Founded the surrealist movement, writing its manifestos in 1924, 1930, and 1934; experimented with automatic writing. Novel: *Nadja*, 1928.

BRUNHOFF, JEAN DE, 1899–1937. French author/illustrator. Wrote and illustrated a popular series of children's books about Babar, the king of the elephants. *The Story of Babar the Little Elephant*, 1931; *Babar's Travels*, 1935; *Babar the King*, 1936.

BUTOR, MICHEL, Sept. 14, 1926 (Mons-en-Barouel, France). French novelist and essayist. *Passage de Milan*, 1954; *Mobile*, 1962; *Répertoire V*, 1982.

CAMUS, ALBERT, Nov. 7, 1913 (Mondovi, Algeria) –Jan. 4, 1960. French philosopher, novelist, dramatist, journalist. Wrote chiefly about the absurd— the meaninglessness of existence; associated with JEAN PAUL SARTRE and the existentialists; awarded Nobel Prize in literature, 1957. *The Stranger*, 1942; *Caligula*, 1944; *The Plague*, 1948; *The Rebel*, 1951; *State of Siege*, 1958.

CHATEAUBRIAND, FRANÇOIS RENÉ, VICOMTE DE, Sept. 4, 1768 (St. Malo, Fr.)–July 4, 1848. French novelist, diplomat. His works helped shape the romantic movement. *Atala*, 1801; *Rene*, 1805; *Les Natchez*, 1826; Memoirs: *Memories from Beyond the Grave*, 1849–1850.

CHRÉTIEN DE TROYES, fl. 1160–1190. French poet. His early Arthurian legends, written in eight-syllable rhymed couplets, incorporated the ideals of the 12th-cent. court to which he was attached; introduced the character Lancelot, courtly love, and the special significance of the Holy Grail. *Erec et Enide; Cligès; Lancelot, or The Knight of the Cart; Percival, or The Story of the Grail*.

CLAUDEL, PAUL, Aug. 6, 1868 (Villeneuve-sur-Fère, Fr.)–Feb. 23, 1955. French dramatist, poet, essayist. Eminent Catholic man of letters. Used religious symbols, exotic backgrounds, pantomime, ballet, music and film techniques in his plays; *Partage de midi* (1906, rev. 1948) and *The Satin Slipper* (1929) are his masterpieces. *Tidings Brought to Mary*, 1912.

COCTEAU, JEAN, July 5, 1889 (Maisons-Lafitte, Fr.)–Oct. 11, 1963. French poet, novelist, playwright, essayist, filmmaker, craftsman, artist. Stood in the forefront of 20th-cent. avant-garde movements. *Orphée*, 1926; *Opéra*, 1927; *Les Enfants Terribles*, 1929; *The Blood of the Poet* (film), 1933; *Beauty and the Beast* (film), 1946.

COLETTE (born Sidonie Gabrielle Colette), Jan. 28, 1873 (St. Sauveur-en-Puisaye, Fr.)–Aug. 3, 1954. French novelist. Her novels about relationships between men and women are noted for their intimate style and deep feeling for nature. *Claudine at School*, 1900; *Chéri*, 1920; *La maison de Claudine*, 1923; *Sido*, 1929; *Gigi*, 1945.

CORNEILLE, PIERRE, June 6, 1606 (Rouen, Fr.)–Sept. 30, 1684. French playwright. He ushered in the great age of Neo-Classical French drama, both with his own tragedies and with his criticism that advocated strict adherence to the "three utilities"

of time, place, and action in drama. *Médée*, 1635; *Le Cid*, 1637; *Horace*, 1640; *Cinna*, 1640; *Polyeucte*, 1643; *Le Menteur*, 1643.

CRÈVECOEUR, MICHEL GUILLAUME JEAN DE (pseud.: Hector Saint-John de Crèvecoeur, J. Hector St. John, Agricola). Jan. 31, 1735 (near Caen, Fr.)–Nov. 12, 1813. French-U.S. essayist. In *Letters from an American Farmer* (1782), painted a vivid picture of 18th-cent. American rural life. *Sketches of Eighteenth Century America*, 1925.

CYRANO DE BERGERAC, SAVINIEN, Mar. 6, 1619 (Paris, Fr.)–July 28, 1655. French novelist, playwright. Wrote fantasies that foreshadow modern science fiction; his fiery temper, dueling skill, and long nose are portrayed in EDMOND ROSTAND's 1897 play, *Cyrano de Bergerac*. *Comical History of the States and Empires of the Moon*, 1656; *Comical History of the States and Empires of the Sun*, 1661.

DAUDET, ALPHONSE, May 13, 1840 (Nimes, Fr.)–Dec. 16, 1897. French novelist, short-story writer. Wrote humorous, sympathetic stories of provincial and Parisian life. *Letters from My Mill*, 1866; *Le petit chose*, 1868; *Tartarin de Tarascon*, 1872; *Contes du Lundi*, 1873.

DU BELLAY, JOACHIM, 1522? (Anjou, France) –Jan 1, 1560. French poet. A founder of the Pléide group of poets: he lived for a time in Rome and wrote of the glories of ancient Rome and the corruption of modern Rome. *Defense and Glorification of the French Language*, 1549; *Antiquities of Rome*, 1558; *Regrets*, 1558.

DUMAS, ALEXANDRE (Dumas père, born Davy de la Pailleterie), July 24, 1802 (Villers-Cotterêts, Fr.)–Dec. 5, 1870. French novelist. Published almost 300 books with a "factory" of collaborators; accused of pilfering plots and rewriting history; best known for his historical novels *The Count of Monte Cristo* (1844) and *The Three Musketeers* (1844). (Father of A. DUMAS, fils.)

DUMAS, ALEXANDRE (Dumas fils), July 27, 1824 (Paris, Fr.)–Nov. 27, 1895. French dramatist, novelist. The illegitimate son of A. DUMAS (père); noted for moralistic works; *La dame aux camélias* (novel, 1848; play, 1852) was the basis for GUISEPPE VERDI's opera *La Traviata*.

DURAS, MARGUERITE, Apr. 4, 1914 (Giadinh, Indochina [now Vietnam]). French novelist, playwright, screenwriter. *The Sea Wall*, 1952; *Hiroshima, Mon Amour* (screenplay), 1959; *The Rapture of L. V. Stein*, 1967.

ÉLUARD, PAUL (born Eugène Grindel), Dec. 14, 1895 (Paris, Fr.)–Nov. 18, 1952. French poet. A major French poet and a founder of the surrealist movement; active in the French Resistance in WW II. *To Die of Not Dying*, 1924; *The Immaculate Conception* (with ANDRE BRETON), 1930; *Cours naturel*, 1938; *Poemes politiques*, 1948.

FEYDEAU, GEORGES, Dec. 8, 1862 (Paris, Fr.)– June 6, 1921. French dramatist. His 39 plays, bedroom farces, comedies of manners, and comedies of character, dominated the Parisien stage for 15 years. *L'Hôtel du libre-Echange*, 1894; *The*

*Lady from Maxim's*, 1907; *Occupe-toi d'Amélie*, 1908.

**FLAUBERT, GUSTAVE,** Dec. 12, 1821 (Rouen, Fr.)–May 8, 1880. French novelist. A master of fiction, extremely influential, and a key proponent of "art for art's sake." The objective, detailed realism of *Madame Bovary* (1857) made it a literary landmark; his story "Un Coeur Simple" (1875–77) is also a classic. *L'Education sentimentale,* 1849, 1869; *La tentation de Saint Antoine,* 1854, 1874; *Salammbô,* 1862.

**FRANCE, ANATOLE** (pseud. of Jacques Anatole Thibault), Apr. 16, 1844 (Paris, Fr.)–Oct. 13, 1924. French novelist, poet, critic. The most prominent and prolific French man of letters of his day; awarded Nobel Prize in literature, 1921. *The Crime of Sylvester Bonnard,* 1881; *The Red Lily,* 1894; *Penguin Island,* 1909.

**GAUTIER, (Pierre Jules) THÉOPHILE,** Aug. 31, 1811 (Hautes-Pyrénées, Fr.)–Oct. 23, 1872. French poet, novelist, critic. A leader of the "art for art's sake" movement in France; a forerunner of the Parnassian school. Novel: *Mademoiselle de Maupin,* 1835; Poetry: *Emaux et Camées,* 1852.

**GENÊT, JEAN,** Dec. 19, 1910 (Paris, Fr.)–Apr. 15, 1986. French novelist, dramatist, essayist, poet. An aesthete, an existentialist, and a pioneer of the theater of the absurd; spent much of his youth in reformatories and prisons, pardoned from life imprisonment after the intervention of ANDRE GIDE, JEAN PAUL SARTRE, JEAN COCTEAU and others. Novels: *Our Lady of the Flowers* (1944), *Querelle of Brest* (1947); his powerful, stylized dramas include *The Maids* (1948), *The Balcony* (1957), and *The Blacks* (1959).

**GIDE, ANDRÉ,** Nov. 22, 1869 (Paris, Fr.)–Feb. 19, 1951. French novelist, essayist. Prolific master craftsman, influential as a moralist, philosopher, and writer; founder of a *Nouvelle Revue Française,* the most important literary journal of its time; awarded Nobel Prize in literature, 1947. *The Immoralist,* 1902; *Strait Is the Gate,* 1924; *Counterfeiters,* 1926; *Travels in the Congo,* 1927; *Return from the USSR,* 1936.

**GIRAUDOUX, JEAN,** Oct. 29, 1882 (Haute-Vienne, Fr.)–Jan. 31, 1944. French dramatist, novelist, diplomat. A prolific writer best known for his early fanciful novels and whimsical plays. Novel: *My Friend from Limousin,* 1922. Plays: *Amphitryon 38,* 1929; *Tiger at the Gates,* 1935; *Ondine,* 1939; *The Madwoman of Chaillot,* 1945.

**GONCOURT, EDMOND LOUIS ANTOINE HUOT DE,** May 26, 1822 (Nancy, Fr.)–July 16, 1896; and his brother **GONCOURT, JULES ALFRED HUOT DE,** Dec. 17, 1830 (Paris, Fr.)–June 20, 1870. French novelists, art critics, historians, diarists. Inseparable personally and professionally, known as *les deux Goncourt;* collaborated on several popular novels, including *Renée Mauperin* (1864), which initiated the naturalistic movement; wrote the *Jounal des Goncourt* (9 vols., 1887–96), featuring accounts of Parisian society; Edmond's

will provided funds for the Goncourt Acad., which annually awards the Goncourt Prize in fiction.

**HUGO, VICTOR,** Feb. 26, 1802 (Besançon, Fr.)–May 22, 1885. French poet, novelist, dramatist. In the forefront of the Romantic movement; best known in France for lyric poetry, elsewhere for novels *The Hunchback of Notre Dame* (1831), and *Les Miserables* (1862). Poetry: *Orientales,* 1829; *Les rayons et les ombres,* 1840; *Les Contemplations,* 1856; *La légende des siècles,* 1859–1883. Plays: *Hernani,* 1830; *Le roi s'amuse,* 1832.

**HUYSMANS, JORIS KARL** (born Charles Huysmans), Feb. 5, 1848 (Paris, Fr.)–May 12, 1907. French novelist. A disciple of Zola; first pres. of Goncourt Acad. *Marthe,* 1876; *Against Nature,* 1884.

**IONESCO, EUGÈNE,** Nov. 13, 1912 (Slatina, Rum.). French playwright. Inaugurated the theater of the absurd with his one-act classic, *The Bald Soprano,* 1950. *The Chairs,* 1952; *Rhinoceros,* 1959; *Exit the King,* 1963.

**JARRY, ALFRED,** Sept. 8, 1873 (Laval, France)–Nov. 1, 1907. French surrealist novelist. *Ubu roi,* 1896; *Le Surmale* (The Supermale), 1902.

**LA BRUYÈRE, JEAN DE,** Aug. 16, 1645 (Paris, Fr.)–May 10, 1696. French satirist. Best known for *Characters of Theophrastus Translated from the Greek, with Characters or the Manners of this Century* (1688–1694), a social satire with more than 1000 character sketches and aphorisms.

**LACLOS, PIERRE CHODERLOS DE,** Oct. 19, 1741 (Amiens, France)–Nov. 5, 1803. French epistolary novelist. *Les Liaisons dangereuses,* 1782.

**LA FAYETTE, MARIE MADELEINE PIOCHE DE LA VERGNE, COMTESSE DE,** Mar. 16, 1634 (Paris, Fr.)–May 25, 1693. French novelist. Held brilliant literary salons; introduced serious historical fiction to French literature with *The Princess of Cleves* (1678).

**LA FONTAINE, JEAN DE,** July 8, 1621 (Chateau-Thierry, Fr.)–Apr. 13, 1695. French poet. Wrote the classic *Selected Fables Versified* (1668–94), 12 books of 238 tales, re-creations of the fables of AESOP and others.

**LAMARTINE, ALPHONSE DE,** Oct. 21, 1790 (Mâcon, Fr.)–Feb. 28, 1869. French poet, novelist, statesman. His *Meditations poetiques* (1820) influenced the French Romantic movement; with *Histoire des Girondins* (1847), helped bring about the Revolution of 1848; headed the short-lived provisional government, before losing out to Napoleon III.

**LA ROCHEFOUCAULD, FRANÇOIS, DUC DE,** Sept. 15, 1613 (Paris, Fr.)–Mar. 16, 1680. French writer. Noted for *Reflexions ou sentences et maximes morales* (5 ed., 1665–93), epigrams based on the belief that behavior derives from self-love.

**LESAGE, ALAIN RENÉ,** May 8, 1668 (Brittany, Fr.)–Nov. 17, 1747. French novelist, dramatist. His masterpiece, the picaresque *Adventures of Gil Blas of Santillane* (1715–35), was influential in the development of the realistic novel. *Turcaret* (play), 1709.

**MALLARMÉ, STEPHANE,** Mar. 18, 1842 (Paris,

Fr.)–Sept. 9, 1898. French poet. Leader of the symbolist movement. *Hérodiade* (begun 1864, never completed); *L'Aprés-midi d'un faune*, 1876 (the inspiration for C. DEBUSSY's orchestral prelude); *Poésies complètes*, 1887.

**MALRAUX, ANDRÉ,** Nov. 3, 1901 (Paris, Fr.)–Nov. 23, 1976. French novelist, art historian, public official. Participated in revolutionary movements in China and Indochina, 1924–27; fought against F. FRANCO in the Spanish Civil War, 1936–39; hero and leader of the French Resistance during WW II; French min. of information, 1945, 1958; min. of cultural affairs, 1959–69. *Man's Fate*, 1933; *Man's Hope*, 1937; *The Voices of Silence*, 1951; *Anti-Mémoirs*, 1967.

**MARTIN DU GARD, ROGER,** Mar. 23, 1881 (Neuilly-sur-Seine, Fr.)–Aug. 22, 1958. French novelist, dramatist. Known for the eight-part cyclical novel, *The World of the Thibaults* (1922–40), a panoramic survey of French society in the early 20th cent.; awarded Nobel Prize in literature, 1937.

**MAUPASSANT, GUY DE,** Aug. 5, 1850 (nr. Dieppe, Fr.)–July 6, 1893. French short-story writer. Master of the short story; from 1880 to 1890, wrote more than 300, including the celebrated "Ball of Fat," "A Piece of String," "The House of Mme. Tellier," "Moonlight," "Mlle. Fifi," "The Necklace," "Jewels," and "The Mask."

**MAURIAC, FRANÇOIS,** Oct. 11, 1885 (Bordeaux, Fr.)–Sept. 1, 1970. French novelist, essayist, dramatist. A major writer in the French Catholic tradition; awarded Nobel Prize in literature, 1952. *The Kiss to the Leper*, 1922; *The Desert of Love*, 1925; *Thérèse*, 1927; *Viper's Tangle*, 1932.

**MAUROIS, ANDRÉ** (born Émile Herzog), July 26, 1885 (Elbeuf, Fr.)–Oct. 9, 1967. French man of letters. Best known for biographies of PERCY BYSSHE SHELLEY, VOLTAIRE, LORD BYRON, VICTOR HUGO, GEORGE SAND, HONORÉ DE BALZAC, MARCEL PROUST, CHARLES DICKENS and IVAN TURGENEV; also wrote histories and novels; elected to French Academy, 1938; knighted by the British Empire, 1938. *Ariel*, 1923; *Byron*, 1930; *Olympio*, 1954; *Lélia*, 1952; *Prometheus, the Life of Balzac*, 1965; *The Quest for Proust*, 1950.

**MÉRIMÉE, PROSPER,** Sept. 28, 1803 (Paris, Fr.)–Sept. 23, 1870. French man of letters. Best known for his restrained, ironic short stories and novellas; elected to French Academy, 1844; made a senator, 1853. *Colomba*, 1841; *Nouvelles*, which includes "Carmen," the basis for GEORGES BIZET's opera, 1852.

**MISTRAL, FRÉDÉRIC,** Sept. 8, 1830 (Maillane, Fr.)–Mar. 25, 1914. French poet. Led the 19th-cent. revival of Provençal language and literature; awarded Nobel Prize in literature, 1904. *Mirèio*, 1859; *Le Rhône*, 1897; *My Origins*, 1906.

**MOLIÈRE** (pseud. of Jean Baptiste Poquelin), baptized Jan. 15, 1622 (Paris, Fr.)–Feb. 17, 1673. French dramatist, actor. The foremost French comic dramatist, whose works range from high comedy to broad farce; championed natural man, ridiculed

the pretensions and hypocrisy of the bourgeoisie. *The School for Wives*, 1662; *Tartuffe*, 1664; *Le misanthrope*, 1666; *The Miser*, 1668; *Le bourgeois gentilhomme*, 1670; *The Imaginary Invalid*, 1673.

**MONTAIGNE, MICHEL DE,** Feb. 28, 1533 (nr. Bordeaux, Fr.)–Sept. 13, 1592. French essayist. With his informal, unpretentious essays, established a new literary form; wrote three volumes of essays (1580, 1588, 1595); advocated a humanistic morality.

**MUSSET, ALFRED DE,** Dec. 11, 1810 (Paris, Fr.)–May 2, 1857. French poet, playwright. Important poet and playwright in French Romantic movement. Poetry: *Contes d'Espagne et d'Italy*, 1829; *Le Spectacle dans un fauteuil*, 1833. Plays: *Lorenzaccio*, 1834; *Il ne faut juver de rien*, 1836. Memoirs: *La Confession d'un enfant du Siècle*, 1836.

**NIN, ANAÏS,** Feb. 21, 1903 (nr. Paris, Fr.)–Jan. 14, 1977. French-U.S. diarist, novelist, short-story writer. Became a cult figure for her poetic novels; won wide readership with her diaries, which spanned 60 years in the U.S. and bohemian Paris. *House of Incest*, 1937; *Winter of Artifice*, 1942; *Diary of Anaïs Nin*, 1966; *Delta of Venus*, 1977.

**PÉGUY, CHARLES,** Jan. 7, 1873 (Orleans, Fr.)–Sept. 5, 1914. French poet, philosopher. Founded the influential journal *Les Cahiers de la quinzaine*, 1900; a Christian, socialist, and strong supporter of ANDRÉ DREYFUS; killed in action in WW I. *Mystère de la charité de Jeanne d'Arc*, 1910; *Ève*, 1913.

**PERRAULT, CHARLES,** Jan. 12, 1628 (Paris, Fr.)–May 16, 1703. French fairy tale writer and critic. *Contes de ma mere l'Oye (Mother Goose Tales)*, 1697.

**PERSE, ST.-JOHN** (pseud. of Marie René Auguste Alexis Léger), May 31, 1887 (Saint-Léger des Feuilles, Guadeloupe)–Sept. 20, 1975. French poet, diplomat. Noted for obscure poetry, exotic words; awarded Nobel Prize in literature, 1960. *Anabase*, 1925; *Exil*, 1942; *Winds*, 1946; *Seamarks*, 1957; *Chronique*, 19670; *Birds*, 1962.

**PRÉVOST, ABBÉ** (born Antoine François Prévost d'Exiles), Apr. 1, 1697 (Hesdin, Fr.)–Nov. 25, 1763. French novelist. Noted for *Histoiré du Chevalier des Grieux et de Manon Lescaut* (1731), a classic "novel of feeling" adapted into the operas *Manon* (1884) by JULES MASSENET and *Manon Lescaut* (1893) by GIACOMO PUCCINI.

**PROUST, MARCEL,** July 10, 1871 (Anteuil, Fr.)–Nov. 18, 1922. French novelist. Known for his seven-volume semiautobiographical novel, *Remembrance of Things Past* (1913–27) one of the major literary works of the 20th century, told as an allegorical search for truth and written in a highly original style. *Swann's Way*, 1913; *Within a Budding Grove*, 1918; *The Guermantes Way*, 1920; *Cities of the Plain*, 1920, 1922; *The Captive*, 1923; *The Sweet Cheat Gone*, 1925; *The Past Recaptured*, 1927.

**RABELAIS, FRANÇOIS,** c.1490 (nr. Chinon, Fr.)–probably Apr. 9, 1533. French novelist. Best known as author of the comic masterpiece *Gargantua and Pantagruel* (4 books, 1532–52); another volume, published after his death, is of questionable authorship); noted for his broad, often ribald humor (adjective *Rabelaisian* means coarsely and boisterously satirical); a monk, later an eminent physician and humanist.

**RACINE, JEAN,** baptized Dec. 22, 1639 (La Ferté-Milon, Fr.)–Apr. 21, 1699. French dramatist. The model of French classicism; supplanted PIERRE CORNEILLE as the foremost French tragic dramatist; a rival of MOLIÈRE; elected to the French Academy, 1673. *Andromaque,* 1667; *Britannicus,* 1669; *Bérénice,* 1670; *Bajazet,* 1672; *Mithridate,* 1673; *Iphigenie en Aulide,* 1674; *Phèdre,* 1677.

**RESTIF DE LA BRETONNE, NICHOLAS EDMÉ,** (born Nicholas-Edmé Restif), Oct. 23, 1734 (Sacy, Fr.)–Feb. 3, 1806. French novelist. "The Rousseau of the gutter" wrote some 250 rambling, coarse, erotic novels about lower-class life. *Le Pied de Fanchette,* 1769; *Le paysan perverti,* 1776; *Monsieur Nicolas,* 1794–97.

**RIMBAUD, ARTHUR,** Oct. 20, 1854 (Charleville, Fr.)–Nov. 10, 1891. French poet. His original, imaginative, dreamlike verse and prose-poems influenced the symbolists and anticipated the surrealists; won lasting renown outside France partly as a rebel and visionary. *Illuminations,* 1886; *The Drunken Boat,* 1871; *A Season in Hell,* 1873.

**ROBBE-GRILLET, ALAIN,** Aug. 18, 1922 (Brest, Fr.). French novelist. Originated the French *nouveau roman,* the "antinovel" of the 1950s, which described images without commentary and was often marked by violence. *The Erasers,* 1953; *The Voyeur,* 1955; *Jealousy,* 1957; *Towards a New Novel,* 1963; *Last Year at Marienbad* (screenplay), 1961.

**ROLLAND, ROMAIN,** Jan. 29, 1866 (Clamecy, Fr.)–Dec. 30, 1944. French novelist, dramatist, biographer, essayist. An apostle of heroic idealism; best known as author of the epic *Jean Christophe* (10 vols., 1904–12), which introduced the *roman fleuve,* or saga novel; a political activist, was involved in the DREYFUS affair; awarded Nobel Prize in literature, 1915. *Life of Beethoven,* 1903; *Life of Michelangelo,* 1905; *The Soul Enchanted,* 1922–23.

**RONSARD, PIERRE DE,** Sept. 11, 1524 (La Possonnière, Fr.)–Dec. 27, 1585. French poet. Leader of the Pléiade, seven writers who advocated adopting the language and literary forms of the classics to French literature. *Les amours,* 1552–55; *Les hymnes,* 1555–56; *Sonnets pour Hélène,* 1578; *La Franciade,* 1572.

**ROSTAND, EDMOND,** Apr. 1, 1868 (Marseilles, Fr.)–Dec. 2, 1918. French dramatist. Best known for his play *Cyrano de Bergerac* (1897), a colorful combination of comedy and pathos. *L'Aiglon,* 1900, was one of actress SARAH BERNHARDT's greatest triumphs.

**SADE, MARQUIS DE** (born Donatien Alphonse François, Comte de Sade), June 2, 1740 (Paris, Fr.)–Dec. 2, 1814. French writer. Wrote licentious prose narratives and plays; imprisoned for scandalous conduct, institutionalized for sexual offenses; during his last confinement, directed inmates in theatrical performances; the word "sadism" is derived from his name. *The One Hundred Days of Sodom* (1785); *Justine* (1791).

**SAGAN, FRANÇOISE** (pseud. of Françoise Quoirez), June 21, 1935 (Carjac, Fr.). French novelist. Author of short works in the tradition of the French psychological novel. *Bonjour Tristesse,* 1945; *A Certain Smile,* 1953; *Do You Like Brahms?,* 1959; *Salad Days,* 1984.

**SAINT-EXUPERY, ANTOINE DE,** June 29, 1900 (Lyons, Fr.)–July 31, 1944. French writer, aviator. Wrote poetic narratives about aviation, but best known for the fable *The Little Prince* (1943), read by both children and adults; lost in action in WW II. *Southern Mail,* 1929; *Night Freight,* 1932; *Wind, Sand, and Stars,* 1939.

**SAND, GEORGE** (pseud. of Amandine Aurore Dupin, Baronne Dudevant), July 1, 1804 (Paris, Fr.)–June 8, 1876. French novelist. Best known for rustic tales of love that transcends convention and class; she led an unconventional life, including liaisons with PROSPER MÉRIMÉE, ALFRED DE MUSSET, FRÉDÉRIC CHOPIN. *Indiana,* 1832; *Valentine,* 1832; *Lélia,* 1833; *La Mare au diable,* 1846; *Histoire de ma vie* (4 vols.), 1854–55; *Tales of a Grandmother,* 1873.

**SEVIGNE, MARIE DE RABUTIN CHANTAL, MARQUISE DE,** Feb. 5, 1626 (Paris, Fr.)–Apr. 17, 1696. French writer. Wrote more than 1,700 letters, in an elegant but unaffected style, which are a model of the epistolary genre and provide a portrait of her age.

**SIMON, CLAUDE,** Oct. 10, 1913 (Tamanmarive, Madagascar). French *Noveau Roman* novelist; awarded 1985 Nobel Prize in literature. *Le Vent (The Wind),* 1957; *Le Palace (The Palace),* 1962; *Historie,* 1967.

**STAËL, GERMAINE DE** (born Anne Louise Germaine Necker), after her marriage, Baronne de Staël-Holstein, Apr. 22, 1766 (Paris, Fr.)–July 14, 1817. French woman of letters. One of the most important liberal intellectuals of her time, she publicized the German Romantic movement, held salons for leading intellectuals in Paris and Geneva. *Delphine,* 1802; *Corinne,* 1807; *D'l'Allemagne,* 1818; *Considérations sur les principaux événéments de la révolution francaise,* 1818.

**STENDAHL** (pseud. of Henri Beyle), Jan. 23, 1783 (Grenoble, Fr.)–Mar. 23, 1842. French novelist. A foremost literary figure of 19th cent. France, best known for two masterpieces of psychological and political insight, *The Red and the Black* (1830) and *The Charterhouse of Parma* (1839).

**SULLY PRUDHOMME** (born René Prudhomme), Mar. 16, 1839 (Paris, Fr.)–Sept. 7, 1907. French poet. Leading member of the anti-Romantic Parnassans; elected to the French Acad., 1881; awarded Nobel Prize in literature, 1901. *Stances et poems,* 1865; *Les épreuves,* 1866; *La justice,* 1878; *Le bonheur,* 1888.

**VALERY, PAUL,** Oct. 30, 1871 (Sete, Fr.)–July 20, 1945. French poet, critic. Associated with the symbolists; elected to the French Acad., 1925. *The*

*Evening with Monsieur Teste*, 1896; *La jeune parque*, 1917; *Charmes* (inc. "The Graveyard by the Sea"), 1922; *Variété*, 5 vols., 1922–44.
VERLAINE, PAUL, Mar. 30, 1844 (Metz, Fr.)– Jan. 8, 1896. French poet. A foremost symbolist, noted for his original, musical poetry; prominent in the bohemian literary life of Paris; his marriage ended because of his liaison with protégé A. RIMBAUD, whom he shot and wounded in a quarrel; sentenced to two years in prison. *Poèmes saturniens*, 1866; *Fêtes galantes*, 1869; *Romances sans paroles*, 1874; *Parallèlement*, 1889.
VIGNY, ALFRED VICTOR, COMTE DE, Mar. 27, 1797 (Loche, Fr.)–Sept. 17, 1863. French man of letters. A leading French Romantic; translated *Othello* (1829) and *The Merchant of Venice* (1829) into French verse; elected to the French Acad., 1845. *Cinq-Mars* (historical novel), 1826; *The Military Necessity* (short stories), 1835; *Chat-*

terton (romantic drama), 1835; *The Fates* (poetry), 1864.
VILLON, FRANÇOIS (born François de Moncorbier or François de Loges), 1431 (Paris, Fr.)–after 1463. French poet. The greatest French medieval poet. A brilliant student who took the name of his patron; led a life of crime, narrowly escaping the gallows in 1463; banished from Paris for 10 years, he disappeared. "Ballade des dames du temps jadis"; "Ballade pur prier Notre Dame"; *Little Testament*, 1456; *Grand Testament*, 1461.
ZOLA, ÉMILE (born Edouard Charles Antoine), Apr. 2, 1840 (Paris, Fr.)–Sept. 29, 1902. French novelist. Leader of the naturalist school; best known for *Les Rougon-macquart* (1871–93), a 20-novel series, including *The Dram-Shop* (1877), *Nana* (1880), and *Germinal* (1885), portraying a family's fortunes under the Second Empire; wrote "J'accuse" (1898), an open letter supporting A. DREYFUS.

## OTHER FOREIGN WRITERS

ACHEBE, CHINUA, Nov. 16, 1930 (Ogidi, Nigeria). Nigerian novelist, poet, short-story writer, and essayist. *Things Fall Apart*, 1958; *A Man of the People*, 1966; *The Trouble With Nigeria*, 1983.
AESCHYLUS, 525? B.C. (Eleusis? Gr.)–456 B.C. Greek playwright. Often called the originator of tragedy; a military hero, said to have fought at Marathon; his plays are heroic, shocking, with epic sweep, broad characterizations, lofty themes; he introduced true dialogue and elaborate costumes; won many firsts in the annual Athenian competition; of some 90 plays only 7 survive: *The Persians, Prometheus Bound, Seven against Thebes, The Oresteia* (inc. *Agamemnon, Choephori*, and *Eumenides*), and *Supplicants.*
AESOP, c.620? B.C.–c.?560 B.C. Greek fabulist. Semilegendary figure credited with composing hundreds of fables in which talking animals illustrate human follies and foibles—*Aesop's Fables*, first collected around 300 B.C.
AGNON, S(hmuel) Y(osef) (pseud. Mazel Tov, Ironi, born Samuel Czaczkes), July 17, 1888 (E. Galicia, Pol.)–Feb. 17, 1970. Israeli novelist, short-story writer. Moved from traditional Hassidic tales to nightmarish stories about the disintegration of social and religious forms; awarded Nobel Prize in literature (shared with NELLY SACHS), 1966. *The Bridal Canopy*, 1937; *The Day Before Yesterday*, 1945; *Days of Awe*, 1948; *A Guest for the Night*, 1968.
AKHMATOVA, ANNA, June 23, 1888 (nr. Odessa, Rus.)–Mar. 5, 1966. Soviet poet. A leader of the acmeist "art for art's sake" movement, along with her first husband, NIKOLAI GUMILEV, and OSIP MANDELSTAM; ostracized by gov't., 1920; "rehabilitated," 1940. *Evening*, 1912; *The Rosary*, 1913; *Anno Domini MCMXXI*, 1921; *The Willow Tree*, 1940.
ALEICHEM, SHOLOM (born Solomon Rabinovitch), Feb. 18, 1859 (Pereyaslav, Ukraine)–May 13, 1916. Russian writer of Yiddish short stories

and plays. "The Yiddish Mark Twain," his three main characters—Tevye, Menachem Mendel, and Mottel—have become Jewish archetypes. *The Old Country*, tr. 1946; *Tevye the Dairyman*, tr. 1949; *Adventures of Mottel, the Cantor's Son*, tr. 1953.
ALEIXANDRE Y MERLO, VICENTE, Apr. 26, 1898 (Seville, Sp.)–Dec. 14, 1984. Spanish poet. Member of the so-called Generation of 1927, writers inspired by Spain's golden age of literature; awarded Nobel Prize in literature, 1977. *Swords as Lips*, 1932; *Shadow of Paradise*, 1944; *Story of the Heart*, 1954; *Dialogues of Insight*, 1974.
AMADO, JORGE, Aug. 10, 1912 (Bahia, Brazil). Brazilian novelist. *O paiz do carnaval* (*Carnival Land*), 1932; *Doña Flor e seus dois maridos* (*Dona Flor and Her Two Husbands*), 1966; *Tieta do agreste*, 1979.
AMICHAI, YEHUDA, 1924 (Germany). Israeli lyric poet, novelist, and short-story writer. *Now and in Other Days* (poems); *Not of This Time, Not of This Place* (novel), 1963; *The World Is a Room and Other Stories*, 1984.
ANACREON, 572? B.C.–? (Teos, Ionia). Greek lyric poet. Hic main themes were wine and love—most of his works have been lost; the tune of an old drinking song about him, "To Anacreon in Heaven," became the tune of "The Star-Spangled Banner."
ANDERSEN, HANS CHRISTIAN, Apr. 2, 1805 (Odense, Den.)–Aug. 4, 1875. Danish fairy-tale writer, poet, novelist. Best known for his 168 fairy tales (1835–1872), including "The Princess and the Pea," "The Little Match Girl," "The Ugly Duckling," and "The Emperor's New Clothes."
ANDRIC, IVO, Oct. 10, 1892 (Travnik, Bosnia, now Yugo.)–Mar. 13, 1975. Yugoslav novelist, short-story writer, poet; awarded Nobel Prize in literature, 1961. *The Bridge on the Drina*, 1945; *The Bosnian Chronicle*, 1945; *Devil's Yard*, 1954.
APOLLONIUS OF RHODES, c.295 B.C. (Alexandria, Egypt)–c.215 B.C. Greek epic poet. He was the director of the Library at Alexandria from 26-

to 247 B.C.; his most famous work, *Argonautica*, was an epic in four books about the story of Jason and the Argonauts.

**APULEIUS, LUCIUS,** c.123 (Madaura, now M'Daourouch, Alg.)–? Latin writer, philosopher. His *Metamorphoses, or The Golden Ass*, the only Latin novel to survive intact, influenced Bocaccio's *Decameron*, Cervantes's *Don Quixote*, and Le Sage's *Gil Blas*.

**ARIOSTO, LUDOVICO,** 1474 (Reggio, Italy)– 1533. Italian poet and dramatist. *Orlando Furioso (Roland Mad)*, 1516.

**ARISTOPHANES,** c.450 B.C. (Athens, Greece)– c.385 B.C. Greek playwright, poet. His 11 extant plays, the only surviving examples of Greek comedy, combine music, dance, word play, political satire, lyric poetry, and fantasy. *The Clouds*, 423 B.C.; *The Wasps*, 422 B.C.; *The Birds*, 414 B.C.; *Lysistrata*, 411 B.C.; *The Frogs*, 405 B.C.

**ASTURIAS, MIGUEL ANGEL,** Oct. 19, 1899 (Guatemala City, Guat.)–June 9, 1974. Guatemalan novelist, poet. His works combine European socio-political realism and surrealistic tales of Guatemala's land and people; awarded Nobel Prize in literature, 1967. *Hombres de Máz*, 1949; *Strong Wind*, 1950; *The Green Pope*, 1954; *Las Ojos de los Enterrados*, 1960; *Mulata de Fol*, 1963.

**BABEL, ISAAC,** July 13, 1894 (Odessa, Rus.)– Mar. 17, 1941. Soviet short-story writer. Wrote ironically humorous tales of Jewish life in Odessa, and realistic war stories; died in a Siberian prison camp. *Odessa Tales*, 1923–24; *Red Cavalry*, 1926.

**BACHMANN, INGEBORG,** June 25, 1926 (Klagenfurt, Austria)–Oct. 16, 1973. Austrian short-story writer, lyric poet, dramatist, and librettist. She began her literary career while she was working at a radio station in Vienna. *Das dreissigste Jahr (The Thirtieth Year)*, 1961; *Anrufung des grossen Baeren (Invocation of the Great Bear)*, 1956; *Malina*, 1971.

**BEMELMANS, LUDWIG,** Apr. 27, 1898 (Meran, Austria)–Oct. 1, 1962. Austrian-U.S. writer, illustrator. Best known for the *Madeline* series of children's books (from 1939); also wrote novels, short stories, essays.

**BENAVANTE Y MARTÍNEZ, JACINTO,** Aug. 12, 1866 (Madrid, Sp.)–July 14, 1954. Spanish playwright. Author of satires of upper-class life, reminiscent of Italian commedia dell'arte; awarded Nobel Prize in literature, 1922. *The Bonds of Interest*, 1907; *Señora Ama*, 1908; *Passion Flower*, 1913.

**BENN, GOTTFRIED,** May 2, 1886 (Mansfeld, Ger.)–July 7, 1956. German poet, critic. Influenced by F. NIETZSCHE, he is best known for early expressionistic poems and poetic dramas; considered by many to be the most influential writer in post-WW II Germany. *Morgue*, 1912; *Fleish* (1916); and *Schutt* (1924).

**BJØRNSON, BJØRNSTJERNE,** Dec. 8, 1832 (Kvikne, Nor.)–Apr. 26, 1910. Norwegian dramatist, short-story writer, novelist, poet, political leader. The national poet of Norway, and one of the "four great ones" of 19th cent. Norwegian literature; Nobel Prize in literature, 1903. *A Happy Boy*

(short stories, 1860); *Sigurd the Bastard* (drama, 1862); *Poems and Songs*, 1870; *Magnhild* (novel, 1877).

**BLOK, ALEKSANDR,** Nov. 28, 1880 (St. Petersburg, Rus.)–Aug. 7, 1921. Russian writer. The most significant Russian poet of the early 20th cent. and the foremost Russian symbolist. *Verses about the Beautiful Lady*, 1904; *The Unknown Woman*, 1906; *The Twelve*, 1918; *The Scythians*, 1920.

**BOBROWSKI, JOHANNES,** April 9, 1917 (Tilsit, East Prussia)–Sept. 2, 1965. East German lyric poet, novelist, and short-story writer. A soldier in the German army during World War II, he was a prisoner of war in the U.S.S.R. *Sarmatische Zeit: Gedichte (Sarmatian Times: Poems)*, 1961; *Levins Muehle (Levin's Mill)*, 1964; *Mauesefest, und andere Erzachlungen (Mouse Feast, and Other Stories)*, 1965.

**BOCCACCIO, GIOVANNI,** 1313 (Paris, Fr.)–Dec. 21, 1375. Italian poet, storyteller. With PETRARCH, a principal precursor of the Italian Renaissance, his masterpiece, the *Decameron* (1348–53), a collection of 100 stories, was influential. *Filostrato; Teseida*.

**BÖLL, HEINRICH,** Dec. 21, 1917 (Cologne, Ger.) –July 16, 1985. German novelist, short-story writer, poet. Left-wing Catholic, critic of modern society; awarded Nobel Prize in literature, 1972. *Traveler, If You Come to Spa...* 1950; *Billiards at Half-Past Nine*, 1962; *Group Portrait with Lady*, 1973.

**BORGES, JORGE LUIS,** Aug. 24, 1899 (Buenos Aires, Arg.). Argentine poet, critic, short-story writer, noted for his highly original fictional narratives. *Historia universal de la infamia*, 1935; *Ficciones*, 1944; *El Aleph*, 1949; *Extraordinary Tales*, 1955; *Labyrinths*, 1962.

**BRECHT, BERTOLT,** Feb. 10, 1898 (Augsburg, Ger.) Aug. 11, 1956. German dramatist, poet. The foremost German playwright of this century. Developed anti-Aristotelian epic theater; founded Berliner Ensemble theater. *A Man's a Man*, 1926; *The Threepenny Opera*, 1928, *Rise and Fall of the City of Mahagonny*, 1929; *Mother Courage and Her Children*, 1939; *The Good Woman of Setzuan*, 1938–40; *The Caucasian Chalk Circle*, 1944–45.

**BULGAKOV, MIKHAIL,** May 15, 1891 (Kiev, Rus.)–Mar. 10, 1940. Soviet novelist, short-story writer, playwright. His sympathetic treatment of Russians hostile to the revolution and his satires on Soviet bureaucracy brought him official criticism. *The Deviliad*, 1925; *The Days of the Turbines*, 1926; *The Master and Margarita*, 1940.

**BUNIN, IVAN,** Oct. 10, 1870 (Voronezh, Rus.)– Nov. 8, 1953. Soviet short-story writer, novelist, poet. A foremost figure in pre-Revolutionary Russian literature; the first Soviet citizen to win a Nobel Prize in literature, 1933. *The Village*, 1910; *The Gentleman from San Francisco*, 1916.

**CALDERON DE LA BARCA, PEDRO,** Jan. 17, 1600 (Madrid, Sp.)–May 25, 1681. Spanish dramatist. After the death of LOPE DE VEGA (1635), the foremost Spanish dramatist and the last great figure in the golden age of Spanish literature. *La Vida es sueño*, 1635; *El Alcalde de Zalamea*, c.1640; *El Mágico prodigioso*, 1637; *El Gran Teatro del Mundo*, c.1635.

CALVINO, ITALO, Oct. 15, 1923 (Santiago de Las Vegas, Cuba)–Sept. 19, 1985. Italian novelist and short-story writer. *Il sentiero dei nidi di ragno (The Path to the Nest of Spiders)*, 1947; *Fiabe italiane (Italian Fables)*, 1956; *Mr. Palomar*, 1985.

CAMÕES (or Camoëns), LUIS VAZ DE, 1524? (Lisbon?, Port.)–June 10, 1580. Portuguese poet. Most celebrated figure in Portuguese literature; led a romantic life, including banishment from court for his romance with the queen's lady-in-waiting; wrote sonnets and lyrics; modeled his epic, *The Lusiads* (1572) on VIRGIL's *Aeneid*.

CANETTI, ELIAS, 1905 (Bulgaria). Bulgarian-British biographer, novelist, and nonfiction writer. Awarded Nobel Prize for literature in 1981. *Die Blendung (Tower of Babel)*, 1935; *Masse und Macht (Crowds and Power)*, 1960; *Die Fackel im Ohr (The Torch in the Ear)*, 1980.

ČAPEK, KAREL, Jan. 9, 1890 (Malé Svatoňovice, Bohemia)–Dec. 25, 1938. Czech novelist, dramatist. Wrote two plays, *R.U.R.* (1921) and *The Insect Play* (1921), with his brother Josef. *Hordubal*, 1933; *Meteor*, 1935; *An Ordinary Life*, 1936.

CARDUCCI, GIOSUÈ, July 28, 1835 (Val di Castello, It.)–Feb. 16, 1907. Italian poet, scholar, critic. First Italian to be awarded Nobel Prize in literature, 1906. "Inno a Satana," 1865; *Giambi ed epodi*, 1867–79; *Rime nuove*, 1861–87; *Odi barbare*, 1877–89; *Rime e ritmi*, 1887–99.

CASANOVA, GIOVANNI GIACOMO, Apr. 2, 1725 (Venice, It.)–June 4, 1798. Italian adventurer, author. A man of learning and taste, led an adventurous life all over Europe as a gambler, spy, seducer; his memoirs, *History of My Life* (12 vols. 1826–38), though an exaggerated account of his erotic exploits, is of historical interest.

CASTIGLIONI, BALDASSARE, Dec. 6, 1478 (Mantua, Italy)–Feb. 7, 1549. Italian diplomat and writer. *Il libro del cortegiano (The Book of the Courtier)*, 1518.

CATULLUS, GAIUS VALERIUS, c.84 B.C. (Verona, It.)–c.54 B.C. Roman lyric poet. Wrote love lyrics, epigrams, elegies, and marriage poems, the last of which became models for SPENSER, JONSON, and HERRICK. "Hail and farewell"; "Let us live and love, My Lesbia"; "I hate and I love"; *Attis; Thetis, Peleus*.

CELAN, PAUL, Nov 23, 1920 (Cernowitz, Romania)–May 1, 1970. Romanian-born French lyric poet who wrote in German. *Speech-Grille*, 1971; *Selected Poems*, 1972; *Nineteen Poems*, 1973.

CERVANTES SAAVEDRA, MIGUEL DE, Sept. 29?, 1547 (Alcalá de Hernares)–Apr. 23, 1616. Spanish novelist, dramatist, poet. Best known for his masterpiece *Don Quixote* (1605), a novel describing the adventures of a country gentleman and his squire. *Novelas Ejemplares* ("12 Tales"), 1613.

CÉSAIRE, AIMÉ, June 25, 1913 (Basse-Pointe, Martinique). Martinique poet, essayist, and drama-

tist. One of the founders of Négritude, a movement to celebrate the accomplishments of blacks. Poems: *Cahier d'un retour du pays natal (Return to My Native Land)*, 1947; Essays: *Discours sur le colonialisme (Discourse on Colonialism)*, 1951; Play: *Une saison au Congo (A Season in the Congo)*, 1966.

CHEKHOV, ANTON, Jan. 29, 1860 (Taganrog, Rus.)–July 14, 1904. Russian dramatist, short-story writer. Author of works characterized by realism, simplicity, compassion, humor, an emphasis on internal life, and the inability to communicate. *Ivanov*, 1889; *Uncle Vanya*, 1897; *The Seagull*, 1896; *the Three Sisters*, 1901; *The Cherry Orchard*, 1904.

CORTÁZAR, JULIO, Aug. 26, 1914 (Brussels, Belgium)–Feb. 12, 1984. Argentine metaphysical novelist. Fled the Perón regime to France. *Los premios (The Winners)*, 1960; *Rayuela (Hopscotch)*, 1963; *Un tal Lucas (A Certain Lucas)*, 1979.

D'ANNUNZIO, GABRIELE, Mar. 12, 1863 (Pescara, It.)–Mar. 1, 1938. Italian novelist, short-story writer, dramatist, poet. Prolific, eccentric writer; led 12,000 men in march on Fiume (Sept. 1919), which he ruled until Jan. 1921, when he declared war on Italy; an enthusiastic fascist, given a hereditary title and made resident of the Royal Academy by BENITO MUSSOLINI. *The Triumph of Death*, 1894; *The Dead City*, 1898; *The Daughter of Jorio*, 1904.

DANTE, ALIGHIERI, May 1265 (Florence, It.)–Sept. 14, 1321. Italian poet. The most famous Italian poet; his masterpiece, *The Divine Comedy* (c.1307– 21), tells the story of his imaginary journey through Hell, Purgatory, and Heaven, guided by VIRGIL, then by Beatrice (probably Beatrice Portinari, whom he idolized). *The New Life*, c.1292.

DAVIES, ROBERTSON, Aug. 28, 1913 (Thamesville, Ont.). Canadian writer. Also an actor. *Leaven of Malice*, 1954; *Fifth Business*, 1970, *The Manticore*, 1972; *World of Wonders*, 1975; *What's Bred in the Bone*, 1985; *The Lyre of Orpheus*, 1988.

DINESEN, ISAK (pseud. of Baroness Karen Blixen), April 17, 1885 (Rungsted, Den.)–Sept. 7, 1962. Danish short-story writer. Wrote mainly in English; noted for her accounts of life on an East African coffee plantation, collected in *Out of Africa* (1937) and *Shadows on the Grass* (1960). *Seven Gothic Tales*, 1934; *Winter's Tales*, 1942.

DOSTOYEVSKY, FYODOR, Nov. 11, 1821 (Moscow, Rus.)–Feb. 9, 1881. Russian novelist. Author of powerful, realistic novels combining psychology and philosophy; his tragic life included four years of hard labor in a Siberian prison camp for association with radical Utopians. *Notes from the Underground*, 1864; *Crime and Punishment*, 1866; *The Idiot*, 1869; *The Possessed*, 1871; *The Brothers Karamazov*, 1880.

DÜRRENMATT, FRIEDRICH, Jan. 5, 1921 (Konolfingen, Switz.). Swiss playwright, novelist. Nicknamed the Helvetian Aristophanes for his humorous treatment of serious subjects. *The Marriage of*

*Mr. Mississippi*, 1952; *The Visit*, 1958; *The Physicists*, 1962.

**ECHEGARAY Y EIZAGUIRRE, JOSÉ,** April 19, 1832 (Madrid, Sp.)–Sept. 14, 1916. Spanish dramatist, mathematician, physicist, economist, politican. Author of technically masterful melodramas; awarded Nobel Prize in literature (with FRÉDÉRIC MISTRAL), 1904. *Folly or Saintliness, 1877; The Great Galeoto*, 1881.

**EHRENBERG, ILYA,** Jan. 27, 1891 (Kiev, Rus.)–Aug. 31, 1967. Soviet novelist, journalist. His novel critical of the post-Stalin period, *The Thaw* (1954), gave that era its name. *People, Years, Life*, 1961–65.

**EICHENDORFF, JOSEPH FREIHERR VON,** Mar. 10, 1788 (near Ratibov, Upper Silesia)–Nov. 26, 1857. German romantic poet, novelist, and historian. *Ahnung und Gegenwart (Presentiment and the Present)*, 1815; *Aus dem Leben eines Taugenichts (From the Life of a Ne'er-Do-Well)*, 1826; *Über die ethische und religiöse Bedeutung der neueren romantischen Poesie in Deutschland (On the Ethical and Religious Importance of Recent Romantic Poetry in Germany)*, 1847.

**EKELÖF, GUNNAR,** Sept. 15, 1907 (Stockholm, Sweden)–March 16, 1968. Swedish poet. Wrote of the obscure and esoteric. *Selected Poems*, 1967; *I Do Best Alone at Night*, 1968; *Selected Poems*, 1972.

**ELYTIS, ODYSSEUS,** Nov. 2, 1911 (Heraklion, Crete). Greek poet. Awarded Nobel Prize for literature in 1979. *To axion esti (The Axion Esti of Odysseus Elytis)*, 1959; *Hexe kai mia typheis ghia ton ouran (Six and One Regrets for the Sky)*, 1960.

**ESENIN, SERGEI,** Oct. 3, 1895 (Konstantinovo [now Esenino], Rus.)–Dec. 27, 1925. Soviet poet. Cult figure in the early Soviet period, connected with the imagists; wrote simple lyrics about rural Russia, an alcoholic, denounced for "hooliganism" and committed suicide at age 30. *Confessions of a Hooligan: Fifty Poems*, 1924; *Tavern Moscow*, 1924. (Second of his three wives was I. DUNCAN.)

**EURIPIDES,** 480 or 485 B.C. (Attica)–406 B.C. Greek playwright. One of the great tragedians; of some 92 plays he wrote, only 18 (possibly 19) plays are extant; called the first realist, he wrote works noted for their psychological insight, religious skepticism, and technical innovations, including expository prologue and the problem-resolving *deus ex machina* device. *Medea*, 431 B.C.; *The Trojan Women*, 415 B.C.; *Electra*, 413 B.C.; *Orestes*, 408 B.C.; *The Bacchae* 406–405; *Iphigenia in Aulis*, 405–404.

**FEDIN, KONSTANTIN,** Nov. 24, 1892 (Saratov, Rus.)–July 17, 1977. Soviet novelist. His novels deal with small-town life before and after the October Revolution. *Early Joys*, 1945; *No Ordinary Summer*, 1948; *The Bonfire*, 1962.

**FEUCHTWANGER, LION,** July 7, 1884 (Munich, Ger.)–Dec. 12, 1958. German novelist, playwright. Noted for his historical romances. *The Ugly Dutchess*, 1923; *Josephus*, 1932; *The Jew of Rome*, 1935; *Josephus and the Emperor*, 1942.

**FIRDOUSI** (born Qāsim Mansur or Hasan), 941? (Tūs, Persia) 1020, Persian epic poet. Spent 35 years writing *Shan-Nama (Book of Kings)*, 1010.

**FONTANE, THEODOR,** Dec. 30, 1819 (Neuruppin, Brandenburg)–Sept. 26, 1898. German realistic novelist. *Irrungen, Wirrungen (Trials and Tribulations)*, 1888; *Frau Jenny Treibel*, 1892; *Effi Briest*, 1894.

**FRISCH, MAX,** May 15, 1911 (Zürich, Switzerland). Swiss dramatist and novelist. Specializes in war and its destructiveness. *Nun singen sie wieder (Now They're Singing Again)*, 1945; *Als der Krieg zu Ende war (When the War Was Over)*, 1949; *Triptychon*, 1978.

**FUENTES, CARLOS,** Nov. 11, 1928 (Mexico City, Mex.). Mexican novelist, playwright, critic. Noted Latin American fiction writer; headed Mexican Dept. of Cultural Relations, 1956–59; Mexican amb. to France, 1975. *Good Conscience*, 1959; *Where the Air Is Clear*, 1958; *Our Land*, 1974.

**GARCÍA LORCA, FEDERICO,** June 5, 1898 (Fuente Vaqueros, Sp.)–Aug. 19, 1936. Spanish poet, dramatist. A major modern Spanish literary figure; his passionate and violent works are derived from the folklore of his native Andalusia; killed by FRANCO's forces during the Spanish Civil War. *House of Bernarda Alba*, 1936; *Lament for the Death of a Bullfighter*, 1937; *Blood Wedding*, 1933; *Gypsy Ballads*, 1928; *The Poet in New York*, 1940.

**GARCÍA MÁRQUEZ, GABRIEL,** Mar. 6, 1928 (Arataca, Colombia). Colombian novelist, short-story writer. A highly imaginative writer, deals with the extraordinary as if it were commonplace; awarded Nobel Prize in literature, 1982. *The Funeral of Mama Grande*, 1962; *No One Writes to the Colonel and Other Stories*, 1968; *One Hundred Years of Solitude*, 1970; *Leaf Storm and Other Stories*, 1972; *Love in the Time of Cholera*, 1985.

**GEORGE, STEFAN,** July 12, 1868 (Büdesheim, Germany)–Dec. 4, 1933. German mythic poet. *Das Jahr der Seele (The Year of the Soul)*, 1897; *Der Stern des Bundes (The Star of the Covenant)*, 1914; *Das neue Reich (The New Kingdom)*, 1928.

**GIBRAN, KAHLIL,** Jan. 6, 1883 (Bechari, Leb.)–Apr. 10, 1931. Syrian-U.S. writer. Best known as author of *The Prophet* (1923), an extremely popular mystical prose-poem.

**GJELLERUP, KARL ADOLF,** June 2, 1857 (Roholte, Den.)–Oct. 11, 1919. Danish poet, novelist. Criticized his times, caricaturing the Danish bourgeoisie; awarded Nobel Prize in literature (with his compatriot Henrik Pontoppidan), 1917. *An Idealist*, 1878; *The Disciple of the Teutons*, 1882; *The Pilgrim Kamanita*, 1906.

**GOETHE, JOHANN WOLFGANG VON,** Aug. 28, 1749 (Frankfurt, Ger.)–Mar. 22, 1832. German poet, dramatist, novelist. Leading *Sturm und Drang* ("Storm and Stress") dramatist; originated Weimar classicism in drama; originated the German novel of character development. *Faust*, 1808, 1832; *The Sorrows of Young Werther*, 1774.

**GOGOL, NIKOLAI,** Apr. 1, 1809 (Sorochintsy,

Rus.)–Mar. 4, 1852. Russian short-story writer, novelist, dramatist. The father of Russian realism, although in some of his best work ("The Overcoat," 1842) he combined realism and fantasy; depression and religious fanaticism led him to burn the second part of his novel *Dead Souls* (1842) and starve himself to death. *The Nose*, 1836; *The Inspector-General*, 1836; *Diary of a Madman*, 1842.

GOLDONI, CARLO, Feb. 25, 1707 (Venice, It.)– Feb. 6, 1793. Italian dramatist. The creator of modern Italian comedy; superseded the commedia dell'arte by eliminating masks and depicting ordinary Venetians realistically, in the manner of MOLIÈRE. *The Mistress of the Inn*, 1753; *The Fan*, 1763; *The Beneficient Bear*, 1771.

GONCHAROV, IVAN, June 18, 1812 (Simbirsk [now Ulyanovsk], Rus.)–Sept. 27, 1891. Russian novelist. Best known for his novel *Oblomov* (1859), about a Russian nobleman from whose name the Russian word *oblomovism* ("indolence") was derived. *A Common Story*, 1847; *The Precipice*, 1869.

GÓNGORA Y ARGOTE, LUIS DE, July 11, 1561 (Córdoba, Spain)–May 23, 1627. Spanish intellectual poet. Founder of Gongorism. *Fábula de Polifemo y Galatea*, 1613?; *Soledades*, 1613; *Las firmezas de Isabela*, 1633.

GORDIMER, NADINE, Nov. 20, 1923 (Springs, South Africa). South African anti-apartheid novelist and short-story writer. *Face to Face*, 1949; *Burger's Daughter*, 1979; *Something Out There*, 1984.

GORKY, MAXIM (pseud. of Aleksei Maximovich Pyeshkov), Mar. 28, 1868 (Nizhny Novgorod [now Gorky], Rus.)–June 18, 1936. Soviet novelist, short-story writer, dramatist. The first proletarian writer; the father of Soviet literature and a founder of Socialist Realism. *The Lower Depths*, 1902; *Mother*, 1907; *Childhood, In the World, My Universities* (autobiographical trilogy) 1913–23.

GRASS, GÜNTER, Oct. 16, 1927 (Danzig [now Gdansk], Pol.). German novelist, playwright. The literary spokesman for Germans who grew up during the Nazi era. *The Tin Drum*, 1959; *Cat and Mouse*, 1961; *Dog Years*, 1965; *Local Anesthetic*, 1970; *From the Diary of a Snail*, 1973.

GRILLPARZER, FRANZ, Jan. 15, 1791 (Vienna, Austria)–Jan. 21, 1872. Austrian dramatist. Although now considered the greatest Austrian dramatist, was not well received in his time and gave up publishing after 1838. *The Golden Fleece*, 1821; *Hero and Leander*, 1831; *A Dream Is Life*, 1834; *The Jewess of Toledo; Family Strife in Hapsburg*, published posthumously.

GRIMM, JACOB LUDWIG CARL, Jan. 4, 1785 (Hanau, Ger.)–Sept. 20, 1863; and his brother WILHELM CARL GRIMM, Feb. 24, 1786 (Hanau, Ger.)–Dec. 16, 1859. German philologists, folklorists, lexicographers. Best known as the coauthors of *Grimm's Fairy-Tales* (1812–15), based on their interviews with peasants; also began to write the great *German Dictionary*, which was not completed until 1954.

GUILLÉN, JORGE, Jan. 18, 1893 (Valladolid,

Spain)–1984. Spanish lyric poet. *Maremágnum*, 1957; *Que van a dar en el mar*, 1960; *A la altura de las circunstancias*, 1963.

GUMILEV, NIKOLAI, Apr. 15, 1886 (Kronstadt, Rus.)–Aug. 25, 1921. Russian poet. With his wife, ANNA AKHMATOVA, a founder of the Acmeist movement, 1912; his poetry reflected his travels in Europe and Africa; executed by the Bolsheviks for alleged conspiracy. *The Pillar of Fire*, 1921.

HĀFIZ, (born Shams-ud-din Muhammad), 1320?– 1390? Persian Poet. Specialist in odes written in five to 15 couplets each. The *Dīvān of Hāfiz*.

HAMSUN, KNUT (born Knut Pedersen), Aug. 4, 1859 (Lom, Norway)–Feb. 19, 1952. Norwegian novelist. Lived as a vagabond in Norway and the U.S. until age 30; gained fame with his first novel, *Hunger* (1899); awarded Nobel Prize in literature, 1920. *Pan*, 1894; *The Growth of the Soil*, 1917.

HAŠEK, JAROSLAV, Apr. 30, 1883 (Prague, Czech.) –Jan. 2, 1923. Czech novelist, short-story writer. Best known for *The Good Soldier Schweik* (4 vols., 1920–23), a hilarious satire on military bureaucracy and an indictment of war.

HAUPTMANN, GERHART, Nov. 15, 1862 (Silesia [now Szczawno Zdrój, Pol.])–June 8, 1946. German dramatist, poet. Foremost German playwright of the pre-WW I period; his first play, *Before Sunrise* (1889), brought naturalism to the German theater; awarded Nobel Prize in literature, 1912. *The Weavers*, 1892; *The Sunken Bell*, 1897.

HAVEL, VÁCLAV, Oct. 5, 1936 (Prague, Czechoslovakia). Czech dramatist, poet, and politician. Uses a satirical and absurdist technique to criticise the dehumanization of language, social institutions, and human relations; was active in the Czech civil rights movement after the Soviet-led invasion of 1968, and was harrassed by the Soviets for years; after the thaw in 1989, elected president of Czechoslovakia. *The Garden Party*, 1963; *The Memorandum*, 1965; *The Increased Difficulty of Concentration*, 1968.

HEBEL, (Christian) FRIEDRICH, March 18, 1813 (Wesselburen, Holstein)–Dec. 13, 1863. German realistic dramatist. *Judith*, 1841; *Maria Magdalena*, 1844; *Die Nibelungen*, 1862.

HEIDENSTAM, VERNER VON, July 6, 1859 (Närke, Swed.)–May 20, 1940. Swedish poet, novelist, essayist. A major Swedish lyric poet, led the reaction against the naturalist movement in Sweden; awarded Nobel Prize in literature, 1916. *Pilgrimage and Wonder-Years*, 1888; *Poems*, 1895; *The Tree of the Folkungs*, 2 vols., 1905–07; *New Poems*, 1915.

HEINE, HEINRICH (born Chaim Harry Heine), Dec. 13, 1797 (Düsseldorf, Ger.)–Feb. 17, 1856. German lyric poet. His poetry has been used in over 3,000 musical works, including those of FRANZ SCHUBERT, ROBERT SCHUMANN, FELIX MENDELSSOHN, F. LISZT. *Buch der Lieder*, 1827; *Neue Gedichte*, 1844; *Reisebilder*, 4 vols., 1826–31.

HERBERT, ZBIGNIEW, 1924 (Poland). Polish lyric poet. Fought with the Polish Resistance against the Nazis in World War II. *Sturna swiatla (A String of*

*Light)*, 1956; *Hermes, pies i gwiazda (Hermes, Dog and Star)*, 1957; *Pan Cogito (Mr. Cogito)*, 1974.

HEREDIA, JOSE MARIA, Dec. 31, 1803 (Santiago, Cuba)–May 2, 1839. Cuban poet. The national poet of Cuba, one of the New World's first Romantic poets. *On the Temple Pyramid of Cholula*, 1820; *Ode to Niagara Falls*, 1824.

HESIOD, eighth and ninth centuries. Greek poet. Founder of didactic poetry. *Works and Days; Theogony.*

HESSE, HERMANN, July 2, 1877 (Württemberg, Ger.)–Aug. 9, 1962. German-Swiss novelist. Wrote lyrical, symbolic, ironic novels; underwent a revival in the 1960s, especially among students; awarded Nobel Prize in literature, 1946. *Demian*, 1919; *Steppenwolf*, 1927; *Magister Ludi*, 1943.

HOFFMAN, E(rnst) T(heodore) A(madeus), Jan. 24, 1776 (Königsberg, Germany)–June 25, 1822. German short-story writer. Three of his stories were used by JACQUES OFFENBACH in his opera *Tales of Hoffman. Fantasiestücke (Fantasy-pieces)*, 1814–1815; *Nachtstücke (Night-pieces)*, 1817; *Die Elixiere des Teufels (The Devil's Elixirs)*, 1816.

HOFFMANNSTHAL, HUGO VON, Feb. 1, 1874 (Vienna, Austria)–July 15, 1929. Austrian dramatist, poet, essayist, and librettist. Wrote librettos for operas by RICHARD STRAUSS, including *Der Rosenkavalier. Der Tod des Tizian (The Death of Titian)*, 1892; *Das kleine Welttheater (The Small World-Theater)*, 1897; *Elektra*, 1903.

HOLBERG, LUDVIG, BARON, Dec. 3, 1684 (Bergen, Nor.)–Jan. 28, 1754. Danish dramatist, essayist, poet. The foremost Scandinavian writer of the Enlightenment, called the Molière of the North; claimed by both Norway and Denmark as the founder of their literatures; his *Pedar Paars* (1719–20), a mock-heroic epic, is the earliest extant Danish-language epic. *The Political Tinker*, 1722.

HÖLDERLIN, FRIEDRICH, March 20, 1770 (Lauffen, Württemberg)–June 7, 1843. German classical lyric poet and novelist. *Hyperion oder Der Eremit in Griechenland (Hyperion, or the Hermit in Greece)*, 1797–1799; "Brod und Wein" ("Bread and Wine"); "Germanien."

HOLUB, MIROSLAV, Sept. 13, 1923 (Pilsen, Czechoslovakia). Czech poet. Although a clinical pathologist, he still finds time to write anti-rhetorical poetry. *Day Duty*, 1958; *Where the Blood Flows*, 1963; *On the Contrary*, 1982.

HOMER, fl. 8th cent. B.C. (Asia Minor, probably Ionia). Greek poet. Although his existence has long been disputed by scholars, it is now generally believed that a single, unifying intelligence, created the *Iliad* and the *Odyssey*—the two epic poems from which all Western literature has developed—from history, folk tales, and legends; blind, according to legend.

HORACE (in full; Quintus Horatius Flaccus), Dec. 8, 65 B.C. (Venusia, Apulia)–Nov. 27, 8 B.C. Roman poet. Great lyric poet, noted especially for his *Odes* (23 B.C.–c.13 B.C.); his poetry reveals much about the Augustan age; adapted Greek meters to Latin; wrote under the patronage of Maecenas

and AUGUSTUS. *Epodes*, 30 B.C.; *Satires*, c.35 B.C.–30 B.C.; *Epistles*, 20 B.C.–c.13 B.C.; *Ars Poetica*, 8 B.C.

HUIDOBRO, VICENTE, Jan. 10, 1893 (Santiago, Chile)–Jan. 27, 1948. Chilean poet, novelist, literary theorist. Father of the avante-garde movements of "creationism" and "ultraism." *I Will Not Serve* (manifesto), 1914; *Tour Eiffel*, 1917; *Satire or the Power of Words*, 1939; *Ultimos poemas*, 1948.

IBSEN, HENRIK, Mar. 20, 1828 (Skien, Nor.) –May 23, 1906. Norwegian dramatist. The father of modern drama; his realistic plays emphasized social problems, characterizations, and psychological conflicts. *Peer Gynt*, 1867; *A Doll's House*, 1879; *Ghosts*, 1881; *An Enemy of the People*, 1882; *The Wild Duck*, 1884; *Hedda Gabler*, 1890; *The Master Builder*, 1892.

JIMÉNEZ, JUAN RAMÓN, Dec. 24, 1881 (Moguer, Sp.)–May 29, 1958. Spanish lyric poet. His early poems reflect French symbolist influence; later, he wrote simplified, concise free verse; awarded Nobel Prize in literature, 1956. *Pastorales*, 1911; *Diary of a Recently Married Poet*, 1917.

JOHNSON, EYVIND, July 29, 1900 (Overlulea, Swe.)–Aug. 25, 1976. Swedish novelist, short-story writer. Best known for his four-volume autobiographical work, *The Novel about Olov* (1934–37); awarded Nobel Prize in literature (with Harry Martinson), 1974. *Rain at Daybreak*, 1933; *Return to Ithaca*, 1946.

JUVENAL, born Decimus Junius Juvenalis, c.60 (Aquinum?)–c.140. Roman poet. Noted for 16 satires in which he denounced the degeneracy of the Empire. *Satires*, 5 books, c.100–127.

KAFKA, FRANZ, July 3, 1883 (Prague, Czech.) –June 3, 1924. German novelist, short-story writer. Wrote visionary tales of guilt-ridden, isolated, anxious men in an aimless, unfathomable world. *The Metamorphosis*, 1915, *In the Penal Colony*, 1919, *The Trial*, 1925; *The Castle*, 1926; *Amerika*, 1927.

KAISER, GEORG, Nov. 25, 1878 (Mägdeburg, Ger.)–June 4, 1945. German playwright. Leading German expressionist playwright. *The Burghers of Calais*, 1914; *From Morn to Midnight*, 1916; *Trilogy: The Corals* (1917), *Gas I* (1918), and *Gas II* (1920).

KĀLIDĀSA (also known as Kamadeva or Kandarpa), late 4th century (Vjjain?, India)–early 5th century. Indian dramatist and poet. Considered to be one of the great Sanskrit poets. *Shākuntalā; Vikramorvashīya; Mālavikāgnimitra.*

KAWABATA YASUNARI, June 14, 1899 (Osaka, Jap.)–Apr. 16, 1972. Japanese novelist. Author of melancholy, impressionistic novels and short stories; the first Japanese to be awarded the Nobel Prize in literature, 1968. *The Izu Dancer*, 1925; *Snow Country*, 1935–1947; *Thousand Cranes*, trans. 1959; *The House of the Sleeping Beauties and Other Stories*, trans. 1969.

KAZANTZAKIS, NIKOS, Feb. 18, 1883? (Crete) –Oct. 26, 1957. Greek poet, novelist. Best known in the U.S. for his novel *Zorba the Greek* (1946), which was made into a successful film. *The Greek*

*Passion*, 1948; *The Odyssey, A Modern Sequel*, 1938; *The Last Temptation of Christ*, 1951.

**KHLEBNIKOV, VELEMIR**, Nov. 9, 1885 (Tundutov, Rus.)–June 28, 1922. Russian poet. Influential avante-garde poet and a founder of futurism in Russia. *Zangezi*, 1922.

**KIELLAND, ALEXANDER LANGE**, Feb. 18, 1849 (Stavanger, Nor.)–Apr. 6, 1906. Norwegian novelist, short-story writer, dramatist. With H. IBSEN, B. BJØRNSON, and J. LIE, one of the "big four" of 19th-cent. Norwegian literature. *Workers*, 1881; *Skipper Worse*, 1882; *St. John's Festival*, 1887.

**KLEIST, HEINRICH VON**, Oct. 18, 1777 (Frankfurt on the Oder, Ger.)–Nov. 21, 1811. German dramatist, writer of novellas. Best known for the historical tragedy *The Prince of Homburg* (1821) and the novella *Michael Kolhaas* (1808); unrecognized in his time, appealed strongly to modern authors; committed suicide. *The Broken Pitcher*, 1805.

**KOESTLER, ARTHUR**, Sept. 5, 1905 (Budapest, Hung.)–Mar. 3, 1983. Hungarian-English novelist, essayist. Spokesman for the ex-communist left; his *Darkness at Noon* (1941) is based on the Moscow trials of the 1930s; *Bricks to Babel* (anthology), 1980; committed suicide with his wife.

**KOSINSKI, JERZY**, June 14, 1933 (Lódź, Pol.). Polish-U.S. novelist. Gained fame for *The Painted Bird* (1965), a horrifying, surrealistic account of a six-year-old boy in Eastern Europe during WW II; came to U.S. in 1957. *Steps*, 1968; *Being There*, 1971; *The Devil Tree*, 1973; *Blind Dates*, 1977; *Pinball*, 1982.

**LAGERKVIST, PÄR**, May 23, 1891 (Växjö, Swe.)–July 11, 1974. Swedish novelist, dramatist, poet. Best known for his humanistic novels, especially *Barabbas* (1950); awarded Nobel Prize in literature, 1951. *The Man without a Soul*, 1936; *The Dwarf*, 1945; *The Sibyl*, 1956.

**LAGERLÖF, SELMA**, Nov. 20, 1858 (Värmland, Swe.)–Mar. 16, 1940. Swedish novelist, short-story writer. Best known for her classic children's stories, such as *The Wonderful Adventures of Nils* (1906); the first woman to win the Nobel Prize in literature, 1909. *Gösta Berling Saga*, 1891; *The Ring of the Löwenskolds* (trilogy), 1925–28, trans. 1931.

**LAMPEDUSA, GIUSEPPE DI, DUKE OF PARMA, PRINCE OF LAMPEDUSA**, Dec. 23, 1896 (Palermo, Sicily)–1957. Italian novelist. Born into a wealthy aristocratic family; noted for *The Leopard* (trans. 1960), a historical novel set in late 19th cent. Sicily.

**LAXNESS, HALLDÓR**, Apr. 23, 1902 (Laxnes, Iceland). Icelandic novelist, poet, playwright. A major figure in modern Icelandic literature; noted for his lyrical novels set in an Icelandic fishing village; awarded Nobel Prize in literature, 1955. *Independent People* (2 vols., 1934–35); *The Light of the World* (4 vols., 1937–40).

**LAYE, CAMARA**, 1928 (Kouroussa, Guinea)–1980. Guinean novelist. *L'Enfant noir (The Dark Child)*, 1953; *Le Regard du roi (The Radiance of the King)*, 1954; *Dramouss (A Dream of Africa)*, 1966.

**LEOPARDI, GIACOMO, CONTE**, June 29, 1798 (Recanati, It.)–June 14, 1837. Italian poet, scholar. Foremost 19th-cent. Italian poet; noted for his lyrical, melancholy, pessimistic poems, written in a classical style. *Canzoni*, 1824; *Versi*, 1826; *Canti*, 1831.

**LERMONTOV, MIKHAIL**, Oct. 15, 1814 (Moscow, Rus.)–July 27, 1841. Rusian poet, novelist. One of the foremost Russian poets of the 19th cent.; progressed from early Romantic poetry to simpler, realistic prose works; led a Byronic life, twice exiled to the Caucasus, where he was killed in a duel. *The Song of the Merchant Kalashnikov*, 1837; *A Hero of Our Time*, 1840; *The Demon*, 1841.

**LESSING, GOTTHOLD EPHRAIM**, Jan. 22, 1729 (Saxony)–Feb. 15, 1781. German dramatist, critic. Influential German exponent of the Enlightenment; a major influence in development of modern German theater. *Miss Sara Sampson*, 1755; *Minna von Barnhelm*, 1767; *Emilia Galotti*, 1772; *Nathan the Wise*, 1779.

**LI PO**, (or Li T'ai-po), 701 (Central Asia)–762. Chinese poet of the T'ang dynasty. China's most famous lyric poet. *The Poetry and Career of Li Po*.

**LISPECTOR, CLARICE**, Dec. 10, 1925 (Chechelnik, U.S.S.R.)–Dec. 9, 1977. Ukranian-born Brazilian novelist and short-story writer. Her existential work includes *Perto do Corofão Salvagem*, 1944; *Laços de familia (Family Ties)*, 1972.

**LONGUS**, 3rd or 4th century AD. Greek pastoral poet. Probably the author of *Daphnis and Cloë*.

**LOUW, N. P. VAN WYK**, June 11, 1906 (Sutherland, Cape Colony)–June 18, 1970. Afrikaans poet, playwright, critic. Leader of the 1930s revival of Afrikaans poetry. *Raka*, 1941; *Germanicus*, 1956; *Tristia*, 1962.

**LUCIAN** (or Lucianus), 120 (Samosata, Syria [now Samsat, Turkey])–after 180. Greek satirist. A major figure in the revival of Greek literature under the Roman Empire; best known for his dialogues. *Dialogues of the Gods; Dialogues of the Dead; The Sale of Lives; How to Write History; The True History.*

**LUCRETIUS** (Titus Lucretius Carus), 98?(Rome)–55 B.C. Roman philosophical poet. *De rerum natura (On the Nature of Things)*.

**MACHADO DE ASSIS, JOACHIM MARIA**, June 21, 1839 (Rio de Janeiro, Brazil)–Sept. 29, 1908. Brazil's greatest novelist and poet. First president of the Brazilian Academy of Letters. *Memórias postumas de braz cubas (Epitaph for a Small Winner)*, 1891; *Quincas borba (Philosopher or Dog?)*, 1891; *Dom Casmurro*, 1900.

**MACHADO Y RUIZ, ANTONIO**, July 26, 1875 (Seville, Spain)–Feb. 8, 1939. Spanish lyric poet. He was on the Republican side in Spain's Civil War and was forced to escape to France, where he died one month later. *Soledades*, 1903; *Campos de Castilla*, 1912; *Juan de Mairena*, 1936.

**MAETERLINCK, MAURICE**, Aug. 29, 1862 (Ghent, Belg.)——May 6, 1949. Belgian poet, playwright, prose writer (in French). Best known for his symbolist masterpiece, *Pelléas et Mélisande* (music by CLAUDE DEBUSSY, 1892); awarded Nobel Prize in literature, 1911. *Hothouses*, 1899; *The Life of the Bee*, 1901; *The Intelligence of Flowers*, 1907; *The Blue Bird*, 1909.

**MAHFOUZ, NAGUIB** (born Abdel Aziz Al-Sabilgi), Dec. 11, 1911? (Cairo, Egypt). Egyptian novelist. Also a civil servant; awarded Nobel Prize for literature, 1988. *Zugag Midagg (Midag Alley)*, 1947; *Hikay at haratina (Fountain and Tomb)*, 1975; *Sabah al-ward*, 1987.

**MANDELSTAM, OSIP**, Jan. 15, 1891 (Warsaw, Pol)–c.Dec. 27, 1938. Russian poet. Member of the acmeist group; died in exile in Siberia. *The Stone*, 1913; *Tristia*, 1922.

**MANN, HEINRICH**, Mar. 27, 1871 (Lübeck, Ger.)–Mar. 12, 1950. German novelist. Critic of authoritarian Germany under Wilhelm II; his novel *Professor Unrat* (1905) became the classic film *The Blue Angel*. *In the Land of Cockaigne*, 1900; *Henri Quatre*, 2 vols., 1935, 1938. (Brother of THOMAS MANN.)

**MANN, THOMAS**, June 6, 1875 (Lübeck, Ger.)–Aug. 12, 1955. German-U.S. novelist. One of the foremost German writers; wrote of the relationship of art to reality; left Nazi Germany, 1933; became a U.S. citizen, 1944; awarded Nobel Prize in literature, 1929. *Buddenbrooks*, 1901; *Tonio Kröger*, 1903; *Death in Venice*, 1912; *The Magic Mountain*, 1924; *Doctor Faustus*, 1947; *The Confessions of Felix Krull*, 1954.

**MANZONI, ALLESANDRO**, Mar. 7, 1785 (Milan, It.)–May 22, 1873. Italian novelist, poet. Best known for his novel *The Betrothed* (3 vols., 1825–27), considered a masterpiece; made a senator of Italy, 1860; GUISEPPE VERDI wrote *Requiem* for him, and it was first performed on the anniversary of his death. *Sacred Hymns*, 1812–15; *Il Conte di Carmagnola*, 1820; *The Fifth of May*, 1822; *Adelchi*, 1822.

**MARINETTI, FILIPPO TOMMASO**, Dec. 22, 1876 (Alexandria, Egypt)–Dec. 2, 1944. Italian poet, novelist, and dramatist. He was the founder of the Futurist movement in 1909, which held that courage, audacity, and rebellion are the essential elements of poetry, and urged the abolition of syntax. *Manifeste du Futurisme*, 1909.

**MARTIAL** (born Marcus Valerius Martialis), Mar 1, 40 (Bilbilus, Sp.)–c.103. Roman poet. Wrote some 1,500 epigrams as social and satiric comment, presenting a vivid picture of Rome in the 1st cent. A.D. *Book on Spectacles*, 80; *Guest Gifts, and Gifts to Take Home*, 84–85; *Epigrams*, 86–102.

**MARTINSON, HARRY EDMUND**, May 6, 1904 (Jaemshoeg, Sweden)–Feb. 11, 1978. Swedish novelist, dramatist, poet, and essayist. A master of Swedish proletarian literature; his novels are about the working class and their search for freedom and integrity; (shared the Nobel Prize in literature with EYVIND JOHNSON in 1974). *Kap Farväl (Cape Farewell)*, 1934; *Vägen till Klockrike (The Road)*, 1948; *Vagnen*, 1960.

**MATSUO BASHŌ** (a.k.a. Bashō, born Matsuo Munefusa), 1644 (Iga Prov., [now Mie Pref.], Jap.)–Nov. 28, 1694. Japanese poet. Foremost Japanese practitioner of haiku, which he developed; influenced by Zen Buddhism. "The Narrow Road to the Deep North," 1694.

**MAYAKOVSKY, VLADIMIR**, July 19, 1893 (Bagdadi, now in Georgian SSR)–Apr. 14, 1930. Soviet poet, dramatist. Foremost poet of the Russian Revolution and early Soviet period; a leading futurist; noted for his original, technically innovative, vigorous, declamatory poetry; committed suicide. "A Cloud in Trousers," 1914–15; "The Backbone Flute," 1915; "Ode to the Revolution," 1918; "Left March," 1919; "150,000,000," 1920; "Vladimir Ilich Lenin," 1924; *The Bathouse*, 1929.

**MCCULLOUGH, COLLEEN**, June 1, 1937 (Wellington, Austrl.). Australian novelist. Noted for her best-selling romantic saga set in Australia, *The Thorn Birds* (1977).

**MENANDER**, 342 B.C. (Athens, Gr.)–292 B.C. Athenian dramatist. Considered by the ancient Greeks to be the greatest poet of New Comedy; works writer later adapted by PLAUTUS and TERENCE, and thereby influenced the development of European comedy. *Dyscolus*; *Perikeiromenē*; *Second Adelphoe*; *Epitrepontes*.

**MICHAUX, HENRI**, May 24, 1899 (Namur, Belgium)–Oct. 17, 1984. Belgian fantastic poet and painter. Produced many self-illustrated books of prose and poetry about the effects of hallucinogenic drugs. *Une Certaine Plume*, 1931; *Les Grandes Epreuves de l'espirit et les innombrables petites (The Major Ordeals of the Mind and the Countless Minor Ones)*, 1966; *Au pays de la magie*, 1977.

**MICKIEWICZ, ADAM**, Dec. 24, 1798 (Zaosie, Lithuania)–Nov. 26, 1855. Polish poet. Considered a voice of Polish national freedom; a romantic, influenced by LORD BYRON and SIR WALTER SCOTT; best known for his poetic epic *Master Thaddeus* (1834), *Poetry I*, 1822; *Poetry II*, 1823; *Crimean Sonnets*, 1826; *Konrad Wallenrod*, 1828.

**MILOSZ, CZESLAW**, June 30, 1911 (Lithuania), Lithuanian-born Polish poet, novelist, essayist who now lives in the U.S. An avant-garde poet who was active in the anti-Nazi **underground** in World War II, and later became an anti-Communist; awarded Nobel Prize in literature in 1980. *Zniewolony umysl (The Captive Mind)*, 1953; *Rodzinna Europa (Native Realm)*, 1959; *The Land of Ulro*, 1984.

**MISHIMA, YUKIO** (pseud. of Kimitake Hiraoka), Jan. 14, 1925 (Tokyo, Jap.)–Nov. 25, 1970. Japanese novelist, short-story writer. Wrote about the conflict between contemporary westernized Japan and the militaristic tradition of the old Japan; created his own private army; committed seppuku. *Confessions of a Mask*, 1948; *The Temple of the Golden Pavilion*, 1959; the tetralogy *Sea of Fertility*, 1969–70.

**MISTRAL, GABRIELA**, Apr. 7, 1889 (Vicuna, Chile)–Jan. 10, 1957. Chilean poet. Founded the modernist movement in Chilean poetry; wrote of her love for children and the downtrodden; the first Latin American woman to win the Nobel Prize in literature, 1945. *Sonnets of Death*, 1914;

*Desolation*, 1922; *Tenderness*, 1925, 1945; *Tala*, 1938.

**MOBERG, VILHELM**, Aug. 20, 1898 (Algutsboda, Swe.)–Aug. 8, 1973. Swedish novelist, dramatist. Best known for his multivolume epic about the Swedish emigration to America in the 1850s: *The Emigrants* (1949–59), *Unto a Good Land* (1952), *The Last Letter Home* (1961).

**MOLNÁR, FERENC**, Jan. 12, 1878 (Budapest, Hung.)–Apr. 1, 1952. Hungarian playwright, novelist, journalist. Wrote plays about salon life in Budapest and moving short stories about the underdog; his play *Liliom* (1909) was adapted by RICHARD RODGERS and OSCAR HAMMERSTEIN into the musical *Carousel*. *The Guardsman*, 1910; *The Swan*, 1920; *The Red Mill*, 1923.

**MONTALE, EUGENIO**, Oct. 12, 1896 (Genoa, It.).–Sept. 12, 1981. Italian poet, translator. A major modern Italian poet; translated SHAKESPEARE, T. S. ELIOT, G. M. HOPKINS, others; awarded 1975 Nobel Prize in literature. *Cuttlefish Bones*, 1925; *Notebook of Translations*, 1948; *The Offender*, 1963.

**MORAVIA, ALBERTO**, Nov. 28, 1907 (Rome, It.). Italian novelist and short-story writer. A social realist who writes about alienation and isolation. *The Time of Indifference*, 1929; *The Woman of Rome*, 1947; *Disobedience*, 1948; *The Conformist*, 1951; *The Empty Canvas*, 1960.

**MÖRIKE, EDUARD**, Sept. 8, 1804 (Ludwigsburg, Germany)–June 4, 1875. German lyric poet and novelist. His deceptively simple lyrics were set to music by ROBERT SCHUMANN, FRANZ SCHUBERT, JOHANNES BRAHMS, and HUGO WOLF. *Mahler Nolten (Painter Nolten)*, 1832; *Gedichte (Poems)*, 1834; *Mozart auf Reise nach Prag (Mozart on his Trip to Prague)*, 1856.

**MUNRO, ALICE**, July 10, 1931 (Wingham, Ont., Canada). Canadian short-story writer. *Dance of the Happy Shades*, 1969; *Something I've Been Meaning to Tell You*, 1974; *The Progress of Love*, 1987.

**MURASAKI, SHIKIBU**, 978?–1026?. Japanese novelist. Author of *Tales of Genji*, generally considered to be the first Japanese novel and notable for its picture of a unique court society and sensitivity to emotions and nature; a lady in the court of Empress Akiko, she also wrote a diary of historical and literary value (1007–1010).

**NAIPAUL, V(**idiadhar**) S(**urajprasad**)**, Aug. 17, 1932 (Trinidad). West Indian novelist, journalist. Noted for his satirical portraits of the vanishing culture of the West Indian in Trinidad. *The Mystic Masseur*, 1957; *A House for Mr. Biswas*, 1961; *In a Free State*, 1971; *Guerrillas*, 1975; *A Bend in the River*, 1979.

**NEKRASOV, NIKOLAI**, Dec. 10, 1821 (Yuzvin, Ukraine)–Jan. 8, 1878. Russian poet, editor. Noted for his original and powerful poems, including "Red-nosed Frost" (1863) and "Who Can Be Happy and Free in Russia?" (1879); edited *The Contemporary* and made it a major literary jour-

nal, 1846–66; edited and published *Annals of the Fatherland*, 1868–78.

**NERUDA, PABLO** (born Neftali Ricardo Reyes Basoalto), July 12, 1904 (Parral, Chile)–Sept. 23, 1973. Chilean poet, diplomat. Considered to be one of the most original poets in Spanish-language literature; served as Chilean ambassador to Mexico, 1940–42; became a militant communist; awarded Nobel Prize in literature, 1971. *Crepusculario*, 1923; *Twenty Love Poems and a Song of Despair*, 1924.

**NESTROY, JOHANN**, Dec. 7, 1801 (Vienna, Austria)–May 25, 1862. Austrian playwright, actor. A major comic dramatist and actor; wrote 50 plays in which he played the major role; his play *Einen Jux will er sich machen* (1842) was adapted by THORNTON WILDER as *The Matchmaker* (1955), and later, as the musical play and movie *Hello, Dolly*. *A Man Full of Nothing*, 1844.

**NGUGI WA THIONG'O** (James Ngugi), Jan. 5, 1938 (Limuru, Kenya). Kenyan novelist, dramatist, and essayist. Bitter and satirical, his attacks on the government resulted in his spending almost a year of imprisonment in 1978–1979. *Weep Not, Child*, 1964; *A Grain of Wheat*, 1967; *Devil on the Cross*, 1982.

**OEHLENSCHLÄGER, ADAM GOTTLOB**, Nov. 14, 1779 (Vesterbo, Den.)–Jan. 20, 1850. Danish poet, dramatist. Danish national poet and a leader of the Romantic movement in Denmark; his poem *The Golden Horns* (1802) marked the beginning of romanticism in Denmark. *Midsummer Night's Play*, 1802; *Poetic Writings*, 1805; *Aladdin*, 1805; *Balder the Good*, 1807; *The Gods of the North*, 1819.

**OKIGBO, CHRISTOPHER**, 1905 (Ojoto, Nigeria)–1967. Nigerian poet. Killed in action during the Nigerian Civil War. *Heavensgate*, 1962; *Limits*, 1964.

**OMAR KHAYYAM**, May 1048? (Nishapur, Persia) –Dec. 1122. Persian poet, mathematician, astronomer. During his lifetime, noted for his accomplishments in astronomy, law, history, medicine, and mathematics—but not poetry; the *Rubaiyat*, attributed to him, was discovered by the English Victorian poet EDWARD FITZGERALD, who freely translated it and arranged the quatrains in a continuous elegy (1859).

**ORCZY, BARONESS**, 1865 (Tarna-Eörs, Hung.) –Nov. 12, 1947. Hungarian novelist. Best known for *The Scarlet Pimpernel* (1902), a novel about the swashbuckling adventures of Sir Percy Blakeney during the French Revolution. *The Elusive Pimpernel*, 1908; *The Way of the Scarlet Pimpernel*, 1933.

**OUSMANE, SEMBEN**, Jan. 8, 1923 (Zigguinchor, Casamance, Senegal). Senegalese novelist, screen writer, and film director. He had been a fireman, a stevedore, a bricklayer, and a soldier in the French Army during World War II. *Le Docker noir (The Black Docker)*, 1956; *Xala (Impotence)*, 1973; *Dernier de l'empire (The Last of the Empire)*, 1981.

**OVID** (born Publius Ovidius Naso), Mar. 20, 43 B.C. (Sulmo [now Sulmona], It.)–A.D. 17. Roman poet. His witty and cosmopolitan works were influential and much-translated; best known for *Metamorphoses*, 15 books of legends about the history of the world; first gained fame for his *Amores* (erotic poems); also wrote *The Art of Love*, three books of instructions on lovemaking.

**OZAKI, KŌYŌ,** Dec. 16, 1867 (Tokyo, Jap.)–Oct. 30, 1903. Japanese novelist, essayist, poet. A pioneer of modern Japanese literature; one of the founders of the influential literary magazine *Ken-yūsha*, 1885. *The Perfumed Pillow*, 1890; *Tears and Regrets*, 1896; *The Heart*, 1903; *The Gold Demon*, trans. 1917.

**PARRA, NICANOR,** Sept. 5, 1914 (Chillan, Chile). Chilean poet and professor of theoretical mechanics. Specialist in "antipoetry." *Cancionero sin nombre*, 1937; *Poemas y antipoemas (Poems and Antipoems)*, 1967.

**PASTERNAK, BORIS,** Feb. 10, 1890 (Moscow, Rus.)–May 30, 1960. Soviet poet, novelist, translator. Best known for his novel *Doctor Zhivago* (1957), which was repressed in the Soviet Union as anti-Soviet but gained international fame when published abroad; declined Nobel Prize in literature, 1958. *Over the Barriers*, 1917; *Childhood*, 1918; *The Year 1905*, 1926.

**PATON, ALAN,** Jan. 11, 1903 (Pietermaritzburg, Natal [now S. A.])–Apr. 12, 1988. South African novelist, political activist. Served as pres. of the Liberal Party of South Africa from its founding in 1953 to its enforced dissolution in 1968. *Cry, The Beloved Country*, 1948; *Too Late the Phalarope*, 1953; *Towards the Mountain*, autobiography, 1980.

**PAVESE, CESARE,** Sept. 9, 1908 (Santo Stefano Belbo, It.)–Aug. 27, 1950. Italian translator, critic, editor, novelist, short-story writer, poet. Fostered appreciation of U.S. literature in Italy through his translations and critical articles; founded and served as editor of the publishing house Einaudi; Pavese Prize in literature established in his honor, 1957. *The Moon and the Bonfires*, 1950; *American Literature, Essays and Opinions*, 1951.

**PAZ, OCTAVIO,** Mar. 31, 1914 (Mexico City, Mex.). Mexican poet, critic, social philosopher. Learned, eclectic, experimental writer, concerned with Mexican identity. *Labyrinth of Solitude*, 1950; *Salamandra*, 1962; *Ladera este*, 1969; *Sun Stone*, 1957; *The Bow and the Lyre*, 1956.

**PERETZ, ISAAC LEIB,** May 18, 1852, 1851 (Zamość, Pol.)–Apr. 3, 1915. Polish poet, short-story writer, dramatist. Father of modern Yiddish literature; leader of the Yiddisheit movement; wrote about the poor Jews of Eastern Europe, introducing Hasidic lore; author of the *Silent Souls* series. *Folktales*, 1909.

**PESSOA, FERNANDO,** June 13, 1888 (Lisbon, Portugal)–Nov. 30, 1935. Portuguese poet. He used many pseudonyms. *Selected Poems*, 1971; *Sixty Portuguese Poems*, 1971; *Fernando Pessoa: Selected Poems*, 1974.

**PETRARCH** (in full, Francesco Petrarca), July 20, 1304 (Arezzo, It.)–July 18–19, 1374. Italian poet, scholar. His work served as a model for Italian literature for three centuries; especially known for his vernacular lyrics inspired by his idealized love for the young Laura; wrote over 300 "Petrarchan" sonnets; crowned "laureate of the civilized world," 1341. *Triumphs; Song Book; Africa; Ecologues; Letters.*

**PETRONIUS ARBITER** (born Titus Petronius Niger), died 66. Roman satirist. Reputed to be author of the *Satyricon*, a prose romance interspersed with verse that is generally considered the first Western European novel.

**PINDAR,** c.518 B.C. (Cynoscephalae, Gr.)–c.438 B.C. Greek poet. Choral lyricist, master of *epinicia*—odes celebrating athletic victory; four books of his *epinicia*, rediscovered in the Renaissance, greatly influenced Western poets.

**PIRANDELLO, LUIGI,** June 28, 1867 (Agrigento, Sicily)–Dec. 10, 1936. Italian playwright, novelist, short-story writer. Important innovator in modern drama; invented "theatre within the theatre" with his play, *Six Characters in Search of An Author* (1921); awarded Nobel Prize in literature, 1934. *Henry IV*, 1922; *The Late Mattia Pascal*, 1904.

**PLAUTUS** (born Titus Maccius Plautus), c.254 B.C. (Umbria)–184 B.C. Roman dramatist. Romanized Greek models and created Latin literary idiom; his comedies featured coarse humor, stock comic figures. *Amphitruo; Asinaria; Casina; Epidicus; Persa; Truculentus.*

**POPA, VASCO,** July 29, 1922 (Grebenac, Yugoslavia) Yugoslav poet. Said to be a master of paradox, his poems are in the folk tradition. *Earth Erect*, 1973; *Homage to the Lame Wolf: Selected Poems of Vasco Popa*, 1979; *Collected Poems*, 1979.

**PUIG, MANUEL,** Dec. 20, 1932 (General Villegas, Argentina). Argentine novelist. He has been a teacher of Spanish and Italian in England and Italy. *Heartbreak Tango*, 1969; *Betrayed by Rita Hayworth*, 1971; *The Kiss of the Spider Woman*, 1976.

**PUSHKIN, ALEXANDER,** June 6, 1799 (Moscow, Rus.)–Feb. 10, 1837. Russian poet, novelist, dramatist, short-story writer. A leading figure in Russian literature; introduced Romanticism with *The Prisoner in the Caucasus* (1822); his works inspired operas by M. P. MOUSSORGSKY and P. I. TCHAIKOVSKY. *Boris Godunov*, 1831; *Eugene Onegin*, pub. 1833; *The Queen of Spades*, 1834.

**QUASIMODO, SALVATORE,** Aug. 20, 1901 (Modica, Sicily)–June 14, 1968. Italian poet, translator, critic. Founder and leader of the Hermetic poets; later poems concerned with contemporary issues; awarded Nobel Prize in literature, 1959. *Acque e terre*, 1930; *Il falso e verdo verde*, 1948; *La terra imparrigiabile*, 1958.

**QUEVEDO Y VILLEGAS, FRANCISCO GÓMEZ DE,** Sept. 26, 1580 (Madrid, Sp.)–Sept. 8, 1645. Spanish satirist, novelist. One of the foremost writers of the golden age of Spanish literature. *The Life of a Scoundrel*, 1626; *Visions*, 1627; *Epístola satirica y censoria*, 1639.

**RADISCHEV, ALEKSANDR,** Aug. 31, 1749 (Moscow, Rus.)–Sept. 24, 1802. Russian writer. Founded the revolutionary tradition in Russian literature; in his fictional journal, *A Journey from St. Petersburg to Moscow* (1790), collected examples of social injustice; spent 10 years in Siberia; committed suicide one year later.

**REMARQUE, ERICH MARIA** (born Erich Paul Remark), June 22, 1898 (Osnabrück, Ger.)–Sept. 25, 1970. German-U.S. novelist. Best known for the WW I novel *All Quiet on the Western Front* (1929), in which he recorded the horrors of war. *The Way Back,* 1931; *Three Comrades,* 1937; *A Time to Love and a Time to Die,* 1954.

**RICHLER, MORDECAI,** Jan. 27, 1931 (Montreal, Que., Can.). Canadian novelist, short-story writer, journalist. "New Generation" Canadian novelist best known for *The Apprenticeship of Duddy Kravitz* (1959). *Son of a Smaller Hero,* 1953; *A Choice of Enemies,* 1957; *The Incomparable Atuk,* 1963; *Joshua Then and Now,* 1980.

**RICHTER, JOHANN** (pseud.: Jean Paul), Mar. 21, 1763 (Bavaria, Ger.)–Nov. 14, 1825. German novelist. Combined idealism with *sturm und drang* in his writing. *Hesperus,* 1795; *Quintus Fixlein,* 1796; *Siebenkas,* 1796–97.

**RILKE, RAINER MARIA,** Dec. 4, 1875 (Prague, Czech.)–Dec. 29, 1926. Austrian-German lyric poet. Noted for his highly individualized style; his poems often are mystical, with God and death as frequent themes. *Stories of God,* 1904; *Poems from the Book of Hours,* 1905; *New Poems,* 2 vols., 1907–08; *Duino Elegies,* 1923.

**RITSÓS, YANNIS,** May 1, 1909 (Monemvasia, Greece). Greek Communist poet. Spent years in prisons and in exile. *Trakter,* 1934; *Romiosyne (Romiosini),* 1947; *Scripture of the Blind,* 1978.

**SACHS, NELLY,** Dec. 10, 1891 (Berlin, Ger.)–May 12, 1970. German poet, dramatist. Escaped to Sweden from Nazi Germany; described her experiences and the sufferings of European Jews; awarded Nobel Prize in literature, (with SHMUEL YOSEF AGNON), 1966. *A Mystery Play of the Sufferings of Israel,* 1951; *The Seeker and Other Poems,* 1966; *Israel's Suffering,* 1969.

**SAPPHO,** fl. early 6th cent. B.C. (Mytilene, Lesbos). Greek lyric poet. Wrote concise, picturesque poetry in the vernacular vocabulary of the local Lesbian-Aeolic dialect; invented Sapphic meter; wrote of the loves and hates in an informal association of upper-class women, of which she was the leading spirit.

**SCHILLER, FRIEDRICH VON,** Nov. 10, 1759 (Marbach, Germany)–May 9, 1805. German dramatist, poet, and historian. With JOHAN WOLFGANG VON GOETHE, he led the movement called Weimar Classicism; although his early work was in the style of *Sturm und Drang* (Storm and Stress), he never lost his idealism. *Die Räuber (The Robbers),* 1782; *Die Götter Griechenlands (The Gods of Greece),* 1788; *Die Geschichte des Dreissigjährigen Krieges (History of the Thirty Years' War),* 1791.

**SCHNITZLER, ARTHUR,** May 15, 1862 (Vienna, Aust.)–Oct. 21, 1931. Austrian playwright, novelist. Wrote psychological dramas about Viennese bourgeois life; along with others opposed to German naturalist drama, started the Young Vienna Group. *Anatol,* 1893; *Light-o'-Love,* 1895; *Reigen,* 1897; *None but the Brave,* 1926; *Flight into Darkness,* 1931.

**SEFERIS, GIORGOS** (pseud. of Giorgos Sefiriades), Mar. 13, 1900 (Izmir, Turk.)–Sept. 20, 1971. Greek poet, translator. His poetry is characterized by symbolic evocations of classical Greek themes; first Greek to win Nobel Prize in literature, 1963. *Strophe,* 1931; *Mithistoríma,* 1935; *Poiïmata,* 1940.

**SENGHOR, LEOPOLD SÉDAR,** Oct. 9, 1906 (Joal, Senegal). Senegalese poet, statesman. In his poetry and essays, asserts black African cultural values, or negritude, a concept he formulated with other African thinkers; first pres. of Senegal, 1960–1980; first African member of the French Acad. of Moral and Political Sciences. *Chants d'Ombre,* 1945; *Hosties Noires,* 1948; *Éthiopiques,* 1956.

**SERVICE, ROBERT W(illiam),** Jan. 16, 1874 (Lancashire, Eng.)–Sept. 11, 1958. Canadian writer, poet. Called the "Canadian Kipling," best known for his verse, including "The Shooting of Dan McGrew." *Songs of a Sourdough,* 1907; *Ballads of Cheechako,* 1909; *Bar Room Ballads,* 1940.

**SHOLOKHOV, MIKHAIL,** May 24, 1905 (Veshenskaya, Rus.)–Feb. 21, 1984. Soviet novelist. Best known for *The Quiet Don* (4 vols., 1928–40), a widely read novel in the USSR, considered a model of socialist realism; awarded Nobel Prize in literature, 1965; first officially sanctioned Soviet laureate.

**SIENKIEWICZ, HENRYK,** May 4, 1846 (Wola Orkrzejska, Pol.)–Nov. 14, 1916. Polish novelist, short-story writer. Wrote colorful historical novels, including a trilogy about the Polish nationalist struggle: *With Fire and Sword* (1883), *The Deluge* (1886), *Pan Michael* (1887–88); awarded Nobel Prize in literature, 1905. *Quo Vadis?,* 1895.

**SILLANPÄÄ, FRANS EEMIL,** Sept. 16, 1888 (Hämeenkyrö, Fin.)–June 3, 1964. Finnish novelist, short-story writer. The first Finnish writer to win the Nobel Prize in literature, 1939. *Meek Heritage,* 1919, *The Maid Silja,* 1931.

**SINYAVSKY, ANDREI** (pseud.: Abram Terts) 1925 (USSR). Soviet short-story writer, critic. Became symbol of the oppressed Soviet artist when he was sentenced (1966) to seven years of hard labor for writings published in the West under the pseudonym Abram Terts. *The Trial Begins,* 1961; *Fantastic Stories,* 1963; *The Makepeace Experiment,* 1965.

**SOLZHENITSYN, ALEXANDER,** Dec. 11, 1918 (Rostov, Rus.). Soviet novelist. Gained international fame for *One Day in the Life of Ivan Denisovich* (1962), about a forced labor camp during the Stalinist era, based on his own imprisonment for writing a letter critical of Stalin in 1945; officially censured from 1963; awarded 1970 Nobel Prize in literature, but could not receive it until 1974, after being exiled to the West for treason. *The First Circle,* 1964; *Cancer Ward,* 1966; *August 1914,* 1972; *The Gulag Archipelago,* 1974.

**SOPHOCLES,** c.496 B.C. (Colonus, Gr.)–406 B.C. Greek playwright, poet. With AESCHYLUS and EURIPIDES, one of the great tragedians of classical

Greece; an innovator, he added a third actor, enlarged the chorus, and replaced the trilogy format with single tragedies; of some 123 dramas, seven complete tragedies, part of satyr play, and over 1,000 fragments survive; born to the leisure class, became treasurer of Athens, an army general, and elder statesman. *Antigone*, c.441 B.C.; *Oedipus Rex*, c.429 B.C.; *Electra*; *Trachinae*; *Philoctetes*, 409 B.C.; *Oedipus at Colonus*, 406 B.C.

SOYINKA, WOLE (pen name of Akinwande Oluwole Soyinka), July 13, 1934 (Abeokuta, Western Nigeria). Nigerian dramatist, short-story writer, novelist, lyric poet, and essayist. Draws on European and African (primarily Yoruba) traditions in his work. *A Dance of the Forests*, 1960; *Death and the King's Horseman*, 1975; *Aké: The Years of Childhood*, 1981. (1986 Nobel Prize in literature)

STORNI, ALFONSINA, May 29, 1892 (Ticino, Switzerland)–May 11, 1938. Argentine lyric poet and novelist. A feminist, she showed resentment toward chauvinism, and eventually committed suicide by drowning. *Dulce daño*, 1918; *El mundo de siete pozos*, 1934; *Mascarilla y trébol (Death-Mask and Clover)*, 1938.

STRINDBERG, AUGUST, Jan. 22, 1849 (Stockholm, Swe.)–May 14, 1912. Swedish playwright, novelist, short-story writer. Innovator who began writing dramas of social criticism in the tradition of HENRIK IBSEN; later, focused on the conflict between the sexes. *The Red Room*, 1879; *The Father*, 1887; *Miss Julie*, 1888; *Creditors*, 1888.

TAGORE, RABINDRANATH, May 7, 1861 (Calcutta, India)–Aug. 7, 1941. Bengali poet, playwright, philosopher, novelist. A prodigious and versatile author, regarded as a guru; set hundreds of poems to music; a leading painter; awarded Nobel Prize in literature, 1913; knighted in 1915, but surrendered it to protest the Amritsar Massacre (1919). *The Golden Boat*, 1893; *Late Harvest*, 1896; *Gitanjali*, 1912; *Sadhana: The Realization of Life*, 1914; *Chitra*, 1913; *Red Oleanders*, 1924.

TASSO, TORQUATO, Mar. 11, 1544 (Sorrento, It.)–Apr. 25, 1595. Italian poet. A major poet of the later Renaissance; periodically confined for delusions of persecution. *Rinaldo*, 1562; *Aminta*, 1573; *Jerusalem Liberated*, 1581; *Jerusalem Conquered*, 1593.

TERENCE (born Publius Terentius Afer), c.195 or 185 B.C. (Carthage, modern Tunisia)–159? B.C. Roman dramatist. Wrote six influential verse comedies freely adapted from the works of MENANDER and others. *The Adrian Girl*, 166 B.C.; *The Mother-in-Law*, 165 B.C.; *The Self-Tormentor*, 163 B.C.; *The Eunuch*, 161 B.C.; *Phormio*, 161 B.C.; *The Brothers*, 160 B.C.

THEOCRITUS, c.310 B.C. (probably Syracuse)–c.250 B.C. Greek poet. Credited with the invention of the pastoral poem. *The Idyls*.

THESPIS, fl.6th cent. B.C. (District of Icaria). Greek poet. The founder of tragic drama; introduced an actor, monologues and dialogues in the existing choruses of hymns to Bacchus and other deities.

TOLSTOY, LEO, COUNT, Sept. 9, 1828 (Yasnaya Polyana, Rus.)–Nov. 20, 1910. Russian novelist, philosopher. Considered to be one of the world's greatest writers; born of noble family, he led a profligate life and married, fathering 13 children; after a spiritual crisis (*A Confession*, 1878–79), became a Christian anarchist, abandoning worldly goods and devoting himself to social reform; became the center of an admiring cult. *War and Peace*, 1865–69; *Anna Karenina*, 1875–77; *The Death of Ivan Ilich*, 1886; *The Devil*, 1889; *Resurrection*, 1899.

TU FU, 712 (Hsiang-yang [now Honan Prov.], China)–770. Chinese poet. Generally considered the greatest Chinese poet of all time; a classicist whose verse decries the tragedy of wars and satirized the luxuries of court life.

TURGENEV, IVAN, Nov. 9, 1818 (Orel, Rus.)–Sept. 3, 1883. Russian novelist, short-story writer. Best known for his controversial masterpiece *Fathers and Sons* (1862); attacked serfdom in a simple but powerful style; a Westerner in his writing, from 1845 he lived abroad, chiefly in Germany and France. *Notes of A Hunter: A Sportsman's Sketches*, 1852; *Rudin*, 1856; *A Nest of Gentlefolk*, 1859; *Poems in Prose*, 1882.

TZARÁ, TRISTAN (pen name of Samuel Rosenfeld), 1896 (Sibiu, Romania)–1963. Romanian-born French poet who founded the DADA movement in 1916; the first dada text was his *La Premiere aventure céleste de M. Antipyrine*, 1916. *L'Homme approximatif (The Approximate Man and Other Writings)*, 1973; *Parler seul*, 1956.

UNAMUNO [Y JUGO], MIGUEL DE, Sept. 29, 1864 (Bilbao, Spain)–Dec. 31, 1936. Spanish philosopher, poet, novelist, dramatist, and essayist. Wrote of the conflict between reason and faith and the tragedy and absurdness of life. *Niebla (Mist, A Tragicomic Novel)*, 1914; *La agonía del cristianismo (The Agony of Christianity)*, 1924; *Cancionero*, 1953.

UNDSET, SIGRID, May 20, 1882 (Kallundborg, Den.)–June 10, 1949. Norwegian novelist. Best known for her three-volume historical novel, *Kristin Lavransdatter* (1920–22), a medieval woman's life story; awarded Nobel Prize in literature, 1928; came to U.S. after the Nazi invasion of Norway, 1940. *Jenny*, 1911; *The Master of Hestviken*, 4 vols., 1925–27; *Return to the Future*, 1942.

VALLEJO, CESAR, March 16, 1892 (Santiago de Chuco, Peru)–1938. Peruvian poet, novelist, short-story writer, essayist. A bitter, anguished writer, he identified with the downtrodden and the politically oppressed. Much of his work was written in prison. *Los heraldos negros (The Dark Messengers)*, 1918; *Trilce*, 1922.

VEGA, LOPE DE, Nov. 25, 1562 (Madrid, Sp.)–Aug. 27, 1635. Spanish dramatist. Foremost dramatist of the golden age of Spanish literature; called the Phoenix of Genius; wrote over 1,500 plays, including tragedies, comedies of manners, and cloak-and-dagger intrigues, of which nearly 500 survive. *The King the Greatest Mayor*, 1620–23; *The Knight of Olmedo,* 1620–25; *Punishment without Revenge,* 1631.

**VERGA, GIOVANNI,** Sept. 2, 1840 (Catania, Sicily) –Jan. 27, 1922. Italian novelist. Founder and leading exponent of the Italian realist school; wrote about Sicilian peasants and fishermen with intensity and lyricism; his story *Cavalleria Rusticana* (1884) was adapted into an opera by PIETRO MASCAGNI. *I Malavoglia,* 1881; *Mastro Don Gesualdo,* 1889.

**VIRGIL** (or Vergil), born Publius Vergilius Maro, Oct. 15, 70 B.C. (nr. Mantua, It.)–Sept. 21, 19 B.C. Roman poet. Dominated Latin literature during its golden age; belonged to the literary circle of Maecenas and AUGUSTUS; wrote Eclogues or Bucolics (42 B.C.–37 B.C.), idealizing rural life, and Georgics (30 B.C.), realistic rural poetry; devoted the remainder of his life to the *Aeneid* (12 books, unfinished), a national epic, sophisticated in style and noble in purpose, relating the adventures of the Trojan warrior Aeneas, whom myths linked to the founding of Rome.

**VOZNESENSKY, ANDREI,** May 12, 1933 (Moscow, USSR). Soviet poet. A popular poet who gave many public readings in the 1960s; a close friend and protégé of BORIS PASTERNAK; writing attacked by anti-modernist campaign, 1963. *Parabola,* 1960; *Mosaic,* 1960; *The Triangular Pear,* 1962; *Nostalgia for the Present,* 1978.

**WEISS, PETER,** Nov. 8, 1916 (Nowawes [now Babelsberg], Ger.)–May 10, 1982. German-Swedish dramatist, novelist. Noted for *The Persecution and Assassination of Jean Paul Marat as Performed by the Inmates of the Asylum of Charenton under the Direction of the Marquis de Sade* (1964) and *The Investigation* (1965); *Duelle,* 1972.

**WEST, MORRIS,** Apr. 26, 1916 (Melbourne, Austrl.). Australian novelist. Best known for his best-selling *The Devil's Advocate* (1959) and *The*

*Shoes of the Fisherman* (1963), which reflect his background as a Christian Brother. *The Summer of the Red Wolf,* 1971; *The Salamander,* 1973; *The Navigator,* 1976; *Lazarus,* 1990.

**WHITE, PATRICK,** May 28, 1912 (London, Eng.). Australian novelist, playwright, short-story writer. His main theme is the quest for meaning and value in 20th-cent. Australia; awarded Nobel Prize in literature, 1973. *Happy Valley,* 1939; *The Tree of Man,* 1955; *Riders in the Chariot,* 1961; *The Eye of the Storm,* 1973.

**WOLFRAM VON ESCHENBACH,** c.1170 (Wolframs Eisenbach, Franconia)–c.1220. German *minnesinger,* or lyric poet. Glorified married love in his verse epics; RICHARD WAGNER made him a major character in his *Tannhäuser. Parzival; Willehalm; Titurel.*

**YEVTUSHENKO, YEVGENY,** July 18, 1933 (Zima, USSR). Soviet poet. Popular spokesman for the post-Stalin generation of Soviet poets; was heavily censored for his *A Precocious Autobiography* (1963; published in France), but allowed to make several trips abroad; best known for "Babi Yar," a poem protesting anti-semitism. *Selected Poems,* 1962; *Bratsk Station,* 1965; *Stolen Apples,* 1971; *Wild Apples,* 1984.

**ZAMYATIN, YEVGENY,** Feb. 1, 1884 (Lebedyan, Rus.)–Mar. 10, 1937. Soviet novelist, playwright. Best known for his anti-utopian novel *We* (1924), circulated but never published in the Soviet Union; inspired A. HUXLEY and G. ORWELL. *The Fires of St. Dominic,* 1922.

**ZEAMI, MOTOKIYO,** 1363 (Japan)–1443. Japanese actor and dramatist. Zeami, as head of a theatrical group, was responsible for raising the Nō drama to a mature art form; some of his Nō plays are still presented in Japan. *Atsumori; Hagoromo (The Robe of Feathers); Utō (The Birds of Sorrow).*

## DETECTIVE, GOTHIC, SUSPENSE WRITERS

**ALLINGHAM, MARGERY,** May 20, 1904 (London, Eng.)–June 30, 1966. English novelist. A leading mystery writer; created the erudite detective Albert Campion. *The Crime at Black Dudley,* 1928; *Mystery Mile,* 1929; *Police at the Funeral,* 1931; *Sweet Danger,* 1933; *Death of a Ghost,* 1934; *Flowers for the Judge,* 1936; *The Fashion in Shrouds,* 1938; *Traitor's Purse,* 1941; *Tiger in the Smoke,* 1963; *The China Governess,* 1963; *The Mind Readers,* 1965.

**AMBLER, ERIC,** June 28, 1909 (London, Eng.). English novelist. Author of literate international-intrigue stories; created TV detective series *Checkmate,* 1960; Mystery Writers of America Grand Master Award, 1975. *A Coffin for Dimitrios,* 1939; *Journey into Fear,* 1940; *Dirty Story,* 1967; *The Levanter,* 1972; *The Care of Time,* 1981; *Here Lies: An Autobiography,* 1985.

**BALL, JOHN DUDLEY,** July 8, 1911 (Schenectady, N.Y.). U.S. mystery-story writer. His mystery novel *In the Heat of the Night* (1965), featuring Virgil Tibbs, one of the first black detective heroes,

was made into an Academy Award-winning film. *Five Pieces of Jade,* 1972; *Then Came Violence,* 1980; *The Kiwi Target,* 1988.

**BERKELEY, ANTHONY** (pseud.: A. B. Cox, Francis Iles), 1893–1970. English journalist, critic, mystery writer; anonymously published *The Layton Court Mystery,* featuring the outrageous Roger Sheringham, 1925; as A. B. Cox, founded London's famous Detective Club in 1928, wrote the classic story *The Avenging Chance* (1929), which he later expanded into a satirical novel, *The Poisoned Chocolates Case* (1929); as Francis Iles, wrote the highly praised *Malice Aforethought* (1931), *Before the Fact* (1932, adapted by ALFRED HITCHCOCK in *Suspicion*), and *Trial and Error* (1937).

**BIGGERS, EARL DERR,** Aug. 26, 1884 (Warren, Ohio)–Apr. 5, 1933. U.S. mystery-story writer, novelist. Author of the Charlie Chan stories, first serialized in the *Saturday Evening Post* and later made into a popular film series of the 1930s and 1940s.

**CARR, JOHN DICKSON** (pseud.: Carter Dickson, Carr Dickson), 1906 (Uniontown, Pa.)–Feb. 27,

1976. U.S. mystery-story writer. Master of the locked-room mystery; created Dr. Gideon Fell. *Hag's Nook*, 1933; *The Bride of Newgate*, 1950; *The Dead Man's Knock*, 1958; *The Arabian Nights Murder*, 1965; *Case of the Constant Suicides*, 1962; *Crooked Hinge*, 1964.

CHANDLER, RAYMOND, July 23, 1888 (Chicago, Ill.)–Mar. 26, 1959. U.S. short-story writer, novelist. Master of the "hard-boiled" crime story; created the tough private detective Philip Marlowe. *The Big Sleep*, 1939; *Farewell, My Lovely*, 1940; *The Lady in the Lake*, 1943; *The Long Goodbye*, 1954; *Playback*, 1958.

CHESTERTON, G(ilbert) K(eith), May 29, 1874 (London, Eng.)–June 14, 1936. English essayist, novelist, journalist, poet. Created detective series with Father Brown as the sleuth; a convert to Catholicism; called the Prince of Paradox for the religious dogma underlying his light style. *Tremendous Trifles*, 1909; *The Innocence of Father Brown*, 1911; *Come To Think of It*, 1930.

CHRISTIE, DAME AGATHA (pseud.: Mary Westmacott), Sept. 15, 1890 (Devon, Eng.)–Jan. 12, 1976. English novelist, playwright. Extremely popular mystery novelist whose books have sold over 100,000,000 copies; created the fastidious Belgian detective Hercule Poirot and eccentric spinster Jane Marple; her play *The Mousetrap* (1952) is still running on the London stage. *The Murder of Roger Ackroyd*, 1926; *Murder at the Vicarage*, 1930; *Death on the Nile*, 1937; *And Then There Were None*, 1940; *Witness for the Prosecution* (play), 1954.

COLES, MANNING (pseud. of Cyril Henry Coles, 1899 [London, Eng.]–Oct. 9, 1965, and Adelaide Manning, 1891 [London, Eng.]–1959). English mystery writers. Invented the character Tommy Hambleton, a high-ranking English intelligence agent. *Drink to Yesterday*, 1940; *No Entry*, 1958.

COLLINS, (William) WILKIE, Jan. 8, 1824 (London, Eng.)–Sept. 23, 1889. English novelist. Wrote what are generally considered to be the first detective novels in English. *The Woman in White*, 1860; *The Moonstone*, 1868.

CONDON, RICHARD, Mar. 18, 1915 (New York, N.Y.). U.S. novelist. *The Manchurian Candidate*, 1959; *A Talent for Loving*, 1961; *Arigato*, 1972; *The Star-Spangled Crunch*, 1974; *Winter Kills*, 1974; *Bandicoot*, 1978; *Prizzi's Honor*, 1982; *Prizzi's Family*, 1986.

CREASEY, JOHN (pseud.: J. J. Marric, Gordon Ashe, Robert Caine, many others), Sept. 17, 1908 (Surrey, Eng.)–June 9, 1973. English mystery writer. Wrote over 600 books using 28 pseudonyms. *Department Z*, series, 1932–68; *The Toff*, series, 1938–68; *Inspector West*, series, 1942–68; *Dr. Palfrey*, series, 1942–68.

CRISPIN, EDMUND (pseud. of Robert Bruce Montgomery), Oct. 2, 1921 (Buckinghamshire, Eng.)–Sept. 15, 1978. English detective novelist, musician, composer. Noted for his short stories and novels about Gervase Fen, an Oxford prof. and crime solver; wrote scores for many British films.

*Obsequies at Oxford*, 1945; *The Moving Toyshop*, 1946; *Buried for Pleasure*, 1949.

CROFTS, FREEMAN WILLIS, June 1879 (Dublin, Ire.)–Apr. 11, 1957. Irish detective-story writer. Creator of Inspector French; introduced police routine to detective fiction; his first book, *The Cask* (1920), is a classic that helped launch the golden age of the detective story. *The Box Office Murders*, 1929; *The Mystery of the Sleeping Car Express*, 1956.

CROSS, AMANDA (pseud. of Carolyn Heilbrun), Jan. 13, 1926 (East Orange, N.J.). U.S. mystery novelist. Created Kate Fansler, a university professor, who detects in academic settings. *In the Last Analysis*, 1964; *The James Joyce Murder*, 1967; *The Question of Max*, 1976; *Death in a Tenured Position*, 1981; *A Trap for Fools*, 1989.

DEIGHTON, LEN, Feb. 18, 1929 (London, Eng.). English mystery and nonfiction writer. Author of complex, wry espionage thrillers. *The Ipcress File*, 1962; *Funeral in Berlin*, 1964; *The Billion Dollar Brain*, 1966; *Spy Story*, 1974; *Goodbye, Mickey Mouse*, 1982; *Berlin Game*, 1983; *Spy Hook*, 1988; *Spy Line*, 1989; *Spy Sinker*, 1990.

DOYLE, SIR ARTHUR CONAN, May 22, 1859 (Edinburgh, Scot.)–July 7, 1930. British novelist. Created Sherlock Holmes, one of the best-known characters in English literature; a physician by profession, he abandoned medicine after the success of the first Holmes story, *A Study in Scarlet* (1887); knighted, 1902. *The Sign of the Four*, 1890; *The Memoirs of Sherlock Holmes*, 1894; *Hound of the Baskervilles*, 1902; *Return of Sherlock Holmes*, 1905.

EBERHART, MIGNON, July 6, 1899 (Lincoln, Nebraska). U.S. mystery novelist. Author of over 50 gothic/mystery novels. *While the Patient Slept*, 1930; *The Cases of Susan Dare*, 1934, *The Bayou Road*, 1979.

FLEMING, IAN, May 28, 1908 (London, Eng.)–Aug. 12, 1964. English writer of adventure novels. Created secret agent 007, James Bond. *Casino Royale*, 1953; *From Russia With Love*, 1957; *Dr. No*, 1958; *Goldfinger*, 1959; *Thunderball*, 1961; *Chitty-Chitty-Bang-Bang* (for children), 1964.

FOLLETT, KENNETH, June 5, 1949 (Cardiff, Wales). British mystery novelist. *The Eye of the Needle*, 1978; *The Man From St. Petersburg*, 1981; *Lie Down With Lions*, 1986.

FORSYTH, FREDERICK, Aug. 1938 (Kent, Eng.). English novelist, journalist. *The Day of the Jackal*, 1971; *The Odessa File*, 1972; *The Dogs of War*, 1974; *The Fourth Protocol*, 1984.

FRANCIS, DICK, Oct. 31, 1920 (nr. Tenby, Wales). Welsh jockey, mystery writer. Raced under the Queen Mother's colors for four years; writes mystery novels about jockeys and pilots. *Dead Cert*, 1962; *Odds Against*, 1965; *Forfeit*, 1969; *High Stakes*, 1975; *In the Frame*, 1977; *Risk*, 1978; *Banker*, 1983; *Hot Money*, 1988; *Straight*, 1989.

FREELING, NICOLAS, 1927 (London, Eng.). English mystery novelist. His mysteries, featuring Inspector van der Valk, are noted for their characterizations and authentic descriptions of Dutch locales.

*Love in Amsterdam*, 1962; *The King of the Rainy Country*, 1966.

**GARDNER, ERLE STANLEY** (pseud.: A. A. Fair, Carleton Kendrake), July 17, 1889 (Malden, Mass.) –May 11, 1970. U.S. detective-story writer. A trial lawyer by profession, he wrote crime stories for magazines, as well as over 100 books; several films and a long-running television series were based on his hero, Perry Mason. *The Case of the Velvet Claws*, 1932.

**GILBERT, MICHAEL**, July 17, 1912 (Lincolnshire, Eng.). English lawyer, detective-story writer. Prolific author of short stories, as well as mystery dramas and novels; editor of *Classics of Adventure and Detection*. *The Claimant*, 1957; *A Clean Kill*, 1960; *Game without Rules*, 1967; *Amateur in Violence*, 1973.

**GILMAN, DOROTHY** (pseud.: Dorothy Gilman Butters), June 25, 1923 (New Brunswick, N.J.). U.S. mystery writer. Created Mrs. Pollifax, the geriatric sleuth; under her pseudonym, writes books for young people. *The Unexpected Mrs. Pollifax*, 1966; *The Amazing Mrs. Pollifax*, 1970; *The Elusive Mrs. Pollifax*, 1971; *Mrs. Pollifax on The China Station*, 1983; *Mrs. Pollifax and The Hong Kong Buddha*, 1985.

**GRIMES, MARTHA**, ? (Garrett City, Md.). U.S. mystery novelist. All of her novels are set in England and the titles are the names of pubs. *The Man With a Load of Mischief*, 1981; *The Old Fox Deceiv'd*, 1982; *The Dirty Duck*, 1984; *The Five Bells and Bladebone*, 1987.

**HAMMETT, (Samuel) DASHIELL**, Mar. 27, 1894 (St. Mary's Co., Md.)–Jan. 10, 1961. U.S. writer. Invented the hard-boiled "private eye" in the first Sam Spade book, *The Maltese Falcon* (1930); his Spade, along with Nick and Nora Charles, were the heroes of many radio and TV shows and films. *The Dain Curse*, 1929; *The Glass Key*, 1931; *The Thin Man*, 1934.

**HIGGINS, JACK** (pseud.: Harry Patterson), July 27, 1929 (Newcastle, Eng.). English author of best-selling suspense novels. *The Eagle Has Landed*, 1975; *Storm Warning*, 1976; *Day of Judgement*, 1979; *Exocet*, 1983; *Night of the Fox*, 1987.

**HIGHSMITH, PATRICIA**, 1921 (Fort Worth, Tex.). U.S. novelist, short-story writer. Author of mystery stories, especially popular in Europe; her *Strangers on a Train* (1950) inspired an ALFRED HITCH-COCK film.

**HILLERMAN, TONY**, May 22, 1925 (Sacred Heart, Okla.). U.S. writer. His mystery novels set against the world of Native Americans turn on questions of cultural identity and tribal beliefs. *People of Darkness*, 1980; *The Dark Wind*, 1982; *Skinwalkers*, 1986; *A Thief of Time*, 1988; *Talking God*, 1989.

**HOLT, VICTORIA** (pseud. of Eleanor Burford Hibbert), 1906 (London, Eng.). English novelist. Prolific author of gothic and romantic fiction. *Mistress of Mellyn*, 1960; *Shivering Sands*, 1969; *Pride of the Peacock*, 1976.

**INNES, MICHAEL** (pseud. of John Innes MacKintosh Stewart), 1906 (nr. Edinburgh, Scot.). Scottish novelist, scholar, mystery writer. Under his own name, author of novels, short stories, biographies, and *Eight Modern Writers* (1963), the final volume of the *Oxford History of English Literature;* as Michael Innes, writes mysteries noted for their erudition, complex plotting, and humor, including *Hamlet, Revenge!* (1937) and *Lament for a Maker* (1938).

**JAMES, P(hyllis) D(orothy)**, Aug. 3, 1920 (Oxford, Eng.). English mystery writer. Created the intelligent, perceptive poet and inspector, Adam Dalgliesh. *Cover Her Face*, 1962; *Unnatural Causes*, 1967; *Shroud for a Nightingale*, 1971; *An Unsuitable Job for a Woman*, 1975; *A Taste for Death*, 1986; *Devices and Desires*, 1989.

**KEMELMAN, HARRY**, Nov. 2, 1908 (Boston, Mass.). U.S. mystery writer. Created a series featuring Rabbi David Small as a detective. *Friday the Rabbi Slept Late*, 1964; *Wednesday the Rabbi Got Wet*, 1976; *Someday The Rabbi Will Leave*, 1985; *One Fine Day, The Rabbi Bought a Cross*, 1987.

**KING, STEPHEN**, Sept. 21, 1947 (Portland, Me.). U.S. novelist. Prolific and best-selling horror-story writer. *Carrie*, 1974; *The Shining*, 1976; *The Dark Half*, 1989.

**LATHEN, EMMA** (pseud. of Mary J. Latis and Martha Hennissart). U.S. mystery writers. Respectively an attorney and economic analyst, they met as graduate students at Harvard U.; created the fictional character John Putnam Thatcher, senior vice-pres. of Sloan Guaranty Trust Co. and amateur detective. *Death Shall Overcome*, 1966; *Murder to Go*, 1969; *Sweet and Low*, 1974; *By Hook or by Crook*, 1975.

**LE CARRÉ, JOHN** (pseud. of David John Moore Cornwell), Oct. 19, 1931 (Dorsetshire, Eng.). English novelist. Noted for his realistic spy stories about aging, weary spies. *The Spy Who Came in from the Cold*, 1963; *Tinker, Tailor, Soldier, Spy*, 1974; *The Honourable Schoolboy*, 1977; *The Little Drummer Girl*, 1983; *The Perfect Spy*, 1986.

**LE FANU, JOSEPH SHERIDAN**, Aug. 28, 1814 (Dublin, Ire.)–Feb. 7, 1873. Irish mystery writer. Founded, owned, and edited the *Dublin Evening Mail*, 1839–58; after his wife's death, withdrew from society and wrote supernatural stories. *Uncle Silas: A Tale of Bartram Haugh*, 1864; *Wylder's Hand*, 1864; *Checkmate*, 1871.

**LEROUX, GASTON**, May 6, 1868 (Paris, Fr.) –Apr. 15, 1927. French journalist, dramatist, mystery writer. His classic thriller *The Phantom of the Opera* (1911) was made into several successful films. *The Mysery of the Yellow Room*, 1907; *The Perfume of the Lady in Black*, 1907.

**LEWIS, CECIL DAY** (pseud.: Nicholas Blake), Apr. 27, 1904 (Ballintubber, Ire.)–May 22, 1972. English poet. Prof. of poetry, Oxford U., 1951–56; poet-laureate of England, 1967–72; wrote detective novels under his pseudonym. *Overtures to Death*, 1938; *Pegasus and Other Poems*, 1957; *The Whispering Roots and Other Poems*, 1970.

**LOCKRIDGE, RICHARD**, Sept. 26, 1898 (St. Joseph, Mo.)–June 19, 1982. U.S. novelist, short-story writer. With his wife Frances Lockridge, wrote 27 civilized, humorous mysteries about a husband-and-wife detective team, the Norths; after his wife's death (1963), wrote several other mystery stories. *The Norths Meet Murder*, 1946; *Death on the Aisle*, 1942; *Murder within Murder*, 1946; *The Tenth Life*, 1977; *The Old Die Young*, 1981.

LUDLUM, ROBERT (pseud.: Jonathan Ryder), May 25, 1927 (New York, N.Y.). U.S. novelist. Author of novels of adventure and intrigue. *The Scarlatti Inheritance*, 1971; *The Osterman Weekend*, 1972; *The Rhinemann Exchange*, 1974; *The Holcroft Covenant*, 1978; *The Matarese Circle*, 1979; *The Bourne Identity*, 1980; *The Parsifal Mosaic*, 1982; *The Icarus Agenda*, 1988.

MACDONALD, JOHN D., July 24, 1916 (Sharon, Pa.)–Dec. 28, 1986. U.S. mystery novelist, short-story writer. Most of his stories and books, including the Travis McGee series, are set in Florida; Mystery Writers of America Grand Master Award, 1972. *The Brass Cupcake*, 1950; *The Deep Blue Good-By*, 1964; *The Last One Left*, 1967; *The Dreadful Lemon Sky*, 1975; *Condominium*, 1977; *The Green Ripper*, 1979.

MACDONALD, ROSS (pseud. of Kenneth Millar; other pseud.: John MacDonald, John Ross Mac-Donald), Dec. 13, 1915 (Los Gatos, Cal.)–July 11, 1983. U.S. novelist, mystery writer. Created private detective Lew Archer. *The Dark Tunnel*, 1944; *The Moving Target*, 1949; *The Chill*, 1964; *The Far Side of the Dollar*, 1965; *The Goodbye Look*, 1969; *The Underground Man*, 1972; *The Blue Hammer*, 1976.

MACINNES, HELEN CLARK, Oct. 7, 1907 (Glasgow, Scot.)–Sept. 30, 1985. Scottish-U.S. novelist. Author of popular espionage novels. *Above Suspicion*, 1941; *While We Still Live*, 1944; *Decision at Delphi*, 1960; *The Snare of the Hunter*, 1974; *The Salzburg Connection*, 1968; *Ride A Pale Horse*, 1984.

MACLEAN, ALISTAIR, 1922 (Glasgow, Scot.). Scottish novelist. Author of adventure novels, many of which have been made into films. *The Guns of Navarone*, 1957; *Ice Station Zebra*, 1963; *Where Eagles Dare*, 1967.

MARSH, DAME (Edith) NGAIO, Apr. 23, 1899 (Christchurch, N.Z.)–Feb. 18, 1982. New Zealand-British novelist, actress, theatrical producer. Known for mysteries featuring Inspector Roderick Alleyn of Scotland Yard; made a dame of the Order of the British Empire, 1948. *A Man Lay Dead*, 1934; *Overture to Death*, 1939; *Death of a Fool*, 1956; *Dead Water*, 1963; *Black as He's Painted*, 1974.

MCCLURE, JAMES, Oct. 9, 1939 (Johannesburg, S.A.). South African crime novelist. *The Steam Pig*, 1971; *The Caterpillar Cop*, 1972; *The Gooseberry Fool*, 1974; *Rogue Eagle*, 1976; *The Sunday Hangman*, 1977.

MCNEILE, HERMAN CYRIL (pseud.: Sapper), Sept. 28, 1888 (Cornwall, Eng.)–Aug. 14, 1937. English novelist. Wrote crime and adventure fiction; under his pseudonym, created series about ex-policeman Bulldog Drummond; after McNeile's death, the series was continued by his friend and biographer Gerard Fairlie, after whom Drummond was modeled in part. *Bulldog Drummond: The Adventures of a Demobilized Officer Who Found Peace Dull*, 1920; *Bulldog Drummond Strikes Back*, 1933.

POE, EDGAR ALLAN, Jan. 19, 1809 (Boston, Mass.)–Oct. 7, 1849. U.S. poet, short-story writer, critic. Best known for his mysterious, macabre stories and poems ("To Helen," 1831; "The Raven," 1845; "Annabel Lee," 1847); invented the modern detective story. "The Masque of the Red Death," 1842; "The Fall of the House of Usher," 1839; "The Pit and the Pendulum," 1842; "The Tell-Tale Heart," 1843; "The Murders in the Rue Morgue," 1841; "The Mystery of Marie Roget," 1842; "The Gold Bug," 1843; "The Purloined Letter," 1844.

PRICE, ANTHONY, Aug. 16, 1928 (Hertfordshire, Eng.). English novelist. Author of historical mysteries. *The Labyrinth Makers*, 1970; *Our Man in Camelot*, 1975; *War Game*, 1976.

QUEEN, ELLERY (pseud. of Manford B. Lee, born Manford Lepofsky, Jan. 11, 1905 [New York, N.Y.]–Apr. 2, 1971; and Frederic Dannay, born Daniel Nathan, Oct. 20, 1905 [New York, N.Y.] –Sept. 3, 1982). U.S. mystery writers. Cousins, they collaborated on novels, novellas, and short stories, using their pseudonym for their detective-hero; edited *Ellery Queen's Mystery Magazine*, from 1941, and over 70 anthologies and critical works. *The Roman Hat Mystery*, 1929.

RADCLIFFE, ANN, July 9, 1764 (London, Eng.) –Feb. 7, 1823. English novelist. Wrote popular, classic Gothic romances set in Italy. *The Romance of the Forest*, 1791; *The Mysteries of Udolpho*, 1794; *The Italian; or, The Confessional of the Black Penitents*, 1797.

RENDELL, RUTH (pseud.: Barbara Vine), Feb. 17, 1930 (England). British mystery novelist. *Live Flesh*, 1986; *Talking to Strange Men*, 1987; *The Veiled One*, 1988. As Barbara Vine: *A Dark-Adapted Eye*, 1986; *A Fatal Inversion*, 1987; *A House of Stairs*, 1988.

RINEHART, MARY ROBERTS, Aug. 12, 1876 (Pittsburgh, Pa.)–Sept. 22, 1958. U.S. novelist. Originated the "Had I But Known" school of detective novels. *The Circular Staircase*, 1908; *The Amazing Adventures of Letitia Carberry*, 1911; *Tish*, 1916; *The Bat* (play), 1920.

ROHMER, SAX (pseud. of Arthur Sarsfield Ward [or Wade]), 1883? (Birmingham, Eng.)–June 1, 1959. English mystery writer. Best known as author of 13-book series about Fu Manchu, the sinister Chinese criminal genius. *Dr. Fu Manchu*, 1913; *Re-enter Fu Manchu*, 1957; *The Return of Fu*, 1959.

SANDERS, LAWRENCE, 1920 (New York, N.Y.). U.S. writer. Noted for his best-sellers in which the heroes possess a touch of perversity. *The Anderson Tapes*, 1970; *The First Deadly Sin*, 1973; *The Sixth Commandment*, 1979; *The Case of Lucy Bending*, 1982; *The Fourth Deadly Sin*, 1985; *The Timothy Files*, 1987.

SAYERS, DOROTHY L(eigh), June 13, 1893 (Oxford, Eng.)–Dec. 17, 1957. English mystery novelist. Wrote sophisticated detective novels; created Lord Peter Wimsey, the aristocratic amateur detective; one of the first women graduates of Oxford U. *Clouds of Witness*, 1926; *Strong Poison*, 1930; *Murder Must Advertise*, 1933; *The Nine Tailors*, 1934.

SHELLEY, MARY WOLLSTONECRAFT, Aug. 30, 1797 (London, Eng.)–Feb. 1, 1851. English novelist. Best known as the author of *Frankenstein; or, The Modern Prometheus* (1818), a novel of terror; daughter of author and political philosopher WILLIAM GODWIN and MARY WOLLSTONECRAFT GODWIN, the first radical feminist; at age 18, eloped with PERCY BYSSHE SHELLEY.

SIMENON, GEORGES, (at least 17 pseudonyms), Feb. 13, 1903 (Liege, Belg.)–Sept. 4, 1989. Belgian-French novelist. Incredibly prolific writer of hundreds of short novels involving acts of violence; created Inspector Maigret of the Paris police. *The Strange Case of Peter the Lett*, 1933; *The Patience of Maigret*, 1939; *The Man Who Watched the Trains Go By*, 1942; *Maigret's Memoirs*, 1963; *The Girl with a Squint*, 1978.

SJÖWALL, MAJ, Sept. 25, 1935 (Stockholm, Swed.). Swedish novelist, poet. With her husband, PER WAHLÖÖ, wrote a series of realistic police procedural novels featuring Martin Beck. *Roseanna*, 1967; *The Laughing Policeman*, 1970; *Murder at the Savoy*, 1971; *The Locked Room*, 1973; *The Terrorists*, 1976.

SMITH, MARTIN CRUZ, Nov. 3, 1942 (Reading, Pa.). U.S. mystery novelist. *Nightwing*, 1977; *Gorky Park*, 1981; *Stallion Gate*, 1984; *Polar Star*, 1989.

SPILLANE, MICKEY (born Frank Morrison Spillane), Mar. 9, 1918 (Brooklyn, N.Y.). U.S. writer of detective novels. As a comic-book writer, one of the originators of Captain Marvel and Captain America; created the tough detective Mike Hammer, whom he played in the 1963 film version of his novel *The Girl Hunters* (1962). *I, the Jury*, 1947; *My Gun Is Quick* 1950; *The Big Kill*, 1951.

STEWART, MARY, Sept. 17, 1916 (Durham, Eng.). English novelist. Author of best-selling romantic suspense novels. *Nine Coaches Waiting*, 1959; *My Brother Michael*, 1960; *The Ivy Tree*, 1961; *The Moon-Spinners*, 1962.

STOKER, BRAM (born Abraham Stoker), 1847 (Dublin, Ire.)–Apr. 20, 1912. Irish novelist. Best known as author of *Dracula* (1897), the classic horror story of a Transylvanian count who was a vampire; managed the actor Sir HENRY IRVIN for 27 years.

STOUT, REX, Dec. 1, 1886 (Noblesville, Ind.)–Oct. 27, 1975. U.S. novelist. Created the eccentric, elephantine detective Nero Wolfe; founder of the Vanguard Press, 1926. *Fer-de-Lance*, 1934; *Too Many Cooks*, 1938; *Some Buried Caesar*,

1939; *Black Orchids*, 1942; *The Black Mountain*, 1954; *The Doorbell Rang*, 1965.

STRATEMEYER, EDWARD (pseuds.: Carolyn Keene, Arthur M. Winfield, Ralph Bonehill, Franklin W. Dixon), Oct. 4, 1862 (Elizabeth, N.J.)–May 10, 1930. U.S. writer of juvenile fiction. Established Stratemeyer Literary Syndicate (1906), which mass-produced such series as the "Tom Swift," "Nancy Drew," "Bobbsey Twins," "Hardy Boys," and "Dana Girls"; from 1942, his daughter Harriet Stratemeyer Adams headed the syndicate.

SYMONS, JULIAN, May 30, 1912 (London, Eng.). English novelist, poet, biographer, critic. Prolific crime novelist specializing in violence behind bland, respectable faces; also a critic of crime novels, a social historian, and a literary critic. *The Immaterial Murder Case*, 1945; *The Progress of a Crime*, 1960.

TEY, JOSEPHINE (pseud. of Elizabeth MacKintosh; pseud.: Gordon Daviot), 1896 (Inverness, Scot.)–Feb. 13, 1952. Scottish mystery novelist, playwright. Created the elegant Scotland Yard investigator Alan Grant. *The Man in the Queue*, 1929; *A Shilling for Candles*, 1936; *Miss Pym Disposes*, 1946; *The Daughter of Time*, 1951; *The Singing Sands*, 1952.

VAN DINE, S. S. (pseud. of William Huntington Wright), Oct. 15, 1888 (Charlottesville, Va.)–Apr. 11, 1939. U.S. mystery writer, editor, critic. Created Philo Vance, a wealthy, sophisticated, pompous detective. *The Benson Murder Case*, 1926; *The Bishop Murder Case*, 1929; *The Gracie Allen Murder Case*, 1938.

WAHLÖÖ, PER, May 8, 1926 (Gothenburg, Swed.)–June 23, 1975. Swedish novelist. As Peter Wahlöö, wrote two crime novels, *The Thirty-first Floor* (1966) and *The Steel Spring* (1970), about Chief Inspector Jensen; with his wife, MAJ SJÖWALL, wrote a series of police procedure novels featuring Martin Beck.

WALLACE, EDGAR, Dec. 1875 (Greenwich, Eng.)–Feb. 10, 1932. English writer, dramatist, journalist. Noted as an author of thrillers. *The Clue of the Twisted Candle*, 1916 (U.S.); *The Green Archer*, 1924 (U.S.); *On the Spot*, 1931 (U.S.); *My Hollywood Diary*, 1932 (U.S.).

WESTLAKE, DONALD, (pseud.: Richard Stark, Tucker Cole), July 12, 1933 (New York, N.Y.). U.S. novelist. After early "hard-boiled" novels, turned to humorous crime fiction. *Killing Time*, 1961; *The Fugitive Pigeon*, 1965; *The Hot Rock*, 1970; *Bank Shot*, 1972; *Jimmy the Kid*, 1974; *Nobody's Perfect*, 1977; *A Likely Story*, 1985; *Trust Me on This*, 1988.

WHITNEY, PHYLLIS, Sept. 9, 1903 (Yokohama, Jap.). U.S. juvenile-story and mystery writer. *Mystery of the Haunted Pool*, 1960; *Secret of the Emerald Star*, 1964; *Seven Tears for Apollo*, 1963; *The Winter People*, 1969; *Spindrift*, 1975; *Rainsong*, 1984; *Feather on the Moon*, 1988.

## SCIENCE FICTION WRITERS

ALDISS, BRIAN, Aug. 18, 1925 (England). British science-fiction writer; author of the critically

acclaimed "Helliconia" series. *Hot House*, 1962; *Greybeard*, 1964; *Frankenstein Un-*

*bound*, 1973; *Brotherhood of the Head*, 1978.
**ANDERSON, POUL WILLIAM**, 1926 (Pennsylvania). U.S. science-fiction writer noted for his humor ("Nicholas Van Rijn" series) and time-travel ideas. *Trader to the Stars*, 1964; *Guardians of Time*, 1960; *Tau Zero*, 1970.
**ASIMOV, ISAAC**, Jan. 2, 1920 (USSR). U.S. science and science-fiction writer. Prof. of biochemistry, Boston U., 1955–    ; prolific (over 200 works) author of fiction and nonfiction; his *Foundation* trilogy (1951–53) and his story "Nightfall" (1940) are regarded as being among the best sci-fi works ever written. *I, Robot*, 1950; *Caves of Steel*, 1954; *The Intelligent Man's Guide to Science*, 2 vols., 1960; *The Gods Themselves*, 1973.
**BLISH, JAMES**, 1921 (Orange, N.J.)–July 30, 1975. U.S. science-fiction writer. Noted especially for the "Cities in Flight" series and for his visions of the satanic; wrote for the *Star Trek* TV series.
**BRADBURY, RAY**, Aug. 22, 1920 (Waukegan, Ill.). U.S. science-fiction writer. Known for well-written stories combining fantasy and social criticism; his *The Illustrated Man* (1951) and *Fahrenheit 451* (1953) were made into films. *The Martian Chronicles* (short stories), 1950; *Dandelion Wine* (short stories), 1957; *The Halloween Tree* (short stories), 1972.
**BROWN, FREDERIC**, Oct. 29, 1906 (Cincinnati, Ohio)–Mar. 11, 1972. U.S. science-fiction writer noted for comedy and satire. *What Mad Universe*, 1949; *Martians, Go Home*, 1955.
**BRUNNER, JOHN**, 1934 (England). English science-fiction writer. Noted for novels about ecological disaster. *Stand on Zanzibar*, 1969; *The Sheep Look Up*, 1972.
**CAMPBELL, JOHN WOOD**, June 8, 1910 (Newark, N.J.)–July 11, 1971. U.S. science-fiction editor, writer. Editor of *Astounding Science Fiction* magazine (now *Analog*), 1937–71; "discovered" ISAAC ASIMOV, ROBERT HEINLEIN, ALFRED VAN VOGT, LESTER DEL REY, others; helped Asimov develop the "Robotic Laws"; his emphasis on "hard" science and technical knowledge made him the midwife of modern sci-fi.; his highly-acclaimed story "Who Goes There?" was made into the film *The Thing* (1951).
**CLARKE, ARTHUR C.**, Dec. 16, 1917 (England). English science and science-fiction writer. Many of his stories are marked by a sense of cosmic unity, as in *Childhood's End* (1953); his *Sentinel* (1951) was the basis for STANLEY KUBRICK's 1968 film *2001—A Space Odyssey;* in many of his nonfiction books, strongly advocates space flight.
**DE CAMP, L(yon) SPRAGUE**, Nov. 27, 1907 (New York, N.Y.). U.S. science-fiction and history writer. Primarily a fantasist known for his *Viagens Interplanetarias* stories; his nonfiction includes *Lest Darkness Fall* (1941), *Divide and Rule* (1948), *The Ancient Engineers* (1963).
**DELANY, SAMUEL**, 1942 (New York, N.Y.). U.S. science-fiction writer. Known for his highly individualistic style and symbolism. *Toromon* trilogy,

1963–65; *Nova*, 1968; *Dahlgren*, 1974.
**DEL REY, LESTER**, June 2, 1915 (Saratoga, Minn.). U.S. science-fiction writer. Known for his vivid writing and sympathetic treatment of characters; his classic novel *Nerves* (1942) prophetically describes a nuclear power plant accident. *The Eleventh Commandment*, 1962.
**DICK, PHILIP K.**, 1928 (Chicago, Ill.)–Mar. 2, 1982. U.S. science-fiction writer. Prolific novelist with a growing cult following. *Time out of Joint*, 1959; *Do Androids Dream of Electric Sheep?*, 1968.
**DICKSON, GORDON**, 1923 (Alberta, Can.). U.S.-Canadian science-fiction writer. Best known for his *Dorsai* trilogy, including *Soldier, Ask Not* (1967). *Delusion World*, 1961; *The Alien Way*, 1965.
**ELLISON, HARLAN**, May 27, 1934 (Cleveland, Ohio). U.S. science-fiction writer. Author of innovative, award-winning science-fiction short stories including "A Boy and His Dog" and "I Have No Mouth and I Must Scream"; noted science-fiction anthologist (*Dark Visions*, collections of 1968, 1972, 1976); writer for "*Star Trek*" and other TV shows.
**FARMER, PHILIP JOSÉ**, 1918 (Indiana). U.S. science-fiction writer. Best known for being one of the first to introduce sex into science fiction; authored the innovative "Riverworld" series. *Lovers*, 1961; *Maker of Universes*, 1965.
**HEINLEIN, ROBERT**, July 7, 1907 (Butler, Mo.). U.S. science-fiction writer. Noted for writing "future history" and for the conservative ideology of his writings. *Farmer in the Sky*, 1950; *Stranger in a Strange Land*, 1961; *Orphans of the Sky*, 1963.
**HERBERT, FRANK**, Oct. 8, 1920 (Tacoma, Wash.). U.S. science-fiction writer. Best known for his *Dune* trilogy, detailing the ecology of a desert world. *Dune*, 1965; *Hellstrom's Hive*, 1973; *Dune Messiah*, 1976; *The Illustrated Dune*, 1978.
**KORNBLUTH, C(yril) M.** (pseud.: Cyril Judd), 1923 (New York, N.Y.)–Mar. 21, 1958. U.S. science-fiction writer. Best known for his collaborations with FREDERIK POHL. *The Syndic*, 1953.
**LE GUIN, URSULA**, Oct. 21, 1929 (Berkeley, Calif.). U.S. science-fiction and fantasy writer. Best known for her *Left Hand of Darkness* (1969); Newberry Award, 1971; National Book Award, 1973. *The Lathe of Heaven*, 1971; *The Dispossessed*, 1974.
**LEM, STANISLAW**, Dec. 9, 1921 (Lvov, Pol.). Polish writer. Best known for the surrealism of his themes and plots. *Solaris*, 1961; *The Invincible*, 1973.
**LOVECRAFT, H(oward) P(hilips)**, Aug. 20, 1890 (Providence, R.I.)–Mar. 15, 1937. U.S. writer. Best known for nightmarish horror stories of demonism; all but one of his books were published after his death. *Dunwich Horror*, 1945.
**NIVEN, LAURENCE** (Larry) **VON COTT**, Apr. 30, 1938 (Los Angeles, Calif.). U.S. science-fiction writer. Best known for *The Mote in God's Eye* (with J. Pournelle, 1974). *Ringworld*, 1970; *Lucifer's Hammer* (with J. Pournelle), 1977.

**PADGETT, LEWIS** (pseud. of Henry Kuttner), 1915 (Los Angeles, Calif.)–Feb. 4, 1958. U.S. science-fiction writer. Best known for his many short stories written in collaboration with his wife, C. L. Moore. *Well of the Worlds,* 1952; *Mutant,* 1953.

**POHL, FREDERIK,** Nov. 26, 1919 (New York, N.Y.). U.S. science-fiction writer. Editor of *Galaxy,* 1962–69; collaborated with C. M. KORNBLUTH on many novels and stories. *The Space Merchants* (with Kornbluth), 1953.

**SILVERBERG, ROBERT,** Jan. 1935 (New York, N.Y.). U.S. science-fiction and nonfiction writer. Prolific novelist and short-story writer. *Nightwings,* 1969; *A Time of Changes,* 1971.

**SMITH, CORDWAINER** (pseud. of Paul Myron Anthony Linebarger), 1913 (Milwaukee, Wisc.) –Aug. 6, 1966. U.S. science-fiction writer. Fantasist with a surreal, elusive style; expert in psychological warfare. *The Planet Buyer,* 1964.

**SMITH, EDWARD ELMER** ("Doc"), 1890 (Sheboygan, Wisc.)–Aug. 31, 1965. U.S. science-fiction writer. Specialized in "space opera"; best known for his Lensman and Skylark series.

**STAPLETON, WILLIAM,** May 10, 1886 (England) –Sept. 6, 1950. English science-fiction writer. Best known for his compendious future histories, such as *Star Maker* (1937), and for *Odd John* (1936), the story of a strange superman.

**STURGEON, THEODORE,** (pseud. of Edward Hamilton Waldo), Feb. 26, 1918 (Staten Is., N.Y.). U.S. science-fiction writer. Best known for his group-mind stories, including *More Than Human* (1953) and *Cosmic Rape* (1958). A script writer for *Star Trek* TV series.

**VAN VOGT, ALFRED,** 1912 (Winnipeg, Man.). Canadian science-fiction writer. Best known for *Slan* (1946), *The World of Null-A* (1948), and *The Weapon Shops of Isher* (1951).

**VERNE, JULES,** Feb. 8, 1828 (Nantes, Fr.)–Mar. 24, 1905. French novelist. Wrote some 50 romantic-adventure and science-fiction stories, many of which were translated and made into plays and films; anticipated many scientific achievements of the 20th cent., including submarines, aqualungs, television, and space travel; made an officer of the Legion of Honor, 1892. *Five Weeks in a Balloon,* 1863; *A Journey to the Center of Earth,* 1864; *Twenty Thousand Leagues under the Sea,* 1870; *Around the World in Eighty Days,* 1873.

**WELLS, H(erbert) G(eorge),** Sept. 21, 1866 (Kent, Eng.)–Aug. 13, 1946. English writer. Prolific and popular author of science fiction, realistic novels, and imaginative social philosophy. *The Time Machine,* 1895; *The Invisible Man,* 1897; *The War of the Worlds,* 1898; *Kipps,* 1905; *Tono-Bungay,* 1909; *Outline of History,* 1920.

**WILLIAMSON, JOHN** ("Jack"), 1908 (Arizona). U.S. science-fiction writer. Best known for *The Humanoids* (1949) and its forerunner, "With Folded Hands"; collaborated with F. POHL on *Reefs of Space* trilogy, 1964–69.

**WYNDHAM, JOHN,** 1903 (England). English science-fiction writer. His *The Midwich Cuckoos* (1957) was filmed as *The Village of the Damned. Day of the Triffids,* 1951.

**ZELAZNY, ROGER,** May 13, 1937 (Cleveland, Ohio). U.S. science-fiction writer. *The Dream Master,* 1966; *And Call Me Conrad,* 1965; *Lord of Light,* 1967.

# Publishers, Editors, and Journalists

**ADLER, JULIUS OCHS,** Dec. 3, 1892 (Chattanooga, Tenn.)–Oct. 3, 1955. U.S. newspaper executive. Vice-Pres. and gen. mgr. of *The New York Times*, 1935–55; credited with development of *Times* as most renowned daily in the world.

**ALEXANDER, SHANA,** Oct. 6, 1925 (New York, N.Y.). U.S. journalist, author. Reporter (1951–61), staff writer (1961–64), and columnist of "The Feminine Eye" (1961–64) for *Life;* editor of *McCall's,* 1969–71; columnist and contributing editor to *Newsweek,* 1972–75; commentator on TV's *60 Minutes,* 1975–79. *Shana Alexander's State-by-State Guide to Women's Legal Rights,* 1975; *Anyone's Daughter,* 1979.

**ALSOP, JOSEPH, JR.** Oct. 11, 1910 (Avon, Conn.) –Aug. 28, 1989. U.S. journalist. With his brother, STEWART ALSOP, wrote the syndicated column "Matter of Fact," for the New York *Herald-Tribune,* 1945–58; also with his brother, wrote *We Accuse* (1955), *The Reporter's Trade* (1958), and *Nixon and Rockefeller* (1960).

**ALSOP, STEWART,** May 17, 1914 (Avon, Conn.) –May 26, 1974. U.S. journalist. With his brother, JOSEPH ALSOP, wrote the syndicated column "Matter of Fact," for the New York *Herald-Tribune,* 1945–58; also with his brother, wrote *We Accuse* (1955), *The Reporter's Trade* (1958), and *Nixon and Rockefeller* (1960). *Stay of Execution,* 1973.

**ANDERSON, JACK,** Oct. 19, 1922 (Long Beach, Calif.). U.S. journalist. Began as staff member for Drew Pearson's column, "Washington Merry-Go-Round"; took over column on Pearson's death, 1969. *The Case Against Congress* (with Pearson), 1969; Pulitzer Prize for national reporting, 1972.

**ASCOLI, MAX,** June 25, 1898 (Ferrara, It.). U.S. writer, publisher. Editor and publisher of *The Reporter,* 1949–1968; author of several books on political economy. *Fascism for Whom,* 1938; *The Power of Freedom,* 1948.

**ATKINSON,** (Justin) **BROOKS,** Nov. 28, 1894 (Melrose, Mass.)–Jan. 13, 1984. U.S. drama critic. Writing for *The New York Times,* exerted tremendous influence on American theater, 1925–42, 1946–60; won Pulitzer Prize in correspondence, 1947. *New Voices in the America Theatre,* 1955; *Broadway,* 1970.

**BAKER, RUSSELL,** Aug. 14, 1925 (Loudoun Co., Va.). U.S. journalist, author. Writes a nationally-syndicated humor column for *The New York Times;* Pulitzer Prize in commentary, 1979. *Growing Up,* 1982.

**BALLANTINE, IAN,** Feb. 15, 1916 (New York, N.Y.). U.S. publishing executive. Instrumental in development of U.S. paperback-book industry as pres. of Bantam Books (1945–52) and as head of his own Ballantine Books (1952–75).

**BEADLE, ERASTUS FLAVEL,** Sept. 11, 1821 (near Cooperstown, N.Y.)–Dec. 18, 1894. U.S. publisher. Publication of his *Dime Song Book* started a new era that climaxed with his publication of the first "dime novel," 1861; his inexpensive books won great popularity and were forerunners of today's paperbacks.

**BEAVERBROOK, LORD** (born William Maxwell Aitken), May 25, 1879 (Maple, Ontario, Canada) –June 9, 1964. British publisher and politician. He became rich with his London *Daily Express,* and he served as a Member of Parliament from 1910 to 1916; in 1917 he was made a peer, and was minister of information in 1918.

**BENNETT, JAMES GORDON, JR.,** May 10, 1841 (New York, N.Y.)–May 14, 1918. U.S. publisher. Became the editor of the *New York Herald* when he was 26, when his father retired; originated the "exclusive" news story and it was he who sent HENRY STANLEY to Africa to find the explorer DAVID LIVINGSTONE; also founded the Paris edition of the *Herald* in 1887.

**BERNSTEIN, CARL,** Feb. 14, 1944 (Washington, D.C.). U.S. journalist, author. As a reporter with the *Washington Post,* with ROBERT WOODWARD played a major role in uncovering and publicizing the Watergate scandal, 1972–74; also with Woodward, wrote *All The President's Men* (1974) and *The Final Days* (1976), accounts of Watergate and its aftermath.

**BISHOP, JIM,** Nov. 21, 1907 (Jersey City, N.J.). U.S. journalist, author. Writer of best-selling, hour-by-hour accounts of the days on which Jesus Christ, Abraham Lincoln and John F. Kennedy were killed. *The Day Lincoln Was Shot,* 1955; *The Day Christ Died,* 1957; *The Day Kennedy Was Shot,* 1968.

**BOMBECK, ERMA,** Feb. 21, 1927 (Dayton, Ohio). U.S. newspaper columnist, author. Her syndicated column, "At Wit's End," deals humorously with her life as a contemporary suburban housewife. *The Grass is Greener over the Septic Tank,* 1976; *If Life Is a Bowl of Cherries, What Am I Doing in the Pits?,* 1978; *Motherhood: The Second Oldest Profession,* 1983.

**BOURKE-WHITE, MARGARET,** June 14, 1906 (New York, N.Y.)–Aug. 27, 1971. U.S. photographer. Noted as an innovator in photo essays; on *Life* magazine staff, 1936–69. *Eyes on Russia,* 1931; *You Have Seen Their Faces,* 1937; *North of the Danube,* 1939.

**BRADLEE, BENJAMIN,** Aug. 26, 1921 (Boston, Mass.). U.S. journalist. He began as a newspaper reporter and then became the press attaché of the United States Embassy in Paris; after a stint as a bureau chief for *Newsweek,* joined the *Washington Post,* eventually becoming executive editor, 1968; he is the author of *That Special Grace,* 1964; and *Conversations with Kennedy,* 1975.

**BRESLIN, JIMMY,** Oct. 17, 1929 (Jamaica, N.Y.). U.S. journalist, novelist. Wrote DAMON RUN-YON-type column for the New York *Herald-Tribune* (1963–65), New York *World-Journal-Tribune* (1965–67), *New York* magazine (1968–71) and currently for the *New York Daily News* and *Newsday. Can't Anybody Around Here Play This Game?,* 1963; *The Gang that Couldn't Shoot Straight,* 1969; *How the Good Guys Finally Won,* 1975; *The World According to Breslin,* 1984.

**BRINKLEY, DAVID,** July 10, 1920 (Wilmington, N.C.). U.S. news commentator. Best known as the partner of Chet Huntley in the popular award-winning NBC-TV *The Huntley-Brinkley Report,* 1956–71; on NBC *Nightly News,* 1976–79; noted for his dry wit and terse style of news analysis; currently on ABC-TV, *This Week with David Brinkley,* 1981– .

**BRODY, JANE E.,** May 19, 1941 (Brooklyn, N.Y.). U.S. journalist. Science writer, personal health columnist, *The New York Times,* 1965– . *Jane Brody's Nutrition Book,* 1981; *Jane Brody's Good Food Book,* 1985.

**BROKAW, TOM,** Feb. 6, 1940 (Webster, S. Dak.). U.S. broadcast journalist. NBC-TV White House corresp., 1973–76; host, *The Today Show,* 1976–82; anchorman, *NBC Nightly News,* 1982– .

**BROUN, HEYWOOD,** Dec. 7, 1888 (Brooklyn, N.Y.)–Dec. 18, 1939. U.S. journalist, novelist. Wrote a liberal-oriented column for several New York City newspapers; helped found the Newspaper Guild, which annually presents an award in his name for reporting. *The Boy Grew Older,* 1922.

**BROWN, HELEN GURLEY,** Feb. 18, 1922 (Green Forest, Ark.). U.S. author, editor. Gained fame as author of the best-selling *Sex and the Single Girl* (1962); editor-in-chief of *Cosmopolitan,* 1965– .

**BROWN, TINA,** Nov. 21, 1953 (Maidenhead, England). British magazine editor, dramatist. Currently editor of *Vanity Fair* magazine; a former writer for *Punch* magazine and editor-in-chief of the *Tatler* magazine in London, she wrote such plays as *Under the Bamboo Tree,* 1973; and *Happy Yellow,* 1978, and such books as *Loose Talk,* 1979; and *Life As a Party,* 1983.

**BUCHANAN, PATRICK,** Nov. 2, 1938 (Washington, D.C.). U.S. journalist. After working on the editorial page of the St. Louis *Globe Democrat,* he became a special assistant to President RICHARD M. NIXON (1969–1973); later he was a columnist and a radio and television political commentator, and presently works for the Cable News Network.

**BUCHWALD, ART,** Oct. 20, 1925 (Mt. Vernon, N.Y.). U.S. columnist, author. Author of a syndicated humor column. *Art Buchwald's Paris,* 1954; *How Much Is That in Dollars?,* 1961; *I Am Not a Crook,* 1974; *Down the Seine and Up the Potomac,* 1977; *While Reagan Slept,* 1983.

**BUCKLEY, WILLIAM F., JR.,** Nov. 24, 1925 (New York, N.Y.). U.S. editor, writer. Well-known U.S. political conservative; founder and editor of *National Review,* 1955– ; host of TV show *Firing Line,* 1966– . *God and Man at Yale,* 1951; *Saving the Queen,* 1976; *Airborne,* 1976.

**CANFIELD, CASS,** Apr. 26, 1897 (New York, N.Y.)–Mar. 27, 1986. U.S. publishing executive. Chm. of the exec. com. and editorial board of Harper and Bros. (1927–61) and Harper & Row (1962–67). *The Publishing Experience,* 1969; *Up and Down and Around,* 1971.

**CERF, BENNETT A.,** May 25, 1898 (New York, N.Y.)–Aug. 27, 1971. U.S. publisher, editor, columnist. Pres. of Modern Library, 1925–71; founder (1927), pres. (1927–65), and chm. (1965–70) of Random House; won landmark court battle ending U.S. censorship ban on JAMES JOYCE's *Ulysses,* 1933; published the works of F. KAFKA, MARCEL PROUST, EUGENE O'NEILL, and WILLIAM FAULKNER; compiled over 20 anthologies of humor; panelist on TV show *What's My Line,* 1952–68.

**CHAMBERS, WHITTAKER,** Apr. 1, 1901 (Philadelphia, Pa.)–July 9, 1961. U.S. journalist. Principal accuser of Alger Hiss in the controversial espionage case, 1948–50; an editor of *New Masses, Daily Worker,* and *Time* magazines. *Witness,* 1952.

**CHANDLER, HARRY,** May 17, 1864 (Landaff, N.H.)–Sept. 23, 1944. U.S. newspaper publisher. Joined and later bought *Los Angeles Times* in 1885, and built circulation from 1,400 to a combined daily and Sunday circulation of over one million by the time of his retirement in 1942. (Grandfather of O. CHANDLER.)

**CHILDS, MARQUIS,** Mar. 17, 1903 (Clinton, Ia.)–June 30, 1990. U.S. journalist. Author of syndicated political column; awarded first Pulitzer Prize in commentary, 1969. *Sweden, the Middle Way,* 1936.

**CHUNG, CONNIE** (Constance), Aug. 20, 1946

(Washington, D.C.). U.S. broadcast journalist. Corresp., CBS, 1976–83; joined NBC, 1983; anchor NBC Nightly News (Sat), 1987– ; won Emmy awards, 1978, 1980, 1987.
CONSIDINE, ROBERT, Nov. 4, 1906 (Washington, D.C.)–Sept. 25, 1975. U.S. journalist. For nearly 40 years worked for Hearst Publications as war correspondent, sportswriter, general-interest columnist, and editor. MacArthur the Magnificent, 1942; The Babe Ruth Story, 1948; Toots, 1969.
COOKE, (Alfred) ALISTAIR, Nov. 20, 1908 (Manchester, Eng.). English-U.S. journalist, broadcaster, U.S. correspondent for the Guardian. Best known as the urbane master of ceremonies for TV's Masterpiece Theater, 1971– ; host of TV's Omnibus, 1952–61; writer and narrator of TV's America: A Personal History of the United States, 1972–73. Six Men, 1977; The Americans, 1979.
COPLEY, HELEN K. Nov. 28, 1922 (Cedar Rapids, Ia.). U.S. newspaper publisher. An exec.-owner with Copley Press, Inc. (1952– ), Copley News Service (1973– ), and San Diego Union—Evening Tribune (1973– ).
COSELL, HOWARD, born Howard William Cohen, Mar. 25, 1918 (Winston-Salem, N.C.). U.S. sportscaster, for ABC-TV, 1956–85; columnist, New York Daily News, 1986– ; known for his abrasive manner and personality. Like It Is, 1974.
COUSINS, NORMAN, June 24, 1915 (Union City, N.J.). U.S. magazine editor; author. Joined Saturday Review of Literature (later dropped "of Literature") (1940), and transformed the struggling literary magazine into the prestigious organ that became synonymous with its name. Present Tense: An American Editor's Odyssey, 1967; Anatomy of an Illness, 1979.
CRONKITE, WALTER, Nov. 4, 1916 (St. Joseph, Mo.). U.S. broadcast journalist. As anchorman of CBS Evening News (1962–81), the preeminent broadcast journalist in the U.S.; worked as a newspaper reporter and wire service correspondent prior to joining CBS.
CROWTHER, BOSLEY, July 13, 1905 (Lutherville, Md.)–Mar. 7, 1981. U.S. film critic. As film critic (1940–67) and critic emeritus (1967–81) of The New York Times, an early champion of foreign films. The Lion's Share: The Story of an Entertainment Empire, 1957; The Great Films: Fifty Golden Years of Motion Pictures, 1967; Vintage Films, 1977.
CURTIS, CHARLOTTE, Dec. 19, 1928 (Chicago, Ill.)–Nov. 7, 1978. U.S. journalist. Noted for her tongue-in-cheek society reporting and for upgrading the family/style section of The New York Times; reporter (1961– ), women's news editor (1965–72), family/style editor (1972–74), associate editor and editor of the Op-Ed page (1974– ), The New York Times. First Lady, 1963; The Rich and other Atrocities, 1976.
CURTIS, CYRUS, June 18, 1850 (Portland, Me.)–June 7, 1933. U.S. publisher, philanthropist. Founded Curtis Publishing Co., 1890; publisher of

Ladies' Home Journal, Saturday Evening Post, and the Philadelphia Ledger.
DANIEL, (Elbert) CLIFTON, JR., Sept. 19, 1912 (Zebulon, N.C.). U.S. journalist. Foreign correspondent, editor, and managing editor of The New York Times, 1964– .
DAVIS, RICHARD HARDING, April 18, 1864 (Philadelphia, Pa.)–April 11, 1916. U.S. journalist. As a foreign correspondent, he reported six wars for New York and London newspapers, and he was the one who made THEODORE ROOSEVELT and his Rough Riders famous during the Spanish-American War; also wrote seven volumes of his memoirs as well as novels, plays, and short stories.
DONALDSON, SAM, Mar. 11, 1934 (El Paso, Tex.). U.S. broadcast journalist. Known for his combative, pushy, and irreverent style; with ABC-TV from 1967; White House correspondent, 1977– . Books: Hold On, Mr. President, 1987.
DOUBLEDAY, FRANK NELSON, Jan. 8, 1862 (Brooklyn, N.Y.)–Jan. 30, 1934. U.S. publisher. Founded the communications empire that bears his name. Founded Doubleday & McClure with SAMUEL S. MCCLURE, 1897; reorganized as Doubleday, Page & Company, 1900; moved firm to Garden City, N.Y., 1910, and started chain of retail book stores; merged into Doubleday, Doran & Company, 1927, and became Doubleday & Company, 1946.
DYSTEL, OSCAR, Oct. 31, 1912 (New York, N.Y.). U.S. publisher. Magazine circulation and promotion expert; editor, Coronet, 1940–42 and 1944–48; managing editor, Collier's, 1948–49; as pres. (1954–78) and chm. and chief operating officer (1978–80) of Bantam Books, credited with developing firm into paperback industry leader.
EPSTEIN, JASON, Aug. 25, 1928 (Cambridge, Mass.). U.S. publishing executive. After working as an editor at Doubleday (1951–1958), he moved to Random House as editorial director in 1958.
EVANS, JONI, April 20, 1942 (New York, N.Y.). U.S. publisher. After a stint as an editor for William Morrow (1966–1974), she moved to Simon & Schuster (1974–1987); in 1987 she was appointed publisher of Random House.
FADIMAN, CLIFTON, May 15, 1904 (Brooklyn, N.Y.). U.S. literary critic, author. Editor at Simon and Schuster, 1929–35; book editor of The New Yorker, 1933–43; member, editorial board of Book-of-The-Month Club, 1944– ; master of ceremonies for the radio program Information Please, 1938–48. Party of One, 1955.
FIELD, MARSHALL, III, Sept. 28, 1893 (Chicago, Ill.)–Nov. 8, 1956. U.S. publisher, philanthropist. Founded the Chicago Sun (later the Chicago Sun-Times), 1941; major stockholder in New York City's ill-fated PM newspaper, 1940–48. (Grandson of MARSHALL FIELD.)
FLANNER, JANET, Mar. 13, 1892 (Indianapolis, Ind.)–Nov. 7, 1978. U.S. journalist. Correspondent for The New Yorker for almost 50 years; wrote the "Letter from Paris" under the byline "Genet"; one

of the few women to be awarded the French Legion of Honor.

**FRANKEL, MAX,** April 3, 1930 (Gera, Germany). U.S. journalist. He joined the staff of *The New York Times* in 1952, was its chief Washington correspondent, Sunday editor, and editorial page editor; in 1986 he became its executive editor; awarded Pulitzer Prize in international reporting, 1973.

**FRENEAU, PHILIP M.,** Jan. 2, 1752 (New York, N.Y.)–Dec. 18, 1832. U.S. poet, journalist. Often called the first professional U.S. journalist; edited the *National Gazette* (a pro-Jefferson organ), 1791–93. Poems: "The British Prison Ship," 1781; "The Wild Honeysuckle," 1786; "The Indian Burying Ground," 1788.

**FRIENDLY, FRED W.,** Oct. 30, 1915 (New York, N.Y.). U.S. communications executive, educator. Collaborated with Edward R. Murrow on *See It Now* (CBS-TV); pres. of CBS News, 1964–66; prof. of broadcast journalism at Columbia U. *Due to Circumstances beyond Our Control,* 1967.

**FURNESS, BETTY,** Jan. 3, 1916 (New York, N.Y.). U.S. broadcast journalist, consumer adviser, actress. Movie actress, 1932–37; on CBS radio in *Dimension of a Woman's World, Ask Betty Furness,* 1961–67; chairperson of President's Com. on Consumer Interests, 1967–69; currently a consumer specialist with NBC News in New York City.

**GILLIATT, PENELOPE,** 1933 (London, Eng.). English film critic, writer. Film critic with *The Observer,* London (1961–67) and *The New Yorker* (1968–79); author of short stories, novels, nonfiction and the screenplay of the film *Sunday, Bloody Sunday* (1971). *Nobody's Business,* 1972; *Splendid Lives,* 1977; *They Sleep Without Dreaming,* 1985.

**GILMER, ELIZABETH,** Nov. 18, 1861 (Woodstock, Tenn.)–Dec. 16, 1951. U.S. journalist. Under the byline "Dorothy Dix," wrote for 55 years a popular syndicated advice column. *How to Hold a Husband,* 1939.

**GODEY, LOUIS ANTOINE,** June 6, 1804 (New York, N.Y.)–Nov. 29, 1878. U.S. publisher. His *Lady's Book,* established in 1830, and eventually known as *Godey's Ladey's Book,* was the leading fashion magazine for 19th-cent. American women.

**GOTTLIEB, ROBERT,** April 29, 1931 (New York, N.Y.). U.S. publisher. After careers as editor-in-chief at Simon & Schuster and Alfred A. Knopf and president of Knopf, he became editor of *The New Yorker* magazine.

**GRAHAM, KATHARINE,** June 16, 1917 (New York, N.Y.). U.S. publisher. Consistently voted to be one of the most influential women in the U.S. Member of editorial staff of the *Washington Post;* pres. of Washington Post Co., 1963–67; publisher of the *Washington Post,* 1968–78; chm. and chief exec. officer of Washington Post Co., 1973– .

**GRAHAM, SHEILAH** (born Lily Sheil) 1905 (England)–Nov. 17, 1989. U.S. journalist. Hollywood gossip columnist and author of several nonfiction books, notably a number of reminiscences about her relationship with F. SCOTT FITZGERALD in his last years. *Beloved Infidel* (with Gerold Frank), 1958; *College of One,* 1967; *The Real F. Scott Fitzgerald,* 1976.

**GRANN, PHYLLIS,** Sept. 2, 1937 (London, England). U.S. publisher. After editorial careers at William Morrow, David McKay, and Simon & Schuster, she became president of G. P. Putnam's and Sons and later of the Putnam Berkley Group.

**GREELEY, HORACE,** Feb. 3, 1811 (Amherst, N.H.)–Nov. 29, 1872. U.S. newspaper editor, reformer. Noted as a crusader against slavery; founder and editor of the New York *Tribune* (1841–72); liberal Republican party presidential candidate, 1872.

**GUMBEL, BRYANT C.,** Sept. 29, 1948 (New Orleans, La.). U.S. broadcaster. Sports host, NBC Sports, NYC, 1975–82; co-host, The Today Show, 1982– ; won Emmy awards, 1976–1977.

**GUNTHER, JOHN,** Aug. 30, 1901 (Chicago, Ill.)–May 29, 1970. U.S. journalist, author. Noted for his popular books on regions of the world, culled from his travels and interviews with political leaders. Overseas correspondent with the Chicago *Daily News,* 1924–36. *Inside Europe,* 1936; *Inside U.S.A.,* 1947.

**HALBERSTAM, DAVID,** Apr. 10, 1934 (New York, N.Y.). U.S. author, journalist. As foreign correspondent covered Congo, Vietnam, and Poland. *The New York Times,* 1960–67; won Pulitzer Prize for international reporting, 1964. *The Best and the Brightest,* 1972; *The Powers That Be,* 1979; *The Summer of 'Forty-Nine,* 1989.

**HEARST, WILLIAM RANDOLPH,** Apr. 29, 1863 (San Francisco, Calif.)–Aug. 14, 1951. U.S. editor, publisher. Creator of Hearst Newspapers, at its peak the largest newspaper chain in the U.S.; used "yellow journalism" (sensationalism, glaring headlines, and exaggerated news) to build sales; transformed the San Francisco *Examiner* into a success; in New York City fought JOSPEH PULITZER with the New York *Journal* and the New York *American;* spent money lavishly, fought for social reform; U.S. rep. (D, N.Y.), 1903–07.

**HEFNER, HUGH,** Apr. 9, 1926 (Chicago, Ill.). U.S. editor, publisher. Founder of *Playboy,* 1953.

**HIGGINS, MARGUERITE,** Sept. 3, 1920 (Hong Kong)–Jan. 3, 1966. U.S. journalist. Only woman correspondent at the Korean War front; reported from Vietnam in the 1960s; awarded Pulitzer Prize in international reporting, 1951. *War in Korea: The Report of a Woman Combat Correspondent,* 1951.

**HOPPER, HEDDA** (born Elda Furry), June 2, 1890 (Hollidaysburg, Pa.)–Feb. 1, 1966. U.S. journalist. Wrote a chatty, caustic syndicated column about Hollywood; noted for her exotic hats and conservative views.

**HOWARD, ROY W.,** Jan. 1, 1883 (Gano, Ohio)–Nov. 20, 1964. U.S. newspaperman. With United Press from 1906; board chairman of UP, Newspaper Enterprise Association and their parent concern, the Scripps-Rae Newspaper chain (now Scripps Howard), 1921–36; pres., 1936–52; chairman of the executive committee, 1953–64.

JENNINGS, PETER C., July 29, 1938 (Toronto, Ont.). Canadian broadcast journalist. London anchor on ABC's *World News Tonight*, 1964–83; anchor, 1983– .

KERR, WALTER, July 8, 1913 (Evanston, Ill.). U.S. journalist, playwright. Drama critic at the New York *Herald-Tribune* (1951–66) and *The New York Times* (1966–83); Pulitzer Prize for criticism, 1978. *Murder in Reverse* (play with wife JEAN KERR), 1935; *How Not to Write a Play*, 1956; *Tragedy and Comedy*, 1967.

KIPLINGER, WILLARD, Jan. 8, 1891 (Bellefontaine, Ohio). U.S. journalist. Founder and editor, *Kiplinger Washington Letters*, 1923. *Washington Is Like That*, 1942.

KNOPF, ALFRED A., Sept. 12, 1892 (New York, N.Y.)–Aug. 11, 1984. U.S. publisher. With wife Blanche W. Knopf, founded Alfred A. Knopf, Inc., publishers, 1915.

KOPPEL, TED, Feb. 8, 1940 (Lancashire, Eng.). U.S. broadcast journalist. With ABC News since the early 1960s; anchor, *ABC News Nightline*, 1980– .

KORDA, MICHAEL, October 8, 1933 (London, England). U.S. editor and novelist. After working in television with the Columbia Broadcasting System, he was named editor-in-chief of Simon & Schuster in 1958. *Male Chauvinism! How It Works*, 1973; *Power! How to Get It, How to Use It*, 1975; *Worldly Goods*, 1982.

KROCK, ARTHUR, Nov. 16, 1887 (Glasgow, Ky.) –Apr. 12, 1974. U.S. journalist. Chief Washington correspondent, *The New York Times* 1932–53; won four Pulitzer Prizes, in 1935 and 1938 for correspondence, a special commendation, and a special citation. *Memoirs: Sixty Years on the Firing Line*, 1970.

LANDERS, ANN (pseud. of Esther P. Lederer), July 4, 1918 (Sioux City, Ia.). U.S. journalist. Syndicated advice columnist, 1955– . *Since You Asked Me*, 1962; *Teenagers and Sex*, 1964; *Truth is Stranger*, 1968. (Twin sister of ABIGAIL VAN BUREN.)

LAWRENCE, DAVID, Dec. 25, 1888 (Philadelphia, Penn.)–Feb. 11, 1973. U.S. publisher. A Washington correspondent from 1910 to 1933, he became president and editor of *U.S. News* (1933–1948); founded the magazine *World Report* and merged with it *U.S. News* in 1948, forming *U.S. News and World Report*, of which he was chairman of the board until his death. *True Story of Woodrow Wilson*, 1924; *The Other Side of Government*, 1929; *Diary of a Washington Correspondent*, 1942.

LEHRER, JAMES, May 19, 1934 (Wichita, Kan.). U.S. broadcast journalist. Co-anchor, *The MacNeil/Lehrer News Hour* (PBS), 1983– .

LERNER, MAX, Dec. 20, 1902 (Minsk, Rus.). U.S. journalist. Syndicated columnist for *New York Post*, 1949– . *It Is Later than You Think*, 1943; *America as Civilization*, 1957; *The Age of Overkill*, 1962.

LEWIS, ANTHONY, Mar. 27, 1927 (New York, N.Y.). U.S. journalist. Reporter, Washington bureau of *The New York Times*, 1955–64; awarded Pulitzer Prize in national reporting, 1955 and 1963; columnist, *The New York Times*, 1969– . *Gideon's Trumpet*, 1964; *Portrait of a Decade: The Second American Revolution*, 1964.

LIPPMANN, WALTER, Sept. 23, 1889 (New York, N.Y.)–Dec. 14, 1974. U.S. journalist. Syndicated political columnist for the New York *Herald-Tribune* (1931–67); awarded special Pulitzer Prize citations for news analysis (1958) and for international reporting (1962); Presidential Medal of Freedom, 1964. *Public Opinion*, 1922; *A Preface to Morals*, 1929; *The Good Society*, 1937; *The Communist World and Ours*, 1952.

LORIMER, GEORGE H. Oct. 6, 1867 (Louisville, Ky.)–Oct. 22, 1937. U.S. editor, writer. As editor of the *Saturday Evening Post*, raised its circulation from 1,800 to 3 million, 1899–1936. *Letters From a Self-made Merchant to His Son*, 1902.

LUCE, HENRY R., Apr. 3, 1898 (Tengchow [now Penglai], China)–Feb. 28, 1967. U.S. editor, publisher. Co-founder of *Time* (1932) and later founder of *Fortune* (1931) and *Life* (1936); one of the most influential publishers in the U.S., and one of the most controversial; believing objective reporting was impossible, encouraged editors to present their own views, even in unsigned articles. (Husband of C. B. LUCE.)

MARQUIS, DONALD, July 29, 1878 (Walnut, Ill.)–Dec. 29, 1937. U.S. journalist, humorist. Wrote the popular columns "The Sun Dial," for the New York *Sun*, and "The Lantern," for the New York *Tribune*; created Archy the cockroach, who reported in first-person lowercase the adventures of Mehitabel, the cat. *the lives and times of archy and mehitabel*, 1940.

MACNEIL, ROBERT, Jan. 19, 1931 (Montreal, Que.). Canadian broadcast journalist. Co-anchor, *The MacNeil/Lehrer News Hour* (PBS), 1983 ; won Emmy award, 1974. *The Story of English* (co-author), 1986.

MARTIN, JUDITH, Sept. 13, 1938 (Washington, D.C.). U.S. columnist. After a career as a reporter and critic on the *Washington Post*, she became a nationally syndicated columnist on etiquette, writing under the pseudonym Miss Manners: Among her books are *The Name on the White House Floor*, 1972; *Miss Manners' Guide to Excruciatingly Correct Behavior*, 1982; *Miss Manners' Guide to Rearing Perfect Children*, 1984, and *Miss Manners' Guide to the Turn-of-The-Millenium*, 1989.

MAXWELL, (Ian) ROBERT, June 10, 1923 (Selo Slatina, Czechoslovakia). British publisher and film producer. He is the chairman of such publishing companies as Pergamon Press, Maxwell Communication Corp., and the Mirror Group Newspapers, Ltd.; also chairman of several television groups, a producer of documentary movies, and served as a Labour member of Parliament (1964–1970).

MCCLURE, SAMUEL S., Feb. 17, 1857 (County Antrim, Ire.)–Mar. 21, 1949. U.S. publisher, editor. Founded McClure's Syndicate, first newspaper syndicate in the U.S., 1894; formed S. S. McClure

Co., publishers of *McClure's* Magazine, a respected literary journal, 1893.

**MCGRAW, JAMES H.,** Dec. 17, 1860 (Panama, N.Y.)–Feb. 21, 1948. U.S. publisher. Merged his industrial-journal publishing firm with the Hill Publishing Co. to form McGraw-Hill, the world's largest publisher of technical books and journals, 1916.

**MCCORMICK, ROBERT RUTHERFORD,** July 30, 1880 (Chicago, Ill,)–April 1, 1955. U.S. publisher. He made the *Chicago Tribune* one of the most powerful newspapers in the world, and built an empire that also included the New York *Daily News* and the *Washington Times-Herald*. (Cousin of J. M. PATTERSON.)

**MCWHIRTER, (Alan) ROSS,** Aug. 12, 1925 (London, Eng.)–Nov. 27, 1975. English editor, author. With his twin brother, NORRIS, compiler and editor of *The Guinness Book of World Records* (1955–75); killed in an IRA terrorist attack.

**MCWHIRTER, NORRIS,** Aug. 12, 1925 (London, Eng.). English editor, author. With his twin brother, ROSS, compiler and editor of *The Guinness Book of World Records* (1955–75; on his own, 1975– ).

**MENCKEN, H(enry) L(ouis),** Sept. 12, 1880 (Baltimore, Md.)–Jan. 29, 1956. U.S. journalist, critic, editor. Controversial editor of *The Smart Set* (1914–23) and *American Mercury* (1924–33); columnist on the Baltimore *Sun* and *Evening Sun*, 1906–56; attacked business, organized religion, and middle-class America; known for his acerbic wit and cynicism. *American Language*, 1919; *Prejudice*, 6 vols., 1919–27; *Happy Days*, 1940; *Newspaper Days*, 1941; *Heathen Days*, 1943.

**MERZ, CHARLES,** Feb. 23, 1893 (Sandusky, Ohio) –Aug. 31, 1977. U.S. editor, author. Editor of *The New York Times*, 1938–61. *The Great American Bandwagon*, 1928; *The Dry Decade*, 1931; *Days of Decision* (ed.), 1941.

**MOYERS, BILL D.,** June 5, 1934 (Hugo, Okla.). U.S. journalist. Personal asst. to LYNDON B. JOHNSON, 1960–67; White House press secy. (to LBJ), 1965–67; editor-in-chief of TV's *Bill Moyers' Journal* (PBS), 1971–76, 1978–81; editor and chief correspondent of TV's *CBS Reports*, 1976–78; senior news analyst, CBS News, 1981–86; executive editor, Public Affairs TV, Inc., 1987– .

**MUDD, ROGER,** Feb. 9, 1928 (Washington, D.C.). U.S. news broadcaster. Reporter for WTOP TV and Radio, Washington, D.C., 1956–61; news broadcaster, with CBS-TV, 1961–80; chief Washington correspondent, NBC, 1980–87; special correspondent, *McNeil/Lehrer News Hour*, 1987.

**MUIR, MALCOLM,** July 19, 1885 (Glen Ridge, N.J.)–Jan. 30, 1979. U.S. publisher. As pres. of McGraw-Hill, Inc. (1928–37), created *Business Week* magazine, 1929; pres., publisher, editor-in-chief and board chm. of Newsweek Inc., 1937–61.

**MURDOCH, (Keith) RUPERT,** March 11, 1931 (Melbourne, Australia). British publisher and media executive. He is the owner and/or publisher of many newspapers, magazines, and television stations in the U.S., the United Kingdom, and Austral-

ia, as well as being the chairman of 20th Century Fox Productions.

**MURROW, EDWARD R.,** April 25, 1908 (near Greensboro, N.C.)–April 27, 1965. U.S. news broadcaster. A war correspondent during the London blitz of World War II, he won fame for his on-the-spot broadcasts of the bombing; narrated the television series *See It Now* and *Person to Person*, starting a new style of TV newscasting with on-the-scene reporting; served as the director of the U.S. Information Agency, 1961–1964.

**NAST, CONDÉ,** Mar. 26, 1874 (New York, N.Y.) –Sept. 19, 1942. U.S. magazine publisher. Worked for *Collier's*, 1900–07; moved on to manage Home Pattern Co., which he had founded in 1904; bought *Vogue* (1909), and started publishing empire that would include *House and Garden* and *Vanity Fair*.

**NEWHOUSE, SAMUEL I.,** May 24, 1895 (New York, N.Y.)–Aug. 29, 1979. U.S. publisher. Founded Newhouse chain of newspapers, magazines, and broadcasting stations when he bought the *Staten Island Advance*, 1921; bought Conde-Nast; a major endower of Syracuse U.'s Newhouse Communications Center. (Father of S. I. NEWHOUSE, JR.)

**NEWHOUSE, S(amuel) I., JR.,** Nov. 7, 1947 (New York, N.Y.). U.S. publisher. As head of Advance Publications, owns Newhouse Publications, Random House, and the Conde Nast magazine publishing empire. (Son of S. I. NEWHOUSE.)

**NEWMAN, EDWIN H.,** Jan. 25, 1919 (New York, N.Y.). U.S. news commentator, author. News commentator with NBC-TV, 1952– ; has narrated many TV specials; a defender of the clear use of the English language. *Strictly Speaking*, 1974; *A Civil Tongue*, 1976.

**NIELSEN, ARTHUR C.,** Sept. 5, 1897 (Chicago, Ill.). U.S. market researcher. Organized A.C. Nielsen Co. to do market research on industrial equipment, 1923; started a food-and-drug research service to record retail sales of products; began a rating service for radio programs using "Nielsen Audimeter," 1941; pioneered TV ratings, 1950.

**OCHS, ADOLPH,** March 12, 1858 (Cincinnati, Oh.)–April 8, 1935. U.S. publisher. He became the owner and publisher of the *Chattanooga Times* in 1878, and was also, beginning in 1896, the owner and publisher of *The New York Times*. (Father-in-law of A. H. SULZBERGER, grandfather of A. O. SULZBERGER.)

**PALEY, WILLIAM S.,** Sept. 28, 1901 (Chicago, Ill.). U.S. communications executive. Pioneer in U.S. broadcasting industry who parlayed fortune from family cigar business into CBS, Inc., the communications conglomerate he founded in 1928; CBS pres. (1928–46) and chm. of the board (1946–83).

**PARSONS, LOUELLA O.,** Aug. 6, 1893 (Freeport, Ill.)–Dec. 9, 1972. U.S. journalist. Syndicated gossip columnist for Hearst Newspapers during Hollywood's golden age; great rival of HEDDA HOPPER. *Tell It to Louella*, 1961.

**PATTERSON, JOSEPH MEDILL,** Jan. 6, 1879 (Chicago, Ill.)–May 26, 1946. U.S. publisher. A war correspondent, he later fought in several battles in France during World War I; co-editor and publisher of the *Chicago Tribune* from 1914 to 1925, he founded the *New York Daily News* in 1919.

**PAULEY, JANE,** Oct. 31, 1950 (Indianapolis, Ind.). U.S. broadcast journalist. Principal writer, reporter, *NBC Nightly News,* 1980–82; co-anchor, *The Today Show,* 1976–90. (Wife of G. TRUDEAU.)

**PEARSON, DREW,** Dec. 13, 1897 (Evanston, Ill.) –Sept. 1, 1969. U.S. columnist. Served as a foreign correspondent in China, France, Cuba, the U.S.S.R., and many other spots; from 1931 until his death, wrote a popular syndicated column, "Washington Merry-Go-Round."

**PERKINS, MAXWELL E.,** Sept. 20, 1884 (New York, N.Y.)–June 17, 1947. U.S. editor. Preeminent editor of his day. At Charles Scribner's Sons, from 1910; edited THOMAS WOLFE's first novels, *Look Homeward Angel* (1929) and *Of Time and the River* (1935), also worked with F. SCOTT FITZGERALD, ERNEST HEMINGWAY, RING LARDNER, TAYLOR CALDWELL, others. *Editor to Author,* 1950.

**PITKIN, WALTER,** Feb. 6, 1878 (Ypsilanti, Mich.) –Jan. 25, 1953. U.S. psychologist, journalist, editor. Best known for writings on pop psychology, especially *Life Begins at Forty* (1932).

**PORTER, SYLVIA,** June 18, 1913 (Patchogue, N.Y.). U.S. journalist. Leading financial columnist with the *New York Post* (1935–77; wrote as S. F. Porter until 1942) and the New York *Daily News* (1978– ). *Sylvia Porter's Income Tax Guide,* published annually since 1960; *Sylvia Porter's Money Book,* 1975.

**POST, EMILY,** Oct. 30, 1873 (Baltimore, Md.) –Sept. 25, 1960. U.S. journalist. Wrote the definitive book on proper social behavior, *Etiquette,* 1921 (in its 10th ed. by the time of her death); wrote a daily syndicated column on etiquette.

**PULITZER, JOSEPH,** Apr. 10, 1847 (Mako, Hung.) –Oct. 29, 1911. U.S. newspaper publisher, often called the father of modern American journalism. After serving the Union in the Civil War, settled in St. Louis as a reporter for a German-language daily, 1868; bought St. Louis *Dispatch* and combined it with St. Louis *Post,* 1878; bought *New York World* in 1883 and made it a leading newspaper, trading heavily on working-class appeal and sensationalism; established (1903) and endowed by his will School of Journalism at Columbia U. and Pulitzer Prizes for journalistic excellence.

**PUTNAM, GEORGE PALMER,** Feb. 7, 1814 (Brunswick, Me.)–Dec. 20, 1872. U.S. publisher. Started first bookseller's trade journal, the *Bookseller's Advertiser;* founded G. P. Putnam and Son (later G. P. Putnam's Sons) book publishers, 1848.

**PYLE, ERNIE,** Aug. 3, 1900 (Dana, Ind.)–Apr. 18, 1945. U.S. journalist. Noted WW II correspondent in Europe, North Africa, and the Pacific; wrote about the experiences of ordinary G.I. Joe; awarded Pulitzer Prize for distinguished correspondence, 1944; killed by Japanese machine-gun fire on Ie Shima,

1945. *Ernie Pyle in England,* 1941. *Here is Your War,* 1943; *Brave Men,* 1944; *Last Chapter,* 1946.

**QUINN, JANE BRYANT,** Feb. 5, 1930 (Niagara Falls, N.Y.). U.S. journalist. Syndicated financial columnist, 1974– ; columnist, *Women's Day,* 1974. *Everyone's Money Book,* 1979.

**RATHER, DAN,** Oct. 5, 1931 (Wharton, Tex.). U.S. broadcast journalist. As CBS-TV White House correspondent (1964, 1966–74); co-anchorman of TV's *60 Minutes* (1975–81); anchorman, *CBS Evening News with Dan Rather,* 1981– . *The Palace Guard* (with Gary Gates), 1974; *The Camera Never Blinks* (with Mickey Herskowitz), 1977.

**REED, JOHN,** Oct. 22, 1887 (Portland, Ore.) –Oct. 19, 1920. U.S. journalist, poet. Radical journalist from a wealthy Portland, Ore., family; was an eyewitness to the 1917 Russian Revolution and became a close associate of LENIN; his account of the revolution, *Ten Days That Shook the World* (1919), is considered the best eyewitness account of the events by a supporter of the Bolsheviks.

**RESTON, JAMES B.,** Nov. 3, 1909 (Clydebank, Scot.). U.S. author, journalist. Joined *The New York Times* in 1939; chief Washington correspondent and columnist, 1953–64; associate editor 1964–68; executive editor, 1968–69; vice-president, New York Times Co., 1969–74; member, bd. of dir., 1973– ; awarded Pulitzer Prize in national correspondence (1945) and in national reporting (1957). *The Artillery of the Press,* 1967; *Sketches in the Sand,* 1967.

**ROONEY, ANDREW** (Andy), Jan. 14, 1919 (Albany, N.Y.). U.S. writer, columnist. Writer, producer, CBS-TV News, since 1959; commentator, *60 Minutes,* 1978– ; syndicated columnist, 1979– ; briefly suspended from *60 Minutes,* over controversial comments in newspaper interview, 1990; won Emmy awards, 1968, 1978, 1981, 1982. *A Few Minutes With Andy Rooney,* 1981.

**ROSS, HAROLD,** Nov. 6, 1892 (Apsen, Col.) –Dec. 6, 1951. Magazine editor. He left high school to become a newspaperman and became an editor of the service publication, *Stars and Stripes,* during World War I; in 1925 founded *The New Yorker* magazine, and edited it until his death.

**ROTHMERE, LORD** (born Esmond Cecil Harmsworth), May 29, 1898 (England)–July 12, 1978. British publisher. He was a long-time chairman of the *London Daily Mail.*

**RUKEYSER, LOUIS R.,** Jan. 30, 1933 (New York, N.Y.). U.S. economic commentator. Sr. corresp., ABC News, 1965–73; *Wall Street Week with Louis Rukeyser* (PBS), 1970; syndicated financial columnist, 1986– . *How to Make Money on Wall Street,* 1974.

**ROYKO, MIKE,** Sept. 19, 1932 (Chicago, Ill.). U.S. journalist. Columnist with Chicago *Daily News* (1959–78) and the Chicago *Sun-Times* (1978– ); awarded Pulitzer Prize in commentary, 1972.

**SAFIRE, WILLIAM,** Dec. 17, 1929 (New York, N.Y.). U.S. journalist, author. Special asst. to Pres. RICHARD M. NIXON, 1969–73; columnist with *The New York Times,* 1973– . *The New Language*

*of Politics*, 1968 (rev. 1972); *Full Disclosure*, 1977; *On Language*, 1980.

**ST. JOHNS, ADELA ROGERS**, May 20, 1894 (Los Angeles, Calif.)–Aug. 10, 1988. U.S. journalist. Started at age 18 as a reporter for *The Los Angeles Herald;* became star reporter for the Hearst papers, covering the Lindbergh baby kidnapping and BRUNO HAUPTMANN trial. *A Free Soul*, 1924; *Final Verdict*, 1962; *Some Are Born Great*, 1974.

**SALANT, RICHARD S.**, Apr. 14, 1914 (New York, N.Y.). U.S. communications executive. Pres. of CBS News, 1961–1979; vice-chm. of NBC Network, 1979– .

**SALINGER, PIERRE**, June 14, 1925 (San Francisco, Calif.). U.S. politician, journalist. Reporter for the San Francisco *Chronicle*, 1946–55; press secy. to Pres. JOHN F. KENNEDY, 1961–63; U.S. sen. (D, Calif.), 1964–65; with ABC News from 1977, chief foreign correspondent, 1983– .

**SALISBURY, HARRISON E.**, Nov. 14, 1908 (Minneapolis, Minn.). U.S. journalist. Editor and writer for *The New York Times*, 1954–73; served as *Times* Moscow correspondent, 1949–54; Pulitzer Prize in international correspondence, 1955. *The Shook-up Generation*, 1958; *Moscow Journal*, 1961; *Russia*, 1965; *The 900 Days: The Siege of Leningrad*, 1969; *To Peking and Beyond*, 1973; *The Gates of Hell*, 1975; *Russia in Revolution*, 1978; *The Long March: The Untold Story*, 1985.

**SARNOFF, DAVID**, Feb. 27, 1891 (Uzlian, Rus.) –Dec. 12, 1971. U.S. communications executive. As a wireless operator, relayed first news of the sinking of the *Titanic*, 1912; joined RCA Corp. in 1919, later service as pres. (1930–47), chief exec. (1947–66), and board chm. (1947– 71); a founder of the NBC network, 1926; a pioneer in TV experimentation. (Father of R. W. SARNOFF.)

**SAWYER, DIANE**, Dec. 22, 1945 (Glasgow, Ky.). U.S. broadcast journalist. With CBS News, 1978–89; co-anchor, *CBS Morning News*, 1981–89; left to join ABC for over $1 million, 1989; hostess of *Prime Time Live* (ABC), 1990– . (Wife of M. NICHOLS.)

**SCRIBNER, CHARLES**, Feb. 21, 1821 (New York, N.Y.)–Aug. 26, 1871. U.S. publisher. In partnership with Isaac D. Baker, founded Baker and Scribner Publishers (Charles Scribner's Sons, from 1878), 1846; at first published philosophical and theological books, then turned to reprints and translations of British and European literary works; founder and publisher of *Scribner's* magazine, 1870–71.

**SCRIPPS, E(dward) W(yllis)**, June 18, 1854 (nr. Rushville, Ill.)–Mar. 12, 1926. U.S. newspaper publisher. Beginning with the *Cleveland Penny Press* (1878), organized the first major chain of newspapers in the U.S., the Scripps-McRae League (now Scripps Howard), 1895; established Newspaper Enterprise Assn. to supply cartoons and features to his chain, 1902; established the UP, 1907.

**SCRIPPS, ELLEN BROWNING**, Oct. 18, 1836 (London, Eng.)–Aug. 3, 1932. U.S. newspaper publisher, philanthropist. A shareholder and active participant in the operations of family-owned newspaper chain (later Scripps Howard), 1867–1930; with brother E. W. SCRIPPS, founded the Marine Biological Assn. of San Diego (later called Scripps Inst. of Oceanography), 1903; founded Scripps C. for Women, 1927.

**SEVAREID, (Arnold) ERIC**, Nov. 26, 1912 (Velva, N.D.). U.S. broadcast journalist. Correspondent with CBS News, 1939–77; commentator on TV's *CBS Evening News*, 1964–77; consultant with CBS News, 1977– . *Not So Wild a Dream*, 1946; *This Is Eric Sevareid*, 1964.

**SHAWN, WILLIAM**, Aug. 31, 1907 (Chicago, Ill.). U.S. editor. He was a reporter and editor for newspapers before he joined *The New Yorker* magazine in 1933, and was made its editor in 1952; forced to resign in 1987, he became a book editor for Farrar, Straus & Giroux.

**SHIRER, WILLIAM L.**, Feb. 24, 1904 (Chicago, Ill.). U.S. journalist and author. As a newspaper reporter he worked for the Paris edition of the *Chicago Tribune* from 1925 to 1933, then with the Universal News Service (1935–1937); switching to radio, he became a war correspondent and commentator for the Columbia Broadcasting System and later the Mutual network until 1949. Books: *Berlin Diary*, 1941; *The Rise and Fall of the Third Reich*, 1960 (National Book Award, 1961); and *The Nightmare Years*, 1984.

**SIMON, RICHARD LEO**, Mar. 6, 1899 (New York, N.Y.)–July 29, 1960. U.S. publisher. With Max L. Schuster, founder of Simon and Schuster, Inc., 1924; introduced Pocket Books, Inc., one of the first enterprises devoted to inexpensive reprints, 1939.

**SMITH, (Albert) MERRIMAN**, Feb. 10, 1913 (Savannah, Ga.)–Apr. 13, 1970. U.S. journalist. Dean of the White House correspondents; UPI correspondent, 1936–70 (covered White House from 1941); awarded Pulitzer Prize in national reporting, 1964; *Thank You, Mr. President*, 1946; *Good New Days*, 1962.

**SMITH, HEDRICK L.**, July 9, 1933 (Kilmalcolm, Scot.). U.S. journalist. With *The New York Times* since 1962; served as foreign correspondent for the *Times* in Moscow, the Middle East, and Vietnam; awarded Pulitzer Prize in international reporting, 1974. *The Russians*, 1976; *The Power Game*, 1988.

**SMITH, HOWARD K.**, May 12, 1914 (Ferriday, La.). U.S. news commentator. Chief European correspondent and European dir. of London Bureau of CBS, 1946–57; correspondent with Washington Bureau of CBS, 1957–61; news analyst for ABC TV, 1962–.

**SMITH, LIZ**, Feb. 2, 1923 (Ft. Worth, Tex.). U.S. columnist. After careers as a book editor and a radio producer, she became a film critic and, finally, a gossip columnist for the Chicago Tribune, New York Daily News Syndicate in 1976; also serves as a New York gossip commentator on television.

**SNYDER, RICHARD E.**, April 6, 1933 (New York, N.Y.). U.S. publishing executive. After a career in marketing and sales for publishing companies, he was made publisher of Simon & Schuster in 1969 and the company president in 1975; he has been the director of the National Book Awards, Inc. since 1986.

**STAHL, LESLEY,** Dec. 16, 1941 (Lynn, Mass.). U.S. broadcast journalist. With NBC News from 1967; news corresp., CBS News, Washington, 1972– ; moderator, *Face the Nation,* 1973– .

**STANTON, FRANK NICHOLS,** Mar. 20, 1908 (Muskegon, Mich.). U.S. communications executive. Pres. (1946–71) and vice-chm. (1971–73) of CBS, Inc.; for many years the number-two man behind WILLIAM S. PALEY at CBS; instrumental in the development of TV segment on CBS, Inc.

**STONE, I(sidor) F(einstein),** Dec. 24, 1907 (Philadelphia, Pa.)–June 18, 1989. U.S. radical journalist. Editorial writer for the *New York Post,* 1933–39; assoc. editor (1938–40) and Washington editor (1940–46) on *The Nation;* editor and publisher of *I. F. Stone's Weekly,* 1953–71.

**STRAUS, ROGER W., JR.,** Jan. 3, 1917 (New York, N.Y.). U.S. publisher. He began as a newspaper reporter and later as a magazine editor; in 1945, he was a co-founder of the publishing house, Farrar, Straus & Co., which is now Farrar, Straus & Giroux; became president of Hill and Wang from 1971 to 1987, and returned as president of Farrar, Straus & Giroux, in 1987.

**SULZBERGER, ARTHUR OCHS,** Feb. 5, 1926 (New York, N.Y.). U.S. newspaper executive. He began with *The New York Times* in 1951, becoming its assistant treasurer (1958–1963) and finally its president and publisher in 1963. (Son of A. H. SULZBERGER).

**SWAYZE, JOHN CAMERON, SR.,** Apr. 4, 1906 (Wichita, Kan.). U.S. news correspondent. Anchorman of NBC-TV's *Camel News Caravan* 1948–56; panelist on the radio show *Who Said That?,* 1948–51.

**SWOPE, HERBERT BAYARD,** Jan. 5, 1882 (St. Louis, Mo.)–June 20, 1958. U.S. journalist. War correspondent with the New York *World,* 1914–16 (awarded Pulitzer Prize in reporting, 1917); as exec. editor (1920–29) of the *World,* known for crusading and fine writing.

**TARBELL, IDA,** Nov. 5, 1857 (Erie Co., Pa.) –Jan. 6, 1944. U.S. journalist. A leading muckraker. *The Early Life of Abraham Lincoln,* 1896; *The Life of Abraham Lincoln,* 1900; *History of the Standard Oil Company,* 1904.

**THOMAS, HELEN,** Aug. 4, 1920 (Winchester, Ky.). U.S. journalist. A reporter for UPI in Washington, D.C., 1943–74; first woman chief of the UPI White House bureau, 1974– .

**THOMAS, LOWELL,** Apr. 6, 1892 (Woodington, Ohio)–Aug. 29, 1981. U.S. author, radio news commentator. A news commentator on radio from 1930; from 1935, filmed and narrated travelogues and written books about his travels; host of TV series *High Adventure,* 1957–59. *The Seven Wonders of the World,* 1956; *With Lawrence in Arabia,* 1924; *Good Evening, Everybody: From Cripple Creek to Samarkand,* 1976.

**THOMPSON, DOROTHY,** July 9, 1894 (Lancaster, N.Y.)–Jan. 31, 1961. U.S. journalist. Syndicated columnist for the New York *Herald-Tribune. The New Russia,* 1928; *I Saw Hitler,* 1932; *Listen, Hans,* 1942; *The Courage to Be Happy,* 1957. (Wife of S. LEWIS, 1928–42.)

**VAN BUREN, ABIGAIL** (pseud. of Pauline Friedman Phillips), July 4, 1918 (Sioux City, Ia.). U.S. journalist. Since 1956, has written "Dear Abby," a syndicated advice column. *Dear Abby,* 1957; *Dear Teenager,* 1959; *Dear Abby on Marriage,* 1962. (Twin sister of A. LANDERS.)

**VANDERBILT, AMY,** July 22, 1908 (Staten Is., N.Y.)–Dec. 27, 1974. U.S. journalist. Wrote daily syndicated column on etiquette. *Amy Vanderbilt's Complete Book of Etiquette,* 1952; *Amy Vanderbilt's Etiquette,* 1972.

**VILLARD, OSWALD GARRISON,** Mar. 13, 1872 (Wiesbaden, Ger.)–Oct. 1, 1949. U.S. editor, journalist. As editor of *The Nation* (1918–32), made it a leading liberal journal; inherited New York *Evening Post,* served as owner and editor, 1897–1918; champion of minority rights, pacifism. *John Brown: A Biography Fifty Years After,* 1910; *Newspapers and Newspaper Men,* 1932. (Grandson of W. L. GARRISON.)

**VREELAND, DIANA,** ? (Paris, France)–Aug. 22, 1989. U.S. publisher. She began her U.S. career as fashion editor of *Harper's Bazaar* magazine in 1939 and joined *Vogue* magazine in 1962, becoming editor-in-chief in that same year, resigning the position to become its consulting editor in 1971.

**WALLACE, DEWITT,** Nov. 12, 1889 (St. Paul, Minn.)–Mar. 30, 1981. U.S. publisher. With his wife, Lila Acheson Wallace, founded the Reader's Digest Assn. in a small Greenwich Village, N.Y., office, 1921; developed firm into a large communications enterprise that publishes books and produces films, as well as the magazine.

**WALLACE, MIKE,** May 9, 1918 (Brookline, Mass.). U.S. TV interviewer, commentator. With CBS-TV since 1951, news correspondent since 1963; on *Mike Wallace Interviews* (1957–58), used aggressive style with which he has become associated; costar and coeditor of *60 Minutes,* 1968– .

**WALTERS, BARBARA,** Sept. 25, 1931 (Boston, Mass.). U.S. newscaster. With ABC since 1976, when she was the first woman to anchor an evening TV news program, joining *ABC Evening News;* with NBC-TV's *Today Show* from 1961, was a panel member (1963–74) and cohost (1974–76). *How To Talk With Practically Anybody About Practically Anything,* 1970.

**WHITE, THEODORE H.,** May 6, 1915 (Boston, Mass.). U.S. journalist, author. Best known for his meticulously detailed chronicles of U.S. presidental campaigns. Chief of China bureau of *Time* magazine, 1939–45; as foreign correspondent, covered Europe, NATO, and American politics, 1955–78. *Thunder Out of China* (with Annalee Jacoby), 1946; *Making of the President 1960,* 1961 (awarded Pulitzer Prize in general nonfiction, 1962); *Making of the President 1964,* 1965; *Making of the Presi-*

*dent 1968, 1969; In Search of History: A Personal Adventure,* 1978.

**WHITE, WILLIAM ALLEN,** Feb. 10, 1868 (Emporia, Kan.)–Jan. 29, 1944. U.S. journalist. Known as "The Sage of Emporia"; as owner and editor, made *The Emporia Gazette* internationally famous as a representative of grass-roots political opinion, 1895–1944; awarded 1923 Pulitzer Prize in editorial writing for "To an Anxious Friend"; awarded 1947 Pulitzer Prize in biography for *The Autobiography of William Allen White* (1946). *The Editor and His People* (collection), 1924.

**WICKER, THOMAS,** June 18, 1926 (Hamlet, N.C.). U.S. journalist, novelist. Chief of the Washington bureau of *The New York Times,* 1964–68; *Times* assoc. editor, 1968–85; retired columnist, 1985– . *Kennedy Without Tears,* 1964; *JFK and LBJ: The Influence of Personality upon Politics,* 1968; *Facing the Lions,* 1973; *A Time to Die,* 1975.

**WILL, GEORGE F.,** 1941 (Champaign, Ill.). U.S. political columnist. Contributing editor to *Newsweek;* commentator on *This Week with David Brinkley,* 1981– ; commentator, *World News Tonight,* 1984– ; won Pulitzer Prize for commentary, 1977.

**WINCHELL, WALTER,** Apr. 7, 1897 (New York, N.Y.)–Feb. 20, 1972. U.S. journalist. Wrote "On Broadway," an internationally famous, much-imitated syndicated gossip column; had a popular, long-running radio gossip program (1930–50).

**WOLFE, TOM** (born Thomas Kennerly Wolfe, Jr.), Mar. 2, 1931 (Richmond, Va.). U.S. journalist. Leading exponent of the so-called New Journalism, which combines fictional techniques with nonfiction reporting in studies of contemporary American culture. *The Kandy-Kolored Tangerine-Flake Streamline Baby,* 1965; *The Electric Kool-Aid Acid Test,* 1968; *Radical Chic and Mau-mauing the Flak Catchers,* 1970; *The Bonfire of the Vanities.*

**WOODWARD, ROBERT,** Mar. 26, 1943 (Geneva, Ill.). U.S. journalist. With *Washington Post* colleague CARL BERNSTEIN, uncovered the Watergate scandal that led to the resignation of Pres. RICHARD NIXON; with Bernstein, wrote *All the President's Men* (1974) and *The Final Days* (1976). *The Brethren* (with Scott Armstrong); *Wired,* 1984; *Veil,* 1987.

**WOOLLCOTT, ALEXANDER,** Jan. 19, 1887 (Phalanx, N.J.)–Jan. 23, 1943. U.S. journalist, critic, actor. Drama critic with *The New York Times* (1914–22), *New York Herald* (1922–24), *New York Sun* (1924–25), and the New York World (1925–28); starred in weekly radio show *The Town Crier,* 1929–49; the model for Sheridan Whiteside in the GEORGE S. KAUFMAN and MOSS HART play *The Man Who Came to Dinner. While Rome Burns,* 1934; *Long Long Ago,* 1943.

**ZENGER, JOHN PETER,** 1697 (Germany)–July 28, 1746. U.S. printer, journalist. As publisher of the *New York Weekly Journal* (founded 1733), the central figure in a famous libel suit (1734–35); his acquittal is regarded as fundamental to the establishment of freedom of the press in America.

# Artists

**ABBOTT, BERENICE,** July 17, 1898 (Springfield, Ohio). U.S. photographer. Photographed literary and artistic social circles, 1920s; teacher at New School for Social Research, New York City. *Changing New York,* 1937.

**ADAMS, ANSEL,** Feb. 20, 1902 (San Francisco, Calif.)–Apr. 22, 1984. U.S. landscape photographer. Used technical and artistic innovations to depict Western wilderness areas and mountain panoramas, emphasizing lighting effects and sharp detail. *This Is the American Earth,* 1960; *This We Inherit,* 1962.

**ADDAMS, CHARLES,** Jan. 7, 1912 (Westfield, N.J.)–Sept. 29, 1988. U.S. cartoonist. His macabre cartoons appeared in *The New Yorker* from 1935. *Drawn and Quartered,* 1942; *Home Bodies,* 1954.

**ALLSTON, WASHINGTON,** Nov. 5, 1779 (nr. Georgetown, S.C.)–July 9, 1843. U.S. painter, author. Considered a pioneer of U.S. romantic landscape painting. Paintings: *The Deluge,* 1804; *Moonlit Landscape,* 1819; *Belshazzar's Feast,* begun 1817. Books: *The Sylphs of the Seasons, with Other Poems,* 1813.

**ARBUS, DIANE,** Mar. 14, 1923 (New York, N.Y.)–July 26/27, 1971. U.S. photographer. Photographed the traumatic experiences of people; won Guggenheim Fellowship, (1963 and 1966) for project entitled "The American Experience"; committed suicide.

**ARNO, PETER,** Jan. 8, 1904 (New York, N.Y.)–Feb. 22, 1968. U.S. cartoonist, writer. His cartoons in *The New Yorker* and other magazines satirized cafe society, from 1925.

**AUDUBON, JOHN JAMES,** Apr. 26, 1785 (Les Cayes, Haiti)–Jan. 27, 1851. U.S. naturalist, painter. Devoted his mature professional years almost entirely to illustrations of U.S. wildlife. *The Birds of America,* 1827–38; *Ornithological Biography* (with William MacGillivray), 1831–39; *The Viviparous Quadrupeds of North America* (with his son John), 1845–48.

**BECK, C**(harles) C(larence), June 8, 1910 (Zumbrota, Minn.)–Nov. 22, 1989. U.S. cartoonist. Humor illustrator with Fawcett's pulp magazines, from 1933; chief artist for *Captain Marvell,* cartoon strip, 1939–54; created Captain Tootsie for Tootsie Roll Candy Co.

**BELLOWS, GEORGE WESLEY,** Aug. 12, 1882 (Columbus, Ohio)–Jan. 8, 1925. U.S. painter. A popular exponent of the U.S. realistic school; painted urban scenes, sports events, and landscapes with forceful brushstrokes; member of the Eight; active in promoting the Armory Show, 1913. Paintings: *Stag at Sharkey's,* 1909; *The Cliff Dwellers,* 1913.

**BENTON, THOMAS HART,** Apr. 15, 1889 (Neosho, Mo.)–Jan. 19, 1975. U.S. painter, muralist. A regionalist painter who specialized in flowing, colorful mythic portrayals of rural American life; opposed abstract art because it was divorced from American traditions. Paintings: *Cotton Pickers,* 1932; *July Hay,* 1943; murals at the Harry S. Truman Library, Independence, Mo., 1959.

**BIERSTADT, ALBERT,** Jan. 3, 1830 (Solingen, Germany)–1902. U.S. romantic landscape painter. Most famous for his panoramas of the western mountains. He fell in love with western scenery while on a surveying expedition, and took photographs which he later turned into paintings.

**BINGHAM, GEORGE CALEB,** Mar. 20, 1811 (Augusta Co., Va.)–July 7, 1879. U.S. painter. Specialized in scenes of Midwestern river life and colorful political campaigns. Paintings: *Fur Traders Descending the Missouri,* 1844; *Stump Speaking,* 1854.

**BLOCK, HERBERT LAWRENCE** ("Herblock"), Oct. 13, 1909 (Chicago, Ill.). U.S. cartoonist. A political cartoonist since 1929; widely known for his liberal views and biting satire; awarded Pulitzer Prize for editoral cartooning, 1942, 1954, and 1979.

**BORGLUM, GUTZON,** Mar. 25, 1871 (nr. Bear Lake, Idaho)–Mar. 6, 1941. U.S. sculptor. Moved from specializing in horse sculptures to large monumental portraits; sculpted the heads of presidents Washington, Jefferson, Lincoln, and T. Roosevelt on Mt. Rushmore, 1927–41.

**BULFINCH, CHARLES,** Aug. 8, 1763 (Boston, Mass.)–Apr. 4, 1844. U.S. architect. Reputedly the first professional U.S. architect; introduced the neoclassical Adam style to the U.S. as the so-called Federal style; designed the Massachusetts State House (1787–88) and the rotunda of the U.S. Capitol (1818–30).

**BURNHAM, DANIEL H.**, Sept. 4, 1846 (Henderson, Mass.)–June 1, 1912. U.S. architect, city planner. Led the so-called City Beautiful movement; guided the redevelopment of Chicago and Washington, D.C., along grand, classical lines; designed the triangular Flatiron Bldg., New York City (1902) and Union Station, Washington, D.C. (1906).

**CALDER, ALEXANDER**, July 22, 1898 (Lawnton, Pa.)–Nov. 11, 1976. U.S. sculptor. One of the inventors of the mobile (suspended sculpture made of separate, moving parts) and the stabile (stationary sheet-metal sculptures); made toys, jewelry, and furniture. Works: *Lobster Trap and Fish Tail*, 1939; *Spiral*, 1958; *Ticket Window*, 1965.

**CANIFF, MILTON**, Feb. 28, 1907 (Hillsboro, Ohio) –Apr. 3, 1988. U.S. cartoonist. Created the comic strips *Terry and the Pirates* and *Steve Canyon*, which pitted American heroes against sinister Orientals.

**CAPP, AL**, Sept. 28, 1909 (New Haven, Conn.) –Nov. 5, 1979. U.S. cartoonist. Created the *"Li'l Abner"* comic strip noted for broad satire of U.S. mores and politics and for voluptuously-drawn female hillbilly citizens of Dogpatch, U.S.A.

**CASSATT, MARY**, May 22, 1844 (Allegheny City, Pa.)–June 14, 1926. U.S. painter, printmaker. Impressionist, worked in France specializing in domestic scenes. Paintings: *Cup of Tea*, 1879; *Reading "Le Figaro,"* 1882; *Woman Bathing*, 1890; *The Coiffure*, 1890; *The Bath*, 1891–92.

**CATLIN, GEORGE**, July 16, 1796 (Wilkes-Barre, Pa.)–Dec. 23, 1872. U.S. painter, engraver, writer. Traveled among the American Indians; painted hundreds of Indian scenes; published travel books, including *Life Among the Indians* (1867).

**CHASE, WILLIAM MERRITT**, Nov. 1, 1849 (Nineveh, Ind.)–Oct. 25, 1916. U.S. painter and art teacher. His work combined flowing brushwork with brilliant colors; much of it contained stylish women in his studio, but he also did sunny coastal landscapes; his famous students included CHARLES SHEELER, EDWARD HOPPER, and GEORGIA O'KEEFFE.

**CHRISTO** (born Christo Vladimirov Javacheff), June 13, 1935 (Gabrovo, Bulg.). U.S. sculptor. Noted for wrapping figures and edifices in fabric, usually white so that they appear to be nearly formless; wrappings range from coastline in Little Bay, Australia, to CLINT EASTWOOD.

**CHURCH, FREDERICK EDWIN**, May 4, 1826 (Hartford, Conn.)–Apr. 7, 1900. U.S. painter. A prominent member of the Hudson River School; achieved dramatic light, water, and sunset effects in his grand, often exotic landscapes such as *Niagara Falls* (1857) and *Heart of the Andes* (1859).

**CLOSE, CHUCK** (born Charles Thomas Close), July 5, 1940 (Monroe, Wash.). U.S. painter. A super-realist; uses a mixture of techniques includ-

ing airbrush, pointillism, and painting from composed photographs "to translate photographic information into paint information."

**COLE, THOMAS**, Feb. 1, 1801 (Bolton-le-Moor, Lancs. Eng.)–Feb. 11, 1848. U.S. painter. Founded the Hudson R. school; painted awesome Romantic landscapes; also painted large allegorical canvases. Paintings: *Voyage of Life* series, 1839–40; *The Oxbow*, 1836; *Schroon Mountain*, 1938.

**COPLEY, JOHN SINGLETON**, July 3, 1738 (probably Boston, Mass.)–Sept. 9, 1815. U.S. painter. Painted realistic, strong portraits of New Englanders with their tools of trade; went to England (1774), where he painted realistic historical scenes. Paintings: *Boy with a Squirrel*, 1765; *Watson and the Shark*, 1778; *Death of Major Peirson*, 1782–84.

**CORNELL, JOSEPH**, Dec. 24, 1903 (Nyack, N.Y.). U.S. sculptor. One of the originators of a sculpture form called assemblage, in which disparate objects are joined together in an unorthodox fashion; one of first American artists to join the surrealist movement.

**CUNNINGHAM, IMOGEN**, Apr. 12, 1883 (Portland, Ore.)–June 24, 1976. U.S. photographer. Known for portraits and photographs of plants. Works: *Marsh at Dawn*, 1901; *Words beyond the World*, 1912; *Two Callas*, 1929.

**CURRIER, NATHANIEL**, Mar. 27, 1813 (Roxbury, Mass.)–Nov. 20, 1888. U.S. lithographer. Partner in Currier and Ives with JAMES MERRITT IVES, from 1857; produced more than 7,000 prints and titles between 1840 and 1890.

**DAVIES, ARTHUR BOWEN**, Sept. 26, 1862 (Utica, N.Y.)–Oct. 24, 1928. U.S. painter, printmaker, tapestry designer. Organized the Ashcan School exhibit, 1908; major figure in organizing the groundbreaking 1913 Armory Show of modern art. Works: *Along the Erie Canal*, 1890; *Crescendo*, 1910; *Dancers*, 1913.

**DAVIS, JIM** (James Robert), July 28, 1945 (Marion, Ind.). U.S. cartoonist. The creator of "Garfield," 1970–  ; has had dozens of best-selling books beginning with *Garfield at Large* (1980).

**DAVIS, STUART**, Dec. 7, 1894 (Philadelphia, Pa.) –June 24, 1964. U.S. abstract artist. Sought inspiration in urban environment—taxis, chain-store fronts, neon signs, etc. Paintings: *Lucky Strike*, 1921; *Egg Beater* series, 1927–30; *Little Giant Still-Life*, 1950.

**DE KOONING, WILLEM**, April 24, 1904 (Rotterdam, Holland). U.S. abstract expressionist artist. Painted linear patterns and violent brushstrokes on canvas, and delicate, refined compositions in oil and pastels; best known for his series, *Women*, in 1953.

**DEMUTH, CHARLES**, Nov. 8, 1883 (Lancaster, Pa.)–Oct. 23, 1935. U.S. painter. Profoundly influenced by work of MARCEL DUCHAMP and the Cubists while visiting Europe, 1907–13; major works are still-lifes, landscapes, and architectural paintings; illustrated HENRY JAMES's *Turn of the Screw*, EDGAR ALLAN POE's "Masque of the Red Death," and EMILE ZOLA's *Nana*.

**DIEBENKORN, RICHARD,** Apr. 22, 1911 (?). U.S. painter. First recognized as an abstract painter, turned to a figurative style in 1955, influencing many younger California artists to return to representationalism.

**DUNCAN, DAVID DOUGLAS,** Jan. 23, 1916 (Kansas City, Mo.). U.S. photojournalist. Photographer for *Life* magazine, 1946–56; photo correspondent in Vietnam for *Life* magazine and ABC-TV, 1967–68. *I Protest*, 1968; *Self-Portrait, U.S.A.*, 1969; *War Without Heroes*, 1970; *Goodbye Picasso*, 1974; *Magic Worlds of Fantasy*, 1978.

**DURAND, ASHER BROWN,** Aug. 21, 1796 (Jefferson Village, N.J.)–Sept. 17, 1886. U.S. painter, engraver, illustrator. A founder (1826) and pres. (1845–61) of the National Acad. of Design; also a founder of the Hudson River School. Works: *Declaration of Independence*, 1823; *Kindred Spirits*, 1849.

**EAKINS, THOMAS,** July 25, 1844 (Philadelphia, Pa.)–Jun. 25, 1916. U.S. artist. Prime exponent of native tradition of realism in American art; known for strong draftsmanship and dramatic compositions. Paintings: *The Surgical Clinic of Professor Gross*, 1875; *The Chess Players*, 1876; *The Concert Singer*, 1892; *The Thinker*, 1900.

**EAMES, CHARLES,** June 17, 1907 (St. Louis, Mo.)–Aug. 21, 1978. U.S. architect and designer. Best known for series of chairs he designed, 1940s; molded plywood furniture, mass-produced by the Herman Miller Furniture Co., 1946; design consultant for IBM, in the 1960s.

**FEIFFER, JULES,** Jan. 26, 1929 (New York, N.Y.). U.S. cartoonist, writer. Cartoonist with the *Village Voice* (1956– ), *Playboy* magazine (1959 ), and the *London Observer* (1958–66 and 1972). *Sick, Sick, Sick*, 1958; *The Great Comic Book Heroes*, 1965; *Feiffer on Nixon: The Cartoon Presidency*, 1974; *Knock, Knock*, 1976; won Pulitzer Prize for editorial cartooning, 1986.

**FRANCIS, SAM,** 1923 (San Mateo, Calif.). U.S. painter. Credited, after JACKSON POLLACK, with bringing a new spatial dimension to the American scene; has had numerous one-man shows, and his works are displayed worldwide.

**FRANKENTHALER, HELEN,** Dec. 12, 1928 (New York, N.Y.). U.S. abstract expressionist painter. Paintings: *Mountains and Sea*, 1952; *Open Wall*, 1953; *The Human Edge*, 1967.

**FRENCH, DANIEL CHESTER,** Apr. 20, 1850 (Exeter, N.H.)–Oct. 7, 1931. U.S. sculptor. Works: *The Minute Man*, 1875; the seated statue of Lincoln in the Lincoln Memorial, Washington, D.C., dedicated in 1922; *John Harvard*, 1884.

**GIBSON, CHARLES DANA,** Sept. 14, 1867 (Roxbury, Mass.)–Dec. 23, 1944. U.S. artist, illustrator. Best known for his "Gibson Girl" drawings; contributed illustrations to *Life* magazine and *Collier's Weekly*; illustrated *London As Seen by C. D. Gibson* (1895–97), *People of Dickens* (1897) and *The Education of Mr. Pipp* (1899); satirical drawings of high society include *Americans*, 1900, *The Social Ladder*, 1907.

**GILBERT, CASS,** Nov. 24, 1859 (Zanesville, Ohio) –May 17, 1934. U.S. architect. Designed the Woolworth Bldg., New York City, 1908–13; U.S. Sup. Ct. Bldg., Washington, D.C., completed 1935; Minnesota State Capitol, St. Paul, 1896–1903.

**GORKY, ARSHILE,** 1905 (Khorkom Vari, Turkish Armenia)–July 21, 1948. Armenian-U.S. painter. Combined European expressionist and U.S. abstract expressionist styles. Paintings: *How My Mother's Embroidered Apron Unfolds in My Life*, 1944; *The Diary of a Seducer*, 1945; *The Betrothal II*, 1947.

**HARRISON, WALLACE K.,** Sept. 28, 1895 (Worcester, Mass.)–Dec. 2, 1981. U.S. architect. With the firm Harrison and Abramovitz, 1945–79; co-designer of Rockefeller Center, New York City, 1929–40; dir. of planning for UN Plaza, New York City, 1947; designed Met. Opera House, Lincoln Center, New York City, 1965; pres. of Architectural League of New York, 1946–47.

**HASSAM, CHILDE,** Oct. 17, 1859 (Boston, Mass.) –Aug. 27, 1935. U.S. impressionist painter, printmaker. Member of "The Ten"; known for his scenes of New York life. Paintings: *Washington Arch, Spring*, 1890; *Southwest Wind*, 1905; *Church at Old Lyme*, 1906; *Allies Day: May, 1917*, 1917.

**HENRI, ROBERT,** June 25, 1865 (Cincinnati, Ohio) –July 12, 1929. U.S. painter. A leader of the modernist Ashcan school of artists; instructor at the Women's School of Design of Philadelphia, 1891–98; teacher at the Art Students' League of New York, 1915–28. Paintings: *Willie Gee*, 1904; *Himself* and *Herself*, 1913.

**HICKS, EDWARD,** Apr. 4, 1780 (Attleboro, now Langhorne Bucks County, Pa.)–Aug. 23, 1849. U.S. folk painter. Known for landscape paintings of Pennsylvania and New York farm country. Paintings: *The Peaceable Kingdom*; *The Cornell Farm*, 1836.

**HOBAN, JAMES,** c.1762 (Callan, Co. Kilkenny, Ire.)–Dec. 8, 1831. U.S. architect. Designed the White House, Washington, D.C., 1793–1801; other works include Grand Hotel (1793–95) and the State and War Offices (1818), both in Washington, D.C.

**HOFMANN, HANS,** Mar. 21, 1880 (Weissenburg, Ger.)–Feb. 16, 1966. U.S. painter. One of the principal inspirations for the style of painting that came to be known as Abstract Expressionism; a major retrospective of his work was held at the Whitney Museum in New York in 1957.

**HOMER, WINSLOW,** Feb. 24, 1836 (Boston, Mass.) –Sept. 29, 1910. U.S. painter. A Romantic painter in the tradition of native American realism; began as a painter of convivial social scenes, then turned to powerful, dramatic depictions of man-versus-the-sea; in his last years, painted atmospheric, impressionistic coastal views. Paintings: *Eight Bells*, 1866; *Snap the Whip*, 1872; *The Gulf Stream*, 1899.

**HOOD, RAYMOND,** Mar. 29, 1881 (Pawtucket, R.I.)–Aug. 14, 1934. U.S. architect. Designer of Neo Gothic skyscrapers in Chicago and New York,

including the McGraw-Hill Bldg., New York, 1930–31 and some of Rockefeller Center, 1929–40.
**HOPPER, EDWARD,** July 22, 1882 (Nyack, N.Y.) –May 15, 1967. U.S. painter. Chiefly depicted city scenes, with photographic realism. Paintings: *Model Reading*, 1925; *Room in Brooklyn*, 1932; *Night-hawks*, 1942; *Second-Story Sunlight*, 1960.
**HUNT, RICHARD M.,** Oct. 31, 1827 (Brattleboro, Vt.)–July 31, 1895. U.S. architect. Established the French Beaux-Arts style in U.S.; a founder of American Inst. of Architects; designed the Tribune Bldg. (1873) and the façade of the Met. Museum of Art (completed 1900–02), both in New York City; Biltmore, Ashville, N.C. (1890–95).
**INNESS, GEORGE,** May 1, 1825 (Newburgh, N.Y.) –Aug. 3, 1894. U.S. painter. A landscapist of the Hudson R. school. Paintings: *The Lackawanna Valley*, 1855; *The Delaware Water Gap*, 1861; *Peace and Plenty*, 1865; *Autumn Oaks*, 1875.
**IVES, JAMES MERRITT,** Mar. 5, 1824 (New York, N.Y.)–Jan. 3, 1895. U.S. painter, lithographer, publisher. Partner with NATHANIEL CURRIER in Currier & Ives lithograph publishers, from 1857.
**JENNEY, WILLIAM LE BARON,** Sept. 25, 1832 (Fairhaven, Mass.)–June 15, 1907. U.S. civil engineer, architect. An innovator in the development of the skyscraper; best known for designing and solving the structural problems in erecting the Home Insurance Bldg., Chicago (1884–85), often considered the first true skyscraper.
**JOHNS, JASPER,** May 15, 1930 (Augusta, Ga.). U.S. artist. A major pop artist known for using numbers, alphabetical letters, flags, targets in his work. Paintings: *Construction with a Piano*, 1954; *Book*, 1957; *Map*, 1961; *Field Painting*, 1964.
**JOHNSON, PHILIP C.,** July 8, 1906 (Cleveland, Ohio). U.S. architect, theorist. One of the principal exponents of the so-called International style of architecture; best-known for functionalist glass-and-steel buildings such as the Glass House, New Canaan, CT, 1949, the New York State Theater, Lincoln Center, NYC, 1964, and the Seagram Bldg. (with M. VAN DER ROHE), New York City, 1958; Dir. of dept. of architecture at the Museum of Modern Art, New York City, 1932–40 and 1946–54. Coauthor (with H. R. Hitchcock) of *The International Style: Architecture Since 1922*, 1932.
**KAHN, ALBERT,** Mar. 21, 1869 (Westphalia, Ger.) –Dec. 8, 1942. U.S. architect. His Detroit firm designed over 2,000 industrial buildings, from 1902. Buildings: Univ. Mich. Hospital, 1920; River Rouge Ford plant, late 1940s.
**KELLY, ELLSWORTH,** May 31, 1923 (Newburgh, N.Y.). U.S. painter, sculptor. Moved from early figurative paintings to abstract collages, and finally to MONDRIAN-like grid painting based on random combinations of colors and shapes; also known for his curvilinear, biomorphic compositions which he started with a 1954–55 series composed almost entirely in black and white.
**KENT, ROCKWELL,** June 21, 1882 (Tarrytown Heights, N.Y.)–Mar. 13, 1971. U.S. painter, illus-

trator. Known for his stark, dramatic lithographs and exotic landscapes. Works: *The Road Roller*, 1909; *North Wind*, 1919; *Wilderness*, 1920.
**KLINE, FRANZ,** May 23, 1919 (Wilkes-Barre, Pa.)–May 13, 1962. U.S. painter. From realism turned to a non-representational style of painting, eventually becoming one of the leaders of the "action painting" movement, a branch of Abstract Expressionism; paintings were black on white or black on gray; added color only near the end of his life.
**LA FARGE, JOHN,** Mar. 31, 1835 (New York, N.Y.)–Nov. 14, 1910. U.S. landscape and figure painter, also worked in stained glass. National Academician at Soc. of American Artists, 1869; painted the altarpiece at St. Peter's Church, New York City, 1863; decorated New York City's Trinity Church. *Lectures on Art*, 1895, *Higher Life in Art*, 1908.
**LANE, FITZ HUGH** (born Nathaniel Rogers Lane), Dec. 19, 1804 (Gloucester, Mass.)–Aug. 14, 1865. U.S. painter. One of the finest marine painters of the 19th-cen. America. Paintings: *Gloucester Harbor from Rocky Neck*, 1844; *Salem Harbor*, 1853.
**LANGE, DOROTHEA,** 1895 (Hoboken, N.J.)–Oct. 11, 1965. U.S. photographer. Came to prominence through her documentary series, "An American Exodus: A Record of Human Erosion" (1939), the result of her selection by the Farm Security Administration to document the migration of the "Oakies" from the dust bowl of the Great Plains region; her "Migrant Mother" was selected as one of the best photographs of the last half-century and hangs in the Library of Congress.
**LARSON, GARY,** Aug. 14, 1950 (Tacoma, Wash.). U.S. cartoonist. Before becoming a syndicated cartoon strip artist, he was a jazz musician, music store clerk, and Humane Society investigator; he started his eerily unconventional cartoon feature, *The Far Side*, in 1979.
**LATROBE, BENJAMIN H.,** May 1, 1764 (Fulneck, Yorkshire, Eng.)–Sept. 3, 1820. U.S. architect. An exponent of the Classical Revival style; appointed architect of the Capitol, Washington, D.C., 1803; rebuilt the Capitol after it was destroyed in the War of 1812; Basilica of the Assumption, Baltimore, MD, 1805–21.
**LICHTENSTEIN, ROY,** Oct. 27, 1923 (New York, N.Y.). U.S. painter. A leader of the pop art movement. Paintings: *Flatten...sandfleas*, 1962; *Preparedness*, 1968.
**MCKIM, CHARLES F.,** Aug. 24, 1847 (Chester Co., Pa.)–Sept. 14, 1909. U.S. architect. A founder (1879) of McKim, Mead and White, the most prestigious U.S. architectural firm of the late 19th cent. and the designers of Boston Public Library (1887–95), the Washington Memorial Arch (New York, 1889), Symphony Hall (Boston, 1901), and the Morgan Library (New York, 1903).
**MIES VAN DER ROHE,** Mar. 27, 1886 (Aachen, Ger.)–Aug. 18, 1969. U.S. architect. An acknowledged master of 20th-cent. architecture; originated the steel and glass skyscraper; directed the Bauhaus school at Dessau, Ger., until it was closed by Nazis

in 1933; emigrated to U.S., 1938. Works: Seagram Building (NYC), 1956 (with PHILIP C. JOHNSON); Chicago Federal Center.

**MILLS, ROBERT,** Aug. 12, 1781 (Charleston, S.C.) –Mar. 3, 1855. U.S. neoclassical architect. Considered the first American-born professional architect; designed the original U.S. Post Office, the Treasury Office, and the Patent Office, all in Washington, D.C., 1836–51; also designed the Washington Monument, 1836.

**MOSES, GRANDMA,** Sept. 7, 1860 (Greenwich, N.Y.)–Dec. 13, 1961. U.S. folk painter. Best known for documentary paintings of U.S. rural life, including *Black Horses* (1941) and *From My Window* (1946). Autobiography: *My Life's History,* 1952.

**MOTHERWELL, ROBERT,** Jan. 14, 1915 (Aberdeen, Wash.). U.S. painter. A founder of abstract expressionism; later adopted surrealist technique of automatism. Paintings: *Poncho Villa, Dead and Alive,* 1943; *Africa,* 1964–65; *Open series,* 1967–69.

**MUYBRIDGE, EADWEARD,** Apr. 9, 1830 (Kingston-on-Thames, Eng.)–May 8, 1904. U.S. photographer. Pioneer in photographic studies of motion and in moving-picture projection; invented zoopraxiscope and motion photography, 1877; did motion studies of humans at the U. of Pennsylvania, 1884–87.

**NAST, THOMAS,** Sept. 27, 1840 (Landau, Ger.) –Dec. 7, 1902. U.S. cartoonist. With *Harper's Weekly,* 1858–86; known for the creation of the Democratic Party Donkey and the Republican Party Elephant, and for his brilliant cartoons savaging the corrupt Tammany Hall political machine and BOSS TWEED.

**NEVELSON, LOUISE,** 1899 (Kiev, Rus.)–Apr. 17, 1988. U.S. sculptor, painter. Known for her large-scale wooden pieces. First exhibition, New York City, 1941. Sculptures: *Sky Cathedral,* 1958.

**NEWMAN, BARNETT,** Jan. 29, 1905 (New York, N.Y.)–July 3, 1970. U.S. abstract expressionist painter. Cofounder (with W. Baziotes, ROBERT MOTHERWELL, and MARK ROTHKO) of the Subject of the Artist school, 1948; best known for his series of 14 paintings titled *Stations of the Cross,* 1966.

**NOGUCHI, ISAMU,** Nov. 17, 1904 (Los Angeles, Calif.)–Dec. 30, 1988. U.S. sculptor, designer. Designed fountain for Ford Pavillion at the New York World's Fair, 1939. Other works: *Kouros,* 1945; garden for UNESCO, Paris, 1958; *Euripides* 1966.

**O'KEEFFE, GEORGIA,** Nov. 15, 1887 (Sun Prairie, Wisc.)–Mar. 6, 1986. U.S. painter. Best known for her semiabstract depictions of natural subjects. Paintings: *Black Iris,* 1926; *Cow's Skull: Red, White and Blue,* 1931; *Sky above Clouds IV,* 1965. (Wife of A. STIEGLITZ.)

**OLDENBURG, CLAES THURE,** Jan. 28, 1929 (Stockholm, Swed.). U.S. sculptor. A representational sculptor, transcended the pop art movement which gave him his start; best known for "soft sculptures"—items representing everyday objects, such as shirts, ice cream cones, and cars; best known works are "The Sheet" and "The Store,"

bundle-like sculptures made of paper, wood, and string.

**OLIPHANT, PAT**(rick), July 24, 1935 (Adelaide, Australia). U.S. editorial cartoonist. Pulitzer Prize for editorial cartooning, 1967. Author: *The Oliphant Book,* 1969; *But Seriously Folks,* 1983; *Up to There in Alligators,* 1987.

**OLMSTED** (or Olmstead), **FREDERICK LAW,** Apr. 26, 1822 (Hartford, Conn.)–Aug. 28, 1903. U.S. landscape architect. Pioneer in urban landscaping; best known for his designs for New York's Central Park (1857) and for the grounds of the 1893 Chicago World's Fair (now Jackson Park); chm. of the first Yosemite commission, 1864–90.

**PARISH, MAXFIELD FREDERICK,** July 25, 1870 (Philadelphia, Pa.)–Mar. 30, 1966. U.S. painter, illustrator. Known for his highly original posters and book illustrations; member of the Natl. Acad. of Design, from 1906. Books illustrated: *Mother Goose in Prose, Knickerbocker's History of New York.* Paintings: *Daybreak.*

**PEALE, CHARLES WILSON,** Apr. 15, 1741 (Queen Annes Co., Md.)–Feb. 22, 1827. U.S. painter. Best known for his portraits of American Revolutionary figures, including GEORGE WASHINGTON, BENJAMIN FRANKLIN, and THOMAS JEFFERSON; founder of the first U.S. museum, the Peale Museum, 1786. Paintings: *Exhuming the Mastodon,* 1806; *The Staircase Group,* 1795.

**PEI, I**(eoh) **M**(ing), Apr. 26, 1917 (Canton, China). U.S. architect. With Webb and Knapp, New York City, 1948–55; formed I. M. Pei and Partners, 1955; known for innovative modernist structures. Buildings: National Airlines Terminal, Kennedy Airport, New York, N.Y., 1960; Herbert F. Johnson Museum of Art, Cornell U., 1973; Natl. Gallery of Art, East Bldg., Washington, D.C., 1978.

**PETERS, MIKE,** Oct. 9, 1943 (St. Louis, Mo.). U.S. political cartoonist. He began his political cartoons at the *Chicago Daily News* and moved to the *Dayton Daily News* in 1969, and has had several anthologies of his cartoons published; also draws comic strip, "Mother Goose and Grim." *The Nixon Chronicles,* 1976; *Clones, You Idiot...I Said Clones,* 1978; *Win One for the Geezer,* 1982.

**PHYFE, DUNCAN,** 1768 (Loch Fannich, Ross and Cromarty, Scotland)–Aug. 16, 1854. U.S. cabinet-maker. Established Duncan Phyfe and Sons, 1837; known for his chairs, settees, tables in the neoclassical style.

**POLLOCK, JACKSON,** Jan. 28, 1912 (Cody, Wyo.) –Aug. 11, 1956. U.S. painter. A leader of the abstract expressionist movement in America and an initiator of the op art movement of the 1950s and 1960s. Paintings: *Mural,* 1944; *Full Fathom Five,* 1947; *Autumn Rhythm,* 1955; *Portrait and a Dream,* 1953.

**PORTER, ELIOT,** Dec. 6, 1901 (Winnetka, Ill.). U.S. photographer. Illustrated books: *American Places,* 1981; *Eliot Porter's Southwest,* 1985; *Maine,* 1986.

**PORTMAN, JOHN C.,** Dec. 4, 1924 (Walhalla, S.C.). U.S. architect. Head of John Portman and

Assoc., 1968–  ; known for distinctly designed hotels, many built for the Hyatt chain. Buildings: Hyatt Regency Hotel, Atlanta; Hyatt Regency, O'Hare Chicago; Bonaventure Hotel, Los Angeles; Peachtree Center Plaza Hotel, Atlanta.

**POWERS, HIRAM,** July 29, 1805 (nr. Woodstock, Vt.)–June 27, 1873. U.S. sculptor. Through his job in the wax works department of a Cincinnati museum discovered his aptitude for modelling figures; made busts of JOHN MARSHALL, ANDREW JACKSON, and DANIEL WEBSTER.

**RAUSCHENBERG, ROBERT,** 1925 (Port Arthur, Tex.). U.S. painter. Created what is believed to be the first pop art painting; artistic signature is marriage of everyday commercial objects (Coke bottles, shopping bags, i.e, the so-called "detritus of society") with paint and canvas.

**RAY, MAN,** Aug. 27, 1890 (Philadelphia, Pa.)–Nov. 18, 1976. U.S. painter, sculptor, photographer. Cofounder (with MARCEL DUCHAMP and Francis Picabia) of the Dada group, 1917; member of dada and surrealist group, Paris, 1924–39; developed the rayograph technique in photography, 1921. Photographs: *Le Violon d'Ingres,* 1924. Films: *Le Retour à la raison,* 1923; *L'Etoile de mer,* 1928–29. Paintings: *Observatory Time—The Lovers,* 1932–34.

**REINHARDT, AD,** 1913–1967. U.S. painter. One of the pioneers of American abstraction, his "ultimate paintings" foreshadowed minimalism.

**REMINGTON, FREDERIC,** Oct. 4, 1861 (Canton, N.Y.)–Dec. 26, 1909. U.S. painter, sculptor, illustrator. Best known for his colorful, exuberant paintings depicting scenes from the Old West. Paintings: *A Dash for the Timber,* 1889; *The Scout: Friends or Enemies,* c.1890. Sculpture: *A Bronco Buster,* 1895.

**RENWICK, JAMES.,** Nov. 3, 1818 (Bloomingdale [now in New York City], N.Y.)–June 23, 1895. U.S. architect. Best known for his Gothic revival designs; buildings include Grace Church (1843–46) and St. Patrick's Cathedral in New York City (dedicated in 1879) and the Smithsonian Inst. (1844–46) and Corcoran Art Gallery now the Renwick (1859) in Washington, D.C.

**RICHARDSON, HENRY H.,** Sept. 29, 1838 (Priestley Plantation, St. James Par., La.)–Apr. 27, 1886. U.S. architect. Worked in neo-Romanesque style; influenced the work of Louis Sullivan and FRANK LLOYD WRIGHT. Buildings: Trinity Church, Boston, 1872–77; Marshal Field Warehouse, Chicago, 1885–87.

**RIPLEY, ROBERT,** Dec. 25, 1893 (Santa Rosa, Calif.)–May 27, 1949. U.S. cartoonist. Best known for his "Believe it or Not" cartoons, first published in 1918 and syndicated in over 300 newspapers all over the world.

**RIVERS, LARRY,** Aug. 17, 1923 (New York, N.Y.). U.S. artist. A forerunner of the pop art movement; among the first to use popular images in his paintings. Paintings: *Double Portrait of Berdie,* 1955.

**ROCKWELL, NORMAN,** Feb. 3, 1894 (New York, N.Y.)–Nov. 8, 1978. U.S. illustrator, painter. Best known for his nostalgic, highly detailed covers for the *Saturday Evening Post. The Four Freedoms,* 1943; Recipient of Presidential Freedom Medal, 1977.

**ROOT, JOHN WELLBORN,** Jan. 10, 1850 (Lumpkin, Ga.)–Jan. 15, 1891. U.S. architect. In partnership with DANIEL H. BURNHAM, 1872–92; consulting architect for the World's Columbian Exposition, 1890. Buildings: Chicago Acad. of Fine Arts, 1882; The Monadnock Building, 1889–91; Chicago Daily News Bldg., 1890.

**ROSENQUIST, JAMES,** Nov. 29, 1933 (Grand Forks, N. Dak.). U.S. painter. In the pop art movement; incorporates everyday images in huge canvases. Paintings: *F-111* (51 panels), 1965.

**ROTHKO, MARK,** Sept. 25, 1903 (Dvinska [now Daugapils], Rus.)–Feb. 25, 1970. U.S. painter. A cofounder of the abstract expressionist group called The Ten, 1935, committed suicide. Works: *Subway* series, late 1930s; *Baptismal Scene,* 1945; *No. 2, 1948,* 1948; *Light, Earth and Blue,* 1954; *Black on Grey,* 1970.

**RYDER, ALBERT PINKHAM,** Mar. 19, 1847 (New Bedford, Mass.)–Mar. 28, 1917. U.S. painter. Best known for his seascapes and allegorical scenes. Paintings: *Toilers of the Sea,* c.1884; *Jonah, Death on a Pale Horse.*

**SAARINEN, EERO,** Aug. 20, 1910 (Kirkkonummi, Fin.)–Sept. 1, 1961. U.S. architect. In partnership with his father, Eliel Saarinen, 1938–50. Buildings: Gen. Motors Technical Center, Warren, Mich., 1948–56; U.S. Embassy, London, 1955–60, T.W.A. Terminal, JFK Airport, N.Y.C., 1962.

**SAINT-GAUDENS, AUGUSTUS,** Mar. 1, 1848 (Dublin, Ire.)–Aug. 3, 1907. U.S. sculptor. Executed both relief and in-the-round works in a Beaux Arts mode; the most famous American sculptor of his day. Works: Monument to Admiral Farragut, 1880; *Amor Caritas,* 1887; Memorial to Mrs. Henry Adams, 1891; Monument to Robert Gould Shaw, 1897; designs for the U.S. $20 gold piece (1907) and the $10 gold piece.

**SARGENT, JOHN SINGER,** Jan. 12, 1856 (Florence, It.)–Apr. 15, 1925. U.S. portrait and genre painter. The most sought-after portraitist of the late-19th and early-20th centuries, in both Europe and the U.S.; a master of composition and surface effects, official war artist WW I. Paintings: *The Daughters of Edward Darly Boit,* 1882; *El Jaleo,* 1882; *Madame X,* 1884; *Carnation, Lily, Lily, Rose,* 1885–86; *Gassed,* 1918; decorative murals for Boston Public Library, 1890–1916.

**SCHULZ, CHARLES M.,** ("Sparky"), Nov. 26, 1922 (Minneapolis, Minn.). U.S. cartoonist. Created syndicated comic strip *Peanuts,* 1950; numerous collections of cartoons published in books, from 1952; won Outstanding Cartoonist award, Natl. Cartoonist Soc., 1956; won Emmy award for *A Charlie Brown Christmas,* 1966.

**SEGAL, GEORGE,** Nov. 26, 1924 (New York, N.Y.). U.S. sculptor. Dissatisfied with his work as a painter turned to sculpture; created sculptures which featured life-size plaster casts of people, most of them friends or relatives. Works: *The Artist in His Studio*, 1968; *The Subway*, 1968; *The Aerial View*, 1970.

**SENDAK, MAURICE**, June 10, 1928 (Brooklyn, N.Y.). U.S. writer and illustrator of children's books. *Kenny's Window*, 1956; *Where the Wild Things Are* (1964 Caldecott medal); *In the Night Kitchen*, 1970; *The Cunning Little Vixen*, 1985.

**SHAHN, BEN**(jamin), Sept. 12, 1898 (Kaunas, Lith. [now USSR])–Mar. 14, 1969. U.S. painter, graphic artist. Worked with DIEGO RIVERA to execute *Man at the Crossroads* at New York City's Rockefeller Center, 1933; did a series of paintings of the trials of Sacco and Vanzetti (1931–32) and of Tom Mooney (1932–33). Other paintings: *Seurat's Lunch*, 1939; *Handball*, 1939.

**SHEELER, CHARLES**, July 16, 1883 (Philadelphia, Pa.)–May 7, 1965. U.S. painter, photographer. Style has become emblematic of the concept of "American Precisionism" a blending of elements of Modernism, photography, and industrial art. Paintings: *Church Street*, 1919; *Upper Deck*, 1929; *Americana*, 1931.

**SKIDMORE, LOUIS**, Apr. 8, 1897 (Lawrenceburg, Mo.)–Sept. 27, 1962. U.S. architect. A partner in Skidmore, Owings and Merrill from 1949, an architectural firm that pioneered in commercial and institutional design and structure. Buildings: Connecticut Gen. Life Insurance Co., Hartford, Conn., 1954–57; U.S. Air Force Acad., 1954–62.

**SLOAN, JOHN F.**, Aug. 2, 1871 (Lock Haven, Pa.)–Sept. 7, 1951. U.S. painter, etcher, lithographer, illustrator. Best known for his depictions of everyday life in New York City; a founder of the Ashcan school, 1908. Works: *Wake of the Ferry*, 1907; *Sunday, Women Drying Their Hair*, 1912; *Backyards, Greenwich Village*, 1914.

**SMITH, DAVID**, Mar. 9, 1906 (Decatur, Ind.)–May 24, 1965. U.S. sculptor. Found career as an artist while working with metal during summer jobs as a riveter and spot welder for the Studebaker plant in South Bend, Ind.; worked mostly with iron and steel, forging, welding and riveting them into increasingly abstract shapes.

**STEICHEN, EDWARD**, Mar. 27, 1879 (Luxembourg)–Mar. 25, 1973. U.S. photographer. With ALFRED STIEGLITZ, founded the Photo-Secession Gallery, 1905; head of WW I U.S. Army Air Corps photography; celebrity photographer, 1923–38; created *The Family of Man* exhibition, 1955.

**STELLA, FRANK**, May 12, 1936 (Malden, Mass.). U.S. painter. Recognized as a leader of the "Minimal Art" movement; first came to prominence as an Abstract Expressionist; has exhibited widely, and was included in Museum of Modern Art's "Sixteen Americans" exhibition, 1959–60.

**STIEGLITZ, ALFRED**, Jan. 1, 1864 (Hoboken, N.J.)–July 13, 1946. U.S. photographer. Known as the father of modern photography; founded Photo-Secession Group, 1902; with EDWARD STEICHEN, opened Photo-Secession Gallery, 1905; known for his 400-print series of his wife, GEORGIA O'KEEFFE.

**STILL, CLIFFORD**, Nov. 30, 1904 (Grandin, N.D.). U.S. painter. Abstract Expressionist painter, considered one of the fathers of the "New York School" of art.

**STONE, EDWARD DURELL**, Mar. 9, 1902 (Fayetteville, Ark.)–Aug. 6, 1978. U.S. architect. Organized his own firm, 1936; one of the designers for the Mus. of Modern Art, 1937. Buildings: U.S. Embassy, New Delhi, 1954; American Pavillion, Brussels World's Fair, 1958; John F. Kennedy Center for the Performing Arts (Washington, D.C.), 1964. *The Evolution of an Architect*, 1962.

**STUART, GILBERT**, Dec. 3, 1755 (N. Kingstown, Kings, R.I.)–July 9, 1828. U.S. painter. Best known for his portraits of early Americans. Painted three portraits of G. WASHINGTON from life, 1795, 1796, and c. 1796. Paintings: *The Skater*, 1782; *Mrs. Richard Yates*, 1793–94.

**SULLIVAN, LOUIS HENRY**, September 3, 1856 (Boston, Mass.)–Apr. 14, 1924. U.S. architect. Founder of "the Chicago School" of architecture, expounded modernism and was opposed to useless tradition; believed that design should be related to use and materials and respond to its milieu; designs included the Auditorium Building Theater and Gage Building in Chicago, and the Wainwright Building, thought to be the first true skyscraper, in St. Louis.

**SULLY, THOMAS**, June 19, 1783 (Horncastle, Lincs. Eng.)–Nov. 5, 1872. U.S. portrait painter. Executed some 2,000 portraits and 500 subject and historical pictures, including *Lady with a Harp* (1818), *The Passage of the Delaware* (1819), and *Col. Thomas Handasyd Perkins* (1831–32).

**TIFFANY, LOUIS COMFORT**, Feb. 18, 1848 (New York, N.Y.)–Jan. 17, 1933. U.S. painter, decorator, designer. Son of the jeweler, CHARLES LEWIS TIFFANY; organized the Soc. of American Artists, 1877; established an interior-decorating studio in New York (1878) that specialized in *favrile* glass, which was executed in irridescent art nouveau style.

**TRUDEAU, GARRY**, 1948 (New York, N.Y.). U.S. cartoonist. Creator of the comic strip *Doonesbury* (1975 Pulitzer Prize for cartooning).

**TRUMBULL, JOHN**, June 6, 1756 (Lebanon, Conn.)–Nov. 10, 1843. U.S. painter, architect, writer. Best known for his paintings of the American Revolutionary era. Pres. of American Acad. of Fine Arts, 1816. Four paintings for Capitol Rotunda, 1818, including *The Declaration of Independence*. (Son of J. TRUMBULL.)

**UPJOHN, RICHARD**, Jan. 22, 1802 (Shaftesbury, Dorset, Eng.)–Aug. 17, 1878. U.S. architect. Best known for his Gothic revival churches; helped to found American Inst. of Architects, 1857. Buildings: St. John's Church, Bangor, Maine, 1837; Trinity Church, New York City, 1839–46. Books: *Upjohn's Rural Architecture*, 1852.

**WARHOL, ANDY**, Aug. 6, 1928 (Pittsburgh or McKeesport, Pa.)–Feb. 21, 1987. U.S. artist. Leader of the pop art movement of the 1960s; known for his paintings of soup cans, sculptures of Brillo Soap Pad boxes; publisher of *Interview* magazine, 1969–1987. Films: *My Hustler*, 1965; *The Chelsea*

*Girls*, 1966. Books: *Andy Warhol's Index*, 1967; *The Philosophy of Andy Warhol from A–B and Back Again*, 1975; *Exposures*, 1979.

**WARREN, WHITNEY**, Jan. 29, 1864 (New York, N.Y.)–Jan. 24, 1943. U.S. architect. With McKim, Mead and White, 1894–98; formed Warren and Wetmore, 1898–1931; a founder of Soc. of Beaux Arts Architects of New York; designed many New York City landmarks, including the N.Y. Yacht Club, Grand Central Station (1913), and the Ritz-Carlton, Vanderbilt, and Biltmore hotels.

**WEST, BENJAMIN**, Oct. 10, 1738 (nr. Springfield, Pa.)–Mar. 11, 1820. U.S. painter. A portrait painter, was the first American to study in Italy, 1860; travelled to England, and was named a charter member of the Royal Academy; appointed painter to the king by George III. Paintings: *Agrippa with the Ashes of Germanicus*, 1763; *Death of Wolfe*, 1771; *Death On a Pale Horse*, 1817.

**WESTON, EDWARD**, Mar. 24, 1886 (Highland Park, Ill.)–Jan. 1, 1958. U.S. photographer. Used only natural light; rarely cropped, enlarged, or retouched his negatives. *California and the West*, 1940; *The Cats of Wildcat Hill*, 1947; *Fifty Photographs*, 1947; *My Camera on Point Lobos*, 1950.

**WHISTLER, JAMES ABBOTT MCNEILL**, July 10, 1834 (Lowell, Mass.)–July 17, 1903. U.S. etcher, painter, lithographer. Expatriate American painter known for his studies in color tones; pres. of Royal Soc. of British Artists, 1886–88; taught at Académie Carmen, Paris, 1898–1901. Works: *Thames* series of etchings, 1860; *At the Piano*, 1859; *Blue Wave*, 1860; *The Little Girl in White*, 1863; *Arrangement in Gray and Black No. 1: The Artist's Mother*, 1871–1872.

**WHITE, STANFORD**, Nov. 9, 1853 (New York, N.Y.)–June 25, 1906. U.S. architect. With McKim,

Mead, and White, 1880–1906; known for his design of the original Madison Square Garden, New York City, 1889; where he was shot to death by H. K. THAW over his alleged affair with E. NESBIT, Thaw's wife.

**WHITNEY, GERTRUDE VANDERBILT**, Apr. 19, 1877 (New York, N.Y.)–Apr. 18, 1942. U.S. sculptor. Conceived and financed the Whitney Museum of American Art, 1931.

**WOOD, GRANT**, Feb. 13, 1892 (nr. Anamosa, Ia.)–Feb. 12, 1942. U.S. painter. Depicted Midwestern rural life of the 1930s; best known for his *American Gothic* (1930).

**WRIGHT, FRANK LLOYD**, June 8, 1867 (Richland Center, Wisc.)–Apr. 9, 1959. U.S. architect, writer. One of the most influential U.S. architects in history; created so-called organic architecture. Buildings: Larkin Bldg., Buffalo, N.Y., 1904–05; Fallingwater, Mill Run, Pa., 1936; Guggenheim Museum, New York City, 1943–59. Books: *An Organic Architecture*, 1939; *An American Architecture*, 1955.

**WYETH, ANDREW**, July 12, 1917 (Chadds Ford, Pa.). U.S. artist. Landscape painter. Award winner: American Academy of Arts and Letters, National Academy, National Institute for Arts and Letters, Carnegie Institute. Works: *Helga Pictures*. (Son of N. C. WYETH, father of J. WYETH.)

**WYETH, JAMES**, July 16, 1946 (Wilmington, Del.). U.S. painter. Most notable exhibit: *An American Vision: Three Generations of Wyeth Art*. (Son of A. WYETH, grandson of N. C. WYETH.)

**WYETH, N**(ewell) **C**(onvers), Oct. 22, 1882 (Needham, Mass.)–Oct. 19, 1945. U.S. painter. A muralist whose work graces many building interiors, he is best known for being the illustrator of 20 juvenile classics. (Father of A. WYETH, grandfather of J. WYETH.)

## FOREIGN ARTISTS

**AALTO, HUGO ALVAR**, Feb. 3, 1898 (Kuortane, Fin.)–May 11, 1976. Finnish architect, city planner, furniture designer. One of the pioneers of 20th-cent. Scandinavian design; used natural materials and irregular forms blended with natural surroundings. Structures: Viipuri Municipal Library, 1930–35; Säynatsälo town hall, 1950–52.

**ADAM, ROBERT**, July 3, 1728 (Kirkcaldy, Scot.)–Mar. 3, 1792. English architect, furniture designer, decorator. Initiated the elegant, airy, neoclassical Adam style; designed rooms at Osterly Park, Middlesex (1761–80), and at Syon House, Middlesex (1762–69).

**ALBERTI, LEON BATTISTA**, Feb. 14, 1404 (Genoa, It.)–Apr. 25, 1472. Italian architect, scholar. A typical Ren. man—poet, art theorist, moral philosopher, and mathematician; worked out scientific system of linear perspective used by most Italian Ren. artists; used classical motifs in his church and secular architectural designs; designed churches of San Sebastiano (1460) and Sant' Andrea (1472), both in Mantua; author of *Della pittura* (On Paint-

ing), 1435; *De re aedificatoria* (On Architecture), 1485.

**ALTDORFER, ALBRECHT**, 1480 (Regensburg, Ger.)–Feb. 12, 1538. German painter, engraver, architect. One of the earliest European landscape artists; member of the Danube school. Paintings: *The Battle of Alexander at Issus*, 1529; *The Fall and Redemption of Man* (a series of 40 engravings).

**ANDREA DEL SARTO** (born Andrea Domenico d'Agnolo di Francesco,) July 16, 1486 (Florence, It.)–Sept. 28, 1531. Italian painter. Known for his draftsmanship and feeling for color and atmosphere; one of the leading fresco painters of the High Ren.; painted frescoes in Florence at the Church of Annunziata (1509 and 1525) and the Chiostro dello Scalzo (John the Baptist series, 1511–26).

**ANGELICO, FRA**, c.1400 (Vicchi, It.)–Feb. 18, 1455. Italian painter. Known for his altarpieces; his use of perspective and sense of form reflected Early Ren. influence, while his use of exclusively religious subjects, unmixed colors, and traditional composition linked him to his medieval predecessors.

ARP, HANS (or Jean), Sept. 16, 1887 (Strasbourg, Ger. [now Fr.])–June 7, 1966. French painter, sculptor, poet. Pioneer abstract painter; one of the founders of Dadaism; became a surrealist, from 1925; wrote experimental poetry.

BACON, FRANCIS, Oct. 28, 1909 (Dublin, Ire.). English painter. Painted expressionist portraits distorted by terror, the subjects often shown screaming. Paintings: *Studies after Velazquez' Portrait of Pope Innocent X*, 1951–53, 1960.

BARTOLOMMEO, FRA, Mar. 28, 1475 (Florence, It.)–October 31, 1517. Italian painter. Painted religious subjects in the classical, monumental style of the High Ren.; introduced use of generalized, rather than contemporary, settings and costumes. Paintings: *Mystic Marriage of St. Catherine*, 1511; *St. Peter* and *St. Paul*, 1515.

BEARDSLEY, AUBREY, Aug. 21, 1872 (Brighton, Eng.)–Mar. 16, 1898. English illustrator. Influential exponent of art nouveau; earned a reputation for decadence with his sinuous, sensual, and often macabre black–and–white drawings; art editor of *Yellow Book* (1894) and *Savoy* (1895); illustrated *Morte d'Arthur* (1893–94) and *Salomé* (1894).

BEATON, CECIL, Jan. 14, 1904 (London, Eng.)–Jan. 18, 1980. English photographer, theatrical designer. His stylish photographic portraits for *Vanity Fair*, *Vogue*, and other magazines stressed decorative, often artificial backgrounds; designed sets and costumes for the musical *My Fair Lady*, 1956.

BECKMANN, MAX, Feb. 12, 1884 (Leipzig, Ger.)–Dec. 27, 1950. German expressionist painter. Used angular, contorted forms and bright, flat colors in his depictions of 20th-cent. savagery. Paintings: *Departure*, 1932–33; *Blindman's Bluff*, 1945.

BELLINI, GENTILE, c.1429 (Venice, It.)–buried Feb. 23, 1507. Italian painter. Painted portraits and narrative panoramas, especially of Venetian life. Paintings: *Portrait of Mohammed II*, c.1480; *Procession in the Piazza of San Marco*, 1496; (Son of J. BELLINI; half brother of GIOVANNI BELLINI.)

BELLINI, GIOVANNI, c.1430 (Venice, It.)–Nov. 1516. Italian painter. His adoption of oils enabled him to develop a style of rich coloring and warm lighting that defined subsequent Venetian art; his detailed settings marked him as a great landscape painter. Paintings: *St. Francis in Ecstasy*, c.1480; *Allegory of Purgatory*, 1480s. (Son of J. BELLINI; half brother of GENTILE BELLINI.)

BELLINI, JACOPO, 1400? (Venice, It.)–1470 or 1471. Italian painter. One of the founders of the Renaissance style of painting in northern Italy; his work shows his interest in linear perspective, which permitted him to give his paintings a more three-dimensional appearance. (Father of GENTILE BELLINI and GIOVANNI BELLINI and father-in-law of A. MANTEGNA.)

BERNINI, GIOVANNI LORENZO, Dec. 7, 1598 (Naples, It.)–Nov. 28, 1680. Italian sculptor, architect, painter, designer. Considered the founder of the Italian baroque style; stressed movement and theatrical effects in his religious and secular works. Sculpture: *Apollo and Daphne*, 1622–24; *Ecstasy*

of *St. Theresa*, 1644–52; tomb of Urban VIII, 1628–47.

BONHEUR, ROSA, 1822 (Bordeaux, Fr.)–1899. French artist. Most famous for her paintings of animals and rural scenes; the most successful female painter of the 1800s, and her most famous work is undoubtedly *The Horse Fair*, 1853–1855.

BONNARD, PIERRE, Oct. 3, 1867 (Fontenay-aux-Roses, Fr.)–Jan. 23, 1947. French painter, printmaker. A postimpressionist who used brilliant colors, warm lighting effects, and decorative patterns in his still-lifes, domestic interiors, and landscapes. Paintings: *The Open Window*, 1921; *The Breakfast Room*, 1930.

BORROMINI, FRANCESCO, Sept. 25, 1599 (Bissone, It.)–Aug. 3, 1667. Italian baroque architect. Used unusual solid geometric shapes for church floor-plans and spiral finials and concave façades as ornamentation; considered idiosyncratic, but strongly influenced late baroque architecture. Buildings: Church of San Carlo alle Quattro Fontane, Rome, 1638–1646; St. Agnese, Rome; Sant'Ivo alla Sapienz, Rome, 1642–60.

BOSCH, HIERONYMUS, c.1450 (s'Hertogen-bosch, Neth.)–c.1516. Flemish painter. His fantastic, subtly colored landscapes and carefully detailed allegorical groups expressed a mystical obsession with sin and punishment. Paintings: *Garden of Earthly Delights*, 1505–10; *Crowning with Thorns*; *The Haywain*.

BOTTICELLI, SANDRO, 1445 (Florence, It.)–May 17, 1510. Italian painter. One of the greatest artists of Early Ren. Florence; his use of relatively flat surfaces, flowing lines, soft lighting, quiet facial expressions, and allegorical details reflect a melancholy spirituality; career divided sharply between early works with classical subjects and later religious paintings. Paintings: *Primavera*, 1474–78; *Birth of Venus*, 1485–88.

BOUCHER, FRANÇOIS, Sept. 29, 1703 (Paris, Fr.)–May 30, 1770. French painter, tapestry and porcelain designer, engraver. His pastel colors, delicate composition, and sensuous treatment of pastoral and mythological subjects epitomized the sophisticated elegance of French rococo. Tapestries: *Pastorales*. Paintings: *Triumph of Venus*, 1740.

BOUTS, DIERIK, c.1400–1415 (Haarlem, Neth.)–May 6, 1475. Dutch painter. His austere religious paintings were characterized by controlled, intense facial expressions. Paintings: *Last Supper*, 1464; *Last Judgement*, 1468.

BRAMANTE, DONATO, 1444 (Monte Asdruvaldo, It.)–Apr. 11, 1514. Italian architect, town planner, writer. Through his many commissions in Milan and Rome, developed the classical High Ren. style in architecture; designed the Church of Sta. Maria delle Grazie (Milan) and the early 16th-cent. plan for rebuilding Rome, including the original design for St. Peter's.

BRANCUSI, CONSTANTIN, Feb. 21, 1876 (Hobita, Rum.)–Mar. 16, 1957. Rumanian–French sculptor. A pioneer in sculpture of abstract figures; stressed form over detail and the peculiar qualities of his various materials, including wood, marble, and polished bronze. Sculpture: *The Kiss*, 1908; *Bird in Space* (variations), 1924–40.

**BRAQUE, GEORGES,** May 13, 1882 (Argenteuil, Fr.)–Aug. 31, 1963. French painter, sculptor, and stage, book, and glass designer. Acknowledged as a principal founder of modern art; with PICASSO, developed cubism; known for his collage technique, still-lifes, and interiors. Paintings: *Houses at L'Estaque*, 1908; *Man with Guitar*, 1911; *The Yellow Tablecloth*, 1937.

**BREUER, MARCEL,** May 21, 1902 (Pécs, Hung.)–July 1, 1981. Hungarian-U.S. architect, furniture designer. Helped develop and popularize the sleek, streamlined International Style in architecture, furniture, and industrial design; invented the tubular metal chair, 1925, designed UNESCO headquarters in Paris (1953–58), St. John's Abbey in Collegeville, Minn. (1953–61), and the Whitney Museum in New York City (1963–66).

**BRONZINO, IL,** Nov. 17, 1503 (Monticelli, It.)–Nov. 23, 1572. Italian painter, poet. Best known for his courtly portraits, whose elongated figures, smooth surfaces, and artificial colors typified Mannerism. Paintings: *Portrait of a Young Man; Venus, Cupid, Folly and Time*, c.1546.

**BROWN, LANCELOT,** ("Capability Brown"), 1715 (Kirkharle, Northumberland, Eng.)–Feb. 6, 1783. English landscape gardener. Led the development of the informal, naturally contoured "English garden" style; responsible for the estates at Kew and Blenheim.

**BRUEGEL** (or Breughel) **THE ELDER, PIETER,** 1525? (nr. Breda, Neth.)–Sept. 5/9, 1569. Flemish painter. Painted vigorous, almost primitive scenes of peasant life and Biblical allegories; his innovative landscapes and detailed crowd scenes are unified by rhythm of movement and warm color. Paintings: Months of the Year series, c.1565; *Tower of Babel*, 1563; *Peasant Dance*, 1565.

**BRUNELLESCHI, FILIPPO,** 1377 (Florence, It.)–Apr. 15, 1446. Italian architect, engineer, inventor, sculptor. One of the founders of Ren. architecture, both esthetically and technologically; the chief developer of the rules of linear perspective in painting; designed the dome of Florence Cathedral (1418), as well as the Ospedale degli Innocenti (1421–55) and the Church of Santa Maria degli Angeli (begun 1434) in Florence.

**BURNE-JONES, EDWARD,** Aug. 28, 1833 (Birmingham, Eng.)–June 17, 1898. English painter, designer. A Pre-Raphaelite painter of carefully drawn, artificially posed medieval and classical narrative scenes; a leader of the "artist-craftsman" movement; created baronet, 1894. Paintings: *The Beguiling of Merlin*, 1872–77; *The Golden Staircase*, 1880. Book illustrations: *Chaucer*, 1896.

**CALLICRATES** (or Kallikrates), fl.5th cent. B.C. Athenian architect. One of the two builders of the Parthenon in Athens, c.440 B.C.; designed the temple of Athena Nike on the Acropolis, 427–424 B.C.

**CAMERON, JULIA MARGARET,** 1815 (Calcutta, India)–1879. British photographer. Pioneer in the field of artistic photography; noted for dramatic close–up photos and portraits of prominent figures.

**CAMPIN, ROBERT,** c.1378 (Tournai, Flanders)–Apr. 26, 1444. Flemish painter. One of the founders of the naturalistic Flemish painting tradition; often identified with the Master of Flémalle; the *Mérode Altarpiece* (c.1428) is attributed to him.

**CANALETTO,** Oct. 28, 1697 (Venice, It.)–Apr. 19, 1768. Italian painter, etcher. A pioneer of colorful, architecturally accurate *vedute* (cityscapes); did animated views of Venice and London. Paintings: *Views of Venice*, 1725–26; *The Old Horse Guards*, 1749.

**CAPA, ROBERT** (born Endre Erno Friedman), Oct. 22, 1913 (Budapest, Hung.)–May 25, 1954. Hungarian photographer. Came to prominence through series of photographs on the Spanish Civil War that appeared in *Life*; his photographs of Japanese invasion of China and from WWII brought him further fame; killed when he stepped on a land mine in Vietnam.

**CARAVAGGIO, MICHELANGELO MERISI DA,** Sept. 28, 1573 (Caravaggio, Lombardy It.)–July 18, 1610. Italian painter. A founder of the Italian baroque; used chiaroscuro (modeling via light and shade) for emotional impact in intensely realistic works. Paintings: *Young Bacchus*, c.1590; *Calling of St. Matthew*, c.1597; *Conversion of St. Paul*, 1600–01.

**CARPACCIO, VITTORE,** 1465? (Venice, It.)–1526?. Italian artist. His paintings combined an almost Flemish precision with a sense of the Venetian scale, and his most famous work was a cycle of paintings—*The Legend of St. Ursula*.

**CARRACCI** (or Caracci) family: **LUDOVICO,** baptized Apr. 21, 1555 (Bologna, It.)–Nov. 13, 1619; **ANNIBALE,** Nov. 3, 1560 (Bologna, It.)–July 15, 1609; **AGOSTINO,** baptized Aug. 16, 1557 (Bologna, It.)–Feb. 23, 1602. Italian family of painters. Among the founders of the Italian baroque; formed the influential Bologna Acad., 1582; joint works include frescoes in Palazzo Farnese (c.1595–1604) in Rome and Palazzo Fava in Bologna (1584).

**CARTIER-BRESSON, HENRI,** Aug. 22, 1908 (Chanteloup, Fr.) French photographer. Best known for his spontaneous, sympathetic portraits and documentary photographs.

**CASTAGNO, ANDREA DEL,** c.1421 (San Martino a Corella, It.)–Aug. 19, 1457. Italian painter. Early Florentine Ren. master; introduced naturalism and perspective into religious scenes. Paintings: *Last Supper*, 1445; *Trinity with St. Jerome*.

**CELLINI, BENVENUTO,** Nov. 1, 1500 (Florence, It.)–Feb. 13, 1571. Italian goldsmith, sculptor, writer. Designed and executed lavishly intricate Mannerist metalworks, ranging from coins to helmets; known for his innovative, picaresque autobiography (1562), which influenced subsequent views of the Ren.; created a gold and enamel saltcellar for Francis I and a bust of *Bindo Altoviti* (1550).

**CÉZANNE, PAUL,** Jan. 19, 1839 (Aix-en-Provence, Fr.)–Oct. 22, 1906. French painter. Perhaps the most influential Western painter since GIOTTO;

his works span the innovative era from impressionism to cubism; evolved a style that dynamically assembled simple masses of color and shape in contrasting planes of still-lifes, landscapes, and figure studies; laid the pictorial and imaginative groundwork for abstract art. Paintings: *Card Players*, 1890–92; *Mont Sainte-Victoire with Large Pine Trees*, 1885–87; *Grandes Baigneuses*, 1898–1905.

**CHAGALL, MARC,** July 7, 1887 (Vitebsk, Rus.)–Mar. 28, 1985. Russian-French painter, graphic artist, theatrical designer. Painted colorful fantasy narratives, usually expressing the mores, religion, and folklore of Eastern European Jews. Paintings: *I and My Village*, 1911; *Over Vitebsk*, 1923; *12 Tribes* (windows at the Hadassah Center in Jerusalem), 1962.

**CHARDIN, JEAN SIMÉON,** Nov. 2, 1699 (Paris, Fr.)–Dec. 6, 1779. French painter. Master of still-life and genre subjects who painted in a serene, sympathetic tone; turned to pastels late in life. Paintings: *Le Bénédicté*, 1740; *Attributes of the Arts* and *Attributes of Music*, 1765.

**CHIRICO, GIORGIO DE,** July 10, 1888 (Volos, Greece). Greek painter. One of the pioneers of 20th-cent. fantastic art and a great influence on the surrealist movement.

**CIMABUE, GIOVANNI,** c.1240 (Florence, It.)–1302. Italian painter, mosaicist. The first great Florentine master; last to work in Byzantine style with strong compositional control and classically dignified poses and faces; known as the teacher of GIOTTO. Paintings: *Madonna and Child Enthroned with Angels and Prophets*, early 1280s.

**CLAUDE LORRAIN,** 1600 (Chamagne, Fr.)–Nov. 23, 1682. French painter. His idealized landscapes of ancient Roman countrysides and harbor views were inspired by classical antiquity. Paintings: *Embarkation of Ulysses*, 1646; *Pastoral Landscape*, 1647; *Rest on the Flight into Egypt*, 1661.

**CLEMENTE, FRANCESCO,** 1952 (Italy). Italian painter. His figurative neo-expressionist style came to prominence in the late 1970s along with the works of Kiefer, Schnabel, and others.

**CONSTABLE, JOHN,** June 11, 1776 (East Bergholt, Suffolk, Eng.)–Mar. 31, 1837. English painter. Noted for his Romantic views of English countryside in which man's works blend with serene nature; his early naturalistic precision gave way to more impressionistic handling. Paintings: *The Haywain*, 1821; *Salisbury Cathedral*, 1823; *Waterloo Bridge*, 1832.

**CORBUSIER, LE,** Oct. 6, 1887 (La Chaux-de-Fonds, Switz.)–Aug. 27, 1965. Swiss architect, city planner. One of the founders of modern functionalist architecture; coined the phrase, "The house is a machine for living." Buildings: Palace of the League of Nations, Geneva, 1927–28; Convent of Sainte-Marie-de-la-Tourette, near Lyons, Fr., 1957–61; National Museum of Western Art, Tokyo, Jap., 1960; Carpenter Visual Art Center, Harvard U., 1964.

**COROT, JEAN BAPTISTE CAMILLE,** July 16, 1796 (Paris, Fr.)–Feb. 22, 1875. French painter.

His freely-painted landscapes, with subtle atmospheric effects, influenced the impressionists; extremely popular in his day. Paintings: *Bridge of Narni*, 1820s; *Souvenir de Mortefontaine*, 1864.

**CORREGGIO,** 1489 or 1494 (Correggio, It.)–Mar. 5, 1534. Italian painter. Founded Ren. Parma school; painted huge, dramatic fresco murals with foreshortened figures and (later) poetic, sensuous works. Paintings: *Mystic Marriage of St. Catherine*, c.1526; dome paintings at the Cathedral of Parma, 1526–30; *Leda*, 1530s.

**COURBET, GUSTAVE,** June 10, 1819 (Ornans, Fr.)–Dec. 31, 1877. French painter. Leader of realist movement in France, rebelling against romantic painting of the day; imprisoned for activities in the Commune, 1871. Paintings: *The Stone Breakers*, 1849; *The Artist's Studio*, 1855.

**CRANACH THE ELDER, LUCAS** (born Lucas Müller), 1472 (Kronach, Ger.)–Oct. 16, 1553. German painter. Court painter at Wittenberg, 1505–50; propagandist for Protestant Ref., from 1517; works include altarpieces, court portraits, portraits of Protestant reformers, women.

**CUYP, ALBERT,** baptized Oct. 20, 1620 (Dordrecht, Neth.)–Nov. 1691. Dutch painter. Best known for landscapes of Dutch countryside. Paintings: *Hilly Landscape with Cows and Shepherds*, 1665; *Castle by a River Bank*, 1645.

**DALI, SALVADOR,** May 11, 1904 (Figueras, Sp.)–Jan. 23, 1989. Spanish painter. Important Surrealist; built Dali's Dream House, N.Y. World's Fair, 1937–39; costume and scenery designer for operas and ballets, 1939–42; elected to French Acad. of Fine Arts, 1979. Films: *Un chien adalou* (1925), *L'age d'or* (1930), with LUIS BUÑUEL. Paintings: *Persistence of Memory*, 1931; *Tuna–Fishing*, 1966–67.

**DAUMIER, HONORÉ,** Feb. 20/26, 1808 (Marseilles, Fr.)–Feb. 11, 1879. French caricaturist, painter, sculptor. Best known for satiric cartoons and lithographs of 19th cent. French politics and society.

**DAVID, JACQUES-LOUIS,** Aug. 30, 1748 (Paris, Fr.)–Dec. 29, 1825. French artist. Official painter to NAPOLEON I; painted portraits and historical subjects in the neoclassical style. Paintings: *The Oath of the Horatii*, 1784; *The Dead Marat*, 1793; *Coronation*, 1808.

**DÉGAS, EDGAR,** July 19, 1834 (Paris, Fr.)–Sept. 27, 1917. French artist. One of the greatest draftsmen of all time; with C. MONET, A. RENOIR, and others, organized the first impressionist exhibition, 1874; closely associated with the impressionist movement, although he rejected the classification; failing eyesight in his later years led him to abandon his precise, compositionally-innovative oil paintings for softer and more colorful pastels. Paintings: *The Cotton Exchange*, 1873; *Absinthe*, 1876; *Prima Ballerina*, c.1876.

**DELACROIX, EUGÈNE,** Apr. 26, 1798 (Charenton-Saint-Maurice, Fr.)–Aug. 13, 1863. French Romantic painter. Known for exotic subjects and vivid colors. Paintings: *Massacre at Chios*, 1824; *Death of Sardanapalus*, 1827; murals in the Palais

Bourbon, 1833; murals in Museum of History at Versailles, 1837.

**DELLA ROBBIA, LUCA,** 1399/1400 (Florence, It.)–Feb. 1482. Italian Ren. sculptor. Founder of family studio; worked in enamelled terra-cotta and marble. Sculpture: *Singing Gallery,* 1431; tabernacle at Peretola, 1441; tomb of Benozzo Federighi, bishop of Fiesole, 1454–57.

**DOMENICHINO,** Oct. 1581 (Bologna, It.)–Apr. 6, 1641. Italian baroque painter. Best known for such landscapes as *The Hunt of Diana* (1617–18) and *The Martyrdom of St. Sebastian* (1628–30).

**DONATELLO,** c.1386 (Florence, It.)–Dec. 13, 1466. Italian sculptor. First postclassical sculptor to render the human body as self-activating and functional; the principal creative genius of the Italian Early Ren. and the acknowledged mentor of MICHELANGELO. Sculpture: *St. George and the Dragon,* 1416–17; *David,* 1430–35; *Gattamelata,* 1447–53.

**DUCCIO DI BUONINSEGNA,** c.1255 (Siena, It.)–c.1318. Italian painter. Founder of the Sienese school of painting; with GIOTTO, one of the key figures in the transition from Gothic to Ren. art; best-known work is the *Maestà* high altar for the Siena Cathedral, 1308–11.

**DUCHAMP, MARCEL,** July 28, 1887 (Blainville, Fr.)–Oct. 2, 1968. French-U.S. painter. Known as an "antiartist" because he eliminated the boundaries between works of art and everyday objects; an important cubist and a founder of Dadaism. Paintings: *Nude Descending a Staircase, No. 2,* 1912. Assemblages: *The Bride Stripped Bare by her Bachelors, Even,* 1915–23.

**DUFY, RAOUL,** June 3, 1877 (Le Havre, Fr.)–Mar. 23, 1953. French painter, designer. Helped to popularize modern art, especially Fauvism. Paintings: *Bois de Boulogne,* 1929; *Deauville,* 1930.

**DÜRER, ALBRECHT,** May 21, 1471 (Nuremberg, Ger.)–Apr. 6, 1528. German painter, graphic artist. The great genius of the Northern Ren.; combined Italian Ren. elements with German expressionism in brilliantly executed altarpieces, religious paintings, self-portraits, and engravings. Paintings: *Self-Portrait,* 1498; *Four Apostles,* 1526. Woodcuts: *Apocalypse* series, 1498. Engravings: *Knight, Death, and the Devil,* 1513; *Melancholia I,* 1514.

**EIFFEL, ALEXANDRE-GUSTAVE,** Dec. 15, 1832 (Dijon, Fr.)–Dec. 28, 1923. French engineer. Known for his design of the Eiffel Tower, 1887–89; built the first aerodynamic laboratory, at Auteuil, 1912.

**ELSHEIMER, ADAM,** Mar. 18, 1578 (Frankfurt-am-Main, Ger.)–Dec. 1610. German painter, etcher. A founder of modern landscape painting; known for small paintings on copper of Biblical and mythological subjects. Paintings: *Flight into Egypt,* 1609; *Philemon and Baucus; The Good Samaritan; St. Paul on Malta;* c.1600.

**ENSOR, JAMES SYDNEY,** Apr. 13, 1860 (Ostend, Belg.)–Nov. 19, 1949. Flemish painter, printmaker. Created expressionist works noted for fantasy and social commentary; member of the progressive Les Vingt group of artists, 1883–88. Paintings: *Woman*

*Eating Oysters,* 1882; *Scandalized Masks,* 1883; *Entry of Christ into Brussels,* 1888; *Masks,* 1890.

**ERNST, MAX,** Apr. 2, 1891 (Brühl, Ger.)–April 1, 1976. German painter, sculptor. Worked in the Expressionistic mode of Surrealism, later converted to Dadaism. Paintings: *The Elephant of the Célèbes,* 1921; *Here Everything Is Still Floating,* 1920; *The Great Forest,* 1927; *The Temptation of St. Anthony,* 1945; *The King Playing with the Queen,* 1944.

**ESCHER, M(aurits) C(ornelius),** June 17, 1898 (Leeuwarden, Neth.)–Mar. 27, 1972. His surreal, yet precisely drawn, images have fascinated generations of mathematicians, poets, and scientists; his work has influenced everything from science fiction writing to design of record album covers.

**EYCK, JAN VAN,** c.1395 (Maaseik, Flanders [now Belg.])–July 9, 1441. Flemish painter. His strongly realistic oil paintings, principally portraits and religious subjects, had a profound influence on later Northern European painters. Paintings: *Ghent Altarpiece: Adoration of the Lamb,* completed 1432; *Giovanni Arnolfini and His Bride,* 1434.

**FABERGÉ, PETER CARL,** May 30, 1846 (St. Petersburg, Rus. [now Leningrad, USSR])–Sept. 24, 1920. Russian goldsmith, jeweler, decorator. Inherited family jewelry business, 1870; commissioned by Tsar Alexander III and Nicholas II to design the ceremonial eggs for his tsarina, 1884.

**FANTIN-LATOUR, HENRI,** Jan. 14, 1836 (Grenoble, Fr.)–Aug. 25, 1904. French painter, printmaker, illustrator. Best known for his realistic still-lifes and portraits. Paintings: *Hommage à Delacroix,* 1864; *Un coin de table,* 1872. Books illustrated: Adolphe Jullien's *Wagner* (1886), and *Berlioz* (1888).

**FRAGONARD, JEAN-HONORÉ,** Apr. 5, 1732 (Grasse, Fr.)–Aug. 22, 1806. French painter. Painted landscapes, portraits, and fêtes-galantes in rococo style; decorated Madame du Barry's Pavillon de Louveciennes with four paintings depicting the *Progress of Love,* 1770. *The Swing,* c.1766.

**FUSELI, HENRY,** Feb. 7, 1741 (Zurich, Switz.)–Apr. 16, 1825. Anglo-Swiss painter. Romantic painter who used eerie, often grotesque imagery; prof. of painting at the Royal Acad., London, from 1799. Paintings: *The Death of Cardinal Beaufort,* 1774; *The Oath of the Rütli,* 1778; *The Nightmare,* 1781.

**GAINSBOROUGH, THOMAS,** baptized May 14, 1727 (Sudbury, Suffolk, Eng.)–Aug. 2, 1788. English painter. Known for his portraits and landscapes of idyllic scenes. *The Blue Boy* (1770), *The Honorable Mrs. Graham,* 1777.

**GAUGUIN, PAUL,** June 7, 1848 (Paris, Fr.)–May 8, 1903. French painter. Post-impressionist artist known for his use of color and "primitive" subject-matter and formats. Paintings: *Self-Portrait,* 1889; *Bonjour, Monsieur Gauguin,* 1889; *Whence Come We? What Are We? Whither Go We?,* 1897–98.

**GÉRICAULT, THÉODORE,** Sept. 26, 1791 (Rouen, Fr.)–Jan. 26, 1824. French Romantic painter whose realistic and freely rendered paintings of historical and animal subjects caused a furor in official French art circles. Paintings: *Mounted Officer of the Impe-*

*rial Guard*, 1812; *The Wounded Cuirassier*, 1814; *The Raft of the Medusa*, 1819.

**GHIBERTI, LORENZO,** 1378 (Pelago, It.)–Dec. 1, 1455. Italian sculptor. A transitional figure between the elegant International Gothic style and the naturalistic Ren. era; his bronze-relief doors for the Baptistery in Florence, (first set, 1403–24; second set, the *Gates of Paradise*, 1425–52) broke new ground in perspective systems and in modeling of the human form.

**GHIRLANDAIO, DOMENICO,** born Domenico di Tommaso Bigordi, 1449 (Florence, It.)–Jan. 11, 1494. Italian painter. One of the principal painters of the Italian Early Ren.; MICHELANGELO studied in his studio. Paintings: fresco series in Sistine Chapel, Rome, 1481–82; two series of frescoes in Sta. Trinità and Sta. Maria Novella, Florence, 1482–94.

**GIACOMETTI, ALBERTO,** Oct. 10, 1901 (Borgonovo, Switz.)–Jan. 11, 1966. Swiss sculptor, painter. Created a skeletal attenuated style; known for sculptures of solitary figures. Sculptures: *Observing Head*, 1927/28; *City Square*, 1948; *Chariot*, 1950.

**GIORGIONE,** c.1477 (Castelfranco, It.)–1510. Italian painter. Venetian High Ren. painter whose luminous colors and deft brushwork had a profound influence on 16th-century Venetian painting. Paintings: *The Tempest*, 1505; *Fête Champetre*, c.1510.

**GIOTTO,** c.1267 (Vespignano, It.)–Jan. 8, 1337. Italian painter, architect. Often called the single most-influential artist in European history; his frescoes introduced the attitudes and concerns that would dominate European painting until the late 19th-cent., including narrative drama, the dignity and beauty of the human form, and the construction of "realistic" pictorial space; inaugurated the great line of Florentine painters that stretched well into the 16th-cent. Paintings: Arena Chapel fresco-cycle, Padua, 1305–06; *Enthroned Madonna*, 1310; *Bardi Chapel fresco cycle*, Florence, 1320s.

**GIRARDON, FRANÇOIS,** baptized Mar. 17, 1628 (Troyes, Fr.)–Sept. 1, 1715. French baroque sculptor. Employed at Versailles under LOUIS XIV; member of French Royal Acad. of Painting and Sculpture, from 1657. Sculpture: *Apollo Tended by the Nymphs*, 1666; equestrian statue of Louis XIV (destroyed), 1683–92; tomb of CARDINAL RICHELIEU, begun 1675.

**GOGH, VINCENT VAN,** Mar. 30, 1853 (Zundert, Neth.)–July 29, 1890. Dutch postimpressionist painter. Noted for powerfully expressive works rendered with thick brushwork and in brilliant colors; committed suicide. Paintings: *The Potato Eaters*, 1885; *Outdoor Cafe at Night, Arles*, 1888; *Sunflowers*, 1888; *Starry Night*, 1889.

**GOYA (y Lucientes), FRANCISCO DE,** Mar. 30, 1746 (Fuendetodos, Sp.)–Apr. 16, 1828. Spanish painter, etcher. First gained fame for his portraits and genre works, later executed powerful, Romantic depictions of the heroes of war; his last paintings are macabre renderings of nightmare subjects. Paintings: *Los Caprichos*, 1796; *May 3, 1808*,

1814–15; *The Witches' Sabbath*. Etchings: *The Disasters of War* series, 1810–13.

**GRECO, EL,** 1541 (Candia [Iráklion], Crete)–Apr. 7, 1614. Greek painter, sculptor, architect; worked in Spain. Known for his unorthodox, elongated treatment of devotional subjects and portraits; became a citizen of Spain, 1577; introduced Ren. and Mannerist elements into Spanish painting. Paintings: *The Burial of Count Orgaz*, 1586; *View of Toledo*.

**GROPIUS, WALTER,** May 18, 1883 (Berlin, Ger.)–July 5, 1969. German architect, educator. Leader in the development of modern architecture; dir. of the Bauhaus, 1919–28; chm. of the architecture dept. at Harvard U., 1938–52. Buildings: Workers' flats, Berlin, 1929; U.S. Embassy, Athens, 1956–61.

**GRÜNEWALD, MATTHIAS,** real name Matthis Gothart (Nithart), c.1470 (Aschaffenburg, Ger.)–1528. German painter. Best known for his highly expressionistic and mystical treatment of religious subjects, especially in his *Isenheim Altarpiece*, begun 1517.

**HALS, FRANS,** 1581/85 (Antwerp, Belg.)–buried Sept. 1, 1666. Flemish painter. A baroque painter known for his brilliant portraits, particularly of the Dutch bourgeoisie of Haarlem. Paintings: *The Laughing Cavalier*, 1624; *The Governors of the Almshouse*, 1664; *Lady Regents of the Almshouse*, 1664.

**HEPWORTH, DAME BARBARA,** Jan. 10, 1903 (Wakefield, Yorks., Eng.)–May 20, 1975. English abstract sculptor. Named Dame of the British Empire, 1965; died in fire which consumed her studio. Sculptures: *Reclining Figure*, 1932; *Wave*, 1943–44; *Winged Figure*, 1962; *Single Form*, 1962–63; *Four-Square*, 1966.

**HILDEBRANDT, JOHANN LUCAS VON,** Nov. 14, 1668 (Genoa, It.)–Nov. 16, 1745. Austrian baroque architect, military engineer. Appointed court engineer; architect to Prince Eugene and court Austrian aristocrats, 1700. Buildings: the Belvedere Palace, 1700–23; Austrian Chancellory, 1717–19.

**HOBBEMA, MEINDERT,** baptized Oct. 31, 1638 (Amsterdam, Neth.)–Dec. 7, 1709. Dutch baroque landscape painter. Paintings: *Water Mill*, c.1665; *The Ruins of Brederode Castle*, 1671; *The Avenue, Middelharnis*, 1689.

**HOCKNEY, DAVID,** July 9, 1937 (Bradford, Eng.) British stage designer. *The Rake's Progress*, 1975; *The Magic Flute*, 1979; *Tristan und Isolde*, 1987.

**HOGARTH, WILLIAM,** Nov. 10, 1697 (London, Eng.)–Oct. 26, 1764. English painter, engraver. Best known for his morality pictures featuring brilliant characterizations and a wealth of detail. Paintings: *The Harlot's Progress* (series), 1732; *The Rake's Progress* (series), 1735; *Marriage à la Mode* (series), 1745.

**HOLBEIN THE YOUNGER, HANS,** 1497/98 (Augsburg, Ger.)–1543. German painter. Court painter of the Northern Ren. period, best known for his well executed and psychologically penetrating portraits. Paintings: *Sir Thomas More*, 1526; *Henry VIII*, 1540.

**HOUDON, JEAN ANTOINE,** Mar. 20, 1741 (Versailles, Fr.)–July 15, 1828. French neoclassical sculptor. Sculptures: *Diana*, 1777; *Voltaire*, 1781; *George Washington*, 1788; also did busts of THOMAS JEFFERSON, JOHN PAUL JONES, MOLIÈRE, ROUSSEAU, NAPOLEON.

**HUNT, HOLMAN,** Apr. 2, 1827 (London, Eng.)–Sept. 7, 1910. English painter. Cofounder (with MILLAIS and ROSSETTI) of the Pre-Raphaelite Brotherhood, 1848; known for his religious works, including *Rienzi* (1849), *The Light of the World* (1854) and *The Scapegoat* (1855); author of *Pre-Raphaelitism and the Pre-Raphaelite Brotherhood*, 2 vols., 1905.

**INGRES, JEAN-AUGUSTE-DOMINIQUE,** Aug. 29, 1780 (Montauban, Fr.)–Jan. 14, 1867. French painter. One of the greatest draftsmen in European art history; known for his highly finished and sensual works; dir. of French Acad. of Rome, 1835–41. Paintings: *Jupiter and Thetis*, 1811; *The Apotheosis of Homer*, 1827.

**JONES, INIGO,** baptized July 19, 1573 (London, Eng.)–June 21, 1652. English architect, painter, designer. Highly influential architect in the Palladian manner; King's surveyor of works, 1615–42. Buildings: Banqueting House, Whitehall, 1619–22; Queen's Chapel at St. James Palace, 1623–27; restoration of the old St. Paul's Cathedral, London, 1634–42.

**KANDINSKY, VASILY,** Dec. 4, 1866 (Moscow, Rus.)–Dec. 13, 1944. Russian painter. Best known for his abstract paintings; founded the Munich group called The Blue Rider, 1911–14; teacher at the Bauhaus School of Design, 1921–33.

**KLEE, PAUL,** Dec. 18, 1879 (Munchenbuchsee, Switz.)–June 29, 1940. Swiss painter, etcher. Surrealist painter influenced by primitive African sculpture; prof. at the Düsseldorf Acad. of Art, 1930–33. Paintings: *Twittering Machine*, 1922; *The Mocker Mocked*, 1930; *Death and Fire*, 1930.

**LA TOUR, GEORGE DE,** Mar. 19, 1593 (nr. Lunéville, Fr.)–Jan. 30, 1652. French painter. A baroque painter famed for portraying subjects in candlelight. Paintings: *The Mocking of Job*, *St. Joseph the Carpenter*, *The Fortune Teller*.

**LÉGER, FERNAND,** Feb. 4, 1881 (Argentan, Fr.)–Aug. 17, 1955. French Cubist painter. Influenced by modern industrial technology. Paintings: *The Cyclist*, *Adam and Eve*.

**LEIDEN, LUCAS VAN** (born Lucas Hugensz), 1489–94 (Leiden, Neth.)–1533. Dutch painter, engraver. Paintings: *Muhammad and the Monk Sergius*, 1508; *Susanna and the Elders*, 1508; *The Poet Vergil Suspended in a Basket*, 1521.

**LE NAIN,** brothers. ANTOINE, 1588–May 25, 1648; LOUIS, c.1593 (Laon, Fr.)–May 23, 1648; MATHIEU, 1607 (Laon, Fr.)–Apr. 20, 1677. French realistic painters of peasant life; all received into the French Acad., 1648.

**L'ENFANT, PIERRE** Aug. 2, 1754 (Paris, Fr.)–June 14, 1825. French engineer, architect, urban designer. Designed basic plan for Washington, D.C.,

1791–92; renovated old City Hall for U.S. Congress as Federal Hall, New York City, 1787.

**LEONARDO DA VINCI,** 1452 (Vinci, It.)–May 2, 1519. Italian painter, sculptor, architect, engineer. The archetypal Ren. Man; brilliant draftsman and colorist who invented *sfumato* (smoky) style of painting; his *Notebooks* are a treasury of art criticism, scientific investigation, and prototype inventions centuries ahead of their time (e.g., the helicopter). Paintings: *The Last Supper*, 1495–97; *Mona Lisa*, 1503–06; *St. John the Baptist*, c.1514.

**LIEBERMANN, MAX,** July 20, 1847 (Berlin, Ger.)–Feb. 8, 1935. German impressionist painter. Known for his study of light and depiction of life of humble people. Paintings: *Women Plucking Geese*, 1872; *Old Folks' Home in Amsterdam*, 1880; *The Flax Spinners*, 1887.

**LIPPI, FRA FILIPPO,** c.1402 (Florence, It.)–Oct. 9, 1469. Italian Ren. painter. Known for his sensual, elegant Madonnas. Paintings: *Madonna and Child*, 1437; *The Coronation of the Virgin*, 1445.

**MAGRITTE, RENÉ,** Nov. 21, 1898 (Lessines, Belg.)–Aug. 15, 1967. Belgian Surrealist painter. Best known for his jolting juxtapositions of unrelated elements in realistic-looking pictures. Paintings: *The Rape*, 1934; *Golconda*, 1953; *The Castle of the Pyrenees*, 1959.

**MANET, EDOUARD,** Jan. 23, 1832 (Paris, Fr.)–Apr. 30, 1883. French painter, printmaker. A forerunner of the impressionists. Paintings: *Le Déjeuner sur L'Herbe*, 1863; *Olympia*, 1863; *Bar at the Folies-Bergere*, 1882.

**MANTEGNA, ANDREA,** 1431 (Mantua, It.)–Sept. 13, 1506. Italian Ren. painter, engraver. Court painter in Mantua, 1459. Paintings: *Camera degli Sposi*, 1474; Ovetari Chapel frescoes, 1448–55; *Triumph of Caesar*, 1486.

**MASACCIO, GUIDI,** Dec. 21, 1401 (Castello San Giovanni di Valdarno, It.)–autumn, 1428. Italian painter. The most important and influential painter of the Early Ren. in Italy; introduced humanism into art. Paintings: *Madonna and Child with St. Anne*, 1424; *The Tribute Money*, c.1427.

**MASSYS, QUENTIN,** c.1466 (Louvain, Flanders)–1530. Flemish painter. Member of painters' guild of Antwerp, 1491–1530. Paintings: *St. Anne Altarpiece*, 1509; *The Money Changer and His Wife*, 1514.

**MATISSE, HENRI,** Dec. 31, 1869 (Le Cateau, Picardy, Fr.)–Nov. 3, 1954. French painter. A leading fauvist, and one of the two most important French painters of the 20th-cent. Paintings: *Woman with the Hat*, 1905; *The Red Studio*, 1911; *Chappelle du Rosaire*, Vence, 1951.

**MEMLING** (or Memlinc), **HANS,** c.1430 (Seligenstadt, Ger.)–Aug. 11, 1494. Flemish painter. Member of the painters' guild, Brussels, from 1467; known for use of color and minute detail. Paintings: *Last Judgement*, 1472–73; *Virgin and Child*, 1487; *Madonna with Angels*, 1490.

**MICHELANGELO,** Mar 6, 1475 (Caprese, It.)–Feb. 18, 1564. Italian painter, sculptor, architect. Giant of the High Ren.; known for monumental style, noble renderings of the human form; epitomized the High Ren. style, presaged baroque art and Mannerism; also wrote sonnets. Sculpture: *Pietà*, 1498; *David*, 1504. Paintings: ceiling of Sistine Chapel, 1508–12; *Last Judgement*, 1534–41. Architecture: Medici Chapel, 1502–34; The Laurentian Library, 1523–59; the Dome of St. Peter's.

**MIES VAN DER ROHE, LUDWIG,** Mar. 27, 1886 (Aachen, Ger.)–Aug. 17, 1969. German architect. A leading practitioner of 20th-cent. functionalist architecture; head of School of Architecture at Chicago's Armour Inst., 1937–58. Buildings: Seagram Bldg., New York City, 1958; Gallery of the Twentieth Century, Berlin, 1968.

**MILLAIS, SIR JOHN EVERETT,** June 8, 1829 (Southhampton, Eng.)–Aug. 13, 1896. English painter, illustrator. A founder of the Pre-Raphaelite Brotherhood; pres. of Royal Acad., 1896. Paintings: *The Return of the Dove to the Ark*, 1851; *The Order of Release*, 1853; *The Blind Girl*, 1856; *Chill October*, 1870. Created baronet 1885.

**MILLET, JEAN-FRANÇOIS,** Oct. 4, 1814 (Gruchy, Fr.)–Jan. 20, 1875. French painter. Known for his romanticized depictions of rural scenes. Paintings: *The Milkmaid*, 1844; *A Peasant Grafting a Tree*, 1855; *The Gleaners*, 1857; *The Man with the Hoe*, 1863.

**MODIGLIANI, AMEDEO,** July 12, 1884 (Leghorn, It.)–Jan. 24, 1920. Italian painter, sculptor. Known for his unique, elongated portraits. Paintings: *Peasant Boy; Portrait of Mme. Modigliani; Woman Seated; Girl with Rose.*

**MONDRIAN, PIET,** Mar. 7, 1872 (Amersfoort, Neth.)–Feb. 1, 1944. Dutch artist. A leader of the Dutch abstract art movement called De Stijl: Cubist phase, 1912–17; neoplastic phase, 1917–20; thereafter American phase. Paintings: *New York City*, 1943; *Broadway Boogie Woogie*, 1943.

**MONET, CLAUDE,** Nov. 14, 1840 (Paris, Fr.)–Dec. 5, 1926. French artist. One of the founders and a principal leader of the impressionist movement. Paintings: *Haystacks*, 1891; *Rouen Cathedral*, 1894; *Waterlilies, Water Landscape*, 1905.

**MOORE, HENRY,** July 30, 1898 (Castleford, Yorks., Eng.)–Aug. 31, 1986. English abstract sculptor. Teacher of sculpture at Royal C. of Art (1925–32) and Chelsea School of Art (1932–39).

**MORISOT, BERTHE,** Jan. 14, 1841 (Bourges, Fr.)–Mar 2, 1895. French impressionist painter, printmaker. Paintings: *The Artist's Sister, Mme. Portillon, Seated on the Grass*, 1873. (Granddaughter of J. H. FRAGONARD).

**MORRIS, WILLIAM,** Mar. 24, 1834 (Walthamstow, Eng.)–Oct. 3, 1896. English craftsman, poet. Associate of EDWARD BURNE-JONES and DANTE GABRIEL ROSSETTI; formed Morris & Co., a firm of decorators that designed wallpaper, furniture, and tapestries that revolutionized Victorian taste; established Kelmscott Press (1890), where he designed type, page borders, and book bindings; his most notable poetic works include *The Defense of Guenevere and Other Poems* (1858), *The Life*

*and Death of Jason* (1862), and *Earthly Paradises* (3 vols., 1868–70).

**MUNCH, EDVARD,** Dec. 12, 1863 (Löten, Norway)–Jan. 23, 1944. Norwegian expressionist painter, printmaker. Influenced the development of German expressionism; known for his shocking, agonized images of psychic traumas. Paintings: *The Shriek*, 1893; *The Kiss*, 1895.

**MURILLO, BARTOLOME,** baptized Jan 1, 1618 (Seville, Sp.)–Apr. 13, 1682. Spanish baroque religious painter. Founder and first pres. of Acad. of Painting, Seville, 1660. Paintings: *Virgin of the Rosary*, 1642; *Immaculate Conception*, 1652; *Vision of St. Anthony*, 1656; *Self-Portrait*, 1675.

**NERVI, PIER LUIGI,** June 21, 1891 (Sorvino, It.)–Jan. 9, 1979. Italian architect, engineer. Prof. at U. of Rome, from 1947; invented *ferrocemento* (reinforced concrete); designed two sports palaces for Rome Olympic games, 1957–60; designed George Washington Bridge Bus Terminal, 1961–62.

**PALLADIO, ANDREA,** Nov. 30, 1508 (Padua, It.)–Aug. 1580. Italian architect. His neoclassical style had a tremendous influence on European domestic architecture; published *Le antichità di Roma* (1554) and *I quattro libri dell'architetura* (1570).

**PHIDIAS,** 500 b.c. (Athens, Gr.)–430 b.c. Greek sculptor. Works: Temple of Theseus; Athena Areia at Plataea; Olympian Zeus; reputedly designed the Parthenon sculptures, the Athena Promachos, and the Athena Parthenos.

**PICASSO, PABLO,** Oct. 25, 1881 (Málaga, Sp.)–Apr. 8, 1973. Spanish painter, sculptor. Seminal modern artist; with BRAQUE, founded Cubist movement, 1907–08. Paintings: *Demoiselles d'Avignon*, 1907; *Three Musicians; Guernica*, 1937; *Woman in White.*

**PIERO DELLA FRANCESCA,** 1410/20 (Borgo San Sepolcro, It.)–Oct. 12, 1492. Italian Ren. painter. Member of the Umbrian school; known for his monumental, architectonic frescos. Paintings: *The Story of the True Cross*, 1452–66.

**PISSARRO, CAMILLE,** July 10, 1830 (St. Thomas, V.I.)–Nov. 13, 1903. French impressionist painter. Best known for his paintings of the boulevards of Paris, streets of Rouen, landscapes of Normandy. Paintings: *Boulevard des Italiens, Paris—Morning Sunlight*, 1897.

**PONTORMO, JACOPO DA,** May 24, 1494 (Pontormo, It.)–Jan. 2, 1557. Italian painter. An initiator of the Florentine Mannerist style. Paintings: altarpiece for Church of Saint Michele, Florence, 1518; *Joseph in Egypt*, 1515.

**POUSSIN, NICHOLAS,** 1594 (Villers, Fr.)–Nov. 19, 1665. French painter. A leader of pictorial classicism in the baroque period.

**PRAXITELES,** fl. 4th century b.c. (Athens, Gr.) Greek sculptor. Best known for his statues of Hermes carrying the infant Dionysus, Aphrodite of Cnidus.

**RAPHAEL,** Apr. 6, 1483 (Urbino, It.)–Apr. 6, 1520. Italian painter. Exemplar of serene, classical High Ren. style. Paintings: *Coronation of the Virgin*, 1503; Vatican stanza, including *The School of Athens*, decorated for Pope Julius II, 1508.

**REMBRANDT VAN RIJN,** July 15, 1606 (Leiden, Neth.)–Oct. 4, 1669. Dutch painter. Greatest practitioner of Northern baroque painting; known for brilliant use of light, revealing portraits. Paintings: *Clemency of Titus,* 1626; *The Anatomy Lesson of Dr. Tulp,* 1632; *Self-Portrait with Saskia,* 1635; *The Deposition,* 1653; *Three Trees,* 1643.

**RENOIR, PIERRE-AUGUSTE,** Feb. 25, 1841 (Limoges, Fr.)–Dec. 3, 1919. French impressionist painter. A leader and founder of the French impressionist movement. Paintings: *Le Moulin de la Galette,* 1876; *Portrait of Mme. Charpentier and Her Children,* 1879.

**REYNOLDS, SIR JOSHUA,** July 16, 1723 (Plympton, Devon, Eng.)–Feb. 23, 1792. English painter. Known for his portraits; pres. of Royal Acad., from 1768; knighted, 1768. Paintings: *Captain John Hamilton,* 1746; *Commodore Augustus Keppel,* 1753; *Duchess of Devonshire and Her Daughter,* 1786.

**RIVERA, DIEGO,** Dec. 8, 1886 (Guanajuato, Mex.) –Nov. 25, 1957. Mexican painter known for bold, leftist murals, helped to begin govt.-sponsored project for the decoration of public buildings with frescos, 1921; with BEN SHAHN, painted *Man at the Crossroads,* mural for RCA Bldg., New York City (subsequently destroyed).

**RODIN, AUGUSTE,** Nov. 12, 1840 (Paris, Fr.)– Nov. 17, 1917. French sculptor. Best known for his *The Thinker* (1880), *Le Baiser* (1886), and *The Burghers of Calais* (1884–86).

**ROUSSEAU, HENRI,** ("Le Douanier"), May 21, 1844 (Laval, Fr.)–Sept. 2, 1910. French painter. Leader of the primitivist school of postimpressionism; a major influence on Cubism. Paintings: *Landscape with Tree Trunks,* 1887; *Myself: Portrait Landscape,* 1890; *The Child among the Rocks,* 1895; *The Sleeping Gypsy,* 1897; *The Repast of the Lion,* 1907; *Tropical Forest with Monkeys,* 1910; *The Dream,* 1910.

**RUBENS, PETER-PAUL,** June 28, 1577 (Siegen, Ger.)–May 30, 1640. Flemish baroque painter. Known for his dynamic colors and well-rounded figures. Paintings: *The Rape of the Sabines,* 1635; *Venus and Adonis,* 1635; *Self-Portrait,* 1639; *Christ on the Cross,* 1635–40.

**RUISDAEL, JACOB VAN,** 1628/29 (Haarlem, Neth.) –Mar. 1682. Dutch baroque painter. Known for his landscapes. Paintings: *Dunes,* 1647; *Bentheim Castle,* 1653; *Jewish Cemetery,* c.1660; *Wheatfields,* 1670.

**SCHWITTERS, KURT,** June 20, 1887 (Hannover, Ger.)–Jan. 8, 1948. German Dada visual artist and poet. He was a specialist in collages and junk sculpture; edited the Dada magazine *Merz* from 1923 to 1932, fleeing Germany to escape the Nazis.

**SEURAT, GEORGES,** Dec. 2, 1859 (Paris, Fr.)– Mar. 29, 1891. French painter. Founder of the 19th-cent. school of neo-impressionism; invented pointillist style. Paintings: *Sunday Afternoon on The Island of La Grande Jatte; Une Baignade, Asnieres.*

**SISLEY, ALFRED,** Oct. 30, 1839 (Paris, Fr.)–Jan.

29, 1899. French painter. Known for his impressionist landscapes. Paintings: *Flood at Port-Marly,* 1876.

**STUBBS, GEORGE,** Aug. 24, 1724 (Liverpool, Eng.)–July 10, 1806. English animal painter, anatomical draftsman; executed 18 etched plates for Dr. John Burton's *Essay Towards a Complete New System of Midwifery,* 1751. Paintings: *Mares and Foals in a Landscape,* 1760–70.

**TERBORCH, GERARD,** 1617 (Zwolle, Neth.)– Dec. 8, 1681. Dutch baroque painter, known for interiors. Paintings: *The Swearing of the Oath of Ratification of the Treaty of Münster,* 1648; *Self-Portrait,* 1670.

**TIEPOLO, GIOVANNI BATTISTA,** Mar. 5, 1696 (Venice, It.)–Mar. 27, 1770. Italian artist. Known for his large-scale frescos; executed frescos for the Residenz, Würzburg, including *Olympus;* painted three ceilings at the Royal Palace, Madrid, for King Carlos III, 1762.

**TINTORETTO,** 1518 (Venice, It.)–May 31, 1594. Italian Mannerist painter of the Venetian school. Paintings: *Vulcan Surprising Venus and Mars,* 1545; *The Last Supper,* 1547.

**TITIAN,** c.1487/90 (Pieve di Cadore, It.)–Aug. 27, 1576. Italian Ren. painter. Venetian painter known for his monumental compositions and sensual use of color. Paintings: *The Assumption,* 1516–18; *The Venus of Urbino,* 1538; *Equestrian Portrait of Charles V,* 1548; *The Death of Actaeon,* 1565.

**TOULOUSE-LAUTREC, HENRI DE,** Nov. 24, 1864 (Albi, Fr.)–Sept. 9, 1901. French artist. Known for his post-impressionist depictions of Parisian night life, such as *La Goulue at the Moulin Rouge* (1891).

**TURNER, J(oseph) M(allord) W(illiam),** Apr. 23, 1775 (London, Eng.)–Dec. 19, 1851. English Romantic painter. Best known for his original use of light and color in his impressionistic landscapes and seascapes. Paintings: *Snow Storm, The Burning of the Houses of Parliament.*

**UCCELLO, PAOLO,** 1397 (Pratovecchio, nr. Florence, It.)–Dec. 12, 1475. Italian Ren. painter. Paintings: *Battle of San Romano,* 1542.

**VAN DYCK, SIR ANTHONY,** Mar. 22, 1599 (Antwerp, Belg.)–Dec. 9, 1641. Flemish artist. Appointed by King Charles I as Painter-in-Ordinary to the English court; his portraits set the style in English portraiture for almost 100 years.

**VASARI, GIORGIO,** July 30, 1511 (Arezzo, It.)– June 27, 1574. Italian Mannerist painter, architect, writer. Designed the Uffizi Palace, Florence, for COSIMO I DE MEDICI, 1560; author of *The Lives of the Most Eminent Italian Architects, Painters and Sculptors,* 1550.

**VELÁZQUEZ, DIEGO,** baptized June 6, 1599 (Seville, Sp.)–Aug. 6, 1660. Spanish painter. Greatest Spanish Baroque painter; known for his technical excellence and highly effective sense of composition. Paintings: *Los Borrachos Bacchus,* 1629; *Surrender at Breda,* 1634; *Juan de Perera,* 1649; *The Rokeby Venus,* c.1651; *Las Meniñas,* 1656.

**VERMEER, JAN,** Oct. 30, 1632 (Delft, Neth.)–

Dec. 15, 1675. Dutch painter. Dean of painters' guild at Delft, 1662–63 and 1670–71; known for his beautifully composed landscapes and interiors. Paintings: *View of Delft*, 1660; *Young Woman with a Water Jug*, 1663; *Artist and Model*, 1663; *Girl with a Red Hat*, 1667.

**VERONESE, PAOLO,** 1528 (Verona, It.)–Apr. 19, 1588. Italian painter of the 16th-cent. Venetian school; known for his devotional themes. Paintings: *Bevilicqua-Lazise Altarpiece*, 1548; *The Temptation of St. Anthony*, 1552.

**VUILLARD, EDOUARD,** Nov. 11, 1868 (Ciuseaux, Fr.)–June 21, 1940. French painter, graphic artist. With PIERRE BONNARD, developed the intimist style of painting; known for his domestic scenes. Paintings: *Self-Portrait*, 1892; *Woman Sweeping*, 1892; *Interior*, 1898.

**WATTEAU, ANTOINE,** Oct. 10, 1684 (Valenciennes, Fr.)–July 18, 1721. French rococo painter. Known for paintings of "fêtes galantes"; elected to French Acad., 1712. Paintings: *The Embarkation for Cythera*.

**WEYDEN, ROGER VAN DER,** 1400 (Tournai, Flanders)–June 16, 1464. Flemish painter. City planner of Brussels, 1435–64; highly influential in the development of Flemish naturalism. Paintings: *Descent from the Cross*, 1435; *Braque tryptych*, 1450–52.

**WREN, SIR CHRISTOPHER,** Oct. 20, 1632 (E. Knoyle, Wilts., Eng.)–Feb. 25, 1723. English architect, astronomer. Prof. of astronomy at Gresham C., 1657; rebuilt over 50 churches, after the Great Fire, including St. Martin's (Ludgate), St. Magnus the Martyr (London Bridge); designed St. Paul's Cathedral and Chelsea Hospital, 1682–85.

**ZURBARÁN, FRANCISCO DE,** baptized Nov. 7, 1598 (Fuente de Cantos, Sp.)–Aug. 27, 1664. Spanish baroque painter. Known for his religious works. Paintings: *Immaculate Conception*, 1616; *Labours of Hercules*, 1634; *A Franciscan Monk*, 1630–32.

# Composers, Concert, Ballet, and Opera Personalities

**AILEY, ALVIN,** Jan. 5, 1931 (Rogers, Tex.)–Dec. 1, 1989. U.S. choreographer, dancer. Incorporated modern, jazz, and academic dance forms in his choreography; his ballets to traditional music include *Blues Suite* (1958) and *Revelations* (1960); formed the Alvin Ailey American Dance Theatre in 1958.

**ALBANESE, LICIA,** July 22, 1913 (Bari, It.). U.S. operatic soprano. Debuted in Parma, It., 1934; debuted at Met. Opera, 1940; sang at the Met. for 25 years, in over 40 roles.

**ANDERSON, MARIAN,** Feb. 17, 1902 (Philadelphia, Pa.). U.S. contralto, concert artist. Has made many internatl. concert tours; the first black to perform in a major role at the Met. Opera (Ulrica in *Un ballo in maschera*), 1955; U.S. del. to the UN, 1958.

**ARRAU, CLAUDIO,** Feb. 6, 1903 (Chillan, Chile). Chilean-U.S. concert pianist. Child prodigy; began to make internatl. tours in 1912; came to the U.S. permanently, 1941; has won many internatl. awards.

**ARROYO, MARTINA,** Feb. 2, 1940 (New York, N.Y.). U.S. operatic soprano. Won Met. Opera "Auditions of the Air," 1958; famed as replacement for BIRGIT NILSSON in *Aida* at Met., 1965; specializes in major dramatic roles in G. VERDI and G. ROSSINI operas.

**BALANCHINE, GEORGE,** Jan. 9, 1904 (St. Petersburg, Rus. [now Leningrad, USSR])–Apr. 30, 1983. Russian-U.S. choreographer. Most influential choreographer of classical ballet in the U.S. Chief choreographer of Ballets Russes, 1925; founded School of American Ballet, 1934; cofounder of Ballet Soc., 1946 (NYCB, from 1948); artistic dir., NYCB, from 1948. Major works: *The Prodigal Son*, 1929; *Agon; The Four Temperaments*, 1946; *Jewels; Vienna Waltzes; Tricolore.*

**BARBER, SAMUEL,** Mar. 9, 1910 (West Chester, Pa.)–Jan. 23, 1981. U.S. composer. Prolific modern composer known for his operas, songs, and string music. Opera: *Vanessa*, 1958 (awarded 1958 Pulitzer Prize). Other works: *Essays for Orchestra*, 1938 and 1942; *First Symphony*, 1936; *Piano Concerto*, 1962 (awarded 1963 Pulitzer Prize).

**BARYSHNIKOV, MIKHAIL,** Jan. 1948 (Riga, USSR). Soviet–U.S. dancer. Leading premiere danseur; member of Kirov Ballet from 1969 until defection to U.S. in 1974; companies worldwide, 1974– ; soloist with ABT, 1974–78; soloist with NYCB, 1978–79; artistic dir. of ABT, 1980–89; choreographed *Nutcracker* for ABT, 1976. Films: *The Turning Point*, 1976; *White Nights*, 1985.

**BATTLE, KATHLEEN,** ? (Portsmouth, Ohio). U.S. operatic soprano. Has appeared with many prominent opera companies and symphony orchestras; won a Grammy Award in 1987 for her recordings.

**BERLIN, IRVING** (born Israel Baline) May 11, 1888 (Russia)–Sept. 22, 1989. U.S. composer. Wrote more than 800 pop songs, as well as scores for Broadway musicals; received Congressional Gold Medal for song "God Bless America." Songs: "Alexander's Ragtime Band"; "A Pretty Girl Is like a Melody"; "All by Myself"; "Easter Parade"; "Cheek to Cheek"; "White Christmas" (AA). Plays scored: *Annie Get Your Gun*, 1946; *Call Me Madam*, 1950.

**BERNSTEIN, LEONARD,** Aug. 25, 1918 (Lawrence, Mass.). U.S. composer, conductor. Immensely popular conductor of the New York Phil., 1958–69; his compositions, of both serious and show music, frequently reflect American themes. Works: *Jeremiah Symphony*, 1942; *Mass*, 1971; *An American Songbook*, 1978. Show music: *On the Town*, 1944; *Candide*, 1956; *West Side Story*, 1957; *Mass*, 1971; *Dybbuk* (ballet), 1974.

**BIGGS, E(dward George) POWER,** Mar. 29, 1906 (Westcliff, Eng.)–Mar. 10, 1977. British-U.S. organist. Concert virtuoso who popularized the organ and, especially, Baroque music, through recitals, records and broadcasts; authority on music of J. S. BACH.

**BOLCOM, WILLIAM E.,** May 26, 1938 (Seattle, Wash.). U.S. composer. A music professor at the University of Michigan, he has composed several symphonies, much chamber music, operas, and other musical works; won the Pulitzer Prize for music, for his "12 New Etudes for Piano", 1988.

**BUMBRY, GRACE,** Jan. 4, 1937 (St. Louis, Mo.). U.S. singer. Operatic mezzo-soprano; joint winner, Met. Auditions, 1958; debuts in Paris (1960), Bayreuth (1961), Covent Garden (1963), Met. Opera (1965).

**CAGE, JOHN, JR.,** Sept. 5, 1912 (Los Angeles, Calif.). U.S. composer. Advocate of indeterminism in music; pieces composed for "prepared piano"; has explored electronic music; music dir. of MERCE CUNNINGHAM and Dance Co., 1944–66.

**CALDWELL, SARAH,** Mar. 6, 1924 (Maryville, Mo.). U.S. conductor and opera producer. Established opera workshop, Boston U., 1948; after reorganization, first chairman of music theater dept., 1954; founder, artistic dir., and conductor of Opera Co. of Boston, 1957; became first woman conductor at New York Met., 1976.

**CALLAS, MARIA** (born Cecilia Sophia Anna Maria Kalogeropoulos), Dec. 3, 1923 (New York, N.Y.)–Sept. 16, 1977. U.S. prima donna operatic soprano. Professional debut with Athens Royal Opera, 1939; vocal and dramatic versatility allowed her to sing both dramatic and lyric roles; sang 43 roles in over 500 performances in all major internatl. opera houses.

**CLIBURN, VAN,** July 12, 1934 (Shreveport, La.). U.S. concert pianist. Concert debut, 1940; internatl. concert tours; gained internatl. fame by winning first prize at the Internatl. Tchaikovsky Piano Competition, Moscow, 1958; established his own piano competition at Ft. Worth, Tex., 1962.

**COPLAND, AARON,** Nov. 14, 1900 (Brooklyn, N.Y.). U.S. composer. Founder (with ROGER SESSIONS) of Copland-Sessions Concerts, 1929–31. Works: *Billy the Kid* (ballet), 1938; *Rodeo* (ballet), 1942; *A Lincoln Portrait*, 1942; *Appalachian Spring*, 1944 (awarded Pulitzer Prize in music, 1945); film score for *The Heiress*, (AA, 1950).

**CUNNINGHAM, MERCE,** Apr. 16, 1922 (Centralia, Wash.). U.S. dancer, choreographer. Developed new forms of abstract dance movement called "choreography by chance"; with MARTHA GRAHAM Co., 1939–45; formed own co., 1952. Works: *Summerspace*, 1958; *Winterbranch*, 1965.

**DAMROSCH, WALTER,** Jan. 30, 1862 (Breslau, Ger. [now Wroclaw, Pol.])–Dec. 22, 1950. U.S. conductor, composer. Specialized in Wagnerian opera; with Met. Opera Co., 1885–91 and 1900–02; founded Damrosch Opera Co., 1894–1900; pioneer of symphonic broadcasting; musical counsel, NBC, 1928–47; composed operas and other works.

**DE MILLE, AGNES,** 1909 (New York, N.Y.). U.S. dancer, choreographer. Toured with humorous mimedancers, 1929–40; choreographed *Rodeo* (1942), first ballet to include tap dancing; choreographed the musicals *Oklahoma* (1943); *Carousel* (1945), *Gentlemen Prefer Blondes* (1949), and *Paint Your Wagon* (1951); won Tony awards in 1947 and 1962; received Capezio Dance Award, 1966.

**DORATI, ANTAL,** Apr. 9, 1906 (Budapest, Hung.)–Nov. 13, 1988. U.S. composer, conductor. Conductor and musical dir. throughout Europe, 1924–40; Ballet Theatre, 1940–44; Dallas Symphony Orch.,

1945–49; Minneapolis Symphony Orch., 1949–60; BBC Symphony Orch., 1962–66; musical dir. of Washington Natl. Symphony, 1969–77; Detroit Symphony Orch., 1977–81.

**DUNCAN, ISADORA,** May 27, 1878 (San Francisco, Calif.)–Sept. 14, 1927. U.S. dancer. Rejected the formality of ballet; one of the first to interpret dance as a free form of art; popularized barefoot dance; found great success in Europe, especially England and Russia.

**DUNHAM, KATHERINE,** June 22, 1910 (Chicago, Ill.). U.S. dancer, choreographer. First to organize a black dance troupe to professional caliber; dance dir. of New York Labor Stage, 1939; established Dunham School of Dance (1945) and Katherine Dunham Dance Co. (1945); received *Dance Magazine* Award, 1968.

**EGLEVSKY, ANDRE,** Dec. 21, 1917 (Moscow, Rus.)–Dec. 4, 1977. Russian-U.S. ballet dancer. One of the greatest male classical dancers; with Ballet Russe (1933–35), Ballet de Monte Carlo (1935–37, 1938–42), American Ballet (1935), New York City Ballet (1951–58); repertoire included *Giselle* and *Swan Lake*; created roles in *Caracole* and *Scotch Symphony*.

**ELLINGTON, DUKE** (born Edward Kennedy Ellington), Apr. 29, 1899 (Washington, D.C.)–May 24, 1974. U.S. musician. Composer, pianist, jazz orchestra leader; a major jazz influence who led his own orchestra, 1923–74. "Mood Indigo"; "Don't Get Around Much Anymore"; "Satin Doll."

**ELMAN, MISCHA,** Jan. 20, 1891 (Talnoye, Ukraine, Russia)–Apr. 5, 1967. U.S. violinist. A student of the legendary Leopold Auer, he made his first concert appearance outside Russia in Berlin in 1904; became a celebrated, world-touring soloist.

**FARRAR, GERALDINE,** Feb. 28, 1882 (Melrose, Mass.)–Mar. 11, 1967. U.S. operatic soprano. With Met. Opera Co., 1906–22; lead roles included Madame Butterfly, Manon, Carmen.

**FARRELL, EILEEN,** Feb. 13, 1920 (Willimantic, Conn.). U.S. operatic soprano. Best known for her roles in Wagnerian operas; sang with San Francisco and Chicago opera cos. before making Met. Opera debut, 1960.

**FARRELL, SUZANNE,** Aug. 16, 1945 (Cincinnati, Ohio). U.S. ballerina. With NYCB, 1961–69 and 1975–   ; created many roles in G. BALANCHINE ballets; received *Dance Magazine* Award, 1976.

**FIEDLER, ARTHUR,** Dec. 17, 1894 (Boston, Mass.)–July 10, 1979. U.S. conductor. Organized and conducted Esplanade concerts, Boston, 1929–79; conducted the Boston Symphony Pops Concerts, 1930–79.

**FIRKUSNY, RUDOLF,** Feb. 11, 1912 (Napajedla, Czech.). Czech-U.S. pianist. Child prodigy who first appeared with Czech Philharmonic orch. in 1922; European concert tours, 1930–39; a U.S. resident since 1950; best known for his interpretations of L. BEETHOVEN and Czech composers.

**FOSTER, STEPHEN,** July 4, 1826 (Lawrenceville, Pa.)–Jan. 13, 1864. U.S. composer. Wrote classic minstrel songs and popular ballads of the mid-19th cent. Songs: "My Old Kentucky Home"; "Oh, Susanna"; "Old Folks at Home"; "Camptown Races"; "Old Black Joe"; "Beautiful Dreamer"; "Jeannie with the Light Brown Hair."

**GERSHWIN, GEORGE,** Sept. 26, 1898 (Brooklyn, N.Y.)–July 11, 1937. U.S. composer. Composed Broadway musicals, concert music, songs with elements of jazz. Works: "Swanee," 1918; *Rhapsody in Blue,* 1924; *Porgy and Bess* (opera), 1925; *Lady Be Good,* 1924; *Funny Face,* 1927; *An American in Paris,* 1928; *Of Thee I Sing,* (first musical to win a Pulitzer Prize), 1931.

**GLASS, PHILIP,** Jan. 31, 1937 (Baltimore, Md.). U.S. composer, musician. Studied at Julliard and with NADIA BOULANGER; a composer of orchestral works, operas, and film and stage scores, he is the founder and performer of the Philip Glass Ensemble; composed the ceremonial music for the 1984 Olympics. Works: *Einstein on the Beach,* 1976.

**GRAHAM, MARTHA,** May 11, 1895 (Pittsburgh, Pa.). U.S. dancer, teacher, choreographer of modern dance. Studied and worked with Denishawn Dancers, 1916–23; founder and artistic dir. of Martha Graham School of Contemporary Dance, 1927; over 150 choreographed works, including *Appalachian Spring* (1944); received 1956 *Dance Magazine* Award and 1960 Capezio Dance Award.

**GREGORY, CYNTHIA,** July 8, 1946 (Los Angeles, Calif.). U.S. ballerina. Soloist with San Francisco Ballet, 1962–65; soloist with American Ballet Theatre, NYC, 1965– .

**HANDY, W(illiam) C(hristopher),** Nov. 16, 1873 (Florence, Ala.)–Mar. 28, 1958. U.S. composer. First to write down and publish "blues" music; established popularity of the blues in band music; ignoring his blindness, conducted own orchestra, 1903–21. Works: "St. Louis Blues," 1914.

**HANSON, HOWARD,** Oct. 28, 1896 (Wahoo, Neb.)–Feb. 26, 1981. U.S. composer, conductor. Dir. of Eastman School of Music at U. of Rochester, 1924–64; works include five symphonies, an opera (commissioned by the Met.); won Prix de Rome, 1921; awarded 1944 Pulitzer Prize in music, for his Fourth Symphony.

**HEIFETZ, JASCHA,** Feb. 2, 1901 (Vilna, Lith. [now USSR])–Dec. 10, 1987. U.S. violin virtuoso. Child prodigy who played F. MENDELSSOHN Concerto at age seven; New York debut at Carnegie Hall, 1917; many internatl. tours; has transcribed works of J. S. BACH and A. VIVALDI for violin; named Chevalier, Legion of Honor, 1926.

**HERBERT, VICTOR,** Feb. 1, 1859 (Dublin, Ire.)–May 26, 1924. Irish-U.S. virtuoso cellist, conductor, composer. Best known for his operattas *Babes in Toyland* (1903) and *Naughty Marietta* (1910); conductor of Pittsburgh Symphony Orch., 1898–1904; cofounder of ASCAP, 1914; wrote music scores for plays, motion pictures (*The Fall of a Nation,* 1916).

**HINDEMITH, PAUL,** Nov. 16, 1895 (Hanau, Ger.)–Dec. 28, 1963. German-U.S. composer, musical theorist. Member of Frankfurt Opera Orch., 1915–

23; his opera *Mathis der Maler* (1934) was banned by Nazis; taught in Europe and the U.S.; works include chamber music, operas, instrumental music.

**HINES, JEROME** (born Jerome Heinz), Nov. 8, 1921 (Hollywood, Calif.). U.S. operatic bass. Made debut, 1941; with Met. Opera, from 1946; at Bayreuth, 1958–63; repertoire includes Mephistopheles, Boris Godunov, Grand Inquisitor (*Don Carlos*), and Swallow (*Peter Grimes*).

**HORNE, MARILYN,** Jan. 16, 1934 (Bradford, Pa.). U.S. operatic mezzo-soprano. Has appeared in most major internatl. opera houses; with Met. Opera, 1970– ; best known for performances in coloratura roles such as *Carmen*; sang leading role on the sound track for the film *Carmen Jones,* 1954.

**HOROWITZ, VLADIMIR,** Oct. 1, 1904 (Kiev, Rus.)–Nov. 5, 1989. U.S. virtuoso pianist. Made internatl. concert tours from 1924; best known for his interpretations of RACHMANINOV, CHOPIN, LISZT, PROKOFIEV, SCRIABIN, SCHUMANN.

**HUMPHREY, DORIS,** Oct. 17, 1895 (Oak Park, Ill.)–Dec. 29, 1958. U.S. dancer, choreographer, teacher. With Denishawn Co. (1917–28); and Humphrey-Weidman School & Co. (1928–44); artistic dir. of JOSÉ LIMON Co., 1942–58; influenced the U.S. modern-dance movement.

**IVES, CHARLES,** Oct. 20, 1874 (Danbury, Conn.) –May 19, 1954. U.S. composer. Known for tonal, rhythmic, and harmonic experimentation; themes drawn from New England; awarded 1947 Pulitzer Prize in music for his *Third Symphony* (*The Camp Meeting*).

**JOFFREY, ROBERT** (born Abdulla Jaffa Anver Bey Khan), Dec. 24, 1930 (Seattle, Wash.)–Mar. 25, 1988. U.S. dancer, choreographer, ballet dir. First choreographed ballet was *Persephone,* 1952; founder and dir. of ballet faculty at American Ballet Center, 1953–65; founder of R. Joffrey Ballet, 1956 (became City Center Joffrey Ballet, 1966).

**JOPLIN, SCOTT,** Nov. 24, 1868 (Texarkana, Tex.) –Apr. 1, 1917. U.S. ragtime pianist, composer. Entertained in vaudeville; ragtime instrumental music includes "Maple Leaf Rag."

**KIRCHNER, LEON,** Jan 24, 1919 (Brooklyn, N.Y.). U.S. composer, pianist. Wrote mainly keyboard and string compositions; won 1967 Pulitzer Prize, for *String Quartet No. 3* (1966).

**KIRKLAND, GELSEY,** Dec. 12, 1952 (Bethlehem, Pa.). U.S. ballerina. With the New York Ballet as a soloist, 1969–72, and principal, 1972–74; with American Ballet Theater, 1974–84. Books: *Dancing on My Grave,* 1986.

**KIRSTEIN, LINCOLN,** May 4, 1907 (Rochester, N.Y.). U.S. ballet promoter. A founder of the School of American Ballet, he received the Presidential Medal of Freedom in 1984; his books include *Flesh Is Heir* (1932), *Dance: A Short History of Theatrical Dancing* (1935), and *Blast at Ballet* (1938).

**KOSTELANETZ, ANDRE,** Dec. 22, 1901 (St. Petersburg, Rus. [now Leningrad, USSR])–Jan. 13, 1980. U.S. conductor. Gained fame with CBS radio broadcasts, from 1928; many concert tours and guest appearances with major internatl. orchs.

**KOUSSEVITZKY, SERGE ALEXANDROVITCH,** July 26, 1874 (Vyshni Volochek, Rus.)–June 4, 1951. Russian–U.S. conductor. With Boston Symphony Orch., 1924–49; founder and dir. of Berkshire Music Festival, 1937; organized Koussevitzky Fndn. (1942) to commission and perform new works; known for his interpretations of works by modern composers.

**LEINSDORF, ERICH,** Feb. 4, 1912 (Vienna, Austria). U.S. conductor. With Met. Orch., 1937–43; music dir. of Phil. Orch. of Rochester (N.Y.) 1947–56; dir. or Met. Opera, 1957–62; music dir. of Boston Symphony Orch., 1962–69; principal conductor, West Berlin Radio Orchestra, 1977–80.

**LEVINE, JAMES,** June 23, 1943 (Cincinnati, Ohio). U.S. conductor, pianist. Asst. conductor of Cleveland Orch., 1964–70; music director of Met. Opera, 1975– ; Salzburg Festival, 1976– .

**LIMÓN, JOSÉ,** Jan. 12, 1908 (Cuiliacán, Mex.)–Dec. 2, 1972. Mexican-U.S. modern dancer, choreographer, teacher. Dancer with Humphrey & Weidman Co., 1930–40; founder of José Limón American Dance Co., 1947; artistic dir. of American Dance Theatre, 1964.

**MAAZEL, LORIN,** Mar. 6, 1930 (Paris, Fr.). U.S. conductor, violinist. Conductor at the Edinburgh, Bayreuth and Salzburg festivals, 1960–70; musical dir., Cleveland Orchestra, 1972–82; dir., Vienna Opera, 1982–84; music dir., Pittsburgh Symphony Orch., 1986– .

**MAKAROVA, NATALIA,** Nov. 21, 1940 (Leningrad, USSR). Soviet-U.S. ballerina. Known for her performances in Romantic roles; after defection (1970) to U.S., with ABT, 1970–72; won Tony in 1984 for "On Your Toes."

**MARTINS, PETER,** Oct. 27, 1946 (Copenhagen, Denmark). U.S. ballet master, choreographer, and dancer. A former principal dancer with the Royal Danish Ballet, he came to the U.S. in 1967; codirector of the New York City Ballet; has choreographed many ballets as well as Broadway musicals.

**MCBRIDE, PATRICIA,** Aug. 23, 1942 (Teaneck, N.J.). U.S. ballerina. With NYCB, from 1959, now principal dancer; repertoire includes *Swan Lake, Harlequinade, Nutcracker, Jewels, Coppelia.*

**MCCORMACK, JOHN,** June 13, 1884 (Athlone, Ire.)–Sept. 16, 1945. U.S. operatic tenor. Made Covent Garden debut, 1907; known for effortless singing, diction, phrasing; sang mostly Italian opera, German lieder, Irish folk songs.

**MCCRACKEN, JAMES,** Dec. 16, 1926 (Gary, Ind.)–Apr. 29, 1988. U.S. operatic tenor. Many roles in major international houses; known for his performances as Otello.

**MELCHIOR, LAURITZ,** Mar. 20, 1890 (Copenhagen, Denmark)–Mar. 18, 1973. U.S. operatic tenor. Debuted as baritone (1913) and as a tenor (1918); specialized in Wagnerian roles, especially Tristan and Siegfried; sang with Metropolitan Opera, 1926–50.

**MERRILL, ROBERT,** June 4, 1919 (Brooklyn,

N.Y.). U.S. operatic baritone. Made debut, 1944; with Met. Opera, 1945–1975; roles include Escamillo (*Carmen*), Germont (*La Traviata*), Marcello (*La Boheme*), Iago (*Otello*); first American to sing 500 performances at Met. Opera.

**MILNES, SHERRILL,** Jan. 10, 1935 (Downers Grove, Ill). U.S. operatic baritone. With Met. Opera, 1965– ; best known for his performances in G. VERDI operas.

**MOFFO, ANNA,** June 27, 1932 (Wayne, Pa.). U.S. operatic soprano. Made U.S. debut, 1957; with Met. Opera, from 1959–1969; repertoire includes *La Boheme, Rigoletto, Madama Butterfly, The Barber of Seville, Tosca.*

**NORMAN, JESSYE,** Sept. 15, 1945 (Augusta, Ga.). U.S. operatic soprano. Made her opera debut in Berlin, West Germany, 1969; well known in lieder, has sung with most of the major opera companies and symphonic orchestras in the world; received Grammys in 1980, 1982, and 1985.

**ORMANDY, EUGENE,** Nov. 18, 1899 (Budapest, Hung.)–Mar. 12, 1985. U.S. conductor, music dir.; at age 5½, the youngest pupil at the Royal State Acad. of Music; toured Europe as child violinist; conductor of Minneapolis Symphony Orch., 1931–36; conductor and music dir. of Philadelphia Orch., from 1936.

**PEERCE, JAN** (born Jacob Pincus Perelmuth), June, 1904 (New York, N.Y.)–Dec. 17, 1984. U.S. operatic tenor. Made his Metropolitan Opera debut (1941) and his Broadway debut in *Fiddler on the Roof* (1971); first American singer to appear at the Bolshoi Opera, USSR.

**PETERS, ROBERTA,** May 4, 1930 (New York, N.Y.). U.S. operatic soprano. Made Met. Opera debut as Zerlina in *Don Giovanni,* 1950; repertoire includes *Rigoletto* and *Magic Flute.*

**PIATIGORSKY, GREGOR,** Apr. 17, 1903 (Ekaterinoslav, Russia)–Aug. 6, 1976. U.S. cello virtuoso. Solo cellist, Imperial Opera, Moscow (1916–19) and Berlin Philharmonic (1923–28); U.S. debut, 1929.

**PISTON, WALTER,** Jan. 20, 1894 (Rockland, Maine)–Nov. 12, 1976. U.S. composer, teacher. Prof. of music, Harvard U., 1944–60; noted for his compositions in neoclassical style with romantic overtones; awarded Pulitzer prizes for Third (1947) and Seventh (1960) symphonies.

**PONS, LILY,** (born Alice Josephine Pons), Apr. 16, 1904 (Draguignan, Fr.)–Feb. 13, 1976. U.S. coloratura soprano. With Met. Opera, 1931–56; repertoire included *Lakme* and *Lucia di Lammermoor*; in the films *I Dream Too Much* (1935) and *That Girl from Paris* (1936).

**PONSELLE, ROSA,** Jan. 22, 1897 (Meriden, Conn.)–May 25, 1981. U.S. operatic soprano. Sang with Metropolitan Opera, 1918–37; repertoire included *La Forza del Destina, Carmen, Aida, La Traviata*; coach and artistic dir., Baltimore Civic Opera Co., from 1954.

**PREVIN, ANDRÉ,** Apr. 6, 1929 (Berlin, Ger.). U.S. composer, conductor. With Houston Symphony (1967–69) and London Symphony Orch. (1968–

79); music dir. of Pittsburgh Symphony, 1976–86; music dir., Royal Philharmonic, 1985– ; music dir., Los Angeles Philharmonic, 1986– ; winner of four AAs.

**PRICE, LEONTYNE,** Feb. 10, 1927 (Laurel, Miss.). U.S. operatic soprano. Made debut with San Francisco Opera, 1957; with Met. Opera, 1961– ; created role of Cleopatra (*Antony and Cleopatra*); also known for her role as Aida; has won over 20 Grammy awards for classical vocal recordings; received Presidential Medal of Freedom, 1964.

**REICH, STEVE,** Oct. 3, 1936 (New York, N.Y.). U.S. composer. Associated with minimalist schools of composition; works include music for unusual combinations of instruments, such as "Four Organs," "Six Pianos," and "Music for Eighteen Musicians."

**REINER, FRITZ,** Dec. 19, 1888 (Budapest, Hung.) –Nov. 15, 1963. Hungarian-U.S. conductor. With Cincinnati Symphony, 1922–31; at Curtis Inst. of Music (Philadelphia), 1931–41; with Pittsburgh Symphony, 1938–48; with Met. Opera, 1948–53; with Chicago Symphony, 1953–62; best known for interpretations of R. WAGNER and R. STRAUSS.

**ROBBINS, JEROME,** Oct. 11, 1918 (New York, N.Y.). U.S. ballet dancer, choreographer. Many Broadway musical appearances; with ABT, 1940–44; assoc. music dir. of NYCB, 1959–89.

**ROBESON, PAUL,** Apr. 9, 1898 (Princeton, N.J.) –Jan. 23, 1976. U.S. dramatic bass-baritone. Performed on stage, in films. Plays: *All God's Chillun Got Wings,* 1924; *The Emperor Jones,* 1924; *Show Boat,* 1928.

**RODGERS, RICHARD,** June 28, 1902 (New York, N.Y.)–Dec. 30, 1979. U.S. composer. Leading composer of American musical theater, noted for his collaborations with LORENZ HART and OSCAR HAMMERSTEIN II. Shows: *Jumbo,* 1935; *Babes in Arms,* 1937; *The Boys from Syracuse,* 1938; *Pal Joey,* 1940; *Oklahoma,* (Pulitzer), 1943; *Carousel,* 1945; *South Pacific* (Tony, Pulitzer), 1949; *Flower Drum Song,* 1958; *The King and I* (Tony), 1951; *The Sound of Music,* 1960; *No Strings* (Tony), 1962; *I Remember Mama,* 1979.

**RODZINSKI, ARTUR,** Jan. 1, 1892 (Spalato, Dalmatia [now Yugo.])–Nov. 27, 1958. U.S. conductor. Organized the NBC Symphony for A. TOSCANINI and conducted many of their concerts, 1937; permanent conductor, New York Philharmonic, 1942–47; permanent conductor, Chicago Symphony, from 1948.

**ROMBERG, SIGMUND,** July 29, 1887 (Szeged, Hung.)–Nov. 9, 1951. U.S. composer. Wrote 40 scores for musicals; best known for his operettas, including *Maytime* (1917), *The Student Prince* (1924), and *The Desert Song* (1926).

**ROSTROPOVICH, MSTISLAV,** Mar. 27, 1927 (Baku, USSR). Soviet-U.S. cello virtuoso, conductor. Made cello debut, 1935; Soviet citizenship revoked, 1978; music dir. of Natl. Symphony Orch., 1977– .

**RUBINSTEIN, ARTHUR,** (or Artur), Jan. 28, 1887 (Lodz, Pol.)–Dec. 20, 1982. U.S. concert pianist. A child prodigy who made U.S. debut in 1906; famed for international concert performances and especially for his interpretations of F. CHOPIN.

**SAINT DENIS, RUTH,** Jan. 20, 1877 (Newark, N.J.)–July 21, 1968. U.S. dancer and choreographer. Began by choreographing dances based on eastern themes; with her husband, TED SHAWN, opened the Denishawn dance company, which toured from 1915 to 1931; among their students were MARTHA GRAHAM, DORIS HUMPHREY, and Charles Weidman.

**SCHIPPERS, THOMAS,** Mar. 9, 1930 (Kalamazoo, Mich.)–Dec. 16, 1977. U.S. conductor. With New York City Opera, 1951–54; with Met. Opera, 1955–77; founder (with GIAN CARLO MENOTTI) of Festival of Two Worlds (Spoleto, It.), 1958.

**SCHNABEL, KARL,** Aug. 6, 1909 (Berlin, Ger.). U.S. concert pianist. Internatl. career, including recitals, broadcasts, concert tours, and solos with major orchs. *Modern Technique of the Pedal,* 1954.

**SCHOENBERG, ARNOLD,** Sept. 13, 1874 (Vienna, Austria)–July 13, 1951. Austrian-U.S. composer, teacher. Invented the 12-tone row, 1921; at Prussian Acad. of Arts, 1925–33; prof. at UCLA, 1936–44. Works: *Verklärte Nacht,* 1889; *Gurrelieder,* 1913; *Pierrot Lunaire,* 1912.

**SERKIN, RUDOLF,** Mar. 28, 1903 (Eger, Bohemia). Austrian-U.S. pianist. A child prodigy who made European debut in 1915; U.S. debut, 1933; dir. of Curtis Inst. of Music, 1968–76; received Presidential Medal of Freedom, 1963.

**SESSIONS, ROGER,** Dec. 28, 1896 (Brooklyn, N.Y.)–Mar 16, 1985. U.S. composer, teacher. With AARON COPLAND, organized Copland-Sessions Concerts for contemporary music, 1928; works include nine symphonies, three operas, string and keyboard pieces, orchestral suites.

**SILLS, BEVERLY** (born Belle Silverman), May 25, 1929 (Brooklyn, N.Y.). U.S. operatic coloratura soprano. With radio's *Major Bowes Capital Family Hour,* 1934–41; with New York City Opera Co. since 1955– , as gen. dir. since 1979; repertoire includes *Manon, La Traviata, Lucia di Lammermoor,* Autobiography: *Bubbles,* 1976; *Beverly,* 1987.

**SOUSA, JOHN PHILIP** ("The March King"), Nov. 6, 1854 (Washington, D.C.)–Mar. 6, 1932. U.S. bandmaster, composer. Led U.S. Marine Band, 1880–92; formed own band, 1892; composed over 100 marches incl. "Stars and Stripes Forever," 1897; "Semper Fidelis," 1888; "The Washington Post," 1889; "The Liberty Bell," 1893; "El Capitán," 1896.

**STADE, FREDERICA VON,** June 1, 1945 (Sommerville, N.J.). U.S. operatic mezzo-soprano. With Metropolitan Opera, 1970– ; has made international opera house appearances; repertoire includes *Marriage of Figaro, Faust,* and *Don Giovanni.*

**STERN, ISAAC,** July 21, 1920 (Kreminiecz, Rus.). U.S. violinist. Made U.S. debut, 1931; many internatl. tours and solo and chamber-music recordings; won Grammy awards in 1971 and 1973; Grammy Lifetime Achievement Award, 1987.

**STEVENS, RISË** (born Risë Steenberg), June 11,

1913 (New York, N.Y.). U.S. operatic mezzo-soprano. Made Metropolitan Opera debut, 1938; repertoire includes *Mignon*, *Carmen*, *Samson et Dalila*, and *Cosi Fan Tutte*; pres., Mannes College of Music, N.Y., 1975–78.

**STOKOWSKI, LEOPOLD**, Apr. 18, 1882 (London, Eng.)–Sept. 13, 1977. U.S. conductor. With Cincinnati Symphony, 1909–12; music dir. of Philadelphia Orch., 1912–36; organized All-American Youth Orch., 1940–41; formed American Symphony Orch., 1962.

**SZELL, GEORGE**, June 7, 1897 (Budapest, Hung.)–July 30, 1970. U.S. conductor. Made piano debut with Vienna Symphony at age 10; conductor of Berlin State Opera, 1924–29; with German Opera, Prague, 1930–33; with Met. Opera, 1942–45; principal conductor of Cleveland Orch., 1946–70.

**TAYLOR, PAUL**, July 29, 1930 (Allegheny County, Pa.). U.S. modern dancer, choreographer. Dancer, Martha Graham Dance Co., 1955–61; dir., choreographer, Paul Taylor Dance Co., 1955– .

**THARP, TWYLA**, July 1, 1941 (Portland, Ind.). U.S. dancer, choreographer. With Paul Taylor Dance Co., 1963–65; freelance choreographer with own modern-dance troupe, 1965– ; major choreography includes *Eight Jelly Rolls* (1971) and *Push Comes to Shove* (1976).

**THOMAS, MICHAEL TILSON**, Dec. 21, 1944 (Hollywood, Calif.). U.S. conductor. Music dir. and conductor of Buffalo Phil. Orch., 1971–79; dir. and conductor of New York Phil. Young People's Concerts (CBS-TV), 1971–77; won Grammy award, 1976; principal conductor, London Symphony, 1988– .

**THOMSON, VIRGIL**, Nov. 25, 1896 (Kansas City, Mo.)–Sept. 30, 1989. U.S. composer, music critic.

Works include chamber music, ballet, symphonies, choral works, operas (*Four Saints in Three Acts*, 1934; *The Mother of Us All*, 1947); music critic with the New York Herald-Tribune, 1940–54; won Pulitzer Prize in music, 1949.

**TRAUBEL, HELEN**, June 20, 1899 (St. Louis, Mo.)–July 28, 1972. U.S. operatic and concert soprano. Made Met. Opera debut, 1939; principal Wagnerian soprano at Met., 1939–53.

**TUCKER, RICHARD** (born Reuben Ticker), Aug. 28, 1914 (Brooklyn, N.Y.)–Jan. 8, 1975. U.S. operatic tenor. With Met. Opera, 1945–75; well-known cantor; repertoire included *Aida*, *Pagliacci*, *La Juive*, *La Boheme*.

**VILLELLA, EDWARD**, Oct. 1, 1936 (Long Isl., N.Y.). U.S. ballet dancer. With NYCB, 1957– ; roles include *Prodigal Son*, *Harlequinade*; has starred in musicals (*Brigadoon*, 1962); won 1957 Emmy for *Harlequinade* (*CBS Festival of Lively Arts*).

**WARREN, LEONARD**, (born Leonard Vaarenov), Apr. 21, 1911 (New York, N.Y.)–Mar. 4, 1960. U.S. operatic baritone. With Met. Opera, 1939–60; popular radio and TV singer; known for roles in G. VERDI operas; died on stage at Met. during *La Forza del Destino*.

**WATTS, ANDRÉ**, June 20, 1946 (Nuremberg, Ger.). U.S. concert pianist. Made debut in Philadelphia Orch. Children's Concerts, 1955; made European debut with London Symphony Orch., 1966; won Grammy award, 1963.

**ZIMBALIST, EFREM**, May 7, 1889 (Rostov-on-Don, Rus.)–Feb. 22, 1985. Russian-U.S. violinist. Made debut in Berlin at age 17; extensive international tours; dir. of Curtis Inst. of Music. 1941–68. (Father of actor E. ZIMBALIST, JR.)

## FOREIGN COMPOSERS, CONCERT, BALLET, AND OPERA PERSONALITIES

**ABBADO, CLAUDIO**, June 26, 1933 (Milan, It.). Italian symphony and opera conductor. Has conducted at many major opera houses and symphonic halls; Conductor at La Scala, 1967–86; currently the music director of the Vienna State Opera (1986– ) and the Vienna Philharmonic Orchestra.

**ALONSO, ALICIA** (born Alicia Ernestina de la Caridad del Cobre Martinez Hoyo), Dec. 21, 1921 (Havana, Cuba). Cuban prima ballerina. Danced with the Ballet Theatre (now ABT), 1941, 1943–48, and 1951; formed Alicia Alonso ballet co. in Havana, 1948; prima ballerina and dir. of Ballet Nac. de Cuba, 1959– ; bouts of blindness have caused temporary interruptions in her career; a pure, classical ballerina whose most famous role is *Giselle*.

**ANSERMET, ERNEST**, Nov. 11, 1883 (Vevey, Switz.)–Feb. 20, 1969. Swiss conductor. Noted for conducting I. STRAVINSKY and other modern composers; conductor for S. DIAGHILEV's Ballets Russes; founded Orchestre de la Swisse Romande, 1918; composed symphonic poem "Fueilles au Printemps."

**ASHKENAZY, VLADIMIR**, July 6, 1937 (Gorky, USSR). Russian pianist. Internatl. concert star; won second prize in Chopin Competition, 1955; winner

of Tchaikovsky Piano Competition, 1962; London debut, 1963; music dir., Royal Philharmonie, 1986– .

**ASHTON, SIR FREDERIC (WILLIAM MALLANDINE)**, Sept. 17, 1906 (Guayaquil, Ecuador). English choreographer. Founder, principal choreographer, and dir. of England's Royal Ballet, 1952–70; has choreographed for many ballet cos. worldwide.

**BACH, CARL PHILIPP EMANUEL**, Mar. 8, 1714 (Weimar, Ger.)–Dec. 14, 1788. German composer. Third son of J. S. BACH; court musician to FREDERICK THE GREAT, 1740–67; prolific composer; a pioneer in sonatas, symphonic orchestrations, and chamber music; wrote "Essay on Keyboard Instruments" (1753), a valuable source on 18th-cent. music technique.

**BACH, JOHANN CHRISTIAN** ("The English Bach"), Sept. 5, 1735 (Leipzig, Ger.)–Jan 1, 1782. German composer, organist. Resident of Milan (and cathedral organist), (1754–59) and London, where he taught music to the royal family (1759–82); composed operas, sonatas, symphonics.

**BACH, JOHANN SEBASTIAN**, Mar. 21, 1685

(Eisenach, Ger.)–July 28, 1750. German composer. Founding father of a music dynasty, pioneer in the playing of and composition for keyboard instruments; musician for royalty and church in native Germany; became totally blind, 1749; wrote keyboard music, cantatas, concertos, masses, hymns. Mass in B Minor, 1724–46; *Brandenburg* Concertos, 1721; *The Goldberg* Variations, 1722; *Well-Tempered Clavier*, 1742.

**BARBIROLLI, SIR JOHN,** Born Giovanni Battista Barbirolli, Dec. 2, 1899 (London, Eng.)–June 29, 1970. British conductor. Musical dir. of British Natl. Opera (1926–27), New York Phil. (1937–43).

**BARENBOIM, DANIEL,** Nov. 15, 1932 (Buenos Aires, Argentina). Israeli symphony conductor and pianist. Made his piano debut at the age of seven and his conducting debut at the age of 20; musical director of the Orchestre de Paris, 1975–  ; appointed to be the musical director of the Chicago Symphony beginning in 1992.

**BARTOK, BÉLA,** Mar. 25, 1881 (Nagyszentmiklos, A.-H. [now Sînnicolau Mare, Rum])–Sept. 26, 1945. Hungarian composer, pianist. Utilized Hungarian folk themes and a chromatic system of 12 tones to produce a variety of string, piano, and choral music. Operas: *Bluebeard's Castle*, 1911. Ballets: *The Wooden Prince*, 1916; *The Wonderful Mandarin*, 1919. Piano collection: *Mikrokosmos*, 1926–39.

**BEECHAM, SIR THOMAS,** Apr. 29, 1879 (St. Helen's, Eng.)–Mar. 8, 1961. British conductor. Introduced Britain to RICHARD STRAUSS (1915), the Ballets Russes (1911) and Chaliapin (1913); founder of British Natl. Opera Co., London Phil. (1932) and Royal Phil. (1946); artistic dir. of Covent Garden, from 1933.

**BEETHOVEN, LUDWIG VAN,** baptized Dec. 17, 1770 (Bonn, Ger.)–Mar. 26, 1827. German composer. The prototypical Romantic composer of symphonies, sonatas, choral works, chamber music, etc.; a child prodigy taught by MOZART (1787) and HAYDN (1792–94); spent most of his career in Vienna; composed many of finest works while almost totally deaf; first composer to make a living without church subsidy. First period (1794–1800): First Symphony. Second period (1801–14): Second-Eighth Symphonies, *Moonlight* Sonata, *Appassionata*, Fourth and Fifth Concerti, *Battle* Symphony, *Fidelio*. Third period (1815–27): Ninth Symphony, string quartets.

**BEHRENS, HILDEGARD,** ? (Oldenburg, West Germany). German operatic soprano. Made her debut in 1971 with the Freiburg Opera; sings with several major opera companies; known for roles as Brünnhilde, Isolde, and Tosca.

**BÉJART, MAURICE** (born Maurice-Jean de Berger), Jan. 1, 1928 (Marseilles, Fr.). French choreographer. Founded Ballet of the XXth Century Company, 1954; known for his radical contemporary interpretations of ballet classicals, produced in a lavish manner.

**BELLINI, VINCENZO,** Nov. 3, 1801 (Catania, Sicily)–Sept. 23, 1835. Italian composer. Prime mover in the composition of bel canto opera. Operas: *La Sonnambula*, 1831; *Norma*, 1831; *I Puritani*, 1835.

**BERG, ALBAN,** Feb. 9, 1885 (Vienna, Austria)–Dec. 24. 1935. Austrian composer. Composer of atonal music, influenced by ARNOLD SCHONBERG; wrote orchestral, chamber music and songs; best known for two operas, *Wozzeck* (1925) and *Lulu* (1937).

**BERIOSOVA, SVETLANA,** Sept. 24, 1932 (Kaunas, Lith [now USSR]). Russian-English ballerina. Prima with many ballet cos. (1948–75) chiefly with Sadler's Wells (now Royal) Ballet in England (1952–75); her Giselle most famous role.

**BERLIOZ, (Louis) HECTOR,** Dec. 11, 1803 (La Côte-Saint Andre, Fr.)–Mar. 8, 1869. French composer. Most important of the French Romantics; noted for symphonies and operas. Works: *Symphonie Fantastique*, 1830; *Romeo and Juliet*, 1839; *La Damnation de Faust*, 1846; *Les Troyens*, 1858–60; "Te Deum," 1849.

**BING, SIR RUDOLPH,** Jan. 9, 1902 (Vienna, Austria). Anglo-Austrian impresario. Held various managerial posts, most notably, gen. mgr. of Met. Opera, 1950–72; cofounder of Edinburgh Festival, 1947.

**BIZET, GEORGES** (born Alexandre Cesar Leopold Bizet), Oct. 25, 1838 (Paris, Fr.)–June 3, 1875. French composer. Known for his dramatic music and the opera *Carmen* (1875). Works: *L'Arlesienne*, 1872; *Jeux d'enfants*, 1871; Symphony in C Major, 1855.

**BJÖRLING, JUSSI** (born Johan Jonaton Björling), Feb. 5, 1911 (Stora Tuna, Swe.)–Sept. 9, 1960. Swedish singer. Operatic tenor; made debut, 1929; debut in U.S., 1937; known for elegant robustness of voice, particularly in VERDI and PUCCINI dramatic roles.

**BÖHM, KARL,** Aug. 28, 1894 (Graz, Austria)–Aug. 14, 1981. Austrian conductor. Gen. music dir. at Darmstadt, 1927–31; dir. of Hamburg Opera, 1931–34; dir. of Dresden Opera, 1934–42; dir. of Vienna Opera, 1943–45; known for interpretations of WAGNER and MOZART.

**BOITO, ARRIGO** (born Enrico Giuseppi Giovanni Boito), Feb. 24, 1842 (Padua, It.)– June 10, 1918. Italian librettist, composer, critic. Wrote libretti for several famous operas of VERDI; as a critic, favored reform of Italian opera, 1860s. *Mefistofele*, 1875. Libretti: *La Giaconda*, 1876; *Simon Boccanegra*, 1881; *Otello*, 1887; *Falstaff*, 1893.

**BORODIN, ALEKSANDR,** Nov. 12, 1833 (St. Petersburg, Rus. [now Leningrad, USSR])–Feb. 27, 1887. Russian composer. A professional scientist and part-time musician, he became one of five influential figures in Russian nationalistic music for his three symphonies and the opera, *Prince Igor*.

**BOULANGER, NADIA,** Sept. 16, 1887 (Paris, Fr.)–Oct. 22, 1979. French music teacher/ conductor. As a teacher of composition, influenced a whole generation of musicians and composers, including PISTON, COPLAND and THOMSON. First woman to conduct Boston Symphony (1938) and N.Y. Philharmonic (1939).

**BOULEZ, PIERRE,** Mar. 26, 1925 (Montbrison, Fr.). French conductor, composer. Conductor of major orchs. worldwide; musical dir. of New York Phil., 1971–77; dir. of research inst. for techniques of modern music in Paris, 1977– . Works: *Sonatine*, 1946; *Structures, Book I*, 1952.

**BOULT, SIR ADRIAN,** Apr. 8, 1889 (Chester, Eng.)–Feb. 23, 1983. English conductor. Musical dir. and conductor of many orchestras, including Birmingham City Orch. (1924–30), the BBC Orch. (1930–42 and 1959–60), London Phil. (1950–57), and the Bach Choir (1928–33).

**BOURNONVILLE, AUGUSTE,** Aug. 21, 1805 (Copenhagen, Denmark)–Nov. 30, 1879. Danish dancer and choreographer. He became the leading dancer of the Royal Danish Ballet and director of its school in 1829; choreographed some 50 ballets during his career.

**BRAHMS, JOHANNES,** May 7, 1833 (Hamburg, Ger.)–Apr. 3, 1897. German composer. Prime exponent of the Romantic school of composition, in symphonies, chamber music, piano works, concerti, choral works, songs, lieder; protégé of R. SCHUMANN. Works: *A German Requiem*, 1868; Hungarian Dances, 1878–93; Violin Concerto in D Major, 1878; "Lullaby," 1868.

**BREAM, JULIAN,** July 15, 1933 (London, Eng.). British guitarist and lutenist. Leading authority on music of 16th–18th cents. for guitar and lute; has own Julian Bream Consort, a performing group; protégé of A. SEGOVIA.

**BRITTEN, (Edward) BENJAMIN,** Nov. 22, 1913 (Lowestoft, Eng.)–Dec. 4, 1976. English composer. Leading figure in mid-20th-cent. chromatic composition, especially opera and religious works. Operas: *Peter Grimes*, 1945; *Rape of Lucretia*, 1946; *Billy Budd*, 1951; *Turn of the Screw*, 1954; *Death in Venice*, 1973. Other works: *The Young Person's Guide to the Orchestra*, 1945; *Curlew River*, 1964; *The Prodigal Son*, 1968.

**BRUCKNER, (Josef) ANTON,** Sept. 4, 1824 (Ansfelden, Austria)–Oct. 11, 1896. Austrian Romantic composer. Noted for nine monumental symphonies and for sacred music; organist at Linz (1856) and Vienna (1868); disciple of R. WAGNER.

**BRUHN, ERIK** (born Belton Evers), Oct. 3, 1928 (Copenhagen, Den.). Danish dancer. Ballet dancer with Royal Danish Ballet (1947–55), ABT (1949, 1955–58, 1960–61, and 1968–69); noted for 19th-cent.-style roles; in recent years, has turned to character roles and modern dance (with JOSÉ LIMON Co.); choreographer for ABT, 1981–83; artistic director, National Ballet of Canada, 1983– .

**BÜLOW, BARON HANS, VON,** Jan 8, 1830 (Dresden, Ger.)–Feb. 12, 1894. German conductor. First modern virtuoso conductor; a champion of R. WAGNER, he conducted the first performances of *Meistersinger* (1868) and *Tristan und Isolde* (1862); first to conduct from memory.

**CABALLÉ, MONTSERRAT,** Apr. 12, 1933 (Barcelona, Sp.). Spanish operatic soprano. Leading bel canto soprano; repertoire also includes W. A. MOZART and R. STRAUSS; Met. Opera debut, 1965.

**CARUSO, ENRICO,** Feb. 25, 1873 (Naples, It.)–

Aug. 2, 1921. Italian operatic lyric tenor. Sang entire French and Italian repertoires; achieved fame singing Rodolfo in *La Bohéme*, in Milan; Covent Garden, 1903–07; Met. Opera Co., 1908–21; first operatic singer to appreciate the potential of phonograph recordings.

**CASADESUS, ROBERT,** Apr. 7, 1899 (Paris, Fr.)–Sept. 19, 1972. French concert pianist and composer. Popular concert artist, 1917–72; gave many concerts with wife Gaby and son Jean; chm. of piano dept. (1935) and dir.-gen. (from 1955) at American Conservatory, Paris; composed piano pieces, symphonies, orchestral suites.

**CASALS, PABLO,** Dec. 29, 1876 (Vendrell, Sp.) –Oct. 22, 1973. Spanish cellist, conductor. Noted for his virtuoso interpretations of J. S. BACH; formed trio with Alfred Corot and Jacques Thibaud, 1905; founded (1919) and conducted (1920) Orquesta Pau Casals, Barcelona; inaugurated annual festivals.

**CHALIAPIN, FYODOR,** Feb. 13, 1873 (Kazan, Russia)–Apr. 12, 1938. Russian operatic bass. With his powerful voice, gusto, and natural acting ability, considered one of opera's greatest performers. Dramatic roles: Boris in *Boris Godunov*; Philip II in *Don Carlos*; Mefistofele in *Faust*. Comic roles: Don Basilio in *Barber of Seville*; Leporello in *Don Giovanni*.

**CHOPIN, FREDERIC,** Mar. 1, 1810 (Zelazowa Wola, Pol.)–Oct. 17, 1849. Polish-French composer and pianist. Child prodigy; Vienna debut, 1829; Paris debut, 1832; London debut, 1837; piano compositions include concertos, sonatas, nocturnes, études, mazurkas, polonaises, waltzes.

**CORELLI, FRANCO,** Apr. 8, 1921 (Ancona, Italy). Italian operatic tenor. Specializes in heroic tenor roles, especially of R. WAGNER; debut, Spoleto, 1951; N.Y. Metropolitan Opera debut, 1961.

**DANILOVA, ALEXANDRA,** ? (Peterhof, Russia). Russian ballerina and choreographer. A member of the Russian State Ballet and the Diaghileff Ballet, she came to the U.S. in 1934; an international star ballet dancer, now teaches at the School of American Ballet.

**DAVIDOVSKY, MARIO,** Mar. 4, 1934 (Buenos Aires, Argentina). Argentine composer. The director of the Electronic Music Center at Princeton and Columbia Universities; has composed chamber music, orchestral works, and works for electronic music; won the Pulitzer Prize in music for his "Synchronisms N. 6", in 1971.

**DEBUSSY, CLAUDE,** Aug. 22, 1862 (St. Germain-en-Laye, Fr.)–Mar. 25, 1918. French Romantic composer. Works: "Prélude à L'Aprèsmidi d'un Faune," 1894; "Clair de lune," 1890–1905; "La Mer," 1905; *Pelléas et Mélisande* (opera), 1902; "Jeux," 1912.

**DE LARROCHA, ALICIA,** May 23, 1923 (Barcelona, Sp.). Spanish concert pianist. Child prodigy who debuted in 1927; known for her interpretation of F. CHOPIN.

**DELIBES, C. P. LÉO,** Feb. 21, 1836 (St.-Germain-du-Val, Fr.)–Jan. 16, 1891. French composer. Known for his operettas, operas, and ballets, including

*Coppelia* (1870) and *Lakme* (1883); accompanist at the Theatre Lyrique (1853) and the Paris Opera (1863); prof. of composition at the Conservatoire, 1881.

DELIUS, FREDERICK, Jan. 29, 1862 (Bradford, Eng.)–June 10, 1934. English composer. Involved in late-19th-cent. revival of English music. Works: *Koanga* (opera), 1904; *Village Romeo and Juliet* (opera), 1907; "Over the Hills and Far Away" (tone poem), 1895.

DE LUCA, GIUSEPPE, Dec. 25, 1876 (Rome, It.)–Aug. 26, 1950. Italian operatic baritone. Best known for his performances in MOZART and VERDI operas; La Scala debut, 1903; sang with Metropolitan Opera, 1915–41.

DE VALOIS, NINETTE (born Edris Stannus), June 6, 1898 (Baltiboys, Ire.). British dancer, choreographer, ballet director. Dancer with Ballets Russes, 1923–25; dir. of ballet at Abbey Theatre, Dublin, 1928–31; dir. of Vic-Wells Ballet, 1931–63 (later Sadler's Wells and Royal Ballet); founder and dir. of Sadler's Wells Ballet School (now Royal Ballet School), 1931.

DIAGHILEV, SERGEI, Mar. 19, 1872 (Novgorod Prov., Russia)–Aug. 19, 1929. Russian ballet, art, music impresario. Artistic dir. of Maryinsky Theatre, 1899–1901; formed Ballets Russes, 1911–29; in producing such innovative ballets as STRAVINSKY's *The Firebird* (1910) and *The Rite of Spring* (1913), revitalized ballet in Western Europe.

DOMINGO, PLACIDO, Jan. 21, 1941 (Madrid, Sp.). Spanish operatic tenor, conductor. Made his U.S. debut, 1961; internationally renowned for his interpretations of VERDI and PUCCINI roles and French and Italian verisimo operas; debuted as conductor, 1973.

DONIZETTI, GAETANO, Nov. 29, 1797 (Bergamo, It.)–Apr. 8, 1848. Italian composer. Composed over 65 operas; gained internatl. fame with *Anna Bolena*, 1830; romantic operas include *L'Elisir d'Amore* (1832), *Lucrezia Borgia* (1833), *Lucia di Lammermoor* (1835); comic operas include *La Fille du Regiment* (1840) and *Don Pasquale* (1843).

DOWELL, ANTHONY, Feb. 16, 1943 (London, Eng.). British ballet dancer. The principal dancer with the Royal Ballet since 1966; became its artistic director, 1986; holds the title of Commander of the Order of the British Empire.

DUKAS, PAUL, Oct. 1, 1865 (Paris, Fr.)–May 17, 1935. French composer. Known for his dramatic and program music, as well as his piano compositions; most popular work: *The Sorcerer's Apprentice*, 1897.

DVOŘÁK, ANTONIN, Sept. 18, 1841 (Nelahozeves, Bohemia)–May 1, 1904. Czech composer. His 19th-cent. Romantic music was influenced by Czech folk songs; wrote chamber music, symphonies, and concertos; dir. of Natl. Conservatory of Music, New York City, 1892–95. Works: Slavonic Dances, 1878; *Symphony No. 9 (from the New World)*, 1893.

ELGAR, SIR EDWARD, June 2, 1857 (Broadheath, Eng.)–Feb. 23, 1934. English composer. Known for his orchestral works. Works: *Enigma*

*Variations*, 1896; *Dream of Gerontius*, 1900; *Pomp and Circumstance* marches, 1901–30.

ELSSLER, FANNY, June 23, 1810 (near Vienna, Austria)–Nov. 27, 1884. Austrian ballerina. Appointed to the corps de ballet of the Vienna Hoftheater when she was but 12 years old; toured the world; excelled in folk dances adapted to ballet.

FALLA, MANUEL DE, Nov. 23, 1876 (Cadiz, Sp.)–Nov. 14, 1946. Spanish composer. Incorporated Spanish folk themes in his music; organized festival of traditional folk songs of southern Spain, 1922; Works: *La Vida Breve* (opera), 1905; *The Three-Cornered Hat* (ballet), 1919.

FAURÉ, GABRIEL, May 12, 1845 (Pamiers, Fr.)–Nov. 4, 1924. French composer. Prof. of composition (1896) and dir. (1905–20) at Paris Conservatory; best known for his *Masse de Requiem*, 1887; wrote over 100 songs, plus piano works, incidental music, and chamber music.

FISCHER-DIESKAU, DIETRICH, May 28, 1925 (Berlin, Ger.). German operatic baritone. Made his debut, 1948; has sung in all major international opera houses; repertoire includes *Don Giovanni, Macbeth, Wozzeck, Almaviva*; noted as a singer of German lieder.

FLAGSTAD, KIRSTEN, July 12, 1895 (Hamar, Nor.)–Dec. 7, 1962. Norwegian operatic soprano. Best known for her roles in Wagnerian operas, especially as Brünnhilde; debut, 1913; Met. Opera debut, 1935; Covent Garden debut, 1936; first dir. of Royal Norwegian Opera, 1958–60.

FOKINE, MICHEL (born Mikhail Mikhaylovich Fokine), Apr. 26, 1880 (St. Petersburg, Rus. [now Leningrad, USSR])–Aug. 22, 1942. Russian-U.S. dancer, choreographer. Influenced the development of modern dance by incorporating mime, music, scenery, and costume into dance; choreographed *The Dying Swan* for ANNA PAVLOVA, 1905; chief choreographer for Ballets Russes, creating *The Firebird* (1910), and *Petrushka* (1911).

FONTEYN, MARGOT (born Margaret Hookham), May 18, 1919 (Reigate, Eng.). English prima ballerina. Has danced all standard classical roles; made debut in *Nutcracker* at Vic-Wells Ballet, 1934; pres. of Royal Acad. of Dancing, from 1954; received *Dance Magazine* Award, 1962. Autobiography: *Margot Fonteyn: An Autobiography*, 1975.

FRACCI, CARLA, Aug. 20, 1936 (Milan, It.). Italian prima ballerina. Best known for her interpretations of romantic roles; with La Scala Ballet, from 1954; principal dancer with ABT, 1967–

FRANCA, CELIA, June 25, 1921 (London, Eng.). English ballet dancer, director, choreographer. Debut, 1936; danced with numerous cos., 1936–59; founder and artistic dir. of Natl. Ballet of Canada, 1951–74; cofounder of Natl. Ballet School, Toronto, 1959.

FRANCK, CÉSAR, Dec. 10, 1822 (Liège, Belg.)–Nov. 8, 1890. French Romantic composer, organist. Organist at St. Clotilde's Church, Paris, from 1858; teacher at Paris Conservatoire, from 1872; known for his Symphony in D Minor, (1886–88).

FURTWÄNGLER, WILHELM, Jan. 25, 1886 (Berlin, Germany)–Nov. 30, 1954. German conductor and composer. Conducted orchestras all over Europe and the United States; permanent conductor of the Berlin Philharmonic Orchestra, 1922–34; renowned for his interpretations of Beethoven, Brahms, and Bruckner, but also promoted modern music.

**GALWAY, JAMES,** Dec. 8, 1939 (Belfast, Ire.). Irish virtuoso flutist. Internationally acclaimed flutist; a member of orchs. all over Europe; principal flutist with Berlin Phil., 1969–75; soloist, from 1975; published *An Autobiography*, 1979.

**GEDDA, NIKOLAI** (born Nikolai Ustinov), July 11, 1925 (Stockholm, Swe.). Swedish operatic tenor. With Paris Opera, Covent Garden (1954), Salzberg, Met. Opera (1957); fluent in six languages; performs works by VERDI, PUCCINI, HAYDN, WAGNER, and others.

**GILELS, EMIL,** Oct. 19, 1916 (Odessa, Russia) –Oct. 14, 1985. Soviet concert pianist. Began his first concert tour in 1945; professor of piano at the Moscow Conservatory, from 1954.

**GLAZUNOV, ALEKSANDR,** Aug. 10, 1865 (St. Petersburg, Rus. [now Leningrad, USSR])–Mar. 21, 1936. Russian composer. Wrote eight symphonies, the symphonic poem "Stenka Razin," the ballets *Raymonda* and *Les Saisons*, as well as concerti; dir. of St. Petersburg Conservatory, 1905–28.

**GLINKA, MIKHAIL,** June 1, 1804 (Novospasskoye, Russia)–Feb. 15, 1857. Russian composer. Founder, Russian National School. Operas: *Life for the Tsar*, 1836; *Ruslan and Ludmila*, 1842.

**GLUCK, CHRISTOPH,** July 2, 1714 (Erasbach, Ger.)–Nov. 15, 1787. German composer. Best known for his operas based on simplicity, including *Orfeo ed Eurydice* (1762), *Alceste* (1767), and *Paride ed Elena* (1770).

**GOBBI, TITO,** Oct. 24, 1915 (Bassano del Grappa, It.)–Mar. 5, 1984. Italian operatic baritone. Made debut, 1937; has appeared throughout the world in all major opera houses; known for his roles in VERDI and PUCCINI operas, especially as Scarpia in *Tosca*.

**GOULD, GLENN,** Sept. 25, 1932 (Toronto, Can.) –Oct. 4, 1982. Canadian concert pianist. Debuted with Toronto Symphony at age 15; known for his interpretations of J.S. BACH and Romantic composers.

**GOUNOD, CHARLES,** June 17, 1818 (Paris, Fr.)–Oct. 18, 1893. French composer. Best known for his operas, including *Faust* (1859) and *Romeo and Juliette* (1867); composed a large amount of sacred music; awarded Prix de Rome, 1839.

**GRIEG, EDVARD,** June 15, 1843 (Bergen, Nor.) –Sept. 4, 1907. Norwegian composer. Founder of Norwegian natl. school; music rooted in Norwegian folk tradition; composed songs, piano, choral and orchestral works; best known for his *Peer Gynt* Suites.

**HAITINK, BERNARD,** Mar. 4, 1929 (Amsterdam, the Netherlands). Dutch symphonic and operatic conductor. The premier conductor of the Concertgebouw Orchestra of Amsterdam, 1964–1988, and the London Philharmonic Orchestra, 1967-1979;

music director of the Royal Opera, Covent Garden, London, 1987– .

**HANDEL, GEORGE,** Feb. 23, 1685 (Halle, Ger.)– Apr. 14, 1759. British composer. Known for operas, oratorios, instrumental music; music dir. to the Elector of Hanover (later King George I of England), 1710. Works: "Acis and Galatea," 1731; "Coronation Anthems," 1727; *Messiah*, 1741; "Water Music," 1740; "Royal Fireworks Music," 1749.

**HARNONCOURT, NIKOLAUS,** Dec. 6, 1929 (Berlin, Ger.). Austrian symphonic conductor. Has led orchestras all over the world; president, the Mozarteum Institute of Musicology and the University of Salzburg, Austria, 1972– .

**HAYDEN, MELISSA** (born Mildred Herman), Apr. 25, 1923 (Toronto, Can.). Canadian dancer. Danced with Ballet Theatre (1946–55) and N.Y.C. Ballet (1949–53; as principal dancer, 1953–73).

**HAYDN, (Franz) JOSEPH,** Mar. 31, 1732 (Rohrau, Austria)–May 31, 1809. Austrian composer. Worked under the patronage of the Esterhazy family, 1761–90; composed masses, chamber music, symphonies, operas, keyboard music; famous oratorios include *The Creation* (1789) and *The Seasons* (1801).

**HESS, DAME MYRA,** Feb. 25, 1890 (London, Eng.)–Nov. 25, 1965. British concert pianist. Best known for her work in chamber music; interpreted BACH, MOZART, BEETHOVEN, and SCHUMANN; named Dame Commander of the British Empire, 1941.

**HOGWOOD, CHRISTOPHER,** Sept. 10, 1941 (Nottingham, Eng.). English conductor, harpsichordist. Noted for "authentic" performances with original instruments, including complete recording of Mozart symphonies; founded Academy of Ancient Music, 1973.

**HOLST, GUSTAV,** Sept. 21, 1874 (Cheltenham, Eng.)–May 25, 1934. English composer, music teacher. Known for Oriental and mystical themes, most popular work is "The Planets" (orchestral suite), 1914–16.

**HONEGGER, ARTUR,** Mar. 10, 1892, (Le Havre, Fr.)–Nov. 27, 1955. French composer. Advocate of polytonality; one of "Les Six" Parisian composers; operas include *Le Roi David* (1921), *Judith* (1926), and *Antigone* (1927); orchestral works include *Pacific 231*, 1924.

**HUMPERDINCK, ENGELBERT,** Sept. 1, 1854 (Sieberg, Ger.)–Sept. 27, 1921. German composer best known for his opera *Hansel und Gretel* (1893).

**ITURBI, JOSÉ,** Nov. 28, 1895 (Valencia, Sp.)– June 28, 1980. Spanish-U.S. conductor, pianist. Conductor of musicals and films; many internatl. piano tours; conducted Rochester Philharmonic, 1936–44.

**JANÁČEK, LEOŠ,** July 3, 1854 (Hukvaldy, Moravia [now Czech.])–Aug. 12, 1928. Czech composer. His music was influenced by Czech folk music; best known for his opera *Jenufa*, 1904.

**JOOSS, KURT,** Jan. 12, 1901 (Wasseralfingen, Ger.)–May 22, 1979. German-British dancer, teacher, choreographer, ballet director. First interl. choreographer to combine classical and modern dance; founder and dir. of Ballets Jooss, 1933–67.

**KARAJAN, HERBERT VON,** Apr. 5, 1908 (Salzburg, Austria)–July 16, 1989. Austrian orchestral and operatic conductor. With Berlin State Opera, 1938–45; dir. and conductor of Vienna State Opera, 1945–64; musical dir. of Berlin Phil., 1954– .

**KHACHATURIAN, ARAM,** June 6, 1903 (Tiflis, Rus. [now USSR])–May 1, 1978. Soviet composer. Uses themes based on Armenian folk music; named People's Artist of the Soviet Union, 1954; known for the "Saber Dance" from the ballet *Gayne*. Other works: "Masquerade Suite," 1944; *Spartacus* (ballet), 1953.

**KLEMPERER, OTTO,** May 14, 1885 (Breslau, Ger. [now Wroclaw, Pol.])–July 6, 1973. German conductor with German Natl. Theatre, Prague, 1907; with Los Angeles Phil., 1933–39; with Budapest Opera, 1947–50; known for his interpretations of BEETHOVEN and MAHLER.

**KODÁLY, ZOLTÁN,** Dec. 16, 1882 (Kecskemet, Hung.)–Mar. 6, 1967. Hungarian composer. Theory and composition teacher at Budapest U., 1907–41; published collections of Magyar folk songs with BELA BARTOK, 1906–1921; style derived from Hungarian folk music. Works: *Psalmus Hungaricus*, 1923; *Hary Janos* (comic opera), 1926.

**KREISLER, FRITZ,** Feb. 2, 1875 (Vienna, Austria) –Jan. 29, 1962. Austrian-U.S. violin virtuoso. His technique capitalized on intensive vibrato and bow economy.

**KUBELIK, RAFAEL,** June 29, 1914 (Bychory, Czech.). Czech-Swiss conductor, composer. With Czech. Phil., 1936–39 and 1941–48; music dir. of Chicago Symphony, 1950–53; music dir. of Covent Garden Opera Co., 1955–58; conductor, Bavarian Radio Symphony, 1961– .

**LALO, EDOUARD,** Jan. 27, 1823 (Lille, Fr.)–Apr. 22, 1892. French composer. Composed impressionist-style music. Works: *Symphonie espagnole*, 1875; Cello Concerto, 1876; *Namouna* (ballet), 1882; Symphony in G Minor, 1887; *Le Roi d'Ys* (opera), 1888.

**LANDOWSKA, WANDA,** July 5, 1879 (Warsaw, Pol.)–Aug. 16, 1959. French harpsichordist. Researched old music and keyboard instruments; founded a school of early-music interpretation, 1925; influenced the modern revival of interest in the harpsichord; known for her recording of BACH's "Well-Tempered Clavier."

**LASSUS, ORLANDE DE** (born Roland de Lassus), 1532 ? (Mons, now Belgium)–June 14, 1594. Flemish composer. Wrote about 500 motets for chorus, plus light-hearted songs; he became the music director for the Duke of Bavaria in Munich, Germany, 1556.

**LEHÁR, FRANZ,** Apr. 30, 1870 (Kemárom, Hung.) –Oct. 24, 1948. Hungarian composer. Best known for his operetta *The Merry Widow* (1905).

**LEHMANN, LILLI,** Nov. 24, 1848 (Wurzburg, Ger.)–May 17, 1929. German operatic soprano, lieder singer. Known for her performances in *Tristan und Isolde* and *Fidelio*; coached by WAGNER for

debut of *Der Ring des Nibelungen*, repertoire included 170 operatic roles and 600 lieder, mostly by Wagner and MOZART.

**LEONCAVALLO, RUGGIERO,** Mar. 8, 1858 (Naples, It.)–Aug. 9, 1919. Italian opera composer, librettist. Reacted against Wagnerian and Romantic Italian opera; best known for *Pagliacci* (1892).

**LIND, JENNY** (born Johanna Maria Lind), Oct. 6, 1820 (Stockholm, Swed.)–Nov. 2, 1887. Anglo-Swedish operatic and oratorio soprano. Known for her vocal purity and control; made debut in Stockholm, 1838; many internatl. concert and stage tours.

**LISZT, FRANZ,** Oct. 22, 1811 (Raiding, Hung.)–July 31, 1886. Hungarian piano virtuoso, composer. Advanced playing techniques and methods of composition for the piano; dir. of music at the Weimar Court, Germany, 1843–61; over 700 compositions, including Préludes (1856) and 200 Hungarian Rhapsodies (1851–86).

**LLOYD WEBBER, ANDREW,** Mar. 22, 1948 (London, Eng.). British composer. His musicals for the stage have brought him international fame and fabulous wealth. *Joseph and His Amazing Technicolor Dreamcoat*, 1968; *Jesus Christ Superstar*, 1976; *Cats*, 1981; *Requiem*, 1984; *Starlight Express*, 1984; *Phantom of the Opera*, 1986.

**LUDWIG, CHRISTA,** Mar. 16, 1928 (Berlin, Ger.). German operatic mezzo-soprano. Known for her lieder singing; sang with N.Y. Met., 1966–71 and 1973–74; resident member, Staatsoper, Vienna, 1958– ; repertoire includes *Norma, Lohengrin, Fidelio,* and *Cosi fan Tutti.*

**LULLY, JEAN-BAPTISTE,** Nov. 28, 1632 (Florence, It.)–Mar. 22, 1687. French composer. Court composer to LOUIS XIV; introduced minuet form to ballet. Works: *Au Clair de la Lune; Alceste* (opera), 1674.

**MACKENZIE, SIR ALEXANDER,** Aug. 22, 1847 (Edinburgh, Scot.)–Apr. 28, 1935. Scottish composer. Helped to revive British music in late 19th-cent.; works include *Scottish Rhapsodies,* cantatas ("The Bride") and operas (*Colomba*). Knighted, 1894.

**MACKERRAS, CHARLES,** Nov. 17, 1925 (Schenectady, N.Y.). Australian symphonic and operatic conductor. Musical director, English National Opera, 1949–1953; musical director, BBC Concert Orchestra, 1954–1956; knighted in 1979; musical director, Welsh National Opera, 1986– .

**MACMILLAN, KENNETH,** Dec. 11, 1929 (Dumfermline, Scotland). British choreographer and ballet director. A founding member and dancer with Sadler's Wells Theatre Ballet in London; the principal choreographer of the Royal Ballet, 1977– ; knighted in 1983.

**MAHLER, GUSTAV,** July 7, 1860 (Kaliště, A.-H.)–May 18, 1911. Austrian composer, conductor. Dir. of Imperial Opera, Vienna, 1897–1907; dir. of Met. Opera, 1907; conductor of N.Y. Phil. Orch., 1909; major works include 10 symphonies, 44 lieder, various song cycles; known for complex

Romantic symphonies employing enormous numbers of musicians and singers.

**MANTOVANI, ANNUNZIO,** Nov. 15, 1905 (Venice, It.)–Mar 29, 1980. Anglo-Italian conductor. Famous for the "Mantovani sound," harmonious orchestral arrangements of classics, light classics, and pop music that make good background music, from 1923.

**MARKOVA, ALICIA** (born Lilian Alicia Marks), Dec. 1, 1910 (London, Eng.). English ballerina. Made debut in DIAGHILEV Ballet at age 14; with Vic-Wells Ballet, 1931–35; dir. (with Anton Dolin) of Markova-Dolin Ballet, 1935–38; dir. of London's Festival Ballet, 1949–52; dir. of Met. Ballet, 1963–69; known for her outstanding performances as Giselle.

**MASCAGNI, PIETRO,** Dec. 7, 1863 (Livorno, It.)–Aug. 2, 1945. Italian composer. In the "Verismo" school; best known for his one-act opera *Cavalleria Rusticana* (1890).

**MASSENET, JULES,** May 12, 1842 (Montaud, Fr.)–Aug. 13, 1912. French composer. Prof. of music at Paris Conservatorie, 1878–1912; composed orchestral and piano music; operas include *Manon* (1884) and *Thaïs* (1894); won 1863 Prix de Rome for his cantata "David Rizzio."

**MASSINE, LEONIDE,** Aug. 8, 1896 (Moscow, Russia)–Mar. 16, 1979. Russian-U.S. dancer, choreographer. Principal dancer, choreographer, Ballet Russe de Monte Carlo, 1932–38; choreographed "Le Sacre du Printemps," "Le Roi David"; danced in and choreographed the films *The Red Shoes* (1948) and *Tales of Hoffmann* (1951).

**MASUR, KURT,** July 18, 1927 (Brieg, Silesia). German conductor. Widely admired for his work with European romantic music; music dir., Leipzig Gewandhaus Orch., 1970–  ; named to succeed ZUBIN MEHTA, beg. in 1992, as music dir., New York Philharmonic, 1990.

**MEHTA, ZUBIN,** Apr. 29, 1936 (Bombay, India). Indian conductor. Musical dir. of Montreal Symphony, 1961–67; music dir. of Los Angeles Phil., 1962–78; music dir. of New York Phil., Israeli Philharmonic, and Covent Garden, 1977–  .

**MELBA, NELLIE** (born Helen Porter Mitchell), May 19, 1861 (Richmond, Austl.)–Feb. 23, 1931. Australian operatic soprano. Made debut, 1887; repertoire included 25 roles; best known for her roles in *Lakmé, Faust,* and *La Traviata*; famous for her pure tone and effortlessness in singing.

**MENDELSSOHN** (-Bartholdy), **FELIX,** Feb. 3, 1809 (Hamburg, Ger.)–Nov. 4, 1847. German composer, pianist. Founder of Leipzig Conservatory of Music, 1843; Works: Overture to *A Midsummer Night's Dream*, 1826; five symphonies; String Octet, 1826; eight books of "Songs without Words."

**MENOTTI, GIAN CARLO,** July 7, 1911 (Cadegliano, It.). Italian composer, librettist, producer. Work includes chamber music, songs, operas (*The Consul, The Saint of Bleecker Street, Amahl and the Night Visitors*); established Festival of Two Worlds (Spoleto, It.), 1958; won 1950 and 1954 Pulitzer Prize in music and 1954 New York Drama Critics Circle award.

**MENUHIN, YEHUDI,** Apr. 22, 1916 (New York, N.Y.). British violin virtuoso. A child prodigy, he performed Mendelssohn *Violin Concerto* at age seven; has made many international concert tours, often with sister, Hephzibah Menuhin, pianist; dir., Bath Festival (now Menuhin Festival), 1959–68.

**MEYERBEER, GIACOMO** (born Jakob Liebmann Meyer Beer), Sept. 5, 1791 (Tasdorf, Ger.)–May 2, 1864. German opera composer. Known for spectacular "grand opera" dramatic style. Works: *Robert le Diable,* 1831; *Les Huguenots,* 1836; *L'Africaine,* 1864.

**MITROPOULOS, DMITRI,** Feb. 18, 1896 (Athens, Greece)–Nov. 2, 1960. Greek symphonic and operatic conductor. Chief conductor of the Minneapolis Symphony, 1937–49; principal conductor, New York Philharmonic, 1949–1958.

**MOISEYEV, IGOR,** Jan. 21, 1906 (Kiev, Ukraine). Soviet ballet dancer, choreographer, director. Dancer, Bolshoi Ballet, 1924–39; dir. of choreography, Moscow Theater for Folk Art, 1936; created State Folk Dance Ensemble, the first Soviet folk dance ensemble, 1937.

**MONTEUX, PIERRE,** Apr. 4, 1875 (Paris, Fr.)–July 1, 1964. French conductor. As conductor of DIAGHILEV's Ballets Russes, led world premieres of STRAVINSKY's *The Rite of Spring* (1913) and RAVEL's *Daphnis et Chloé* (1912); founder and dir. of Paris Symphony, 1929–38; led San Francisco Symphony, 1936–52.

**MONTEVERDI, CLAUDIO,** baptized May 15, 1567 (Cremona, It.)–Nov. 29, 1643. Italian composer. Founder of Italian opera; developed orchestration; music dir. at St. Mark's Cathedral, Venice from 1613; works include madrigals, sacred music, and operas (*Favola d'Orfeo,* 1607; *L'incoronazione di Poppea,* 1642).

**MOUSSORGSKY, MODEST,** Mar. 21, 1839 (Karevo, Rus.)–Mar. 28, 1881. Russian composer. A founder of realistic natl. music in Russia; best known works include *Boris Godunov* (opera, 1874), *Pictures from an Exhibition* (piano suite, 1874), and *Night on Bald Mountain* (1872).

**MOZART, WOLFGANG AMADEUS,** Jan. 27, 1756 (Salzburg, Austria)–Dec. 5, 1791. Austrian composer. A child prodigy (violin), patronized by archbishop of Salzburg, 1775–81; chamber music composer to Emperor Joseph II, 1787; composed over 600 works, including chamber music, piano concerti, symphonies, operas (*The Marriage of Figaro* [1786], *Don Giovanni* [1787], *The Magic Flute* [1791]); one of the great musical geniuses of all time.

**MUNCH, CHARLES,** Sept. 26, 1891 (Strasbourg, Fr.)–Nov. 6, 1968. French conductor. Best known for his interpretations of BRAHMS, DEBUSSY, RAVEL; cofounder and conductor, Paris Philharmonic Orchestra, 1935–38; conductor, Boston Symphony Orch. (1949–62); director, Tanglewood Berkshire Music Center (1951–62); formed Orchestre de Paris, 1962.

**MUTI, RICCARDO,** July 28, 1941 (Naples, Italy). Italian symphonic conductor. Both a symphonic and operatic conductor; musical director of the Philadelphia Orchestra, (1981–   ) and the London Philharmonic Orchestra (1973–82); musical dir., La Scala, 1986–   .

**NIJINSKY, VASLAV,** Mar. 12, 1890 (Kiev, Rus.)– Apr. 8, 1950. Russian ballet dancer. Leading dancer with Maryinsky Theatre, 1907–11; with Ballets Russes, 1909–13; created roles in *Les Sylphides, Le Spectre de la Rose, Scheherazade*; choreographed *L'Après-midi d'un Faune* (1912) and *The Rite of Spring* (1913).

**NILSSON, BIRGIT,** May 17, 1918 (Karup, Swe.). Swedish operatic soprano. Made Met. Opera debut, 1959; known for roles in WAGNER and VERDI operas; repertoire includes Brunnhilde, Isolde, Salomé, Elektra, Turandot, Tosca, Lady Macbeth.

**NOVERRE, JEAN-GEORGES,** Apr. 29, 1727 (Paris, Fr.)–1810. French ballet dancer and choreographer. After making his ballet debut at the age of 16, he was named ballet master of the Opéra Comique in Paris at the age of 20; served as ballet master at the Paris Opéra, 1760–1767.

**NUREYEV, RUDOLF,** Mar. 18, 1938 (Irkutsk, Rus.). Soviet–British ballet dancer. Soloist with Leningrad Kirov Ballet, 1958; following his defection from USSR, made Paris and U.S. debut, 1962; permanent guest artist at Royal Ballet, London; known for suspended leaps and fast turns; roles include *Swan Lake, Giselle, Don Quixote,* and *Romeo and Juliet.*

**OFFENBACH, JACQUES** (born Jakob Eberst), June 20, 1819 (Cologne, Ger.)–Oct. 5, 1880. French composer. Wrote over 100 operettas; organized and directed the Bouffes-Parisiens, 1855–66; operettas included *Orpheus in the Underworld* (1859) and *La Perichole* (1868); only grand opera is *The Tales of Hoffmann,* unfinished at his death.

**OZAWA, SEIJI,** Sept. 1, 1935 (Hoten, Manchuria). Japanese conductor. Asst. conductor of New York Phil., 1961–62; music dir. of Ravinia Festival, 1964–69; conductor of Toronto Symphony Orch., 1965–69; music dir. of San Francisco Symphony Orch., 1970–76; music dir. of Boston Symphony Orch., 1973–   .

**PAGANINI, NICCOLO,** Oct. 27, 1782 (Genoa, It.)–May 27, 1840. Italian composer, violin virtuoso. Composed 24 Capricci for unaccompanied violin, 1801–07; European tours, 1828–32; known for brilliant violin technique, pizzicato, fingering, improvisation.

**PALESTRINA, GIOVANNI PIERLUIGI DA,** c.1525 (Palestrina, It.)–Feb. 2, 1594. Italian composer. Chapelmaster at St. John Lateran (1555–60) and St. Maria Maggiore (1561–71), Rome; composed three masses (1565), setting the standard for ecclesiastical music; works include over 100 masses and 250 motets, plus lamentations and litanies.

**PASTA, GIUDITTA,** Apr. 9, 1798 (Saronno, It.)– Apr. 1, 1865. Italian operatic soprano. Known for her large vocal range; BELLINI's *Norma* (1831) and DONIZETTI's *Anna Bolena* (1830) were written for her.

**PAVAROTTI, LUCIANO,** Oct. 12, 1935 (Modena, It.). Italian lyric tenor. The outstanding lyric tenor of his generation; made debut as Rodolfo (*La Bohème*), 1961; Met. Opera debut, 1968; roles included Edgardo (*Lucia di Lammermoor*) and the Duke (*Rigoletto*).

**PAVLOVA, ANNA,** Jan. 31, 1882 (St. Petersburg, Rus. [now Leningrad, USSR])–Jan. 23, 1931. Russian ballerina. With Maryinsky Theatre from 1899, as prima ballerina, 1906–13; with Ballets Russes tour, 1909; debut with Met. Opera, 1909; remembered for dancing in *The Dying Swan.*

**PETIPA, MARIUS,** Mar. 11, 1818 (Marseilles, Fr.) –July 14, 1910. French dancer, choreographer. Greatly influenced modern classical Russian ballet; choreographed over 60 ballets; collaborated with TCHAIKOVSKY on *The Nutcracker* (1892) and *Sleeping Beauty* (1889).

**PINZA, EZIO,** May 18, 1892 (Rome, It.)–May 9, 1957. Italian operatic bass. Made debut in Rome, 1921; with Met. Opera, 1926–48; many Broadway musicals (*South Pacific,* 1949), and films.

**PLISETSKAYA, MAYA,** Nov. 20, 1925 (Moscow, USSR). Soviet prima ballerina. Soloist with Bolshoi Ballet, from 1945; known for her fine technique; created the role of Carmen in *Carmen Suite,* 1967.

**POULENC, FRANCIS,** Jan. 7, 1899 (Paris, Fr.)– Jan. 30, 1963. French composer. Known for his sophisticated, comic style; sacred music includes *Mass in G Major,* 1937. Operas: *Les Mamelles de Tiresias,* 1947; *Dialogues of the Carmelites,* 1953–56.

**PROKOFIEV, SERGEI,** Apr. 23, 1891 (Sontsovka, Rus.)–Mar. 5, 1953. Soviet composer. Influenced the development of Soviet and modern music; works include collaborations on the film *Aleksandr Nevsky* (1938) and the ballets *Romeo and Juliet* (1935–36) and *Peter and the Wolf* (1936); numerous symphonies, piano concerti.

**PUCCINI, GIACOMO,** Dec. 22, 1858 (Lucca, It.)– Nov. 29, 1924. Italian opera composer. Works include *La Bohème,* (1896), *Tosca,* (1900), *Madama Butterfly* (1904), and *Turandot* (left unfinished at death).

**PURCELL, HENRY,** c.1659 (London, Eng.)–Nov. 21, 1695. English composer. Composer to King Charles II from 1677; Chapel Royal organist, from 1682; known for his works *Dido and Aeneas* (opera, 1689) and *The Fairy Queen,* and for his incidental music to *A Midsummer Night's Dream.*

**RACHMANINOFF, SERGEI,** Apr. 1, 1873 (Oneg. Rus.)–Mar. 28, 1943. Russian-U.S. piano virtuoso, composer. Composed in the Romantic style; works include three symphonies and four piano concerti, as well as chamber music and other piano works.

**RAMBERT, MARIE,** Feb. 20, 1888 (Warsaw, Pol.) –June 12, 1982. British dancer. After opening a ballet school in London in 1920, she formed the Ballet Club, later called Ballet Rambert, in 1926; made a Dame of the British Empire, 1962.

**RAMPAL, JEAN-PIERRE,** Jan. 7, 1922 (Marseilles, Fr.). French flutist. Has appeared internationally since 1945; founded French Wind Quintet (1945) and Paris Baroque ensemble (1953).

**RAVEL, MAURICE,** Mar. 7, 1875 (Ciboure, Fr.)–

Dec. 28, 1937. French composer. Known for impressionist style and form. Works: *Pavanne for a Dead Infanta*, 1899; *Daphnis et Chloé* (ballet), 1912; *Boléro*, 1928.

**RICHTER, SVYATOSLAV,** Mar. 20, 1915 (Zhitomir, Ukraine). Russian pianist. Stands in the front rank of modern pianists; gave his first recital at the age of 19, and made his American debut with the Chicago Symphony in 1960.

**RIMSKY-KORSAKOV, NIKOLAI,** Mar. 18, 1844 (Tikhvin, Rus.)–June 21, 1908. Russian composer, teacher, editor. Composed Romantic music. Operas: *The Snow Maiden*, 1882; *Sadko*, 1898; *Le Coq d'or*, 1909. Other works: *Scheherazade*, 1888; *Capriccio espagnol*, 1887; *Russian Easter Festival Overture*, 1888.

**ROSSINI, GIOACCHINO,** Feb. 29, 1792 (Pesaro, It.)–Nov. 13, 1868. Italian opera composer. Wrote 39 operas, including *The Barber of Seville* (1816), *The Siege of Corinth* (1826), and *William Tell* (1829).

**RUBINSTEIN, ANTON,** Nov. 28, 1829 (Podolia Prov., Russia [now in Moldavian SSR])–Nov. 20, 1894. Russian composer, pianist. Founder and dir. of St. Petersburg Conservatory of Music, 1862–67, 1887–1891; instituted the Rubinstein Prizes for piano playing and composition; works include symphonies, operas, oratorios, piano pieces.

**SAINT-SAËNS, (Charles) CAMILLE,** Oct. 9, 1835 (Paris, Fr.)–Dec. 16, 1921. French composer, pianist. Organist at Church of the Madelaine, Paris, 1857–77; helped to found Société Nationale de Musique, 1871. Works: five symphonies; *Samson et Dalila* (opera), 1877; *Carnival of the Animals* (concerti).

**SATIE, ERIK,** May 17, 1866 (Honfleur, Fr.)–July 1, 1925. French composer. Composed unconventional, witty music; influenced Les Six; composed chiefly piano works. Works. *Sarabandes*, 1887; *Gymnopédies*, 1888; *Socrate*, 1918; *Les Mariés de la tour Eiffel* (ballet), 1921.

**SCARLATTI, ALESSANDRO,** May 2, 1660 (Palermo, It.)–Oct. 24, 1725. Italian composer. Influenced the development of classical harmony; works include operas, sacred music, chamber music; wrote over 600 cantatas, 100 operas, 200 masses.

**SCARLATTI, (Giuseppe) DOMENICO,** Oct. 26, 1685 (Naples, It.)–July 23, 1757. Italian composer, harpsichordist. Noted for his keyboard sonatas (over 600) and, especially, his music which aided the technical and musical development of the harpsichord.

**SCHUBERT, FRANZ,** Jan. 31, 1797 (Himmelpfortyrund, [now Alsergrund] Austria)–Nov. 19, 1828. Austrian composer. Combined classical and Romantic styles; created German lieder in 1814, when he set J.W. GOETHE'S poem "Gretchen am Spinnrade" to music; works include lieder, song cycles, chamber music, symphonies, and piano music.

**SCHUMANN, ROBERT,** June 8, 1810 (Zwickau, Ger.)–July 29, 1856. German composer. Founder and editor of *Neue Zeitschrift für Musik*; dir. of music at Düsseldorf, 1850–53; known for piano music and song cycles (*Carnaval, Myrthen, Liederkreise* [1840]).

**SCHWARZKOPF, ELISABETH,** Dec. 9, 1915 (Jarotschin, Poland). German operatic soprano. Has sung at Vienna Staats Opera (1943–48), Covent Garden (1947–50), La Scala (1948–63), and N.Y. Metropolitan Opera (1964–66); roles include Manon, Violetta, Cio-Cio-San, Mimi, Donna Elvira; has made concert tours singing German lieder.

**SCOTTO, RENATA,** Feb. 24, 1933 (Savona, It.). Italian operatic soprano. At La Scala, from 1954; at Covent Garden, 1962; with Met. Opera, from 1965; repertoire includes *La Bohème, Manon, Don Giovanni*, and *Madama Butterfly*.

**SCRIABIN, ALEKSANDR,** Jan. 6, 1872 (Moscow, Rus.)–Apr. 27, 1915. Russian composer, pianist, teacher. Moscow Conservatory, 1898–1903; European concert tours, from 1892; works include piano and orchestral music; experimented with harmony.

**SEGOVIA, ANDRÉS,** Feb. 17, 1894 (Linares, Sp.)–June 2, 1987. Spanish classical-guitar virtuoso. Made debut in Granada, Sp., 1909; extensive international tours; has adapted for guitar the works of BACH, HAYDN, MOZART; awarded Spain's Gold Medal for meritorious work, 1967.

**SHEARER, MOIRA,** Jan. 17, 1926 (Dunfermline, Scot.). Scottish ballerina. With Sadler's-Wells Ballet, 1942; danced in films *The Red Shoes* (1948) and *Tales of Hoffmann* (1951); retired 1954.

**SHOSTAKOVICH, DIMITRI,** Sept. 25, 1906 (St. Petersburg, Rus. [now Leningrad, USSR])–Aug. 9, 1975. Soviet composer. Compositions include 15 symphonies, chamber music, concerti, film scores; awarded numerous Stalin Prizes and Lenin Prizes.

**SIBELIUS, JEAN,** Dec. 8, 1865 (Hameenlinna, Fin.)–Sept. 20, 1957. Finnish composer. Principal creator of Finnish natl. music; known for seven symphonies, tone poems ("Tapiola" [1925] and "Finlandia" [1900]), orchestral suites ("The Swan of Tuonela" [1893]), violin music.

**SLEZAK, LEO,** Aug. 18, 1873 (Sumperk, Moravia [now Czech.])–June 1, 1946. Austrian operatic tenor. Sang with Vienna Staats Opera, 1901–26; made Covent Garden debut (1909) and Metropolitan Opera debut (1909–13); known for his Wagnerian roles.

**SMETANA, BEDŘICH,** Mar. 2, 1824 (Leitomischl, Bohemia [now Czech.])–May 12, 1884. Czech composer. Conductor with Natl. Theater, Prague, 1866–74; best known for his cycle of six symphonic poems (*My Country*) and his opera *The Bartered Bride*, (1866).

**SOLTI, SIR GEORG,** Oct. 21, 1912 (Budapest, Hung.). British conductor. With Budapest Opera House, 1933–39; with Munich Opera, 1952–60; music dir. of Covent Garden, 1961–71; with Chicago Symphony Orch., 1969–91; artistic dir. and conductor of London Phil., 1979–83.

**STRAUSS (The Younger), JOHANN** ("The Waltz

King"), Oct. 25, 1825 (Vienna, Austria)–June 3, 1899. Austrian composer. Combined father's band with his (1849) and toured Europe, Russia and England, to 1874; wrote 400–500 pieces, mostly dance music and several operas. Works: *The Blue Danube*, 1867; *Artist's Life*, 1867; *Tales from the Vienna Woods*, 1868; *Wine, Women and Song*, 1869; *Wiener Blut*, 1871; *Die Fledermaus*, 1874.

STRAUSS, RICHARD, June 11, 1864 (Munich, Ger.)–Sept. 8, 1949. German composer. Known chiefly for operas (*Der Rosenkavalier*, 1911; *Salomé*, 1905; *Elektra*, 1909; *Ariadne auf Naxos*, 1912) and tone poems ("Don Juan," 1889; "Thus Spake Zarathustra," 1896); pres. of Reichsmusikkammer (Nazi govt. music agency), 1933–35.

STRAVINSKY, IGOR, June 17, 1882 (Oranienbaum, Rus.)–Apr. 6, 1971. Russian composer. Best known for his ballets, including *The Firebird* (1910), *Petrouchka* (1911), and *The Rite of Spring* (1913); works also include chamber music, concerti, orchestral music.

SULLIVAN, SIR ARTHUR S(eymour), May 13, 1842 (London, Eng.)–Nov. 22, 1900. English composer, conductor. Most noted for collaboration with W. S. GILBERT (1871–1896), which produced enduringly popular satiric operas. Works: *Trial by Jury*, 1875; *H.M.S. Pinafore*, 1878; *The Pirates of Penzance*, 1880; *The Mikado*, 1885.

SUTHERLAND, DAME JOAN, Nov. 7, 1926 (Sydney, Austrl.). Australian coloratura soprano. Best known for heroine roles in BELLINI and DONIZETTI operas; repertoire includes *Lucia di Lammermoor, La Traviata, Julius Caesar, Norma, Tales of Hoffmann*; named Dame of the British Empire, 1979.

TAGLIONI, MARIE, Apr. 23, 1804 (Stockholm, Swe.)–Apr. 24, 1884. Swedish–Italian ballet dancer. Popularized dancing on pointe; bell-like skirt worn in *La Sylphide* (1832) became accepted uniform for classical dancers; initiated system of ballet examination at Paris Opéra.

TCHAIKOVSKY, PETER ILYICH, May 7, 1840 (Votkinsk, Rus.)–Nov. 6, 1893. Russian composer. Advocate of Western style of music composition with Slavic character; known for classical ballet scores, including *Sleeping Beauty* (1890), *Swan Lake* (1877), and *The Nutcracker* (1892); composed six symphonies, eleven operas (*Eugene Onegin*, 1879), and many orchestral works (*Marche Slav* [1876], *1812 Overture* [1880], *Capriccio Italien* [1880]).

TEBALDI, RENATA, Feb. 1, 1922 (Pesaro, It.). Italian lyric soprano. Made debut, 1944; at La Scala, 1946; made U.S. debut (San Francisco), 1950; with Met. Opera, 1955; repertoire includes *La Bohème, Madama Butterfly, Tosca*.

TE KANAWA, KIRI, Mar. 6, 1944 (Gisborne, New Zealand). British operatic soprano. Joined the Royal Opera House in London, 1971; appears regularly in all major European and American opera houses; became a British dame when she was decorated in 1983.

TELEMANN, GEORG PHILIPP, Mar. 14, 1681 (Magdeburg, Ger.)–June 25, 1767. German baroque composer. Music dir. at Frankfurt (1712–21) and Hamburg (1721–67); works include 40 operas and 600 overtures, as well as sacred music, vocal and instrumental music, and chamber music.

TETRAZZINI, LUISA, June 29, 1871 (Florence, It.)–Apr. 28, 1940. Italian operatic coloratura soprano. Made debut, 1890; at Covent Garden, 1907; at Met. Opera, 1911; after WW I, gave recitals and taught; the dish Chicken Tetrazzini is named after her.

TOSCANINI, ARTURO, Mar. 25, 1867 (Parma, It.)–Jan. 16, 1957. Italian conductor. Music dir. of La Scala, from 1898; conductor of New York Phil., 1928–36; dir. of NBC Symphony Orch., 1937–54; known for energetic interpretations of VERDI operas, BEETHOVEN symphonies, WAGNER's music; conducted from memory.

TUDOR, ANTONY, born William Cook, Apr. 4, 1909 (London, Eng.)–Apr. 19, 1987. English dancer, choreographer, teacher. Dir. and choreographer with Marie Rambert's Ballet Club, 1930–38; a founder of London Ballet, 1938; with ABT, 1939–87; known for the development of the psychological ballet.

ULANOVA, GALINA, Jan. 8, 1910 (St. Petersburg, Rus. [now Leningrad, USSR]). Russian prima ballerina. With Kirov Ballet, from 1934; with Bolshoi Ballet, 1944–62; presently ballet mistress and coach of Bolshoi Ballet; known for personality and warmth of dance in *Giselle, The Dying Swan, The Red Poppy*; author of *The Bolshoi Ballet Story* (1959).

VAUGHN WILLIAMS, RALPH, Oct. 12, 1872 (Down Ampney, Eng.)–Aug. 26, 1958. English composer. Founder of nationalist movement in English music; musical themes draw upon English folk songs of Tudor period. Works: *A London Symphony*, 1914; *A Pastoral Symphony*, 1922; Sixth Symphony, 1948.

VERDI, GIUSEPPE, Oct. 10, 1813 (Le Roncole, It.)–Jan. 27, 1901. Italian opera composer. Composed 27 operas, including *Nabucco* (1842), *Rigoletto* (1851), *Il Trovatore* (1853), *La Traviata* (1853), *Aida* (1872) *Otello* (1887), and *Falstaff* (1892); also known for his Requiem Mass (1874) and other sacred music.

VICKERS, JON, Oct. 29, 1926 (Prince Albert, Sask., Can.). Canadian operatic tenor. Made Covent Garden debut, 1957; Met. Opera debut, 1960; repertoire includes both lyrical and dramatic roles.

VILLA-LOBOS, HEITOR, Mar. 5, 1887 (Rio de Janeiro, Braz.)–Nov. 17, 1959. Brazilian composer, music educator. Proponent of Brazilian nationalism in music. Works: *Chôros*, 1920–29 (14 works), twelve symphonies, 1920–58.

VIVALDI, ANTONIO, Mar. 4, 1678 (Venice, It.) –July 28, 1741. Italian composer, violin virtuoso. Composed instrumental music of late baroque period; composed over 450 concerti for solo instruments accompanied by string orchestra; most famous work is *The Four Seasons*.

WAGNER, RICHARD, May 22, 1813 (Leipzig, Ger.)–Feb. 13, 1883. German opera composer. Opera themes derived from medieval legends; involved in German revolution of 1848; forced into exile in 1849. Operas: *The Flying Dutchman*, 1843; *Tannhäuser*, 1845; *Lohengrin*, 1848; *Der Ring des Nibelungen*, 1876; *Tristan und Isolde*, 1857; *Parsifal*, 1882.

**WALTER, BRUNO** (born B. W. Schlesinger), Sept. 15, 1876 (Berlin Ger.)–Feb. 17, 1962. German conductor. With Vienna Opera, 1901– 12; conducted premier of MAHLER's Ninth Symphony, 1912; with Met. Opera, from 1941; with New York Phil., 1947–49.

**WEBER, CARL MARIA VON,** Nov. 18, 1786 (Eutin, Ger.)–June 5, 1826. German composer. Founder of German natl. opera; works include compositions, chamber music, operas (*Euryanthe*, 1823; *Oberon*, 1826); dir. of Dresden Opera, 1817.

**WEBERN, ANTON VON,** Dec. 3, 1883 (Vienna, Austria)–Sept. 15, 1945. Austrian composer. Influenced 20th-cent. music by adopting the 12–tone system of composition of his teacher. A. SCHOEN-

BERG; his music was banned by Nazi regime.

**WEILL, KURT,** Mar. 2, 1900 (Dessau, Ger.)–Apr. 3, 1950. German composer. Wrote several of the most popular operas of the 20th-cent. and was a major force in the musical theater; husband of LOTTE LENYA, the legendary cabaret singer, he wrote much of his greatest music for her; a frequent collaborator with BERTOLT BRECHT. Works: *The Rise and Fall of the City of Mahagonny*, 1927; *Threepenny Opera*, 1928; *Knickerbocker Holiday*, 1938; *Lady in the Dark*, 1941; *One Touch of Venus*, 1943; *Street Scene*, 1947; *Lost in the Stars*, 1949.

**WOLF, HUGO,** Mar. 13, 1860 (Windischgraz, Austria)–Feb. 22, 1903. Austrian composer. A master of the *lied*; composed about 300 of these songs; many were music set to the poetry of JOHANN GOETHE, HEINRICH HEINE, HENRIK IBSEN, and MICHELANGELO.

# Philosophers and Religious Leaders

## U.S. PHILOSOPHERS AND RELIGIOUS LEADERS

**ADLER, FELIX,** Aug. 13, 1851 (Alzey, Ger.)– Apr. 24, 1933. U.S. educator, ethical reformer. Founded and lectured at the New York Society for Ethical Culture, 1876; professor of political and social ethics, Columbia U. 1902–33. *Creed and Deed*, 1877; *Life and Destiny*, 1905; *Religion of Duty*, 1905; *An Ethical Philosophy of Life*, 1918.

**ALCOTT, AMOS BRONSON,** Nov. 29, 1799 (Wolcott, Conn.)–Mar. 4, 1888. U.S. philosopher, teacher, reformer. A leader of the New England Transcendentalist group; started several innovative schools; founded Fruitlands, a cooperative Utopian community, 1844–45; directed the Concord School of Philosophy, 1879–88; a nonresident member of Brook Farm. *Conversations with Children on the Gospels* (2 vols., 1836–37). (Father of L. M. ALCOTT.)

**ASBURY, FRANCIS,** Aug. 20, 1745 (Handsworth, Staff., Eng.)–Mar. 31, 1816. U.S. bishop. His efforts did much to assure the continuance of the Methodist Episcopal Church in the new world; supt. of the church, 1784; bishop, 1785; church membership grew from 300 to over 200,000 at the time of his death.

**BAKKER, JAMES,** Jan. 2, 1940 (Muskegon, Mich.). U.S. evangelist. The leader of the power ful PTL ministry; admitted in 1987 that he had had sex with a young admirer in 1980, and resigned his post; he was convicted of fraud and conspiracy in connection with the misuse of PTL funds, and was sentenced to 45 years in prison, 1989.

**BLAKE, EUGENE CARSON,** Nov. 7, 1906 (St. Louis, Mo.)–July 31, 1985. U.S. Presbyterian churchman, ecumenical leader. Pres., National Council of the Churches of Christ in the U.S.A., 1954–57; general secy., World Council of Churches, 1966–72; pres., Bread for the World, 1974–78.

**BOYD, MALCOLM,** June 8, 1923 (Buffalo, N.Y.). U.S. Episcopal priest, author. Priest-activist involved in civil and gay rights; experimented with new ways of communicating the gospel through music and theater. *Are You Running with Me Jesus?*,

1965; *Free to Live, Free to Die*, 1967; *Gay Priest: An Inner Journey*, 1986.

**BREWSTER, WILLIAM,** 1567 (Nottinghamshire, Eng.)–Apr. 10, 1644. English lay elder. Sailed to America on the *Mayflower* (1620) and became the spiritual leader of the Plymouth Colony; heavily influenced the formulation of the colony's doctrines, worship, and practices.

**CABRINI, SAINT FRANCIS XAVIER,** ("Mother Cabrini"), July 15, 1850 (Sant' Angelo Lodigiano, It.)–Dec. 22, 1917. Italian-U.S. religious worker who founded the Missionary Sisters of the Sacred Heart, 1880; first U.S. citizen to be canonized, 1946.

**CARROLL, JOHN,** Jan. 8, 1735 (Upper Marlboro, Md.)–Dec. 3, 1815. U.S. clergyman. The first R.C. bishop in the U.S., 1789; founded Georgetown U., 1789; accompanied BENJAMIN FRANKLIN on a fruitless mission to persuade Canada to join the revolutionary cause; archbishop of Baltimore, 1808–15.

**COFFIN, WILLIAM SLOANE, JR.,** June 1, 1924 (New York, N.Y.). U.S. clergyman. A leader in the Vietnam War peace movement; chaplain, Yale U., 1958–76; pastor, Riverside Church (New York City), 1977–87.

**COHEN, MORRIS RAPHAEL,** July 25, 1880 (Minsk, Rus.)–Jan. 28, 1947. U.S. philosopher, author. Prof. of philosophy, C. of the City of New York, 1912–38; first U.S. philosopher to work extensively on legal philosophy; a major contributor to logic and the philosophy of science and history. *Reason and Nature*, 1931; *Law and the Social Order*, 1933; *Preface to Logic*, 1944; *The Faith of a Liberal*, 1945.

**COOKE, TERENCE JAMES,** Mar. 1, 1921 (New York, N.Y.)–Oct. 6, 1983. U.S. R.C. cardinal (from 1969). Archbishop of New York, from 1968; has distinguished himself in areas of finance, fundraising, and supervision of building programs.

**COTTON, JOHN,** Dec. 4, 1584 (Derby, Derbyshire, Eng.)–Dec. 23, 1652. English Puritan leader of the Massachusetts Bay Colony in America. Influenced the Congregational Church immensely and pushed it in a theocratic direction; responsible for the expulsion of ANNE HUTCHINSON (1637) and ROGER WILLIAMS (1635) from the colony. *Spiritual Milk for Babies*, 1645. (Grandfather of C. MATHER.)

**COUGHLIN, CHARLES E.,** Oct. 25, 1891 (Hamilton, Ont., Can.)–Oct. 27, 1979. U.S. R.C. priest. Gained prominence in 1930s through his radio addresses bitterly opposing administration of Pres. FRANKLIN D. ROOSEVELT, 1936; his magazine, *Social Justice* (1936–42), was banned from U.S. mails for violation of the Espionage Act.

**CUSHING, RICHARD J.,** Aug. 24, 1895 (Boston, Mass.)–Nov. 2, 1970. U.S. R.C. cardinal, from 1958. Archbishop of Boston, 1944–70; highly successful director of the Boston office of the Society for the Propagation of the Faith; was called "the most pervasive social force" in Boston in the late 1940s and early 1950s.

**DAVENPORT, JOHN,** baptized Apr. 9, 1597 (Coventry, Eng.)–Mar. 11, 1670. American colonial clergyman. Led the settlers of the colony of New Haven, 1638; served as pastor there, 1638–1668.

**DEWEY, JOHN,** Oct. 20, 1859 (Burlington, Vt.)–June 1, 1952. U.S. philosopher, educator. Adherent of pragmatism as formulated by WILLIAM JAMES; helped inaugurate the theories and practice of progressive education. *The School and Society*, 1899; *Democracy and Education*, 1916; *Experience and Nature*, 1925.

**DOUGLASS, TRUMAN B.,** July 15, 1901 (Grinnell, Ia.)–May 27, 1969. U.S. clergyman. A moving spirit in the unification of the Congregational, Evangelical, and Reformed denominations into the United Church of Christ, 1957; his early concern for blacks, problems of urban living, and ethics in mass communication profoundly affected modern Protestantism.

**DURANT, WILLIAM JAMES,** Nov. 5, 1885 (North Adams, Mass.)–Nov. 7, 1981. U.S. philosopher. Critic of popular philosophy and history; attempted to humanize knowledge by grounding the story of speculative thinking in the lives of great philosophers. *The Story of Philosophy*, 1926; *The Story of Civilization*, 11 vols. 1935–75 (last five volumes with wife Ariel.)

**EDDY, MARY BAKER,** July 16, 1821 (Bow, N.H.)–Dec. 3, 1910. U.S. religious leader, founder of the Christian Science movement. Attempting to relieve a chronic spinal malady, became interested in health; after a fall (1866) was healed by reading the New Testament (Matt. 9:1–8); developed a system of thought based on her experience and the Bible; organized first Christian Science Church, 1879; founded the *Christian Science Journal*, 1883; also *Christian Science Sentinel*, 1898; *Christian Science Monitor*, 1903; substituted a "lesson-sermon" for a sermon preached from the pulpit. *Science and Health*, 1875; *Retrospection and Introspection*, 1891.

**EDWARDS, JONATHAN,** Oct. 5, 1703 (East Windsor, Conn.)–Mar. 22, 1758. American colonial theologian, philosopher. The greatest theologian of American Puritanism; a leader of the Great Awakening of the 1740s; fought against the current theological stream of thought by emphasizing man's dependence on God, the role of love in religion, and the need for genuine faith in obtaining church membership. *History of the Work of Redemption*, 1737; *Freedom of the Will*, 1754; *Treatise on Religious Affections*, 1746. (Grandfather of A. BURR.)

**ELIOT, JOHN,** ("Apostle to the Indians"), Aug. 1604 (Widford, Herts., Eng.)–May 21, 1690. English Puritan missionary in colonial America. His translation of the Bible into the Algonquin language (1661–63) was the first Bible printed in North America; his work set a pattern for Indian missions for the next two centuries.

**ERHARD, WERNER,** Sept. 5, 1935 (Philadelphia, Pa.). U.S. cult leader. Founder of est training, which stresses the power of the human being to transform the quality of his or her life.

**FALWELL, JERRY L.,** Aug. 11, 1933 (Lynchburg, Va.). U.S. clergyman. Founder and pastor of Thomas Road Baptist Church, Lynchburg, Va., 1956– ; founder and pres. of Moral Majority (now called Liberty Foundation), 1979– .

**FARRAKHAN, LOUIS,** May 11, 1933 (New York, N.Y.). U.S. religious leader. U.S. muslim leader and a minister of the Nation of Islam; despite his anti-semitic rhetoric and controversial statements considered by many a strong leader and potential successor to MALCOLM X.

**FOSDICK, HARRY EMERSON,** May 24, 1878 (Buffalo, N.Y.)–Oct. 5, 1969. U.S. clergyman. Liberal Prot. minister who stood at the center of the Prot. liberal-fundamentalist controversies; pastor, Riverside Church (New York City) 1926–46; preached on the *National Vespers* nationwide radio program, 1926–46.

**GRAHAM, WILLIAM** ("Billy"), Nov. 17, 1918 (Charlotte, N.C.). U.S. clergyman. Southern Baptist evangelist who first came to national attention with his Los Angeles campaign, 1949; his continued success has created a large organization that he leads on preaching tours worldwide. *Revival in Our Times*, 1950; *The Seven Deadly Sins*, 1956; *Facing Death and The Life After*, 1987.

**HARRIS, WILLIAM TORREY,** Sept. 10, 1835 (North Killingly, Conn.)–Nov. 5, 1909. U.S. philosopher. Leading U.S. Hegelian; interpreter of German philosophical thought to America; editor of the *Journal of Speculative Philosophy*, 1867–93; U.S. commissioner of education, 1889–1906; editor-in-chief of *Webster's New Internatl. Dictionary*, first edition, 1909. *Introduction to the Study of Philosophy*, 1889; *Psychologic Foundation of Education*, 1898.

**HECK, BARBARA,** 1734 (Ballingrane, County Limerick, Ire.)–Aug. 17, 1804. Irish-American religious leader. Organized first Methodist church in America, in New York City, 1768; called the Mother of Methodism in the U.S.

**HESBURGH, THEODORE M.,** May 25, 1917 (Syracuse, N.Y.). U.S. educator, religious leader.

Ordained as R.C. priest, 1943; pres., Notre Dame U., 1952–87; under his chairmanship (1969–72), U.S. Commission on Civil Rights issued a report (1970) critical of the government's failure to enforce civil rights legislation. Awarded Presidential Medal of Freedom, 1964.

**HOCKING, WILLIAM E.,** Aug. 10, 1873 (Cleveland, Ohio)–June 12, 1966. U.S. philosopher. Prof. of philosophy, Harvard U., 1914–43; an idealist philosopher who attempted to discern speculative issues in the practical problems of living. *The Meaning of God in Human Expeience,* 1912; *The Spirit of World Politics,* 1932; *The Coming World Civilization,* 1956.

**HOFFER, ERIC,** July 25, 1902 (New York, N.Y.)– May 21, 1983. U.S. author, migrant worker, longshoreman, social philosopher. *The True Believer,* 1951; *The Passionate State of Mind,* 1955; *Reflections on the Human Condition,* 1972; *Truth Imagined,* 1983.

**HOOKER, THOMAS,** July 7, 1586 (Marfield, Leics., Eng.)–July 19, 1647. English clergyman. Founded Hartford, Conn., 1636; one of the drafters of the Fundamental Orders, the Constitution of Conn., one of the first documents of American democracy, 1639.

**HUBBARD, L. RON**(ald), Mar. 13, 1911 (Tilden, Neb.)–Jan. 24, 1986. U.S. religious leader, founder of Scientology. A science-ficton writer until 1950; formulated dianetics, a method of achieving mental and physical health, 1938; in the early 1950s, founded Scientology, a religious movement based on dianetics; withdrew from the directorship of the Church of Scientology, 1966. *Dianetics: The Modern Science of Mental Health,* 1950; *Battlefield Earth,* 1982.

**HUTCHINSON, ANNE,** baptized July 20, 1591 (Alford, Lincolnshire, Eng.)–Aug. or Sept. 1643. American colonial religious liberal. Banished from the Massachusetts Bay Colony for her religious views, which opposed those of the New England Puritans and Calvinists, 1637; emigrated with her family to Rhode Island; killed in an Indian massacre.

**JAMES, HENRY,** June 3, 1811 (Albany, N.Y.)– Dec. 18, 1882. U.S. theologian. Rebelled against Calvinism; influenced by SWEDENBORG and in social philosophy, by FOURIER. (Father of W. JAMES and novelist H. JAMES.) *Christianity: The Logic of Creation,* 1857.

**JAMES, WILLIAM,** Jan. 11, 1842 (New York, N.Y.)–Aug. 26, 1910. U.S. philosopher, psychologist. The first distinguished American psychologist and a leading philosopher of pragmatism; his functional psychology, experimental religious philosophy, and pragmatism function as an interrelated whole; his lively writing style spurred the influence and popularity of his ideas. *Principles of Psychology,* 1890; *The Varieties of Religious Experience,* 1902; *Pragmatism,* 1907; *Essays in Radical Empiricism,* 1912. (Son of theologian H. JAMES; brother of novelist H. JAMES.)

**KOHLER, KAUFMANN,** May 10, 1843 (Fürth, Bavaria, Ger.)–Jan. 28, 1926. U.S. rabbi. Leader of Reformed Judaism; pres., Hebrew Union C., 1903– 21; scholar and rabbi of Temple Beth-El (New York City), 1879–1903, elected hon. min. for life, 1903; an editor of *The Jewish Encyclopedia. Backwards or Forwards: Lectures on Reform Judaism,* 1885; *The Origins of the Synagogue and the Church,* 1929.

**KUHLMAN, KATHRYN,** 1910 ? (Concordia, Mo.) –Feb. 20, 1976. U.S. religious leader, faith healer. Preached the Holy Spirit's power to cure; set up an organization devoted to missionary churches, drug rehabilitation, and the education of blind children; used radio and TV programming. *I Believe in Miracles,* 1962.

**LAMY, JOHN BAPTIST** (born Jean Baptiste l'Amy), Oct. 11, 1814 (Lempdes, Puy de Dôme, Fr.)–Feb. 13, 1888. U.S. R.C. priest. Archbishop of southwestern U.S., 1875–85; established the first school to teach English in Santa Fe, N.M.; successfully extended the R.C. faith to the Indians and whites of the Southwest; the model for WILLA CATHER's protagonist in *Death Comes for the Archbishop.*

**LANGDON, WILLIAM CHAUNCEY,** Aug. 19, 1831 (Burlington, Vt.)–Oct. 28, 1895. U.S. Episcopal clergyman. One of the early organizers of the Young Men's Christian Association in the U.S.; active in the ecumenical movement.

**MARCUSE, HERBERT,** July 19, 1898 (Berlin, Ger.)–July 29, 1979. German-U.S. political philosopher. Fled Nazi Germany, 1933; his ideas, notably that modern American society was repressive, became popular with American student radicals in the 1960s; taught at Columbia, Harvard, Brandeis, and the U. of California. *Eros and Civilization,* 1958; *One-Dimensional Man,* 1964; *Counterrevolution and Revolt,* 1972.

**MARSHALL, PETER,** May 27, 1902 (Coatbridge, Scot.)–Jan. 25, 1949. U.S. Presbyterian clergyman. Chaplain to the U.S. Senate, 1947–49; known for his deft phraseology; subject of the book *A Man Called Peter* (by his wife, CATHERINE MARSHALL), as well as a film of the same name.

**MATHER, COTTON,** Feb. 12, 1663 (Boston, Mass.) –Feb. 24, 1728. American colonial clergyman. Pastor, Second Church of Boston, 1723–28; a prolific writer, helped establish New England as a cultural center; his interest in science led him to advocate inoculation for smallpox and the use of scientific evidence in witchcraft trials. *Magnalia Christi Americana,* 1702. (Son of I. MATHER, grandson of J. COTTON.)

**MATHER, INCREASE,** June 21, 1639 (Dorchester, Mass.)–Aug. 23, 1723. American colonial clergyman. Pastor of the Second Church of Boston, 1664–1723; pres. of Harvard C., 1685–1701; after Massachusetts' loss of its charter, obtained a new charter from King William, 1688; wrote the most outspoken and earliest public utterance in New England against the practices of the witchcraft— *Cases of Conscience Concerning Evil Spirits* (1693). (Father of C. MATHER.)

**MCPHERSON, AIMEE SEMPLE** (born A. Elizabeth Kennedy), Oct. 9, 1890 (Ingersoll, Ont., Can.)–

Sept. 27, 1944. U.S. religious leader. Best-known woman evangelist of her day. Itinerant revivalist, 1916–23; founded the International Church of the Foursquare Gospel and built the Angelus Temple in Los Angeles, serving as its minister, 1923–44.

MOODY, DWIGHT, Feb. 5, 1837 (East Northfield, Mass.)–Dec. 22, 1899. U.S. evangelist, popular urban revivalist. Worked for YMCA; with Ira Sankey, wrote hymns and led highly successful evangelist campaigns in Great Britain, 1873–75, 1881–84; founded in Chicago two secondary schools and the Bible Inst. for Home and Foreign Missions (1889).

MOTT, JOHN RALEIGH, May 25, 1865 (Livingston Manor, N.Y.)–Jan. 31, 1955. U.S. evangelist, Methodist layman. Student secy., International Committee of the YMCA, 1888–1915; organized World Missionary Conference, 1910; pres., World's Alliance of YMCAs, 1926–37; shared Nobel Peace Prize with EMILY G. BALCH, for his work in international church and missionary movements, 1946.

MUHAMMAD, ELIJAH (born Elijah Poole), Oct. 10, 1897 (nr. Sandersville, Ga.)–Feb. 25, 1975. U.S. black nationalist leader. An automobile assembly-line worker, became follower of Wali Farad, who had founded Temple of Islam in Detroit; upon Farad's disappearance (1934), took over leadership of movement, which became known as the Nation of Islam or the Black Muslims; calling himself the "Messenger of Allah," preached that only salvation for U.S. black people was withdrawal into an autonomous state.

MUHLENBERG, HEINRICH M., Sept. 6, 1711 (Einbeck, Hanover, Ger.)–Oct. 7, 1787. U.S. Lutheran clergyman, often called the patriarch of Lutheranism. Led all Lutheran groups in the colonies; organized first Lutheran synod in America, 1748; helped prepare a uniform liturgy, a hymnal, and an ecclesiastical constitution.

NEUMANN, SAINT JOHN NEPOMUCENE, Mar. 28, 1811 (Prachatice, Bohemia [now Czech.])–Jan. 5, 1860. U.S. R.C. bishop. As fourth bishop of Philadelphia, oversaw much building and an expansion of membership, 1852–60; helped establish the Sisters of the Third Order of St. Francis (1855); beatified, 1963; canonized, 1977.

NIEBUHR, REINHOLD, June 21, 1892 (Wright City, Mo.)–June 1, 1971. U.S. theologian, one of the most influential of the 20th-cent. Prof., Union Theological Seminary (New York City), 1928–60; a critic of theological liberalism; proposed a Christian Realism that recognized the persistence of evil and the egotism and pride of nations and other social groups; political activist. *The Nature and Destiny of Man*, 1941, *Moral Man and Immoral Society*, 1932.

O'CONNOR, JOHN JOSEPH, Jan. 15, 1920 (Philadelphia, PA.). U.S. Roman Catholic leader. Served for 27 years as a U.S. naval chaplain; ordained bishop, 1979; archbishop of New York City, 1984– ; opposed New York Gov. MARIO CUOMO on abortion issue.

O'HAIR, MADALYN MURRAY, Apr. 13, 1919 (Pittsburgh, Pa.). U.S. lawyer. Well-known atheist, the principal in the U.S. Supreme Court case (1963) that removed Bible reading and prayer recitation from public schools. Originated *American Atheist Magazine*, 1965; dir. of the American Atheist Center, 1965–73; pres. 1973–86; founder of the United World Atheists, 1970. *Why I Am an Atheist*, 1965.

OLCOTT, HENRY STEEL, Aug. 2, 1832 (Orange, N.J.)–Feb. 17, 1907. U.S. farmer, lawyer. A founder of the Theosophical Society, which he served as pres., 1875–1907. *A Buddhist Catechism*, 1881; *Theosophy, Religion and Occult Science*, 1885.

PAINE, THOMAS, Jan. 29, 1737 (Thetford, Norfolk, Eng.)–June 8, 1809. American colonial political philosopher, pamphleteer. His *Common Sense* (1776), advocating immediate independence from England, was widely considered the best argument for the cause; published *Crisis* (16 issues), upholding the colonial cause, 1776–83; in *Rights of Man* (1791, 1792), inspired by the French Revolution, proposed to end poverty, illiteracy, unemployment, and war; published *Age of Reason* (2 vols., 1794 and 1796), a philosophical discussion of his deist beliefs.

PEALE, NORMAN VINCENT, May 31, 1898 (Bowersville, Ohio). U.S. clergyman. Prominent religious author and radio preacher on the national program *The Art of Living*; minister, Marble Collegiate Reformed Church (New York City), 1932–84. *You Can Win*, 1939; *The Power of Positive Thinking*, 1952; awarded Presidential Medal of Freedom, 1984.

PEIRCE, CHARLES S., Sept. 10, 1839 (Cambridge, Mass.)–Apr. 19, 1914. U.S. philosopher, logician. A founder of pragmatism; did valuable work in mathematics, pendulum work, and logic; considered the effects of an object to be part of its conception as a principle of method. *Collected Papers of Charles Sanders Peirce*, 8 vols., 1931–58.

PIKE, JAMES A., Feb. 14, 1913 (Oklahoma City, Okla.)–Sept. 21, 1969. U.S. Episcopalian priest, lawyer. As dean of Cathedral of St. John the Divine in New York City (1952–58), spoke out against McCarthyism, advocated civil rights and planned parenthood; bishop of California, 1958–66; joined Center for Democratic Institutions, 1966; renounced church to form Fndn. for Religious Transition, 1968; died on an expedition to the Judean desert.

PRIESAND, SALLY, June 27, 1946 (Cleveland, Ohio). U.S. rabbi. The first U.S. woman to be ordained as a rabbi, 1972; asst. rabbi (1972–77) and associate rabbi (1977–79) of New York City's Stephen Wise Free Synagogue; rabbi, Temple Beth-El, Eliz. N.J.; 1979–81; Monmouth Reform Temple, Tintorn Falls, N.J., 1981– .

RAPP, (Johann Georg) GEORGE, Nov. 1, 1757 (Iptingen, Ober amt Maulbronn Württemberg, Ger.)–Aug. 7, 1847. German-U.S. religious leader, founder of the Harmonists. Emigrated to Pennsylvania with a group of followers who literally interpreted the bible, 1803; established a settlement called Harmony, where they lived communally and in celibacy; sold property to ROBERT OWEN and formed other settlements and continued as spiritual head of Harmonists until his death.

**ROBERTS, (Granville) ORAL,** Jan. 24, 1918 (nr. Ada, Okla.). U.S. evangelist. Evangelist, 1936–41; began worldwide evangelistic ministry through crusades, radio, TV, and print media, 1947; established Oral Roberts Evangelistic Assn., 1948; founded Oral Roberts U., Tulsa, Okla., 1963. *If You Need Healing, Do These Things,* 1947; *God's Formula for Success and Prosperity,* 1956; *The Miracle Book,* 1972.

**ROBERTSON, PAT** (born Marion Gordon Robertson), Mar. 22, 1930 (Lexington, Va.). U.S. religious leader, televangelist. Ordained in Southern Baptist Church, 1959; set up nation's first Christian television station in Portsmouth, Va., in 1960, and built it into the Christian Broadcasting Network (CBN), today one of the largest cable networks in the U.S.; ran for the U.S. president, 1988.

**ROYCE, JOSIAH,** Nov. 20, 1855 (Grass Valley, Calif.)–Sept. 14, 1916. U.S. idealist philosopher who stressed individuality, will and loyalty. *The Religious Aspect of Philosophy,* 1885; *The World and the Individual,* (2 vols.) 1900–01; *The Philosophy of Loyalty,* 1908.

**RUSSELL, CHARLES TAZE,** Feb. 16, 1852 (Pittsburgh, Pa.)–Oct. 31, 1916. U.S. religious leader. Founded the Intl. Bible Students Assn. or Russellites, a sect of millennialists; founded the journal *The Watchtower,* 1879; his sect formed the nucleus for the Jehovah's Witnesses.

**RUTHERFORD, JOSEPH FRANKLIN** ("Judge"), Nov. 8, 1869 (nr. Booneville, Mo.)–Jan. 8, 1942. U.S. religious leader, author. Pres., Jehovah's Witnesses (called Russellites before 1925), 1917–42; indicted for obstructing the war effort by counseling people to be conscientious objectors, 1917.

**SANTAYANA, GEORGE,** (orig. Jorge Agustín Nicolás Santayana), Dec. 16, 1863 (Madrid, Sp.)–Sept. 26, 1952. U.S. philosopher, poet. Taught philosophy at Harvard U. (1889–1912), then resided chiefly in Europe; in early work, applied the psychological approach to life of the mind, later turned to a more classical philosophical approach. *The Sense of Beauty,* 1896; *The Life of Reason,* 1905–06; *Scepticism and Animal Faith,* 1923; *The Realms of Being,* 4 vols., 1927–1940.

**SCHULLER, ROBERT H.,** Sept. 16, 1926 (Alton, Ia.). U.S. clergyman, author. Founder and sr. pastor, Garden Grove (Calif.). Community Church, 1955–  ; pres. and founder, Hour of Power TV Ministry, 1970; has written dozens of books.

**SHEEN, FULTON JOHN** (born Peter John Sheen), May 8, 1895 (El Paso, Ill.)–Dec. 9, 1979. U.S. R.C. bishop. Outstanding orator, well–known as a radio broadcaster from 1930; known for his attacks on communism and Freudianism. *The Cross and the Crisis,* 1938; *Communism and the Conscience of the West,* 1948.

**SMITH, JOSEPH,** Dec. 23, 1805 (Sharon, Vt.)–

June 27, 1844. U.S. religious leader. Founder of the Church of Jesus Christ of Latter-day Saints, usually called the Mormon Church; at age 14 had a revelation; later visions told him of buried plates, which he allegedly received from an angel (1827) and translated into *The Book of Mormon* (1830); founded church at Fayette, N.Y., 1830; moved colony to Ohio, Missouri, then Illinois; ruled despotically; arrested by non-Mormons, taken from jail in Carthage, Ill., by mob and assassinated.

**SPELLMAN, FRANCIS JOSEPH,** May 4, 1889 (Whitman, Mass.)–Dec. 2, 1967. U.S. religious leader. Roman Catholic cardinal from 1946; archbishop of New York, 1939–67; interests lay in education and charities; an advocate of state aid to parochial schools.

**STAPLETON, RUTH,** Aug. 7, 1929 (Plains, Ga.)–Sept. 26, 1983. U.S. evangelist. A nondenominational Christian evangelist; based at "Holovita" (whole life), a retreat near Dallas, Tex. *The Gift of Inner Healing,* 1976; *The Experience of Inner Healing,* 1977. (Sister of J. CARTER.)

**SUNDAY, WILLIAM** ("Billy"), Nov. 19, 1862 (Ames. Ia.)–Nov. 6, 1935. U.S. revivalist, professional baseball player. As an urban revivalist, possessed a theatrical mastery of idiomatic language; supported Prohibition; accepted the support of the Ku Klux Klan; conducted more than 300 revivals with an estimated attendance of 100 million.

**THOREAU, HENRY DAVID,** July 12, 1817 (Concord, Mass.)–May 6, 1862. U.S. essayist, poet, naturalist. Best known for his book *Walden* (1854), in which he described his solitary life in a cabin near Walden Pond; a member of the Transcendentalist group of the mid-19th-cent. and a friend of RALPH WALDO EMERSON; as an ardent abolitionist, came to the defense of JOHN BROWN's raid on Harper's Ferry, 1859. "Civil Disobedience," 1845.

**SWAGGART, JIMMY,** 1935 (Ferriday, La.). U.S. evangelist. A gospel singer and evangelist, his television ministry was one of the most successful in the world until 1988, when he admitted to the TV viewers that he had committed an unnamed sin, and resigned from his organization.

**TILLICH, PAUL,** Aug. 20, 1886 (Starzeddel, Kreis Guben, Prussia)–Oct. 22, 1965. German-U.S. philosopher, theologian. A Protestant thinker who attempted to bring Christianity and contemporary culture together; an opponent of the Nazi movement, he was barred from German universities and came to Union Theological Seminary (New York City), 1933; used a method of "correlation between the human questions of the times and the divine answers of Christian revelation." *The Courage to Be,* 1952; *Dynamics of Faith,* 1957; *Systematic Theology,* (3 vols.) 1951–1963.

**TURNER, HENRY MCNEAL,** Feb. 1, 1834 (Newberry Court House, S.C.)–May 8, 1915. U.S. Methodist Episcopal bishop, government worker. One of the principal advocates of the return of black people to Africa; the first black chaplain commissioned in the U.S., 1863; bishop of the African Methodist Episcopal Church, 1880–92.

**VINCENT, JOHN HEYL,** Feb. 23, 1832 (Tuscaloosa, Ala.)–May 9, 1920. U.S. Methodist bishop. Attempted to improve teaching methods used in Sunday schools; organized a Sunday-school teachers' institute at Chautauqua, N.Y., which grew into the Chautauqua movement, 1874; became a bishop in the American Methodist Church, 1888.

**WATTS, ALAN WITSON,** Jan. 6, 1915 (Chislehurst, Kent, Eng.)–Nov. 16, 1973. U.S. writer, lecturer on philosophy. For almost 40 years, interpreted Eastern thought to the West; gained considerable popularity in the late 1950s and 1960s as interest in the East grew in the U.S. *The Spirit of Zen,* 1936; *This Is It,* 1960.

**WHITE, ELLEN GOULD,** Nov. 26, 1827 (Gorham, Me.)–July 16, 1915. U.S. religious leader. As leader of the Seventh-Day Adventists, probably influenced the movement more than any other individual; her interpretation of Scripture did much to shape orthodoxy.

**WILLIAMS, ROGER,** c.1603 (London, Eng.)–March? 1683. English clergyman. Founder of Rhode Island Colony in America; became embroiled in dispute with the Massachusetts Colony over his claim that civil magistrates should have no authority over the consciences of men; banished in 1635; founded Providence, R.I., 1636; received charter from England for Rhode Island Colony, 1644. *The Bloudy Tenent of Persecution for Cause of Conscience,* 1644.

**WISE, ISAAC MAYER,** Mar. 29, 1819 (Steingrub, Bohemia [now Czech.])–Mar. 26, 1900. German-U.S. rabbi. Organizer of Reform Judaism in the U.S.; tried to unify U.S. synagogues and give them common standards; founded Hebrew Union C., 1875; pres., 1875–1900; edited *The American Israelite* and *Die Deborah.*

**YOUNG, BRIGHAM,** June 1, 1801 (Whitingham, Vt.)–Aug. 29, 1877. U.S. Mormon leader. Joined church, 1832; directed Mormon removal to Nauvoo, Ill., 1838; he led the great migration west to the settlement at Salt Lake City, Utah, 1846–47; built the settlement into a prosperous one; gov. of state of Deseret, later Utah territory, 1849–57, resigned when defied the U.S. government against attacks on the Mormons; accused of polygamy.

## FOREIGN PHILOSOPHERS AND RELIGIOUS LEADERS

**ABELARD, PIERRE,** c.1079 (Le Pallet, nr. Nantes, Brittany Fr.)–Apr. 21, 1142. French philosopher, theologian. A leading figure of medieval scholasticism; affair with a student, HELOISE, led to his castration by ruffians hired by her uncle; espousal of nominalist doctrines led to his persecution. *Sic et Non.*

**ABRAHAM,** fl. 1800? B.C. (Ur, Mesopotamia). First patriarch of the Jews. A central ancestral figure in Judaism, Islam, and Christianity; the model of a man of faith, tested by God; his journey to Canaan from Haran, his treatment of his nephew Lot, and his willingness to sacrifice his son Isaac expressed his devotion to God; received the promise of Canaan as the land of his people; began the tradition of circumcision.

**ANAXAGORAS,** c.500 B.C. (Clazomenae, Anatolia [now Turkey])–428 B.C. Greek philosopher. The first to introduce a dualistic explanation of the universe; gave first known explanation of moon phases and moon and sun eclipses; taught Pericles, EURIPIDES, and possibly SOCRATES.

**ANAXIMANDER,** 611 B.C. (Miletus)–547 B.C. Greek astronomer and philosopher. Generally credited with the discovery of obliquity of the ecliptic, the introduction of the sun dial, the idea of *apeiron,* and the invention of geographic maps; formulated the doctrine of a single-world principle, the starting point and origin of the cosmic process that he called "the infinite."

**ANGELA MERICI, SAINT,** Mar. 21, 1474 (Desenzano, Rep. of Venice)–Jan. 27, 1540. Italian nun. Founded the Ursulines, the first religious order for the teaching of young girls, 1531; worked to increase the Christian influence on the family; canonized, 1807.

**ANTISTHENES,** 444? B.C. (Athens, Gr.)–c.370 B.C. Greek philosopher. Established own school of philosophy from which Cynics evolved; in the quest for virtue, taught the importance of disregarding external goods, such as social convention and pleasure, and of looking to internal values, such as truth and knowledge of the soul.

**ARISTOTLE,** 384 B.C. (Stageira Macedonia, Gr.)–322 B.C. Greek philosopher. Studied under PLATO at the Athens Academy; tutor of ALEXANDER THE GREAT; taught in Athens as head of the Peripatetic school; the first proponent of the scientific method, and the first Western thinker to set forth coherent theories of logic and causality. *Prior Analytics; Posterior Analytics; Metaphysics; Physics; On the Soul; Generation; Nicomachean Ethics; Politics; Poetics; Rhetoric; On the Heavens; On Beginning and Perishing.*

**AUGUSTINE OF HIPPO, SAINT** (orig. Aurelius Augustinus), Nov. 13, 354 (Tagaste, Numidia [now Souk–Ahras, Algeria])–Aug. 28, 430. Early Christian church Father, philosopher. Through sermons, books, and pastoral letters, he exerted a tremendous influence in the Christian world; stood forth as a champion of orthodoxy against the Manicheans, Donatists, and Pelagians; fused the religion of the New Testament with the Platonic tradition of Greek philosophy. *The City of God,* 413–426; *Confessions,* 397–401.

**AUGUSTINE OF CANTERBURY, SAINT,** d.604?. English religious leader. Responsible for the Christianization of England; he became the first archbishop of Canterbury in 601.

**AVERROËS,** 1126 (Cordoba, Sp.)–Dec. 10, 1198. Islamic philosopher. Integrated Islamic traditions and Greek thought; defended the philosophical study of religion against the philosophers; wrote commentaries on most of ARISTOTLE's works and on PLATO's *Republic.*

**AVICENNA,** 980 (Bukhara, Persia)–1037. Islamic physician, philosopher, scientist. The most famous philosopher and scientist of medieval Islam; his medical writings enjoyed immense prestige for hundreds of years; interpreted ARISTOTLE's writings in a Neoplatonic fashion. *Canon of Medicine.*

**BA'AL-SHEM-TOV** (born Israel ben Eliezer), c.1700 (nr. Tluste, Ukraine)–1760. Jewish teacher, tavern keeper, founder of modern Hasidism. His emphasis on the joy of religious devotion and repudiation of the prevailing asceticism gained him a considerable following; taught that learning was not necessary for salvation; spent his time with simple people, dressing like them—a highly controversial practice.

**BACON, SIR FRANCIS, BARON VERULAM, VISCOUNT ST. ALBANS,** Jan. 22, 1561 (London, Eng.)–Apr. 9, 1626. English philosopher, essayist, statesman. An early advocate of inductive reasoning from intensive observation; his prestige made empirical science respectable and fashionable; knighted, 1603; made baron, 1618; made viscount, 1621; chan. of England, 1618–21. *Novum Organum* 1620; *New Atlantis; Essays,* 1597–1625.

**BACON, ROGER,** c.1214 (Eng.)–1294. English philosopher, friar. Considered natural science complementary to faith, not opposed to it, and battled for placing the sciences in the curriculum of university studies; knew how to make gunpowder. *Opus majus; Opus minus* (or *secundum*); *Opus tertium.*

**BARTH, KARL,** May 10, 1886 (Basel, Switz.)–Dec. 9, 1968. Swiss theologian. Reasserted the principles of the Reformation in modern theology; developed a "theology of the word of God" in opposition to the anthropocentric theological writings of the 19th cent.; led church opposition against Hitler's Third Reich. *Der Römerbrief,* 1919; *Kirchliche Dogmatik,* 1932–62.

**BENEDICT, SAINT,** 480 (Nursia, It.)–547. Italian monk, the father of Western monasticism. Founded the monastery at Monte Cassino; his monastic rule, which included a year of probation and a vow of obedience, became the norm for monastic living throughout Europe.

**BENTHAM, JEREMY,** Feb. 15, 1748 (London, Eng.)–June 6, 1832. English philosopher, economist. Founded utilitarianism, the first systematic effort to describe and evaluate all human acts, institutions, and laws in terms of immediate sensible pleasures and pains; a pioneer in prison reform; proposed a scientific discipline for achieving solutions to social problems. *Introduction to the Principles of Morals and Legislation,* 1789.

**BERDYAEV, NIKOLAI,** Mar. 6, 1874 (Kiev, Rus.)–Mar. 23, 1948. Russian philosopher, religious thinker. A former Marxist, he was leading thinker of Russian Orthodox Christianity; exiled in 1922, he lived in Berlin and Paris, where he wrote extensively, criticizing Russian communism and developing a Christian existentialist philosophy. *Freedom and the Spirit,* 1927; *The Destiny of Man,* 1931.

**BERGSON, HENRI,** Oct. 18, 1859 (Paris, Fr.)–Jan. 4, 1941. French philosopher. One of the first "process" philosophers, he proposed a theory of evolutionary vitalism and fought against a spacialized conception of time by stressing its quality of duration; Nobel Prize for Lit., 1927. *Time and Free Will,* 1910; *Matter and Memory,* 1911; *Creative Evolution,* 1911.

**BERKELEY, GEORGE,** Mar. 12, 1685 (Dysert Castle, Cty. Kilkenny, Ire.)–Jan. 14, 1753. Anglo-Irish philosopher, churchman. A subjective idealist, he argued that all qualities of the world are in the mind; Anglican bishop of Cloyne, 1734–53. *An Essay Towards a New Theory of Vision,* 1709; *A Treatise Concerning the Principles of Human Knowledge,* 1710.

**BERNADETTE, SAINT** (born Marie-Bernarde Soubirous), Jan. 7, 1844 (Lourdes, Fr.)–Apr. 16, 1879. French visionary. A peasant girl who at age 14 claimed to see the Virgin Mary in a grotto near Lourdes on several occasions; became a Sister of Charity; canonized, 1933.

**BESANT, ANNIE,** Oct. 1, 1847 (London, Eng.)–Sept. 20, 1933. British social reformer, theosophist, Indian independence leader. A former Christian, she went through an atheist stage in the 1880s, when she advocated birth control and became a prominent Fabian socialist; converted to theosophy, 1889; pres., Theosophical Society, 1907–1933; went to India in 1916, establishing the Indian Home Rule League and promoting Jiddu Krishnamurti as the new messiah.

**BIDDLE, JOHN,** 1615 (Wotton-under-Edge, Glos., Eng.)–Sept. 22, 1662. British lay theologian. The father of English Unitarianism, often imprisoned for his antitrinitarian views. *Twelve Arguments Against the Deity of the Holy Ghost,* 1644.

**BLAVATSKY, HELENA,** 1831 (Yekaterinoslav, now Dnepropetrovsk, Rus.)–1891. Russian spiritualist, author. A cofounder of the Theosophical Society; fused Vedantic thought and Egyptian serpent worship into an occult system based on the belief in a pantheistic evolutionary process. *Isis Unveiled,* 1877; *The Secret Doctrine,* 1888; *Key to Theosophy,* 1889.

**BOEHME, JAKOB,** 1575 (Alts Seidenberg, Saxony, Ger.)–Nov. 21, 1624. German Christian mystic, metaphysician. Out of a religious experience, developed a mystical strain of thought that employed a dialectical method; merged Renaissance naturemysticism with Biblical religion. *The Aurora,* 1612; *The Way to Christ,* 1624; *The Great Mystery,* 1623.

**BRUNNER, EMIL,** Dec. 23, 1889 (Winterthur, Switz.)–Apr. 6, 1966. Swiss theologian. As professor of theology, U. of Zurich (1924–53), became the leading theologian in the Reformed tradition; opposed rational and liberal Christianity with a theology of revelation and divine encounter; in leaving some room for natural theology in his system, distinguished himself from KARL BARTH. *The Divine Imperative,* 1932; *Justice and the Social Order,* 1945; *Natural Theology,* 1946.

**BUBER, MARTIN,** Feb. 8, 1878 (Vienna, Aust.)–June 13, 1965. Jewish philosopher of encounter. Distinguished two fundamental relationships, "I-it" and "I-thou"; his relational thought led him to new insights into the Bible; edited the magazine *Der Jude* (1916–24). *I and Thou*, 1923; *The Eclipse of God*, 1952.

**BUDDHA, GAUTAMA** (born Siddhartha), c.566 B.C. (Kapilavastu, India)–486? B.C. Indian philosopher, religious leader, founder of Buddhism. Renounced wealthy heritage to lead an ascetic life; taught for 45 years and founded monastic orders; his teaching offered a prescription to cure suffering; considered everything impermanent; preached rigorous disciplines for overcoming dependency; Buddhist movement played a central role in the entire Eastern world.

**CALVIN, JOHN**, July 10, 1509 (Noyon, Picardy, Fr.)–May 27, 1564. French theologian, ecclesiastical statesman. Founder of Calvinsim; promulgated the doctrine of divine election and gave a preeminent place to the Holy Spirit; wrote his views with a clarity and force that did much to propel the Prot. movement; originated the form of church government called a presbytery. *Institutes of the Christian Religion*, 1536.

**CAMPION, BLESSED EDMUND**, c.1540 (London, Eng.)–Dec. 1, 1581. English Roman Catholic martyr. He was born in Elizabethan times, and was a devout member of the Anglican Church; gave up his job as a teacher at Oxford, went to Spain, and joined the Roman Catholic Jesuit Order; returning to England in 1580, he was arrested for treason, tortured, hanged, drawn, and quartered; his most important writing was *History of Ireland*, 1571.

**COMTE, AUGUSTE**, Jan. 19, 1798 (Montpellier, Fr.)–Sept. 5, 1857. French philosopher, social reformer. Founded positivism and modern sociology; devised a scheme of social evolution, relating it to the stages of science. *The Course of Positive Philosophy*, 1830–42; *System of Positive Polity*, 1851–54.

**CONDORCET, MARIE JEAN, MARQUIS DE**, Sept. 17, 1743 (Ribemont, Picardy, Fr.)–Mar. 29, 1794. French mathematician, philosopher. A leading thinker of the Enlightenment, he contributed to the theory of probability; took part in the French Revolution; devised a system of state education. *Sketch for a Historical Picture of the Human Mind*, 1795.

**CONFUCIUS**, (born K'ung Ch'iu), c.551 B.C. (state of Lu [now Shantung Prov.], China)–479 B.C. Chinese philosopher. Most influential philosopher in Chinese history; spent his life teaching and seeking a government post through which to implement his ideas; his teachings emphasized moral character as the source of social order; wanted to reform men and thereby government; considered the founder of a new class in China, the literati; valued filial piety, loyalty, reciprocity, and sincerity; although his teachings were ignored by the rulers of his time, they survived and were used by generations of subsequent rulers.

**CRANMER, THOMAS**, July 2, 1489 (Aslacton, Notts., Eng.)–Mar. 21, 1556. English churchman. The first Prot. archbishop of Canterbury, 1533–56; one of the principal authors of the *Book of Com-*

*mon Prayer*, 1549; as legal adviser to HENRY VIII, found legal rationales for the king's divorces; after the accession of MARY I, convicted of heresy and burned.

**CROCE, BENEDETTO**, Feb. 25, 1866 (Pescasseroli, It.)–Nov. 20, 1952. Italian idealist philosopher who constructed a so-called Philosophy of the Spirit; a committed opponent of MUSSOLINI's fascism in Italy. *Philosophy of the Spirit*, 1902–17 (4 vols.); *History as the Story of Liberty*, 1938.

**DALAI LAMA** (born Tenzin Gyatso), July 6, 1935 (Taktser, Tibet). Tibetan religious leader. He was enthroned as Dalai Lama XIV in 1940, but fled to India in 1959 after an abortive revolution by the Tibetan people against the Communist Chinese occupying the country. *My Land and My People*, 1962; *Key to the Middle Way*, 1971; *A Human Approach to World Peace*, 1984.

**DAMIEN, FATHER** (born Joseph de Veuster), Jan. 3, 1840 (Tremeloo, Belg.)–Apr. 15, 1889. Belgian priest. As R.C. missionary to the leper colony in Molokai, Hawaii (1873–1889), cared for the physical and spiritual needs of 600 persons; when his character came under attack, ROBERT LOUIS STEVENSON wrote *Father Damien: An Open Letter to the Reverend Dr. Hyde*, 1890.

**DEMOCRITUS**, ("The Laughing Philosopher"). c.460 B.C. (Abdera, Thrace, Gr.)–370 B.C. Greek philosopher. The first developer of the atomic theory of the universe, holding that reality consists ultimately of atoms and the space between them; anticipated the distinction between primary and secondary qualities of matter later made by J. LOCKE.

**DESCARTES, RENÉ**, Mar. 31, 1596 (La Haye, Touraine, Fr.)–Feb. 1, 1650. French philosopher, mathematician, scientist. Founder of modern philosophical rationalism; inventor of analytic geometry; made many advances in optics; crusaded to apply mathematical methods to all fields of knowledge; beginning with radical skepticism, attempted to prove through deductive steps the existence of the world and of God. *Discourse on Method*, 1637; *Meditations Concerning Primary Philosophy*, 1641; *Principles of Philosophy*, 1644.

**DIDEROT, DENIS**, Oct. 5, 1713 (Langres, Fr.) –July 30, 1784. French philosopher, writer. Chief editor (1745–72) of the *Encyclopédie*, a comprehensive compendium of knowledge and a symbol and stimulant of the Enlightenment; in his battle against censorship of the *Encyclopédie*, figured in the movement toward tolerance and freedom of expression. *Le père de famille*, 1758; *Elements of Physiology*, 1774–80; *Jacques le fataliste*, 1796.

**DIOGENES**, c.412 B.C. (Sinope, Gr. [now Turkey]) –323 B.C. Greek philosopher. Leader of the Cynics, a group that believed in self-sufficiency and disregard of luxuries; his high moral standards resulted in his famous search, with a lantern in daylight, for an honest man.

**ECKHARD** (or Eckart, Eckardt, Eccard, or Eckehart), **JOHANNES** (known as Meister Eckhard), 1260? (Hochheim, Ger.)–1327? German Dominican theo-

logian, mystic, preacher. Founded German mysticism; the father of German philosophical language. **EMPEDOCLES,** c.495 B.C. (Acragas, [now Agrigento] Sicily)–c.435 B.C. Greek pre-Socratic philosopher. Postulated that the world is composed of four elements, (air, water, earth, fire) and two forces (love and strife); considered physical motion the only kind of change possible.
**EPICTETUS,** c.50 (Hierapolis, Asia Minor)–c.138. Greek Stoic philosopher. Valued self-control and selflessness; believed that the will was the sole source of value; influenced Christian thinkers.
**EPICURUS,** 341 B.C. (Samos)–270 B.C. Greek philosopher. Considered pleasure to be the only good and the end of all morality, but it must be honorable, prudent, and just.
**ERASMUS, DESIDERIUS** (born Gerhard Gerhards), Oct 26/27, 1466 (Rotterdam, Neth.)–July 12, 1536. Dutch humanist. Represented the northern Renaissance. The first editor of the Greek version of the New Testament; edited Greek and Latin classics; defended reason, tolerance, and faith; attacked MARTIN LUTHER's position on predestination. *Praise of Folly,* 1509; *The Education of a Christian Prince,* 1515.
**EUCKEN, RUDOLPH,** Jan. 5, 1846 (Aurich, E. Friesland, Ger.)–Sept. 15, 1926. German philosopher. Developed a philosophy of ethical activism, a metaphysical-idealistic philosophy of life; an interpreter of ARISTOTLE; awarded Nobel Prize in literature, 1908. *The Truth of Religion,* 1901; *The Life of the Spirit,* 1909; *Knowledge and Life,* 1913.
**FÉNELON, FRANÇOIS DE SALIGNAC DE LA MOTHE,** Aug. 6, 1651 (Château de Fénelon, Périgord, Fr.)–Jan. 7, 1715. French theologian. The archbishop of Cambrai (from 1695), his liberal views on politics and education faced a concerted opposition from church and state. *Traité de l'education des filles,* 1687; *Explications des maximes des saints,* 1697; *Les overtures de Télémaque,* 1699; *Lettre à l'Académie,* 1714.
**FEUERBACH, LUDWIG,** July 28, 1804 (Landshut, Ger.)–Sept. 13, 1872. German philosopher. Abandoned Hegelian idealism for naturalistic materialism; attacked orthodox religion and immortality; concluded that God is the outward projection of man's inner nature; influenced MARX. *The Essence of Christianity,* 1841.
**FICHTE, JOHANN,** May 19, 1762 (Rammenau, Ger.)–Jan. 27, 1814. German philosopher. The successor to IMMANUEL KANT, he developed the first idealist system (ethical idealism) out of Kant's work; influential as a patriot and liberal. *Science of Knowledge,* 1794; *The Vocation of Man,* 1800.
**FOX, GEORGE,** July 1624 (Fenny Drayton, Leics., Eng.)–Jan. 13, 1691. English religious leader. Founded the Society of Friends, also known as the Quakers, 1668; on the basis of a personal religious experience, emphasized a God-given "light within" as the source of authority and revelation; fought against slavery and war. *Journal,* 1694.
**FRANCIS OF ASSISI, SAINT,** 1182 (Assisi, It.)–Oct. 3, 1226. Italian religious leader. After his

conversion to holy life, he attempted to live literally by the Gospel, renouncing material goods and family ties; wandering as a street preacher, he gathered a large following, leading to the establishment of the Franciscan order of priests (formally chartered 1223); canonized, 1228. *Canticle of the Sun,* 1224.
**GHAZALI, AL-** (or Al-Gazel), c.1058 (Tūs, now Mashhad, Iran)–Dec. 18, 1111. Islamic philosopher. A mystical ascetic, he opposed the use of rational methods in pursuing religious truths; influential in suppressing Moslem rationalism. *Destruction of the Philosophers.*
**GODWIN, WILLIAM,** Mar. 3, 1756 (Wisbech, Isle of Ely, Cambs. Eng.)–Apr. 7, 1836. English philosopher. Champion of atheism, anarchism, and personal freedom; defended the power of reason in making choices. *An Enquiry Concerning Political Justice...,* 1793; *Things as They Are, or, The Adventures of Caleb Williams,* 1794. (Husband of M. WOLLSTONECRAFT; father of M. SHELLEY.)
**GREGORY XIII** (born Ugo Buoncompagni), June 7, 1502 (Bologna, It.)–Apr. 10, 1585. Italian pope, (1572–85). Reformed the Julian calendar, creating the Gregorian calendar, 1582; founded several colleges and universities, including Gregorian U., 1572; attempted to implement the decrees of the Council of Trent; built Quirinal Palace.
**HÄRING, BERNARD,** Nov. 10, 1912 (Böttingen, Württemberg, Ger.). German theologian. R.C. moral theologian influential in the reforms of Vatican II. *The Law of Christ,* 1956.
**HEGEL, GEORG W.,** Aug. 27, 1770 (Stuttgart, Ger.)–Nov. 14, 1831. German idealist philosopher. Constructed a grand system that deeply influenced the modern movements of existentialism, Marxism, positivism, and analytical philosophy; believing that the limits IMMANUEL KANT placed on reason were wrong, he saw reason operating in history as a World Spirit infusing order in various areas of culture and society. *The Phenomenology of the Spirit,* 1807; *The Science of Logic,* 1812–16; *Philosophy of Right and Law,* 1820.
**HEIDEGGER, MARTIN,** Sept. 26, 1889 (Messkirch, Ger.)–May 26, 1976. German philosopher. The major German philosopher of existentialism; greatly influenced European culture between the World Wars; placed being or ontology at the center of his philosophy; coined his own terms in an attempt to revitalize philosophical terminology; brought the awareness of death into philosophical focus. *Being and Time,* 1927; *What is Metaphysics?,* 1929.
**HERACLITUS,** c.540 B.C. (Ephesus, Anatolia, now Turkey)–c.480 B.C. Greek philosopher. A cosmologist who taught that everything is in a state of flux; believed that everything carries within itself its opposite (life carries the potential of death, etc.); taught that fire is the underlying reality transformed into various manifestations.
**HERDER, JOHANN G.,** Aug. 25, 1744 (Mohrungen, East Prussia [now Morag, Pol.])–Dec. 18, 1803. German philosopher. Founder of German

Romanticism; a leader of the *Sturm und Drang* literary movement; considered language and poetry to be natural human expressions; developed a profound philosophy of history emphasizing the unique contributions of each era and an integrated view of culture. *On the Origin of Language*, 1772; *Folk Songs*, 1778–79; *Outlines of a Philosophy of the History of Man*, 1784–91.

**HOBBES, THOMAS,** Apr. 5, 1588 (Malmesbury, Wilts., Eng.)–Dec. 4, 1679. English philosopher. An influential political philosopher who applied the mechanistic and scientific world view to society; had a pessimistic view of human nature; argued for absolutist government. *Leviathan*, 1651.

**HUME, DAVID,** May 7, 1711 (Edinburgh, Scot.)–Aug. 25, 1776. Scottish philosopher. A philosophical skeptic, he questioned the existence of causality and substance; his writings jarred IMMANUEL KANT from his "dogmatic slumber" and challenged many others to deepen their thinking. *A Treatise of Human Nature*, 1739–40; *An Enquiry Concerning Human Understanding*, 1748; *Dialogues Concerning Natural Religion*, 1779.

**HUSS, JOHN** (Czech: Jan Hus), 1372 (Husinec, Bohemia, now Czech.)–July 6, 1415. Czech religious reformer. A forerunner of the Prot. Reformation, he was influenced by the writings of JOHN WYCLIFFE; proclaimed the ultimate authority of the Scriptures over the church, and proposed that the state had the right to rule the church; burned at the stake.

**IGNATIUS OF LOYOLA, SAINT** (born Iñigo de Lopez y Loyola), Dec. 24, 1491 (Loyola, nr. Azpeitia, Sp.)–July 31, 1556. Spanish priest. Founded the Jesuit order; after being wounded in battle, reoriented his life in a spiritual direction, attempting to imitate the life of Christ; underwent a 12-year education; in 1540, founded an order, the Society of Jesus (Jesuits), that renounced some of the traditional forms of religious life, such as penitential garb, and stressed mobility, flexibility, and learning; canonized, 1622. *Spiritual Exercises*, 1548; *Constitutions*.

**INGE, WILLIAM,** June 6, 1860 (Crayke, Yorkshire, Eng.)–Feb. 26, 1954. English theologian. Explored the mystical aspects of Christianity; known for his originality and pessimism; dean of St. Paul's Cathedral, 1911–34. *The Church in the World*, 1927; *Mysticism in Religion*, 1948.

**ISAIAH,** fl. 8th century B.C. (Jerusalem). Hebrew prophet. Called to prophecy c.742 B.C.; saw the advancement of Assyria as a divine warning, reputed to have suffered a martyr's death; Book of Isaiah in the Old Testament is named after him.

**JASPERS, KARL,** Feb. 23, 1883 (Oldenburg, Ger.)–Feb. 26, 1969. German philosopher. Considered a prominent existentialist thinker, though he himself rejected the classification because it placed him within a restricted school of thought. *General Psychopathology*, 1913; *Man in the Modern Age*, 1933.

**JEREMIAH,** c.650 B.C. (Anathoth, Judah)–c.585 B.C. Hebrew prophet. His life and teaching are recorded in the book of Jeremiah in the Old Testament; denounced social injustice and false worship in Judah; saw Babylonian invasion and capture of Jerusalem as a punishment from God; urged people to make peace and believe in God, teaching that they could preserve their worship even in disaster and in exile.

**JEROME, SAINT** (born Eusebius Hieronymus Sophronius), c.342 (Stridon, [now in Yugo.])–Sept. 30, 420. Christian Biblical scholar. A Father of the Roman Catholic Church; his preparation of a standard text of the Gospels for Latin-speaking Christians and new translation of the Psalms and Old Testament was the basis for the Vulgate, or authorized Latin text of the Bible.

**JESUS CHRIST,** c.6 B.C. (Bethlehem, Judea)–c.30 A.D. The founder of Christianity. Son of Joseph the carpenter, but believed, by his followers, to have been miraculously conceived by his mother, the VIRGIN MARY; a wandering rabbi, gathered a large following drawn by his healing powers, teaching in parables, and authority; gathered 12 disciples; his attacks on hypocrisy offended privileged classes; betrayed by one of his disciples, Judas Iscariot, and seized by Roman soldiers and convicted of blasphemy; crucified; believed by his followers to have risen from the dead.

**JOAN OF ARC** (in French, Jeanne D'Arc), Jan. 1412 (Domremy, Champagne, Fr.)–May 30, 1431. French saint, national heroine. Called the "Maid of Orleans"; heard voices exhorting her to aid the dauphin (later King Charles VII), who furnished her with troops; defeated English at Patay, 1429; captured by Burgundians at Compiègne and sold to English, who turned her over to Ecclesiastical Court at Rouen; tried for heresy and witchcraft by French clerics supporting the English; turned over to secular court; burned at the stake; trial annulled, 1456; beatified, 1909; canonized, 1920.

**JOHN OF THE CROSS, SAINT** (born Juan de Yepes y Alvarez), June 24, 1542 (Fontiveros, Sp.)–Dec. 14, 1591. Spanish monk, Doctor of the Church. A great lyric poet and profound mystic; founded the Discalced Carmelites, 1579; a close friend of ST. THERESA OF AVILA; his reforms of the order led to his imprisonment (1577–78) during which time he wrote his greatest poetry; beatified, 1675; canonized, 1726. *The Dark Night of the Soul*; *The Ascent of Mount Carmel*.

**JOHN PAUL I** (born Albino Luciani), Oct. 17, 1912 (Forno di Canale, [now Canaled'Agordo] Italy)–Sept. 28, 1978. Italian pope, for 34 days in 1978. A long-time pastor, taught the rural poor; vice rector, Bellumo Seminary, 1937–47; patriarch of Venice, 1969–78; cardinal of Venice, 1973–78.

**JOHN PAUL II** (born Karol Wojtyla), May 18, 1920 (Wadowice, Pol.). Polish pope (elected Oct. 16, 1978), the first non-Italian to be elevated to the papacy in 455 years. Prof. of Moral Theology, U. of Cracow and Lublin, 1953–58; archbishop of Cracow, 1964–78; cardinal, 1967–78. *Love and Responsibility*, 1962; *Person and Work*, 1969; *The Future of the Church*, 1979.

**KANT, IMMANUEL,** Apr. 22, 1724 (Königsberg,

E. Prussia [now Kalingrad, USSR])–Feb. 12, 1804. German philosopher. One of the foremost thinkers of the Enlightenment, he attempted to reconcile two previously divergent trends in philosophy—rationalism and empiricism; using a new method he called "transcendental," showed that "concepts without percepts are empty, percepts without concepts are blind." *Critique of Pure Reason*, 1781; *Prolegomena to Any Future Metaphysics*, 1783; *Critique of Practical Reason*, 1788; *Critique of Judgement*, 1790; *Metaphysics of Morals*, 1797.

**KIERKEGAARD, SØREN,** May 5, 1813 (Copenhagen, Den.)–Nov. 11, 1855. Danish philosopher, the father of existentialism. Developed a body of thought that stressed the primacy of personal experience and choice; a critic of official Christianity, laid out a tortuous version of an authentic religious life. *Either/Or*, 1843; *Fear and Trembling*, 1843; *The Concept of Dread*, 1844; *Concluding Unscientific Postscript*, 1846.

**KNOX, JOHN,** c.1514 (Haddington, East Lothian, Scot.)–Nov. 24, 1572. Scottish religious leader. The founder of Scottish Presbyterianism; zealously led the Prot. battle to win Scotland from the R.C. Church; a stirring preacher, he disseminated Prot. ideas and then fought the political establishment that resisted them. *Book of Common Order*, 1566; *History of the Reformation in Scotland*, first printed, 1587.

**LAO-TZU,** c.600 B.C. (Honan, China). Chinese philosopher. His life is shrouded in obscurity, but he was probably a recluse who shunned worldly life; a scholar at the Chou court; traditionally considered to be the author of the *Tao-te Ching*, a text of tremendous importance to Chinese cultural life.

**LATIMER, HUGH,** c.1485 (Thurcaston, Leics., Eng.)–Oct. 16, 1555. English priest, Prot. leader. His popular preaching and his martyrdom (1555) during counter-Reformation did much to further Prot. cause in England; attacked the superstitions of the clergy and the wealth of the R.C. Church.

**LEE, ANN** (Mother Ann), Feb. 29, 1736 (Manchester, Eng.)–Sept. 8, 1784. English religious leader, founder of American sect of Shakers. Joined the "Shaking Quakers" in England, 1758; founded the first Shaker settlement at Niskeyuna, now Watervliet, N.Y., 1776.

**LEFEBVRE, MARCEL,** Nov. 29, 1905 (Turcoing, Fr.). Roman Catholic archbishop. Outspoken champion of defeated minority of Vatican II, renounces council openness to the modern world; ordained four bishops against Vatican wishes, resulting in immediate excommunication and placement of him and his followers in a state of schism, 1988.

**LEIBNIZ, GOTTFRIED,** July 1, 1646 (Leipzig, Ger.)–Nov. 14, 1716. German philosopher and mathematician who made major contributions to mathematics, logic, and metaphysics. Invented, independently of ISAAC NEWTON, differential and integral calculus, 1684; based his metaphysics on the theory of monads (distinct simple substances);

also contributed to symbolic logic. *Theodicy*, 1710; *Monadology*, 1714.

**LOCKE, JOHN,** Aug. 29, 1632 (Wrington, Somerset, Eng.)–Oct. 28, 1704. English philosopher, founder of British empiricism; leading proponent of liberalism. His theory of knowledge, in an attempt to account for the rise of modern science, stressed the role of sensations on the blank mind (*tabula rasa*); his political philosophy argued for social contract, consent, the protection of property, and the separation of legislative and executive powers; greatly influenced the framers of the U.S. Constitution. *Essay Concerning Human Understanding*, 1690; *Two Treatises on Civil Government*, 1690.

**LOMBARD, PETER,** c.1100 (Novara, It.)–Aug. 21/22, 1160. Italian theologian. Best known for a series of four books, *Sentences*, which were the source of Catholic theology until replaced by T. AQUINAS's *Summa theologica*.

**LUTHER, MARTIN,** Nov. 10, 1483 (Eisleben, Ger.)–Feb. 18, 1546. German religious reformer, leader of the Prot. Reformation. As an Augustinian friar, he grappled with his own religious anxieties, developing his own reading of the Scriptures; feeling disgust at the prevailing ecclesiastical laxity, protested the sale of indulgences by posting his 95 theses at Wittenberg, Ger., 1517; as his breach with Rome widened, he attacked the authority of the priesthood to mediate between man and God and rejected the sacraments except as visible signs of an unseen grace; advocated salvation by faith alone; translated the Bible into German, which had great influence on German lit.; Lutheran religion named after him.

**MAHAVIRA** ("The Great One", born Vardhamāna); c.599 B.C. (Ksatriyakundagrāma, India)–527 B.C. Indian ascetic, a founder of Jainism. Organized earlier Jaina doctrines and established the rules for the Jaina religious order, or *sangha*; practiced extreme asceticism and developed the doctrine of *ahimsa* (nonviolence); the five great vows of renunciation have been attributed to him.

**MAIMONIDES, MOSES,** Mar. 30, 1135 (Cordoba, Sp.)–Dec. 13, 1204. Jewish philosopher, jurist, physician. Organized and clarified the Torah, the Jewish oral law; attempted to develop a more rational philosophy of Judaism by reconciling Aristotle, the Bible, and Jewish tradition. *Guide for the Perplexed; Mishneh Torah.*

**MANI** (also Manes or Manichaeus), Apr. 24, 216 (Ecbatana, South Babylonia)–274? Persian religious leader, founder of the Manichaean religion. After a religious experience, traveled to northwest India, where he preached a dualistic doctrine of good and evil; advocated ascetic practices to liberate oneself from matter; died as a captive of Persian Zoroastrian priests.

**MARCUS AURELIUS** (born Marcus Annius Verus), Apr. 20, 121 (Rome, It.)–Mar. 17, 180. Roman emperor (161–180), Stoic philosopher. His *Meditations* are a classic and beautiful expression of Stoic philosophy; as emperor, repressed countless rebellions, implemented many reforms, and persecuted Christians.

MARITAIN, JACQUES, Nov. 18, 1882 (Paris, Fr.)–Apr. 28, 1973. French philosopher. An influential Catholic neo-Thomist thinker who defended the scholastic use of reason and fought against modern subjectivism. *Art and Scholasticism*, 1920; *True Humanism*, 1936; *Men and the State*, 1951.

MARY, also SAINT MARY or VIRGIN MARY. The Mother of Jesus. A figure of tremendous religious and cultural importance to Roman Catholic, Orthodox, and Anglican Christianity; considered a religious figure in her own right, as a mediator of grace.

MENCIUS (born Meng K'o), c.371 B.C. (Tsou [modern Shantung Prov.], China)–c.289 B.C. Chinese philosopher, one of the greatest early Confucians. Stressed the innate goodness of human nature and the obligation of rulers to provide for the common people; known as the Second Sage.

MINDSZENTY, JOZSEF (born Jozsef Pehm), Mar. 29, 1892 (Szombathely, Hung.)–May 6, 1975. Hungarian Roman Catholic cardinal from 1946. Became a stirring symbol of resistance in his fight against fascism and communism in Hungary; arrested by fascist Hungarian government, 1944; arrested by communist government, 1948; granted protection in U.S. embassy from 1956 to 1971, when he obeyed the Vatican order to leave Hungary.

MOHAMMED, 570 (Mecca)–June 8, 632. Arabian prophet and founder of Islam. Called the Prophet of Allah; a wealthy merchant, he received a call from God (c.610); began to preach, but received with hostility in Mecca; learning of a plot to murder him, fled to Medina, an event called the *hegira*, 622; established a theocracy in Medina, from which his empire grew; victory over the Meccans at Badr increased his prestige; conquered Mecca (630) making all Arabia Islamic; each of his military victories was seen as confirming evidence of divine sanction for his message and mission.

MONTESQUIEU, CHARLES-LOUIS DE SECONDAT, BARON DE LA BRÈDE ET DE, Jan. 18, 1689 (Château de la Brède, nr. Bordeaux, Fr.)–Feb. 10, 1755. French liberal political philosopher. His writings inspired the Declaration of the Rights of Man and the U.S. Constitution; reclassified governments according to their manner of conducting policy; developed theory of the separation of powers; a social figure and satirist. *Persian Letters*, 1721; *Considerations on the Causes of Greatness of the Romans and Their Decline*, 1734; *The Spirit of the Laws*, 1748.

MOSES, c.1350? B.C. (Egypt)–c.1250? B.C. Hebrew prophet, Jewish religious leader, founder of the Hebrew nation. Called by God, who revealed himself as a burning bush; directed by God to lead his people, the Hebrews, out of bondage in Egypt, took them across the desert to the edge of Canaan; received the Ten Commandments from God on top of Mt. Sinai; died after seeing Canaan from Mt. Nebo.

NEWMAN, JOHN H., Feb. 21, 1801 (London,

Eng.)–Aug. 11, 1890. English churchman, cardinal (from 1879). A leader of the Oxford movement in the Church of England, and after his conversion, in the R.C. church. *Loss and Gain*, 1848; *The Idea of a University*, 1852; *Apologia pro vita sua*, 1864; *Grammar of Assent*, 1870.

NIETZSCHE, FRIEDRICH, Oct. 15, 1844 (Röcken, Ger.)–Aug. 25, 1900. German philosopher. A highly influential critic of his culture, he disparaged Christianity, conformism, and nationalism, displaying a remarkable psychological understanding for his time; saw the will-to-power as underlying many phenomena. *The Birth of Tragedy*, 1872; *Thus Spoke Zarathrusta*, 1883–91; *Beyond Good and Evil*, 1886.

OCKHAM, (or Occam), WILLIAM OF, c.1285 (Ockham, Surrey, Eng.)–c.1349. English philosopher. Made two fundamental contributions to the philosophy of science by denying the reality of PLATO's ideal forms in favor of immediately perceived phenomena and by devising "Ockham's razor," a rule of thought that forbids unnecessary complexity.

ORTEGA Y GASSET, JOSÉ, May 9, 1883 (Madrid, Sp.)–Oct. 18, 1955. Spanish philosopher. Perhaps the foremost Spanish thinker of the 20th cent., he sought to bring Spain out of its intellectual isolation; his main concern was to fashion a philosophy that brought reason and life together. *Revolt of the Masses*, 1930; *Concord and Liberty*, 1946.

PARMENIDES, fl. 450 B.C. (born at Elea, now in Italy). Greek pre-Socratic philosopher. The first Western thinker to use a rigorous logical method; postulated that reality is one, eternal, perfect being knowable only through the intellect.

PASCAL, BLAISE, June 19, 1623 (Clermont, Ferrand, Fr.)–Aug. 19, 1662. French philosopher, mathematician, physicist. Formulated the modern theory of probability; invented the first digital calculator (1642–44), the syringe, and the hydraulic press; discovered a law of atmospheric pressure; midway through his life, after a brush with death, turned to religion; his delineation of the "reasons of the heart" for having faith influenced modern existentialism. *Provincial Letters*, 1656; *Pensées*, 1670.

PATRICK, SAINT, c.385 (Bannavem Taburniae nr. the Severn, Britain)–461. Christian missionary. The patron saint of Ireland, also called the Apostle of Ireland; known for his successful conversion of Ireland to Christianity, after a vision called him to preach there; consecrated missionary bishop to Ireland, 432; introduced the Roman alphabet to Ireland. *Confessio; Epistola.*

PAUL, SAINT (born Saul) ? (Tarsus, Asia Minor)–c.67. Christian missionary, theologian. Converted on the road to Damascus from a life of persecuting Christians; his preaching was influential in launching the Christian movement; his letters to outposts of Christianity indelibly stamped Christian thinking; wrote the following New Testament books: Romans, 1 and 2 Corinthians, Galatians, Philippians, Colossians, and 1 Thessalonians.

PICO DELLA MIRANDOLA, COUNT GIOVAN-

**NI,** Feb. 24, 1463 (Mirandola, nr. Ferrara, It.)–Nov. 17, 1494. Italian humanist, philosopher. An eminent Renaissance thinker who championed human dignity and free will; developed a syncretic philosophy; used Kabbalistic doctrine to defend Christian theology. *Oration on the Dignity of Man,* 1486.

**PLATO,** 427? B.C. (Athens, Gr.)–347? B.C. Greek philosopher who attempted to show the rational relationship between the soul, the state, and the cosmos. A student of SOCRATES; founded a school, the Academy, where he taught; traveled to Syracuse, Sicily, twice in a vain attempt to implement his political ideals; poetically presented the rational pursuit for truth and then demonstrated it with brilliance in all fields of knowledge; wrote in dialogue form, the dialectic method he considered the royal road to truth. *Republic; Phaedo; Symposium; Phaedrus; Timaeus; Apology; Meno.*

**PLOTINUS,** 205 (Lycopolis, Egypt?)–270. Roman Neoplatonist philosopher. Transformed a revival of Platonism in the Roman Empire into what is now called Neoplatonism; although opposed to Christianity, his teaching affected Christian thought and influenced the Islamic world.

**PRABHUPADA, SWAMI** (born A. C. Bhaktivedanta Swami Prabhupada), 1896 (Calcutta, Ind.)–Nov. 14, 1977. Indian spiritual leader. Founder of the Hare Krishna movement in the U.S., 1965; set up 108 temples in major cities around the world; wrote 52 books on ancient Vedic culture. *The Bhagavad-Gita As It Is,* 1972.

**PROTAGORAS,** c.485 B.C. (Abdera, Gr.)–c.410 B.C. Greek philosopher. Known as the first of the Sophists; his philosophy is summed up in the familiar dictum, "Man is the measure of all things"; generally credited with being the first to systematize the study of grammar.

**PYTHAGORAS,** c.582 B.C. (Samos, Gr.)–c.497 B.C. Greek philosopher, mathematician, astronomer. Discovered the basic principles of musical pitch; his emphasis on the importance of numbers in the universe sparked much early mathematics, including the Pythagorean theorem on the length of the hypotenuse of a right triangle; the first to note that the morning and evening star were one planet; founded a mystical cult that lasted to about 350 B.C.

**ROUSSEAU, JEAN JACQUES,** June 28, 1712 (Geneva, Switz.)–July 2, 1778. French philosopher. A highly influential 18th-cent. thinker; in his political thought, went beyond the economic liberalism of social-contract theorists such as JOHN LOCKE to recognize the role of the general will of the people; his philosophy of education with its freely accepted "contract" between teacher and pupils inspired modern educational theory; the father of romantic sensibility in his longing for closeness with nature; contributor to the Encyclopédie. *Discours sur l'origine de l'inégalité des hommes,* 1754; *La nouvelle Héloïse,* 1761; *Contrat social,* 1762; *Émile,* 1762; *Du confessions,* 1782.

**RUSSELL, BERTRAND, 3rd EARL,** May 18, 1872 (Trelleck, Monmouthshire, Wales)–Feb. 2, 1970. British philosopher, mathematician, essayist. Beyond his eminent philosophical contributions, wrote popular books for the laymen and took controversial stands on public issues; made major contributions to symbolic logic; began as an idealist, but became a realist and logical atomist; arrested for resisting conscription in WW I and later for his activity against the arms race; O.M., 1949. Nobel Prize in Literature, 1950. *Principia Mathematica,* with ALFRED N. WHITEHEAD, 3 vols. 1910–13; *Mysticism and Logic,* 1918; *History of Western Philosophy,* 1945.

**SARTRE, JEAN-PAUL,** June 21, 1905 (Paris, Fr.)–Apr. 15, 1980. French writer, philosopher. Leading thinker in the existentialist movement; active in the Resistance movement in WW II; one of the major playwrights and novelists of the 20th-cent.; won and declined Nobel Prize for Lit., 1964. *Nausea,* 1938; *Being and Nothingness,* 1943; *No Exit,* 1944; *The Words,* 1964.

**SCHELLING, FRIEDRICH VON,** Jan. 27, 1775 (Leonberg, Württemberg, Ger.)–Aug. 20, 1854. German idealist philosopher. Laid the foundation for much of HEGEL's philosophy; identified reality with the necessary movement of thought; his philosophy of nature was very influential. *System of Transcendental Idealism,* 1800.

**SCHLEGEL, FRIEDRICH VON,** Mar. 10, 1772 (Hanover, Ger.)–Jan. 12, 1829. German writer, critic. Conceived many of the ideas of the early Romantic movement in Germany; founded Oriental studies in Germany with his work on India. *Über die Sprache und Weischeit der Inder,* 1808; *Vorlesungen zur Philosophie der Geschichte,* 2 vols. 1829.

**SCHLEIERMACHER, FRIEDRICH,** Nov. 21, 1768 (Breslau, Ger. [now Wroclaw, Pol.])–Feb. 12, 1834. German Prot. theologian, philosopher. Stressed the integrity of religion and located its distinctiveness in the awareness of absolute dependence. *On Religion: Speeches to its Cultured Despisers,* 1799; *The Christian Faith,* 1821–22.

**SCHOPENHAUER, ARTHUR,** Feb. 22, 1788 (Danzig, Ger. [now Gdansk, Pol.])–Sept. 21, 1860. German philosopher. Stressed the irrational impulses of life arising from the will over the predominantly rational emphasis of thought in vogue at the time; a pessimist, his world was characterized by conflict and unsatisfied desires; concluded that the renunciation of desire was the only possible escape from madness. *The World as Will and Representation,* 1819.

**SENECA THE YOUNGER** (Lucius Annaeus Seneca), c.3 B.C. (Corduba [now Cordoba, Sp.])–65. Roman philosopher, dramatist, statesman. The tutor of Nero, was very powerful at the beginning of Nero's reign; wrote brilliantly on Stoic doctrines; wrote nine tragedies; out of favor, took his own life on the orders of Nero. *Consolationes,* 41.

**SERRA, JUNÍPERO** (born Miguel José Serra), Nov. 24, 1713 (Petra, Majorca)–Aug. 28, 1784. Spanish Franciscan missionary in Mexico and California.

Founded the first mission in upper California, at San Diego, 1769, the guiding spirit behind the establishment of many other missions in the West; known for his asceticism and preaching; beatified, 1988.

**SOCRATES,** c.470 B.C. (Athens, Gr.)–399 B.C. Greek philosopher who introduced the Socratic method (eliciting truth through question-and-answer dialogue) to philosophy. Left no writings, known chiefly through the works of his pupil, PLATO; pursued his method in the marketplace, constantly challenging people to back up their ideas; emphasized moral conduct and ethics; believed in the unity of knowledge and virtue; conceived of the soul as the seat of moral character; brought to trial for corrupting youth, condemned, and forced to drink hemlock.

**SPENCER, HERBERT,** Apr. 27, 1820 (Derby, Derbyshire, Eng.)–Dec. 8, 1903. English naturalist philosopher. Primary formulator of the doctrines of Social Darwinism and popularizer of the idea of "survival of the fittest"; helped establish sociology as a discipline; developed an individualistic doctrine of utilitarianism. *Social Statics,* 1851; *First Principles,* 1862; *The Study of Sociology,* 1872; *The Man Versus the State,* 1884; *The Synthetic Philosophy,* 1896.

**SPINOZA, BARUCH,** Nov. 24, 1632 (Amsterdam, Neth.)–Feb. 21, 1677. Dutch philosopher. Influenced by RENÉ DESCARTES and the geometrical method; deduced the rationally-necessary character of reality; deep religious feeling animated his system; one of the first to raise questions of higher criticism of the Bible. *Theological-Political Treatise,* 1670; *Ethics,* 1677.

**SWEDENBORG, EMANUEL,** Jan. 29, 1688 (Stockholm, Swe.)–Mar. 29, 1772. Swedish scientist, mystic, philosopher, theologian. Wrote scientific treaties on the brain, psychology, and the animal kingdom; a 1745 revelation led him to spiritual matters; rejected many traditional docrines, such as the Trinity, original sin, and eternal punishment; taught that gradual redemption occurs through stages, that heaven and hell are not places but states. *Principia rerum naturalium,* 1734; *Arcana coelestia,* 1749–56.

**TAINE, HIPPOLYTE ADOLPHE,** Apr. 21, 1828 (Vouziers, Ardennes, Fr.)–Mar. 5, 1893. French critic, philosopher. An influential French positivist who attempted to apply the scientific method to the humanities; prof. of aesthetics at École des Beaux-Arts, 1864–84. *The Origins of Contemporary France,* 5 vols., 1876–93; *On Intelligence,* 2 vols., 1870.

**TEILHARD DE CHARDIN, PIERRE,** May 1, 1881 (Sarcenat, Fr.)–Apr. 10, 1955. French R.C. priest, paleontologist, philosopher. Forged a synthesis between Christianity and contemporary theories of evolution; while working as a paleontologist in China, became involved in discovery of Peking Man's skull, 1923–46. *The Phenomenon of Man,* 1938–40; *The Appearance of Man,* 1956; *The Divine Milieu,* 1960.

**TERESA, MOTHER** (born Agnes Gonxha Bojaxhiu), 1910 (Skopje, Yugoslavia). Yugoslav-born Roman Catholic nun called the "saint of the gutters" for her work with the poor of Calcutta, India; founded a religious order in 1950 in Calcutta, called the Missionaries of Charity—providing food, medical care, education, and shelters for lepers and the dying poor; awarded Nobel Peace Prize in 1979.

**TERESA OF AVILA, SAINT** (born Teresa de Cepeda y Ahumda), Mar. 28, 1515 (Gotarrendura, nr. Avila, Sp.)–Oct. 4, 1582. Spanish reformer, author. Reformed the Carmelite order, returning it to its original austerity of total withdrawal; established 17 convents; wrote beautiful mystical literature; canonized, 1628. *The Way of Perfection,* 1583; *The Interior Castle,* 1588; *Life of the Mother Teresa of Jesus,* 1611.

**THALES,** c.624 B.C. (Miletus, Ionia, now Turkey)–c.546 B.C. Greek philosopher. The first recorded Western philosopher to give a rational rather than a mythological answer to the nature of the universe considered water to be the basic constituent of the universe; according to belief, introduced geometry into Greece and predicted an eclipse of the sun.

**THOMAS À BECKET** (Saint Thomas Becket) c.1118 (London, Eng.)–Dec. 29, 1170. English ecclesiastic, confidant and chancellor to King Henry II. Became archbishop of Canterbury, 1162; fought Henry over the church's right to use ecclesiastical courts in trying clergy for secular offenses and other issues; killed in Canterbury Cathedral by four of the king's barons for refusing to withdraw some censures; canonized, 1173.

**THOMAS À KEMPIS** (Thomas Hämmerlein or Hämmerken) c.1379 (Kempen, Ger.)–Aug. 8, 1471. German monk, theologian. Reputed to be author of the *Imitation of Christ,* a great devotional work; copied and wrote at the Mt. St. Agnes convent; a representative of the *devotio moderna* movement of the late Middle Ages.

**THOMAS AQUINAS, SAINT,** c.1224 (Roccasecca, It.)–Mar. 7, 1274. Italian theologian philosopher, Doctor of the Church. Devised one of the most powerful and comprehensive Roman Catholic systems of thought; the greatest figure of Scholasticism; building on ARISTOTLE, defended the place of reason as a harmonious adjunct to faith; his synthesis was made the official R.C. philosophy in 1879; canonized 1323. *Summa theologica,* 1267–73.

**TORQUEMADA, TOMÁS DE,** 1420 (Valladolid, Sp.)–Sept. 16, 1498. Spanish Dominican friar. First Grand Inquisitor in Spain, from 1483; confessor to King FERDINAND V and Queen ISABELLA I, whom he convinced to expel all Jews refusing to be baptized, leading to expulsion of about 170,000 Jews, 1492; centralized the Inquisition and pronounced its guidelines.

**UNAMUNO Y JUGO, MIGUEL DE,** Sept. 29, 1864 (Bilbao, Sp.)–Dec. 31, 1936. Spanish philosopher, writer, educator. Concerned with immortality and the problems of modern Spain; father of the modern Spanish essay; lost many university posts because of his political involvement. *The Tragic Sense of Life in Men and in Peoples,* 1913.

**URBAN II** (born Odo of Lagery), c.1035 (Lagery, Fr.)–July 29, 1099. French pope (1088–99). Launched the Crusade movement, 1095; strengthened the papacy and reformed the church, building on the reforms started by Pope Gregory VII; centralized the administrative power of the Papacy; attempted to clarify the church-state relationship; excommunicated King Philip I of France for repudiating his wife.

**VOLTAIRE (François Marie Arouet)**, Nov. 21, 1694 (Paris, Fr.)–May 30, 1778. French philosopher, writer. Attacked tyranny, bigotry, and cruelty; fought against religious fanaticism and worked for political reform; imprisoned several times for his remarks, crusaded against persecution; wrote poetry, plays, novels, and letters; wrote first modern historical treatises using a critical method. *Le Siècle de Louis XIV*, 1751; *Essai sur les mouers*, 1753, 1756; *Candide*, 1759.

**WEIL, SIMONE**, Feb. 3, 1909 (Paris, Fr.)–Aug. 24, 1943. French mystic, social philosopher, and activist in French Resistance during WW II. *Waiting for God*, 1951; *Gravity and Grace*, 1952; *The Need for Roots*, 1952; *Oppression and Liberty*, 1958.

**WESLEY, JOHN**, June 17, 1703 (Epworth, Lincs., Eng.)–Mar. 2, 1791. English evangelist, theologian, a founder of the Methodist movement. Ordained an Anglican priest, 1728; led study group at Oxford called methodists, 1729; journeyed on mission to Georgia in America, 1735; upon return to England experienced a spiritual conversion; set up Methodist societies and became an influential revivalist, developing a theology suitable to revivals; rejected Calvinist doctrine of election.

**WHITEHEAD, ALFRED NORTH**, Feb. 15, 1861 (Ramsgate, Kent, Eng.)–Dec. 30, 1947. English mathematician, philosopher. Made important contributions to mathematics, logic, the philosophy of science, and metaphysics; late in life, developed a philosophy of organism that stressed the linkage of matter, space, and time. *Principia Mathematica*, with BERTRAND RUSSELL, 1910–13; *Science and the Modern World*, 1925; *Process and Reality*, 1929.

**WILLEBRANDS, JOHANNES**, Sept. 4, 1909 (Bovenkarspel, Neth.). Dutch cardinal (since 1969). Founded the Catholic Conference for Ecumenical Questions, 1952; pres., Secretariat for the Union of Christians, 1969; archbishop of Utrecht, 1975–83.

**WITTGENSTEIN, LUDWIG JOSEF JOHANN**, Apr. 26, 1889 (Vienna, Austria)–Apr. 19, 1951. Austrian–English philosopher, teacher. Prof., Cambridge U., 1939–47; molded the modern discipline of philosophy with his logical theories and philosophy of language; pioneered in the philosophical study of ordinary language. *Tractatus Logicophilosophicus*, 1921; *Philosophical Investigations*, 1953.

**WYCLIFFE, JOHN**, c.1320 (Hipswell?, North Riding of Yorkshire, Eng.)–Dec. 31, 1384. English theologian, church reformer. A forerunner of the Reformation; challenged Church authority by claiming supreme authority for the Scriptures and holding that the Church did not have the only access to grace; promoted a notable translation of the Bible.

**ZENO**, c.490 B.C. (Elea, now in Italy)–c.430 B.C. Greek philosopher. Defended PARMENIDES by demonstrating, with his famous paradoxes, that motion and multiplicity are logically impossible; attempts to resolve his paradoxes sparked major mathematical and physical–science developments for the next 2,000 years.

**ZOROASTER**, c.660 B.C. (Rhages, Medea [now Rayy, Iran])–c.583 B.C. Persian religious reformer, prophet, founder of Zoroastrianism, or Parsiism. After a revelation from Ahura Mazda, the Wise Lord, he preached his belief and converted King Vishtaspa; his teachings were monotheistic, although polytheism and a pronounced dualism were present; emphasized the vanquishing of the spirit of evil.

**ZWINGLI, HULDRYCH**, Jan. 1, 1484 (Wildhaus in the Toggenburg, Sankt Gallen, Switz.)–Oct. 11, 1531. Swiss Prot. reformer, a leader of the Prot. Reformation. Preached his new views by means of scriptural study; his lectures on the New Testament sparked the Reformation in Switzerland, 1522. *Commentary on True and False Religion*, 1525; *67 Proofs*, 1522.

# Historians, Economists, and Other Scholars

ACTON, JOHN EMERICH, BARON ACTON, Jan. 10, 1834 (Naples, It.)–June 19, 1902. English historian. A Christian liberal who edited *The Rambler*, a Roman Catholic monthly; opposed doctrine of papal infallibility promulgated at first Vatican Council, 1870; as prof. of modern history at Cambridge U. (1895–1902), planned the great *Cambridge Modern History*; created baron, 1869.

ADAMS, BROOKS, June 24, 1848 (Quincy, Mass.)–Feb. 13, 1927. U.S. historian and social critic. Believed that commercial civilizations rise and fall predictably, coming together in large cities and later throw off spiritual and creative values. *The Law of Civilization and Decay*, 1895; *America's Economic Supremacy*, 1900. (Son of C. F. ADAMS and grandson of J. Q. ADAMS.)

ADAMS, HENRY BROOKS, Feb. 16, 1838 (Boston, Mass.)–Mar. 27, 1918. U.S. historian, novelist. Edited the *North American Review*, 1870–76; prof. of history, Harvard U., 1870–77. *History of the United States*, 9 vols., 1889–91; *Mont-Saint-Michel and Chartres*, 1904; *The Education of Henry Adams*, pub. 1907. (Son of C. F. ADAMS; grandson of J. Q. ADAMS; great-grandson of J. and A. ADAMS.)

ADLER, ALFRED F., Feb. 7, 1870 (Vienna, Austria) –May 28, 1937. Austrian psychiatrist. Founded the school of individual psychology. Postulated that a feeling of inferiority was the source of all personality difficulties and was compensated for with a need for power or self-assertion.

ALLAIS, MAURICE, May 31, 1911 (Paris, Fr.). French economist. Noted for theories showing how a monopoly could set prices for such products as coal or electricity at the best level for society; awarded Nobel Prize in economics, 1988.

ANGELL, SIR NORMAN THOMAS (born Ralph Norman Angell Lane), Dec. 26, 1874 (Holbeach, Lincolnshire, Eng.)–Oct. 7, 1967. English economist, author. Rancher, prospector, and journalist in western U.S., to 1898; editor of *Foreign Affairs*, 1928–31; in his antiwar book, *The Great Illusion* (1910), argued that common economic interests of nations made war futile; awarded Nobel Peace Prize, 1933; knighted, 1931.

ARENDT, HANNAH, Oct. 14, 1906 (Hanover, Ger.)–Dec. 4, 1975. German-U.S. political scientist, philosopher. Political theorist known for her study of totalitarianism and writings on Jewish affairs; a refugee from Nazi Germany. *The Origins of Totalitarianism*, 1951; *Eichmann in Jerusalem*, 1963.

BABBITT, IRVING, Aug. 2, 1865 (Dayton, Ohio) –July 15, 1933. U.S. scholar, educator, literary critic. With Paul Elmer Moore, founded modern humanistic movement; a foe of Romanticism and its offshoots, realism and naturalism, he championed the classical values of restraint and moderation. *Rousseau and Romanticism*, 1919; *Democracy and Leadership*, 1924.

BAGEHOT, WALTER, Feb. 3, 1826 (Langport, Somerset, Eng.)–Mar. 24, 1877. English economist, editor, literary critic, political analyst. As editor of *The Economist*, helped build its reputation, 1860–77; applied the concept of evolution to political societies. *The English Constitution*, 1867; *Physics and Politics*, 1872; *Lombard Street*, 1873; *Literary Studies*, 1879.

BANCROFT, GEORGE, Oct. 3, 1800 (Worcester, Mass.)–Jan. 17, 1891. U.S. diplomat, historian. Called the "Father of American History" for his 10-volume *A History of the United States* (1834–74). U.S. secy. of the navy, 1845–46; U.S. min. to England, 1846–49; min. to Prussia, 1867–71; min. to German Emp., 1871–74.

BARTLETT, JOHN, June 14, 1820 (Plymouth, Mass.)–Dec. 3, 1905. U.S. editor, bookseller. Compiled the famous *Familiar Quotations* (1855) that has become the standard reference work in its field.

BEARD, CHARLES A., Nov. 27, 1874 (nr. Knightstown, Ind.)–Sept. 1, 1948. U.S. historian. Noted for his economic interpretation of U.S. institutional development; analyzed motivational factors in the founding of institutions; criticized scientific certitude in historical research. *An Economic Interpretation of the Constitution, 1913.*

**BEDE, THE VENERABLE,** 672–73 (nr. Narrow, Northumbria, [now Co. Dunham], Eng.)–May 25, 735. English historian, monk. His *Ecclesiastical History of the English People* (731) remains an indispensable source for the conversion of the Anglo-Saxon tribes to Christianity; set the example in England for dating events from the birth of Christ (A.D. and B.C.)

**BENEDICT, RUTH,** June 5, 1887 (New York, N.Y.)–Sept. 17, 1948. U.S. anthropologist. Demonstrated the role of culture in individual personality formation; a student and colleague of FRANZ BOAS at Columbia U. *Patterns of Culture,* 1934; *The Chrysanthemum and the Sword: Patterns of Japanese Culture,* 1946.

**BETTLEHEIM, BRUNO,** Aug. 28, 1903 (Vienna, Austria)–Mar. 13, 1990. Austrian-U.S. psychologist, educator. Authority on children, especially emotionally disturbed children. Taught educational psychology and headed Sonia Shankman Orthogenic School, at U. of Chicago, 1944–73. *Love Is Not Enough,* 1950; *The Informed Heart,* 1960; *The Children of the Dream,* 1969; *The Uses of Enchantment,* 1976; *A Good Enough Parent,* 1987.

**BILLINGTON, JAMES H.,** June 1, 1929 (Bryn Mawr, Pa.). U.S. historian. A specialist in Russian studies, taught at Harvard and Princeton; 13th librarian of Congress, 1987– . *The Icon and the Axe,* 1966.

**BLACKSTONE, SIR WILLIAM,** July 10, 1723 (London, Eng.)–Feb. 14, 1780. English jurist, writer. Best known for his *Commentaries on the Laws of England* (4 vols., 1765–69); appointed to the Court of King's Bench and knighted, 1770; an advocate of prison reform.

**BLOOM, ALLEN,** Sept. 14, 1930 (Indianapolis, Ind.). U.S. philosopher. Prof. of Philosophy at Univ. of Chicago; in his surprise bestseller, *The Closing of the American Mind* (1987), argued that universities no longer teach students how to think and that those who want a liberal education can no longer get one.

**BOAS, FRANZ,** July 9, 1858 (Minden, Ger.)– Dec. 22, 1942. German-U.S. anthropologist. As the first professor of anthropology, at Columbia U. (from 1899), exerted a great influence on the field; trained many important U.S. anthropologists, including MARGARET MEAD; founded relativistic, culture-centered anthropology; specialist in the cultures and languages of American Indians. *The Mind of Primitive Man,* 1911 (rev. 1938); *Primitive Art,* 1927; *Race, Language and Culture,* 1940.

**BOORSTIN, DANIEL J.,** Oct. 1, 1914 (Atlanta, Ga.) U.S. historian. A prolific writer on American history. Dir. of Smithsonian Inst.'s Museum of History and Technology, 1969–73; librarian of Congress, 1975–87. *The Americans,* 3 vols., 1958–74.

**BOYD ORR, JOHN, BARON BOYD ORR OF BRECHIN MEARNS,** Sept. 23, 1880 (Kilmaurs, Ayrshire, Scot.)–June 25, 1971. British nutritionist, agricultural scientist. A major contributor to the solution of world food problems and an advocate of world govt.; dir.-gen. of UN Food and Agri. Org., 1945–48; awarded Nobel Peace Prize, 1949; knighted, 1935; created baron, 1949. *Food and the People,* 1943; *The White Man's Dilemma,* 1953.

**BRINTON, (Clarence) CRANE,** Feb. 12, 1898 (Winsted, Conn.)–Sept. 7, 1968. U.S. historian. An authority on the history of ideas and an expert on the theory of revolution. Taught at Harvard U., 1923–68. *The Anatomy of Revolution,* 1938.

**BRONOWSKI, JACOB,** Jan. 18, 1908 (Poland)– Aug. 22, 1974. U.S. historian, mathematician. A writer on science and human value; his *The Ascent of Man* (1973) was made into a popular TV series detailing the breakthroughs in human civilization. Senior fellow at Salk Inst. of Biological Studies, 1946–74. *Science and Human Values,* 1958.

**BROOKS, VAN WYCK,** Feb. 16, 1886 (Plainfield, N.J.)–May 2, 1963. U.S. literary critic, cultural historian. Viewed literature as an outgrowth of a natl. culture. *The Wine of the Puritans,* 1909; *America's Coming of Age,* 1915; *The Flowering of New England, 1815–65,* 1936 (Pulitzer Prize in history, 1937.

**BUCHANAN, JAMES M.,** Oct. 12, 1919 (Murfreesboro, Tenn.). U.S. economist. Pioneered in development of new methods of analyzing economic and political decision-making; awarded Nobel Prize in economics, 1986.

**BURCKHARDT, JACOB,** May 25, 1818 (Basel, Switz.)–Aug. 8, 1897. Swiss cultural historian. Famous for his pioneering study in Ren. Italy; saw individualistic modern man as originating at the Ren. and being threatened by industrialization. *The Civilization of the Renaissance in Italy,* 1860.

**BURKE, EDMUND,** Jan. 12, 1729 (Dublin, Ire.)– July 9, 1797. British political writer, statesman. A prominent conservative political theorist and a reformer in Parliament; worked for a more conciliatory policy with the American colonies; considered unrestricted rationalism to be destructive in human affairs. *Reflections on the Revolution in France,* 1790.

**CARLYLE, THOMAS,** Dec. 4, 1795 (Ecclefechan, Dumfriesshire, Scot.)–Feb. 4, 1881. Scottish essayist, historian. Noted for his spiritual autobiography, *Reminisences* (written 1866, pub. 1881) and *The French Revolution* (1837). Stressed the need for a strong paternalistic govt.; believed certain "heroes" molded history.

**CASTAÑEDA, CARLOS,** Dec. 25, 1931 (São Paulo, Braz.) U.S. anthropologist. Author of popular books about his experiences as the apprentice to a Yaqui Indian sorcerer. *The Teachings of Don Juan,* 1968; *Journey to Ixtlan,* 1972; *Tales of Power,* 1974.

**CATTON, BRUCE,** Oct. 8, 1899 (Petoskey, Mich.)– Aug. 28, 1978. U.S. historian, editor, journalist. Noted for his works on the military history of the Civil War. Editor (1954–59) and senior editor (1959–78), *American Heritage;* awarded Presiden-

tial Medal of Freedom, 1977. *A Stillness at Appomattox*, 1953 (Pulitzer Prize in history, 1954.)
**CHAMPOLLION, JEAN-FRANÇOIS,** Dec. 23, 1790 (Figeac, Fr.)–Mar. 4, 1832. French archeologist. Founded the science of Egyptology. Using the Rosetta Stone, established the principles for deciphering Egyptian hieroglyphics.
**CHOMSKY, NOAM,** Dec. 7, 1928 (Philadelphia, Pa.). U.S. linguist, writer, political activist. Founded transformational or generative grammar, which revolutionized the scientific study of language; a prolific propagandist for radical causes. *Cartesian Linguistics*, 1966.
**COLES, ROBERT,** Oct. 12, 1929 (Boston, Mass.). U.S. child psychiatrist, educator, writer. Has written extensively about people caught up in the turmoil of social crisis; as activist working extensively with women and children in crisis. *Children of Crisis*, 1967–77 (1973 Pulitzer Prize for volumes II & III); *Moral Life of Children*, 1985; *Call of the Stories*, 1989.
**COMFORT, ALEX,** Feb. 10, 1920 (London, Eng.). English fiction and nonfiction writer. A. Ph.D. in biochemistry and dir. of research in gerontology at University C., London. Best known for *The Joy of Sex: A Gourmet's Guide to Love Making* (1972) and *More Joy* (1974).
**COMMAGER, HENRY STEELE,** Oct. 25, 1902 (Pittsburgh, Pa.). U.S. historian. Prolific writer on a wide range of topics; a Jeffersonian liberal. *The American Mind*, 1950.
**DEBREU, GERARD,** July 4, 1921 (Calais, Fr.). U.S. economist. Studied how prices operate to balance what producers supply with what buyers want; awarded Nobel Prize in economics, 1983. *The Theory of Value: An Axiomatic Analysis of Economic Equilibrium*, 1959.
**DEUTSCH, HELENE,** Oct. 9, 1884 (Przemysl, A.-H. [now Poland])–Mar. 29, 1982. U.S. psychoanalyst. A pioneer in the Freudian movement and last of the original Freudians. *The Psychology of Women*, 2 vols., 1944 (U.S.).
**DE VOTO, BERNARD A.** Jan. 11, 1897 (Ogden, Ut.)–Nov. 13, 1955. U.S. editor, critic, historian, novelist. Noted for his works on U.S. literature and the American frontier; wrote the "Easy Chair" column for *Harper's*, 1935–52. *Across the Wide Missouri*, 1947 (awarded Pulitzer Prize in history, 1948).
**DEWEY, MELVIL,** Dec. 10, 1851 (Adams Center, N.Y.)–Dec. 26, 1931. U.S. librarian. Devised the Dewey Decimal System of classification for library cataloging; founded the first training school for librarians, a founder of the *Library Journal* and American Library Assn.
**DU PONT DE NEMOURS, PIERRE SAMUEL,** Dec. 14, 1739 (Paris, Fr.)–Aug. 6, 1817. French economist. The main writer of the Physiocratic school of economics; an important figure in the Constituent Assembly during the French Revolution; emigrated to U.S., 1800; his two sons VICTOR MARIE and ÉLEUTHÈRE IRÉNÉE, founded the two U.S. branches of the family.

**DURKHEIM, EMILE,** Apr. 15, 1858 (Epinal, Fr.)–Nov. 15, 1917. French sociologist. One of the founders and leaders of modern sociology; formulated a rigorous methodology for sociology; founded *L'Année Sociologique*, 1896; conducted studies on suicide, moral education, population density, the division of labor, and primitive religion.
**EISELEY, LOREN COREY,** Sept. 3, 1907 (Lincoln, Neb.)–July 9, 1977. U.S. anthropologist, naturalist. A major interpreter of CHARLES DARWIN and poetic popularizer of biological science. *The Immense Journey*, 1957; *Darwin's Century*, 1958; *All the Strange Hours*, 1975.
**ELLIS, (Henry) HAVELOCK,** Feb. 2, 1859 (Croydon, Surrey, Eng.)–July 8, 1939. English scientist, man of letters. Pioneer writer on the psychology of sex; conducted the first study of homosexuality; wrote extensively about masturbation; an advocate of sex education. *Studies in the Psychology of Sex*, 1897–1928.
**EVANS, BERGEN (BALDWIN),** Sept. 19, 1904 (Franklin, Ohio)–Feb. 4, 1978. U.S. grammarian, critic. Prof. of English at Northwestern U., 1932–75; wrote the column "Skeptic's Corner" in *The American Mercury*, 1946–50; author of "The Last Word," a daily syndicated newspaper feature; host of several language-oriented TV shows. *Natural History of Nonsense*, 1946; *Dictionary of Contemporary American Usage*, 1957; *Dictionary of Quotations*, 1968.
**FELDSTEIN, MARTIN E.,** Nov. 25, 1939 (New York, N.Y.). U.S. economist. At Harvard Univ. from 1967, full prof. of economics, 1969– . *The American Economy in Transition* (ed.).
**FIEDLER, LESLIE,** Mar. 8, 1917 (Newark, N.J.). U.S. literary critic. Controversial critic who had applied Freudian and Jungian concepts to American literature and social thought. Prof. of English at State Univ. of New York at Buffalo, 1965– . *Love and Death in the American Novel*, 1959.
**FRASER, LADY ANTONIA** (now married to HAROLD PINTER) Aug. 27, 1932 (London, Eng.). English biographer. *Mary, Queen of Scots*, 1969; *Cromwell: The Lord Protector*, 1973; *Royal Charles*, 1979; *The Weaker Vessel*, 1984.
**FRAZER, SIR JAMES,** Jan. 1, 1854 (Glasgow, Scot.)–May 7, 1941. Scottish anthropologist, classicist. Author of *The Golden Bough: A Study in Magic and Religion* (1890), a masterpiece on primitive culture; devised a theory of divine kingship and a theory of psychic development; knighted, 1914.
**FRIEDMAN, MILTON,** July 31, 1912 (Brooklyn, N.Y.). U.S. economist. Known for his work in monetary economics; supports laissez-faire economic policies, floating exchange rates, and a stable Federal Reserve policy; prof. at U. of Chicago, 1946– ; awarded Nobel Prize in economics, 1976. *Capitalism and Freedom*, 1962.
**FROMM, ERICH,** Mar. 23, 1900 (Frankfurt, Ger.)–Mar. 18, 1980. Ger.-U.S. psychoanalyst. Emphasized the role of social and cultural pressures on individ-

uals. *Escape from Freedom*, 1941; *Man for Himself*, 1947; *The Art of Loving*, 1956.

**GALBRAITH, JOHN KENNETH,** Oct. 15, 1908 (Iona Sta., Ontario, Can.). U.S. economist. Author of popular books on the U.S. economy; involved in several Democratic presidential campaigns, including those of ADLAI STEVENSON, JOHN F. KENNEDY, and GEORGE MCGOVERN; U.S. amb. to India, 1961–63; chm. of Americans for Democratic Action, 1967–69. *The Affluent Society*, 1958; *The New Industrial State*, 1967.

**GIBBON, EDWARD,** May 8, 1737 (Putney, Surrey, Eng.)–Jan. 16, 1794. British historian. Best known as the author of *The History of the Decline and Fall of the Roman Empire* (1776–88); considered the greatest English historian of his century.

**GOODALL, JANE,** Apr. 3, 1934 (London, Eng.). British ethologist. An authority on chimpanzees, discovered that they are not strict vegetarians and are crude toolmakers; has studied great apes at the Gombe Stream Game Reserve, Tanzania, from 1960. *My Friends the Wild Chimpanzees*, 1967; *In the Shadow of Man*, 1971.

**HAAVELMO, TRYGVE,** ? (Norway). Norwegian economist. Pioneered in methods for testing economic theories, which helped prepare the way for modern economic forecasting; awarded Nobel Prize in economics, 1989.

**HALL, GRANVILLE STANLEY,** Feb. 1, 1844 (Ashfield, Mass.)–Apr. 24, 1924. U.S. psychologist. Founded American experimental psychology; pioneer in child and educational psychology; a major exponent of SIGMUND FREUD's work. *Adolescence*, 1904.

**HANDLIN, OSCAR,** Sept. 29, 1915 (Brooklyn, N.Y.). U.S. historian. Influential in the field of U.S. social history; noted for his work on immigration to the U.S., *The Uprooted*, 1951 (Pulitzer Prize in history, 1952).

**HARRINGTON, MICHAEL,** Feb. 24, 1928 (St. Louis, Mo.)–July 31, 1989. U.S. writer. Noted leftist author of *The Other America* (1963), which played a major role in awakening the U.S. to the problem of American poverty. *Twilight of Capitalism*, 1976; *Taking Sides*, 1985.

**HAYEK, FRIEDRICH AUGUST VON,** May 8, 1899 (Vienna, Austria). Anglo-Austrian economist. Leading speaker for the Austrian school of economics, which favors a free-market economy and opposes govt. management; awarded Nobel Prize in economics (with GUNNAR MYRDAL), 1974. *Prices and Production*, 1931; *The Pure Theory of Capital*, 1941; *The Road to Serfdom*, 1944.

**HERODOTUS,** c.485 B.C. (Halicarnassus [now Bodrum, Turk.])–c.430 B.C. Greek historian. As author of the first history of the ancient world, called the "Father of History"; wrote primarily about the Persian wars; though his history lacks accuracy, it is comprehensive and has a charming, anecdotal style.

**HITE, SHERE D.** (born Shirley Diana Gregory) Nov. 2, 1942 (St. Joseph, Mo.). U.S. author, cultural historian. Dir. of Natl. Org. of Women's Female Sexuality Project, 1972– . *Sexual Honesty: By Women for Women*, 1974; *The Hite Report: A Nationwide Study of Female Sexuality*, 1976; *The Hite Report on Male Sexuality*, 1981; *The Hite Report: Women and Love; A Cultural Revolution in Progress*, 1987.

**HOFSTADTER, RICHARD,** Aug. 6, 1916 (Buffalo, N.Y.)–Oct. 24, 1970. U.S. historian. Author of popular and controversial books on American social and intellectual history. *The American Political Tradition*, 1948; *The Age of Reform: From Bryan to F.D.R.*, 1955 (Pulitzer Prize for history, 1955); *Anti-Intellectualism in American Life* (Pulitzer Prize in general non-fiction, 1964), 1964.

**HORNEY, KAREN,** Sept. 16, 1885 (Hamburg, Ger.)–Dec. 4, 1952. Norwegian-German psychoanalyst, writer, teacher. Asst. dir., the American Institute for Psychoanalysis; stressed social and environmental factors in determining personality; studied the behavior of children. *The Neurotic Personality of Our Time*, 1937; *Neurosis and Human Growth*, 1950.

**HOWE, IRVING,** June 11, 1920 (New York, N.Y.). U.S. literary and social critic. A vocal radical; editor of *Dissent*, 1955– ; prof. of English at Hunter C., 1963– . *Sherwood Anderson*, 1951; *World of Our Fathers*, 1976 (National Book Award, 1977); *Socialism in America*, 1985.

**HULME, T(homas) E(rnest),** Sept. 16, 1883 (Endon, Staffordshire, Eng.)–Sept. 28, 1917. English critic, philosopher, poet. Theorist of the Imagist movement, whose ideas were popularized by T. S. ELIOT and EZRA POUND. *Speculations*, 1924; *Notes on Language and Style*, 1929; *Further Speculations*, 1955.

**JANEWAY, ELIOT,** Jan. 1, 1913 (New York, N.Y.). U.S. economist, author. Economic advisor to many firms; author of syndicated newspaper column on the nation's business. *The Economics of Crisis*, 1968; *What Shall I Do with My Money?*, 1970.

**JUNG, CARL GUSTAV,** July 26, 1875 (Kesswil, Switz.)–June 6, 1961. Swiss psychologist, psychiatrist. Founder of analytic psychology. Differentiated people according to attitude types, extroverted and introverted; conducted studies in mental association; an associate of S. FREUD, split with him over the question of libido. *The Psychology of Dementia Praecox*, 1909; *The Psychology of the Unconscious*, 1916.

**KAZIN, ALFRED,** June 5, 1915 (Brooklyn, N.Y.). U.S. critic, writer. *On Native Grounds*, 1942; *Walker in the City*, 1951; *Starting Out in the Thirties*, 1965; *Bright Book of Life*, 1973.

**KEYNES, JOHN MAYNARD,** June 5, 1883 (Cambridge, Eng.)–Apr. 21, 1946. British economist. The most influential modern economist, whose ideas on the causes of prolonged unemployment demanded a greater role for govt. in the economy; argued that private and public expenditure determines the levels of income and employment. *Economic Consequences of the Peace*, 1919; *The General Theory of*

*Employment, Interest, and Money,* 1935; created baron, 1942.

**KINSEY, ALFRED CHARLES,** June 23, 1894 (Hoboken, N.J.)–Aug. 25, 1956. U.S. zoologist. Author of studies of the sexual life of human beings based on 18,500 personal interviews; founded Institute for Sex Research, 1947. *Sexual Behavior in the Human Male,* 1948; *Sexual Behavior in the Human Female,* 1953.

**KLEIN, LAWRENCE R.,** Sept. 14, 1920 (Omaha, Neb.). U.S. economist. Noted for his research dealing with the construction and analysis of empirical models of business fluctuations; awarded Nobel Prize in economics, 1980.

**KRAFFT-EBBING, RICHARD, BARON,** Aug. 14, 1840 (Mannheim, Germany)–Dec. 22, 1902. German neurologist, psychiatrist. Initiated study of sexual deviation; coined the words *paranoia, sadism, masochism. Psychopathia Sexualis,* 1886.

**LAROUSSE, PIERRE,** Oct. 23, 1817 (Toucy, Fr.)–Jan. 3, 1875. French lexicographer, encyclopedist. Publisher of many of best education and reference books of 19th-cent. France, including the *Grand dictionnaire universel du XIX siècle* (15 vols., 1866–76).

**LASKI, HAROLD,** June 30, 1893 (Manchester, Eng.)–Mar. 24, 1950. English political scientist, educator. Beginning as a pluralist, became a Marxist during the troubled 1930s. Prof. at London School of Economics, 1926–50; member of Executive Com. of the Labour Party, 1936–49. *The Grammar of Politics,* 1925.

**LEAKEY, LOUIS,** Aug. 7, 1903 (Kabete, Kenya)–Oct. 1, 1972. British archeologist, anthropologist. Made fossil discoveries in E. Africa that proved that humans existed much earlier than previously thought and that human evolution was centered in Africa, not Asia. *Stone-Age Africa,* 1936; *White African,* 1937; *Olduvai Gorge,* 1952. (Husband of M. LEAKEY; father of R. LEAKEY.)

**LEAKEY, MARY,** Feb. 6, 1913 (London, Eng.). English anthropologist. Her discovery of *zinjanthropus* (1959) and fossils in Laetoli, Tanzania (1975), helped push back the dates of the first true man to almost four million years ago. *Disclosing the Past,* 1984. (Wife of L. B. LEAKEY; mother of R. LEAKEY.)

**LEAKEY, RICHARD E.,** Dec. 19, 1944 (Nairobi, Kenya.). English anthropologist. Based on his discoveries in Koobi Fora in Kenya, he argued that three humanlike forms existed of which two died out and the third, *Homo habilis,* evolved into *Homo erectus,* the direct ancestor of *Homo sapiens;* dir. of Natl. Museum of Kenya, 1968– . *Origins* (with Roger Lewin), 1977; *People of the Lake* (with Roger Lewin), 1978; *Human Origins,* 1982. (Son of L. and M. LEAKEY.)

**LEONTIEF, WASSILY W.,** Aug. 5, 1906 (St. Petersburg, Rus. [now Leningrad, USSR]). U.S. economist. Originated the input-output analysis used in economic planning and in forecasting output and growth requirements. Prof. at Harvard U., 1931–75;

prof. at N.Y.U., 1975–  ; awarded Nobel Prize in economics, 1973.

**LEVI-STRAUSS, CLAUDE,** Nov. 28, 1908 (Brussels, Belg.). French anthropologist. Founder of structural anthropology; prof. at Institut d'Ethnologie, U. of Paris, 1948–59; prof. at College de France, 1959–  ; elected to French Acad., 1973. *Tristes Tropiques,* 1955; *Structural Anthropology,* 1958; *From Honey to Ashes,* 1966.

**LEWIS, OSCAR,** Dec. 25, 1914 (New York, N.Y.)–Dec. 16, 1970. U.S. anthropologist. Noted for his theory that poverty creates an identifiable culture that transcends national differences. *Five Families,* 1959; *The Children of Sanchez,* 1961; *La Vida,* 1966; *Anthropological Essays,* 1970.

**LEWIS, W. ARTHUR,** Jan. 23, 1915 (St. Lucia, B.W.I.). British economist. Widely regarded for his work on developmental economies; awarded Nobel Prize in economics (shared with T. SCHULTZ), 1979. *The Theory of Economic Growth.*

**LIDDELL HART, SIR B(asil) H(enry),** Oct. 31, 1895 (Paris, Fr.)–Jan. 29, 1970. English military historian and strategist. Developed the "expanding torrent" method of attack; advocate of mechanized warfare, surprise attack, mobility, and airpower; military correspondent for the *Daily Telegraph* (1925–35) and *The Times* (1935–39); knighted, 1966. *The Remaking of Modern Armies,* 1927; *Strategy of Indirect Approach,* 1929.

**LIFTON, ROBERT JAY,** May 16, 1926 (New York, N.Y.). U.S. psychiatrist, author. Working as an air force psychiatrist developed material for several major studies linking psychiatry with ethics and history. *Thought Reform and the Psychology of Totalism,* 1961; *Death in Life,* 1969 (Natl. Book Award); *Indefensible Weapons,* 1982.

**LIVY** (in full, Titus Livius), c.59 B.C. (Patavium [now Padua, It.])–A.D. 17. Roman historian. The most famous of the ancient Roman historians; his *The Annals of the Roman People* consisted of 142 books covering the period 753 B.C. to 9 B.C.; only 35 survive.

**MACAULAY, THOMAS B., BARON MACAULAY OF ROTHLEY,** Oct. 25, 1800 (Rothley Temple, Leicestershire, Eng.)–Dec. 28, 1859. English historian. His *History of England from the Accession of James the Second* (5 vols., 1849–61) is considered one of the great works of the 19th century; published poetry and essays, especially in *Edinburgh Review;* member of Parliament, 1830, 1831, 1839–47, and 1852–56; secy. of war, 1839–41; buried in Westminster Abbey; created Baron, 1857.

**MALTHUS, THOMAS R.,** Feb. 14, 1766 (Dorking, Surrey, Eng.)–Dec. 23, 1834. English political economist. Pioneer in modern population-theory who warned that poverty was inevitable since population increases by geometrical ratio, while means of subsistence increase only arithmetically; F.R.S., 1819. *Essay on the Principles of Population,* 1798.

**MEAD, MARGARET,** Dec. 16, 1901 (Philadelphia, Pa.)–Nov. 15, 1978. U.S. anthropologist. Noted for her work on childhood and adolescence, the cultural conditioning of sexual behavior, national character, and culture change. Outspoken on contemporary social issues. Asst. curator (1926–42), assoc. curator (1942–64), and curator (1964–69) of ethnology at American Museum of Natural History. *Coming of Age in Samoa*, 1928; *Male and Female*, 1949; *Culture and Commitment*, 1970.

**MENNINGER, KARL A.,** July 22, 1893 (Topeka, Kan.)–July 18, 1990. U.S. psychiatrist. A cofounder of the Menninger Fndn., a major center for the study and treatment of mental-health problems, 1941; a pioneer in the modern reform of mental hospitals; Menninger Clinic founded, 1919.

**MICHELET, JULES,** Aug. 21, 1798 (Paris, Fr.)–Feb. 9, 1874. French historian. Great historian of the Romantic school, evoked the Middle Ages with brilliance. Work marred by his bias against the clergy, the nobility, and the monarchic institutions. *Historie de France*, 1833–46.

**MILL, JOHN STUART,** May 20, 1806 (London, Eng.)–May 8, 1873. English economist, philosopher. Influential utilitarian who examined the rule of induction and who urged reform and expanded democracy; applied the principles of utility to political theory. *A System of Logic*, 1843; *The Principles of Political Economy* (2 vols.), 1848; *On Liberty*, 1859; *Subjection of Women*, 1869; *Autobiography*, 1873.

**MILLER, PERRY GILBERT,** Feb. 25, 1905 (Chicago, Ill.)–Dec. 9, 1963. U.S. historian. A leader in American intellectual history who wrote extensively on the colonial period; argued that religion rather than economics was the primary motive behind the settling of New England. *The New England Mind*, (2 vols.), 1939, 1953; *Errand into the Wilderness*, 1956.

**MILLS, C. WRIGHT,** Aug. 28, 1916 (Waco, Tex.)–Mar. 20, 1962. U.S. sociologist. Argued that social scientists should be activists rather than disinterested observers. *White Collar*, 1951; *The Power Elite*, 1956; *The Sociological Imagination*, 1959.

**MONNET, JEAN,** Nov. 9, 1888 (Cognac, Fr.)–Mar. 16, 1979. French economist, govt. official. The architect of the European Common Market; played a leading role in the financial reconstruction of Poland, Austria, and Rumania following WW I; recapitalized the Diamond Match Co., after the scandal involving IVAR KREUGER; sent as the League of Nations representative to China, 1933; through his posts within the French govt., developed the Schuman Plan, the first step to organizing European economic life, embodied in treaty which created European Coal and Steel Community, which later became the Common Market, 1950.

**MONTAGU, (Montague Francis) ASHLEY,** June 28, 1905 (London, Eng.). British-U.S. anthropologist, author. Writes prolifically for the layman. *Man's Most Dangerous Myth: The Fallacy of Race*, 1942; *The Natural Superiority of Women*, 1953, 1958; *The Prevalence of Nonsense*, 1967.

**MORISON, SAMUEL ELIOT,** July 9, 1887 (Boston, Mass.)–May 15, 1976. U.S. historian. Prof. at Harvard U., 1925–55; official historian of Harvard U. and official U.S. naval historian for WW II. *The*

*Growth of the American Republic* (with H. S. COMMAGER), 1930; *Admiral of the Ocean Sea*, 1942 (Pulitzer Prize in biography, 1943); *John Paul Jones*, 1958 (Pulitzer Prize in biography, 1959).

**MUMFORD, LEWIS,** Oct. 19, 1895 (Flushing, N.Y.)–Jan. 26, 1990. U.S. social critic. Wrote on architecture and the city. *Sticks and Stone*, 1924; *The Brown Decades: A Study of the Arts in America, 1861–95*, 1931; *The Culture of Cities*, 1938; *The City in History*, 1961.

**MYRDAL, GUNNAR,** Dec. 6, 1898 (Gustafs, Swe.)–May 17, 1987. Swedish economist, sociologist, public official. Involved in the development of Swedish welfare state and the United Nations; awarded Nobel Prize in economics (with F. VON HAYEK), 1974. *Beyond the Welfare State*, 1960; *Asian Drama*, 3 vols., 1968.

**NAISBITT, JOHN H.,** ? U.S. trend analyst. Developed technique of using content analysis to determine trends; best known for his influential and best-selling book, *Megatrends* (1982), which he co-authored with his wife Patricia Aburdene; founder, Urban Research Corp. (now Naisbitt Group), 1968.

**NEARING, SCOTT,** Aug. 6, 1883 (Morris Run, Pa.)–Aug. 24, 1983. U.S sociologist. Well-known radical who fought against child labor, war, and big business; retired to become a homesteader in Maine. *Poverty and Riches*, 1916; *War*, 1931; *Living the Good Life*, 1954; *The Making of a Radical*, 1972.

**NEVINS, ALLAN,** May 20, 1890 (Camp Point, Ill.)–Mar. 5, 1971. U.S. historian. Prolific writer, noted for his masterful political biographies. As prof. of history at Columbia U. (1931–58), established Columbia's oral-history program. *Grover Cleveland—A Study in Courage*, 1932 (Pulitzer Prize in biography, 1933); *Hamilton Fish*, 1936 (Pulitzer Prize in biography, 1937).

**NOVAK, MICHAEL, JR.,** Sept. 9, 1933 (Johnstown, Pa.). U.S. social philosopher. Resident scholar in religion and public policy, American Enterprise Inst., 1978– .

**OGDEN, ROBERT MORRIS,** July 6, 1877 (Binghampton, N.Y.)–Mar. 2, 1959. U.S. psychologist, educator. As prof. of education at Cornell U. (1917–39), introduced Gestalt psychology to the U.S. *Psychology and Education*, 1926.

**PACKARD, VANCE,** May 22, 1914 (Granville Summit, Pa.). U.S. nonfiction writer. Author of popular sociological tracts. *The Hidden Persuaders*, 1957; *The Status Seekers*, 1959; *The Waste Makers*, 1960; *The Naked Society*, 1964; *The People Shapers*, 1977.

**PARETO, VILFREDO,** Aug. 15, 1848 (Paris, Fr.)–Aug. 19, 1923. Italian sociologist, economist. Attempted to establish a theory applying mathematical analyses to economic and social phenomena; devised the "circulation of elites" concept; his ideas were largely incorporated into Italian fascism. *The Mind and Society*, 4 vols., trans. 1935.

**PARSONS, TALCOTT,** Dec. 13, 1902 (Colorado Springs, Col.)–May 8, 1979. U.S. sociologist.

Attempted to construct a theoretical framework for classifying societies and their parts. Prof. at Harvard U., 1927–73. *The Social System*, 1951.

PARTRIDGE, ERIC, Feb. 6, 1894 (Gisborne, N.Z.) –June 1, 1979. British lexicographer, author. Expert on the English language and prolific author of popular books on slang, catch phrases, punctuation, clichés, correct usage and other miscellany. *Usage and Abusage*, 1942; *A Dictionary of Underworld*, 1950; *A Dictionary of Slang and Unconventional English*, 1937; *A Charm of Words*, 1960.

PASSY, FREDERIC, May 20, 1822 (Paris, Fr.) –June 12, 1912. French economist. A pacifist, founded the International League for Permanent Peace (1867) and served as its gen. secy. until 1889. Awarded, with J. Dunant, first Nobel Peace Prize, 1901. *Leçons d'économie politique*, 1860–61; *La question de la paix*, 1891.

PETER, LAWRENCE J., Sept. 16, 1919 (Vancouver, B.C., Can.)–Jan. 12, 1990. Canadian-U.S. educator, author. Formulated the "Peter Principle" on the level of competence in organizations. *The Peter Principle: Why Things Always Go Wrong*, 1969.

PIAGET, JEAN, Aug. 9, 1896 (Neuchâtel, Switz.) –Sept. 16, 1980. Swiss psychologist. Known for his theory on child cognition and intellectual development, which showed that a child thinks differently from an adult and that its cognitive development proceeds in genetically determined stages. Prof. at U. of Lausanne, 1937–54. *The Language and Thought of the Child*, 1926; *Biology and Knowledge*, 1971.

PLINY THE ELDER (in full Gaius Plinius Secundus), c.23 (Novum Comum Cisalpine Gaul [now Como, Italy])–Aug. 24, 79. Roman naturalist. Noted for one surviving work, *Historia naturalis*, an encyclopedia of natural science, some of which is now known to be incorrect; authority on scientific matters up to Middle Ages; died in the eruption of Vesuvius.

PLUTARCH, 46? (Chaeronea, Boetia) c.120. Greek essayist, biographer. Deeply influenced early modern letters; attempted to portray character in his biographies of Roman soldiers, legislators, orators, and statesmen. *The Parallel Lives: Moralia*.

REUBEN, DAVID R., Nov. 29, 1933 (Chicago, Ill.). U.S. psychiatrist, author. *Everything You Always Wanted to Know about Sex*, 1969; *Any Woman Can!*, 1971; *How to Get More out of Sex*, 1974; *The Save-Your-Life Diet*, (with Barbara Reuben), 1976; *Everything You Always Wanted to Know about Nutrition*, 1978; *Dr. David Reuben's Mental First Aid Manual*, 1982.

RHINE, JOSEPH BANKS, Sept. 29, 1895 (Waterloo, Pa.)–Feb. 20, 1980. U.S. parapsychologist. A pioneer in advocating scientific practices, particularly the use of statistics, in the study of telepathy, clairvoyance and other psychic phenomena.

RICARDO, DAVID, Apr. 19, 1772 (London, Eng.) –Sept. 11, 1823. English political economist. One of the first systematic economists; proposed an "iron law of wages," stating that wages tend to stabilize around the subsistence level; developed a theory of value and of comparative advantage in internatl. trade. *On the Principles of Political Economy and Taxation*, 1817.

RORSCHACH, HERMANN, Nov. 8, 1884 (Zurich, Switz.)–Apr. 2, 1922. Swiss psychiatrist. Developed the Rorschach ink-blot test (1921), as an aid in psychiatric diagnosis.

SAMUELSON, PAUL A., May 15, 1915 (Gary, Ind.). U.S. economist. Noted for his widely-used introductory textbook, *Economics: An Introductory Analysis* (1948) and for important contributions to the mathematical structure of economic theory. Prof. at M.I.T., 1940– ; awarded Nobel Prize in economics, 1970.

SCHLESINGER, ARTHUR M., JR., Oct. 15, 1917 (Columbus, Ohio). U.S. historian, public official. Prof. at Harvard U. (1946–62) and City U. of N.Y. (1966– ); cofounder of Americans for Democratic Action, 1947. *The Age of Jackson*, 1945 (Pulitzer Prize in history, 1946); *A Thousand Days*, 1965 (Pulitzer Prize in biography, 1966).

SCHLIEMANN, HEINRICH, Jan. 6, 1822 (Neubukow, Mecklinburg-Schwerin, Ger.)–Dec. 26, 1890. German archeologist. Noted as the discoverer of the ruins of Troy. A successful businessman who retired to devote himself to archeology out of his love for HOMER; discovered four superimposed towns, including Troy, at Hissarlik, Turkey, 1871; excavated at Mycenae (1876), Ithaca (1878), Boeotia (1881–82) and Tiryns (1884–85). *Troy and Its Remains*, 1875.

SCHULTZ, THEODORE W., Apr. 30, 1902 (nr. Arlington, S.D.). U.S. economist. Noted for his work on developmental economies; awarded Nobel Prize in economics (shared with L. ARTHUR), 1979.

SCHUMPETER, JOSEPH (JOSEF ALOIS), Feb. 8, 1883 (Triesch, Moravia A –H [now Czech ]) –Jan. 8, 1950. Austrian-U.S. economist. Developed theories of capitalist development and business cycles, predicted that capitalism would perish from its success. *Capitalism, Socialism, and Democracy*, 1942.

SHIRER, WILLIAM L., Feb. 23, 1904 (Chicago, Ill.). U.S. nonfiction writer. *Berlin Diary*, 1941; *The Rise and Fall of the Third Reich: a History of Nazi Germany*, 1960; *The Rise and Fall of Adolf Hitler*, 1961; *The Collapse of the Third Republic, an Inquiry into the Fall of France in 1940*, 1969.

SKINNER, B(urrhus) F(rederic), Mar. 20, 1904 (Susquehanna, Pa.). U.S. behavioral psychologist who made major contributions to understanding of "instrumental learning" and the role of "reinforcement." *Walden Two*, 1948; *Verbal Behavior*, 1957; *Beyond Freedom and Dignity*, 1971.

SMITH, ADAM, baptized June 5, 1723 (Kirkcaldy, Fife, Scot.)–July 17, 1790. Scottish economist, philosopher. Noted as the author of *An Inquiry into the Nature and Causes of the Wealth of Nations* (1776), in which he postulated that wealth resides in labor; argued for the beneficent effect of the division of labor and a self-regulating free market in which an "invisible hand" turns private gain into public welfare. *Theory of Moral Sentiments*, 1759.

**SOLOW, ROBERT M.**, Aug. 23, 1924 (Brooklyn, N.Y.). U.S. economist. Noted for seminal contributions to the theory of economic growth, including a mathematical model illustrating that long-term growth depends on technological progress as well as increases in capital and labor; awarded Nobel Prize in economics, 1987.

**SONTAG, SUSAN**, Jan. 16, 1933 (New York, N.Y.). U.S. critic, essayist, novelist. Best known for her critical essays on 1960s avant-garde culture, especially "Camp"; also has written experimental fiction. *Against Interpretation*, 1966; *The Benefactor* (novel), 1963; *Styles of Radical Will*, 1969; *On Photography*, 1977; *Illness as a Metaphor*, 1978.

**SPENGLER, OSWALD**, May 29, 1880 (Blankenburg-am-Harz, Ger.)–May 8, 1936. German writer on philosophy of history. Proposed in *The Decline of the West* (1918–22) that world history follows definite laws of growth and that Western culture had passed through a life cycle and was in a period of decline.

**SPINGARN, JOEL E.**, May 17, 1875 (New York, N.Y.)–July 26, 1939. U.S. educator, literary critic. An exponent of the aesthetic school of criticism; prof. of comparative literature at Columbia U., 1899–1911; a founder of Harcourt, Brace and Co., 1919; pres. of the NAACP, 1930–39; established the NAACP Spingarn Medal for the black person of greatest service to his people. *A History of Literary Criticism in the Renaissance*, 1899; *The New Criticism*, 1911.

**STEPHEN, SIR LESLIE**, Nov. 28, 1832 (London, Eng.)–Feb. 22, 1904. English author, critic. The first serious critic of the novel; editor of *The Dictionary of Natl. Biography*, 1882–91; as editor of *Cornhill* magazine (1871–82), encouraged writers. *History of English Thought in the Eighteenth Century*, 2 vols., 1876; *The English Utilitarians*, 3 vols., 1900; knighted, 1902. (Father of V. WOOLF.)

**STIGLER, GEORGE J.**, Jan. 17, 1911 (Renton, Wash.). U.S. economist. Noted for research on the working of industry and the role of government regulation in the economy; awarded Nobel Prize in economics, 1982.

**STONE, RICHARD**, Aug. 13, 1913 (London, Eng.). British economist. Noted for his work in developing systems for measuring the performance of national economies that are now used widely and are pivotal in the work of organizations such as the UN, IMF, and World Bank; awarded Nobel Prize in economics, 1984.

**STRABO**, c.63 B.C. (Amaseia, [now Amasya] Pontus [near northern coast of modern Turk.])–c.23. Greek geographer. His 17-volume *Geography*, provided a detailed description of the ancient world and a record of previous geographers' work (since lost).

**STRACHEY, (Giles) LYTTON**, Mar. 1, 1880 (London, Eng.)–Jan. 21, 1932. English biographer. Transformed the art of writing biography by writing brief, critical biographies; member of the Bloomsbury group. *Eminent Victorians*, 1918; *Queen Victoria*, 1921; *Portraits in Miniature*, 1931.

**SUETONIUS**, (in full, Gaius Suetonius Tranquillus), c.69 (Hippo Regius, N. Africa)–c. 140. Roman biographer. Wrote lively biographies that deeply influenced history's view of Rome until the modern discovery of nonliterary evidence. *The Twelve Caesars* (trans. by ROBERT GRAVES, 1957); *Concerning Illustrious Men*.

**TACITUS, (Gaius Publius) CORNELIUS**, c.56 (Gallia Narbonensis [now Narbonne, Fr.])–c.120. Roman historian, orator, public official. Probably the greatest Roman historian, *Historiae*; *Dialogue on Orators*; *Life of Agricola*; *Germania*; *Annales*.

**TATE, ALLEN**, Nov. 19, 1899 (Winchester, Ky.)–Feb. 9, 1979. U.S. critic, poet, novelist. Major critic of the so-called "New Criticism"; regionalist advocate of the agrarian, conservative South. *Stonewall Jackson: The Good Soldier*, 1928; *Mr. Pope and Other Poems*, 1928; *The Fathers*, 1938.

**THOMAS, LEWIS**, Nov. 25, 1913 (Flushing, N.Y.). U.S. physician, educator. Noted for explaining scientific phenomena in terms which will not daunt the average reader. *Lives of a Cell*, 1974.

**THUCYDIDES**, c.455 B.C. (Athens, Gr.)–c.400 B.C. Greek historian. In writing the *History of the Peloponnesian War*, became the earliest critical historian in antiquity; placed speeches in mouths of people in order to show their motives.

**TOBIN, JAMES**, Mar. 5, 1918 (Champaign, Ill.). U.S. economist. Noted for his analyses of financial markets and their effect on how businesses and families spend and save money; awarded Nobel Prize in economics, 1981.

**TOCQUEVILLE, ALEXIS DE**, July 29, 1805 (Verneuil, Fr.)–Apr. 16, 1859. French writer, politician. Noted as the author of a perceptive study of the young U.S., *Democracy in America* (2 vols., 1835; 1940), in which he noted the distinctiveness of American institutions and the results of unprecedented equality. *L'Ancien Régime et la Révolution*, 1856.

**TOYNBEE, ARNOLD**, Apr. 14, 1889 (London, Eng.)–Oct. 22, 1975. English historian. Noted as author of the monumental *A Study of History* (12 vols., 1934–61), in which he analyzed the cyclical development and decline of civilizations. Prof. at London School of Economics, 1925–56.

**TREITSCHKE, HEINRICH VON**, Sept. 15, 1834 (Dresden, Ger.)–Apr. 28, 1896. German historian. Advocated German unification under Prussian leadership; an anti-Semitic and nationalist writer; editor of *Preussiche Jahrbucher*, 1866–89. *History of Germany in the Nineteenth Century*, 7 vols., 1879–94.

**TREVELYAN, GEORGE MACAULAY**, Feb. 16, 1876 (Welcombe, Eng.)–July 21, 1962. English historian. Noted for his three-volume study of G. GARIBALDI (1907–11), for *British History in the Nineteenth Century, 1782–1901* (1922), and for *England Under Queen Anne* (3 vols., 1930–34). Prof. at Cambridge U., 1927–51.

**TRILLING, LIONEL**, July 4, 1905 (New York,

N.Y.)–Nov. 5, 1975. U.S. critic, author. Noted for his essays combining social, psychological, and political insights with literary criticism. *The Liberal Imagination*, 1950; *The Opposing Self*, 1955; *A Gathering of Fugitives*, 1956.

**TUCHMAN, BARBARA**, Jan. 30, 1912 (New York, N.Y.)–Feb. 6, 1989. U.S. historian. Noted for her best-selling historical books. *The Guns of August* (Pulitzer Prize in history, 1963), 1962; *Stillwell and the American Experience in China, 1911–45* (Pulitzer in history, 1972), 1971; *A Distant Mirror*, 1978; *The First Salute*, 1988.

**UNTERMEYER, LOUIS**, Oct. 1, 1885 (New York, N.Y.)–Dec. 18, 1977. U.S. poet, editor, anthologist. Best known for his anthologies, especially *Modern American Poetry* (1919), *Modern British Poetry* (1920), and *A Treasury of the World's Great Poems* (1942).

**VAN DOREN, CARL**, Sept. 10, 1885 (Hope, Ill.)–July 18, 1950. U.S. author, editor. Member of group that established American literature and history as a central part of university curriculums; prof. of English at Columbia U., 1911–30; literary editor of *The Nation* (1919–22), *Century* (1922–25), and *Literary Guild* (1926–34). *Benjamin Franklin*, 1938 (Pulitzer Prize in biography, 1939). (Brother of M. VAN DOREN.)

**VAN DOREN, MARK**, June 13, 1894 (Hope, Ill.)–Dec. 10, 1972. U.S. critic, poet, educator. Prof. at Columbia U., 1920–59; literary editor (1924–28) and film critic (1935–38) for *The Nation. Collected Poems*, 1922–28 (Pulitzer Prize in poetry, 1940), 1939. (Brother of C. VAN DOREN.)

**VEBLEN, THORSTEIN B.**, July 30, 1857 (Cato Twp, Manitowoc Cty., Wisc.)–Aug. 3, 1929. U.S. economist, social critic. Coined the phrases "conspicuous consumption" and "pecuniary emulation" in his attempt to understand the emergence of big business in the U.S. *The Theory of the Leisure Class*, 1899; *The Theory of Business Enterprise*, 1904.

**VELIKOVSKY, IMMANUEL**, June 10, 1895 (Vitebsk, Rus.)–Nov. 17, 1979. Russian U.S. writer. Proponent of the catastrophe theory of cosmology in a series of books that achieved worldwide popular success but were met with skepticism or hostility by the scientific community. *Worlds in Collision*, 1950; *Earth in Upheaval*, 1955; *Ages in Chaos*, 1952; *Oedipus and Akhnaton*, 1960; *Mankind in Amnesia*, 1982.

**VOLCKER, PAUL A.**, Sept. 5, 1927 (Cape May, N.J.). U.S. economist. Chmn., bd. of gov., Federal Reserve Board, 1979–87; currently chmn., James D. Wolfensohn Co.

**WARD, BARBARA, BARONESS JACKSON OF LODSWORTH**, May 23, 1914 (York, Eng.)–May 31, 1981. English economist. Noted for writings on political and economic affairs; counseled European economic unity and a liberal approach to the underdeveloped world; created baroness, 1976. *The Rich Nations and the Poor Nations*, 1962; *Nationalism and Ideology*, 1966; *Spaceship Earth*, 1966; *Progress for a Small Planet*, 1979.

**WEBER, MAX**, Apr. 21, 1864 (Erfurt, Ger.)–June 14, 1920. German sociologist. A founder of modern sociology, credited with first noting the importance of bureaucracy in modern life; developed the famous thesis that the Protestant Ethic decisively influenced the rise of Western capitalism. *Protestant Ethic and the Spirit of Capitalism*, 1930. (in trans., orig. 1904–5).

**WEBSTER, NOAH**, Oct. 16, 1758 (West Hartford, Conn.)–May 28, 1843. U.S. lexicographer, writer. Known for his *American Spelling Book* (1783), which helped to standardize American spelling; agitated for U.S. copyright law. *American Dictionary of the English Language*, 1828.

**WILSON, EDMUND**, May 8, 1895 (Red Bank, N.J.)–June 12, 1972. U.S. literary and social critic. Noted for his influential critical writings on ERNEST HEMINGWAY, JOHN DOS PASSOS, F. SCOTT FITZGERALD, WILLIAM FAULKNER, and the symbolists, as well as his social studies of European revolutionary tradition and the American Depression. *Axel's Castle*, 1931; *American Jitters*, 1932; *To the Finland Station*, 1940; *The Boys in the Back Room*, 1941; *Patriotic Gore*, 1962; *The Bit between My Teeth*, 1965.

**WITTE, EDWIN E.**, Jan. 4, 1887 (Jefferson Co., Wisc.) May 20, 1960. U.S. economist. Leading prof. of economics at U. of Wisconsin, 1920–57; while serving on President's Com. on Economic Security (1934–35), authored Social Security Act of 1935, first govt.-sponsored old-age pension in U.S. history.

**WOODSON, CARTER G.**, Dec. 19, 1875 (nr. New Canton, Va.)–Apr. 3, 1950. U.S. educator, historian. Devoted his life to research and publication in the field of black history; organized Chicago Assn. for the Study of Negro Life and History, 1915; founded and edited the *Journal of Negro History*, 1916–50; founder (1921) and pres. (1921–50) of Associated Publishers, Inc., devoted to publishing books on blacks. *The Education of the Negro Prior to 1861*, 1915; *Negro Makers of History*, 1928; *African Heroes and Heroines*, 1939.

**XENOPHON**, c.431 B.C. (Athens, Gr.)–c.350 B.C. Greek historian. A disciple of SOCRATES; led a long retreat from the battle of Cunaxa (401 B.C.), which he described in *Anabasis. Memorabilia* (Recollections of Socrates); *Hellenica; De re equestri*.

**YERKES, ROBERT MEARNS**, May 26, 1876 (Breadysville, Pa.).–Feb. 3, 1956. U.S. psychologist. One of the first comparative psychologists to work with animals in a laboratory setting; while at Yale U.'s Inst. of Psychology, founded experimental station near Orange Park, Fla. (1929), later named Yerkes Laboratories of Primate Biology and the nucleus of the present Yerkes Regional Primate Research Center. *The Great Apes: A Study of Anthropoid Life* (with A.W. Yerkes), 1929.

**ZAMENHOF, LUDWIK LEJZER**, ("Dr. Esperanto"), Dec. 15, 1859 (Bialystok, Pol.)–Apr. 14, 1917. Polish linguist. Creator of Esperanto, an internatl. language based on Indo-European languages, especially those of Western Europe. *Lingvo Internacia*, 1887; *Fundamento de Esperanto*, 1905.

# Educators

**ADLER, CYRUS,** Sept. 13, 1863 (Van Buren, Ark.) –Apr. 7, 1940. U.S. educator, editor, Conservative Jewish leader. First pres., Dropsie C. for Hebrew and Cognate Learning, 1908–40; pres., Jewish Theological Seminary, 1924–40; founded American Jewish Historical Soc., 1892; planned and edited the *American Jewish Yearbook*, 1899–1905.

**ANGEL, JAMES BURRILL,** Jan. 7, 1829 (Scituate, R.I.)–Apr. 1, 1916. U.S. educator. Pres., U. of Vermont, 1866–71; as pres., U. of Michigan (1871–1909), elevated that school to academic prominence.

**ARNOLD, THOMAS** ("Arnold of Rugby"), June 13, 1795 (West Cowes, Isle of Wight)–June 12, 1842. English educator. As headmaster at Rugby (1828–42), set the pattern for the English public-school system. *History of Rome,* 3 vols., 1838–43; *Lectures on Modern History,* 1842. (Father of M. ARNOLD.)

**BAKER, GEORGE PIERCE,** Apr. 4, 1866 (Providence, R.I.)–Jan. 6, 1935. U.S. teacher. Started Harvard U. class for playwrights called "47 Workshop," 1905; students included EUGENE O'NEILL, PHILIP BARRY, THOMAS WOLFE, and JOHN DOS PASSOS; founded Yale Drama School, 1925.

**BARNARD, FREDERICK,** May 5, 1809 (Sheffield, Mass.)–Apr. 27, 1889. U.S. educator. Pres., U. of Mississippi, 1856–61; as pres., Columbia U., established Barnard C. for women, 1864–89.

**BEECHER, CATHARINE ESTHER,** Sept. 6, 1800 (East Hampton, N.Y.)–May 12, 1878. U.S. educator who promoted higher education for women. (Daughter of L. BEECHER; sister of H. B. STOWE.)

**BELL, ANDREW,** Mar. 27, 1753 (St. Andrews, Scot.)–Jan. 27, 1832. Scottish educator, clergyman. Originated a system of education (Bell or Madras) in which the older students instruct the younger.

**BENNETT, WILLIAM,** July 3, 1943 (Brooklyn, N.Y.). U.S. education official. Chmn., National Endowment for the Humanities, 1981–85; U.S. secy. of education, 1985–8?.

**BETHUNE, MARY McLEOD,** July 10, 1875 (Mayesville, S.C.)–May 18, 1955. U.S. educator. Founded Daytona Normal and Industrial Inst. for Negro Girls, 1904; merged school with Cookman Inst. (1923), to form Bethune-Cookman C., of which she was pres., 1923–42 and 1946–47; founded National Council of Negro Women, 1937; awarded Spingarn Medal (NAACP), 1935.

**BLAIR, JAMES,** 1655 (Scot.)–Apr. 18, 1743. Colonial clergyman, educator. Established the C. of William and Mary, the second-oldest institution of higher learning in the U.S.

**BOK, DEREK C.,** May 22, 1930 (Ardmore Pa.). U.S. educator. Dean, Harvard Law School, 1968–71; pres., Harvard U., 1971– .

**BORK, ROBERT H.,** Mar. 1, 1927 (Pittsburgh, Pa.). U.S. jurist, educator. Prof. of law, Yale Univ., 1962–81; U.S. solicitor gen., 1973–77; judge, U.S. Court of Appeals (D.C. circuit), 1982–88; nominated to U.S. Supreme Court but rejected in bitter Senate confirmation battle over his conservative stances on censorship, abortion, and affirmative action, 1987; currently resident scholar at American Enterprise Inst.

**BRADEMAS, JOHN,** Mar. 2, 1927 (Mishawaka, Ind.). U.S. university president. U.S. rep. (D, Ind.), 1959–81; majority whip, 1977–81; pres., New York Univ., 1981–91.

**BREWSTER, KINGMAN,** June 17, 1919 (Longmeadow, Mass.)–Nov. 8, 1988. U.S. educator, diplomat. Prof. of law at Harvard U. (1950–60) and Yale U. (1961–63); pres. of Yale U., 1963–77; chm. of Natl. Policy Panel of the UN, 1968; U.S. amb. to Great Britain, 1977–81; Master, University College, Oxford, 1986–88.

**BUSCAGLIA, LEO**(nardo), Mar. 31, 1924 (Los Angeles, Calif.). U.S. educator, author. Joined education dept. at UCLA from 1965; prof. of education, 1975– ; frequent lecturer. *Because I Am Human,* 1972; *Living, Loving, and Learning,* 1982; *Loving Each Other,* 1984.

**BUTLER, NICHOLAS MURRAY,** Apr. 2, 1862 (Elizabeth, N.J.)–Dec. 4, 1947. U.S. educator. Pres., Columbia U., 1902–45; helped establish Carnegie Endowment for International Peace and served as pres., 25–45; won Nobel Peace Prize, 1931.

**COMENIUS, JOHN AMOS** (born Jan Amos

Komensky), Mar. 28, 1592 (Nivnice, Moravia) –Nov. 15, 1670. Czech churchman, educator. Attempted to reform educational methods and advocated universal education; wanted knowledge organized systematically and in vernacular language; called the "grandfather" of modern education. *The Great Didactic,* 1628–32.

CONANT, JAMES BRYANT, Mar. 26, 1893 (Dorchester, Mass.)–Feb. 11, 1978. U.S. educator, diplomat. Pres. of Harvard U., 1933–53; U.S. amb. to W. Germany, 1955–57. *The Chemistry of Organic Compounds,* 1923.

DOBIE, JAMES FRANK, Sept. 26, 1888 (Live Oak Co., Tex.)–Sept. 18, 1964. U.S. teacher, folklorist. Prof. of English, U. of Texas, 1933–47; wrote some 30 books chronicling the legends and stories of Texas and the Southwest.

DORIOT, GEORGES F., Sept. 24, 1899 (Paris, Fr.)–June 2, 1987. U.S. business executive, educator. Asst. dean (1926–31) and prof. of industrial management (1926–66) at Harvard Business School; through his course on manufacturing, credited with creating the professional management corps of U.S. business; pres. of American Research and Development Co., 1947–72.

DUNSTER, HENRY, 1609 (Lancashire, Eng.)–Feb. 16, 1659. U.S. educator. First pres. of Harvard C., 1640–54.

EISENHOWER, MILTON STOVER, Sept. 15, 1899 (Abilene, Kan.)–May 2, 1985. U.S. educator. Pres., Kansas St. U., 1943–50; pres., Pennsylvania St. U., 1950–56; pres., Johns Hopkins U., 1956–67 and 1971–72. (Brother of D. D. EISENHOWER.)

ELIOT, CHARLES WILLIAM, Mar. 20, 1834 (Boston, Mass.)–Aug. 22, 1926. U.S. educator. Pres., Harvard U., 1869–1909; introduced electives into curriculum and balance of arts and sciences.

FRANCKE, AUGUST HERMANN, Mar. 22, 1663 (Lübeck, Ger.)–June 8, 1727. German clergyman, educator. Principal promoter of Pietism; founded a charity school in Halle (1698) that later became the Francke Inst.

FROEBEL (or Fröbel), FRIEDRICH WILHELM, Apr. 21, 1782 (Oberweissbach, Ger.)–June 21, 1852. German educator. Founded the kindergarten system, 1837.

GALLAUDET, THOMAS HOPKINS, Dec. 10, 1787 (Philadelphia, Pa.)–Sept. 10, 1851. U.S. educator. Established the first free school for the deaf in the U.S., 1817; Gallaudet C. is named for him.

GIAMATTI, A(ngelo) BARTLETT, Apr. 4, 1938 (Boston, Mass.)–Sept. 1, 1989. U.S. educator. Pres., Yale U., 1978–86; pres., of National League, 1986–89; commissioner of major league baseball, 1989.

GOHEEN, ROBERT FRANCIS, Aug. 15, 1919 (Vengurla, India). U.S. educator, diplomat. Pres., Princeton U., 1957–72; U.S. amb. to India, 1977–80.

GRAY, HANNA HOLBORN, Oct. 25, 1930 (Heidelberg, Ger.). U.S. educator. Provost and prof. of history (1974–78) and acting pres. (1977–78) of Yale U.; pres., U. of Chicago, 1978– .

HARPER, WILLIAM RAINEY, July 26, 1856 (New Concord, Ohio)–Jan. 10, 1906. U.S. educator,

Hebraist. First pres., U. of Chicago, 1891–1906.

HARVARD, JOHN, baptized Nov. 29, 1607 (London, Eng.)–Sept. 14, 1638. American colonial clergyman. Left his library and half of his estate to a newly founded college that was renamed in his honor, 1639.

HERBART, JOHANN FRIEDRICH, May 4, 1776 (Oldenburg, Ger.)–Aug. 14, 1841. German philosopher, educator. Noted for coordinating philosophy (realism) and morality in devising educational systems and methods.

HOPKINS, MARK, Feb. 4, 1802 (Stockbridge, Mass.) –June 17, 1887. U.S. educator, moral philosopher. Noted for his ability to arouse students to express their own thoughts and natures; pres. of Williams C., 1836–72.

HUNTER, THOMAS, Oct. 18, 1831 (Ardglass, Ire.)–Oct. 14, 1915. U.S. educator. Organized and headed Normal C. of the City of New York, 1870–1906; college renamed after him, 1914.

KALLEN, HORACE MEYER, Aug. 11, 1882 (Silesia, Ger.)–Feb. 16, 1974. U.S. educator, philosopher. Prof. of philosophy, New School for Social Research, 1919–52. *William James and Henri Bergson,* 1914.

LANCASTER, JOSEPH, Nov. 25, 1778 (London, Eng.)–Oct. 24, 1838. English educator. Developed "Lancasterian schools," a system of mass education in which brighter children (monitors) taught other children under the direction of an adult; emigrated to the U.S. (1818), where he established many such schools.

LA SALLE, SAINT JEAN BAPTISTE DE, Apr. 30, 1651 (Reims, Fr.)–Apr. 7, 1719. French educator, Roman Catholic saint. Founded the Brothers of the Christian Schools, 1680–84; canonized, 1900.

LINCOLN, MARY JOHNSON, July 8, 1844 (S. Attleboro, Mass.)–Dec. 2, 1921. U.S. educator, author. Dir., Boston Cooking School, 1879–85; wrote several cookbooks, including *Mrs. Lincoln's Boston Cook Book,* (1884) and *Boston School Kitchen Textbook* (1887).

LYON, MARY, Feb. 28, 1797 (Buckland, Mass.) –Mar. 5, 1849. U.S. educator. Founded Mt. Holyoke C., the first women's college in the U.S., 1837.

MACKENZIE, JAMES CAMERON, Aug. 15, 1852 (Aberdeen, Scot.)–May 10, 1931. U.S. educator. Noted for raising scholarship standards in U.S. secondary schools; founded Wilkes-Barre (Pa.) Academy (1878), Lawrenceville (N.J.) School (1882), and MacKenzie (N.Y.) school (1901); at Lawrenceville, introduced English house system, honor system, athletic fields, and golf links.

MACY, ANNE SULLIVAN, Apr. 14, 1866 (Feeding Hills, Mass.)–Oct. 20, 1936. U.S. teacher. Best known as the teacher and companion of HELEN KELLER. Her eyesight was seriously weakened by a childhood illness, but was restored through a series of operations; studied at the Perkin's Inst. for the Blind; accompanied Keller through her education at Perkins, Cambridge School for Young Ladies, and Radcliffe C., 1900–1904.

MANN, HORACE, May 4, 1796 (Franklin, Mass.)

–Aug. 2, 1859. U.S. educator, public official. Known as "the Father of American public education"; as the first secy. of the Massachusetts Board of Education, 1837–48, established public-school system that became model for the nation; U.S. rep. (Whig, Mass.), 1849–53; pres., Antioch C., 1853–59.

MASON, LOWELL, Jan. 8, 1792 (Medfield, Mass.) –Aug. 11, 1872. U.S. educator, hymn writer. Organized Boston Academy of Music, 1832; devised system of musical instruction for children; wrote "Nearer, My God, to Thee."

MCGUFFEY, WILLIAM HOLMES, Sept. 23, 1800 (Claysville, Pa.)–May 4, 1873. U.S. educator. Author of *Eclectic Readers*, known popularly as "McGuffey's Readers," six volumes published between 1836 and 1857 that served as standard texts in 19th–cent. U.S. public schools.

MCLUHAN, HERBERT MARSHALL, July 21, 1911 (Edmonton, Alta., Can.)–Dec. 31, 1980. Canadian educator, author, expert on mass media. *Understanding Media*, 1964; *The Medium is the Massage*, 1967.

MONTESSORI, MARIA, Aug. 31, 1870 (nr. Ancona, It.)–May 6, 1952. Italian educator. Originated the Montessori method of education, especially for preschool and early elementary school, which stresses development of initiative, and sense and muscle training, as well as the freedom of the child; opened her first school, in Rome, 1907.

NEILSON, WILLIAM ALLEN, Mar. 28, 1869 (Doune, Scot.)–Feb. 13, 1946. U.S. educator, editor, author. Pres., Smith C., 1917–39; editor in chief, *Webster's New International Dictionary*, 2nd edition, 1934; editor, Cambridge edition of *Shakespeare's Works*, 1906 and 1942. *Essentials of Poetry*, 1912.

PATTERSON, FREDERICK DOUGLAS, Oct. 10, 1901 (Washington, D.C.). U.S. educator. Pres. of Tuskegee Normal and Industrial Inst., 1935–53; organized United Negro C. Fund, 1943.

PEABODY, ELIZABETH PALMER, May 16, 1804 (Billerica, Mass.)–Jan. 3, 1894. U.S. educator. Founded first kindergarten in the U.S., Boston, 1860; published elementary-school textbooks in grammar and history; participant in the Transcendental movement.

PESTALOZZI, JOHANN HEINRICH, Jan. 12, 1746 (Zurich, Switz.)–Feb. 17, 1827. Swiss educational reformer. Stressed the importance of accurate observation of actual objects for clear, accurate thinking; influenced methods of instruction in elementary schools in Europe and the U.S.

PHILLIPS, JOHN, Dec. 6, 1719 (Andover, Mass.) –Apr. 21, 1795. U.S. merchant, educational benefactor. Founded Phillips Exeter Academy, at Exeter, N.H., 1781; helped found Phillips Academy, at Andover, Mass., 1778.

RAIKES, ROBERT, Sept. 14, 1735 (Gloucester, Eng.)–Apr. 5, 1811. British philanthropist. Pioneer of the Sunday-school movement.

SCHMIDT, BENNO C., JR., Mar. 20, 1942 (Washington, D.C.). U.S. educator. Dean, Columbia Univ.

Law School, 1969–86; pres., prof. of law, Yale Univ., 1986–  .

SCOPES, JOHN T., 1900 (Salem, Ill.)–Oct. 21, 1970. U.S. schoolteacher. Taught the theory of evolution in defiance of a Tennessee state law, precipitating the "Scopes Trial," July 1925; convicted and fined, but rulings were later reversed.

SETON, ELIZABETH ANN, ("Mother Seton"), Aug. 28, 1774 (New York, N.Y.)–Jan. 4, 1821. U.S. educator, religious leader. Founded the Sisters of St. Joseph, a teaching order instrumental in the establishment of the parochial school system in the U.S., 1809; canonized as the first U.S.-born saint, 1975.

STURM, JOHANNES VON, Oct. 1, 1507 (Schleisden, Ger.)–Mar. 3, 1589. German educator. Founded a school in Strasbourg that emphasized maintenance of strict discipline and mastery of the classics, 1537.

THOMAS, MARTHA CAREY, Jan. 2, 1857 (Baltimore, Md.)–Dec. 2, 1953. U.S. educator, prominent suffragist. First woman college faculty member to hold the title "dean"; pres., Bryn Mawr C., 1894–1922. *The Higher Education of Women*, 1900.

VITTORINO DA FELTRE (born Vittorino Ramboldini [or dei Ramboldoni]), 1378 (Feltre, It.)–Feb. 2, 1446. Italian educator, humanist. Founded a school that admitted both noble and poor boys and girls, in Mantua, 1423; set the pattern for Renaissance schools.

WASHINGTON, BOOKER T., Apr. 5, 1856 (Franklin Co., Va.)–Nov. 14, 1915. U.S. educator, social reformer. Established Tuskegee Inst., 1881, and headed it until his death; an educational leader and principal spokesman of black Americans (1895–1915).

WHEELOCK, ELEAZAR, Apr. 22, 1711 (Windham, Conn.)–Apr. 24, 1779. U.S. educator. Tutored American Indians, from 1743; founded Dartmouth C. and served as its first pres., 1770–79.

WHITE, ANDREW DICKSON, Nov. 7, 1832 (Homer, N.Y.)–Nov. 4, 1918. U.S. educator, diplomat. A founder (with EZRA CORNELL) of Cornell U. (1865), which he served as pres., 1868–85; U.S. min. to Germany (1879–81) and Russia (1892–94); U.S. amb. to Germany (1897–1902).

WIGGIN, KATE DOUGLAS, Sept. 28, 1856 (Philadelphia, Pa.)–Aug. 24, 1923. U.S. educator, writer. Founded, with her sister Nora, the California Kindergarten Training School, 1880. *Rebecca of Sunnybrook Farm*, 1903.

WILLARD, EMMA, Feb. 23, 1787 (Berlin, Conn.) –Apr. 15, 1870. U.S. educator. Pioneer in the field of higher education for women; established the Emma Willard School, 1821.

WYTHE, GEORGE, 1726 (Elizabeth Co., Va.) –June 8, 1806. U.S. lawyer, educator. A member of the Continental Congress and signer of the Declaration of Independence; first prof. of law in the U.S., at William and Mary, 1779–89; taught THOMAS JEFFERSON, JOHN MARSHALL, and HENRY CLAY.

# Scientists, Physicians, and Inventors

## U.S. SCIENTISTS, PHYSICIANS, AND INVENTORS

**ABBE, CLEVELAND,** Dec. 3, 1838 (New York, N.Y.)–Oct. 28, 1916. U.S. astronomer, meteorologist. Initiated daily weather bulletins, 1869; the first meteorologist of U.S. Weather Bureau; instrumental in initiating use of standard time zones.

**ADAMS, WALTER SYDNEY,** Dec. 20, 1876 (Syria)–May 11, 1956. U.S. astronomer. Developed a method of spectroscopic parallax that enabled calculation of distances of far–away stars, 1914; first discoverer of a white dwarf star, 1915.

**AGASSIZ, LOUIS,** May 28, 1807 (Môtier-en-Vully, Switzerland)–Dec. 14, 1873. U.S. zoologist, geologist, naturalist. By examining modern glaciers and their effects on the land, discovered (c.1840) that glaciers and ice had once covered large parts of northern Europe and America (the Ice Age); made significant studies on the classification of animals; prominent antievolutionist.

**AIKEN, HOWARD HATHAWAY,** Mar. 9, 1900 (Hoboken, N.J.) Mar. 14, 1973. U.S. mathematician. Invented Mark I, first modern digital computer (completed 1944), which weighed 35 tons, was 51 ft. long, had a memory, and did only arithmetic.

**ALEXANDERSON, ERNST F.,** Jan. 25, 1878 (Sweden)–May 14, 1975. U.S. electrical engineer. Developed a high-frequency alternator able to produce continuous radio waves, thus revolutionizing radio communications, 1906; invented modern radio-tuning device, 1916; developed an early automatic-control system for sensitive manufacturing processes (the amplidyne); early TV pioneer, demonstrating it privately in 1927.

**ALTMAN, SIDNEY,** (Montreal, Que.). Canadian–U.S. chemist. Discovered that the crucial genetic substance RNA was not merely a passive carrier of genetic information, but could actively aid chemical reactions in the cells; awarded Nobel Prize in chemistry (shared with T. CECH), 1989.

**ALVAREZ, LUIS W.,** June 13, 1911 (San Francisco, Calif.)–Sept. 1, 1988. U.S. physicist. His discovery of "resonance particles" led to major modern theories of subatomic particles (after 1945); made major contributions to aviation radar, including ground-control approach (GCA) landing systems, 1940–44; worked on development of atomic bomb at the Los Alamos Lab, N.M.; awarded Nobel Prize in physics, 1968.

**ANDERSON, CARL D.,** Sept. 3, 1905 (New York, N.Y.). U.S. physicist. Discovered and named the positron, the first known particle of antimatter, 1932; discovered and named the first mesotron (shortened to meson and later to mu meson, or muon), 1935; awarded Nobel Prize for physics, 1936.

**ANDERSON, PHILIP W.,** Dec. 13, 1923 (Indianapolis, Ind.). U.S. physicist. Noted for his basic studies of the electrical and magnetic properties of noncrystalline solids; awarded Nobel Prize in Physics (with J. H. VAN VLECK and N. F. MOTT), 1977.

**ANFINSEN, CHRISTIAN B.,** Mar. 26, 1916 (Monessen, Pa.). U.S. biochemist. Studied how the structure of enzymes and other proteins relate to their physiological function; awarded Nobel Prize in chemistry (with S. MOORE and W. H. STEIN), 1972. *The Molecular Basis of Evolution,* 1959.

**ANGLE, EDWARD H.,** June 1, 1855 (Herrick, Pa.)–Aug. 11, 1930. U.S. orthodontist. Founded modern orthodontia as the first specialist in field, c.1886; founded first School of Orthodontia, in St. Louis, 1895; initiated idea of normal occlusion (bite) of the teeth.

**ARMSTRONG, EDWIN H.,** Dec. 18, 1890 (New York, N.Y.)–Feb. 1, 1954. U.S. inventor. Invented regenerative circuit, the first amplifying receiver and reliable transmitter, 1914; invented superheterodyne circuit, the basis for most modern radio, TV, and radar reception, 1918; invented FM (frequency modulation) broadcasting system, 1933; in long fight to defend his primary role in these inventions, lost to L. DE FOREST on the regenerative circuit and committed suicide in midst of suit over FM.

**AXELROD, JULIUS,** May 30, 1912 (New York, N.Y.). U.S. biochemist. Discovered two ways in which noradrenaline activity in the nervous system is stopped; awarded Nobel Prize in physiology or medicine (with B. KATZ and U. S. VON EULER), 1970.

**BAEKELAND, LEO H.,** Nov. 14, 1863 (Belgium)–Feb. 23, 1944. Belgian-U.S. chemist. Invented Bakelite, one of the first plastics with widespread applications, 1909; invented Velox, the first commercially successful photographic paper; founded Bakelite Corp., now part of Union Carbide, 1910.

**BAILEY, LIBERTY HYDE,** Mar. 15, 1858 (South Haven, Mich.)–Dec. 25, 1954. U.S. horticulturist, botanist, educator. Established first distinctively horticultural laboratory in the U.S., 1888; leader in establishment of agricultural-extension courses in rural areas.

**BALTIMORE, DAVID,** Mar. 7, 1938 (New York, N.Y.). U.S. microbiologist, virologist. Conducted research into the process by which a virus can change the genetic makeup of a cell; demonstrated the existence of "reverse transcriptase," a viral enzyme that reverses the normal DNA-to-RNA process, 1970; awarded Nobel Prize in physiology or medicine (with R. DULBECCO and H. TEMIN), 1975.

**BANNEKER, BENJAMIN,** Nov. 9, 1731 (Ellicott's Mills, Md.)–Oct. 1806. U.S. astronomer, mathematician. A self-taught black scientist who published an annual almanac and astronomical ephemeris for years 1792–1802 for mid-Atlantic states, one of the most accurate and sophisticated in the world at that time; assisted in 1789 survey of District of Columbia; wrote essays and pamphlets against slavery and war.

**BARDEEN, JOHN,** May 23, 1908 (Madison, Wis.). U.S. physicist. First person to win two Nobel Prizes in one field; a discoverer (with W. B. S. SHOCKLEY and W. H. BRATTAIN) of the transistor, c.1948; with L. N. COOPER and J. R. SCHRIEFFER, developed the BCS theory, which explains superconductivity according to fundamental physics, 1957; awarded 1956 Nobel Prize in physics (with Brattain and Shockley) and 1972 Nobel Prize in physics (with Cooper and Schrieffer).

**BEADLE, GEORGE W.,** Oct. 22, 1903 (Wahoo, Neb.). U.S. geneticist. Pioneer in the study of the chemical functions of genes in the production of enzymes, 1940s; awarded Nobel Prize in physiology or medicine (with E. L. TATUM and J. LEDERBERG), 1958.

**BEAUMONT, WILLIAM,** Nov. 21, 1785 (Lebanon, Conn.)–Apr. 25, 1853. U.S. surgeon. First to use an artificial opening (fistula) in a living body to study body processes; observed and made experiments in the process of digestion of a man whose stomach had been opened by a shotgun blast, 1822–33.

**BEEBE, WILLIAM,** July 29, 1877 (Brooklyn, N.Y.)–June 4, 1962. U.S. naturalist, explorer, inventor. Invented the bathysphere; was the first man to descend in the ocean beyond a few hundred ft.—3,028 ft., 1934.

**BELL, ALEXANDER GRAHAM,** Mar. 3, 1847 (Edinburgh, Scot.)–Aug. 2, 1922. Scot.-U.S.-Can. inventor. Opened a school in Boston for training teachers of the deaf, 1872; first to patent and commercially exploit the telephone, 1876; in addition to other inventions and improvements, supported other researchers; founded the journal *Science*, 1883; a founding member of the National Geographic Society, 1888; his famous first words on the telephone: "Watson, please come here. I want you."

**BENACERRAF, BARUJ,** Oct. 29, 1920 (Caracas, Venez.). U.S. physician. Noted for his work in making tissue typing possible and shedding new light on the body's immune system; awarded Nobel Prize in medicine or physiology (shared with G. SNELL and J. DAUSSET), 1980.

**BERG, PAUL,** June 30, 1926 (New York, N.Y.). U.S. biochemist. Developed methods that make it possible to map in detail the function and structure of DNA; awarded Nobel Prize in chemistry (shared with W. GILBERT and F. SANGER), 1980.

**BISHOP, J. MICHAEL,** Feb. 22, 1936 (York, Pa.). U.S. medical researcher. Noted for research in cancer; awarded Nobel Prize in physiology or medicine (shared with H. VARMUS), 1989.

**BERLINER, EMILE,** May 20, 1851 (Germany)–Aug. 3, 1929. U.S. inventor. Invented the flat, "platter," phonograph record and a gramaphone; worked on improvements in the telephone and airplane motors; a leading advocate of compulsory pasteurization of milk.

**BJERKNES, JACOB,** Nov. 2, 1897 (Sweden)–July 7, 1975. Norwegian-U.S. meteorologist. With father, Vilhelm, worked out the theory of polar and tropical air masses and weather fronts, the basic ideas of modern meteorology.

**BLACKWELL, ELIZABETH,** Feb. 3, 1821 (England)–May 31, 1910. English-U.S. physician. First woman in U.S. to gain an M.D. degree, 1849; founded New York Infirmary (1857) and London School of Medicine for Women (1875).

**BLOCH, FELIX,** Oct. 23, 1905 (Zurich, Switz.)–Sept. 10, 1983. U.S. physicist. Devised methods for the study of magnetism in atomic nuclei (c.1945–46) that opened the way to more precise knowledge of nuclear structure, to very sensitive magnetometers, and to new techniques in analytic chemistry; first dir.-genl. of CERN, a multinational nuclear lab in Geneva, Switz.; awarded Nobel Prize in physics (with E. M. PURCELL), 1952.

**BLOCH, KONRAD,** Jan. 21, 1912 (Neisse, Ger.). U.S. biochemist. Traced the construction of cholesterol out of the simple two-carbon compound acetic acid, 1946–58; awarded Nobel Prize in physiology or medicine (with F. Lynen), 1964.

**BLOEMBERGEN, NICOLAAS,** Mar. 11, 1920 (Dordrecht, Neth.). U.S. physicist. Noted for work in developing technologies with lasers and other devices that can seek out the innermost secrets of complex forms of matter; awarded Nobel Prize in physics (shared with K. SIEGBAHN and A. SCHAWLOW), 1981.

**BORDEN, GAIL,** Nov. 9, 1801 (Norwich, N.Y.)–Jan. 11, 1874. U.S. inventor. Invented process for condensing milk (1853) and a variety of juice concentrates; father of the "instant food" industry.

BRATTAIN, WALTER H., Feb. 10, 1902 (Amoy, China)–Oct. 13, 1987. U.S. physicist. One of the discoverers of the transistor, 1948; researched semiconductors; awarded Nobel Prize in physics (with W. SHOCKLEY and J. BARDEEN), 1956.

BRAUN, WERNHER VON, Mar. 23, 1912 (Germany)–June 16, 1977. German-U.S. engineer. Early pioneer of rocketry; led development of Germany's V-2 missiles in WW II (1938–45) and of U.S. rocket-engine program that culminated in manned flight to the moon (1950s–60s); instrumental in development of first U.S. satellite, Explorer I.

BREASTED, JAMES HENRY, Aug. 27, 1865 (Rockford, Ill.)–Dec. 2, 1935. U.S. archaeologist. Became one of the world's leading authorities on the archaeology and history of ancient Egypt; founder of the Oriental Institute of the University of Chicago. History of Egypt from the Earliest Times to the Persian Conquest, 1905; The Conquest of Civilization, 1926; The Dawn of Conscience, 1933.

BRIDGMAN, PERCY WILLIAMS, Apr. 21, 1882 (Cambridge, Mass.)–Aug. 20, 1961. U.S. physicist. Pioneer in development of high-pressure chambers for study of matter at extreme pressures; a philosopher of science; awarded Nobel Prize in physics, 1946.

BRONK, DETLEV W., Aug. 13, 1897 (New York, N.Y.)–Nov. 17, 1975. U.S. biophysicist, physiologist, and educator. Founded biophysics, the application of physics to biological processes; headed Rockefeller Inst., 1953–68.

BROTHERS, JOYCE D., Sept. 20, 1928 (New York, N.Y.). U.S. psychologist. Had several TV programs in the 1960s and 1970s, including Ask Dr. Brothers (1965–75); syndicated columist, 1972– ; columnist, Good Housekeeping, 1962. How to Get Whatever You Want Out of Life, 1982; What Every Woman Should Know About Love and Marriage, 1984.

BROWN, HERBERT C., May 22, 1912 (London, Eng.). U.S. chemist. Recognized for his work in organic synthesis; awarded Nobel Prize in chemistry (shared with G. WITTIG), 1979.

BROWN, MICHAEL S., Apr. 13, 1941 (New York, N.Y.). U.S. geneticist. Discovered that the cells of the human body have receptors on their surfaces that trap and absorb blood-stream particles containing cholesterol, 1973; awarded Nobel Prize in medicine or physiology (shared with J. GOLDSTEIN), 1985.

BRUSH, CHARLES FRANCIS, Mar. 17, 1849 (Euclid, Ohio)–June 15, 1929. U.S. inventor, manufacturer. Invented a long-lasting arc light; installed first electric store-lighting in Wanamaker's of Philadelphia (1878), and first electric arc street-lighting, in Cleveland, Ohio (1879).

BRYCE, JAMES W., Sept. 5, 1880 (New York, N.Y.)–Mar. 27, 1949. U.S. inventor. Working at IBM from 1917 on, a major pioneer in the application of electronics to business machines, acquiring more than 500 patents; led in the development of visual display tubes.

BURBANK, LUTHER, Mar. 7, 1849 (Lancaster, Mass.)–Apr. 11, 1926. U.S. botanist. Pioneer in improving food plants through grafting, hybridization, etc.; developed a new potato (Burbank or Idaho) and new varieties of plums and berries; also developed new flowers, including the Shasta daisy.

BUSH, VANNEVAR, Mar. 11, 1890 (Everett, Mass.)–June 28, 1974. U.S. electrical engineer. Built the first analog computer, 1925; as chm. of the U.S. Office of Scientific Research and Development in early 1940s, headed U.S. scientific war effort and early uranium research for the atomic bomb; instrumental in founding Manhattan Project (1942), which developed the fission bomb.

BUSHNELL, DAVID, 1742? (Saybrook, Conn.)–1824. U.S. inventor. Invented the first submarine, known as the "Turtle," a one-man craft designed to attach a mine to an enemy hull, 1776.

CALDERONE, MARY S., July 1, 1904 (New York, N.Y.). U.S. physician. Med. dir., Planned Parenthood-World Population, 1953–64; pres., Sex Information Education Council, U.S., 1964–82. Release From Sexual Tensions, 1960.

CALVIN, MELVIN, Apr. 8, 1911 (St. Paul, Minn.). U.S. biochemist. Worked out the steps of the photosynthesis process, the formation of food and oxygen from sunlight, carbon dioxide, water, and minerals, 1949–57; awarded Nobel Prize in chemistry, 1961.

CANNON, ANNIE JUMP, Dec. 11, 1863 (Dover, Del.)–Apr. 13, 1941. U.S. astronomer. Called the "Census Taker of the Sky," she cataloged and classified some 400,000 astronomical objects, many of them appearing in the Henry Draper Catalogue, 1897–1930; first woman to receive an honorary doctorate from Oxford U., 1925.

CAROTHERS, WALLACE H., Apr. 27, 1896 (Burlington, Ia.)–Apr. 29, 1937. U.S. chemist. Invented the first form of nylon (1935) and neoprene (a synthetic rubber).

CARVER, GEORGE WASHINGTON, 1864 (nr. Diamond Grove, Mo.)–Jan. 5, 1943. U.S. agricultural chemist, educator. Born a slave, he revolutionized Southern agriculture by advocating planting peanuts and sweet potatoes, which enrich the soil, to replace cotton and tobacco, which impoverish it; developed over 300 byproducts of peanuts and sweet potatoes; headed Dept. of Agriculture at Tuskegee Inst., 1896–1943; refused offers of work from T. A. EDISON, HENRY FORD, and the USSR; took no personal profit from his discoveries; awarded Roosevelt Medal, 1939; his birthplace is a national monument.

CECH, THOMAS R., Dec. 8, 1947 (Chicago, Ill.). U.S. chemistry and biochemistry educator. Discovered that the crucial genetic substance RNA was not merely a passive carrier of genetic information, but could actively aid chemical reactions in the cells; awarded Nobel Prize in chemistry (shared with S. ALTMAN), 1989.

CHAMBERLAIN, OWEN, July 10, 1920 (San Francisco, Calif.). U.S. physicist. With EMILIO SEGRÈ, discovered the antiproton, 1955; awarded Nobel Prize in physics (with Segrè), 1959.

**CHANDRASEKHAR, SUBRAHMANYAN,** Oct. 19, 1910 (Lahore, Pak.). U.S. astrophysicist. Studied the evolution of stars, how they were born and what they were made of; awarded Nobel Prize in physics (shared with W. FOWLER), 1979.

**COBLENTZ, WILLIAM W.,** Nov. 20, 1873 (North Lima, Ohio)–Sept. 15, 1962. U.S. physicist. An early pioneer in infrared spectrophotometry, which enables detection of atomic groupings within molecules; founded radiometry section of Natl. Bureau of Standards; major figure in establishment of internatl. radiation standards.

**COHEN, STANLEY,** Nov. 17, 1922 (Brooklyn, N.Y.). U.S. biochemist. Noted for major contributions to the understanding of substances that influence cell growth and the orderly development of tissues, including the nervous system; awarded Nobel Prize in physiology or medicine (shared with R. LEVI-MONTALCINI), 1986.

**COLT, SAMUEL,** July 19, 1814 (Hartford, Conn.)–Jan. 10, 1862. U.S. inventor. Invented Colt revolver, 1835 (introduced, 1852); founded Colt's Armory in Hartford, Conn. (1842), which made extensive use of assembly-line techniques and interchangeable parts.

**COMMONER, BARRY,** May 28, 1917 (Brooklyn, N.Y.). U.S. biologist, environmentalist. A major advocate of environmental protection and the use of solar energy. *Science and Survival,* 1966; *The Politics of Energy,* 1979.

**COMPTON, ARTHUR H.,** Sept. 10, 1892 (Wooster, Ohio)–Mar. 15, 1962. U.S. physicist. Discovered and named the photon, the particle unit of light, thus giving confirmation to MAX PLANCK's quantum theory, 1923; first to prove that cosmic rays were particles, not electromagnetic forces; awarded Nobel Prize in physics (with C. T. R. WILSON), 1927.

**COOLIDGE, WILLIAM D.,** Oct. 23, 1873 (Hudson, Mass.)–Feb. 3, 1975. U.S. physical chemist. Developed a method of making fine wire (filament) from tungsten (1908), making possible the mass production of long-lived light bulbs, radio tubes, etc.; also developed a tungsten-using x-ray tube ("Coolidge tube") that made mass production possible, 1913.

**COOPER, LEON N.,** Feb. 28, 1930 (New York, N.Y.). U.S. physicist. With J. BARDEEN and J. R. S. SCHRIEFFER, developed an effective theory of superconductivity, 1957; awarded Nobel Prize in physics (with Bardeen and Schrieffer), 1972.

**CORI, CARL F.,** Dec. 5, 1896 (Prague, Czech.)–Oct. 20, 1984; and **GERTY T. CORI,** Aug. 15, 1896 (Prague, Czech.)–Oct. 26, 1957. U.S. biochemists. Worked out details of glycogen breakdown and resynthesis through use of phosphates; discoverers of "Cori ester," the basic phosphate of this process, which is essential to the understanding of muscular energy; awarded Nobel Prize in physiology or medicine (with B. A. HOUSSAY), 1947.

**CORMACK, ALLAN MACLEOD,** Feb. 23, 1924 (Johannesburg, S. Africa). U.S. physicist. Developed computed axial tomography, the CAT scan, a revolutionary x-ray technique (shared with G. HOUNSFIELD), 1979.

**CRAM, DONALD J.,** Apr. 22, 1919 (Chester, Vt.). U.S. chemistry educator. A pioneer in wide-ranging research, including the creation of artificial molecules; awarded Nobel Prize in chemistry (shared with C. PEDERSEN and J. LEHN), 1987.

**CRONIN, JAMES W.,** Sept. 29, 1931 (Chicago, Ill.). U.S. physicist. Noted for discoveries concerning the symmetry of subatomic particles; awarded Nobel Prize in physics (shared with V. FITCH), 1980.

**CURTISS, GLENN H.,** May 21, 1878 (Hammondsport, N.Y.)–July 23, 1930. U.S. aviator, inventor. Pioneer in aviation who built his first successful plane in 1908; his major contributions were the aileron and the development of powerful, lightweight engines; held a variety of air records, 1908–10; invented the amphibious plane, 1911.

**DAVISSON, CLINTON J.,** Oct. 22, 1881 (Bloomington, Ill.)–Feb. 1, 1958. U.S. physicist. By diffracting an electron beam with a nickel crystal, demonstrated that an electron has a wave motion, 1927; awarded Nobel Prize in physics (with G. P. THOMSON), 1937.

**DEBAKEY, MICHAEL,** Sept. 7, 1908 (Lake Charles, La.). U.S. surgeon. First surgeon to perform operations to correct aneurysms and obstructive lesions of major arteries; performed first aortocoronary artery bypass, using part of a vein from the patient's leg, 1964.

**DEBYE, PETER J. W.,** Mar. 24, 1884 (Maastricht, Netherlands)–Nov. 2, 1966. Dutch-U.S. physical chemist. Developed basic theory of dipole movements, fundamental to the understanding of chemical bonds (the unit of dipole moment is called a debye) and contributed to the Debye-Hückel theory of ion behavior in solutions; awarded Nobel Prize in chemistry, 1936.

**DE FOREST, LEE,** Aug. 26, 1873 (Council Bluffs, Ia.)–June 30, 1961. U.S. inventor. Invented the triode, the basis of the first electronic-sound amplification before transistors, 1906; invented first sound-on-film system, 1923; owned over 300 patents.

**DEHMELT, HANS G.,** Sept. 9, 1922 (Germany). U.S. experimental physicist. Developed methods to isolate atoms and subatomic particles for study; awarded Nobel Prize in physics (shared with W. PAUL and N. RAMSEY), 1989.

**DELBRÜCK, MAX,** Sept. 4, 1906 (Berlin, Ger.)–Mar. 9, 1981. U.S. biologist, physicist. A founder of molecular biology through his basic discoveries in bacterium and virus reproduction and mutation, 1940; awarded Nobel Prize in physiology or medicine (with A. D. HERSHEY and S. E. LURIA), 1969.

**DEVRIES, WILLIAM C.,** Dec. 19, 1943 (Brooklyn, N.Y.). U.S. surgeon. Dir., artificial heart project, Humana Hospital, Louisville, Ky.

**DICK, ALBERT BLAKE,** Apr. 16, 1856 (Bureau Co., Ill.)–Aug. 15, 1934. U.S. inventor. Invented the mimeograph process and machines, c.1887;

founded A. B. Dick Co., a duplicator manufacturer, 1887.

DREW, CHARLES RICHARD, June 3, 1904 (Washington, D.C.)–Apr. 1, 1950. U.S. surgeon. An expert on blood plasma who organized and operated the first blood bank (1940, in New York City); the segregation rules of that time forbade Dr. Drew, a black, to donate his own blood to the bank; awarded Spingarn Medal, 1944.

DULBECCO, RENATO, Feb. 2, 1914 (Cantanzaro, Italy). U.S. molecular biologist. Developed laboratory techniques for the study of animal viruses; awarded Nobel Prize in physiology or medicine (with D. BALTIMORE and H. TEMIN), 1975.

DUNNING, JOHN R., Sept. 24, 1907 (Shelby, Neb.)–Aug. 25, 1975. U.S. physicist. First to demonstrate fission of uranium-235, 1940; developed gas-diffusion method of concentrating U-235.

DU PONT, FRANCIS IRÉNÉE, Dec. 3, 1873 (Wilmington, Del.)–Mar. 16, 1942. U.S. chemist, financier. Made basic discoveries in the field of smokeless powder and minerals-separation processes; founded F. I. du Pont & Co., investment bankers, 1931.

DU VIGNEAUD, VINCENT, May 18, 1901 (Chicago, Ill.)–Dec. 11, 1978. U.S. biochemist. Synthesized penicillin (1946) and two hormones; awarded Nobel Prize in chemistry, 1955.

EASTMAN, GEORGE, July 12, 1854 (Waterville, N.Y.)–Mar. 14, 1932. U.S. inventor. Invented photographic emulsion gel (1878) and its application to paper (1884) to make film; patented celluloid film, 1889; developed the Kodak, the first lowprice, popularly available camera; pioneer in such business practices as sickness benefits, employee life insurance, and pensions.

EDELMAN, GERALD M., July 1, 1929 (New York, N.Y.). U.S. biochemist. First to work out the structure of an antibody molecule (1969), independently of R. R. PORTER; awarded Nobel Prize in physiology or medicine (with Porter), 1972.

EDISON, THOMAS ALVA, Feb. 11, 1847 (Milan, Ohio)–Oct. 18, 1931. U.S. inventor. Invented stock ticker (1869), phonograph (1877), the first electric light bulb (1879), and nearly 1,300 other items; made major contributions to the development of motion pictures, telephones, electrical generating systems; discovered the "Edison effect," the basis of modern electronics, 1883; the total value of his inventions was estimated at $25 billion before his death.

EINSTEIN, ALBERT, Mar. 14, 1879 (Ulm, Württemberg, Ger.)–Apr. 18, 1955. U.S.-Swiss-German physicist. Revolutionized cosmology and physics with his special (1905) and general (1915) theories of relativity, the former containing the equation $E = mc^2$, the basis of atomic power, and the latter revealing that gravity bends light; showed that I. NEWTON's physics did not apply on the subatomic and cosmic level; awarded 1921 Nobel Prize in physics for his explanation of the photoelectric effect (1905), which verified M. PLANCK's quantum theory.

ELION, GERTRUDE B., Jan. 23, 1918 (New York, N.Y.). U.S. drug researcher. Developed a series of drugs that have become essential in treating heart disease, peptic ulcers, gout, and leukemia; awarded Nobel Prize in physiology or medicine (shared with G. H. HITCHINGS and J. BLACK), 1988.

ENDERS, JOHN F., Feb. 10, 1897 (West Hartford, Conn.)–Sept. 8, 1985. U.S. microbiologist. Discovered a method to culture viruses outside of living bodies, the first step in the development of the polio vaccine, 1948–49; awarded Nobel Prize in physiology or medicine (with T. H. WELLER and F. C. ROBBINS), 1954.

ERLANGER, JOSEPH, Jan. 5, 1874 (San Francisco, Calif.)–Dec. 5, 1965. U.S. physiologist. Using an oscillograph to study nerve impulses, showed the velocity of impulse varied directly with the thickness of nerve fiber (1920s); awarded Nobel Prize in physiology or medicine (with H. S. GASSER), 1944.

EWING, WILLIAM M., May 12, 1906 (Lockney, Tex.)–May 4, 1974. U.S. geologist. Pioneer in studies of the ocean floor; discovered that the midAtlantic ridge continues into the Pacific and Indian oceans and that there is a chasm running along the center of the ridge; proposed theory of polar warming and the melting of Arctic ice with consequent increase in temperate-zone snow, to explain the Ice Age.

FEYNMAN, RICHARD P., May 11, 1918 (New York, N.Y.)–Feb. 15, 1989. U.S. physicist. Worked out the behavior of electrons with greater mathematical precision than ever before (quantum electrodynamics); awarded Nobel Prize in physics (with J. S. SCHWINGER and S. I. TOMONAGA), 1965.

FITCH, JOHN, Jan. 21, 1743 (Windsor, Conn.) –July 2, 1798. U.S. inventor. Built the first steamboat to carry passengers (between Trenton, N.J. and Philadelphia), 1790.

FITCH, VAL L., Mar. 10, 1923 (Merriman, Neb.). U.S. physics educator. Noted for discoveries concerning the symmetry of subatomic particle; awarded Nobel Prize in physics (shared with J. CRONIN), 1980.

FOWLER, WILLIAM A., Aug. 9, 1911 (Pittsburgh, Pa.). U.S. astrophysicist. Studied the evolution of stars, how they were born and what they were made of; awarded Nobel Prize in physics (shared with S. CHANDRASEKHAR), 1983.

FRANCK, JAMES, Aug. 26, 1882 (Hamburg, Ger.) –May 21, 1964. U.S. physicist. With G. HERTZ, demonstrated an aspect of M. PLANCK's quantum theory by bombarding gases with electrons to induce light emission; awarded Nobel Prize in physics (with G. Hertz), 1925.

FULLER, R(ichard) BUCKMINSTER, July 12, 1895 (Milton, Mass.)–July 1, 1983. U.S. engineer, architect, author. Developer of the geodesic dome (c.1940), which utilizes his *Dymaxion* principle of maximum output for minimum input. (Great nephew of S. M. FULLER.) *Operating Manual for Spaceship Earth*, 1969; *Utopia or Oblivion*, 1969; *Synergetics*, 1975.

FULTON, ROBERT, Nov. 14, 1765 (Little Britain

[now Fulton], Pa.)–Feb. 24, 1815. U.S. inventor. First to develop a profitable, practical steamship, 1807.

GAMOW, GEORGE, Mar. 4, 1904 (Odessa, Rus.) –Aug. 19, 1968. U.S.-Russian physicist. Made fundamental contributions to early nuclear theory, from 1928 on; a major formulator of "Big Bang" theory of the origin of the universe; with E. TELLER, worked out theory of the nature of red giant stars, an early step in understanding stellar evolution, 1942; worked out process by which elements were created in the "Big Bang," 1948; suggested idea of "genetic code" in arrangement of components of DNA, 1954.

GARAND, JOHN C., Jan. 1, 1888 (St. Remi, Que., Can.)–Feb. 16, 1974. U.S. gun designer. Patented the Garand semiautomatic rifle (M-1), 1934, and it was adopted by the U.S. Army, 1936.

GASSER, HERBERT S., July 5, 1888 (Platteville, Wisc.)–May 11, 1963. U.S. physiologist. With J. ERLANGER, showed that different nerve fibers carry specific impulses, such as those for pain or heat; awarded Nobel Prize in physiology or medicine (with Erlanger), 1944.

GATLING, RICHARD J., Sept. 12, 1818 (Winton, N.C.)–Feb. 26, 1903. U.S. inventor. Invented the first machine-gun, which had rotating barrels, 1862; improved agricultural machines, including steam plow; his name is the origin of the slang word gat, meaning a gun.

GELL-MANN, MURRAY, Sept. 15, 1929 (New York, N.Y.). U.S. physicist. Received his Ph.D. at age 22; introduced concept of "strangeness" to nuclear-particle theory, 1953; proposed the "Eightfold Way," a system of grouping nuclear particles, one of which was found in 1964; introduced idea of "quarks," particles with fractional electric charges, as basic building blocks of matter; awarded Nobel Prize in physics, 1969.

GESELL, ARNOLD L., June 21, 1880 (Alma, Wisc.) –May 29, 1961. U.S. psychologist. Made a major contribution to the description and understanding of the normal mental development of infants and children, from 1911. Atlas of Infant Behavior (with collaborators), 1934; The Child from Five to Ten (with collaborators), 1946; Youth: The Years from Ten to Sixteen, 1956.

GIAEVER, IVAR, Apr. 5, 1929 (Bergen, Nor.). U.S. physicist. Made basic discoveries in the phenomenon of electron "tunneling" and superconductivity, 1960; awarded Nobel Prize in physics (with L. ESAKI and B. D. JOSEPHSON), 1973.

GIAUQUE, WILLIAM F., May 12, 1895 (Niagara Falls, Ont., Can.)–Mar. 28, 1982. U.S. chemist. Discovered the isotopes of oxygen, 1929; devised a new method for achieving temperatures very near to absolute zero, 1926 (first successful use, 1935); awarded Nobel Prize in chemistry, 1949.

GIBBS, JOSIAH W., Feb. 11, 1839 (New Haven, Conn.)–Apr. 28, 1903. U.S. physicist. Worked out most of the details of chemical thermodynamics and statistical mechanics, in the 1870s; F.R.S.,

1897; his work was virtually ignored for over a decade.

GILBERT, WALTER, Mar. 21, 1932 (Boston, Mass.) U.S. molecular biologist. Developed methods that make it possible to map in detail the function and structure of DNA; awarded Nobel Prize in chemistry (shared with P. BERG and F. SANGER), 1980.

GLASER, DONALD A., Sept. 21, 1926 (Cleveland, Ohio). U.S. physicist. Invented the bubble chamber, vital to recent study of high-energy particles, 1952; awarded Nobel Prize in physics, 1960.

GLASHOW, SHELDON L., Dec. 5, 1932 (New York, N.Y.). U.S. physicist. Known for his work toward the discovery of a unified field theory; awarded Nobel Prize in physics (shared with S. WEINBERG and A. SALAM), 1979.

GODDARD, ROBERT HUTCHINGS, Oct. 5, 1882 (Worcester, Mass.)–Aug. 10, 1945. U.S. physicist. Father of modern rocketry; tested first liquid-fueled rocket engine, 1923; devised prototypes of many modern rocket systems, including combustion chambers, steering mechanisms, and multistages; his work, ignored by the U.S. govt., was financed by the Smithsonian Institution and the Guggenheim Foundation at C. LINDBERGH's urging; the U.S. finally "discovered" his work when German rocket experts acknowledged Goddard as the master, 1945.

GOEPPERT-MAYER, MARIE, June 28, 1906 (Kattowitz, Poland [then part of Germany])–Feb. 20, 1972. German-U.S. physicist. Proposed idea of nuclear shells, independently of H. D. JENSEN, 1949; awarded Nobel Prize in physics (with Jensen and E. P. WIGNER), 1963.

GOETHALS, GEORGE WASHINGTON, June 29, 1858 (Brooklyn, N.Y.)–Jan. 21, 1928. U.S. engineer. Chief engineer for and administrator of the Panama Canal project, 1907–14.

GOLDMARK, PETER C., Dec. 2, 1906 (Budapest, Hung.)–Dec. 7, 1977. U.S. inventor. Developed color television (1940) and the first commercially successful long-playing record (1948); also developed electronic video recording system.

GOLDSTEIN, JOSEPH L., Apr. 18, 1940 (Sumter, S.C.). U.S. geneticist. Discovered that the cells of the human body have receptors on their surfaces that trap and absorb blood-stream particles containing cholesterol, 1973; awarded Nobel Prize in medicine and physiology (shared with M. BROWN), 1985.

GOODYEAR, CHARLES, Dec. 29, 1800 (New Haven, Conn.)–July 1, 1860. U.S. inventor. Invented the vulcanized-rubber process, patented in 1844; died a pauper.

GORGAS, WILLIAM C., Oct. 3, 1854 (Mobile, Ala.)–July 3, 1920. U.S. surgeon. Organized antimosquito controls in the Panama Canal Zone, ending malaria and yellow-fever epidemic and thus making the construction of the canal possible without massive loss of life from disease, 1904.

GRAY, ASA, Nov. 18, 1810 (Sauquoit, N.Y.)–Jan. 30, 1888. U.S. botanist. The major contributor to knowledge of North American plants; a major early supporter of C. DARWIN in the U.S.; named to Hall of Fame for Great Americans, 1900. *Gray's Manual of Botany*, 1848.

GRINNELL, GEORGE BIRD, Sept. 20, 1849 (Brooklyn, N.Y.)–Apr. 11, 1938. U.S. naturalist. Founder of the Audubon Soc., 1886; originated the idea of Glacier Natl. Park, 1885; a pioneer conservation advocate and expert in Plains Indian folklore.

GUILLEMIN, ROGER, Jan. 11, 1924 (Dijon, Fr.). U.S. physiologist. Isolated the hormone stomatostatin (1973) and (with A. SCHALLY) the hormone TRH (1968–69), important in the treatment of some pituitary deficiencies, discovered endorphins; awarded Nobel Prize in physiology or medicine (with Schally and R. S. YALOW), 1977.

GUTTMACHER, ALAN F., May 19, 1898 (Baltimore, Md.)–Mar. 18, 1974. U.S. physician. Called the "Father of birth control in the U.S."; as pres. of Planned Parenthood Federation of America (1962–74), advocated unlimited access to contraceptive information and liberal abortion regulations; chief of obstetrics and gynecology at Mt. Sinai Hospital in New York City, 1952–62.

HALE, GEORGE E., June 29, 1868 (Chicago, Ill.)–Feb. 21, 1938. U.S. astronomer. Prime mover behind the Yerkes Observatory and Yerkes telescope (largest refracting telescope in the world), the Mount Wilson observatory (1908), and the Mount Palomar observatory (1948); invented the spectroheliograph, 1889.

HALL, CHARLES M., Dec. 6, 1863 (Thompson, Ohio)–Dec. 27, 1914. U.S. chemist. Independently of P. L. T. Héroult, discovered an inexpensive way of refining aluminum by electrolysis, thus making the metal available for widespread use, 1886.

HALSTED, WILLIAM S., Sept. 23, 1852 (New York, N.Y.)–Sept. 7, 1922. U.S. surgeon. Discovered that blood, once aerated, could be reinfused into a patient's body, 1881; developed local anesthesia, 1885; the first to use rubber gloves in surgery, 1890; founded first surgical school in the U.S., at Johns Hopkins, c.1890; his techniques and demands for careful work laid the basis for modern surgery.

HARKINS, WILLIAM D., Dec. 28, 1873 (Titusville, Pa.)–Mar. 7, 1951. U.S. chemist. Predicted the existence of the neutron and deuterium; introduced idea of "packing fraction" and from that idea, hypothesized the process of nuclear fusion as the source of solar energy.

HARTLINE, HALDAN KEFFER, Dec. 22, 1903 (Bloomsburg, Pa.)–Mar. 7, 1983. U.S. physiologist. Made major advances in the study of individual retinal cells; awarded Nobel Prize in physiology or medicine (with G. WALD and R. A. Granit), 1967.

HAUPTMAN, HERBERT A., Feb. 14, 1917 (New York, N.Y.). U.S. mathematician. Developed mathematical techniques through which x-ray crystallography can be used directly to deduce the three-dimensional structure of natural substances vital to the chemistry of the human body and of drugs that can be used to treat various ailments; awarded Nobel Prize in chemistry (shared with J. KARLE), 1985.

HENCH, PHILIP S., Feb. 28, 1896 (Pittsburgh, Pa.)–Mar. 30, 1965 U.S. physician. Discovered that cortisone, a hormone, alleviated arthritis, 1948; awarded Nobel Prize in physiology or medicine (with E. C. KENDALL and T. REICHSTEIN), 1950.

HENRY, JOSEPH, Dec. 17, 1797 (Albany, N.Y.)–May 13, 1878. U.S. physicist. Made major contributions to the development of electromagnets, 1829–31; the major contributor to the invention of the telegraph, 1831–37; the first to describe (but not to make) an electric motor, 1831; discovered self-induction, 1832; invented the electric relay, 1835; first secy. of the Smithsonian Inst., 1846; originated the gathering of weather reports that grew into the U.S. Weather Bureau; unit of inductance, the "henry," named for him.

HERSCHBACH, DUDLEY, June 18, 1932 (San Jose, Calif.). U.S. chemist. Noted for helping to create the first detailed understanding of chemical reactions; awarded Nobel Prize in chemistry (shared with Y. LEE), 1986.

HERSHEY, ALFRED D., Dec. 4, 1908 (Owosso, Mich.). U.S. biologist. Confirmed earlier indications that nucleic acid in cells was the material basis of the genetic code; awarded Nobel Prize in physiology or medicine (with M. DELBRUCK and S. E. LURIA), 1969.

HERSKOWITZ, IRA, July 14, 1946 (St. Louis, Mo.). U.S. molecular biologist. Noted for research in the molecular basis for gene control in viruses and yeast.

HILLIER, JAMES, Aug. 22, 1915 (Brantford, Ont., Can.). Canadian-U.S. physicist. Designed and constructed the first practical electron microscope, 1937.

HITCHINGS, GEORGE H., Apr. 18, 1905 (Hoquiam, Wash.). U.S. biochemist. Developed a series of drugs that have become essential in treating heart disease, peptic ulcers, gout, and leukemia; awarded Nobel Prize in physiology or medicine (shared with G. ELION and J. BLACK), 1988.

HOFFMANN, ROALD, July 18, 1937 (Zloczow, Pol.). U.S. chemist. Noted for work in explaining chemical reactions; awarded Nobel Prize in chemistry (shared with K. FUKUI), 1981.

HOFSTADTER, ROBERT, Feb. 5, 1915 (New York, N.Y.). U.S. physicist. Did basic studies in the structure of neutrons and protons, 1961; predicted the existence of massive mesons; awarded Nobel Prize in physics (with R. L. MOSSBAUER), 1961.

HOLLEY, ROBERT W., Jan. 28, 1922 (Urbana, Ill.). U.S. chemist. Isolated three varieties of transfer-RNA (1962) and worked out the structure of one (1965); awarded Nobel Prize in physiology or medicine (with H. G. KHORANA and M. W. NIRENBERG), 1968.

HOWE, ELIAS, July 9, 1819 (Spencer, Mass.)–Oct. 3, 1867. U.S. inventor. Invented the first practical sewing machine, the first modern invention to lighten the load of women's household chores, by placing the eye near the needle's point and using two threads, 1846; sold the English rights for $1,250;

U.S. patent, confirmed in 1854, finally brought him license fees from competitors.

**HUBBLE, EDWIN P.,** Nov. 20, 1889 (Marshfield, Mo.)–Sept. 28, 1953. U.S. astronomer. Discovered that nebulae (other galaxies) were far removed from the sun's galaxy, 1924; showed that these nebulae were receding at a speed directly proportional to their distance (Hubble's constant, 1929), thus establishing the idea of the expanding universe.

**HUBEL, DAVID H.,** Feb. 27, 1926 (Windsor, Ont.). U.S. physiologist. Noted for research vital to understanding the organization and functioning of the brain; awarded Nobel Prize in medicine or physiology (shared with T. WIESEL and R. SPERRY), 1981.

**HUGGINS, CHARLES B.,** Sept. 22, 1901 (Halifax, N.S., Can.). Canadian-U.S. surgeon. First to show that some cancers could be controlled by chemicals, in this case the female sex hormone for male prostate cancer, 1943; awarded Nobel Prize in physiology or medicine (with F. P. ROUS), 1966.

**HYATT, JOHN W.,** Nov. 28, 1837 (Starkey, N.Y.)–May 10, 1920. U.S. inventor. Invented and named celluloid, the first synthetic plastic, 1869; also filter for moving water in sugarcane refining and textiles; invented method for solidifying hardwoods for bowling balls, golf clubs, etc.

**IPATIEFF, VLADIMIR,** Nov. 21, 1867 (Moscow, Rus.)–Nov. 29, 1952. Russian-U.S. chemist. Determined the structure of isoprene, the basic molecule of rubber, 1897; discovered high-temperature catalytic reactions in hydrocarbons, 1900; developed the process for making low-grade gasoline into "high octane," 1930s.

**JANSKY, KARL G.,** Oct. 22, 1905 (Norman, Okla.)–Feb. 14, 1950. U.S. radio engineer. First to detect and determine the source of radio waves from outside the solar system, the beginning of radio astronomy, 1932; unit of radio-wave emission strength, the "jansky" named for him.

**JARVIK, ROBERT K.,** May 11, 1946 (Midland, Mich.). U.S. biomedical research scientist. Inventor of Jarvik-7, a total artificial heart powered by electro-hydraulic energy; first Jarvik-7 was implanted in Barney Clark, a retired dentist, December 1982; asst. research prof. of surgery, U. of Utah, 1979– .

**KAMEN, MARTIN D.,** Aug. 27, 1913 (Toronto, Ont., Can.). Canadian-U.S. biochemist. Discovered carbon-14 isotope, a basic tool of biochemical and archaeological research, 1940; the first to show that in photosynthesis, the liberated oxygen comes from water, not carbon dioxide.

**KARLE, JEROME,** June 18, 1918 (New York, N.Y.). U.S. research physicist. Developed mathematical techniques through which x-ray crystallography can be used directly to deduce the three-dimensional structure of natural substances vital to the chemistry of the human body and of drugs that can be used to treat various ailments; awarded Nobel Prize in chemistry (shared with H. HAUPTMAN), 1985.

**KENDALL, EDWARD C.,** Mar. 8, 1886 (S. Norwalk, Conn.)–May 4, 1972. U.S. biochemist. Isolated thyroxine, the basic substance of the thyroid hormone, 1916; isolated most of the hormones produced by the adrenal cortex, 1930s; awarded Nobel Prize in physiology or medicine (with P. S. HENCH and T. REICHSTEIN), 1950.

**KENNELLY, ARTHUR E.,** Dec. 17, 1861 (Bombay, India)–June 18, 1939. English-U.S. electrical engineer. Chief-assistant to T. A. EDISON, 1887–1894. Independently of O. HEAVISIDE, hypothesized the existence of the Kennelly-Heaviside layer of charged particles in the upper atmosphere that makes long-distance radio transmission possible, 1902.

**KHORANA, H. GOBIND,** Jan. 9, 1922 (Raipur, India). Indian-U.S. chemist. Worked out most of the genetic code, independently of M. W. NIRENBERG; awarded Nobel Prize in physiology or medicine (with Nirenberg and R. W. HOLLEY), 1968.

**KOOP, C(harles) EVERETT,** Oct. 14, 1916 (Brooklyn, N.Y.). U.S. physician. As U.S. surgeon general (1982–89), became a leading spokesman in the first against AIDS, stressing education as the only way to control it.

**KRAFT, CHRISTOPHER COLUMBUS,** Feb. 28, 1924 (Phoebus, Va.). U.S. aeronautical engineer. Flight dir. of U.S. manned space-flight program, 1959–70.

**KÜBLER-ROSS, ELISABETH,** c.1926 (Zurich, Switz.). Swiss-U.S. physician. International consultant in the care of the dying and medical pioneer in the study of how people die; board chm. of Shanti-Nilaya, a healing and growth center in Escondido, Calif. *On Death and Dying,* 1969; *Death—The Final Stage of Growth,* 1975; *Living with Death,* 1981; *Aids: The Ultimate Challenge,* 1987.

**KUIPER, GERARD P.,** Dec. 7, 1905 (Harenkarspel, Neth.)–Dec. 23, 1973. U.S. astronomer. Detected the atmosphere of Saturn's moon Titan; discovered and named Miranda (1948), a moon of Uranus, and Nereid (1949), a moon of Neptune; proposed the theory that planets and moons are formed by independent condensations, 1951.

**LAND, EDWIN H.,** May 7, 1909 (Bridgeport, Conn.). U.S. inventor. Invented the Polaroid lens, 1932; discovered a method of producing the full spectrum by using only two colors; invented the instant (Land) camera, 1947; also motion-picture system (Polavision), in which a movie could be viewed immediately after being taken, demonstrated 1977.

**LANDSTEINER, KARL,** June 14, 1868. (Vienna, Austria)–June 26, 1943. U.S. physician. Discovered human blood groups, thus making transfusions safe, 1900; the first to isolate the polio virus, 1908; helped discover Rh factor in blood, 1940; awarded Nobel Prize in physiology or medicine, 1930.

**LANGLEY, SAMUEL PIERPONT,** Aug. 22, 1834 (Roxbury, Mass.)–Feb. 27, 1906. U.S. astronomer, inventor. Invented a bolometer capable of measuring minute quantities of heat, 1881; a pioneer in development of the airplane, he worked out basic aerodynamic principles and built several unsuccessful planes, until one equipped with a powerful engine flew in 1914; founded Smithsonian Astrological Observatory, 1890, and National Zoological Park.

LANGMUIR, IRVING, Jan. 31, 1881 (Brooklyn, N.Y.)–Aug. 16, 1957. U.S. chemist. Made a basic improvement in light bulbs by filling them with nitrogen; invented a hydrogen blowtorch capable of temperatures close to 6,000°C (10,700°F); the first to study mononuclear films; awarded Nobel Prize in chemistry, 1932. F.R.S., 1935.

LARSON, JOHN A., Dec. 11, 1892 (Shelburne, Nova Scotia, Can.). U.S. psychiatrist. Invented the "lie detector" or polygraph, 1921.

LAWRENCE, ERNEST O., Aug. 8, 1901 (Canton, S.D.)–Aug. 27, 1958. U.S. physicist. Invented the cyclotron to increase vastly the energy of charged particles bombarding atomic nuclei, thus making possible most major advances in recent nuclear physics, 1930; invented and patented color-tv picture tube; lawrencium (element 103) named in his honor; awarded Nobel Prize in physics, 1939.

LEDERBERG, JOSHUA, May 23, 1925 (Montclair, N.J.). U.S. geneticist. With E. L. TATUM, discovered sexual reproduction in bacteria, thus expanding the value of bacteria in genetic research, c.1947; showed that some viruses could transfer genetic material from one bacterium to another, 1952; awarded Nobel Prize in physiology or medicine (with Tatum and G. W. BEADLE), 1958.

LEDERMAN, LEON M., July 15, 1922 (New York, N.Y.). U.S. physicist. Noted for work on a collaborative experiment that led to the development of a new tool for studying the weak nuclear force, which affects the radioactive decay of atoms; awarded Nobel Prize in physics (shared with M. SCHWARTZ and J. STEINBERGER), 1988.

LEE, TSUNG-DAO, Nov. 24, 1926 (Shanghai, China). U.S. physicist. With C. N. YANG, showed that the principle of conservation of parity (mirror equivalence of right- and left-handedness) did not apply in "weak" nuclear interactions; awarded Nobel Prize in physics (with Yang), 1957.

LEE, YUAN T., Nov. 29, 1936 (Hsin-chu, Taiwan). U.S. chemist. Noted for helping to create the first detailed understanding of chemical reactions; awarded Nobel Prize in chemistry (shared with D. HERSCH BACH), 1986.

LEVI-MONTALCINI, RITA, Apr. 23, 1909 (Turin, It.). Italian-U.S. developmental biologist. Noted for major contributions to the understanding of substances that influence cell growth and the orderly development of tissues, including the nervous system; awarded Nobel Prize in physiology or medicine (shared with S. COHEN), 1986.

LEY, WILLY, Oct. 2, 1906 (Berlin, Ger.)–June 24, 1969. U.S. engineer. Founded the German Rocket Soc. (1972) and introduced WERNHER VON BRAUN to rocketry; his strong advocacy of rocketry prepared the U.S. for space exploration in the 1960s.

LIBBY, WILLARD F., Dec. 17, 1908 (Grand Valley, Col.)–Sept. 8, 1980. U.S. chemist. Discovered and developed the carbon-14 dating technique, 1947; awarded Nobel Prize in chemistry, 1960.

LIPMANN, FRITZ A., June 12, 1899 (Königsberg, Ger. [now Kaliningrad, USSR])–July 24, 1986. U.S. biochemist. Made fundamental discoveries about the function of phosphates in animal metabolism; discovered coenzyme A, a basic catalyst in animal metabolism; awarded Nobel Prize in physiology or medicine (with H. A. KREBS), 1953. F.R.S., 1962.

LOEWI, OTTO, June 3, 1873 (Frankfurt-am-Main, Ger.)–Dec. 25, 1961. U.S. physiologist. Discovered acetylcholine, a chemical transmitter of nerve impulses, 1921; studied diabetes, and action of digitalis; devised Loewi's test of detection of pancreatic disease; awarded 1936 Nobel Prize in physiology or medicine (With H. H. DALE), but was forced to turn over his prize money to the Nazis in 1938 as the price for emigration. F.R.S., 1954.

LOWELL, PERCIVAL, Mar. 13, 1855 (Boston, Mass.)–Nov. 12, 1916. U.S. astronomer. Established Lowell observatory in Arizona, 1894; predicted the existence of the planet Pluto prior to its 1930 discovery; proponent of theory that intelligent life existed on Mars. (Brother of the poet A. LOWELL.)

LURIA, SALVADOR, Aug. 13, 1912 (Turin, It.). Italian-U.S. biologist. Made basic discoveries in mutation of bacteria and viruses, 1940s; awarded Nobel Prize in physiology or medicine (with M. DELBRUCK and A. D. HERSHEY), 1969.

MARSH, OTHNIEL C., Oct. 29, 1831 (Lockport, N.Y.)–Mar. 18, 1899. U.S. paleontologist. The first prof. of paleontology in the U.S., at Yale C., 1866–99; led fossil-finding expedition in American West, guided by W. F. CODY; discovered the pterodactyl, 1871; discovered some 1,000 fossil vertebrates; through fossils of extinct horses, traced a complete evolutionary line, thus giving powerful support to CHARLES DARWIN's evolutionary theory.

MASTERS, WILLIAM H., Dec. 27, 1915 (Cleveland, Ohio). U.S. physician, educator. Noted for his important research in the field of sex therapy, with wife Virginia E. Johnson; with Johnson, wrote Human Sexual Response (1966), Human Sexual Inadequacy (1970), The Pleasure Bond (1975), Homosexuality in Perspective (1979), and Human Sexuality (1982).

MAYO, WILLIAM J., June 29, 1861 (Le Sueur, Minn.)–July 28, 1939 and his brother MAYO, CHARLES H., July 19, 1865 (Rochester, Minn.)–May 26, 1939. U.S. surgeons. Cofounders of the Mayo Clinic and Fndn. for Medical Education and Research (1915) with a contribution to the U. of Minnesota of $2,800,000.

MCCLINTOCK, BARBARA, June 16, 1902 (Hartford, Conn.). U.S. cytogeneticist. Discovered that genes can move from one spot to another on the chromosomes of plants and change the future generations of plants; awarded Nobel Prize in medicine or physiology, 1983.

MCCORMICK, CYRUS H., Feb. 15, 1809 (Rockbridge Co., Va.)–May 13, 1884. U.S. inventor. Invented the first reaper to combine effectively all the basic elements of the modern reaper, 1831; established a farm-machine business (1848) on expiration of reaper patent that later (1902) became the Internatl. Harvester Co.

**MCMILLAN, EDWIN M.,** Sept. 18, 1907 (Redondo Beach, Calif.). U.S. physicist. Discovered the first transuranium element, neptunium, 1940, also plutonium; devised improvements in the cyclotron to create the synchrotron, vastly increasing the energy to which particles could be accelerated; awarded Nobel Prize in chemistry (with G. T. SEABORG), 1951.

**MERGENTHALER, OTTMAR,** May 11, 1854 (Hachtel, Württemburg, Ger.)–Oct. 28, 1899. U.S. inventor. Invented the Linotype machine (1885), which mechanized typesetting.

**MERRIFIELD, R. BRUCE,** July 15, 1921 (Ft. Worth, Tex.). U.S. biochemist. Noted for research revolutionizing the study of proteins and leading to the development of significant new drugs; awarded Nobel Prize in chemistry, 1984.

**MICHELSON, ALBERT ABRAHAM,** Dec. 19, 1852 (Strelno, Prussia [now Poland])–May 9, 1931. U.S. physicist. Progressively refined the measure of the speed of light to within 5.5 km per second of the presently accepted value, 1882–1927; with E. W. MORLEY, failed to show that light moved more rapidly if projected in the direction of earth's motion, thus throwing great doubt on the then-prevailing theory of light waves (1887) and initiating the revolution in physics by K. LORENZ, M. PLANCK, and A. EINSTEIN; the first to measure the width of a star by interferometry, 1920; awarded Nobel Prize in physics, (the first U.S. winner), 1907.

**MILLIKAN, ROBERT A.,** Mar. 22, 1868 (Morrison, Ill.)–Dec. 19, 1953. U.S. physicist. In subtle experiments with ionized oil droplets, determined the value of the charge on a single electron, proving beyond doubt that electricity consists of particles, 1910; verified A. EINSTEIN's photoelectric explanation experimentally and derived a value for Planck's constant, 1916; invented the term *cosmic rays*, 1925; awarded Nobel Prize in physics, 1923.

**MODIGLIANI, FRANCO,** June 18, 1918 (Rome, It.). Italian-U.S. economist. Noted for his pioneering work in analyzing the behavior of household savers and the functioning of financial markets; awarded Nobel Prize in economics, 1985.

**MOORE, STANFORD,** Sept. 4, 1913 (Chicago, Ill.)–Aug. 23, 1982. U.S. biochemist. Made a basic contribution to the development of chromatographic techniques in the study of protein structures; with W. H. STEIN, determined the constituents of enzyme ribonuclease; awarded Nobel Prize in chemistry (with C. B. ANFINSEN and Stein), 1972.

**MORGAN, THOMAS H.,** Sept. 25, 1866 (Lexington, Ky.)–Dec. 4, 1945. U.S. geneticist. Established and completed the work of G. MENDEL by mapping gene positions on the chromosomes of fruit flies and discovering the "crossing-over" phenomenon by which gene-linkage on a specific chromosome is occasionally broken, 1907–26; awarded Nobel Prize in physiology or medicine, 1933. *The Theory of the Gene,* 1926.

**MORLEY, EDWARD WILLIAMS,** Jan. 29, 1838 (Newark, N.J.)–Feb. 24, 1923. U.S. chemist. Collaborated with A. A. MICHELSON in the famous experiments with light that began the modern revolution in physics.

**MORSE, SAMUEL F.,** Apr. 27, 1791 (Charlestown, Mass.)–Apr. 2, 1872. U.S. inventor and painter. With great assistance from J. HENRY, invented the first practical telegraph (1840), which was first built in 1844; devised "Morse code" for use with the telegraph, 1838; one of founders of National Academy of Design.

**MORTON, WILLIAM T.,** Aug. 9, 1819 (Charlton City, Mass.)–July 15, 1868. U.S. dentist. First to patent and publicize the use of ether as an anesthetic, during tooth extraction, 1846.

**MUIR, JOHN,** Apr. 21, 1838 (Dunbar, East Lothian, Scot.)–Dec. 24, 1914. U.S. naturalist. The primary force behind the first U.S. land-conservation laws and establishment of Yosemite and Sequoia natl. parks; explored most of the Sierra (1868–74) and a large portion of Alaska and the Yukon.

**MULLER, HERMAN N. J.,** Dec. 21, 1890 (New York, N.Y.)–Apr. 5, 1967. U.S. biologist. Discovered the mutagenic effects of X rays, thus speeding up the process of mutation for genetic studies, 1926; when study of mutations revealed that most are lethal, became an early advocate of limiting exposure to X rays and the use of sperm banks to conserve healthy genes; awarded Nobel Prize in physiology or medicine, 1946.

**NATHANS, DANIEL,** Oct. 30, 1928 (Wilmington, Del.). U.S. biologist. Found that the restriction enzyme discovered by H. O. SMITH could break up the DNA of a cancer virus, leading to a complete mapping of the genetics of the virus, 1971; awarded Nobel Prize in physiology or medicine (with Smith and W. ARBER), 1978.

**NEUMANN, JOHN VON,** Dec. 28, 1903 (Budapest, Hung.)–Feb. 8, 1957. U.S. mathematician. Developed "game theory," 1926–44; directed construction of computers that helped solve problems in engineering the H-bomb; did major advanced work in mathematical physics; received Fermi Award, 1956.

**NIRENBERG, MARSHALL W.,** Apr. 10, 1927 (New York, N.Y.). U.S. biochemist. First to produce enzyme trypsin in the lab, also a crystalline form of diptheria toxin, 1941; first to discover an element of the genetic code, relating a particular group of three DNA nucleotides to the building of a particular amino acid, 1961; awarded Nobel Prize in physiology or medicine (with H. G. KHORANA and R. W. HOLLEY), 1968.

**NORTHROP, JOHN HOWARD,** July 5, 1891 (Yonkers, N.Y.)–May 27, 1987. U.S. biochemist. His work, from 1930, in enzyme crystallization and analysis proved conclusively that enzymes are proteins; awarded Nobel Prize in chemistry (with J. B. SUMNER and W. M. STANLEY), 1946.

**OCHOA, SEVERO,** Sept. 24, 1905 (Luarca, Spain). U.S. biochemist. First to synthesize RNA, 1955; awarded Nobel Prize in physiology or medicine (with Arthur Kornberg), 1959.

OPPENHEIMER, J(ulius) ROBERT, Apr. 22, 1904 (New York, N.Y.)–Feb. 18, 1967. U.S. physicist. His basic theoretical work led to the discovery of the positron and to advances in neutron bombardment; headed Los Alamos, N.M., laboratories during the development of the first A-bombs, 1943–45; chm. of the gen. advisory com. of the AEC, 1947–53; proclaimed a security risk for his reluctance to proceed with H-bomb development, 1954; received Fermi Award, 1963.

OTIS, ELISHA GRAVES, Aug. 3, 1811 (Halifax, Vt.)–Apr. 8, 1861. U.S. inventor. Invented the first elevator with a reliable safety device to prevent its falling if the cable were to break, 1852.

PALADE, GEORGE EMIL, Nov. 19, 1912 (Iaşi, Rumania). U.S. physiologist. Discovered the function of ribosomes as the sites of protein manufacture, 1956; awarded Nobel Prize in physiology or medicine (with A. CLAUDE and C. R. De Duve), 1974.

PAPANICOLAOU, GEORGE N., May 13, 1883 (Coumi, Greece)–Feb. 19, 1962. U.S. physiologist. Devised a simple test (Pap smear) for early discovery of cervical cancer, 1928; work was ignored until 1940.

PAUL, WOLFGANG, Aug. 10, 1913 (Lorenzkirch, E. Ger.). U.S. physicist. Developed methods to isolate atoms and subatomic particles for study; awarded Nobel Prize in physics (shared with H. DEHMELT and N. RAMSEY), 1989.

PAULI, WOLFGANG, Apr. 25, 1900 (Vienna, Austria)–Dec. 15, 1958. U.S.-Austrian physicist. Pronounced the "Pauli exclusion principle," a fundamental explanation of the behavior of a class of atomic particles, 1925; the first to postulate the existence of the neutrino, 1931; awarded Nobel Prize in physics, 1945.

PAULING, LINUS C., Feb. 28, 1901 (Portland, Ore.). U.S. chemist. Made basic theoretical contributions to understanding the structure of molecules and the nature of chemical bonds, 1939; first to suggest a helical structure for protein molecules, early 1950s; a major advocate of nuclear disarmament and an end to nuclear testing; a major advocate of large doses of vitamin C to prevent the common cold; awarded Nobel Prize in chemistry, 1954; awarded Nobel Peace Prize, 1962.

PEDERSEN, CHARLES J., Oct. 3, 1904 (Pusan, Korea). U.S. research chemist. A pioneer in wideranging research, including the creation of artificial molecules; awarded Nobel Prize in chemistry (shared with D. CRAM and J. LEHN), 1987.

PENZIAS, ARNO, Apr. 26, 1933 (Munich, Ger.). U.S. physicist. With R. W. WILSON, discovered the cosmic background-radiation theoretically left over from the "Big Bang" that began the universe, 1964; awarded Nobel Prize in physics (with R. W. Wilson and P. L. KAPITSA), 1978.

PINCUS, GREGORY, Apr. 9, 1903 (Woodbine, N.J.)–Aug. 22, 1967. U.S. biologist. Invented the birth-control pill, 1955.

PURCELL, EDWARD M., Aug. 30, 1912 (Taylorville, Ill.). U.S. physicist. Discovered, independently of F. BLOCH, nuclear magnetic resonance and used it to devise methods for the study of magnetism in atomic nuclei and new techniques in analytic chemistry; in radio astronomy, discovered the radio emission of neutral hydrogen in interstellar space, 1951; awarded Nobel Prize in physics (with Bloch), 1952.

RABI, ISIDOR ISAAC, July 29, 1898 (Rymanóv, A.-H. [now Ukrainian S.S.R.])–Jan. 11, 1988. U.S. physicist. Developed technique of using molecular beams (see O. STERN) as a means to measure magnetic properties of atoms and molecules, from 1933; worked on the development of radar and the A-bomb; chairman of the scientific advisory com. of the AEC, 1952–56; awarded Nobel Prize in physics, 1944.

RAINWATER, JAMES, Dec. 9, 1917 (Council, Ida.)–May 31, 1986. U.S. physicist. Proposed that some atomic nuclei can be asymmetrical, not spherical, and suggested why, 1949; awarded Nobel Prize in physics (with B. R. MOTTELSON and A. N. BOHR), 1975.

RAMSEY, NORMAN F., Aug. 27, 1915 (Washington, D.C.). U.S. physicist. His work led to the development of the atomic clock, which measures the vibrations of atoms to create a time standard used around the world; awarded Nobel Prize in physics (shared with H. DEHMELT and W. PAUL), 1989.

REBER, GROTE, Dec. 22, 1911 (Wheaton, Ill.). U.S. radio astronomer. Built the first radio telescope (1937) and was the only radio astronomer in the world from 1937 to 1945; mapped high-frequency sources (1938–42) and low-frequency sources (from 1951).

REED, WALTER, Sept. 13, 1851 (Belroi, Va.)–Nov. 23, 1902. U.S. bacteriologist. Led the commission that tracked the carrier of yellow fever to a particular mosquito, 1900; proved the cause was a filterable virus, 1901; his discoveries contributed greatly to the successful construction of the Panama Canal.

REMSEN, IRA, Feb. 10, 1846 (New York, N.Y.)–Mar. 4, 1927. U.S. chemist. Discovered the chemical sweetener later named saccharin, 1879.

RICHARDS, THEODORE W., Jan. 31, 1868 (Germantown, Pa.)–Apr. 2, 1928. U.S. chemist. Determined the atomic weight of most elements as accurately as possible with purely chemical means; confirmed by chemical means F. SODDY's prediction of the existence of isotopes, c.1915; awarded Nobel Prize in chemistry, 1914.

RICHTER, BURTON, Mar. 22, 1931 (Brooklyn, N.Y.). U.S. physicist. Independently of S. C. C. TING, discovered the J-(psi) particle, 1974; his discovery helped confirm the theory of charmed quarks; awarded Nobel Prize in physics (with Ting). 1976.

RICHTER, CHARLES F., Apr. 26, 1900 (Butler Co., Ohio)–Sept. 30, 1985. U.S. seismologist. Developed a method for calculating the severity of earthquakes and a scale to measure earthquake intensity (Richter scale).

ROBBINS, FREDERICK C., Aug. 25, 1916 (Auburn, Ala.). U.S. microbiologist. With J. ENDERS and T. WELLER, discovered (1952) how to cultivate viruses in tissue culture, which contributed directly to the development of a polio vaccine; awarded Nobel Prize in physiology or medicine (with Enders and Weller), 1954.

ROEBLING, JOHN A., June 12, 1806 (Mühlhausen, Thuringia, Prussia)–July 22, 1869. U.S. engineer. First to recognize the strength and resilience of steel wire and to weave wire into cable, about 1841; pioneered in the design and construction of suspension bridges, including the Brooklyn Bridge.

ROUS, PEYTON, Oct. 5, 1879 (Baltimore, Md.)–Feb. 16, 1970. U.S. physician. The first to isolate a cancer-causing virus, 1910; worked on development of blood-preserving techniques which made blood banks possible in WW I; awarded Nobel Prize in physiology or medicine (with C. B. HUGGINS), 1966.

RUSSELL, HENRY N., Oct. 25, 1877 (Oyster Bay, N.Y.)–Feb. 18, 1957. U.S. astronomer. Independently of E. HERZSPRUNG, devised a scale of stellar types on which the life-cycle of stars could be plotted, 1913; did pioneering work in determining the sun's composition, 1929.

SABIN, ALBERT B., Aug. 26, 1906 (Bialystok, Rus. [now Pol.]). U.S. microbiologist. Developed the oral vaccine for polio, using "attenuated" live viruses, 1959.

SAGAN, CARL, Nov. 9, 1934 (New York, N.Y.). U.S. astronomer. Specializes in planetary surfaces and atmospheres; advocates the search for extraterrestrial intelligence; a science popularizer. *The Dragons of Eden*, 1977 (Pulitzer prize in non-fiction, 1978); *Broca's Brain*, 1979; *Cosmos*, 1980 (based on his television series).

SALK, JONAS E., Oct. 28, 1914 (New York, N.Y.). U.S. microbiologist. Developed the first polio vaccine, using dead viruses, 1952–55; awarded Presidential Medal of Freedom, 1977.

SCHALLY, ANDREW V., Nov. 30, 1926 (Wilno, Pol.). U.S. biochemist. Isolated the hormone LHRH (1971), vital to human ovulation, and independently of R. GUILLEMIN, the vital pituitary hormone TRH (1968–69); awarded Nobel Prize in physiology or medicine (with Guillemin and R. S. YALOW), 1977.

SCHAWLOW, ARTHUR L., May 5, 1921 (Mt. Vernon, N.Y.). U.S. physicist. Noted for work in developing technologies with lasers and other devices that can seek out the innermost secrets of complex forms of matter; awarded Nobel Prize in physics (shared with N. BLOEMBERGEN and K. SIEGBAHN), 1981.

SCHLEIDEN, MATTHIAS JACOB, April 5, 1804 (Hamburg, Germany)–June 23, 1881. German botanist. Formulated the cell theory—that all plants are composed of these basic building blocks; discovery was made independently of THEODOR SCHWANN, who posited the same theory for the animal kingdom.

SCHRIEFFER, JOHN R., May 31, 1931 (Oak Park, Ill.). U.S. physicist. With J. BARDEEN and L. N. COOPER, developed an effective theory of superconductivity, 1957; awarded Nobel Prize in physics (with Bardeen and Cooper), 1972.

SCHWARTZ, MELVIN, Nov. 2, 1932 (New York, N.Y.). U.S. physicist. Noted for work on a collaborative experiment that led to the development of a new tool for studying the weak nuclear force, which affects the radioactive decay of atoms; awarded Nobel Prize in physics (shared with L. LEDERMAN and J. STEINBERGER), 1988.

SCHWINGER, JULIAN S., Feb. 12, 1918 (New York, N.Y.). U.S. physicist. Made a basic theoretical contribution to the development of quantum electrodynamics; awarded Nobel Prize in physics (with R. P. FEYNMAN and S. I. TOMONAGA), 1965.

SEABORG, GLENN T., Apr. 19, 1912 (Ishpeming, Mich.). U.S. physicist. Made basic discoveries in the physics and chemistry of transuranian elements, from 1940; chm. of the AEC, 1961–71; awarded Nobel Prize in chemistry (with E. M. MCMILLAN), 1951.

SEGRÈ, EMILIO G., Feb. 1, 1905 (Tivoli, Italy)–Apr. 22, 1989. U.S. physicist. Discovered element 43, technetium, the first artificially produced element, 1937; with O. CHAMBERLAIN, demonstrated the existence of the antiproton, 1955; awarded Nobel Prize in physics (with Chamberlain), 1959.

SEMMELWEIS, IGNAZ PHILIPP, July 1, 1818 (Buda, Hungary)–Aug. 13, 1865. Hungarian-born Austrian physician. First to use antiseptic methods during childbirth; urged his fellow doctors to clean their hands in order not to spread puerperal fever; though ridiculed, he published his work *The Etiology, Concept and Prophylaxis of Childbirth Fever*, in 1860; his theory was finally proved in the year of his death when JOSEPH LISTER performed his antiseptic operations.

SHANNON, CLAUDE E., Apr. 30, 1916 (Gaylord, Mich.). U.S. mathematician. The founder of information theory, which has had a major impact on computer development, communications technology, biology, and other fields. *Mathematical Theory of Communications*, 1949.

SHOCKLEY, WILLIAM, Feb. 13, 1910 (London, Eng.)–Aug. 12, 1989. U.S. physicist. A major contributor to the invention of the transistor and development of semiconductor technology; awarded Nobel Prize in physics (with J. BARDEEN and W. H. BRATTAIN), 1956.

SIKORSKY, IGOR, May 25, 1889 (Kiev, Rus.)–Oct. 26, 1972. U.S. aviation engineer. Built and flew the first multimotored plane, 1913; developed the early transoceanic amphibian plane; developed the first successful helicopter, 1939.

SMITH, HAMILTON O., Aug. 23, 1931 (New York, N.Y.). U.S. biochemist. Discovered a restriction enzyme that always breaks certain DNA molecules at the same place, 1970; developed new techniques to isolate and purify restriction enzymes;

awarded Nobel Prize in physiology or medicine (with D. NATHANS and W. ARBER), 1978.

SNELL, GEORGE, Dec. 19, 1903 (Bradford, Mass.). U.S. geneticist. Noted for his work in making tissue typing possible and shedding new light on the body's immune system; awarded Nobel Prize in medicine or physiology (shared with J. DAUSSET and B. BENACERRAF), 1980.

SPERRY, ELMER A., Oct. 12, 1860 (Cortland, N.Y.)–June 16, 1930. U.S. inventor. Developed the gyroscopic compass, 1896–1910; obtained over 400 patents for a wide variety of electrical devices and industrial processes; a founder of the Sperry-Rand Corp.

SPERRY, ROGER W., Aug. 20, 1913 (Hartford, Conn.). U.S. neurobiologist. Noted for research vital to understanding the organization and functioning of the brain; awarded Nobel Prize in medicine or physiology (shared with D. HUBEL and T. WIESEL), 1981.

SPITZER, LYMAN, June 26, 1914 (Toledo, Ohio). U.S. astronomer. His research on the formation of stars out of interstellar gas in magnetic fields led to work on hydrogen fusion and one of the first suggestions that fusion reactions could be contained in magnetic "bottles."

SPOCK, BENJAMIN M., May 2, 1903 (New Haven, Conn.). U.S. pediatrician and psychiatrist. A major influence on modern U.S. child-rearing practices and health care; ran for U.S. pres. on People's party ticket, 1972; his Common Sense Book of Baby and Child Care (1946) has sold over 24 million copies.

STANLEY, FRANCIS E., June 1, 1849 (Kingfield, Me.)–July 31, 1918; and his twin brother FREELAN O. STANLEY, June 1, 1849 (Kingsfield, Me.)–Oct. 2, 1940. U.S. inventors. Invented the Stanley Steamer, a steam-powered automobile, 1897.

STANLEY, WENDELL M., Aug. 16, 1904 (Ridgeville, Ind.)–June 15, 1971. U.S. biochemist. First to crystallize a virus (1935), thus opening the way to understanding their molecular structure; developed influenza vaccine during WWII; awarded Nobel Prize in chemistry (with J. NORTHROP and J. SUMNER), 1946.

STEIN, WILLIAM H., June 25, 1911 (New York, N.Y.)–Feb. 20, 1980. U.S. biochemist. With S. MOORE, determined the constituents of ribonuclease and developed automated techniques for analysis of amino acids in enzymes; awarded Nobel Prize in chemistry (with C. B. ANFINSEN and Moore), 1972.

STEINBERGER, JACK, May 25, 1921 (Bad Kissingen, Ger.). U.S. physicist. Noted for work on a collaborative experiment that led to the development of a new tool for studying the weak nuclear force, which affects the radioactive decay of atoms; awarded Nobel Prize in physics (shared with L. LEDERMAN and M. SCHWARTZ), 1988.

STEINMETZ, CHARLES P., Apr. 9, 1865 (Breslau, Ger. [now Wroclaw, Pol.])–Oct. 26, 1923. U.S. electrical engineer. Established the mathematical methods of electrical engineering; worked out the

necessary mathematics to predict the efficiency of electrical motors (1892) and alternating-current circuits (1893); designed a generator able to produce an electrical discharge of immense power in order to study effects of lightning.

SUMNER, JAMES B., Nov. 19, 1887 (Canton, Mass.)–Aug. 12, 1955. U.S. biochemist. First to crystallize an enzyme and to prove that enzymes were proteins, 1926; awarded Nobel Prize in chemistry (with J. H. NORTHROP and W. M. STANLEY), 1946.

SUTHERLAND, EARL W., JR., Nov. 19, 1915 (Burlingame, Kan.)–Mar. 9, 1974. U.S. biochemist. Conducted basic studies in roles of enzymes and hormones in carbohydrate metabolism; awarded Nobel Prize in physiology or medicine, 1971.

SZILARD, LEO, Feb. 11, 1898 (Budapest, Hung.)–May 30, 1964. U.S. physicist. Developed the first method of separating isotopes of radioactive elements, 1934; ghosted the famous letter from A. EINSTEIN to Pres. F. D. ROOSEVELT advocating development of an atomic bomb, 1939; worked with E. FERMI in building the first nuclear reactor, 1942; did basic research in biophysics, after 1946; received Atoms for Peace award, 1959.

TATUM, EDWARD L., Dec. 14, 1909 (Boulder, Col.)–Nov. 5, 1975. U.S. biochemist. With G. W. BEADLE, did basic research in genetic mutation and the study of the chemical function of genes in the production of enzymes; helped create field of molecular genetics; awarded Nobel Prize in physiology or medicine (with Beadle and J. LEDERBERG), 1958.

TAYLOR, FREDERICK W., Mar. 20, 1856 (Philadelphia, Pa.)–Mar. 21, 1915. U.S. engineer. Father of scientific management; conducted the first time-and-motion studies to improve efficiency, 1881.

TELLER, EDWARD, Jan. 15, 1908 (Budapest, Hung.). U.S. physicist. Called the "Father of the H-bomb" for devising a secret element that made the device practical and leading the H-bomb project as administrator (1949–52); received Fermi Award, 1962.

TEMIN, HOWARD M., Dec. 10, 1934 (Philadelphia, Pa.). U.S. molecular biologist. Conducted research into the process by which a virus can change the genetic makeup of a cell; awarded Nobel Prize in physiology or medicine (with D. BALTIMORE and R. DULBECCO), 1975.

TESLA, NIKOLA, July 9, 1856. (Smiljan, Croatia, [now Yugoslavia])–Jan. 7, 1943. U.S. electrical engineer. Regarded by many as one of the most brilliant men in history; developed (by 1885) the principles and devices that made alternating current practical and dominant in the U.S.; his wide-ranging experiments in electricity contributed to most developments in electronics.

TING, SAMUEL C. C., Jan. 26, 1936 (Ann Arbor, Mich.). U.S. physicist. Discovered the J(-psi) particle, independently of BURTON RICHTER, 1974; his discovery helped confirm the theory of charmed quarks; awarded Nobel Prize in physics (with Richter), 1976.

TOWNES, CHARLES H., July 28, 1915 (Greenville, S.C.). U.S. physicist. An inventor of the maser, 1953; contributed to the theory of the laser, 1958; awarded Nobel Prize in physics (with A. M. PROKHOROV and N. G. BASOV), 1964.

UREY, HAROLD C., Apr. 29, 1893 (Walkerton, Ind.)–Jan. 5, 1981. U.S. chemist. Proved the existence of deuterium, or heavy hydrogen, 1931; did basic research in isotope separation essential to the development of the A-bomb, 1930s; developed the basic theories of evolution of the elements in stellar activity, c.1950; major advocate of the condensation theory of planet formation; awarded Nobel Prize in chemistry, 1934.

VAN ALLEN, JAMES A., Sept. 7, 1914 (Mount Pleasant, Ia.). U.S. physicist. Helped develop the proximity fuse, c.1942; a major advocate of the space program, 1945–58; pioneered in the use of rockets and satellites for scientific purposes; discovered the magnetosphere (or Van Allen radiation belts) around the earth, 1958.

VAN VLECK, JOHN H., Mar. 13, 1899 (Middletown, Conn.)–Oct. 28, 1980. U.S. physicist. Made basic contributions to the understanding of magnetic forces within and between atoms; awarded Nobel Prize in physics (with N. F. MOTT and P. W. ANDERSON), 1977.

VARMUS, HAROLD E., Dec. 18, 1939 (Oceanside, N.Y.). U.S. microbiologist. Noted for research in cancer; awarded Nobel Prize in physiology or medicine (shared with J. BISHOP), 1989.

WAKSMAN, SELMAN A., July 22, 1888 (Priluka, Ukraine, Russia)–Aug. 16, 1973. U.S. microbiologist. Discovered streptomycin, a breakthrough in the search for antibiotics, 1943; coined the word *antibiotics*; awarded Nobel Prize in physiology or medicine, 1952.

WALD, GEORGE, Nov. 18, 1906 (New York, N.Y.). U.S. chemist. Did basic research in the chemistry of vision, in the 1940s and 1950s; in the late 1960s became a spokesman for the anti-Vietnam War movement and later, anti-nuclear power groups; awarded Nobel Prize in physiology or medicine (with H. K. HARTLINE and R. A. Granit), 1967.

WALKER, MARY, Nov. 26, 1832 (Oswego, N.Y.) –Feb. 21, 1919. U.S. physician. Graduated from Syracuse Medical C. (1855), six years after E. BLACKWELL became the first U.S. female physician; asst. surgeon in Union Army; first woman ever to receive Medal of Honor, 1865; arrested several times for wearing a frock coat and trousers on the street, a custom she had picked up during the Civil War, in the late 1860s; active in The Mutual Dress Reform and Equal Rights Assn.

WATSON, JAMES D., Apr. 6, 1928 (Chicago, Ill.). U.S. biochemist. With F. H. C. CRICK, worked out the molecular structure of DNA; awarded Nobel Prize in physiology or medicine (with Crick and M. H. F. WILKINS), 1962.

WATSON, JOHN B., Jan. 9, 1878 (Greenville, S.C.)–Sept. 25, 1958. U.S. psychologist. Founded behaviorist psychology, the study of human behavior as almost entirely the product of conditioned response and learning.

WEINBERG, STEVEN, May 3, 1933 (New York, N.Y.). U.S. physicist. Recognized for his work toward the discovery of a unified field theory; awarded Nobel Prize in physics (shared with S. GLASHOW and A. SALAM), 1979.

WELLER, THOMAS H., June 15, 1915 (Ann Arbor, Mich.). U.S. microbiologist. With J. F. ENDERS and F. C. ROBBINS, devised methods to cultivate viruses in the laboratory, 1948–49; awarded Nobel Prize in physiology or medicine (with Enders and Robbins), 1954.

WESTINGHOUSE, GEORGE, Oct. 6, 1846 (Central Bridge, N.Y.)–Mar. 12, 1914. U.S. engineer. Invented the air brake, patented 1869; developed many important railroading devices and systems for piping gas; founded Westinghouse Electric Co., 1886; bought N. TESLA's patents in alternating current and made it the standard form of electrical transmissions in the U.S.

WHITNEY, ELI, Dec. 8, 1765 (Westboro, Mass.) –Jan. 8, 1825. U.S. inventor. Invented the cotton gin, which made cotton-growing highly profitable, 1793; devised precision-machining methods that made musket parts interchangeable, c.1801; the first to use assembly-line methods in industry.

WIENER, NORBERT, Nov. 26, 1894 (Columbia, Mo.)–Mar. 18, 1964. U.S. mathematician. Made fundamental contributions to mathematics, 1930s; founder of cybernetics, the science of communication and control within and between machines, animals, and organizations, on which much modern automation is based. *Cybernetics*, 1948.

WIESEL, TORSTEN N., June 3, 1924 (Upsala, Swed.). U.S. neurobiologist. Noted for research vital to understanding the organization and functioning of the brain; awarded Nobel Prize in medicine or physiology (shared with D. HUBEL and R. SPERRY), 1981.

WIGNER, EUGENE P., Nov. 17, 1902 (Budapest, Hung.). U.S. physicist. Worked out the theory of neutron absorption, essential to reactor operation, 1936; worked out the theory of parity conservation; helped in construction of the first atomic reactor, 1942; awarded Nobel Prize in physics (with M. GOEPPERT-MAYER and J. D. H. JENSEN), 1963.

WILSON, KENNETH G., June 8, 1936 (Waltham, Mass.). U.S. physics research administrator. Noted for his method of analyzing the basic changes in matter under the influence of pressure and temperature; awarded Nobel Prize in physics, 1982.

WILSON, ROBERT WOODROW, Jan. 10, 1936 (Houston, Tex.). U.S. physicist. With A. A. PENZIAS, discovered the cosmic radiation background that tends to support the Big Bang theory of the origin of the universe; awarded Nobel Prize in physics (with Penzias and P. L. KAPITSA), 1978.

WOODWARD, ROBERT B., Apr. 10, 1917 (Boston, Mass.)–July 8, 1979. U.S. chemist. Made fundamental contributions to the processes of molecular-structure determination, leading to his synthesis of quinine (1944), cholesterol (1951), strychnine (1954), reserpine (1956), and others; worked out the structures of many substances, including penicillin (1945); F.R.S., 1956; awarded the Nobel Prize in chemistry, 1965.

**WRIGHT, WILBUR,** Apr. 16, 1867 (Millville, Ind.)–May 30, 1912; and his brother, **ORVILLE WRIGHT,** Aug. 19, 1871 (Dayton, Ohio)–Jan. 30, 1948. U.S. inventors. Made the first powered, controlled, and sustained airplane flight, Dec. 17, 1903; invented ailerons; designed internal-combustion engines with lower weight-to-horsepower ratios; developed the first practical airplane, 1905.

**YALOW, ROSALYN,** July 19, 1921 (New York, N.Y.). U.S. medical physicist. Made a major contribution to the development of radioimmunoassay techniques for measuring concentrations of biological substances in the body, 1950s–60s; awarded

Nobel Prize in physiology or medicine (with R. GUILLEMIN and A. SCHALLY), 1977.

**YANG, CHEN NING,** Sept. 22, 1922 (Hofei, Anhwei, China). U.S. physicist. with T.-D. LEE, proved that the law of parity conservation did not hold true in "weak" nuclear interactions, 1956; awarded Nobel Prize in physics (with Lee), 1957.

**ZINN, WALTER H.,** Dec. 10, 1906 (Kitchener, Ont., Can.). U.S. physicist. Developed the first so-called breeder reactor, 1951; won Fermi Award, 1969.

**ZWORYKIN, VLADIMIR K.,** July 30, 1889 (Mourom, Russia)–July 29, 1982. U.S. physicist. The father of electronic TV; invented the iconoscope (1923), or TV transmitter, and the kinescope (1924), or TV receiver; developed the first practical TV system, 1938; his innovations made practical the electron microscope, 1939; also the sniperscope and snooperscope in WW II.

## BRITISH SCIENTISTS, PHYSICIANS, AND INVENTORS

**ABEL, SIR FREDERICK AUGUSTUS,** July 17, 1827 (Woolwich, London, England)–Sept. 6, 1902. English chemist. Pioneered in smokeless powders; with SIR JAMES DEWAR, invented cordite, c.1889; knighted 1883; created baronet, 1893.

**ADRIAN, EDGAR DOUGLAS, (first) BARON ADRIAN OF CAMBRIDGE,** Nov. 30, 1889 (London, Eng.)–Aug. 4, 1977. English physiologist. Conducted research on the electrical activity of sensory and muscular nerve cells and in the brain; awarded Nobel Prize in physiology or medicine, (with C. S. SHERRINGTON), 1932; created baron, 1955; O.M. 1942.

**APPLETON, SIR EDWARD V.,** Sept. 6, 1892 (Bradford, Yorks., England)–Apr. 21, 1965. English physicist. Discovered the Appleton, or F, layer of the ionosphere, a reliable reflector of the shorter shortwave radio waves, thus making possible more dependable long-distance radio communication and aiding development of radio, 1926; knighted, 1941; awarded Nobel Prize in physics, 1947.

**ASTON, FRANCIS W.,** Sept. 1, 1877 (Harborne, Birmingham, England)–Nov. 20, 1945. English chemist, physicist. Developed the mass spectrograph, which accurately distinguishes atoms of the same element with minutely different masses (isotopes), 1920; discovered many isotopes; awarded Nobel Prize in chemistry, 1922.

**BABBAGE, CHARLES,** Dec. 26, 1792 (Teignmouth, Devon, England)–Oct. 18, 1871. English mathematician, inventor. Created the first reliable actuarial tables; showed that a flat fee for postage made more money than fees based on distance, c.1835; developed the first speedometer; invented skeleton keys and the cow-catcher; one of first to conceive of and try to build a computer, after 1822.

**BAIRD, JOHN L.,** Aug. 13, 1888 (Helensburgh, Dunbarton, Scotland)–June 14, 1946. Scottish engineer. First man to demonstrate television of objects in motion, 1926; first demonstrated television, 1924; went on to work on color and stereoscopic television; his early system used mechanical scan-

ners, not the electronic scanners of modern television.

**BARTON, SIR DEREK H. R.,** Sept. 18, 1918 (Gravesend, Kent, Eng.). English organic chemist. Father of conformational analysis in organic chemistry, the study of molecular structure in three dimensions, 1949; developed theory of phenol and alkaloid structure (1956) that simplified understanding of the biosynthesis of these complex substances; awarded Nobel Prize in chemistry (with O. Hassel), 1969; knighted, 1972.

**BAYLISS, SIR WILLIAM M.,** May 2, 1860 (Wednesbury, Staffordshire, England)–Aug. 27, 1924. English physiologist. With E. H. STARLING, discovered hormones, 1902; discovered intestinal hormone, secretin, and peristaltic wave; used saline injections to treat surgical shock during WW I; knighted, 1922. *Principles of General Physiology*, 1914.

**BESSEMER, SIR HENRY,** Jan. 19, 1813 (Charlton, Herts., England)–Mar. 15, 1898. English metallurgist, inventor. Discovered "blast furnace" method of making steel directly from cast iron by blowing air directly on molten iron to burn off carbon impurities; reduced the cost of high-grade steel by ten times, making modern steel construction possible, 1856–1860; knighted in 1879.

**BLACK, SIR JAMES W.,** June 14, 1924 (Uddingston, Scot.). British pharmacologist. Developed a series of drugs that have become essential in treating heart disease, peptic ulcers, gout, and leukemia; awarded Nobel Prize in physiology or medicine (shared with G. ELION and G. HITCHINGS), 1988.

**BLACKETT, PATRICK M. S., BARON BLACKETT OF CHELSEA,** Nov. 18, 1897 (London, Eng.)–July 13, 1974. English physicist. Improved upon and made extensive use of the Wilson cloud chamber to get the first photographs and precise knowledge of subatomic particle reaction (1925) and cosmic rays (1932); did basic work in tracing changes in earth's magnetic field; dir. of British Naval Operations Research in WW II; awarded Nobel Prize in physics, 1948; made a life peer, 1969.

**BOOLE, GEORGE,** Nov. 2, 1815 (Lincoln, England) –Dec. 8, 1864. English mathematician. Originated Boolean algebra, the basis of symbolic logic and the beginning of the attempt to place mathematics on a firm logical basis, 1854. *An Investigation of the Laws of Thought,* 1854.

**BOYLE, ROBERT,** Jan. 25, 1627 (Lismore, Cty. Waterford, Ireland)–Dec. 30, 1691. Anglo-Irish physicist, chemist. A major founder of modern science in his firm advocacy of careful experimentation, thorough description and publication of findings; major advocate of the idea that elements were irreducible material substances, not mystical properties; did major experimental work in the study of vacuums and gases; discovered Boyle's law (volume of gas changes in simple inverse proportion to pressure), 1661; first to distinguish between acids, bases, and neutral substances. *The Sceptical Chemist,* 1661.

**BRADLEY, JAMES,** Mar. 1693 (Sherborne, Gloucs., England)–July 13, 1762. English astronomer. Discovered "aberration of light," the first observational proof of the heliocentric theory, 1728; first to calculate with relative accuracy the speed of light; discovered "nutation," the shift in the earth's axis caused by lunar gravity, succeeded E. HALLEY as Astronomer Royal, 1742.

**BRAGG, SIR WILLIAM H.,** July 2, 1862 (Wigton, Cumb., England)–Mar. 12, 1942. English physicist. With his son, W. L. BRAGG, pioneered in the study of molecular structures by x-ray diffraction in crystals, which made possible the analysis of the structure of such substances as DNA; awarded Nobel Prize in physics (with W. L. BRAGG), 1915; knighted, 1920.

**BRAGG, SIR WILLIAM L.,** Mar. 31, 1890 (Adelaide, Austrl.)–July 1, 1971. Australian-English physicist. With his father, W. H. BRAGG, pioneered in x-ray crystallography; became dir. of Cavendish Lab. at Cambridge (replacing ERNEST RUTHERFORD), 1938; awarded Nobel Prize in physics (with W. H. BRAGG), 1915 (the youngest man ever to win a Nobel); knighted, 1941.

**BRAID, JAMES,** 1795 (Rylawhouse, Fife, Scotland)–Mar. 25, 1860. Scottish surgeon. Established the reality of and named hypnotism, c.1842.

**BRIGGS, HENRY,** Feb. 1561 (Warleywood, Yorks., England)–Jan. 26, 1630. English mathematician. Invented common logarithmic notation; worked out logarithmic tables for numbers from 1 to 20,000, 1624; invented modern method of long division. *Trigonometria Britannica,* 1633.

**CAVENDISH, HENRY,** Oct. 10, 1731 (Nice, France) –Feb. 24, 1810. English chemist, physicist. Discovered hydrogen, c.1766; first to measure weights of gases to determine density; first to show that hydrogen, when burned, produces water; discovered argon, 1785; first to work out the constant of gravitational force and to compute accurately the mass and density of the Earth, 1798; an eccentric, he published few of his findings and much of his work remained unknown for many years; F.R.S., 1760.

**CAYLEY, SIR GEORGE,** Dec. 27, 1773 (Scarborough, Yorks., England)–Dec. 15, 1857. English engineer. Built the first successful glider, 1853; founded science of aerodynamics, developing the basic elements (fixed wings, tail with elevators and rudder, etc.) of modern airplanes; invented the caterpillar tractor.

**CHADWICK, SIR JAMES,** Oct. 20, 1891 (Manchester, England)–July 24, 1974. English physicist. Discovered the neutron, a major step in the development of atomic fission; awarded Nobel Prize in physics, 1935; knighted, 1945; F.R.S., 1927.

**CHAIN, SIR ERNST B.,** June 19, 1906 (Berlin, Ger.)–Aug. 14, 1979. English biochemist. With H. W. FLOREY, the first to isolate penicillin, during 1940s; awarded Nobel Prize in physiology or medicine (with H. W. FLOREY and A. FLEMING), 1945; knighted in 1969.

**COCKCROFT, SIR JOHN D.,** May 27, 1897 (Todmorden, Yorks., England)–Sept. 18, 1967. English physicist. Pioneered in development of particle accelerators, with E. T. S. WALTON; first to cause a nuclear reaction without using natural radioactivity, 1932; knighted, 1948; awarded Nobel Prize in physics (with Walton), 1951.

**CRAPPER, THOMAS,** 1837 (England)–1910. English sanitary engineer, inventor. Invented the valve-and-siphon arrangement that made the modern flush toilet possible.

**CRICK, FRANCIS H. C.,** June 8, 1916 (Northampton, England). English biochemist, physicist. With J. D. WATSON, discovered the double-helix structure of DNA, the basic substance of the chromosome and thus of heredity, 1953; awarded Nobel Prize in physiology or medicine (with Watson and M. H. F. WILKINS), 1962; *Of Molecules and Men,* 1966.

**CROOKES, SIR WILLIAM,** June 17, 1832 (London, Eng.)–Apr. 4, 1919. English physicist. Discovered thallium, 1861; invented radiometer, 1875; was a major pioneer in development and study of the vacuum electron tube, which led to x-ray tubes, cathode-ray tubes, and display tubes used in television and radar, 1875; knighted, 1897; invented spinthariscope, a device for monitoring alpha particles, 1903.

**DALTON, JOHN,** Sept. 6?, 1766 (Eaglesfield, Cumb., England)–July 27, 1844. English chemist. First to propound the modern view of the theory that elements are composed of atoms, 1803; the first to devise a table of atomic weights; a pioneer in meteorology, keeping detailed weather records from 1787 to his death; the first to describe color-blindness, 1794. *New System of Chemical Philosophy,* 1808, 1810.

**DARWIN, CHARLES R.,** Feb. 12, 1809 (Shrewsbury, England)–Apr. 19, 1882. English naturalist. Developed the theory of organic evolution through natural selection (1844–58), sparking the revolution in biological sciences, after a five-year voyage (1831–36) on the H.M.S. *Beagle* to South America and the Galapagos Is.; his study of finch species (Darwin's finches) on the islands and his reading (1838) of T. MALTHUS's *Essay on the Principle of Population* provided the basis of the evolutionary theory, which was firmly established before his death. *The Origin of Species*, 1859; *The Descent of Man*, 1871.

**DARWIN SIR GEORGE H.**, July 9, 1845 (Down, Kent, England)–Dec. 7, 1912. English astronomer. Discovered that the rate of the earth's rotation and angular momentum were decreasing because of tidal friction and that the moon's distance from Earth was increasing, 1879, knighted, 1905. (Son of C. DARWIN.)

**DAVY, SIR HUMPHREY**, Dec. 17, 1778 (Penzance, Cornwall, Eng.)–May 29, 1829. English chemist. Discovered potassium, sodium (1807), barium, magnesium, strontium, calcium (1808); correctly identified chlorine as an element, named it, and discovered that it supported combustion; discovered nitrous oxide (1800), the first chemical anesthetic (laughing gas); invented the Davy lamp, which decreased danger of gas explosions in mines, 1815; F.R.S., 1803; knighted, 1812; created baronet, 1815.

**DEWAR, SIR JAMES**, Sept. 20, 1842 (Kincardine-on-Forth, Scotland)–Mar. 27, 1923. Scottish physicist and chemist. First to liquefy (1898) and then solidify (1899) hydrogen, reaching a temperature of only 14 degrees above absolute zero; his research in low-temperature preservation led to the Thermos bottle; with F. ABEL, invented cordite, the first practical smokeless powder; F.R.S., 1897; knighted, 1901.

**DIRAC, PAUL A. M.**, Aug. 8, 1902 (Bristol, England)–Oct. 24, 1984. English physicist, mathematician. His development of the hypothesis of wave mechanics of electrons led to the hypothesis of antiparticles, 1930; F.R.S., 1930; awarded Nobel Prize in physics (with E. SCHRÖDINGER), 1933.

**DUNLOP, JOHN BOYD**, Feb. 5, 1840 (Dreghorn, Ayrshire, Scotland)–Oct. 23, 1921. Scottish veterinary surgeon. Invented the pneumatic tire, c.1887.

**FARADAY, MICHAEL**, Sept. 22, 1791 (Newington, Surrey, England)–Aug. 25, 1867. English physicist, chemist. Discovered benzene, 1825; first to define the laws of electrolysis, 1832; first to convert electromagnetic forces into continuous mechanical motion, 1821; invented the transformer and electric generator, 1831; discovered electrical induction; the first to hypothesize electromagnetic "lines of force," a beginning of field theory; the key pioneer in the development of modern electricity; F.R.S., 1824; refused knighthood.

**FLAMSTEED, JOHN**, Aug. 19, 1646 (Derby, Derbyshire, England)–Dec. 31, 1719. English astronomer. Created first great star maps using telescopic observations, 1675–1719; first Astronomer Royal, 1675; established observatory at Greenwich that later marked the prime meridian; F.R.S., 1677.

**FLEMING, SIR ALEXANDER**, Aug. 6, 1881 (Lochfield, Ayr, Scotland)–Mar. 11, 1955. Scottish bacteriologist. Discovered penicillin by accident (1928) and demonstrated that it killed some bacteria and did no harm to human cells; knighted, 1944; awarded Nobel Prize in physiology or medicine (with E. B. CHAIN and H. W. FLOREY), 1945.

**FLOREY, HOWARD W., BARON FLOREY OF ADELAIDE**, Sept. 24, 1898 (Adelaide, Austrl.)–Feb. 22, 1968. Australian-English pathologist. With E. B. CHAIN, isolated penicillin from the mold in which it was discovered by A. FLEMING; awarded Nobel Prize in physiology or medicine (with Chain and Fleming), 1945; knighted, 1944; awarded life peerage, 1965.

**GABOR, DENNIS**, June 5, 1900 (Budapest, Hung.)–Feb. 8, 1979. British physicist. Invented holography, a technique of three-dimensional photography based on creating an interference pattern of two light beams on film, 1947; F.R.S., 1956; awarded Nobel Prize in physics, 1971.

**GALTON, SIR FRANCIS**, Feb. 16, 1822 (Birmingham, Eng.)–Jan. 17, 1911. English anthropologist. Founded modern technique of weather mapping, 1863; began a system of fingerprint identification; studied the hereditary basis of intelligence and coined the term *eugenics*, 1883; knighted, 1909.

**GILBERT, WILLIAM**, May 24, 1544 (Colchester, Essex, England)–Dec. 10, 1603. English physician, physicist. Pioneer in research into magnetism and electric phenomena; coined the terms *electric* and *magnetic poles*; the first to suggest that the earth was like a magnet and that heavenly bodies were kept in place by magnetism; court physician to ELIZABETH I and JAMES I. *De Magnete...*, 1600.

**GRAHAM, THOMAS**, Dec. 20, 1805 (Glasgow, Scot.)–Sept. 16, 1869. Scottish chemist. Discovered "Graham's law" of gas diffusion, 1831; discovered and named the processes of dialysis and osmosis, 1861; founded colloid chemistry.

**HALDANE, JOHN BURDON**, Nov. 5, 1892 (Oxford, England)–Dec. 1, 1964. English-Indian geneticist. Conducted basic studies of sex-linkage in chromosomes and of mutation rate; contributed to development of the heart-lung machine; used himself as subject in experiments on the human body under stress; determined safe gas mix for underwater breathing, 1941; F.R.S., 1932. *Science and Ethics*, 1928; *Biochemistry of Genetics*, 1953.

**HALLEY, EDMUND**, Nov. 8, 1656 (Shoreditch, nr. London, England)–Jan. 14, 1742. English astronomer and mathematician. First to predict the appearance of a comet (now named for him) in 1758, on the basis of his study of records of comet sightings, 1705; first professional astronomer to catalogue southern hemisphere stars; first to prepare mortality tables, 1693; first to produce a meteorological chart, 1686; became Astronomer Royal, 1720; devised method of determining longitude at sea, by means of lunar observation; F.R.S., 1678; a close friend of I. NEWTON.

**HAMILTON, SIR WILLIAM R.**, Aug. 4, 1805 (Dublin, Ire.)–Sept. 2, 1865. Irish mathematician. Discovered quaternions, an essential element of the mathematics of three-dimensional space, 1843; his work in optics and dynamics presaged the appearance of quantum mechanics, 1835; knighted, 1835.

**HARDEN, SIR ARTHUR**, Oct. 12, 1865 (Manchester, England)–June 17, 1940. English biochemist. Discovered the coenzyme, a nonprotein necessary to the function of enzymes, c.1904; his discovery of enzymes' use of phosphates began the study of intermediate metabolism; F.R.S., 1909; awarded Nobel Prize in chemistry (with H. VON EULER-CHELPIN), 1929; knighted, 1936.

HARVEY, WILLIAM, Apr. 1, 1578 (Folkestone, Kent, England)–June 3, 1657. English physician. The father of modern physiology, through his discovery of the circulation of the blood, 1616; adapted GALILEO's experimental approach to physiology and ended the influence of GALEN on medical studies; appointed physician extraordinary to King James I (1618) and Charles I (1625).

HAWKING, STEPHEN, Jan. 8, 1942 (Eng.). British physicist. Has used black holes as a stepping stone to seek the relationship between physical laws that govern the universe. *A Brief History of Time: From the Big Bang to Black Holes*, 1987.

HAWORTH, SIR WALTER N., Mar. 19, 1883 (Chorley, Lancs., England)–Mar. 19, 1950. English chemist. Conducted basic studies of sugars; devised modern ring form of representing sugar molecules; one of the first to synthesize vitamin C, and coined the name *ascorbic acid*, 1934; awarded Nobel Prize in chemistry (with Paul Karrer), 1937; knighted, 1947.

HEAVISIDE, OLIVER, May 13, 1850 (London, Eng.)–Feb. 3, 1925. English physicist. Did basic work in the application of mathematics to electrical engineering and electromagnetic theory; shortly after A. E. KENNELLY in 1902, predicted the existence of an electrically charged layer in the upper atmosphere now called the Kennelly-Heaviside layer; F.R.S., 1891.

HERSCHEL, SIR JOHN FREDERICK, Mar. 7, 1792 (Slough, Bucks., England)–May 11, 1871. English astronomer. Continued the work of his father, W. HERSCHEL, with double stars and nebulae; completed E. HALLEY's catalogue of the stars of the southern hemisphere, 1847; the first to identify the Magellanic Clouds as star clusters; the first to measure accurately the brightness of stars; coined terms *positive* and *negative* in photography; developed protographic processes, including use of sodium thiosulfate or "hypo" as fixer; F.R.S., 1813; knighted, 1831; created baronet, 1837.

HERSCHEL, SIR WILLIAM, Nov. 15, 1738 (Hanover, Ger.)–Aug. 25, 1822. German-English astronomer. With his sister Caroline, built the best telescope of his time, 1774; discovered Uranus, the first new planet found since ancient times, 1781; the first to determine that many double stars were not simply line-of-sight pairs, but revolved about each other, 1793; the first to hypothesize that the sun was in motion, 1805; the first to hypothesize other galaxies; discovered infrared radiation, 1800; F.R.S., 1781; knighted, 1816.

HEWISH, ANTONY, May 11, 1924 (Fowey, Cornwall, England). English radio astronomer. Discovered pulsars, 1967; awarded Nobel Prize in physics (with M. Ryle), 1974.

HINSHELWOOD, SIR CYRIL N., June 19, 1897 (London, Eng.)–Oct. 9, 1967. English physical chemist. Conducted basic studies in kinetics (rate at which chemical reactions occur at various temperatures); deduced bacteria will develop resistance against action of antibodies; F.R.S., 1929; awarded Nobel Prize in chemistry (with N. N. SEMENOV), 1956; knighted, 1948.

HINTON, CHRISTOPHER, LORD HINTON OF BANKSIDE, BARON OF DULWICH, May 12, 1901 (Tisbury, Wilts., England)–June 22, 1983. English nuclear engineer. Built the first large-scale nuclear power plant (Calder Hall, Eng., 1956); F.R.S., 1954; knighted, 1957; created life peer, 1965.

HODGKIN, SIR ALAN L., Feb. 5, 1914 (Banbury, Oxon., England). English physiologist. With A. F. HUXLEY, discovered the "sodium pump" action of nerve-cell impulse transmission, 1952; F.R.S., 1948; awarded Nobel Prize in physiology or medicine (with A. F. Huxley and J. C. ECCLES), 1963; knighted, 1972.

HOOKE, ROBERT, July 18, 1635 (Freshwater, Isle of Wight, Eng.)–Mar. 3, 1703. English physicist, astronomer. Discovered Hooke's law of elasticity (1678), and worked from this to devise the hairspring of modern watches; built first Gregorian reflecting telescope, suggested Jupiter rotates on axis; early proponent of evolution, considered fossils remains of organic creatures; F.R.S., 1663; coined the word *cell*, 1665.

HOPKINS, SIR FREDERICK G., June 30, 1861 (Eastborne, Sussex, England)–May 16, 1947. English biochemist. Discovered the first "essential amino acid," tryptophan, 1900; suggested the necessity of trace substances in the diet, 1906; F.R.S., 1905; awarded Nobel Prize in physiology or medicine (with C. Eijkman), 1929; knighted, 1925; O.M., 1935.

HOUNSFIELD, GODFREY N., 1919 (Nottinghamshire, Eng.). British electronic engineer. Developed computed axial tomography, the CAT scan, a revolutionary X-ray technique; awarded Nobel Prize in medicine or physiology (shared with A. CORMACK), 1979.

HUGGINS, SIR WILLIAM, Feb. 7, 1824 (London, Eng.)–May 12, 1910. English astronomer. The first to discover a "red shift" in the spectrum of a receding star, 1868; the first to devise a method of photographic spectroscopy in astronomy, 1875; the first to consistently use spectroscopy in astronomy; F.R.S., 1865; knighted, 1897.

HUTTON, JAMES, June 3, 1726 (Edinburgh, Scot.)–Mar. 26, 1797. Scottish geologist. Founded the science of geology; formulated principle of "uniformitarianism," that the forces now slowly changing the earth's surface had always operated in the same way at the same rate (as opposed to "catastrophism"), 1785; anticipated Darwin in idea of organic evolution by natural selection, 1797.

HUXLEY, SIR ANDREW F., Nov. 2, 1917 (London, Eng.). English physiologist. With A. L. HODGKIN, discovered the "sodium pump" action of nerve-cell impulse transmission, 1952; Nobel Prize in physiology or medicine (with A. L. Hodgkin and J. C. ECCLES), 1963; knighted, 1974.

HUXLEY, THOMAS H., May 4, 1825 (Ealing, Middlesex, England)–June 29, 1895. English biologist. Primary advocate of CHARLES DARWIN's natural selection theory (from 1858 on), and a major science popularizer; expert on jellyfish, named phylum Coelenterata; F.R.S., 1851; coined the word *agnostic*. (Grandfather of A. and A. F. HUXLEY.)

JEANS, SIR JAMES H., Sept. 11, 1877 (London, Eng.)–Sept. 16, 1946. English mathematician, astronomer. First to suggest the "continuous creation" theory of the origin of the universe, 1928; popularizer of astronomy; F.R.S., 1906; knighted, 1928. *Universe around Us*, 1929; *The Mysterious Universe*, 1930; *Through Space and Time*, 1934.

JENNER, EDWARD, May 17, 1749 (Berkeley, Glos., England)–Jan. 26, 1823. English physician. Discovered and named the process of vaccination for prevention of smallpox, the first disease to be conquered by modern medicine, 1796; F.R.S., 1789.

JERNE, NIELS KAI, Dec. 23, 1911 (London, Eng.). British-Danish immunologist. Widely regarded for three important theories in immunology; awarded Nobel Prize in medicine or physiology (shared with C. MILSTEIN and G. KOHLER), 1984.

JOSEPHSON, BRIAN D., Jan. 4, 1940 (Cardiff, Wales). British physicist. Noted for his basic research in electron "tunneling" and superconductivity, 1962; F.R.S., 1970; awarded Nobel Prize in physics (with I. GIAEVER and L. ESAKI), 1973.

JOULE, JAMES P., Dec. 24, 1818 (Salford, Lancs , England)–Oct. 11, 1889. English physicist. Credited with the accurate determination of the mechanical equivalent of heat, a fundamental contribution to understanding the law of conservation of energy, 1847; with William Thomson (LORD KELVIN), discovered the Joule-Thomson effect (the cooling of expanding gas in a vacuum), essential to low-temperature studies, 1852; F.R.S., 1850; the electrical unit of work is named after him.

KATZ, SIR BERNARD, Mar. 26, 1911 (Leipzig, Ger.). British physiologist. Conducted basic research on nerve function and transmission of nerve impulses to muscular fiber; F.R.S., 1952; knighted, 1969; awarded Nobel Prize in physiology or medicine (with J. AXELROD and U. S. VON EULER), 1970.

KELVIN, WILLIAM THOMSON, 1ST BARON KELVIN OF LARGS., June 26, 1824 (Belfast, Ire.)–Dec. 17, 1907. British physicist, mathematician. Devised the Kelvin scale of temperature, based on absolute zero; argued correctly that gas has no energy or motion at absolute zero, 1848; coined term *kinetic energy*, 1856; made major contributions to thermodynamics, mathematics of electricity and magnetism, and law of energy conservation; made many practical inventions, including a receiver that made the transatlantic cable useful; F.R.S., 1851; knighted, 1866; raised to peerage, 1892.

KREBS, SIR HANS A., Aug. 25, 1900 (Hildesheim, Germany)–Nov. 22, 1981. British biochemist. In basic studies of carbohydrate metabolism, discovered

and outlined the Krebs cycle, which creates the body's energy through complex processes of carbon dioxide breakdown and oxygen-hydrogen combination; F.R.S., 1947; awarded Nobel Prize in physiology or medicine (with F. A. LIPMANN), 1953; knighted, 1958.

LISTER, JOSEPH, BARON LISTER OF LYME REGIS, Apr. 5, 1827 (Upton, Essex, England)–Feb. 10, 1912. English surgeon. Introduced the use of antiseptic practices in surgery and in hospitals, 1867; F.R.S., 1860; created baronet, 1883; raised to peerage, 1897.

LOCKYER, SIR JOSEPH NORMAN, May 17, 1836 (Rugby, England)–Aug. 16, 1920. English astronomer. A pioneer in solar spectroscopy, 1860s; with P. Janssen, discovered helium by studying solar spectra, 1868; F.R.S., 1869; knighted after helium was discovered on earth, 1897.

LOVELL, SIR ALFRED C. B., Aug. 31, 1913 (Oldland Common, Gloucestershire, Eng.). English astronomer. A leader in the development of radio astronomy and a major force behind the construction of the Jodrell Bank radio telescope (completed 1957), the first major radio telescope in the world; F.R.S., 1955; knighted, 1961.

LYELL, SIR CHARLES, Nov. 14, 1797 (Kinnordy, Forfarshire [now Angus], Scotland)–Feb. 22, 1875. British geologist. Verified and popularized the geological views of J. HUTTON, establishing uniformitarianism as the basis of modern geology; defined four geologic epochs of tertiary period; arranged publication of DARWIN and WALLACE; F.R.S., 1826; knighted, 1848; created baronet, 1864. *The Principle of Geology*, 1830–33.

MACLEOD, JOHN J. R., Sept. 6, 1876 (Cluny, Perth,. Scotland)–Mar. 16, 1935. Scottish physiologist. With F. G. BANTING, credited for first isolation of insulin; he had merely lent his lab to Banting and C. H. Best, but as the senior and most prestigious, took credit for the work; F.R.S., 1923; awarded Nobel Prize in physiology or medicine, (with F. G. Banting), 1923.

MARTIN, ARCHER J. P., Mar. 1, 1910 (London, Eng.). English biochemist. With R. L. M. SYNGE, developed paper chromatography, a method of separating and identifying the parts of such complex substances as protein, which has led to major advances in research in chemistry, biology, and medicine; awarded Nobel Prize in chemistry (with Synge), 1952.

MAXIM, SIR HIRAM STEVENS, Feb. 5, 1840 (Brockway's Mills, Me.)–Nov. 24, 1916. English inventor. Invented the first fully automatic machine gun (1883), which was adopted by the British army in 1889; knighted, 1901.

MAXWELL, JAMES CLERK, Nov. 13, 1831 (Edinburgh, Scot.)–Nov. 5, 1879. Scottish mathematician, physicist. Worked out the mathematics that expressed and united electricity and magnetism, discovering that an electromagnetic field moved outward at the speed of light and postulating that light itself was an electromagnetic radiation far beyond the light spectrum; developed the Maxwell-

Boltzmann kinetic theory of gases, which proved heat to be a form of motion, 1860; played leading role in establishment of Cavendish Laboratory; F.R.S., 1861.

**MEDAWAR, SIR PETER B.**, Feb. 28, 1915 (Rio de Janeiro, Braz.)–Oct. 2, 1987. British biologist. Discovered that immunity is acquired in the embryo stage or in very early infancy, c.1950; F.R.S., 1949; awarded Nobel Prize in physiology or medicine (with F. M. BURNET), 1960; knighted, 1965; O.M., 1981.

**MICHELL, JOHN**, 1724 (Nottinghamshire, England)–Apr. 21, 1793. English geologist. Considered to be the father of seismology for suggesting the existence of earthquake waves and that timing the waves could reveal the center of the quake; F.R.S., 1760.

**MILSTEIN, CESAR**, Oct. 8, 1927 (Bahia Blanca, Arg.). Argentine-British immunologist. Discovered a laboratory technique for antibody production that is now used virtually universally; awarded Nobel Prize in medicine or physiology (shared with N. JERNE and G. KOHLER), 1984.

**MOSELEY, HENRY G. J.**, Nov. 23, 1887 (Weymouth, Dorset, Eng.)–Aug. 10, 1915. English physicist. Developed the concept of the atomic number, based on his postulation of a positive nuclear charge characteristic of each element that could be determined by finding the X-ray radiation wavelength characteristic of each element, 1914; his X-ray analysis technique was a major advance in chemical analysis; killed in the Gallipoli campaign in WW I.

**MOTT, SIR NEVILL F.**, Sept. 30, 1905 (Leeds, Eng.). English physicist. Conducted basic studies of electrical conduction in noncrystalline solids; F.R.S., 1936; knighted, 1962; awarded Nobel Prize in physics (with P.W. ANDERSON and J. H. VAN VLECK), 1977.

**NAPIER, JOHN**, 1550 (Merchiston Castle, nr. Edinburgh, Scotland)–Apr. 4, 1617. Scottish mathematician. Discovered the usefulness of exponential notation; worked out the first tables of logarithms (a word he coined), thus vastly simplifying routine calculations, 1614; introduced the use of the decimal point.

**NEWTON, SIR ISAAC**, Jan. 4, 1642 (Woolsthorpe, nr. Grantham, Lincs., England)–Mar. 31, 1727. English scientist, mathematician. One of the greatest scientific minds in history, from whose work stems all modern science and technology; first to demonstrate that white light was a combination of all colors, 1666; developed the calculus independently of G. LEIBNIZ, 1670–85; devised the reflecting telescope, 1668; first enunciated the three laws of motion and the law of universal gravitation, 1687; F.R.S., 1674; knighted, 1708. *Philosophiae naturalis principia mathematica*, 1687.

**NICHOLSON, WILLIAM**, 1753 (London, Eng.)–May 21, 1815. English chemist. Discovered electrolysis, the making of a chemical reaction by applying an electric current, 1790.

**NIGHTINGALE, FLORENCE** ("The Lady with the Lamp"), May 12, 1820 (Florence, It.)–Aug. 13, 1910. English nurse. Raised nursing standards and status of profession in Eng.; a pioneer in the development of civil and military nursing and hospital care; O.M. 1907.

**NORRISH, RONALD G. W.**, Nov. 9, 1897 (Cambridge, Eng.)–June 7, 1978. English chemist. With G. PORTER, made studies of chemical reactions that take place in as little as one-billionth of a second, 1949–55; awarded Nobel Prize in chemistry (with Porter and M. EIGEN), 1967.

**OUGHTRED, WILLIAM**, Mar. 5, 1575 (Eton, Bucks., England)–June 30, 1660. English mathematician, minister. Invented the slide rule, 1622; introduced the multiplication sign and the trigonometry abbreviations sin, cos, and tan.

**OWEN, SIR RICHARD**, July 20, 1804 (Lancaster, Eng.)–Dec. 18, 1892. English zoologist. Made primary contributions to comparative anatomy; coined the term *dinosaur* (1842) and made major advances in understanding the extinct reptiles; involved in development of British Museum (Nat. Hist.); discovered the parathyroid glands, 1852; the most virulent opponent of C. DARWIN's theory of evolution; F.R.S., 1834; knighted, 1884.

**PARSONS, SIR CHARLES ALGERNON**, June 13, 1854 (London, Eng.)–Feb. 11, 1931. English engineer. Made the first practical steam turbine (1884) and adapted it for use in steamships (1890s); *Turbinia* (1897) reached speed of 34.5 knots; F.R.S., 1898; knighted, 1911; O.M., 1927.

**PERKIN, SIR WILLIAM HENRY**, Mar. 12, 1838 (London, Eng.)–July 14, 1907. English chemist. Discovered aniline purple or mauve, the first synthetic dye, 1856; discovered the first synthetic aromatic for use in perfume, 1868; first to synthesize an amino acid (glycine), 1858; discovered the important chemical reaction named for him, 1867; F.R.S., 1866; knighted, 1906.

**PERUTZ, MAX F.**, May 19, 1914 (Vienna, Austria). British biochemist. Worked out the structure of hemoglobin, 1960; made a basic contribution to the technique of X-ray diffraction analysis, 1953; F.R.S., 1954; awarded Nobel Prize in chemistry (with J. C. Kendrew), 1962.

**PORTER, SIR GEORGE**, Dec. 6, 1920 (Stainforth, Yorks., England). English chemist. With R. G. W. NORRISH, worked on ultrafast chemical reactions; awarded Nobel Prize in chemistry (with Norrish and M. EIGEN), 1967; knighted, 1972.

**PORTER, RODNEY R.**, Oct. 8, 1917 (England)–Sept. 6, 1985. English biochemist. First to work out the chemical structure of an antibody molecule (1969), independently of G. M. EDELMAN; awarded Nobel Prize in physiology or medicine (with Edelman), 1972.

**POWELL, CECIL F.**, Dec. 5, 1903 (Tonbridge, Kent, England)–Aug. 9, 1969. English physicist. Developed the process for registering the tracks and interactions of atomic particles directly on a photographic emulsion, 1930s; discovered the pimeson, or pion, 1947; F.R.S., 1949; awarded Nobel Prize in physics, 1950.

**PRIESTLEY, JOSEPH,** Mar. 13, 1733 (Birstall Fieldhead, Yorks., England)–Feb. 6, 1804. English chemist, political theorist, clergyman. His basic studies in gases resulted in the discovery of ammonia, sulphur dioxide, hydrogen chloride, and most notably, oxygen (1774); invented carbonated water, 1773; F.R.S., 1776; a radical in religion and politics, his outspoken sympathy with the French Revolution forced him to flee to the U.S., 1794; also made major contributions to education (de-emphasizing the classics) and to liberal theology and political theory.

**RAMSAY, SIR WILLIAM,** Oct. 2, 1852 (Glasgow, Scot.)–July 23, 1916. Scottish chemist. Discovered argon (with J. W. S. RAYLEIGH, 1894), helium on earth (1895), and neon, krypton, xenon (1898), and radon (1910); F.R.S., 1888; knighted, 1902; awarded Nobel Prize in chemistry, 1904.

**RANKINE, WILLIAM J. M.,** July 5, 1820 (Edinburgh, Scot.)–Dec. 24, 1872. Scottish physicist, engineer. A fundamental contributor to modern engineering who consistently related scientific theory to practical engineering issues; basic work in metal fatigue (1843), applied mechanics (1858), systematic theory of steam engines (1859), and soil mechanics; F.R.S., 1853.

**RAYLEIGH, JOHN W., 3RD BARON,** Nov. 12, 1842 (Langford Grove, nr. Maldon, Essex, England)–June 30, 1919. English physicist. His basic research in waves led to advances in measurements of electricity and magnetism; made fundamental discoveries in optics and acoustics; succeeded to title, 1873; with W. RAMSAY, discovered the first inert gas (argon), 1894; F.R.S., 1893; awarded Nobel Prize in physics, 1904.

**RICHARDSON, SIR OWEN W.,** Apr. 26, 1879 (Dewsbury, Yorks., England)–Feb. 15, 1959. English physicist. Worked out the mathematics of ion emission from heated substances, thus contributing directly to the development of electronic-tube technology; F.R.S., 1913; awarded Nobel Prize in physics, 1928; knighted in 1939.

**ROSS, SIR RONALD,** May 13, 1857 (Almora, India)–Sept. 16, 1932. English bacteriologist. Discovered the cause and carrier of malaria, 1898; F.R.S., 1901; awarded Nobel Prize in physiology or medicine, 1902; knighted, 1911.

**RUMFORD, BENJAMIN THOMPSON, COUNT,** Mar. 26, 1753 (Woburn, Mass.)–Aug. 21, 1814. English-U.S. physicist. Pioneer of central steam and hot water heating; first to conclude that heat was a form of motion, not a fluid, and to attempt to derive a value for the mechanical equivalent of heat, 1798; introduced J. WATT's steam engine to Europe; founded the Royal Inst., for the dissemination of scientific information, 1799; F.R.S., 1779; knighted (by George III), 1784; made a count of the Holy Roman Empire by the elector of Bavaria, for whom he worked, 1791.

**RUTHERFORD, ERNEST, 1ST BARON RUTHERFORD OF NELSON,** Aug. 30, 1871 (Spring Grove [now Brightwater], nr. Nelson, New Zealand)–Oct. 19, 1937. British physicist. Discovered and named alpha, beta (1897), and gamma (1900) radiation; discovered and named the "half-life" phenomenon of radioactivity, c.1902; discovered nuclear structure of atom, 1911; the first to achieve a manmade nuclear reaction, turning nitrogen atoms into oxygen by bombarding them with alpha particles, 1917; awarded Nobel Prize in chemistry, 1908; instrumental in rescuing many Jewish scientists from Nazi Germany; knighted, 1914; raised to peerage, 1931; O.M. 1925; buried in Westminster Abbey.

**SANGER, FREDERICK,** Aug. 13, 1918 (Rendcomb, Eng.). British molecular biologist. Developed methods that make it possible to map in detail the function and structure of DNA; awarded Nobel Prize in chemistry (shared with P. BERG and W. GILBERT), 1980.

**SHERRINGTON, SIR CHARLES S.,** Nov. 27, 1857 (London, Eng.)–Mar. 4, 1952. English neurologist. Pioneer in neurophysiology; did basic studies in reflexes (c.1906), the kinetic sense (c.1894), and the motor areas of the brain; F.R.S., 1893; knighted, 1922; awarded Nobel Prize in physiology or medicine (with E. D. ADRIAN), 1932.

**SIEMENS, SIR WILLIAM,** Apr. 4, 1823 (Lenthe, Prussia, Germany)–Nov. 18, 1883. English inventor of the open-hearth steel-making process, 1861; F.R.S., 1862; knighted, 1883.

**SIMPSON, SIR JAMES YOUNG,** June 7, 1811 (Bathgate, Linlithgowshire, Scotland)–May 6, 1870. Scottish physician. A founder of modern gynecology; the first to use anesthesia in childbirth, 1847; introduced iron wire sutures and acupressure to arrest hemorrhages; appointed official physician to Queen VICTORIA, 1847; created baronet, 1866.

**SMITHSON, JAMES,** 1765 (Paris, France)–June 26, 1829. English chemist, mineralogist. Published 27 scientific papers; elected to Royal Acad. at age 22; provided funds for the founding of the Smithsonian Inst., Washington, D.C.; the mineral smithsonite (carbonate of zinc) is named after him.

**SODDY, FREDERICK,** Sept. 2, 1877 (Eastbourne, Sussex, England)–Sept. 22, 1956. English chemist. With E. RUTHERFORD, worked out an explanation of radioactive breakdown, c.1902; worked out the theory of isotopes and coined that term, 1912; awarded Nobel Prize in chemistry, 1921.

**STARLING, ERNEST HENRY,** Apr. 17, 1866 (London, Eng.)–May 2, 1927. English physiologist. With W. M. BAYLISS, discovered and named hormones, from 1902.

**STEPHENSON, GEORGE,** June 9, 1781 (Wylam, Northumberland, England)–Aug. 12, 1848. English inventor of the first practical and commercially-successful steam locomotive, 1825.

**SWAN, SIR JOSEPH WILSON,** Oct. 31, 1828 (Sunderland, Durham, England)–May 27, 1914. English chemist, inventor. Invented "dry plate" photography (1871) and bromide paper for photographic prints (1879); invented one of the first light bulbs (1860) and developed a practical one (1880) independently of T. A. EDISON; made lamps that lit Savoy Theatre for R. D'OYLY-CARTE, 1881; knighted, 1904.

**SYNGE, RICHARD L. M.**, Oct. 28, 1914 (Liverpool, Eng.). English biochemist. With A. J. P. MARTIN, developed paper chromatography techniques, 1944; F.R.S., 1950; awarded Nobel Prize in chemistry (with Martin), 1952.

**THOMSON, SIR GEORGE P.**, May 3, 1892 (Cambridge, Eng.)–Sept. 10, 1975. English physicist. Discovered electron diffraction, independently of C. J. DAVISSON; F.R.S., 1930; awarded Nobel Prize in physics (with Davisson), 1937; knighted, 1943. (Son of J. J. THOMSON.)

**THOMSON, SIR JOSEPH J.**, Dec. 18, 1856 (Cheetham Hill, nr. Manchester, England)–Aug. 30, 1940. English physicist. Discovered the electron, 1897; opened the field of subatomic physics; awarded Nobel Prize in physics, 1906; many of his students, including his son, G. P. THOMSON, won Nobel Prizes; knighted, 1908.

**TINBERGEN, NIKOLAAS**, Apr. 15, 1907 (The Hague, Neth.)–Dec. 24, 1988. English ethologist. Conducted fundamental studies of the social behavior of animals; also human behavioral disorders, particularly autism; F.R.S., 1962; awarded Nobel Prize in physiology or medicine (with K. Z. LORENZ and K. VON FRISCH), 1973.

**TODD, ALEXANDER R., BARON TODD OF TRUMPINGTON**, Oct. 2, 1907 (Glasgow, Scot.). Scottish biochemist. His basic research in and synthesis of nucleic acid components (1940s) prepared the way for fine-structure analysis of DNA; awarded Nobel Prize in chemistry, 1957; knighted, 1954; created life peer, 1962; O.M., 1977.

**TREVITHICK, RICHARD**, Apr. 13, 1771 (Illogan, Cornwall, England)–Apr. 22, 1833. English engineer. Made a major contribution to the development of high-pressure steam engines; built the first locomotive, 1803.

**TYNDALL, JOHN**, Aug. 2, 1820 (Leighlin Bridge, Cty. Carlow, Ireland)–Dec. 4, 1893. Irish physicist. His investigations of light-scattering by colloidal particles provided the explanation for why the sky is blue, c.1870; demonstrated the Tyndall effect, the diffusion of light by large molecules and dust; popularized the idea of heat as motion and the law of conservation of energy.

**VANE, JOHN R.**, Mar. 29, 1927 (Worcestershire, Eng.). British pharmacologist. Noted for discoveries in controlling prostaglandins, a natural substance implicated in a wide range of human and animal illnesses; awarded Nobel Prize in medicine or physiology (shared with B. SAMUELSSON and K. S. BERGSTROM), 1982.

**WALLACE, ALFRED R.**, Jan. 8, 1823 (Usk, Monmouthshire, Wales)–Nov. 7, 1913. English naturalist. Simultaneously with, but independently of C. R. DARWIN, proposed the theory of evolution by natural selection, 1858; F.R.S., 1893; O.M. 1910.

**WALTON, ERNEST T. S.**, Oct. 6, 1903 (Dungarvan, Cty. Waterford, Ireland). Irish physicist. With J. D. COCKROFT, devised the voltage-multiplier particle accelerator (1929) and obtained the first nuclear reaction with artificially accelerated particles, 1932; awarded Nobel Prize in physics (with Cockroft), 1951.

**WATSON-WATT, SIR ROBERT**, Apr. 13, 1892 (Brechin, Angus, Scotland)–Dec. 5, 1973. Scottish physician. Invented the first practical radar, c.1935.

**WATT, JAMES**, Jan. 19, 1736 (Greenock, Renfrewshire, Scotland)–Aug. 19, 1819. Scottish engineer. Father of the Industrial Revolution; created the first efficient steam engines with addition of separate condenser (1769) and the first reciprocal steam engine (c.1771); was the first to use a steam engine to turn a wheel (1781); invented pressure gauge, 1790; invented the first automatic governor, to regulate the flow of steam; invented and defined the idea of horsepower; F.R.S., 1785.

**WHEATSTONE, SIR CHARLES**, Feb. 6, 1802 (Gloucester, Eng.)–Oct. 19, 1875. English physicist. Anticipated S. F. B. MORSE in the invention of the telegraph, 1837; the first to use and popularize the Wheatstone bridge, a device for precision measurement of electrical resistance, 1843; F.R.S., 1836; knighted, 1868.

**WILKINS, MAURICE H. F.**, Dec. 15, 1916 (Pongaroa, New Zealand). English physicist. His X-ray diffraction studies of DNA provided J. WATSON and F. CRICK with essential data for determining DNA's structure, 1953; awarded Nobel Prize in physiology or medicine (with Crick and Watson), 1962.

**WILKINSON, SIR GEOFFREY**, July 14, 1921 (England). English chemist. Conducted basic research in organometallic compounds; awarded Nobel Prize in chemistry (with E. O. FISCHER), 1973.

**WILLIAMSON, ALEXANDER W.**, May 1, 1824 (London, Eng.)–May 6, 1904. English chemist. First to provide an understanding of reversible chemical reactions, to describe clearly dynamic equilibrium, and to explain the function of a catalyst, 1854; his studies of ethers and alcohols laid important groundwork for later understanding of chemical structure.

**WILSON, CHARLES T. R.**, Feb. 14, 1869 (Glencorse, Midlothian, Scotland)–Nov. 15, 1959. Scottish meteorologist, physicist. His basic research in cloud formation led to his invention of the Wilson cloud chamber (1911), an essential device in the study of nuclear radiation until 1952; awarded Nobel Prize in physics (with A. H. COMPTON), 1927.

**YOUNG, THOMAS**, June 13, 1773 (Milverton, Somerset, England)–May 10, 1829. English physicist. Discovered how the lens of the eye changes shape to focus at different distances; discovered the cause of astigmatism, 1801; provided conclusive evidence of the wave nature of light, 1803; first to state the three-color theory; one of the first to decipher Egyptian hieroglyphics, c.1815; F.R.S., 1794.

## GERMAN SCIENTISTS, PHYSICIANS, AND INVENTORS

**AGRICOLA, GEORGIUS** (born Georg Bauer), Mar. 24, 1494 (Glauchau, Saxony)–Nov. 21, 1555. German mineralogist, physician. Called the father of mineralogy because of his written descriptions of

Saxon mining knowledge and machinery, *De re metallica* (published 1556); also wrote first mineralogy text, *De natura fossilium*.

**ALBERTUS MAGNUS, SAINT** (Albert the Great), born Albert, Count von Bollstädt, c.1193 (Lauingen, Bavaria, Germany)–Nov. 15, 1280. German botanist, chemist, alchemist, philosopher. Introduced Aristotelian natural philsophy to northern Europe, 1245–54; a teacher of THOMAS AQUINAS in Paris; an early advocate of personal observation and skepticism in the sciences; beatified, 1622; sanctified, 1931.

**ALDER, KURT**, July 10, 1902 (Königshütte, Germany)–June 20, 1958. German organic chemist. With OTTO DIELS, worked out (1928) the Diels-Alder reaction that became the basis of many modern synthetic products, ranging from rubber to many plastics and insecticides; awarded Nobel Prize in chemistry (with Diels), 1950.

**BAEYER, ADOLF JOHANN VON**, Oct. 31, 1835 (Berlin, Ger.)–Aug. 20, 1917. German chemist. Discovered barbituric acid (basis of barbituates), 1864; synthesized indigo, 1880; developed "strain" theory to explain why small carbon rings commonly hold only five or six carbon atoms, 1886; awarded Nobel Prize in chemistry, 1905.

**BEHRING, EMIL A. VON**, Mar. 3, 1854 (Hansdorf, Prussia, Germany)–Mar. 31, 1917. German bacteriologist. Discovered antitoxin serums against tetanus and diphtheria; awarded first Nobel Prize in physiology or medicine, 1901.

**BENDORZ, JOHANES GEORG**, May 16, 1950 (W. Ger.). West German physicist. Noted for pioneering work in superconductivity; awarded Nobel Prize in physics (shared with K. MULLER), 1987.

**BENZ, KARL FRIEDRICH**, Nov. 25, 1844 (Karlsruhe, Baden, Germany)–Apr. 4, 1929. German engineer. Designed and built first feasible automobile with internal combustion engine, 1885.

**BERGIUS, FRIEDRICH**, Oct. 11, 1884 (Goldschmieden, nr. Breslau, Germany)–Mar. 30, 1949. German chemist. Using high-pressure processes, developed methods of making gasoline from coal and heavy oil; discovered ways to break down wood molecules to produce alcohol and sugar; his processes played vital role in German economy during WW II; awarded Nobel Prize in chemistry (with Carl Bosch), 1931.

**BESSEL, FRIEDRICH WILHELM**, July 22, 1784 (Minden, Brandenburg, Prussia)–Mar. 17, 1846. Prussian astronomer. Brought modern precision to processes of measurement in astronomy and geodetics; established exact positions of some 50,000 stars; first to accurately measure the distance of a star from the earth, thus multiplying by many times the idea of the size of the universe; first to hypothesize the existence of binary stars and of Neptune.

**BETHE, HANS A.**, July 2, 1906 (Strasbourg, Ger. [now France]). German-U.S. physicist. Developed modern view of stellar energy as the result of combining hydrogen atoms to form helium, with resulting conversion of some hydrogen mass into

energy, 1938; contributed to development of atomic weapons and energy; awarded Fermi Prize, 1961; awarded Nobel Prize in physics, 1967.

**BINNIG, GERD**, July 20, 1947 (Frankfurt, W. Ger.). West German physicist. Noted for pioneering work in developing the scanning tunneling microscope; awarded Nobel Prize in physics (shared with H. ROHRER and E. RUSKA), 1986.

**BOTHE, WALTHER**, Jan. 8, 1891 (Oranienburg, nr. Berlin, Ger.)–Feb. 8, 1957. German physicist. Devised a method of studying cosmic rays ("coincidence counting") that permitted measurement of extremely brief time-intervals (less than a billionth of a second) and demonstration of the law of conservation of energy and momentum at the atomic level; awarded Nobel Prize in physics (with Max Born), 1954.

**BRAUN, KARL F.**, June 6, 1850 (Fulda, Hesse-Kassel, Germany)–Apr. 20, 1918. German physicist. Invented the oscillograph, 1897; helped develop use of crystals in radios, c.1875; awarded Nobel Prize in physics (with G. MARCONI), 1909.

**BUCHNER, EDUARD**, May 20, 1860 (Munich, Ger.)–Aug. 13, 1917. German chemist. While attempting to demonstrate that dead yeast could not turn sugar into alcohol, proved the opposite, ending serious debate over whether life must be present to cause certain chemical reactions, 1896; awarded Nobel Prize in chemistry, 1907; killed in action in WW I.

**BUNSEN, ROBERT WILHELM**, March 31, 1811 (Göttingen, Westphalia, Germany)–Aug. 16, 1899. German chemist, inventor. Pioneer in study of arsenic, gas analysis methods, heat measurement; first to demonstrate that burning magnesium could make a very bright light; did not invent Bunsen burner, but popularized it; invented spectroscopy (with G. R. KIRCHHOFF), 1859.

**BUTENANDT, ADOLF F. J.**, Mar. 24, 1903 (Bremerhaven-Lehe, Germany). German chemist. Pioneer in isolation and analysis of sex hormones; isolated estrone, androsterone, and progesterone; synthesized testosterone; awarded Nobel Prize in chemistry (with L. Ruzicka), 1939, but was forced by Nazi government to refuse the prize (finally accepted it in 1949).

**CHLADNI, ERNST**, Nov. 30, 1756 (Wittenberg, Germany)–Apr. 3, 1827. German physicist. Founded the science of acoustics, by working out the quantitative rules of the transmission of sound, c.1809; determined the speed of sound in many gases; invented the euphonium, 1789.

**CLAUSIUS, RUDOLF**, Jan. 2, 1822 (Köslin, Prussia, Germany [now Poland])–Aug. 24, 1888. German physicist. Discovered second law of thermodynamics, "heat cannot of itself pass from a colder to a hotter body," 1850; coined the word *entropy*.

**DAIMLER, GOTTLIEB WILHELM**, Mar. 17, 1834 (Schorndorf, Wüttenberg, Germany)–Mar. 6, 1900. German inventor. Invented the high-speed, gasoline-burning internal-combustion engine that made the automobile practical, 1883; by installing such an engine on a bicycle, made the first motorcycle, 1885; founded Daimler motor company (1890), and developed the Mercedes automobile.

**DIELS, OTTO P. H.,** Jan. 23, 1876 (Hamburg, Ger.)–Mar. 7, 1954. German chemist. With KURT ALDER, discovered Diels-Alder reaction, essential to the synthesis of many complex compounds, 1928; awarded Nobel Prize in chemistry (with Alder), 1950.

**DIESEL, RUDOLF,** Mar. 18, 1858 (Paris, Fr.)–Sept. 30, 1913. German inventor. Invented the diesel engine (1897).

**DIESENHOFER, JOHANN,** Sept. 30, 1943 (Zusamaltheim, Bav. [now W. Ger.]). West German biochemist. Noted for research that revealed the three-dimensional structure of closely-linked proteins essential to photosynthesis; awarded Nobel Prize in chemistry (shared with R. HUBER and H. MICHEL), 1988.

**EHRLICH, PAUL,** Mar. 14, 1854 (Strehlen, Silesia, Germany)–Aug. 20, 1915. German bacteriologist. Discovered "silver bullets," chemicals that act primarily on disease-causing organisms without affecting healthy cells, for sleeping sickness and syphilis (1909), thus founding modern chemotherapy; made major contributions to studies of immunization and serum therapy; awarded Nobel Prize in physiology or medicine (with I. I. MECHNIKOFF), 1908.

**EIGEN, MANFRED,** May 9, 1927 (Bochum, Germany). German physicist. Made major contributions to the study of chemical reactions that take place in as little as a billionth of a second; awarded Nobel Prize in chemistry (with R. G. NORRISH and G. PORTER), 1967.

**FAHRENHEIT, DANIEL GABRIEL,** May 24, 1686 (Danzig, Ger. [now Gdansk, Pol.])–Sept. 16, 1736. German-Dutch physicist. Invented mercury thermometer, 1714; devised Fahrenheit scale.

**FISCHER, EMIL,** Oct. 9, 1852 (Euskirchen, Prussia, Germany)–July 15, 1919. German chemist. Pioneer in stereochemistry, the study of the three-dimensional structure of complex compounds (during 1880s), conducted nucleic acid research and protein-structure and synthesis studies (1907); awarded Nobel Prize in chemistry, 1902.

**FISCHER, ERNST OTTO,** Nov. 10, 1918 (Munich, Ger.). German chemist. Noted for his fundamental research in organo-metallic chemistry, in the 1950s and 1960s; awarded Nobel Prize in chemistry (with G. WILKINSON), 1973.

**FISCHER, HANS,** July 27, 1881 (Hochst, nr. Frankfurt-am-Main, Germany)–Mar. 31, 1945. German chemist. Worked on the composition and structure of the heme molecule, a vital part of the blood, 1929; did the same for chlorophyll, in the late 1930s; awarded Nobel Prize in chemistry, 1930.

**FLEMMING, WALTHER,** April 21, 1843 (Sachsenberg, Mecklenberg, Germany)–Sept. 5, 1905. German anatomist. Discovered chromosomes and the details of mitosis (process of cell division), c.1881.

**FORSSMANN, WERNER,** Aug. 19, 1904 (Berlin, Germany)–June 1, 1979. German surgeon. Demonstrated (on himself) that a catheter introduced at a vein in the elbow could safely be pushed through to the heart (1929), making possible new techniques in diagnosis and therapy; awarded Nobel Prize in physiology or medicine (with A. Cournand and D. W. Richards), 1956.

**GAUSS, KARL FRIEDRICH,** Apr. 30, 1777 (Brunswick, Germany) –Feb. 23, 1855. German mathematician. Discovered method of least-squares, c.1795; developed concept of complex numbers and proved the fundamental theorems of algebra (1799) and arithmetic (1801); made major contributions to calculations of asteroid orbits; calculated location of the earth's magnetic poles; devised units of measurement for magnetic phenomena, 1832; the unit of magnetic flux was named for him.

**GEIGER, (Johannes) HANS WILHELM,** Sept. 30, 1882 (Neustadt an der Haardt, Germany)–Sept. 24, 1945. German physicist. Introduced the Geiger counter, the first successful device for detecting and measuring radioactivity, 1913; redesigned it with the help of A. Müller, 1928.

**GEISSLER, HEINRICH,** May 26, 1814 (Igelshieb, Thuringia, Germany)–Jan. 24, 1879. German inventor. Invented a pump that could produce most thorough vacuum possible in tubes (now called Geissler tubes), which made possible basic advances in atomic physics, 1855.

**GUERICKE, OTTO VON,** Nov. 20, 1602 (Magdeburg, Prussian Saxony, Germany)–May 11, 1686. German physicist. Invented the first air pump, 1650; the first to create a vacuum.

**GUTENBERG, JOHANNES,** c.1398 (Mainz, Ger.)–1468. German inventor. Invented movable type and the printing press, enabling a revolution in the spread of learning and ideas, c.1454.

**HAECKEL, ERNST,** Feb. 16, 1834 (Potsdam, Prussia)–Aug. 8, 1919. German biologist. Popularized the phrase "ontogeny recapitulates phylogeny"; a supporter of C. DARWIN; coined the term *ecology*.

**HAHN, OTTO,** Mar. 8, 1879 (Frankfurt-am-Main, Germany)–July 28, 1968. German physical chemist. Discovered uranium fission, 1938; with L. MEITNER, discovered protactinium (1918) and nuclear isomers (1921); awarded Nobel Prize in chemistry, 1944.

**HEISENBERG, WERNER KARL,** Dec. 5, 1901 (Würzburg, Germany)–Feb. 1, 1976. German physicist. Discovered the "uncertainty principle," which stated that the position and momentum of a particle could not be known simultaneously at one instant of time, thus introducing the element of chance into modern physics and weakening the deterministic cause-and-effect view, 1927; awarded Nobel Prize in physics, 1932.

**HELMHOLTZ, HERMANN,** Aug. 31, 1821 (Potsdam, Prussia)– Sept. 8, 1894. German physiologist, physicist. Did basic studies in the function of the eye and ear; made a basic contribution to the law of conservation of energy, 1847.

**HERTZ, GUSTAV LUDWIG,** July 22, 1887

(Hamburg, Ger.)–Oct. 30, 1975. German physicist. With J. FRANCK, demonstrated an aspect of M. PLANCK's quantum theory by bombarding gases with electrons to stimulate light emissions; awarded Nobel Prize in physics (with J. Franck), 1925; (a nephew of H. R. HERTZ.)

HERTZ, HEINRICH RUDOLF, Feb. 22, 1857 (Hamburg, Ger.)–Jan. 1, 1894. German physicist. The first to observe the photoelectric effect, 1888; demonstrated the existence of electromagnetic waves (1888), confirming J. C. MAXWELL's hypothesis, and demonstrated that they obeyed the same laws as light; discovered "long waves," the basis of radio; unit of electromagnetic frequency is named after him.

HEVELIUS, JOHANNES, (Ger. Johann Hewel or Höwelcke; Pol. Jan Heweliusz) Jan. 28, 1611 (Danzig [now Gdansk], Pol.)–Jan. 28, 1687. German astronomer. An early mapper of the moon's surface; his names for the moon's mountains and "seas" are still in use; discovered comets; F.R.S., 1664.

HOPPE-SEYLER, ERNST FELIX, Dec. 26, 1825 (Freiburg an der Unstrut, Halle, Ger.)–Aug. 10, 1895. German biochemist. Established biochemistry as a distinct discipline, 1872–1877; discovered the enzyme invertase (1871) and lecithin; constructed the present system of classifying proteins.

HUBER, ROBERT, Feb. 20, 1937 (Munich, Ger.). West German biochemist. Noted for research that revealed the three-dimensional structure of closely-linked proteins essential to photosynthesis; awarded Nobel Prize in chemistry (shared with J. DIESEN HOFER and H. MICHEL), 1988.

HUMBOLDT, FRIEDRICH, FREIHERR VON, Sept. 14, 1769 (Berlin, Ger.)–May 6, 1859. German naturalist, explorer. Traveled throughout Europe, the Americas, and Russian Asia, collecting plants, studying rivers, ocean currents, volcanoes, and temperature changes, and measuring geomagnetism; suggested building the Panama Canal; made the first isothermic and isobaric maps; wrote Kosmos, a five-volume review of astronomy and earth sciences, 1835–60; during his life, contributed his entire fortune to the advancement of science.

JENSEN, J(ohannes) HANS DANIEL, June 25, 1907 (Hamburg, Ger.)–Feb. 11, 1973. German physicist. Proposed the idea of nuclear shells, independently of M. GOEPPERT-MAYER, 1949; awarded Nobel Prize in physics (with Goeppert-Mayer and E. P. WIGNER), 1963.

KEKULÉ VON STRADONITZ, FRIEDRICH AUGUST, Sept. 7, 1829 (Darmstadt, Ger.)–July 13, 1896. German chemist. Suggested ideas of Kekulé structures (the representation of molecules as specific patterns of atoms) and tetravalent carbon, 1858; proposed "ring" theory for benzene structure, 1865; his ideas provided the foundation of modern advances in organic chemistry; F.R.S., 1875.

KEPLER, JOHANNES, Dec. 27, 1571 (Weilder Stodt, Württemberg, Germany)–Nov. 15, 1630. German astronomer. Discovered that the orbits of the planets are ellipses with the sun at one focus, 1609; did fundamental work in optics; developed tables of planetary motion based on data collected by T. BRAHE. Mysterium cosmographicum, 1596; As tronomia Nova, 1609.

KIRCHHOFF, GUSTAV ROBERT, Mar. 12, 1824 (Königsberg, Prussia [now Kalingrad, USSR])–Oct. 17, 1887. German physicist. With R. W. BUNSEN, invented spectroscopy, 1859; discovered cesium (1860) and rubidium (1861); developed techniques of solar spectroscopy; first to propose the idea of "black body" radiation; F.R.S., 1875.

KLITZING, KLAUS VON, June 28, 1943 (Schroda, Pol.). West German computer expert. Dir., Max Planck Institute, Stuttgart, W. Ger.; developed an exact way of measuring electrical conductivity; awarded Nobel Prize in physics, 1985.

KOCH, (Heinrich Hermann) ROBERT, Dec. 11, 1843 (Clausthal, Germany)–May 27, 1910. German bacteriologist. Developed basic modern techniques and rules of bacteriology; pioneered in the use of gels as culture mediums; discovered the causative agents of anthrax (1876), tuberculosis (1882), and cholera (1883); discovered the louse and tsetse fly vectors of bubonic plague and sleeping sickness, 1897–1906; awarded Nobel Prize in physiology or medicine, 1905.

KOHLER, GEORGES J. F., Apr. 17, 1946 (Munich, W. Ger.). West German immunologist. Discovered a laboratory technique for antibody production that is now used virtually universally; awarded Nobel Prize in medicine or physiology (shared with C. MILSTEIN and N. JERNE), 1984.

KOLBE, ADOLPH W. H., Sept. 27, 1818 (Elliehausen, nr. Göttingen, Germany)–Nov. 25, 1884. German chemist. A pioneer in the synthesis of organic compounds from inorganic substances; developed new methods of synthesis, one of which made possible the mass production of acetylsalicylic acid (aspirin), 1859; F.R.S., 1877.

KOSSEL, ALBRECHT, Sept. 16, 1853 (Rostock, Mecklenburg, Germany)–July 5, 1927. German biochemist. First to isolate and begin analysis of nucleic acid (DNA and related substances), discovering it contained adenine, guanine, cytosine and thymine—now known to be the elements of the genetic code; also made extensive studies of proteins; awarded Nobel Prize in physiology or medicine, 1910.

LAMBERT, JOHANN HEINRICH, Aug. 26, 1728 (Mulhouse, Alsace [now France])–Sept. 25, 1777. German mathematician, physicist. Proved pi to be an irrational number; did basic studies of light reflection and coined the term albedo, 1760; the first to measure light intensities accurately; lambert, a measurement of light intensity, named in his honor.

LAUE, MAX VON, Oct. 9, 1879 (Pfaffendorf, nr. Koblentz, Germany)–Apr. 23, 1960. German physicist. Discovered X-ray diffraction by crystals, making it possible to determine the wavelengths of X rays and the atomic structures of crystals; awarded Nobel Prize in physics, 1914; F.R.S., 1949.

LINDE, KARL P. G. VON, June 11, 1842 (Berndorf, Bavaria, Ger.)–Nov. 16, 1934. German engineer, chemist. Developed the first efficient refrigerator; devised new method of liquefying gases in quantity, 1895; discovered how to separate large quantities of pure liquid oxygen from liquid air, thus sparking advances in high-temperature industrial processes, 1901.

**MAYER, JULIUS ROBERT, VON** Nov. 25, 1814 (Heilbronn, Württemberg, Germany)–Mar. 20, 1878. German physicist. In advance of J. P. JOULE and H. HELMHOLTZ, respectively, worked out the mechanical equivalent of heat and the law of conservation of energy, 1842; the first to argue that all energy on earth ultimately derived from the sun; his contributions went unrecognized until the 1860s.

**MESMER, FRANZ** (or Friedrich) **ANTON,** May 23, 1734 (Iznang, am Bodensee, Aus.)–Mar. 5, 1815. Austrian physician. The modern discoverer of cure by suggestion in certain cases, which he attributed to "magnetic" force; his work, though discredited (1784), prepared the way for the discovery of hypnotism and the investigation of hysterical symptoms.

**MESSERSCHMITT, WILHELM,** June 26, 1898 (Frankfurt-am-Main, Ger.)–Sept. 15, 1978. German aviation engineer and designer. Designed the Me-262, the first jet to fly in combat, 1944; also designed the Me-109, the major German fighter in WW II.

**MICHEL, HARMUT,** July 18, 1948 (Ludwigsburg, W. Ger.). West German biochemist. Noted for research that revealed the three-dimensional structure of closely-linked proteins essential to photosynthesis; awarded Nobel Prize in chemistry (shared with J. DIESENHOFER and R. HUBER), 1988.

**MÖBIUS, AUGUST FERDINAND,** Nov. 17, 1790 (Schulpforta, Saxony, Germany)–Sept. 26, 1868. German mathematician, astronomer. Made basic contributions to mathematics, especially analytical geometry; a founder of topology; best known for discovering and analyzing the Möbius strip, a three-dimensional band with one edge and one surface that remains whole even when split down the middle.

**MOHS, FRIEDRICH,** Jan. 29, 1773 (Gernrode, Germany)–Sept. 29, 1839. German mineralogist. Devised the Mohs scale of comparative mineral hardness, ranging from talc at 1 to diamond at 10.

**MÖSSBAUER, RUDOLF L.,** Jan. 31, 1929 (Munich, Ger.). German physicist. Discovered the so-called Mössbauer effect, describing the behavior of gamma waves emitted and absorbed by crystals under particular conditions, 1958; this effect permitted the first laboratory test of A. EINSTEIN's general theory of relativity; awarded Nobel Prize in physics (with R. HOFSTADTER), 1961.

**NERNST, WALTHER H.** June 25, 1864 (Briesen, Prussia)–Nov. 18, 1941. German physical chemist. Discovered the third law of thermodynamics, that entropy nears zero at a temperature of absolute zero, 1906; explained why a chlorine-and-hydrogen mixture will explode on exposure to light, thus making clear the existence of chemical "chain reactions," 1918; awarded Nobel Prize in chemistry, 1920; F.R.S., 1932.

**NICHOLAS OF CUSA** (or Nicholaus Cusanus), born Nicholas Krebs, 1401 (Kues, Trier, Germany) –Aug. 11, 1464. German philosopher. On intuition alone, hypothesized that the earth turned on its axis and revolved around the sun, that space was infinite, and that the stars were other suns and had planets, 1440; invented concave-lens spectacles for the near-sighted; became a cardinal, 1448.

**OHM, GEORG SIMON,** Mar. 16, 1789 (Erlangen, Bavaria, Germany)–July 7, 1854. German physicist. Defined the relationships between the difference in potential, the resistance of the conductor, and the amount of electric current that would flow through a wire, 1827; both the ohm (the unit of resistance) and the mho (the unit of conductance), are named for him.

**OSTWALD, WILHELM,** Sept. 2, 1853 (Riga, Lat. [now USSR])–Apr. 4, 1932. German physical chemist. A major founder of modern physical chemistry; made basic contributions to the understanding of how catalysts work; awarded Nobel Prize in chemistry, 1909.

**OTTO, NIKOLAUS AUGUST,** June 10, 1832 (Holzhausen, Nassau, Germany)–Jan. 26, 1891. German inventor. First to build a four-stroke internal combustion engine, the type used almost universally today, 1876.

**PLANCK, MAX K. E. L.,** Apr. 23, 1858 (Kiel, Schleswig, Ger.)–Oct. 3, 1947. German physicist. Began modern physics with his proposal of the quantum theory, which states that electromagnetic radiation consists of quanta (particles of energy) directly proportional in size to the frequency of the radiation; awarded Nobel Prize in physics, 1918; F.R.S., 1926.

**PRANDTL, LUDWIG,** Feb. 4, 1875 (Freising, Germany)–Aug. 15, 1953. German physicist. Often considered the father of aerodynamics; his discovery of the "boundary layer" led to understanding of streamlining, 1904; made fundamental contributions to wing theory and turbulence studies.

**REGIOMONTANUS** (born Johann Müller), June 6, 1436 (Königsberg, Franconia, Germany)–July 6, 1476. German astronomer. His updated tables of planetary motion were widely used by explorer-navigators, including C. COLUMBUS; completed revised Latin translation of PTOLEMY's *Almagest*, inspiration to COPERNICUS; the first to observe and study the comet later called Halley's; the primary exponent in his day of a stationary, nonspinning earth.

**RIEMANN, GEORG F. B.,** Sept. 17, 1826 (Breselenz, Hanover, Germany)–July 20, 1866. German mathematician. A major creative source of mathematics in modern theoretical physics through his development of a non-Euclidean geometry of curved space, 1854; F.R.S., 1866.

**RITTER, JOHANN WILHELM,** Dec. 16, 1776 (Samitz bei Haynau, Silesia, Ger. [now Pol.])–Jan. 23, 1810. German physicist. Discovered the ultraviolet end of the light spectrum, 1801; discovered the electroplating process, 1800; built first dry cell, 1802.

ROENTGEN, WILHELM KONRAD, Mar. 27, 1845 (Lennup, Prussia [now Remscheid, W. Ger.], Germany)–Feb. 10, 1923. German physicist. Discovered X rays while experimenting with cathode rays (1895)—a discovery that revolutionized medicine, led directly to the discovery of radioactivity, and is often considered the beginning of modern physics; awarded the first Nobel Prize in physics; 1901; the unit of X-radiation is named after him.

RUSKA, ERNEST, Dec. 25, 1906 (Heidelberg, Ger.)–May 27, 1988. German physicist. Noted for pioneering work in developing the scanning tunneling microscope; awarded Nobel Prize in physics (shared with G. BINNIG and H. ROHRER), 1986.

SCHWABE, SAMUEL HEINRICH, Oct. 25, 1789 (Dessau, Anhalt, Germany)–Apr. 11, 1875. German pharmacist, astronomer. Discovered the sunspot cycle, after 18 years of observation and recordkeeping, 1843; made first detailed drawing of great Red spot of Jupiter, 1831; F.R.S., 1868.

SCHWANN, THEODOR, Dec. 7, 1810 (Neuss, Prussia, Germany)–Jan. 11, 1882. German physiologist. The primary developer of the cell theory of life, 1839; the first to isolate an animal enzyme (pepsin), 1836.

SPEMANN, HANS, June 27, 1869 (Stuttgart, Württemberg, Ger.)–Sept. 12, 1941. German zoologist. His basic research in embryology revealed the role of hormones in organizing the development of embryo cells, 1920s; coined term metabolism; awarded Nobel Prize in physiology or medicine, 1935.

STAHL, GEORG ERNST, Oct. 21, 1660 (Ansbach, Franconia, Germany)–May 14, 1734. German chemist. Father of "phlogiston theory" of combustion (1700), which held that some materials contained "phlogiston" that was used up in the combustion process; his theory dominated chemical thought until A. LAVOISIER.

STERN, OTTO, Feb. 17, 1888 (Sohrau, Germany)–Aug. 17, 1969. German-U.S. physicist. Developed molecular beams as a tool for studying the structure of molecules; measured the magnetic moment of the proton, 1933; awarded Nobel Prize in physics, 1943.

STRUVE, FRIEDRICH G. W. VON, Apr. 15, 1793 (Altona, Ger.)–Nov. 23, 1864. German-Russian astronomer. Established binary-star studies with a catalogue of over 3,000 binaries, 1837; discovered parallax of Vega (1840), a breakthrough in precise measurement of stellar distance.

VIRCHOW, RUDOLPH, Oct. 13, 1821 (Schivelbein, Pomerania [now Swidwin, Poland], Prussia)–Sept. 5, 1902. German pathologist and political leader. Founder of cellular pathology, 1858; first to describe leukemia, 1845; entered politics to fight for social reforms as a first step in preventing disease, 1861; dug with SCHLIEMANN at Troy.

WALDEYER, HEINRICH W. G. VON, Oct. 6, 1836 (Hehlen, Germany)–Jan. 23, 1921. German anatomist. Proposed the theory that the nervous system is made up of discrete cells, c.1870; coined the words *neuron* and *chromosome*.

WALLACH, OTTO, Mar. 27, 1847 (Königsberg, Prussia [now Kaliningrad, USSR])–Feb. 26, 1931.

German organic chemist. His basic research on the molecular structure of terpenes (such as menthol and camphor) contributed to the development of the perfume industry and understanding of steroids; awarded Nobel Prize in chemistry, 1910.

WARBURG, OTTO HEINRICH, Oct. 8, 1883 (Freiburg im Breisgau, Baden, Ger.)–Aug. 1, 1970. German biochemist. His basic research in the details of cell respiration helped to clarify the functions of several vitamins and enzymes, 1920s and 1930s; awarded Nobel Prize in physiology or medicine, 1931.

WASSERMAN, AUGUST VON, Feb. 21, 1866 (Bamberg, Ger.)–Mar. 16, 1925. German bacteriologist. Developed the prevalent diagnostic test for syphilis, 1906.

WEBER, ERNST HEINRICH, June 24, 1795 (Wittenberg, Ger.)–Jan. 26, 1878. German physiologist. Developed the theory of the "just noticeable difference," a way of measuring the acuity of the senses and the foundation of experimental psychology, 1830s; his ideas were popularized by G. T. Fechner.

WEIZSÄCKER, CARL FRIEDRICH, FREIHERR (BARON) VON, June 28, 1912 (Kiel, Ger.). German astronomer. Originated the modern nebular hypothesis for the origin of the solar system, 1944.

WIELAND, HEINRICH OTTO, June 4, 1877 (Pforzheim, Germany)–Aug. 5, 1957. German chemist. Did basic research in the structure of steroids, 1912–20; conducted basic research in how food is converted to energy, 1920s; awarded Nobel Prize in chemistry, 1927.

WIEN, WILHELM, Jan. 13, 1864 (Gaffken, E. Prussia [now Poland])–Aug. 30, 1928. German physicist. His basic research in black-body radiation proved that the wavelength of radiation shortens as the temperature of the emitting body increases, 1893; awarded Nobel Prize in physics, 1911

WINDAUS, ADOLF O. R., Dec. 25, 1876 (Berlin, Ger.)–June 9, 1959. German chemist. Worked out the structure of cholesterol, 1901–31; synthesized histamine, 1907; did basic research in steroids; awarded Nobel Prize in chemistry, 1928.

WITTIG, GEORG, 1897 (Berlin, Ger.)–Aug. 26, 1987. German chemist. Widely regarded for his work in organic synthesis; awarded Nobel Prize in chemistry (shared with H. BROWN), 1979.

WUNDT, WILHELM MAX, Aug. 16, 1832 (Neckerau, Baden, Germany)–Aug. 31, 1920. German physiologist. Founded the science of experimental psychology, 1862; established the first psychology laboratory, in Leipzig, 1879.

ZEPPELIN, FERDINAND, GRAF VON, July 8, 1838 (Constance, Baden, Germany)–Mar. 8, 1917. German inventor, military officer. Invented the rigid dirigible, which made the first directed flight by man, July 2, 1900.

ZSIGMONDY, RICHARD A., Apr. 1, 1865 (Vienna, Austria)–Sept. 23, 1929. German chemist. Pioneer in colloid studies with the slit ultramicroscope (which he helped develop, 1903); awarded Nobel Prize in chemistry, 1925.

## FRENCH SCIENTISTS, PHYSICIANS, AND INVENTORS

**AMPÈRE, ANDRÉ-MARIE,** Jan. 22, 1775 (Lyons, France)–June 10, 1836. French mathematician, physicist. Founded the study of electromagnetics (then called electrodynamics), 1820; stated the basic concept of the solenoid (which he named); stated Ampère's law, which describes mathematically the magnetic force between two electric currents; the unit of rate of motion of electric current was named an *ampere* by W. T. KELVIN, 1883.

**BECQUEREL, ANTOINE HENRI,** Dec. 15, 1852 (Paris, Fr.)–Aug. 25, 1908. French physicist. Discovered radioactivity, showing that atoms were composed of still smaller charged particles; awarded Nobel Prize in physics (with M. and P. CURIE), 1903.

**BERTHELOT, PIERRE EUGÈNE MARCELLIN,** Oct. 27, 1827 (Paris, France)–Mar. 18, 1907. French chemist. Synthesized methyl alcohol, ethyl alcohol, methane, benzene, acetylene; first to synthesize organic compounds that do not occur in nature; did extensive studies of the heat of chemical reaction; French senator, 1881–1907; minister of foreign affairs, 1895–96; secy. of Académie des Sciences, 1889–1907.

**BINET, ALFRED,** July 8, 1857 (Nice, France)–Oct. 18, 1911. French physiologist. Inventor of standardized tests for general intelligence.

**BLÉRIOT, LOUIS,** July 1, 1872 (Cambrai, France)–Aug. 2, 1936. French aviator, inventor. First to fly an airplane across the English Channel, July 25, 1909; invented auto lights.

**BUFFON, GEORGE-LOUIS LECLERC, COMTE DE,** Sept. 7, 1707 (Montbard, France)–Apr. 16, 1788. French naturalist. Wrote first 36 volumes of *Natural History* (1749-88), an attempt at a complete description of nature (eight more volumes appeared after his death); first to develop theory of geological eras, 1778; first to theorize the earth might be older than the biblically determined 6,000 years; first to propose idea of organic evolution.

**CAILLETET, LOUIS PAUL,** Sept. 21, 1832 (Châtillon-sur-Seine, France)–Jan. 5, 1913. French physicist. Independently of R. P. Pictet, was first to liquify oxygen, nitrogen, and carbon monoxide by compressing and cooling them, then allowing them to expand to further decrease their temperatures to the critical point.

**CARNOT, NICOLAS-LEONARD SADI,** June 1, 1796 (Paris, Fr.)–Aug. 24, 1832. French physicist. First to compute mathematically the relation between heat and work, thus founding study of thermodynamics.

**CARREL, ALEXIS,** June 28, 1873 (Sainte-Foy-lès-Lyon, Fr.)–Nov. 5, 1944. French-U.S. surgeon. Developed method for suturing blood vessels end-to-end, 1902; pioneer in the preservation of body organs by perfusion and in design of early "artificial heart" machines; awarded Nobel Prize in physiology or medicine, 1912.

**CHARCOT, JEAN-MARTIN,** Nov. 29, 1825 (Paris, Fr.)–Aug. 16, 1893. French neurologist. A pioneer in the study of neurological disease and in determining areas of the nervous system responsible for specific functions; a pioneer in the study of hysteria and in the use of hypnosis for such studies.

**CHARDONNET, LOUIS-MARIE-HILAIRE BERNIGAUD,** May 1, 1839 (Besançon, France)–Mar. 12, 1924. French chemist. Invented rayon ("Chardonnet silk"), the first common artificial fiber, 1884.

**CHARLES, JACQUES ALEXANDRE CÉSAR,** Nov. 12, 1746 (Beaugency, France)–Apr. 7, 1823. French physicist. First to express the law that the volume of a gas is proportional to its absolute temperature where pressure is held constant (called Charles's law or Gay-Lussac's law); constructed first hydrogen balloon, 1783.

**CORIOLIS, GUSTAVE-GASPARD DE,** May 21, 1792 (Paris, Fr.)–Sept. 19, 1843. French physicist. Worked out the mathematics of motion on a spinning surface (Coriolis forces), essential to meteorology, ballistics, rocket launches, etc., c.1840; first to give the exact modern definitions of kinetic energy and work.

**COULOMB, CHARLES AUGUSTIN DE,** June 14, 1736 (Angoulême, France)–Aug. 23, 1806. French physicist. Discovered Coulomb's law (of the force of electrical attraction and repulsion), 1785.

**CURIE, MARIE,** Nov. 7, 1867 (Warsaw, Pol.)–July 4, 1934. Polish-French chemist. Using piezoelectric phenomena to measure intensity of radiation, determined that uranium was the source of radio activity in uranium compounds; discovered polonium and radium (1898) as further sources of radioactivity in compounds; coined word *radioactive*; awarded Nobel Prize in physics (with husband P. CURIE and A. H. BECQUEREL), 1903; awarded Nobel Prize in chemistry in 1911, for discovery of radium and thallium; was excluded from French Acad. by one vote, because of her sex.

**CURIE, PIERRE,** May 15, 1859 (Paris, Fr.)–Apr. 19, 1906. French chemist. With his brother, discovered and named piezoelectric phenomenon, the basis of microphones and record players, 1880; was first to measure heat and radioactivity; made other discoveries under the guidance of his wife, MARIE CURIE; awarded Nobel Prize in physics, with Marie Curie and A. H. BECQUEREL.

**CUVIER, BARON GEORGES** Aug. 23, 1769 (Montbéliard, France)–May 13, 1832. French anatomist. Founded comparative anatomy and paleontology; developed principles of classification still in use, with emphasis on internal structure rather than outward appearance.

**DAGUERRE, LOUIS,** Nov. 18, 1789 (Cormeilles, France)–July 12, 1851. French inventor, artist. One of the inventors of photography; used copper plates and silver salts to achieve photographic image, 1837.

**DAUSSET, JEAN,** Oct. 19, 1916 (Toulouse, Fr.).

French immunologist. Highly regarded for his work in making tissue typing possible and shedding new light on the body's immune system; awarded Nobel Prize in medicine or physiology (shared with G. SNELL and B. BENACERRAF), 1980.

**FERMAT, PIERRE DE**, Aug. 17, 1601 (Beaumont-de-Lomagne, France)–Jan. 12, 1665. French mathematician. Founded modern number theory and, with BLAISE PASCAL, the probability theory.

**FOUCAULT, JEAN-BERNARD-LÉON**, Sept. 18, 1819 (Paris, Fr.)–Feb. 11, 1868. French physicist. The first to arrive at an almost precise measure of the speed of light and to demonstrate that light-speed slowed down in water, 1850; the first to demonstrate the rotation of the earth, using the Foucault pendulum, 1851; invented the gyroscope, 1852.

**FOURIER, JEAN-BAPTISTE-JOSEPH, BARON**, Mar. 21, 1768 (Auxerre, Fr.)–May 16, 1830. French mathematician and Egyptologist. Discovered Fourier's theorem of periodic oscillation, fundamental to the study of any wave phenomenon and the basis of dimensional harmonic analysis, 1807; made a baron by NAPOLEON I.

**GASSENDI, PIERRE**, Jan. 22, 1592 (Champtercien, Provence, France)–Oct. 24, 1655. French physicist, philosopher. The first to observe a transit of Mercury, 1631; studied velocity of sound; an early advocate of atomism and mechanistic view of nature; opponent of RENÉ DESCARTES.

**GAY-LUSSAC, JOSEPH-LOUIS**, Dec. 6, 1778 (Saint-Leonard-de-Noblat, France)–May 9, 1850. French chemist. Showed that all gases expand equally with rise in temperature, 1802; propounded law of combining volumes, or Gay-Lussac's law, 1808; isolated boron, 1808; showed iodine to be an element, 1813; made two balloon ascensions for scientific purposes, reaching a then-record altitude of 23,018 ft., 1804; his careful techniques made a major contribution to analytic chemistry.

**GRIGNARD, VICTOR**, May 6, 1871 (Cherbourg, France)–Dec. 13, 1935. French chemist. Discovered Grignard reagents, magnesium compounds vital to the development of many synthetics, 1900; awarded Nobel Prize in chemistry (with P. SABATIER), 1912.

**JACOB, FRANÇOIS**, June 17, 1920 (Nancy, France). French biologist. With J. MONOD, demonstrated that the function of some genes is to regulate the action of others; also with Monod, proposed the existence of messenger RNA, which regulates the building of enzymes, 1961; awarded Nobel Prize in physiology or medicine (with Monod and A. M. LWOFF), 1965.

**JOLIOT-CURIE, JEAN-FRÉDÉRIC**, Mar. 19, 1900 (Paris, Fr.)–Aug. 14, 1958; and his wife, **IRÈNE JOLIOT-CURIE**, Sept. 12, 1897 (Paris, Fr.)–Mar. 17, 1956. French physicists. Discovered "artificial radioactivity," the creation of radioactive isotopes of common elements by atomic-particle bombardment, 1934; the major contributors to France's independent development of nuclear power; awarded Nobel Prize in chemistry, 1935.

**JOUFFROY D'ABBANS, CLAUDE-FRANÇOIS-DOROTHÉE, MARQUIS DE**, 1751 (Roches-sur-Rognon, France)–1832. French engineer who built first practical steamboat, 1783.

**LAËNNEC, RENÉ**, Feb. 17, 1781 (Quimper, Brittany, France)–Aug. 13, 1826. French physician. Invented and named the stethoscope, 1819; developed anatomical-clinical method of diagnosing diseases of the chest.

**LAGRANGE, JOSEPH LOUIS, COMTE DE**, (originally Giuseppe Luigi Lagrangia), Jan. 25, 1736 (Turin, Sardinia-Piedmont, It.)–Apr. 10, 1813. French mathematician, astronomer. The basic contributor to mathematical analysis and number theory and to analytic and celestial mechanics; his work on the gravitational relations among three bodies resulted in the discovery of "Lagrange points" at which a very small body maintains a stable orbit while under the influence of two much larger bodies; instrumental in the establishment of the metric system; his *Analytic Mechanics* (1788) laid the basis of this field of mathematics; F.R.S., 1791.

**LAMARCK, JEAN BAPTISTE PIERRE ANTOINE DE MONET, CHEVALIER DE**, Aug. 1, 1744 (Bazentin-le-Petit, Picardy, France)–Dec. 18, 1829. French naturalist. Did the basic work of classifying invertebrates, 1801–22; first to fully develop a theory of evolution which, though based on false ideas of inheritance of acquired characteristics, pushed the problem of evolution into the forefront of biological science.

**LAPLACE, PIERRE SIMON, MARQUIS DE**, Mar. 28, 1749 (Beaumont-en-Auge, Normandy, Fr.)–Mar. 5, 1827. French mathematician, astronomer. Did basic work in celestial mechanics; with J. LAGRANGE, showed that planetary orbits are extraordinarily stable; his work in probability theory modernized that subject, 1812–20; proposed nebular hypothesis of solar system formation; pres. of French Acad., 1817, during Fr. Rev. helped establish metric system; minister of interior, 1799; Academie Française, 1816; F.R.S., 1789.

**LAVOISIER, ANTOINE LAURENT**, Aug. 26, 1743 (Paris, Fr.)–May 8, 1794. French chemist. The father of modern chemistry through his emphasis on precise measurements; disproved G. E. STAHL's phlogiston theory of combustion (1774) and defined the role of oxygen, which he named (1779); based on similar work with hydrogen, concluded that human energy derived from oxidation of hydrogen and carbon; instrumental in establishing chemical nomenclature, 1787; wrote *Elementary Treatise on Chemistry*, first modern textbook on the subject, 1789; entered Acad. of Sciences at age 24, 1768; F.R.S., 1788; executed by guillotine during Reign of Terror.

**LEHN, JEAN-MARIE**, Sept. 30, 1939 (Rosheim, Fr.). French chemist. A pioneer in wide-ranging research, including the creation of artificial molecules; awarded Nobel Prize in chemistry (shared with D. CRAM and C. PEDERSEN), 1987.

**LWOFF, ANDRÉ**, May 8, 1902 (Aulnay-le-Chateau, France). French microbiologist. Discovered lysogeny, in which viral DNA incorporates itself into chromosomes of bacteria and is thereafter passed on to future generations of bacteria; awarded Nobel Prize in physiology or medicine (with J. MONOD and F. JACOB), 1965; F.R.S., 1958.

MAGENDIE, FRANÇOIS, Oct. 15, 1783 (Bordeaux, Fr.)–Oct. 7, 1855. French physiologist. Laid the groundwork for modern nutritional studies in experiments showing the dietary necessity of a variety of foods containing nitrogen (protein); experimented with the effects of drugs on the human system; his spinal-cord studies of the 1820s showed the functions of sensory and motor nerveroots; established the first medical school laboratory, early 1830s.

MESSIER, CHARLES JOSEPH, June 26, 1730 (Badonviller, Lorraine, France)–Apr. 11, 1817. French astronomer. In a fanatical search for comets, compiled a list of over 100 blurry celestial objects that he determined were not comets; these objects much later were found to be nebulas, galaxies, and star clusters, now often referred to by their so-called Messier number; Acad. of Sci., 1770; F.R.S., 1764.

MONOD, JACQUES, Feb. 9, 1910 (Paris, Fr.)–May 31, 1976. French biochemist. With F. JACOB, proposed the existence of messenger RNA, which regulates the building of enzymes, 1961; also with Jacob, found that some genes serve only to regulate the function of other genes; wrote the best-seller Chance and Necessity, (1970), in which he argued that human life was no more than a chance collection of atoms; awarded Nobel Prize in physiology or medicine (with Jacob and A. M. LWOFF), 1965.

MONTGOLFIER, JOSEPH MICHEL, Aug. 26, 1740 (Vidalon-les-Annonay, France)–June 26, 1810; and his brother JACQUES ÉTIENNE MONTGOLFIER, Jan. 7, 1745 (Vidalon-les-Annonay, France)–Aug. 2, 1799. French inventors. Invented the hot-air hydrogen balloon, 1783; conducted first untethered and manned (Nov. 21, 1783) flights.

NÉEL LOUIS, Nov. 22, 1904 (Lyon, Fr.). French physicist. Made fundamental contributions to the understanding of the varieties and properties of magnetism, in the 1930s and 1940s; awarded Nobel Prize in physics (with H. O. G. Alfven), 1970.

PARÉ, AMBROISE, 1510 (Bourg-Hersent, France) –Dec. 22, 1590. French surgeon. Often considered the father of modern surgery; made several advances in the treatment of wounds and in improving cleanliness; devised artificial limbs, numerous surgical and orthopedic devices.

PASTEUR, LOUIS, Dec. 27, 1822 (Dôle, Jura, France)–Sept. 28, 1895. French chemist. Proposed the "germ" theory of disease, perhaps the greatest single advance in the history of medicine, late 1860s; discovered "pasteurization," gentle heating to kill harmful bacteria in wine and milk, 1860s; proved that total sterility was possible in the labo-

ratory, 1864; discovered the process of using "attenuated" germs in inoculations against some diseases (1881), leading to the prevention of rabies (1885); made basic discoveries in polarimetry, 1848–58; elected to French Acad. of Med., 1873; French Acad., 1882; F.R.S., 1869; the first head of the Pasteur Inst., founded for him by the French govt. in 1888.

PEREGRINUS DE MARICOURT, PETRUS, c.1220–? French crusader and scholar. The first to describe the modern compass, suggesting it be mounted on a pivot and encircled by a scale denoting directions, 1269; author of the first significant work describing magnetism, Epistola de Magnete.

PINEL, PHILIPPE, Apr. 20, 1745 (Saint-André, Tarn, France)–Oct. 25, 1826. French physician. A primary founder of psychiatry; the first to identify insanity with disease (rather than demons) and to propose that extreme stress, physiological damage, or heredity might be the cause, c.1790; described many psychotic systems and invented the term alienation for mental disorder. Treatise on Mental Alienation, 1801.

POINCARÉ, HENRI, Apr. 29, 1854 (Nancy, Fr.) –July 17, 1912. French mathematician. Made important contributions in most areas of mathematics, especially the three-body problem and tidal forces; F.R.S., 1894; Acad. Franc., 1908. (Cousin of R. POINCARÉ.)

POISSON, SIMÉON-DENIS, June 21, 1781 (Pithiviers, France)–Apr. 25, 1840. French mathematician. Made major contributions to the application of mathematics to electromagnetics and mechanics and to the development of the mathematics of probability.

RÉAUMUR, RENÉ DE, Feb. 28, 1683 (La Rochelle, Fr.)–Oct. 17, 1757. French physicist and entomologist. Proved that digestion was a process of chemical dissolving and not mechanical grinding, 1752; devised the Réaumur thermometer and temperature scale, 1731; the first to demonstrate the importance of carbon in steel-making.

SABATIER, PAUL, Nov. 5, 1854 (Carcassone, France)–Aug. 14, 1941. French chemist. Discovered nickel catalysis, which made possible the mass production from inedible vegetable oils of margarine, shortening, and other edible fats; F.R.S., 1918; awarded Nobel Prize in chemistry (with F. A. V. GRIGNARD), 1912.

SCALIGER, JOSEPH JUSTUS, Aug. 5, 1540 (Agen, France)–Jan. 21, 1609. French scholar. Father of modern chronology; founder of the Julian Day system, 1583.

VIETA, FRANCISCUS, (François Viète) 1540 (Fontenoy-le-Comte, Poitou, France)–Dec. 13, 1603. French mathematician. Considered the father of modern algebra; introduced the use of letters for unknowns and constants, 1591.

## OTHER FOREIGN SCIENTISTS, PHYSICIANS, AND INVENTORS

ANGSTRÖM, ANDERS JONAS, Aug. 13, 1814 (Lögdö, Medelpad, Sweden)–June 21, 1874. Swedish physicist, astronomer. A pioneer in astronomical

spectrosopy, he discovered the sun was made of hydrogen and other elements, 1862; first to use $10^{-10}$ meter as a unit to measure wavelengths of light (this unit was named after him in 1905). **ARBER, WERNER,** June 3, 1929 (Gränichen, Switzerland). Swiss microbiologist. Noted for his basic contributions to the study and isolation of a restriction enzyme that cuts or cleaves DNAs at specific points, 1968; awarded Nobel Prize in physiology or medicine (with D. NATHANS and H. O. SMITH), 1978.

**ARCHIMEDES,** c.287 B.C. (Syracuse, Sicily)–c.212 B.C. Greek mathematician, engineer. Discovered principle of buoyancy while in a bathtub (and shouted "Eureka!"); developed the mathematical principles of the lever; derived more accurate value for "pi."

**ARRHENIUS, SVANTE A.,** Feb. 19, 1859 (Vik, Sweden)–Oct. 2, 1927. Swedish chemist. Founded modern physical chemistry through his theory that some atoms (ions) carry electric charges, c.1884; awarded Nobel Prize in chemistry, 1903.

**AVOGADRO, AMADEO, CONTE DI QUAREGNA,** June 9, 1776 (Turin, Piedmont, It.)–July 9, 1856. Italian physicist. Coined the word *molecules* and was the first to draw the distinction between molecules and atoms, 1811; his ideas were not accepted until about 1858.

**BANTING, SIR FREDERICK G.,** Nov. 14, 1891 (Alliston, Ont., Can.)–Feb. 21, 1941. Canadian physiologist. First to isolate insulin (1922), thus providing an effective treatment for diabetes; awarded Nobel Prize in physiology or medicine, (with J. J. R. MACLEOD), 1923; knighted in 1934.

**BARNARD, CHRISTIAAN N.,** Nov. 8, 1922 (Beaufort West, South Africa). South African surgeon. Performed first successful heart transplant, Dec. 3, 1967; patient lived 18 days after the operation; 2nd patient lived 594 days.

**BASOV, NIKOLAI GENNADIEVICH,** Dec. 14, 1922 (Voronezh, USSR). Soviet physicist. With ALEKSANDR PROKHOROV, worked out theoretical principles of the maser (microwave amplification by stimulated emission of radiation); awarded Nobel Prize in physics, (with Prokhorov and CHARLES H. TOWNES), 1964.

**BERGSTROM, K. SUNE,** Jan. 10, 1916 (Stockholm, Swed.). Swedish biochemist. Noted for discoveries in controlling prostaglandins, a natural substance implicated in medicine or physiology (shared with J. VANE and B. SAMUELSSON), 1982.

**BERNOULLI, DANIEL,** Feb. 8, 1700 (Groningen, Netherlands)–Mar. 17, 1782. Swiss mathematician. Discovered Bernoulli's principle, that fluid pressure decreases as velocity of flow increases, c.1733; also made major contributions to study of behavior of gases and to differential calculus.

**BERZELIUS, BARON JÖNS JAKOB,** Aug. 20, 1779 (nr. Linköping, Sweden)–Aug. 7, 1848. Swedish chemist. Devised first relatively accurate list of atomic weights, 1828; devised atomic symbols, 1813; discovered selenium (1818), silicon (1824), and thorium (1829); dominated world of chemistry from 1830 to his death; created baron in 1835.

**BOHR, AAGE NIELS,** June 19, 1922 (Copenhagen, Denmark). Danish physicist. Discovered the connection between collective motion and particle motion in atomic nuclei by work on problem of asymmetrical nuclei, 1950–53; awarded Nobel Prize in physics (with J. RAINWATER and B. MOTTELSON), 1975. (Son of N. BOHR.)

**BOHR, NIELS,** Oct. 7, 1885 (Copenhagen, Den.)–Nov. 18, 1962. Danish physicist. A major theoretician and administrative force in modern physics; revolutionized physics by combining elements of M. PLANCK's quantum theory with classic mechanics to explain electromagnetic radiation, 1913; framed "principle of complimentarity," allowing subatomic phenomena to be viewed in two contradictory ways, with each valid in its own terms, 1927; brought to U.S. the news that uranium would apparently undergo fission when bombarded by neutrons, and predicted that the fissionable isotope was U-235, 1939; played major role in rescue of many Danish Jews from Hitler, 1940–43; worked on U.S. atom bomb project, 1943–45; organized first Atoms for Peace conference, 1955; awarded Nobel Prize in physics, 1922.

**BORDET, JULES-JEAN-BAPTISTE-VINCENT,** June 13, 1870 (Soignies, Belgium)–Apr. 6, 1961. Belgian bacteriologist. His discoveries in immunology (1895 and later) laid the basis for most modern work in the field, including the Wasserman test for syphilis; discovered and developed a vaccine against the whooping cough bacillus, 1906; awarded Nobel Prize in physiology or medicine, 1919.

**BOVET, DANIELE,** Mar. 23, 1907 (Neuchâtel, Switz.). Swiss–Italian pharmacologist. With others, discovered sulphanilamide, 1936; discovered the first antihistamines (1937–44), and the use of curare as a muscle relaxant in surgery; awarded Nobel Prize in physiology or medicine, 1957.

**BRAHE, TYCHO** (born Tyge), Dec. 14, 1546 (Knudstrup, Scania, Denmark [now Sweden])–Oct. 24, 1601. Danish astronomer. The last naked-eye astronomer; observed first recorded exploding star seen in Europe and named the phenomenon a "nova," 1572; built first major astronomical observatory, 1580; made first scientific observations of a comet; his research made Gregorian calendar reform possible; his data became basis for the laws of planetary motion devised by his pupil and asst. J. KEPLER.

**BURNET, SIR FRANK MACFARLANE,** Sept. 3, 1899 (Traralgon, Austrl.)–Aug. 31, 1985. Australian physician. First to perceive that immunological resistance to foreign proteins might not be inborn, but might be developed very early in life; awarded Nobel Prize in physiology or medicine (with P. B. MEDAWAR), 1960; knighted in 1951.

**CANDOLLE, AUGUSTINE PYRAME DE,** Feb. 4, 1778 (Geneva, Switz.)–Sept. 9, 1841. Swiss botanist. Began a 21-volume encyclopedia of plants; coined *taxonomy* for science of classification; taxonomic system for plants still commonly used.

**CASSINI, GIOVANNI DOMENICO** (Jean Dominique), June 8, 1625 (Perinaldo, Republic of Genoa)–Sept. 11, 1712. French–Italian astronomer. Determined rotation periods of Mars and Jupiter, 1665–66; discovered four of Saturn's satellites,

1671–84; discovered Cassini's diversion, the gap in Saturn's rings, 1675; first to arrive at a close approximation of the sun's true distance from earth, 1672.

**CELSIUS, ANDERS,** Nov. 27, 1701 (Uppsala, Sweden)–Apr. 25, 1744. Swedish astronomer. Devised the Celsius or centigrade scale of temperature with 100° between the freezing and boiling points of water.

**CHERENKOV, PAVEL,** Aug. 10, 1904 (Voronezh, Russia). Soviet physicist. First to observe Cherenkov radiation, a glow caused by the movement of elementary particles through a medium, such as water, at a rate faster than the speed of light in that medium, 1934; awarded Nobel Prize in physics (with I. M. FRANK and I. J. TAMM), 1958.

**CLAUDE, ALBERT,** Aug. 24, 1898 (Langlier, Belgium)–May 22, 1983. Belgian-U.S. microbiologist. Made fundamental discoveries in the anatomy of cells (including mitochondria) and developed centrifuge techniques for separating the parts of cells; awarded Nobel Prize in physiology or medicine (with G. E. PALADE and C. De Duve), 1974.

**COPERNICUS, NICOLAS,** Feb. 19, 1473 (Thorn [Torun], Poland)–May 24, 1543. Polish astronomer. Worked out the mathematics of a heliocentric solar system, beginning in 1512; first to explain precission of equinoxes as caused by earth's wobbling on its axis; his ideas were quietly circulated among scholars from about 1530, and first published in 1543; his work began the scientific revolution.

**DE VRIES, HUGO MARIE,** Feb. 16, 1848 (Haarlem, Netherlands)–May 21, 1935. Dutch botanist. Independently discovered the Mendelian laws of heredity (1900) and recovered GREGOR MENDEL's original work of a generation earlier; first proposed the theory of mutation, 1901.

**DOPPLER, CHRISTIAN JOHANN,** Nov. 29, 1803 (Salzburg, Austria)–Mar. 17, 1853. Austrian physicist. The first to explain the Doppler effect, the change in pitch as a sound source approaches and moves away from a listener; correctly predicted a similar effect for light waves.

**DUBOIS, MARIE,** Jan. 28, 1858 (Eisden, Netherlands)–Dec. 16, 1940. Dutch paleontologist. The first to discover a "missing link" between ape and man—*Pithecanthropus erectus,* or Java man—1894.

**ECCLES, SIR JOHN CAREW,** Jan. 27, 1903 (Melbourne, Austrl.). Australian physiologist. Made a major contribution to the study of chemical transfer of nerve impulses across the synapse; F.R.S., 1941; knighted, 1958; awarded Nobel Prize in physiology or medicine (with A. L. HODGKIN and A. F. HUXLEY), 1963.

**ERATOSTHENES,** c.276 B.C. (Cyrene [now in Libya])–c.195 B.C. Greek astronomer. Determined a relatively accurate value for the circumference of the earth that was not bettered until J. Picard's calculations.

**ESAKI, LEO** (born Esaki Reiona), Mar. 12, 1925 (Osaka, Jap.). Japanese physicist. Conducted basic research in electron "tunneling" in semiconductors; discovered the tunnel diode, 1957; awarded Nobel

Prize in physics (with I. GIAEVER and B. D. JOSEPHSON), 1973.

**EUCLID,** fl. 305–285 B.C. Greek mathematician. Compiled and arranged logically the geometrical knowledge of his time, some number theory, and problems of ratio and proportion. *Elements.*

**EULER, LEONHARD,** Apr. 15, 1707 (Basel, Switz.)–Sept. 18, 1783. Swiss mathematician. Made major contributions in all areas of mathematics and to the application of mathematics to work in physics; established many of the mathematical notations used today.

**EULER(-CHELPIN), ULF SVANTE VON,** Feb. 7, 1905 (Stockholm, Swe.)–Mar. 9, 1983. Swedish physiologist. Noted for his basic research on the action of hormones in the nervous system and the discovery of the key role of noradrenaline as the impulse transmitter in the sympathetic nervous system; awarded Nobel Prize in physiology or medicine (with B. KATZ and J. AXELROD), 1970. (Son of H. EULER-CHELPIN.)

**EULER-CHELPIN, HANS,** Feb. 15, 1873 (Germany)–Nov. 7, 1964. German-Swedish chemist. Contributed to knowledge of the structure of several vitamins; first to work out the structure of a coenzyme; awarded Nobel Prize in chemistry (with A. HARDEN), 1929. (Father of U. EULER.)

**FERMI, ENRICO,** Sept. 29, 1901 (Rome, It.)–Nov. 28, 1954. U.S.-Italian physicist. Pioneer in the study of neutrons and neutron bombardment, beginning in 1932; led the group which achieved the first manmade nuclear chain reaction, Dec. 2, 1942, in Chicago; awarded Nobel Prize in physics, 1938.

**FIBONACCI, LEONARDO** (or Leonard da Pisa), c.1170 (Pisa, It.)–c. 1240. Italian mathematician. Primarily responsible for European adoption of Arabic numerals, which he explained in *Liber abbaci* (1202).

**FRANK, ILYA,** Oct. 23, 1908 (St. Petersburg, Rus. [now Leningrad, USSR]). Soviet physicist. With I. Y. TAMM, explained Cherenkov radiation as caused by the passage of high-energy particles through water or other mediums at a speed greater than light in that medium, 1937; awarded Nobel Prize in physics (with Tamm and P. CHERENKOV), 1958.

**FREUD, SIGMUND,** May 6, 1856 (Freiburg, Moravia [now Příbor, Czech.])–Sept. 23, 1939. Austrian neurologist. As the founder of psychoanalysis, made an incalculable impact on modern thought with his theories of neuroses stemming from childhood relationships with parents and with his stress on the importance of sexuality in both normal and abnormal development. *Studies in Hysteria,* with J. Breur, 1895; *The Interpretation of Dreams,* 1900.

**FRISCH, KARL VON,** Nov. 20, 1886 (Vienna, Austria)–June 12, 1982. Austrian-German zoologist. Discovered that the "dances" of bees convey the direction and distance of food sources (1923) and that bees can orient themselves by the direction of light polarization (1949); awarded Nobel Prize in physiology or medicine (with K. LORENZ and N. TINBERGEN), 1973.

**FRISCH, OTTO ROBERT,** Oct. 1, 1904 (Vienna, Austria)–Sept. 22, 1979. Austrian-British physicist. Collaborated with his aunt, L. MEITNER, on a paper proposing that changes observed in uranium bombarded with neutrons were caused by fission; before publication (1939), told N. BOHR, who told U.S. physicists, thereby initiating the development of the A-bomb.; F.R.S., 1948.

**FUKUI, KENICHI,** Oct. 4, 1918 (Nara, Japan). Japanese chemist. Noted for work in explaining chemical reactions; awarded Nobel Prize in chemistry (shared with R. HOFFMANN), 1981.

**GALEN,** c.130 (Pergamum [now Bergama, Tur.])– c.200. Greek physician. The leading medical authority in Europe until the 17th cent.; made basic discoveries in anatomy; court physician to MARCUS AURELIUS.

**GALILEO** (born Galileo Galilei), Feb. 15, 1564 (Pisa, It.)–Jan. 8, 1642. Italian physicist, astronomer. Established mechanics as a science, discovering the law of uniformly accelerated motion (1604) and the law of parabolic fall; invented the astronomical telescope (1609) and discovered four of Jupiter's moons, the period of the sun's rotation, and the phases of Venus; his discoveries ended the influence of ARISTOTLE and PTOLEMY on astronomy; the first to systematically pursue experimentation and quantitative methods; forced by religious authorities to recant Copernican view, June 22, 1633. *Dialogue on the Two Chief World Systems,* 1632; *Discourse Concerning Two New Sciences,* 1638.

**GALVANI, LUIGI,** Sept. 9, 1737 (Bologna, It.)– Dec. 4, 1798. Italian anatomist. Conducted studies of the effects of electric impulses on muscle, from 1771; galvanic electric processes were named after him.

**GÖDEL, KURT,** Apr. 28, 1906 (Brünn, Aust.-H [now Brno, Czech.])–Jan. 14, 1978. Austrian-U.S. mathematician. Author of "Gödel's proof" (1931), showing that no logically certain basis can be established for any logical mathematical system, ending nearly 100 years of search for such a basis and freeing mathematics for greater advances.

**GOLDHABER, MAURICE,** Apr. 18, 1911 (Lemberg, Aust.-H.). Austrian-U.S. physicist. Discovered that the nucleus of deuterium contains a proton and a neutron; discovered the nuclear photoelectric effect, 1934; demonstrated the usefulness of photographic emulsions for particle studies; demonstrated that beta rays are electrons; discovered that beryllium was a good moderator, an essential contribution to nuclear reactor technology, 1940.

**GOLGI, CAMILLO,** July 7, 1843 (Corteno, Italy) –Jan. 21, 1926. Italian histologist. Did the basic work on the fine structure of the nervous system, discovering silver nitrate staining, the Golgi cells and the Golgi complex, and demonstrating the existence of the synapses; awarded Nobel Prize in physiology or medicine (with S. RAMÓN Y CAJAL), 1906.

**GUILLAUME, CHARLES É.,** Feb. 15, 1861. (Fleurier, Switzerland)–June 13, 1938. Swiss-French physicist. Dir. of Bureau of Internatl. Weights and Measures, 1915–36; did basic work in increasing precision of measurements; discovered invar, an iron-nickel alloy essential to accurate time measurement, 1896; awarded Nobel Prize in physics, 1920.

**HALLER, ALBRECHT VON,** Oct. 16, 1708 (Bern, Switz.)–Dec. 12, 1777. Swiss physiologist, poet. Father of experimental physiology and neurology; the first to understand the mechanics of respiration (1747) and to recognize the autonomous operation of the heart and the function of bile; his extensive experiments proved that nerves, not tissues, were the channels of sensation and muscular stimulation, 1766; F.R.S., 1739.

**HERTZSPRUNG, EJNAR,** Oct. 8, 1873 (Frederiksberg, Denmark)–Oct. 21, 1967. Danish astronomer. Devised the notion of stars' absolute magnitude and related that to their color, devising a scale of stellar types basic to modern astronomy, 1905 and 1907; devised a luminosity scale for Cepheid variable stars, 1913, the first step in the process of determining the shape of the galaxy and the sun's place in it.

**HEVESY, GEORG,** Aug. 1, 1885 (Budapest, Hung.)– July 5, 1966. Hungarian-Danish chemist. The first to use radioactive tracers to study biological processes, 1923; discovered hafnium, 1923; F.R.S., 1939; awarded Nobel Prize in chemistry, 1943.

**HIPPARCHUS,** c. 190 B.C. (Nicea [now Iznik, Tur.])–c.120 B.C. Greek astronomer. Often considered the father of trigonometry, which he used to compute the moon's distance with relative accuracy; created an accurate map of over 1,000 stars; established the idea of the latitude and longitude grid on earth; discovered the "precession of the equinoxes"; devised the basic outlines of the present star-magnitude scale; worked out the basic mathematics of the geocentric (Ptolemaic) system of astronomy.

**HIPPOCRATES,** 460 B.C. (Cos, Gr.)–c.370 B.C. Greek physician. The father of medicine; founded the most famous medical school of the ancient world; established rational, cautious, ethical standards for medical practice.

**HOUSSAY, BERNARDO A.,** Apr. 10, 1887 (Buenos Aires, Arg.)–Sept. 21, 1971. Argentine physiologist. Demonstrated the importance of the pituitary gland to sugar metabolism; awarded Nobel Prize in physiology or medicine (with CARL F. and GERTY T. CORI), 1947.

**HUYGENS, CHRISTIAAN,** Apr. 14, 1629 (The Hague, Neth.)–June 8, 1695. Dutch physicist, astronomer, mathematician. Wrote first formal treatise on probability, 1657; discovered first satellite of Saturn and Saturn's rings, 1656; invented the pendulum clock, 1656; the first major advocate of the wave theory of light; F.R.S., 1663.

**INGENHOUSZ, JAN,** Dec. 8, 1730 (Breda, Netherlands)–Sept. 7, 1799. Dutch physician, plant physiologist. First to show clearly that green plants consume carbon dioxide and exude oxygen in light and do the opposite in the dark, thus discovering photosynthesis, 1779; F.R.S., 1769.

KAMERLINGHONNES, HEIKE, Sept. 21, 1853 (Groningen, Netherlands)–Feb. 21, 1926. Dutch physicist. First to liquefy helium, 1908; discovered superconductivity (loss of electrical resistance in some metals at low temperatures); pioneering work in cryogenics; awarded Nobel Prize in physics, 1913.

KAPITSA, PYOTR, July 8, 1894 (Kronstadt, Russia)–Apr. 8, 1984. Soviet physicist. Discovered superfluidity of helium II, 1941; made major contributions to the development of high-powered magnetic fields (1924), to the Soviet space program (1957), and to nuclear fusion studies (1969); F.R.S., 1929; awarded Nobel Prize in physics (with A. PENZIAS and R. WILSON), 1978.

KITASATO, SHIBASABURO, BARON, Dec. 20, 1852 (Oguni, Kumamoto, Japan)–June 13, 1931. Japanese bacteriologist. Isolated the causative agents of tetanus (1889), bubonic plague (1894), and dysentery (1898); made a baron, 1924.

KLUG, AARON, Aug. 11, 1926 (Lithuania). South African biological chemist. Noted for research revealing the most detailed structures of viruses and some of the most important components within living things; awarded Nobel Prize in chemistry, 1982.

KOCHER, EMIL T., Aug. 25, 1841 (Berne, Switz.)–July 27, 1917. Swiss surgeon. Advanced surgical techniques for many operations; received 1909 Nobel Prize in physiology or medicine for his work on the physiology, pathology, and surgery of the thyroid gland. *Chirurgische Operationslehre*, 1892.

KURCHATOV, IGOR, Jan. 12, 1903 (Sim, Russia)–Feb. 7, 1960. Soviet physicist. The prime mover of Soviet fission research (1943–60), leading the Soviet groups which developed the A-bomb (1949), H-bomb (1953), and an experimental nuclear-power station (1954).

LANDAU, LEV, Jan. 22, 1908 (Baku, Azerbaijan, Rus.)–Apr. 3, 1968. Soviet physicist. Did fundamental theoretical work in low-temperature physics, predicting properties for a rare helium isotope that scientists are still trying to verify; F.R.S., 1960; awarded Nobel Prize in physics, 1962.

LEEUWENHOEK, ANTON VAN, Oct. 24, 1632 (Delft, Neth.)–Aug. 26, 1723. Dutch biologist. A pioneer in precision lens-grinding and microscopy; discovered protozoa, 1674; described spermatozoa, 1677; described bacteria, 1683; F.R.S., 1680.

LENOIR, JEAN JOSEPH ÉTIENNE, Jan. 12, 1822 (Mussy-la-Ville, Belgium)–Aug. 4, 1900. Belgian inventor. Devised the first workable and commercially successful internal-combustion engine (1859), which he attached to a vehicle for a six-mile trip (1860); also attached his invention to a boat.

LINNAEUS, CAROLUS (born Carl Linné) later von Linné, May 23, 1707 (Råshult, Småland, Sweden)–Jan. 10, 1778. Swedish botanist. Founded modern taxonomy by devising a methodical system of classification (the "two name"—genera and species—method), developing classes and orders, and precisely describing differences between species, 1735; named *Homo sapiens*; the first to use male and female symbols ($\delta$, $\female$) *Systema Naturae*, 1735; granted patent of nobility, 1761, antedated to 1757; F.R.S., 1753.

LIPPERSHEY, HANS, c.1587 (Wesel, Netherlands)–c.1619. Dutch optician who invented the telescope, 1608.

LOMONOSOV, MIKHAIL, Nov. 9, 1711 (nr. Archangel, Rus.)–Apr. 5, 1765. Russian chemist, author. The first major Russian scientist, although most of his work remained unknown for decades in the West; with L. EULER, founded U. of Moscow, 1755; wrote poetry, plays; introduced reforms into the Russian language, 1755.

LORENTZ, HENDRIK A., July 18, 1853 (Arnhem, Neth.)–Feb. 4, 1928. Dutch physicist. One of the first to theorize that charged particles in the atom produced visible light, c.1890; introduced idea of local time, 1895; first to show that an electron's mass at the speed of light must be infinite (Lorentz transformations, the basis of ALBERT EINSTEIN's special theory of relativity), 1904; awarded Nobel Prize in physics (with P. ZEEMAN), 1902.

LORENZ, KONRAD, Nov. 7, 1903 (Vienna, Austria)–Feb. 27, 1989. Austro-German ethologist. The major pioneer of modern ethology, the study of animal behavior; proposed the theory that all animal behavior is explicable in terms of adaptive evolution; described imprinting, 1935; awarded Nobel Prize in physiology or medicine (with K. VON FRISCH and N. TINBERGEN), 1973. *On Aggression*, 1966.

LYSENKO, TROFIM, Sept. 29, 1898 (Karlovka, Ukraine, Rus.)–Nov. 20, 1976. Soviet biologist. A major modern proponent of the idea of the inheritance of acquired characteristics, in opposition to mainstream biology and genetics; received strong political support from J. STALIN and was dir. of the Soviet Inst. of Genetics, 1940–65.

MACH, ERNST, Feb. 18, 1838 (Chirlitz-Turas, Moravia A.-H.)–Feb. 19, 1916. Austrian physicist. Best known for his studies of airflow and the discovery (1887) of sudden change of airflow over an object moving at close to the speed of sound; the speed of sound in air is named for him.

MALPIGHI, MARCELLO, Mar. 10, 1628 (Crevalcore, nr. Bologna, Italy)–Nov. 30, 1694. Italian physiologist. First to make extensive use of the microscope, 1650s; discovered capillaries, thus filling in the gap between the venous and arterial systems; discovered that blood flows over the lungs; the first to observe many physiological elements of plant and insect life; F.R.S., 1669.

MARCONI, GUGLIELMO, MARCHESE, Apr. 25, 1874 (Bologna, Italy)–July 20, 1937. Italian physicist. Invented the radio, 1894–1901; received his first patent, 1896; transmitted signals across the Atlantic, Dec. 12, 1901; made a major contribution to the development of short-wave radio; awarded Nobel Prize in physics (with K. F. Braun), 1909.

MEITNER, LISE, Nov. 7, 1878 (Vienna, Austria)–Oct. 17, 1968. Austrian-Swedish physicist. The first to make public the probability that uranium fission had occurred in the laboratory; worked with O. HAHN for 30 years and collaborated in many achievements credited to him; F.R.S., 1955. (Aunt of O. FRISCH.)

**MENDEL, GREGOR JOHANN,** July 22, 1822 (Heinzendorf [now Hynčice] Lower Silesia, A.-H. [now Czech.])–Jan. 6, 1884. Austrian botanist, monk. Discovered the basic laws of biological inheritance, including the statistical probability of dominant and recessive trait-reproduction, early 1860s; his work explained the mechanisms of natural selection, but was ignored and forgotten by other scientists until discovered by H. M. DE VRIES in 1900.

**MENDELEEV, DMITRI,** Feb. 7, 1834 (Tobolsk, Siberia, Rus.)–Feb. 2, 1907. Russian chemist. Created the periodic table of elements (1869), leaving gaps in the table to fit his schema and predicting (1871) the gaps would be filled by yet undiscovered elements, three of which he described in detail; all three new elements were discovered by 1885; participated in early development of Russian oil fields; though he won worldwide acclaim, he missed receiving the 1906 Nobel Prize in chemistry by one vote.

**MERCATOR, GERARDUS** (born Gerhard Kremer), Mar. 5, 1512 (Rupelmonde, Flanders)–Dec. 2, 1594. Flemish geographer. Invented the Mercator projection system of mapmaking, still the most common projection for world maps, 1568; a founder of modern geography; introduced term atlas for collection of maps.

**METCHNIKOFF, ÉLIE,** May 15, 1845 (Ivanouka, nr. Kharkov, Ukraine, Rus.)–July 15, 1916. Russian French bacteriologist. Discovered white corpuscles in living cells, identifying them as phagocytes of alien bacteria and an important factor in resistance to disease and infection; studied aging and death; succeeded L. PASTEUR as dir. of the Pasteur Inst.; awarded Nobel Prize in physiology or medicine (with P. EHRLICH), 1908.

**MONIZ, ANTÓNIO,** Nov. 29, 1874 (Avanca, Portugal)– Dec. 13, 1955. Portuguese surgeon, statesman. Foreign min. of Portugal, 1917–19; invented prefrontal lobotomy for hopelessly disturbed mental patients, thus beginning the field of psychosurgery, 1935; awarded Nobel Prize in physiology or medicine (with W. R. Hess), 1949.

**MORGAGNI, GIOVANNI BATTISTA,** Feb. 25, 1682 (Forlì, Italy)–Dec. 5, 1771. Italian anatomist. The father of medical pathology; from early work on anatomy and diseases of the ear (1704), went on to seek the causes of disease through autopsies. *On the Seats and Causes of Diseases,* 1761.

**MOTTELSON, BEN ROY,** July 9, 1926 (Chicago, Ill.). Danish physicist. With A. BOHR, discovered relationship of motion of parts of the nucleus to motion of the whole, 1950–53; awarded Nobel Prize in physics (with J. RAINWATER and A. Bohr), 1975.

**MULLER, K(arl) ALEX,** Apr. 20, 1927 (Basel, Switz.). Swiss physicist. Noted for pioneering work in superconductivity; awarded Nobel Prize in physics (shared with J. BEDNORZ), 1987.

**MÜLLER, PAUL,** Jan. 12, 1899 (Olten, Switzerland)–Oct. 12, 1965. Swiss chemist. Discovered the value of DDT as an insecticide (1939) in time to stop two threatening typhus epidemics (Naples, 1944; Japan, 1945); awarded Nobel Prize in physiology or medicine, 1948.

**OERSTED, HANS CHRISTIAN,** Aug. 14, 1777 (Rudkøping, Denmark) Mar. 9, 1851. Danish physicist. First to demonstrate a connection between electricity and magnetism, 1819; first to make metallic aluminum, 1825.

**PARACELSUS** (born Theophrastus Phillipus Aureolus Bombastus von Hohenheim), May 1, 1493 (Einsiedln, Switzerland)–Sept. 24, 1541. Swiss physician. His work marks the transition from alchemy to chemistry; introduced a questioning, experimental approach to medicine.

**PAVLOV, IVAN,** Sept. 26, 1849 (Ryazan, Russia) –Feb. 27, 1936. Russian physiologist. Made basic discoveries in the way autonomic nerves control the digestive process, 1889; did basic studies of the nature and development of conditional reflexes, early 1890s; awarded Nobel Prize in physiology or medicine, 1904.

**PICCARD, AUGUSTE,** Jan. 28, 1884 (Basel, Switz.)– Mar. 24, 1962. Swiss physicist. Developed enclosed balloon gondolas to carry men into the stratosphere, reaching a height of 55,500 ft., 1932; invented the bathyscaphe to carry men to ocean depths, 1946; one of his bathyscaphes reached 35,800 ft., 1960.

**PREGL, FRITZ,** Sept. 3, 1869 (Laibach, Austria [now Ljubljana, Yugo.])–Dec. 13, 1930. Austrian chemist. The father of microchemistry; developed methods for performing chemical analysis of substances in quantities of only 3 mg; awarded Nobel Prize in chemistry, 1923.

**PROKHOROV, ALEKSANDR,** July 11, 1916 (Atherton, Queensland, Australia). Soviet physicist. Made basic contributions to the theories that led to the development of the maser and the laser, 1955; awarded Nobel Prize in physics (with N. G. BASOV and C. H. TOWNES), 1964.

**PTOLEMY** (Claudius Ptolemaeus), c.75 (Alexandria, Egypt)–? Greek or Egyptian astronomer. Using the system of HIPPARCHUS, established the geocentric view of the universe; named 48 constellations; preserved some ancient trigonometry; his views dominated astronomy for 1,400 years. *Megale mathematica syntaxis (Almagest* in Arabic).

**PURKINJE** (or Purkyne), **JAN EVANGELISTA,** Dec. 17, 1787 (Libochovice, Bohemia [now Czech.]) –July 28, 1869. Czech physiologist. An expert in microscopy, for which he devised several improvements in technique; made many basic discoveries in histology, brain and heart function, and other areas; founded German system of lab training for university students; discovered Purkinje nerve cells in the brain (1837) and the Purkinje nerve fibers in the heart (1839); coined the word *protoplasm,* 1839; remembered in Czechoslovakia more for his poetry, his translations of J. GOETHE and F. SCHILLER, and his nationalism.

**PYTHEAS,** fl. c.300 B.C. (Massalia [now Marseilles, Fr.]). Greek explorer, astronomer. Explored and described the western and northern coasts of Europe and the eastern coast of England; discovered that the Pole Star is not precisely at the pole; the first to attribute tidal motion to the moon's influence.

**RAMAN, SIR CHANDRASEKHARA V.,** Nov. 7, 1888 (Trichinopoly, Madras, India)–Nov. 21, 1970. Indian physicist. Proved that visible light changed wavelengths when scattered, thus adding to the particle theory of light, 1928; the primary founder of higher education in science in India; knighted, 1929; awarded Nobel Prize in physics, 1930.

**RAMÓN Y CAJAL, SANTIAGO,** May 1, 1852 (Petilla de Aragón, Spain)–Oct. 18, 1934. Spanish histologist. His basic studies of the nervous system revealed the connection between the cells in the brain and the spinal cord, 1889; worked out the structure of the retina; established the neuron theory of the brain; awarded Nobel Prize in physiology or medicine (with C. GOLGI), 1906.

**REICHSTEIN, TADEUSZ,** July 20, 1897 (Wtoctawek, Poland). Swiss chemist. A synthesizer of vitamin C, 1933; independently of E. C. KENDALL, isolated many corticoid compounds, 1930s; awarded Nobel Prize in physiology or medicine (with Kendall and P.S. HENCH), 1950; F.R.S., 1952.

**RICCI** (-Curbastro), **GREGORIO,** Jan. 12, 1853 (Lugo, It.)–Aug. 6, 1925. Italian mathematician. Primary developer of tensor analysis (Absolute differential calculus), and indispendable tool for EINSTEIN's formulation of the theory of general relativity.

**ROHRER, HEINRICH,** June 6, 1933 (Switz.). Swiss physicist. Noted for pioneering work in developing the scanning tunneling microscope; awarded Nobel Prize in physics (shared with G. BINNIG and E. RUSKA), 1986.

**RUBBIA, CARLO,** Mar. 31, 1934 (Gorizia, It.). Italian physicist. Discovered three sub-atomic particles, considered a crucial step in developing a single theory to account for all natural forces; awarded Nobel Prize in physics (shared with S. VAN DER MEER), 1984.

**SALAM, ABDUS,** Jan. 29, 1926 (Jhang, Pak.). Pakistani physicist. Noted for his work toward the discovery of a unified field theory; awarded Nobel Prize in physics (shared with S. WEINBERG and S. GLASHOW), 1979.

**SAMUELSSON, BENGT,** May 21, 1934 (Halmstad, Swed.). Swedish medical chemist. Noted for discoveries in controlling prostaglandins, a natural substance implicated in a wide range of human and animal illnesses; awarded Nobel Prize in medicine or physiology (shared with J. VANE and K. S. BERGSTROM), 1982.

**SCHEELE, KARL WILHELM,** Dec. 9, 1742 (Stralsund, Pomerania [now Ger.])–May 21, 1786. Swedish chemist. Discovered a wide variety of compounds and played a role in the discovery of several elements, including oxygen, which he discovered (1772)

before J. PRIESTLEY but failed to announce; the mineral scheelite is named after him.

**SCHIAPARELLI, GIOVANNI VIRGINIO,** Mar. 14, 1835 (Savigliano, Piedmont, Italy)–July 4, 1910. Italian astronomer. The "discoverer" of Mars's "canals," an illusion of a system of straight lines that gave rise to the speculation about life on the planets, 1881.

**SCHRÖDINGER, ERWIN,** Aug. 12, 1887 (Vienna, Austria)–Jan. 4, 1961. Austrian physicist. His work in wave mechanics put quantum theory on a firm mathematical base and clarified the modern view of atomic structure; awarded Nobel Prize in physics (with P. DIRAC), 1933.

**SEMENOV, NIKOLAY,** Apr. 15, 1896 (Saratov, Rus.)–Sept. 28, 1986. Soviet physical chemist. In basic work on chemical chain reactions and thermal explosions, developed the theory of branched chain reactions, 1920s; awarded Nobel Prize in chemistry (with C. N. HINSHELWOOD), 1956; F.R.S., 1958.

**SIEGBAHN, KAI,** Apr. 20, 1918 (Lund, Sweden). Swedish physicist. Developed technologies with lasers and other devices that can seek out the innermost secrets of complex forms of matter; awarded Nobel Prize in physics, 1981.

**SIEGBAHN, KARL M.G.,** Dec. 3, 1886 (Örebro, Sweden)–Sept. 30, 1978. Swedish physicist. The major contributor to the development of X-ray spectroscopy, from 1916; the first to demonstrate X-ray refraction; awarded Nobel Prize in physics, 1924.

**SPALLANZANI, LAZZARO,** Jan. 12, 1729 (Modena, Italy)–Feb. 11, 1799. Italian physiologist. Did basic experiments to disprove ideas of spontaneous generation of life, 1767–68; the first successfully to try artificial insemination, 1785; experimented with tissue regeneration and transplantation, 1767–68; F.R.S., 1768.

**STEVINUS, SIMON** (born Simon Stevin), 1548 (Bruges, Flanders [now Belg.])–1620. Flemish mathematician. Established the use of decimal fractions, 1585; first to demonstrate that all bodies fall at the same rate regardless of weight, 1586; founded modern science of hydrostatics, 1586.

**SVEDBERG, THEODOR H. E.,** Aug. 30, 1884 (Fleräng, Valbo, nr. Gävle, Sweden)–Feb. 26, 1971. Swedish chemist. Developed the untracentrifuge to separate colloids and large molecules, particularly proteins, 1923; developed electrophonetic methods to separate proteins; awarded Nobel Prize in chemistry, 1926.

**SZENT-GYÖRGYI** (von Nagryapolt), **ALBERT,** Sept. 16, 1893 (Budapest, Hung.)–Oct. 22, 1986. Hungarian–U.S. biochemist. First to isolate vitamin C, although he failed to identify it as such, c.1928; did basic research in oxidation of nutrients by cells (1930s) and the chemical processes of muscle contraction (1940s); awarded Nobel Prize in physiology or medicine, 1937.

**TAMM, IGOR,** July 8, 1895 (Vladivostok, Rus.)–Apr. 12, 1971. Soviet physicist. With I. M. FRANK, found the explanation for Cherenkov radiation,

1937; suggested the "pinch effect" for magnetic containment of plasma in fusion reactions; awarded Nobel Prize in physics (with Frank and P.A. CHERENKOV), 1958.

TAUBE, HENRY, Nov. 30, 1915 (Neudorf, Sask). Canadian chemist. Discovered how electrons transfer between molecules in chemical reactions; awarded Nobel Prize in chemistry, 1983.

TOMONAGA, SIN-ITIRO, Mar. 31, 1906 (Tokyo, Jap.)–July 8, 1979. Japanese physicist. Worked out the basic theory of quantum electrodynamics, making it consistent with A. EINSTEIN's special theory of relativity, independently of J.S. SCHWINGER and R.P. FEYNMAN; awarded Nobel Prize in physics (with Schwinger and Feynman), 1965.

TONEGAWA, SUSUMU, Sept. 5, 1939 (Nagoya, Jap.). Japanese molecular biologist. Discovered how the body can suddenly marshal its immunological defenses against millions of different disease agents it has never previously encountered; awarded Nobel Prize in physiology or medicine, 1987.

TORRICELLI, EVANGELISTA, Oct. 15, 1608 (Faenza, Romagna, Italy)–Oct. 25, 1647. Italian physicist, mathematician. GALILEO's secretary. Invented the barometer and created the first man-made sustained vacuum, 1643; his work in geometry contributed to the development of integral calculus, 1644.

TSAI LUN, c.50 (China)–c.118. Chinese court official. Invented paper, which he made from bamboo pulp, c.105.

TSVETT, MIKHAIL, May 14, 1872 (Asti, Italy)–June 26, 1919. Russian botanist. Invented chromatography (1906), a technique of separating fine substances in the laboratory (later reinvented by R. Willstätter).

TSIOLKOVSKY, KONSTANTIN, Sept. 17, 1857 (Izhevskoye, Russia)–Sept. 19, 1935. Soviet physicist. Father of the Soviet space effort; a pioneer in rocket theory, from 1895.

VAN DER MEER, SIMON, Nov. 24, 1925 (The Hague, Neth.). Dutch physicist. Discovered three sub-atomic particles, considered a crucial step in developing a single theory to account for all natu-

ral forces; awarded Nobel Prize in physics (shared with C. RUBBIA), 1984.

VAN DER WAALS, JOHANNES D., Nov. 23, 1837 (Leiden, Neth.)–Mar. 9, 1923. Dutch physicist. Worked out the mathematics of the acutal behavior of gases and liquids under varying temperatures and pressures, making possible modern low-temperature physics studies, 1881; awarded Nobel Prize in physics, 1910.

VAN'T HOFF, JACOBUS H., Aug. 30, 1852 (Rotterdam, Neth.)–Mar. 1, 1911. Dutch physical chemist. Explained optical activity and asymmetry of organic compounds in solution by introducing the three-dimensional view of chemical bonds; did basic research on the behavior of materials in solutions, 1886; awarded the first Nobel Prize in chemistry, 1901.

VESALIUS, ANDREAS, Dec. 31, 1514 (Brussels, Flanders [now Belg.])–Oct. 15, 1564. Flemish anatomist. Father of modern anatomy; wrote the first accurate text on human anatomy, with superb illustrations, De humani corporis fabrica libri septem, 1543.

VOLTA, ALESSANDRO GIUSEPPE ANTONIO ANASTASIO, CONTE, Feb. 18, 1745 (Como, It.)–Mar. 5, 1827. Italian physicist. Invented the (voltaic) pile) first electric battery, 1800; developed the basic elements for the condenser, 1775; made a count by NAPOLEON, 1801.

YUKAWA, HIDEKI, Jan. 23, 1907 (Tokyo, Jap.)–Sept. 8, 1981. Japanese physicist. Predicted the existence of mesons (1935) and the process of "K capture" (1936); awarded Nobel Prize in physics, 1949.

ZEEMAN, PIETER, May 25, 1865 (Zonnemaire, Zeeland, Netherlands)–Oct. 9, 1943. Dutch physicist. Discovered the Zeeman effect, by which the spectral lines of a light source in a strong magnetic field are split into three components, 1896; F.R.S., 1921; awarded Nobel Prize in physics (with H.A. LORENTZ), 1902.

ZWICKY, FRITZ, Feb. 14, 1898 (Varna, Bulgaria)–Feb. 8, 1974. Swiss astronomer. Made basic contributions to the understanding of supernovas; discovered 18 supernovas, 1937–41; invented many essential elements of earliest jet engines, 1943–49.

# Explorers

U.S. EXPLORERS

**ALDRIN, EDWIN E., JR.** ("Buzz"), Jan. 20, 1930 (Montclair, N.J.). U.S. astronaut. Participated in *Gemini 12* flight (1966) and *Apollo 11* flight (1969); the second man to set foot on the moon, 1969.

**ANDREWS, ROY CHAPMAN,** Jan. 26, 1884 (Beloit, Wisc.)–Mar. 11, 1960. U.S. naturalist, explorer, author. Led scientific expeditions to Alaska (1909), northern Korea (1911–12), Tibet, southwestern China, and Burma (1916–17), northern China and Outer Mongolia (1919). In Central Asia, discovered first known dinosaur eggs, a skull, and other parts of the Baluchitherium, the largest known land animal, along with other evidence of prehistoric human life; director, American Museum of Natural History, 1935–42.

**ARMSTRONG, NEIL A.,** Aug. 5, 1930 (Wapakonea, Ohio). U.S. astronaut. Served as command pilot of *Gemini 8*, 1966; on *Apollo 11* mission, became the first man to step on the moon, stating, "That's one small step for a man, one giant leap for mankind," 1969.

**AUSTIN, STEPHEN,** Nov. 3, 1793 (Austinville, Va.)–Dec. 27, 1836. U.S. colonizer, public official. Founded English-speaking settlements in Texas in the 1830s; a leader in the fight for Texas independence from Mexico.

**BALCHEN, BERNT,** Oct. 23, 1899 (Tveit, Nor.) –Oct. 17, 1973. Norwegian-U.S. aviator. Piloted the first flight over the South Pole, Nov. 29, 1929; chief pilot for RICHARD BYRD (1928–30) and LINCOLN ELLSWORTH (1933–35) polar expeditions; U.S. Air Force officer in WW II.

**BARTLETT, ROBERT ABRAM,** Aug. 15, 1875 (Brigus, Nfld.)–Apr. 28, 1946. Canadian-U.S. explorer. Commanded ROBERT PEARY's expedition ship, 1905–09; commanded *Karluk*, which was crushed by ice near Wrangle I., reached Siberia, 1914; headed expeditions to Greenland, Baffin I., and Labrador, 1926–34.

**BECKNELL, WILLIAM,** c.1796 (Amherst Co., Va.) –Apr. 30, 1865. U.S. fur trader and explorer. Blazed the Santa Fe Trail from Franklin, Mo., to Santa Fe, N.M. 1821.

**BINGHAM, HIRAM,** Nov. 19, 1875 (Honolulu, Haw.)–June 6, 1956. U.S. explorer. On his explorations in South America early in this century, discovered the Inca cities of Vitcos and Machu Picchu; later he became governor of Connecticut and resigned the post to serve in the United States Senate. *Journal of an Expedition Across Venezuela and Colombia,* 1909; *Across South America,* 1911; *Lost City of the Incas,* 1948.

**BORMAN, FRANK,** Mar. 14, 1928 (Gary, Ind.). U.S. astronaut, airline executive. Made *Gemini 7* flight, 1965; made *Apollo 8* flight, the first manned flight around the moon, 1968; pres. and chief executive officer (1975–76), and chairman of the board (1976–86), Eastern Airlines; vice-chairman and director, Texas Air Corp., 1986–   .

**BYRD, RICHARD E.,** Oct. 25, 1888 (Winchester, Va.)–Mar. 11, 1957. U.S. admiral, aviator, explorer. Made first flight over the North Pole (1926) and over the South Pole (1929); conducted five Antarctic exploration expeditions, pioneering the aerial mapping and scientific investigation of the continent, 1928–56.

**CARPENTER, MALCOLM SCOTT,** May 1, 1925 (Boulder, Col.). U.S. astronaut, oceanographer. Completed three-orbit space flight mission of *Aurora 7,* Project Mercury, 1962.

**CARSON, KIT** (born Christopher Carson), Dec. 24, 1809 (Madison Co., Ky.)–May 23, 1868. U.S. frontiersman, soldier, Indian agent. Guided JOHN C. FREMONT's expeditions into Wyoming and California, 1842–46; U.S. scout in the Mexican War, 1846–48; Indian agent at Taos, N.M., 1853–60; Union Army officer in the Civil War.

**CHISHOLM, JESSE,** 1806–c.1868. U.S. frontiersman. Gave his name to the Chisholm Trail which ran from the Mexican border to Abilene, Kan., and was used for cattle drives from 1867 to the 1880s.

**CLARK, WILLIAM,** Aug. 1, 1770 (Caroline Co., Va.)–Sept. 1, 1838. U.S. frontiersman, explorer, mapmaker. With MERIWETHER LEWIS, led an expedition to the Pacific Northwest, giving the first comprehensive description of that vast area, 1804–06.

COCHRAN, JACQUELINE, c.1910 (Pensacola, Fla.) –Aug. 9, 1980. U.S. aviator, cosmetics executive. Piloted bomber to England, 1941; organized Women's Air Force Service Pilots, 1943; first woman to exceed the speed of sound, 1953; set numerous world speed records; owned her own cosmetics firm, 1935–63.

CODY, WILLIAM F. ("Buffalo Bill"), Feb. 26, 1846 (Scott Co., Ia.)–Jan. 10, 1917. U.S. buffalo hunter, army scout, Indian fighter, showman. His exploits were fictionalized by dime novelists, including NED BUNTLINE; starred as himself in Buntline's drama, *Scouts of the Prairies*, 1872; organized his own Wild West Exhibitions, featuring fancy shooting, a buffalo hunt, ANNIE OAKLEY, and Chief SITTING BULL, from 1883.

COLLINS, MICHAEL, Oct. 31, 1930 (Rome, It.). U.S. astronaut. Copiloted *Gemini 10* space flight, 1966; on *Apollo 11* flight, piloted command module during the first moon landing, 1969.

CONRAD, CHARLES, JR., June 2, 1930 (Philadelphia, Pa.). U.S. astronaut. Copiloted *Gemini 5* space flight, 1962; command pilot of *Gemini 11* space flight, 1966; commander of *Apollo 12* moon flight, 1969.

COOK, FREDERICK, A., June 10, 1865 (Callicoon Depot, N.Y.)–Aug. 5, 1940, U.S. explorer. Claimed that he had discovered the North Pole in April, 1908, but ROBERT E. PEARY disputed the claim in 1909; his claim that he had reached the summit of Mount McKinley, Alaska, was also disputed.

COOPER, L. GORDON, JR., Mar. 6, 1927 (Shawnee, Okla.). U.S. astronaut. Command pilot of *Gemini 5* space flight, 1965.

CROCKETT, DAVEY (born David Crockett), Aug. 17, 1786 (Limestone, Tenn.)–Mar. 6, 1836. U.S. frontiersman, politician. One of the legendary heroes of frontier America. Fought in Creek War (1813–14) under ANDREW JACKSON; elected to Tennessee leg., 1821 and 1823; U.S. rep. (D, Tenn.), 1827–31 and 1833–35; joined Texas independence forces and was killed at the Alamo. *Autobiography* (with Thomas Chilton), 1834.

DU SABLE, JEAN BAPTISTE POINT (also de Sable, de Saible, Sable, Point du Sable), c.1745 (prob. Sainte-Domingue [now Haiti])–Aug. 28, 1818. U.S. pioneer. Called the "Father of Chicago," on whose site he built the first house and opened the first trading post, in the 1770s.

EARHART, AMELIA, July 24, 1898 (Atchison, Kan.)–disappeared July 2, 1937. U.S. aviatrix. The first woman to make a solo flight across the Atlantic, 1932; made solo flight from Hawaii to California, 1935; disappeared in the South Pacific while attempting to fly around the world, 1937.

ELLSWORTH, LINCOLN, May 12, 1880 (Chicago, Ill.)–May 26, 1951. U.S. polar explorer, scientist. Led first trans-Arctic (1926) and trans-Antarctic (1935) air crossings; with UMBERTO NOBILE, made first crossing of the Polar Basin, a 3,393-mi. journey from Spitsbergen to Alaska, 1926; made an 800-mile canoe trip through central Labrador, 1931; claimed some 300,000 sq. mi. of Antarctic terrain for the U.S.

FREMONT, JOHN C., Jan. 21, 1813 (Savannah, Ga.)–July 13, 1890. U.S. explorer, public official, Union general, mapmaker. Led three expeditions into the Far West, 1842–46; mapped out the Oregon Trail and the South Pass in the Rockies, helping make possible the western expansion of the mid-19th cent.; first Republican presidential candidate, 1856; territorial governor of Arizona, 1878–83.

GIST, CHRISTOPHER, c.1706 (Maryland)–c.1759. U.S. explorer, scout. The first white American to explore the Ohio Valley, 1750; rescued GEORGE WASHINGTON from drowning, 1753; guided EDWARD BRADDOCK's ill-fated expedition against Ft. Duquesne, 1755.

GLENN, JOHN H., JR., July 18, 1921 (Cambridge, Ohio). U.S. astronaut, politician. The first American to orbit the Earth, Feb. 20, 1962; U.S. senator (D, Ohio), 1975– .

GRAY, ROBERT, May 10, 1755 (Tiverton, R.I.)–1806. U.S. sailor, explorer. Captained the first U.S. ship to circumnavigate the world, 1787–90; discovered the Columbia R. in Oregon, 1792.

GREELY, ADOLPHUS W., Mar. 27, 1844 (Newburyport, Mass.)–Oct. 20, 1935. U.S. explorer, soldier. Headed expedition to establish Arctic Meteorological Station 1881; established Ft. Conger on Ellesmere Isl.; reached most northerly point yet, and explored Ellesmere and northern Greenland.

GRISSOM, VIRGIL I. ("Gus"), Apr. 3, 1926 (Mitchell, Ind.)–Jan. 27, 1967. U.S. astronaut. The third man to enter space, 1961; the first man to return to space, 1965; killed during a simulation of the *Apollo 1* launching, 1967.

HENSON, MATTHEW A., 1866 (Charles Co., Md.)–Mar. 9, 1955. U.S. explorer who accompanied Adm. PEARY on all of his polar expeditions; placed U.S. flag at the North Pole, 1909.

LEWIS, MERIWETHER, Aug. 18, 1774 (Albemarle Co., Va.)–Oct. 11, 1809. U.S. explorer. With WILLIAM CLARK, led expedition into the Pacific Northwest, 1804–06; private secy. to Pres. THOMAS JEFFERSON, 1801–03; the first gov. of the Louisiana Territory, 1807–09.

LINDBERGH, CHARLES A. ("The Lone Eagle"), Feb. 4, 1902 (Detroit, Mich.)–Aug. 26, 1974. U.S. aviator. Made the first solo nonstop trans-Atlantic flight, New York–Paris, 1927; his infant son kidnapped and murdered, 1932; spokesman for isolationism, 1939–41; flew combat missions in the Pacific during WW II; awarded Pulitzer Prize for his biography, *The Spirit of St. Louis*, 1953.

LOVELL, JAMES A., JR., Mar. 25, 1928 (Cleveland, Ohio). U.S. astronaut. Participated in the following space flights: *Gemini 7*, 1965; *Gemini 12*, 1966; *Apollo 8*, the first flight around the moon, 1968; *Apollo 13*, 1970.

MACMILLAN, DONALD B., Nov. 10, 1874 (Provincetown, Mass.)–Sept. 7, 1970. U.S. Arctic explorer. Went with ROBERT PEARY on Arctic expedition, 1908–09; led numerous expeditions to Arctic lands, 1913–37.

**PALMER, NATHANIEL BROWN,** Aug. 8, 1799 (Stonington, Conn.)–June 21, 1877. U.S. explorer, sea captain. Sighted Palmer Peninsula (named in his honor), becoming the first man to lay eyes on the Antarctic continent, 1820; aided in the discovery of the South Orkney Is., 1822.

**PEARY, ROBERT E.,** May 6, 1856 (Cresson, Pa.) –Feb. 20, 1920. U.S. Arctic explorer, admiral. Led the first expedition to reach the North Pole (1909), though his claim is still disputed by some; explored the Greenland ice cap several times.

**PIKE, ZEBULON MONTGOMERY,** Jan. 5, 1779 (Lamberton, N.J. )–Apr. 27, 1813. U.S. Army officer, explorer. Led wilderness expedition into the northern portions of the Louisiana Purchase to seek Mississippi R. headwaters, 1805–06; led journey through Southwest, sighting Pike's Peak (named after him), 1806–07; served in War of 1812, killed during attack on York (now Toronto), Can., 1813.

**POST, WILEY,** Nov. 22, 1899 (Grand Saline, Tex.)– Aug. 15, 1935. U.S. aviator. Made the first solo around-the-world flight, proving the value of navigation instruments, including the automatic pilot, July 15–22, 1933; killed, with WILL ROGERS, in a plane crash in Alaska, 1935.

**RIDE, SALLY,** May 26, 1951 (Los Angeles, Cal.). U.S. Astronaut. On-orbit capsule communicator in STS-2 and STS-3 missions, 1983; Mission specialist STS-7 mission, 1983.

**SACAGAWEA** or **SACAJAWEA** ("Bird Woman"), c.1787 (Montana or Idaho)–Dec. 12, 1812 or Apr. 9, 1884. Shoshone Indian guide. Interpreted for LEWIS and CLARK on their expedition to the Pacific Northwest, 1804–06; death date in doubt because an old woman claiming to be Sacagawea turned up in 1875 and lived until 1884.

**SCHIRRA, WALTER M., JR.,** Mar. 12, 1923 (Hackensack, N.J.). U.S. astronaut. Only one of original seven astronauts to fly all three manned spacecraft (Mercury, Gemini, and Apollo); manned Mercury *Sigma 7* space flight, 1962; commanded *Gemini 6* (1965) and *Apollo 7* (1968) space flights.

**SHEPARD, ALAN B., JR.,** Nov. 18, 1923 (East Derry, N.H.). U.S. astronaut. One of the original seven astronauts, the first to travel in space, suborbital flight, May 5, 1961; commanded *Apollo 14* space flight, 1971.

**SMITH, JEDEDIAH STRONG,** Jan. 6, 1799 (Jericho, now Bainbridge, N.Y.)–May 27, 1831. U.S. explorer and fur trader, a leading explorer of the West and Pacific Northwest; opened South Pass through the Rocky Mts., 1824; crossed Mojave Desert to California, then made first west-to-east

crossing over the Sierra Nevadas and Great Salt Desert to Salt Lake, 1826; opened overland trail from Colorado Riv. to California, 1828.

**STAFFORD, THOMAS P.,** Sept. 17, 1930 (Weatherford, Okla.). U.S. astronaut. Participated in the following space flights: *Gemini 6* (1965), *Gemini 9* (1966), and *Apollo 10* (1969); commanded U.S. flight in Apollo-Soyuz test, 1975.

**STEFANSSON, VILHJALMUR,** Nov. 3, 1879 (Arnes, Man., Can.)–Aug. 26, 1962. Canadian-U.S. explorer, ethnologist. Explored vast areas of the Canadian Arctic, 1908–12; after adapting himself to the Eskimo way of life, led expedition that discovered new lands in the Arctic archipelago and destroyed many myths about the inhospitality of the Far North, 1913–16. *My Life with the Eskimos*, 1913; *The Friendly Arctic*, 1921.

**SUTTER, JOHN AUGUSTUS,** Feb. 15, 1803 (Kandern, Baden, Ger.)–June 18, 1880. U.S. pioneer. Colonized California, establishing settlement called Neuva Helvetia on the site of present-day Sacramento, 1839; discovery of gold on his land precipitated the California gold rush, 1848.

**WHITMAN, MARCUS,** Sept. 4, 1802 (Rushville, N.Y.)–Nov. 29, 1847. U.S. Congregational missionary, pioneer, physician. A missionary to the Indians of Washington and Oregon and prominent pioneer in opening up the Pacific Northwest to settlement; along with wife and children, massacred by the Cayuse Indians, which led to early passage of a bill to organize the Oregon Territory (1848).

**WILKES, CHARLES,** Apr. 3, 1798 (New York, N.Y. )–Feb. 8, 1877. U.S. naval officer, explorer. Led round-the-world expedition that explored Antarctic area now known as Wilkes Land, 1838–42; as a Union Navy officer in the Civil War, stopped a British ship, precipitating the so-called *Trent* Affair, 1861.

**WINNEMUCCA, SARAH,** c.1844 (Humboldt Sink, Nev.)–Oct. 16, 1891. American Indian scout. A member of the Paiute tribe, she voluntarily scouted more than 100 miles of hostile territory for the U.S. Army, 1878; lectured across the U.S., collecting thousands of signatures requesting the govt. to give land to the Paiutes. *Life Among the Paiutes; Their Wrongs and Claims*, 1883.

**YEAGER, CHARLES** ("Chuck"), Feb. 13, 1923 (Myra, W. Va.). U.S. brigadier general and aviator. The first person to break the sound barrier on Oct. 14, 1947.

**YOUNG, JOHN W.,** Sept. 24, 1930 (San Francisco, Calif.). U.S. astronaut. Participated in the following space flights: *Gemini 3* (1965), *Gemini 10* (1966), *Apollo 10* (1969), and *Apollo 16* (1972); commanded first space shuttle, *Columbia* (1981).

## FOREIGN EXPLORERS

**ADAMS, WILLIAM,** 1564 (Gillingham, Kent, England)–May 16, 1620. English navigator, adventurer. As the first Englishman in Japan (1600) made a nobleman by the shogun (ruler); prototype

for the character Blackthorn in JAMES CLAVELL's novel *Shogun* (1975).

**AMUNDSEN, ROALD** (Engelbregt Gravning), July 16, 1872 (Borge, Nor.)–June 1928. Norwegian polar explorer. Commanded the first ship to complete the Northwest Passage, east to west, 1903–06; the first man to reach the South Pole, 1911; one of the first to cross the Arctic by dirigible, 1926; disappeared during attempted rescue of NOBILE.

**BAFFIN, WILLIAM,** c.1584 (England)–Jan. 23, 1622. British navigator. Searched for the Northwest Passage and gave his name to Baffin I. and Baffin Bay.

**BAKER, SIR SAMUEL WHITE,** June 8, 1821 (London, Eng.)–Dec. 30, 1893. British explorer. Helped locate the sources of the Nile, 1861–64; knighted, 1866.

**BALBOA, VASCO NÚÑEZ DE,** c.1475 (Jerez de los Caballeros, Extremadura Prov., Sp.)–Jan. 1519. Spanish conquistador, explorer. The first European to sight the Pacific Ocean, Sept. 1513.

**BARENTS, WILLEM,** c.1550 (Terschelling, Neth.) –June 20, 1597. Dutch navigator. In search of the Northwest Passage, made three voyages, 1594–97, into what would later be called the Barents Sea.

**BERING, VITUS JONASSEN,**1681 (Horsens, Den.)– Dec. 19, 1741. Danish navigator. Employed by Russia to discover if N. America and Asia were connected (1725–41), he discovered the Bering Sea and Bering Strait.

**BIENVILLE, SIEUR DE** (real name, Jean Baptiste le Moyne), Feb. 23, 1680 (Ville-Marie [now Montreal], Quebec, Canada)–March 7, 1768. French-Canadian explorer, prominent in the settlement of the province of Louisiana; served as governor of the province four times; also founded New Orleans, Mobile, and Biloxi.

**BOUGAINVILLE, LOUIS ANTOINE DE,** Nov. 11, 1729 (Paris, Fr.)– Apr. 31, 1811. French navigator. Headed the first French naval force to circumnavigate the globe, 1766–69; fought in the latter part of the French and Indian wars; bougainvillea, a tropical flowering vine, named after him Voyage autour du monde, 1771.

**BRULE, ETIENNE,** c.1592 (Champigny-sur-Marne, Fr.) c.1632. French explorer. Explored the Great Lakes, 1610–26; interpreted Indian languages for SAMUEL DE CHAMPLAIN; betrayed the French to the British, leading to the capture of Quebec, 1629.

**BURTON, SIR RICHARD FRANCIS,** Mar. 19, 1821 (Torquay, Devon, Eng.)–Oct. 20, 1890. British scholar, explorer. The first European to discover Lake Tanganyika, 1858; the first European to enter the forbidden city of Harar, in present-day Ethiopia, 1854; wrote 43 volumes on his explorations and translated some 30 volumes of Eastern writings, including *The Book of The Thousand Nights and One Night* (10 vols, 1885–88).

**CABEZA DE VACA, ALVAR NÚÑEZ,** c.1490 (Extremadura Prov., Sp.)–c.1560. Spanish explorer. Spent eight years in the gulf region of present-day Texas, 1528–36; his accounts of the legendary Seven Golden Cities of Cibola inspired extensive exploration of U.S. South and Southwest by HERNANDO DE SOTO and FRANCISCO DE CORONADO.

**CABOT, JOHN,** c.1450 (Genoa, It.)–c.1499. Italian navigator, explorer. Employed by the British, he reached North America, laying the groundwork for British claim to Canada, 1497; sailed again for N. America, 1498; details of last voyage are obscure— he may have died at sea or returned to England. (Father of S. CABOT.)

**CABOT, SEBASTIAN,** c.1482 (Venice, It.)–1557. Italian explorer, cartographer. Served England and Spain; his efforts to find a Northwest Passage led to the development of trade between England and Russia. (Son of J. CABOT.)

**CABRAL, PEDRO ALVAREZ,** c.1467 (Belmonte, Port.)–1520. Portuguese navigator. Generally credited with the discovery of Brazil, 1500.

**CABRILLO, JUAN RODRIGUEZ,** ?(Portugal?)– Jan 3, 1543. Portuguese soldier-explorer in the employ of Spain. Discovered California, entering San Diego Bay, 1542.

**CADILLAC, ANTOINE DE LA MOTHE, SIEUR DE,** Mar. 5, 1658 (Les Laumets, Fr.)–Oct. 15, 1730. French fur trader and explorer. Founded Detroit, 1701; gov. of Louisiana, 1710–16.

**CANO, JUAN SEBASTIAN DEL,** c.1460 (Guetaria, Sp.)–Aug. 4, 1526. Spanish navigator. Sailed with FERDINAND MAGELLAN, after whose death Cano commanded the first expedition to circumnavigate the globe, 1522.

**CARTIER, JACQUES,** 1491 (St. Malo, Fr.)–Sept. 1, 1557. French explorer. His explorations (1534–42) of the North American coast and St. Lawrence R. laid the basis for later French claims to Canada, although his pessimistic reports discouraged French exploration in North America for over half a century.

**CHAMPLAIN, SAMUEL DE,** c.1567 (Brouage, Fr.) –Dec. 25, 1635. French explorer. Mapped New England coast as far as Cape Cod, 1605–07; founded Quebec, the first white settlement in New France, 1608; discovered Lake Champlain, 1609; surrendered Quebec to the British, 1629.

**COLUMBUS, CHRISTOPHER,** c.1451 (Genoa, It.) May 20, 1506. Italian explorer, navigator. In the service of Spain, made the first historically verifiable European discovery of the New World, sighting San Salvador on Oct. 12, 1492; discovered South America (1498) and Central America (1502); his four voyages to the New World opened the way for European exploration and colonization and changed the course of history.

**COOK, JAMES,** Oct. 27, 1728 (Marton-in-Cleveland, Yorks., Eng.)–Feb. 14, 1779. British navigator. Led scientific voyage to Tahiti, 1768–71; surveyed coast of New Zealand, charted eastern coast of Australia, naming it New South Wales, and claimed it for England, 1770; mapped much of southern hemisphere, sailing farther south than anyone before him, 1772–75; discovered Sandwich (Hawaiian) Is., 1778.

**CORONADO, FRANCISCO VÁSQUEZ DE,** c.1510 (Salamanca, Sp.)–Sept. 22, 1554. Spanish explorer. Explored the U.S. Southwest, 1540–42; he or his lieutenants discovered many noted physical landmarks, including the Grand Canyon.

**CORTES, HERNAN** (or Hernando Cortez), 1485 (Medellin, Sp.)–Dec. 2, 1547. Spanish conquistador. Aided in conquest of Cuba, 1511; conquered Aztec Empire in Mexico, 1518–21.

COUSTEAU, JACQUES, June 11, 1910 (Sainte-Andre-de-Cubzac, Fr.). French explorer of the oceans, filmmaker, author. Famed for extensive undersea investigations. Invented the aqualung, making possible the sport of scuba diving, 1943; designed underwater structures that house men for prolonged periods of time; commanded research ships, *Calypso* and *Alcyone*. Books: *The Silent World*, 1953; *The Living Sea*, 1963; *Life and Death in a Coral Sea*, 1971. Films: *World Without Sun*, 1964; *Desert Whales*, 1970.

DAMPIER, WILLIAM, May 1652 (East Coker, Somerset, Eng.)–Mar. 1715. British buccaneer and explorer. One of the first Englishmen to see Australia, 1686.

DAVIS (or Davys), JOHN, c.1550 Sandridge, Devonshire, Eng.)–Dec. 29/30, 1605. British navigator, Arctic explorer. Searching for a Northwest Passage, pushed through Davis Strait (named for him) into Baffin Bay, 1587; discovered Falkland Isl, 1592; invented the quadrant, used through 18th cent. for navigation.

DE SOTO, HERNANDO, c.1499 (Extremadura Prov., Sp.)–May 21, 1542. Spanish explorer. Explored coastal and interior areas of Central America, 1516–20; helped conquer Nicaragua and Peru; headed an expedition that explored much of southeastern U.S., probably being the first Europeans to sight the Mississippi R., 1539–42.

DRAKE, SIR FRANCIS, c. 1540 (Devonshire, Eng.) –Jan. 28, 1596. British admiral. The most renowned seaman of the Elizabethan age; circumnavigated the globe, 1577–80; knighted, 1580; played an important role in the defeat of the Spanish Armada, 1588.

ERICSON (also Ericsson, Eriksson), LEIF, 971 (Iceland)–c.1015. Norse explorer. Made landfall on North American coast, c.1000, calling landing place Vinland; according to speculation, Vinland could have been present-day Newfoundland, Nova Scotia, or Cape Cod; converted to Christianity, proselytized in Iceland. (Son of ERIC THE RED.)

ERIC THE RED, c.950 (Norway)–c.1000. Norse explorer who established first European settlement on Greenland, c.986. (Father of LEIF ERICSON.)

FRANKLIN, SIR JOHN, April 16, 1786 (Spinsby, Lincolnshire, England)–June 11, 1847. British explorer. Explored in the Arctic; he was killed, as was all his crew, on his third Arctic exploration in search of a Northwest Passage—a northern water route across North America.

FROBISHER, SIR MARTIN, 1535 (Yorkshire, Eng.) –Nov. 22, 1594. British navigator. Early explorer of Canada's northeastern coast, 1576–78; played a prominent role in the campaign against the Spanish Armada, 1588; knighted, 1588.

GAGARIN, YURI, Mar. 9, 1934 (nr. Gzhatsk [now Gagarin], USSR)–Mar. 27, 1968. Soviet cosmonaut. First man to travel into space, Apr. 12, 1961; awarded Order of Lenin; died in an airplane crash on a routine training flight.

GAMA, VASCO DA, 1460 (Sines, Port.)–Dec. 24, 1524. Portuguese navigator. Led expedition around Africa to India, opening a sea route to Asia, 1497–99; Port. viceroy to India, 1524.

GILBERT, SIR HUMPHREY, c.1537 (Greenway, Devon, Eng.)–Sept. 9, 1583. British explorer. Attempted to start first English colony in America, at present-day St. John's, Nfld., 1583; knighted, 1570. (Step-brother of SIR W. RALEIGH.)

HENRY THE NAVIGATOR, (HENRIQUE OF PORTUGAL), Mar 4, 1394 (Porto, Port.)–Nov. 13, 1460. Portuguese prince. Sponsored voyages of discovery that led to the foundation of the Portuguese Empire.

HEYERDAHL, THOR, Oct. 6, 1914 (Larvik, Nor.). Norwegian ethnologist, adventurer. Led "*Kon-Tiki*" expedition from South American Pacific coast to Polynesia, establishing the possibility that Polynesians may have originated in South America, 1947; led *Ra* expedition from Morocco to within 600 miles of Central America, confirming the possibility that pre-Columbian cultures may have been influenced by Egyptian civilization, 1970. *Kon-Tiki*, 1950; *Aku-Aku: The Secret of Easter Island*, 1958; *The Ra Expeditions*, 1971.

HILLARY, SIR EDMUND, July 20, 1919 (Auckland, N.Z.). New Zealand mountain climber, Antarctic explorer. The first, with Tenzing Norgay, to reach the summit of Mt. Everest, May 19, 1953; led the New Zealand group in the British Commonwealth Trans-Antarctic expedition, 1955–58; knighted, 1953.

HUDSON, HENRY, fl. 1607–1611. English explorer. Explored the Hudson R. for the Dutch East India Co., establishing the basis of Dutch claims to New York, 1609; in the service of England, sailed through Hudson Strait into Hudson Bay and James Bay, where his mutinous crew set him adrift to die, 1610–11.

IBERVILLE, PIERRE LE MOYNE, SIEUR D', July 16, 1661 (Montreal, Quebec, Can.)–July 9, 1706. French-Canadian soldier, explorer. Founded the first permanent settlement in the French territory of Louisiana at Mobile Bay, 1699; led West Indian fleet in attacks on Nevis and St. Kitts islands, forcing British surrender, 1706.

JOLLIET (or Joliet), LOUIS, Sept. 21, 1645 (Beaupré, Quebec, Can.)–c.May 1700. French-Canadian explorer, cartographer. The first white man, with JACQUES MARQUETTE, to traverse the Mississippi R. from its confluence with the Fox R. in present-day Wisconsin to the Arkansas R. in present-day Arkansas, 1673; traveled to Hudson Bay, charted Labrador coast, 1694.

LA SALLE, ROBERT CAVELIER, SIEUR DE, Nov. 21, 1643 (Rouen, Normandy, Fr.)–Mar. 19, 1687. French explorer, fur trader. Led the first expedition to the mouth of the Mississippi R., establishing France's claim to the Mississippi Valley and Louisiana, 1681–82.

LE MOYNE, CHARLES, Aug, 1626 (Dieppe, France) –Feb. 1685. French-Canadian colonist. Founded the city of Longueuil; lived at a Jesuit mission when he arrived in Canada, learned several Indian dialects, and became a fur trader, farmer, and soldier; French government honored him with many titles and large grants of land. (Father of SIEUR DE BIENVILLE and SIEUR DE IBERVILLE).

**LEONOV, ALEKSEI,** May 30, 1934 (nr. Kemerovo, USSR). Soviet cosmonaut. On the *Voshod 2* space flight, was the first man to climb out of a ship in space, 1965.

**LIVINGSTONE, DAVID,** Mar. 19, 1813 (Blantyre, Scot.)–May 1, 1873. British missionary, physician, explorer. Accomplished extensive exploration of Africa, then the "dark continent"; discovered Victoria Falls, 1855; searched for source of Nile, 1866; attempted to end the slave trade; the famous greeting, "Dr. Livingstone, I presume," addressed to him by HENRY M. STANLEY, who found him on a rescue mission, 1871. *Missionary Travels and Researches in Africa,* 1857.

**MACKENZIE, SIR ALEXANDER,** 1755 (Stornoway, Is. of Lewis, Outer Hebrides)–Mar. 11, 1820. Scottish fur trader, explorer. Journeyed from Ft. Chipewyan along Slave and Mackenzie rivers to the Arctic Ocean, 1789; crossed the Rocky Mts. to the Pacific coast at present-day British Columbia, the first known transcontinental crossing of America north of Mexico, 1793.

**MAGELLAN, FERDINAND,** 1480 (Porto, Port.)–1521. Portuguese navigator in the service of Spain. Often called the first circumnavigator of the globe, although he died before the voyage was completed; sailed through the strait that was to bear his name, 1520; reached the Philippines (1521), becoming the first European to command an expedition across the Pacific from east to west and establishing a new route between Europe and Asia.

**MARQUETTE, JACQUES** ("Père Marquette"), June 1, 1637 (Laon, Fr.)–May 18, 1675, French Jesuit missionary, explorer. Traveled with LOUIS JOLLIET down the Mississippi R. and reported the first accurate data on its course, 1673; one of the first white men to live near present-day Chicago.

**MENDOZA, PEDRO DE,** c. 1487 (Guadix, Sp.)–June 23, 1537. Spanish colonizer and explorer. Founded the first colony at Buenos Aires, Arg., 1536.

**NANSEN, FRIDTJOF,** Oct. 10, 1861 (Christiana [now Oslo] Norway)–May 13, 1930. Norwegian polar explorer. With five others crossed Greenland from east to west, 1888, and made several other expeditions; Norwegian minister to Great Britain, 1906–1908; returned to become a professor at the University of Christiana, and went on several other polar expeditions; awarded the 1922 Nobel Peace Prize for his efforts to return German and Soviet war prisoners to their homelands.

**NICOLET, JEAN,** 1598 (Cherbourg, Fr.)–Nov. 1, 1642. French explorer. The first European to discover Lake Michigan and the area that now comprises Wisconsin and Michigan, 1634.

**NOBILE, UMBERTO,** Jan. 21, 1885 (Lauro, It.)–July 29, 1978. Italian aeronautical engineer, pioneer in Arctic aviation. Flew over the North Pole in dirigible, *Norge,* with ROALD AMUNDSEN and LINCOLN ELLSWORTH, from Spitsbergen to Alaska, 1926.

**PINZON, MARTIN ALONSO,** c. 1441 (Palos, Seville, Sp.)–1493. Spanish explorer. Part-owner of the *Pinta,* and *Niña* of CHRISTOPHER COLUMBUS's 1492 fleet; his suggestion, as commander of the *Pinta,* resulted in landfall in the Bahamas, Oct. 12, 1492. (Brother of V. PINZÓN.)

**PINZÓN, VICENTE YÁNEZ,** c. 1460 (Palos, Seville, Sp.)–c. 1523. Spanish navigator. Commanded *Niña* in CHRISTOPHER COLUMBUS's expedition, 1492–93; discovered Amazon R. estuary and present-day Costa Rica, c. 1500; gov. of Puerto Rico, 1505. (Brother of M. A. PINZÓN.)

**PIZARRO, FRANCISCO,** 1475 (Trujillo, Extremadura, Sp.)–June 26, 1541. Spanish conquistador. Accompanied VASCO BALBOA on his discovery of the Pacific Ocean, 1513; conquered the Inca Empire in Peru, 1531–33; founded city of Lima, Peru, 1535. (Half-brother of G. PIZARRO.)

**PIZARRO, GONZALO,** c.1502 (Trujillo, Sp.)– Apr. 10, 1548. Spanish explorer. Aided his half brother FRANCISCO PIZARRO in the conquest of Peru, 1531–33; led anti-royalist forces in Peru and won the Battle of Anaquito, 1546; was captured and executed.

**PONCE DE LEÓN, JUAN,** 1460 (Tierra de Campos Palencia, Leon, Sp.)–1521. Spanish explorer. Sailed with CHRISTOPHER COLUMBUS on his second voyage to the New World, 1493; explored Puerto Rico, founding colony near present-day San Juan, 1508–09; gov. of Puerto Rico, 1509–12; discovered Florida while searching for the mythical fountain of youth, 1513.

**PORTOLA, GASPAR DE,** c.1723 (Balaguer, Catalonia, Sp.)–c.1784. Spanish explorer. Commanded expedition to colonize upper California, 1767–70; honored as founder of San Diego.

**RADISSON, PIERRE ESPRIT,** c.1636 (St. Malo, Fr.)–c.1710. French explorer, fur trader, in service of England. Explored Hudson Bay and the wilderness west of the Great Lakes; his activities led to formation of the Hudson's Bay Co., 1670

**RASMUSSEN, KNUD,** July 7, 1879 (Jakobshaven, Greenland)–Dec. 21, 1933. Danish explorer. Made several Arctic explorations, and founded Thule, an Eskimo trading post which is often the base for exploration. Books: *Greenland Along the Polar Sea,* 1922; *Across Arctic America,* 1927; and *Eskimo Poems from Canada and Greenland,* 1973.

**RIBAUT, JEAN,** c.1520 (Dieppe, Fr.)–Oct. 23, 1565. French explorer. Founded first French colony in America, at present-day Port Royal, S.C., 1562; executed by Spanish in Florida as heretic.

**SCOTT, ROBERT F.,** June 6, 1868 (Devonport [now part of Plymouth], Devon, Eng.)–c. Mar. 29, 1912. British Antarctic explorer. As leader of expedition to the South Pole (1910–13), arrived (Jan. 1912) only to find R. AMUNDSEN had already been there; plagued by sickness and ill weather, entire party died by end of March. *Scott's Last Expedition* (2 vols., 1913).

SHACKLETON, SIR ERNEST, Feb. 15, 1874 (Kilkee, Co. Kildare, Ire.)–Jan. 5, 1922. British Antarctic explorer. Made three expeditions to the Antarctic; reached within 97 miles of South Pole, sent parties to the summit of Mt. Erebrus, 1908, and went to magnetic South Pole, 1909; knighted, 1909. *Heart of the Antarctic*, 1909; *South*, 1919.

SPEKE, JOHN, May 4, 1827 (nr. Ilminster, England) –Sept. 18, 1964. British explorer. The first European to reach Lake Victoria in Africa, 1858; named the lake and later found that it was the source of the Nile River.

STANLEY, HENRY M., Jan. 28, 1841 (Denbigh, Denbighshire, Eng.)–May 10, 1904. English-U.S. journalist, explorer. As a journalist for the New York *Herald*, was commissioned to find African explorer DAVID LIVINGSTONE; when he finally reached Livingstone (1871), greeted him with the words, "Dr. Livingstone, I presume?"; led a second expedition, furthering Livingstone's explorations, 1874–77; on third expedition, laid foundation for Congo Free State, 1879–84; on last expedition, relieved Emin Pasha, during Mahdist advance in Sudan, 1887–89; knighted, 1899. *How I Found Livingstone*, 1872; *In Darkest Africa*, 2 vols., 1890.

TABEI, JUNKO, 1940 (nr. Tokyo, Japan). Japanese mountain climber. The first woman to reach the top of Mt. Everest, 1975; part of a 15-member all-female Japanese expedition.

TERESHKOVA, VALENTINA, Mar. 6, 1937 (Maslennikovo, USSR). Soviet cosmonaut. The first woman to travel into space; completed 48 orbits in 71 hours aboard *Vostok 6*, June 16, 1963.

THOMPSON, DAVID, Apr. 30, 1770 (London, Eng.)–Feb. 10, 1857. British-Canadian explorer, geographer. The first European to explore the Columbia R., 1807–11; made the first definitive map of western Canada and portions of northwestern U.S.; served on commission that surveyed the U.S.-Canadian border, 1816–26; died in obscurity.

THORFINN KARLSEFNI, c. 980 (Iceland)–? Scandinavian explorer. Believed to be the first European to attempt colonization of North America, probably on Newfoundland, 1002.

VANCOUVER, GEORGE, June 22, 1757 (King's Lynn, Norfolk, Eng.)–May 10, 1798. British navigator. Surveyed Pacific coast of North America from the vicinity of San Francisco to present-day British Columbia, 1792–94; Vancouver I. and Vancouver, B.C., were named for him. *A Voyage of Discovery to the North Pacific Ocean and 'round the World* (3 vols. and atlas, 1798).

VÉRENDRYE, PIERRE GAULTIER DE VARENNES, SIEUR DE LA, Nov. 17, 1685 (Trois-Rivières, Que., Can.)–Dec. 5, 1749. French-Canadian fur trader, explorer. Built a string of trading posts from Rainy Lake, Ont., to Winnipeg, Man., breaking the Hudson's Bay Co. monopoly and strengthening French claims in North America, 1731–39; pushing farther west than any other previous white man, claimed present-day S.D., for France, 1743.

VERRAZANO (or Verrazzano), GIOVANNI DA, c. 1485 (nr. Florence, It.)–c.1528. Italian navigator in the service of France. Explored North American coast from Cape Fear, N.C., to Cape Breton, N.S., becoming the first European to sight New York and Narragansett bays, 1524.

VESPUCCI, AMERIGO, 1454 (Florence, It.)–Feb. 22, 1512. Italian navigator, explorer. Made voyages in the service of Spain (1499–1500) and Portugal (1501–02); explored 6,000 miles of the S. American coast, observing that it was not Asia, but a new continent; Martin Waldseemüller, a geographer, issued a map showing the new continent (now S. America) and proposed naming it after its discoverer; in time, name was applied to the N. American continent as well.

WEDDELL, JAMES, Aug. 24, 1787 (Ostend, Belg.)–Sept. 9, 1834. British explorer. Penetrated farther south than any previous explorer, reaching present-day Weddell Sea in the Antarctic, 1823. *A Voyage Toward the South Pole*, 1825.

WILKINS, SIR GEORGE HUBERT, Oct. 31, 1888 (Mount Bryan East, Austrl.)–Dec. 1, 1958. Australian explorer and aviator. Advanced use of the airplane and pioneered use of the submarine for polar research; captained the submarine *Nautilus*, 1931, and navigated it under the Arctic Ocean; managed Lincoln Ellsworth's Antarctic expedition, 1933–39; knighted, 1928.

WRANGEL (Vrangel or Wrangell), FERDINAND, BARON VON, Jan. 9, 1797 (Pskov, Rus.)–June 6, 1870. Russian explorer. Mapped northeastern coast of Siberia, locating present-day Wrangel I., 1820–24.

# Rulers, Statesmen, and Political Leaders

## U.S. RULERS, STATESMEN, AND POLITICAL LEADERS

**ABZUG, BELLA,** July 24, 1920, (New York, N.Y.). U.S. politician, lawyer. Helped found Women Strike for Peace (1961), and served as its legislative dir., (1961–70); a founder of the New Democratic Coalition, 1968; U.S. rep. (D, N.Y.), 1971–77; a leader of the anti-Vietnam War movement; a leader of the feminist movement. *Gender Gap* (w/Mim Kelber) 1984.

**ACHESON, DEAN, G.,** Apr. 11, 1893 (Middletown, Conn.)–Oct. 12, 1971. U.S. lawyer, statesman. As secy. of state (1949–53), principal creator of the U.S. foreign policy aimed at containment of communist expansion after WW II; helped create NATO; awarded Pulitzer Prize in history for *Present at the Creation,* 1970.

**ADAMS, JOHN,** Oct 30, 1735 (Braintree, Mass.)–July 4, 1826. U.S. president, lawyer, diplomat. Delegate to 1st Continental Congress; helped draft Declaration of Independence, 1776; helped draft Treaty of Paris that ended Revolutionary War, 1783; served as diplomat in France, Netherlands, and Great Britain, 1777–88; v.-pres., 1789–97; as 2nd U.S. pres. (1797–1801), prevented war with France (1798) and approved the Alien and Sedition Acts (1798). (Father of J.Q. ADAMS; husband of A. ADAMS.)

**ADAMS, JOHN QUINCY,** July 11, 1769 (Braintree, Mass.)–Feb. 23, 1848. U.S. president, lawyer, diplomat, political writer. As U.S. secy. of state under JAMES MONROE, helped prepare Monroe Doctrine, 1823; negotiated Treaty of Ghent, ending War of 1812, 1814; min. to the Netherlands (1794), Prussia (1797–1801), Russia (1809–14), and Great Britain (1815–17); U.S. Rep. (MA), 1831–48; 6th U.S. pres., 1825–29. (Son of J. and A. ADAMS.)

**ADAMS, SAMUEL,** Sept. 27, 1722 (Boston, Mass.)–Oct. 2, 1803. American Revolutionary patriot, statesman. Helped plan the Boston Tea Party, 1773; pamphleteered against the British and helped organize the Sons of Liberty, early 1770s; member of the Continental Cong., 1774–81; signer of the Declaration of Independence, 1776; gov. of Massachusetts, 1794–97.

**ADAMS, SHERMAN,** Jan. 8, 1899 (East Dover, Vt.)–Oct. 27, 1986. U.S. politician, lumber-industry exec. U.S. rep. (R, NH), 1945–47; gov. (R) of New Hampshire, 1949–53; asst. to Pres. D. D. EISENHOWER, 1953–58. *First Hand Report,* 1961.

**AGNEW, SPIRO,** Nov. 9, 1918 (Baltimore, Md.). U.S. vice-pres., lawyer. Baltimore Co. exec., 1962–67; as Maryland gov. (R), implemented progressive policies, 1967–68; known for outspokenness as U.S. vice-pres. (R, 1969–73); resigned as vice-pres. when faced with federal income-tax charge, 1973; disbarred 1974.

**ALBERT, CARL,** May 10, 1908 (McAlester, Okla.). U.S. lawyer, politician. U.S. rep. (D, Okla.), 1947–77; Democrat House whip, 1955–62; House majority leader, 1962–71; House Speaker, 1971–77.

**ALDEN** (or Aldin; **JOHN,** 1599? (England)–Sept. 12, 1687. English gov. official in colonial America. One of the Pilgrim Fathers, a founder of Plymouth Colony, serving as assistant gov. intermittently between 1633 and 1686; founded Duxbury, Mass.; married PRISCILLA MULLINS, after, according to legend, failing to win her hand for MILES STANDISH; last surviving signer of Mayflower Compact (1620).

**ARTHUR, CHESTER ALAN,** Oct. 5, 1829 (Fairfield, Vt.)–Nov. 18, 1886. U.S. pres., lawyer. Collector of the port of New York, 1871–78; U.S. vice pres. 1881; on death of Pres JAMES GARFIELD became 21st pres. (R, 1881–85); supported the Civil Service Reform Act of 1883 and vetoed a Chinese exclusion bill.

**ASPIN, LES,** July 21, 1938 (Milwaukee, Wis.). U.S. politician. U.S. rep. (D. Wisc.), 1971– ; former chairman of John F. Kennedy's Council of Economic Advisors and chairman of the House Armed Services Committee.

**ATTUCKS, CRISPUS,** c.1723 (Framingham, Mass.)–Mar. 5, 1770. American colonial anti-British agitator. Ex-slave; leader of the demonstration that resulted in the Boston massacre, in which he died.

**ATWATER, LEE,** Feb. 27, 1951 (Atlanta, Ga). U.S. political consultant. Managed George Bush for

President campaign; named chairman of the Republican Committee after the election—the first professional political consultant to hold that job, 1988- .

BACON, NATHANIEL, Jan. 2, 1647 (Suffolk, Eng.)–Oct. 1676. American colonial leader. An English aristocrat who led angry frontiersmen in the short-lived Bacon's Rebellion in colonial Virginia, 1676.

BAKER, HOWARD, JR., Nov. 15, 1925 (Huntsville, Tenn.) U.S. politician, lawyer. U.S. Sen. (R, Tenn.), 1967–85; Senate minority leader, 1977–81; member of Senate Select Com. on Presidential Activities, Foreign Relations Com., and Public Works Com., White House Chief of Staff, 1987–89.

BAKER, JAMES A. III, April 28, 1930 (Houston, Tex.). U.S. politician. Chief of the White House staff and secretary of the treasury under Ronald Reagan; secretary of state, 1988- .

BARKLEY, ALBEN W., Nov. 24, 1877 (Graves Co. Ky.)–Apr. 30, 1956. U.S. vice-pres., lawyer. A major contributor to the Democratic New Deal of the 1930s; U.S. rep (D, Ky.) 1913–27; U.S. sen. (D, Ky.), 1927–49, 1954–56; U.S. vice-pres. (D), 1949–53.

BARTLETT, JOSIAH, Nov. 21, 1729 (Amesbury, Mass.)–May 19, 1795. American Revolutionary patriot. A signer of the Declaration of Independence, 1776; chief justice of the New Hampshire state sup. ct., 1788–89; first gov. of New Hampshire 1792–94.

BAYH, BIRCH, Jan. 22, 1928 (Terre Haute, Vigo Co. Ind.). U.S. politician, lawyer, farmer. U.S. sen. (D, Ind.), 1963–81; chm. of Senate Rights of Americans, Transportation Appropriations, and Construction sub coms.

BENNETT, WILLIAM J., July 3, 1943 (Brooklyn, N.Y.). U.S. statesman. A leader in the war on drugs; a former secretary of education under Ronald Reagan, he was appointed head of the office of National Drug Control Policy by George Bush in January, 1989.

BENTON, THOMAS HART, Mar. 1, 1782 (Harts Mill, N.C.)–Apr. 10, 1858. U.S. politician, lawyer, teacher, editor, author. Vigorous advocate of the opening up of the West and of a hard money (gold over silver) policy, and an opponent of the extension of slavery into the territories. Editor of the St. Louis Enquirer, 1818–20; U.S. sen. (D, Mo.), 1821–51; served as Democratic leader in the Senate. Thirty Years' View, 1854–56. (Father-in-law of J.C. FRÉMONT).

BENTSEN, LLOYD, JR., Feb. 11, 1921 (Mission, Tex.). U.S. politician, businessman. U.S. rep. (D, Tex.), 1948–54; pres. of Lincoln Consolidated, a financial holding company, and dir. of a number of corporations, 1955–70; U.S. sen. (D, Tex.), 1971- ; member of Senate Finance, Environment, Public Works, and Joint Economic coms; Democratic Candidate for v.p., 1988.

BIDEN, JOSEPH R., JR., Nov. 20, 1942 (Scranton, Pa.). U.S. politician. U.S. senator (D. Delaware)

1973- ; chairman of the Senate Judiciary Committee.

BIRCH, JOHN, killed Aug. 25, 1945. U.S. soldier. U.S. intelligence officer in China, killed by the Communist Chinese ten days after V-J Day; name adopted by a U.S. anticommunist political organization, The John Birch Society, which honors him as the first hero of the Cold War.

BIRD, ROSE ELIZABETH, Nov. 2, 1936 (Tucson, Ariz.). U.S. jurist. As California secy. of agric. (1975–77), drafted a controversial farm-labor law that restored peace to California farming; chief justice of California Sup. Ct., 1977–87.

BLACK, HUGO, Feb. 27, 1886 (Harlan, Ala.)–Sept 25, 1971. U.S. jurist, lawyer. U.S. sen. (D, Ala.), 1927–37; as U.S. Sup. Ct. assoc. justice (1937–71), opposed Congressional and state violation of free speech and due process, led activists on the court, advocated court-enforced legislative reapportionment, wrote the opinion forbidding prayers in public schools, worked for procedural simplicity and enforcement of antitrust laws.

BLACKMUN, HARRY A., Nov. 12, 1908 (Nashville, Ill.). U.S. jurist, lawyer. Federal cir. ct. judge, 1959–70; as U.S. Sup. Ct. assoc. justice (1970- ), noted for his scholarly opinions, and for his generally conservative stands (except in civil-rights cases).

BLAINE, JAMES G., Jan. 31, 1830 (West Brownsville, Pa.)–Jan. 27, 1893. U.S. politician, newspaper editor. A leading Republican politician during the latter half of the 19th cen., he attempted to foster closer relations with Latin American countries, began the Pan-American movement, originated the idea of reciprocal tariff treaties. U.S. rep, (R, Me.), 1863–76; speaker, 1868; U.S. sen. (R, Me.), 1876–80; U.S. secy. of state, 1881, 1889–92; Republican presidential candidate, 1884.

BOGGS, CORINNE ("Lindy"), Mar. 13, 1916 (Brunswick Plantation, La.). U.S. politician. Elected U.S. rep. (D, La.) to fill seat vacated by the death of her husband, 1973- ; member of House Appropriations Com.; chairman of Democratic National convention, 1976.

BOHLEN, CHARLES E. ("Chip"), Aug. 30, 1904 (Clayton, N.Y.)–Jan 2, 1974. U.S. diplomat. Specialist in Soviet affairs; served as Russian interpreter for U.S. presidents at the Teheran (1943) and Yalta (1945) conferences; U.S. amb. to the USSR, 1953–57; U.S. amb. to the Philippines, 1957–59; U.S. amb. to France, 1962–68. Witness to History, 1973.

BOND, JULIAN, Jan. 14, 1940 (Nashville, Tenn.). U.S. politician, poet, television commentator. Gained national prominence at the 1968 Democratic National Convention in Chicago, where he cochaired the challenge delegation from Georgia that fought in opposition to then-gov. LESTER MADDOX's handpicked delegation; Georgia state rep., 1967–74; Georgia state sen., 1975–78.

BORAH, WILLIAM E., June 29, 1865 (Fairfield, Ill.)–Jan. 19, 1940. U.S. politician, lawyer. U.S. sen. (R, Idaho), 1907–40; an isolationist, he played a major role in preventing the U.S. from joining the League of Nations and the World Court.

**BOWLES, CHESTER,** Apr. 5, 1901 (Springfield, Mass.)–May 25, 1986. U.S. diplomat, advertising executive. Co-founder of Benton and Bowles advertising agency, 1929; gov. (D) of Connecticut, 1949–51; U.S. amb. to India, 1951–53, 1963–69; U.S. undersecy. of state, 1961–63. *Tomorrow without Fear,* 1946; *Promises to Keep,* 1971; *The Conscience of a Liberal,* 1962.

**BRADFORD, WILLIAM,** Mar. 1590 (Austerfield, Yorkshire, Eng.)–May 19, 1657. English leader in colonial America. A framer of the Mayflower Compact, 1620; as gov. of Plymouth Colony (intermittently 1621–56), played a major role in the colony's survival, dealt cleverly with the economic hardships of the colony, treated the Indians fairly. *History of Plymouth Plantation,* 1620–47 (pub. 1856).

**BRADLEY, BILL,** July 28, 1943 (Crystal City, Mo). U.S. politician, basketball player. A Rhodes scholar from Princeton U., who played professional basketball for the N.Y. Knickerbockers, 1967–77; U.S. sen. (D, N.J.), 1979– . Books: *Life on The Run,* 1976; *The Fair Tax,* 1984.

**BRADLEY, THOMAS,** Dec. 29, 1917 (Calvert, Tex.). U.S. politician, lawyer, policeman. First black mayor of a predominantly white city; a member of the Los Angeles Police Dept., 1940–62; mayor of Los Angeles, 1973– ; cochairperson of Democratic National Convention, 1976.

**BRANDEIS, LOUIS D.,** Nov. 13, 1856 (Louisville, Ky.)–Oct. 5, 1941. U.S. jurist, lawyer. As assoc. justice of U.S. Sup. Ct., (1916–39) was a judicial liberal; the first to devise a brief in which economic and sociological data are used to buttress legal propositions; fought monopolies and defended individual rights, state legislative power, and economic legislation.

**BRECKINRIDGE, JOHN CABELL,** Jan. 21, 1821 (nr. Lexington, Ky.)–May 17, 1875. U.S. politician, lawyer, railroad executive, soldier. U.S. rep. (D, KY) 1851–55; As U.S. vice-pres. (D), he presided over the U.S. Senate during the troublesome years prior to the Civil War, 1857–61; unsuccessfully supported by Southern Democrats for the presidency, 1860; a gen. in the Confederate Army, 1861–65; sec. of state C.S.A., 1865.

**BRENNAN, WILLIAM J., JR.,** Apr. 25, 1906 (Newark, N.J.). U.S. jurist, lawyer. As assoc. justice of U.S. Sup. Ct., (1956–90), he has written many majority opinions, particularly in the areas of obscenity and antitrust; known for strong defense of Bill of Rights.

**BROOKE, EDWARD WILLIAM,** Oct. 26, 1919 (Washington, D.C.). U.S. politician, lawyer. U.S. sen. (R, Mass.), 1967–79; served on Senate Banking, Housing and Urban Affairs, and Appropriations coms., and on the Senate Special Com. on aging; headed Nat'l. Low-Income Housing Coalition 1979– ; first black senator since Reconstruction. *The Challenge of Change,* 1966.

**BROWDER, EARL R.,** May 20, 1891 (Wichita, Kan.)–June 27, 1973. U.S. political leader. Led the U.S. Communist party from 1921 to 1946, when he was ousted, then expelled, for being a "right deviationist"; imprisoned for refusing the draft, 1919–20; U.S. Communist party candidate for U.S. pres., 1936 and 1940.

**BROWN, EDMUND G. ("Pat"),** Apr. 21, 1905 (San Francisco, Calif.) U.S. politician, lawyer. California atty. gen. (D), 1950–58; gov. (D) of California, 1959–66; chm. of National Commission for the Reform of Federal Criminal Codes and of the California Council on the Environment and Economic Balance. (Father of E.G. BROWN, JR.)

**BROWN, EDMUND G., JR. ("Jerry"),** Apr. 7, 1938 (San Francisco, Calif.). U.S. politician, lawyer. Member of Los Angeles Co. Crime Commission, 1969–70; California secy. of state (D), 1971–75; Gov. (D) of California, 1975–83. (Son of E.G. BROWN.)

**BRUCE, DAVID K.E.,** Feb. 12, 1898 (Baltimore, Md.)–Dec. 5, 1977. U.S. diplomat. U.S. amb. to France (1949–52), West Germany (1957–59), Great Britain (1961–69); headed U.S. delegation to Paris peace talks on Vietnam, 1970–71; head of U.S. liaison office in Peking, 1973–74; U.S. amb. to NATO, 1947–76.

**BRYAN, WILLIAM JENNINGS,** Mar. 19, 1860 (Salem, Ill.) July 26, 1925. U.S. politician, orator, lawyer, editor. Political leader of the agrarian and silver forces in the late 19th cent. U.S. rep (D, Neb.), 1891–95; won Democratic presidential nomination with his famous "Cross of Gold" speech, 1896 (also received 1900 and 1908 Democratic presidential nominations); as U.S. secy. of state, advocated arbitration to prevent war, 1913–15; took part in the prosecution at the Scopes trial, 1925.

**BRZEZINSKI, ZBIGNIEW,** Mar. 28, 1928 (Warsaw, Pol.). U.S. gov. official, political scientist. Prof. and dir. of research at Inst. for International Change of Columbia U., 1960–77; dir. of Trilateral Com., 1973–77; asst. to the U.S. pres. for national security affairs, 1977–81. *Soviet Bloc: Unity and Conflict,* 1960; *Fragile Blossom: Crisis and Change in Japan,* 1972; *Power Principle,* 1983; *Game Plan,* 1986.

**BUCHANAN, JAMES,** Apr. 23, 1791 (Cove Gap, Pa.)–June 1, 1868. U.S. pres., lawyer. U.S. rep. (Fed., Pa.), 1821–31; U.S. sen. (D, Pa.), 1834–45; U.S. secy. of state, 1845–49; as U.S. min. to Great Britain, 1853–56; as 15th U.S. pres. (D, 1857–61), attempted to find a compromise in the conflict between the North and the South, but failed to prevent civil war.

**BULLITT, WILLIAM C.,** Jan. 25, 1891 (Philadelphia, Pa.)–Feb. 15, 1967. U.S. diplomat. As member of the U.S. delegation to the peace talks at the end of WW I, unsuccessfully recommended recognition of the USSR; first U.S. amb. to the USSR, 1933–36; U.S. amb. to France, 1936–41. *It's Not Done,* 1926; *The Great Globe Itself,* 1946.

**BUMPERS, DALE,** Aug. 12, 1925 (Charleston, Ark.). U.S. politician, lawyer. Gov. (D) of Arkansas, 1971–75; U.S. sen. (D, Ark.), 1975– .

**BUNCHE, RALPH,** Aug. 7, 1904 (Detroit, Mich.)–Dec. 9, 1971. U.S. diplomat, educator. After teaching political science at Howard U. (From 1928), entered UN as director of the Trusteeship Council, 1946; became principal secy. of UN Palestine Com., 1947; awarded 1950 Nobel Peace Prize for mediating Palestine conflict of 1948–49; U.S. undersecy. for special political affairs, 1958–70; UN special rep. to the Congo, 1960; UN under secy. gen. 1967–71. *An American Dilemma* (with GUNNAR MYRDAL), 1944.

**BUNDY, WILLIAM P.,** Sept. 24, 1917 (Washington, D.C.). U.S. gov. official, lawyer. U.S. asst. secy of def. for internal security affairs, 1961–63; U.S. asst. secy. of state for East Asian and Pacific affairs, 1964–69; visiting prof. at M.I.T., 1969–71; editor of *Foreign Affairs*, 1972–84.

**BUNKER, ELLSWORTH,** May 11, 1894 (Yonkers, N.Y.)–Sept. 27, 1984. U.S. diplomat, businessman. Dir. of National Sugar Refining Co., 1927–66; U.S. amb. to India (1956–61), Org. of American States, (1964–66), South Vietnam (1967–73); U.S. amb.-at-large, 1966–67 and 1973–77.

**BURGER, WARREN E.,** Sept. 17, 1907 (St. Paul, Minn.). U.S. jurist, lawyer. Justice of U.S. Ct. of Appeals for the Dist. of Columbia, 1955–69; chief justice of U.S. 1969–1986; considered a strict constructionist in criminal law matters.

**BURNS, ARTHUR F.,** Apr. 27, 1904 (Stanislau, Austria)–June 26, 1987. U.S. gov. official, economist. Prof. of economics at Columbia U., 1941–69; pres. of National Bureau of Economic Research, 1957–67; counselor to the U.S. pres., 1969–70; chm. of the board of governors of the Federal Reserve System, 1970–78.

**BURR, AARON,** Feb. 6, 1756 (Newark, N.J.)–Sept. 14, 1836. U.S. politician. U.S. sen. (D, N.Y.), 1791–97; in 1800 election, lost U.S. presidency to THOMAS JEFFERSON on 36th ballot; U.S. vice-pres., 1801–05; after losing 1804 race for New York gov., held ALEXANDER HAMILTON responsible, challenged him to a duel, and killed him, 1804; conspired with Gen. JAMES WILKINSON to invade Mexico and set up an independent gov.; arrested, tried for treason, acquitted, 1807.

**BURTON, HAROLD H.,** June 22, 1888 (Jamaica Plain, Mass.)–Oct. 28, 1964. U.S. jurist, lawyer. Reform mayor of Cleveland, Ohio, 1935– 40; U.S. sen. (R, Ohio), 1941–45; as assoc. justice, U.S. Sup. Ct. (1945–58), known as an advocate of judicial restraint, and voted to uphold noncommunist-oath requirement of the Taft-Hartley Act.

**BURTON, PHILLIP,** June 1, 1926 (Cincinnati, Ohio)–Apr. 10, 1983. U.S. politician, lawyer. U.S. rep. (D, Calif.), 1964–83; member of House Interior and Insular Affairs, Education, and Labor Coms.

**BUSH, GEORGE HERBERT WALKER,** June 12, 1924 (Milton, Mass.). U.S. politician, diplomat. U.S. rep. (R, Tex.), 1967–71; U.S. amb. to the UN, 1971–73; chm.. of Republican National Com., 1973–74; chief of U.S. Liaison Office, Peoples' Republic of China, 1974–75; dir. of CIA, 1976–77; candidate for 1980 Republican presidential nomi-

nation; v.p. under RONALD REAGAN, 1981–1989, 41st U.S. pres., 1989– .

**BYRD, HARRY F. JR.,** Dec. 20, 1914 (Winchester, Va.). U.S. politician. Pres. and editor of Winchester (Va.) *Evening Star*, 1935– ; U.S. sen. (Ind, Va.), 1965–83; second person in the history of the Senate to be elected as an independent; reelected for third term with largest vote ever given to any Virginia candidate, 1976.

**BYRD, ROBERT C.** (born Cornelius Calvin Sale), Nov. 20, 1917 (North Wilkesboro, N.C.). U.S. politician, lawyer. Widely considered one of the most influential political leaders in the U.S.; U.S. rep. (D, W.Va.), 1952–58; U.S. sen. (D, W.Va.), 1958– ; Senate majority whip, 1971–76; Senate majority leader, 1977– .

**BYRNES, JAMES F.,** May 2, 1879 (Charleston, S.C.)–Apr. 9, 1972. U.S. politician, lawyer, editor. U.S. rep (D, S.C.) 1911–25; U.S. sen. (D, S.C.), 1931–41; assoc. justice of U.S. Sup. Ct., 1941–42; during WW II, served as dir. of economic stabilization (1942) and dir. of war mobilization (1943–45); secy. of state, 1945–47; gov. (D) of South Carolina, 1951–55 *All in One Lifetime*, 1958.

**CALHOUN, JOHN C.,** Mar. 18, 1782 (Abbeville dist. S.C.)–Mar. 31, 1850. U.S. politician, lawyer, political philosopher. A leading Southern politician who championed states' rights, opposed the prohibition of slavery in newly admitted states, defended the interest of the Southern aristocracy, and promoted Southern unity. U.S. rep. (D, S.C.), 1811–17; U.S. secy. of war, 1817–25; U.S. vice-pres. (D), 1824–32; U.S. sen. (D, S.C.), 1832–44, 1845–50.

**CALIFANO, JOSEPH A. JR.,** May 15, 1931 (Brooklyn, N.Y.). U.S. govt. official, lawyer. Special asst. to Pres. LYNDON JOHNSON, 1965–69; U.S. secy of HEW, 1977–79. *The Student Revolution*, 1969; *A Presidential Nation*, 1975; *The Media and the Law* (with Howard Simons), 1976.

**CANNON, CLARENCE,** Apr. 11, 1879 (Elsberry, Mo.)–May 12, 1964. U.S. politician, lawyer, history prof. U.S. rep. (D, Mo.), 1922–64; chm. of powerful House Appropriations com., 1941–47, 1949–53, 1955–64; a noted parliamentarian.

**CANNON, JOSEPH** ("Uncle Joe"), May 7, 1836 (New Garden, N.C.)–Nov. 12, 1926. U.S. politician, lawyer. U.S. rep., (R, Ill.), 1873–91, 1893–1913, 1915–23; through his chairmanship of the House Rules Com. and then as Speaker of the House (1903–11), ruled that body despotically; noted leader of reactionary Republicans.

**CARAWAY, HATTIE W.,** Feb. 1, 1878 (Bakerville, Tenn.)–Dec. 21, 1950. U.S. politician, teacher. The first woman elected to the U.S. Senate (D, Ark.) and twice reelected, 1932–45; supported Prohibition, antilobbying bills, equal rights for women, and most New Deal legislation.

**CARDOZO, BENJAMIN N.,** May 24, 1870 (New York, N.Y.)–July 9, 1938. U.S. jurist, lawyer. Judge of the New York Ct. of Appeals, 1914–32; as assoc. justice of U.S. Sup. Ct. (1932–38), a foremost spokesman for sociological jurisprudence, concerned with the relationship between law and social change; influenced the U.S. appellate toward more involvement in public issues.

**CAREY, HUGH L.,** Apr. 11, 1919 (Brooklyn, N.Y.). U.S. politician, lawyer. As U.S. rep. (D, N.Y.; 1960–74), and gov. (D) of New York (1975–83), worked to solve the financial difficulties of New York City; holder of Bronze Star and Croix de Guerre with Silver Star war decorations.

**CARR, WILBUR JOHN,** Oct. 31, 1870 (Hillsboro, Ohio)–June 26, 1942. U.S. diplomat. Called the "Father of the U.S. Foreign Service," in recognition of his role in making it an honorable career based on merit, not political patronage; U.S. asst. secy. of state, 1924–37; U.S. min. to Czechoslovakia, 1937–39.

**CARROLL** (of Carrollton), **CHARLES,** Sept. 19, 1737 (Annapolis, Md.)–Nov. 14, 1832. American Revolutionary leader. Helped draft Maryland constitution, 1776; U.S. sen. (Fed, Md.), 1789–92; the only Roman Catholic signer of the Declaration of Independence and the last signer to die.

**CARTER, JIMMY** (born James Earl Carter), Oct. 1, 1924 (Plains, Ga.). U.S. president, peanut farmer, nuclear engineer. Georgia state sen. (D), 1963–67 gov. (D) of Georgia, 1971–75; 39th pres. (D, 1977–81), the first pres. elected from the deep South since before the Civil War; as pres., initiated a human-rights campaign in foreign policy; negotiated treaty to end U.S. sovereignty over the Panama Canal Zone by the year 2000; led negotiations on Egyptian-Israeli conflict, leading to a major breakthrough, 1978. *Keeping Faith,* 1982.

**CASEY, WILLIAM J.,** March 13, 1913 (Elmhurst, Queens, N.Y.)–May 6, 1987. U.S. government official. A lawyer, he held various federal posts; director of the Central Intelligence Agency, 1981–1987; author of *Lawyers Desk Book,* 1965, and others.

**CELLER, EMANUEL,** May 6, 1888 (Brooklyn, N.Y.)–Jan. 15, 1981. U.S. politician, lawyer. U.S. rep. (D, N.Y.), 1923–73; noted for his support of the New Deal and opposition to Sen. JOSEPH MCCARTHY; served as chairman or ranking party leader on the House Judiciary Com., 1949–72; coauthored Celler-Kefauver Anti-Merger Act of 1950, and numerous civil rights bills.

**CHASE, SALMON P.,** Jan. 13, 1808 (Cornish Township, N.H.)–May 7, 1873. U.S. jurist, lawyer, teacher. A determined foe of slavery; active in the Free Soil movement, elected sen. (FS-D, Ohio; 1849–55, 1860–61) and gov. of Ohio (1855–59); as U.S. treas. secy. (1861–64), originated national banking system, 1863; as chief justice of U.S. Sup. Ct. (1864–73), presided over the trial of Pres. ANDREW JOHNSON.

**CHASE, SAMUEL,** Apr. 17, 1741 (Princess Anne, Md.)–June 19, 1811. U.S. jurist, lawyer. Signer of the Declaration of Independence, 1776; assoc. justice of U.S. Sup. Ct., 1796–1811; his acquittal in an impeachment trial increased the independence of the judiciary, 1805.

**CHENEY, RICHARD B.,** Jan. 30, 1941 (Lincoln, Neb.). U.S. politician. U.S. representative (R, Wyo.), 1978–89; secretary of defense, 1989– .

**CHISHOLM, SHIRLEY,** Nov. 30, 1924 (Brooklyn, N.Y.) U.S. politician, nursery-school teacher. New York st. assemblywoman (D), 1964–68; U.S. rep. (D, N.Y.), 1969–83; candidate for the presidency, 1972; chairwoman, Nat. Polit Cong. Black Women. *Unbossed and Unbought,* 1970; *The Good Fight,* 1973.

**CHURCH, FRANK,** July 25, 1924 (Boise, Idaho)–Apr. 7, 1984. U.S. politician, lawyer. U.S. sen. (D, Ida.), 1957–81; chm. of Senate Intelligence and Aging coms.; ranking member Senate Foreign Relations Com. and Energy and Natural Resources Com.

**CLARK, CHAMP,** Mar. 7, 1850 (nr. Lawrenceburg, Ky.)–Mar. 12, 1921. U.S. politician. As U.S. rep. (D, Mo.; 1893–95 and 1897–1921), became Democratic leader (1907), organized successful fight (1910) against House Speaker JOSEPH CANNON and his arbitrary control of legislative procedure, and served as House Speaker (1911–19).

**CLARK, THOMAS C.,** Sept. 23, 1899 (Dallas, Tex.)–June 13, 1977. U.S. jurist. As assoc. justice of U.S. Sup. Ct. (1949–67), wrote opinion upholding constitutionality of the 1964 Civil Rights Act stipulation requiring desegregation of public accommodations; often upheld the government position in antitrust, internal security, and criminal procedure cases; U.S. Atty. Gen., 1945–49. (Father of R. CLARK.)

**CLARK,** (William) **RAMSEY,** Dec. 18, 1927 (Dallas, Tex.). U.S. lawyer, government official. A strong supporter of civil rights and opponent of the death penalty. Asst. atty. gen., U.S. Justice Dept., 1961–65; U.S. dep. atty. gen. 1965–67; as U.S. atty. gen. (1967–69), refused to use wiretaps except in cases of national security. *Crime in America,* 1970. (Son of T. CLARK.)

**CLAY, HENRY,** Apr. 12, 1777 (Hanover Co., Va.)–June 29, 1852. U.S. politician, lawyer. Influential figure of the pre-Civil War decades, called the "Great Pacificator" for his role as drafter of the Missouri Compromise (1820); advocated economic expansion, laid the foundations for Pan-Americanism; made significant contribution in attempt to avoid civil war, in the Compromise of 1850; U.S. sen. (Ky.), 1806–07, 1810–11, 1831–42, and 1849–52; U.S. rep. (Ky.), 1811–21, 1823–25; speaker (same years, except 1821); U.S. secy. of state, 1825–29.

**CLEVELAND,** (Stephen) **GROVER,** Mar. 18, 1837 (Caldwell, N.J.)–June 24, 1908. U.S. pres., politician. As gov. (D) of New York (1883–84), opposed Tammany Hall; as 22nd and 24th U.S. pres. (D, 1885–89 and 1893–97), attempted to lower the tariff and supported the Civil Service Commission.

**CLINTON, DEWITT,** Mar. 2, 1769 (Napanock, N.Y.)–Feb. 11, 1828. U.S. political leader, lawyer, historian. Mayor of New York City, 1803–15 (intermittently); gov. of New York, 1817–23, 1825–28; a patron of the arts and supporter of public education; responsible for promoting the idea of an Erie Canal. (Nephew of G. CLINTON).

**CLINTON, GEORGE,** July 26, 1739 (Little Britain, N.Y.)–Apr. 20, 1812. U.S. politician, soldier, lawyer. Gov. of New York, 1777–95 and 1800–04;

U.S. vice-pres., 1805–12; opposed adoption of the U.S. Constitution as a threat to state power. (Uncle of D. CLINTON.)

COHEN, WILLIAM, Aug. 28, 1940 (Bangor, Me.). U.S. politician, lawyer. U.S. rep. (R, Me.), 1973–77; U.S. sen. (R, Me.), 1979–  ; gained national attention during the 1974 impeachment hearings as one of the first Republican members of the House Judiciary committee to call for Pres. R. M. NIXON's ouster.

COLFAX, SCHUYLER, Mar. 23, 1823 (New York, N.Y.)–Jan. 13, 1885. U.S. politician, newspaper editor. Editor of St. Joseph Valley (Ind.) *Register*, a Whig paper, 1845–63; U.S. rep. (R, Ind.), 1855–69; spkr. of the hse., 1863–69; U.S. vice-pres. (R) 1869–73; involvement in Credit Mobilier scandal terminated his political career.

COLSON, CHARLES W., Oct. 16, 1931 (Boston Mass.). U.S. lawyer. As special counsel to Pres. R. M. NIXON (1969–73), became involved in the Watergate scandal; assoc. of Fellowship House (Washington, D.C.). 1975–  .

CONABLE, BARBER B., JR., Nov. 2, 1922 (Warsaw, N.Y.). U.S. politician, lawyer. Senator and congressman (R, New York), 1965–85; lawyer and president of the International Bank for Reconstruction and Development, 1986–  .

CONKLING, ROSCOE, Oct. 30, 1829 (Albany, N.Y.)–Apr. 18, 1888. U.S. politician. New York State political boss who controlled federal patronage; U.S. rep. (R, N.Y.) 1858–64, 1865–67; U.S. sen. (R, N.Y.) 1867–81; opposed JAMES T. BLAINE for Republican presidential nomination, 1876; resigned Senate seat in protest against policies of Pres. JAMES A. GARFIELD.

CONNALLY, JOHN B., Feb. 27, 1917 (Floresville, Tex.). U.S. politician, lawyer. Gov. (D) of Texas, 1963–69; switched to Republican party, 1973; special adviser to pres. R. M. NIXON, 1973; acquitted of bribery charges in effort to raise federal milk price supports, 1975; U.S. secy. of the treas., 1971–72.

COOLIDGE, (John) CALVIN, July 4, 1872 (Plymouth Notch, Vt.)–Jan. 5, 1933. U.S. pres., lawyer. Gov. (R) of Massachusetts, 1919–20; U.S. vice-pres. (R), 1921–23; succeeded to U.S. presidency upon death of WARREN G. HARDING, 1923; reelected by huge majority, 1924; as 30th pres. (1923–29), twice vetoed farm-relief bills because of their price-fixing features.

COOPER, JOHN SHERMAN, Aug. 23, 1901 (Somerset, Ky.). U.S. politician, lawyer. U.S. sen. (D, Ky.), 1946–48, 1952–54, 1956–72; U.S. amb. to India and Nepal (1955–56) and to East Germany (1974–77).

COX, ARCHIBALD, May 17, 1912 (Plainfield, N.J.). U.S. lawyer, professor. Named Watergate special prosecutor, then fired by Pres. R. M. NIXON when he rejected an admin. compromise on the disputed Watergate tapes (Oct. 20, 1973). Prof. at Harvard Law School, 1946–76; U.S. solicitor gen., 1961–65. *The Warren Court*, 1968; *Role of the Supreme Court in American Government*, 1976.

CRANSTON, ALAN M., June 19, 1914 (Palo Alto, Calif.). U.S. politician. U.S. sen. (D, Calif.) 1969–  ; Democratic whip, 1977–  ; member of Senate Budget Com. and Nutrition and Human Needs Com.; chm. of Democratic Credentials Com.

CRITTENDEN, JOHN J., Sept. 10, 1787 (nr. Versailles, Ky.)–July 26, 1863. U.S. politician, lawyer. U.S. sen. (Whig, Ky.), 1817–19, 1835–41, 1842–48, and 1855–61; gov. of Kentucky, 1848–50; noted for Crittenden Compromise on the slavery issue that he proposed in the Senate prior to the Civil War.

CUOMO, MARIO, June 15, 1932 (Queens, N.Y.). U.S. politician. Democratic gov. of New York, 1983–  ; gained national attention with his stirring keynote speech at the 1984 Democratic National Convention.

CURTIS, BENJAMIN R., Nov. 4, 1809 (Watertown, Mass.)–Sept. 15, 1874. U.S. jurist, lawyer. As assoc. justice of the U.S. Sup. Ct. (1851–57), wrote one of the two dissenting opinions in the Dred Scott case (1857); chief counsel to Pres. ANDREW JOHNSON at his impeachment (1868).

CURTIS, CHARLES, Jan. 25, 1860 (N. Topeka, Indian terr., later Kan.)–Feb. 8, 1836. U.S. politician, lawyer. U.S. rep. (R, Kan.), 1893–1907; U.S. sen. (R, Kan.), 1907–13 and 1915–29; Republican whip, 1915–24; majority leader, 1924–29; U.S. vice-pres. (R.), 1929–33.

DALEY, RICHARD J., May 15, 1902 (Chicago, Ill.)–Dec. 20, 1976. U.S. politician. A Democrat, he was mayor of Chicago from 1955 until his death; as head of the Cook County Democratic organization, he was one of the most powerful political leaders in the United States, and an advisor to presidents JOHN F. KENNEDY and LYNDON B. JOHNSON. (Father of R. M. DALEY.)

DALEY, RICHARD M., April 24, 1942 (Chicago, Ill.). U.S. political leader. Mayor of Chicago (1989–  ) and former state's attorney of Illinois. (Son of R.J. DALEY.)

DAVIS, JEFFERSON, June 3, 1808 (Fairview, Ky.) –Dec. 6, 1889. U.S. political leader, soldier-farmer. U.S. sen. (D, Miss.), 1847–51 and 1857–61; U.S. secy. of war, 1853–57; pres. of the Confederate States of America, 1861–65; his firm rule as CSA pres. conflicted with the states'-rights sentiment behind the South's secession; disapproved of Gen. ROBERT E. LEE's surrender; imprisoned and indicted for treason, but case dropped. *Rise and Fall of the Confederate Government, 1881.*

DAWES, CHARLES G., Aug. 27, 1865 (Marietta, Ohio)–Apr. 23, 1951. U.S. politician, diplomat, financier. Working for the Allied Reparations Commission, developed Dawes Plan to stabilize post-WW I finances; awarded Nobel Peace Prize, 1925; U.S. vice-pres., 1925–29; U.S. amb. to Great Britain, 1929–1932.

DAYTON, JONATHAN, Oct. 16, 1760 (Elizabethtown [now Elizabeth] N.J.)–Oct. 9, 1824. U.S. politician, lawyer, soldier. Del. to Constitutional Convention and youngest signer of the U.S. Constitution; U.S. rep. (Fed, N.J.), 1791–99; U.S. sen.

(Fed, N.J.), 1799–1805; indicted (1807) for conspiracy with A. BURR, but never brought to trial. Dayton, Ohio is named after him.

**DEAN, JOHN W. 3rd,** Oct. 14, 1938 (Akron, Ohio). U.S. lawyer. Counsel to Pres. RICHARD M. NIXON, 1971–73; key prosecution witness in the Watergate hearings. *Lost Honor,* 1983; *Blind Ambition,* 1976; disbarred.

**DEANE, SILAS,** Dec. 24, 1737 (Groton, Conn.)– Sept 23, 1789. U.S. diplomat, lawyer, merchant. The first American diplomat sent abroad, he procured French aid for the Revolutionary cause, 1776; accused of irregularities, investigated (1778), fled into exile (1780); posthumously vindicated by Congress.

**DEWEY, THOMAS E.,** Mar. 24, 1902 (Owosso, Mich.)–Mar. 16, 1971. U.S. politician, lawyer. "Racket-busting" prosecuting atty. for New York City, 1935–37; dist. atty. of New York Co., 1938–43; gov. (R) of New York, 1943–55; Republican candidate for president, 1944 and 1948.

**DICKINSON, JOHN,** Nov. 8, 1732 (Talbot Co., Md.)–Feb. 14, 1808. American patriot, lawyer. Conservative patriot of the American Revolutionary era, called the "Penman of the Revolution." Drafted declaration of rights and grievances of the Stamp Act Congress, 1765; voted against the Declaration of Independence, 1776; member of Constitutional Convention, 1787. *Letters from a Farmer in Pennsylvania,* 1767–68.

**DIES, MARTIN,** Nov. 5, 1901 (Colorado, Tex.)– Nov. 14, 1972. U.S. politician. U.S. rep. (D, Tex.), 1931–45 and 1953–59; first chm. of the House Com. on Un-American Activities, 1938–45; claimed that the New Deal and the Congress of Industrial Organizations were infiltrated by communists. *The Martin Dies Story,* 1963.

**DIRKSEN, EVERETT MCKINLEY,** Jan. 4, 1896 (Pekin, Ill.)–Sept. 7, 1969. U.S. politician. U.S. sen. (R, Ill.), 1951–69; Senate Republican minority leader, 1959–69; played a critical role in the passage of the 1965 Voting Rights Act and the 1968 Fair Housing Act; noted as an excellent orator.

**DOLE, ROBERT J.,** July 22, 1923 (Russell, Kan.). U.S. politician, lawyer. U.S. sen. (R, Kan.), 1969– ; chm. of Republican National Com., 1971–73; Republican vice-presidential candidate, 1976.

**DOUGLAS, HELEN GAHAGAN,** Nov. 25, 1900 (Boonton, N.J.)–June 28, 1980. U.S. politician, actress, U.S. rep. (D, Cal.), 1945–51; ran against R. M. NIXON for California Senate seat and lost, at which time she was called "the most courageous fighter for Liberalism in Congress" by *The New Republic.* (Wife of M. DOUGLAS.)

**DOUGLAS, PAUL H.,** Mar. 26, 1892 (Salem, Mass.) –Sept. 24, 1976. U.S. politician, educator. Prof. of economics at U. of Chicago, 1925–39; adviser to the National Recovery Administration, 1930s; as U.S. Sen. (D, Ill.), concentrated on labor, banking, and social security legislation 1948–66. *In the Fullness of Time,* 1972.

**DOUGLAS, STEPHEN A.,** Apr. 23, 1813 (Brandon, Vt.)–June 3, 1861. U.S. politician, lawyer,

U.S. rep. (D, Ill.), 1843–47; U.S. sen. (D, Ill.), 1847–61; advocated popular sovereignty on the issue of slavery in the territories; as chm. of the Senate com. on territories was instrumental in the passage of the Compromise of 1850 and the Kansas-Nebraska Act of 1854; a great orator noted for his debates with A. LINCOLN during 1858 Senate campaign; defeated by Lincoln for the presidency, 1860.

**DOUGLAS, WILLIAM O.,** Oct. 16, 1898 (Maine, Minn.)–Jan. 19, 1980. U.S. jurist. As assoc. justice of the U.S. Sup. Ct. (1939–75), advocated a strong interpretation of the Bill of Rights, often voted for a broad exercise of the court's powers; author of many works on business law, outdoor life, and travel, including *Of Men and Mountains* (1950), *Russian Journey* (1956), *A Living Bill of Rights* (1961).

**DUKAKIS, MICHAEL,** Nov. 3, 1933 (Brookline, Mass.). U.S. politician. Governor of Massachusetts, 1975–1979, 1983– ; in 1988 he received the Democratic Party's nomination for president, and was defeated by GEORGE BUSH.

**DULLES, ALLEN,** Apr. 7, 1893 (Watertown, N.Y.)– Jan. 29, 1969. U.S. govt. official, diplomat, lawyer. Chief of Near Eastern Affairs Div. at U.S. State Dept., 1922–26; chief of Office of Strategic Services in Switzerland and Germany, 1942–45; dir. of CIA, 1953–61. (Brother of J. F. DULLES.)

**DULLES, JOHN FOSTER,** Feb. 25, 1888 (Washington, D.C.)–May 24, 1959. U.S. govt. official, diplomat, lawyer. U.S. del. to the UN Gen. Assembly, 1946–50; U.S. amb.-at-large, 1951; U.S. secy of state, 1953–59; the prime architect of the U.S. policy of containment of communism, he believed in developing military forces to make possible "massive retaliation." (Brother of A. DULLES.)

**EAGLETON, THOMAS F.,** Sep. 4, 1929 (St. Louis, Mo.). U.S. politician, lawyer Atty. Gen. (1961–65) and lt. gov. (1965–68) of Missouri (D); U.S. sen. (D, Mo.), 1968–87; forced to withdraw from Democratic vice-presidential nomination after confirmed reports that he had undergone psychiatric examinations, 1972. *War and Presidential Power; A Chronicle of Congressional Surrender,* 1974.

**EASTLAND, JAMES O.,** Nov. 28, 1904 (Doddsville, Miss.)–Feb. 19, 1986. U.S. politician, lawyer, farmer. U.S. sen. (D, Miss.), 1941–78; pres. pro tem of the Senate, 1972–78; chm. of Senate Judiciary Com.; member of Senate Agriculture, Nutrition and Forestry Com. and of Democratic Policy Com.

**EHRLICHMAN, JOHN D.,** Mar. 20, 1925 (Tacoma, Wash.). U.S. govt. official, lawyer. As domestic-affairs asst. to Pres. R. M. NIXON (1969–73) and exec. dir. of the Domestic Council, played a major role in the Watergate scandal; convicted (1975), imprisoned (1976), and released (1978). *The Company,* 1976.

**EISENHOWER, DWIGHT DAVID** ("Ike"), Oct. 14, 1890 (Denison, Tex.)–Mar. 28, 1969. U.S. pres., soldier. As supreme commander of the Allied Expeditionary Force in Europe during WW II, led the invasion that forced Germany's surrender,

1943–45; U.S. Amry chief of staff, 1945–48; pres. of Columbia U., 1948–50; supreme commander of NATO, 1951–52; as 34th U.S. pres. (R, 1953–61), ended the Korean War; sent federal troops to Little Rock, Ark., to force compliance with desegregation orders; suffered difficulties passing domestic legislation; extended aid to S. Vietnam.

**ELLSBERG, DANIEL,** Apr. 7, 1931 (Chicago, Ill.). U.S. govt. official, political activist. Noted for leaking the Pentagon Papers to *The New York Times,* 1971. Staff member at Rand Corp., 1959–64 and 1967–70; member of R. MCNAMARA study group on the history of U.S. decision-making in Vietnam 1967–69.

**ERVIN, SAMUEL J. JR.,** Sept. 17, 1896 (Morgantown, N.C.)–Apr. 23, 1985. U.S. politician, lawyer. U.S. sen. (D, N.C.), 1954–75; as head of the Senate Select Com. on Presidential Campaign Activities investigating the Watergate scandal, fought Pres. R. M. NIXON's efforts to withhold evidence and testimony on the grounds of executive privilege, 1973–74.

**FALL, ALBERT B.,** Nov. 26, 1861 (Frankfort, Ky.)–Nov. 30, 1944. U.S. politician, lawyer, rancher. U.S. sen (R, N.M.) 1912–21; as U.S. secy. of the int. (1921–23), involved in the Teapot Dome and Elk Hills oil-leasing scandals; convicted (1929) of accepting a $100,000 bribe and jailed (1931–32).

**FARLEY, JAMES A.,** May 30, 1888 (Grassy Point, N.Y.)–June 9, 1976. U.S. political leader, businessman. Managed Pres. F. D. ROOSEVELT'S 1932 and 1936 presidential campaigns; chm. of Democratic National Com., 1932–40; U.S. postmaster gen., 1933–40.

**FAUBUS, ORVAL,** Jan. 7, 1910 (Combs, Ark.). U.S. politician, teacher, editor. Gov. (D) of Arkansas, 1955–67; the only state gov. to serve six times; called out the National Guard to block integration of Little Rock Central High School, 1957.

**FESSENDEN, WILLIAM PITT,** Oct. 16, 1806 (Boscawen, N.H.)–Sept. 8, 1869. U.S. politician, lawyer. A Whig politician who played a major role in the founding of the Republican party, 1856; U.S. sen. (Whig-R, Me.), 1854–64 and 1865–69; a great debater, he cast the deciding vote for acquittal of impeached Pres. ANDREW JOHNSON, 1868.

**FEINSTEIN, DIANNE,** June 22, 1933 (San Francisco, Cal.). U.S. politician. Mayor of San Francisco, 1978–1988; a recipient of many awards for her civic achievements, she has been prominent in the Task Force on AIDS.

**FILLMORE, MILLARD,** Jan. 7, 1800 (Locke Township, N.Y.)–Mar. 8, 1874. U.S. pres., lawyer. U.S. vice pres., 1849–50; upon Pres. Z. TAYLOR'S death became 13th U.S. pres. (Whig, 1850–53); worked for compromise on the slavery issue, but his support of the Fugitive Slave Act of 1850 alienated the North and funded his political career.

**FISH, HAMILTON,** Aug. 3, 1808 (New York, N.Y.)–Sept. 6, 1893. U.S. politician, lawyer. as U.S. secy. of state (1869–77), negotiated the Treaty of Washington (1871) with Britain, settling the *Alabama* claims; fought graft in the administration

of Pres. U.S. GRANT; opposed intervention on behalf of Cuba against Spain.

**FITZGERALD, JOHN** ("Honey Fitz"), Feb. 11, 1863 (Boston, Mass.)–Oct. 2, 1950. U.S. newspaper publisher, banker, insurance broker. A power in the Massachusetts Democratic party; U.S. rep. (D, Mass.), 1895–1901; mayor (D) of Boston, 1906–07, and 1910–14. (Grandfather of J., R., and E. KENNEDY.)

**FOLEY, THOMAS, S.,** March 6, 1929 (Spokane, Wash.). U.S. politician. U.S. rep. (D, Wash.) 1965–  ; House majority leader, 1986–89; House speaker, 1989–  .

**FORD, GERALD R.** (born Leslie King, Jr.), July 14, 1913 (Omaha, Neb.). U.S. pres., politician. U.S. rep. (R, Mich.), 1949–73; Republican minority leader, 1965–73; appointed vice-pres. by Pres. R. M. NIXON, 1973; became 38th U.S. pres. (R, 1974–76) after Nixon's resignation; attempted to heal the wounds of Watergate by conducting an open administration; in a controversial move, pardoned Nixon, Sept. 9, 1974; a fiscal conservative who vetoed many Congressional legislative initiatives.

**FORRESTAL, JAMES V.** Feb. 15, 1892 (Beacon, N.Y.)–May 22, 1949. U.S. govt. official. Pres. of Dillon, Read and Co., 1937–40; as undersecy. (1940–43) and secy. (1944–46) of the navy, responsible for meeting the need for the massive deployment of naval power during WW II; first U.S. secy. of def., 1947–49; resigned from office; committed suicide.

**FORTAS, ABE,** June 19, 1910 (Memphis, Tenn.)–Apr. 5, 1982. U.S. jurist, lawyer. As assoc. justice of U.S. Sup. Ct., (1965–69), considered a liberal; nominated to be chief justice, but accusations of bribery and political resistance to the nomination forced him to resign from the court, 1969.

**FRANKFURTER, FELIX,** Nov. 15, 1882 (Vienna, Austria)–Feb. 22, 1965. U.S. jurist. Prof. at Harvard Law School, 1914–39; helped found American Civil Liberties Union, 1920; as assoc. justice of U.S. Sup. Ct. (1939–62), a liberal who advocated judicial restraint; an active U.S. Zionist.

**FRANKLIN, BENJAMIN,** Jan. 17, 1706 (Boston, Mass.)–Apr. 17, 1790. U.S. statesman, diplomat, inventor, scientist, printer. Published *Poor Richard's Almanack* (1732–57) and the *Pennsylvania Gazette;* helped draft and signed the Declaration of Independence, 1776; min. to France, 1778–85; as a del. to the Federal Constitutional Convention (1787), helped formulate compromise that resulted in the Constitution; proved the existence of electricity in lightning, invented the Franklin stove, bifocal spectacles, and lightning rod.

**FULBRIGHT, J(ames) WILLIAM,** Apr. 9, 1905 (Sumner, Mo.). U.S. politician, lawyer, teacher. As U.S. sen. (D, Ark.), 1945–75; a defender of congressional prerogatives in the conduct of U.S. foreign affairs and an articulate critic of U.S. Vietnam policy; chm. of Senate Foreign Relations Com. (1959–75) and Banking and Currency com. (1955–59); founded the Fulbright scholarship program.

GALLATIN, ALBERT, Jan. 29, 1761 (Geneva, Switz.)–Aug. 12, 1849. U.S. politician, banker, farmer. U.S. secy. of the treasury, 1801–14; played a crucial role in negotiating an end to the War of 1812; U.S. min. to France (1816–23) and Great Britain (1826–27); helped found New York U. and the American Ethnological Soc.

GARFIELD, JAMES A., Nov. 19, 1831 (nr. Orange, Ohio)–Sept. 19, 1881. U.S. pres., college pres., lay preacher. U.S. rep. (R, Ohio), 1863–80; 20th U.S. pres. (R), Mar. 4–Sept. 19, 1881; shot after only four months in office, he lay ill for 80 days before dying.

GARNER, JOHN NANCE, Nov. 22, 1868 (Red River Co., Tex.)–Nov. 7, 1967. U.S. politician, lawyer. U.S. rep. (D, Tex.) 1903–33, speaker, 1931–33; U.S. vice-pres, (D), 1933–41.

GEPHARDT, RICHARD A., Jan. 31, 1941 (St. Louis, Mo.). U.S. politician, lawyer. U.S. rep. (D, Mo.), 1977– ; a candidate for the Democratic nomination for president in 1988.

GERRY, ELBRIDGE, July 17, 1744 (Marblehead, Mass.)–Nov. 23, 1814. U.S. statesman, exporter/importer. Signer of the Declaration of Independence (1776) and Articles of Confederation (1781); U.S. rep., 1789–93; member of the XYZ diplomatic mission to France, 1797; gov. of Massachusetts, 1810–11; U.S. vice-pres., 1812–14; his support of a partisan redistricting bill gave rise to the term *gerrymander*.

GLASS, CARTER, Jan. 4, 1858 (Lynchburg, Va.)–May 28, 1946. U.S. politician. As U.S. rep. (D, Va.; 1902–19), helped draft Federal Reserve Bank Act of 1913; U.S. treas. secy., 1918–20; as U.S. sen. (D, Va.; 1920–46,) was one of the sponsors of the Glass-Steagall Act of 1933, which created the Federal Deposit Insurance Corp.; a determined opponent of most New Deal legislation.

GOLDBERG, ARTHUR J., Aug. 8, 1908 (Chicago, Ill.)–Jan. 19, 1989 U.S. govt. official, jurist, lawyer. A prominent labor lawyer who played an important role in the 1955 merger of the CIO and AFL unions and led fight to expel the teamsters from the AFL.; U.S. secy. of labor, 1961–62; assoc. justice of U.S. Sup. Ct., 1962–65; U.S. del. to the UN, 1965–68, ran for gov. N.Y., 1970.

GOLDWATER, BARRY M., Jan. 1, 1909 (Phoenix, Ariz.). U.S. politician. A widely respected conservative Republican leader. U.S. sen. (R, Ariz.), 1953–64 and 1969–87; as Republican presidential candidate (1964), urged total victory over world communism and a drastic reduction of federal powers. *Conscience of a Conservative*, 1960.

GORE, ALBERT A., Dec. 26, 1907 (Granville, Tenn.). U.S. coal-industry exec., politician. U.S. rep. (D, Tenn.), 1939–53; as U.S. sen. (D, Tenn.; 1953–70), principal author of the 1956 Interstate Highways Act; chm. of Creek Coal Co., 1972– . (Father of A. GORE, JR.)

GORE, ALBERT, JR., March 31, 1948 (Washington, D.C.). U.S. politician. U.S. sen. (D, Tenn.), 1985– ; a former newspaper reporter, he campaigned for the Democratic nomination for president in 1988. (Son of A. GORE.)

GRANT, ULYSSES SIMPSON (born Hiram Ulysses Grant) Apr. 27, 1822 (Point Pleasant, Ohio)–July 23, 1885. U.S. pres., soldier. As Union Army gen., scored first major Union victory of the Civil War, at Ft. Donelson, Tenn., 1862; as commander of the Army of the Tennessee, conducted a brilliant campaign to capture Vicksburg, 1863; as commander in chief of Union Army (1864–65), he forced and accepted Gen. R. E. LEE's surrender; elected 18th pres. (R, 1869–77), his admin. was characterized by corruption and bitter partisan politics.

GREENSPAN, ALAN, March 6, 1926 (New York, N.Y.). U.S. economist. Chairman of Board of Governors of the Federal Reserve System, 1987– .

GRIFFIN, ROBERT P., Nov. 6, 1923 (Detroit, Mich.). U.S. politician, lawyer. U.S. rep. (R, Mich.), 1957–66; U.S. sen. (R, Mich.), 1966–79; Senate minority whip, 1969–77.

GRIFFITHS, MARTHA, Jan. 29, 1912 (Pierce City, Mo.) U.S. politician. As U.S. rep. (D, Mich.; 1955–74), devised the strategy that got the Equal Rights Amendment out of com. and through Congress (1972), and was the first woman to serve as a member of both the Joint Economic Com. and the House Ways and Means Com; Lieut.-gov. (D, Mich; 1983– ).

GRUENING, ERNEST, Feb. 6, 1887 (New York, N.Y.)–June 26, 1974. U.S. politician, journalist, editor. As gov. (D) of Alaska (1939–53), attempted to develop wisely the state's natural resources; lobbied for statehood for Alaska, U.S. sen. (D, Alas.; 1959–69).

GUFFEY, JOSEPH F., Dec. 29, 1870 (Guffey's Landing, Pa.)–Mar. 6, 1959. U.S. politician, utilities exec., oil producer. As U.S. sen. (D, Pa.), opposed poll taxes and supported antilynching laws, 1935–47; credited with coining the term "unholy alliance" to describe the alliance of Southern Democrats whose purpose was to defeat New Deal measures.

GWINNETT, BUTTON, baptized Apr. 10, 1735 (Down Hatherley, Glospa, Eng.)–May 16, 1777. American patriot, planter. Del. to Continental Congress, 1776–77; a signer of the Declaration of Independence, 1776; pres. of the state of Georgia, 1777.

HAIG, ALEXANDER, Dec. 2, 1924 (Philadelphia, Pa.). U.S. statesman, business executive, military leader. A much-decorated army general; the Supreme Allied Commander of European SHAPE, 1974–1979; CEO of United Technologies Corporation 1979–1981; U.S. Secretary of State, 1981–1982.

HALDEMAN, H(arry) R., Oct. 27, 1926 (Los Angeles, Calif.). U.S. govt. official, advertising exec. Chief of staff of R. M. NIXON's presidential campaign, 1968; asst. to Pres. Nixon, 1969–73; convicted (1975) for his involvement in the Watergate scandal and jailed, 1977–78. *The Ends of Power*, 1978.

HALLECK, CHARLES A., Aug. 22, 1900 (De Motte, Ind.)–Mar. 3, 1986. U.S. politician. As U.S.

rep. (R, Ind.; 1935–68), a leader of the conservative coalition that dominated the House in the 1950s and early 1960s, defeating many J. F. KENNEDY admin. bills; House majority leader, 1947–48 and 1953–54; House minority leader, 1959–68.

HAMILTON, ALEXANDER, Jan. 11, 1755 (Nevis, B.W.I.)–July 12, 1804. U.S. statesman, lawyer, author. Federalist party leader who wrote (with JOHN HAY and JAMES MADISON) *the Federalist Papers;* as first secy. of the treas. (1789–95), created the Bank of the United States, 1791; killed by AARON BURR in a duel.

HAMLIN, HANNIBAL, Aug. 27, 1809 (Paris Hill, Me.)–July 4, 1891. U.S. politician, lawyer, farmer. A prominent antislavery advocate who switched from the Democratic to the Republican party over that issue; U.S. sen. (D, Me.), 1848–57; U.S. vice-pres., 1861–65; as U.S. sen. (R, Me.), was a radical reconstructionist, 1869–81.

HANCOCK, JOHN, Jan. 12, 1737 (Braintree, Mass.) –Oct. 8, 1793. American patriot and Revolutionary leader, merchant. Pres. of Continental Congress, 1775–77; the first signer of the Declaration of Independence, 1776; gov. of Massachusetts, 1780–85 and 1787–93.

HANNA, MARCUS A. ("Mark"), Sept. 24, 1837 (New Lisbon [now Lisbon], Ohio)–Feb. 15, 1904. U.S. political leader, businessman, banker. Republican kingmaker who backed WILLIAM MCKINLEY, playing the crucial role in his election to the presidency, 1896; U.S. sen. (R, Ohio), 1897–1904; represented the alliance of big business and politics to further economic policy.

HANSON, JOHN, Apr. 13, 1721 (Mulberry Grove, Md.)–Nov. 22, 1783. U.S. politician, farmer. As first pres. under the Articles of Confederation (1781–82), sometimes considered the first pres. of the U.S.

HARDING, WARREN G. Nov. 2, 1865 (Blooming Grove, Ohio)–Aug. 2, 1923. U.S. president, teacher, newspaperman. U.S. sen. (R, Ohio), 1915–21 as 29th a pres. (R, 1921–23), promised a "return to normalcy"; his administration was plagued by corruption and scandals; died in office.

HARLAN, JOHN, M., June 1, 1833 (Boyle Co., Ky.)–Oct. 14, 1911. U.S. jurist, lawyer. As assoc. justice of U.S. Sup. Ct. (1877–1911), noted as a great dissenter; supporter of black rights, which he argued, were guaranteed by the Constitutional amendments passed after the Civil War.

HARRIMAN, W(illiam) AVERELL, Nov. 15, 1891 (New York, N.Y.)–July 26, 1986. U.S. statesman, diplomat, banker. A prominent U.S. diplomat who served a succession of presidents during his long career. Lend-Lease coordinator, 1941–43; U.S. amb. to USSR (1943–46) and Great Britain (1946); U.S. secy. of commerce, 1946–48; gov. (D) of New York, 1955–58; U.S. amb.-at-large, 1961 and 1965–75; as U.S. undersecy. of state for political affairs, 1963–65, negotiated limited nuclear test ban treaty; conducted Paris peace negotiations with N. Vietnam, 1968–69.

HARRIS, PATRICIA ROBERTS, May 31, 1924 (Mattoon, Ill.)–Mar. 23, 1985 U.S. govt. official, lawyer. Prof. of law at Howard U., 1961–65, 1967–69; U.S. amb. to Luxembourg, 1965–67; U.S. secy. of HUD, 1977–79; U.S. secy. of HEW, 1979; U.S. secy. Health and Human Services, 1979–81; first black woman to reach both ambassadorial and cabinet rank.

HARRISON, BENJAMIN, Aug. 20, 1833 (North Bend, Ohio)–Mar. 13, 1901. U.S. pres., lawyer. U.S. sen. (R, Ind.), 1881–87; as 23rd U.S. pres. (R, 1889–93), oversaw enactment of McKinley Tariff Act (1890) and Sherman Silver Purchase Act and Sherman Anti-trust Act (1890). (Grandson of W.H. HARRISON.)

HARRISON, WILLIAM HENRY, Feb. 9, 1773 ("Berkeley" plantation, Charles City Co., Va.)– Apr. 4, 1841. U.S. pres., soldier. A major gen. in the War of 1812; U.S. sen. (Whig, Ohio), 1825–28; the first to use public relations in a presidential campaign; as 9th U.S. pres. (Whig, 1841), served in office for one month before his death from pneumonia. (Grandfather of B. HARRISON.)

HART, PHILIP A., Dec. 10, 1912 (Bryn Mawr, Pa.)–Dec. 26, 1976. U.S. politician, lawyer. As U.S. sen. (D, Mich.), 1959–76, worked for civil rights, consumer, and antitrust legislation; outspoken critic of Vietnam War.

HARTKE, (Rupert) VANCE, May 31, 1919 (Stendal, Ind.). U.S. politician. Mayor (D) of Evansville, Ind., 1956–58; as U.S. sen. (D, Ind.), worked for civil rights and flood-control legislation, 1959–77. *The American Crisis in Vietnam,* 1968; *You and Your Senator,* 1970.

HATCHER, RICHARD G., July 10, 1933 (Michigan City, Ind.). U.S. politician, lawyer. Mayor (D) of Gary, Ind., 1967–87; co-convenor of National Black Political Convention, 1972; pres. of National Black Political Council, 1973– .

HATFIELD, MARK O., July 12, 1922 (Dallas, Ore.). U.S. politician, political scientist. Secy. of state (1956–58) and gov. (R) of Oregon, 1959–67; U.S. sen. (R, Ore.), 1967– .

HAY, JOHN, Oct. 8, 1838 (Salem, Ind.)–July 1, 1905. U.S. statesman, diplomat, author. Private secy. to ABRAHAM LINCOLN, 1861–65; U.S. amb. to Great Britain, 1897–98; served as U.S. secy. of state (1898–1905) during the critical period when the U.S. emerged as a world power, promoting Open Door policy with China and signing treaties opening the way for the Panama Canal. *Abraham Lincoln: A History,* 1890.

HAYAKAWA, SAMUEL I., July 18, 1906 (Vancouver, B.C., Can.). U.S. politician, educator. As Pres. of San Francisco St. C., was noted for his stand against student protesters, 1968–73; U.S. sen. (R, Cal.), 1977–83.

HAYDEN, CARL, Oct. 2, 1877 (Hayden's Ferry [now Tempe], Ariz.)–Jan. 25, 1972. U.S. politician who served in the U.S. Congress for 56 years (1912–69), the longest term in the nation's history. U.S. rep. (D, Ariz.), 1912–27; U.S. sen. (D, Ariz.).

1927–69; Senate pres. pro tem, 1957 69; chm. of Senate Appropriations Com., 1957–69.

HAYDEN, TOM, Dec, 11, 1939 (Royal Oak, Mich.). U.S. political activist. A co-founder of Students for a Democratic Society; served as a California state legislator. *Rebellion in Newark*, 1967; *Rebellion and Repression*, 1969; *The American Future*, 1980. (Former husband of J. FONDA.)

HAYES, RUTHERFORD B., Oct. 4, 1822 (Delaware, Ohio)–Jan. 17, 1893. U.S. pres., politician. Gov. (R.) of Ohio, 1868–72 and 1876–77; as the 19th U.S. pres. (R, 1877–81), ended the Reconstruction period in the South, attempted to establish higher standards of integrity in the government, fought for civil service reform, and sent troops to suppress the railroad strike of 1877.

HELMS, JESSE A., Oct. 18, 1921 (Monroe, N.C.). U.S. politician, newspaper editor. Exec. vice-pres. of WRAL-TV and Tobacco Radio Network, 1960–72; U.S. sen. (R, N.C.), 1972– ; ranking Republican on Senate Foreign Relations Committee.

HENRY, PATRICK, May 29, 1736 (Studley plantation, Hanover cty., Va.)–June 6, 1799. American patriot, lawyer, merchant. Del. to Continental Congress, 1774–76; gov. of Virginia, 1776–79 and 1784–86; great orator of the American Revolution, whose stirring call to arms against the British brought many to the cause; a radical leader who argued against the Stamp Act, advocated individual liberties, opposed to Federal Constitution because he feared it infringed upon states' rights; remembered for his words, "…give me liberty or give me death."

HERTER, CHRISTIAN A., Mar. 28, 1895 (Paris, Fr.)–Dec. 30, 1966. U.S. diplomat, journalist. Gov. (D) of Massachusetts, 1953–57; as U.S. secy. of state (1959–61), built a firm defense of Berlin and stronger U.S.-European ties, chief U.S trade negotiator in the J. F. KENNEDY and L. B. JOHNSON admins.

HILLS, CARLA, Jan. 3, 1934 (Los Angeles, Cal.). U.S. lawyer, educator and civil rights leader. Sec. of Housing and Urban Development, 1975–77; U.S. trade representative, 1989– .

HISS, ALGER, Nov. 11, 1904 (Baltimore, Md.), U.S. public official. The central figure in a sensational spy case, accused by WHITTAKER CHAMBERS of being part of a communist espionage ring in Washington, D.C.; convicted of perjury in 1950, imprisoned for five years, released still claiming his innocence. U.S. State Dept. official, 1936–46; pres. of Carnegie Endowment for Peace, 1946–49.

HOBBY, OVETA CULP, Jan. 19, 1905 (Killeen, Tex.). U.S. govt. official, newspaper publisher. Participated in planning Women's Army Corps, becoming its first dir., 1942; awarded Distinguished Service Medal for her work with WAC; first U.S. secy. of HEW, 1953–55; pres. and editor (1955–65) and chm. of the board (1965– ) of the Houston *Post*.

HOLMES, OLIVER WENDELL, JR., Mar. 8, 1841 (Boston, Mass.)–Mar. 6, 1935. U.S. jurist. An assoc. justice of U.S. Sup. Ct. (1902–32), known as the

"Great Dissenter"; developed the "clear and present danger" rule of the First Amendment, believed in "judicial restraint," proposed new conceptions of the origin of the nature of law. (Son of poet O.W. HOLMES.)

HOLTZMAN, ELIZABETH, Aug. 11, 1941 (Brooklyn, N.Y.). U.S. politician, lawyer. U.S. rep. (D, N.Y.), 1973–81; member of the House Judiciary Com. who gained national attention during the 1974 Nixon impeachment hearings; Dist. Atty, Brooklyn, 1982– .

HOOVER, HERBERT, C., Aug. 10, 1874 (West Branch, Ia.)–Oct. 20, 1964. U.S. pres., engineer. Head of allied relief operations during WW I; U.S. secy. of commerce, 1921–29; as 31st U.S. pres. (R. 1929–33), led the U.S. through the early years of the Depression, worked through the Federal Farm Bureau and the Reconstruction Finance Corp. to relieve suffering; defeated for reelection, 1932; participated in famine relief work in Europe after WW II.

HOOVER, J(ohn) EDGAR, Jan. 1, 1895 (Washington, D.C.)–May 2, 1972. U.S. govt. official, lawyer, criminologist. As dir. of the FBI (1926–72), established a fingerprint file, a scientific crime-detection laboratory, and the FBI National Acad.; contributed greatly to higher standards of police work; freed the FBI from political control; became known for his anticommunist views; criticized toward the end of his career for his authoritarianism and overzealousness.

HOPKINS, HARRY L., Aug. 17, 1890 (Sioux City, Ia.)–Jan. 29, 1946. U.S. govt. administrator, social worker. A close friend and adviser to Pres. F. D ROOSEVELT; administrator of Federal Emergency Relief, 1933–35; organized Civil Works Admin.; head of Works Progress Admin., 1935–38; U.S. secy. of commerce, 1938–40; Pres. H.S. TRUMAN's representative to Moscow to settle the Polish question, 1945.

HOPKINS, STEPHEN, Mar. 7, 1707 (Scituate, R.I.)–July 13, 1785. American patriot, farmer, merchant. Signer of the Declaration of Independence, 1776; member of Continental Congress, 1774–80; gov. of Rhode Island, 1755, 1756, 1758–61, 1763, 1764, and 1767. *The Rights of the Colonies Examined*, 1765.

HOPKINSON, FRANCIS, Oct. 2, 1737 (Philadelphia, Pa.)–May 9, 1791. American patriot, lawyer, author. Signer of the Declaration of Independence, 1776; claimed design of the U.S. flag. *Miscellaneous Essays and Occasional Writings*, 1792; *A Pretty Story*, 1774; *The New Roof*, 1787; composer, *Seven Songs* (First book of music published by an American composer, 1788.)

HOUSE, EDWARD M. ("Colonel"), July 26, 1858 (Houston, Tex.)–Mar. 28, 1938. U.S. statesman, diplomat. As confidential advisor to Pres. WOODROW WILSON (1913–19), played an important role in peace negotiations at the end of WW I; primarily interested in foreign affairs, he yielded to Allied pressure for harsh measures against Germany following WW I, for which he was dismissed by Wilson.

HOUSTON, SAM(uel), Mar. 2, 1793 (nr. Lexington, Va.)–July 26, 1863. U.S. politician, soldier, lawyer. Leader of the fight with Mexico for control of Texas. A Tennessee politician, he moved to Oklahoma, later Texas; commanded forces of provisional Texas govt. in brilliant victory over SANTA ANNA at San Jacinto, 1836; pres. of Rep. of Texas, 1836–38 and 1841–44; after admission of Texas to the Union, served as an antisecessionist Union Democrat U.S. sen. (1846–59) and Texas gov. (1859–61).

HUGHES, CHARLES EVANS, Apr. 11, 1862 (Glens Falls, N.Y.)–Aug. 27, 1948. U.S. jurist, lawyer. As chief justice of U.S. (1930–41), resisted attempts to "pack" the court with justices favorable to Pres. F. D. ROOSEVELT. Gov. (R) of New York, 1907–10; assoc. justice of U.S. Sup. Ct., 1910–16, Republican presidential nominee, 1916; U.S. secy. of state, 1921–25.

HULL, CORDELL, Oct. 2, 1871 (Byrdstown, Tenn.) –July 23, 1955. U.S. statesman, diplomat, lawyer. As U.S. secy. of state (1933–44), initiated a reciprocal trade program, developed the Good Neighbor policy with Latin America, promoted cooperation with the Soviet Union against Hitler, obtained support in Congress and internationally for starting the UN; awarded Nobel Peace Prize, 1945.

HUMPHREY, HUBERT H., May 27, 1911 (Wallace, S.D.)–Jan. 13, 1978. U.S. politician, pharmacist. Outstanding liberal and Democratic party leader. Mayor (D) of Minneapolis, 1945–48; as U.S. sen. (D, Minn.; 1949–65 and 1971–78), helped achieve bipartisan support for the Nuclear Test Ban Treaty (1963) and the Civil Rights Act (1964); as U.S. vice-pres. (1965–69), defended U.S. Vietnam policy; Democratic presidential candidate, 1968.

HUNT, E. HOWARD, JR., Oct. 9, 1918 (Hamburg, N.Y.). U.S. govt. official. A 21-year veteran of the CIA, was serving as a consultant to CHARLES W. COLSON when he was caught during the Watergate break-in, 1972; pleaded guilty to all charges, 1973; author of 42 short stories and spy novels under several pseudonyms.

HUTCHINSON, THOMAS, Sept. 9, 1711 (Boston, Mass.)–June 3, 1780. Colonial American administrator. As colonial gov. of Massachusetts (1771–74), resisted the Boston revolutionaries and helped to inflame them; refused to allow tea-laden ships to leave Boston harbor before the tea was unloaded, precipitating the Boston Tea Party, 1773.

INGALLS, JOHN JAMES, Dec. 29, 1833 (Middleton, Mass.)–Aug. 16, 1900. U.S. politician, lawyer, farmer. U.S. sen. (R, Kan.), 1873–91; well-known orator who "waved the bloody shirt" during the Reconstruction era.

INOUYE, DANIEL K., Sept. 7, 1924 (Honolulu, Haw.). U.S. politician, lawyer. U.S. rep. (D. Haw.), 1959–62; U.S. sen. (D. Haw.), 1963– ; Senate asst. majority whip, 1963–76; chm. of Senate Select Com. on Intelligence, 1976–84.

JACKSON, ANDREW ("Old Hickory"), Mar. 15, 1767 (Waxhaw, S.C.)–June 8, 1845. U.S. pres., soldier, lawyer, planter. As 7th U.S. pres. (D,

1829–37), the first to be elected by a mass base of voters, rewarded the men of his Democratic party with jobs, and fought the Bank of the United States. U.S. rep. (D, Tenn.), 1796–97; U.S. sen. (D, Tenn.), 1797–98; a military hero of the War of 1812 for his victory at New Orleans (1815).

JACKSON, HENRY M., May 31, 1912 (Everett, Wash.)–Sept. 1, 1983. U.S. politician, lawyer. Influential Democratic party leader, authority on national defense, supporter of Israel, conservationist. U.S. sen. (D, Wash.), 1952–83; chm. of Senate Energy and Natural Resources Com.; unsuccessfully sought Democratic presidential nomination in 1972 and 1976.

JACKSON, JESSE, Oct. 8, 1941 (Greenville, S.C.). U.S. politician clergyman. Founder of such public assistance organizations as Operation Breadbasket, Operation PUSH, and the National Rainbow Coalition; twice a candidate for the Democratic Party nomination for president, 1984 and 1988.

JACKSON MAYNARD, Mar. 23, 1938 (Dallas, Tex.). U.S. politician, lawyer. Mayor (D) of Atlanta, 1974–82; member of Democratic National Com.

JACKSON, ROBERT H., Feb. 13, 1892 (Spring Creek, Pa.)–Oct. 9, 1954. U.S. jurist, lawyer. As assoc. justice of U.S. Sup. Ct. (1941–54), opposed monopolies, believed in judicial restraint, supported civil liberties; U.S. rep. and chief counsel at the Nuremberg war crimes trials, 1945–46.

JARVIS, HOWARD A., Sept. 22, 1902 (Magna, Ut.)–Aug. 12, 1986. U.S. tax reformer. A co-sponsor (with Paul Gann) and vocal supporter of Proposition 13, a California primary-ballot initiative to cut property taxes 57% (passed in June 1978); exec. dir. of Apartment Assn. of Los Angeles Co. and of the United Org. of Taxpayers.

JAVITS, JACOB K., May 18, 1904 (New York, N.Y.)–Mar. 7, 1986. U.S. politician, lawyer. U.S. rep. (R, N.Y.), 1946–54; U.S. sen. (R, N.Y.), 1956–86; member of Senate Select Com. on Small Business, Joint Economic Com., Foreign Relations Com., Govt. Operations Com., and Labor and Public Welfare Com.

JAWORSKI, LEON, Sept. 19, 1905 (Waco, Tex.)– Dec. 9, 1982. U.S. lawyer. Dir. of Office of the Watergate Special Prosecution Force, 1973–74; special counsel to House Com. on Standards for Official Conduct, for its investigation of the Korean lobbying scandal, 1977–78; member, President's Commission on the Causes and Prevention of Violence, 1968–69. *The Right and the Power*, 1976.

JAY, JOHN, Dec. 12, 1745 (New York, N.Y.)– May 17, 1829. U.S. jurist, lawyer, statesman. Pres. of Continental Congress, 1778–1779; negotiated the Treaty of Paris with Great Britain, 1783; negotiated the Jay Treaty, a controversial commercial treaty, 1794; as first chief justice of U.S., played an important role in formation of the court's procedures, 1789–95; wrote (with J. MADISON and A. HAMILTON) *The Federalist Papers*.

JEFFERSON, THOMAS, Apr. 13, 1743 ("Shadwell," Goochland, [now Albemarle Co.], Va.)– July 4, 1826. U.S. pres., lawyer, educator, architect, inventor. The principal intellectual force behind the founding of the Rep. of the U.S. Author of the Declaration of Independence, 1776; U.S. secy. of state, 1790–93; as 3rd U.S. pres. (1801–09), negotiated Louisiana Purchase for the U.S. (1803), and kept the U.S. out of the Napoleonic Wars; founded the U. of Virginia, 1819.

JOHNSON, ANDREW, Dec. 29, 1808 (Raleigh, N.C.)–July 31, 1875. U.S. pres., politician, tailor. Military gov. of Tennessee, 1862–64; succeeded the assassinated ABRAHAM LINCOLN to become 17th U.S. pres. (D), 1865–69; made enemies by executing a mild Reconstruction program; survived impeachment attempt by Congress, 1868.

JOHNSON, HIRAM W., Sept. 2, 1866 (Sacramento, Calif.)–Aug. 6, 1945. U.S. politician, lawyer. A founder of the Progressive party and an isolationist who voted against U.S. entry into WW I and sponsored the Neutrality Acts of the 1930s. Reform gov. of California, 1911–17; U.S. sen. (R, Calif.), 1917–45.

JOHNSON, LYNDON BAINES, Aug. 27, 1908 (Gillespie Co., Tex.)–Jan. 22, 1973. U.S. president, teacher. A protégé of Rep. SAM RAYBURN; as U.S. sen. (D, Tex.), was a highly successful majority leader, 1954–61; succeeded the assassinated Pres. JOHN F. KENNEDY to become 36th U.S. pres., 1963–69; as pres., exercised his political skill in passing legislation, especially in areas of civil rights, tax reduction, antipoverty programs, and conservation; escalated U.S. involvement in South Vietnam; anti-Vietnam War sentiment caused him to decide not to seek renomination in 1968.

JORDAN, BARBARA, Feb. 21, 1936 (Houston, Tex.) U.S. politician, lawyer. As Texas state sen. (D, 1967–72), the first black woman to serve in the Texas leg. in the 20th cent.; U.S. rep. (D, Tex.), 1972–78; as a member of House Judiciary Comm. during 1974 Nixon impeachment hearings, supported Pres. R. M. NIXON's impeachment; as keynote speaker, ignited the 1976 Democratic National Convention.

JORDAN, HAMILTON, Sept. 21, 1944 (Charlotte, N.C.). U.S. govt. official. Campaign manager during JIMMY CARTER's race for Georgia gov., 1970; exec. secy. to Gov. Carter, 1970–74; asst. to Pres. Carter 1977–79; chief of staff, 1979–81.

KEFAUVER, ESTES, July 26, 1903 (Monroe Co., Tenn.)–Aug. 10, 1963. U.S. politician, lawyer. U.S. rep. (D, Tenn., 1939–49); U.S. sen. (D, Tenn.), 1949–63; attracted nationwide attention as chm. of Senate com. investigating organized crime, 1950–52; Democratic party nominee for vice-pres., 1956.

KELLOGG, FRANK B., Dec. 22, 1856 (Potsdam, N.Y.)–Dec. 21, 1937. U.S. politician, diplomat, lawyer. Originally a trustbusting lawyer who helped break up the Standard Oil Co.; U.S. sen. (R, Minn.), 1917–23; U.S. amb. to Great Britain, 1923–25; as U.S. secy. of state (1925–29), negotiated the antiwar Kellogg-Briand Pact (1928); awarded Nobel Peace Prize, 1929.

KEMP, JACK, July 13, 1935 (Los Angeles, Cal.).

U.S. politician. A former professional football quarterback, served in the United States House of Representatives (R, N.Y.), 1970–80; candidate for the Republican nomination for president, 1988, U.S. secy. of Housing and Urban Development, 1989– .

KENNAN, GEORGE F. Feb. 16, 1904 (Milwaukee, Wisc.). U.S. diplomat, historian. Influential in forming the U.S. policy of "containment" of the Soviet Union following WW II; prof. at Inst. for Advanced Study, 1956, 1963–74. Awarded 1957 Pulitzer Prize in history for *Russia Leaves the War* (1956) and 1968 Pulitzer Prize in biography for *Memoirs 1925–50* (1967).

KENNEDY, EDWARD M. ("Ted"), Feb. 22, 1932 (Brookline, Mass.). U.S. politician, lawyer. As U.S. sen. (D, Mass.) 1963– , has worked for national health insurance and tax reduction; Senate asst. majority leader, 1968–71; ranking Democrat, Labor and Human Resources Comm., 1981– ; his political future was temporarily blighted when he left the scene of an accident on Chappaquiddick I., 1969. (Brother of J.F. and R.F. KENNEDY.)

KENNEDY, JOHN F., May 29, 1917 (Brookline, Mass.)–Nov. 22, 1963. U.S. pres., politician. WW II hero; U.S. rep. (D, Mass.), 1947–53; U.S. sen. (D, Mass.), 1953–60; as 35th U.S. pres (D, 1961–63), the first Roman Catholic to hold the office; took responsibility for the Bay of Pigs Invasion of Cuba, 1961; started the Alliance for Progress with Latin America and the Peace Corps, 1961; forced the USSR to remove missiles from Cuba, 1962; negotiated a limited test-ban treaty, 1963; assassinated in Dallas, Tex. Awarded 1957 Pulitzer Prize in history for *Profiles in Courage* (1956). (Brother of R.F. and E.M. KENNEDY.)

KENNEDY, ROBERT F., Nov. 20, 1925 (Brookline, Mass.)–June 6, 1968. U.S. politician, lawyer. As U.S. atty. gen. (1961–64), aggressive fighter for civil rights and a leading adviser to brother Pres. JOHN F. KENNEDY; U.S. sen. (D, N.Y.), 1965–68; assassinated in the midst of his campaign for the 1968 Democratic presidential nomination. (Brother of E.M. KENNEDY.)

KERR, ROBERT S., Sept. 11, 1896 (Ada, Okla.)–Jan. 1, 1963. U.S. politician, oilman. Gov. (D) of Oklahoma, 1943–47; as U.S. Sen. (D, Okla.), 1949–63, a powerful defendant of the domestic oil business and influential in securing passage of much of Pres. JOHN F. KENNEDY's legislation.

KERREY, JOSEPH ROBERT, Aug. 27, 1943 (Lincoln, Neb.). U.S. politician. A navy hero during the Vietnam War, he won the Congressional Medal of Honor and other citations; gov. (D, Neb.), 1970–78; U.S. sen., 1979– .

KING, RUFUS. Mar. 24, 1755 (Scarborough, Mass., now Me.)–Apr. 29, 1827. U.S. politician, diplomat, lawyer. Eloquent U.S. sen. (Fed, N.Y., 1789–96 and 1813–25) who argued for a strong central govt. at the 1787 Constitutional Convention; U.S. min. to Great Britain, 1796–1803 and 1825–26; unsuccessful Federalist candidate for vice-pres. In 1804 and 1808, and for pres. in 1816.

KISSINGER, HENRY, May 27, 1923 (Fürth, Ger.).

U.S. govt. official, scholar. As adviser for national security affairs (1969–75) and U.S. secy. of state (1973–77), heavily influenced U.S. foreign policy, particularly in the negotiations that ended the U.S. role in Vietnam; prof. of govt. at Harvard U., 1962–69; initiated the SALT talks, 1969; attempted to negotiate an Arab-Israeli peace agreement, 1973–75; awarded (with LE DUC THO) Nobel Peace Prize, 1973. *Nuclear Weapons and Foreign Policy*, 1957; *Years of Upheaval*, 1982.

**KNOWLAND, WILLIAM F.**, June 26, 1908 (Alameda, Calif.)–Feb. 23, 1974. U.S. politician, publisher. U.S. sen. (R, Calif.), 1945–58; Senate minority leader (1955–58) and majority leader (1953–54); publisher of the Oakland *Tribune*, 1965–74.

**KNOX, PHILANDER CHASE**, May 6, 1853 (Brownsville, Pa.)–Oct. 12, 1921. U.S. politician, lawyer. U.S. atty gen., 1901–04; U.S. sen. (R, Pa.), 1904–09 and 1917–21; as U.S. secy. of state (1909–13), extended the Monroe Doctrine to include Asian nations and started "dollar diplomacy."

**KOCH, EDWARD I.**, Dec. 12, 1924 (New York, N.Y.). U.S. politician, lawyer. U.S. rep. (D, N.Y.), 1969–77; mayor (D) of New York City 1977–90. *Mayor*, 1984.

**LA FOLLETTE, PHILIP F.**, May 8, 1897 (Madison, Wisc.)–Aug. 18, 1965. U.S. politician, lawyer. As gov. (Prog.) of Wisconsin (1931–33 and 1935–39), passed the nation's first unemployment legislation. (Son of R. M. LA FOLLETTE; brother of R. M. LA FOLLETTE, JR.)

**LA FOLLETTE, ROBERT M.**, June 14, 1855 (Primrose, Wisc.)–June 18, 1925. U.S. politician, lawyer. Leader of the U.S. Progressive movement, championed the little guy against established interests. U.S. rep. (R, Wisc.), 1885–91; reform gov. (R) of Wisconsin, 1900–06; U.S. sen. (R-Prog., Wisc.), 1907–25; founded *La Follette's Weekly* (later called *The Progressive*), 1909; Progressive party presidential candidate, 1924. (Father of P.F. LA FOLLETTE and R.M. LA FOLLETTE, JR.)

**LA FOLLETTE, ROBERT MARION, JR.**, Feb. 6, 1895 (Madison, Wisc.)–Feb. 24, 1953. U.S. politician, publishing and broadcasting executive. Like his father, ROBERT LA FOLLETTE, an independent Progressive Republican, elected to succeed his father as U.S. sen. (Wisc.), 1925–47; an isolationist and advocate of unemployment legislation; defeated by JOE MCCARTHY. (Brother of P.F. LA FOLLETTE.)

**LAGUARDIA, FIORELLO H.** ("The Little Flower"), Dec. 11, 1882 (New York, N.Y.)–Sept. 20, 1947. U.S. politician. U.S. rep. (R, N.Y.), 1917–19 and 1922–33; as New York City mayor (1933–45), known for his honesty and nonpartisanship; obtained a new charter for the city (1938), promoted building in the city, and improved the efficiency of city govt.

**LAIRD, MELVIN R.** Sept. 1, 1922 (Omaha, Neb.). U.S. politician, govt. official. As U.S. secy. of def. (1967–73), reduced the U.S. armed forces by 1 million men, laid plans for an all-volunteer army, and marshaled support for the continuing presence of U.S. armed forces in Vietnam. U.S. rep. (R, Wisc.), 1953–69; domestic affairs counselor to U.S. pres., 1973–74.

**LANCE, BERT**, June 3, 1931 (Gainesville, Ga.). U.S. banker, govt. official. Pres. (1963–74) and chm. (1974–77, 1981–86) of Calhoun (Ga.) First National Bank; dir. of U.S. Office of Management and the Budget, 1977; forced to resign because of questionable banking practices.

**LANDON, ALF**(red), Sept. 9, 1887 (West Middlesex, Pa.)–Oct. 12, 1987. U.S. politician, oilman. Gov. (R) of Kansas, 1933–37; Republican presidential candidate, 1936.

**LANDRIEU, MOON**, July 23, 1930 (New Orleans, La.). U.S. politician, lawyer. Mayor (D) of New Orleans, 1970–78; U.S. secy. of HUD, 1979–81.

**LAXALT, PAUL**, Aug. 2, 1922 (Reno, Nev.). U.S. politician, lawyer. Gov. (R) of Nevada, 1967–71; U.S. sen. (R, Nev.), 1975–87; chm. of RONALD REAGAN's presidential campaign, 1976, 80, 84.

**LEE, FRANCIS LIGHTFOOT**, Oct. 14, 1734 ("Stratford," Westmoreland Co., Va.)–Jan. 11, 1797. U.S. political leader. Member, Virginia House of Burgesses, 1758–76; a signer of the Declaration of Independence, 1776; member, second Continental Congress, 1775–79; fought for ratification of the Constitution. (Brother of R.H. LEE.)

**LEE, RICHARD HENRY**, Jan. 31, 1732 ("Stratford," Westmoreland Co., Va.)–June 19, 1794. American Revolutionary patriot, lawyer. Proposed a resolution for the independence of the colonies that was passed by the Second Continental Congress, July 2, 1776; a signer of the Declaration of Independence, 1776; U.S. sen. (Va.), 1789–92. (Brother of F.L. LEE.)

**LIDDY, G. GORDON**, Nov. 30, 1930 (New York, N.Y.). U.S. lawyer, govt. official. The most flamboyant of the original defendants in the Watergate break-in, 1972; served as counsel for the Com. to Re-elect the President (1971) and its Finance Com. (1971); convicted on six counts for his involvement, 1973; imprisoned, 1973; 20-year sentence commuted by Pres. J. CARTER, released 1977. *Will*, 1980.

**LINCOLN, ABRAHAM**, Feb. 12, 1809 (Hardin Co. [now Larue Co.] Ky.)–Apr. 15, 1865. U.S. pres., lawyer. As 16th U.S. pres. (1861–65) led the Union during the Civil War, published the Emancipation Proclamation (1863), delivered the famous Gettysburg Address (1863); widely hailed as the savior of the Union, he was assassinated by J.W. BOOTH. U.S. rep. (Whig, Ill.), 1847–49; joined Republican party and chosen to oppose STEPHEN A. DOUGLAS in the 1858 Senate race, which he lost despite his brilliant performance in debates with Douglas.

**LINDSAY, JOHN V.**, Nov. 24, 1921 (New York, N.Y.). U.S. politician, lawyer, author. U.S. rep. (R, N.Y.), 1959–65; as mayor of New York City (1966–74), the first Republican elected to that post in 20 years, he was plagued with labor unrest, increased crime, and rising welfare costs; switched to Democratic party and unsuccessfully campaigned for presidential nomination in 1972. *Journey into Politics*, 1966; *The Edge*, 1976.

**LIVINGSTON, PHILIP,** Jan. 15, 1716 (Albany, N.Y.)–June 12, 1778. American patriot, merchant. A signer of the Declaration of Independence, 1776; played a crucial role in organizing New York's boycott of British goods, 1768; represented New York in the first and second Continental Congresses, 1774–78.

**LIVINSTON, ROBERT, R.,** Nov. 27, 1746 (New York, N.Y.)–Feb. 26, 1813. U.S. diplomat, lawyer. Member of the Com. of Five who drafted the Declaration of Independence, 1776; administered the oath of office to Pres. GEORGE WASHINGTON, 1789; partner with ROBERT FULTON in building the first steamboat; as U.S. min. to France (1801–1804), helped negotiate the Louisiana Purchase (1803).

**LODGE, HENRY CABOT,** May 12, 1850 (Boston, Mass.)–Nov. 9, 1924. U.S. politician, historian. As U.S. sen. (R, Mass.), 1893–1924, led the successful Congressional opposition to U.S. participation in the League of Nations following WW I. *Life and Letters of George Cabot*, 1877. (Grandfather of H.C. LODGE, JR.)

**LODGE, HENRY CABOT, JR.,** July 5, 1902 (Nahant, Mass.)–Feb. 27, 1985. U.S. politician, diplomat. U.S. sen. (R, Mass.), 1937–44 and 1947–53; U.S. del. to the UN, 1953–60; Rep. vice-presidential candidate, 1960; U.S. amb. to S. Vietnam, 1963–64 and 1965–67; Pres. RICHARD M. NIXON's rep. at the Paris Peace Talks on Vietnam, 1969. (Grandson of H.C. LODGE.)

**LONG, EARL,** Aug. 25, 1895 (Winnfield, La.)–Sept. 5, 1960. U.S. politician. He preached the same sort of "share the wealth" doctrine that his brother Huey Long used to win the governorship of Louisiana; elected governor of the state three times—1939–1940, 1948–1952, and 1956–1960, since the governor of Louisiana could not succeed himself; died in a mental institution. (Brother of H. LONG, uncle of R. LONG.)

**LONG, HUEY P.** ("The Kingfish"), Aug. 30, 1893 (Winn Parish, La.)–Sept. 10, 1935. U.S. politician, lawyer. Demagogic political leader in Louisiana politics who commanded a nationwide following in the 1930s. As gov. (D) of Louisiana (1928–32) and U.S. sen. (D, La., 1932–35), fought established interests for benefits for the poor; assassinated. (Father of R.B. LONG.)

**LONG, RUSSELL B.,** Nov. 3, 1918 (Shreveport, La.). U.S. politician, lawyer. U.S. sen. (D, La.) 1948–86; Senate majority whip, 1965–69; asst. Senate majority leader, 1965–68; chm. of Senate Finance com., 1966–81. (Son of H.P. LONG.)

**LUCE, CLARE BOOTHE,** Apr. 10, 1903 (New York, N.Y.)–Oct. 9, 1987. U.S. politician, journalist, diplomat. Assoc. editor of *Vogue*, 1930; assoc. and managing editor of *Vanity Fair*, 1933–34; U.S. rep. (R, Conn.), 1943–47; keynote speaker at 1944 Republican National Convention; U.S. amb. to Italy, 1953–57. *Stuffed Shirts*, 1931; *The Women*, 1937; *Kiss the Boys Goodbye*, 1938. (Wife of H. LUCE.)

**LUGAR, RICHARD G.,** Apr. 4, 1932 (Indianapolis, Ind.). U.S. politician, stockfarmer. Mayor (R) of Indianapolis, Ind., 1968–75; U.S. sen. (R, Ind.), 1977– ; chm., Foreign Relations Committee, 1985–87; member of National Advisory Commission on Criminal Justice Standards and Goals.

**MADDOX, LESTER,** Sept. 30, 1915 (Atlanta, Ga.). U.S. politician. Gained notoriety by driving blacks from his Pickrick restaurant in defiance of federal civil-rights laws and closing the restaurant rather than desegregating it, 1964; although elected gov. (D) of Georgia (1967–71) as an avowed segregationist with Ku Klux Klan support, was unable to stop desegregation; Ga. lt. gov., 1971–75.

**MADISON, JAMES,** Mar. 16, 1751 (Port Conway, Va.)–June 28, 1836. U.S. pres., political theorist. Influential in the framing of the Constitution; contributed to the *Federalist* papers; sponsored the first ten amendments (Bill of Rights) to the Constitution; U.S. secy. of state, 1801–09; 4th U.S. pres., 1809–17.

**MAGNUSON, WARREN G.,** Apr. 12, 1905 (Moorhead, Minn.)–May 20, 1989. U.S. politician, lawyer. U.S. sen. (D, Wash.), 1944–81; chm. of Senate Appropriations Com.; 1978–81.

**MAGRUDER, JEB STUART,** Nov. 5, 1934 (Staten I., N.Y.). U.S. govt. official. As dep. dir. of the Committee to Re-elect the President (1971–72), was involved in the Watergate scandal; pleaded guilty, 1974; imprisoned, 1974–75. *An American Life*, 1974.

**MANSFIELD, MIKE,** Mar. 16, 1903 (New York, N.Y.). U.S. politician, diplomat, engineer. U.S. rep. (D, Mont.), 1943–53; U.S. sen. (D, Mont.), 1953–77; asst. Senate majority leader, 1957–61; Senate majority leader, 1961–77; U.S. amb. to Japan, 1977– .

**MARCY, WILLIAM L.** Dec. 12, 1786 (Southbridge, Mass.)–July 4, 1857. U.S. politician. Known as the champion of the "spoils system," credited with the remark, "To the victor belong the spoils of the enemy." U.S. sen. (D, N.Y.), 1831–33; gov. (D) of New York, 1833–39; U.S. secy. of war, 1845–49; U.S. secy. of state, 1853–57.

**MARSHALL, JOHN,** Sept. 24, 1755 (Germantown, Va.)–July 6, 1835. U.S. jurist. As 4th chief justice of U.S. (1801–35), influential in molding the Court and establishing its function; founder of the U.S. system of Constitutional law and doctrine of judicial review. Special commissioner to France in the XYZ Affair, 1797–98; U.S. secy. of state, 1800–01.

**MARSHALL, THOMAS R.,** Mar. 14, 1854 (N. Manchester, Ind.)–June 1, 1925. Democratic party wit known for the slogan, "What this country needs is a good five-cent cigar." Gov. of Indiana, 1909–13; U.S. vice-pres., 1913–21.

**MARSHALL, THURGOOD,** July 2, 1908 (Baltimore, Md.). U.S. jurist, lawyer. As assoc. justice of U.S. Sup. Ct. (1967– ), the first black to serve on the Court. Chief of the legal staff of NAACP, 1940–61; argued the case of *Brown vs. Board of*

*Education of Topeka* before the U.S. Sup. Ct., 1954; U.S. solicitor gen., 1965–67.

**MARTIN, WILLIAM MCCHESNEY, JR.,** Dec. 17, 1906 (St. Louis, Mo.). U.S. govt. official, financier. The first salaried pres. of the New York Stock Exchange, 1938–41; dir. of Export-Import Bank, 1945–50; asst. secy. of the U.S. treas., 1949–51; as chm. of Federal Reserve Board (1951–70), favored a "hard money" policy and tight control over the money supply.

**MCADOO, WILLIAM G.,** Oct, 31, 1863 (nr. Marietta, Ga.)–Feb. 1, 1941. U.S. govt. official, lawyer. As U.S. secy. of the treas. (1913–18), successfully floated $18 billion worth of loans to finance WW I allied forces; a founder and chm. of the Federal Reserve Board, 1913. (Son-in-law of W. WILSON.)

**MCCARRAN, PATRICK A.,** Aug. 8, 1876 (Reno, Nev.)–Sept. 28, 1954. U.S. politician, lawyer, farmer. U.S. sen. (D, Nev.), 1933–54; chm. of Senate Judiciary Com., 1943–46 and 1949–53; sponsored a bill for the registration of communists and an alien immigration act that tightened loyalty regulations (1952).

**MCCARTHY, EUGENE,** Mar. 29, 1916 (Watkins, Minn.). U.S. politician, teacher. U.S. rep. (D, Minn.), 1949–59; U.S. sen. (D, Minn.), 1959–70; ran against Pres. LYNDON JOHNSON for the Democratic nomination in the 1968 state primaries, calling for disengagement from and negotiated peace in Vietnam; Liberal Indep. cand. for pres, 1976.

**MCCARTHY, JOSEPH R.,** Nov. 14, 1908 (Grand Chute, Wisc.)–May 2, 1957. U.S. politician, lawyer, farmer. As U.S. sen. (R, Wisc.; 1947–57), conducted highly publicized investigations of alleged communists, using his chairmanship of the Senate Permanent Subcom. on Investigations to pursue his witch hunt; censured by the Senate (1954) for contempt and abuse, after which his influence declined.

**MCCLELLAN, JOHN L.,** Feb. 25, 1896 (Sheridan, Ark.)–Nov. 27, 1977. U.S. politician, lawyer. U.S. rep. (D, Ark.), 1935–39; U.S. sen. (D, Ark.), 1943–77; chm. of Senate Appropriations Com. 1972–77; as chm. of the Senate Select Com. on Improper Activities in the Labor or Management Field (late 1950s), investigated unions, especially the Teamsters.

**MCCLOSKEY, PAUL N., JR.,** ("Pete"), Sept. 29, 1927 (San Bernardino, Calif.). U.S. politician, lawyer. U.S. rep. (R, Calif.), 1967–83; ran unsuccessfully for the 1972 Republican presidential nomination.

**MCCORD, JAMES W., JR.,** July 26, 1924 (Texas). U.S. govt. official. CIA employee, 1951–71; was working as security coordinator for the R. M. NIXON reelection com. and Republican Natl. Com. when arrested as one of the burglars in the Watergate break-in (1972); convicted, 1973; imprisoned, March–May 1975.

**MCCORMACK, JOHN W.,** Dec. 21, 1891 (Boston, Mass.)–Nov. 22, 1980. U.S. politician, lawyer. U.S. rep. (D, Mass.). 1928–71; House majority leader, 1940–47, 1949–53, and 1955–61; Speaker of the House, 1962–71.

**MCGOVERN, GEORGE S.,** July 19, 1922 (Avon, S.D.). U.S. politician, historian. Dir. of Food for Peace Program, 1961–62; U.S. rep. (D, S.D.), 1957–61; U.S. sen. (D, S.D.), 1963–81; as Democratic presidential candidate in 1972 and 1984, campaigned for an immediate end to the Vietnam War and a broad program of social change.

**MCKINLEY, WILLIAM,** Jan. 29, 1843 (Niles, Ohio)–Sept. 14, 1901. U.S. pres., politician. As U.S. rep. (R, Ohio; 1877–83 and 1885–91), advocated tariff protectionism and opposed free silver; as 25th U.S. pres. (R, 1897–1901), led the U.S. through the Spanish-American War; assassinated by L. CZOLGOSZ an anarchist.

**MCMAHON, BRIEN,** Oct. 6, 1903 (Norwalk, Conn.)–July 28, 1952. U.S. politician, lawyer. As U.S. sen. (D, Conn; 1944–52), played a major role in the formation of U.S. atomic energy policy; an advocate of civilian control of atomic development, sponsored McMahon Act of 1946 that established the AEC; chm. of Joint Congressional Com. on Atomic Energy, 1948–52.

**MCNAMARA, ROBERT S.,** June 9, 1916 (San Francisco, Calif.). U.S. govt. official, banker, business executive. Exec. of Ford Motor Co., 1946–61; as U.S. secy. of def. (1961–68), caused controversy by applying modern managerial concepts; pres. of International Bank for Reconstruction and Development, 1968–81.

**MEESE, EDWIN, III,** Dec. 2, 1931 (Oakland, Cal.). U.S. statesman. A deputy district attorney of Alameda County, California, he became secretary of legal affairs for Governor RONALD REAGAN; went back to private practice and teaching and then became counselor to Pres. Reagan (1981–1985), later serving under him as Attorney General (1985–1988).

**MILLER, G. WILLIAM,** Mar. 9, 1925 (Sapulpa, Okla.). U.S. govt. official, lawyer, business exec. Pres. and chm. of the board (1960–74) of Textron, Inc.; chm. of Federal Reserve Board, 1978–79; U.S. secy. of the treasury, 1979–81.

**MINUIT (or Minnewit), PETER,** 1580 (Wesel, Ger.)–June 1638. Dutch administrator in colonial America. Dir.-gen. of colony of New Netherland, 1626–31; purchased Manhattan I. from the Indians for the equivalent of $24; in the service of Sweden, established New Sweden (later Wilmington, Del.), 1638.

**MITCHELL, GEORGE, J.,** Aug. 20, 1933 (Waterville, Me.). U.S. politician. Served as executive assistant to Senator EDMUND MUSKIE; U.S. sen. (D, Me.), 1981–  .

**MITCHELL, JOHN N.,** Sept. 15, 1913 (Detroit, Mich.)–Nov. 9, 1988. U.S. govt. official, lawyer. As U.S. atty. gen. (1969–72), played a major role in the Watergate scandal; directed Pres. R. M. NIXON's Com. for the Reelection of the President, 1972; convicted of conspiracy, obstruction of justice, and perjury (1975)—the first member of any cabinet to be imprisoned, 1977–79.

**MONDALE, WALTER F.** ("Fritz"), Jan. 5, 1928 (Ceylon, Minn.). U.S. politician, lawyer. U.S. sen.

(D, Minn.), 1964–77, U.S. vice-pres. (D, 1977–81); Dem. cand. for pres. 1984.

MONROE, JAMES, Apr. 28, 1758 (Westmoreland Co., Va.)–July 4, 1831. U.S. pres., diplomat. U.S. sen. (Va.), 1790–94; U.S. min. to France, 1794–96; as special envoy to France (1802–03), participated in negotiations for the Louisiana Purchase; U.S. secy. of state, 1811–17; as fifth U.S. pres. (1817–25), established Monroe Doctrine, warning Europe not to interfere in the Western Hemisphere, and approved the Missouri Compromise (1820).

MORGENTHAU, HENRY, JR., May 11, 1891 (New York, N.Y.)–Feb. 6, 1967. U.S. govt. official, farmer, conservationist. Editor of *American Agriculturist*, 1922–33; head of Farm Credit Admin., 1933; as U.S. secy. of the treas. (1934–45), raised and spent the incredibly large amount of money the New Deal and WW II demanded.

MORRIS, GOUVERNEUR, Jan. 31, 1752 (Morrisania [now part of New York City], N.Y.)–Nov. 6, 1816. American Revolutionary patriot, govt. official. One of the authors of New York's first state constitution, 1776; del. to Continental Congress, 1777–79; as U.S. min. of finance (1781–85), devised the decimal coinage plan; U.S. sen. (Fed, N.Y.), 1800–03. *Observations on the American Revolution*, 1779; *Diary of the French Revolution*, 1939 (edited and published by his great-grand daughter.).

MORRIS, ROBERT, Jan. 31, 1734 (Liverpool, Eng.)–May 8, 1806. U.S. financier, Revolutionary patriot. A successful shipper to the W. Indies, 1755–1806; del. to Second Continental Congress, 1775–78, and a signer of the Declaration of Independence, 1776; purchasing agent for Continental Army troops, 1778–79; a founder of the Bank of Pennsylvania, first U.S. bank, 1780; founded Bank of North America, 1782; colonial supt. of finance, 1781–1784; personally financed a large part of Revolutionary War effort; del. to Constitutional Congress, 1787; first U.S. sen. from Pennsylvania, 1789–95.

MORSE, WAYNE, Oct. 20, 1900 (Madison, Wisc.)–July 22, 1974. U.S. politician, lawyer. Elected to U.S. Senate (Ore.), as a Republican in 1944; refused to support D. D. EISENHOWER for the presidency (1952) and declared himself an independent; formally became a Democrat (1954), serving as such until 1969; noted for his outspokenness; opposed Vietnam War from the outset.

MORTON, ROGERS C. B., Sept. 19, 1914 (Louisville, Ky.)–Apr. 19, 1979. U.S. politician, farmer, businessman. U.S. rep. (R, Md.), 1963–71; chm. of Republican National Com., 1969–71; U.S. secy. of the int. 1971–75; U.S. secy. of commerce, 1975–76. (Brother of T.B. MORTON.)

MORTON, THRUSTON B., Aug. 19, 1907 (Louisville, Ky.)–Aug. 14, 1982. U.S. politician, businessman. U.S. rep. (R, Ky.), 1946–52; U.S. asst. secy. of state, 1953–56; U.S. sen. (R, Ky.), 1957–69. (Brother of R.C.B. MORTON.)

MOSES, ROBERT, Dec. 18, 1888 (New Haven, Conn.)–July 29, 1981. U.S. public official. As a New York state official, dominated state politics in his time and built many highways, parks, and public works. NYC parks commissioner, 1934–60; chm. of Consolidated Triborough Bridge and New York Tunnel Authority, 1946–48; chm. of Power Authority of the State of New York, 1954–63.

MOYNIHAN, DANIEL PATRICK, Mar. 16, 1927 (Tulsa, Okla.). U.S. politician, professor, Prof. of education and urban politics at Harvard U., 1966–72 and 1975– ; U.S. amb. to India (1973–74) and the UN (1975–76); U.S. sen. (D, N.Y.), 1977– . *Beyond the Melting Pot*, 1963, *Maximum Feasible Misunderstanding*, 1969.

MUHLENBERG, FREDERICK AUGUSTUS CONRAD, Jan. 1, 1750 (New Providence [now Trappe], Pa.)–June 4, 1801. U.S. statesman, Lutheran clergyman. Del. to Continental Congress, 1779–80; U.S. rep. (Pa.), 1789–97; first Speaker of the House, 1789–97. (Son of H. M. MUHLENBERG.)

MUSKIE, EDMUND S., Mar. 28, 1914 (Rumford, Me.). U.S. politician, lawyer. Gov. (D.) of Maine, 1955–59; U.S. sen. (D, Me.), 1959–81; chm. of Senate Budget com., 1974–80; Democratic vice presidential candidate, 1968; ran unsuccessfully for Democratic presidential nomination, 1972; sect. of state 1980–81.

NELSON, GAYLORD A., June 4, 1916 (Clear Lake, Wisc.). U.S. politician. Gov. (D) of Wisconsin, 1958–62; U.S. sen. (D, Wisc.), 1963–80; chm. of Senate Select Com. on Small Business.

NIXON, RICHARD M., Jan. 9, 1913 (Yorba Linda, Calif.). U.S. president, lawyer. U.S. rep. (R, Calif.), 1947–50; U.S. sen. (R, Calif.) 1950–53; U.S. vice-pres. (R), 1953–61; as 37th U.S. pres. (1969–74), reopened relations with the People's Republic of China after a 21-year estrangement (1972), attempted wage and price controls (1971–73), ended U.S. involvement in Vietnam (1973); implicated in the Watergate scandal, became the first president to resign office, Aug. 9, 1974; pardoned by Pres. GERALD FORD, Sept. 8, 1974.

NORRIS, GEORGE W. July 11, 1861 (Sandusky Co., Ohio)–Sept. 2, 1944. U.S. politician, lawyer. As U.S. rep. (R, Neb.; 1903–13), led fight against absolute control of House Speaker JOSEPH CANNON, 1910; as U.S. sen. (R-Ind., Neb.; 1913–43), wrote the 20th Amendment and was influential in passage of bills creating the Tennessee Valley Authority, 1933.

NORTON, ELEANOR HOLMES, June 13, 1937 (Washington, D.C.). U.S. govt. official, lawyer. Asst. legal dir. of ACLU, 1965–70; exec. asst. to mayor of NYC, 1971–74; chm. of Equal Employment Opportunities Commission 1977–83.

NUNN, SAM, Sept. 8, 1938 (Perry, Ga.). U.S. politician. U.S. sen. (D, Ga.), 1973– ; chairman, Senate Armed Services Committee.

O'BRIEN, LAWRENCE, July 7, 1917 (Springfield, Mass.). U.S. politician. Prominent political adviser and strategist. Key figure in JOHN F. KENNEDY's Senate (1952 and 1958) and presidential (1960) campaigns; U.S. postmaster gen., 1965–68; chm.

of Democratic National Com., 1968–72; commissioner of the National Basketball Assn., 1975–84.
**OGLETHORPE, JAMES E.,** Dec. 22, 1696 (London, Eng.)–July 1, 1785. English founder of the colony of Georgia in America. A member of Parliament interested in prison reforms, he conceived of founding a colony for debtors; received charter for colony in Georgia, 1732; founded Savannah; repulsed Spanish attack on Georgia, 1742.
**O'NEILL, THOMAS P., JR.** ("Tip"), Dec. 9, 1912 (Cambridge, Mass.) U.S. politician. U.S. rep. (D, Mass.), 1953–87; House majority leader, 1973–76; Speaker of the House, 1977–87.
**OTIS, JAMES,** Feb. 5, 1725 (W. Barnstable, Mass.)–May 23, 1783. American Revolutionary leader. Developed a powerful legal rationale for the rights of the colonies; argued against British-imposed writs of assistance in the Superior Ct. in Boston, 1761; member of Stamp Act Congress, 1765. *A Vindication of the Conduct of the House of Representatives of the Province of Massachusetts Bay,* 1762.
**PASSMAN, OTTO E.,** June 27, 1900 (Washington Par., La.)–Aug. 13, 1988. U.S. politician. As U.S. rep. (D, La; 1946–76), worked for the reduction of foreign aid and foreign operations in order to reduce the growing federal debt; chm. of House Subcom. on Foreign Operations for many years.
**PATMAN, WRIGHT,** Aug. 6, 1893 (Patman's Switch, Tex.)–Mar. 7, 1976. U.S. politician, lawyer. U.S. rep. (D, Tex.), 1929–76, sponsored the legislation that created the Small Business Administration; chm. of House Banking Com., 1963–75.
**PELL, CLAIBORNE,** Nov. 22, 1918 (New York, N.Y.). U.S. politician, business exec. U.S. sen. (D, R.I.), 1960–     . *Megalopolis Unbound,* 1966; *Power and Policy,* 1972.
**PENN, WILLIAM,** Oct. 24, 1644 (Ruscombe, Berks., Eng.)–Aug. 30, 1718. English Quaker leader. Champion of religious toleration who founded Pennsylvania; in England, engaged in political campaigns, fighting for religious toleration, 1675–80; received grant in America from Crown, 1681; sailed for America, laid out city of Philadelphia, 1682; returned to England, where he drafted the first plan for a union of American colonies, 1696; returned to Pennsylvania, 1699–1701. *The Great Case of Liberty of Conscience,* 1670.
**PERCY, CHARLES H.,** Sept. 27, 1919 (Pensacola, Fla.). U.S. politician, business exec. Pres. of Bell and Howell, 1949–61; as U.S. sen. (R, Ill.; 1976–85), suggested appointment of a Watergate special prosector (1973) and asked for the end of the U.S. embargo of Cuba (1975); chairman, Inst. of Intl. Ed., 1985–     .
**PERKINS, FRANCES,** Apr. 10, 1882 (Boston, Mass.)–May 14, 1965. U.S. govt. official. Member (1923–26) and chm. (1926–29) of New York St. Industrial Board; New York St. industrial commissioner, 1929–33; as U.S. secy. of labor (1933–45), the first woman to serve in a presidential cabinet and an important contributor to New Deal legislation.
**PIERCE, FRANKLIN,** Nov. 23, 1804 (Hillsbo-

rough, N.H.)–Oct. 8, 1869. U.S. pres., lawyer. As 14th U.S. pres. (D, 1853–57), mishandled the sectional controversy over slavery, and oversaw passage of the Kansas-Nebraska Bill (1854) and the Gadsden Purchase (1853).
**PINCKNEY, CHARLES,** Oct. 26, 1757 (Charleston, S.C.)–Oct. 29, 1824. U.S. politician, diplomat, lawyer. As a delegate to the Constitutional Convention, submitted "Pinckney Draught" (1787), influential plan for the final U.S. Constitution; gov. of South Carolina, 1789–92, 1796–98, 1806–1808; U.S. sen. (D, S.C.), 1798–1801; U.S. min. to Spain, 1801–04. (Second cousin of C.C. PINCKNEY).
**PINCKNEY, CHARLES C.,** Feb. 25, 1746 (Charleston, S.C.)–Aug. 16, 1825. U.S. statesman, diplomat. Prominent soldier in the American Revolution; active participant in the drafting of the Constitution; took part in the XYZ affair with France, 1798; Federal party presidential candidate, 1804 and 1808. (Second cousin of C. PINCKNEY.)
**POLK, JAMES K.,** Nov. 2, 1795 (Mecklenburg Co., N.C.)–June 15, 1849. U.S. pres., lawyer. Eleventh U.S. pres. (D, 1845–49), the first "dark horse" candidate to be elected; reluctantly led U.S. in war against Mexico, which resulted in annexation of U.S. Southwest.
**POWELL, ADAM CLAYTON, JR.,** Nov. 29, 1908 (New Haven, Conn.)–Apr. 4, 1972. U.S. politician, minister. Prominent black leader. Min. at Abyssinian Baptist Church of New York City, 1937–71; founder and editor of *The People's Voice,* 1942; U.S. rep. (D, N.Y.), 1945–67 and 1969–70; excluded from the House for alleged improper acts, 1967. *Is This a White Man's War?,* 1942.
**POWELL, LEWIS F., JR.,** Sept. 19, 1907 (Suffolk, Va.). U.S. jurist, lawyer. Pres. of American Bar Assn., 1964–65; member of National Commission on Law Enforcement and Admin. of Justice, 1965–67; assoc. justice of U.S. Sup. Ct. 1972–87.
**PROXMIRE, WILLIAM,** Nov. 11, 1915 (Lake Forest, Ill.). U.S. politician. U.S. sen. (D, Wisc.), 1957–88; chm., Senate Banking, Housing and Urban Affairs Com. (1975–81) and House-Senate Joint Com. on Defense Production; a critic of bureaucratic waste, periodically awards a "Golden Fleece" to persons or groups he deems guilty of such waste.
**RAINEY, JOSEPH H.,** June 21, 1832 (Georgetown, S.C.)–Aug. 2, 1887. U.S. politician, banker, broker. The son of slaves who had purchased their freedom, the first black to serve in the U.S. House (R, S.C.), 1870–79.
**RANDOLPH, EDMUND,** Aug. 10, 1753 (Williamsburg, Va.)–Sept. 12, 1813. U.S. politician, lawyer. Influential in drafting and ratification of U.S. Constitution. The first U.S. atty. gen., 1789–94; served as secy. of state (1794–95), during the negotiations of the Jay Treaty; chief defense counsel at the treason trial of AARON BURR, 1807.
**RANDOLPH, JOHN,** June 2, 1773 (Prince George Co., Va.)–May 24, 1833. U.S. politician, planter. As U.S. rep. (Va.; 1799–1813, 1815–17, 1819–25 and 1827–29) and U.S. sen. (Va.; 1825–27), a brilliant advocate of states' rights who opposed a

national bank and protective tariffs and resisted the Missouri Compromise of 1820.

**RANDOLPH, PEYTON,** Sep., 1721 (Williamsburg, Va.)–Oct. 22, 1775. American colonial political leader. As a member of the Virginia House of Burgesses (1748–49 and 1752–75), wrote the protest against the proposed Stamp Act, 1764; first pres. of the Continental Congress, 1774, 1775.

**RANKIN, JEANETTE,** June 11, 1880 (nr. Missoula, Mont.)–May 18, 1973. U.S. politician, social worker. First woman U.S. rep. (R, Mont.), 1917–19 and 1941–43; an active suffragist and pacifist who voted against U.S. entrance into both world wars; opposed U.S. involvement in the Vietnam War.

**RAY, DIXY LEE,** Sep. 3, 1914 (Tacoma, Wash.). U.S. politician, marine biologist. Member (1972–75) and chairperson (1973–75) of AEC; U.S. asst. secy. of state for oceans and international environment and science affairs, 1975; gov. (D) of Washington, 1977–81.

**RAYBURN, SAM** ("Mr. Democrat"), Jan. 6, 1882 (Roane Co., Tenn.)–Nov. 16, 1961. U.S. politician, lawyer. U.S. rep. (D, Tex.), 1913–61; Speaker of the House (1940–46, 1949–53, and 1955–61); a congressional power who was responsible for passage of a great part of the New Deal legislation.

**REAGAN, RONALD,** Feb. 6, 1911 (Tampico, Ill.). U.S. pres., actor. Co-chm. of Calif. Republicans for Goldwater, 1964; as gov. (R) of California (1967–75) sought to reverse the growth of state govt.; sought Republican presidential nomination, 1968 and 1976; 40th U.S. pres. (1981–1989); while administration beset by budget deficit, Irangate and Contragate scandals, personal popularity remained high.

**REHNQUIST, WILLIAM,** Oct. 1, 1924 (Milwaukee, Wisc.). U.S. jurist, lawyer. U.S. asst. atty. gen., 1967–71; assoc. justice of U.S. Sup. Ct., 1972–86; chief justice, 1986–.

**REUSS, HENRY S.,** Feb. 22, 1912 (Milwaukee, Wisc.). U.S. politician, lawyer. U.S. rep. (D, Wisc.), 1954–87; chm. of House Banking, Currency, and Housing Com. *Revenue Sharing,* 1970.

**REVELS, HIRAM R.,** Sept. 1, 1822 (Fayetteville, N.C.)–Jan. 16, 1901. U.S. politician, teacher, minister. The first black to be elected to U.S. Senate (R, Miss.), 1870–71; backed legislation to restore the right to vote and hold office to all ex-Confederates.

**RHODES, JOHN J.,** Sept 18, 1916 (Council Grove, Kan.). U.S. politician, lawyer. U.S. rep. (R, Ariz.), 1953–83; House minority leader, 1973–81. *The Futile System,* 1976.

**RIBICOFF, ABRAHAM A.,** Apr. 9, 1910 (New Britain, Conn.). U.S. politician, lawyer. U.S. rep. (D, Conn.), 1949–53, gov. (D) of Connecticut, 1955–61; U.S. secy. of HEW, 1961–62; U.S. sen. (D, Conn.), 1963–81; chm. of Senate Governmental Affairs com.

**RICHARDSON, ELLIOT,** July 20, 1920 (Boston, Mass.). U.S. govt. official, diplomat. U.S. secy. of HEW, 1970–73; U.S. secy. of defense, 1973; U.S. atty. gen., 1973, resigned rather than firing Watergate Special Prosecutor Archibald Cox; U.S. amb. to Great Britain 1975–76; U.S. amb.-at-large, 1977–80.

**RIVERS, L. MENDEL,** Sept. 28, 1905 (Berkeley Co., S.C.)–Dec. 28, 1970. U.S. politician. U.S. rep (D, S.C.), 1941–70; chm. of House Armed Services Com., 1965–70.

**ROCKEFELLER, JOHN DAVISON, IV** ("Jay"), June 18, 1937 (New York, N.Y.). U.S. politician, college pres. West Virginia secy. of state (D), 1969–72, pres. of West Virginia Wesleyan C., 1973–75; gov. (D) of West Virginia, 1977–85; U.S. sen (D, W. Va) 1985– (Great-grandson of J.D. ROCKEFELLER; grandson of J.D. ROCKEFELLER, JR.; and son of J. D. Rockefeller III.).

**ROCKEFELLER, NELSON A.,** July 8, 1908 (Bar Harbor, Me.)–Jan. 26, 1979. U.S. politician, art patron. As gov. (R) of New York (1959–73), tremendously expanded the state university system and oversaw much public construction; refused to negotiate with inmates involved in the Attica prison uprising, 1971; U.S. vice-pres. (R) 1974–76. (Grandson of J.D. ROCKEFELLER; son of J.D. ROCKEFELLER, JR.; brother of D. ROCKEFELLER.)

**RODINO, PETER W., JR.,** June 7, 1909 (Newark, N.J.). U.S. politician, lawyer. U.S. rep. (D, N.J.), 1948–74; as chm. of the Housing Judiciary com. chaired the Nixon Impeachment hearings, 1973–74

**RODNEY, CAESAR,** Oct. 7, 1728 (Dover, Del.)–June 26, 1784. American Revolutionary leader. A signer of the Declaration of Independence, 1776; del. to Stamp Act Congress, 1765; pres. of Delaware, 1778–82.

**ROGERS, WILLIAM P.,** June 23, 1913 (Norfolk, N.Y.). U.S. statesman, lawyer. He began his federal service in 1947 as a council to the United States Senate War Investigating Committee; chief council to the U.S. Senate Investigations Sub-committee of the Executive Expenditures Committee, 1948–1950; after private law practice, served as U.S. attorney general, 1958–1961; secy. of state, 1969–1973; currently a partner in a law firm.

**ROOSEVELT, FRANKLIN DELANO,** Jan. 30, 1882 (Hyde Park, N.Y.) Apr. 12, 1945 As 32nd U.S, pres., (1933–45), brought the U.S. out of Depression and led it through WW II; initiated many reforms and expanded the govt.'s powers through New Deal programs aimed at bringing about economic recovery; played a major role in creating an alliance among the U.S., the USSR, and Great Britain during WW II; died in office. Asst. secy. of the Navy, 1913–20; stricken with polio, 1921; gov. (D) of New York, 1929–33.

**ROOSEVELT, THEODORE,** Oct. 27, 1858 (New York, N.Y.)–Jan. 6, 1919. U.S. pres. Led "Rough Riders" in Cuba during the Spanish-American War, 1898; gov. (R) of New York, 1899–1900; U.S. vice-pres., 1901; as 26th U.S. pres. (1901–09), aggressively broke up trusts and regulated business, attempted to conserve national resources, acquired the Panama Canal Zone (1903), and intervened in Latin American affairs; awarded Nobel Peace Prize, 1906; organized Progressive (or Bull Moose) party and ran as its presidential candidate, 1912. *The Winning of the West,* (1889–96).

ROOT, ELIHU, Feb. 15, 1845 (Clinton, N.Y.)–Feb. 7, 1937. U.S. govt. official. U.S. secy. of war, 1899–1904; U.S. secy. of state, 1905–09; U.S. sen. (R, N.Y.), 1909–15; member of Hague Tribunal, 1910; pres. of Carnegie Endowment for International Peace, 1912; awarded Nobel Peace Prize, 1912.

ROSS, NELLIE TAYLOE, Nov. 29, 1876 (St. Joseph, Mo.)–Dec. 19, 1977. U.S. politician, govt. official. First woman in U.S. to serve as gov. (D) of a state (Wyoming, 1925–27); dir. of the U.S. Mint (also the first woman to hold the position), 1933–53.

ROSTENKOWSKI, DAN, Jan. 2, 1928 (Chicago, Ill). U.S. politician. U.S. rep. (D, Ill.) 1959– ; served as chairman of the Democratic caucuses in the 90th and 91st Congresses, and is currently the chairman of the House Ways and Means Committee.

RUSH, BENJAMIN, Jan. 4, 1746 (Byberry, Pa. [now part of Philadelphia])–Apr. 19, 1813. U.S. physician, chemist. First prof. of chemistry at an American university (C. of Philadelphia, 1769); signer for Pennsylvania of the Declaration of Independence, 1776; helped start the Conway Cabal, 1777; established first free dispensary in the U.S., 1786; sometimes considered the father of the Women's Christian Temperance Union.

RUSK, DEAN, Feb. 9, 1909 (Cherokee Co., Ga.). U.S. govt. official. Pres. of Rockefeller Fndn., 1952–61; as U.S. secy. of state (1961–69) became a defender of U.S. involvement in Vietnam.

RUSSELL, RICHARD B., Nov. 2, 1897 (Winder, Ga.)–Jan. 21, 1971. U.S. politician, lawyer. As U.S. sen. (D, Ga.; 1933–71), led the Southern bloc; chm. of Senate Armed Forces Com., 1951–69; pres. pro tem of the Senate, 1969–71.

RUTLEDGE, EDWARD, Nov. 23, 1749 (Charleston, S.C.)–Jan. 23, 1800. U.S. politician. A signer of the Declaration of Independence, 1776; member of S. Carolina leg., 1782–96; gov. of S. Carolina, 1798–1800.

SCALIA, ANTONIN, March 11, 1936 (Trenton, N.J.). U.S. Supreme Court justice. A former assistant attorney general and justice of the United States Court of Appeals, he was appointed to the Supreme Court in 1986.

SCHLESINGER, JAMES R., Feb. 15, 1929 (New York, N.Y.). U.S. govt. official, economist. Chm. of AEC, 1971–73; dir. of CIA, 1973; U.S. secy. of defense, 1973–75; U.S. secy. of energy, 1977–79.

SCHMITT, HARRISON ("Jack"), July 3, 1935 (Santa Rita, N.M.). U.S. politician, geologist, astronaut. Scientist at NASA, 1965–73; piloted Apollo 17 lunar module, 1972; U.S. sen. (R, N.M.), 1977–83.

SHULTZ, GEORGE P., Dec. 13, 1920 (New York, N.Y.). U.S. secretary of state. A former dean of the school of business at the University of Chicago; secy. of labor, 1969–1970; secy. of the treasury, 1972–1974; secy. of state, 1982–1989.

SCHULTZE, CHARLES, Dec. 12, 1924 (Alexandria, Va.). U.S. government official, economist. Dir. of U.S. Bureau of the Budget, 1965–68; senior fellow at Brookings Inst., 1968–76, 1981–87; dir.

Econ. Studies, Brookings Inst., 1987– ; chm. of Council of Economic Advisors, 1977–81.

SCHURZ, CARL, Mar. 2, 1829 (Liblar, Germany)–May 14, 1906. U.S. statesman, orator, writer, lawyer. Political reformer who led the Liberal Republicans and the Mugwumps. U.S. sen. (R, Mo.), 1869–75; U.S. secy. of the int., 1877–81; editor of the New York *Evening Post*, 1881–84.

SCHWEIKER, RICHARD S., June 1, 1926 (Norristown, Pa.). U.S. politician. U.S. rep. (R, Pa.), 1961–69; U.S. sen. (R, Pa.), 1969–81; sec. Health and Human Servs., 1981–83; ranking minority member of Senate Labor-HEW Subcom., Labor and Human Resources Com. and its Health Subcom.

SCOTT, HUGH D., JR., Nov. 11, 1900 (Fredericksburg, Va.). U.S. politician, lawyer. U.S. rep. (R, Pa.), 1941–45 and 1947–59; chm. of Republican National Com., 1948–49; as U.S. sen. (R, Pa.; 1959–76), served as Senate minority leader (1969–76) and defended Pres. R. M. NIXON's Vietnam policy.

SCRANTON, WILLIAM W., July 19, 1917 (Madison, Conn.). U.S. politician, lawyer, diplomat. Gov. (R) of Pennsylvania, 1963–67; chm. of President's Commission on Campus Unrest, 1970; amb. to the U.S. mission to the UN, 1976.

SEWALL, SAMUEL, Mar. 28, 1652 (Bishopstoke, Eng.)–Jan. 1, 1730. American colonial jurist. Presided over the Salem witchcraft trials (1692), but later publicly confessed his error and guilt in the condemnations (1697); chief justice of Mass. Sup. Ct., 1718–28; his diary, (1674–1729) is an invaluable record of his times first pub'd. 1878–82. Also *The Selling of Joseph*, 1700, antislavery tract.

SEWARD, WILLIAM H., May 16, 1801 (Florida, N.Y.)–Oct. 10, 1872. U.S. politician, statesman. As U.S. secy. of state (1861–69), kept the European nations out of the Civil War and acquired Alaska from Russia. Gov. (Whig) of New York, 1838–42; U.S. sen. (Whig-R, N.Y.), 1849–61; severely wounded in assassination attempt as part of LINCOLN conspiracy, 1865.

SHERMAN, JOHN, May 10, 1823 (Lancaster, Ohio)–Oct. 22, 1900. U.S. politician, govt. official. A leading expert on finance who helped plan the national banking system, opposed free coinage of silver, and supported the Specie Resumption Act (1875). U.S. sen. (R, Ohio), 1861–77 and 1881–97; U.S. secy. of the treas., 1877–81; U.S. secy. of state, 1897–98. (Brother of W.T. SHERMAN.)

SHERMAN, ROGER, Apr. 19, 1721 (Newton, Mass.)–July 23, 1793. U.S. statesman, lawyer, surveyor. Signer of the Declaration of Independence, Articles of Association, Articles of Confederation, and the Constitution—the only person to sign all four. As del. to the Constitutional Convention (1787), proposed the Connecticut Compromise setting up a bicameral Congress; mayor of New Haven, 1784–93; U.S. rep. (CT), 1789–91; U.S. sen. (Conn.), 1791–93.

SHRIVER, R. SARGENT, JR., Nov. 9, 1915 (Westminster, Md.). U.S. govt. official, diplomat. Dir. of Peace Corps, 1961–66; dir. of Office of Economic Opportunity, 1964–68; U.S. amb. to

France, 1968–70; Democratic vice-presidential candidate, 1972.

SIMON, WILLIAM E., Nov. 27, 1927 (Paterson, N.J.). U.S. govt. official, financier. Partner in Salomon Bros., 1964–72; administrator of Federal Energy Office, 1973–74; U.S. secy. of the treas., 1974–77.

SIRICA, JOHN J., Mar. 19, 1904 (Waterbury, Conn.). As chief judge of U.S. Dist. Ct., Dist. of Columbia (1971–74), presided over the Watergate scandal trials, 1973–74. *To Set the Record Straight,* 1979.

SMITH, ALFRED E., Dec. 30, 1873 (New York, N.Y.)–Oct. 4, 1944. U.S. politician. As gov. (D) of New York (1919–20 and 1923–28), effective in pushing his reform programs through a Republican-controlled leg.; first Roman Catholic to seek the Presidency (as Democratic candidate), 1928.

SMITH, JOHN, baptized Jan. 8, 1580 (Willougby, Lincolnshire, Eng.)–June 21, 1631. English soldier, explorer and colonist in America. A leader of the first permanent English settlement in N. America, at Jamestown, Va., 1607; traditionally saved from death by POCAHONTAS; developed trade for corn with Indians; returned to England, 1609; on second voyage, mapped the New England coast, 1614. *A True Relation of…Virginia Since the First Planting of That Colony,* 1608; *A Description of New England,* 1616.

SMITH, MARGARET CHASE, Dec. 14, 1897 (Skowhegan, Me.). U.S. politician, columnist, U.S. rep. (R, Me.), 1940–49; as U.S. sen. (R, Me.; 1949–73), served longer than any other woman; sought Republican presidential nomination, 1964; one of the first to criticize sen. JOSEPH MCCARTHY.

SPARKMAN, JOHN J., Dec. 20, 1899 (Hartselle, Ala.)–Nov. 16, 1985. U.S. politician, lawyer. U.S. rep. (D, Ala), 1937–46; U.S. sen. (D, Ala), 1946–79; as chm. of Senate Banking, Housing, and Urban Affairs com.; supported U.S. military and defense policy in the 1960s.

STANS, MAURICE H., Mar. 22, 1908 (Shakopee, Minn.). U.S. govt. official. Dir. of Bureau of the Budget, 1958–61; chm. of Nixon for President Com., 1968; as chm. of Finance Com. to Reelect the President (1972), became involved peripherally in the Watergate scandal; U.S. secy. of commerce, 1969–72. *The Terrors of Justice,* 1978.

STANTON, EDWIN M., Dec. 19, 1814 (Steubenville, Ohio)–Dec. 24, 1869. U.S. statesman. As U.S. secy. of war (1862–68), competently administered the Union Army during the Civil War; dismissed by Pres. ANDREW JOHNSON for advocating stricter Reconstruction measures than Johnson wanted.

STASSEN, HAROLD E., Apr. 13, 1907 (W. St. Paul, Minn.). U.S. lawyer, politician. Gov. (R) of Minnesota, 1938–43; pres. of U. of Pa., 1948–53; special asst. to U.S. pres., with cabinet rank, to direct studies of U.S. and world disarmament, 1955–58; unsuccessful candidate for Republican presidential nomination, 1948, 1952, 1964, and 1968.

STENNIS, JOHN C., Aug. 3, 1901 (Kemper Co., Miss.). U.S. politician, lawyer. U.S. sen. (D, Miss.), 1947–89; chm. of Senate Armed Services com., 1969–80; supporter of a strong national defense.

STEPHENS, ALEXANDER H., Feb. 11, 1812 (Crawfordsville, Ga.)–Mar. 4, 1883. U.S. political leader, lawyer. U.S. rep. (Ga.), 1843–59 and 1873–82; as vice-pres. of the Confederacy (1861–65), opposed use of extraordinary war powers by Pres. JEFFERSON DAVIS because of his concern for states' rights and civil liberties. *A Constitutional View of the Late War between the States,* 2 vols., 1868–70.

STETTINIUS, EDWARD R., JR., Oct. 22, 1900 (Chicago, Ill.)–Oct. 31, 1949. U.S. statesman, industrialist. Chm. of the board of U.S. Steel, 1938; chm. of War Resources Board, 1939; administrator of Lend-Lease, 1941–43; U.S. secy. of state, 1944–45; an adviser to FDR at the Yalta Conference, 1945; chm. of U.S. delegation to UN conference in San Francisco and first U.S. del. to UN (1945–46).

STEVENS, JOHN PAUL, Apr. 20, 1920 (Chicago, Ill.). U.S. jurist. Judge of U.S. Ct. of Appeals for the Seventh Cir. (Chicago, Ill.), 1970–75; as assoc. justice of U.S. Sup. Ct. (1975–  ), considered a legal centrist.

STEVENS, THEODORE F., Nov. 18, 1923 (Indianapolis, Ind.). U.S. politician, lawyer. U.S. sen. (R, Alaska), 1968–  ; Senate asst. minority leader, 1977–80; asst. majority ldr, 1981–85.

STEVENSON, ADLAI E., Oct. 23, 1835 (Christian Co., Ky.)–June 14, 1914. U.S. politician. U.S. rep. (D, Ill.), 1875–76 and 1879–80; U.S. vice-pres. (D), 1893–97. (Grandfather of A.E. STEVENSON II.)

STEVENSON, ADLAI E. II, Feb. 5, 1900 (Los Angeles, Calif.)–July 14, 1965. U.S. statesman, diplomat, lawyer. Participant at foundation of UN at San Francisco Conference, 1946; gov. (D) of Illinois, 1948–52; Democratic presidential candidate, 1952 and 1956; U.S. del. to the UN, 1946–47, 1961–65. (Grandson of A.E. STEVENSON; Father of A.E. STEVENSON III.)

STEVENSON, ADLAI E. III, Oct. 10, 1930 (Chicago, Ill.). U.S. politician, lawyer. Illinois treas. (D), 1967–70; U.S. sen. (D, Ill.), 1970–81; ran for gov. of Illinois, 1982. (Son of A.E. STEVENSON II.)

STEWART, POTTER, Jan. 23, 1915 (Jackson, Mich.)–Dec. 7, 1985. U.S. jurist, lawyer. Judge of U.S. Ct. of Appeals, Sixth Cir., 1954–58; as assoc. justice of U.S. Sup. Ct. (1958–81), known as an independent and a moderate.

STIMSON, HENRY L., Sept. 21, 1867 (New York, N.Y.)–Oct. 20, 1950. U.S. govt. official. U.S. secy. of war, 1911–13 and 1940–45; U.S. secy. of state, 1929–33; following Japanese invasion of Manchuria (1931) advocated nonrecognition of Japanese rule (the "Stimson Doctrine"); recommended use of the atom bomb on Japan, 1945.

STONE, HARLAN FISKE, Oct. 11, 1872 (Chesterfield, N.H.)–Apr. 22, 1946. U.S. jurist. As assoc. justice (1925–41) and chief justice (1941–46) of U.S. Sup. Ct., a liberal who believed in judicial restraint; contributed to legal though on the power of the state to regulate interstate commerce and the power of the national govt. to make basic changes in society.

**STORY, JOSEPH,** Sept. 18, 1779 (Marblehead, Mass.)–Sept. 10, 1845. U.S. jurist. Prof. of Law at Harvard C., 1829–45; a pioneer in founding and directing Harvard Law School; as assoc. justice of U.S. Sup. Ct., (1811–45), wrote opinion putting the highest state courts under the appellate authority of the Sup. Ct. in cases involving federal law; wrote famous series of nine commentaries, 1832–45.

**STRAUSS, ROBERT S.,** Oct. 19, 1918 (Lockhart, Tex.). U.S. govt. official, lawyer. Pres. of Strauss Broadcasting Co., 1964–  ; chm. of Democratic National Com. 1972–77; U.S. special rep. for trade negotiations (with rank of amb.) 1977–79; U.S. amb.-at-large to the Middle East, 1979.

**STUYVESANT, PETER** (or Petrus), c.1592 (Scherpenzeel, Friesland, Neth.)–Feb. 1672. Dutch colonial gov. in America. Lost his leg in campaign against St. Martin I., 1644; gov. of New Netherland (later New York), 1646–64; aroused great discontent in the colony with his dictatorial rule.

**SUMNER, CHARLES,** Jan. 6, 1811 (Boston, Mass.)–Mar. 11, 1874. U.S. politician. As U.S. sen. (D-Free Soil-R, Mass.; 1851–74), a powerful opponent of slavery; attacked Kansas-Nebraska Bill of 1854 with his famous "Crime against Kansas" speech (1856), led radical Republicans in their opposition to Pres. ANDREW JOHNSON's moderate Reconstruction program for the South; chm. of Senate Foreign Relations com., 1861–71.

**SYMINGTON, STUART,** June 26, 1901 (Amherst, Mass.)–Dec. 14, 1988. U.S. politician, businessman. Pres. of Emerson Electric Manufacturing Co., 1938–45; U.S. secy. of the air force, 1947–50; as U.S. sen. (D, Mo.; 1953–77), opposed waste in the defense budget and the Vietnam War.

**TAFT, ROBERT A.** ("Mr. Republican"), Sept. 8, 1889 (Cincinnati, Ohio)–July 31, 1953. U.S. politician. As U.S. sen. (R, Ohio; 1939–53), advocated isolationism prior to WW II, helped write Taft-Hartley Act (1947), opposed centralization of power in the federal govt., and opposed U.S. membership in NATO; unsuccessfully sought Republican presidential nomination, 1952. (Son of W.H. TAFT.)

**TAFT, WILLIAM HOWARD,** Sept. 15, 1857 (Cincinnati, Ohio)–Mar. 8, 1930. U.S. pres., jurist. Pres. of Philippine Commission, 1900–01; first civilian gov., 1901–04; U.S. secy. of war, 1904–08; as 27th U.S. pres. (R; 1909–13), vigorously enforced antitrust legislation, began postal savings bank (1910), created dept. of labor (1911); chief justice of U.S. Sup. Ct., 1921–30. (Father of R.A. TAFT.)

**TALMADGE, HERMAN E.,** Aug. 9, 1913 (McRae, Ga.) U.S. politician, lawyer. Gov. (D) of Georgia, 1948–55; U.S. sen. (D, Ga.), 1957–1981; chm. of Senate Agr., Nutrition, and Forestry Com.

**TANEY, ROGER B.,** Mar. 17, 1777 (Calvert Co., Md.)–Oct. 12, 1864. U.S. jurist, lawyer. As U.S. atty. Gen. (1831–32), fought against the federal bank; as chief justice of U.S. Sup. Ct. (1836–64),

upheld federal supremacy over state authorities, but in the Dred Scott case (1857), held that Congress could not forbid slavery in the territories and that slaves were not citizens.

**TAYLOR, ZACHARY** ("Old Rough and Ready"), Nov. 24, 1784 ("Montebello," Orange Co., Va.)–July 9, 1850. U.S. president, soldier. The hero of the U.S.-Mexican War (1846–48), he commanded army at the Texas border and won Northern Mexico at the Battle of Buena Vista (1847); as 12th pres. (Whig, 1849–50), favored admission of California into the Union, which led to Compromise of 1850; faced charges of corruption in his cabinet; died in office.

**THOMPSON, JAMES R.,** May 8, 1936 (Chicago, Ill.). U.S. politician, lawyer. U.S. atty. for Northern Illinois Dist, 1971–75; gov. (R) of Illinois, 1977–  .

**THORNBURGH, RICHARD,** July 16, 1932 (Pittsburgh, Pa.). U.S. statesman. After a few years of private law practice, he was a U.S. attorney in western Pennsylvania, 1969–1975; he was an asst. atty. gen., U.S. dept. of justice, 1975–77; taught at Harvard University; U.S. atty. gen. 1988–  .

**THURMOND, STROM,** Dec. 5, 1902 (Edgefield, S.C.). U.S. politician, farmer, lawyer. Gov. (D) of South Carolina, 1947–51; States'-Rights presidential candidate, 1948; U.S. sen. (D-R, S.C.), 1954–  ; switched from Democrat to Republican party, 1964; has often been the rallying point for Southern conservatism in the Senate.

**TILDEN, SAMUEL J.,** Feb. 9, 1814 (New Lebanon, N.Y.)–Aug. 4, 1886. U.S. politician, lawyer. A leader in the overthrow of the Tweed Ring, 1871; gov. (D) of New York, 1875–76; the 1876 Democratic presidential candidate, lost by one electoral vote to R. B. HAYES in a highly disputed election; donated his vast estate to establish a free public library in New York City.

**TOWER, JOHN GOODWIN,** Sept. 29, 1925 (Houston, Tex.). U.S. politician, political scientist. U.S. sen. (R, Tex.), 1961–85.

**TRUMAN, HARRY S.,** May 8, 1884 (Lamar, Mo.)–Dec. 26, 1972. U.S. pres., politician. U.S. sen. (D, Mo.), 1935–45; as 33rd U.S. pres. (D, 1945–53), made decision to drop the atom bomb on Japan, decided to go to war against Korea, propounded a doctrine of containment of communism.

**TRUMBULL, JONATHAN,** Oct. 12, 1710 (Lebanon, Conn.)–Aug. 17, 1785. American colonial leader. As gov. of Connecticut (1769–84), the only colonial gov. to advocate the Revolutionary cause.

**TWEED, WILLIAM MARCY** ("Boss"), Apr. 3, 1823 (New York, N.Y.)–Apr. 12, 1878. U.S. politician. Democratic political boss who plundered New York City of over $30 million. New York St. senator, 1867–71, a sachem (1857) and grand sachem (1868) in Tammany Hall; charged with corruption by *The New York Times* and THOMAS NAST's powerful cartoons, 1870; pursued legally by SAMUEL J. TILDEN, arrested (1871) and convicted (1873).

**TYDINGS, MILLARD E.,** Apr. 6, 1890 (Havre de

Grace, Md.)–Feb. 9, 1961. U.S. politician, civil engineer. U.S. rep. (D, Md.), 1923–27; as U.S. sen. (D, Md.), 1927–51, opposed much of the New Deal legislation and some of Pres. F. D. ROOSEVELT's foreign policy; headed Senate subcom. investigating Sen. JOSEPH R. MCCARTHY's allegations of communist infiltration in the U.S. State Dept. (1950); the com. cleared the dept. and denounced McCarthy as a liar.

TYLER, JOHN, Mar. 29, 1790 (Charles City Co., Va.)–Jan. 18, 1862. U.S. pres. As 10th U.S. pres. (Whig, 1841–45), twice vetoed a national bank bill, annexed Texas, and reorganized the U.S. navy; the first vice-pres. to attain presidency upon the death of a pres., W. H. HARRISON.

UDALL, MORRIS K. ("Mo"), June 15, 1922 (Saint Johns, Ariz.). U.S. politician, lawyer. U.S. rep. (D, Ariz.), 1961– ; chm. of House Interior and Insular Affairs Com. and Energy and Environment Subcom.; sought Democratic presidential nomination, 1976. (Brother of S.L. UDALL.)

UDALL, STEWART L., Jan. 31, 1920 (Saint Johns, Ariz.). U.S. politician, govt. official. U.S. rep. (D, Ariz.), 1955–61. As U.S. secy. of the int. (1961–69), launched Parks for America, establishing many new wildlife refuges and ranges; syndicated columnist, 1970– . The Quiet Crisis, 1963; National Parks of America, 1972. (Brother of M. UDALL.)

VALLANDIGHAM, CLEMENT L., July 29, 1820 (New Lisbon, Ohio)–June 17, 1871. U.S. politician, lawyer. A leader of the Peace Democrats, or Copperheads, during the Civil War. U.S. rep. (D, Ohio), 1857–63; convicted for alleged treasonable utterances (1863) and banished to the Confederacy; following the Civil War, worked for national unity.

VAN BUREN, MARTIN, Dec. 5, 1782 (Kinderhook, N.Y.)–July 24, 1862. U.S. pres. U.S. sen. (D, N.Y.), 1821–28; U.S. secy. of state, 1829–31; vice-pres., 1833–37; as 8th pres. of the U.S. (1837–41), known for his political cunning; attempting to deal with the Panic of 1837, recommended an independent treas. system.

VANCE, CYRUS R., Mar. 27, 1917 (Clarksburg, W. Va.). U.S. govt. official. U.S. secy. of the army, 1962–64; U.S. dep. secy. of def., 1964–67; U.S. negotiator at Paris Peace Conference on Vietnam, 1968–69; U.S. secy. of state, 1977–80.

VANDENBERG, ARTHUR H., Mar. 22, 1884 (Grand Rapids, Mich.)–Apr. 18, 1951. U.S. politician, editor. As U.S. sen. (R, Mich; 1928–51), progressed from isolationism to a leading backer of Pres. HARRY TRUMAN's anticommunist foreign policy; chm. of Senate Foreign Relations com., 1947–49; played an important role in the formation of the UN; marshaled congressional support for NATO and the Marshall Plan.

VINSON, FREDERICK M., Jan. 22, 1890 (Louisa, Ky.)–Sept. 8, 1953. U.S. politician, jurist. As U.S. rep. (D, Ky.; 1923–29 and 1931–38), became known as a fiscal expert; dir. of Office of Economic Stabilization, 1943–45; dir. of Office of War Mobilization and Reconversion and sec. treas., 1945; as

chief justice of U.S. Sup. Ct. (1946–53), frequently upheld the powers of the federal govt. versus individual rights.

VOLSTEAD, ANDREW J., Oct. 31, 1860 (Goodhue Co., Minn.)–Jan. 20, 1947. U.S. politician, lawyer. As U.S. rep. (R, Minn.) (1903–23), authored the Volstead Act (1919), which enforced prohibition; chm. of House Judiciary Com., 1919-23.

WAGNER, ROBERT F., June 8, 1877 (Nastätten, Hesse-Nassau, Ger.)–May 4, 1953. U.S. politician, lawyer. Known as the "Legislative Pilot of the New Deal." As U.S. sen. (D, N.Y.; 1927–49), directed the Congressional career of the National Labor Relations Act (1935) and worked for the extension of federal housing, unemployment insurance bill. (Father of R.F. WAGNER, JR.)

WAGNER, ROBERT F., JR., Apr. 20, 1910 (New York, N.Y.) U.S. politician, diplomat. As mayor (D) of New York City (1954–66) and pres. of the Borough of Manhattan (1949–53) accomplished significant reforms in education and housing; U.S. amb. to Spain, 1968–69; envoy to Vatican, 1978–80; (Son of R. F. WAGNER.)

WALKER, JAMES J. ("Jimmy"), June 19, 1881 (New York, N.Y.)–Nov. 18, 1946. U.S. politician, lawyer. As mayor of New York City (1925–32), developed the transit system, created the Sanitation Dept; administration investigated for civic corruption; resigned; very popular figure, noted as dapper and debonair.

WALLACE, GEORGE C., Aug. 25, 1919 (Clio, Ala.). U.S. politician, lawyer. Leader of the South's fight against federally ordered racial integration in the 1960s. Gov. (D) of Alabama, 1963–67, 1971–74, 1975–78 and 83–87; attempted to block enrollment of black students at the U. of Alabama, 1963; American Independent party presidential candidate, 1968; sought Democratic presidential nomination, 1972 and 1976; shot while campaigning and paralyzed from the waist down, 1972.

WALLACE, HENRY A., Oct. 7, 1888 (Adair Co, Ia.)–Nov. 18, 1965. U.S. politician, editor, agricultural expert. As U.S. secy. of agric. (1933–40), led the New Deal farm program; U.S. vice-pres. (D, 1941–45); editor of The New Republic, 1946–47; Progressive party presidential candidate, 1948.

WARNER, JOHN W., Feb. 18, 1927 (Washington, D.C.). U.S. politician, lawyer. U.S. secy. of the navy, 1972–74; administrator of American Revolution Bicentennial Adm., 1974–76; U.S. sen. (R, Va.), 1979– .

WARNKE, PAUL C., Jan. 31, 1920 (Webster, Mass.). U.S. govt. official, lawyer. U.S. asst. secy. of def. for internal security affairs, 1967–69; dir. of Arms Control and Disarmament Agency, 1977–78; chief negotiator at SALT talks, 1977–78.

WARREN, EARL, Mar. 19, 1891 (Los Angeles, Calif.)–July 9, 1974. U.S. politician, jurist. Gov. (R) of California, 1943–53; as chief justice of U.S. Sup. Ct. (1953–69), presided over a period of great change in civil rights, wrote the decision regarding school desegregation in Brown v. Board of Education of Topeka, Kans., 1954, led Court to expand the rights of the accused, headed the official investigation into the assassination of Pres. J.F. KENNEDY.

**WASHINGTON, GEORGE,** Feb. 22, 1732 ("Wakefield", Westmoreland Co., Va.)–Dec. 14, 1799. U.S. pres., soldier, farmer, surveyor. As commander in chief of the Continental forces during the American Revolution, provided steady and inspirational leadership that kept the Revolutionary Army in being, 1775–83; as first U.S. pres. (1789–97), did much to shape the office, warned against the dangers of party politics and foreign alliances.

**WEAVER, ROBERT C.,** Dec. 29, 1907 (Washington, D.C.). U.S. govt. official, economist. As U.S. secy. of HUD (1966–68), the first black to serve in the U.S. cabinet; prof. of urban affairs at Hunter C., 1970–78. *The Negro Ghetto,* 1948.

**WEBSTER, DANIEL,** Jan. 18, 1782 (Salisbury, N.H.)–Oct. 24, 1852. U.S. politician, lawyer, orator. U.S. rep. (Fed, N.H.), 1813–17 and (Fed, Mass.) 1823–27; as U.S. sen. (Whig, Mass; 1827–41 and 1845–50), gained fame as an orator; backed the Compromise of 1850 in his devotion to the survival of the Union; defended the industrial interests of his region; U.S. secy. of state, 1841–43 and 1850–52.

**WEBSTER, WILLIAM H.,** Mar. 6, 1924 (St. Louis, Mo.). U.S. statesman, lawyer. Dir. Federal Bureau of Investigation, 1978–1987; dir, Central Intelligence Agency, 1987–  .

**WEICKER, LOWELL P., JR.,** May 16, 1931 (Paris, Fr.). U.S. politician, lawyer. U.S. sen. (R, Conn.), 1971–89; as a member of the Senate Watergate Com., played a prominent role in the investigation of the Watergate scandal, 1973–74.

**WEINBERGER, CASPAR W.,** Aug. 18, 1917 (San Francisco, Cal.). U.S. statesman, lawyer. After practicing law and serving in the California Legislature, he became dir. of the U.S. office of management and budget, 1970–72; secy. of health, education and welfare, 1973–1975; secy. of defense, (1981–1987); publisher, *Forbes,* 1989–  .

**WELLES, SUMNER,** Oct. 14, 1892 (New York, N.Y.)–Sept. 24, 1961. U.S. diplomat. As U.S. undersecy. of state (1937–43), a major architect of the "Good Neighbor Policy" toward Latin America.

**WHEELER, BURTON K.,** Feb. 27, 1882 (Hudson, Mass.)–Jan. 7, 1975. U.S. politician, lawyer. U.S. sen. (D, Mont.), 1923–47; a leader of the isolationist movement prior to WW II; Progressive party vice-presidential running-mate of ROBERT M. LA FOLLETTE, 1924.

**WHIPPLE, WILLIAM,** Jan. 14, 1730 (Kittery, Me.)–Nov. 10, 1785. American Revolutionary leader, legislator, soldier. A signer of the Declaration of Independence, 1776; member of Continental Congress, 1776–79; a brigadier gen. in the Revolutionary army.

**WHITE, BYRON R.** ("Whizzer") June 8, 1917 (Ft. Collins, Col.). U.S. athlete, jurist. An All-American football player at U. of Colorado, played professional football with the Pittsburgh Pirates (now Steelers), and with the Detroit Lions; U.S.

dep. atty. gen., 1961–62; as assoc. justice of U.S. Sup. Ct. (1962–  ), a "swing" justice who has written many dissenting opinions in rights of criminal defendants and the protection of First Amendment guarantees; elected to the Football Hall of Fame, 1954.

**WHITE, EDWARD D.,** Nov. 3, 1845 (Lafourche Par., La.)–May 19, 1921. U.S. jurist. As assoc. justice (1894–1910) and chief justice (1910–21) of U.S. Sup. Ct., read the "rule of reason" into the antitrust laws, made decisions in favor of federal emergency powers, formulated concept of the "incorporation" of territories acquired by the U.S. in 1898.

**WILLKIE, WENDELL L.,** Feb. 18, 1892 (Elwood, Ind.)–Oct. 8, 1944. U.S. politician, business exec., lawyer. Pres. of Commonwealth and Southern Corp., 1933–40; a major critic of the New Deal; Republican presidential candidate, 1940; fought isolationism during WW II. *One World,* 1943.

**WILSON, PETE,** Aug. 23, 1933 (Lake Forest, Ill.). U.S. politician. Mayor of San Diego, Cal., 1971–83; U.S. sen., 1984–  ; noted for his work in the fights against retinitis pigmentosa and Alzheimer's disease.

**WILSON, WOODROW,** Dec. 28, 1856 (Staunton, Va.)–Feb. 3, 1924. U.S. pres., politician scientist, educator. Pres. of Princeton U., 1902–10; gov. (D) of New Jersey, 1911–13; as 28th U.S. pres. (D, 1913–21), worked for creation of the Federal Reserve System (1913) and the FTC (1914), opposed imperialism, attempted to maintain U.S. neutrality in WW I; after WW I, put forward peace plan based on "Fourteen Points," attended Paris Peace Conference (1919), and labored tirelessly for the League of Nations; awarded Nobel Peace Prize, 1919.

**WINTHROP, JOHN,** Jan. 23, 1588 (Edwardstone, Suffolk, Eng.)–Mar. 26, 1649. American colonial leader. A leader of the Massachusetts Bay Colony, serving as its gov. 12 times between 1629 and 1649; led effort to oust ANNE HUTCHINSON and the Antinomians, 1637; attempted to make the colony into a theocratic society.

**WITHERSPOON, JOHN,** Feb. 5, 1723 (Yester, Scot.)–Nov. 15, 1794. Scottish-U.S. Presbyterian clergyman. Pres., C. of New Jersey (later Princeton U.), 1768–94; a signer of the Declaration of Independence (1776) and delegate to the Continental Congress (1776–82).

**WOLCOTT, OLIVER,** Nov. 20, 1726 (Windsor, Conn.)–Dec. 1, 1797. American Revolutionary leader. Helped negotiate the neutrality of the pro-British Six Nations Indians prior to the Revolution, 1775; a signer of the Declaration of Independence, 1776; during the Revolution, in charge of the defense of the Connecticut coast against British raids; gov. of Connecticut, 1796–97.

**WOODCOCK, LEONARD F.,** Feb. 15, 1911 (Providence, R.I.). U.S. govt. and labor-union official. Succeeded WALTER REUTHER as pres. of United Automobile Workers, 1970–77; chief of mission, with rank of U.S. amb., to China, 1977–78; full amb. to China, 1979–81.

WRIGHT, JAMES C., JR., Dec. 22, 1922 (Ft. Worth, Tex.). U.S. politician. A member of the Texas Legislature, 1947–1949; mayor of Weathersford, Texas 1950–1954; U.S. rep. (D, Texas), from 1954; elected House Speaker, 1987; in 1989, in the face of serious ethical charges, he resigned from Congress.

YOUNG, ANDREW, Mar. 12, 1932 (New Orleans, La.). U.S. politician, minister. As U.S. rep. (D, Ga.) 1973–77, the first black to win a Democratic nomination for Congress from the South in 100 years;

U.S. amb. to the UN, 1977–79; major of Atlanta 1982–1990.

YOUNG, COLEMAN A., May 24, 1918 (Tuscaloosa, Ala.). U.S. politician. Mayor (D) of Detroit, Mich., 1974– .

YOUNG, MILTON R., Dec. 6, 1897 (Berlin, N.D.) –May 31, 1983. U.S. politician, farmer. Republican dean of the Senate. U.S. sen. (R, N.D.), 1945–81; as secy. of Senate Republican Conference Com. (1946–71), served for longest period ever in a leadership position in the Senate.

## BRITISH RULERS, STATESMEN, AND POLITICAL LEADERS

ALBERT, OF SAXE-COBURG-GOTHA, PRINCE, August 26, 1819 (Rosenau, Ger.)–Dec. 14, 1861. Prince consort of England (From 1857), husband of QUEEN VICTORIA (from 1840) and her most trust counselor; upon his death at age 42, mourned by Victoria for the remaining years of her reign.

ALFRED THE GREAT, 849 (Wantage, Berks., Eng.)–Apr. 26, 899. Saxon king, soldier, scholar. As king of the West Saxons (871–99), saved England from Danish conquest; strengthened the English military; led a great revival of learning; translated many major works of the time; organized a court school; issued his own code of laws; translated *Consolations* of Boethius and Bede's *History.*

ASQUITH, HERBERT HENRY, EARL OF OXFORD AND ASQUITH, Sept. 12, 1852 (Morley, Yorkshire, Eng.)–Feb. 15, 1928. English statesman. As Liberal party prime min. (1908–16), put through the Parliament Act of 1911 limiting the power of the House of Lords, and also enacted much social legislation. K.G., 1925, created earl, 1925.

ASTOR, NANCY, VISCOUNTESS, May 19, 1879 (Danville, Va.)–May 2, 1964. English politician. The first woman to sit in the British House of Commons, 1919–1945; advocate of women's rights, temperance; an opponent of socialism. *My Two Countries*, 1923.

ATTLEE, CLEMENT, VISCOUNT PRESTWOOD, Jan. 3, 1883 (London, Eng.) Oct. 8, 1967. English politician. Leader of the Labour party, 1935–55; as prime min. (1945–51), led Great Britain during a period of economic austerity and development of a welfare state; O. M., 1951; K. G., 1956; created earl and viscount, 1955.

BALFOUR, ARTHUR, (first) EARL OF BALFOUR, July 25, 1848 (Whittingehame, East Lothian, Scot.) –Mar. 19, 1930. British statesman. A major force in the Conservative party for 50 years; prime min., 1902–05; as foreign secy. (1916–19), known for the Balfour Declaration (1917) expressing official British approval of Zionism; opponent of Irish home rule; O.M., 1916; K.G., 1922; created earl 1922.

BEAVERBROOK, LORD, (William Maxwell Aitken) May 25, 1879 (Maple, Ont., Can.)–June 9, 1964. British publisher, statesman, financier. As owner of several British newspapers, including the *Daily Express, Sunday Express,* and *Evening Standard,* played a major role in building the popular press in

Great Britain; entered govt. during WW II as min. of aircraft production (1940–41) and min. of supply (1941–42); lord privy seal (1943–45); created baronet, 1916; baron, 1917.

BEVIN, ERNEST, Mar. 9, 1881 (Winsford, Somerset, Eng.)–Apr. 14, 1951. English statesman, labor leader. Powerful British union leader who merged several unions to form the Transport and General Workers' Union, 1921; as min. of labor (1940–45), mobilized manpower for WW II; as foreign min. (1945–51), helped lay the basis of NATO; helped establish Organization for European Economic Cooperation, 1948.

BOLEYN, ANNE, 1507? (Blickling Hall, Norfolk, Eng.?)–1536. English queen (1533–36), second wife of HENRY VIII and mother of ELIZABETH I. Her refusal to be Henry's mistress led him to start proceedings to annul his marriage to Catherine of Aragon; secretly married to Henry, 1533; her failure to provide a male heir turned Henry away; beheaded for treason (adultery with several men, including her brother), 1536.

BOLINGBROKE, HENRY ST. JOHN, (first) VISCOUNT, Sept. 16, 1678 (Wiltshire?, Eng.)–Dec. 12, 1751. English politician, historian, philosopher. The leading political leader in the reign of Queen Anne, 1702–14. As secy. of state (1710–14), negotiated the Treaty of Utrecht (1713).

CALLAGHAN, JAMES, BARON, Mar. 27, 1912 (Portsmouth, Hants., Eng.). English politician. Member of Parliament, 1945–87; chan. of the exchequer, 1964–67; home secy., 1967–70; as foreign secy. (1974–76), renegotiated the terms for British membership in the European Economic Community; prime min., 1976–79; K.G., 1987; created baron (Life Peer), 1987. *A House Divided,* 1973.

CECIL LORD ROBERT GASCOYNE, (first) VISCOUNT CECIL OF CHELWOOD, Sept. 14, 1864 (London, Eng.)–Nov. 24, 1958. English statesman. Collaborator in drafting of the League of Nations Covenant, 1916, and ardent backer of the league; awarded Nobel Peace Prize, 1937; raised to peerage, 1923.

CHAMBERLAIN, SIR JOSEPH, Oct. 16, 1863 (Birmingham, Eng.)–Mar. 16, 1937. English statesman. As foreign secy. (1924–29), played a major role in the Locarno Pact (1925); lost political favor after the failure of the Geneva Conference on naval limitations, 1927; awarded Nobel Peace Prize (with

C.G. DAWES), 1925; K.G., 1925. (Half brother of N. CHAMBERLAIN).

**CHAMBERLAIN, NEVILLE,** Mar. 18, 1869 (Birmingham, Eng.)–Nov. 9, 1940. English statesman. As prime min. (1937–40), became symbol of appeasement when he signed the Munich Pact (1938) that granted most of A. HITLER's demands and left Czechoslovakia defenseless; resigned on Hitler's invasion of Lowlands. (Half-brother of J.A. CHAMBERLAIN).

**CHARLES, PRINCE,** Nov. 14, 1948 (London, England). British prince. The heir apparent to the British throne, he has been a leader in the movement to return to the basics in architecture; holds titles as Prince of Wales and Earl of Chester, Duke of Cornwall, Duke of Rothesay, Earl of Carrick, Baron of Renfrew, Lord of the Isles, and Great Steward of Scotland.

**CHURCHILL, LORD RANDOLPH,** Feb. 13, 1849 (Blenheim Palace, nr. Woodstock, Ox., Eng.)–Jan. 24, 1895. English politician. Independent Conservative Party leader, advocate of "Tory Democracy"; secy. of state for India (1885–86) during the annexation of Burma; chan. of the exchequer and leader of the House of Commons, 1886. (Father of W. CHURCHILL.)

**CHURCHILL, SIR WINSTON,** Nov. 30, 1874 (Blenheim Palace, nr. Woodstock, Ox., Eng.)–Jan. 24, 1965. English statesman, author. As prime min. (1940–45 and 1951–55), gave Britain inspiring leadership during WW II; visited battlefronts, attended internatl. conferences, and provided stirring oratory for his struggling nation. Secy. of war 1919–21; head of colonial office, 1921–22; knighted, 1953; awarded 1953 Nobel Prize in literature for his *The Second World War* (6 vols., 1948–53); O.M., 1946; K.G., 1953. (Son of R. CHURCHILL.)

**CLIVE, ROBERT** (Baron Clive of Plassey), Sept. 29, 1725 (Styche, Shropshire, Eng.)–Nov. 22, 1774. English administrator, soldier. Conqueror of Bengal and first British administrator in India with East India Co.; as gov. of British territories in Bengal (1758–59), ran a corrupt admin.; returned to England and honored for his conquests (Plassey, 1757), 1760; serving again as gov. (1765–67), secured East India Co.'s rule over Bengal and Bihār and corrected many abuses; committed suicide after debate in Parliament over his conduct; created baron in Irish peerage, 1762.

**CROMWELL, OLIVER,** Apr. 25, 1599 (Huntingdon, Huntingdonshire, Eng.)–Sept. 3, 1658. English statesman, soldier. Led the parliamentary forces in the English Civil War; waged war against Ireland and Scotland, 1649–51; dissolved Parliament, 1652; installed as lord protector of England, Scotland and Ireland, 1653–58; led a war against the Dutch and Spain.

**CROMWELL, THOMAS,** (Earl of Essex) c.1485 (London, Eng.)–July 28, 1540. English statesman. As adviser to HENRY VIII (1532–40), drafted the acts that brought the Ref. to England; suppressed the monasteries; negotiated Henry VIII's marriage

to Anne of Cleves, 1539; accused of treason and executed; created earl, 1540.

**CURZON, GEORGE NATHANIEL, (first) BARRON and (first) MARQUESS CURZON OF KEDLESTON,** Jan. 11, 1859 (Kedleston Hall, Derbyshire, Eng.)–Mar. 20, 1925. English statesman. As viceroy of India (1898–1905), instituted many reforms and pacified the northern frontier; lord privy seal, 1915–16; foreign secy., 1919–24; presided over the Conference of Lausanne, 1922–23; K.G., 1916; created earl, 1911; marquess, 1921.

**DE VALERA, EAMON,** Oct 14, 1882 (New York, N.Y.)–Aug. 29, 1975. Irish statesman. Fought for Irish independence from England in the Easter Rising of 1916; pres. of the Sinn Fein party, 1917–26; launched new party, Fianna Fáil, 1926; prime min., 1937–48, 1951–54, and 1957–59; pres., 1959–73.

**DEVLIN, BERNADETTE,** April 23, 1947 (Cookstown, Co. Tyrone, N. Ire.) Irish civil-rights leader. Leader of Northern Ireland's civil-rights movement in the late 1960s; at age of 21, youngest woman ever elected to the British Parliament, 1969; imprisoned for four months in 1970 for her part in Londonderry demonstrations, 1969; defeated for reelection, 1974; member of the Irish Republican Socialist Party, 1975–76. *The Price of My Soul,* 1969.

**DISRAELI, BENJAMIN, EARL OF BEACONS FIELD,** Dec. 21, 1804 (London, Eng.)–Apr. 19, 1881. British statesman. Founder of the modern Conservative party; brilliant parliamentarian; elected to House of Commons, 1837; instrumental in passage of Reform Bill of 1867; as prime min. (1868, 1874–80), instituted many reforms in housing, public health, and factory legislation; checked Russian imperialism in Turkey and the Balkans. Novels: *Vivian Grey,* 1826; *Coningsby,* 1844; K.G., 1878; created earl, 1876.

**EDEN, SIR ANTHONY, (first) EARL OF AVON,** June 12, 1897 (Windlestone Hall nr. Bishop Auckland, Durham, Eng.)–Jan. 14, 1977. English statesman. Foreign secy., 1935–38, 1940–45, and 1951–55; as prime min. (1955–57), took part in the Indochina settlement in Geneva (1954), helped establish the Southeast Asia Treaty Org., played a key (and controversial) role in the Anglo-French Suez expedition (1956); K.G., 1954; created earl, 1961.

**EDWARD VIII** (after his abdication, **DUKE OF WINDSOR**), June 23, 1894 (Richmond, Eng.)–May 18, 1972. King of Great Britain and Ireland, Jan. 20–Dec. 10, 1936. Abdicated in order to marry the twice-divorced American Mrs. Wallis Warfield Spencer Simpson (DUCHESS OF WINDSOR); following the abdication, lived mainly in France. *A King's Story,* 1951.

**ELIZABETH I,** Sept. 7, 1533 (Greenwich, Eng.) –Mar. 23, 1603. Queen of England (1558–1603). Led her country during one of its greatest periods; instituted the religious settlement of 1559, which enforced the religious settlement by law and tolerated Catholics for the sake of national unity; restored the currency; encouraged interest in exploration of the New World; fought Spain's world empire, notably defeating the Spanish Armada (1588); passed "poor laws" in an attempt to eradicate widespread poverty; her reign was marked by a brilliant English literary renaissance, led by W. SHAKESPEARE and F. BACON.

**ELIZABETH II,** Apr. 21, 1926 (London, Eng.). Queen of Great Britain and Northern Ireland, 1952– . Trained as a junior subaltern in A.T.S. during WW II; married Philip Mountbatten, duke of Edinburgh, 1947; as queen, joined Pres. D. D. EISENHOWER in the opening of the St. Lawrence Seaway, 1959; had audience with Pope JOHN XXIII, 1961; allowed televised reports of the royal family's domestic life, 1970.

**FOX, CHARLES** Jan. 24, 1749 (London, Eng.)– Sept. 13, 1806. English statesman, orator. Fought for liberal reform and opposed King GEORGE III's policies, especially the coercive polices against the American colonies; helped to end British slave trade; favored the French Revolution and Catholic Emancipation; secured passage of Libel Bill (1792), which upheld full rights of juries in libel cases.

**GAITSKELL, HUGH,** April 9, 1906 (London, Eng.) –Jan. 18, 1963. British politician leader. Entered House of Commons, 1945; min. of state for economic affairs, 1950, chan. of the exchequer, 1950–51; as Labour Party leader (1955–63), persuaded the party to reverse its decision in favor of unilateral disarmament; opposed British entry in E.E.C.

**GLADSTONE, WILLIAM,** Dec. 29, 1809 (Liverpool, Eng.)–May 19, 1898. British statesman. As prime min. (1868–74, 1880–85, 1886, and 1892–94) and Liberal Party leader, powerfully affected the political life of his era; crusaded for Irish Home Rule, despite its political unpopularity; injected a high moral tone into Victorian politics; reformed the British Civil Service; took anti-imperialist stand; attempted to extend suffrage; reorganized the courts.

**GREY, CHARLES, (second) EARL,** Mar. 13, 1764 (Falloden, Northumberland, Eng.)–July 17, 1845. English statesman. A liberal Whig, part of the opposition to the Tory admin. of WILLIAM PITT; advocate of Catholic Emancipation; foreign secy., 1806–07; as prime min. (1830–34), fought for extension of the franchise, leading to the Reform Act of 1832.

**GREY, LADY JANE,** Oct. 1537 (Bradgate, Leicestershire, Eng.)–Feb. 12, 1554. Queen of England for nine days in 1553. Married to Lord Guildford Dudley and put on the throne by unscrupulous politicians; sentenced to death and executed for treason under MARY I in part for her father's participation in Wyatt's Rebellion.

**HALIFAX, EARL OF** (Edward Frederick Lindley Wood), Apr. 16, 1881 (Powderham, Devon, Eng.) –Dec. 23, 1959. English statesman, diplomat. Viceroy of India, 1925–31; as foreign secy. (1938–40), identified with an appeasement policy toward Nazi Germany; amb. to the U.S., 1941–46; K.G., 1931; O.M., 1946; succeeded to peerage as viscount, 1934, created earl, 1944. *Fullness of Days,* 1957.

**HAROLD II,** c. 1020 (Godwinson)-Oct. 14, 1066.

The last Anglo-Saxon king of England. Ruled for nine months until his death at the Battle of Hastings.

**HASTINGS, WARREN,** Dec. 6, 1732 (Churchill, nr. Daylesford, Oxfordshire, Eng.)–Aug. 22, 1818. English administrator. With East India Co, from 1750; as the first gov.-gen. of British India (1773–85), revitalized the British presence in India with his aggressive rule; suppressed banditry; involved Britain more deeply in Indian politics, both in conquered and unconquered provinces; impeached (1788) for maladministration and acquitted (1795).

**HEATH, EDWARD,** July 9, 1916 (Broadstairs, Kent, Eng.) English statesman. As lord privy seal (1960–63), negotiated British entry into the European Economic Community; Conservative party leader, 1965–75; as prime min. (1970–74), his admin. was hurt by bad inflation and a threatened miners' strike.

**HENRY VII,** Jan. 28, 1457 (Pembroke, Pembrokeshire, Eng.)–Apr. 21, 1509. King of England, 1485–1509. Founded the Tudor dynasty, thereby ending the dynastic Wars of the Roses; as king, kept England at peace; promoted trade and internal, law and order.

**HENRY VIII,** June 28, 1491 (Greenwich, Eng.)– Jan. 28, 1547. King of England, 1509–47. Played a major role in the break of the English church from Rome and the growth of Protestantism in England. Wanting to divorce his wife Catherine, fought against the church to gain papal assent; because of continued conflict, with Parliament's backing created a national church separate from the Roman Catholic Church and proclaimed himself its head in Act of Supremacy; dissolved the monasteries; also brought unity to England, built up the navy, and increased parliamentary powers. (Wives: CATHERINE OF ARAGON [1509–1533], ANNE BOLEYN [1533–1536], Jane Seymour [1536–1537], Anne of Cleves [Jan.-July, 1540], Catherine Howard [1540–1542], Katherine Parr [1543–1547].)

**HOWE, GEOFFREY,** Dec. 20, 1926 (United Kingdom). British statesman. A member of Parliament; British secretary of state for foreign and commonwealth affairs; knighted, 1970.

**HYDE, EDWARD, (first) EARL OF CLARENDON,** Feb. 18, 1609 (Dinton, Wiltshire, Eng.)–Dec. 9, 1674. English statesman, historian. Entered Parliament, 1640; worked to create a bridge between CHARLES I and Parliament; after English Civil War brought OLIVER CROMWELL to power, followed Prince Charles into exile, 1646; following Cromwell's death, helped negotiate restoration of the monarchy under CHARLES II, 1660; fell from grace for his criticism of king's immorality; lived in France until his death; created baron, 1660; viscount and earl, 1661. *History of the Rebellion,* 1670.

**JOHN, (John Lackland),** Dec. 24, 1167 (Oxford, Eng.)–Oct. 19, 1216. King of England (1199–1216). Forced by the English barons to sign the Magna Carta (June 12, 1215) after he violated the traditional feudal relationships with the nobility; lost all Normandy and most of Poitou, 1204–05 (Brother of RICHARD I; son of ELEANOR OF AQUITAINE.)

**KINNOCK, NEIL,** March 28, 1942 (Tredegar, Wales). British statesman. The youngest leader in the history of the Labour Party; known for his dramatic speech-making style.

**LAW, ANDREW BONAR,** Sept. 16, 1858 (Kingston, N.B., Can.)–Oct. 30, 1923. British politician. Leader of British Conservative party, 1911–21 and 1922–23; British chan. of the exchequer (1916–19) and prime min. (1922– 23); a supporter of tariff reform and an opponent of home rule for Ireland.

**LAWSON, SIR NIGEL,** March 11, 1932 (London, England). British statesman. A newspaperman and BBC broadcaster, has been a member of Parliament since 1974; chancellor of the exchequer, 1983– .

**LLOYD GEORGE, DAVID,** Jan. 17, 1863 (Manchester, Eng.)–Mar. 26, 1945. British statesman. As prime min. (1916–22), laid the foundations of the modern welfare state. Chan. of the exchequer, 1908–15; worked for a nonvindictive treaty at Versailles, 1919; negotiated Irish independence, 1921; O.M., 1919; created Earl Lloyd George, and Viscount Gwynedd, 1945.

**MACBRIDE, SEAN,** Jan. 26, 1904 (Paris, Fr.)–Jan. 15, 1988. Irish internatl. civil servant. Secy. gen. of Internatl. Com. of Jurists, 1963–70; UN commander for Namibia, 1973–76; chm. of Amnesty Internatl., 1970–73; awarded Nobel Peace Prize, 1974; Lenin Peace Prize, 1977. (Son of M. GONNE).

**MACMILLAN, HAROLD,** Feb. 10, 1894 (London, Eng.)–Dec. 29, 1986. English statesman. Min. to Allied Hq. in N. Africa, 1942–45; chan. of the exchequer, 1955–57; as Conservative party prime min. (1957–63), failed to gain British entry into the European Economic Community and suffered setback of the Profumo scandal; achieved Nuclear Test-Ban Treaty, 1963; created Earl of Stockton, 1984.

**MARY, QUEEN OF SCOTS,** born Mary Stuart, Dec. 7, 1542 (Linlithgow Palace, Lothian, Scot.)–Feb. 8, 1587. Queen of Scotland, 1542–67. Inherited throne at age of six days; queen consort of François II of France, 1559–60; returned to Scotland to rule, 1561; faced hostility because of her Roman Catholicism; married (1565) Lord Darnley, a generally unpopular choice; then allegedly conspired in Darnley's murder, 1567; married Earl of Bothwell, provoking rebellion of Scottish nobles; imprisoned, forced to abdicate, 1567; fled to England, 1568, where she was imprisoned by ELIZABETH I; held for 18 years then tried for her part in Babington conspiracy and executed.

**MARY I** ("Bloody Mary"), Feb. 18, 1516 (Greenwich, Eng.)–Nov. 17, 1558. Queen of England, 1553–58. The first English queen to rule in her own right; married to Philip II of Spain, 1554; persecuted Protestants in an attempt to restore Roman Catholicism in England; lost Calais, last English continental possession, 1558.

**MORE, SIR, THOMAS,** Feb. 7, 1477 (London, Eng.)–July 6, 1535. English statesman, humanist. A leading humanist whose *Utopia* (1516) formulated an ideal state based on reason. Entered service of

**HENRY VIII,** 1518; knighted, 1521; succeeded Cardinal WOLSEY as lord chan., 1529–32; enraged Henry by refusing to attend ANNE BOLEYN's coronation, 1533; arrested and imprisoned, 1534; refused to accept Act of Supremacy making Henry head of the Church of England; beheaded for treason. A saint of the Roman Catholic Church; canonized, 1935.

**MOSELY, SIR OSWALD,** Nov. 16, 1896 (London, Eng.)–Dec 2, 1980. British fascist leader. Leader of British Union of Fascists (1932–40) and its successor, the Union movement (1948–66); member of House of Commons, 1918–31; interned, 1940–43.

**NORTH, FREDERICK, LORD, (second) EARL OF GUILFORD,** Apr. 13, 1732 (London, Eng.)–Aug. 5, 1792. English statesman. Served as prime min. during the American Revolution, 1770–82; partially repealed the Townshend Acts, 1770; passed the Intolerable Acts (1774), including the Boston Port Bill; became convinced the king's policy toward the colonies was mistaken and attempted to convince Parliament not to tax the colonies; resigned; K.G., 1772, succeeded to earldom, 1790.

**O'CONNELL, DANIEL** ("The Liberator"), Aug. 6, 1775 (Cahirciveen, County Kerry, Ire.)–May 15, 1847. Irish nationalist leader in the British House of Commons, 1829–40 and 1844–47. United Irish Roman Catholics into a league to press for Irish claims; his election to Parliament (1828) forced British govt. to accept Emancipation Act of 1829, which allowed Roman Catholics to sit in Parliament and hold office; lord mayor of Dublin, 1841–43.

**PARNELL, CHARLES STEWART,** June 27, 1846 (Avondale, Co. Wicklow, Ire.)–Oct. 6, 1891. Irish nationalist leader. First pres. of Natl. Land League of Ireland, 1879; as member of Parliament, 1875–91, obstructed parliamentary business in order to bring attention to Irish Home Rule; advocated a boycott against landlords and land agents; politician career ruined by a scandal involving himself and a colleague's wife, 1889.

**PEEL, SIR ROBERT,** Feb. 5, 1788 (Bury Lancashire, Eng.)–July 2, 1850. English political leader, a major founder of the Conservative Party. Chief secy. for Ireland, 1812–18; as home secy. (1822–27, 1828–30), founded the London Police Force (1829) and sponsored a bill enabling Roman Catholics to sit in the House of Commons (1829); as British prime min. (1834–35 and 1841–46), reorganized the Bank of England, launched a policy of reform in Ireland (1845), and repealed the Corn Laws (1846) that had restricted grain imports; suceeded to title, 1830.

**PITT** (the Elder), **WILLIAM, EARL OF CHATHAM,** ("The Great Commoner"), Nov. 15, 1708 (Westminster, London, Eng.)–May 11, 1778. English statesman. As secy. of state (1756–61) and prime min. (1766–68), extremely influential in making England into an imperial power; led England during the Seven Years' War (1756–63), which won vast territory for England, including Canada;

worked for conciliation with the American colonies, just short of independence.

**PITT** (the Younger), **WILLIAM**, May 28, 1759 (Hayes, Kent, Eng.)–Jan. 23, 1806. English statesman. As prime min. (1783–1801, 1804-06), led England during the French Revolutionary wars and Napoleonic Wars; widely considered to be England's greatest prime min.; implemented financial reforms; during French Revolutionary wars, clamped down on radical agitation; worked for Catholic emancipation in Ireland.

**RHODES, CECIL**, July 5, 1853 (Bishop's Stortford, Hertfordshire, Eng.)–Mar. 26, 1902. English statesman, financier. Based on the fortune he had cleverly amassed in diamonds, built an empire in S. Africa; formed the De Beers Mining Co., 1888; prime min. of Cape Colony, 1890–96; established the Rhodes Scholarships at Oxford U.; Rhodesia named for him.

**RICHARD I** ("The Lion-Heart"), Sept. 8, 1157 (Oxford, Eng.)–Apr. 6, 1199. King of England, 1189–99. Known for his chivalry, the subject of many romantic legends; started on the Third Crusade, 1189; conquered Cyprus, 1191; recaptured Acre, 1191 and Jaffa from Saladin, 1192; on his return, captured in Austria (1192) and held for ransom; ransomed and returned to England, 1194. (Brother of JOHN, son of ELEANOR OF AQUITAINE.)

**RICHARD III**, Oct. 2, 1452 (Fotheringay Castle, Northamptonshire, Eng.)–Aug. 22, 1485. King of England, 1483–85. On the death of his brother, Edward IV, assumed protectorship of young Edward V; placed Edward and his brother, the duke of York, in the Tower of London, then a royal palace and had himself crowned king; the mysterious deaths of the two young princes traditionally has been attributed to Richard, although modern research has cast doubt on his guilt; killed at Bosworth Field, thereby ending War of Roses, 1485.

**ROBERT I**, or Robert the Bruce, July 11, 1274 (prob. Ayrshire, Scot.) June 7, 1329. King (1305–29) and liberator of Scotland. Initially paid homage to Edward I of England, 1296; crowned king of Scotland, he rebelled but was defeated, 1306; upon returning from refuge in Ireland, reconquered most of Scotland from England, 1307-09; defeated Edward II's army at Bannockburn, 1314; fought the English repeatedly until Edward III recognized the independence of Scotland, 1328.

**SHAFTESBURY, ANTHONY ASHLEY COOPER,** (first) **EARL OF SHAFTESBURY,** (first) **BARON ASHLEY**, July 22, 1621 (Winborne, St. Giles, Dorset, Eng.)–Jan. 21, 1683. English statesman. A leading politician of his time, served as a cabinet min. both under OLIVER CROMWELL and after the Restoration of Charles II; opposed Charles's pro-Roman Catholic policies; pres. of Council of Trade and Foreign Plantations, 1672–74, helped to found the Carolinas; created baron, 1661; earl, 1672.

**STRAFFORD, SIR THOMAS WENTWORTH,**

**EARL OF,** Apr. 13, 1593 (London, Eng.)–May 12, 1641. English statesman. From an influential family of the north, initially opposed King Charles I, but became one of his chief supporters with appointment as lord pres. of the north (1628) and privy councillor (1629); supported king's authoritarian rule; as lord dep. of Ireland (1633–39), sought to strengthen royal power there; his failed attempt to quell Scottish revolt of 1639–40 brought impeachment by Parliament; attainted and executed with consent of Charles; knighted, 1611; succeeded as 2nd baronet, 1614; created baron and viscount, 1628; created earl, 1640.

**THATCHER, MARGARET**, Oct. 13, 1925 (Grantham, England). British stateswoman. A member of the Conservative Party; elected to the House of Commons, 1959; in 1975, became the first woman to head a British political party; prime minister, 1979–   ).

**VICTORIA** (in full, Alexandrina Victoria), May 24, 1819 (London, Eng.)–Jan. 22, 1901. Queen of Great Britain and Ireland (1837-1901) and empress of India (1876–1901). Through her long reign, enjoyed great popularity and restored dignity to her crown; very devoted to her husband Prince ALBERT, on whom she conferred the title Prince Consort; had nine children; had great interest in the British colonies, especially India.

**WALPOLE, ROBERT**, Aug. 26, 1676 (Houghton Hall, Norfolk, Eng.)–Mar. 18, 1745. English statesman. Regarded as the first British prime min. (1721–42); made the cabinet system effective and powerful for the first time; successfully handled the South Sea Bubble financial problem, 1720; encouraged trade; cultivated friendship with France; managed Parliament brilliantly, enforcing party discipline, K.G., 1726; created Earl of Orford, 1742.

**WILLIAM I** ("the Conqueror"), c. 1028 (Falaise, Normandy, Fr.)–Sept. 9, 1087. King of England (1066–87) and duke of Normandy (1035–87). Conquered England (the Norman Conquest), 1066; replaced old English nobility with his followers; made a survey of England (Domesday Book), 1085; established the primacy of loyalty to the king rather than to subordinate lords; instituted continental system of feudalism upon Anglo-Saxon England.

**WILSON, SIR HAROLD** (Baron Wilson of Rievaulx), Mar. 11, 1916 (Huddersfield, Yorkshire, Eng.). English statesman, economist. As prime min. (1964–70, 1974–76), attempted unsuccessfully to impose economic sanctions against the white supremacist regime in Rhodesia; plagued by economic problems in England. *New Deal for Coal*, 1945. K.G., 1976, created baron, 1983.

**WOLSEY, THOMAS**, c. 1475 (Ipswich?, Suffolk, Eng.)–Nov. 29, 1530. English cardinal, statesman. Dominated the English govt. during the reign of HENRY VIII, 1515-1529; named lord chancellor, 1515; appointed papal rep., 1518; used his power to amass wealth second only to that of the king; failed in attempt to persuade the pope to annul Henry's marriage to Catherine of Aragon.

## FRENCH RULERS, STATESMEN, AND POLITICAL LEADERS

**BARRE, RAYMOND,** Apr. 12, 1924 (Saint-Denis, Réunion, Fr.). French politician. Vice-Pres. of the Comm. of European Communities, 1967–72; min. of economy and finance, 1976–78; prime min. 1976-81. *Economie politique,* 1957.

**BRIAND, ARISTIDE,** Mar. 28, 1862 (Nantes, Fr.) –Mar. 7, 1932. French statesman. With Jean Jaurès, founded *L'Humanitè,* 1904; served as prime min. seven times, 1909-1932; as foreign min. (1925-32), responsible for the Locarno treaties (1925) and the Kellogg-Briand Pact (1927–28) to renounce war; awarded Nobel Peace Prize (with G. STRESEMANN), 1926.

**CAPET, HUGH,** c. 938–Oct. 14, 996. Founder of the Capetian line of French monarchs. Battled with Charles, the Carolingian contender, to defend his rule; secured his election as king, 987.

**CASSIN, RENE,** Oct. 5, 1887 (Bayonne, Fr.) –Feb. 20, 1976. French jurist. As pres. of UN Human Rights Comm. (1946–68), the principal author of the UN Declaration of the Rights of Man (adopted 1948); awarded Nobel Peace Prize, 1968.

**CATHERINE DE MEDICIS,** Apr. 13, 1519 (Florence, It.)–Jan. 5, 1589. Queen consort of HENRY II of France, then regent of France (1560–74). Deeply involved in the Catholic-Huguenot wars, at first tried to reconcile the two sides, then joined the Catholics; after religious war broke out, helped plan the St. Bartholomew's Day massacre (1572). (Granddaughter of LORENZO DE MEDICI.)

**CHARLEMAGNE** (or Charles the Great, Charles I), Apr. 2, c. 742 (Aix-la-Chapelle, now Aachen, Ger.)–Jan. 28, 814. French ruler. King of the Franks, 768–814; conquered the united almost all of the Christian lands of W. Europe and ruled as emperor (800–814); reformed admin. by the use of personal reps.; nurtured a renaissance in learning; preserved classical literature and established schools; began a monometallic system of currency; introduced the capitulary as a form of legal promulgation, 779.

**CHARLES VII,** Feb. 22, 1403 (Paris, Fr.)–July 22, 1461. King of France, 1422–61. Inspired and aided by JOAN OF ARC, waged war against the English occupation of northern France; captured Orléans and crowned at Reims, 1429; concluded peace with the Burgundians, 1435; recovered all French lands from the English, except Calais, 1437–53; reorganized admin., undermined the power of the nobility.

**CHIRAC, JACQUES,** Nov. 29, 1932 (Paris, France). French leader. Served as prime minister of France 1974–76; elected mayor of Paris, 1977; prime minster, 1986– .

**CLEMENCEAU, GEORGES,** Sept. 28, 1841 (Mouilleron-en-Pareds, Fr.)–Nov. 24, 1929. French statesman and journalist. Helped LÉON GAMBETTA in overthrowing the empire of Napoleon III, 1870; a defender of A. DREYFUS; as premier (1906–09 and 1917–20), extended French interests in Morocco and strengthened the alliance with England,

then revitalized the French war effort during WW I; framer of the treaty of Versailles, 1919.

**COLBERT, JEAN BAPTISTE,** Aug. 29, 1619 (Reims, Fr.)–Sept. 6, 1683. French govt. official, businessman. As finance min. to LOUIS XIV (1665–83), oversaw economic reconstruction of France; followed doctrines of mercantilism; encouraged tariff protection; built French navy, 1669–72; initiated state manufactures.

**CORDAY, CHARLOTTE,** July 27, 1768 (Saint-Saturin, Normandy, Fr.)–July 17, 1793. French patriot. An aristocrat inspired by the Girondist cause, she assassinated the French revolutionary JEAN PAUL MARAT because she saw him as the persecutor of the Girondists, 1793.

**DALADIER, EDOUARD,** June 18, 1884 (Carpentras, Fr.)–Oct. 10, 1970. French politician. Member of Chamber of Deputies, 1919–40; as premier (1933, 1934, and 1938–40), signed the Munich Pact (1938); imprisoned by Vichy govt., 1940–45; served in National Assembly, 1946–58.

**DANTON, GEORGES,** Oct. 26, 1759 (Champagne, Fr.)–Apr. 5, 1794. French revolutionary leader. Led the Cordeliers in the early days of the revolution; participated in the overthrow of the monarchy; dominated the first Com. of Public Safety, 1793; became critical of the revolutionary govt. for its excesses; executed for treason.

**ELEANOR OF AQUITAINE,** c.1122-Apr. 1, 1204. Queen consort of Louis VII of France (1137–52) and HENRY II of England (1154–89). Heiress of duchy of Aquitaine; went on the Second Crusade, 1147–49; helped her sons, RICHARD I and JOHN, to rule England; a patroness of the arts.

**GAMBETTA, LÉON,** Apr. 2, 1838 (Cahors, Fr.)–Dec. 31, 1882. French political leader. One of the chief founders of the Third Republic. Pres. of Chamber of Deputies, 1879–81; premier, 1881–82.

**DE GAULLE, CHARLES,** Nov. 22, 1890 (Lille, Fr.)–Nov. 9, 1970. French statesman, soldier, writer. Distinguished himself as a soldier in WW I; leader of the French govt.-in-exile during WW II and symbol of the French Resistance; critical of the Fourth Republic, retired to private life; returned as pres. of the Fifth Republic (1958–69); solved Algerian crisis by granting independence, 1962; attempted to build a powerful France; formed a foreign policy independent of the USSR and the U.S..

**GISCARD D'ESTAING, VALÉRY,** Feb. 2, 1926 (Coblenz, Ger.). French political leader. Elected to the National Assembly, 1956; to UN Gen. Assembly, 1956–58; founded Independent Republican party, 1962; min. for finance and economic affairs, 1962–66, 1969; pres., 1974–81.

**HENRY IV** (or Henry of Navarre), Dec. 13, 1553 (Pau, Fr.)–May 14, 1610. King of Navarre (as Henry III) (1572–89) and king of France (1589–1610). The first of the Bourbon line; brought an end to the religious wars in France. Raised a Calvinist, renounced Protestantism for Catholicism when he became king; defeated the Catholic League and other opposition; with the Edict of Nantes (1598), established toleration of the Protestants; encouraged economic prosperity in France.

**LAVAL, PIERRE,** June 28, 1883 (Châteldon, Fr.)– Oct. 15, 1945. French politician. Leader of the Vichy govt.'s collaboration with the Germans during WW II; executed for treason.

**LOUIS XIV** ("The Sun King"), Sept. 5, 1638 (Saint-Germain-en-Laye, Fr.)–Sept. 1, 1715. King of France (1643–1715). Made the state an absolute monarchy and led France during a period of greatness. Unified France; made the nobility financially dependent upon him; through wars, expanded France territorially, 1667–97; persecuted the Huguenots; built the palace at Versailles; patron of the arts; military reverses in later wars and the ruinous expenditures on the armed forces left France exhausted and poor at his death.

**LOUIS XVI,** Aug. 23, 1754 (Versailles, Fr.)–Jan. 21, 1793. King of France (1774–93). His reforms failed to prevent the French revolution (1789); once the revolution was underway, he failed to hold the confidence of its leadership; imprisoned, convicted of treason, guillotined. (Husband of MARIE-ANTOINETTE.)

**MACMAHON, COMTE MARIE EDME PATRICE MAURICE DE,** July 13, 1808 (Sully, Fr.)–Oct. 17, 1893. French politician, soldier. A marshal of France, monarchist. As pres. of the French Republic (1873–79), suffered a constitutional crisis that resulted in parliamentary rather than presidential control of the republic.

**MAGINOT, ANDRÉ** (-Louis-René), Feb. 17, 1877 (Paris, Fr.)–Jan. 7, 1932. French statesman. As min. of war (1922–24, 1926–29, 1929–31), largely responsible for the construction of the Maginot Line, a defense barrier along the eastern border of France.

**MARAT, JEAN PAUL,** May 24, 1743 (Boudry, Switz.)–July 13, 1793. French revolutionary. Well-known writer and advocate of extreme violence during the French Revolution; editor of *Ine Friend of the People,* 1789; del. to the Natl. Convention, 1792; leader of the radical Montagnard faction; helped DANTON and ROBESPIERRE overthrow the Girondists; assassinated by C. CORDAY while in his bath.

**MARIE ANTOINETTE,** Nov. 2, 1755 (Vienna, Austria)–Oct. 16, 1793. Austrian queen-consort of LOUIS XVI of France, 1774–93. Attempted to strengthen French ties with Austria, an unpopular policy in France; surrounded herself with a dissipated clique; found guilty of treason by French Revolutionary forces and guillotined. (Daughter of MARIA-THERESA.)

**MAZARIN, JULES,** born Guilio Mazarini, July 14, 1602 (Pescina, It.)–Mar. 9, 1661. French cardinal, statesman. The successor to RICHELIEU, he continued to strengthen France. Became chief min., 1642; won a war with Austria; defeated the Fronde (revolt of the nobility) with clever diplomacy, 1648–53; negotiated the favorable Peace of the Pyrenees at the end of war with Spain, 1659.

**MENDÈS-FRANCE, PIERRE,** Jan. 11, 1907 (Paris, Fr.)–Oct. 18, 1982. French political leader, economist. Leader of the Radical-Socialist Party; as premier (1954–55), withdrew France from Indochina and aided the formation of the Western European Union; opposed the return of DE GAULLE to power.

**MITTERRAND, FRANÇOIS.** Oct. 26, 1916 (Jarnac, France). French statesman. The leader of the Socialist Party, 1981–  ; elected the country's first leftist president since 1958, favored expanding the government's control in business; re-elected, 1988.

**NAPOLEON I** (Napoleon Bonaparte), Aug. 15, 1769 (Ajaccio, Corsica)–May 5, 1821. French soldier and emperor. Became an army officer, 1785; fought during the French Revolution; promoted to brig. gen., 1793; commanded the Army of Italy in several victories, 1796–97; defeated in Egypt and Syria, 1798–99; in coup, brought to supreme power as first consul, 1799; made reforms in education and govt., formulation the Napoleonic Code that remains the basis of the French legal system; defeated the Austrians, 1800; went to war against Great Britain, 1803; had himself crowned emperor, 1804; disastrously invaded Russia, 1812; defeated by Allied coalition, 1814; exiled to Elba, 1814; returned, regained power, defeated at Waterloo, 1815; exiled to St. Helena.

**POINCARÉ, RAYMOND,** Aug. 20, 1860 (Bar-le-Duc, Fr.)–Oct. 15, 1934. French statesman. As prime min. and foreign min. (1912), strove to increase French security, supporting entente with Britain and alliance with Russia; as pres. (1913–20), sought national unity during WW I and pressed for harsher measures for Germany after the war.

**POMPADOUR, MADAME DE** (Marquise de), Dec. 29, 1721 (Paris, Fr.)–Apr. 15, 1764. France mistress of Louis XV of France. Exerted much control over French policies and decorative arts; encouraged France's alliance with Austria, which involved France in the Seven Years' War (1756–63); a patron of the anticlerical philosophers; a friend of VOLTAIRE; created marquise 1711.

**POMPIDOU, GEORGES** (Jean-Raymond) July 5, 1911 (Montboudif, Fr.)–Apr. 2, 1974. French statesman. WW II aide to CHARLES DE GAULLE; as premier (1962–68), was a prominent negotiator during the 1968 strikes and riots; as pres. of the Fifth Republic (1969–74), ended France's opposition to Great Britain's entry into the European Common Market.

**REYNAUD, PAUL,** Oct. 15, 1878 (Barcelonette, Fr.)–Sept. 21, 1966. French statesman. As min. of finance (1938–40), devalued the franc to help pay for a better defense; as prime min. (1940), tried unsuccessfully to save France from German occupation. *In the Thick of the Fight, 1930–45,* 1955.

**RICHELIEU, ARMAND JEAN DU PLESSIS, DUC DE,** Sept. 9, 1585 (Richelieu, Poitou, Fr.)–Dec. 4, 1642. French cardinal, statesman. As chief min. to Louis XIII (1624–42), built France into a great power; centralized the govt. suppressing the Huguenots and the great nobles; made alliances with the Netherlands and the German Protestant powers, increasing France's power to the detriment of Spain's.

**ROBESPIERRE, MAXIMILIEN FRANÇOIS MARIE ISIDORE DE,** May 6, 1758 (Arras, Fr.)–July 28, 1794. French revolutionary leader. Jacobin leader and a major figure of the Reign of Terror of the French Revolution; elected to the Estates-Gen., 1789; leader of the radical Montagnard faction in the Natl. Convention; dominated the Com. of Public Safety (1793), which ruled during the Reign of Terror; overthrown and killed in the Thermidorian Reaction of 1794.

**SCHUMAN, ROBERT,** June 29, 1886 (Luxembourg)–Sept. 4, 1963. French statesman. Founder of the European Coal and Steel Community (1952) and proponent of European unity; as French foreign min. (1948–52), proposed the Schuman Plan (1950) for European economic and political unity; pres. of European Parliament Assembly, the consultive arm of the Common Market, 1958–60.

**SILHOUETTE, ÉTIENNE DE,** 1709–1767. French government official. As controller general of finances (1759), attempted to enforce stringent economies, causing the nobility to apply his name to a mere outline profile drawing, i.e., a "silhouette."

**TALLEYRAND-PÉRIGORD, CHARLES MAURICE DE, PRINCE DE BÉNÉVET,** Feb. 2, 1754 (Paris, Fr.)–May 17, 1838. French statesman, diplomat. The leading French politician of his time. Min. of foreign affairs under NAPOLEON I, 1797–1807; aided in the restoration of the Bourbons; negotiated the Treaty of Paris; represented France brilliantly at the Congress of Vienna, 1814; helped organize the Quadruple Alliance, 1834.

**THIERS, LOUIS ADOLPHE,** Apr. 15, 1797 (Marseilles, Fr.)–Sept. 3, 1877. French statesman, historian. A founder and the first pres. of the Third Republic (1871–73); suppressed the Paris Commune, 1871. *Histoire de la révolution française,* 10 vols., 1823–27.

## OTHER FOREIGN RULERS, STATESMEN, AND POLITICAL LEADERS

**ABU BAKR** (*As-Siddīg* "The Upright"), c.573 (Mecca, Arabia)–Aug. 23, 634. First Moslem Caliph (632–34) and successor to MOHAMMED. Father-in-law of Mohammed and his only companion on the hegira; began the amazing expansion of Islam as a world religion.

**ADENAUER, KONRAD** ("der Alte"), Jan. 5, 1876 (Cologne, Ger.)–Apr. 19, 1967. German statesman. As first chan. of the Federal Republic of Germany (1949–63), responsible for the nation's amazing economic recovery and political independence after WW II. Mayor of Cologne, 1917–33; twice imprisoned by the Nazis, 1934 and 1944.

**ALARIC,** c.370 (Peuce I. [now Rumania])–410. Chief of the Visigoths (from 395). Captured and sacked Rome, 410.

**ALEXANDER NEVSKY,** c.1220 (Vladimir, Rus.)–Nov. 14, 1263. Prince of Kiev, grand prince of Vladimir. Halted the Swedish (1240) and Teutonic Knights (1242) invasions of Russia; canonized by the Russian Orthodox Church; 1547; united Russian principalities under Mongolian yoke, pursued policy of cooperation with Mongols.

**ALEXANDER THE GREAT** (or Alexander III), 356 B.C. (Pella, Macedonia)–June 13, 323 B.C. King of Macedonia, 336–323 B.C. Taught by ARISTOTLE; conquered Thrace and Illyria and gained control over all Greece, 335; conquered Persia (334), Tyre, Gaza, occupied Egypt and founded Alexandria (332); invaded India (327); died of fever and fatigue at age 33.

**ALLENDE GOSSENS, SALVADOR,** July 26, 1908 (Valparaiso, Chile)–Sept. 11, 1973. Chilean politician, physician. As the first Marxist pres. of Chile (1970–73), nationalized several foreign-owned industries and pushed agrarian reform; besieged by crippling strikes and economic problems, overthrown by a military coup (1973); reported to have committed suicide.

**AMIN DADA, IDI,** 1925? (Koboko, Uganda). Ugandan military and political leader. As pres. of Uganda, (1971–79), ordered almost all Asians expelled, 1972; in attempt to purge Lango and Acholi tribes, caused deaths of an estimated 90,000 persons, 1971–74; chaired Org. of African Unity, 1975–76; survived many assassination attempts; ousted by Tanzanian-led invasion, 1979.

**ANDREOTTI, GIULIO,** Jan. 14, 1919 (Rome, It.). Italian politician, journalist. Editor of *Concretezza,* 1954–76; chm. of Christian Democratic party 1968–72; minister of foreign affairs, 1983–89; prime min. 1972–73, 1976–79 and 89– .

**ANTONESCU, ION,** June, 15, 1882 (Pitești, Rum.) –June 1, 1946. Rumanian statesman, soldier. As dictator of the pro-German govt. during WW II (1940–44), declared war on the USSR, 1941; initiated domestic reform programs; fostered emergence into power of the fascist Iron Guard, then suppressed it, 1941; lost support with increasing losses on the Russian front and overthrown, 1944; executed as a war criminal.

**ANTONY, MARC** (in Latin, Marcus Antonius), c.82 B.C.–Aug., 30 B.C. Roman triumvir, general. After J. CAESAR's death, formed with Octavian (Later AUGUSTUS) and Lepidus the second triumvirate, 43 B.C.; defeated BRUTUS and Cassius at Philippi, 42 B.C.; lived with CLEOPATRA in Alexandria, from c.40 B.C.; committed suicide after naval defeat at Actium by Octavian's forces.

**ARAFAT, YASIR,** Aug. 24, 1929 (Jerusalem, Palestine [now Israel]). Palestinian political and guerrilla leader. Helped found the al-Fatah *fedayeen,* 1956; head of Palestine Liberation Org., 1968– ; addressed UN in historic address seeking recognition of the PLO, 1974.

**ARIAS SÁNCHEZ, OSCAR,** Sept. 13, 1941 (Costa Rica). Costa Rica statesman. President, 1986– ; awarded the Nobel Peace Prize in 1987 for his efforts to bring peace and harmony to the Central American countries.

**ASOKA** ("The Great"), 273–c.232 B.C. Indian emperor of the Maurya dynasty (c.259–c.232 B.C.) who united most of India for the first time and spread Buddhism widely, elevating it to a world religion.

**ASSAD, HAFEZ AL–**, 1928 (Qardaha, Syria). Syrian political leader. The president of Syria, from 1971, known for hard-line pro-Moscow stance in the Middle East.

**ATATÜRK, KEMAL** (Mustafa Kemal), 1881 (Salonika, Turkish Macedonia, now Greece)–Nov. 10, 1938. Turkish statesman, reformer, soldier. As founder and first pres. of the Turkish Republic (1923–38), abolished the caliphate, closed religious courts and schools, instituted modern law (1926), decreed use of Latin rather than Arabic letters (1928), and extended the franchise to women (1934).

**AUGUSTUS, GAIUS JULIUS CAESAR OCTAVIANUS** (Octavian), Sept. 23, 63 B.C.–Aug. 19, 14. First Roman emperor (27 B.C.–14). The adopted son of JULIUS CAESAR, went to Rome to avenge his death, 44 B.C.; in an alliance with ANTONY and Lepidus (the Second Triumvirate), defeated his enemies; as emperor, centralized power; spread the army throughout the empire; supported the arts; introduced the Pax Romana, an era of peace; made taxation more equitable; accomplished much construction.

**AURANGZEB** (or Aurungzeb, Aurungzebel), Oct. 24, 1618 (Ahmandnagar, India)–Mar. 3, 1707. Moghul emperor of India (1658–1707). Under his rule the empire reached its greatest size; his fanatical devotion to Islam alienated the Hindus and his empire disintegrated after his rule. (Son of SHAH JEHAN.)

**BAKUNIN, MIKHAIL**, May 30, 1814 (Torzhok, Rus. [now Kalinin, USSR])–July 1, 1876. Russian anarchist. An opponent of KARL MARX; participated in the German revolutions of 1848–49; active in the First Internatl., 1868; believed in complete freedom and that destruction of the existing order was necessary. *God and the State*, 1882.

**BATISTA Y ZALDIVAR, FULGENCIO**, Jan. 16, 1901 (Banes, Cuba)–Aug. 6, 1973. Cuban dictator, soldier. As dictator of Cuba (1933–44), built a strong, efficient govt.; in his second term (1952–59) turned brutal and corrupt; ousted by FIDEL CASTRO, 1959.

**BAUDOUIN**, Sept. 7, 1930 (Stuyvenberg Castle, nr. Brussels, Belg.). Belgian political leader. King of Belgium, 1951– ; proclaimed the independence of the Belgian Congo (now Zaire), 1960; helped form five coalition govts., 1958–68.

**BEGIN, MENACHEM**, Aug. 16, 1913 (Brest-Litovsk, Rus.). Israeli political leader. Headed Betar Zionist Youth Movement in Poland, 1939; arrested by Soviet govt. and held in a Siberian concentration camp, 1940–41; in Palestine, took command of underground Irgun Zvai Leumi extremist organization, 1942; founded Herut (Freedom) Movement in Israel, 1948; joint chm. of Likud (Unity) Party, 1973– ; prime min. of Israel, 1977–83; negotiated with SADAT for peace in Middle East; with Sadat won Nobel Peace Prize, 1978.

**BENEŠ, EDUARD**, May 28, 1884 (Kožlány, Bohemia [now Czech.])–Sept. 3, 1948. Czechoslovak statesman. A founder of modern Czechoslovakia; min. of foreign affairs, 1918–35; pres. 1935–38; fled in 1938 to lead a Czech exile regime in London during WW II; returned in 1945 and served as pres. until forced to succumb to communist takeover, 1948.

**BEN-GURION, DAVID**, Oct. 16, 1886 (Plonsk, Pol.)–Dec. 1, 1973. Israeli statesman. The first prime min. of Israel (1948–52 and 1954–63), often called the "Father of the Nation,"; a young Zionist who emigrated to Palestine in 1906; expelled by Turks, but returned when British took over rule; founded Histadrut (General Org. of Jewish Labor), 1920; chaired World Zionist Org. during the struggle to create the state of Israel.

**BERIA, LAVRENTI**, Mar. 29, 1899 (Merkheuli, Georgia, Rus.)–Dec. 22, 1953. Soviet political leader. As head of Soviet internal security (NKVD) (1938–53), purged many of J. STALIN's opponents and administered labor camps; killed in power struggle to succeed Stalin.

**BETANCOURT, RÓMULO**, Feb. 22, 1908 (Guatiré, Ven.)–Sept. 28, 1981. Venezuelan leader. Helped found the Accion Democratia, an anticommunist party, 1941; as pres. (1945–48 and 1959–64), instituted many reforms.

**BHUTTO, BENAZIR**, 1953 (Karachi, Pakistan). Pakistani leader. Forced to go into exile in London, (1984), but returned to her country to head the Pakistan People's Party in 1986, and was elected prime minister in 1988, becoming the first woman to head an elected government in an Islamic nation.

**BISMARCK, OTTO VON** ("The Iron Chancellor"), Apr. 1, 1815 (Schönhausen, Brandenburg) –July 30, 1898. German statesman. Founder and first chan. of the German Empire; unified the German states into one empire under Prussian leadership, 1871; developed a common currency, a central bank, and a single code of commercial and civil law; first European statesman to devise a comprehensive scheme of Social Security; presided over the Congress of Berlin, 1878.

**BOLIVAR, SIMÓN** ("The Liberator"), July 24, 1783 (Caracas, Ven.)–Dec. 17, 1830. S. American statesman, soldier. Leader in the liberation of northern S. America from Spanish imperial control, leading to independence for Colombia (1819), Venezuela (1821), Ecuador (1822), Peru (1824), and Bolivia (1825); pres. of Colombia, 1819–30; pres. of Peru, 1824–27; his attempts to form a Hispanic-American union under his control failed.

**BORGIA, CESARE**, c.1475 (Rome?, It.)–Mar. 12, 1507. Italian leader, soldier. Powerful papal lieutenant who was idealized by N. MACHIAVELLI in *The Prince*; the son of Pope Alexander VI, became duke of the Romagna and captain-gen. of the armies of the Church; murdered his brother; through intrigue and military victory became lord of large territory in central Italy and spread terror throughout the country.

**BORGIA, LUCREZIA,** Duchess of Ferrara, Apr. 18, 1480 (Rome, It.)–June 24, 1519. Italian noblewoman. Long associated with crimes and the moral excesses of her father, Rodrigo Borgia (later Pope Alexander VI), and brother CESARE BORGIA, she has been largely cleared by recent research; married three times into prominent families for reasons of political expediency; after her father's death (1503), led an exemplary life, making Ferrara an artistic and literary center of the Italian Renaissance.

**BRANDT, WILLY** Dec. 18, 1913 (Lubeck, Ger.). German politician. Member of Bundestag, 1949–57; mayor of W. Berlin, 1957–66; chan. of Federal Republic of Germany, 1969–74; resigned after a spy scandal; member of Euro. Parl., 1979–83; awarded Nobel Peace Prize in 1971 for his work in improving relations between W. Germany and the Soviet Union.

**BREZHNEV, LEONID,** Dec. 19, 1906 (Kamenskoye, Rus. [now Dneprodzerzhinsk, USSR])–Nov. 10, 1982, Soviet political leader. First Soviet leader to hold simultaneously the posts of secy. gen. of Soviet Communist party (1964–82) and chm. of the Presidium of the Supreme Soviet; while in power, applied scientific management to domestic problems and some forceful measures to foreign-policy problems.

**BRIAN BORU** (or Boramham, Boraimbe), 940? (nr. Killaloe, County Clare, Ire.)–1014. King of Ireland (963–1014, high king from 1002). Increased his territory through conquest and broke Norse power in Ireland forever.

**BRUTUS, MARCUS JUNIUS,** 85 B.C.–42 B.C. Roman politician, soldier. Remembered chiefly as one of the conspirators who assassinated JULIUS CAESAR, 44 B.C.; his army was defeated by MARK ANTONY, 42 B.C.; committed suicide.

**BUKHARIN, NIKOLAI,** Oct. 9, 1888 (Moscow, Rus.)–Mar. 13, 1938. Russian communist leader. A member of the Bolshevik wing of the Social Democratic party who became a member of the Central Com. of the Russian Communist party following the 1917 Revolution; member of the Soviet Politburo, 1924–29; head of Third Internatl., 1926–29; advocated slow agricultural collectivization and industrialization; expelled from party (1929), readmitted (1934), tried for treason and executed (1938).

**BULGANIN, NIKOLAI,** June 11, 1895 (Nizhni-Novgorod, Rus. [now Gorki, USSR])–Feb. 24, 1975. Soviet leader. Mayor of Moscow, 1931–37; chm. of the State Bank, 1937–41; became a full member of the Politburo, 1948; defense min., 1947–49 and 1953–55; premier, 1955–58.

**BÜLOW, BERNHARD, PRINCE VON,** May 3, 1849 (Klein-Flottbek, Ger.)–Oct. 28, 1929. German statesman. As chan. (1900–09), aggressively pursued Germany's interests, in the process strengthening the Triple Entente among Great Britain, France, and Russia.

**CAESAR, GAIUS JULIUS,** July 12, 100 B.C. (Rome,

It.)–Mar. 15, 44 B.C. Roman general, statesman, orator, writer. Formed the first triumvirate, with Pompey and Crassus, 60 B.C.; conquered all Gaul (modern France and Belgium), 58–49 B.C.; invaded Britain, 54 B.C., ruled as Roman dictator, 49–44 B.C.; reformed the calendar, 46 B.C.; assassinated by BRUTUS, Cassius and others in the Senate house. *Commentaries (De bello Gallico and De bello civili)*.

**CALIGULA, (GAIUS CLAUDIUS CAESAR),** Aug. 31, 12 (Antium [now Anzio]. It.)–Jan. 24, 41. Roman emperor, 37–41. After a short period of rule marked by moderation, resorted to cruelty and tyranny; reputed to have suffered from insanity; murdered by a member of the Praetorian Guard.

**CARL XVI GUSTAF,** Apr. 30, 1946 (Stockholm, Swed.). King of Sweden, 1973– .

**CASTRO, FIDEL,** Aug. 13, 1927 (Near Birán, Cuba). Cuban political leader. As premier of Cuba (1959– ), has transformed his nation into the first communist state in the Western Hemisphere; led the 26th of July Movement, a guerrilla campaign, to overthrow the F. BATISTA regime, 1959; collectivized agriculture, expropriated all native and foreign industry; held absolute authority until Dec. 1976, when assemblies with limited power were created.

**CATHERINE II** ("The Great"), May 2, 1729 (Stettin, Ger. [now Szczecin, Pol.])–Nov. 17, 1796. Russian empress, 1762–1796. With help of the palace guard, overthrew her husband, Tsar Peter Ill; extended Russian territory greatly; through her diplomacy, increased Russian power and prestige; annexed Crimea from the Turks, 1783; divided Poland among Russia, Austria, and Prussia, 1795; a patron of the arts who corresponded with VOLTAIRE and was a disciple of the French Encyclopedists.

**CATHERINE OF ARAGON,** Dec. 16, 1485 (Alcala de Henares, Sp.)–Jan. 7, 1536. Spanish princess. First wife of King HENRY VIII of England; Henry wanted a legitimate male successor and after six of Catherine's children died and only one female (Queen Mary) lived, the couple separated, 1531; the annulment of their marriage by the archbishop of Canterbury (1533) brought about the break between Henry and Rome and led to the English Reformation. (Daughter of FERDINAND of Aragon and ISABELLA of Castile.)

**CATO, THE ELDER, MARCUS PORCIUS,** 234 B.C. (Tusculum, It.)–149 B.C. Roman statesman, soldier, writer. Fought in the Second Punic War (218–201 B.C.) and First Syrian War (192–189 B.C.); crucial in defeat of Antiochus at Thermopylae, 191 B.C.; as Roman censor (elected 184), defended traditional Roman values; the first Latin prose writer of importance. *De agricultura* (On Farming), 160 B.C.

**CAVOUR, CAMILLO BENSO, CONTE DE,** Aug. 10, 1810 (Turin, It.)–June 6, 1861. Italian statesman. Primarily responsible for the unification of Italy; founded the liberal daily *Il Risorgimento*, 1847; as premier of Sardinia (1852–59 and 1860–61), modernized and industrialized the state; with help from the French, liberated Italy from Austrian domination; with diplomatic maneuvering and G. GARIBALDI's military successes, molded a unified Italy, 1861.

CEAUSESCU, NICOLAE, Jan. 26, 1918 (Oltenia, Rum.)–Dec. 25, 1989. Rumanian political leader. Deputy min. of the Armed Forces, 1950–54; member of Politburo of Rumanian Communist party, 1955–89; as leader of the Rumanian Communist party (1967–89), asserted independence of Rumania from Soviet domination; first pres. of the Socialist Republic of Rumania, 1974–89; assassinated in aftermath of the Rumanian liberalization movement.

CHAMORRO, VIOLETA BARRIOS DE, 1929 (Rivas, Nicaragua). Nicaraguan leader. A member of the National Opposition Union in Nicaragua; defeated the Sandanista president, DANIEL ORTEGA, in February, 1990.

CHARLES V, Feb. 24, 1500 (Ghent, Flanders) –Sept. 21, 1558. Holy Roman emperor (1519–56) and (as Charles I) king of Spain (1516–56). Attempted to establish a universal Christian empire; tried to stop the Turkish invasion of Europe; struggled against the Protestant Ref.; hampered by economic problems as well as the new nationalism.

CHARLES XIV JOHN (Jean-Baptiste Jules Bernadotte, Prince of Ponte Corvo), Jan. 26, 1763 (Pau, Fr.)–Mar. 8, 1844. French marshal and king of Sweden and Norway, 1818–44. A gen. in the French Army and brilliant administrator under NAPOLEON I; chosen by the Swedish monarchy to succeed an aging king, 1810; united Norway with Sweden by marching on Denmark, forcing the Danes to cede Norway, 1814; ruled well, promoting many internal improvements.

CHARLES MARTEL ("The Hammer"), 688–Oct. 22, 741. Frankish ruler. The mayor of the palace of Austrasia who united the Frankish realm under his rule; stopped the Muslim invasion of Europe by his victory over the Moors of Spain in the Battle of Tours (or Poitiers), 732; supported missionary efforts directed at the German tribes he conquered.

CHEOPS (Khufu), fl.c.2680 B.C. Egyptian king, second pharaoh of the fourth dynasty. Builder of the great Pyramid at Giza.

CHIANG KAI-SHEK (Jiang Kaishek), Oct. 31, 1887 (Chekiang Prov., China)–Apr. 5, 1975. Chinese statesman, soldier. Fought against the Manchus (1911) and then joined SUN YAT-SEN; commander in chief of the Revolutionary Army, 1925; established himself as Chinese head of state, 1928–49; fought both the Chinese communists and the Japanese; defeated by communists, 1949; resumed presidency of China in exile on Taiwan, 1949–75.

CHOU EN-LAI (Zhou Enlai), 1898 (Huaian, Kiangsu Prov., China)–Jan. 8, 1976. Chinese communist leader. Became a communist in France, 1920–24; participated in national revolution in China led by the Kuomintang; succeeded MAO TSE-TUNG as political commissar of the Red Army, 1932; chief negotiator of Chinese Communist party with noncommunist Chinese against Japan and with the U.S. at the end of WW II; foreign min. 1949–58;

premier, 1949–76; sided with moderates in the Cultural Revolution of the 1960s; normalized relations with the West in the 1970s in face of the growing Soviet threat.

CHU TEH, Dec. 18, 1886 (I-lung, Szechwan Prov., China)–July 6, 1976. Chinese military leader. Founder of the Communist Chinese army and a great military leader of China; took part in the Nanking uprising, 1927; led the Red Army through the Long March of 1934–35 and to victory over the Nationalists in 1949; remained in command of the People's Liberation Army until 1954.

CICERO, MARCUS TULLIUS, 106 B.C. (Arpino, It.)–Dec. 7, 43 B.C. Roman statesman, scholar, orator. Upheld republican values during the civil wars of the Roman Republic; as consul of Rome (63) executed Catiline and his conspirators; exiled by his political enemies, 58; recalled by Pompey, 57 B.C.; opposed JULIUS CAESAR; defended rule of law and constitutional govt. *Philippics; De oratore; De republica; De legibus; De natura deorum.*

CLAUDIUS I, Aug. 1, 10 B.C. (Lugdunum [now Lyon, Fr.])–Oct. 13, 54. Roman emperor. Made Britain a Roman province; implemented administrative reforms, including increased reliance on freedmen; extended Roman rule over N. Africa; built many roads; thought to have been killed by his wife Agrippina.

CLEOPATRA VII (or VI), 69 B.C. (Egypt)–30 B.C. Egyptian queen (51–49 and 48–30 B.C.). Noted in history and drama as a *femme fatale*; engaged in civil war with her brother, Ptolemy XIII, over the Egyptian throne for 30 years; after his arrival (48) won over JULIUS CAESAR, who defeated her brother (47); joined Caesar in Rome (c.46), remaining until his death (44); captivated his successor, MARK ANTONY whom she married (37), ruining his popularity in Rome; defeated with Antony, 31 at Battle of Actium; fled to Egypt, committed suicide.

CONSTANTINE I ("the Great"), c.280 (Naissus, Upper Moesia [now Nis, Yugo])–May 22, 337. Roman emperor (306–337). Made Christianity the empire's lawful religion and moved the capital to Byzantium, which was rebuilt as Constantinople; converted to Christianity just before the Battle of Milvian Bridge, 312; emerged after civil wars as sole ruler; convened the church council at Nicea (325); strengthened and unified the empire.

CRAXI, BETTINO, February 24, 1934 (Milan, Italy). Italian political leader. A member of the Socialist Party, has served in the Italian chamber of deputies since 1968; prime minister, 1983–87.

CYRUS THE GREAT, 600? B.C.–529 B.C. Persian king (559-529 B.C.). Conquered much of the Near East and founded the Achaemenid (Persian) empire; noted for respecting the autonomy and local customs of the lands he conquered.

DARIUS I, 550 B.C.–486 B.C. King of Persia, 521–486 B.C. One of the greatest rulers of the Achaemenid dynasty; revised and increased satrapies (territories) in the admin. of his empire; promoted trade; built great buildings; led numerous military campaigns; noted as a lawgiver; instituted new gold coinage; defeated by the Greeks at the Battle of Marathon, 490 B.C.

**DAVID,** 11th cent. B.C. (Bethlehem, Israel)–c.973 B.C. Second king of Israel, 1013?–973? B.C. Symbol of the ideal king in the Jewish tradition; successor to SAUL; unified the tribes into a nation; as king of the southern kingdom of Judah, fought for the liberation of the northern tribes from the Philistines; made Jerusalem the capital of the united kingdom; completed the conquest of the Promised Land.

**DE GASPERI, ALCIDE,** Apr. 3, 1881 (Pieve Tesino, Aus. [now in Italy])–Aug. 19, 1954. Italian politician. As prime min. (1945–53), led the reconstruction of Italy after WW II, brought Italy into NATO (1951), began long-term land reform, helped establish the European Coal and Steel Comm. (1951).

**DE KLERK, F**(rederik) **W**(illem), March 18, 1936 (South Africa). South African statesman. Has served in the South African parliament since 1972; elected president, 1989; the most significant act he performed after his election was to free NELSON MANDELA.

**DEMOSTHENES,** 384 B.C. (Athens, Gr.)–Oct. 12, 322 B.C. Greek orator, statesman. Greatest of the Greek orators, roused Athens to oppose Philip of Macedon and ALEXANDER the Great with orations, known as Philippics; leader of the democratic faction in Athens.

**DESAI, MORARJI,** Feb. 29, 1896 (Bhadeli, Gujarat Prov., India). Indian statesman. A disciple of MAHATMA GANDHI; finance min., 1958–63; deputy prime min., 1967–69; resigned in break with INDIRA GANDHI and the Congress party and formed, with other former Congress leaders, another Congress party (INC-O); imprisoned by Gandhi for vocal opposition, 1975–77; helped form the Janata party, a new political coalition that he headed; prime min., 1977–79.

**DIAZ, PORFIRIO,** Sept. 15, 1830 (Oaxaca, Mex.)–July 2, 1915. Mexican statesman. As pres. (1876–80 and 1884–1911), an absolute ruler who brought peace and prosperity to Mexico; played his opponents off one another; welcomed foreign capital.

**DIEFENBAKER, JOHN,** Sept. 18, 1895 (Neustadt, Grey Co., Ont., Can.)–Aug. 16, 1979. Canadian statesman. Leader of the Progressive Conservative party, 1956–67; as prime min. (1957–63), obtained Agricultural Rehabilitation Development Act (ARDA) of 1961; suffered downfall in crisis over proposed manufacture of nuclear weapons.

**DIEM, NGO DINH,** Jan 3, 1901 (Quang Binh Prov., Vietnam)–Nov. 2, 1963. Vietnamese leader. As pres. of the Republic of Vietnam (1955–63), ruled as a dictator, backed by the U.S.; assassinated by his generals in a coup d'état.

**DIOCLETIAN** (born Gaius Aurelius Valerius Diocletianus) 245 (Salonae, Dalmatia [now Yugo.])–316. Roman emperor, 284–305. Split empire into four administrative divisions and subdivided them; reorganized the army; failed in an attempt to control prices; persecuted Christians.

**DOLLFUSS, ENGELBERT,** Oct. 4, 1892 (Kirnberg-an der Mank, Austria)–July 25, 1934. Austrian statesman. As chan. and dictator of Austria (1932–34), destroyed the Austrian Republic; obtained support from B. MUSSOLINI; took military action against Austrian socialists; assassinated by rebelling Austrian Nazis.

**DUARTE, JOSÉ NAPOLEÓN,** Nov. 23, 1925 (San Salvador, El Salvador)–Feb. 23, 1990. Salvadoran statesman. An organizer of the Christian Democratic Party 1960; served as president of his country, 1984–1989, developing a program of economic reform.

**DUNANT, JEAN HENRI,** May 8, 1828 (Geneva, Switz.)–Oct. 30, 1910. Swiss philanthropist. Founder of the Red Cross, 1864; a founder of the World's Young Men's Christian Assn.; took part in the first Geneva Convention, 1864; awarded first Nobel Peace Prize (with F. PASSY), 1901.

**DUVALIER, FRANÇOIS** ("Papa Doc"), Apr. 14, 1907 (Port-au-Prince, Haiti)–Apr. 21, 1971. Haitian leader. Entered politics as a reformer and .black nationalist; as pres. (1957–71), consolidated power into a regime marked by terror and corruption; succeeded by his son, Jean-Claude Duvalier (Baby Doc).

**ECHEVERRIA ALVAREZ, LUIS,** Jan. 17, 1922 (Mexico City, Mex.). Mexican lawyer and politician. Member of Institutional Revolutionary party; as secy. of the interior (1963–69), quelled the 1969 student riots in Mexico City; as pres. (1970–76), promoted agricultural technical-assistance programs.

**EICHMANN, ADOLF,** Mar. 19, 1906 (Solingen, Ger.)–May 31, 1962. German Nazi official. The principal technician in the execution of millions of Jews during WW II; seized by Israeli agents in Argentina, 1960; convicted by Israeli court (1961), and executed.

**ERHARD, LUDWIG,** Feb. 4, 1897 (Fürth, Ger.)–May 5, 1977. German statesman., economist. As federal economics min. (1949–63), the chief architect of West Germany's post-WW II economic recovery; introduced the currency reform (1948) that started West Germany's economic recovery; chan., 1963–66.

**FAISAL,** c. 1906 (Riyadh, al-Quaysumah [now Saudi Arabia])–Mar. 25, 1975. King of Saudi Arabia, 1964–75. Worked for Islamic unity and to improve the lot of his people; assassinated by his nephew.

**FARUK** (or Farouk), Feb. 11, 1920 (Cairo, Egypt)–Mar. 18, 1965. King of Egypt, 1936–52. Clashed with the Wafd party; suffered imposition of a pro-British premier during WW II; met a humiliating defeat in the 1949 Arab-Israeli conflict; toppled by military coup, led by G. NASSER, 1952.

**FERDINAND V** (of Castile) or Ferdinand II (of Aragon), Mar. 10, 1452 (Sos, Sp.)–Jan 23, 1516. King of Aragon. Brought about the unification of Spain by his marriage to ISABELLA I, queen of Castile, 1469; expelled Jews and Moors from Spain; initiated the search for American gold; converted large agricultural areas into grazing lands for the benefit of the wool industry; began the Spanish Inquisition.

**FRANCIS FERDINAND, ARCHDUKE,** Dec. 18,

1863 (Graz, Austria)–June 28, 1914. Austrian archduke. The nephew of Francis Joseph and heir to the Austrian throne whose assassination (June 28, 1914) at Sarajevo was the immediate cause of WW I.

**FRANCO, FRANCISCO,** Dec. 4, 1892 (El Ferrol, Sp.)–Nov. 20, 1975. Spanish dictator. Led the Nationalist forces that overthrew the Spanish democratic republic in the Spanish Civil War, 1936–39; as gen. and dictator of Spain (1936–75), kept Spain neutral during WW II; obtained U.S. economic aid in exchange for allowing U.S. military bases; relaxed his iron grip in the 1950s and 1960s only to reassert it in the 1970s.

**FRASER, MALCOLM,** May 21, 1930 (Melbourne, Austrl.). Australian politician. Min. of education and science, 1968–69 and 1971–72; min. of def., 1969–71; prime min., 1975–83.

**GANDHI, INDIRA,** Nov. 19, 1917 (Allahabad, India)–Oct. 31, 1984. Indian politician. As prime min. (1966–77) and Congress party leader, attempted to hold the two wings of the party together in a coalition; worked for economic planning and social reform; convicted of election-law violation, declared state of emergency and suspended civil liberties, 1975; re-elected prime minister, 1980; assassinated, 1984; succeeded by her son RAJIV GANDHI. (Daughter of J. NEHRU.)

**GANDHI, MOHANDAS K.,** known as Mahatma, Oct. 2, 1869 (Porbandar, India)–Jan. 30, 1948. Indian political leader. Leader of Indian nationalist movement against British rule; espoused a doctrine of nonviolence to achieve political and social progress; led civil disobedience campaign in S. Africa against anti-Hindu discrimination, 1893–1914; in Indian independence movement, called for revival of home industries and the abolition of untouchability; threatened "fasts unto death," which were effective because of his prestige; unified the Indian National Congress, 1925; shot to death by a Hindu fanatic.

**GANDHI, RAJIV,** Aug. 20, 1944 (Bombay, India). Indian statesman. A mechanical engineer and airplane pilot, replaced his mother, INDIRA GANDHI, as prime minister after her assassination in 1984.

**GARIBALDI, GIUSEPPE,** July 4, 1807 (Nice, Fr.)–June 2, 1882. Italian military leader in the movement for Italian unification and independence, influenced by GUISEPPE MAZZINI; conquered the Kingdom of the Two Sicilies (1860), capturing Naples, and thus paving the way for Italian unification (1861); defeated in attempt to capture Rome, 1862 and 1867.

**GENGHIS KHAN** (born Temujin), c.1162 (nr. Lake Baikal, Mongolia)–Aug. 18, 1227. Mongol warrior and ruler. Amassed a huge empire stretching from Eastern Europe to the Sea of Japan; consolidated tribes in Mongolia and eliminated his enemies; acknowledged supreme ruler, 1206; conquered northern China, southern Russia and Iran; administered his wide empire well; in military campaigns, brilliantly used flying horse columns and feigned retreats.

**GENSCHER, HANS-DIETRICH,** March 21, 1927 (Reideburg, Germany). German statesman. A member of the Free Democratic Party; vice-chancellor of West Germany, 1974– .

**GIEREK, EDWARD,** Jan. 6, 1913 (Porabka, Pol.). Polish communist leader. Involved in the Belgian underground during WW II; a specialist in economics and heavy industry; secy. of Central Communist Comm. of Poland, 1970–80; expelled from Communist Party, 1981.

**GODFREY** (Godefroy) **DE BOUILLON,** c.1060 (Baisy, Brabant)–July 18, 1100. Leader of the First Crusade. Duke of Lower Lorraine; first Latin ruler of Jerusalem (elected 1099); a great hero, the subject of many legends.

**GODUNOV, BORIS,** 1552–Apr. 23, 1605. Tsar of Russia, 1598–1605. A favorite of Tsar IVAN IV and chief adviser to Fyodor I, Ivan's son, virtually ruling Russia (1584–98); succeeded as tsar; strengthened the power of state officials at the expense of the boyars; recolonized Siberia; made peace with Sweden and Poland; rule undermined by famine.

**GOEBBELS, JOSEPH,** Oct. 29, 1897 (Rheydt, Ger.)–May 1, 1945. German Nazi official. As Nazi min. of propaganda (1928–45), controlled the press, radio, films, publications, theater, and music, and was responsible for creating a favorable image of the Nazi regime to the German people; killed his wife and six children and committed suicide in the Berlin bunker at the end of WW II.

**GOERING, HERMANN,** Jan. 12, 1893 (Rosenheim, Ger.)–Oct. 15, 1946. German Nazi leader. A WW I flying ace who rebuilt the German Air Force in the 1930s; organized the Gestapo (secret police); virtually dictated the German economy until 1943; Hitler's designated successor; committed suicide in jail.

**GORBACHEV, MIKHAIL,** March 2, 1931 (Privolnoye, U.S.S.R.). Soviet political leader. Became general secretary, or head, of the Communist Party of the Soviet Union, 1985; instituted the policies of *perestroika* (restructuring) and *glasnost* (a call for more openness); appointed president, 1990.

**GROTIUS, HUGO,** Apr. 10, 1583 (Delft, Neth.)–Aug. 28, 1645. Dutch jurist, scholar. Called the "Father of modern internatl. law," made major contributions in the field. *On the Law of Prize and Booty,* 1604; *On the Law of War and Peace,* 1625.

**GUEVARA, CHE** (Ernesto Guevara De La Sema); June 14, 1928 (Rosario, Arg.)–Oct. 9, 1967. Latin American guerrilla and revolutionary theoretician and tactician who played a major role in the Cuban Revolution (1956–59). Became a trusted aide of FIDEL CASTRO and min. of industry; disappeared in 1965, reappeared in Bolivia in 1966, where he established a guerrilla base. *Guerrilla Warfare,* 1961.

**HADRIAN** (or Adrian), Jan. 24, 76 (Spain)–July 10, 138. Roman emperor, 117–138. Although he did not expand the empire, it reached its height during his reign; excellent administrator; strengthened fortifications and frontier defenses; did extensive building; reorganized law and civil service; patron of the arts; suppressed a Jewish rebellion, 134.

HAILE SELASSIE ("The Lion of Judah"), July 23, 1892 (Harar Prov., Ethiopia)–Aug. 27, 1975. Emperor of Ethiopia, 1930–74. Emancipated the slaves and brought Ethiopia into League of Nations, 1924; led troops against Italian invasion, 1935; fled to Britain but returned (1941) to reclaim power with British help; established Natl. Assembly, 1955; crushed domestic rebellion, 1960; overthrown in military coup, 1974.

HAMMARSKJÖLD, DAG, July 29, 1905 (Jönköping, Swe.)–Sept. 18. 1961. Swedish diplomat, political economist. As secy. gen. of UN (1953–61), played an important role in the resolution of the Suez Canal crisis; sent UN troops to suppress civil strife in the Congo, 1960; built up prestige of the UN and established its independence from the U.S.; awarded Nobel Peace Prize, 1961. *Markings*, 1964.

HAMMURABI (or Hammurapi), before 1792 B.C. (Babylon)–1750 B.C. Babylonian ruler. The sixth ruler of the first dynasty of Babylon, 1792–1750 B.C.; known for his set of laws, once considered to be oldest promulgation of laws in history; brought all of Mesopotamia under one rule.

HASSAN II, July 9, 1929 (Rabat, Morocco). King of Morocco, 1961– . Succeeded his father; in foreign affairs, has followed a policy of nonalignment; has attempted to expand education and make it more Arabic; suspended attempts to institute a democratic constitution after riots ensued, 1965, 1970, 1972.

HAWKE, ROBERT, Dec. 9, 1929 (Bordertown, South Australia). Australian statesman. Became prime minster when the Labour Party won the election, 1983; has worked to create jobs through government spending.

HEROD THE GREAT 73? B.C. (Palestine)–4 B.C. King of Judea under the Romans, 47–4 B.C. A tyrannical ruler who expanded Judea; destroyed traditional Jewish institutions; attempted to Hellenize the country; used brutal police methods.

HERZL, THEODOR, May 2, 1860 (Budapest, Hung.)–July 3, 1904. Hungarian-born journalist, founder of Zionism. Correspondent with *Neue Freie Presse* (Vienna), 1891–95; founded Congress of the Zionist Orgs., 1897; established the Zionist newspaper *Die Welt*; negotiated with Turkey and Britain for a mass Jewish settlement in Palestine. *Der Judenstaat* (The Jewish State), 1896.

HEYDRICH, REINHARD, Mar. 7, 1904 (Halle, Ger.)–June 4, 1942. German Nazi official. Nazi specialist in terror. As dep. chief of SS, involved in June 1934 purges; administered Nazi concentration camps; head of Reich Central Security Office, 1939–42; assassinated by Czech patriots.

HIMMLER, HEINRICH, Oct. 7, 1900 (Munich, Ger.)–May 23, 1945. German Nazi official. The second most powerful man in the Third Reich; participated in the Munich Putsch, 1923; became head of the SS, 1929; commander of all police forces, 1936; established first concentration camp, at Dachau; organized the extermination camps in Eastern Europe; dismissed by HITLER for his involvement in a conspiracy to succeed him, 1945.

HINDENBURG, PAUL VON, Oct. 2, 1847 (Posen, Prussia [now Poznan, Pol.])–Aug. 2, 1934. German statesman, soldier. As field marshal during WW I, scored some brilliant victories on the Eastern Front; as second pres. of the Weimar Republic (1925–34), his power dwindled as the economy worsened and he was pressured into appointing HITLER as chan., 1933.

HIROHITO (reign name, Showa), Apr. 29, 1901 (Tokyo, Jap.)–Jan. 7, 1989. Emperor of Japan, 1926–89. Helped convince Japanese govt. to surrender to the Allies, 1945; publicly renounced the idea of imperial divinity, 1946; attempted to bring the throne close to the people; visited the U.S., 1975.

HITLER, ADOLF, Apr. 20, 1889 (Braunau am Inn, Austria)–Apr. 30, 1945. German dictator. Leader of the National Socialist Workers' (Nazi) Party (1921–45) and dictator of Germany (1933–45); gained political power in the early 1930s, playing on people's fears and the worsening economic situation; named chan., 1933; on death of HINDENBURG, united offices of pres. and chan., (taking title Der Führer); concentrated on territorial expansion; initiated policy of anti-semitism; annexed Austria (1938), the Sudentenland (1938), and Czechoslovakia (1939); invaded Poland, starting WW II, 1939; became poor strategist as war turned against him; committed suicide. *Mein Kampf* (Eng. trans.), 1933.

HO CHI MINH, May 19, 1890 (Hoang Tru, Vietnam)–Sept. 3, 1969. Vietnamese leader. One of the most influential communist leaders in the 20th cent. Joined French Communist party 1920; founded the Communist party of Vietnam, 1930; organized the Vietminh, which fought the Japanese in Vietnam and China (1945); as pres. of Vietnam (1946–54) during the First Indochina War sought negotiations with France, thereby playing an indirect role in the Geneva Accords (1954), which created two Vietnams; pres. of Democratic Republic of Vietnam (North Vietnam), 1954–69. *Notebook from Prison.*

HORTHY, MIKLOS, June 18, 1868 (Kenderes, Hung.)–Feb. 9, 1957. Commanded the Austro-Hungarian fleet in WW I; ousted Béla Kun regime and became regent of Hungary (1920– 44); during WW II, acquiesced to alliance with the Axis powers, but later rebelled.

HUA KUO-FENG (Hua Guofeng), c.1920 (Shansi Prov., China). Chinese political leader. An ardent Maoist, identified with the moderates; dep. prime min. and min. of public security, 1975; premier of Chinese People's Republic and first dep. chm. of Chinese Communist party, 1976–81; vice-chm., 1981–82; mem. cen. comm. 1982– .

HUERTA, VICTORIANO, Dec. 23, 1854 (Colotlan, Mex.)–Jan. 13, 1916. Mexican revolutionary, politician. Took part in revolution that raised PORFIRIO DIAZ to power; provisional pres. of Mexico, 1913–14.

HUSÁK, GUSTÁV, Jan. 10, 1913 (Bratislava, Slovakia [now Czech.]). Czechoslovak communist leader. Took part in the Slovak National Rising,

1944; member of Natl. Assembly, 1945–51; following the Soviet invasion of Czechoslovakia (Aug. 1968), succeeded A. Dubcek as gen. secy. of the Czechoslovak Communist party (1969–75); pres., 1975–89.

**HUSSEIN TALAL IBN,** Nov. 14, 1935 (Amman, Trans Jordan [now Jordan]). King of Jordan (1953–    ). His generally pro-western policies have met with criticism from the Arab League and Arab refugees from Israeli-occupied territory.

**IBARRURI, DELORES** ("La Pasionaria") Dec. 9, 1895 (Gallarta, nr. Bilbaö, Spain)–Nov. 12, 1989. Spanish communist leader. Joined (1920) the Spanish Communist party and became one of its most influential members; during Spanish Civil War, gave radio speeches urging Spaniards to resist the forces of Gen F. FRANCO; at war's end, fled to Soviet Union to head the exiled Spanish Communist party, 1939; when Communist party was legalized in Spain by King JUAN CARLOS, returned to Spain, 1977. *El único camino,* 1962.

**IBN SAUD,** c.1880 (Riyadh, Saudi Arabia)–Nov. 9, 1953. King of Saudi Arabia, 1932–53. Founder of the kingdom of Saudi Arabia. Captured Riyadh, the ancestral capital, 1902; continued to capture and defend his territory until he created Saudi Arabia, 1932; signed the first agreement for oil exploration, 1933; played only a minor role in Arab-Israeli hostilities.

**IEYASU** (Iyeyasn), Jan. 31, 1543 (Okazaki, Jap.)–June 1, 1616. Japanese dictator, gen. As founder of the Tokugawa shogunate, unified Japan against the feudal barons and the Buddhist monasteries, defeated his rivals in the battle of Sekigahara, 1600; built up and strengthened the state; encouraged foreign trade.

**IKHNATON** (Akhenaton, originally Amenhotep IV), (Thebes, Egypt) ruled. 1379–1362 B.C. Pharaoh of Egypt. Noted for his introduction of a monotheistic form of worship centered on Aten, the sun god; this redirection to sun-irradiated nature encouraged artists to become more naturalistic; founded the new capital of Akhetaton (now Tell-el-Amarna); empire declined due to his negligence.

**ISABELLA I** ("The Catholic"), Apr. 22, 1451 (Madrigal de las Altas Torres, Castile, Sp.)–Nov. 26, 1504. Queen of Castile (1474–1504) who married Ferdinand II of Aragon, 1469, and ruled jointly with him as Isabella I and FERDINAND V of Castile and Aragon (1479–1504). Helped unify Spain; conquered the Moorish kingdom of Grenada; expelled the Moors; reestablished the Inquisition; encouraged the arts; patron of CHRISTOPHER COLUMBUS. (Mother of CATHERINE OF ARAGON.)

**ITO, PRINCE HIROBUMI,** Sept. 2, 1841 (Choshu, Jap.)–Oct. 26, 1909. Japanese statesman. An important figure in the emergence of modern Japan; drafter of the Meiji constitution, 1889; served as prime min. four times, 1886–1901; created prince, 1907; first pres. of the Seiyuhai party; assassinated by a Korean fanatic.

**IVAN IV** ("the Terrible"), Aug. 25, 1530 (Kolo-

menskoye, nr. Moscow, Rus.)–Mar. 18, 1584. Ruler of Russia (1547–84) and grand prince of Moscow, 1533–84. Established the tsarist autocracy; surrounded himself with commoners rather than boyars (nobles); started the eastward expansion of Russia; grew gloomy and suspicious, terrorizing the country with murder; killed his son, Ivan, in a fit of fury.

**JOHN III SOBIESKI,** Aug. 17, 1629 (Olesko, Pol.) –June 17, 1696. King of Poland, 1674–96. Built Poland into a great country in a short period of time; distinguished himself as a soldier in wars against Sweden and Russia; saved Vienna from the Turks, 1683.

**JUAN CARLOS I,** Jan. 5, 1938 (Rome, It.). King of Spain, 1975–   . Designated by F. FRANCO as his successor, 1969; encouraged revival of political parties; deflected possible military coup, 1981.

**JUAREZ, BENITO,** Mar. 21, 1806 (San Pablo Guelatao, Mex.)–July 18, 1872. Mexican leader and revolutionary hero. Led the rebellion against SANTA ANNA, 1855; chief justice of Mexican Sup. Ct., 1857; as pres. (1958–59, 1861–63, and 1867–72), fought French (1864–67) and reduced the privileges of the army and the clergy.

**JUDAS MACCABAEUS,** died c.160 B.C. Jewish patriot. Leader of the Jewish revolt against Antiochus IV, king of Syria; reconsecrated the Temple of Jerusalem (165 B.C.), in memory of which the festival of Hanukkah is celebrated; prevented imposition of Hellenism upon Judea, preserved Jewish religion.

**JUSTINIAN I** (the Great), born Petrus Sabbatius, Flavius Justinianus when adopted by uncle Justin I, 483 (Tauresium [now in Yugo.])–Nov. 14, 565. Byzantine emperor (527–65). Extended the empire in Africa and Italy under BELISARIUS insisted on the supremacy of the emperor over the church; commissioned extensive construction, including the rebuilding of Hagia Sophia; codified Roman law into the *Corpus Juris Civillis* (body of civil law); reorganized administration. Codex Justinianus, 534.

**KARAMANLIS, KONSTANTINE,** Mar. 8, 1907 (Prote, nr. Serra, Macedonia, Greece.) Greek politician. As premier (1955–63 and 1974–80), has maintained a pro-Western foreign policy; restored the 1952 constitution; granted political amnesty; pres., 1980–85.

**KAUNDA, KENNETH,** Apr. 28, 1924 (Lubwa nr. Chinsali, N. Rhodesia, now Zambia). Zambian leader. As the first pres. of Zambia (1964–   ), has supported African unity and pressed economic development. Helped organize the African Natl. Congress (ANC) of No. Rhodesia, 1949; assumed leadership of the United Natl. Independence party, 1960.

**KENYATTA, JOMO,** c.1894 (Ichaweri, British East Africa, now Kenya)–Aug. 22, 1978. Kenyan leader. The first pres. of the Republic of Kenya, 1964–78. Pres. of Kenya African Union, 1947; imprisoned for allegedly leading Mau Mau terrorism, 1953–61; helped negotiate Kenya's independence at London Conference, 1962; as pres., attempted to strengthen ties among E. African states.

**KERENSKY, ALEXANDER,** Apr. 22, 1881 (Simbirsk, Rus. [now Ulyanovsk, USSR])–June 11, 1970. Russian revolutionary leader. A moderate socialist who, following the first Russian Revolution (Feb. 1917), headed the provisional govt. From July to Oct. 1917, when he was overthrown by the Bolsheviks.

**KHALID BIN ABDUL AZIZ,** 1913 (Riyadh, Saudi Arabia)–June 13, 1982. King of Saudi Arabia, 1975–82. Earlier, as vice-pres. of Council of Ministers (1962–75), represented his nation at various internatl. conferences.

**KHOMEINI, RUHOLLAH,** c.1901 (Khumain, Iran) –June 3, 1989. Iranian ayatollah (Moslem religious leader). In exile since 1963, returned to Iran after overthrow of the Shah, proclaimed new regime, marked by return to Islamic fundamentalism, deliberately reversed SHAH's pro-western orientation, 1979–89.

**KHRUSHCHEV, NIKITA,** Apr. 17, 1894 (Kalinkova, Ukraine, Rus.)–Sept. 11, 1971. Soviet communist leader. As first secy. of the Soviet Communist party (1953–64) and premier (1958–64), initiated a program of destalinization; failed to achieve the sixth five-year plan; enunciated a policy of peaceful coexistence with the Western powers; became involved in an increasingly bitter struggle with China; withdrew missiles from Cuba, 1962; removed from power for failures in agricultural production and other problems.

**KIM IL-SUNG,** Apr. 15, 1912 (nr. Pyongyang, Korea). Korean communist leader. Organized Korean armed resistance to the Japanese occupation in the 1930s; following WW II, with the help of the USSR, took control of the northern part of Korea; attempted to conquer the south, 1950–53; has maintained friendly relations with the USSR; premier 1948–72; pres. 1972– .

**KING, WILLIAM LYON MACKENZIE,** Dec. 17, 1874 (Berlin [now Kitchener], Ont., Can.)–July 22, 1950. Canadian statesman. Leader of the Liberal party, 1919–48; as prime min. (1921–26, 1926–30, and 1935–48), signed an agreement to help the U.S. build up defense production during WW II; signed the Washington Declaration on Nuclear Power, 1945; handled the French-Canadian problem skillfully. *Industry and Humanity,* 1918.

**KOSSUTH, LAJOS,** Sept. 19, 1802 (Monok, Hung.) –Mar. 20, 1894. Hungarian statesman. Principal figure in the Hungarian revolution of 1848; became pres. of the independent Republic of Hungary (1848), but forced to flee when the insurrection was crushed (1849).

**KOHL, HELMUT,** April 3, 1930 (Ludwigshafen, Germany). German statesman. Chancellor of West Germany, 1982– ; a member of the Christian Democratic Union; advocates a close union with the countries of the Western World.

**KOSYGIN, ALEXEI,** Feb. 20, 1904 (St. Petersburg, Rus. [now Leningrad, USSR])–Dec. 18, 1980, Soviet communist leader. As premier (1964–1980), led the Soviet effort at economic modernization in the 1960s, but receded into the background in the

1970s; member of the Soviet Communist party, 1927–1980); deputy chm. of Council of Ministers, 1957–64; negotiated India-Pakistan ceasefire, 1966; met with L. B. JOHNSON at Glassboro N.J. 1967; headed Soviet mission to Czechoslovakia, 1968.

**KREISKY, BRUNO,** Jan. 22, 1911 (Vienna, Austria). Austrian political leader. Min. of foreign affairs, 1959–66; chm. of Socialist party of Austria, 1967–83; federal chan. of Austria, 1970–83.

**KRUGER, PAUL** ("Oom Paul"), Oct. 10, 1825 (Cradock district, Cape Colony)–July 14, 1904. South African leader. Leader of Dutch South African (or Transvaal) movement for independence; a leader of Boer rebellion (1880), helped negotiate peace (1881); pres., Transvaal Republic, 1883–1900; fled to Europe during the Boer War, 1900.

**KUBLAI KHAN** (or Kubla Khan), 1216–1294. Mongol leader. Grandson of GENGHIS KHAN; subdued northern China (1260s) and by 1279 controlled southern China as well, thus becoming the first foreign conqueror to rule all of China; became famous in the West through accounts of his empire written by MARCO POLO.

**LANDSBERGIS, VYTAUTAS,** Oct. 18, 1932 (Kaunas, Lithuania). Lithuanian statesman. A music professor, a member of the pro-independence movement before his country broke its ties with the Soviet Union; elected president in 1990.

**LASSALLE, FERDINAND,** Apr. 11, 1825 (Breslau, Ger. [now Wroclaw, Pol.])–Aug. 31, 1864. German socialist leader. Founder of the German Social Democratic party; a disciple of MARX, from 1848; propagandist for and champion of the working classes; founded the General German Workers' Assn. to promote use of political power by workers, 1863.

**LENIN, VLADIMIR, ILYICH** (original surname, Ulyanov), April 22, 1870 (Simbirsk; Rus. [now Ulyanovsk, USSR])–Jan. 21, 1924. Russian communist leader, founder of Bolshevism, and architect of the first Soviet state. Converted to Marxism, 1889; exiled to Siberia, 1897; went to Switzerland (1900), where he founded *Iskra* (Spark), a revolutionary journal; split Russian Socialist party into two factions, taking up leadership of Bolshevik faction, 1903; returned to Russia after Feb. 1917 revolution, assumed control of revolutionary movement, and overthrew the provisional government (Nov. 1917); declared all power to be vested in the Soviets; became premier (1918–24), establishing the dictatorship of the proletariat; led Russia through civil war with counter-revolutionaries, 1918–21; eliminated all opposition; instituted far-reaching social and economic reforms; founded the Third Internatl., 1919. *What Is to Be Done?,* 1902; *The State and the Revolution,* 1917.

**LESSEPS, FERDINAND, VICOMTE DE,** Nov. 19, 1805 (Versailles, Fr.)–Dec. 7, 1894. French diplomat, engineer. Best known as the builder of the Suez Canal; persuaded Egyptian viceroy to allow construction of the canal, 1854; organized the Suez Canal Co., raised necessary capital, and oversaw the construction, 1859–69; headed French co. formed to build Panama Canal, but gave up the project because of financial difficulties, 1881–89

**LIE, TRYGVE**, July 16, 1896 (Cristiania, now Oslo, Nor.)–Dec. 30, 1968. Norwegian govt. official. As first secy.-gen. of the UN (1946–52), dealt with Arab intervention in Israel, N. Korea's invasion of S. Korea, and accusations that the UN employed U.S. communists. *In the Cause of Peace,* 1954.

**LIEBKNECHT, KARL**, Aug. 13, 1871 (Leipzig, Ger.)–Jan. 15, 1919. German socialist leader. Founder of the Spartacus League, the precursor of the German Communist party; elected to Reichstag, 1912; played an important role in the Spartacist Revolt, 1919; arrested (with ROSA LUXEMBURG) and killed.

**LI HUNG-CHANG**, Feb. 25, 1823 (Hofei, China)–Nov. 7, 1901. Chinese diplomat. Leading diplomat of the late 19th cent. who advocated the self-strengthening of China; negotiated peace treaty (1895) that ended first Sino-Japanese war (1894); prime min. 1895–98; negotiated with foreigners in the Boxer Rebellion, 1900.

**LILIUOKALANI, LYDIA KAMEKEHA**, Sept. 2, 1838 (Honolulu, Haw.)–Nov. 11, 1917. Hawaiian queen (1891–93). The last sovereign to rule before the annexation of the islands; composed "Aloha Oe."

**LIN PIAO** (Lin Biao), Dec. 5, 1907 (Huang-kang, Hupeh Prov., China)–Sept. 13, 1971. Chinese communist military leader. Pres. of the Red Acad., 1936; field commander of the Red Army against Japan and the Nationalist Chinese; def. min., 1959; supporter of the Cultural Revolution, 1966–9; disappeared mysteriously in a plane crash.

**LI PENG**, Oct. 1928 (Chengdu, People's Republic of China). Chinese leader. An electrical engineer, has been a member of the Chinese politburo since 1985; premier, 1988– .

**LUMUMBA, PATRICE**, July 2, 1925 (Oualua, Belgian Congo [now Zaïre])–Jan. 17, 1961. Congolese leader. As the first prime min. of the Congo (1960), a national hero; founded Congolese Natl Movement, 1958; fled following the Jan. 1959 uprising against the Belgians; a leading negotiator with Belgium for independence; as premier, met opposition over his determination to end Belgian-backed secession of Katanga Prov.; removed from office and killed.

**LUTHULI, ALBERT**, 1898 (nr. Bulawayo, Rhodesia)–July 21, 1967. S. African reformer. Member of African Natl. Congress, 1945; led passive-resistance campaign against apartheid, 1952; arrested, 1956; awarded Nobel Peace Prize for his nonviolent opposition to racial discrimination, 1960. *Let My People Go,* 1962.

**LUXEMBURG, ROSA**, Mar. 5, 1871 (Zamość, Pol.)–Jan. 15, 1919. German socialist revolutionary. Took part in the Russian Revolution of 1905; confounder (with KARL LIEBKNECHT), of the Spartacus; advocated the general strike as a revolutionary weapon; involved in Spartacist uprising (1919), arrested, and killed on the way to prison.

**MACDONALD, SIR JOHN**, Jan. 11, 1815 (Glasgow, Scot.)–June 6, 1891. Canadian statesman. A powerful figure in the unification of the British N. American provinces; as first prime min. of Canada (1867–73 and 1878–91), advocated reciprocal trade agreements with the U.S., worked for strong bonds with Great Britain, oversaw building of the Canadian Pacific RR. knighted, 1867.

**MACHIAVELLI, NICCOLÒ**, May 3, 1469 (Florence, It.)–June 22, 1527. Italian statesman, writer. Best known for *The Prince* (1513), a work outlining his pragmatic theory of govt. and maxims of practical statecraft. *The Discourses on the First Ten Books of Livy,* 1519; *The Art of War,* 1519–20.

**MAKARIOS III** (born Mikhail Khristodolou Mouskos), Aug. 3, 1913 (Pano, Panayia, Paphos, Cyprus)–Aug. 3, 1977. Cypriot leader. The first pres. of Cyprus (1959–74), and archbishop of the Orthodox Church of Cyprus (1950–77); led the struggle for *énosis* (union) with Greece during the British occupation, in the 1950s; as pres., worked for integration of the Greek and Turkish communities on Cyprus; following Turkish invasion (1974), resisted partition of the island.

**MANDELA, NELSON**, 1918 (Umtata, South Africa). South African black leader. A lawyer, joined the African National Congress, a group opposed to apartheid; charged with treason, he was acquitted in 1961; but in 1962 he was arrested and later convicted of sabotage and conspiracy and sentenced to life imprisonment; not released until 1990.

**MAO TSE-TUNG** (Mao Zedong), Dec. 26, 1893 (Hunan Prov., China)–Sept. 9, 1976. Chinese communist leader and prime theorist of Chinese communism. Organized peasant and industrial unions in the 1920s; broke with CHIANG KAI-SHEK and led the Red Army on the Long March, 1934–35; fought the Nationalists and Japanese, winning control of China, 1949; became chm. of the Chinese Communist party (1949–76) and chm. of the People's Republic of China (1949–59); attempted to decentralize the economy with the Great Leap Forward, 1957; reasserted control through the Cultural Revolution, 1966–69.

**MARCOS, FERDINAND E.**, Sept. 11, 1917 (Sarrat, Luzon, Philippines)–Sept. 28, 1989. Philippine leader. As pres. of the Philippines (1966–86), supported U.S. policy in Vietnam, imposed martial law to quell mounting internal disturbances in the 1970s; political power weakened by spoils system; manipulated vote counting to gain victory over CORAZON AQUINO, who claimed victory for herself; in face of eroding support at home and in U.S., fled, 1986; died without facing charges of looting Philippine treasury and defrauding U.S. banks.

**MARCOS, IMELDA**, July 2, 1931 (Tolosa, Leyte, Philippines). Philippine political leader. The wife of Philippine Pres. FERDINAND MARCOS and second-most powerful figure in the country; escaped assassination attempt, 1972; appointed gov. of metropolitan Manila; indicted but acquitted by a U.S. court on charges she and her late husband had looted the Philippine treasury and used the money to buy expensive U.S. property for themselves.

**MARIA THERESA,** May 13, 1717 (Vienna, Austria)–Nov. 29, 1780. Empress of Holy Roman Empire (1740–80), archduchess of Austria, queen of Hungary and Bohemia. Ousted the pretender Charles VII and crowned queen, 1742; obtained election of husband Francis I as Roman emperor and coregent, 1745; fought Seven Year's War with FREDERICK THE GREAT of Prussia, 1756–63; known for her diplomatic skill; instituted governmental reforms affecting taxes and fiscal matters, and enlarged central admin. of the Austrian Empire. (Mother of MARIE ANTOINETTE.)

**MARTI, JOSÉ,** Jan. 28, 1853 (Havana, Cuba)–May 19, 1895. Cuban poet, patriot. Leader of the Cuban struggle for independence and noted Spanish-American writer. Deported for his political activities on behalf of independence, 1871 and 1879; helped organize the Cuban Revolutionary party, 1892; led an invasion of Cuba, in which he died, 1895. *Neustra América,* 1891; *Bolívar,* 1893.

**MASARYK, JAN GARRIGUE,** Sept. 14, 1886 (Prague, Czech.)–Mar. 10, 1948. Czech statesman. Min. to Great Britain, 1925–38; foreign min., 1940–48; vice-premier of Czechoslovak Provisional Govt. in London, 1941–45; allegedly committed suicide after the communist takeover of Czechoslovakia. (Son of T. G. MASARYK.)

**MASARYK, TOMÁŠ GARRIGUE,** Mar. 7, 1850 (Hodonin, Moravia [now Czech.])–Sept. 14, 1937. Czech statesman, philosopher. Chief founder and first pres. (1918–35) of the Czechoslovak Republic; prof. of philosophy at Charles U., 1882–1911; member of Austrian Parliament, 1891–93 and 1907–14; formed Czechoslovak national council in Paris during WW I; as pres., instituted extensive land reform, brought minorities together, and tried to reconcile church and state. (Father of J. G. MASARYK.)

**MAXIMILIAN** (in full, Ferdinand Maximilian Joseph), July 6, 1832 (Vienna, Austria)–June 19, 1867. Austrian archduke, emperor of Mexico (1864–67). Given the Mexican throne by Mexican conservatives and French Emperor Napoleon III, he ruled poorly, alienating many with his liberal plans; with withdrawal of French troops, his empire collapsed and he was executed.

**MAZZINI, GIUSEPPE,** June 22, 1805 (Genoa, It.)–Mar. 10, 1872. Italian patriot, revolutionary. Fought for Italian unity and independence, even though in exile much of his life; founded Giovine Italia (Young Italy), a secret revolutionary society, in exile, 1832; returned during the upheavals of 1848, and became a member of the Republic of Rome (1849), but returned to exile with reestablishment of papal control; took part in various rebellions and aided in organizing GARIBALDI's revolutionary expeditions, 1860, 1862, and 1867.

**MBOYA, TOM,** Aug. 15, 1930 (Kilima Mbogo, nr. Nairobi, Central Province, Kenya)–July 5, 1969. Kenyan political leader. A leader in the Kenyan struggle for independence; gen. secy., Kenya Feder-

ation of Labour (KLF), 1953–63; founder-member, Kenya African National Union party, 1960; Kenyan min. for economic planning, 1964–69; assassinated.

**MEDICI, COSIMO I DE** ("the Great"), June 12, 1519–Apr. 21, 1574. Florentine statesman. As grand duke of Tuscany (1569–74) and duke of Florence (1537–69), guided Florence to the peak of its political importance and prosperity; a cruel but effective tyrant; conquered Siena, 1555.

**MEDICI, LORENZO DI** ("the Magnificent"), Jan. 1, 1449 (Florence, It.)–Apr. 8, 1492. Florentine statesman, merchant prince, patron of the arts. As ruler of Florence (1469–92), a major figure in the Italian Ren.; engaged in a struggle with supporters of the pope, with whom he made peace, 1480; though his rule was tyrannical, Florence prospered under him.

**MEIR, GOLDA,** May 3, 1898 (Kiev, Rus.)–Dec. 8, 1978. Israeli stateswoman. The first woman premier of Israel, 1969–74; emigrated to Palestine from Milwaukee, Wisc., where she had grown up, 1921; worked with the Histadrut (Federation of Labor); a leader in the fight for a state of Israel, 1948; min. of labor (1949–56) and foreign affairs (1956–66); as premier, worked to achieve a peace with the Arabs through diplomacy, but eruption of the fourth Arab-Israeli War (1973) eroded her support. *My Life,* 1975.

**MENES,** fl. 3100 B.C. First king of the first dynasty of Egypt. Unified Upper and Lower Egypt into a single monarchy; founded the capitol of Memphis; tomb discovered at Negadr, 1897.

**METAXAS, IOANNIS,** Apr. 12, 1871 (Ithaca, Greece)–Jan. 29, 1941. Greek statesman, general. As dictator of Greece (1936–41), led Greece into war with Italy and Germany; a royalist, he distinguished himself in the Balkan wars, 1912–13.

**METTERNICH, KLEMENS W. N. L.,** May 15, 1773 (Coblenz, Ger.)–June 11, 1859. Austrian diplomat, statesman. As min. of foreign affairs (1809–48), made Austria a leading power and built a stable internatl. order in Europe; a voice of conservatism; one of the leaders of the Allies against Napoleon; the dominant influence at the Congress of Vienna, 1814–15; the years 1815– 1848 have been called the Age of Metternich because of his role in maintaining a balance of power during that era.

**MIRANDA, FRANCISCO,** Mar. 28, 1750 (Caracas, Ven.)–July 14, 1816. Venezuelan revolutionist. A precursor of the Latin American independence struggles; gained support from many foreign leaders for the liberation of S. and Central America from Spanish domination; became dictator of Venezuela when it gained independence, 1811; fought in vain against royalists, forced to sign treaty ceding control, imprisoned (1812).

**MOLOTOV, VYACHESLAV,** Mar. 9, 1890 (Kukarka, Rus.)–Nov. 8, 1986. Soviet communist leader. Editor and confounder of *Pravda,* 1912; chm. of Council of People's Commissars, 1930–41; as foreign min. (1939–49 and 1953–56), negotiated the German-Soviet Nonaggression Pact (1939).

**MORO, ALDO,** Sept. 23, 1916 (Maglie, It.)– May 9, 1978. Italian statesman. Secy. of Christian Democratic party, 1959–63; as prime min. in five governments (1963–68 and 1974–76), brought about a coalition between Socialists and Christian Democrats for the first time; kidnapped and killed by the *Brigata Rossa*, Italian leftist terrorists, 1978.

**MUAWIYAH I** (or Moawiyah), c.602 (Mecca, Arabia)–Apr./May 680. first ruler of Islam (661–80) after the legitimate caliphs. Founder of the Umayyad dynasty; governor of Syria; centralized admin.; made continual raids beyond his borders; practiced religious toleration within conquered provinces.

**MULRONEY, BRIAN,** March 20, 1939 (Baie-Comeau, Quebec, Canada). Canadian statesman. A lawyer and business executive; member of the Conservative Party in Canada; prime minster, 1984– .

**MUÑOZ MARÍN, LUIS,** Feb. 18, 1898 (San Juan, P.R.)–Apr. 30, 1980. Puerto Rican statesman. Founder of the Commonwealth of Puerto Rico. Gov. of Territory of Puerto Rico (1948–52) and Commonwealth of Puerto Rico (1952–65); senator-at-large, 1932 and 1965–72; initially an advocate of Puerto Rican independence, later worked for progress under U.S. governance.

**MUSSOLINI, BENITO** ("Il Duce") July 29, 1883 (Predappio, It.)–Apr. 28, 1945. Italian fascist leader. Founded the Italian Fascist Party, in Milan, 1919; led fascists in march on Rome, 1922; when cabinet resigned, was asked to form a government; as prime min. (1922–43), assured fascist control of govt., assuming dictatorial powers; attacked Ethiopia, 1935; made an alliance with HITLER, 1939; entered WW II with the fall of France, June 1940; after Allied invasion of Italy, lost support, dismissed by King, arrested, rescued by Germans, 1943; killed by Italian partisans.

**MUTSUHITO** (reign name, Meiji), Nov. 3, 1852 (Kyoto, Jap.)–July 30, 1912. Emperor of Japan, 1867–1912. A unifying symbol during a period of great transformations, delegating much authority and allowing change while standing for traditional values; oversaw many reforms, including the abolition of feudalism; granted a constitution, 1889.

**NAGY, IMRE,** June 7, 1896 (Kaposvar, Hung.)– June 16, 1958. Hungarian communist leader. As premier (1953–55), forced out of office, denounced for "Titoism" as his "new course" loosened controls and he became increasingly critical of Soviet control; recalled as premier of the new govt. in the Hungarian revolution, 1956; as revolution began to fail, appealed to West for help; when revolution was crushed, arrested, tried, and executed.

**NASSER, GAMAL ABDEL,** Jan. 15, 1918 (Alexandria, Egypt)–Sept. 28, 1970. Egyptian leader. As the first pres. of Egypt (1954–58) and of the United Arab Republic (1958–70), a symbol of Arab nationalism and an advocate of Arab unity; led the coup d'état against King Faruk, 1952; as pres., began construction of the Aswan Dam, forced Britain to evacuate its troops from the Suez Canal (1956), accepted Soviet arms, lost Six-Day war with Israel (1967), inaugurated land reform.

**NEBUCHADNEZZAR II,** 630–562 B.C. King of Babylonia (605 562 B C.) Made many conquests; built the city of Babylon, constructing its famous hanging gardens; destroyed Jerusalem (586 B.C.) and deported many of the survivors into the 70 Years' Captivity.

**NEHRU, JAWAHARLAL,** Nov. 14, 1889 (Allahabad, India)–May 27, 1964. Indian statesman. The first prime min. of independent India, 1947–64; associated with M. GANDHI and the Indian Natl. Congress, of which he became pres. in 1929; imprisoned frequently for civil disobedience in opposition to British colonialism; as prime min., attempted to pursue a policy of nonalignment in foreign affairs; loved by the Indian people, but criticized for his handing of Communist China. (Father of I. GANDHI.)

**NKRUMAH, KWAME,** Sept. 1909 (Nkroful, Gold Coast [now Ghana])–Apr. 27, 1972. Ghanian leader. The first prime min. of Ghana, 1957–66. Formed Convention People's party to fight for self-government of Gold Coast, 1949; elected prime min. of Gold Coast, 1952; after independence, pursued a pan-African policy, increasingly suppressed dissent; overthrown; awarded Lenin Peace Prize. 1962.

**NORIEGA MORENO, MANUEL,** Feb. 11, 1940 (Panama City, Panama). Panamanian leader. A soldier, rose to general; became the leader of the armed forces of Panama, 1983; ousted and replaced President Devalle when he tried to fire him, 1988; in 1989, claimed presidency in what was probably a stolen election; later that year, under drug charges in the United States, surrendered to invading U.S. troops and was extradited to Florida.

**OLAV V,** July 2, 1903 (Sandringham, Norfolk, Eng.). King of Norway, 1957– . Headed Norwegian armed forces, 1944; spent WW II in exile in England; regent 1945, 1955–57.

**ORTEGA, DANIEL,** 1945 (La Libertad, Nicaragua). Nicaraguan leader. A member of the Sandinista Liberation Front; elected president of Nicaragua in 1984; defeated in 1990 in a bid for re-election by VIOLET BARRIO DE CHAMARRO.

**PADEREWSKI, IGNACE,** Nov. 18, 1860 (Kurylowka, Pol.)–June 29, 1941. Polish statesman, pianist, composer. Leader of the movement to restore Poland as a nation; as Polish rep. to U.S. during WW I, influenced Pres. W. WILSON to include Polish independence as one of his "14 Points"; prime min. of Poland, 1919; a master pianist.

**PAHLAVI, MOHAMMED REZA,** Oct. 26, 1919 (Teheran, Persia [now Iran])–July 27, 1980. Shah of Iran, 1941–79. Pursued a course of rapid industrialization that led to unrest and his eventual overthrow; in early 1950s, struggled with Premier Mohammed Mosaddeq, a zealous nationalist, for control; when Mosaddeq was overthrown, assumed control, 1953; implemented land reform; developed dam and irrigation projects; tolerated no political opposition, causing thousands to be arrested in the 1970s; under attack from Moslem rightists, he was forced into exile.

**PARK CHUNG HEE,** Sept. 30, 1917 (Sangmo,

Korea)–Oct. 26, 1979. S. Korean leader, military officer. Led coup d'état that overthrew the Second Republic, 1961; as S. Korean pres (1963–79), maintained close relations with the U.S., grew more dictatorial, declared martial law (1972), altered constitution to give himself unlimited power, assassinated.

**PEARSON, LESTER,** Apr. 23, 1897 (Toronto, Ont., Can.)–Dec. 27, 1972. Canadian statesman, diplomat. Headed Canadian delegation to the UN, 1948–57; awarded 1957 Nobel Peace Prize for his work on the Suez Crisis of 1956; prime min., 1963–68.

**PEDRO I,** (or Pedro IV of Portugal), known as Dom Pedro, born Dom Antonio Pedro de Alcantara Bourbon, Oct. 12, 1798 (Lisbon, Port.)–Sept. 24, 1834. Portuguese founder of the Brazilian Empire and first emperor of Brazil (1822–31). Fled to Brazil when NAPOLEON conquered Portugal; made Brazilian regent, 1821; sided with Brazilians against Portuguese reactionary policy; declared Brazilian independence, crowned emperor, 1822; proclaimed king of Portugal in 1826, but ousted in 1828; abdicated as Brazilian emperor, 1831.

**PEREZ DE CUELLAR, JAVIER,** Jan. 19, 1920 (Lima, Peru). Peruvian statesman. Rose through ranks of Peruvian diplomatic corps; permanent rep. to UN, 1971–79; under sec.-gen. for special political affairs, 1979–81; sec.-gen., 1982; played key role in arranging formal cease-fire and starting talks between Iran and Iraq, 1988.

**PERON, EVA DUARTE DE** ("Evita"), May 7, 1919 (Los Toldos, Arg.)–July 26, 1952. Argentine political figure. As a teenager, one of the most popular radio and film stars in Argentina; married JUAN PERÓN (1945), and campaigned actively for his election as Argentine pres., (1946); virtually cogoverned during the first six years of Peron's admin.; credited with the introduction of compulsory religious education in Argentina; amassed a large popular following; died of cancer.

**PERÓN SOSA, JUAN,** Oct. 8, 1895 (Lobos, Arg.)–July 1, 1974. Argentine political leader. As pres. (1946–55 and 1973–74), a strongly nationalistic leader who attempted to make Argentina self-sufficient economically; repressed opposition; overthrown and forced into exile, 1955; his popularity, fostered by a Peronista movement, continued; returned following victory of his party in gen. elections; succeeded by his wife, ISABEL PERÓN.

**PERÓN, ISABEL** (Martinez Cartas) DE, Feb. 4, 1931 (La Rioja, Arg.). Argentine political leader, dancer. Succeeded her husband, JUAN PERÓN, as pres. of Argentina, 1974–76; deposed in a military coup.

**PETER I** ("the Great"), June 9, 1672 (Moscow, Rus.)–Feb. 8, 1725. Tsar (1682–1725) and emperor (1721–25) of Russia. Through wars with Turkey (1695–96) and Sweden (1700–21), obtained access for Russia to the Baltíc and Black seas; brought Russia closer to Europe by pushing modernization; reformed the calendar; formed a regular army; created a navy; established technical schools;

moved the capitol to a new city he built as a "window to the West," St. Petersburg (now Lenin grad).

**PIECK, WILHELM,** Jan. 3, 1876 (Guben, Ger.)–Sept. 7, 1960. German communist leader. One of the foremost communist leaders of Europe; a leader in Spartacist movement, the forerunner of the German Communist party; pres. of the German Democratic Republic (E. Germany), 1949–60.

**PILATE, PONTIUS.** d after AD 36. Roman procurator of Judea (26–36) under TIBERIUS; handed JESUS CHRIST over to Jewish authorities to be crucified.

**PILSUDSKI, JOZEF,** Dec. 5, 1867 (Zulow, Pol. [now USSR])–May 12, 1935. Polish statesman. Poland's first chief of state (1918–22) and virtual dictator (1926–28 and 1930); fought against Russian domination, arrested, exiled to Siberia (1887); joined Polish Socialist party, 1892; fought against Germany during WW I.

**PINOCHET UGARTE, AUGUSTO,** Nov. 25, 1915 (Valparaiso, Chile). Chilean leader, military officer. Army chief of staff, 1972; leader of the military junta that overthrew the Socialist govt. of Pres. SALVADOR ALLENDE, 1973; pres., 1973–90.

**PLEKHANOV, GEORGI,** Dec. 11, 1856 (Gudalovka, Tambob Prov., Rus.)–May 30, 1918. Russian revolutionist, social philosopher, founder of Russian Marxism. Broke with Land and Liberty Org. because of his opposition to political terror, 1879; fled to Geneva and helped found the League for the Emancipation of Labor, 1883; started *Iskra*, a revolutionary journal (with V. I. LENIN), 1900; in Russian Socialist party split (1903), his political thinking provided basis of the Menshevik faction. *Socialism and Political Struggle,* 1883.

**EL-QADDAFI** (or al-Quaddafi, al-Khadafy), MUAMMAR, 1942 (Misratah, Libya). Libyan leader. Led a military coup against King Idris, 1969; as prime min. (1970– ), removed U.S. and British military bases (1970), nationalized foreign-owned petroleum assets (1973); has supported Palestinian, Pan-Arab, and revolutionary causes.

**QUEZON Y MOLINA, MANUEL LUIS,** Aug. 19, 1878 (Baler, Tayabas Prov., Philippines)–Aug. 1, 1944. Philippine statesman. First pres. of the Commonwealth of the Philippines, 1935–44; fought for independence from the U.S., 1899; resident commissioner for the Philippines to the U.S. Congress, 1909–16; as pres., expanded his power and strengthened defense; went into exile in the U.S. during Japanese occupation.

**QUIDDE, LUDWIG,** Mar. 23, 1858 (Bremen, Ger.)–Mar. 5, 1941. German peace activist. Leader of the German peace movement; pres. of German Peace Soc., 1914–29; awarded Nobel Peace Prize (with F. E. Buisson), 1927.

**QUISLING, VIDKUN,** July 18, 1887 (Fyresdal, Nor.)–Oct. 24, 1945. Norwegian politician. Formed the fascist National Union party, 1933; collaborated in German conquest of Norway, 1940; head of state during German occupation during WW II,

1940–45; tried for treason, executed; name has become synonymous with "traitor."

**RASPUTIN, GRIGORI** ("the Debauched"), c.1873 (Pokrovskoye, Rus.)–Dec. 30/31, 1916. Russian monk. A powerful figure at the court of Emperor Nicholas II and Empress Alexandra; notorious for his debauchery; interfered in church and secular politics; his influence at court led to incompetency in the govt; killed by a conspiracy of nobles.

**RHEE, SYNGMAN,** Apr. 26, 1875 (Whanghae, Korea)–July 19, 1965. Korean statesman. Pres., of Korean provisional govt. in exile, 1919–39. As the first pres. of the Republic of Korea (S. Korea), ruled dictatorially, 1948–60; forced out of office by popular uprising sparked by election fraud and other abuses.

**RIBBENTROP, JOACHIM VON,** Apr. 30, 1893 (Wesel, Ger.)–Oct. 16, 1946. German diplomat. Amb. to Great Britain, 1936–38; as foreign min. (1938–45), negotiated the German-Soviet Nonaggression Pact of 1939; played key roles in forming the Rome Berlin Axis and planning the German attack on Poland that started WW II; executed as war criminal.

**RURIK,** died c.879. Reputed founder of the Russian empire. A prince of the Scandinavian Vikings; probably conquered Novgorod, c.862; the Rurik dynasty reigned until 1598.

**EL-SADAT, ANWAR,** Dec. 25, 1918 (Talah Minufiya, Egypt)–Oct. 6, 1981. Egyptian leader. Served time in prison for antigovt. activities, 1940s; participated in the overthrow of King FARUK, 1952; served in the govt. under G. NASSER; as pres. (1970–81), ousted Soviet advisers and technicians (1972), attacked the Israelis across the Suez Canal (1973), traveled to Israel to promote peace (1977), and signed a peace agreement with Israel (1979); rec'd Nobel Peace Prize, 1978, with M. BEGIN; assassinated.

**SALADIN,** c.1138 (Takrit, Mesopotamia, [now Iraq])–Mar. 4, 1193. Sultan of Egypt and Syria, from c.1174. Most famous Moslem hero; tried to drive the Christians from Palestine; captured Jerusalem, 1187; after forestalling RICHARD I's attempt to reconquer Jerusalem, negotiated a truce with the Crusaders, 1192.

**SALAZAR, ANTÓNIO DE OLIVEIRA,** Apr. 28, 1889 (Vimieiro, Port.)–July 27, 1970. Portuguese leader. Prof. of economics at U. of Coimbra, 1918–26; helped form the Catholic Center Party; min. of finance, 1928; as prime min. (1932–68), ruled ruthlessly as virtual dictator, was chiefly responsible for draft of a new constitution (1932), improved public finances, and made alliance with Spain (1942).

**SAN MARTIN, JOSÉ DE,** Feb. 25, 1778 (Yapeyu, vice royalty of La Plata, now in Arg.)–Aug. 17, 1850. S. American statesman, soldier. With SIMON BOLIVAR, leader of S. America's independence movement; served as an officer in the Spanish army for 20 years; trained guerrillas in Argentina, 1812; led an army over the Andes (1817), defeating the Spanish at Chacabuco and Maipo (1818); es-

tablished independence of Chile; won over Peruvians, taking Lima (1821) and proclaiming an independent Peru; proclaimed the Protector of Peru.

**SANTA ANNA, ANTONIO LÓPEZ DE,** Feb. 21, 1794 (Jalapa, Mex.)–June 21, 1876. Mexican statesman, army officer. Led several revolts against Spanish rule, 1822–32; pres. of Mexico, 1833–35 and 1841–42, 1842–43, 1844–1847; in attempt to crush Texan Revolution, seized Alamo but was defeated at San Jacinto and captured by SAM HOUSTON, 1836; commanded Mexican Army against U.S., 1846–47; defeated at Buena Vista, Cerro Gordo, and Puebla; exiled, 1848; recalled and made pres., 1853–55; exiled, 1855.

**SATO, EISAKU,** Mar. 27, 1901 (Tabuse, Jap.)–June 3, 1975. Japanese statesman. Worked as lawyer in the ministry of railways, 1924–47; elected as a Liberal Democrat to Diet, 1949; min. of finance, 1958–60; as prime min. (1964–72), signed treaty with U.S. returning Ryukyu Islands to Japan (1969) and oversaw the increasing prosperity of Japan; awarded Nobel Peace Prize (with S. MAC-BRIDE), 1974.

**SAUL,** fl.1025–1000 B.C. First king of Israel, c.1021–1000 B.C. Anointed king by Samuel; reigned over the hill country of Judah; defended Israel against the Philistines; killed by the Philistines in battle of Mount Gilboa and succeeded by DAVID.

**SCHMIDT, HELMUT,** Dec. 23, 1918 (Hamburg, Ger.). German political leader. Defense min. 1969–72; finance min. 1972–74; chanc., 1974–82.

**SEYSS-INQUART, ARTHUR,** July 22, 1892 (Stannern, Bohemia [now Czech.])–Oct. 16, 1946. Austrian Nazi leader. Austrian chan. (1938–39), when Austria was annexed by Germany (1938); German high commissioner of the Netherlands, 1940–45; executed as a war criminal.

**SHAH JEHAN,** Jan. 5, 1592 (Lahore, India [now Pak.])–Jan. 22, 1666. Mogul emperor in India (1628–58) and builder of the Taj Mahal. Restored Islam as a state religion; conquered much of S. India; carried Mogul empire to the height of its wealth and glory.

**SHEVARDNADZE, EDUARD,** Jan. 25, 1928 (Mamati, Lauchkhutsky, U.S.S.R.). Soviet statesman. Entered politics in his native Georgia S.S.R. in 1964; was named the U.S.S.R. foreign minister, 1985– .

**SHIH HUANG TI** (or Ch'in Shih Huang Ti), c.259 B.C. (Ch'in, China)–210 B.C. Chinese emperor (c.247–210 B.C.), the fourth ruler of the Ch'in dynasty. Created the first unified Chinese empire, 221; built a system of roads and canals; developed a centralized admin.; standardized coinage and weights and measures; connected local walls into the Great Wall of China; ordered the burning of books in China to suppress dissent, 213.

**SIHANOUK, NORODOM,** Oct. 31, 1922 (Phnom Penh, Cambodia). Cambodian leader. Named king at age of 18, 1940; obtained independence for Cambodia from France, 1953; abdicated, 1955; in 1960, named chief of state, but was overthrown, 1970; from 1975 to 1976, again served as chief of state, but in 1976 was overthrown and placed under house arrest.

SMITH, IAN, Apr. 8, 1919 (Selukwe, Southern Rhodesia [now Zimbabwe]). Rhodesian political leader. Elected to Southern Rhodesian assembly, 1948; founded right-wing Rhodesian Front, 1961; as prime min. of Rhodesia (1964–79), unilaterally declared his nation's independence rather than negotiate a constitution that would have given power to the black majority, 1965; after elections giving blacks majority rule (1979), remained in cabinet as min. without portfolio.

SMUTS, JAN CHRISTIAAN, May 24, 1870 (Borenplaats, nr. Riebeeck West, Cape Colony [now S.A.]) –Sept. 11, 1950. South African statesman, soldier. Boer guerrilla leader in the S. African War, 1899–1902; played a major role in the formation of the Union of S. Africa as a self-governing part of the British Empire, 1910; as prime min. of S. Africa (1919–24 and 1939–48), aided in the British-Irish problem, supported the League of Nations, and took part in the organization of the UN.

SOARES, MARIO, Dec. 7, 1924 (Lisbon, Port.). Portuguese political leader. A Socialist who was imprisoned 12 times on political grounds under Portugal's repressive govt.; in exile in Paris, 1970–74; returned following the April 1974 coup; min. of foreign affairs, 1974–75; prime min., 1976–78, 1983–85; pres. 1986– .

SOMOZA-GARCIA, ANASTASIO, Feb. 1, 1896 (San Marcos, Nicar.)–Sept. 29, 1956. Nicaraguan leader. As pres. (1937–47 and 1950–56), ruled harshly, amassed a fortune, exiled most of his opponents, was assassinated. (Father of A. SOMOZA-DEBAYLE.)

SOMOZA-DEBAYLE, ANASTASIO, Dec. 5, 1925 (Leon, Nicar.)–Sept. 17, 1980. Nicaraguan political leader. Leader of the Liberal National party; pres., 1967–72 and 1974–79; forced to resign by Sandinist rebels after a protracted civil war and went into exile in the U.S., 1979, assassinated. (Son of A. SOMOZA-GARCIA.

SPAAK, PAUL HENRI, Jan. 25, 1899 (Schaerbeek, Belg.)–July 31, 1972. Belgian statesman. Premier, 1938–39, 1946, and 1947–49; first pres. of UN Gen. Assembly, 1946; participated in formation of the European Coal and Steel Community, also NATO, 1949, Benelux, 1948 and the EEC, 1957; Belgian foreign min., 1954–57 and 1961–66; secy. gen. of NATO, 1957–61.

SPINOLA, ANTONIO DE, Apr. 11, 1910 (Estremoz, Port.). Portuguese leader, army officer. Leader of the military junta that overthrew Portugal's repressive govt, 1974; served as provisional pres., May–Sept., 1974. *Portugal and the Future*, 1974.

STALIN, JOSEPH (Iosif Vissarionovich Dzhugashvili), Dec. 21, 1879 (Gori, Georgia, Rus.)–Mar. 5, 1953. Soviet political leader. As the virtual dictator of the Soviet Union (1924–53), built the nation into a world power; joined the Social Democratic party, 1903; became a close advisor of V. I. LENIN; eliminated his rivals to become Lenin's successor, using his position as secy. gen. of Central Com. of

the Soviet Communist Party as a power base; as unopposed ruler, started intensive industrialization, forced collectivization of agric., purged the party several times during the 1930s, concluded a nonaggression pact with Germany (1939); took control of the military after Hitler invaded; was a key figure in the post-WW II Cold War.

STRESEMANN, GUSTAV, May 10, 1878 (Berlin, Ger.)–Oct. 3, 1929. German statesman. As foreign min. (1923–29) and chan. (1923) of the Weimar Republic, restored Germany's prestige after WW I; formed the German People's party, 1918; brought Germany into the League of Nations, 1926; signed the Kellogg-Briand Pact, 1928; awarded Nobel Peace Prize (with A. BRIAND), 1926.

SUAREZ the Duke of GONZALES, ADOLFO, Sept. 25, 1932 (Cebreros, Sp.). Spanish political leader. Civil gov. of Segovia, 1968–69; Spanish prime min. and pres. of the council of ministers, 1976–81; leader of Union Centro Democrátio (UCD), 1977–81; founded Centro Democratico y Social (CDS), 1982; created Duke, 1981.

SUHARTO, (also Soeharto), June 8, 1921 (Kemusu Argamulja, Batavia [now Djakarta], Indonesia). Indonesian leader, military officer. As a major-gen. in charge of army strategic command, put down an alleged communist coup d'etat and overthrew Pres. SUKARNO; as pres. (1967–   ), has worked for economic progress and a cooperative foreign policy.

SUI WEN TI (born Yang Chien), 541 (China)–604. Chinese emperor (581–604). Founder of Sui dynasty, who reunified China after it had been divided for hundreds of years; laid foundations for the great T'ang dynasty; took census, simplified taxation, started construction of the Grand Canal, which connects China's two greatest rivers; instituted civil-service examinations for the selection of govt. officials.

SUKARNO, June 6, 1901 (Surabaja, Java, Dutch East Indies, [now Indonesia])–June 21, 1970. Indonesian statesman. Leader of the Indonesian independence movement and his nation's first pres. (1949–67); helped found the Indonesian Nationalist party, 1928; exiled, 1933–42; led struggle against the Dutch, 1945–49; as pres., ignored economic problems in the quest for internatl. prestige, worked for friendly relations with China, opposed U.S. influence; toppled by a military coup, 1965.

SUN YAT-SEN, Nov. 12, 1866 (Hsiang-shan, Kwangtung Prov., China)–Mar. 12, 1925. Chinese revolutionary leader and national hero. Worked to overthrow the Ch'ing dynasty; in exile (1895–1911), organized the Revolutionary Alliance, 1905; participated in several abortive uprisings; planned revolution against Manchus, finally accomplishing it in 1911; formed Kuomintang, or Nationalist party (1912) and served as provisional Chinese pres. for two months; disagreed with dictatorial policies of his successor Yuan Shi-k'ai, elected head of self-proclaimed S. Chinese Republic, 1921; fought to conquer and unite China.

TANAKA, KAKUEI, May 4, 1918 (Futuda, now Nishiyama, Jap.). Japanese statesman. Rose through the ranks of the Liberal Democratic party to min.

of finance (1962–64) and min. of international trade (1971–72); as prime min. (1972–74), established diplomatic relations with Communist China; forced to leave office amid charges he had used it to amass a personal fortune; convicted on charges of bribery.

**TENG HSIAO-PING** (Deng Xiaoping), Aug. 22, 1904 (Kuang-an Szechwan Prov., China). Chinese political leader. Although only vice-chm. of the Chinese Communist party central com. and vice-premier, seems to be China's real administrator; took part in the Long March, 1934–35; appointed secy. of Central Comm. Communist party, 1949; vice-premier, 1956; purged during Cultural Revolution (1966–69) for revisionism; reinstated (1973), then purged again by radical "gang of four" as a "capitalist roader," 1976; reemerged after MAO TSE-TUNG's death and purge of "gang of four," 1976; chf. dep. prem. 1980, retired, but maintained political influence.

**THANT, U,** Jan. 22, 1909 (Pantanaw, Maubin Dist., Burma)–Nov. 25, 1974. Burmese diplomat. Chairman of Burmese delegation of UN, 1947–52; rep. to UN, 1953–61; as secy.-gen. of UN (1961–71), deeply involved in internatl. peacekeeping and led UN into concentrating on social and economic development of Third World countries.

**TIBERIUS** (in full Tiberius Claudius Nero Caesar), Nov. 16, 42 B.C. (Rome, It.)–Mar. 16, 37. Second Roman emperor, 14–37. Succeeding to principate on the death of his stepfather, father-in-law, and adopter AUGUSTUS, ruled with moderation, strengthening the principate and leaving the state stronger than when he inherited it; vilified by Roman historians as a vicious tyrant.

**TITO** (Josip Broz), May 7, 1892 (Kumrovec, Croatia, now in Yugo.)–May 4, 1980. Yugoslav communist leader, creator of the Yugoslav state. Led the Yugoslav partisans against the German invaders in WW II, assuming military control by war's end; as Yugoslav prime min. (1943–53), was first communist national leader to defy Soviet control, 1948; as pres. (1953–80), developed relations with Western nations, attempted to form a neutralist bloc with Egypt and India, worked for conciliation of Yugoslavia's different nationalities.

**TOGLIATTI, PALMIRO,** Mar. 26, 1893 (Genoa, It.)–Apr. 21, 1964. Italian political leader. A leader of the Italian Communist party from 1924 until his death; worked for a national, democratically-oriented communism; became a member of Central com. of the Italian Communist party, 1924; vice-premier of Italy, 1945; the Soviet city of Stavrapol (now Tolyatti) was renamed after him, 1964.

**TOJO HIDEKI,** Dec. 30, 1884 (Tokyo, Jap.)–Dec. 23, 1948. Japanese leader, military officer. As prime min. (1941–44), ordered the attack on Pearl Harbor, pushed the Japanese offensive in China, Southeast Asia, and the Pacific; hanged as a war criminal.

**TORRIJOS-HERRERA, OMAR,** Feb. 13, 1929 (Santiago de Veragua Pan.)–July 31, 1979. Panamanian leader, soldier. As pres. (1969–1981), pushed Panama's claim to the Canal Zone, resulting

in an agreement with the U.S. for its gradual release (1977); worked for social and economic reform; killed in plane crash.

**TOUSSAINT L'OUVERTURE, FRANÇOIS,** 1743 (Bréda, Saint-Dominque [now Haiti])–Apr. 7, 1803. Haitian liberator, soldier. Leader of the Haitian independence movement during the French Revolution; joined a slave revolt, 1791; formed his own guerrilla band to fight against the Spanish and British; gained control over the entire island and freed the slaves, 1801; surrendered to French invaders, died in prison.

**TRAJAN,** Sept. 15?, 53 (Italica [now Santiponce, Sp.])–Aug. 8, 117. Roman emperor, 98–177. Led the last major expansion of the Roman Empire; conquered Dacia (modern Rumania) and most of the Parthian empire; an excellent ruler and administrator.

**TROTSKY, LEON** (Lev Bronstein), Nov. 7, 1879 (Yanovka, Ukraine, Rus.)–Aug. 20, 1940. Soviet communist leader, one of the founders of the Soviet state. Collaborated with V.I. LENIN on the revolutionary journal *Iskra* in Switzerland; returned to Russia during the Revolution of 1905; advocated the theory of permanent revolution; a leader in the October Revolution, 1917; commissar of foreign affairs and of war, 1917–25; engaged in power struggle with J. STALIN; banished from the Soviet Union, 1929; lived in exile, writing against Stalin; assassinated in Mexico.

**TRUDEAU, PIERRE ELLIOTT** (Ives), Oct. 18, 1919 (Montreal, Que., Can.). Canadian political leader. As prime min. (1968–79, 1980–84), took a strong stand against terrorists of the Front de Liberation du Quebec (1970); led Canada to recognize Communist China, 1970; presented anti-inflationary budgets; oversaw the institution of French and English as dual official languages in federal offices; reformed Canadian constitution.

**TRUJILLO MOLINA, RAFAEL L.,** Oct. 24, 1891 (San Cristobal, D.R.)–May 30, 1961. Dominican political leader, army officer. Seized power in a revolt against Pres. Horacio Vasquez, 1930; ruled with absolute power as dictator (1930–61), placing family members in office; stabilized his nation; assassinated by military officers.

**TSHOMBE, MOISE K.,** Nov. 10, 1919 (Musumba, Belgian Congo [now Zaire])–June 29, 1969. Congolese political leader. Worked for a loose federation within the Congo after its independence (1960); when he failed, declared his province of Katanga independent; served as pres. of the secessionist state, 1960–1963; finally forced to capitulate (1963) by UN forces and went into exile; returned to be premier in a govt. of national reconciliation, 1964; exiled again after charges of treason, 1965.

**TUTANKHAMEN,** reigned 1361–52 B.C. Egyptian pharaoh. His reign witnessed the return of traditional religion and art following Akhenaton's "revolution"; his intact tomb was discovered by Howard Carter, 1922.

**ULBRICHT, WALTER,** June 30, 1893 (Leipzig, Ger.)–Aug. 1, 1973. E. German Communist party leader. Joined German Communist party in the 1920s; fled to Soviet Union under the Third Reich; influential in the formation of the E. German state after WW II; as chm. of the council of state (1960–73), ruled ruthlessly, suppressing opposition and keeping E. Germany a close ally of the USSR.

**VARGAS, GETÚLIO DORNELES,** Apr. 19, 1883 (São Borja, Braz.)–Aug. 24, 1954. Brazilian leader. As pres. (1930–45 and 1951–54), ruled Brazil as a benevolent dictator; centralized fiscal control; enfranchised laborers and women; enacted social-security laws; reformed education; overthrown by democratic movement, 1945; returned (1950) as pres., but following govt. scandal, committed suicide.

**VENIZELOS, ELEUTHERIOS,** Aug. 23, 1864 (Mournies, Crete)–Mar. 18, 1936. Greek states-man, diplomat. Played a major role in Crete's uprising against Ottoman rule, 1897; as prime min. of Greece (1910–15, 1917, 1924, 1928–32), doubled the area and population of the state during the Balkan Wars and led Greece into WW I on the allied side, opposed the royalists.

**VERWOERD, HENDRIK F.,** Sept. 8, 1901 (Amsterdam, Neth.)–Sept. 6, 1966. South African leader, educator. As min. of native affairs (1950–58), responsible for pushing through much of the apartheid legislation; as prime min. (1958–66), vigorously applied apartheid policy and led South Africa out of the Commonwealth of Nations, 1961; assassinated.

**VLADIMIR II,** Monomachus (Monomakh), 1053 (Kiev, Rus.)–May 19, 1125. Grand prince of Kiev, 1113–25. Won many campaigns against the Germans; led Kiev to the peak of its power; founded the city of Vladimir.

**VORSTER, BALTHAZAR JOHANNES,** Dec. 13, 1915 (Jamestown, Cape Province, S.A.)–Sept. 10, 1983. S. African political leader. Imprisoned for his opposition to the Allies in WW II, 1942–44; as min. of justice (1961–66), repressed opponents of apartheid; as prime min. (1966–78), developed a more conciliatory foreign policy and personified Afrikaaner values of determination and rectitude; pres., 1978–79; resigned on charges of previous irregularities.

**WALDHEIM, KURT,** Dec. 21, 1918 (near Vienna, Austria). Austrian statesman. Served as secretary-general of the United Nations, 1972–1982; elected president of Austria in 1986 despite the discovery that he may have been involved in the murders of Jews during World War II.

**WALESA, LECH,** Sept. 29, 1943 (Popow, Poland). Polish political leader. An electrician, by trade, became the leader of Poland's labor movement, in 1980; negotiated with the Communist government until Solidarity, an organization of about 50 labor unions, was recognized—the first time that a Com-munist country recognized a labor organization that was independent of the country's Communist Party; elected chairman of Solidarity in 1981; was imprisoned that year when the government suspended Solidarity's operations; released in 1982, led the movement that led to election of almost all Solidarity-endorsed candidates to parliament, 1989.

**WEIZMANN, CHAIM,** Nov. 27, 1874 (Motol, Rus.)–Nov. 9, 1952. Zionist leader, biochemist. Participated in the negotiations leading to the Balfour Declaration of 1917; pres. of World Zionist Org., 1920–29 and 1935–46; first pres. of Israel, 1949–52. As biochemist, discovered a process of synthesizing acetone that aided British munitions during WW I.

**WITTE, SERGEI COUNT,** June 29, 1849 (Tiflis, Rus. [now Tbilisi, USSR])–Mar. 13, 1915. Russian political leader. A great exponent of Russian mod-ernization as the first constitutional prime min. of tsarist Russia, 1905–06; as minister of finance (1892–1903), oversaw completion of Trans-Siberian railway.

**XERXES,** c.519 B.C.–465 B.C. King of Persia, 486–465 B.C. Son of DARIUS THE GREAT; in-vaded Greece; defeated Leonidas and his 300 Spartans at Thermopylae, occupied Athens, his fleet was destroyed at Salamis, 480 B.C.

**YELTSIN, BORIS,** Feb. 1, 1931 (Sverdlorsk, USSR). Soviet political leader. A political maverick, cham-pions ordinary people and greater democracy; elected pres. of Russian SSR, and resigned Communist Party membership, 1990; a rival for power of MIKHAIL GORBACHEV.

**ZAPATA, EMILIANO,** Aug. 8, 1883 (Anenecuilco, Mex.)–Apr. 10, 1919. Mexican leader. Revolution-ary leader of a Mexican agrarian movement. Supported Francisco Madero's overthrow of POR-FIRIO DIAZ, 1911; seized land with an army of Indians; outlined the Plan of Ayala (1911) for agrarian reform and dropped support of Madero; occupied Mexico City three times, 1914–15; assas-sinated.

**ZHDANOV, ANDREI,** Feb. 14, 1896 (probably Mariupol, Ukraine, Rus. [now Zhdanov, USSR]) –Aug. 31, 1948. Soviet govt. and Communist par-ty official. A close associate of J. STALIN, directed the post-WW II Cold War policy called Zhdanovism, which severely restricted cultural activities and pro-moted an anti-Western bias in policy.

**ZINOVIEV, GRIGORI** (born Ovsel Gershon Aronov Radomylsky), Sept. 23, 1883 (Yelizavetgrad, Ukraine, Rus. [now Kirovgrad, USSR])–Aug. 25, 1936. Sovi-et political leader. Worked closely with V. I. LENIN in the Bolshevik party before the 1917 revolution; following Lenin's death (1924), briefly involved in a ruling triumvirate with J. STALIN and L. Kamenev; a victim of Stalin's Great Purge.

# Military and Naval Leaders

**ABRAMS, CREIGHTON W.**, Sept. 15, 1914 (Springfield, Mass.)–Sept. 4, 1974. U.S. Army general. As a WW II tank commander, broke through German lines to relieve U.S. troops at Bastogne, 1944; commanded U.S. forces in Vietnam, implemented program of gradual withdrawal, (Vietnamization); 1968–72; chief of staff, U.S. Army, 1972–74.

**ALLEN, ETHAN**, Jan. 21, 1738 (Litchfield, Conn.) –Feb. 12, 1789. American Revolutionary soldier, politician. Commanded the "Green Mountain Boys"; captured Ft. Ticonderoga, 1775; taken prisoner by the British at Montreal and held in captivity, 1775–78; worked for Vermont statehood.

**ANDREWS, FRANK M.**, Feb. 3, 1884 (Nashville, Tenn.)–May 3, 1943. U.S. Army Air Force general. An early advocate of strategic air power; credited with development of Boeing B-17 bomber, commander, U.S. forces in Europe, Feb.–May 1943.

**ARNOLD, BENEDICT**, Jan. 14, 1741 (Norwich, Conn.)–June 14, 1801. American Revolutionary general. Fought with ETHAN ALLEN at Ft. Ticonderoga, 1775; failed to capture Quebec, 1775; victorious at Valcour Island, 1776; played a major role in American victory at Saratoga, 1777; attempted to surrender West Point to the British for 20,000, 1780; led British forces in raids in Virginia and Connecticut, 1780–81.

**ARNOLD, HENRY** ("Hap"), June 25, 1886 (Galdwyne, Pa.)–Jan. 15, 1950. U.S. Army Air Force general. As commanding general, U.S. Army Air Force (1941–46), built world's largest air force; planned strategic bombing of Germany and Japan in WW II; created general of the army, 1944. *Global Mission*, 1949.

**BANKS, NATHANIEL**, Jan. 30, 1816 (Waltham, Mass.)–Sept. 1, 1894. Union Army general, public official. Served as U.S. rep. nine times in period 1853–91; speaker of the house, 1856–57; gov. of Massachusetts, 1858–61; captured Port Hudson on the Mississippi R., 1863; led disastrous Red River campaign, 1864.

**BARRY, JOHN**, c.1745 (Co. Wexford, Ire.)–Sept. 13, 1803. American Revolutionary naval officer. Often called the "Father of the U.S. Navy"; won numerous sea battles during the Revolution.

**BEAUREGARD, PIERRE**, May 28, 1818 (St. Bernard Par., La.)–Feb. 20, 1893. Confederate Army general. Ordered bombardment of Ft. Sumter to open Civil War; victorious at the First Battle of Bull Run, 1861. *Principles and Maxims of the Art of War*, 1863.

**BLACK HAWK**, 1767 (Ill.)–Oct. 3, 1838. Sauk Indian leader. His defeat at Bad Axe R. (1832) led to first Indian cession of lands in Iowa.

**BOWIE, JAMES**, 1796 (Burke Co., Ga.)–Mar. 6, 1836. U.S. frontiersman, soldier. Popular hero of the Texas Revolution; killed at the Alamo, 1836; his name is associated with the Bowie knife, invented by James or his brother, Rezin.

**BRADLEY, OMAR N.**, Feb. 12, 1893 (Clark, Mo.) –Apr. 8, 1981. U.S. general of the army (appointed 1950), Commander, U.S. II Corps, North Africa and Sicily, 1943; led U.S. ground troops in the Normandy invasion, 1944; commander, 12th Army Group, 1944–45; chairman, Joint Chiefs of Staff, 1949–53. *A Soldier's Story*, 1951.

**BRAGG, BRAXTON**, Mar. 22, 1817 (Warrenton, N.C.)–Sept. 27, 1876. Confederate Army general. Victorious at Chickamauga, 1863; defeated at Chattanooga, 1863; military advisor to JEFFERSON DAVIS, 1864–65.

**BROWN, GEORGE S.**, Aug. 17, 1918 (Montclair, N.J.)–Dec. 5, 1978. U.S. Air Force general. U.S. Air Force chief of staff, 1973–74; chairman, Joint Chiefs of Staff, 1974–78; sparked controversy by suggesting that U.S. Jews exert undue influence in U.S. affairs (1974), and by calling Israel a "burden" to U.S. (1976); awards include Silver Star, Legion of Merit, and Distinguished Flying Cross.

**BUCKNER, SIMON BOLIVAR**, Apr. 1, 1823 (nr. Munfordville, Ky.)–Jan. 8, 1914. Confederate Army general, politician. Surrendered Ft. Donelson, Tenn., to Gen. U.S. Grant, 1862; gov. of Kentucky, 1887–91. (Father of S. B. BUCKNER, JR.).

**BUCKNER, SIMON BOLIVAR, JR.**, July 18, 1886 (Munfordville, Ky.)–June 18, 1945. U.S. Army general. Led successful invasion of Japanese-held Ryukyu Is., 1945, killed in action. (Son of S. B. BUCKNER).

**BUFORD, JOHN,** Mar. 4, 1826 (Woodford Co., Ky.)–Dec. 16, 1863. Union Army general. Led cavalry of the Army of the Potomac, 1862–63; fought at 2nd Manassas (1862), Gettysburg (1863).

**BURNSIDE, AMBROSE,** May 23, 1824 (Liberty, Ind.)–Sept. 13, 1881. Union Army general, political leader. Credited with originating side whiskers (sideburns); defeated at Antietam, Fredericksburg, 1862; commanded Army of the Potomac, (Nov. 1862-Jan. 1863); mishandled operations at Petersburg, Va., 1864, and forced to resign; gov. of Rhode Island, 1866–69; U.S. senator (R, R.I.), 1875–81.

**BUTLER, BENJAMIN FRANKLIN,** Nov. 5, 1818 (Deerfield, N.H.)–Jan. 11, 1893. Union Army general, public official. As military gov. of New Orleans (1862) outraged public sensibilities by his dictatorial rule and was recalled by Pres. LINCOLN; U.S. rep. (R, Mass.), 1867–75, 1877–79; led impeachment movement against ANDREW JOHNSON, 1868; Greenback Party presidential candidate, 1884.

**CARLSON, EVANS FORDYCE,** Feb. 26, 1896 (Sidney, N.Y.)–May 27, 1947. U.S. Marine Corps general. Led commando force in the Pacific (the Gilberts and Guadalcanal), known as Carlson's Raiders, whose battle cry was "Gung Ho," during WW II.

**CHAFFEE, ADNA ROMANZA,** Apr. 14, 1842 (Orwell, Ohio)–Nov. 1, 1914. U.S. Army officer. His career extended from the Civil War through the Boxer Rebellion (1900), in which he commanded U.S. contingent; U.S. Army chief of staff, 1904–06. (Father of A.R. CHAFFEE, JR.)

**CHAFFEE, ADNA ROMANZA, JR.,** Sept. 23, 1884 (Junction City, Kan.)–Aug. 22, 1941. U.S. Army officer who was a prime mover behind the development of the U.S. armored force. (Son of A.R. CHAFFEE.)

**CHENNAULT, CLAIRE,** Sept. 6, 1890 (Commerce, Tex.)–July 27, 1958. U.S. Army Air Force general. Created and led "Flying Tigers" in China in WW II; commanded U.S. Army Air Force in China, 1942–45.

**CLARK, GEORGE R.,** Nov. 19, 1752 (nr. Charlottesville, Va.)–Feb. 13, 1818. U.S. frontiersman, army general. Captured Vincennes, 1779; saved St. Louis, 1780; involved in scheme to found colony west of Mississippi. (Brother of W. CLARK.)

**CLARK, MARK,** May, 1, 1896 (Madison Barracks, N.Y.)–Apr. 17, 1984. U.S. Army general. Commanded 5th Army in Italy, 1943–44; commanded United Nations forces in Korea, 1952–53. *Calculated Risk,* 1950.

**CLAY, LUCIUS,** Apr. 23, 1897 (Marietta, Ga.)–Apr. 16, 1978. U.S. Army general. Commander-in-chief, U.S. forces in Europe, 1947–49; administered Berlin airlift, 1948–49.

**COCHISE,** c.1812 (probably Ariz.)–June 9, 1874. Chiricahua Apache leader. Led war against white settlers in Southwest, 1861–72.

**CRAZY HORSE,** c.1845 (nr. Rapid City, S.D.)

–Sept. 5, 1877. Oglala Sioux chief. Led resistance against white encroachments in Black Hills; one of the Indian leaders in the victory at the Little Bighorn, 1876; surrendered May 6, 1877.

**CROOK, GEORGE,** Sept. 23, 1829 (Dayton, Ohio) –Mar. 21, 1890. U.S. Army general, Indian fighter. Fought in Civil War and Sioux War, 1876; captured GERONIMO, 1883.

**CUSTER, GEORGE ARMSTRONG,** Dec. 5, 1839 (New Rumley, Ohio)–June 25, 1876. U.S. cavalry officer. Outstanding record in the Civil War; defeated and killed at Battle of Little Bighorn (1876), the worst defeat in the Indian campaigns, often called Custer's Last Stand. *My Life on the Plains,* 1874.

**DAVIS, BENJAMIN O.,** July 1, 1877 (Wash., D.C.) –Nov. 26, 1970. U.S. Army general. First black general in U.S. Army, 1940; lieut, Spanish-Amer. War, 1898; U.S. military attaché in Liberia, 1909–11. (Father of B.O. DAVIS, JR.)

**DAVIS, BENJAMIN O., JR.,** Dec. 18, 1912 (Wash., D.C.). U.S. Air Force general. First black graduate of West Point, 1936; WW II pilot; organized and commanded 99th Fighter Sqd. and 333 Fighter Group in WW II; first black general in the Air Force, 1954; asst. sec. of treas., 1971. (Son of B.O. DAVIS.)

**DECATUR, STEPHEN,** Jan. 5, 1779 (Sinepuxent, Md.)–Mar. 22, 1820. U.S. naval commodore. Hero of the Barbary Wars, 1804–05, 1815; fought in War of 1812; famed for toast, "Our country, right or wrong"; killed in a duel.

**DEWEY, GEORGE,** Dec. 26, 1837 (Montpelier, Vt.)–Jan. 16, 1917. U.S. admiral. Defeated Spanish fleet at Manila Bay during the Spanish-American War, 1898; admiral of the navy, 1899; famed for command, "You may fire when you are ready, Gridley."

**DONOVAN, WILLIAM** ("Wild Bill"), Jan. 1, 1883 (Buffalo, N.Y.)–Feb. 8, 1959. U.S. Army general, public official. Director, Office of Strategic Services, 1942–45.

**DOOLITTLE, JAMES H.** ("Jimmy"), Dec. 14, 1896 (Alameda, Calif.). U.S. Army Air Corps general. Led first U.S. WW II bombing raid on Tokyo, 1942.

**EARLY, JUBAL,** Nov. 3, 1816 (Franklin Co., Va.)– Mar. 2, 1894. Confederate Army general. Raided close to Washington, D.C., causing panic and forcing Gen. U.S. GRANT to divert forces to repel him, 1864.

**EDMONDS SARAH,** Dec. 1841 (York Co., New Brunswick, Can.)–Sept. 5, 1898. Union Army soldier. Disguised as a man, fought at the First Battle of Bull Run (1861), the Peninsular campaign (1862), and Fredericksburg (1862); spied behind Confederate lines "disguised" as a woman; granted a veteran's pension by Congress; nurse and spy in the Union Army, 1865.

**FARRAGUT, (James) DAVID GLASGOW,** July 5, 1801 (nr. Knoxville, Tenn.)–Aug. 14, 1870. Union admiral. The first admiral in U.S. history; seized New Orleans, 1862; captured Mobile Bay, 1864, bellowing, "Damn the torpedoes: full speed ahead!" (Adopted by D. PORTER.)

FLETCHER, FRANK, Apr. 29, 1885 (Marshall town, Ia.)–Apr. 25, 1973. U.S. admiral. Led naval forces in Pacific in WW II; fought at Coral Sea and Midway, 1942.

FORREST, NATHAN BEDFORD, July 13, 1821 (nr. Chapel Hill, Tenn.)–Oct. 29, 1877. Confederate cavalry general. Noted for daring cavalry raids that disrupted Union supply lines; first Grand Wizard of the original Ku Klux Klan (disbanded, 1869).

GALVIN, JAMES R., May 13, 1929 (Wakefield, Mass.). U.S. army general. As supreme allied commander Europe heads all military units in Europe assigned to NATO; a four-star general. *The Minute Men*, 1967.

GATES, HORATIO, c.1728 (Maldon, Essex, Eng.)–Apr. 10, 1806. American Revolutionary general. As a British soldier, engaged in French and Indian War, 1754–63; moved to America (1772) and joined Continental Army; won the Battle of Saratoga, 1777; blamed for disastrous defeat at Camden (1780), and relieved of command.

GAVIN, JAMES M., Mar. 22, 1907 (Brooklyn, N.Y.)–Feb. 23, 1990. U.S. Army general, diplomat. Engaged at Normandy and the Battle of the Bulge during WW II; U.S. ambassador to France, 1961–62; critic of U.S. military strategy during the Vietnam War. *War and Peace in the Space Age*, 1958. *On to Berlin*, 1978.

GERONIMO, June 1829 (No-Doyohn Canyon, Ariz.)–Feb. 17, 1909. Chiricahua Apache Indian chief. Led raids in Mexico and U.S.; surrendered to U.S. troops, 1886.

GREENE, NATHANAEL, Aug. 7, 1742 (Potowomut [now Warwick] R.I.)–June 19, 1786. American Revolutionary general. Ranked second to Gen. GEORGE WASHINGTON, as military strategist. Defeated British in Southern campaign, 1780–81.

GROVES, LESLIE RICHARD, Aug. 17, 1896 (Albany, N.Y.)–July 13, 1970. U.S. Army general. Headed Manhattan Project, which developed the atomic bomb, 1942–47. *Now It Can Be Told: The Story of the Manhattan Project*, 1962.

HAIG, ALEXANDER M., JR., Dec. 2, 1914 (Bala-Cynwyd, Pa.). U.S. Army general, presidential assistant. Chief of White House staff, 1973–74; NATO Supreme Allied Commander, Europe, 1974–79; Sect. of State, 1981–82.

HALE, NATHAN, June 6, 1755 (Coventry, Conn.)–Sept. 22, 1776. American Revolutionary hero. Hanged by British as a spy, he gained immortality with his last words: "I only regret that I have but one life to lose for my country."

HALLECK, HENRY WAGER, Jan. 16, 1815 (Westernville, N.Y.)–Jan. 9, 1872. U.S. military officer. General in chief of the Union Army, 1862–64; known as an excellent administrator but poor strategist.

HALSEY, WILLIAM F., JR., ("Bull"), Oct. 30, 1882 (Elizabeth, N.J.)–Aug. 16, 1959. U.S. admiral. Commander in So. Pacific during WW II; helped turn back Japanese at Guadalcanal, 1942;

played a major role in the destruction of the Japanese battle fleet at Battle of Leyte Gulf (the largest sea battle in history), 1944; directed final major operations of WW II, around Okinawa, 1945.

HAMPTON, WADE, Mar. 28, 1818 (Charleston, S.C.)–Apr. 11, 1902. Confederate cavalry general, public official. Fought at Antietam (1862), Gettysburg (1863); governor of South Carolina, 1877–79; U.S. senator (D, S.C.), 1879–91.

HANCOCK, WINFIELD SCOTT, Feb. 14, 1824 (Montgomery Co., Pa.)–Feb. 9, 1886. Union Army general. Served in Peninsular campaign, 1862; prepared defensive positions on Cemetery Ridge at Gettysburg, 1863; Democratic presidential candidate, 1880.

HERRES, ROBERT T. Dec. 1, 1932 (Denver, Colo.) U.S. Army general. Commander in chief North American Aerospace Command, 1984–85; first commander in chief, U.S. Space Command, 1985–87; first vice chm., Joint Chiefs of Staff, 1987–90.

HERKIMER, NICHOLAS, 1728 (nr. present day Herkimer, N.Y.)–Aug. 16, 1777. American Revolutionary general. Led militiamen at Battle of Oriskany, where he was mortally wounded; home town named in his honor.

HERSHEY, LEWIS B., Sept. 12, 1893 (nr. Angola, Steuben Co., Ind.)–May 20, 1977. U.S. Army general. Directed Selective Service System under six presidents, overseeing the draft of some 14.5 million Americans, 1941–70.

HODGES, COURTNEY H., Jan. 5, 1887 (Perry, Ga.)–Jan. 16, 1966. U.S. Army general. Commanded 1st Army, the first to enter Paris and to cross the Siegfried Line, 1944.

HOOD, JOHN BELL, June 1, 1831 (Owingsville, Ky.)–Aug. 30, 1879. Confederate general. Wounded at Gettysburg and Chickamauga; as commander, Army of Tennessee, failed to repel the forces of Gen. WILLIAM T. SHERMAN at Atlanta, 1864; suffered disastrous defeat at Battle of Nashville, Dec. 1864.

HOOKER, JOSEPH ("Fighting Joe"), Nov. 13, 1814 (Hadley, Mass.)–Oct. 31, 1879. Union Army general. Commander, Army of the Potomac, 1863; defeated at Battle of Chancellorsville, May 2–4, 1863; won "Battle Above the Clouds," Lookout Mt., Tenn., Nov. 24, 1863.

HOPKINS, ESEK, Apr. 26, 1718 (Scituate, R.I.)–Feb. 26, 1802. American Revolutionary naval commander. Commanded Continental Navy, 1775–77; suspended from command following his defeat on Long Island Sound.

HOWARD, OLIVER OTIS, Nov. 8, 1830 (Leeds, Me.)–Oct. 26, 1909. U.S. Army general, educator. Saw action at the First Battle of Bull Run (1861), Peninsular campaign (1862), Antietam (1862), and Fredericksburg (1862) during the Civil War; headed Freedman's Bureau, 1865–72; founder and third pres., Howard U., 1869–74; negotiated peace with CHIEF JOSEPH, 1877. Supt. of West Point, 1880–82.

HULL, ISAAC, Mar. 9, 1773 (Derby, Conn.)–Feb. 13, 1843. U.S. naval commodore. Commanded

U.S.S. *Constitution* (nick-named "Old Ironsides") in victory over British frigate *Guerrière*, (1812), a battle that helped unite the nation behind the war effort and destroyed the legend of British naval invincibility. (Nephew of W. HULL.)

HULL, WILLIAM, June 24, 1753 (Derby, Conn.) –Nov. 29, 1825. U.S. Army general. Surrendered Detroit to British with no resistance, 1812; court-martialed and sentenced to death for cowardice; sentence remitted by Pres. JAMES MADISON. (Uncle of I. HULL.)

INGERSOLL, ROYAL E., June 20, 1883 (Washington, D.C.)–May 20, 1976. U.S. admiral. Commander of the Atlantic Fleet, 1942–44.

JACKSON, THOMAS ("Stonewall"), Jan. 21, 1824 (Clarksburg, Va., now in W.Va.)–May 10, 1863. Confederate Army general. Won acclaim at the First Battle of Bull Run (1861), when General Bee shouted, "There stands Jackson like a stone wall! Rally behind the Virginians!", victorious in Shenandoah campaign, 1862; his flanking movement led to Confederate victory at Chancellorsville, where he was mortally wounded, 1863.

JAMES, DANIEL, JR., ("Chappie"), Feb. 11, 1920 (Pensacola, Fla.)–Feb. 25, 1978. U.S. Army general. The first black to achieve four-star rank in the U.S. armed forces when he was promoted to Lt. gen., 1973.

JOHNSTON, JOSEPH EGGLESTON, Feb. 3, 1807 (nr. Farmville, Va.)–Mar. 21, 1891. Confederate Army general. Helped win first important Southern victory at the First Battle of Bull Run, 1861; commander, Army of No. Virginia, 1861–62; failed to stop Gen. W. T. SHERMAN's advance on Atlanta, 1864; U.S. rep, (D, VA) 1879–81.

JONES, JOHN PAUL, July 6, 1747 (Kirkbean, Kirkcudbright, Scot.)–July 18, 1792. Naval hero of the American Revolution. Captured eight British ships, sank eight others, 1776; commanded *Bonhomme Richard* in celebrated victory over *Serapis* (when asked to surrender, replied, "Sir, I have not yet begun to fight"), 1779; as admiral in Russian navy, won victories over Turks, 1788; died in Paris; remains transferred to U.S. Naval Acad. at Annapolis, 1913.

JOSEPH (Chief Joseph), c.1840 (Wallowavalley, Ore.)–Sept. 21, 1904. Nez Percé Indian leader. Led his band in flight to Canada, traveling 1,600 miles through Idaho and Montana and fighting brilliant rearguard action before surrender, 1877.

KEARNY, STEPHEN, Aug. 30, 1794 (Newark, N.J.)–Oct. 31, 1848. U.S. Army general. Commanded Army of the West in the Mexican War, 1846–48; captured New Mexico, helped win California.

KENNEY, GEORGE C., Aug. 6, 1889 (Yarmouth, N.S., Can.)–Aug. 9, 1977. U.S. Army Air Force general. Headed Gen. DOUGLAS MACARTHUR's air forces in the Pacific during WW II. *General Kenney Reports*, 1948.

KIMMEL, HUSBAND EDWARD, Feb. 26, 1882 (Henderson, Ky.)–May 14, 1968. U.S. admiral. Commander of Pearl Harbor naval base at the time

of the Japanese attack, 1941; was relieved of his command 10 days later, charged with errors of judgement. *Admiral Kimmel's Story*, 1955.

KING, ERNEST J., Nov. 23, 1878 (Lorain, Ohio) –June 25, 1956. U.S. admiral. Commander-in-chief of U.S. Fleet (1941–45) and chief of Naval Operations (1942–45), the first to hold both jobs at the same time; principal architect of the Allied victory at sea in WW II.

KIRBY-SMITH, EDMUND, May 16, 1824 (St. Augustine, Fla.)–Mar. 28, 1893. Confederate Army officer. Last Confederate commander to surrender, 1865. Pres. of U. of Nashville, 1870–75.

KRUEGER, WALTER, Jan. 26, 1881 (Flatow, W. Prussia, now Zlotów, Pol.)–Aug. 20, 1967. U.S. Army general. Headed Southern Defense Command, 1941–43; commander, 6th Army, 1943–46; his troops invaded New Britain, occupied Hollandia; advanced 2,000 miles to the Philippine Islands, occupied Japan.

LAWRENCE, JAMES, Oct. 1, 1781 (Burlington, N.J.)–June 4, 1813. U.S. naval captain. Commander of the U.S.S. *Chesapeake* when it was defeated by the British frigate *Shannon* in battle off Boston, 1813; famed for his dying words, uttered during the battle: "Don't give up the ship."

LEAHY, WILLIAM D., May 6, 1875 (Hampton, Ia.)–July 20, 1959. U.S. admiral. Served as personal chief of staff for Pres. FRANKLIN D. ROOSEVELT during WW II and to Pres. HARRY S. TRUMAN, 1945–49.

LEE, CHARLES, 1731 (Dernhall, Cheshire, Eng.) –Oct. 2, 1782. American Revolutionary general. Held captive by the British, 1776–78 (letters found in 1858 in papers of WILLIAM HOWE indicated Lee had treasonable negotiations with the British during his captivity); failed at the Battle of Monmouth, 1778; court-martialed and suspended, dismissed after writing an insulting letter to Congress, 1780.

LEE, HENRY ("Light-Horse Harry"), Jan. 29, 1756 (Leesylvania, Prince William Co., Va.)–Mar. 25, 1818. American Revolutionary cavalry officer, public official. Captured British post at Paulus Hook, N.J., 1779; engaged in Carolina campaign; served in Continental Congress, 1785–88; governor of Virginia, 1792–95. (Father of R.E. LEE.)

LEE, ROBERT E., Jan. 19, 1807 (Stratford, Westmoreland Co., Va.)–Oct. 12, 1870. Confederate Army general, the South's outstanding military leader. Supt., U.S. Military Academy, 1852–55; refused command of Union armies, resigned U.S. commission, 1861; military adviser to JEFFERSON DAVIS, 1861–62; led Army of Northern Virginia, 1862–65; commander-in-chief of all Confederate armies, 1865; victorious at Seven Days' Battle (1862), Second Manassas (1862), Fredericksburg (1862), Chancellorsville (1863); defeated at Gettysburg, 1863; surrendered at Appomattox Courthouse, 1865. (Son of H. LEE.)

LEMAY, CURTIS E., Nov. 15, 1906 (Columbus, Ohio). U.S. Air Force general, pioneer of strategic bombing concepts in WW II. Commander in chief,

Strategic Air Command, 1948–57; chief of staff, U.S. Air Force, 1961–65; American Independent Party v.-pres. candidate (ran with GEORGE WALLACE), 1968.

**LEMNITZER, LYMAN**, Aug. 29, 1899 (Honesdale, Pa.)–Nov. 12, 1989. U.S. Army general. Engaged in WW II and Korean War; chief of staff, U.S. Army, 1959–60; chairman, Joint Chiefs of Staff, 1960–62; commander, U.S. forces in Europe, 1962; Supreme Allied Commander, 1963.

**LONGSTREET, JAMES**, Jan. 8, 1821 (Edgefield Dist., S.C.)–Jan. 2, 1904. Confederate Army general. Held important commands at the First and Second battles of Manassas (1861, 1862), Peninsular campaign (1862), Antietam (1862), Fredericksburg (1862), Gettysburg (1863), Chickamauga (1863), and the Wilderness campaign (1864); made a scapegoat in the South after the war for the defeat at Gettysburg, partly because he joined the Republican party. *From Manassas to Appomattox*, 1896.

**MACARTHUR, ARTHUR**, June 2, 1845 (Chicopee Falls, Mass.)–Sept. 5, 1912. U.S. Army officer. Fought for the Union in the Civil War, winning the Congressional Medal of Honor for heroism at battle of Missionary Ridge 1863; in Spanish-American War, helped capture Manila, 1898; ranking officer in the U.S. Army at retirement, 1909. (Father of D. MACARTHUR.)

**MACARTHUR, DOUGLAS**, Jan. 26, 1880 (nr. Little Rock, Ark.)–Apr. 5, 1964. U.S. Army officer. Commander of 42nd (Rainbow) Division, WW I; army chief of staff and military advisor to Philippines prior to WW II; resigned 1937; recalled, 1941; withdrawn from Corregidor, fled 3,000 miles to Australia, saying, "I have come through, I shall return," 1941; made supreme allied commander in SW Pacific 1941; launched counterattack; liberated Philippines, 1944–45; accepted Japanese surrender, 1945; commander of occupation forces in Japan, 1945–50; commander in chief of UN forces in Korea, 1950–51; dismissed when he publicly challenged Pres. TRUMAN's conduct of the war; returned to U.S. to hero's welcome, saying "Old soldiers never die, they just fade away." (Son of A. MACARTHUR.)

**MAHAN, ALFRED THAYER**, Sept. 27, 1840 (West Point, N.Y.)–Dec. 1, 1914. U.S. admiral, naval historian and theorist. Wrote some 20 books on naval history and global strategy, which were instrumental in shaping the policies of the great powers in the late-19th and early-20th cent., his doctrines influenced the enlargement of the U.S. Navy after 1880, the annexation of Hawaii, and the digging of the Panama Canal. *The Influence of Sea Power upon History, 1660–1783*, 1890.

**MARION, FRANCIS** ("The Swamp Fox"), c.1732 (Winyah, S.C.)–Feb. 27, 1795. American Revolutionary general. Led guerrilla actions against British in South Carolina, 1780–81.

**MARSHALL, GEORGE C.**, Dec. 31, 1880 (Uniontown, Pa.)–Oct. 16, 1959. U.S. Army general, statesman. As U.S. Army chief of staff in WW II, was the principal organizer of the U.S. war effort, 1939–45;

presidential envoy to China, 1945–47; U.S. secretary of state, 1947–49; U.S. secretary of defense, 1950–51; proposed Marshall Plan for postwar European relief, for which he won the Nobel Peace Prize, 1953.

**MCAULIFFE, ANTHONY C.**, July 2, 1898 (Washington, D.C.)–Aug. 11, 1975. U.S. Army general famed for his reply to German surrender demand at Bastogne, 1944–"Nuts!"

**MCCAULEY, MARY**, ("Molly Pitcher"), Oct. 13, 1754 (Trenton, N.J.)–Jan. 22, 1832. American Revolutionary heroine. Carried water and fired cannon at Battle of Monmouth, 1778.

**MCCLELLAN, GEORGE, B.**, Dec. 3, 1826 (Philadelphia, Pa.)–Oct. 29, 1885. Union Army general, public official. Commander, Army of the Potomac, 1861–62; his indecisiveness led to Union defeats in the Peninsular campaign and Seven Days' Battles and to the bloody draw at Antietam, 1862; relieved of command, 1862; Democratic presidential candidate, 1864; gov. of New Jersey, 1878–81.

**MEADE, GEORGE**, Dec. 31, 1815 (Cadiz, Sp.)–Nov. 6, 1872. Union Army general. Commander, Army of the Potomac 1863–65; victor at Gettysburg, 1863.

**MILES, NELSON APPLETON**, Aug. 8, 1839 (Westminster, Mass.)–May 15, 1925. U.S. Army general. Most noted for his role in wars with the Western Indians; drove SITTING BULL into Canada, 1876; captured CHIEF JOSEPH, 1877; put down the Ghost Dance uprising that ended with Battle of Wounded Knee, 1890; led invasion of Puerto Rico, 1898.

**MITCHELL, WILLIAM** ("Billy"), Dec. 29, 1879 (Nice, Fr.)–Feb. 19, 1936. U.S. Army Air Corps general, aviation pioneer. WW I aviation hero; an ardent advocate of air power who warned of inadequate U.S. defenses in regard to Japan; his attack against the Navy and War departments for their neglect of air power led to guilty verdict in court-martial for insubordination, 1925; resigned his commission, 1926; vindicated by events of WW II. *Winged Defense*, 1925.

**MITSCHER, MARC A.**, Jan. 26, 1887 (Hillsboro, Wisc.)–Feb. 3, 1947. U.S. admiral. Commanded U.S.S. *Hornet* in the Battle of Midway, 1942; commanded Task Force 58, the principal carrier strike force in the Pacific; led successful air strikes in the battles of the Philippine Sea, Leyte Gulf, Iwo Jima, and Okinawa, 1944–45.

**MONTGOMERY, RICHARD**, 1738 (Swords, Co. Dublin, Ire.)–Dec. 31, 1775. American Revolutionary general. Served in British army, 1756–72; commanded Quebec campaign for Continental Army; killed during assault on Quebec, 1775.

**MOORER, THOMAS, H.** Feb. 9, 1912 (Mount Willing, Ala.). U.S. admiral. Chief of Naval Operations, 1967–70; chairman, Joint Chiefs of Staff, 1970–74.

**MORGAN, DANIEL**, 1736 (Hunterdon Co., N.J.)–July 6, 1802. American Revolutionary general. Fought at Quebec, 1775, Saratoga, 1777; victorious at Battle of Cowpens, 1781; U.S. rep (F, VA) 1797–99.

**MOULTRIE, WILLIAM,** Dec. 4, 1730 (Charleston, S.C.)–Sept. 27, 1805. American Revolutionary general. Held fort on Sullivan's I., near Charleston, S.C., against heavy British attack, 1776; surrendered Charleston after 2 mos. siege, 1780; gov. 1785–87, 1794–96.

**MUHLENBERG, JOHN,** Oct. 1, 1746 (Trappe, Pa.)–Oct. 1, 1807. American Revolutionary general, clergyman, congressman. Fought at Brandywine, Monmouth, Yorktown; served three times as U.S. rep. from Pennsylvania, 1789–1801. (Son of Lutheran leader H. M. MUHLENBERG, brother of F. A. C. MUHLENBERG).

**NIMITZ, CHESTER W.,** Feb. 24, 1885 (Fredericksburg, Tex.)–Feb. 20, 1966. U.S. admiral. Commanded U.S. naval forces in the Pacific during WW II; directed the battles of Coral Sea and Midway, 1942; directed landings on the Solomons, Gilberts, Marshalls, Marianas, Philppines, Iwo Jima, and Okinawa, 1942–45; chief of Naval Operations, 1945–47.

**O'HARE, EDWARD H.** ("Butch"), Mar. 13, 1914 (St. Louis, Mo.)–Nov. 20, 1943 (killed in action). U.S. Navy officer, aviator. Credited with saving U.S.S. *Lexington* in heroic air battle, shooting down five Japanese bombers and damaging three others, 1942; Chicago's O'Hare Airport named in his honor.

**PATTON, GEORGE S., JR.** ("Old Blood and Guts"), Nov. 11, 1885 (San Gabriel, Calif.)–Dec. 21, 1945. U.S. army officer, armored-warfare tactician. Led U.S. Army II Corps in N. Africa, 1942–43; led 7th Army assault on Sicily, 1943; caused homefront furor by slapping a hospitalized GI and cursing others as malingerers in Sicilian field hospital, 1943; led 3rd Army invasion of German occupied Europe, 1944; made political statements that often embarrassed superiors and was relieved of command, 1945.

**PERRY, MATTHEW C.,** Apr. 10, 1794 (So. Kingston, R.I.)–Mar. 4, 1858. U.S. Navy commodore. Helped capture Veracruz, 1847; helped prepare first curriculum for the U.S. Naval Academy; negotiated Treaty of Kanagawa, which opened U.S. trade with Japan, 1853–54. (Brother of O.H. PERRY.)

**PERRY, OLIVER HAZARD,** Aug. 20, 1785 (So. Kingston, R.I.)–Aug. 23, 1819. U.S. Navy captain. Won the decisive Battle of Lake Erie in the War of 1812, 1813. (Brother of M. PERRY.)

**PERSHING, JOHN J.** ("Black Jack"), Sept. 13, 1860 (Laclede, Mo.)–July 15, 1948. U.S. Army general. Commanded Mexican border campaign, 1916–17; commanded American Expeditionary Force in Europe in WW I; named by Congress general of the armies, 1919; chief of staff, U.S. Army, 1921–24; won 1932 Pulitzer Prize in history for *My Experiences in the World War*, 1931.

**PICKETT, GEORGE E.,** Jan. 25, 1825 (Richmond, Va.)–July 30, 1875. Confederate Army general. His name is linked with disastrous Pickett's Charge at

Gettysburg, 1863, although he did not command the overall attack.

**PONTIAC,** c.1720 (Ohio)–Apr. 20, 1769. Ottawa Indian tribal chief. Forged an alliance of 18 Indian tribes; led uprising against the British following the French surrender in the French and Indian War; laid siege to Detroit; victorious at Battle of Bloody Run, 1763; signed peace treaty, 1766.

**POPE, JOHN,** Mar. 16, 1822 (Louisville, Ky.) –Sept. 23, 1892. Union Army general. Suffered disastrous defeat at the Second Battle of Bull Run, 1862.

**PORTER, DAVID,** Feb. 1, 1780 (Boston, Mass.)– Mar. 3, 1843. U.S. Navy commodore. Commanded frigate *Essex* during War of 1812, capturing numerous British whaling vessels in the Pacific; captured, 1814; headed Mexican Navy, 1826–29; U.S. chargé d'affaires, minister to Turkey, 1831–43. (Father of D.D. PORTER; adopted D. FARRAGUT.)

**PORTER, DAVID DIXON,** June 8, 1813 (Chester, Pa.)–Feb. 13, 1891. U.S. admiral. Helped seize New Orleans (1862), Vicksburg (1863), and Ft. Fisher (1865) for the Union during the Civil War; headed Naval Academy, 1865–69. (Son of D. PORTER; foster brother of D. FARRAGUT.)

**PORTER, FITZ-JOHN,** Aug. 31, 1822 (Portsmouth, N.H.)–May 21, 1901. Union Army general. Fought in Peninsular campaign; court-martialed and cashiered for disobedience at Second Battle of Bull Run, 1862; later vindicated.

**POWELL, COLIN J.,** Apr. 5, 1937 (New York, N.Y.) U.S. army general. Asst. to the pres. for national security affairs, 1987–89; chm., joint chiefs of staff, 1989–  .

**POWERS, FRANCIS GARY,** Aug. 17, 1929 (Jenkins, Ky.)–Aug. 1, 1977. U.S. pilot. Precipitated major diplomatic incident when his high-altitude reconnaissance plane (U-2) was shot down over the USSR and he was imprisoned, 1960; exchanged for Soviet spy RUDOLF ABEL, 1962.

**PRESCOTT, WILLIAM,** Feb. 20, 1726 (Groton, Mass.)–Oct. 13, 1795. American Revolutionary officer. Remembered as the hero of the Battle of Bunker Hill, 1775.

**PULLER, LEWIS B.** ("Chesty"), June 26, 1898 (West Point, Va.)–Oct. 11, 1971. U.S. Marine Corps general. Won four Navy Crosses in WW II; led first Marine regiment ashore at Inchon, Korea, 1950; won fifth Navy Cross in Korean War.

**PUTNAM, ISRAEL,** Jan. 7, 1718 (Salem Village, now Danvers, Mass.)–May 29, 1790. American Revolutionary general. Helped plan the fortifications for the Battle of Bunker Hill, where he warned his troops as the British approached, "Don't fire until you see the whites of their eyes."

**QUANTRILL, WILLIAM C.,** July 31, 1839 (Canal Dover, now Dover, Ohio)–June 6, 1865. Confederate Army guerrilla leader who led Aug. 21, 1863, raid on Lawrence, Kan., razing the town and killing 180 persons.

**RADFORD, ARTHUR, W.,** Feb. 27, 1896 (Chicago, Ill.)–Aug. 17, 1973. U.S. admiral. Commanded Northern Carrier Group in campaigns in Gilbert and Marshall Is.; chairman, Joint Chiefs of Staff, 1953–57.

**REVERE, PAUL,** Jan. 1, 1735 (Boston, Mass.)–May 10, 1818. American patriot, silversmith. An organizer of the Boston Tea Party, 1773; famed for his ride to warn of the British march on Concord, 1775; commanded Fort William in Boston harbor, 1778–79; designed and printed first Continental money.

**RICKENBACKER, EDWARD** ("Eddie"), Oct. 8, 1890 (Columbus, Ohio)–July 23, 1973. U.S. aviator, airline executive. The most celebrated U.S. air ace in WW I, in which he won Medal of Honor; headed Eastern Airlines, 1938–63; while touring military bases in the South Pacific during WW II, his plane crashed at sea and he spent over three weeks in a life raft before being rescued. *Fighting the Flying Circus,* 1919; *Seven Came Through,* 1946.

**RICKOVER, HYMAN G.,** Jan. 27, 1900 (Makov, Russia, now Maków, Poland)–July 8, 1986. U.S. admiral, educator. Called "Father of the atomic submarine," he supervised construction of the first nuclear submarine, U.S.S. *Nautilus,* 1947–54; helped develop first U.S. full-scale experimental nuclear power plant, 1956–57; influential in upgrading U.S. education in mathematics and science.

**RIDGWAY, MATTHEW B.,** Mar. 3, 1895 (Ft. Monroe, Va.). U.S. Army general. Directed U.S. airborne assaults on Sicily (1943) and Europe (1944–45); commander, UN forces in Korea, 1951–52; supreme commander, Allied Forces in Europe, 1952–53; chief of staff, U.S. Army, 1953–55.

**ROGERS, ROBERT,** Nov. 7, 1731 (Methuen, Mass.)–May 18, 1795. Colonial military officer. Led Rogers Rangers, forerunners of modern commandos, during French and Indian War, 1755–63.

**ROSECRANS, WILLIAM STARKE,** Sept. 6, 1819 (Kingston Township, Ohio)–Mar. 11, 1898. Union Army general. Victorious at Stones River, 1862–63; drove Confederates out of central Tennessee, 1863; defeated at Chickamauga and relieved 1863; U.S. rep (D, Calif.) 1881–85.

**ST. CLAIR, ARTHUR,** Mar. 23, 1734 (Thurso, Caithness, Scot.)–Aug. 31, 1818. American Revolutionary general, public official. Abandoned Ft. Ticonderoga, 1777; served in Continental Congress, 1785–87 (pres., 1787); gov. of the Northwest Territory, 1787–1802; defeated by Miami Indians, 1791.

**SCOTT, WINFIELD** ("Old Fuss and Feathers"), June 13, 1786 (nr. Petersburg, Va.)–May 29, 1866. U.S. Army general. Defeated British at Chippewa Creek, 1814; general in chief, U.S. Army, 1841–61; led U.S. forces in Mexican War, 1846–48; Whig party presidential candidate, 1852.

**SEMMES, RAPHAEL,** Sept. 27, 1809 (Charles Co., Mo.)–Aug. 30, 1877. Confederate naval commander. His raider, *Alabama,* seized or sank over 64 Union vessels during the Civil War.

**SHAYS, DANIEL,** c.1747 (Hopkinton, Mass.)–Sept. 29, 1825. American Revolutionary soldier. Served at Bunker Hill, Ticonderoga, and Saratoga, his name is associated with "rebellion" in western Mass., in which he played a prominent part, 1786–87.

**SHERIDAN, PHILIP,** Mar. 6, 1831 (Albany, N.Y.)–Aug. 5, 1888. Union Army general. Commanded Army of the Shenandoah, 1864–65; cut off GEN. ROBERT E. LEE's line of retreat at Appomattox, 1865; campaigned against Indians, 1868–69; 1871–83.

**SHERMAN, WILLIAM TECUMSEH,** Feb. 8, 1820 (Lancaster, Ohio)–Feb. 14, 1891. Union Army general. Held important commands at Shiloh (1862), Vicksburg (1863), Chattanooga (1863); led advance on Atlanta and the "March to the Sea," 1864; commanding general of the army, 1869–83; known for observation, "War is hell"; halted Republican party attempt (1884) to nominate him for the presidency by saying, "If nominated, I will not accept. If elected, I will not serve." (Brother of J. SHERMAN.)

**SIGSBEE, CHARLES D.,** Jan. 16, 1845 (Albany, N.Y.)–July 19, 1923. U.S. admiral. Commander of the U.S.S. *Maine* when it was sunk at Havana harbor, 1898; "Remember the *Maine*" became the catch phrase of the Spanish-American War.

**SIMS, WILLIAM S.,** Oct. 15, 1858 (Port Hope, Ont., Can.)–Sept. 28, 1936. U.S. admiral. Promoted convoy system that contributed to Allied victory in WW I; won Pulitzer Prize for history for *The Victory at Sea,* 1920.

**SITTING BULL,** c.1831 (S.D.)–Dec. 15, 1890. Hunkpapa Sioux Indian leader, medicine man. Organized resistance leading to the Battle of Little Bighorn ("made medicine," took no part in fighting), 1876; toured with BUFFALO BILL's Wild West show; a leader in Ghost Dance uprising leading to Battle of Wounded Knee, 1890.

**SMITH, HOLLAND M.** ("Howlin' Mad Smith"), Apr. 20, 1882 (Seale, Ala.)–Jan. 12, 1967. U.S. Marine Corps general who helped plan WW II Marine assaults on Gilbert and Marshall Is., Saipan, Guam, Iwo Jima, and Okinawa, 1943–45. *Coral and Brass,* 1949.

**SPAATZ, CARL,** June 28, 1891 (Boyertown, Pa.)–July 14, 1974. U.S. Air Force general. As commander of U.S. Strategic Air Forces in Europe, directed strategic bombing of Germany, and later Japan, in WW II; chief of staff, U.S. Air Force, 1947–48.

**SPRUANCE, RAYMOND A.,** Jan. 3, 1886 (Baltimore, Md.)–Dec. 13, 1969. U.S. admiral. Victor at Midway Island, 1942; commanded U.S. 5th Fleet in the Pacific, 1944–45; headed Naval War College, 1945–48; U.S. ambassador to the Philippines, 1952–55.

**STANDISH, MILES** (or MYLES) c.1584 (Lancashire, Eng.)–Oct. 3, 1656. British officer. Military leader of Plymouth Colony, 1620–25; asst. gov., treas. of colony, 1644–49; his role in LONGFELLOW's poem "The Courtship of Miles Standish" is not based on historical evidence.

**STARK, JOHN,** Aug. 28, 1728 (Londonderry, N.H.)–May 8, 1822. American Revolutionary general.

Fought at Bunker Hill, 1775; defeated Hessians at Bennington, 1777; played an important role in the victory at Saratoga, 1777.

**STEWART, CHARLES,** July 28, 1778 (Philadelphia, Pa.)–Nov. 6, 1869. U.S. naval officer. Commanded U.S.S. *Constitution* during the War of 1812. (Grandfather of C.S. PARNELL.)

**STILWELL, JOSEPH W.** ("Vinegar Joe"), Mar. 19, 1883 (Palatka, Fla.)–Oct. 12, 1946. U.S. Army general. Commanded U.S. forces in the China-Burma-India theater during WW II; also served as chief of staff to Chinese pres. CHIANG KAI-SHEK; his disagreement with Chiang over the role of Chinese forces led to his being relieved of command by Pres. FRANKLIN D. ROOSEVELT, 1944.

**STUART, J(ames) E(well) B(rown),** Feb. 6, 1833 (Patrick Co., Va)–May 12, 1864. Confederate cavalry commander. Played a major role in numerous Southern victories; mortally wounded at Yellow Tavern, 1864.

**TAYLOR, MAXWELL D.,** Aug. 26, 1901 (Keytesville, Md.)–April 19, 1987. U.S. general, diplomat. Commanded 101st Airborne Division in WW II; supt., U.S. Military Academy, 1945–49; commanded U.S. 8th Army in Korean War; chairman, Joint Chiefs of Staff, 1962–64; U.S. ambassador to South Vietnam, 1964–65. *An Uncertain Trumpet,* 1959.

**TECUMSEH,** Mar. 1768 (Old Piqua, nr. Springfield, Greene Co., Ohio)–Oct. 5, 1813. Shawnee Indian chief. Tried to unite tribes to resist westward expansion of the white man; thwarted by U.S. victory at Tippecanoe, 1811; allied with British forces in War of 1812; killed at Battle of the Thames.

**THAYER, SYLVANIUS,** June 9, 1785 (Braintree, Mass.)–Sept. 7, 1872. U.S. general, educator. As supt. of U.S. Military Academy (1817–33), upgraded training and curriculum.

**THOMAS, GEORGE H.** ("The Rock of Chickamauga"), July 31, 1816 (Southhampton Co., Va.)–Mar. 28, 1870. Union Army general. Saved Union Army of the Tennessee at Chickamauga, 1863; victorious at Battle of Nashville, 1864.

**TRAVIS, WILLIAM BARRET,** Aug. 9, 1809 (Red Banks, S.C.)–Mar. 6, 1836. Texas Revolutionary army officer, lawyer. Commanded forces that defended the Alamo, 1836.

**TURNER, STANSFIELD,** Dec. 1, 1923 (Chicago, Ill.). U.S. admiral. Commander, U.S. 2nd Fleet, 1974–75; commander-in-chief, Allied Forces, Southern Europe (NATO), 1975–77; director, Central Intelligence Agency, 1977–81.

**TWINING, NATHAN FARRAGUT,** Oct. 11, 1897 (Monroe, Wis.)–May 29, 1982. U.S. Air Force general. Directed air assaults against Solomon Islands and New Guinea in WW II; chairman, Joint Chiefs of Staff, 1957–60.

**UNCAS,** c.1588 (?)–c.1683. Pequot Indian sachem. Split from tribe with followers known as Mohecans; joined Eng. settlers and Narragansetts in Pequot War, 1637; fought Narragansett tribe, 1643–47; attacked Massasoit, 1661.

**VANDEGRIFT, ALEXANDER A.,** Mar. 13, 1887 (Charlottesville, Va.)–May 8, 1973. U.S. Marine Corps general. Distinguished himself at Guadalcanal, 1942; oversaw landings at Bougainville, 1943; commandant of Marine Corps, 1944–48.

**WAINWRIGHT, JONATHAN M.** ("Skinny"), Aug. 23, 1883 (Walla Walla, Wash.)–Sept. 2, 1953. U.S. Army general. Defended Corregidor, forced to surrender, and taken as prisoner of war, 1942; rescued in Manchuria, 1945.

**WALKER, WALTON H.,** Dec. 3, 1899 (Belton, Tex.)–Dec. 23, 1950. U.S. army officer. Commanding XX U.S. Army Corps, captured Reims and liberated Buchenwald concentration camp, 1944–45; led S. Korean and UN forces in Korea, 1950.

**WARREN, JOSEPH,** June 10, 1741 (Roxbury, Mass.)–June 17, 1775. American Revolutionary patriot, militia officer and physician. Sent PAUL REVERE and William Dawes on their famous rides, killed at Bunker Hill, 1775.

**WAYNE, ANTHONY** ("Mad Anthony"), Jan. 1, 1745 (nr. Paoli, Chester Co., Pa.)–Dec. 15, 1796. American Revolutionary general. Captured Stony Point, 1779; defeated Indians at the Battle of Fallen Timbers, which helped open the Northwest Territory to settlement, 1794.

**WESTMORELAND, WILLIAM C.,** Mar. 26, 1914 (Spartanburg Co., S.C.). U.S. Army general. Commanded U.S. forces in Vietnam, 1964–68; chief of staff, U.S. Army, 1968–72. *A Soldier Reports,* 1976.

**WHEELER, EARLE GILMORE,** Jan. 13, 1908 (Washington, D.C.)–Dec. 18, 1975. U.S. Army general. Chairman, Joint Chiefs of Staff, 1964–70; directed secret bombings over Cambodia on orders of Pres. RICHARD M. NIXON, 1969–70.

**WHEELER, JOSEPH** ("Fighting Joe"), Sept. 10, 1836 (nr. Augusta Ga.)–Jan. 25, 1906. U.S. and Confederate Army general. Engaged for the confederacy at Chattanooga and Chickamauga (1863), and in the Atlanta campaign (1864); served as U.S. rep. (D, Ala.), 1881–1900; as corp commander (U.S. Army), fought at San Juan and Las Guasimas during the Spanish-American War.

**WILKINSON, JAMES,** 1757 (Calvert Co., Md.)–Dec. 28, 1825. U.S. Revolutionary general, double-agent intriguer. Involved in "Conway Cabal" against GEORGE WASHINGTON and forced to resign his commission, 1778; appointed clothier-general of Continental Army, but forced to resign because of irregularity in his accounts, 1781; agent of Spain, 1787–1806; implicated in AARON BURR conspiracy, 1805–07, but acquitted by court-martial, 1811; mishandled Montreal expedition, but acquitted by court-martial, 1813.

**WILSON, JAMES HARRISON,** Sept. 2, 1837 (nr. Shawneetown, Ill.)–Feb. 23, 1925. Union Army general. Captured Selma, Montgomery, Columbus, Macon, and CSA Pres. JEFFERSON DAVIS, 1865; served in the Spanish-American War (1898–99) and the Boxer Rebellion (1900).

**WOOD, LEONARD,** Oct. 9, 1860 (Winchester, N.H.)–Aug. 7, 1927. U.S. Army general. A close friend of THEODORE ROOSEVELT, helped raise and organize the Rough Riders, 1898; chief of staff, U.S. Army, 1910–14; governor-general of the Philippines, 1921–27.

YORK, ALVIN, Dec. 13, 1887 (Pall Mall, Tenn.) –Dec. 2, 1964. U.S. soldier. One of the most decorated heroes of WW I, received 50 medals, including the Congressional Medal of Honor; film *Sergeant York*, 1941, was his story.

ZUMWALT, ELMO R., JR., Nov. 29, 1920 (Tulare, Cal.). U.S. admiral. Noted for personnel reforms and for initiating warship modernization to meet the growing challenges posed by the Soviet navy; commanded U.S. naval forces in Vietnam, 1968–70; chief of Naval Operations, 1970–74. *On Watch: a memoir*, 1976.

## FOREIGN MILITARY AND NAVAL LEADERS

ABEL, RUDOLF, c.1902 (Moscow, Rus.)–Nov. 15, 1971. Soviet intelligence officer. Convicted in U.S. for conspiring to transmit military secrets to the USSR, 1957; exchanged for FRANCIS GARY POWERS, 1962.

ABERCROMBIE (or Abercromby), JAMES, 1706 (Scot.)–Apr. 28, 1781. British general. Commanded forces in N. America during the French and Indian War; defeated at Ticonderoga, 1758.

ABERCROMBY, SIR RALPH, Oct. 7, 1734 (Tullibody, Clackmannan, Scotland)–Mar. 28, 1801. British general. Defeated French army at Alexandria, Egypt, where he was mortally wounded, 1801; knighted, 1795.

ALEXANDER, HAROLD, (first) EARL ALEXANDER OF TUNIS ("Alex"), Dec. 10, 1891 (London, Eng.)–June 16, 1969. British general, field marshal. Commanded British forces at Dunkirk, supervising the evacuation of 300,000 troops, 1940; commander in chief, Allied forces in Italy, 1943–44; gov.-gen. of Canada; 1946–52; minister of defence, 1952–54; knighted 1942; created Viscount Alexander of Tunis, 1946; earl, 1952.

ALLENBY, EDMUND, (first) VISCOUNT ALLENBY, Apr. 23, 1861 (Brackenhurst, Notts., Eng.)– May 14, 1936. British field marshal. Served in Boer War and WW I; led 3rd Army (Egyptian Expeditionary Force), capturing Gaza and Jerusalem (1917) and Megiddo (1918); created Viscount Allenby of Megiddo and Felixstowe, 1919.

ALVARADO, PEDRO DE, c.1485 (Badajoz, Sp.)– July 4, 1541. Spanish conquistador who helped conquer Mexico and Central America for Spain, 1519–34, 1539–1541.

AMHERST, JEFFREY, BARON AMHERST, Jan. 29, 1717 (Sevenoaks, Kent, Eng.)–Aug. 3, 1797. British Army commander. Captured Canada for Great Britain, 1758–60; gov. general British North America, 1760–63; commander in chief of British Army, 1772–95; Amherst College and several U.S. towns are named after him; knighted, 1761; created baron, 1776, field marshal, 1796.

ANDRÉ, JOHN, May 2, 1750 (London, Eng.)–Oct. 2, 1780. British Army officer. Negotiated with BENEDICT ARNOLD for surrender of West Point; captured with incriminating papers and executed, 1780.

ATTILA, KING OF THE HUNS, c.406 (Central Asia)–453. Barbarian ruler. Known as the "Scourge of God"; attacked the Roman Empire, destroying towns and cities, 441–43; invaded Gaul, conducting campaign against Romans and Visigoths, 451; invaded Italy, 452.

BAGRATION, PRINCE PYOTR, 1765 (Kizlyar, Rus.)–Sept. 25, 1812. Russian Army general, hero of the Napoleonic Wars. Captured Brescia, 1799; captured Aaland I., 1808; killed at Borodino, 1812.

BALBO, ITALO, June 6, 1896 (nr. Ferrar, It.) –June 28, 1940. Italian air marshal and fascist leader. Developed BENITO MUSSOLINI's air force.

BELISARIUS, c.505 (Germania, now in Greece) –Mar. 565. Byzantine general. The leading military figure in the time of Byzantine emperor Justinian I; shattered Vandal kingdom in North Africa, 533; began reconquest of Italy.

BLIGH, WILLIAM, Sept. 9, 1754 (Cornwall, Eng.)– Dec. 7, 1817. British admiral. As captain of the H.M.S. *Bounty* at the time of the celebrated mutiny, Apr. 28, 1789, cast adrift with 18 others in an open boat and sailed nearly 4,000 miles, reaching Timor, East Indies, June 14; as captain of H.M.S. *Director*, again put ashore in a mutiny, 1797; as Gov. of New South Wales (from 1805) his oppressive behavior led to mutiny, 1808.

BLÜCHER VON WAHLSTATT, GEBHARD LIBERECHT, Dec. 16, 1742 (Rostock, Mecklenburg-Schwerin, now E. Ger.)–Sept. 12, 1819. Prussian field marshal. Victorious at the Battle of Leipzig, 1813; played an important role in the defeat of Napoleon at Waterloo, 1815.

BRADDOCK, EDWARD, 1695 (Perthshire, Scot.) –July 13, 1755. British general. Commanded British forces in North America during early stages of French and Indian War, 1755; on expedition against Ft. Duquesne (Pittsburgh, Pa.), surprised by French and their Indian allies and mortally wounded.

BRAUCHITSCH, HEINRICH VON, Oct. 4, 1881 (Berlin, Ger.)–Oct. 18, 1948. German field marshal. As commander in chief of German Army, directed campaigns against Poland, the Netherlands, Belgium, France, the Balkans, and USSR, 1938–41; made the scapegoat for German failure to capture Moscow; resigned command, 1941.

BROOKE, ALAN FRANCIS, (first) VISCOUNT ALANBROOKE, July 23, 1883 (Bagnères-de-Bigorre, Fr.)–June 17, 1963. British field marshal. Principal military adviser to WINSTON CHURCHILL during WW II; created baron, 1945; viscount, 1946.

BUDENNY, SEMYON, Apr. 25, 1883 (Kozyvirn, Voronezh Province, Rus.)–Oct. 27, 1973. Soviet marshal. Commanded Soviet calvary corps during the Russian civil war; defeated by Germans at Kiev, 1941.

BURGOYNE, JOHN, ("Gentleman Johnny"), 1722 (Sutton, Bedfordshire, Eng.)–Aug. 4, 1792. British general, dramatist. Recaptured Ft. Ticonderoga, 1777;

defeated at Saratoga (Oct. 1777), and returned to England to face severe criticism. Plays: *The Heiress,* 1786; *The Maid of the Oaks,* 1774.

CANARIS, WILHELM, Jan. 1, 1887 (Aplerbeck, Westphalia, Ger.)–Apr. 9, 1945. German admiral. Chief of military intelligence (Abwehr) (1935–44), and a leader among anti-Hitler conspirators; executed by SS.

CARRANZA, VENUSTIANO, Dec. 29, 1859 (Cuatro Ciénegas, Coahuila, Mex.)–May 21, 1920. Mexican revolutionist, political leader. Played a leading role in civil war following overthrow of PROFIRIO DIAZ, 1911; successfully opposed VICTORIANO HUERTA (1914), and proclaimed "first chief"; provisional pres., 1915–17; elected pres., 1917–20; murdered.

CHAUVIN, NICOLAS. French soldier. His simple-minded devotion to Napoleon and all things military led to the coining of the word *chauvinism.*

CHUIKOV, VASILII, Feb. 21, 1900 (Russia)–Mar. 18, 1982. Soviet field marshal. Military adviser to CHIANG KAI-SHEK, 1926–37; in command of the 62nd Soviet Army, defended Stalingrad, 1942; led his army to recapture Odessa (1944) and in the assault on Berlin (1945); became commander of Soviet occupation forces in Germany; supreme commander of land forces, 1960–64. *The Beginning of the Road,* 1962.

CHURCHILL, JOHN, (first) DUKE OF MARL-BOROUGH, May 26, 1650 (Ashe, Devon, Eng.)–June 16, 1722. British general, political figure. Supported William of Orange in the Glorious Revolution, 1688; led British and Allied armies against LOUIS XIV in the War of the Spanish Succession, gaining victories at Blenheim (1704), Ramillies (1706), Oudenaarde (1708), and Malplaquet (1709); created Earl Marlborough, 1689; duke 1702.

CID, EL, c.1043 (Vivar, Sp.)–July 10, 1099. Spanish military leader and national hero. Commander under Castilian king in 1065; then served Moslem rulers of Saragossa; conquered Valencia, 1094; his role in history is the subject of much controversy among historians.

CINCINNATUS, LUCIUS QUINCTIUS, c.519 B.C.–?. Roman general, statesman. Supported the patricians in the struggle against the plebians, 462–454 B.C.; appointed dictator, defeated the Aequians, and resigned, all in the span of 16 days, 458 B.C.; second dictatorship against Spurius Maelius, 439 B.C.

CLAUSEWITZ, KARL VON, June 1, 1780 (Burg, Ger.)–Nov. 16, 1831. Prussian Army general, military strategist. His books on the philosophy of war influenced military events up to the nuclear age. *Von Kriege* (On War), 1833.

CLINTON, SIR HENRY, 1738 (Newfld., Can.)–Dec. 23, 1795. British general. Commander in chief, British forces in America, 1778–1781; developed British strategy in the successful Southern campaign, 1780; blamed for British defeat at Yorktown; knighted, 1777.

COLLINS, MICHAEL, Oct. 16, 1890 (Clonakilty, County Cork, Ire.)–Aug. 22, 1922. Irish revolu-

tionary and military leader. Pioneered modern urban guerrilla warfare in the Anglo-Irish War, 1919–21; commanded Free State Army during Irish civil war, 1921–22; became head of government on death of Arthur Griffith (Aug. 12, 1922); shot to death in ambush ten days later.

CONWAY, THOMAS, Feb. 27, 1735 (Ire.)–c.1800. Irish soldier. Served in American Revolution; fought at Brandywine and Germantown, 1777; name associated with "Conway Cabal" against GEORGE WASHINGTON (1777–78), although he was its least culpable participant.

CORNWALLIS, CHARLES, (first) MARQUIS CORNWALLIS, Dec. 31, 1738 (London, Eng.)–Oct. 5, 1805. British general. Victorious at Brandywine (1777) and Guilford Courthouse (1781); surrendered at Yorktown, 1781; as gov.-gen. of India, established many legal and administrative reforms, 1786–93, 1805; viceroy of Ireland, 1798–1801; succeeded father as earl, 1762; created marquis, 1792.

DAYAN, MOSHE, May 20, 1915 (Deganya Alef, Pal., now Israel)–Oct. 16, 1981. Israeli general, public official. Led invasion of Sinai Pen., 1956; agriculture minister, 1959–64; defense minister, 1967–74; led forces to victory in Six Day War, 1967; foreign minister, 1977–79.

DENIKIN, ANTON, Dec. 16, 1872 (Nr. Warsaw, Pol.)–Aug. 8, 1947. Russian general. Led white (anti-Bolshevik) forces on the Southern front during Russian civil war, 1918–20.

DOENITZ, KARL, Sept. 16, 1891 (Grünau, Ger.)–Dec. 24, 1980. German admiral. As commander-in-chief of the German Navy (1943–45), led the U-boat offensive against Allied shipping during WW II; as chan. of Germany after A. HITLER's death (1945), surrendered unconditionally to the Allies.

DOWDING, HUGH CASWALL (first) BARON, DOWDING, Apr. 24, 1882 (Moffat, Dumfries shire, Scot.)–Feb. 15, 1970. British air field marshall. Headed Fighter Command, 1936–42; defeated German Luftwaffe in the Battle of Britain, 1940; knighted, 1933; created baron 1943.

DREYFUS, ALFRED, Oct. 19, 1859 (Mulhouse, Fr.)–July 11, 1935. French Army officer of Jewish parentage. The center of a political controversy tied to anti-Semitism, anticlericalism, and antirepublicanism under the Third Republic of France; convicted of treason (1894) and imprisoned on Devil's I. (1895); investigation (1898), following massive campaign, led chiefly by EMILE ZOLA, proved evidence had been forged; retried and again found guilty, 1899; conviction set aside, 1906; awarded Legion of Honor, promoted to major, 1906

ESTERHAZY, MARIE CHARLES, ("COMTE DE VOILEMENT"), 1847 (Aus.)–May 21, 1923. Austrian officer in the French Army. As a German spy, forged documents that incriminated ALFRED DREYFUS (1894).

FABIUS MAXIMUS VERRUCOSUS, QUINTUS ("Cunctator" [The Delayer]), c. 265 (Rome)–203 B.C. Roman soldier. Best known as the opponent of HANNIBAL during 2nd Punic War, 218–201B.C.; used "Fabian" tactics (a waiting policy), keeping his army always near, never attacking, but continually harassing Hannibal; relieved (216) from command, leading to Hannibal's great victory at Cannae; elected consul five times.

FOCH, FERDINAND, Oct. 2, 1851 (Tarbes, Fr.)– Mar. 20, 1929. French marshal. Helped win the First Battle of the Marne, 1914; commander in chief of the Allied armies, 1918.

FREDERICK II (Frederick the Great), Jan. 24, 1712 (Berlin, Ger.)–Aug. 17, 1786. Prussian king (1740–86), military leader. Led Prussia in the Seven Years War, 1756–63.

FULLER, JOHN FREDERICK, Sept. 1, 1878 (Chichester, Sussex, Eng.)–Feb. 10, 1966. British soldier and military theoretician. Recognized the importance of mechanized warfare during WW I; his ideas, published in Tanks in the Great War (1920) and On Future Warfare (1928), had a great influence on military thinking in Europe, particularly in Germany and the USSR.

GAGE, THOMAS, 1721 (Firle, Sussex, Eng.)–Apr. 2, 1787. British general. Commander in chief of all British forces in North America, 1763–74; military gov. of Massachusetts, 1774–75; instrumental in closing Port of Boston, quartering of troops in private houses and Mass. Govt. Acts.

GORDON, CHARLES G. ("Chinese Gordon"; "Gordon of Khartoum"), Jan. 28, 1833 (Woolwich, Eng.)–Jan. 26, 1885. British general. Became a national hero for his exploits in China, 1859–65; killed at the siege of Khartoum, 1885.

GRASSE, FRANCOIS, MARQUIS DE GRASSE-TILLY, COMTE DE, Sept. 13, 1722 (Alpes-Maritimes, Fr.)–Jan. 11, 1788. French admiral. Reinforced French and American forces at Yorktown and won Battle of Chesapeake Bay, 1781.

GUDERIAN, HEINZ, June 17, 1888 (Kulm, Prussia, now Chetmno, Pol.)–May 15, 1954. German general and tank theorist. A principal architect of armored and "blitzkrieg" warfare; led panzer forces in Poland (1939), France (1940), and Russia (1941–42) during WW II; chief of German Army general staff, 1944–45.

GUSTAVUS II, known as Gustavus Adolphus ("Lion of the North"; "Snow King"), Dec. 9, 1594 (Stockholm, Swe.)–Nov. 16, 1653. King of Sweden, 1611–32. Instituted sweeping legal, administrative and educational reforms, including the establishment of secondary schools; ended war with Denmark (1613) and Russia (1617); hoping to increase Sweden's control of the Baltic, entered Thirty Years' War; defeated A. WALLENSTEIN at Lützen, but died in the battle, 1632.

HAIG, DOUGLAS, (first) EARL HAIG, June 19, 1861 (Edinburgh, Scot.)–Jan 29, 1928. British field marshal. His strategy as commander in chief of the British armies in France (1915–18), resulted in huge British casualties; knighted, 1909, created earl, 1919.

HANNIBAL, 247 B.C. (N. Africa)–183 B.C. Car-thaginian soldier. One of the foremost military commanders in history; took command of Carthaginian forces in Spain, 221 B.C.; with 35,000 select troops, plus elephants, crossed the Alps into Italy; won brilliant victories at Ticinus and Trebia, 218; in his greatest victory, wiped out Roman forces at Cannae, 216; lacking support from Carthage, was unable to take Rome; recalled to Carthage, 203; defeated by SCIPIO AFRICANUS at Zama, 202; governed Carthage, c.202–196; forced to flee by enemies; committed suicide.

HAWKINS (or Hawkyns), SIR JOHN, 1532 (Plymouth, Devon, Eng.)–Nov. 12, 1595. British naval commander, administrator. One of the foremost seamen of 16th-cent. England; chief shaper of the Elizabethan navy.

HOWE, RICHARD, EARL HOWE, Mar. 8, 1726 (London, Eng.)–Aug. 5, 1799. British Admiral. Commanded British forces in N. America, 1776–78; commanded Channel fleet in "Glorious First of June" victory against the French, 1794; created viscount, 1782; earl, 1788. (Brother of W. HOWE.)

HOWE, WILLIAM, (fifth) VISCOUNT HOWE, Aug. 10, 1729 (Plymouth, Eng.)–July 12, 1814. British general. Distinguished himself in the French and Indian War, 1754–63; commander in chief of the British army in N. America, 1776–78; occupied New York, but failed to destroy GEORGE WASHINGTON's crippled army, 1776; victorious at Brandywine and Germantown and occupied Philadelphia, 1777; succeeded to title on death of brother, 1799. (Brother of R. HOWE.)

JODL, ALFRED, May, 10, 1890 (Wurzburg, Ger.) –Oct. 16, 1946. German general. Headed armed forces operations staff, 1939–45; helped plan most of Germany's WW II military campaigns; signed surrender of German armed forces, May 7, 1945; convicted as a war criminal at Nuremberg trials and executed, 1946.

JOFFRE, JOSEPH, Jan. 12, 1852 (Rivesaltes, Pyrénées-Orientales, Fr.)–Jan. 3, 1931. French marshal. Commander in chief of French armies on the Western Front in WW I, 1914–16; victorious in the First Battle of the Marne, 1914; created marshal, 1916.

KEITEL, WILHELM, Sept. 22, 1882 (Helmscherode, Ger.)–Oct. 16, 1946. German field marshal. Headed armed forces high command during WW II; generally considered a weak officer who served as ADOLF HILTER's lackey; convicted as a war criminal at Nuremberg trials and executed, 1946.

KESSELRING, ALBERT, Nov. 20, 1885 (Markstedt, Ger.)–July 16, 1960. German field marshal. Commanded air fleets in Poland, France, and the Battle of Britain, 1939–41; helped direct North African campaign, 1941–42; directed defensive action in Italy for over a year, 1943–45; commander in chief, Western Front, 1945.

KITCHENER, HORATIO HERBERT, (first) EARL KITCHENER OF KHARTOUM, June 24, 1850 (nr. Listowel, County Kerry, Ire.)–June 5, 1916. British field marshal, imperial administrator. Commander in chief of the Egyptian Army, 1892– , won Battle of Omdurman and occupied Khartoum, 1898; broke power of Boer guerrillas, 1900–01; commander in chief in India, 1902–09; ruled Egypt and the Sudan, 1911–14; secy. of state for war, 1914–16; created baron, 1898; created viscount, 1902; created earl, 1914.

**KLUCK, ALEXANDER VON,** May 20, 1846 (Münster, Ger.)–Oct. 19, 1934. German Army general. Headed 1st Army in siege of Paris, 1914; lost First Battle of the Marne, 1914.

**KOLCHAK, ALEKSANDR,** 1873 (St. Petersburg, Rus., now Leningrad)–Feb. 7, 1920. Russian admiral. Ruled the White (counter-revolutionary) forces in Russia, 1918–20; captured and executed by the Bolsheviks.

**KORNILOV, LAVRENTI,** July 30, 1870 (Ust-Kamenogorsk, Siberia, Rus.)–Apr. 13, 1918. Russian general. Commander in chief of the Russian Army, 1917; led counter-revolutionary march on Petrograd, 1917; led makeshift army in assault on Ekaterinodar, mortally wounded, 1918.

**KOSCIUSZKO, TADEUSZ,** Feb. 4, 1746 (Mereczowszczyzna, Pol., now Belorussian SSR)–Oct. 15, 1817. Polish general and national hero. Served rebels in American Revolution; fortified West Point, 1778–80; chief engineer in Gen. NATHANAEL GREENE's Southern campaign, 1780–81; led unsuccessful uprising against Russian, Prussian, and Austrian occupiers of Poland, 1794; promoted Poland's cause for independence in the U.S. and Europe, 1797–1817.

**KUTUZOV, MIKHAIL,** Sept. 16, 1745 (St. Petersburg, Rus.)–Apr. 28, 1813. Russian field marshal. Engaged in Russo-Turkish war, 1787–91; victorious over French at Durrenstein, defeated at Austerlitz, 1805; commander in chief of Russian forces at Battle of Borodino, defeated and withdrew, allowing NAPOLEON to enter Moscow, 1812; harried retreating French army and destroyed it; pursued French forces into Poland and Prussia.

**LAFAYETTE, MARIE JOSEPH PAUL YVES ROCH GILBERT DU MOTIER, MARQUIS DE,** Sept. 6, 1757 (Chavaniac, Fr.)–May 20, 1834. French soldier, statesman, hero of the American Revolution. Fought at Brandywine, 1777; wintered at Valley Forge, 1777–78; negotiated French military support for the American cause, 1779; aided victory at Yorktown, 1781; representative of nobility to Estates-General, 1789; presented first draft Rights of Man, 1789; fled to Austria after overthrow of French monarchy.

**LAWRENCE, THOMAS, E.** ("Lawrence of Arabia"), Aug. 15, 1888 (Tremadoc, Wales)–May 19, 1935. British archeologist, military strategist, author. Aided Arab revolt against Turks during WW I; led Arab army to assist Gen. EDMUND ALLENBY in conquest of Palestine, 1918; agitated for Arab independence after WW I; his reputation as a military genius is the subject of much controversy. *The Seven Pillars of Wisdom,* 1926; *Revolt in the Desert,* 1926; *The Mint,* 1955.

**LEONIDAS I,** fl. early 5th century B.C. King of Sparta, 490?–480 B.C. Remembered for his defense of the pass of Thermopylae against a vast Persian army of XERXES; refused to flee, killed with his 300-man royal guard; evoked as the epitome of bravery against overwhelming odds.

**LUDENDORFF, ERICH,** Apr. 9, 1865 (Kruszewnia, Prussian Pol.)–Dec. 20, 1937. German general. Victorious at Tannenberg, 1914; with PAUL VON HINDENBURG, directed German war effort, 1916–18; launched unlimited submarine warfare that drew U.S. into the war, 1917; formulated the German-Russian treaties of Brest-Litovsk, 1918; marched with ADOLF HITLER in Munich Putsch, 1923.

**MANNERHEIM, CARL, BARON VON,** June 4, 1867 (Villnas, Fin.)–Jan. 27, 1951. Finnish field marshal, public official. Commanded White (counter-revolutionary) forces in suppression of Finnish Workers' Republic, 1918; directed first Winter War against USSR, 1939-41; pres. of Finland, 1944–46.

**MASSÉNA, ANDRÉ, PRINCE D'ESSLING, DUC DE RIVOLI,** May 6, 1758 (Nice, Fr.)–Apr. 4, 1817. French marshal. A leading figure in the French Revolutionary and Napoleonic wars. Victor at Rivoli, 1797 and Zurich, 1799; blamed for French defeat in the Peninsular War, 1808–14; made marshal, 1804; duke, 1808; prince 1810.

**MEDINA-SIDONIA, (seventh) DUQUE DE (ALONSO PEREZ DE GUZMAN),** 1550?–1619? Spanish admiral. Commanded the Spanish Armada when it was destroyed by the English, 1588; responsible for the loss of Cadiz (1596) and Gibraltar (1606).

**MOLTKE, HELMUTH J. L. GRAF VON** ("Moltke the Younger"), May 25, 1848 (Gersdorff, Ger.)–June 18, 1916. German general. Chief of general staff, 1906–14; replaced after defeat at the First Battle of the Marne, 1914. (Nephew of H. K. B. VON MOLTKE.)

**MOLTKE, HELMUTH K. B., GRAF VON,** Oct. 26, 1800 (Parchim, Mecklenburg) –Apr. 24, 1891. Prussian field marshal. As head of general staff (1858–88), reorganized Prussian Army; victorious in war against Denmark (1864), the Austro-Prussian War (1866), and Franco-Prussian War (1870–71), paving the way for German unification. (Uncle of H. J. L. VON MOLTKE.)

**MONTCALM-GROZON, LOUIS JOSEPH DE, MARQUIS DE SAINT-VERAN,** Feb. 28, 1712 (Chateau de Candiac, Fr.)–Sept. 14, 1759. French general. Commander in chief of French forces in Canada, 1756–59; captured Ft. Oswego, 1756; successfully defended Ft. Ticonderoga, 1758; killed defending Quebec, 1759.

**MONTGOMERY, BERNARD LAW, (first) VISCOUNT OF ALAMEIN,** Nov. 17, 1887 (London, Eng.)–Mar. 24, 1976. British field marshal. Defeated Gen. ERWIN ROMMEL at El Alamein, 1942; forced Axis surrender in Tunisia, 1943; aided successful Allied invasion of Sicily, 1943; commanded Allied landings in Normandy, 1944; led Allied forces across northern France, Belgium, the Netherlands, and Germany, 1944–45; chief of imp. gen. staff, 1946–48; knighted, 1942; created viscount, 1946.

**MOREAU, JEAN,** Feb. 14, 1763 (Morlaix, Fr.) –Sept. 2, 1813. French Revolutionary general. Participated in French Revolution, 1792–99; became bitter opponent of Napoleon.

**MURAT, JOACHIM,** Mar. 25, 1767 (La Bastide-Fortunière, Fr.)–Oct. 13, 1815. French cavalry leader, marshal. Instrumental in NAPOLEON's victories at Marengo (1800), Austerlitz (1805), and Jena (1806); in Russian campaign, distinguished himself at Borodino, 1812; made significant contribution to foundation of Italian unity as king of Naples, 1808–15.

**NAGANO, OSAMI,** June 15, 1880 (Kochi, Jap.)–Jan 5, 1947. Japanese admiral. Naval chief of staff, 1941–44; planned and ordered attack on Pearl Harbor, 1941.

**NAGUMO, CHUICHI,** 1887?–June 1944. Japanese admiral. Commanded carrier fleet that carried out attack on Pearl Harbor, 1941; his defeat at Midway reversed the balance of naval power in the Pacific, 1942.

**NAPIER, ROBERT CORNELIS, (first) BARON NAPIER OF MAGDALA,** Dec. 6, 1810 (Colombo, Ceylon, now Sri Lanka)–Jan. 14, 1890. British field marshal, administrator. Engaged in Sikh Wars, 1845–49; commanded military expeditions to Abyssinia and China; commander in chief in India, 1870–76; gov. of Gibraltar, 1876–82. Knighted, 1858; created baron, 1868.

**NELSON, HORATIO, VISCOUNT,** Sept. 29, 1758 (Burnham Thorpe, Norfolk, Eng.)–Oct. 21, 1805. British naval commander. Served in wars with Revolutionary and Napoleonic France; defeated French in Battle of the Nile, 1798; attacked Copenhagen, 1801; killed during the Battle of Trafalgar, in which the French fleet was destroyed; his long romance with Emma, Lady Hamilton caused scandal; knighted 1797; created baron, 1798; viscount, 1801.

**NEY, MICHEL, DUC D'ELCHINGEN, PRINCE DE LA MOSKOWA,** Jan. 10, 1769 (Sarrelouis, Fr.)–Dec. 7, 1815. French marshal. The most famous of NAPOLEON's marshals, he served with Napoleon in Switzerland, Austria, Germany, Spain, and Russia; helped induce Napoleon to abdicate, 1814; rejoined Napoleon after his return from Elba, and shared in defeat at Waterloo, 1815; executed for treason by the Bourbon regime, 1815.

**PAULUS, FRIEDRICH,** Sept. 23, 1890 (Breitenau, Ger.)–Feb. 1, 1957. German field marshal. Commanded 6th Army on the Eastern Front, 1942–1943; surrounded by Russians at Stalingrad, surrendered, 1943.

**PÉTAIN, HENRI PHILIPPE,** Apr. 24, 1856 (Cauchy-à-la-Tour, Fr.)–July 23, 1951. French marshal, chief of state. His defense of Verdun made him a national hero, 1916; as French premier in 1940, negotiated armistice with Germany; headed Vichy government of unoccupied France until 1944; imprisoned for life as a collaborator after the war.

**PLUMER, HERBERT CHARLES, (first) VISCOUNT PLUMER,** Mar. 13, 1857 (Torquay, Eng.) –July 16, 1932. British field marshal. Led successful offensive on Messines Ridge, 1917; gov. of Malta, 1919–25; high commissioner for Palestine, 1925–28; the model for cartoonist David Low's "Colonel Blimp"; knighted 1906; created viscount, 1929.

**PULASKI, COUNT CASIMIR,** Mar. 4, 1747. (Winiary, Mazovia, Pol.)–Oct. 11, 1779. Polish cavalry general in the American Revolution. Aide to Gen. GEORGE WASHINGTON at Brandywine and Valley Forge, 1777–78; mortally wounded leading a cavalry charge near Savannah, Ga., 1779.

**RADETZKY, JOSEPH WENZEL, COUNT RADETZKY VON RADETZ,** Nov. 2, 1766 (Trebnice, Bohemia, now Czech.)–Jan. 5, 1858. Austrian field marshal, national hero. Engaged in Turkish and French Revolutionary wars; helped plan Allied Leipzig campaign, 1813; invaded France, 1814; put down Italian revolt, 1848–49.

**RAEDER, ERICH,** Apr. 24, 1876 (Wandsbek, Ger.) –Nov. 6, 1960. German admiral. Naval commander in chief, 1928–43. In the 1930s, advocated construction of submarines and fast cruisers in contravention of Versailles Treaty; planned and executed invasion of Denmark and Norway, 1940.

**RAGLAN, FITZROY JAMES HENRY SOMERSET, (first) BARON RAGLAN,** Sept. 30, 1788 (Badminton, Eng.)–June 28, 1855. British field marshal. As commander in chief of British forces during the Crimean War (1853–55), criticized for his uninspired leadership; his ambiguous order at Battle of Balaklava led to the disastrous "Charge of the Light Brigade," 1854; his improvisation with slit potato sacks to provide uniforms for his troops gave rise to a sleeve that follows the natural contours of the shoulder—the raglan sleeve; created baron, 1852.

**RAMSAY, SIR BERTRAM HOME,** Jan. 20, 1883 (Hampton, Eng.)–Jan. 2, 1945. British admiral. Directed Dunkirk evacuation, 1940; planned invasion of N. Africa, 1942; led British naval task force in assault on Sicily, 1943; Allied naval commander in chief for Normandy invasion, 1944; knighted, 1940.

**RICHTHOFEN, MANFRED VON** ("The Red Baron"; "The Red Knight"), May 2, 1892 (Breslau, Ger., now Wroclaw, Pol.)–Apr. 21, 1918. German aviator, national hero. As WW I fighter ace, shot down 80 enemy aircraft; killed in action, 1918.

**ROCHAMBEAU, JEAN BAPTISTE DONATIEN DE VIMEUR, COMTE DE,** July 1, 1725 (Vendôme, Fr.)–May 10, 1807. French marshal. In American Revolution commanded French forces that helped defeat the British at Yorktown, 1781.

**RÖHM, ERNST,** Nov. 28, 1887 (Munich, Ger.) –June 30, 1934. German officer, Nazi leader. Headed ADOLF HITLER's storm troops, the SA or "Brownshirts"; murdered on Hitler's orders, 1934.

**ROKOSSOVSKI, KONSTANTIN,** Dec. 21, 1896

(Warsaw, Pol.)–Aug. 3, 1968. Soviet marshal. Commanded victorious forces at Stalingrad, 1942–43; led Russian armies through Poland, 1944–45.

**ROMMEL, ERWIN,** ("The Desert Fox"), Nov. 15, 1891 (Heidenheim, Ger.)–Oct. 14, 1944. German field marshal. Led Afrika Korps to numerous victories, 1941–42; defeated by MONTGOMERY at El Alamein, 1942; ordered to take poison to avoid public trial when suspected of being in contact with anti-Hitler conspirators, 1944.

**RUNDSTEDT, GERD VON,** Dec. 12, 1875. (Aschersleben, Ger.)–Feb. 24, 1953. German field marshal. Led forces in Poland (1939), France (1940), and USSR (1941); directed Battle of the Bulge, 1944.

**SAMSONOV, ALEKSANDR,** 1859?–Aug 29, 1914. Russian WW I general who was defeated at Tannenberg, 1914.

**SCHLIEFFEN, ALFRED, GRAF VON,** Feb. 28, 1833 (Berlin, Ger.)–Jan. 4, 1913. German field marshal. As chief of general staff (1891–1905), developed the Schlieffen Plan, used, with modifications, in invasion of Belgium and France at the outbreak of WW I.

**SCIPIO AFRICANUS, PUBLIUS CORNELIUS,** 236 B.C. (Rome, It.)–183 B.C. Roman soldier. Commanded the Roman invasion of Carthage; his successes necessitated the recall of HANNIBAL, whom he defeated in the Battle of Zama (202), ending the Second Punic War.

**SLIM, WILLIAM JOSEPH, (first) VISCOUNT SLIM,** Aug. 6, 1891 (Bristol, Glos., Eng.)–Dec. 14, 1970. British field marshal. Repelled Japanese invasion of India, 1944; defeated Japanese in Burma, 1945; chief Imp. Gen. Staff, 1948–52; gov.-gen. of Australia, 1953–60; knighted, 1944, created viscount; 1960. *Defeat into Victory,* 1950.

**SPEE, MAXIMILIAN, GRAF (Count) VON,** June 22, 1861 (Copenhagen, Den.)–Dec. 8, 1914. German admiral. Commanded German forces in battles of Coronel, and the Falkland Islands, 1914, where flagship *Scharnhorst* was sunk with all hands.

**STEUBEN, FRIEDRICH, BARON,** Sept. 17, 1730 (Magdeburg, Prussia)–Nov. 28, 1794. German-born American Revolutionary general who trained Continental Army troops; wrote *The Regulations for the Order and Discipline of the Troops of the United States,* used until 1812.

**SUVOROV, ALEKSANDR; GRAF (Count) SUVOROV RIMNIKSY, KNYAZ (Prince) ITOLSKY, REICHSGRAF (Imperial Count),** Nov. 29, 1729 (Moscow, Rus.)–May 18, 1800. Russian field marshal. Noted for his achievements during the Russo-Turkish War, 1787–91, and in the French Revolutionary wars, 1798–99; created count 1789, prince and reichsgrat, 1799.

**TEDDER, ARTHUR WILLIAM, (first) BARON TEDDER,** July 11, 1890 (Glenguin, Sterling, Scot.) –June 3, 1967. British air marshal. Contributed to German defeat in N. Africa 1942–43; played key role in successful Allied landings in Sicily (1943), Italy (1943), and Normandy (1944); knighted, 1942; created baron, 1946. *With Prejudice,* 1966.

**THEMISTOCLES,** c.524 B.C? (Athens. Gr.)–c.460 B.C. Athenian politician and naval strategist. Enlarged Athenian fleet; induced Sparta and other Peloponnesian communities to adopt his naval strategy; responsible for Greek victory over King XERXES I's Persian fleet off Salamis, 480 B.C.

**TIMOSHENKO, SEMYON,** Feb. 18, 1895 (Furmank, Ukrainian SSR)–Mar. 31, 1970. Soviet marshal. Served in Russo-Finnish war, 1939–40; named marshal, 1940; failed to halt the German advance into the Crimea and toward Stalingrad, 1942.

**TIRPITZ, ALFRED VON,** Mar. 19, 1849 (Kustrin, Prussia, now Kostrzyn, Pol.)–Mar. 6, 1930. German admiral. Naval secy., 1897–1916; created formidable High Seas Fleet; enobled, 1900.

**TOGO, COUNT HEIHACHIRO,** Jan. 27, 1848 (Satsuma, now Kagoshima Pref., Jap.)–May 30, 1934. Japanese admiral. Won naval victories in Russo-Japanese war; blockaded Port Arthur for 10 mos., forcing its surrender, 1905; destroyed Russian fleet in the Tsushima Strait, ending the war, 1905.

**TORSTENSON, COUNT LENNART,** Aug. 17, 1603 (Forstena, Swe.)–Apr. 7, 1651. Swedish field marshal. Called the "Father of Field Artillery," he won important victories in the Thirty Years' War (1618–48), and Sweden's war against Denmark (1643–45); created count, 1647.

**TRENCHARD (of Wolfeton), HUGH MONTAGUE, (first) VISCOUNT TRENCHARD,** Feb. 3, 1873 (Taunton, Somerset, Eng.)–Feb. 10, 1956. British air marshal. The principal organizer of the Royal Air Force, 1918; comm. London Metro. Police, 1931–35; knighted 1918, created baronet, 1919, baron, 1930, viscount, 1936.

**TURENNE, HENRI DE LA TOUR D'AUVERGNE, VICOMTE DE,** Sept. 11, 1611 (Sedan, Fr.)–July 27, 1675. French marshal. Distinguished himself in the Thirty Years' War (1618–48), the civil war of the Fronde (1648–53), the Franco-Spanish war (1650s), and the Third Dutch War (1672–78); killed in action.

**VAUBAN, SEBASTIEN LE PRESTRE DE,** May 15, 1633 (St. Leger de Foucherest, now St.-Léger-Vauban, Fr.)–Mar. 30, 1707. French military engineer and theorist. Revolutionized the art of defensive fortifications.

**VILLA, FRANCISCO** ("Pancho Villa"), born Doroteo Arango, June 5, 1878 (Hacienda de Río Grande, San Juan del Rio, Mex.)–June 20, 1923. Mexican guerrilla leader, revolutionary. Joined Madero uprising against DIAZ; executed 16 Americans in Mexico, attacked Columbus, N.M., provoking the U.S. government to send a military expedition under PERSHING in an unsuccessful attempt to arrest him, 1916.

**VOROSHILOV, KLIMENT,** Feb. 4, 1881 (Verkhneye, Ukraine)–Dec. 2, 1969. Soviet Army marshal, political leader. Fought in the Russian civil war, Winter War with Finland (1939–40), and WW II; a leader in an unsuccessful attempt to oust KHRUSHCHEV, 1957; pres. of the USSR, 1953–60.

**WALLENSTEIN, ALBRECHT WENZEL VON, DUKE OF FRIEDLAND AND MECKLENBURG,**

PRINCE OF SAGAN, Sept. 24, 1583 (Hermanice [now in Czech.])–Feb. 25, 1634. Austrian general. Loyalty to Holy Roman Emperor Ferdinand II during the Bohemian rebellion (1618–23) led to high appointments; generalissimo during the Thirty Years War, 1625–30 and 1632–34; defeated by GUSTAVUS ADOLPHUS at Lützen, 1632; his ambition for power brought charges of treason; murdered.

WAVELL, ARCHIBALD PERCIVAL, (first) EARL WAVELL, May 5, 1883 (Colchester, Eng.)–May 24, 1950. British field marshal. Commander in chief for Middle East armies in N. Africa and E. Africa, 1940–41; as commander in chief in S.E. Asia, lost Malaya, Singapore, and Burma, 1941–43; viceroy of India, 1943–47; knighted, 1939, created viscount, 1943, earl, 1947. Generals and Generalship, 1941.

WELLINGTON, ARTHUR WELLESLEY, (first) DUKE OF, May 1, 1769 (Dublin, Ire.)–Sept. 14, 1852. British marshal, politician. Successful in Peninsular War against the French, 1808–14; defeated NAPOLEON at Waterloo, 1815; British prime minister, 1828–30; worked for Catholic Emancipation; knighted 1804, created viscount Wellington, 1809; Marquess, 1812, Duke, 1813.

WINGATE, ORDE CHARLES, Feb. 26, 1903 (Naini Tal, India)–Mar. 24, 1944. British general. Led "Chindits," or "Wingate's Raiders," against Japanese Army in northern Burma during WW II.

WOLFE, JAMES, Jan. 2, 1727 (Westerham, Kent, Eng.)–Sept. 13, 1759. British general. Commanded army at capture of Quebec from French, the victory that led to British supremacy of Canada, 1759; killed in action.

WRANGEL, BARON PETER, Aug. 27, 1878 (Novo-Aleksandrovsk, Lith.)–Apr. 25, 1928. Russian general. Led White (counter-revolutionary) forces, 1920.

YAMAGATA, ARITOMO, April 22, 1838 (Hagi, Choshu, Jap.)–Feb. 1, 1922. Japanese general and statesman. Played a major role in Japan's emergence as a military power at the beginning of the 20th century; prime min. 1889–91, 1898–1900; chief of staff, 1904–05.

YAMAMOTO, ISOROKU, Apr. 4, 1884 (Nagaoka, Jap.)–Apr. 18, 1943. Japanese admiral. Planned and led attack on Pearl Harbor, 1941; planned attack on Midway, 1942; killed in aircrash.

YAMASHITA, TOMOYUKI, Nov. 8, 1885 (Kochi Pref., Jap.)–Feb. 23, 1946. Japanese general. Conquered Malaya and Singapore, 1941–42; hanged as a war criminal, 1946.

ZHUKOV, GEORGI, Dec. 1, 1896 (Kaluga Province, Rus.)–June 18, 1974. Soviet marshal, political figure. Directed defense of Moscow, 1941; made marshal, 1943, commanded final assault on Berlin, 1945; minister of defense, 1955–57; the first military figure to become a member of the Presidium, 1957.

# Social Reformers

**ABBOTT, GRACE,** Nov. 17, 1878 (Grand I., Neb.)–June 19, 1939. U.S. social worker, public administrator. Attacked exploitation of immigrants in newspaper articles and books; as dir. of U.S. Children's Bureau (1921–34), worked for a constitutional amendment aagainst child labor; a close assoc. of JANE ADDAMS. *The Immigrant and the Community,* 1917; *The Child and the State,* 2 vols., 1938.

**ABEL, I(orwith) W(ilbur),** Aug. 11, 1908 (Magnolia, Ohio)–Aug. 10, 1987. U.S. labor leader. A leading union organizer of the steel industry. Staff member of Steel Workers Organizing Com. (later, United Steel Workers of America), 1937–42; dist. dir., 1942–52; secy.-treasurer, 1953–65; pres., 1965–77; elected vice-pres. of AFL-CIO, 1965.

**ABERNATHY, RALPH,** Mar. 11, 1926 (Linden, Ala.)–Apr. 17, 1990. U.S. civil-rights leader, clergyman. A deputy of MARTIN LUTHER KING, JR., in the Southern Christian Leadership Conference, of which he became pres. after King's assassination, 1968–77. With King, organized Montgomery Improvement Assn. (1955), initiated Montgomery bus boycott (1955), and organized the SCLC (1957). *And the Walls Came Tumbling Down,* 1989.

**ADDAMS, JANE,** Sept. 6, 1860 (Cedarville, Ill.)–May 21, 1935. U.S. social reformer, social worker. With Ellen Gates Starr, founded Hull House, in Chicago, one of the first social settlements in N. America, 1889; active in the pacifist and woman-suffrage movements; worked for social reforms, including the first juvenile-court law, factory inspection, and workmen's compensation. Awarded Nobel Peace Prize (with N. M. BUTLER), 1931, named to Hall of Fame for Great Americans, 1965. *The Spirit of Youth and the City Streets,* 1909; *Twenty Years at Hull House,* 1910.

**ALINSKY, SAUL,** Jan. 30, 1909 (Chicago, Ill.)–June 12, 1972. U.S. social activist. A self-termed "professional radical" who organized poor communities to use picketing, sitdowns, strikes, and boycotts to exert pressure on the business establishment, landlords, and local political machines. *John L. Lewis, A Biography,* 1949; *The Professional Radical* (with Marion K. Sanders), 1970; *Rules for Radicals,* 1971.

**ANTHONY, SUSAN B.,** Feb. 15, 1820 (Adams, Mass.)–Mar. 13, 1906. U.S. social reformer and pioneer crusader for woman suffrage. Pres. of Natl. Woman Suffrage Assn., 1892–1900; organized Internatl. Council of Women (1888) and Internatl. Woman Suffrage Alliance (1904); with E. STANTON, secured first laws in New York State guaranteeing women rights over their children and control of property and wages; named to Hall of Fame for Great Americans, 1950. *The History of Woman Suffrage* (with Stanton and M. J. Gage), 3 vols., 1881–86.

**BADEN-POWELL** (of Gilwell), **ROBERT STEPHENSON SMYTH BADEN-POWELL, BARON,** Feb. 22, 1857 (London, Eng.)–Jan. 8, 1941. English founder of the Boy Scouts, 1907; with sister Agnes, founded Girl Guides, 1910 (in U.S. called Girl Scouts, from 1912); founded Wolf Cubs, 1916 (in U.S. called Cub Scouts, from 1916). National hero for his part in defense of Mafeking 1899–1900 in the Boer War; created baronet, 1922; baron, 1929. *Scouting for Boys,* 1908; *Scouting and Youth Movements,* 1929.

**BALCH, EMILY GREENE,** Jan. 8, 1867 (Jamaica Plain [now Boston], Mass.)–Jan. 9, 1961. U.S. economist, social scientist, pacifist. Prof. of economics and sociology at Wellesley C., 1896–1918; a founder and internatl. secy. of Women's Internatl. League for Peace and Freedom, 1919–22, 1934–35, helped found Boston's Denison House Settlement, Women's Trade Union League; awarded Nobel Peace Prize (with J. MOTT), 1946. *Public Assistance of the Poor in France,* 1893; *Toward Human Unity,* 1952.

**BALDWIN, ROGER N.,** Jan. 21, 1884 (Wellesley, Mass.)–Aug. 26, 1981. U.S. lawyer, reformer. Dir. of American Civil Liberties Union, 1920–50; ACLU natl. chm., 1950–55. *Liberty under the Soviets,* 1928.

**BARTON, CLARA,** Dec. 25, 1821 (Oxford, Mass.)

–Apr. 12, 1912. U.S. humanitarian, founder of the American Red Cross. Called "Angel of the Battlefield" during Civil War for establishing a service of supplies for soldiers in army camps and on the battlefield; worked for U.S. signing of the Geneva Agreement for care of war wounded, 1882; founded American Red Cross and served as its pres., 1881–1904. *History of the Red Cross*, 1882; *The Red Cross in Peace and War*, 1899.

BEARD, DAN(iel), June 21, 1850 (Cincinnati, Ohio) –June 11, 1941. U.S. illustrator, naturalist. A founder of the Boy Scouts in America (1910), he served as national scout commissioner until his death. Illustrated many books, including the first edition of M. TWAIN's *A Connecticut Yankee at King Arthur's Court* (1889). *The America Boys' Handy Book*, 1882; *American Boys' Book of Wild Animals*, 1921.

BEECHER, HENRY WARD, June 24, 1813 (Litchfield, Conn.)–Mar. 8, 1887. U.S. Congregational clergyman, abolitionist. Famed as orator and leader in the antislavery movement; an advocate of woman suffrage; sued for adultery by Theodore Tilton (1874), exonerated by two church tribunals, but civil trial ended in jury disagreement. *Seven Lectures to Young Men*, 1844; *Evolution and Religion*, 1885. (Son of L. BEECHER; brother of H. B. STOWE and C. E. BEECHER.)

BEECHER, LYMAN, Oct. 12, 1775 (New Haven, Conn.)–Jan. 10, 1863. U.S. Presbyterian clergyman. Influential abolitionist and anti-Roman Catholic theologian; pres. of Lane Theological Seminary of Cincinnati, 1832–50. (Father of C. E. BEECHER, H. B. STOWE, and H. W. BEECHER among others.)

BISSELL, EMILY PERKINS, May 31, 1861 (Wilmington, Del.)–Mar. 8, 1948. U.S. welfare worker. Headed the first Christmas seal drive (to aid tubercular children) in the U.S., designing, printing and selling the seals, 1907.

BLACK, JAMES, Sept. 23, 1823 (Lewisburg, Pa.)–Dec. 16, 1893. U.S. temperance advocate. The first Natl. Prohibition Party presidential candidate, winning over 5,000 votes, 1872; owned world's largest collection of temperance literature, now in New York Public Library. *The Necessity for the Prohibition Party*, 1876; *The History of the National Prohibition Party*, 1893.

BLACKWELL, ANTOINETTE BROWN, May 20, 1825 (Henrietta, N.Y.)–Nov. 5, 1921. U.S. clergywoman. First ordained woman min. in the U.S. (Congregational; later, Unitarian), 1853. One of first U.S. women to receive a college education; active feminist, abolitionist, temperance advocate. *The Sexes Throughout Nature*, 1875. (Sister-in-law of H. B. BLACKWELL and E. BLACKWELL.)

BLACKWELL, HENRY BROWNE, May 4, 1825 (Bristol, Eng.)–Sept. 7, 1909. U.S. social reformer. Distinguished activist in the woman-suffrage movement; with wife LUCY STONE, helped organize American Woman Suffrage Assn.; 1869; campaigned for suffrage in over 25 states; editor of *Woman's Journal*, 1870–1909. (Brother of E. BLACKWELL; brother-in-law of A. L. BLACKWELL.)

BLANC, (Jean Joseph Charles) LOUIS, Oct. 29, 1811 (Madrid, Sp.)–Dec. 6, 1882. French utopian socialist. Considered the founder of state socialism; founded *Revue de Progrès* (1839), in which he published his seminal work, "The Organization of Labor" (1839); influential in the "banquet" campaign for political reform, 1847; member of provisional govt. of the Second Republic, following 1848 Revolution; after defeat of workers' revolt, lived in exile in England, 1848–70.

BLOOMER, AMELIA, May 27, 1818 (Homer, N.Y.)–Dec. 30, 1894. U.S. social reformer. Campaigned for temperance and women's rights; published biweekly paper, *The Lily*, 1849–54; recommended and adopted full trousers (introduced by Elizabeth Smith Miller) that became known as "bloomers."

BOOTH, BALLINGTON, July 28, 1859 (Brighouse, Eng.)–Oct. 5, 1940. British-U.S. reformer. Son of WILLIAM BOOTH, founder of the Salvation Army; following rift with his father, founded a similar body, the Volunteers of America, 1896. (Brother of E. C. BOOTH.)

BOOTH, EVANGELINE CORY, Dec. 25, 1865 (London, Eng.)–July 17, 1950. English social reformer. The daughter of W. BOOTH, founder of the Salvation Army; was a leader in the movement's work in England; credited with winning repeal of bylaws forbidding open-air preaching; commander of U.S.S.A., 1904–34; elected gen. of international org., 1934. *The War Romance with the Salvation Army* (with G. L. Hill), 1919. (Sister of B. BOOTH.)

BOOTH, WILLIAM, Apr. 10, 1829 (Nottingham, Notts., Eng.)–Aug. 20, 1912. English social reformer. Founder (1878) and first gen. of the Salvation Army; an ordained minister of the Methodist New Connexion (1852), resigned (1861) to become an itinerant evangelist; with wife, founded mission (1865) that became S.A. *In Darkest England and the Way Out* (with W. T. Stead), 1890. (Father of E. C. and B. BOOTH.)

BRECKINRIDGE, SOPHONISBA PRESTON, Apr. 1, 1866 (Lexington, Ky.)–July 30, 1948. U.S. social reformer, social worker, educator. Prominent activist for woman suffrage, child welfare, prison reform, labor legislation, internatl. peace; taught at the Chicago School of Civics and Philanthropy, 1907. *Marriage and the Civic Rights of Women: Separate Domicile and Independent Citizenship*, 1931; *Women in the Twentieth Century: A Study of their Political, Social and Economic Activities*, 1933.

BRENT, MARGARET, c.1600 (Gloucestershire, Eng.)–c.1671. American colonial landowner and administrator. The first woman lawyer in the colonies and probably the first feminist. Through family connections, received the first land grant ever vested in a woman; through other acquisitions, became one of the largest landowners in the colonies, earning title of Lord, right to conduct business and sign contracts; acted as attorney for friends and neighbors.

**BROWN, JOHN,** May 9, 1800 (Torrington, Conn.)–Dec. 2, 1859. U.S. abolitionist. With 21 followers, raided federal arsenal at Harper's Ferry, Va., 1859; captured and tried for treason; his dignity and high moral tone in court won Northern sympathy; when convicted and hanged, became martyr to the anti-slavery cause.

**BROWNMILLER, SUSAN,** Feb. 15, 1935 (New York, N.Y.). U.S. feminist. Noted as the author of *Against Our Will: Men, Women and Rape* (1975), a comprehensive study of rape, also *Femininity*, (1984).

**CARMICHAEL, STOKELY,** June 29, 1941 (Port-of-Spain, Trinidad). U.S. black militant. As chm. of Student Nonviolent Coordinating Com. (1966), responsible for the controversial Black Power concept; resigned (1967) to become prime min. of the Black Panther Party; resigned and moved to Guinea, 1969. *Black Power* (with Charles V. Hamilton), 1967. (Husband of M. MAKEBA.)

**CATT, CARRIE CHAPMAN,** Jan. 9, 1859 (Ripon, Wisc.)–Mar. 9, 1947. U.S. women's-rights leader. A leader in the campaign for woman suffrage for more than 25 years, culminating in adoption of 19th Amendment (1920); reorganized Natl. Woman Suffrage Assn. (1905–15), and served as its pres. (1915–47), later transformed it into the League of Women Voters; also founded the Internatl. Woman Suffrage Alliance (1902) and Com. on the Cause and Cure of War (1925). *Woman Suffrage and Politics, the Inner Study of the Suffrage Movement,* (with N. R. Shuler), 1923.

**CHAVEZ, CESAR,** Mar. 31, 1927 (Yuma, Ariz.). U.S. labor-union organizer. Founder and first pres. of United Farm Workers, AFL-CIO, the first viable agricultural union in the U.S.; used nonviolent tactics, including fasts, marches, long-term strikes, and boycotts.

**COXEY, JACOB S.,** Apr. 16, 1854 (Selinsgrove, Pa.)–May 18, 1951. U.S. reformer. Leader of the famous 1894 march of the unemployed on Washington, D.C., from Massillon, Ohio; remained one of the nation's most colorful personalities, perennially a candidate for offices ranging from mayor to U.S. pres.; only elective office held was as mayor of Massillon, Ohio, 1931–33.

**DAVIS, ANGELA,** Jan. 26, 1944 (Birmingham, Ala.). U.S. black militant, communist activist. Acting prof. of philosophy at U. of California at Los Angeles; acquitted on charges of kidnapping, murder, and conspiracy in connection with the 1970 shootout at Marin Co. (Calif.) courthouse, 1972.

**DAY, DOROTHY,** Nov. 8, 1897 (New York, N.Y.). U.S. reformer. A founder (with Peter Maurin) and head of the pacifist Catholic Worker movement, 1933; publisher of *Catholic Worker,* 1933– ; jailed numerous times in the 1950s for protests against preparations for nuclear war. *From Union Square to Rome,* 1938; *House of Hospitality,* 1939; *The Long Loneliness,* 1952.

**DEBS, EUGENE V.,** Nov. 5, 1855 (Terre Haute, Ind.)–Oct. 20, 1926. U.S. socialist leader, labor organizer. First pres. of the American Railway Un-ion, which gained natl. fame with its successful strike against the Great Northern RR (1894), and participated in the Pullman strike (1894); as Socialist party presidential candidate five times (1900–20), received his highest popular vote in 1920, while imprisoned for criticizing the govt. "Unionism and Socialism," 1904; *Walls and Bars,* 1927.

**DIX, DOROTHEA L.,** Apr. 4, 1802 (Hampden, Me.)–July 17, 1887. U.S. social reformer. Pioneer in the movement for specialized treatment of the insane; her crusades resulted in the establishment of state hospitals for the insane in more than 15 states and Canada.

**DOUGLASS, FREDERICK** (born Frederick Augustus Washington Bailey), Feb. 7, 1817 (Tuckahoe, Md.)–Feb. 20, 1895. U.S. abolitionist, orator, journalist. Born into slavery, escaped to Massachusetts (1838) where he joined Massachusetts Anti-Slavery Society; British admirers bought his freedom and raised money for him to start an abolitionist weekly, *North Star* (1847); aided in recruiting black troops for the Union Army. *Narrative of the Life of Frederick Douglass,* 1845.

**DUBINSKY, DAVID,** Feb. 22, 1892 (Brest-Litovsk, Pol.)–Sept. 17, 1982. U.S. labor leader. Pres. of Internatl. Ladies Garment Workers' Union, 1932–66; a founder of the Labor party in New York State, 1936; resigned party when it came under communist influence; helped organize Liberal party, 1942; awarded Presidential Medal of Freedom, 1969.

**DUBOIS, W(illiam) E(dward) B(urghardt),** Feb. 23, 1868 (Great Barrington, Mass.)–Aug. 27, 1963. U.S. civil-rights leader, author. Advocate of civil, political, and economic equality; a founder of the Natl. Negro Com., later the Natl. Assn. for the Advancement of Colored People, 1909; editor of *Crisis,* NAACP magazine, 1910–32; prof. of economics and history at Atlanta U., 1897–1910 and 1932–44; joined Communist party (1961), moved to Ghana and renounced U.S. citizenship. *The Souls of Black Folk,* 1903.

**ENGELS, FRIEDRICH,** Nov. 28, 1820 (Barmen, Prussia, Ger.)–Aug. 5, 1895. German philosopher, businessman. Cofounder (with K. MARX), of modern communism; with Marx, wrote *The Communist Manifesto* (1848); played a leading role in the First and Second Internatls. *The Condition of the Working Class in England in 1844,* 1845; *The Origin of the Family, Private Property and the State,* 1884.

**EVERS, JAMES C.,** Sept. 11, 1922 (Decatur, Miss.). U.S. political, civil-rights leader. Led a biracial coalition that unseated an all-white Mississippi delegation at the 1968 Democratic National Convention; first black to run for gov. of Mississippi, 1971; mayor of Fayette, Miss., 1969– .

**FARMER, JAMES L.,** Jan. 12, 1920 (Marshall, Tex.). U.S. civil-rights activist, union organizer, lecturer. Helped found (1942) Congress of Racial Equality, which he served as natl. dir. (1961–66); leader of 1961 Freedom Ride; U.S. asst. secy. of HEW, 1969–70 and 1972–75. *Freedom—When?,* 1965.

FLANAGAN, EDWARD J., July 13, 1886 (Roscommon, Ire.)–May 15, 1948. U.S. Roman Catholic priest. Founder of Boys Town, 1922; attempted to develop character in the boys by supplementing vocational training with religious and social education.

FLYNN, ELIZABETH GURLEY, Aug. 7, 1890 (Concord. N.H.)–Sept. 5, 1964. U.S. communist leader. Took part in the bitter textile strikes at Lawrence, Mass. (1912), and Paterson, N.J. (1913); joined U.S. Communist party in 1937; became chairperson of the party's National Com. in 1961, the first woman to hold that post; a founder and board member of the American Civil Liberties Union, expelled (1940) for being a communist. *I Speak My Own Piece*, 1955.

FOSTER, WILLIAM ZEBULON, Feb. 25, 1881 (Taunton, Mass.)–Sept. 1, 1961. U.S. political leader. U.S. communist leader; took part in organizing steelworkers for the strike of 1919; U.S. Communist party presidential candidate in 1924, 1928, and 1932. *Towards Soviet America, From Bryan to Stalin*, 1937.

FOURIER, (François Marie) CHARLES, Apr. 7, 1772 (Besançon, Fr.)–Oct. 10, 1837. French social theorist. Propounded a type of utopian socialism in which agrarian society would be reorganized into communal groups of producers known as *phalanges* (phalanxes); failed to produce any such assns. himself, although his followers attempted to do so in the U.S. at Brook Farm (1841–46) and NA Phalanx, Red Bank, N.J.

FRIEDAN, BETTY, Feb. 4, 1921 (Peoria, Ill.). U.S. feminist, writer. As author of *The Feminine Mystique* (1963), helped revive the feminist movement in the U.S.; a founder and pres. of Natl. Org. for Women, 1966–70. *It Changed My Life: Writings on the Women's Movement*, 1976; *The Second Stage*, 1981.

FULLER, SARAH MARGARET, MARCHESA OSSOLI, May 23, 1810 (Cambridgeport, Mass.) –July 19, 1850. U.S. journalist, writer, educator. Often called the first professional U.S. newspaper woman; an advocate of women's rights; leader in classes of "conversations" for women on various topics; editor of *Dial*, 1840–42; literary critic with the *New York Herald-Tribune*, 1844–46; covered Italy (from 1848–49), becoming first U.S. woman foreign correspondent; married Marchese Angelo Ossoli, with whom she took part in Italian Revolution of 1848. *Woman in the Nineteenth Century*, 1845. (Great-aunt of B. FULLER.)

GARDNER, JOHN W., Oct. 8, 1912 (Los Angeles, Calif.). U.S. psychologist, educator, public official. Founder and chm. of Common Cause, a nonpartisan citizen's lobby, 1970–77. Pres. of Carnegie Fndn. for the Advancement of Teaching, 1955–56; U.S. secy. of HEW, 1965–68; chm. of Urban Coalition, 1968–70.

GARRISON, WILLIAM LLOYD, Dec. 12, 1805 (Newburyport, Mass.)–May 24, 1879. U.S. journalist. Abolitionist leader who published *The Liberator* (1831–65), in which he advocated his uncompromising opposition to slavery; active in organizing the New England Anti-Slavery Soc., 1832; believed that moral persuasion, rather than force or the ballot, was the method needed to achieve abolition; also campaigned for woman suffrage and Prohibition.

GARVEY, MARCUS, Aug. 17, 1887 (St. Ann's Bay, Jamaica)–June 10, 1940. U.S. black nationalist leader. Advocated separatism and racial pride; promoted a "Back to Africa" movement; established the Universal Negro Improvement Assn., 1914; editor of *Negro World*, 1918–23.

GELDORF, BOB, Oct. 5, 1953? (Dublin, Ire.). Irish musician, activist. Member of the Dublin-based rock group The Boomtown Rats who gained worldwide recognition for organizing the 1985 transAtlantic Live Aid concert to help starving people in Africa.

GEORGE, HENRY, Sept. 2, 1839 (Philadelphia, Pa.)–Oct. 29, 1897. U.S. economist, journalist. Famed as the proponent of a single tax. Shocked by the inequalities of wealth in New York, he attempted to find a fair means of redistribution; enjoyed such immense popularity that he nearly won the 1886 New York City mayoral election; his *Poverty and Progress* (1879) greatly increased interest in economics. (Grandfather of A. DEMILLE.)

GOMPERS, SAMUEL, Jan. 27, 1850 (London, Eng.)–Dec. 13, 1924. U.S. labor leader. A founder and the first pres. of the AFL, 1886–1924; stressed business unionism, written contracts, craft autonomy, and voluntarism; marshalled labor support for WW I.

GRIMKÉ, ANGELINA EMILY, Feb. 20, 1805 (Charleston, S.C.)–Oct. 26, 1879; and her sister SARAH MOORE GRIMKÉ, Nov. 26, 1792 (Charleston, S.C.)–Dec. 23, 1873. U.S. reformers, abolitionists. Worked in abolition movement, 1835–38; also lectured and wrote on behalf of women's rights.

GUESDE, JULES (pseud. of Mathieu Basile), Nov. 12, 1845 (Paris, Fr.)–July 28, 1922. French socialist. Leader of the Marxist wing of the French labor movement; founded *L'Égalité*, a Socialist weekly, 1877; member of the Chamber of Deputies, 1893–98 and 1906–22.

HAMER, FANNIE LOU, 1917 (Montgomery Co., Miss.)–Mar. 14, 1977. U.S. civil-rights leader. As a field worker and leader of Student Nonviolent Coordinating Com. (1962–77), helped found the black-led Mississippi Freedom Democratic party; spoke before the 1964 Democratic Convention.

HAYNES, GEORGE E., May 11, 1880 (Pine Bluff, Ark.)–Jan. 8, 1960. U.S. sociologist, civil-rights leader. Cofounder and first exec. dir. of Natl. Urban League, 1910–16; developed the Interracial Clinic, whose methods for dealing with racial tensions were put into effect in more than 30 U.S. cities; organized social science dept. of Fisk U., 1910–12; first black to receive a Ph.D. at Columbia U., 1912.

HILLMAN, BESSIE, May 15, 1889 (Grodno, Rus.)–Dec. 23, 1970. U.S. labor leader. A founder of the Amalgamated Clothing Workers of America, 1914;

v.p., 1946–70; for 20 years, the only female union leader in the clothing industry; led a strike against Hart, Schaffner, and Marx (Chicago), 1910. (Wife of S. HILLMAN.)
**HILLMAN, SIDNEY,** Mar. 23, 1887 (Zagare, Lith.) –July 10, 1946. U.S. labor leader. First pres. of Amalgamated Clothing Workers of America, 1914–46; a founder of the CIO; an advisor to Pres. F. D. ROOSEVELT, held several posts in New Deal orgs. (Husband of B. HILLMAN.)
**HOOKS, BENJAMIN L.,** 1925 (Memphis, Tenn.). U.S. civil rights leader. First black member of the Federal Communications Commission, 1972–79; exec. dir., NAACP, 1977– .
**HOWE, SAMUEL G.,** Nov. 10, 1801 (Boston, Mass.)–Jan. 9, 1876. U.S. humanitarian, physician, educator. First dir. of Perkins School for the Blind, 1832–76; a pioneer in printing books for the blind; established first U.S. school for the mentally retarded. (Husband of J. W. HOWE.)
**HUERTA, DOLORES,** April 10, 1930 (Dawson, N.M.). U.S. labor leader. With CESAR CHAVEZ, worked to unionize farm workers and to prevent takeover of the union by the Teamsters; vice-pres. of United Farm Workers, 1977– ; organized Community Service Org., 1955–62.
**JOHNSON, WILLIAM E.** ("Pussyfoot Johnson"), Mar. 25, 1862 (Coventry, N.Y.)–Feb. 2, 1945. U.S. reformer. A militant Prohibitionist; chief special officer of the Indian Service, 1908–11; known as "Pussyfoot" for his methods of pursuing lawbreakers in the Indian Ter.; managing editor for Anti-Saloon League publications, 1912–16; publicity dir. of league, 1916–18.
**JONES, MARY** ("Mother Jones"), May 1, 1830 (Cork, Ire.).–Nov. 30, 1930. U.S. labor leader. Gained fame as an agitator for Appalachian coal miners; led a children's march from Kensington, Pa., to Sagamore Hill, the N.Y. home of Pres. THEODORE ROOSEVELT, to dramatize the evils of child labor, 1903.
**JOUHAUX, LEON,** July 1, 1879 (Paris, Fr.)–Apr. 28, 1954. French socialist and labor leader. Secy.-gen. of Gen. Confederation of Labor, 1909–47; attempted an antimilitaristic pact with German labor leaders prior to WW I; a founder of the Internatl. Labor Org.; his split with the communist majority in his union (1947) is considered to have saved French labor unions from communism; awarded Nobel Peace Prize, 1951.
**KELLER, HELEN,** June 27, 1880 (Tuscumbia, Ala.) –June 1, 1968. U.S. educator, author. As a deaf and blind woman who graduated from college, became a public figure as an example of achievement in spite of handicaps; taught by ANNE SULLIVAN MACY, via manual alphabet pressed into her hand; traveled and spoke widely on behalf of the physically handicapped. *The Story of My Life,* 1903.
**KENNEDY, THOMAS,** Nov. 2, 1887 (Lansford, Pa.)–Jan. 19, 1963. U.S. labor leader. As a leader of the United Mine Workers of America (1925–63), led the fight to force the AFL to endorse Social

Security and government responsibility for unemployment.
**KING, CORETTA SCOTT,** Apr. 27, 1927 (Marion, Ala.). U.S. civil-rights leader, lecturer, writer, concert singer. The widow of MARTIN LUTHER KING, JR., she has continued his work for social justice; pres. of Martin Luther King, Jr., Center for Social Change; chairperson of Commission on Economic Justice for Women; cochairperson of Natl. Com. on Full Employment.
**KING, MARTIN LUTHER, JR.,** Jan. 15, 1929 (Atlanta, Ga.)–Apr. 4, 1968. U.S. civil-rights leader, clergyman. Leader of the U.S. civil-rights movement from mid-1950s until his death; led black boycott in Montgomery, Ala., against segregated city bus lines, 1955; advocated nonviolent resistance; organized Southern Christian Leadership Conference, 1957; organized massive civil-rights march on Washington, D.C., 1963; announced a "Poor People's Campaign," 1968; assassinated in Memphis, Tenn.; awarded Nobel Peace Prize, 1964. *Stride Toward Freedom* 1958; *Why We Can't Wait,* 1964.
**KIRKLAND, (Joseph) LANE,** Mar. 12, 1922 (Camden, S.C.). U.S. labor official. With AFL-CIO since 1961; pres.; 1979– .
**KRUPSKAYA, NADEZHDA,** Feb. 26, 1869 (St. Petersburg, Rus. [now Leningrad, USSR])–Feb. 27, 1939. Russian revolutionary, educator. Secy. of Bolshevik faction of the Social Democratic party, 1901–17; married V. I. LENIN, 1898, after whose death she exerted great influence in matters of education.
**KUHN, MARGARET** ("Maggie"), Aug. 3, 1905 (Buffalo, N.Y.). U.S. social worker. Organizer of the Gray Panthers, a group dedicated to improving conditions for senior citizens, 1970.
**LATHROP, JULIA,** June 29, 1858 (Rockford, Ill.)– Apr. 15, 1932. U.S. social worker. First chief of the U.S. Children's Bureau, 1912–21; surveyed the problem of infant mortality; worked for legal protection of children born out of wedlock.
**LEARY, TIMOTHY,** Oct. 22, 1920 (Springfield, Mass.). U.S. psychologist, educator, drug cult leader. A leader of the 1960s drug culture; an advocate of the ingestion of LSD; dismissed as prof. at Harvard U. for involving students in drug experiments. *Politics of Ecstasy,* 1968; *Flashbacks,* 1983.
**LEWIS, JOHN L.,** Feb. 12, 1880 (nr. Lucas, Ia.)– June 11, 1969. U.S. labor leader. As pres. of United Mine Workers of America (1920–60), built that union into one of the most powerful in the U.S.; successfully organized mass-production industries, but broke with the AFL to form the CIO, which he served as pres. (1936–40).
**MALCOLM X** (born Malcolm Little), May 19, 1925 (Omaha, Neb.)–Feb. 21, 1965. U.S. militant black leader. Spoke for racial pride and black nationalism in the early 1960s; joined Black Muslims and rose to a position of leadership; suspended (1964) for an inflammatory statement, he formed his own Org. for Afro-American Unity; assassinated. *The Autobiography of Malcolm X* (with ALEX HALEY), 1965.

MARX, KARL, May 5, 1818 (Trier, Ger.)–Mar. 14, 1883. German social philosopher. Chief theorist of modern socialism and communism; also a founder of economic history and sociology; spent the majority of his life studying in the British Museum (London), from 1849; joined the Communist League (1847) and with FRIEDRICH ENGELS wrote its *Communist Manifesto* (1848); after failure of the revolutions of 1848, worked for formation of revolutionary parties; helped found Internatl Workingmen's Assn., 1864. *Das Kapital*, 3 vols., 1867, 1885, and 1895.

MCBRIDE, F(rancis) SCOTT, July 29, 1872 (Carroll Co., Ohio)–Apr. 23, 1955. U.S. temperance leader. As gen. supt. of the Anti-Saloon League of America (1924–36), led the temperance forces in their fight to prevent repeal of the 18th Amendment.

MCNICHOLAS, JOHN T., Dec. 15, 1877 (Treenkeel, County Mayo, Ire.)–Apr. 22, 1950. U.S. Roman Catholic archbishop. Founder of the Natl. Legion of Decency (1934) to boycott motion pictures considered immoral or obscene; archbishop of Cincinnati, Ohio, 1925–50.

MEANY, GEORGE, Aug. 16, 1894 (New York, N.Y.)–Jan. 10, 1980. U.S. labor leader. Pres. of AFL-CIO, 1955–79. Helped reunify the U.S. labor movement by bringing together the AFL and CIO; led the fight after WW II to keep U.S. labor out of the Soviet-dominated World Federation of Trade Unions; has worked against labor corruption; awarded Presidential Medal of Freedom, 1964.

MILLETT, KATE (Katherine), Sept. 14, 1934 (St. Paul, Minn.). U.S. feminist, sculptor, teacher. Lectures and writes extensively on behalf of women's liberation. *Sexual Politics*, 1970; *Flying*, 1974; *Going to Iran*, 1982; *Loony-Bin Trip*, 1990.

MITCHELL, JOHN, Feb. 4, 1870 (Braidwood, Ill.)–Sept. 9, 1919. U.S. labor leader. Played a major role in the United Mine Workers' first successful national strike, 1897; as UMW pres. (1898–1908), organized a 1902 strike of anthracite miners that gained him greatest labor leader of his time; vice-pres. of American Federation of Labor, 1899–1914. *The Wage Earner and His Problems*, 1913.

MORRIS, ESTHER, Aug. 8, 1814 (Tioga Co., N.Y.)–Apr. 2, 1902. U.S. suffragist. Instrumental in winning the right for women to vote in Wyoming (1869), the first state to provide for women's suffrage in its constitution; as justice of the peace in South Pass City, Wyo., the first woman in the U.S. to hold the post, 1870; her statue stands in Statuary Hall of the U.S. Capitol.

MOTT, LUCRETIA, Jan. 3, 1793 (Nantucket, Mass.)–Nov. 11, 1880. U.S. abolitionist, feminist, Quaker minister. Refused recognition by the World Anti-Slavery Convention in London (1840), along with all other women delegates; lectured widely for the rights of women; with ELIZABETH CADY STANTON, a founder of the organized women's-rights movement in the U.S., at Seneca Falls, N.Y., 1848; made her home a sanctuary for runaway slaves.

MURRAY, PHILIP, May 25, 1886 (Blantyre, Lanark, Scot.)–Nov. 9, 1952. U.S. labor leader. As pres. of CIO (1940–52), led the expulsion of several communist-dominated unions, 1949–50; helped organize the steelworkers; pres. of United Steelworkers of America, 1942–52.

NATION, CARRY, Nov. 25, 1846 (Garrard Co., Ky.)–June 9, 1911. U.S. temperance advocate. Famed for entering saloons and wrecking them with a hatchet; lectured widely; supported woman suffrage; was an imposing figure at six ft. and 175 lbs.

OWEN, ROBERT, May 14, 1771 (Newtown, Montgomeryshire, Wales)–Nov. 17, 1858. Welsh manufacturer, socialist. As a manager of a cotton mill, attempted to improve the lot of his employees, leading to the development of a social philosophy; developed a socialist theory in which work and the enjoyment of its results would be shared; believed man's character is molded by his environment; set up several communities based on his plan including New Harmony, Ind. *A New View of Society*, 1813. (Father of R. D. OWEN.)

OWEN, ROBERT DALE, Nov. 9, 1801 (Glasgow, Scot.)–June 24, 1877. U.S. social reformer. A founder of *The Free Enquirer*, a Socialist publication, 1829; as U.S. rep. (D, Ind.; 1843–47), instrumental in founding the Smithsonian Inst. (1845); an active abolitionist and spiritualist. (Son of R. OWEN.)

PANKHURST, EMMELINE, July 4, 1858 (Manchester, Eng.)–June 14, 1928. English suffragist. A militant suffragist who founded her own movement, the Women's Social and Political Union, 1903; imprisoned numerous times, conducted hunger strikes in her cell; tactics of her group included window-smashing, arson, and bombings. *My Own Story*, 1914.

PARKS, ROSA, Feb. 4, 1913 (Tuskegee, Ala.). U.S. civil-rights leader. Initiated the bus boycott in Montgomery, Ala., thereby sparking the beginning of the concerted civil-rights movement, 1955; subsequently a staff asst. to U.S. rep. John Conyers (D, Mich.).

PAUL, ALICE, Jan. 11, 1885 (Moorestown, N.J.)–July 9, 1977. U.S. feminist, lawyer. A leader of the woman-suffrage movement and then the Equal Rights Amendment movement, early 1900s; natl. chairperson of Natl. Woman's Party, 1942; a founder of World Women's Party; known for her radical, confrontation tactics.

POTOFSKY, JACOB S. Nov. 16, 1894 (Radomisl, Ukraine, Rus.)–Aug. 5, 1979. U.S. labor leader. Took part in the historic garment strike (1910) that led to the formation of the Amalgamated Clothing Workers of America, which he served as pres. (1946–72).

PROUDHON, PIERRE JOSEPH, July 15, 1809 (Besançon, Fr.)–Jan. 16, 1865. French social theorist. The first to formulate the doctrines of philosophical anarchism; condemned the abuses of private property; attempted to found a bank with the goal of abolishing interest and ending capital, 1849; prosecuted and tried for his revolutionary opinions. *What is Property?* 1840.

**RANDOLPH, A(sa) PHILIP,** Apr. 15, 1889 (Crescent City, Fla.)–May 16, 1979. U.S. black labor leader. Organized the Brotherhood of Sleeping Car Porters (1925) and continued to work for job rights for blacks; persuaded Pres. FRANKLIN D. ROOSEVELT to issue a fair-employment-practices exec. order, 1941; directed the massive civil-rights march on Washington, D.C., 1963.

**REUTHER, WALTER P.,** Sept. 1, 1907 (Wheeling, W. Va.)–May 9, 1970. U.S. labor leader. As pres. of the United Auto Workers (1946–70) and pres. of the CIO (1952–55), an effective negotiator; a leading labor anticommunist; an architect of the 1955 merger of the AFL and the CIO.

**RIIS, JACOB A.,** May 3, 1849 (Ribe, Den.)–May 26, 1914. U.S. journalist, reformer, author. Crusader for urban reforms; as police reporter for the New York *Tribune* (1877–88), gained wide attention with his exposes of city slums and life among the urban poor. *How the Other Half Lives,* 1890; *The Making of an American,* 1901; *Children of the Tenements,* 1903.

**RIPLEY, GEORGE,** Oct. 3, 1802 (Greenfield, Mass.) –July 4, 1880. U.S. journalist, social reformer. Pastor of Purchase St. Church in Boston, Mass., 1826–41; founded *Dial,* the prototypical little magazine, 1840; organized and directed Brook Farm, the famous utopian community, 1841–47; literary editor of the New York *Tribune,* 1849–80; founder of *Harper's New Monthly Magazine,* 1850.

**RUSTIN, BAYARD,** Mar. 17, 1910 (West Chester, Pa.)–Aug. 24, 1987. U.S. civil-rights activist. Special asst. to Dr. MARTIN LUTHER KING, JR., 1955–60; organized March on Washington for Jobs and Freedom, 1963; pres. of A. Philip Randolph Inst. 1966–79. *Down the Line,* 1971; *Strategies for Freedom,* 1976.

**SAKHAROV, ANDREI,** May 21, 1921 (Moscow, USSR)–Dec. 14, 1989. Soviet political dissident, physicist. A leader of the dissident movement in the Soviet Union; author of an essay advocating atomic disarmament and intellectual freedom in the USSR; awarded Nobel Peace Prize, 1975. *My Country and the World,* 1975.

**SANGER, MARGARET,** Sept. 14, 1883 (Corning, N.Y.)–Sept. 6, 1966. Founder of the birth-control movement in the U.S. Founded the American Birth Control League, 1921; opened the nation's first birth-control clinic, in Brooklyn, N.Y., 1916; organized the first American Birth Control Conference, New York City, 1921; served as first pres. of the Internatl. Planned Parenthood Fnd. (founded 1953). *What Every Mother Should Know,* 1917.

**SAVONAROLA, GIROLAMO,** Sept. 21, 1452 (Ferrara, It.)–May 23, 1498. Italian reformer, Dominican monk. Preached against church and state corruption; became the spiritual and political leader of Florence (1494) and defied the pope; excommunicated (1497), but continued to rule; tried for sedition and heresy, tortured and hanged.

**SCHLAFLY, PHYLLIS,** Aug. 15, 1924 (St. Louis, Mo.). U.S. political activist, author. Chairwoman of Stop ERA, 1972–82; author of a monthly newsletter, *Phyllis Schlafly Report,* 1967– . *A Choice, Not an Echo,* 1964; *Safe—Not Sorry,* 1967; *The Power of the Positive Woman,* 1977.

**SCHNEIDERMAN, ROSE,** Apr. 6, 1884 (Poland) –Aug. 11, 1972. U.S. labor leader. One of the best-known U.S. trade unionists; only eastern organizer of the Women's Trade Union League, 1917–19; elected natl. pres. of Natl. Women's Trade Union League, 1928; secy. of New York State Dept. of Labor, 1937–44.

**SCHWEITZER, ALBERT,** Jan. 14, 1875 (Kaysersberg, Alsace [now France])–Sept. 4, 1965. French theologian, musician, medical missionary. An inspiring figure who gave up the life of a brilliant scholar and musician to become a medical missionary in Africa; set up a native hospital at Lambaréné in French Equatorial Africa, 1913; espoused a philosophy of "reverence for life"; a great organist who wrote a biography of J. S. BACH, 1905.

**SCOT, DRED,** 1795? (Southampton Co.,)–Sept. 17, 1858. U.S. black slave. Sued for his freedom (1846), claiming that his residence in a free state and a free territory had made him a free man; U.S. Sup. Ct. ruled against him in a decision that made slavery legal in the territories and inflamed passions on both sides of the issue.

**SEQUOYA** (or Sequoyah), c. 1770 (Taskigi, Tenn.)– Aug. 1843. American Indian scholar. In 1821, created the Cherokee syllabary (86 characters) that enabled many Cherokees to read and write; sequoia tree and Sequoia Natl. Park are named after him.

**SHANKER, ALBERT,** Sept. 14, 1928 (New York, N.Y.). U.S. labor union official. Pres., United Federation of Teachers (NYC), 1964–85; pres., America Federation of Teachers (Washington, D.C.), 1974– .

**SHCHARANSKY,** (Anatoly) **NATAN,** Jan. 20, 1948. Soviet dissident. A long-time human rights activist and ardent campaigner for the right of Soviet Jews to emigrate; was imprisoned in 1977 for treason, espionage, and anti-Soviet agitation; freed and allowed to emigrate, 1986.

**SIEYES, EMMANUEL JOSEPH,** called Abbé Sieyes, May 3, 1748 (Frejus, Fr.)–June 20, 1836. French Revolutionary leader. Author of "What Is the Third Estate?" (1789), delineating a concept of popular sovereignty that fueled the bourgeois revolt; one of the chief organizers of the coup d'etat that brought NAPOLEON BONAPARTE to power, 1799.

**SMITH, ROBERT H.,** Aug. 8, 1879 (St. Johnsbury, Vt.)–Nov. 16, 1950. U.S. physician, reformer. With WILLIAM G. WILSON, founded Alcoholics Anonymous, a self-help organization, 1935.

**SPARTACUS,** ? (Thrace)–71 B.C. Roman slave. Leader of the Gladiatorial War (73–71 B.C.), in which he gathered an army of slaves and overran southern Italy, before he was finally defeated and killed.

**STANTON, ELIZABETH CADY,** Nov. 12, 1815 (Johnstown, N.Y.)–Oct. 26, 1902. U.S. reformer. A leader of the woman-suffrage movement who helped organize the Seneca Falls, N.Y., convention (1848), the first to deal with women's rights; insisted that suffrage was the key to all other rights for women; editor of *Revolution*, a militant feminist publication, 1868–70; pres. of Natl. Woman Suffrage Assn., 1868–70; associated with L. MOTT and S. B. ANTHONY. *The History of Women's Suffrage* (6 vols.), 1881–1922, (with Matilda Joslyn Gage).

STEINEM, GLORIA, Mar. 25, 1934 (Toledo, Ohio). U.S. feminist, writer, lecturer. A founder of the Women's Political Caucus (1971) and Women's Action Alliance (1970); a founder and editor of *Ms.* magazine, 1972–87.

STONE, LUCY, Aug. 13, 1818 (W. Brookfield, Mass.)–Oct. 18, 1893. U.S. reformer. A leader in the women's rights movement; lectured widely against slavery; helped establish the American-Woman Suffrage Assn., whose strategy was to gain suffrage for women by state legislation, 1869; founded *Woman's Journal*, 1870; refused to give up her name when she married. (Wife of H. B. BLACKWELL.)

SZOLD, HENRIETTA, Dec. 21, 1860 (Baltimore, Md.)–Feb. 13, 1945. U.S. Zionist leader. Founding pres. of Hadassah (1912), a U.S. women's Zionist org. dedicated to health work in Palestine (now Israel) and the largest women's org. in the U.S. today.

TAYLOR, GRAHAM, May 2, 1851 (Schenectady, N.Y.)–Sept. 26, 1938. U.S. clergyman, sociologist. Innovator in social work in Chicago, Ill.; founded the forerunner of the U. of Chicago School of Social Work; professor of social economics, Chicago Theological Seminary; founded Chicago Commons, an early social settlement, 1894.

TERRELL, MARY CHURCH, Sept. 23, 1863 (Memphis, Tenn.)–July 24, 1954. U.S. educator, civil-rights leader. The first black woman to serve on the Dist. of Columbia Board of Ed., 1895–1901, 1906–11; first pres. of National Assn. of Colored Women, 1896–1901; challenged several discriminatory organizations, including America Assn. of U.S. Women, opening them up to blacks.

THOMAS, NORMAN M., Nov. 20, 1884 (Marion, Ohio)–Dec. 19, 1968. U.S. socialist leader, reformer, editor, minister. Codir. of League for Industrial Democracy, 1922–33; helped found ACLU, 1920; socialist candidate for pres., 1928, 1932, 1936, 1940, 1944, and 1948; a pacifist. *America's Way Out—A Program for Democracy*, 1930.

TOBIN, DANIEL J., Apr. 3, 1875 (County Clare, Ire.)–Nov. 14, 1955. U.S. labor leader. As pres. of Internatl. Brotherhood of Teamsters, Chauffeurs, Warehousemen and Helpers of America (1907–52), oversaw massive growth of the union into the largest in the U.S.; worked for labor reunification; prominent in the AFL and the Democratic party.

TOWNSEND, FRANCIS E., Jan. 13, 1867 (Fairbury, Ill.)–Sept. 1, 1960. Originator and head of Old-Age Revolving Pensions, Inc. (1934), an old-age pension plan that gained immense popular support and helped win support for a federal Social Security program.

TOWNSEND, WILLARD, Dec. 4, 1895 (Cincinnati, Ohio)–Feb. 3, 1957. U.S. labor leader. As international pres. of United Transport Service Em-

ployees of America (1940–57), was the first black on the CIO exec. board and first black exec. of a national union that included whites.

TRUTH, SOJOURNER (legally, Isabella Van Wagener), c.1797 (Ulster Co., N.Y.)–Nov. 26, 1883. U.S. abolitionist, reformer. A freed slave, she traveled widely in the North preaching emancipation and women's rights; a moving orator who claimed divine inspiration; renamed herself Sojourner Truth as a reflection of the message she preached.

TUBMAN, HARRIET, c.1820 (Dorchester Co., Md.)–Mar. 10, 1913. U.S. abolitionist. Called the "Moses of Her People," a black slave who became a prominent abolitionist prior to the Civil War; as a leader of the "Underground RR," helped more than 300 slaves to escape.

WALD, LILLIAN D., Mar. 10, 1867 (Cincinnati, Ohio)–Sept. 1, 1940. U.S. social worker, nurse. The founder of New York City's Henry Street Settlement, 1893; initiated the first city school-nurse service, 1902; encouraged establishment of U.S. Children's Bureau (founded 1912). *The House on Henry Street*, 1915; *Windows on Henry Street*, 1934.

WEBB, BEATRICE, Jan. 22, 1858 (Gloucester, Eng.)–Apr. 30, 1943, and husband SIDNEY JAMES WEBB, (first) Baron Passfield, July 13, 1859 (London, Eng.)–Oct. 13, 1947. English socialists, economists. Coauthored many works on labor history and economics; founded the London School of Economics, 1895; founded the *New Statesman*, 1913; leaders of the Fabian Soc. and the Labor movement. *The Cooperative Movement in Great Britain* (Beatrice alone), 1891; *Facts for Socialists* (Sidney alone), 1887; *The History of Trade Unionism*, 1894; *Industrial Democracy*, 1897; created baron, 1929.

WHITE, WALTER, July 1, 1893 (Atlanta, Ga.)–Mar. 21, 1955. U.S. black leader, author. As exec. secy. of NAACP (1931–55), waged a long campaign against lynching of blacks by white mobs. *Fire in the Flint*, 1924; *Rope and Faggot: A Biography of Judge Lynch*, 1929; *A Man Called White*, 1948.

WILKINS, ROY, Aug. 30, 1901 (St. Louis, Mo.)–Sept. 8, 1981. U.S. civil rights leader. Considered the senior statesman of the U.S. civil-rights movement; ed. *Crisis*, 1934–49; as exec. dir. of NAACP (1965–77), sought equal rights via legal redress.

WILLARD, FRANCES, Sept. 28, 1839 (Churchville, N.Y.)–Feb. 18, 1898. U.S. reformer. Pres. of Women's Christian Temperance Union, 1879–98; founder and first pres. of World's Women's Christian Temperance Union, 1883; a leader of the Natl. Prohibition Party.

WILSON, WILLIAM G., Nov. 26, 1895 (E. Dorset, Vt.)–Jan. 24, 1971. U.S. reformer. Cofounded (with R. H. SMITH), Alcoholics Anonymous, a self-help organization, 1935; his wife, Lois Burnham Wilson, founded Al-Anon for spouses of alcoholics and Alateen for children of alcoholics.

WITTENMYER, ANNIE TURNER, Aug. 26, 1827 (Sandy Springs, Ohio)–Feb. 2, 1906. U.S. social reformer. Headed Union Army kitchens during the

Civil War and ministered to the sick and wounded; established and edited *The Christian Woman*, 1871–82; first pres. of the Natl. Woman's Christian Temperance Union, 1874–79. *History of the Woman's Temperance Crusade*, 1882.

**WOLD, EMMA,** Sept. 29, 1871 (Norway [now Menno], S.D.)–July 21, 1950. U.S. lawyer, reformer. Women's-rights activist, affiliated with the National Woman's Party from 1920; authority on women's rights in the Americas. *A Comparison of the Political and Civil Rights of Men and Women in the United States*, 1936.

**WOLLSTONECRAFT, MARY,** Apr. 27, 1759 (nr. London, Eng.)–Sept. 10, 1797. English writer, feminist. An early advocate of women's rights. *Vindication of the Rights of Women* (1792). (Wife of W. GODWIN; mother of M. SHELLEY.)

**WOODHULL, VICTORIA,** Sept. 23, 1838 (Homer, Ohio)–June 10, 1927. U.S. social reformer. An unconventional reformer, claimed to experience visions (from 1841), gave spiritualistic exhibitions in Ohio; with her sister Tennessee, opened stock-brokerage office supported by CORNELIUS VAN-

DERBILT, 1868; founded *Woodhull & Claflin's Weekly* advocating equal rights for women, free love, and single moral standard, 1870; first woman candidate for U.S. pres. (Equal Rights party), 1872. *Origin, Tendencies and Principles of Government*, 1871; *The Human Body; The Temple of God*, 1890.

**WRIGHT, FRANCES** ("Fanny"), Sept. 6, 1795 (Dundee, Scot.)–Dec. 13, 1852. Scottish-U.S. reformer. Noted as the author of one of the most celebrated travel memoirs of the 19th cent., *Views of Society and Manners in America* (1821); a close friend of the MARQUIS DE LAFAYETTE, whom she joined in a triumphal 1824–25 tour of the U.S.; first woman lecturer in the U.S.; edited *The New Harmony Gazette & Free Enquirer* with R. D. OWEN.

**YOUNG, WHITNEY M., JR.,** July 31, 1921 (Lincoln Ridge, Ky.)–Mar. 11, 1971. U.S. civil-rights leader. As exec. dir. of the Natl. Urban League (1961–1971), promoted its programs to improve opportunities for blacks in housing, employment, and social welfare.

# Business Leaders

**AKERS, JOHN F.**, Dec. 28, 1934 (Boston, Mass.). U.S. computer industry executive. With IBM since 1960; pres., dir., 1983– ; CEO, 1985– ; chmn., 1986– .

**ALLERTON, SAMUEL W.**, May 26, 1828 (Amenia Union, N.Y.)–Feb. 22, 1914. U.S. financier. With John B. Sherman, founded Chicago Union Stockyards, 1865; a leader in the development of modern Chicago.

**ANDERSON, SWAN F.**, Jan. 2, 1879 (Tedaholm, Swe.)–Mar. 12, 1963. U.S. manufacturer and inventor. As exec. with Anderson Bros. Mfg. Co. (1915–63), developed dairy-product packaging machinery, including a machine for producing Eskimo Pies.

**ARDEN, ELIZABETH** (born Florence Nightingale Graham), Dec. 31, 1878 (Woodbridge Ontario, Can.)–Oct. 18, 1966. U.S. cosmetics exec. Founder and sole owner of Elizabeth Arden, Inc.; operated salons throughout the U.S., Canada, and Europe; sought to improve the safety of cosmetics.

**ARKWRIGHT, SIR RICHARD**, Dec. 23, 1732 (Preston, Lancs., Eng.)–Aug. 3, 1792. English textile manufacturer. Through his use of power-driven machinery, developed cotton-cloth manufacture as principal industry in northern England in late 1770s; invented machinery for spinning cotton yarn that revolutionized textile industry; knighted, 1786.

**ARMOUR, PHILIP D.**, May 16, 1832 (Stockbridge, N.Y.)–Jan. 6, 1901. U.S. meatpacking exec. Pres. of Armour & Co. of Chicago, 1875–1901; introduced on-premise slaughtering and utilization of animal waste; one of first to use refrigerator cars to transport meat cross-country and to make canned-meat products.

**ASH, MARY KAY**, May 12, 19? (Hot Wells, Tex.). U.S. cosmetics executive. Founder and chmn., Mary Kay Cosmetics, 1963– .

**ASTOR, JOHN JACOB**, July 17, 1763 (Waldorf, nr. Heidelberg, Ger.)–Mar. 29, 1848. U.S. businessman. Founder of an American financial and social dynasty; after emigration to U.S. in 1784, amassed a fortune trading furs all over North America; at his death, the richest man in the U.S.

**AUSTIN, HERBERT**, Nov. 8, 1866 (Little Missenden, Bucks., Eng.)–May 23, 1941. English automaker. Worked in Australia as an engineer, 1883–90; returned to England and designed first 3-wheel car, Wolseley, 1895; formed the automaking concern that would become Austin-Healey, makers of sports cars, 1905.

**AYER, FRANCIS W.**, Feb. 4, 1848 (Lee, Mass.)–Mar. 5, 1923. U.S. advertising pioneer. Founded advertising firm N.W. Ayer & Son, 1869; first to do market research for clients; pioneer in use of trademarks, slogans, and ad copy.

**AYER, HARRIET**, June 27, 1849 (Chicago, Ill.)–Nov. 23, 1903. U.S. manufacturer, writer. After collapse of her husband's business, began to manufacture her own skin cream, Recamier, for which she wrote advertising using testimonials from well-known entertainers and socialites; in plot by financial backers to discredit her and seize business, she was sued, slandered, and kept in an insane asylum; upon release, lectured on "14 Months in a Madhouse"; wrote beauty column for newspapers. *Harriet Hubbard Ayer's Book of Health and Beauty*, 1899.

**BACHE, HAROLD L.**, June 17, 1894 (New York, N.Y.)–Mar. 14, 1968. U.S. stockbroker. Senior partner in J. S. Bache and Co., 1945–68.

**BAER, GEORGE F.**, Sept. 26, 1842 (Somerset Co., Pa.)–Apr. 26, 1914. U.S. railroad exec. Close financial adviser to J. P. MORGAN; pres. of Reading Railway Co. and Central Railway Co., from 1901; prominent figure in 1902 coal strike, the first test of the nascent United Mine Workers.

**BAMBERGER, LOUIS**, May 15, 1855 (Baltimore, Md.)–Mar. 11, 1944. U.S. retailer. Founded L. Bamberger & Co. dept. stores (now a division of Macy's) in Newark, N.J., 1892; founded New York City radio station WOR, 1922; founded Princeton U.'s Inst. for Advanced Study, 1933.

**BARTON, BRUCE**, Aug. 5, 1886 (Robbins, Tenn.)–July 5, 1967. U.S. advertising exec. A founder of Batten, Barton, Durstine & Osborne (1919), which he built into an industry leader; as U.S. rep. (R, N.Y.; 1937–41), a leader of opposition to Pres. F.

D. ROOSEVELT's New Deal policies. *The Man Nobody Knows*, 1925; *The Book Nobody Knows*, 1926.

BARTON, ENOS M., Dec. 2, 1842 (Lorraine, N.Y.)–May 3, 1916. U.S. manufacturer. With Elisha Gray and Anson Stager, founded Western Electric Co., 1872.

BARUCH, BERNARD M., Aug. 19, 1870 (Camden, S.C.)–June 20, 1965. U.S. financier, public official. Made fortune in stock market (1889–1913), then devoted himself to public service; respected adviser to every president from W. WILSON to J. F. KENNEDY; author of the Baruch Plan for international development and control of atomic energy, 1946.

BASSETT, HARRY H., Sept. 11, 1875 (Utica, N.Y.)–Oct. 17, 1926. U.S. auto manufacturer. As pres. of Buick Motor Co. (1920–26), developed firm into number two automaker in the U.S.

BAY, JOSEPHINE H., Aug. 10, 1900 (Anamosa, Idaho). U.S. stockbroker. In 1956, as pres. and chm. of A. M. Kidder and Co., became first woman ever to head member firm of NYSE.

BEECH, OLIVE ANN, Sept. 25, 1903 (Waverly, Kan.). U.S. aircraft industry exec. With husband W. H. BEECH, founded Beech Aircraft Corp., 1932; following her husband's death (1950), became pres., board chm., and chief exec. officer of Beech; under her guidance, sales rose from $74 million in 1963 to $267 million in 1975; retired, 1968, remains active in day-to-day operations. (Wife of W. H. BEECH.)

BEECH, WALTER H., Jan. 30, 1891 (Pulaski, Tenn.)–Nov. 29, 1950. U.S. manufacturer. Founder and pres. of Beech Aircraft Corp. (1936–50), which manufactures planes for commercial and private use. (Husband of O. A. BEECH.)

BEHN, SOSTHENES, Jan. 30, 1882 (St. Thomas, V. I.)–June 6, 1957. U.S. telephone exec. Founder, pres., and chm. of the board of ITT, 1920–56.

BELMONT, AUGUST, Feb. 18, 1853 (New York, N.Y.)–Dec. 10, 1924. U.S. banker. Through family banking firm, financed much of construction of New York City's IRT subway system, 1900; financed Cape Cod Canal, 1914; a renowned horseman, owned illustrious horses including MAN O' WAR; Belmont Stakes and Belmont Racetrack named in his family's honor.

BENDIX, VINCENT, Aug. 12, 1881 (Moline, Ill.)–Mar. 27, 1945. U.S. inventor, industrialist. Pioneer automotive and aviation manufacturer; invented an automobile self-starter; founder, Bendix Aviation Corp., 1929; founder of the Trascontinental Air Race (1931) and donor of the Bendix Trophy.

BERNBACH, WILLIAM, Aug. 31, 1911 (New York, N.Y.)–Oct. 2, 1982. U.S. advertising exec. Founded Doyle-Dane-Bernbach advertising agency, 1949; credited with introducing low-pressure, uncluttered advertising; responsible for Avis Rent-a-Car slogan, "Where you're only number two, you try harder."

BICH, MARCEL, July 29, 1914 (Turin, It.). U.S. manufacturer. Founder, pres., and chm. of the board

of Bic Pen Corp., manufacturers of inexpensive ballpoint pens and lighters, 1953– .

BIDDLE, NICHOLAS, Jan. 8, 1786 (Philadelphia, Pa.)–Feb. 27, 1844. U.S. financier. After pursuing careers as lawyer, diplomat, and publisher, appointed (1819) by Pres. JAMES MONROE as a dir. of the U.S. Bank, which he served as pres. (1823–39) during period when the government withdrew its deposits (1833), setting off banking "war."

BIGELOW, ERASTUS B., Apr. 2, 1814 (W. Boylston, Mass.)–Dec. 6, 1879. U.S. textile manufacturer, inventor. Invented several types of power looms for specialty work, especially the manufacture of carpets; founded Bigelow carpet mills, c.1850; a founder of MIT.

BIRCH, STEPHEN, Mar. 24, 1872 (New York, N.Y.)–Dec. 29, 1940. U.S. mining exec. As pres. of Kennecott Copper Corp. (1915–33), developed firm into one of the world's largest mining concerns.

BIRDSEYE, CLARENCE, Dec. 9, 1886 (Brooklyn, N.Y.)–Oct. 7, 1956. U.S. businessman, inventor. Invented a quick-freeze process, an infrared heat lamp, and other items; founded Gen. Seafoods, later Gen. Foods Corp.

BISHOP, HAZEL GLADYS, Aug. 17, 1906 (Hoboken, N.J.). U.S. chemist, cosmetics manufacturer. Founded Hazel Bishop, Inc., and marketed first "no-smear" lipstick, 1950; financial analyst of cosmetic and health-related stocks, 1968–81; head, cosmetic marketing program, Fashion Institute of Technology, 1978– ; first to occupy Revlon Chair, FIT, 1979.

BISSELL, GEORGE H., Nov. 8, 1821 (Hanover, N.H.)–Nov. 19, 1884. U.S. oil man. Organized Pennsylvania Rock Oil Co., first oil company in the U.S., to develop Pennsylvania's Oil Creek region, 1854; the first to suggest drilling for oil, rather than surface mining.

BISSELL, RICHARD M., June 8, 1862 (Chicago, Ill.)–July 18, 1941. U.S. insurance exec. Organized more successful insurance companies than anyone else in the industry (Aetna, Connecticut Gen.); pres. of Hartford Insurance Co., 1913–41; a founder of Chicago Symphony Orchestra, 1891.

BLOOMINGDALE, JOSEPH B., Dec. 22, 1842 (New York, N.Y.)–Nov. 21, 1904. U.S. merchant. With his brother, Emanuel W. Bloomingdale, founded Bloomingdale's dept. store, 1872; a progressive turn-of-the-cent. employer, he instituted a 10-hour work-day and a half-day off per week.

BLOUGH, ROGER M., Jan. 19, 1904 (Riverside, Pa.)–Oct. 8, 1985. U.S. corp. lawyer, steel exec., philanthropist. Chm. of the board and chief exec. officer of U.S. Steel Corp., 1955–69; member of U.S. Steel Corp. exec. comm., 1956–76.

BOUTELLE, RICHARD S., July 4, 1898 (Vincennes, Ind.)–Jan. 15, 1962. U.S. aircraft exec. At Fairchild Aviation, originated the WW II C-82 "Flying Boxcar" airplane, 1944.

BRADY, JAMES B., ("Diamond Jim"), Aug. 12, 1856 (New York, N.Y.)–Apr. 13, 1917. U.S. financier and bon vivant. Noted for his ample girth and lavish life-style; as exclusive agent for Fox Pressed

Steel Car Truck Co., amassed a fortune in commissions in 1888; organized Pressed Steel Car Co. and Standard Steel Car Co.

**BRECK, JOHN H.,** June 5, 1877 (Holyoke, Mass.)–Feb. 16, 1965. U.S. cosmetics manufacturer. Researched hair and scalp conditions to produce shampoos and other hair-care products sold through John H. Breck Co., founded 1908.

**BROOKINGS, ROBERT S.,** Jan. 22, 1850 (Cecil Co., Md.)–Nov. 15, 1932. U.S. manufacturer, philanthropist. In woodenware business, St. Louis, 1867–96; a benefactor of Washington U. and pres. of the corporation, 1867–1928; provided funds that led to creation of the Brookings Inst. for research in public affairs, 1928.

**BROWN, JOHN Y.,** Dec. 28, 1933 (Lexington, Ky.). U.S. restauranteur. Instrumental in founding Kentucky Fried Chicken, Inc., served as pres. (1964–71) and chm. of the bd. (1971–74); also owns Lum's and Ollie's Trolley restaurants; owner, Boston Celtics, 1978–79; gov. of Kentucky, (D) 1979–85.

**BRYANT, LANE** (born Lena Himmelstein), Dec. 1, 1879 (Lithuania)–Sept. 26, 1951. U.S. merchant. Began as seamstress of maternity clothes and lingerie; opened store that became flagship of Lane Bryant chain, first to sell ready-to-wear stout-women's and maternity clothes, 1910.

**BUDD, RALPH,** Aug. 20, 1879 (Waterloo, Iowa)–Feb. 2, 1962. U.S. railroad exec. Introduced first diesel-powered, streamlined passenger trains, 1934; pres. of both Great Northern (1919–32) and Burlington (1932–49) RRs.

**BULOVA, ARDE,** Oct. 24, 1889 (New York, N.Y.)–Mar. 19, 1958. U.S. manufacturer. Developed family-owned Bulova Watch Co., chmn., 1930–58; standardized numerous aspects of watchmaking process, began manufacturing portable radios in early 1930s; originated spot advertising on radio, 1926; a leader in rehabilitation training.

**BURPEE, DAVID,** Apr. 5, 1893 (Philadelphia, Pa.)–June 24, 1980. U.S. seed-products exec. Chief exec. officer of family-owned Atlee Burpee Seed Co., 1915–70; as plant breeder, created and introduced numerous new hybrid flowers and vegetables, including Fordhook lima beans, Spencer sweet peas, and Dutch tulip bulbs. (Son of W. A. BURPEE.)

**BURPEE, WASHINGTON A.,** Apr. 5, 1858 (Sheffield, N.B., Can.)–Nov. 26, 1915. U.S. seed-products exec. Founded first successful mail-order seed business, 1878; first to introduce bush lima beans, 1890; responsible for developing cultivation of many new hybrid vegetables and flowers. (Father of D. BURPEE.)

**BUSCH, ADOLPHUS,** July 10, 1839 (Mainz, Ger.)–Oct. 10, 1913. U.S. brewery exec. With father-in-law Eberhard Anheuser, founded Anheuser-Busch brewery in St. Louis, 1861; pioneered pasteurization of beer, making long-distance unrefrigerated shipping possible.

**CANDLER, ASA G.,** Dec. 30, 1851 (nr. Villa Rica, Ga.)–Mar. 12, 1929. U.S. businessman. Originally a pharmacist, he purchased formula for Coca-Cola

(1887), introduced some changes in the process, and sold it to soda fountains; its phenomenal success allowed him by 1890 to concentrate full-time on Coca-Cola, which grew to be one of most prosperous companies in the South; mayor of Atlanta, Ga., 1917–18; a major benefactor of Emory U.

**CARLAW, BOGART,** Mar. 28, 1904 (Minneapolis, Minn.)–Feb. 12, 1979. U.S. advertising exec. Associated with several major advertising agencies including J. Walter Thompson, and Foote, Cone, Belding, and Ted Bates & Co., 1925–66; originated "Umm, umm good" slogan for Campbell's Soup, among other product slogans.

**CARLTON, RICHARD P.,** Dec. 20, 1893 (Minneapolis, Minn.)–June 17, 1953. U.S. manufacturer. Rose through ranks of Minnesota Mining & Manufacturing to become pres., 1949–53; helped introduce Scotch tape, Scotch magnetic tape, and Scotchlite reflector tape.

**CARNEGIE, ANDREW,** Nov. 25, 1835 (Dunfermline, Fife, Scot.)–Aug. 11, 1919. U.S. industrialist, philanthropist. Though poor and poorly educated, rose quickly from position as a Pittsburgh telegraph-office messenger to superintendent of the Pittsburgh div. of Pennsylvania RR; formed Keystone Bridge Co., 1865; became chief owner of Homestead Steel Works (1888) and controlled seven other steel manufacturers, all of which he consolidated into Carnegie Steel Co., 1899; sold out to U.S. Steel, for $250 million, 1901; endowed over 2,800 libraries, Carnegie Fndn. (1905), Carnegie Endowment (1910), and Carnegie Corp. (1911). *The Gospel of Wealth,* 1889.

**CESSNA, CLYDE VERNON,** Dec. 5, 1879 (Hawthorne, Ia.)–Nov. 20, 1954. U.S. aircraft manufacturer. Built first cantilever airplane, 1927; founded Cessna Airplane Co., 1927; supplied airplanes to Curtiss Flying Service, an early airline.

**CHENEY, BENJAMIN P.,** Aug. 12, 1815 (Hillsborough, N.H.)–July 23, 1895. U.S. business exec. Beginning as a New England stagecoach driver in 1830s, parlayed an express-company run between Boston and Montreal into a business that grew into the American Express Co., 1879.

**CHILDS, SAMUEL S.,** Apr. 4, 1863 (Basking Ridge, N.J.)–Mar. 17, 1925. U.S. restauranteur. With only $1,600 in capital, founded nationwide Childs Restaurant chain, 1888; introduced such innovations as waitresses and calorie-counts on menus.

**CHRYSLER, WALTER P.,** Apr. 2, 1875 (Wamego, Kan.)–Aug. 18, 1940. U.S. industrialist. By introducing (1924) a six-cylinder auto, turned the economically-troubled Maxwell Car Co. into the highly prosperous Chrysler Corp.; built Chrysler Bldg. in New York City, 1930.

**COFFIN, CHARLES A.,** Dec. 30, 1844 (Somerset Co., Me.)–July 14, 1926. U.S. manufacturer. In 1892, merged two firms to create Gen. Electric, which he headed until 1922; credited with development of electrical industry in U.S.

**COHEN, OTTO,** 1883 (New York, N.Y.)–Apr. 25, 1979. U.S. cosmetics exec. One of the founders of the Charles of the Ritz Cosmetics Co., 1927;

credited with being the first to put quality cosmetics into dept. stores, and with creating special training for salespeople to promote the cosmetics.
**COLGATE, WILLIAM,** Jan. 25, 1783 (Hollingbourne, Kent, Eng.)–Mar. 25, 1857. U.S. manufacturer, philanthropist. Founded soap-and-perfume firm that became the Colgate-Palmolive Co., 1806; one of the founders of the American Bible Union, 1850; contributed land to Madison U., which was renamed Colgate U. (1890) in honor of his family.
**COLLIER, BARRON G.,** Mar. 23, 1873 (Memphis, Tenn.)–Mar. 13, 1939. U.S. business exec., financier. Founder of Barron G. Collier, Inc., advertising agency, 1900; first to place advertising placards in subways in major cities; leader in reclamation of Florida Everglades swampland and completion of the Tamiami Trail.
**COOKE, JAY,** Aug. 10, 1821 (Sandusky, Ohio)–Feb. 18, 1905. U.S. financier. Partner in Philadelphia investment-banking firm, 1842–58; formed Jay Cooke & Co. banking house, 1861; floated $3 million Civil War loan to Pennsylvania; sold a $500 million U.S. bond issue (1862) and an $830 million U.S. bond issue (1865), to aid Union in the Civil War; his financial failure in 1873 precipitated severe financial panic; recouped fortune in Utah mining investments.
**COONEY, JOAN GANZ,** Nov. 30, 1920 (Phoenix, Ariz.). U.S. broadcasting executive. Pres., Children's Television Workshop (producer of *Sesame Street* and *Electric Company*), 1970– .
**COOPER, PETER,** Feb. 12, 1791 (New York, N.Y.)–Apr. 4, 1883. U.S. inventor, manufacturer, philanthropist. Built (1828) Canton ironworks in Baltimore, Md., where he designed and constructed first U.S. steam locomotive, the "Tom Thumb," 1830; built first rolling mill, in New York City, 1836; made first iron structural beams, at Trenton, N.J., mill, 1854; first to use Bessemer process, 1856; active in laying first transatlantic cable; founded Cooper Union educational institution, 1859.
**COREY, WILLIAM E.,** May 4, 1866 (Braddock, Pa.)–May 11, 1934. U.S. industrialist. Second pres. of U.S. Steel Corp., 1903–11; instrumental in building city of Gary, Ind., and making U.S. Steel the largest steel-producer in the U.S.
**CORMACK, GEORGE,** June 17, 1870 (Aberdeen, Scot.)–Sept. 26, 1953. U.S. cereal manufacturer. As head miller at Washburn Crosby Co. (predecessor of Gen. Mills), invented Wheaties, 1924.
**CORNELL, EZRA,** Jan. 11, 1807 (Westchester Landing, N.Y.)–Dec. 9, 1874. U.S. capitalist, philanthropist. Organized Western Union Telegraph Co., 1855; founded Cornell U., 1865.
**COWEN, JOSHUA LIONEL,** Aug. 25, 1880 (New York, N.Y.)–Sept. 8, 1965. U.S. business exec., inventor. Invented toy electric train, 1900; headed Lionel Corp., 1945–65; developed the flashlight, a detonator, and one of the first dry-cell batteries.
**CROCKER, CHARLES,** Sept. 16, 1822 (Troy, N.Y.)–Aug. 14, 1888. U.S. railroad exec. Sought gold in California, 1849–50; joined LELAND STANFORD, Collis P. Huntington, and MARK HOPKINS to

head construction of Central Pacific RR, 1863–69; pres. of Southern Pacific RR, 1871–88; effected merger of Central Pacific and Southern Pacific RRs, 1884.
**CROSLEY, POWEL, JR.,** Sept. 18, 1886 (Cincinnati, Ohio)–Mar. 28, 1961. U.S. industrialist. Manufactured the vacuum-tube socket, the first popularly-priced piece of radio equipment; invented and manufactured Crosley autos; pres., The Crosley Corp., 1921–45; pres., Cincinnati Reds, 1934–61; pres., Crosley Motors, 1945–52.
**CUDAHY, EDWARD A.,** Feb. 1, 1860 (Milwaukee, Wisc.)–Oct. 18, 1941. U.S. meat packer. Associated with his brother M. CUDAHY in Armour & Co. 1875–87; pres. (1910–1926) and chm. (1926–41) of Cudahy Packing Co.
**CUDAHY, MICHAEL,** Dec. 7, 1841 (Callan, Co. Kilkenny, Ire.)–Nov. 27, 1910. U.S. meat-packer. Partner in Armour & Co., 1875; instrumental in first use of refrigeration in meat-packing industry; formed Armour-Cudahy (1887), which became Cudahy Packing Co. (1890) when it parted from Armour. (Brother of E. CUDAHY.)
**CULLEN, HUGH R.,** July 3, 1881 (Denton Co., Tex.)–July 4, 1957. U.S. oilman. Discovered and developed much of the oil resources in the Houston, Tex. area (including the fabulously rich Thompson field, 1930) for Humble Oil, Gulf Oil, and other companies.
**CUNARD, SIR SAMUEL,** Nov. 21, 1787 (Halifax, N.S., Can.)–Apr. 28, 1865. Canadian shipowner. Founded British steamship company bearing his name, 1839; inaugurated first regular trans-Atlantic mail service, 1840; created baronet, 1859.
**CURRAN, JOSEPH E.,** Mar. 1, 1906 (New York, N.Y.)–Aug. 14, 1981. U.S. labor leader. Organizer and first pres. of the National Maritime Union, 1937–73.
**DALY, MARCUS,** Dec. 5, 1841 (Ireland)–Nov. 12, 1900. U.S. mining exec. His discovery of copper (c.1876) in Anaconda silver mine led to formation of Anaconda Mining Co.; a major figure in Montana politics, 1888–1900.
**DAMON, RALPH S.,** July 6, 1897 (Franklin, N.H.)–Jan. 4, 1956. U.S. airline exec. Pres. of Curtiss-Wright Airplane Co., 1935; pres. of Trans World Airlines, 1949–56; developed the Condor airplane, the first "skysleeper," 1933.
**DAWES, HENRY M.,** Apr. 22, 1877 (Marietta, Ohio)–Sept. 29, 1952. U.S. oil exec. U.S. comptroller of the currency, 1921–24; pres. and chm. of Pure Oil Co., 1924–52. (Brother of C. G. DAWES.)
**DE BENEDETTI, CARLO,** Nov. 14, 1934 (Turin, It.). Italian businessman. Noted as the man who rescued and brought back Olivetti & Co.; took over Olivetti, then losing $6 million, invested $17 million of his own money, 1978; Olivetti showed net profit $160 million, 1983; AT&T acquired 25 percent of Olivetti, 1984, and now it is Europe's leading personal computer company.
**DILLER, BARRY,** Feb. 2, 1942 (San Francisco, Calif.). Worked for ABC, 1971–74; chmn., Paramount Pictures, 1974–84; pres., Gulf & Western

Entertainment Group, 1983–84; chmn., CEO, Twentieth Century Fox Film, 1984–  ; Fox Inc., 1985–  .

DODGE, HORACE ELGIN, May 17, 1868 (Niles, Mich.)–Dec. 10, 1920. U.S. manufacturer. Engineering genius of the Dodge Co., he is credited with developing the first midrange, midprice automobile. (Brother of J. F. DODGE.)

DODGE, JOHN F., Oct. 25, 1864 (Niles, Mich.)–Jan. 14, 1920. U.S. manufacturer. The business and organizational genius behind the creation of the Dodge Co. (Brother of H. E. DODGE.)

DODGE, JOSEPH M., Nov. 18, 1890 (Detroit, Mich.)–Dec. 2, 1964. U.S. banker, govt. official. As financial adviser to U.S. military govt. in Germany, initiated plans for reform of German currency and establishment of a West German central bank, 1945–46; in a similar capacity, helped rebuild and reorganize Japan's economy.

DOHENY, EDWARD L. Aug. 10, 1856 (Fond du Lac, Wisc.)–Sept. 8, 1935. U.S. oilman. A major figure in Teapot Dome oil leasing scandal of 1921–24; with H. SINCLAIR of Sinclair Oil, obtained a lease of public lands in Wyoming and drilled for oil for their own benefit; Secy. of Interior A. FALL was forced to resign as a result of granting the lease.

DOHERTY, HENRY L., May 15, 1870 (Columbus, Ohio)–Dec. 26, 1939. U.S. industrialist. In 1910, created Cities Service Co., which eventually controlled the oil, natural gas, and electric-power properties in 33 states and several foreign countries.

DONNELLEY, THOMAS E., Aug. 18, 1867 (Chicago, Ill.)–Feb. 6, 1955. U.S. printer. Developed family firm R. R. Donnelley & Sons into major printing firm, introducing an apprentice-training program, incentives for employees, and the first cost-accounting system in the U.S. printing industry.

DOUGLAS, DONALD W., Apr. 6, 1892 (Brooklyn, N.Y.)–Feb. 1, 1981. U.S. aircraft manufacturer. Founded Douglas Aircraft, 1920; produced the Cloudster, the first streamlined plane and the first plane featuring gas-dump valves and an effective instrument panel, 1920; produced the DC series for commercial airlines and bombers for U.S. govt.

DOW, HERBERT H., Feb. 26, 1866 (Belleville, Ont., Can.)–Oct. 15, 1930. U.S. chemist. Founded the Dow Chemical Co. (1890) upon developing a new method for manufacturing bromine from brine; founded Midland Chemical Co. (1890), which became Dow in 1897.

DRAKE, EDWIN L., Mar. 29, 1819 (Greenville, N.Y.)–Nov. 8, 1880. U.S. oil-industry pioneer. Became first person to tap an oil reservoir by drilling when he struck oil at 69 ft. in Titusville, Pa., Aug. 27, 1859.

DREYFUS, PIERRE, Nov. 18, 1907 (Paris, Fr.). French industrialist. Pres. of Regie Nationale des Usine Renault, manufacturers of Renault automobiles, 1955–75; Min. for Ind., 1981–82.

DRUCKER, PETER F., Nov. 19, 1909 (Vienna, Aust.). U.S. management consultant. Has been an influential force in business management since 1940. *The Concept of the Corporation*, 1946; *Management: Tasks, Responsibilities, Practices*, 1974; *Innovation and Entrepreneurship*, 1985.

DUKE, BENJAMIN N., Apr. 27, 1855 (Durham, N.C.)–Jan. 8, 1929. U.S. tobacco-products manufacturer, philanthropist. Principal exec. of W. Duke & Sons (1885–1929) and American Tobacco Co. (1890–1929); a major benefactor of Duke U. (Brother of J. B. DUKE.)

DUKE, JAMES BUCHANAN, Dec. 23, 1856 (nr. Durham, N.C.)–Oct. 10, 1925. U.S. tobacco-products manufacturer. With his brother B. N. DUKE, founded tobacco-manufacturing firms that became (1890) American Tobacco Co., which he served as pres. from 1890 until 1911, when U.S. Supr. Ct. ordered break-up of the huge combine; a major benefactor of Duke U.

DU PONT, ÉLEUTHÈRE IRÉNÉE, June 24, 1771 (Paris, Fr.)–Oct. 31, 1834. French-U.S. manufacturer. Worked under A. LAVOISIER at French royal gunpowder works in Essone, 1788–91; operated family publishing house, 1788–91; built E. I. Du Pont de Nemours, a gunpowder manufacturing plant, nr. Wilmington, Del., 1802; sold his first gunpowder in 1804 and thereafter was extremely successful; chief powdermaker for U.S. in War of 1812 and after. (Son of P. S. DU PONT DE NEMOURS; great grandfather of T. C. DU PONT and P. S. DU PONT.)

DU PONT, PIERRE SAMUEL, Jan. 15, 1870 (Wilmington, Del.)–Apr. 5, 1954. U.S. industrialist. Pres. (1915–19) and chm. of the board (1919–40) of E. I. Du Pont de Nemours; codeveloper of smokeless shotgun powder, 1893. (Great grandson of E. I. DU PONT.)

DU PONT, THOMAS C., Dec. 11, 1863 (Louisville, Ky.)–Nov. 11, 1930. U.S. manufacturer. Consolidated all companies controlled by E. I. Du Pont de Nemours into one corp. (1902–15), developing it into one of the largest trusts in the U.S.; U.S. Sen. (R, DE) 1921–28. (Great grandson of E. I. DU PONT.)

DURANT, THOMAS C., Feb. 6, 1820 (Lee, Mass.)–Oct. 5, 1885. U.S. railroad magnate. Constructed Michigan Southern RR and other Midwest lines; a chief organizer of the Union Pacific RR, (1862), which he served as pres. until his involvement in Credit Mobilier stock scandal forced him from office in 1867 and off the board of directors in 1869.

DURANT, WILLIAM C., Dec. 8, 1861 (Boston, Mass.)–Mar 18, 1947. U.S. auto manufacturer. A founder of Durant-Dort Carriage Co., 1886; organized Buick Motor Co. (1905), Gen. Motors Co. (1908), and Chevrolet (1915); held controlling interest in GM, 1915–20; founded Durant Motors, Inc., 1921.

EATON, CYRUS S., Dec. 27, 1883 (Pugwash, N.S., Can.)–May 9, 1979. U.S. industrialist. Protégé of J. D. ROCKEFELLER; parlayed a Canadian power-plant franchise into a fortune; developed Continental Gas and Electric, 1912; entered steel industry, taking over Trumbull Steel (1925) and helping to bring about the formation of Republic

Steel (1930); lost $100 million of his personal fortune in stock-market crash of 1929; known for his strong advocacy of friendly relations with USSR and other communist countries for business purposes and to maintain world peace.

**ECCLES, MARRINER S.**, Sept. 9, 1890 (Logan, Utah)–Dec. 18, 1977. U.S. financier, govt. official. Headed family-owned investment firm in Utah, 1929–71; member (1936–51) and chm. (1936–48) of Federal Reserve Board.

**EISNER, MICHAEL**, Mar. 7, 1942 (New York, N.Y.). U.S. entertainment industry executive. During 10 years at ABC was credited with taking the network to first place in ratings; as pres. and COO at Paramount (1976–1984) oversaw production of *Saturday Night Fever, The Raiders of the Lost Ark,* and *Terms of Endearment;* chairman and CEO, Walt Disney Productions (renamed Walt Disney Co. in 1986), 1984– .

**FARGO, WILLIAM G.**, May 20, 1818 (Pompey, N.Y.)–Aug. 3, 1881. U.S. transportation exec. Founder of American Express Co. (1844) and Wells Fargo & Co. (1852).

**FERGUSON, HOMER L.**, Mar. 6, 1873 (Waynesville, N.C.)–Mar. 14, 1953. U.S. shipbuilder. As pres. of Newport News Shipbuilding and Dry Dock Co., built many famous ships, including S.S. *America,* S.S. *United States,* and the carriers U.S.S. *Yorktown,* U.S.S. *Ticonderoga,* U.S.S. *Hornet,* U.S.S. *Midway,* and U.S.S. *Forrestal.*

**FERRARI, ENZO**, Feb. 20, 1898 (Modena, It.) –Aug. 14, 1988. Italian auto manufacturer. As a sports-car racer, associated with Alfa-Romeo; founded his own auto-making firm, 1940; has produced some of the world's fastest racers and fanciest sports cars.

**FIELD, CYRUS W.**, Nov. 30, 1819 (Stockbridge, Mass.)–July 12, 1892. U.S. businessman, science promoter. Spent his fortune laying the first transatlantic cable, 1866.

**FIELD, MARSHALL**, Aug. 18, 1834 (Conway, Mass.)–Jan. 16, 1906. U.S. merchant, philanthropist. Founder of Marshall Field & Co., Chicago's premier dept. store, 1881; introduced first in-store restaurant for customers; left a large part of his $125 million estate to the U. of Chicago and the Field Museum of Natural History. (Grandfather of M. FIELD III.)

**FILENE, EDWARD A.**, Sept. 3, 1860 (Salem, Mass.) –Sept. 26, 1937. U.S. merchant, philanthropist. With his brother Lincoln, developed family store into Filene's, a leading Boston dept. store; founded Massachusetts Credit Union Assn. (1917) and the Twentieth Century Fund (1919); with T. A. EDISON, developed simultaneous translating device.

**FIRESTONE, HARVEY S.**, Dec. 20, 1868 (Columbiana, Ohio)–Feb. 7, 1938. U.S. tire manufacturer. Founded Firestone Tire & Rubber Co. in 1900, and served as its pres. and chm. until 1938; pioneered a method of making tires in continuous lengths; made first detachable tire rims; started auto supply/service chain, 1928.

**FLECK, SIR ALEXANDER**, Nov. 11, 1889 (Glas-

gow, Scot.)–Aug. 6, 1968. Scottish industrialist. Chm. of Imperial Chemical Industries, Ltd., a major British chemical manufacturing concern, 1953–60; instrumental in developing polyethylene and Dacron. Knighted, 1955.

**FOLGER, HENRY CLAY**, June 18, 1857 (New York, N.Y.)–June 11, 1930. U.S. industrialist, philanthropist. An exec. with Standard Oil Co. of New York and New Jersey, 1923–28; a collector of Shakespeariana, he built the Folger Shakespeare Library in Washington, D.C., to house his vast collection.

**FOLSOM, FRANCIS M.** (Frank), May 14, 1894 (Sprague, Wash.)–Jan. 12, 1970. U.S. electronics exec. As pres. of RCA (1948–57), presided over much of firm's development in color-TV manufacture and in broadcasting.

**FORBES, MALCOLM S.**, Aug. 19, 1919 (New York, N.Y.)–Feb. 24, 1990. U.S. publisher, motor cyclist, hot air balloonist. Pub., editor in chief, Forbes, 1957–90; v.p., Forbes, Inc., 1947–64, pres., 1964–80; chmn., CEO, 1980–90; first person to fly coast-to-coast in U.S. in hot air balloon; made first ever motorcycle tour of China, 1972; set six world records in hot air ballooning, 1973. *The Sayings of Chairman Malcolm,* 1978.

**FORD, EDSEL BRYANT**, Nov. 6, 1893 (Detroit, Mich.)–May 26, 1943. U.S. auto exec. The only child of H. FORD, he served as president of Ford Motor Co. from 1919 to 1943; the ill-fated Edsel automobile was named after him. (Son of HENRY FORD; father of H. FORD II.)

**FORD, HENRY**, July 30, 1863 (nr. Dearborn, Wayne Co. Mich.)–Apr. 7, 1947. U.S. auto manufacturer, the father of the mass-produced automobile. Started career as a machinist and engineer; organized Detroit Automobile Co., 1899; oganized Ford Motor Co., 1903; introduced Model T, 1908; using mass-production technique, produced a car that sold for $500, 1913; bought out stockholders, becoming sole owner of Ford Motor Co., 1917; introduced Model A, 1927; introduced first V-8 engine, 1932; signed first union-shop contract in auto industry, 1941. *My Life and Work,* 1922. (Father of E. B. FORD; grandfather of H. FORD II.)

**FORD, HENRY II**, Sept. 4, 1917 (Detroit, Mich.) –Sept. 29, 1987. U.S. auto exec. Chief exec. officer of Ford Motor Co., 1960–80. (Grandson of H. FORD; son of E. B. FORD.)

**FREER, CHARLES L.**, June 25, 1856 (Kingston, N.Y.)–Sept. 25, 1919. U.S. industrialist, philanthropist. Made his fortune manufacturing railroad cars; retired, 1899; collected art, chiefly Chinese, amassing a collection of some 8,000 pieces that he donated to Smithsonian Inst. for display in the Freer Gallery of Art, 1906; patron of painter J. A. M. WHISTLER.

**FRICK, HENRY CLAY**, Dec. 19, 1849 (W. Overton, Pa.)–Dec. 2, 1919. U.S. industrialist. Chm. of the Carnegie Steel Co. during Homestead Strike of 1892, as a result he was shot and stabbed by an anarchist, Alexander Berkman; made a fortune through stock options when he left Carnegie and doubled it when U.S. Steel Corp. absorbed Carnegie in 1901; endowed Frick Museum of Art in NYC (once his home).

**FRUEHAUF, HARVEY C.**, Dec. 15, 1893 (Detroit, Mich.)–Oct. 14, 1968. U.S. manufacturer. A founder (1916) and chm. of the board (1949–53) of Fruehauf Trailer Co., builders of one of the first "semi" trailers for hauling cargo.

**FUGGER, JAKOB II** ("Jakob the Rich"), 1459 (Augsburg, Ger.)–1525. German financier. Scion of the German family that owned the largest trading, mining, and banking house in 15th and 16th cent. Europe; chief financial supporter of German Emperor Maximilian I, 1490; made large loan to HENRY VIII of England, 1516.

**FULLER, ALFRED C.**, Jan. 13, 1885 (Weisford, Kings Co., N.S., Can.)–Dec. 4, 1973. U.S. manufacturer. Founder of Fuller Brush Co., 1906; invented the "twisted wire" brush and the door-to-door sales approach that made his firm a leader in the industry.

**GAMBLE, JAMES N.**, Aug. 9, 1836 (Cincinnati, Ohio)–July 2, 1932. U.S. business exec. Became partner in family-owned Procter & Gamble Co. in 1862, later serving as a vice-pres., 1890–1932; responsible for development of Ivory soap, the first floating soap.

**GARY, ELBERT H.**, Oct. 8, 1846 (nr. Wheaton, Ill.)–Aug. 15, 1927. U.S. lawyer, financier. An organizer of U.S. Steel Corp., 1901; Gary, Ind., the industrial city built (1906–08) by U.S. Steel, was named in his honor.

**GERBER, DANIEL F.**, May 6, 1898 (Fremont, Mich.)–Mar. 16, 1974. U.S. manufacturer. Pres. and chm. of Gerber Products, a family-owned baby-food manufacturing firm, 1945–64; introduced strained baby food into U.S. (Son of F. GERBER.)

**GERBER, (Daniel) FRANK**, Jan. 12, 1873 (Douglas, Mich.)–Oct. 7, 1952. U.S. manufacturer. Pres. (1917–1945) and chm. (1945–52) of the firm that became Gerber Products (1941); entered the baby-food business, 1928. (Father of D. F. GERBER.)

**GETTY, J(ean) P(aul)**, Dec. 15, 1892 (Minneapolis, Minn.)–June 6, 1976. U.S. oil man. With his father, George Franklin Getty, formed the Getty Oil Co. of Oklahoma, 1916; during Depression, purchased shares of other oil companies, including Skelly Oil Co. and Tidewater Oil; negotiated oil concessions in Saudi Arabia and Kuwait, 1950; merged holdings into Getty Oil Co., 1956; reputed to be world's richest man, leaving over $1 billion at his death.

**GIANNINI, AMADEO P.**, May 6, 1870 (San Jose, Calif.)–June 3, 1949. U.S. banker. Organized California's Bank of Italy, 1904; a pioneer in branch-banking system; banks consolidated into Bank of America, 1930–34; founded Transamerica Corp., 1928. (Father of L. M. GIANNINI.)

**GIANNINI, LAWRENCE M.**, Nov. 25, 1894 (San Francisco, Calif.)–Aug. 19, 1952. U.S. banker. The son of A. P. GIANNINI, he worked for the Bank of America from 1918 to 1952, serving as pres.,

1936–52; built the internatl. div. of the bank; pres. of Transamerica Corp., 1930–32.

**GILLETTE, KING CAMP**, Jan. 5, 1855 (Fond du Lac, Wisc.)–July 9, 1932. U.S. inventor, manufacturer. Invented the safety razor and blade, c.1900; founded the Gillette Co. 1901.

**GIMBEL, BERNARD F.**, Apr. 10, 1885 (Vincennes, Ind.)–Sept. 29, 1966. U.S. retailer. As pres. (1927–53) and chm. (1953–66) of Gimbel Bros., responsible for the store's growth to nationwide chain; responsible for purchase of Sak's Fifth Avenue, 1925.

**GOODRICH, BENJAMIN F.**, Nov. 4, 1841 (Ripley, N.Y.)–Aug. 3, 1888. U.S. manufacturer. Founded (1880) B. F. Goodrich Rubber Co., the makers of the first solid rubber tires and first pneumatic auto tires. (Father of D. M. GOODRICH.)

**GOODRICH, DAVID M.**, June 22, 1876 (Akron, Ohio)–May 17, 1950. U.S. manufacturer. The son of B. F. GOODRICH; active in research into rubber, he directed the B. F. Goodrich Rubber Co.'s research in synthetic rubber in the 1930s.

**GOULD, JAY** (born Jason Gould), May 27, 1836 (Roxbury, N.Y.)–Dec. 2, 1892. U.S. financier, railroad exec. A shrewd and unscrupulous investor whose speculation in gold caused the Black Friday panic of Sept. 24, 1869; invested in Erie RR in struggle for control against C. VANDERBILT; invested in Union Pacific and Missouri Pacific RRs; controlled Western Union Telegraph Co. and the New York Elevated Railways.

**GRACE, EUGENE G.**, Aug. 27, 1876 (Goshen, N.J.)–July 25, 1960. U.S. industrialist. As pres. (1916–45) and chm. (1945–57) of Bethlehem Steel Corp., expanded firm into a major supplier of munitions, ships, and steel to the U.S. military.

**GRACE, J. PETER**, May 25, 1913 (Manhasset, N.Y.). U.S. business exec. Pres. (1945–89) of W. R. Grace & Co., a major U.S. manufacturer and processor of chemicals and owner of a major shipping line (Grace Line).

**GROSS, ROBERT E.**, May 11, 1897 (Boston, Mass.)–Sept. 3, 1961. U.S. industrialist. Purchased Lockheed Aircraft Corp. in 1932 for $40,000, and developed it into huge manufacturer of passenger and military aircraft and missiles; introduced jet power for commercial aviation; developed Polaris missile.

**GROSSINGER, JENNIE**, June 16, 1892 (Vienna, Austria)–Nov. 20, 1972. U.S. hotelier. With her parents, founded Grossinger's Hotel in the Catskill Mts. of New York (1914), and developed it into an internationally known resort.

**GRUMMAN, LEROY R.**, Jan. 4, 1895 (Huntington, N.Y.)–Oct. 4, 1982. U.S. aircraft manufacturer. Built his airplane-repair shop into Grumman Aircraft Engineering Corp., a major manufacturer of U.S. military aircraft, particularly amphibious flying craft.

**GUGGENHEIM, DANIEL**, July 9, 1856 (Philadelphia, Pa.)–Sept. 28, 1930. U.S. industrialist. A founder (1901) of American Smelting & Refining Co., one of the world's largest mining operations; endowed

the Daniel Guggenheim Fund for Promotion of Aeronautics, 1926. (Son of M. GUGGENHEIM.)
GUGGENHEIM, MEYER, Feb. 1, 1828 (Langnau, Switz.)–Mar. 15, 1905. U.S. industrialist. Formed (1877) M. Guggenheim's Sons, a smelting and mining operation that in 1901 joined the Smelter Trust, which Guggenheim headed. (Father of D. GUGGENHEIM.)
GUTT, CAMILLE A., Nov. 14, 1884 (Brussels, Belg.)–June 7, 1971. Belgian internatl. banker. As head of the Internatl. Monetary Fund (1946–51), one of the originators of the Benelux customs union and responsible for putting Belgium on a sound financial basis after WW II.
HAAS, WALTER A., 1889 (San Francisco, Calif.)–Dec. 7, 1979. U.S. manufacturer. Credited with transforming the family-owned Levi-Strauss Co. into a major clothing manufacturer, which he served as pres. (1928–56), chm. (1956–70), and chm. emeritus, 1970–79.
HALL, JOYCE C., Aug. 29, 1891 (David City, Neb.)–Oct. 29, 1982. U.S. manufacturer. Founder (1913), pres. (1913–66), and chm. of the board (1913–82) of Hallmark Cards, Inc., foremost greeting-card maker in U.S.
HAMMER, ARMAND, May 21, 1898 (New York, N.Y.). U.S. oil exec., art patron. Chm. and chief exec. officer of Occidental Petroleum Corp., Los Angeles-based oil firm, 1957– ; renowned art collector, co-owner of New York City's Knoedler Gallery, 1972– ; owner of Hammer Galleries, Inc. 1930– ; organized Soviet exhibition of modern French painting that toured U.S., 1972–73.
HARRIMAN, EDWARD H., Feb. 25, 1848 (Hempstead, L. I., N.Y.)–Sept. 9, 1909. U.S. railroad magnate. Owner and dir. of Union Pacific, Illinois Central, Delaware & Hudson, Erie, Georgia Central, Northern Pacific, and other railroads; lost out to J. P. MORGAN and J. J. HILL in epic struggle to control Burlington RR, a battle that set off the stock-market panic of 1901; organized first Boys Club, 1876. (Father of diplomat W. A. HARRIMAN.)
HAVEMEYER, HENRY OSBORNE, Oct. 18, 1847 (New York, N.Y.)–Dec. 4, 1907. U.S. business exec., art collector. With his brother, Theodore Havemeyer, merged 15 New York City and Brooklyn refining plants into Sugar Refineries Co. (later American Refinery Co.), 1887; produced one half of all sugar used in the U.S. by 1907; bequeathed his art collection to New York City's Metropolitan Museum of Art.
HEINZ, HENRY JOHN, Oct. 11, 1844 (Pittsburgh, Pa.)–May 14, 1919. U.S. food-products manufacturer. Founded H. J. Heinz Co., 1876 (incorporated 1905); coined slogan "57 varieties" to describe his products, 1896. (Grandfather of H. J. HEINZ II.)
HEINZ, HENRY JOHN II, July 10, 1908 (Sewickley, Pa.)–Feb. 23, 1987. U.S. food-products manufacturer. Pres. (1941–59) and CEO (1941–66) of H. J. Heinz Co. (Grandson of H. J. HEINZ).
HERSHEY, MILTON S., Sept. 13, 1857 (Hock-

ersville, Pa.)–Oct. 13, 1945. U.S. manufacturer. Founded Hershey Chocolate Corp., world's largest firm devoted solely to the manufacture of cocoa and chocolate, 1893; built Hershey, Pa., out of his factory and surrounding property, from 1903.
HEWITT, ABRAM S., July 31, 1822 (Haverstraw, N.Y.)–Jan. 18, 1903. U.S. iron-works operator, politician. Introduced first open-hearth furnace in U.S. (1862) and made first U.S.-made steel (1870); mayor of New York City, 1886–88; U.S. rep. (D, N.Y.), 19875–79 and 1881–86.
HIGGINS, ANDREW JACKSON, Aug. 28, 1886 (Columbus, Neb.)–Aug. 1, 1952. U.S. shipbuilder. His company, Higgins Industries (founded 1930), served as largest manufacturer of PT boats and landing craft for U.S. military during WW II.
HILL, JAMES J., Sept. 16, 1838 (Rockwood, Ont., Can.)–May 29, 1916. U.S. railroad magnate. Organized system that became the Great Northern RR, 1878; reorganized the Northern Pacific RR (1893) and the Chicago, Burlington & Quincy RR (after epic battle with E. H. HARRIMAN), 1901; his attempt, along with Harriman and J. P. MORGAN, to combine all three railroads under the Northern Securities Co. was broken up when the U.S. Sup. Ct. invoked the Sherman Anti-trust Act, 1904. *Highways of Progress*, 1910.
HILTON, CONRAD N., Dec. 25, 1887 (San Antonio, N.M.)–Jan. 3, 1979. U.S. hotelier. Began buying hotels in 1919 and founded Hilton Hotels Corp. in 1946; at his death, his corp. owned 125 hotels worldwide, valued at $500 million. *Be My Guest*, 1957.
HIRSHHORN, JOSEPH H., Aug. 11, 1899 (Mitau, Latvia)–Aug. 31, 1981. U.S. financier, art collector. Speculator in securities and uranium; donated his art collection to the U.S. govt. in 1966, leading to the building of the Hirshhorn Museum of the Smithsonian Inst. in Washington, D.C.
HOBBS, LEONARD S. ("Luke"), Dec. 20, 1896 (Carbon, Wyo.)–Nov. 1, 1977. U.S. aircraft manufacturer, engineer. Engineer and exec. with Pratt-Whitney Aircraft (now a division of United Aircraft Corp.), 1927–58; developed J-57 split-compressor turbojet engine (first with 10,000-pound thrust), 1948–52; awarded Collier Trophy, presented by Pres. D. D. EISENHOWER for the development of the J-57 jet engine, 1953.
HOFFA, JAMES R., Feb. 14, 1913 (Brazil, Ind.)–disappeared July 30, 1975, presumed dead. U.S. labor leader. During his tenure as pres. of Internatl. Teamster Union (1957–71), extensive corruption was uncovered in union, leading to its expulsion from the AFL-CIO (1957); indicted for accepting illegal payments from a trucking concern, case ended in mistrial; convicted of jury tampering and fraud in union benefits, 1964; imprisoned until sentence commuted by Pres. R. M. NIXON, 1967–71; worked for prison reform, 1971–75; last seen in parking lot of a Michigan restaurant prior to lunch with three alleged mob figures.
HOLLEY, GEORGE M., Apr. 11, 1878 (Port Jervis, N.Y.)–June 27, 1963. U.S. industrialist. His Holley

Motor Co. manufactured the first practical motor cycle (1899) and was a major supplier of carburetors for the Model A Ford and many other autos.

**HOMER, ARTHUR B.**, Apr. 14, 1896 (Belmont, Mass.)–June 18, 1972. U.S. industrialist. Beginning in 1919 in Bethlehem Steel Corp.'s shipbuilding subsidiary became Bethlehem's pres. and chief exec. officer, 1945–64; led Bethlehem during the U.S. govt.'s temporary takeover of steel companies, 1952.

**HONDA, SOICHIRO**, Nov. 17, 1906 (Shizuoka Prefecture, Japan). Japanese business leader. Noted as the founder of the Honda Motor Co.; ignored Japanese managerial traditions by placing unprecedented responsibilities on employees to urge them to use their own creativity; established Honda Technical Research Institute after WW II and first Honda motorcycle appeared on the market in 1949; retired in 1972.

**HOPKINS, JOHN JAY**, Oct. 15, 1893 (Santa Ana, Calif.)–May 3, 1957. U.S. business exec. During his tenure as pres. and board chm. of Gen. Dynamics Corp. (1947–57), built the *Nautilus*, the first nuclear-powered submarine.

**HOPKINS, MARK**, Sept. 1, 1813 (Henderson, N.Y.)–Mar. 29, 1878. U.S. capitalist. An organizer and treasurer of Central Pacific RR, 1861–78; prominent in California gold rush politics.

**HORLICK, WILLIAM**, Feb. 23, 1846 (Ruardean, Glos., Eng.)–Sept. 25, 1936. U.S. manufacturer. Discovered and produced malted milk as pres. and gen. mgr. of Horlick's Malted Milk Corp., 1878–1936.

**HORMEL, GEORGE A.**, Dec. 4, 1860 (Buffalo, N.Y.)–June 5, 1946. U.S. meat packer. As founder and pres. (1892–1928) of Geo. A. Hormel & Co., produced first canned hams in the U.S.; bd. chmn., 1928–46.

**HOUSER, THEODORE V.**, Sept. 8, 1892 (Kansas City, Mo.)–Dec. 17, 1963. U.S. retail industry exec. As an exec. with Sears, Roebuck & Co. (from 1928), directed firm's entry into retail stores (1928) and insurance (1931); developed Sears-owned "brands"; Sears chm. of the board, 1954–58.

**HUGHES, HOWARD R., JR.**, Dec. 24, 1905 (Houston, Tex.)–Apr. 5, 1976. U.S. industrialist. Considered during his lifetime to be one of the world's richest men; inherited (1924) patent rights to an oil tool drill, which, manufactured by Hughes Tool Co., laid the basis for his financial empire; founded Hughes Aircraft Co.; went to Hollywood to produce films, including *Hell's Angels* (AA, 1930), *Scarface*, (1932), and *The Outlaw* (1941); designed and flew airplanes, setting world landspeed record (352.46 mph) on Sept. 12, 1935, and transcontinental flight record on Jan. 19, 1937; went into seclusion, 1950; sold his 78% share of Trans World Airlines stock for $500 million, 1966; bought hotels and casinos in Las Vegas, Nev.

**HUNT, H(aroldson) L(afayette)**, Feb. 7, 1889 (nr. Vandalia, Ill.)–Nov. 29, 1974. U.S. oilman. Considered during his lifetime to be one of the richest men in the world; drilled first major East Texas oilfield, 1930; a conservative advocate of free enterprise, he financed *Life Line* (previously *Facts Forum*), an anticommunist radio program.

**HUNTINGTON, HENRY E.**, Feb. 27, 1850 (Oneonta, N.Y.)–May 23, 1927. U.S. capitalist. Organized and financed the Los Angeles transit system and Pacific Light & Power Co., c.1900–1911; renowned book collector.

**IACOCCA, LEE** (born Lido Anthony Iacocca), Oct. 5, 1924 (Allentown, Pa.). U.S. automotive manufacturing executive. With Ford from 1946, rose through ranks to be pres., Ford Motor Co., 1970–78; pres., COO, Chrysler, 1978–79; chmn. of bd., CEO, 1979– ; chmn., Statue of Liberty-Ellis Island Centennial Commission. *Iacocca: An Autobiography*, 1984.

**ICAHN, CARL C.**, 1936 (Queens, N.Y.). U.S. business executive. An expert in arbitrage and options; chmn., pres., Icahn & Co., 1968– ; dir., chmn., TWA, 1986– .

**INGERSOLL, CHARLES H.**, Oct. 29, 1865 (Delta, Mich.)–Sept. 21, 1948. U.S. manufacturer. With brother R. H. INGERSOLL, founded Robert H. Ingersoll & Bro. Watch Co., makers of the famous one-dollar Ingersoll watch, 1887.

**INGERSOLL, ROBERT H.**, Dec. 26, 1859 (Delta, Mich.)–Sept. 4, 1928. U.S. manufacturer. With brother C. H. INGERSOLL, founded Robert H. Ingersoll & Bro. Watch Co., makers of the famous one-dollar Ingersoll watch, 1887.

**JACK, WILLIAM S.**, Nov. 24, 1888 (Cleveland, Ohio)–June 4, 1960. U.S. industrialist. As head of Jack & Heinz (founded 1940), manufacturers of aircraft parts, made large profits on WW II contracts, which he distributed in extraordinary employee benefits.

**JOBS, STEPHEN P.**, 1955. U.S. computer industry executive, designer. Designed video games for Atari; cofounded, with Stephen Wozniak, Apple Computer Inc. in his parents' garage, 1975; co-designed Apple I; resigned as chairman of Apple, 1985; pres., NeXT, Inc. 1985– .

**JOHNSON, TOM L.**, July 18, 1854 (Georgetown, Ky.)–June 10, 1911. U.S. manufacturer, govt. official. A public transportation-system developer who invented the transparent fare-box, 1873; U.S. rep. (D, Ohio), 1890–94; reform mayor of Cleveland, Ohio, 1901–09.

**KAHN, OTTO H.**, Feb. 21, 1867 (Mannheim, Ger.)–Mar. 29, 1934. U.S. banker, philanthropist. Partner in Kuhn, Loeb & Co., 1897–1934; a noted patron of the arts; chmn. and pres. of the Metropolitan Opera, 1911–1931.

**KAISER, HENRY J.**, May 9, 1882 (Sprout Brook [nr. Canajoharie], N.Y.)–Aug. 24, 1967. U.S. industrialist. As pres. of Bridge Builders, Inc., built S.F. Bay Bridge (1933), Bonneville Dam (1934), and Grand Coulee Dam (1939); turning to shipbuilding, bought yards (1942) in California and Oregon and developed prefabrication and assembly methods that greatly reduced ship construction time; built some 1,490 ships during WW II, most of them famed Liberty-class cargo vessels; to facilitate getting steel for construction, built first steel plant on the Pacific coast, 1942; established Permanente (later Kaiser) Foundation, a non-profit health plan and facilities for his workers.

**KALMUS, HERBERT T.**, Nov. 9, 1881 (Chelsea, Mass.)–July 11, 1963. U.S. business exec. One of the developers of the Technicolor process for making color movies, 1915; head of Technology, Inc., 1922–63.

**KEITH, MINOR C.**, Jan. 19, 1848 (Brooklyn, N.Y.)–June 14, 1929. U.S. financier. Constructed cross-Costa Rica railroad, 1871–1890; through his extensive holdings in banana plantations in Costa Rica, became leader in Central American banana trade by 1899; merged with his chief rival, Boston Fruit Co., to form United Fruit Co., 1899.

**KELLOGG, JOHN HARVEY**, Feb. 26, 1852 (Tyrone, Mich.)–Dec. 14, 1943. U.S. physician. As dir. of a sanitarium, his experiments with health foods and dry breakfast cereals inspired brother W. K. KELLOGG to found the W. K. Kellogg Co., 1906.

**KELLOGG, WILL KEITH**, Apr. 7, 1860 (Battle Creek, Mich.)–Oct. 6, 1951. U.S. food-products manufacturer. Founded W. K. Kellogg Co., manufacturer of cereal products, and introduced cornflakes, 1906. (Brother of J. H. KELLOGG.)

**KENNEDY, JOSEPH P.**, Sept. 6, 1888 (Boston, Mass.)–Nov. 18, 1969. U.S. financier, diplomat, who founded the Kennedy political dynasty. First chm. of SEC, 1934–35; U.S. amb. to Great Britain, 1937–40. (Father of J. F. KENNEDY, R. F. KENNEDY and E. M. KENNEDY.)

**KING, HENRIETTA**, July 21, 1832 (Boonville, Mo.)–Mar. 31, 1925. U.S. cattlewoman, ranch owner. Married R. KING (1854), and upon his death in 1885, inherited and ran King Ranch; added to holdings, building ranch to 1,280,000 acres (the size of Delaware) by the time of her death.

**KING, RICHARD**, July 10, 1825 (Orange Co., N.Y.)–Apr. 14, 1885. U.S. cattleman. Acquired some 500,000 acres of land near Corpus Christi, Tex., thus creating the King Ranch, a major cattle-producing operation in Texas, 1852–85; ran steamboats on the Rio Grande R., 1850–72; built San Diego, Corpus Christi and Rio Grande RRs, 1876–80. (Husband of H. KING.)

**KIRBY, FRED M.**, Oct. 30, 1861 (Jefferson Co., N.Y.)–Oct. 16, 1940. U.S. merchant. His chain of 96 Kirby "five-and-ten cent" stores (founded 1887) merged with F. W. Woolworth Co. in 1912 to form a reorganized and enlarged chain.

**KRAFT, CHARLES H.**, Oct. 17, 1880 (Ft. Erie, Ont., Can.)–Mar. 25, 1952. U.S. food-products manufacturer. Joined brother in 1906 in Chicago cheese-sales firms and instituted manufacture of cheese; his firm became J. L. Kraft Co. in 1909 and Kraft Foods in 1945; a pioneer in development of blended and pasteurized cheese.

**KRESS, SAMUEL H.**, July 23, 1863 (Cherryville, Pa.)–Sept. 22, 1955. U.S. merchant, philanthropist. Founded S. H. Kress & Co. dime-store chain, 1907; established Samuel H. Kress Fndn. for purchase and donation of great works of art to museums, 1929.

**KREUGER, IVAR**, Mar. 2, 1880 (Kalmar, Swe.)–Mar. 12, 1932. Swedish financier. Originally a building contractor, became involved in the manufacture of matches, 1907; by the end of WW I controlled three-quarters of the world's matches; made govt. loans in exchange for monopolies; committed suicide after it was discovered that he had looted his vast trust, 1932.

**KROC, RAY A.**, Oct. 5, 1902 (Chicago, Ill.)–Jan. 14, 1984. U.S. restauranteur. Founded (1955) McDonald's Corp., a pioneering fast-food hamburger chain, which he has served as pres. (1955–68) and board chm. (1968–77); owner of the San Diego Padres baseball team, 1974–79.

**KROGER, BERNARD H.**, Jan. 24, 1860 (Cincinnati, Ohio)–July 21, 1938. U.S. grocer. Founded the business that became the Kroger grocery-store chain, first to operate its own bakeries and meat-packing operations, 1883; pres. and chm. of Provident Savings Bank and Trust Co. of Cincinnati, 1901–38.

**KRUPP, ALFRED**, Apr. 26, 1812 (Essen, Ger.)–July 14, 1887. German armaments manufacturer. Considered the father of modern armaments. Converted family cast-steel manufacturing firm to the manufacture of weapons; Krupp cast-steel cannon highlighted London's Crystal Palace Exhibition, 1851; during Franco-Prussian War of 1870–71, supplied field guns to Prussians, aiding them in winning the war; by 1887, supplied armaments to 46 nations.

**LANE, SIR ALLEN** (born Allen Lane Williams), Sept. 21, 1902 (Bristol, Eng.)–July 7, 1970. English publisher. With his two brothers, founded Penguin Books, Ltd., the first British publishers of paperback books, 1935–36; knighted, 1952.

**LASKER, ALBERT D.**, May 1, 1880 (Freiburg, Ger.)–May 30, 1952. U.S. advertising exec. As owner of the Lord & Thomas advertising agency (1908–42), credited with being the first to create ads telling consumers why they should buy products; founder, with his wife, of Albert and Mary Lasker Fndn., 1942.

**LAUDER, ESTEE**, ? (New York, N.Y.). U.S. cosmetics executive. Introduced her first line of Lauder products to retail stores, 1946; although she has turned over day-to-day control to her son, remains chmn. of the bd. of Estee Lauder, Inc.

**LAWRENCE, ABBOTT**, Dec. 16, 1792 (Groton, Mass.)–Aug. 18, 1855. U.S. manufacturer, govt. official. Associated with brother in Lowell, Mass., cotton mill and other ventures; U.S. representative (Whig-Mass.), 1835–37 and 1839–40; settled northeast Mass. (Maine) boundary dispute with British, 1842; U.S. amb. to Great Britain, 1849–52. (Uncle of A. A. LAWRENCE.)

**LAWRENCE, AMOS A.**, July 31, 1814 (Groton, Mass.)–Aug. 22, 1886. U.S. merchant, philanthropist. Made fortune in family firm of textile manufacture; established Lawrence U. in Appleton, Wisc., 1847; contributed to settlement of Kansas, where town of Lawrence is named in his honor; founded U. of Kansas. (Nephew of A. LAWRENCE.)

**LAWRENCE, MARY WELLS,** May 25, 1928 (Youngstown, Ohio). U.S. advertising exec. Cofounder of Wells, Rich, and Greene, Inc., an innovative New York City advertising agency, 1966; best known for complete restyling of Braniff Airlines—painting the planes in wild colors and dressing the stewardesses in uniforms designed by PUCCI.

**LAWSON, THOMAS W.,** Feb. 26, 1857 (Charleston, Mass.)–Feb. 8, 1925. U.S. financier, author. A financial wizard who amassed a personal fortune of $10 million before age 30; participated in merger of Anaconda and other companies in Amalgamated Copper Co., 1897; wrote "Frenzied Finance," an exposé of shady dealings in the Amalgamated merger, 1904.

**LEFRAK, SAMUEL J.,** Feb. 12, 1918 (New York, N.Y.). U.S. real-estate exec. Pres. and board chm. of Lefrak Org., builders of Lefrak City apartment development in New York City, 1948–  .

**LEIGH, DOUGLAS,** May 24, 1907 (Anniston, Ala.). U.S. advertising exec. Pioneer in neon-sign field; his oversized creations adorned the Times Square area of New York City, most notably the Coca-Cola weather sign (1937) and the smoking-man sign for Camel cigarettes (1941).

**LELAND, HENRY M.,** Feb. 16, 1843 (Danville, Vt.)–Mar 26, 1932. U.S. manufacturer, auto-industry pioneer. As pres. and gen. mgr. of Cadillac Motor Co. (1904–17) and Lincoln Motor Co. (1917–22), responsible for development of the Cadillac and Lincoln motor cars; with Charles Kettering, developed first electric starter, 1911; developed first eight-cylinder motor, 1914.

**LETOURNEAU, ROBERT G.,** Nov. 30, 1888 (Richford, Vt.)–June 1, 1969. U.S. business exec. A heavy-equipment manufacturer whose R. G. LeTourneau, Inc. (founded 1929) supplied over 70% of all earth-moving equipment for the U.S. armed forces during WW II.

**LEVERHULME, WILLIAM H. LEVER, VISCOUNT,** Sept. 19, 1851 (Bolton, Lancashire, Eng.)–May 7, 1925. English manufacturer. With brother James Darcy Lever, leased a financially-ailing soap factory, 1884; began to make Sunlight soap from vegetable oil, 1885; the enterprise, Lever Brothers, Inc., began to expand to cover the country; built model town called Port Sunlight, 1888; started many employee-benefits programs; created baronet, 1911; baron, 1917; viscount, 1922.

**LEVITT, WILLIAM J.,** Feb. 11, 1907 (Brooklyn, N.Y.). U.S. building exec. Founder and chm. of Levitt & Sons, Inc. (1929–  ), home builders who created the developed communities of Levittown, N.Y. (1947), and Levittown, Pa., among others.

**LEWISOHN, ADOLPH,** May 27, 1849 (Hamburg, Ger.)–Aug. 17, 1938. U.S. financier, philanthropist. A metals broker active in Montana copper; noted for philanthropies, chiefly Lewisohn Stadium at City C. of New York (dedicated 1915), and his devotion to child labor reform and prison reform; founded ORT, a Jewish welfare org., 1922.

**LILLY, ELI,** Apr. 1, 1885 (Indianapolis, Ind.)–Jan. 24, 1977. U.S. drug manufacturer, philanthropist. Pres. (1932–48) and board chm. (1948–66) of Eli Lilly & Co., the pharmaceutical firm founded by his grandfather; founded (1937) Lilly Endowment, which had donated over $250 million to charity by the time of his death.

**LIPTON, SIR THOMAS J.,** May 10, 1850 (Glasgow, Scot.)–Oct. 2, 1931. British merchant. Opened a small grocery store in Glasgow that became the basis for Thomas J. Lipton Co., tea and other foods merchants, 1898; maintained his own tea, coffee, and cocoa plantations to provide inexpensive products for his shops; knighted, 1901; created baronet, 1902.

**LITCHFIELD, PAUL W.,** July 26, 1875 (Boston, Mass.)–Mar. 18, 1959. U.S. industrialist. Associated with Goodyear Tire & Rubber Co. from 1900, he developed the first "straight-side" tire, first airplane tire, and the first pneumatic truck tire; Goodyear chm. of the board, 1930–58.

**LOEB, CARL M.,** Sept. 28, 1875 (Frankfurt-am-Main, Ger.)–Jan. 3, 1955. U.S. investment banker. Pres. of American Metal Co., 1914–29; founded Carl M. Loeb, Rhoades & Co., one of the largest brokerage houses in the U.S., 1931.

**LORENZO, FRANK,** May 19, 1940 (New York, N.Y.). U.S. transportation industry executive. Known as a hard-nosed union-buster; founded Texas Air Corp. (TAC), 1980, and serves as its chairman; created New York Air, 1981; won control of Continental Airlines and merged it with TAC, 1981; acquired Eastern Airlines and People Express, for 20 percent share of U.S. market, 1986.

**LOVE, JAMES S.,** July 6, 1896 (Cambridge, Mass.)–Jan. 20, 1962. U.S. textile exec. Developed small, family-owned cotton mill into Burlington Industries, Inc., founded 1923; first manufacturer of rayon, 1924.

**MACK, JOSEPH S.,** Nov. 27, 1870 (Mount Cobb, Pa.)–July 25, 1953. U.S. manufacturer. A silk manufacturer who joined with brothers Augustus, William, and John M. to form Mack Bros. Wagon Co., 1889; built first successful gas-powered bus and truck, 1900; formed company that manufactured Mack trucks, 1911.

**MARCUS, HAROLD S.,** Apr. 20, 1905 (Dallas, Tex.). U.S. retailer. Joined family firm, Nieman-Marcus Co., in 1926; served as pres. 1950–72; originated fashion shows for which the store became famous, 1926; originated Nieman-Marcus fashion awards, 1938. *Minding the Store,* 1974; *His and Hers,* 1982.

**MARRIOTT, JOHN W.,** Sept. 17, 1900 (Marriott, Utah)–Aug. 13, 1985. U.S. hotel and restaurant exec. From a small chain of Marriott Hot Shoppes restaurants, developed and founded Marriott hotel and restaurant chain, 1927; Marriott's pres. (1928–64) and board chm. (1964–85); a leading conservative Republican and R. M. NIXON supporter.

**MARTIN, GLENN L.,** Jan. 17, 1886 (Macksburg, Ia.)–Dec. 4, 1955. U.S. aircraft manufacturer. His Glenn L. Martin Co. (founded 1918) manufactured the first successful twin-engine plane, the Martin Bomber, 1918; manufactured the first American metal monoplane, 1922.

**MAYER, OSCAR F.,** Mar. 29, 1859 (Kaesingen, Württemberg)–Mar. 11, 1955. U.S. meat-packer. Converted a small Chicago meat market and sausage shop into a major meat-packing firm, Oscar Mayer & Co., 1888 (incorporated 1919); pres. and board chm. of Oscar Mayer, 1919–55.

**MAYTAG, ELMER H.,** Sept. 18, 1883 (Newton, Ia.)–July 20, 1940. U.S. manufacturer. Converted a family-owned farm-implement business into a major manufacturer of washing machines, the Maytag Co., which produced its first machines in 1907; pres., treasurer, and board chm. of Maytag, 1926–40. (Son of F. L. MAYTAG.)

**MAYTAG, FREDERICK L.,** July 14, 1857 (Elgin, Ill.)–Mar. 26, 1937. U.S. manufacturer. Cofounder (1893) of Parson Band Cutter and Self-Feeder Co., the company that became the Maytag Co. (1907), washing-machine manufacturers. (Father of E. H. MAYTAG.)

**MCELROY, NEIL H.,** Oct. 30, 1904 (Berea, Ohio)–Nov. 30, 1972. U.S. manufacturer. Pres. (1948–57) and board chm. (1959–72) of Procter & Gamble; instrumental in firm's introduction of "Prell" shampoo, as well as "Dreft" (the first synthetic detergent), "Joy," "Cheer," and "Lilt" products; U.S. secy. of def., 1957–59.

**MCGILL, JAMES,** Oct. 6, 1744 (Glasgow, Scot.)–Dec. 19, 1813. Scottish-Canadian fur trapper, philanthropist. Based in Montreal as a fur trader from 1774; left the bulk of his estate to found McGill U. (opened 1829).

**MCNEELY, EUGENE J.,** Nov. 1, 1900 (Jackson, Mo.)–Dec. 27, 1973. U.S. communications exec. Associated with AT&T since 1922, serving as pres. from 1961 to 1964; instrumental in development of Telstar, the first communications satellite, 1962.

**MELLON, ANDREW W.,** Mar. 24, 1855 (Pittsburgh, Pa.)–Aug. 26, 1937. U.S. financier, govt. official, philanthropist. Joined his father in family banking business, 1874; founded Union Trust Co. (Pittsburgh), which became the center of his financial activities, 1889; developed extensive interests in coal, coke, railroads, steel, oil, water power; as U.S. secy. of the treas. (1921–32), substantially reduced natl. debt; U.S. amb. to Great Britain, 1932–33; donated the first building to house Natl. Gallery of Art, Washington, D.C., along with his art collection, 1937. (Father of P. MELLON.)

**MELLON, PAUL,** June 11, 1907 (Pittsburgh, Pa.). U.S. philanthropist. Son and heir of A. W. MELLON; art connoisseur; pres. and trustee of Natl. Gallery of Art; trustee of Mellon Fndn.; received Natl. Inst. of Arts and Letters award for distinguished service to the arts, 1962.

**MERRILL, CHARLES E.,** Oct. 19, 1885 (Green Cove Springs, Fla.)–Oct. 6, 1956. U.S. investment banker. As founder (1914) of the firm that became Merrill-Lynch brokers, pioneered the stockbroking business; first to pay brokers with salaries rather than commissions; first in brokerage business to

provide financial counseling; first to advertise in popular publications, aiming at the small investor.

**MOORE, WILLIAM H.,** Oct. 25, 1848 (Utica, N.Y.)–Jan. 11, 1923. U.S. financier. Formed Natl. Biscuit Co. from several competing firms, 1898; organized and consolidated several early steel firms that were absorbed by U.S. Steel Corp., 1901; acquired Rock Island RR, 1901.

**MORGAN JOHN PIERPONT,** Apr. 17, 1837 (Hartford, Conn.)–Mar. 31, 1913. U.S. financier, philanthropist. Partner (1871) in Drexel, Morgan & Co. (J. P. Morgan and Co. from 1895), which he built into one of the world's most influential banking firms; formed syndicate that ended J. COOKE's monopoly of treasury notes, 1873; began railroad reorganization, 1885; averted financial crisis by forming syndicate to restore depleted gold to U.S. Treas., 1895; financed several companies that became U.S. Steel, 1901; financed Internatl. Harvester Co., 1902; donated art collection to New York City's Metropolitan Museum of Art, 1918.

**MORTON, JOY,** Sept. 27, 1855 (Detroit, Mich.)–May 9, 1934. U.S. manufacturer. Founder (1885) and pres. (1885–1934) of the Morton Salt Co. (incorporated 1910).

**NASH, CHARLES W.,** Jan. 28, 1864 (DeKalb Co., Ill.)–June 6, 1948. U.S. manufacturer. Automotive pioneer. Pres. of Buick Motor Co. (1910–16) and Gen. Motors (1912–16); founded Nash Motor Co., 1916; merged with Kelvinator Corp. (appliance manufacturers) in 1937, and ran the merged corp., Nash-Kelvinator Corp., until his death.

**NECKER, JACQUES,** Sept. 30, 1732 (Geneva, Switz.)–Apr. 4, 1804. Swiss banker. A dir. of the French East India Co.; min. of finance for King LOUIS XVI of France, 1777–81, 1788–90; attempted unsuccessful fiduciary reforms to save France from bankruptcy. *Compte rendu du roi,* 1781 (Father of G. DE STAEL.)

**NIARCHOS, STAVROS S.,** July 3 1909 (Athens, Gr.). Greek shipping exec. Founded (1939) Niarchos Group Cos., which eventually became the world's largest privately-owned fleet of tankers; brother-in-law of A. ONASSIS; renowned art collector.

**NICHOLS, WILLIAM H.,** Jan. 9, 1852 (Brooklyn, N.Y.)–Feb. 21, 1930. U.S. manufacturer, chemist. In 1871, founded firm that became (1905) Nichols Copper Co., one of the largest copper refiners in the world; formed (1899) Gen. Chemical Co., a leading manufacturer of heavy chemicals that introduced catalytic method of sulphuric-acid manufacture.

**NIDETCH, JEAN,** Oct. 12, 1923 (Brooklyn, N.Y.). U.S. business executive. Founded Weight Watchers, 1963. *Weight Watchers Cookbook,* 1966.

**NOBEL, ALFRED B.,** Oct. 21, 1833 (Stockholm, Swe.)–Dec. 10, 1896. Swedish industrialist, inventor, philanthropist. Discovered and perfected dynamite, 1867; developed blasting gelatin, 1876; left the bulk of his estate for establishment of Nobel prizes for peace, literature, physics, chemistry, and medicine (first prizes awarded in 1901).

NOBLE, EDWARD J., Aug. 8, 1882 (Gouverneur, N.Y.)–Dec. 28, 1958. U.S. business exec. Bought Life Savers candy from its inventor in 1913, and sold it nationwide; merged Life Savers, Inc. with Beech-Nut, Inc., 1956; bought Blue Network from RCA in 1943, and when it became ABC, Inc., continued as principal stockholder and chm. of the board until 1958.

NORDHOFF, HEINZ, Jan. 6, 1889 (Hildesheim, Ger.)–Apr. 12, 1968. German auto executive. Chosen to head Volkswagen Co. by British occupation authorities in Germany, 1948; developed firm into one of world's major automakers; introduced Volkswagen to U.S., 1952; headed firm until 1968.

NORTHCLIFFE, LORD ALFRED CHARLES WILLIAM HARMSWORTH, VISCOUNT NORTHCLIFFE, July 15, 1865 (Chapelizod, County Dublin, Ire.)–Aug. 14, 1922. British newspaper publisher. With brother LORD ROTHERMERE, founded British newspaper empire that included *Answers* (1888), *London Evening News* (1894), *London Daily Mail* (1896), *Daily Mirror* (1903), and the *Times* (1906); created baronet, 1904; baron, 1905; viscount, 1918.

NORTHROP, JOHN K., Nov. 10, 1895 (Newark, N.J.)–Feb. 18, 1981. U.S. aircraft manufacturer. An aircraft engineer who formed Lockheed Aircraft, 1927; formed Northrup Corp., 1932 (became Northrup Aircraft, 1939); designed many pioneering planes, including Vega (1927), Alpha (1930), Flying Wing (1940), and Black Widow (1940).

NORTON, OLIVER W., Dec. 17, 1839 (Allegany Co., N.Y.)–Oct. 1, 1920. U.S. manufacturer. With his brothers, founded Norton Bros., first manufacturer of tin cans for food preservation, 1872; an organizer of the American Can Co., which bought out Norton Bros. in 1901.

OBICI, AMEDEO, July 15, 1877 (Oderzo, Treviso, It.)–May 21, 1947. U.S. manufacturer. With partner Mario Peruzzi, established (1906) Planter Peanut Co. (later the Planters Nut and Chocolate Co.), makers of Planters nuts, peanut candies, and chocolate-covered peanut products; discovered process of roasting peanuts so that they could be skinned without breaking in half.

OGILVY, DAVID M., June 23, 1911 (W. Horsley, Surrey, Eng.). U.S. advertising exec. A founder of Hewitt, Ogilvy, Benson, and Mather (later Ogilvy & Mather) advertising agency, 1948; created Hathaway Shirt man with eyepatch and Commander Whitehead of Schweppes, among other advertising characters. *Blood, Beer and Brains*, 1978.

OLDS, RANSON E., June 3, 1864 (Geneva, Ohio) –Aug. 26, 1950. U.S. inventor, auto manufacturer. Began designing automobiles, 1886; manufactured first Oldsmobile in 1892 and second, more successful Oldsmobile in 1897; his firm became Olds Motor Works in 1899, featuring first U.S. factory especially designed for automaking and first assembly line.

OLIN, JOHN M. Nov. 10, 1892 (East Alton, Ill.)–Sept. 8, 1982. U.S. manufacturer. Credited with a number of innovations in manufacture of ammunition and guns; head (1944–54) and board chm. (1954–57) of Olin Matheson Chemical Corp.

ONASSIS, ARISTOTLE, Jan. 15, 1906 (Smyrna [now Izmir], Turk.)–Mar. 15, 1975. Greek shipping exec. At age 16 sent to Buenos Aires with $60; by age 25 made his first $1 million in the tobacco business; bought first six ships, 1932; started in oil tanker business, 1935; built large fleet of cargo and passenger ships; operated Olympic Airways, 1956–74; married JACQUELINE KENNEDY, 1968.

PACKARD, JAMES W., Nov. 5, 1863 (Warren, Ohio)–Mar. 20, 1928. U.S. manufacturer. Designed and built first Packard auto, 1899; with brother William Doud Packard, organized Packard Motor Car Co., 1903.

PALMER, POTTER, May 20, 1826 (Albany Co., N.Y.)–May 4, 1902. U.S. merchant. Founded (1852) Chicago dept. store that became Marshall Field & Co. in 1881; originated many retailing firsts, including allowing a customer to return or exchange goods and to try goods on approval at home; from 1867 on, devoted his talents to real estate, building, and speculation; credited with shifting business-center of Chicago to State Street.

PARKER, GEORGE S., Dec. 12, 1866 (Salem, Mass.)–Sept. 26, 1952. U.S. games manufacturer. Founder (1888), pres. (1901–33), and board chm. (1933–52) of Parker Bros.; popularized many games, notably Monopoly.

PATIÑO, SIMÓN ITURRI, June 1, 1862 (Cochabamba, Bol.)–Apr. 20, 1947. Bolivian mining exec. Pioneer in Bolivian tin mining; began in 1897 with the small Espiritu Santo mine and developed numerous concessions in the same area, eventually finding 46 main and 1,000 branch veins in the area, making it the world's richest tin mine.

PATTERSON, JOHN H., Dec. 13, 1844 (nr. Dayton, Ohio)–May 7, 1922. U.S. manufacturer. At age 40, bought a cash-register company for $6,500; through an innovative sales technique, built firm into the National Cash Register Co., which he served as pres., 1884–1922; credited with instigating the widespread use of cash registers in business.

PEABODY, GEORGE, Feb. 18, 1795 (S. Danvers, [now Peabody] Mass.)–Nov. 4, 1869. U.S. merchant, philanthropist. Partner in Baltimore dry-goods business, 1814–37; negotiated $8 million loan from Great Britain to save Maryland from bankruptcy, 1835; founded and operated (1836–64) Geo. Peabody & Co., a London banking firm that became the basis of J. P. MORGAN's financial empire; funded Peabody Inst. (Baltimore), Peabody museums at Yale and Harvard, and Peabody Education Fund; birthplace, S. Danvers, was renamed Peabody in his honor, 1868.

PEABODY, GEORGE F., July 27, 1852 (Columbus, Ga.)–Mar. 4, 1938. U.S. banker, philanthropist. Dir. of Federal Reserve Bank of New York, 1914–22; donated his estate, Yaddo, at Saratoga Springs, N.Y., for an arts center, 1926; Peabody Awards for excellence in broadcasting were named in his memory.

**PENNEY, JAMES C.**, Sept. 16, 1875 (Hamilton, Mo.)–Feb. 12, 1971. U.S. merchant. In 1902 purchased a store in Kemmerer, Wyo., that became the J. C. Penney Co., a nationwide chain of dept. stores; served as pres. (1913–17), board chm. (1917–58), and a dir. (1958–71) of what is now J. C. Penney Co., Inc.

**PETERSEN, DONALD E.**, Sept. 4, 1926 (Pipestone, Minn.). U.S. automotive industry executive. With Ford since 1949; chmn., CEO, Ford Motor Co., 1985– .

**PHILLIPS, FRANK**, Nov. 28, 1873 (Scotia, Neb.)–Aug. 23, 1950. U.S. oilman. In partnership with his brothers, formed (1917) Phillips Petroleum Co.; as pres. (1917–1938) and board chm. (1938–49), expanded Phillips's operations into refining.

**PHIPPS, HENRY**, Sept. 27, 1839 (Philadelphia, Pa.)–Sept. 22, 1930. U.S. manufacturer, philanthropist. A manufacturer of iron products, he associated himself with A. CARNEGIE from 1867; dir. of U.S. Steel Corp., 1901–30; benefactor of several medical research clinics.

**PICKENS, T(homas) BOONE, JR.**, May 22, 1928 (Holdenville, Okla.). U.S. businessman. One of the most successful and controversial corporate raiders, often making huge profits when raids fail (Cities Service, 1982; General American Oil, 1983; Unocal, 1985); founder, pres., chmn., Mesa Petroleum Co., 1964– .

**PILLSBURY, CHARLES A.**, Dec. 3, 1842 (Warner, N.H.)–Sept. 17, 1899. U.S. milling executive. Founder (1872) of Charles A. Pillsbury & Co., which built largest mills in the world; sold to English syndicate, 1889, and helped organize the Washburn-Pillsbury Mills (later the Pillsbury Company) in partnership; initiated one of the first employee profit-sharing plans.

**PINKERTON, ALLAN**, Aug. 25, 1819 (Glasgow, Scot.)–July 1, 1884. U.S. detective-agency founder. Spurred to detective work by a chance discovery of a nest of counterfeiters, 1846; worked for the Kane Co. and Cook Co., Ill., sheriffs, 1846–50; founded Pinkerton National Detective Agency to catch railway thieves, 1850; responsible for plan that got Pres. A. LINCOLN safely to his 1861 inauguration; founded first secret service for U.S. govt., 1861.

**PIPER, WILLIAM T.**, Jan. 8, 1881 (Knapps Creek, N.Y.)–Jan. 15, 1970. U.S. aircraft manufacturer. Turned a failing aircraft firm into the Piper Aircraft Corp., the first successful mass-producer of small, inexpensive airplanes; designed the Piper Cub airplane, 1931.

**PITCAIRN, JOHN**, Jan. 10, 1841 (Johnstone, Renfrewshire, Scot.)–July 22, 1916. U.S. manufacturer. As a young telegraph clerk, was put in charge of the train that secretly carried Abraham Lincoln to his 1861 inauguration after rumors of an assassination conspiracy; after a career as an oil producer and railwayman, organized New York City Plate Glass Co. (later Pittsburgh Plate Glass), 1883; founded Swedenborgian community at Bryn Athyn, Pa.

**POST, CHARLES W.**, Oct. 26, 1854 (Springfield, Ill.)–May 9, 1914. U.S. food-products manufacturer. While an invalid for eight years (1884–91), developed Grape-Nuts breakfast cereal; founded Postum Cereal Co., 1897; developed Postum beverage.

**POWERS, JOHN R.**, Sept. 14, 1896 (Easton, Pa.)–July 19, 1977. U.S. model-agency pioneer. Founded John Robert Powers Agency, 1921; started chain of modeling schools, 1929.

**PRATT, CHARLES**, Oct. 2, 1830 (Watertown, Mass.)–May 4, 1891. U.S. oilman, philanthropist. One of the first oil operators in the rich Pennsylvania oil fields; sold his refining firm to Standard Oil, 1874; founded Pratt Inst. in Brooklyn, N.Y., 1887.

**PRINCE, WILLIAM H.**, Feb. 7, 1914 (St. Louis, Mo.). U.S. business exec. Heir to Prince manufacturing fortune. Responsible for $2 million revitalization of Chicago Union Stockyards (1949–57) and $3 million reconstruction of Chicago's Internatl. Amphitheatre (1952); pres. (1957–61) and board chm. (1961– ) of Armour & Co. meat packers (a major family holding).

**PROCTER, WILLIAM C.** Aug. 25, 1862 (Glendale, Ohio)–May 2, 1934. U.S. manufacturer. Pres. (1907–30) and board chm. (1930–34) of Procter & Gamble Co.; one of the first employers to give one-half day off on Saturdays and to institute profit-sharing.

**PULLMAN, GEORGE M.**, Mar. 3, 1831 (Brocton, N.Y.)–Oct. 19, 1897. U.S. manufacturer. Constructed first "palace" (e.g., one that could be used night and day) sleeping car, "The Pioneer," 1865; organized Pullman Palace Car Co. (later the Pullman Co.), 1867; founded and built Pullman, Ill., a company town nr. Chicago, for his employees, 1880.

**QUANT, MARY**, Feb. 11, 1934 (Blackheath, Kent, Eng.). English fashion designer. Credited with developing the "Chelsea look" in fashion in the 1960s; designed line of clothes and cosmetics that developed into multimillion-dollar internatl. fashion empire; named officer of the Order of the British Empire (first woman fashion designer to be so honored), 1966. *Quant by Quant*, 1966.

**QUEENY, JOHN F.**, Aug. 17, 1859 (Chicago, Ill.)–Mar. 19, 1933. U.S. chemicals manufacturer. Founded Monsanto Chemical Co., 1901; first to manufacture saccharin, phenol (carbolic acid) in U.S. and to develop other coal-tar products.

**RACKMIL, MILTON R.**, Feb. 12, 1903 (New York, N.Y.). U.S. business exec. A founder of Decca Records, Inc. (1934), he served Decca as treasurer (1934–46), vice-pres. (1946–49) and pres. 1949–52; when Decca bought Universal Pictures in 1951, served as pres. of Universal Pictures, 1952–72.

**RAND, JAMES H.**, May 29, 1859 (Tonawanda, N.Y.)–Sept. 15, 1944. U.S. business-equipment manufacturer. Devised first visible-ledger system; formed company that became Remington-Rand, Inc., 1890.

**RATHENAU, EMIL**, Dec. 11, 1838 (Berlin, Ger.)–June 20, 1915. German industrialist. Founded Deutsche Edison-Gesellschaft, manufacturer of electrical products based on Edison patents, 1883; firm eventually became (in partnership with WERNER VON SIEMENS) Telefunken, the leading electronic manufacturer in Germany, 1903; first to produce aluminum in Germany.

**REED, JOHN S.**, Feb. 7, 1939 (Chicago, Ill.). U.S. banker. With Citibank N.A. since 1965; chmn., CEO, dir., Citicorp (parent), 1984– .

**REMINGTON, ELIPHALET**, Oct. 27, 1793 (Suffield, Conn.)–Aug. 12, 1861. U.S. manufacturer. With his father, began to manufacture rifles and other guns, 1828; formed E. Remington & sons, which manufactured a cultivator for farming as well as weapons, 1856.

**REUTER, PAUL JULIUS, BARON VON** (born Israel Beer Josaphat), July 21, 1816 (Kassell, Ger.)–Feb. 25, 1899. German-British media executive. Founded a telegraph and carrier-pigeon bureau that collected and sent news between Germany and France, 1849; expanded service to London, 1851; extended operation (now called the Reuters News Agency) to the U.S., 1865; created baron, 1871.

**REVSON, CHARLES H.**, Oct. 11, 1906 (Boston, Mass.)–Aug. 24, 1975. U.S. cosmetics manufacturer. With a $300 investment, founded (1932) Revlon, Inc., the world's largest cosmetics and fragrance manufacturer, which he served as pres. (1932–62) and chm. and chief exec. officer (1962–75).

**RICE, WILLIAM M.**, Mar. 14, 1816 (Springfield, Mass.)–Sept. 23, 1900. U.S. merchant, philanthropist. Settled in Houston, Tex., where he amassed a considerable fortune as a dry-goods merchant, importer, and land speculator; left endowment for a higher-education institution founded as Rice Inst. (later Rice U.), 1912.

**ROCKEFELLER, DAVID**, June 12, 1915 (New York, N.Y.). U.S. banker, philanthropist. An exec. with Chase Natl. Bank of New York from 1948 until 1955, when it merged to form Chase Manhattan Bank; with CMB, served as exec. vice-pres. (1955–57), vice-chm. of the board (1957–61), pres. and chm. of exec. com. (1961–69), and chm. and chief exec. officer (1969–80); serves as trustee of the Rockefeller Bros. Fund, Museum of Modern Art, and Rockefeller Family Fund. (Son of J. D. ROCKEFELLER, JR.; brother of John D. III, L., N., and Winthrop ROCKEFELLER.)

**ROCKEFELLER, JOHN D.**, July 8, 1839 (Richford, N.Y.)–May 23, 1937. U.S. financier, philanthropist. Founder of the political and financial dynasty that bears his name; founded an oil-refining business (1863) that became Standard Oil of Ohio in 1870; consolidated firm with many others to form Standard Oil Trust, 1882; Ohio Sup. Ct. deemed illegal and dissolved the trust, 1892; founded U. of Chicago, 1889; founded Rockefeller Fndn., 1913. (Father of J. D. ROCKEFELLER, JR. and E. R. MCCORMICK.)

**ROCKEFELLER, JOHN D., JR.**, Jan. 29, 1874 (Cleveland, Ohio)–May 11, 1960. U.S. philanthropist. Son of J. D. ROCKEFELLER, he devoted his life to philanthropic use of family fortune; philanthropies included Rockefeller Inst. for Medical Research (1901), Gen. Education Board (1902),

Rockefeller Foundation (1913), and Internatl. Education Board (1923); built Rockefeller Center (begun 1931) and Radio City in New York City; also gave major financial support to Sleepy Hollow Restorations, Inc. (now Historic Hudson Valley, Inc.), Cmdr. BYRD's Arctic and Antarctic expeditions, the Cloisters (1938), restoration of Colonial Williamsburg, Va. (1926–60) and Lincoln Center for the Performing Arts, New York City. (Father of D., John D. III, L., N. A. and Winthrop ROCKEFELLER.)

**ROCKEFELLER, LAURANCE S.**, May 26, 1910 (New York, N.Y.). U.S. exec., conservationist. Chm. of Rockefeller Center, Inc., 1953–56 and 1958–66; pres. of Rockresorts, Inc.; chm. of Citizen's Advisory Commission on Environmental Quality, 1969–73. (Son of J. D. ROCKEFELLER, JR.; brother of D., John D. III, N. A., and Winthrop ROCKEFELLER.)

**ROGERS, HENRY H.**, Dec. 29, 1840 (Mattapoisett, Mass.)–May 19, 1909. U.S. financier. Standard Oil of New Jersey exec., 1892–1909; organized Amalgamated Copper Co., which consolidated copper industry (including Anaconda mines), 1899; managed MARK TWAIN's finances and financed HELEN KELLER's education.

**ROLLS, CHARLES S.**, Aug. 28, 1877 (London) –July 12, 1910. English automaker, aviator. With F. H. ROYCE, formed Rolls-Royce, Ltd., 1906; first aviator to fly across the English Channel, 1910; one month later, became first English air fatality.

**ROTHERMERE, LORD HAROLD SIDNEY HARMSWORTH, VISCOUNT ROTHMERE**, Apr. 26, 1868 (Hampstead, London, Eng.)–Nov. 26, 1940. Irish newspaper publisher. With brother LORD NORTHCLIFFE, founded British newspaper empire that included the *London Daily Mail* (launched 1896) and *Times* (bought 1908); British air min., 1917–18; endowed chairs at Oxford and Cambridge to honor his sons, who were killed in WW I; created baronet, 1910; baron, 1914; viscount, 1919.

**ROTHSCHILD, LIONEL NATHAN**, Nov. 22, 1808 (London, Eng.)–June 3, 1879. English banker. First Jewish member of Parliament, 1858–74; made Irish famine loan (1847) and Crimean War loans (1856). (Son of N. M. ROTHSCHILD; grandson of M. ROTHSCHILD.)

**ROTHSCHILD, MAYER (or Meyer) ANSELM (or Amschel)**, Feb. 23, 1743 (Frankfurt, Ger.)–Sept. 19, 1812. German banker, financier. Founded the House of Rothschild financial dynasty; began as a money lender in Jewish ghetto of Frankfurt; became a banker and, as financial agent (from 1801) for William, Elector of Hesse-Cassell, preserved William's sizable fortune from the 1806 French invasion; in gratitude for his efforts, was allowed free use of the money for a time and, thereby, laid the cornerstone for his own fortune. (Father of N. M. ROTHSCHILD; grandfather of L. N. ROTHSCHILD.)

**ROTHSCHILD, NATHAN MAYER (Meyer) 1ST BARON**, Sept. 16, 1777 (Frankfurt, Ger.)–July 28,

1836. German-British financier. The son of M. A. ROTHSCHILD, extended family financial operation to England; opened banking firm, 1805; subsidized much of British action against NAPOLEON I; made loans to govts. in Europe and S. America; raised 15 million for British govt. to compensate West Indies slave owners, 1835 (Father of L. N. ROTHSCHILD.)

ROTHSCHILD, WALTER NATHAN, Apr. 28, 1892 (New York, N.Y.)–Oct. 8, 1960. U.S. merchant. Entered family firm, Abraham & Straus dept. store, 1913; as pres. (1937–55) and chm. (1955–60) of A&S, directed expansion of store into chain; a founder and exec. of Federated Dept. Stores, a nationwide group that includes A&S, Filene's, Foley's, Bloomingdale's, and Lazarus dept. store, 1929–60.

ROYCE, SIR FREDERICK H., Mar. 27, 1863 (Alwalton, Huntingdonshire, Eng.)–Apr. 22, 1933. English automaker. Built three experimental cars in 1904 and interested C. S. ROLLS, a car dealer, in selling them; their firms merged to form Rolls-Royce, Ltd., 1906. Created baronet, 1930.

RUBICAM, RAYMOND, June 16, 1892 (Brooklyn, N.Y.)–May 8, 1978. U.S. advertising exec. Copywriter at N. W. Ayer & Sons, 1919–23; with John Orr Young, organized (1923) Young & Rubicam advertising agency, which he served as chief exec. officer until his retirement in 1944; first in advertising to engage G. GALLUP to conduct market research, 1932.

RUBINSTEIN, HELENA, Dec. 25, 1870 (Cracow, Pol.)–Apr. 1, 1965. U.S. cosmetics exec. Entered beauty business in Australia, 1902; by 1918, her cosmetics line was renowned in the U.S.; founder and pres. of Helena Rubinstein, Inc.

RUPPERT, JACOB, Aug. 5, 1867 (New York, N.Y.)–Jan. 13, 1939. U.S. brewery exec. Pres. of Jacob Ruppert Brewery (founded by his father, 1867), 1915–39; U.S. Rep. (NY-D) 1899–1907; owner of the New York Yankees baseball team, 1914–39.

RUSSELL, WILLIAM H., Jan. 31, 1812 (Burlington, Vt.)–Sept. 10, 1872. U.S. pioneer in express business. Organized several freight lines in the West; founded Pony Express between St. Joseph, Mo., and Sacramento, Calif., 1860.

RYAN, JOHN D., Oct. 10, 1864 (Hancock, Mich.)–Feb. 11, 1933. U.S. industrialist. An organizer of Amalgamated Copper Co., 1899; as head of Anaconda copper div. (1903–33), developed it into world's foremost copper producer; in 1912, merged several firms to form Montana Power Co., which he served as pres. until his death.

RYAN, THOMAS F., Oct. 17, 1851 (Lovingston, Nelson Co., Va.)–Nov. 23, 1928. U.S. financier. Formed first holding company in the U.S. with his promotion of the New York City transit system, 1886; one of the reorganizers of the American Tobacco Co., 1898; controlled many banks, 1898–1928.

SAGE, MARGARET OLIVIA, Sept. 8, 1828 (Syracuse, N.Y.)–Nov. 4, 1918. U.S. philanthropist. Widow of financier R. SAGE, she founded Russell Sage Fndn. (1907) with $10 million for the purpose of improving social and living conditions; founded Russell Sage C. for Women, 1916; her vast gifts to charities have been attributed to an attempt to counteract her husband's reputation as a skinflint.

SAGE, RUSSELL, Aug. 4, 1816 (Verona Twp., [Oneida Cty.], N.Y.)–July 22, 1906. U.S. financier. Operated successful grocery in Troy, N.Y., 1839–57; U.S. rep. (Whig, N.Y.), 1853–57; went to New York City to engage in stock speculation, 1863; became associated with J. GOULD in the control of several Western railroads; left his fortune to his wife, M. O. SAGE.

SCHACHT, HJALMAR (Horace Greeley), Jan. 22, 1877 (Tingleff, Ger. [now in Den.])–June 4, 1970. German financier. Financial expert noted for stopping the terrible inflation in the Weimar Republic, 1922–23; pres. of Reichsbank, 1923–30; min. of economics under the Third Reich, 1934–37.

SCHAEFER, RUDOLPH J., Feb. 21, 1863 (New York, N.Y.)–Nov. 9, 1923. U.S. brewery exec. Joined family-owned F & M Schaefer Brewing Co., 1882; introduced first bottled beer, 1891.

SCHICK, JACOB, Sept. 16, 1877 (Des Moines, Iowa)–July 3, 1937. U.S. manufacturer. Invented and manufactured Pencilaid pencil sharpener (1921), Schick magazine razor (1923), and "Shick dry shaver," the first successful electric shaver (1924).

SCHNERING, OTTO Y., Oct. 9, 1891 (Chicago, Ill.)–Jan. 10, 1953. U.S. manufacturer. Established small candymaking firm (became Curtiss Candy Co., 1919), 1916; pioneer of "nickel" candy bars; first to present brand-name, individually-wrapped candy bars, including "Baby Ruth"and "Butterfingers."

SCHWAB, CHARLES M., Feb. 18, 1862 (Williamsburg, Pa.)–Sept. 18, 1939. U.S. manufacturer. "Boy wonder" of the steel industry; pres. of Carnegie Steel Corp., 1897–1901; first pres. of U.S. Steel Corp., 1901–03; as pres. (1903–1913) and chm. of the bd. (1913–39) of Bethlehem Steel Corp., moved firm to major leadership role in metals manufacture.

SCRANTON, GEORGE W., May 11, 1811 (Madison, Conn.)–Mar. 24, 1861. U.S. manufacturer. Developed manufacturing process to smelt iron ore with anthracite coal, 1842; Scranton, Pa., named in his honor.

SCULLEY, JOHN, Apr. 6, 1939 (New York, N.Y.). U.S. computer company executive. With Pepsi-Cola from 1967 was pres. of Pepsico, 1974–77, and pres. and CEO, 1977–83; pres., CEO, Apple Computer Co., 1983–  ; chmn., 1986–  .

SEARS, RICHARD W., Dec. 7, 1863 (Stewartville, Minn.)–Sept. 28, 1914. U.S. merchant. Pioneered mail-order business; founded Sears, Roebuck & Co., 1893; Sears pres., 1893–1909.

SELFRIDGE, HARRY G., Jan. 11, 1864 (Ripon, Wisc.)–May 8, 1947. U.S.-British merchant. Partner in Marshall Field & Co. (to 1904); went to London and founded Selfridge & Co., Ltd., a major British dept. store, 1909.

SHEDD, JOHN G., July 20, 1850 (Alstead, N.H.)

–Oct. 22, 1926. U.S. merchant. Became partner of M. FIELD, 1893; as pres. of Marshall Field & Co. (1906–22), developed firm into retail chain; first Chicago merchant to give half-day holiday on Saturday to employees; endowed Shedd Aquarium in Chicago's Grant Park.

SHIELD, LANSING P., Apr. 8, 1896 (Linlithgo, N.Y.)–Jan. 6, 1960. U.S. business exec. Associated with Jones Bros. Tea Co., which merged to form Grand Union Co. grocery chain; pres. of Grand Union, 1947–60; invented Food-O-Mat food dispensing system, 1947.

SHREVE, HENRY M., Oct. 21, 1785 (Burlington Co., N.J.)–Mar. 6, 1851. U.S. river-transport pioneer. Started first trade by water between Philadelphia and St. Louis, 1807; pioneer of Mississippi R. transport, 1810–15; U.S. supt. of Western river improvements, 1827–41; Shreveport, La., named for him, 1839.

SIEMENS, ERNST WERNER VON, Dec. 13, 1816 (Lenthe, Ger.)–Dec. 6, 1892. German manufacturer, inventor. Invented the dial telegraph, 1846; founded Siemens and Halske, manufacturer of electrical equipment, 1847; built the first telegraph line in Germany, 1848; proposed Siemens unit of electrical resistance.

SINCLAIR, HARRY F., July 6, 1876 (Wheeling, W. Va.)–Nov. 10, 1956. U.S. oilman. Founder of Sinclair Oil Corp., 1901 (incorporated 1916); a major figure in Teapot Dome scandal, 1923–24.

SKODA, EMIL VON, Nov. 19, 1839 (Plzen, Bohemia [now Czech.])–Aug. 8, 1900. Czech industrialist. Took over family-owned machine works in Pilsen and developed it into the Skoda Works, famed for the manufacture of munitions, 1869 (incorporated, 1899).

SLATER, SAMUEL, June 9, 1768 (Belper, Derbyshire, Eng.)–Apr. 21, 1835. U.S. manufacturer. Manfactured first American-made yarn and founded American cotton-spinning industry, 1793; founded S. Slater Sons, textile manufacturers, 1798; built cotton mills all over New England.

SLOAN, ALFRED P., JR., May 23, 1875 (New Haven, Conn.)–Feb. 17, 1966. U.S. auto exec. Worked for Hyatt Roller Bearing (1895–1916) until it merged into United Motors Corp., which he served as pres. until 1918, when United Motors became part of Gen. Motors Co.; GM pres. (1923–37), and board chm. (1937–56); founded Alfred P. Sloan Fndn., which started Sloan-Kettering Inst. for Cancer Research, 1945.

STANFORD, A(masa) LELAND, Mar. 9, 1824 (Watervliet, N.Y.)–June 21, 1893. U.S. financier, philanthropist, major California pioneer. Financed and constructed Central Pacific RR, 1863–69; CP pres. and dir. 1863–93; gov. of California, 1861–63; U.S. sen. (R, Cal.), 1885–93; pres. of Southern Pacific RR, 1885–90; founded Stanford U. in memory of his son, 1885.

STEINWAY, HENRY E., Feb. 15, 1797 (Wolfshagen, Brunswick, Ger.)–Feb. 7, 1871. German-U.S. manufacturer. Made pianos in Germany,

1825–48; founded Steinway and Sons piano manufacturers, 1853. (Father of W. STEINWAY.)

STEINWAY, WILLIAM, Mar. 5, 1835 (Seesen, Ger.)–Nov. 30, 1896. U.S. manufacturer. With his father and two brothers, founded Steinway & Sons piano makers, 1853; a skilled piano-maker, oversaw financial and business matters for the firm. (Son of H. E. STEINWAY.)

STONE, AMASA, Apr. 27, 1818 (Charlton, Mass.) –May 11, 1883. U.S. philanthropist, builder. Formed partnership with Azariah Boody to build bridges and railroads; built Cleveland, Columbus & Cincinnati RR, 1849; built Chicago & Milwaukee RR, 1858; endowed Western Reserve U.

STRAUS, ISIDOR, Feb. 6, 1845 (Otterberg, Rhenish Bavaria, Ger.)–Apr. 15, 1912. U.S. merchaant. With his brother, N. STRAUS, became an owner of R. H. Macy Co. dept. store, 1896; U.S. rep. (D, N.Y.), 1894–95; went down on the *Titanic*. (Father of J. I. and P. S. STRAUS.)

STRAUS, JACK ISIDOR, Jan. 13, 1900 (New York, N.Y.)–Sept. 19, 1985. U.S. merchant. The third generation of his family to be associated with the R. H. Macy & Co. dept. stores, serving as pres. (1939–56), chm. of the board and chief exec. officer (1956–68), chm. of exec. com. (1968–76), and honorary chm. and dir. emeritus (1976–85). (Son of JESSE I. STRAUS; nephew of P. S. STRAUS.)

STRAUS, JESSE ISIDOR, June 25, 1872 (New York, N.Y.)–Oct. 4, 1936. U.S. merchant. Joined R. H. Macy Co., 1896; became partner when his father, ISIDOR STRAUS, a senior partner, went down on the *Titanic*, 1912; as pres. (1919–33), developed Macy's into "world's largest store"; U.S. amb. to France, 1933–36. (Father of JACK I. STRAUS.)

STRAUS, NATHAN, Jan. 31, 1848 (Otterberg, Ger.)–Jan. 11, 1931. U.S. merchant. With his brother, I. STRAUS, became an owner of R. H. Macy & Co. dept. store, 1896; a prominent Zionist; initiated campaign for compulsory pasteurization of milk, 1892.

STRAUS, PERCY SELDEN, June 27, 1876 (New York, N.Y.)–Apr. 6, 1944. U.S. merchant. Associated with R. H. Macy dept. store from 1897, serving as pres. (1933–39) and board chm. (1939–44); responsible for flagship store's move to present Herald Sq. location in New York City, 1902. (Son of I. STRAUS; brother of J. I. STRAUS.)

STRAUSS, LEVI, c.1829 (?)–1902. U.S. manufacturer. Little known about his life; left New York City for California to prospect for gold, c.1850; sold cloth to earn money for prospecting; used a spare bolt of canvas to create pants for a miner who had complained about the cheapness of cloth, thus inventing "denim jeans"; founded Levi-Strauss Co. in San Francisco and manufactured Levi pants until his death.

STUART, ELBRIDGE A., Sept. 10, 1856 (Guilford Co., N.C.)–Jan. 14, 1944. U.S. manufacturer. Established and ran a Texas wholesale and retail grocery business, 1881–93; organized firm that produced Carnation evaporated milk (later the Carnation

Co.), 1899; Carnation pres. (1899–1932) and board chm. (1932–44).

**STUBER, WILLIAM G.,** Apr. 9, 1864 (Louisville, Ky.)–June 17, 1959. U.S. business exec. Succeeded G. EASTMAN as pres. of Eastman Kodak Co., 1925–34; EK board chm., 1934–41; made many technical advances in Kodak's sensitized products, including X-ray film (introduced 1914).

**STUDEBAKER, CLEMENT,** Mar. 12, 1831 (nr. Gettysburg, Pa.)–Nov. 27, 1901. U.S. manufacturer. Cofounder of H. and C. Studebaker blacksmith and wagon-making firm, 1852; firm became Studebaker Bros. Manufacturing Co., 1868; as pres. (1868–1901), made Studebaker the largest wagon and carriage manufacturer in U.S.; firm later made Studebaker autos.

**SWIFT, GUSTAVUS F.,** June 24, 1839 (nr. Sandwich, Mass.)–Mar. 29, 1903. U.S. meat packer. Started as a butcher in Massachusetts, moved to Chicago; instrumental in development of refrigerated railroad car, 1875; incorporated Swift & Co. meat-packing firm, 1885.

**THOMPSON, J(ames) WALTER,** Oct. 28, 1847 (Pittsfield, Mass.)–Oct. 16, 1928. U.S. advertising exec. Started as advertising-space salesman for William J. Carlton, 1867; bought out Carlton and formed J. Walter Thompson advertising agency, 1878; brought respectability to advertising industry; famous clients included Pabst Breweries, Kodak, and Prudential Insurance; sold his agency and retired, 1916.

**THOMSON OF FLEET, ROY HERBERT, THOMSON, BARON,** June 5, 1894 (Toronto, Ont., Can.)–Aug. 4, 1976. Canadian-British publishing exec. Parlayed a small Ontario radio station into one of the world's largest media empires, the Thomson Organization, Ltd.; acquired controlling interest in *The Times* of London, 1967. Created baron, 1964.

**THYSSEN, FRITZ,** Nov. 9, 1873 (Mülheim, Ger.)–Feb. 8, 1951. German industrialist. An early supporter of A. HITLER; controlled 15% of Vereinigte Stahlwerke, the world's largest mining trust; had major falling out with Nazis, fled to Switzerland, losing all his money and property, 1939.

**TIFFANY, CHARLES L.,** Feb. 15, 1812 (Killingly, Conn.)–Feb. 18, 1902. U.S. merchant. Founded (1837) a business that became (1868) Tiffany & Co. jewelers. (Father of L.C. TIFFANY.)

**TINKER, GRANT A.,** Jan. 11, 1926 (Stamford, Conn.). U.S. broadcasting executive. Pres., Mary Tyler Moore (MTM) Enterprises, 1970–81; chmn. of bd., CEO, NBC, 1981–86; now an independent producer.

**TILYOU, GEORGE C.,** Feb. 3, 1862 (New York, N.Y.)–Nov. 30, 1914. U.S. amusement-park operator. A real-estate pioneer in the Coney Is., N.Y., area; beginning with Tilyou's Surf Theatre in 1890, built an amusement-park empire that included the Coney Is. boardwalk and Steeplechase amusement park.

**TISCH, LAURENCE A.,** Mar. 15, 1923 (Brooklyn, N.Y.). U.S. business leader. With brother Robert founded Tisch Hotels, Inc., 1959; took control of

Loews Theaters and merged it into Loews Corp., 1986; emerged from bloody takeover battle of CBS in charge, 1988.

**TREES, JOE C.,** Nov. 10, 1869 (Trees Mills, Pa.)–May 19, 1943. U.S. oilman. In partnership with Michael L. Benedum (1896–1943), discovered more oil than any individual or group in history, including first oil in Illinois (1899), the Caddo pool in Louisiana (1909), and the Big Lake field in western Texas (1924).

**TRIPPE, JUAN,** June 27, 1899 (Seabright, N.J.)–Apr. 3, 1981. U.S. aviation exec. A WW I naval aviator who formed Long Island Airways, 1922; a founder of Colonial Air Transport (New York City–Boston), one of first domestic carriers, 1924; a founder of airline that became Pan American Airways, Inc., in 1927; as Pan Am pres. (1927–68) and honorary chm. (1968–81), started first U.S. internatl. air mail service, using Pam Am planes (1927) and started first transatlantic passenger service (1939).

**TRUMP, DONALD J.,** 1946 (New York, N.Y.). U.S. real estate developer. Known for his mega projects and immense wealth; projects include Trump Tower (1983) and at least 4 casinos in Atlantic City, including the Taj Mahal (1990); bought failing Eastern Shuttle and renamed it the Trump Shuttle, 1989.

**UEBERROTH, PETER,** Sept. 2, 1937 (Evanston, Ill.). U.S. business executive. Began as an executive in the travel industry; pres., Los Angeles Olympic Organizing Commission, 1979–84; major league baseball comissioner, 1984–89.

**VAIL, THEODORE N.,** July 16, 1845 (nr. Minerva, Ohio)–Apr. 16, 1920. U.S. communications exec. Launched U.S. govt.'s fast mail service, 1875; gen. mgr. of Bell Telephone Co., 1878–87; founded Western Union Telegraph Co., 1881; pres. of A.T. & T., 1885–87 and 1907–19; as pres. of Western Union (1909–13), revitalized firm; influential in laying first transcontinental telephone cable, 1915.

**VAN CAMP, GILBERT C.,** Dec. 25, 1817 (Brookville, Ind.)–Apr. 4, 1900. U.S. food-products exec. While associated with an Indianapolis grocery firm, built first cold-storage warehouse in U.S. ; originated process of canning foods and organized (1862) Van Camp Packing Co., serving as pres. until 1898.

**VANDERBILT, CORNELIUS** ("Commodore"), May 27, 1794 (Stapleton, Staten Is., N.Y.)–Jan. 4, 1877. U.S. financier, transport exec. Started passenger and freight ferry service between Staten Is. and Manhattan, 1810; in association with Thomas Gibbons, captained ferry line between New Brunswick, N.J. and New York City; formed his own Hudson R. steamboat line in 1829, and by 1846 was a millionaire; owned a New York-to-California steamship line, 1850–58; bought controlling interest in New York and Harlem RR, New York Central RR, and Hudson R. RR, 1862–67; left $100 million at his death. (Father of W. H. VANDERBILT; grandfather of W. K. VANDERBILT.)

**VANDERBILT, WILLIAM H.,** May 8, 1821 (New Brunswick, N.J.)–Dec. 8, 1885. U.S. financier. Oldest son of C. VANDERBILT; succeeded his father as pres. of New York Central RR in 1877 and expanded holdings to include Chicago and Northwestern, and Nickel Plate RRs; donated $100,000 for erection of Cleopatra's Needle in New York City's Central Park. (Father of W. K. VANDERBILT.)

VANDERBILT, WILLIAM K., Dec. 12, 1849 (New Dorp, Staten Island, N.Y.)–July 22, 1920. U.S. financier. Grandson of C. VANDERBILT; financed many railroad consolidations and expansions; pres. of New York & Harlem RR, 1899–1920; a philanthropist who bequeathed his collections of paintings to New York City's Metropolitan Museum of Art, 1920. (Son of W. H. VANDERBILT.)

VAUCLAIN, SAMUEL M., May 18, 1856 (Philadelphia, Pa.)–Feb. 4, 1940. U.S. manufacturer, inventor. Associated with Baldwin Locomotive works, 1883–1940; invented first compound locomotive (1889), wrought iron center for railroad tracks (1889), and rack and rail locomotive, 1896.

VILLARD, HENRY (born Ferdinand Heinrich Gustav Hilgard), Apr. 10, 1835 (Speyer, Bavaria)–Nov. 12, 1900. U.S. railroad magnate. Fled Bavaria to avoid military service; worked as journalist in New York City, 1858–65; formed (1881) a pool that bought the Northern Pacific RR, which he served as pres. (1881–84) and board chm. (1888–93); gave financial support to T. A. EDISON; founded Edison Gen. Electric Co., 1889.

WALLER, FREDERIC, Mar. 10, 1886 (Brooklyn, N.Y.)–May 18, 1954. U.S. manufacturer, inventor. Through his firm, which manufactured and designed optical equipment for movies, invented and developed the Cinerama process, 1938–54.

WANAMAKER, JOHN, July 11, 1838 (Philadelphia, Pa.)–Dec. 12, 1922. U.S. merchant, govt. official. Cofounder of Oak Hall, a Philadelphia clothing store, 1861; founded in 1869 a men's store bearing his name, converting it to a dept. store in 1877; U.S. postmaster gen., 1889–93.

WARBURG, FELIX M., Jan. 14, 1871 (Hamburg, Ger.)–Oct. 20, 1937. U.S. financier, philanthropist. Partner in Kuhn, Loeb & Co., internatl. bankers, 1897–1937; helped secure first legislation for probation for juvenile offenders, 1902; worked in Henry St. Settlement House in New York City, 1919–37; founded and served as officer with several Jewish charities, including Jewish Relief Com. (1914) and Council of the Jewish Agency for Palestine (1929). (Uncle of J. P. WARBURG.)

WARBURG, JAMES P., Aug. 18, 1896 (Hamburg, Ger.)–June 3, 1969. U.S. banker, govt. official, author. A member of Pres. F. D. ROOSEVELT's "Brain Trust," 1932–34. *The Money Muddle,* 1934; *Our War and Our Peace,* 1941; *Germany—Bridge or Battleground,* 1947. (Nephew of F. M. WARBURG.)

WARD, (Aaron) MONTGOMERY, Feb. 17, 1843 (Chatham, N.J.)–Dec. 7, 1913. U.S. merchant. In partnership with George P. Thorne, founded Montgomery Ward & Co., first U.S. mail-order house, 1872.

WARNER, ALBERT (born Albert Eichelbaum),

July 23, 1884 (nr. Warsaw, Poland)–Nov. 26, 1967. U.S. film exec. Founded Warner Bros. Pictures, Inc., with his brothers Harry M., Sam, and J. L. WARNER, 1923; Warner's vice-pres. and treasurer, 1923–56; known for his honesty in business.

WARNER, JACK L. (born Jack Eichelbaum), Aug. 2, 1892 (London, Ont., Can.)–Sept. 9, 1978. U.S. movie exec. With his brothers, Harry, Sam, and A. WARNER, founded Warner Brothers Pictures, Inc., 1923; introduced first film with soundtrack, 1926; introduced first film with spoken sound, 1927; as head of production for the studio, credited with discovery of many stars and directors and with instituting a development program for contract players.

WASHBURN, WILLIAM D., Jan. 14, 1831 (Livermore, Me.)–July 29, 1912. U.S. manufacturer, govt. official. Founded Minneapolis & St. Louis RR, 1870; founded Pillsbury-Washburn flour mills, 1879; U.S. rep. (R, Minn.), 1879–1885; U.S. sen. (R, Minn.), 1889–95.

WATSON, THOMAS J., Feb. 17, 1874 (Campbell, N.Y.)–June 19, 1956. U.S. industrialist. Converted financially ailing Computing-Tabulating-Recording Co., makers of business machines, into an international giant, Internatl. Business Machines Corp. (named changed to IBM, 1924); introduced many firsts, including printing tabulator (1920), electric typewriter (1935–41), electronic calculator (1946), and electronic data-processing system (1952); pres. and dir. (1914–49) and chm. bd. and chief exec. off. (1949–56), IBM. (Father of T. J. WATSON, JR.)

WATSON, THOMAS J., JR., Jan. 8, 1914 (Dayton, Ohio). U.S. business exec. Son of T. J. WATSON, the founder of IBM, which he joined as junior salesman, 1937; succeeded his father as pres., 1952–79; U.S. amb. to the USSR, 1979–81.

WELCH, JOHN F., JR., Nov. 19, 1935 (Peabody, Mass.). U.S. utility industry executive. With General Electric from 1960; vice chmn., CEO, 1979–81; chmn., 1981– .

WELLS, HENRY W., Dec. 12, 1805 (Thetford, Vt.)–Dec. 10, 1878. U.S. transportation exec. In partnership with W. G. FARGO, established Western Express, 1844; firm consolidated with other companies to form American Express Co., 1850; American Express pres., 1850–68; also with Fargo, formed Wells Fargo & Co., 1852; founded Wells Sem. (now Wells College) 1868.

WHARTON, JOSEPH, Mar. 3, 1826 (Philadelphia, Pa.)–Jan. 11, 1909. U.S. metals producer. First producer of nickel in U.S., 1873; founded Bethlehem Steel Corp., 1873; founded Wharton School of Finance and Political Economy at U. of Pennsylvania, 1881.

WHITE, ALFRED T., May 28, 1846 (Brooklyn, N.Y.)–Jan. 29, 1921. U.S. merchant, philanthropist. Associated with family firm, W. A. & A. M. White, merchants, 1865–1921; in 1876, built Tower & Homes tenements in Brooklyn, N.Y., the first planned, decent low-income housing in U.S., which spurred tenement reform. *Improved Dwellings for the Laboring Class,* 1879.

**WHITE, WILLIAM,** Feb. 3, 1897 (Midland Park, N.J.)–Apr. 6, 1967. U.S. railroad exec. Often called the "railroader's railroader"; pres. of Delaware, Lackawanna & Western RR, 1941–52; pres. of New York Central RR, 1952–54; pres. of Delaware & Hudson RR, 1954–63, chmn., 1963–67; pres. of Erie-Lackawanna RR, 1963–67.

**WICKMAN, CARL E.,** Aug. 7, 1887 (Vamhus, Swe.)–Feb. 5, 1954. U.S. transportation exec. Pioneered bus lines in Minnesota, 1914–25; formed holding company for several Midwest bus lines, Motor Transit Corp., 1926; company name changed to Greyhound Corp., 1930; as pres. (1930–46) and board chm. (1946–51), developed Greyhound into nationwide bus system.

**WILLARD, DANIEL,** Jan. 28, 1861 (North Hartland, Vt.)–July 6, 1942. U.S. railroad exec. As pres. of Baltimore & Ohio RR, (1910–41), expanded and improved service, encouraged development of labor unions; effectively headed off a nationwide rail strike, 1917; negotiated temporary 10% industrywide worker layoffs to save U.S. railroads an estimated $400 million at the height of the Depression, 1932.

**WILLYS, JOHN N.,** Oct. 25, 1873 (Canandaigua, N.Y.)–Aug. 26, 1935. U.S. manufacturer, diplomat. In 1908, reorganized failing Overland Auto Co. into Willys-Overland, which he served as pres., 1908–29 and 1935; U.S. amb. to Poland, 1930–32.

**WILSON, CHARLES E.,** July 18, 1890 (Minerva, Ohio)–Sept. 26, 1961. U.S. industrialist, govt. official. As an engineer with the Westinghouse Corp. (1909–19), designed firm's first auto starter (1912); joined Delco, a subsidiary of Gen. Motors Co., 1919; GM pres., 1941–53; U.S. secretary of def., 1953–57.

**WILSON, KEMMONS,** Jan. 5, 1913 (Osceola, Ark.). U.S. hotelier. A Memphis, Tenn., realtor since 1945, opened his first Holiday Inn motel there, 1952; founded Holiday Inn chain, 1953; chm. of the board of Holiday Inns, Inc., 1953–79.

**WINSTON, HARRY,** Mar. 1, 1896 (New York, N.Y.)–Dec. 8, 1978. U.S. jeweler. Founded the renowned gem dealership Harry Winston, Inc., 1932; purchased many famous jewels, including the Hope Diamond, which he gave to the Smithsonian Inst., 1958.

**WITTEMAN, CHARLES R.,** Sept. 15, 1884 (Staten I., N.Y.)–July 8, 1967. U.S. manufacturer, aviation pioneer. Designed and developed first commercially-sold biplane-type gliders, 1903; designed and built Baldwin Red Devil airplane, 1908; developed first automatic-pilot systems for aircraft, 1916–18.

**WOOD, ROBERT E.,** June 13, 1879 (Kansas City, Mo.)–Nov. 6, 1969. U.S. merchant, soldier. Served with distinction in WW I; vice-pres. of Montgomery Ward, 1919–24; joined Sears, Roebuck & Co. in 1924, serving as pres. (1928–39) and board chm. (1939–54); developed Sears from strictly mail-order to retail business; a leader of America First movement prior to WW II.

**WOOLWORTH, FRANK W.,** Apr. 13, 1852 (Rodman, N.Y.)–Aug. 8, 1919. U.S. merchant. Opened his first successful store, selling only five- and ten-cent merchandise, in Lancaster, Pa., June 1879; founded F. W. Woolworth Co., 1912; built network of over 1,000 stores in North America by the time of his death; built Woolworth Bldg. in New York City, 1913.

**WRIGLEY, P(hillip) K(night),** Dec. 5, 1894 (Chicago, Ill.)–Apr. 12, 1977. U.S. manufacturer. Pres. (1925–61) and chm. of the bd. of dirs. (1961–77), William Wrigley & Co., world's largest chewing-gum manufacturer; owner of the Chicago Cubs baseball team. (Son of W. WRIGLEY, JR.)

**WRIGLEY, WILLIAM, JR.,** Sept. 30, 1861 (Philadelphia, Pa.)–Jan. 26, 1932. U.S. manufacturer. Founded the Chicago-based chewing-gum firm bearing his name, 1891; served as pres. until 1932. (Father of P.K. WRIGLEY.)

**WURLITZER, RUDOLPH,** Jan. 31, 1831 (Schoneck, Ger.)–Jan. 14, 1914. U.S. manufacturer. Began making trumpets and drums in Cincinnati, Ohio in 1861, branching out into pianos in 1868; introduced first automatically-played, electric, coin-operated instruments, 1892.

**YALE, ELIHU,** Apr. 5, 1649 (Boston, Mass.)–July 8, 1721. U.S. philanthropist. Made fortune with British East India Co., 1671–99; gov. of Madras, 1687–92; donated monetary gifts and books (1714–18) to Collegiate School, which became Yale C.

**ZECKENDORF, WILLIAM,** June 30, 1905 (Paris, Ill.)–Sept. 3, 1976. U.S. business exec. Noted for his interests in urban development; joined Webb & Knapp, Inc., internatl. realtors in 1938, rising to pres. and chm. of the board, 1947–65; sold property for UN headquarters to JOHN D. ROCKEFELLER, JR., 1946; managed Astor family holdings, 1941–46; built business developments in Los Angeles (Century City) and L'Enfant Plaza in Washington, D.C.

# Sports Personalities

**AARON, HENRY,** Feb. 5, 1934 (Mobile, Ala.). U.S. baseball player, executive. Milwaukee/Atlanta Braves (1954–74), Milwaukee Brewers (1975–76) outfielder; holds major-league record for most career home runs (755), RBIs (2,297), games played (3,298), at bats (12,364), total bases (6,856); NL batting champ, 1956, 1959; NL home-run leader, 1957, 1963, 1966, and 1967; NL RBI leader, 1957, 1960, 1963, and 1966; holds record for most NL career hits (3,771); elected to Hall of Fame, 1982.

**ABDUL-JABBAR, KAREEM** (born Lew Alcindor), Apr. 16, 1947 (New York, N.Y.). U.S. basketball player. Led UCLA to three consecutive NCAA titles 1967–69; NBA scoring leader 1971, 1972; NBA MVP 1971, 1972, 1974, 1976, 1977, 1980; all-time NBA scoring leader with 37,639 points and games played, 1,486 (through 1988); led Milwaukee Bucks to NBA Championship in 1971, and Los Angeles Lakers to championships in 1980, 1982, 1985, 1987 and 1988.

**ALEXANDER, GROVER CLEVELAND,** Feb. 26, 1887 (St. Paul, Neb.)–Nov. 4, 1950. U.S. baseball pitcher. Won 373 major-league games, third on the all-time list; elected to Baseball Hall of Fame, 1938.

**ALI, MUHAMMAD** (born Cassius Clay), Jan. 18, 1942 (Louisville, Ky.). U.S. boxer. First boxer to hold heavyweight title three times, 1964–67, 1974–78, 1978–79; light-heavyweight gold medalist, 1960 Olympics; stripped of pro title by World Boxing Assn. and other groups after refusing military induction (1967), then reinstated after U.S. Sup. Ct. ruling (1971); leader in Black Muslim faith.

**ALLEN, MARCUS,** Mar. 26, 1960 (San Diego, Calif.). U.S. football player. Running back for Los Angeles Raiders, 1982– ; led NFL in rushing, 1985; set NFL record for combined yards in a season, 1985; Super Bowl MVP, 1984; Heisman Trophy, 1981.

**ALLEN, MEL,** Feb. 14, 1913 (Birmingham, Ala.). U.S. sports broadcaster. Broadcasted for N.Y. Yankees, 1939–64; Fox *Movietone News* commentator, 1946–64; elected to National Sportswriters and Broadcasters Hall of Fame, 1972.

**ALLISON, BOBBY,** Dec. 3, 1937 (Miami, Fla.). U.S. auto racer. Won Daytona 500 race, 1978, 1982, and 1988.

**ALSTON, WALTER,** Dec. 1, 1911 (Venice, Ohio) –Oct. 1, 1984. U.S. baseball manager. Managed Brooklyn/Los Angeles Dodgers, 1954–76; team won seven NL titles and four World Series (1955, 1959, 1963, 1965); inducted into Baseball Hall of Fame, 1983.

**ALWORTH, LANCE,** Aug. 3, 1940 (Houston, Tex.). U.S. football player. Pass receiver with AFL San Diego Chargers and NFL Dallas Cowboys; led AFL in receptions, 1966, 1968–69; scored 85 pro TDs on pass receptions; elected to Football Hall of Fame, 1978.

**ANDERSON, O(ttis) J(erome),** Nov. 19, 1957 (W. Palm Beach, Fl.). U.S. football player. Running back, St. Louis Cardinals, 1979–86; New York Giants, 1986– ; gained over 1,000 yards rushing six times.

**ANDRETTI, MARIO,** Feb. 28, 1940 (Montona, Italy). U.S. auto racer. American Automobile Assn. champ., 1965, 1966, 1969. Won Indy 500, 1969; World Grand Prix champion, 1978.

**ANSON, ADRIAN** ("Cap"), Apr. 11, 1851 (Marshalltown, Ia.)–Apr. 14, 1922. U.S. baseball player. Pioneer baseball player/manager with Chicago White Stockings, 1876–97 (manager, 1879–97); led NL in batting, 1879, 1881, 1887, 1888; elected to Baseball Hall of Fame, 1939.

**ARBOUR, AL(ger),** Nov. 1, 1932 (Sudbury, Ont., Can.). Canadian hockey player, coach. NHL defenseman, 1953–71; coach, St. Louis Blues, 1970–72; New York Islanders, 1973–87, 1988– ; led team to four consecutive Stanley Cup championships, 1980–83.

**ARCARO, EDDIE,** Feb. 19, 1916 (Cincinnati, Ohio). U.S. jockey. Won 4,779 races in career, including five Kentucky Derbies, six Preaknesses, six Belmont

Stakes; rode Triple Crown winners Whirlaway (1941) and Citation (1948).

**ARMSTRONG, HENRY,** Dec. 12, 1912 (Columbus, Miss.). U.S. boxer. Held feather-, bantam-, and lightweight titles simultaneously, 1937–38; elected to Boxing Hall of Fame, 1954.

**ASHE, ARTHUR,** July 10, 1943 (Richmond, Va.). U.S. tennis player, sports consultant. First black to make top rank in men's competition. U.S. singles champion, 1968; Wimbledon champion, 1975.

**ASHFORD, EVELYN,** Apr. 15, 1957 (Shreveport, La.). U.S. track and field star. A sprinter, she won the Olympic gold medal in the 100 meters, 1984.

**AUSTIN, TRACY,** Dec. 2, 1962 (Rolling Hills, Calif.). U.S. tennis player. U.S. champ, 1979, 1981.

**BANKS, ERNIE,** Jan. 31, 1931 (Dallas, Tex.). U.S. baseball player. Led NL in home runs, 1958 and 1960; NL MVP, 1958 and 1959; elected to Baseball Hall of Fame, 1977; hit 512 homers in the major leagues; inducted into Hall of Fame, 1977.

**BANNISTER, ROGER,** Mar. 23, 1929 (Harrow, Eng.). British athlete, physician. First to run a mile in under four minutes (3:59.4), May 6, 1954.

**BARBER, RED,** Feb. 17, 1908 (Columbus, Miss.). U.S. sports broadcaster. Covered Brooklyn Dodgers and New York Yankees baseball games from 1930s to 1960s.

**BARKLEY, CHARLES,** Feb. 20, 1963 (Leeds, Ala.). U.S. basketball player. Forward for the Philadelphia 76ers, 1984–  ; led NBA in rebounding, 1987.

**BARRY, RICK,** Mar. 28, 1944 (Elizabeth, N.J.). U.S. basketball player, broadcaster. NCAA scoring leader, 1965; NBA Rookie of the Year, 1966; NBA scoring leader, 1967; ABA scoring leader, 1969.

**BAUGH, SAMUEL** ("Slingin' Sammy"), Mar. 17, 1914 (Temple, Tex.). U.S. football player. Held numerous NFL passing and punting records at 1952 retirement, after 16 pro seasons; elected to Football Hall of Fame, 1963.

**BAYI, FILBERT,** June 23, 1953 (Karratu, Tanganyika). Tanzanian runner. Set, 1,500-m world record (3:32.2) in 1974.

**BAYLOR, ELGIN,** Sept. 16, 1934 (Washington, D.C.). U.S. basketball player, coach, executive. A 10-time NBA All-Star; elected to Basketball Hall of Fame, 1976; head coach of New Orleans Jazz, 1974–79; gen. mgr. Los Angeles Clippers, 1986–  .

**BECKER, BORIS,** Nov. 22, 1967 (Leiman, W. Ger.). West German tennis player. Won U.S. Open, 1989; Wimbledon champion, 1985–86, 1989.

**BELIVEAU, JEAN,** Aug. 31, 1931 (Three Rivers, Que., Can.). Canadian hockey player. Montreal Canadiens center (1953–71); NHL leading scorer, 1956; NHL MVP, 1956 and 1964; Smythe trophy, 1965.

**BELL, GEORGE,** Oct. 21, 1959 (San Pedro de Macoris, Dom. Rep.). Dominican baseball player. Outfielder for Toronto Blue Jays, 1983–  ; led AL in RBIs, MVP, 1987.

**BENCH, JOHNNY,** Dec. 7, 1947 (Oklahoma City, Okla.). U.S. baseball player. Cincinnati Reds catcher; NL Rookie of the Year, 1968; NL homerun leader, 1970 and 1972; NL RBI leader, 1970, 1972

and 1974; NL MVP, 1970 and 1972; inducted into Hall of Fame, 1989.

**BERG, PATTY,** Feb. 13, 1918 (Minneapolis, Minn.). U.S. golfer. Won over 80 tournaments; Female Athlete of the Year, 1938, 1943, 1955.

**BERRA, YOGI,** May 12, 1925 (St. Louis, Mo.). U.S. baseball player, manager, coach. As New York Yankees catcher (1946–63), played in 14 World Series; AL MVP, 1951, 1954, and 1955; managed N.Y. Yankees to AL pennant, 1964; New York Mets to NL pennant, 1973; inducted into Hall of Fame, 1972.

**BERRY, RAY**(mond), Feb. 27, 1933 (Corpus Christi, Tex.). U.S. football player, coach. Baltimore Colts, 1955–67; head coach New England Patriots, 1984.

**BING, DAVE,** Nov. 24, 1943 (Washington, D.C.). U.S. basketball player. NBA leading scorer, 1968; averaged 20.3 points per game during career (1967–78); inducted into Hall of Fame, 1990.

**BIONDI, MATT,** Oct. 8, 1965 (Moraga, Calif.). U.S. swimmer. Won seven medals at 1988 Olympic games, including five golds.

**BIRD, LARRY,** Dec. 7, 1956 (West Baden, Ind.). U.S. basketball player. Boston Celtics forward, 1979–  ; NBA MVP, 1984–86; first-team NBA all-star, 1980–88; NBA rookie of the year, 1980; playoff MVP, 1984, 1986; set record for most points in playoffs, 1984.

**BLANDA, GEORGE,** Sept. 17, 1927 (Youngwood, Pa.). U.S. football player. Quarterback-kicker for Chicago Bears (1949–58), Houston Oilers (1960–66) and Oakland Raiders (1967–69 and 1970–74); scored record 2,002 points in 26-year pro career.

**BLUE, VIDA,** July 28, 1949 (Mansfield, La.). U.S. baseball player. Pitcher for Oakland A's, San Francisco Giants; 20-game winner three times; AL MVP, 1971; won AL Cy Young Award, 1971.

**BLYLEVEN, (Rik) BERT,** Apr. 6, 1951 (Zeist, Holland). U.S. baseball player. Pitcher with Minnesota Twins, 1970–76, 1985–88; Texas Rangers, 1976–77; Pittsburgh Pirates, 1978–80; Cleveland Indians, 1981–85; California Angels, 1988–  ; struck out over 3,500 batters.

**BOGGS, WADE,** June 15, 1958 (Omaha, Neb.). U.S. baseball player. Third baseman for Boston Red Sox, 1982–  ; lead AL in batting, 1981, 1983, 1985–88; had over 200 hits, 1983–89.

**BOITANO, BRIAN,** Oct. 22, 1963 (Sunnyvale, Cal.). U.S. figure skater. Won Olympic gold medal, 1988; U.S. champion, 1985–88; world champion, 1986, 1988.

**BORG, BJORN,** June 6, 1956 (Södertalje, Swe.). Swedish tennis player. Led Sweden to first Davis Cup win, 1975; Wimbledon champ, 1976, 1977, 1978, 1979, 1980.

**BOROS, JULIUS,** Mar. 3, 1920 (Fairfield, Conn.). U.S. golfer. U.S. Open champion, 1952 and 1963; PGA champion, 1968.

**BOSSY, MIKE,** Jan. 22, 1957 (Montreal, Que., Can.). Canadian hockey player. N.Y. Islanders right wing, 1977–87; won Smythe trophy, 1982.

**BOURQUE, RAY,** Dec. 28, 1960 (Montreal, Que.). Canadian hockey player. Boston Bruins defenseman, 1980– ; Rookie of the Year, 1980; won Norris Trophy, 1987, 1988; first-team all-star, 1980, 1982–85, 1987–88.

BRABHAM, JACK, Apr. 2, 1926 (Sydney, Austrl.). Australian auto racer, builder. Grand Prix champ, 1959, 1960, 1966; first to win a driving championship with a car of his own construction.

BRADLEY, PAT, Mar. 24, 1951 (Westford, Mass.). U.S. golfer. Led the LPGA in money won, 1986.

BRADSHAW, TERRY, Sept. 2, 1948 (Shreveport, La.). U.S. football player, commentator. Quarterback for Pittsburgh Steelers, whom he led to Super Bowl championships in 1975, 1976, 1979 and 1980.

BRETT, GEORGE, May 15, 1953 (Glendale, W. Va.). U.S. baseball player. Kansas City Royals third baseman (1973– ); won AL batting title, 1976, 1980; AL MVP, 1980.

BROCK, LOU, June 18, 1939 (El Dorado, Ark.). U.S. baseball player. Chicago Cubs (1961–64), St. Louis Cardinals (1964–79) outfielder; stole 118 bases, 1974; led NL in stolen bases eight times; holds major-league record for stolen bases, 938; inducted into Baseball Hall of Fame, 1985.

BROOKS, HERB, Aug. 5, 1937 (St. Paul, Minn.). U.S. hockey coach. Coached U.S. gold-medal winning hockey team, 1980; New York Rangers, 1981–85; Minnesota North Stars, 1987–88.

BROWN, JIM, Feb. 17, 1936 (St. Simon's, Ga.). U.S. football player, actor. As Cleveland Browns fullback (1957–65), rushed for 12,312 career yards (5.2 yds./carry); had 106 career touchdowns; named NFL Player of the Year, 1958 and 1963; starred in numerous action films, 1960, 1970.

BROWN, LARRY, Sept. 14, 1940 (New York, N.Y.). U.S. basketball player, coach. Lead ABA in assists three times; coached Carolina, 1972–74; Denver, 1975–79; UCLA, 1980–81; New Jersey, 1982–83; Kansas Univ., 1984–88 (NCAA championship, 1988); San Antonio, 1988– .

BROWN, PAUL, Sept. 7, 1908 (Norwalk, Ohio). U.S. football coach, executive. One of the most innovative football coaches of all time; coached Cleveland Browns, 1946–62; coached Cincinnati Bengals, 1968–76; elected to Pro Football Hall of Fame, 1967.

BRUNDAGE, AVERY, Sept. 28, 1887 (Detroit, Mich.)–May 8, 1975. U.S. sports figure. Pres. of U.S. Olympic Assoc., 1929–53; pres. of International Olympic Com., 1952–72.

BRYANT, PAUL ("Bear"), Sept. 11, 1913 (Moro Bottom, Ark.)–Jan. 26, 1983; U.S. football coach. Coach of U. of Alabama, 1958–82; won Div.-I Record 323 games.

BUDGE, DON, June 13, 1915 (Oakland, Calif.). U.S. tennis player. Won tennis Grand Slam, 1938; inducted into Tennis Hall of Fame, 1963.

BUENO, MARIA, Oct. 11, 1939 (São Paulo, Braz.). Brazilian tennis player. U.S. singles champ, 1959, 1963, 1964, 1966; Wimbledon champ three times.

BUNNING, JIM, Oct. 23, 1931 (Southgate, Ky.). U.S. baseball player. Played with Detroit Tigers and Phillies, 1955–71; pitched 2 no-hitters, includ-

ing perfect game against New York Mets, June 21, 1964; U.S. Representative from Kentucky, 1987– .

BUTKUS, DICK, Dec. 9, 1942 (Chicago, Ill.). U.S. football player, actor, sports commentator. Chicago Bears linebacker, 1965–73; chosen best NFL defensive player in 1969 and 1970.

BUTTON, DICK, July 18, 1929 (Englewood, N.J.). U.S. figure skater, broadcaster. Olympic gold medalist in figure skating, 1948 and 1952; world titlist, 1948–52; now sports commentator for ABC.

CAMP, WALTER, Apr. 17, 1859 (New Britain, Conn.)–Mar. 14, 1925. U.S. football player, coach, athletic director. Often called the father of American football, developed game and established many rules; promoted All-American designations.

CAMPANELLA, ROY, Nov. 19, 1921 (Philadelphia, Pa.). U.S. baseball player. Brooklyn Dodgers catcher, 1948–57; NL MVP, 1951, 1953, and 1955; inducted into Baseball Hall of Fame, 1969; crippled in accident, 1958.

CAMPBELL, EARL, Mar. 29, 1955 (Tyler, Tex.). U.S. football player. As U. of Texas running back, awarded 1977 Heisman Trophy; with NFL Houston Oilers, Rookie of Year, 1978, AFC's leading rusher, MVP, 1978, 1979.

CANSECO, JOSE, July 2, 1964 (Havana, Cuba). U.S. baseball player. Outfielder for Oakland A's, 1985– ; led NL in home runs, RBIs, 1988; chosen AL MVP, 1988; hit over 40 home runs, stole 40 bases in season, 1988.

CAREW, ROD, Oct. 1, 1945 (Gatun, Panama). U.S. baseball player. AL batting champ seven times; .335 lifetime batting avg.; 200 or more hits, four times; hit .388 in 1977; AL MVP, 1977.

CARLTON, STEVE, Dec. 22, 1944 (Miami, Fla.). U.S. baseball player. As St. Louis Cardinals (1965–71) and Philadelphia Phillies (1972–86) pitcher; NL Cy Young Award, 1972, 1977, 1980 and 1982, won 329 games, struck out 4,136 batters.

CARNER, JOANNE, Mar. 4, 1939. U.S. golfer. U.S. Women's Open champ, 1971 and 1976; U.S. Women's Amateur champ, five times.

CARTER, GARY ("The Kid"), Apr. 8, 1954 (Culver City, Calif.). U.S. baseball player. Catcher with Montreal Expos, 1974–84; New York Mets, 1985–89; San Francisco Giants, 1990; led NL in RBIs, 1984.

CASPER, BILLY, June 24, 1931 (San Diego, Calif.). U.S. golfer. U.S. Open champ, 1959 and 1966; PGA Player of the Year, 1966, 1968, and 1970.

CAULKINS, TRACY, Jan. 11, 1963 (Winona, Minn.). U.S. swimmer. Set world records in 200- and 400-m individual medley, 1978; Sullivan Award Winner, 1978.

CHADWICK, FLORENCE, May, 1918 (San Diego, Calif.). U.S. distance swimmer. The first woman to swim the English Channel in both directions, from France to England (1950) and from England to France (1951).

CHAMBERLAIN, WILT ("The Stilt"), Aug. 21, 1936 (Philadelphia, Pa.). U.S. basketball player. Center with Philadelphia/San Fancisco Warriors and Los Angeles Lakers; NBA scoring leader, 1960–66;

scored 31,419 points; record 100 points in one game, Mar. 2, 1962; scored a record 50.4 points per game, 1962; holds NBA career records of 30.1 points per game and 23,924 rebounds.

**CHELIOS, CHRIS,** Jan. 25, 1962 (Chicago, Ill.). U.S. hockey player. Defenseman for Montreal Canadiens, 1983–  ; won Norris Trophy, 1989.

**CLARK, WILL,** Mar. 17, 1964 (New Orleans, La.). U.S. baseball player. First baseman for San Francisco Giants, 1987–  ; led NL in RBIs, 1988.

**CLARKE, BOBBY,** Aug. 13, 1949 (Flin Flon, Man., Can.). Canadian hockey player, executive. Center for the Philadelphia Flyers, 1969–84; led team to Stanley Cup championship in 1975 and 1976; named NHL MVP, 1973, 1975, and 1976.

**CLEMENS,** (William) **ROGER,** Aug. 4, 1962 (Dayton, Oh.). U.S. baseball player. Pitcher for Boston Red Sox, 1984–  ; AL Cy Young Award winner, 1986, 1987; AL MVP, 1986.

**CLEMENTE, ROBERTO,** Aug. 18, 1934 (Carolina, P.R.)–Dec. 31, 1972. Puerto Rican baseball player. Pittsburgh Pirates outfielder, 1955–72; NL batting champ, 1961, 1964, 1965, and 1967; MVP, 1966; compiled lifetime batting avg. of .317; inducted into Baseball Hall of Fame, 1973; killed in plane crash.

**COBB, TY** ("Georgia Peach"), Dec. 18, 1886 (Narrows, Ga.)–July 17, 1961. U.S. baseball player. As Detroit Tigers (1905–26) and Philadelphia A's (1927–28) outfielder, often called the greatest player in baseball history; held major-league career records for batting avg. (.367) and most batting titles won (12), most consecutive batting titles won (nine, 1907–15); inducted into Baseball Hall of Fame, 1936.

**COE, SEBASTIAN,** Sept. 29, 1956 (Yorkshire, Eng.). British runner. Set three world records in 1979: 800-m (1:42.4), mile (3:49) and 1,500-m (3:32.1).

**COFFEY, PAUL,** June 1, 1951 (Weston, Ont.). Canadian hockey player. Defenseman for Edmonton Oilers, 1980–87; Pittsburgh Penguins, 1987–  ; won Norris Trophy, 1985, 1986; set NHL record for regular season goals by a defenseman, 48, in 1985–86 season; scored over 100 points in a season four times.

**COLEMAN, VINCE,** Sept. 22, 1961 (Jacksonville, Fla.). U.S. baseball player. Outfielder for St. Louis Cardinals, 1985–  ; led NL in stolen bases, 1985–89.

**COMANECI, NADIA,** Nov. 12, 1961 (Onesti, Rom.). Romanian gymnast. Petite winner of three gold medals in 1976 Olympics, where she earned 7 perfect scores; defected to U.S., 1989.

**CONNOLLY, MAUREEN** ("Little Mo"), Sept. 17, 1934 (San Diego, Calif.)–June 21, 1969. U.S. tennis player. U.S. singles champ, 1951–53; won tennis Grand Slam, 1953; Wimbledon champ, 1952–54; AP Woman Athlete of the Year, 1952–54.

**CONNORS, JIMMY,** Sept. 2, 1952 (E. St. Louis, Ill.). U.S. tennis player. U.S. singles champ, 1974, 1976, and 1978, 1982, 1983. Wimbledon champ, 1974, 1982.

**CORBETT, JAMES J.** ("Gentleman Jim"), Sept. 1, 1866 (San Francisco, Calif.)–Feb. 18, 1933. U.S.

boxer. Credited with being first scientific boxer, he was heavyweight champ from 1892 to 1897.

**CORDERO, ANGEL, JR.,** May 8, 1942 (Santurce, P.R.). Puerto Rican jockey. Rode Kentucky Derby winners Cannonade (1974), Bold Forbes (1976), and Spend a Buck (1985), leading money-winning jockey, 1976, 1982–83.

**COUBERTIN, PIERRE, BARON DE,** Jan. 1, 1863 (Paris, France)–Sept. 1, 1937; French sportsman. Revived Olympic Games, 1894; pres. of the Internatl. Olympic Com., 1894–1925.

**COURT, MARGARET SMITH,** July 16, 1942 (Albury, Austrl.). Australian tennis player; won Grand Slam 1970. U.S. singles champ five times; Wimbledon champ, three times.

**COUSY, BOB,** Aug. 9, 1928 (New York, N.Y.). U.S. basketball player, coach. As Boston Celtics guard (1951–1963), led team to six NBA championships; 10-time NBA all-star; inducted into Basketball Hall of Fame, 1971.

**COWENS, DAVE,** Oct. 25, 1948 (Newport, Ky.). U.S. basketball player, coach. Boston Celtics center (1970–80), and player-coach (1979); NBA MVP, 1973.

**CRAIG, ROGER,** July 10, 1960 (Davenport, Ia.). U.S. football player. Running back for San Francisco 49ers, 1983–  ; set NFL record for most pass receptions by a running back (92), 1985; Thorpe Trophy (MVP), 1988.

**CRUM, DENNY,** Mar. 2, 1937 (San Fernando, Calif.). U.S. basketball coach. Coach, Louisville Univ., 1971–  ; led team to NCAA championship, 1980, 1986.

**CSONKA, LARRY,** Dec. 25, 1946 (Stow, Ohio). U.S. football player. Rushed for over 7,000 yds. in his career with Miami Dolphins (1968–74, and 1979–  ) and New York Giants (1976–78).

**CUNNINGHAM, RANDALL,** Mar. 27, 1963 (Santa Barbara, Calif.). U.S. football player. Quarterback for Philadelphia Eagles, 1985–  .

**DANTLEY, ADRIAN,** Feb. 28, 1956 (Washington, D.C.). U.S. basketball player. NBA forward, since 1976; NBA Rookie of the Year, 1977; NBA leading scorer, 1981, 1984.

**DAVIS, AL,** July 4, 1929 (Brockton, Mass.). U.S. football coach. Coach, general manager, Oakland Raiders, 1963–66; owner (now Los Angeles Raiders), 1966–  .

**DAVIS, ERIC,** May 29, 1962 (Los Angeles, Calif.). U.S. baseball player. Outfielder for Cincinnati Reds, 1984–  .

**DAVIS, MARK,** Oct. 19, 1960 (Livermore, Calif.). U.S. baseball player. Relief pitcher for San Francisco Giants, 1983–87; San Diego Padres, 1987–89; Kansas City Royals, 1990–  ; NL Cy Young Award, 1989.

**DAWSON, ANDRE,** July 10, 1954 (Miami, Fla.). U.S. baseball player. Outfielder for Montreal Expos, 1976–86; Chicago Cubs, 1987–  ; led NL in home runs, RBIs, 1987; NL MVP, 1987.

**DAWSON, LEN,** June 20, 1935 (Alliance, Ohio). U.S. football player, broadcaster. As Kansas City

Chiefs quarterback (1963–75) passed for 28,711 career yds.

**DEAN, DIZZY,** Jan. 16, 1911 (Lucas, Ark.)–July 17, 1974. U.S. baseball player, broadcaster. Pitcher for St. Louis Cardinals (1930–37), Chicago Cubs (1938–41); won 30 games, 1934; NL MVP, 1934; inducted into Baseball Hall of Fame, 1953.

**DEBUSSCHERE, DAVE,** Oct. 16, 1940 (Detroit, Mich.). U.S. basketball player, exec. Basketball forward for Detroit Pistons (1964–68) and New York Knicks (1968–74); NBA All-Defensive team, 1969–74; ABA commissioner, 1975–76; prof. baseball pitcher for Chicago White Sox, 1962–63.

**DEMPSEY, JACK** ("The Manassa Mauler"), June 24, 1895 (Manassa, Colo.)–May 31, 1983. U.S. boxer. Heavyweight champ, 1919–26; lost title to GENE TUNNEY.

**DENT, RICHARD,** Dec. 13, 1960 (Atlanta, Ga.). U.S. football player. Defensive end, Chicago Bears, 1983– .

**DICKERSON, ERIC,** Sept. 2, 1960 (Sealy, Tex.). U.S. football player. Running back for Los Angeles Rams, 1983–87; Indianapolis Colts, 1987– ; led NFL in rushing yardage, 1983, 1984, 1986, 1988; set NFL record for most yards rushing (1,808) and TDs (18) as a rookie, 1983; set NFL record for most yards rushing in a season (2,105), 1984.

**DIMAGGIO, JOE** ("The Yankee Clipper," "Jolting Joe"), Nov. 25, 1914 (Martinez, Calif.). U.S. baseball player. Famed New York Yankees outfielder, 1936–51; batted safely in record 56 consecutive games, 1941; AL batting champ, 1939–40; AL home-run leader, 1937 and 1948; inducted into Baseball Hall of Fame, 1955. (One-time husband of M. MONROE.)

**DITKA, MIKE,** Oct. 18, 1939 (Carnegie, Pa.). U.S. football player, coach. Tight end with Chicago Bears, 1961–66; Philadelphia Eagles, 1967–68; Dallas Cowboys, 1969–72; inducted in Hall of Fame, 1988; coach, Chicago Bears, 1982– ; led team to Super Bowl championship, 1986.

**DORSETT, TONY,** Apr. 7, 1954 (Aliquippa, Pa.). U.S. football player. As U. of Pittsburgh running back, awarded 1976 Heisman Trophy; with NFL Dallas Cowboys, 1977–88; Denver Broncos, 1988–89; NFL Rookie of Year, 1977.

**DOUBLEDAY, ABNER,** June 26, 1819 (Ballston Spa, N.Y.)–Jan. 26, 1893. U.S. sportsman, soldier. Credited for many years with inventing baseball (now considered untrue); Baseball Hall of Fame established where he attended school, in Cooperstown, N.Y.; commanded Ft. Sumter gunners who fired first shots of Civil War.

**DRYSDALE, DON**(ald Scott), July 23, 1936 (Van Nuys, Calif.). U.S. baseball player. Brooklyn, Los Angeles Dodgers pitcher, 1956–69; led NL in strikeouts three times; Cy Young Award winner, 1962.

**DUMARS, JOE,** May 24, 1963 (Shreveport, La.). U.S. basketball player. Guard for Detroit Pistons, 1986– ; NBA playoff MVP, 1989.

**DURAN, ROBERTO,** June 16, 1951 (Panama City, Panama). Panamanian boxer. World lightweight champ, 1972–79; noted for three bouts with SUGAR RAY LEONARD.

**DUROCHER, LEO** ("The Lip"), July 27, 1906 (W. Springfield, Mass.). U.S. baseball player, manager. Outspoken manager famed for comment "Nice guys finish last"; played for 17 years and managed several NL teams; managed N.Y. Giants to World Series win, 1954.

**EARNHARDT,** (Robert) **DALE,** Apr. 29, 1952 (Kannapolis, N.C.). U.S. racing car driver. NASCAR driver, won Winston Cup championship, 1986–87.

**EDERLE, GERTRUDE,** Oct. 23, 1906 (New York, N.Y.). U.S. swimmer. The first woman to swim the English Channel, 1926.

**ELLIOTT, BILL,** Oct. 8, 1955 (Dawsonville, Ga.). U.S. auto racer. NASCAR champion, 1988; won Daytona 500, 1985, 1987.

**ELWAY, JOHN,** June 28, 1960 (Granada Hills, Calif.). U.S. football player. Quarterback for Denver Broncos, 1983– .

**EMERSON, ROY,** Nov. 3, 1936 (Kingsway, Austrl.). Australian tennis player. U.S. singles champ, 1961 and 1964; Wimbledon champ, 1964 and 1965.

**ENGLISH, ALEX,** Jan. 5, 1954 (Columbia, S.C.). U.S. basketball player. Has played in the NBA, since 1976; led NBA in scoring, 1983.

**ERVING, JULIUS** ("Dr. J."), Feb. 22, 1950 (Roosevelt, N.Y.). U.S. basketball player. ABA leading scorer, three times; NBA MVP, 1981.

**ESIASON,** (Norman) **BOOMER,** Apr. 17, 1961 (W. Islip. N.Y.). U.S. football player. Quarterback for Cincinnati Bengals, 1984– ; led NFL in passing, 1986, 1988, 1989.

**ESPOSITO, PHIL,** Feb. 20, 1942 (Sault Ste. Marie, Can.). Canadian hockey player, executive. Leading NHL scorer 1969, 1971–74; NHL MVP, 1969–74; Gen. mgr., New York Rangers, 1987–89. Center for the Chicago Black Hawks, (1964–67); Boston Bruins, (1968–76); New York Rangers (1976–78); NHL leading scorer five times; NHL MVP, 1969 and 1974.

**EVANS, JANET,** Aug. 28, 1971 (Placentia, Calif.). U.S. swimmer. Won three gold medals at the 1988 Olympic games; Sullivan Trophy, 1989.

**EVANS, DWIGHT** ("Dewey"), Nov. 3, 1951 (Santa Monica, Calif.). U.S. baseball player. Outfielder with Boston Red Sox, 1972– .

**EVERT, CHRIS,** Dec. 21, 1954 (Ft. Lauderdale, Fla.). U.S. tennis player. U.S. singles champion, 1975–78, 1980, 1982; Wimbledon champion, 1974 and 1976, 1981.

**EWBANK, WEEB,** May 6, 1907 (Richmond, Ind.). U.S. football coach. Head coach, Baltimore Colts, 1954–62; as head coach (1963–73) led New York Jets to Super Bowl championship in 1969.

**EWING, PATRICK,** Aug. 5, 1962 (Kingston, Jamaica). Jamaican basketball player. New York Knick center, 1985– ; NBA Rookie of the Year, 1986; led Georgetown Univ. to NCAA championship, named MVP, 1985.

**EWRY, RAY,** Oct. 14, 1873 (Lafayette, Ind.)–Sept. 29, 1937. U.S. athlete. Track-and-field standout who won eight gold medals in 1900, 1904, and 1908 Olympics.

**FELLER, ROBERT** ("Rapid Robert"), Nov. 3, 1918 (Van Meter, Ia.). U.S. baseball player. As pitcher for Cleveland Indians (1936–56), a six-time 20-game winner; AL strikeout leader seven times; pitched three no-hitters and 12 one-hitters; won 266 games; inducted into Baseball Hall of Fame, 1962.

**FINGERS, ROLLIE,** Aug. 25, 1946 (Steubenville, Ohio). U.S. baseball player. One of game's premier relief pitchers with the Oakland A's (1968–76) and San Diego Padres (1977–81); World Series MVP 1974.

**FINLEY, CHARLES, O.,** Feb. 22, 1918 (Birmingham, Ala.). U.S. baseball executive. Colorful owner of the Oakland A's (1960–80), known for feuds with the commissioner, other owners, and players; built A's team that won three consecutive World Series, 1972–74.

**FISCHER, ROBERT** ("Bobby"), Mar. 9, 1943 (Chicago, Ill.). U.S. chess player. The first American to hold the world chess title, defeating Boris Spassky in 1972 (held title through 1975).

**FLEISCHER, NAT,** Nov. 3, 1887 (New York, N.Y.)–June 25, 1972. U.S. boxing expert, publisher, author. Founded *The Ring* magazine, 1922; wrote over 50 books on boxing and wrestling.

**FLEMING, PEGGY,** July 27, 1948 (San Jose, Calif.). U.S. figure skater. Olympic gold medalist, 1968; world champion, 1966–68.

**FORD, WHITEY** (born Edward Charles Ford), Oct. 21, 1928 (New York, N.Y.). U.S. baseball player. As N.Y. Yankees pitcher (1950–67), won 10 World Series games; career 2.74 ERA; Cy Young Award winner, 1961; inducted into Baseball Hall of Fame, 1974.

**FOREMAN, GEORGE,** Jan. 10, 1949 (Marshall, Tex.). U.S. boxer. Olympic heavyweight champ, 1968; world pro heavyweight champ, 1973–74.

**FOSBURY, DICK,** Mar. 6, 1947 (Portland, Ore.). U.S. high jumper. Won 1968 Olympic gold medal; developed "Fosbury Flop" maneuver.

**FOSTER, GEORGE,** Dec. 1, 1948 (Tuscaloosa, Ala.). U.S. baseball player. Outfielder for San Francisco Giants, Cincinnati Reds and New York Mets; led NL in home runs, 1977–78; NL MVP, 1977.

**FOX, NELLIE,** Dec. 25, 1927 (St. Thomas, Pa.)–Dec. 1, 1975. U.S. baseball player. Infielder for Philadelphia A's (1947–49), Chicago White Sox (1950–63), and Houston Astros (1964–65); led AL in hits four times; AL MVP. 1959.

**FOXX, JIMMIE** ("Double X"), Oct. 22, 1907 (Sudlersville, Md.)–July 21, 1967. U.S. baseball player. As outfielder for Philadelphia A's (1925–35), Boston Red Sox (1936–42), others, hit 534 home runs and compiled a .325 career batting avg.; won AL Triple Crown, 1933; AL batting champ, 1933 and 1938; AL home run leader, 1932, 1933, 1935, and 1939; hit 58 home runs in 1932; inducted into Baseball Hall of Fame, 1951.

**FOYT, A**(nthony) **J**(ames), Jan. 16, 1935 (Houston, Tex.). U.S. auto racer. Won Indianapolis 500

in 1961, 1964, 1967, and 1977; USAC champion seven times.

**FRASER, DAWN,** Sept. 4, 1937 (Balmain, Austrl.). Australian swimmer. Won Olympic gold medals in 100-m freestyle in 1956, 1960, and 1964.

**FRAZIER, WALT** ("Clyde"), Mar. 29, 1945 (Atlanta, Ga.). U.S. basketball player, broadcaster. Guard for New York Knicks (1967–77) and Cleveland Cavaliers (1977–79); key player on Knicks championship teams of 1970 and 1973.

**FRISCH, FRANKIE** ("The Fordham Flash"), Sept. 9, 1898 (New York, N.Y.)–Mar. 12, 1973. U.S. baseball player and manager. Played with New York Giants (1919–26) and St. Louis Cardinals (1927–37); .316 career batting avg.; hit over .300 13 times; NL MVP, 1931; elected to Baseball Hall of Fame, 1947.

**FUHR, GRANT,** Sept. 28, 1962 (Spruce Grove, Alta.). Canadian hockey player. Goaltender for Edmonton Oilers, 1982–  ; Vezina Trophy, 1988.

**GAINEY, BOB,** Dec. 13, 1953 (Peterborough, Ont., Can.). Canadian hockey player. Forward-defenseman with Montreal Canadiens, 1973–89; won Selke Trophy (outstanding defensive forward), 1978–81; won Smythe Trophy (MVP in playoffs), 1979.

**GARVEY, STEVE,** Dec. 22, 1948 (Tampa, Fla.). U.S. baseball player. First basemen for Los Angeles Dodgers, San Diego Padres, 1969–86; NL MVP, 1974.

**GEHRIG,** (Henry) **LOU**(is), June 19, 1903 (New York, N.Y.)–June 2, 1941. U.S. baseball player. N.Y. Yankees great (1923–39) who played a major-league record 2,130 consecutive games; career .340 batting avg.; AL batting champ, 1934; AL home-run champ, 1931, 1934, and 1936; AL MVP, 1927, 1931, 1934, and 1936; inducted into Baseball Hall of Fame, 1939; died of muscle wasting disease that bears his name.

**GERVIN, GEORGE** ("The Iceman"), Apr. 27, 1952 (Detroit, Mich.). U.S. basketball player. Guard for San Antonio Spurs, 1975–85; NBA scoring leader, 1978 and 1979; avg. 26.2 PPG during career.

**GIBBS, JOE,** Nov. 25, 1940 (Mocksville, N.C.). U.S. football coach. Coach, Washington Redskins, 1981–  ; led team to Super Bowl championship, 1983.

**GIBSON, ALTHEA,** Aug. 25, 1927 (Silver, S.C.). U.S. tennis player. First black to win a major tournament; U.S. and Wimbledon singles champ, 1957 and 1958.

**GIBSON, BOB,** Nov. 9, 1935 (Omaha, Neb.). U.S. baseball player. As St. Louis Cardinals pitcher (1959–75), compiled NL single-season record ERA of 1.12, 1968; NL Cy Young Award winner, 1968 and 1970; NL MVP, 1968; inducted into Hall of Fame, 1981.

**GIBSON, JOSH,** Dec. 21, 1911 (Buena Vista, Ga.)–Jan. 20, 1947. U.S. baseball player. Legendary slugger in Negro leagues; inducted into Baseball Hall of Fame, 1972.

**GIBSON, KIRK,** May 18, 1957 (Pontiac, Mich.). U.S. baseball player. Outfielder for Detroit Tigers,

1979–87; Los Angeles Dodgers, 1988–  ; NL MVP, 1988.

**GIFFORD, FRANK**, Aug. 16, 1930 (Santa Monica, Calif.). U.S. football player, broadcaster. Running back and kicker for the NFL New York Giants, 1952–65; NFL MVP, 1956; associated with *Monday Night Football* games, 1971–  ; elected to Football Hall of Fame, 1977.

**GILMORE, ARTIS**, Sept. 21, 1949 (Chipley, Fla.). U.S. basketball player. Center with ABA Kentucky Colonels (1972–76), Chicago Bulls, San Antonio Spurs.

**GONZALEZ, RICHARD** ("Pancho"), May 9, 1928 (Los Angeles, Calif.). U.S. tennis player, coach. Member of U.S. teams that won Davis Cup, 1949; turned pro, 1949; world pro tennis champion eight times between 1953 and 1962.

**GOODEN, DWIGHT** ("Doc"), Nov. 16, 1964 (Tampa, Fla.). U.S. baseball player. Pitcher for New York Mets, 1984–  ; NL Rookie of the Year, 1984; NL Cy Young Award, 1985.

**GOOLAGONG, EVONNE CAWLEY**, July 31, 1951 (Griffith, Austl.). Australian tennis player. Wimbledon champ, 1971, 1980.

**GOWDY, CURT**(is), 1919 (Green River, Wyo.). U.S. sportscaster. Broadcast N.Y. Yankee (1949–51) and Boston Red Sox (1951–66) games; all-purpose sports announcer; named sportscaster of the year, 1965 and 1967.

**GRAF, STEFFI**, June 14, 1969 (Bruehl, W. Ger.). West German tennis player. Won "grand slam," 1988; U.S. champion, 1988, 1989; Wimbledon champion, 1988, 1989.

**GRAHAM, OTTO**, Dec. 6, 1921 (Waukegan, Ill.). U.S. football player, coach. Quarterback with Cleveland Browns, 1946–55; inducted into Pro Football Hall of Fame, 1965.

**GRANGE, HAROLD** ("Red," "The Galloping Ghost"), June 13, 1903 (Forksville, Pa.). U.S. football player. All-American running back at U. of Ill., 1923–25; played for NFL Chicago Bears, 1925–35; inducted into Pro Football Hall of Fame, 1963.

**GREENBERG, HANK**, Jan. 1, 1911 (New York, N.Y.)–Sept. 4, 1986. U.S. baseball player. First baseman, outfielder for the Detroit Tigers, 1930–46; led AL in homers and RBIs four times; 331 career homers; AL MVP 1935, 1940; elected to Baseball Hall of Fame, 1956.

**GREENE, JOE** ("Mean Joe Greene"), Sept. 24, 1946 (Temple, Tex.). U.S. football player. Defensive lineman with Pittsburgh Steelers, 1969–81; named NFL's outstanding defensive player, 1972 and 1974.

**GRETZKY, WAYNE** ("The Great One"), Jan 26, 1961 (Brantford, Ont.). Canadian hockey player. Edmonton Oilers, 1978–88; Los Angeles Kings, 1988–  ; became NHL all-time leading scorer, 1989; led NHL in scoring, 1980–87, 1990. NHL MVP, 1980–87; Conn Smythe Trophy, 1985, 1988; set NHL regular season records for goals (92), 1981–82, and points (215), 1985–86; set playoff record for points (47), 1984–85.

**GRIESE, BOB**, Feb. 3, 1945 (Evansville, Ind.). U.S.

football player, broadcaster. All-American quarterback at Purdue U.; with NFL Miami Dolphins 1967–81; NFL MVP, 1971.

**GRIFFITH, EMILE**, Feb. 3, 1938 (Virgin Is.). U.S. boxer. Welterweight champ three times in period 1961–66; middleweight champ twice in period 1966–68.

**GRIFFITH JOYNER**, (Delorez) **FLORENCE** ("Flo Jo"), Dec. 21, 1959 (Los Angeles, Calif.). U.S. track and field star. A sprinter, she won three 1988 Olympic gold medals; set world record in the 200-meter run; Sullivan Award winner, 1988.

**GROVE, LEFTY**, Mar. 6, 1900 (Lonaconing, Md.)–May 22, 1975. U.S. baseball player. As Philadelphia A's (1925–33) and Boston Red Sox (1934–41) pitcher, won 300 games in career; had a 31–4 record in 1931; 20–game winner eight times; lowest AL ERA nine times; inducted into Baseball Hall of Fame, 1947.

**GUERRERO, PEDRO**, June 29, 1956 (San Pedro de Macros, Dom. Rep.). Dominican baseball player. Slugger with Los Angeles Dodgers, 1978–88; St. Louis Cardinals, 1988–

**GUIDRY, RON**(ald), Aug. 28, 1950 (Lafayette, La.). U.S. baseball player. Pitcher for New York Yankees (1975–88); had 25-3 record with 1.74 ERA in 1978; AL Cy Young Award winner, 1978.

**GUTHRIE, JANET**, Mar. 7, 1938 (Iowa City, Ia.). U.S. auto racer. The first woman to qualify for and race in the Indianapolis 500, 1977.

**GWYNN, TONY**, May 9, 1960 (Los Angeles, Calif.). U.S. baseball player. Outfielder for San Diego Padres 1983–  ; led NFL in batting, 1984, 1987–89.

**HAGEN, WALTER**, Dec. 21, 1892 (Rochester, N.Y.)–Oct. 5, 1969. U.S. golfer. PGA champ, 1921 and 1924–27; British Open champ, 1922, 1924, 1928, and 1929.

**HALAS, GEORGE**, Feb. 2, 1895 (Chicago, Ill.)–Oct. 31, 1983. U.S. football player, coach, executive. Founder-coach of Chicago Bears and one of the founders of the NFL; inducted into Pro Football Hall of Fame, 1963.

**HAMILTON, SCOTT**, Aug. 28, 1958 (Bowling Green, Oh.). U.S. figure skater. Won gold medal at 1984 Olympics; world, U.S. singles champion, 1981–84.

**HARRIS, FRANCO**, Mar. 7, 1950 (Ft. Dix, N.J.). U.S. football player. As Pittsburgh Steelers running back rushed for 12,120 career yards.

**HARTACK, BILL**, Dec. 9, 1932 (Colver, Pa.). U.S. jockey. Rode record five Kentucky Derby winners, 1957, 1960, 1962, 1964, 1969.

**HAUGHTON, BILL**, Nov. 2, 1923 (Gloversville, N.Y.)–July 15, 1986. U.S. harness-racing driver. Drove Hambletonian winner four times; drove Little Brown Jug winner five times, 1955, 1964, 1968, and 1969.

**HAVLICEK, JOHN**, Apr. 8, 1940 (Martin's Ferry, Ohio). U.S. basketball player. Boston Celtics forward-guard, 1962–78; scored 26,395 career points.

**HAWERCHUK, DALE**, Apr. 4, 1963 (Toronto, Ont.). Canadian hockey player. With the Winnipeg

Jets, 1982–  ; youngest player to have 100-point season, 1981–82; 100-point scorer six times; NHL rookie of the year, 1982.

**HAYES, ELVIN,** Nov. 17, 1945 (Rayville, La.). U.S. basketball player. With Baltimore/Washington Bullets; NBA leading scorer, 1969; scored 27,313 career points, 16,279 rebounds; inducted into Hall of Fame, 1990.

**HAYES, WAYNE** ("Woody"), Feb. 4, 1913 (Clifton, Ohio)–Mar. 12, 1987. U.S. football coach. Controversial head coach of Ohio State football team, 1951–78; led team to 13 big 10 championships and four Rose Bowl victories.

**HEIDEN, ERIC,** June 14, 1958 (Madison Wis.). U.S. speed skater. Won five Olympic gold medals, 1980.

**HENDERSON, RICKEY,** Dec. 25, 1958 (Chicago, Ill.). U.S. baseball player. Outfielder for Oakland A's, 1978–84; New York Yankees, 1985–89; Oakland A's, 1989–  ; stole major league-record 130 bases, 1982; led AL in stolen bases nine times.

**HENIE, SONJA,** Apr. 8, 1912 (Oslo, Norway) –Oct. 12, 1969. U.S. figure skater. Olympic gold medalist, 1928, 1932, and 1936; world champion, 1927–36; leading box-office attraction in 10 movies, 1937–45.

**HERNANDEZ, KEITH,** Oct. 20, 1953 (San Francisco, Calif.). U.S. baseball player. First baseman for St. Louis Cardinals, 1974–1983; New York Mets, 1983–89; Cleveland Indians, 1990–  ; NL batting champ, co-MVP, 1979; won 11 Gold Glove awards.

**HERSHISER, OREL,** Sept. 16, 1958 (Buffalo, N.Y.). U.S. baseball player. Pitcher for Los Angeles Dodgers, 1983–  ; won 23 games, Cy Young Award, 1988; World Series MVP, 1988.

**HERZOG,** (Dorrell) **WHITEY,** Nov. 9, 1931 (New Athens, Ill.). U.S. baseball manager. Played for several major league teams, 1956–63; manager, Texas Rangers, 1973; California Angels, 1974–75; Kansas City Royals, 1975–79; St. Louis Cardinals, 1980–  .

**HEXTALL, RON,** May 3, 1964 (Winnipeg. Man., Can.). Canadian hockey player. Goalie for Philadelphia Flyers, 1987–  ; won Conn Symthe Trophy, 1987; set NHL record for penalty minutes by goalies, 1987; became first goalie to score a goal during Stanley Cup play, May 11, 1989.

**HILL, GRAHAM,** Feb. 15, 1929 (London, Eng.) –Nov. 29, 1975. British auto racer. Won Grand Prix championship 1962, 1968; won Indianapolis 500, 1966.

**HODGES, GIL**(bert), Apr. 4, 1924 (Princeton, Ind.) –Apr. 2, 1972. U.S. baseball player, manager. With Brooklyn/Los Angeles Dodgers (1943–61) and New York Mets (1962–63). Managed New York Mets to World Series win, 1969.

**HOGAN,** (William) **BEN**(jamin), Aug. 13, 1912 (Dublin, Tex.). U.S. golfer. Winner of U.S. Open, 1948, 1950, 1951, and 1953; Masters champ, 1951 and 1953; PGA champ, 1946 and 1948; inducted into PGA Hall of Fame, 1953.

**HOLMES, LARRY,** Nov 3, 1949 (Cuthbert, Ga.). U.S. boxer. WBC heavyweight champ, 1978–83.

**HOLTZ, LOU,** Jan. 6, 1937 (Fallansbee, W. Va.). U.S. football coach. Coach, William and Mary 1969–71; North Carolina State, 1972–75; New York Jets, 1976; Arkansas, 1977–83; Minnesota, 1983–85; Notre Dame, 1986–  .

**HOPPE, WILLIE,** Oct. 11, 1887 (Cornwall-on-the-Hudson, N.Y.)–Feb. 1, 1959. U.S. billiards player. Won some 50 world billiard titles.

**HORNSBY, ROGERS** ("The Rajah"), Apr. 27, 1896 (Winters, Tex.)–Jan. 5, 1963. U.S. baseball player and manager. Infielder with several teams, principally the St. Louis Cardinals (1915–26) and Chicago Cubs (1929–33); batted record .424 in 1924; won NL Triple Crown, 1922 and 1925; NL batting champ, 1920–25 and 1928; .358 lifetime batting avg. is NL record; inducted into Baseball Hall of Fame, 1942.

**HORNUNG, PAUL** Dec. 23, 1935 (Louisville, Ky.). U.S. football player. Heisman Trophy winner at Notre Dame, 1956; runner-placekicker with NFL Green Bay Packers, 1957–66; scored NFL record 176 points in 1960.

**HOWE, GORDIE,** Mar. 31, 1928 (Floral, Sask., Can.). Canadian hockey player. Forward with the Detroit Red Wings (1947–71); also played in World Hockey Assn.; held many NHL scoring records at retirement; NHL leading scorer, 1951–54, 1957, 1963; NHL MVP 6 times; NHL first team all-star 11 times.

**HUBBARD, CAL,** Oct. 31, 1900 (Keytesville, Mo.) –Oct. 17, 1977. U.S. football lineman, baseball umpire. Only man inducted into both Pro Football (1963) and Baseball (1976) halls of fame.

**HUBBELL, CARL** ("King Carl," "The Meal Ticket"), June 22, 1903 (Carthage, Mo.)–Nov. 21, 1988. U.S. baseball player. As New York Giants pitcher (1928–43), won 253 games; won at least 20 games per season, 1933–37; inducted into Baseball Hall of Fame, 1947.

**HUGGINS, MILLER,** Mar. 27, 1879 (Cincinnati, Ohio)–Sept. 25, 1929. U.S. baseball manager. As New York Yankees manager (1918–29), won six AL pennants and three World Series, 1923, 1927, 1928; inducted into Baseball Hall of Fame, 1964.

**HULL, BOBBY,** Jan. 3, 1939 (Point Anne, Ont., Can.). Canadian hockey player. Forward with the Chicago Black Hawks [NHL] (1958–72) and Winnepeg Jets [WHA] (1973–80); NHL leading scorer, 1960, 1962, 1966; NHL MVP, 1965 and 1966. (Father of BRETT HULL.)

**HULL, BRETT,** Feb. 2, 1969 (Belleville, Ont.). Canadian hockey player. Right wing with Calgary Flames, 1986–88; St. Louis Blues, 1988–  ; became first father-son combo to score 50 NHL goals in a season, 1990; scored NHL-leading 72 goals, 1990. (Son of BOBBY HULL.)

**HUNTER, JAMES** ("Catfish"), Apr. 8, 1946 (Hertford, N.C.). U.S. baseball player. Pitcher with Kansas City/Oakland A's (1965–74) and New York Yankees (1975–79); pitched perfect game against Minnesota Twins on May 8, 1968; a 20-game winner, 1971 75; AL Cy Young Award winner, 1974.

**HUTSON, DON,** Jan. 31, 1913 (Pine Bluff, Ark.). U.S. football player. With the Green Bay Packers, 1935–45; led NFL in scoring, 1940–44; led NFL in pass receiving eight times; led NFL in touchdowns, 1935–38 and 1941–44; inducted into Pro Football Hall of Fame, 1963.

**ISSEL, DAN,** Oct. 25, 1948 (Batavia, Ill.). U.S. basketball player. Center with ABA Kentucky Colonels (1971–75) and NBA Denver Nuggets (1976–85); ABA Rookie of the Year and leading scorer, 1971; avg. 20.4 PPG in NBA career.

**JACKSON, REGGIE,** May 18, 1946 (Wyncote, Pa.). U.S. baseball player, broadcaster. Outfielder with Kansas City/Oakland A's (1967–75), Baltimore Orioles (1976), and New York Yankees (1977–81); California Angels, 1982–86, Oakland A's, 1987; led AL in home runs, 1973, 1975, 1980, 1982; hit five World Series home runs, 1977 (3 in one game); AL MVP, 1973.

**JACKSON, (Vincent) BO,** Nov. 30, 1962 (Bessemer, Ala.). U.S. baseball and football player. Outfielder for Kansas City Royals, 1986– ; running back for Los Angeles Raiders, 1987– ; won Heisman Trophy, 1985.

**JACOBS, HELEN HULL,** Aug. 6, 1908 (Globe, Ariz.). U.S. tennis player. U.S. singles champ, 1932–35; Wimbledon champ, 1936.

**JENKINS, FERGUSON ("Fergie"),** Dec. 13, 1943 (Chatham, Ont., Can.). Canadian baseball player. Pitcher chiefly with Chicago Cubs, 1966–73; won at least 20 games per season, 1967–72; NL Cy Young Award, 1971.

**JENNER, BRUCE,** Oct. 28, 1949 (Mt. Kisco, N.Y.). U.S. athlete. Winner of decathlon in 1976 Olympics; Sullivan Trophy winner, 1976; AP Athlete of the Year, 1976.

**JOHN, TOMMY,** May 22, 1943 (Terre Haute, Ind.). U.S. baseball player. Pitcher with several major league teams; won 286 major league games.

**JOHNSON, DENNIS,** Sept. 18, 1954 (San Pedro, Calif.). U.S. basketball player. Guard for Seattle Supersonics, 1977–80; Phoenix Suns, 1980–83; Boston Celtics, 1983– ; member of 1979, 1984, 1986 championship teams; NBA playoff MVP, 1979.

**JOHNSON, DAVEY,** Jan. 30, 1943 (Orlando, Fla.). U.S. baseball manager. Major league second baseman, 1965–78; manager, New York Mets, 1984–90; led team to World Series championship, 1986.

**JOHNSON, JACK,** Mar. 31, 1878 (Galveston, Tex.) –June 10, 1946. U.S. boxer. First black to hold world heavyweight title, 1908–1915.

**JOHNSON, RAFER,** Aug. 18, 1935 (Hillsboro, Tex.). U.S. athlete. Winner of decathlon in 1960 Olympics; one of persons who captured assassin of ROBERT KENNEDY, 1968.

**JOHNSON, KEVIN,** Mar. 4, 1966 (Sacramento, Calif.). U.S. basketball player. Guard for Phoenix Suns, 1988– .

**JOHNSON, (Earvin) MAGIC,** Aug. 14, 1959 (Lansing, Mich.). U.S. basketball player. Los Angeles Lakers guard, 1979– ; NBA MVP, 1987, 1989;

NBA all-star, 1983–89; playoff MVP, 1980, 1982, 1987; member of five NBA championship teams; led NBA in assists four times; NCAA Division 1 championship tournament MVP, 1979.

**JOHNSON, WALTER ("The Big Train"),** Nov. 6, 1887 (Humboldt, Kan.)–Dec. 10, 1946. U.S. baseball player. As a pitcher with the Washington Senators (1907–27), won 413 career games; 20-game winner 12 times; pitched 110 career shutouts; inducted into Baseball Hall of Fame, 1936.

**JONES, BOBBY,** Mar. 17, 1902 (Atlanta, Ga.) –Dec. 18, 1971. U.S. golfer. The dominant force in golf in the 1920s; won Grand Slam, 1930; won four U.S. Opens (1923, 1926 and 1929–30), five U.S. Amateurs (1924–25, 1927–28, 1930) and three British Opens (1926–27 and 1930); helped found the Masters Tournament, 1934.

**JONES, DAVID ("Deacon"),** Dec. 9, 1938 (Eatonville, Fla.). U.S. football player. Defensive lineman with Los Angeles Rams, 1961–71; named NFL outstanding defensive player, 1967 and 1968.

**JONES, ED ("Too Tall"),** Feb. 23, 1951 (Jackson, Tenn.). U.S. football player. Defensive lineman with Dallas Cowboys, 1974– .

**JORDAN, MICHAEL ("Air"),** Feb. 17, 1963 (New York, N.Y.). U.S. basketball player. Chicago Bulls guard, 1984– ; NBA Rookie of the Year, 1985; led NBA in scoring, 1987–90; NBA MVP, 1988; NBA defensive player of the year, 1988; set playoff record for points (63), 1986.

**JOYNER-KERSEE, JACKIE,** Mar. 3, 1962 (E. St. Louis, Ill.). U.S. track and field star. Won 1988 Olympic gold medals in the long jump and heptathlon; set world record in heptathlon.

**JURGENSON, SONNY,** Aug. 23, 1934 (Wilmington, N.C.). U.S. football player. Quarterback for the Philadelphia Eagles (1957–64) and Washington Redskins (1964–74); led NFL in passing, three times.

**KAHANAMOKU, DUKE PAOA,** Aug. 26, 1890 (Waikiki, Haw.)–Jan. 22, 1968. Hawaiian swimmer. Olympic champion in 100-m freestyle, 1912 and 1920.

**KALINE, AL,** Dec. 19, 1934 (Baltimore, Md.). U.S. baseball player. Played with Detroit Tigers, 1953–74; .297 career batting avg.; led AL in batting, 1955; inducted into Baseball Hall of Fame, 1980.

**KAROLYI, BELA,** Sept. 13, 1942 (Cluj, Romania). Romania-U.S. gymnastic coach. Coach of the Romanian gymnastics team who defected to the U.S. in 1981; coached NADIA COMANECI, MARY LOU RETTON, and Phoebe Mills.

**KARRAS, ALEX,** July 15, 1935 (Gary, Ind.). U.S. football player, broadcaster, actor. Defensive lineman for Detroit Lions, 1958–71; Outland Award, 1957; starred in "Webster" TV series, 1983–86.

**KEELER, WILLIE ("Wee Willie"),** March 13, 1872 (Brooklyn, N.Y.)–Jan. 1, 1923. U.S. baseball player. Played chiefly with Baltimore (1894–98), Brooklyn (1899–1902) and New York (1903–10); .345 career batting avg.; credited with saying, "I hit 'em where they ain't"; elected to Baseball Hall of Fame, 1939.

**KERR, TIM,** Jan. 5, 1930 (Windsor, Ont.). Canadian hockey player. Philadelphia Flyers forward, 1981–  ; 50-goal scorer four times; scored NHL-record 35 power play goals, 1986.

**KILLEBREW, HARMON,** June 29, 1936 (Payette, Idaho). U.S. baseball player. With Washington Senators/Minnesota Twins (1954–74) and Kansas City Royals (1975); led AL in home runs, 1959, 1962–64, 1967, and 1969; AL MVP, 1969; hit 573 career home runs.

**KILLY, JEAN-CLAUDE,** Aug. 30, 1943 (St. Cloud, Fr.). French skier. Olympic champ in downhill, slalom, giant slalom, 1968; World Cup champ, 1967, 1968,

**KINER, RALPH,** Oct. 27, 1922 (Santa Rita, N.M.). U.S. baseball player, broadcaster. Outfielder, principally with the Pittsburgh Pirates, 1946–53; led NL in home runs, 1946–52; hit 54 home runs, 1949; inducted into Baseball Hall of Fame, 1975.

**KING, BILLIE JEAN,** Nov. 22, 1943 (Long Beach, Calif.). U.S. tennis player. U.S. singles champ, 1967, 1971–72, and 1974; Wimbledon champ, 1966–68, 1972–73, and 1975; AP Female Athlete of the Year, 1967 and 1973.

**KITE, TOM,** Dec. 9, 1949 (Austin, Tex.). U.S. golfer; PGA leading money winner, 1981, 1989.

**KORBUT, OLGA,** May 16, 1955 (Grodno, USSR). Soviet gymnast. Petite gold medalist (three medals) in 1972 Olympics; credited with popularizing gymnastics in U.S.

**KOUFAX, SANDY,** Dec. 30, 1935 (Brooklyn, N.Y.). U.S. baseball player. Pitcher with Brooklyn/Los Angeles Dodgers, 1955–66; pitched perfect game against Chicago, 1965; pitched four no-hitters; lowest NL ERA, 1962–65; won 27 games with 1.73 ERA, 1966; struck out 382 batters, 1965; NL MVP, 1963; Cy Young Award winner, 1963, 1965, 1966; inducted into Baseball Hall of Fame, 1972.

**KRAMER, JACK,** Aug. 1, 1921 (Las Vegas, Nev.). U.S. tennis player, promoter. U.S. singles champ, 1946–47; Wimbledon champ, 1946–47; organized pro tours, from 1948.

**KUBEK, TONY,** Oct. 12, 1936 (Milwaukee, Wisc.). U.S. baseball player, broadcaster. Shortstop with N.Y. Yankees, 1957–65; played in six World Series.

**KURRI, JARI,** May 18, 1960 (Helsinki, Finland). Finnish hockey player. Forward for Edmonton Oilers, 1981–  ; led Stanley Cup playoffs in goals, 1984, 1985, 1987; Lady Byng Trophy, 1985.

**LAFLEUR, GUY,** Sept. 20, 1951 (Thurso, Que., Can.). Canadian hockey player. Forward with Montreal Canadiens, 1972–85; NHL leading scorer, 1976–78; NHL MVP, 1977 and 1978; MVP in 1977 playoffs; inducted into Hall of Fame, 1988; made comeback with New York Rangers, 1988, Quebec Nordiques, 1989.

**LAJOIE, NAPOLEON,** Sept. 5, 1875 (Woonsocket, R.I.)–Feb. 7, 1959. U.S. baseball player. Infielder with several teams, chiefly the Cleveland Indians, 1903–14; won AL batting crown, 1901–04; had 3,242 career hits for a .338 batting avg.; inducted into Baseball Hall of Fame, 1937.

**LAMBEAU, CURLY,** Apr. 9, 1898 (Green Bay,

Wisc.)–June 1, 1965. U.S. football coach. Founder of Green Bay Packers (1919), whom he led to six NFL championships, 1929, 1930–31, 1936, 1939, 1944; inducted into Pro Football Hall of Fame, 1963.

**LANDIS, KENESAW MOUNTAIN,** Nov. 20, 1866 (Millville, Ohio)–Nov. 25, 1944. U.S. jurist, sports executive. First baseball commissioner, 1920–44; inducted into Baseball Hall of Fame, 1944.

**LANDRY, TOM,** Sept. 11, 1924 (Mission, Tex.). U.S. football coach. Head coach of NFL Dallas Cowboys, 1960–88; led team to Super Bowl victory in 1972, 1978.

**LANGSTON, MARK,** Aug. 20, 1960 (San Diego, Calif.). U.S. baseball player. Pitcher with Seattle Mariners, 1984–89; Montreal Expos, 1989; California Angels, 1990–  ; led AL in strikeouts three times.

**LANGWAY, ROD,** May 3, 1957 (Taiwan). U.S. hockey player. Defenseman for the Montreal Canadiens, 1980–82; Washington Capitals, 1983–  ; won Norris Trophy, 1983, 1984.

**LANIER, BOB,** Sept. 10, 1948 (Buffalo, N.Y.). U.S. basketball player. Center with the NBA Detroit Pistons, 1972–80; has career scoring avg. of 20.1 PPG.

**LANSFORD, CARNEY,** Feb. 7, 1957 (San Jose, Calif.). U.S. baseball player. Third baseman with California Angels, 1978–80; Boston Red Sox,1981–82; Oakland A's, 1983–  ; led AL in batting, 1981.

**LARSEN, DON,** Aug. 7, 1929 (Michigan City, Ind.). U.S. baseball player. While pitching for the New York Yankees, hurled the only perfect game in World Series history, against Brooklyn Dodgers on Oct. 8, 1956.

**LAUDA, NIKI,** Feb. 22, 1949 (Austria). Austrian auto racer. World Grand Prix champ, 1975, 1977, 1984.

**LAVER, ROD,** Aug. 9, 1938 (Rockhampton, Austrl.). Australian tennis player. Won tennis Grand Slam, 1962 and 1969; U.S. singles champ, 1962, 1969; Wimbledon champ, 1961–62, 1968–69.

**LEMIEUX, MARIO,** Oct. 5, 1965 (Montreal, Que.). Canadian hockey player. With Pittsburgh Penguins, 1984–  ; led NHL in scoring, 1988, 1989; NHL MVP, 1988.

**LEMON, BOB,** Sept. 22, 1920 (San Bernardino, Calif.). U.S. baseball player, manager. As Cleveland Indians pitcher (1946–58), won 20 or more games seven times; managed New York Yankees to World Series victory, 1978; inducted into Baseball Hall of Fame, 1976.

**LENDL, IVAN,** Mar. 7, 1970 (Ostrava, Czech.). U.S. tennis player. Won U.S. open, 1985–87; French Open, 1984, 1986–87.

**LENGLEN, SUZANNE,** May 24, 1899 (Compiègne, Fr.)–July 4, 1938. French tennis player. Called the "Pavlova of Tennis," she dominated the game between 1919 and 1926.

**LEONARD, RAY** ("Sugar Ray"), May 17, 1956 (Wilmington, N.C.). U.S. boxer. Won Olympic lt.-

welterweight gold medal, 1976; has held titles in several divisions since 1979.

LEWIS, CARL, July 1, 1961 (Birmingham, Ala.). U.S. track and field star. Won four gold medals at the 1984 Olympics, two gold medals at 1988 Olympics; set world record at 100 meters, 1987.

LILLY, BOB, July 26, 1939 (Olney, Tex.). U.S. football player. Defensive lineman with Dallas Cowboys, 1961–75; rated as a top defensive lineman; earned all-pro honors seven times at defensive tackle.

LINDSAY, TED, July 29, 1925 (Renfrew, Ont., Can.). Canadian hockey player. Forward, mostly with Detroit Red Wings.

LIQUORI, MARTY, Sept. 11, 1949 (Montclair, N.J.). U.S. athlete. Leading miler and distance runner of 1970s.

LOMBARDI, VINCE, June 11, 1913 (Brooklyn, N.Y.)–Sept. 3, 1970. U.S. football coach. As Green Bay Packers head coach (1959–67), led team to Super Bowl championships in 1967 and 1968; won NFL championships, 1961, 1962, 1965–67; inducted into Pro Football Hall of Fame, 1971.

LONG, HOWIE, Jan. 6, 1960 (Somerville, Mass.). U.S. football player. Defensive end, Los Angeles Raiders, 1981– .

LOPEZ, NANCY, Jan. 6, 1957 (Torrance, Calif.). U.S. golfer. Won an unprecedented five consecutive tournaments on LPGA circuits, 1978; LPGA leading money winner, 1978, 1979, 1985.

LOUGANIS, GREG, Jan. 29, 1960 (?). U.S. diver. Won 47 national championships and 13 world titles; Olympic Gold Medalist in 3-meter springboard and 10-meter platform, 1984, 1988.

LOUIS, JOE ("The Brown Bomber"), born Joseph Louis Barrow, May 13, 1914 (Lexington, Ala.)–Apr. 12, 1981. U.S. boxer. World heavyweight champ, 1937–49 (longest reign in history); inducted into Boxing Hall of Fame, 1954.

LUCKMAN, SID, Nov. 21, 1916 (Brooklyn, N.Y.). U.S. football player. Quarterback for Chicago Bears, 1939–50; led team to NFL championships, 1940–41, 1943, and 1946; passed for seven touchdowns in one game, 1943; inducted into Pro Football Hall of Fame, 1965.

MACINNIS, AL, July 11, 1963 (Inverness, N.S.). Canadian hockey player. Defenseman for the Calgary Flames, 1982– ; led Stanley Cup playoffs with 31 points, won Conn Smythe Trophy, 1989.

MACK, CONNIE, Dec. 22, 1862 (E. Brookfield, Mass.)–Feb. 8, 1956. U.S. baseball owner, manager. Owned and managed Philadelphia A's, 1901–50; won nine AL pennants, five world championships; inducted into Baseball Hall of Fame, 1937.

MADLOCK, BILL, Jan. 12, 1951 (Memphis, Tenn.). U.S. baseball player. Led NL in batting, 1975, 1976, 1981, 1983.

MALONE, KARL ("Mailman"), July 24, 1963 (Summerfield, La.). U.S. basketball player. Forward for Utah Jazz, 1986– ; NBA all-star MVP, 1989.

MALONE, MOSES, Mar. 23, 1955 (Petersburg, Va.). U.S. basketball player. Entered ABA directly from high school, 1974; NBA MVP, 1979, 1982,

1983; playoff MVP, 1983; Led NBA in rebounding 6 times.

MANTLE, MICKEY, Oct. 20, 1931 (Spavinaw, Okla.). U.S. baseball player. New York Yankees outfielder who hit 536 career home runs; won AL triple crown, 1956; led AL in home runs, 1955–56, 1958, 1960; hit 54 home runs in 1961; hit record 18 World Series home runs; AL MVP, 1956–57, 1962; inducted into Baseball Hall of Fame, 1974.

MARAVICH, PETER ("Pistol Pete"), June 22, 1948 (Aliquippa, Pa.)–Jan. 5, 1988. U.S. basketball player. Guard who averaged an NCAA record 44.2 points per game at LSU, 1968–70; led NBA in scoring, 1977.

MARBLE, ALICE, Sept. 28, 1913 (Plumas Co., Calif.). U.S. tennis player. U.S. singles champ, 1936, 1938–40; Wimbledon singles champ, 1939.

MARCIANO, ROCKY, Sept. 1, 1923 (Brockton, Mass.)–Aug. 31, 1969. U.S. boxer. World heavyweight champ, 1952–56; retired undefeated after 49 pro fights; inducted into Boxing Hall of Fame, 1959; killed in plane crash.

MARINO, DAN, Sept. 15, 1961 (Pittsburgh, Pa.). U.S. football player. Quarterback with Miami Dolphins, 1983– ; led NFL in yards gained passing four times, TD passes three times; Thorpe Trophy (MVP), 1984; set NFL record for most TD passes (48), yards gained passing (5,084), passes completed (378), 1984.

MARIS, ROGER, Sept. 10, 1934 (Hibbing, Minn.) –Dec. 14, 1985. U.S. baseball player. As New York Yankee outfielder, hit record 61 home runs in 1961; AL MVP, 1960–61.

MARTIN, BILLY, May 16, 1928 (Berkeley, Calif.)– Dec. 25, 1989. U.S. baseball player and manager famed for brawls, feuds, and firings; after playing career chiefly with the New York Yankees (1950–57), managed Minnesota Twins (1969), Detroit Tigers (1971–73), and Texas Rangers (1973–75), Oakland A's (1980–82); as New York Yankees manager (1975–78), won pennants in 1976 and 1977 and World Series in 1977; fired and rehired five times by the Yankees.

MATHEWS, EDDIE, Oct. 13, 1931 (Texarkana, Tex.). U.S. baseball player. Chiefly with the Milwaukee/Atlanta Braves 1953–66; led NL in home runs, 1953 and 1959; hit 512 career homers; elected to Baseball Hall of Fame, 1978.

MATHEWSON, CHRISTY ("Big Six"), Aug. 12, 1880 (Factoryville, Pa.)–Oct. 7, 1925. U.S. baseball player. As New York Giants (1900–16) and Cincinnati Reds (1916) pitcher, won 373 games in career; won 30 or more games, 1904–05, 1908; inducted into Baseball Hall of Fame, 1936.

MATTINGLY, DON, Apr. 20, 1961 (Evansville, Ind.). U.S. baseball player. First baseman for New York Yankees, 1983– ; AL leading batter, 1984; led AL in RBIs, 1985; AL MVP, 1985; led AL in doubles three times.

MAYS, WILLIE ("Say Hey Kid"), May 6, 1931 (Westfield, Ala.). U.S. baseball player. As New York/San Francisco Giants (1951–72) and New York Mets (1972–73) outfielder, hit 660 career

home runs; led NL in home runs, 1955, 1962 and 1964–5; NL MVP, 1954, 1965; NL leading batter, 1954; inducted into Baseball Hall of Fame, 1979.
**MCADOO, BOB,** Sept. 25, 1951 (Greensboro, N.C.). U.S. basketball player. Forward-center with several NBA teams: with Buffalo (1972–76) and New York Knicks (1977–79); leading scorer in NBA, 1974–76; NBA MVP, 1975.
**MCCOVEY, WILLIE** ("Stretch"), Jan. 10, 1938 (Mobile, Ala.). U.S. baseball player. First baseman with San Francisco Giants (1959–73, 1977–80) and San Diego Padres (1974–76); led NL in home runs, 1963 and 1968–69; hit 521 career home runs; inducted into Hall of Fame, 1986.
**MCENROE, JOHN,** Feb. 16, 1959 (Wiesbaden, W. Ger.). U.S. tennis player. U.S. singles champ, 1979, 1980, 1981, 1984; Wimbledon singles champ, 1981, 1983, 1984.
**MCGRAW, JOHN** ("Little Napoleon"), Apr. 7, 1873 (Truxton, N.Y.)–Feb. 25, 1934. U.S. baseball player, manager. As New York Giants manager (1902–32), led team to ten pennants and three world championships, 1905, 1921, and 1922; inducted into Baseball Hall of Fame, 1937.
**MCGUIRE, AL,** Sept. 7, 1931 (New York, N.Y.). U.S. basketball player, coach, broadcaster. Coached Marquette U., 1964–77; won NCAA championship, 1977.
**MCGWIRE, MARK,** Oct. 1, 1963 (Claremont, Calif.). U.S. baseball player. First baseman for Oakland A's, 1986—  ; led AL in homers, 1987.
**MCHALE, KEVIN,** Dec. 19, 1957 (Hibbing, Minn.). U.S. basketball player. Forward for Boston Celtics, 1981—  ; member of 1981, 1984, 1986 championship teams; led NBA in field goal percentage, 1987, 1988.
**MCKAY, JIM,** Sept. 24, 1921 (Philadelphia, Pa.). U.S. sportscaster-commentator. Host of ABC's *Wide World of Sports,* 1961—  ; covered numerous Olympics; won 10 Emmy awards.
**MEDWICK, JOE** ("Ducky"), Nov. 24, 1911 (Carteret, N.J.)–Mar. 21, 1975. U.S. baseball player. Outfielder with several teams, chiefly St. Louis Cardinals (1932–40; 1947–48); won NL Triple Crown, 1937; hit NL record 64 doubles, 1936; career batting avg. of .324; inducted into Baseball Hall of Fame, 1968.
**MEREDITH, DON** ("Dandy Don"), Apr. 10, 1938 (Mt. Vernon, Tex.). U.S. football player, sports caster. Dallas Cowboys quarterback, 1960–69; fixture on ABC *Monday Night Football* for many years.
**MEYER, DEBBIE,** Aug. 14, 1952 (Haddonfield, N.J.). U.S. swimmer. Won gold medals in 200-, 400-, and 800-m freestyle at 1968 Olympics.
**MIKAN, GEORGE,** June 18, 1924 (Joliet, Ill.). U.S. basketball player, executive. Played with Minneapolis Lakers, 1946–56; NBA scoring leader, 1949–51, 1952; selected by AP (1950) as greatest basketball player of the era 1900–50; ABA commissioner, 1968–69 season.
**MIKITA, STAN,** May 20, 1940 (Sokolce, Czech.). Canadian hockey player. Center with Chicago Black

Hawks, 1959–80; NHL leading scorer, 1964–65, 1967–68; NHL MVP, 1967–68; won Lady Byng Trophy, 1967–78.
**MITCHELL, KEVIN,** Jan. 13, 1962 (San Diego, Calif.). U.S. baseball player. Played for New York Mets (1986), San Diego Padres (1987), San Francisco Giants (1988—  ); led in home runs, RBIs, 1989; NL MVP, 1989.
**MONROE, EARL** ("The Pearl"), Nov. 21, 1944 (Philadelphia, Pa.). U.S. basketball player. Played with Baltimore Bullets (1967–72) and New York Knicks (1972–80); averaged over 18 PPG; inducted into Hall of Fame, 1990.
**MONTANA, JOE,** June 11, 1956 (New Eagke, Pa.). U.S. football player. Quarterback for San Francisco 49ers, 1979—  ; MVP in Super Bowl, 1982, 1985, 1990; led NFL in TD passes, 1982, 1987.
**MOORE, ARCHIE,** Dec. 13, 1913 (Benoit, Miss.). U.S. boxer. World light-heavyweight champion, 1952–62.
**MORENZ, HOWIE,** 1902 (Mitchell, Ont., Can.) –Mar. 8, 1937. Canadian hockey player. Played with the Montreal Canadiens, 1924–34; NHL MVP, 1928, 1931–32; chosen in Canadian Press Poll as outstanding hockey player of first half of century, 1950.
**MORGAN, JOE,** Sept. 19, 1943 (Bonham, Tex.). U.S. baseball player, broadcaster. Second baseman for Houston Astros (1964–71; 1980–81), Cincinnati Reds (1971–80), Philadelphia Phillies (1982–83), Oakland A's (1983–84); NL MVP, 1975 and 1976.
**MORPHY, PAUL,** June 22, 1837 (New Orleans, La.)–July 10, 1884. U.S. chessmaster. Defeated world's best players, 1857; first to rely on principle of development before attack.
**MORRIS, JACK,** May 16, 1955 (St. Paul, Minn.). U.S. baseball player. Pitcher for Detroit Tigers, 1977—  ; 20-game winner, 1983, 1986; pitched no-hitter, 1984.
**MOSCONI, WILLIE,** June 21, 1913 (Philadelphia, Pa.). U.S. billiards player. World pocket billiards champ, numerous in the 1940s and 1950s.
**MOSES, EDWIN,** Aug. 31, 1953 (Dayton, Ohio). U.S. hurdler. Won Olympic gold medal in 400-m hurdles, 1976, 1984; set world record in his event (47.02 sec.), 1983.
**MULLIN, JOE,** Feb. 26, 1957 (New York, N.Y.). U.S. hockey player. Hockey forward for St. Louis Blues, 1982–86; Calgary Flames, 1986—  ; set NHL record for most points by U.S.-born player, 110 in 1989; led Stanley Cup playoffs in goals, 1986, 1989; Lady Byng Trophy, 1987.
**MUNOZ, (Michael) ANTHONY,** Aug. 19, 1958 (Ontario, Calif.). U.S. football player. Offensive tackle, Cincinnati Bengals, 1980—  .
**MUNSON, THURMAN,** June 7, 1947 (Akron, Ohio)–Aug. 2, 1979. U.S. baseball player. Catcher with New York Yankees, 1969–79; AL Rookie of the Year, 1970; hit .300 five times; AL MVP, 1976; killed in plane crash.
**MURPHY, CALVIN,** May 9, 1948 (Norwalk, Conn.). U.S. basketball player. A 5'9" guard who

has been with the Houston Rockets in NBA, 1970–83.

**MURPHY, DALE,** Mar. 12, 1956 (Portland, Ore.). U.S. baseball player. With the Atlanta Braves, 1976– ; led NL in home runs, 1984, 1985; led NL in RBIs, 1982, 1983; NL MVP, 1982, 1983.

**MURRAY, EDDIE,** Feb. 24, 1956 (Los Angeles, Calif.). U.S. baseball player. First baseman for Baltimore Orioles, 1977–88; Los Angeles Dodgers, 1989– ; batted in over 100 runs in a season five times.

**MUSIAL, STAN** ("The Man"), Nov. 21, 1920 (Donora, Pa.).–U.S. baseball player. St. Louis Cardinals outfielder, 1941–63; NL batting leader, 1943, 1946, 1948, 1950–52, 1957; hit 475 career homers; had .331 career batting avg.; NL MVP, 1943, 1946, 1948; inducted into Baseball Hall of Fame, 1969.

**NAGURSKI, BRONISLAW** ("Bronko"), Nov. 3, 1908 (Rainy River, Ont., Can.)–Jan. 6, 1990. Canadian football player. Fullback and tackle with Chicago Bears, 1930–37 gaining over 4,000 yards rushing; inducted into Football Hall of Fame, 1963.

**NAISMITH, JAMES,** Nov. 6, 1861 (Almonte, Ont., Can.)–Nov. 28, 1939. Canadian educator. Teacher of phys. ed. who invented the game of basketball, 1891.

**NAMATH, JOE** ("Broadway Joe"), May 31, 1943 (Beaver Falls, Pa.). U.S. football player, actor, sportscaster. Quarterback with the New York Jets (1965–77) and Los Angeles Rams (1977–78); led New York Jets to Super Bowl victory, 1969.

**NASTASE, ILIE** ("Nasty"), July 19, 1946 (Bucharest, Rom.). Romanian tennis player. Famed for on-court temper tantrums; U.S. singles champ, 1972.

**NAVRATILOVA, MARTINA,** Oct. 10, 1956 (Prague, Czech.). Czech-U.S. tennis player. Wimbledon champ, 1978 and 1979, 1982–87, 1990; U.S. champ, 1983, 1984, 1986, 1987.

**NELSON, BYRON,** Feb. 4, 1912 (Ft. Worth, Tex.). U.S. golfer. Masters champ, 1937, 1942; U.S. Open champ, 1939; PGA champ, 1940, 1945; inducted into Golf Hall of Fame, 1953.

**NEWCOMBE, JOHN,** May 23, 1943 (Sydney, Austrl.). Australian tennis player. U.S. singles champ, 1967, 1973; Wimbledon champ, 1967, 1970, and 1971.

**NICHOLAS, BERNIE,** June 24, 1961 (Haliburton, Ont.). Canadian hockey player. Forward for Los Angeles Kings, 1981–90; New York Rangers, 1990– ; scored 70 goals, 150 points, 1989.

**NICKLAUS, JACK** ("The Golden Bear"), Jan. 21, 1940 (Columbus, Ohio). U.S. golfer. Ranked by many as the greatest golfer of all time. U.S. Open champ, 1962, 1967, 1972, 1980; Masters champ, 1963, 1965–66, 1972, 1975; PGA champ, 1963, 1971, 1973, 1974, 1980; leading PGA Tour money-winner seven times.

**NIEUWENDYK, JOE,** Sept. 10, 1966 (Oshana, Ont.). Canadian hockey player. Calgary Flames player, 50-goal scorer, 1988, 1989; rookie of the year, 1988.

**NOLL, CHUCK,** Jan. 5, 1931 (Cleveland, Ohio).

U.S. football coach. Head coach of Pittsburgh Steelers, 1969– ; led team to Super Bowl championships, 1975, 1976, 1979, and 1980.

**NORMAN, GREG,** Feb. 10, 1955 (Queensland, Aust.). Australian golfer. PGA leading money winner, 1986; British Open champ, 1986.

**NURMI, PAAVO** ("The Flying Finn"), June 13, 1897 (Turku, Fin.)–Oct. 2, 1973. Finnish distance runner. Won seven Olympic Gold Medals, 1920, 1924, and 1928; held world record for mile 1923–31.

**OERTER, AL,** Sept. 19, 1936 (New York, N.Y.). U.S. discus thower. Won gold medal at four consecutive Olympics, 1956–68.

**OH, SADAHARU,** May 20, 1940 (Tokyo, Jap.). Japanese baseball player. Known as the "Babe Ruth of Japan"; hit 868 home runs in 22 seasons.

**OLAJUWON, AKEEM,** Jan. 21, 1963 (Lagos, Nigeria). Nigerian basketball player. Center for Houston Rockets, 1985– ; NCAA tournament MVP, 1983; All-NBA first team, 1987, 1988, 1989; led NBA in rebounding, 1989.

**OLDFIELD, BARNEY,** Jan. 29, 1878 (Wauseon, Ohio)–Oct. 4, 1946. U.S. auto racer. First to travel at the speed of a mile a minute, June 5, 1903.

**OLIVA, TONY,** July 20, 1940 (Pinar del Rio, Cuba). U.S. baseball player. Outfielder with Minnesota Twins, 1962–76; led AL in batting, 1964–65 and 1971; AL Rookie of the Year, 1964.

**OLSEN, MERLIN,** Sept. 15, 1940 (Logan, Ut.). U.S. football player, sports broadcaster, actor. Defensive lineman with L.A. Rams, 1962–76; appeared in films, TV series incl. *Little House on the Prairie*.

**ORR, BOBBY,** Mar. 20, 1948 (Parry Sound, Ont., Can.). Canadian hockey player. Defenseman with Boston Bruins (1967–76) and Chicago Black Hawks (1977–1979); NHL Rookie of the Year, 1967; first defenseman to be NHL leading scorer, 1970 and 1975; NHL first team all-star, 1968–75; won Norris Trophy (best defenseman), 1968–75; scored record (for defenseman) 46 goals, 1975; career shortened by five knee operations.

**OTT, MEL**(vin), Mar. 2, 1909 (Gretna, La.)–Nov. 21, 1958. U.S. baseball player. N.Y. Giants outfielder, 1926–47; first to hit 500 home runs in NL; led NL in home runs, 1932, 1934, 1936–38, and 1942; inducted into Baseball Hall of Fame, 1951.

**OWENS, JESSE,** Sept. 12, 1913 (Danville, Ala.)–Mar. 31, 1980. U.S. athlete. Won four gold medals in track and field at 1936 Olympics in Berlin.

**PAIGE, LEROY** ("Satchel"), July 7, 1906 (Mobile, Ala.). U.S. baseball player. Legendary pitcher in Negro leagues; joined Cleveland Indians, 1948; inducted into Baseball Hall of Fame, 1971.

**PALMER, ARNOLD,** Sept. 10, 1929 (Youngstown, Pa.). U.S. golfer. First $1 million-winner in game; Master's champ, 1958, 1960, 1962, and 1964; U.S. Open champ, 1960.

**PALMER, JIM,** Oct. 15, 1945 (New York, N.Y.). U.S. baseball player, broadcaster. Baltimore Orioles pitcher, 1969–84; 20-game winner eight times; most AL games won, 1975–77; lowest AL ERA, 1973, 1975; AL Cy Young Award winner, 1973, 1975–76.

PARCELLS, DUANE ("Bill"), Aug. 22, 1941 (Englewood, N.J.). U.S. football coach. Head coach, New York Giants, 1983– ; led team to Super Bowl championship, 1986.

PARISH, ROBERT, Aug. 30, 1953 (Shreveport, La.). U.S. basketball player. Center for Golden State, 1977–80; Boston Celtics, 1980– ; member of 1981, 1984, and 1986 championship teams.

PARKER, DAVE, June 9, 1951 (Jackson, Miss.). U.S. baseball player. With the Pittsburgh Pirates, 1973–83; Cinn. Reds 1984–87; Oakland A's, 1988–89; Milwaukee Brewers, 1990– ; led NL in batting, 1977–78; named NL MVP, 1978.

PARSEGHIAN, ARA, May 21, 1923 (Akron, Ohio). U.S. football coach, commentator. Coached Northwestern, 1956–63; coached Notre Dame (1964–75), leading it to a national championship, 1966.

PATERNO, JOSEPH, Dec. 21, 1926 (Brooklyn, N.Y.). U.S. football coach. Head coach of Penn St. 1966– ; led team to national championship, 1982, 1986.

PATTERSON, FLOYD, Jan. 4, 1935 (Waco, N.C.). U.S. boxer. World heavyweight champion, 1956–59 and 1960–62; first to regain title after losing it.

PAYTON, WALTER, July 25, 1954 (Columbia, Miss.). U.S. football player. Chicago Bears running back, 1976–87; NFL MVP, 1977, 1985; NFL leading rusher, 1977–80; rushed for NFL record 16,726 yds.; rushed for NFL record 110 TDs.

PELÉ, Oct. 23, 1940 (Tres Coracoes, Braz.). Brazilian soccer player. Led Brazilian National team to three World Cup championships, 1958, 1962, and 1970; played for New York Cosmos (1975–77).

PERRY, GAYLORD, Sept. 15, 1938 (Williamston, N.C.). U.S. baseball player. Pitcher with several teams, chiefly San Francisco Giants (1962–71); has led both NL (1970 and 1978) and AL (1972) in wins; AL Cy Young Award winner, 1972; NL Cy Young Award winner, 1978. Won 314 major league games.

PERRY, WILLIAM ("The Refrigerator"), Dec. 16, 1962 (Aiken, S.C.). U.S. football player. Chicago Bears (1985– ) lineman whose size and personality made him one of the most popular sports figures of the 1980s.

PETTIT, BOB, Dec. 12, 1932 (Baton Rouge, La.). U.S. basketball player. As a forward with the St. Louis Hawks, was the first player to score 20,000 points in the NBA; led NBA scoring, 1956, 1959; NBA MVP, 1956, 1959; inducted into Basketball Hall of Fame, 1970.

PETTY, RICHARD, July 2, 1937 (Randleman, N.C.). U.S. auto racer. Won Daytona 500 in 1964, 1966, 1971, 1973, 1974, 1979, 1981; NASCAR champ in 1964, 1967, 1971–72, 1974–75, 1979.

PHELPS, RICHARDS ("Digger"), July 4, 1941 (Beacon, N.Y.). U.S. basketball coach. Coach of Fordham U., 1970–71; coach of Notre Dame 1971– .

PINCAY, LAFFIT, JR., 1946 (Panama). Panamanian jockey. Leading money-winning jockey, 1970–74, 1979.

PLANTE, JACQUES, Jan. 17, 1929 (Shawinigan Falls, Que., Can.)–Feb. 26, 1986. Canadian hockey player. Goalie, principally with Montreal Canadiens, 1953–63; first goalie to wear a mask in a game; NHL MVP, 1962; won Vezina Trophy (best goalie), 1956–60, 1962, 1969.

PLAYER, GARY, Nov. 1, 1935 (Johannesburg, S.A.). S. African golfer. PGA champ, 1962 and 1972; U.S. Open champ, 1965; British Open champ, 1959, 1968, and 1974; Master's champ, 1961, 1974, and 1978.

POTVIN, DENIS, Oct. 29, 1953 (Hull, Ont., Can.). Canadian hockey player. Defenseman with N.Y. Islanders, 1973–87; NHL Rookie of the Year, 1974; won Norris Trophy (best defenseman), 1976, 1978, and 1979.

PROELL, ANNEMARIE, Mar. 27, 1953 (Kleinarl, Austria). Austrian skier. Won World Cup championship, 1971–75, 1979.

PUCKETT, KIRBY, Mar. 14, 1961 (Chicago, Ill.). U.S. baseball player. Outfielder for Minnesota Twins, 1984– ; led AL in batting, 1989.

RAINES, TIM, Sept. 16, 1959 (Sanford, Fla.). U.S. baseball player. Outfielder for Montreal Expos, 1980– ; NL batting champ, 1986.

REED, WILLIS, June 25, 1942 (Hico, La.). U.S. basketball player, coach, executive. With New York Knicks as a player (1964–74) and as coach (1977–79); named NBA Rookie of the Year, 1965; named MVP in NBA playoffs, 1970 and 1973; coach New York Mets, 1988–89.

RETTON, MARY LOU, Jan. 24, 1968 (Fairmont, W. Va.). U.S. gymnast. Won the all-around gold medal at the 1984 Olympics.

REUSCHEL, RICK ("Big Daddy"), May 16, 1949 (Quincey, Ill.). U.S. baseball player. Pitcher for several major league teams, mostly Chicago Cubs and San Francisco Giants.

REYNOLDS, (Harry) BUTCH, June 8, 1964 (Akron, Oh.). U.S. track and field star. Set world record at 400 meters (43.29 seconds), 1988.

RICE, (Henry) GRANTLAND, Nov. 1, 1880 (Murfreesboro, Tenn.)–July 13, 1954. U.S. sportswriter for N.Y. Tribune, later syndicated columnist. Selected All-American football teams for Collier's magazine; named football's "Four Horsemen," 1924, and Red Grange the "Galloping Ghost"; wrote that success was measured not by whether "you won or lost but how you played the game."

RICE, JERRY, Oct. 13, 1962 (Sparkville, Miss.). U.S. football player. Wide receiver for San Francisco 49ers, 1985– ; Super Bowl MVP, 1989; led NFL in TD receptions, 1986, 1987; Thorpe Trophy (MVP), 1987; set NFL record with TD receptions. 1987.

RICE, JIM, Mar. 8, 1953 (Anderson, S.C.). U.S. baseball player. An outfielder with the Boston Red Sox, 1974–89; led AL in home runs, 1977–78, 1984; led AL in RBIs, 1978, 1984; named AL MVP, 1978.

RICHARD, MAURICE ("Rocket"), Aug. 4, 1924 (Montreal, Que., Can.). Canadian hockey player, was the first to score 500 NHL goals. Forward with Montreal Canadiens, 1942–60; NHL MVP, 1947.

**RICKEY, BRANCH,** Dec. 20, 1881 (Stockdale, Ohio)–Dec. 9, 1965. U.S. baseball executive. Instituted farm system, 1919; as pres. of the Brooklyn Dodgers (1942–50), signed JACKIE ROBINSON to one of the Dodgers' farm teams, thus breaking baseball color barrier, 1946.

**RILEY, PAT,** Mar. 20, 1945 (Rome, N.Y.). U.S. basketball player, coach. Coach, Los Angeles Lakers, 1982–  ; won NBA championships, 1982, 1985, 1987, 1988.

**ROBERTSON, OSCAR** ("Big O"), Nov. 24, 1938 (Charlotte, Tenn.). U.S. basketball player. A three-time All-American at the U. of Cincinnati, 1958–60; played in NBA for Cincinnati (1960–70) and Milwaukee (1970–74); averaged 25.7 points per game in career; NBA record 9,887 career assists; named NBA MVP, 1964.

**ROBINSON, BROOKS,** May 18, 1937 (Little Rock, Ark.). U.S. baseball player. Rated one of game's best fielding third basemen; with Baltimore Orioles, 1955–77; played in four World Series; named AL MVP, 1964.

**ROBINSON, DAVID,** Aug. 6, 1965 (Key West, Fla.). U.S. basketball player. Center for San Antonio Spurs, 1989–  ; Sporting News college player of the year, 1987.

**ROBINSON, FRANK,** Aug. 31, 1935 (Beaumont, Tex.). U.S. baseball player, manager. Played with Cincinnati Reds (1956–65) and Baltimore Orioles (1966–71); won AL Triple Crown, 1966; first black to manage a major league team (Cleveland Indians), 1975; hit 586 career home runs; named NL MVP, 1961; named AL MVP, 1966; named AL manager-of-year with Baltimore, 1989, inducted into Hall of Fame, 1982.

**ROBINSON, JACK**(ie), Jan. 31, 1919 (Cairo, Ga.)–Oct. 24, 1972. U.S. baseball player. First black to enter major leagues with the Brooklyn Dodgers (1947), breaking pro sports color line; played with Dodgers until 1956; NL leading batter, 1949; named NL MVP, 1949; .311 lifetime batting average; inducted into Hall of Fame, 1962; in later years, a civil-rights activist.

**ROBINSON, JOHN,** July 25, 1935 (Chicago, Ill.). U.S. football coach. Coach, USC, 1976–82; Los Angeles Rams, 1983–  .

**ROBINSON, LARRY,** June 2, 1951 (Winchester, Ont.). Canadian hockey player. Defenseman for Montreal Canadiens, 1973–89; Los Angeles Kings 1989–  ; won Norris Trophy, 1977, 1980; won Symthe Trophy, 1978.

**ROBINSON,** ("Sugar") **RAY,** May 3, 1920 (Detroit, Mich.)–Apr. 12, 1989. U.S. boxer. Welterweight champ, 1946–51; middleweight champ five times, 1951–60.

**ROCKNE, KNUTE,** Mar. 4, 1888 (Voss, Nor.)–Mar. 31, 1931. U.S. football coach. As coach (1918–31), built Notre Dame into a football powerhouse; in 13 seasons, team won 105 games, lost 12, tied 5 and went undefeated in 1919, 1920, 1924, 1929, and 1930 seasons.

**ROONEY, ART,** Jan. 27, 1901 (Coulter, Pa.)–Aug. 25, 1988. U.S. football exec. Founder of the NFL Pittsburgh Steelers, 1933; inducted into Football Hall of Fame, 1964.

**ROSE, PETE,** Apr. 14, 1941 (Cincinnati, Ohio). U.S. baseball player. Played with Cincinnati Reds (1963–78), player-mgr. (1984–89), and Philadelphia Phillies (1979–83), Montreal Expos (1984); named NL rookie of the year, 1963; NL leading batter, 1968, 1968, 1973; hit safely in NL record 44 consecutive games, 1978; named NL MVP, 1973; played ML-record 3,562 games, and had ML-record 4,256 hits. Suspended from baseball for gambling, 1989.

**ROSEWALL, KEN,** Nov. 2, 1934 (Sydney, Austrl.). Australian tennis player. U.S. singles champ, 1956 and 1970.

**ROTH, MARK,** Apr. 10, 1951 (New York, N.Y.). U.S. bowler. PBA player of the year, 1977–79, 1984; Hall of Fame, 1987.

**ROY, PATRICK,** Oct. 5, 1965 (Quebec City, Que.). Canadian hockey player. Goalie for Montreal Canadiens, 1985–  ; won Conn Smythe Trophy, 1986; won Vezina Trophy, 1989.

**ROZELLE, ALVIN** ("Pete"). March 1, 1926 (South Gate, Calif.). U.S. football exec. Gen. mgr. of NFL Los Angeles Rams, 1957–60; NFL commissioner, 1960–89.

**RUDOLPH, WILMA,** June 23, 1940 (St. Bethlehem, Tenn.). U.S. sprinter. Won three gold medals in 1960 Olympics, in the 100- and 200-meter dashes and the 400-meter relay.

**RUPP, ADOLPH,** Sept. 2, 1901 (Halstead, Kan.)–Dec. 10, 1977. U.S. basketball coach. Coached Kentucky U. (1930–77) to record 875 wins and national championships in 1948, 1949, 1951, and 1958; inducted into Basketball Hall of Fame, 1968.

**RUSSELL, BILL,** Feb. 12, 1934 (Monroe, La.). U.S. basketball player, coach, sportscaster, executive. First black to coach major pro sports team (Boston Celtics), 1965–69; playing for Boston (1956–69), five-time NBA MVP, 1958, 1961–63, 1965; revolutionized game by stressing defensive play; inducted into Basketball Hall of Fame, 1974.

**RUTH, GEORGE HERMAN** ("Babe," "Sultan of Swat," "The Bambino"), Feb. 6, 1895 (Baltimore, Md.)–Aug. 16, 1948. U.S. baseball player. Played with Boston Red Sox (1914–19), New York Yankees (1920–34) and Boston Braves (1935); led AL in homers 11 times; hit AL record 708 home runs (714 in career); had .342 lifetime batting avg.; played in ten World Series; led AL in RBIs eight times; held over 50 records on retirement; inducted into Baseball Hall of Fame, 1936.

**RYAN, NOLAN,** Jan. 31, 1947 (Refugio, Tex.). U.S. baseball player. Pitcher with the New York Mets (1966–71), California Angels (1972–79), Houston Astros (1980–88) and Texas Rangers (1989–  ); struck out record 383 batters, 1973; pitched no-hitters in 1973, 1974, 1975, 1977, and 1981; holds ML record for strikeouts (5,076 at end of 1989 season); won 300 games, 1990.

**RYUN, JIM,** Apr. 29, 1947 (Wichita, Kan.). U.S.

runner. Set world records (since broken) in the mile (3:51.3) and 1,500-m races, 1967.

**SABERHAGEN, BRET,** Apr. 11, 1964 (Chicago Hts., Ill.). U.S. baseball player. Pitcher for K.C. Royals, 1984– ; won AL Cy Young Award, 1985, 1989; World Series MVP, 1985.

**SANDBERG, RYNE,** Sept. 18, 1959 (Spokane, Wash.). U.S. baseball player. Second baseman for Chicago Cubs, 1982– ; NL MVP, 1984.

**SAWCHUCK, TERRY,** Dec. 28, 1929 (Winnipeg, Man., Can.)–May 31, 1970. Canadian hockey player. Goalie, principally with Detroit Red Wings, NHL Rookie of the Year, 1951; won Vezina Trophy (best goalie), 1952, 1953, and 1965; NHL-record 103 career shutouts.

**SAYERS, GALE,** May 30, 1943 (Wichita, Kan.). U.S. football player. Running back with the NFL Chicago Bears, 1965–72; led NFC in rushing, 1966 and 1969; inducted into Football Hall of Fame, 1977.

**SCHMIDT, MIKE,** Sept. 27, 1949 (Dayton, Ohio). U.S. baseball player. Infielder with the Philadelphia Phillies, 1972–89; led NL in home runs, 1974–76, 1980–81, 1983–84, 1986; hit 548 ML home runs. Chosen NL MVP 1980, 1981, 1986.

**SCOTT, MIKE,** Apr. 26, 1955 (Santa Monica, Calif.). U.S. baseball player. Pitcher for New York Mets, 1978–82; Houston Astros, 1983– ; NL Cy Young Award winner, 1986; pitched no-hitter, 1986.

**SCULLY, VIN**(cent), Nov. 29, 1927 (Bronx, N.Y.). U.S. sportscaster. Announcer for Brooklyn/Los Angeles Dodgers, 1950– .

**SEAVER, (George) THOMAS,** Nov. 17, 1944 (Fresno, Calif.). U.S. baseball player, sportscaster. Pitcher with New York Mets (1967–77) and Cincinnati Reds (1977–82); 20-game winner five times; named NL Rookie of the Year, 1967; won NL Cy Young Award, 1969, 1973, 1975; NL lowest ERA, 1970–71, 1973; won 311 ML games; struck out record 19 in one game, 1970.

**SHOEMAKER, WILLIE,** Aug. 19, 1931 (Fabens, Tex.). U.S. jockey. Rode Kentucky Derby winner, 1955, 1959, 1965; rode Belmont Stakes winner five times; first jockey to ride over 8,000 winners; leading money-winning jockey ten times.

**SHORE, EDDIE,** Nov. 25, 1902 (Ft. Qu'appelle, Sask., Can.)–Mar. 16, 1985. Canadian hockey player, executive. Defenseman with Boston Bruins, 1926–40; NHL MVP, 1933, 1935, 1936, and 1938; first team all-star seven times.

**SHORTER, FRANK,** Oct. 31, 1947 (Munich, Ger.). U.S. distance runner. Won gold medal in marathon at 1972 Olympics; won Sullivan Award, 1972.

**SHULA, DON,** Jan. 4, 1930 (Grand River, Ohio). U.S. football coach. As coach of the NFL Miami Dolphins (1970– ), led team to Super Bowl championships in 1973 and 1974.

**SIERRA, RUBEN,** Oct. 6, 1965 (Rio Piedras, P.R.). Puerto Rican baseball player. Texas Rangers outfielder, 1986– ; lead AL in RBIs, 1989.

**SIMMONS, AL,** May 22, 1902 (Milwaukee, Wis.)–May 26, 1956. U.S. baseball player. Outfielder with many teams, the longest with Philadelphia Athletics; led AL in batting, 1930–31; had .334 career batting average; inducted into Baseball Hall of Fame, 1953.

**SIMMS, PHIL,** Nov. 3, 1956 (Lebanon, Ky.). U.S. football player. Quarterback for New York Giants, 1979– ; Super Bowl MVP, 1987.

**SIMPSON, O**(renthal) **J**(ames), July 9, 1947 (San Francisco, Calif.). U.S. football player, actor, sports commentator; won 1968 Heisman Trophy while at USC; running back with NFL Buffalo Bills (1969–78), and San Francisco 49ers (1978–79); rushed for 100 or more yds. a record 11 times, 1973; named NFL MVP, 1973; AFC leading rusher, 1972–73 and 1975–76; actor in action films in the 1970s.

**SINGLETARY, MIKE,** Oct. 9, 1958 (Houston, Tex.). U.S. football player. Linebacker for Chicago Bears, 1981– ; Pro Bowl, 1983–89.

**SISLER, GEORGE,** Mar. 24, 1893 (Manchester, Ohio)–Mar. 26, 1973. U.S. baseball player. Played with St. Louis, 1915–27; AL leading batter, 1920 and 1922; had .420 batting avg., 1922; had record 257 hits, 1920; had .340 lifetime batting avg.; inducted into Baseball Hall of Fame, 1939.

**SMITH, DEAN,** Feb. 28, 1931 (Emporia, Kan.). U.S. basketball coach. Head basketball coach, Univ. of North Carolina, 1961– ; led team to NCAA championship, 1982; Hall of Fame, 1982.

**SMITH, OZZIE** ("Wizard of Oz"), Dec. 26, 1954 (Mobile, Ala.). U.S. baseball player. Shortstop for San Diego Padres, 1978–81; St. Louis Cardinals, 1981– ; won 10 Gold Glove awards.

**SNEAD, ("Slammin'") SAM,** May 27, 1912 (Hot Springs, Va.). U.S. golfer. PGA champ, 1942, 1949, 1951; Master's champ, 1949, 1952, 1954; inducted into Golf Hall of Fame, 1953.

**SNELL, PETER,** Dec. 17, 1938 (Opunake, N.Z.). New Zealand runner. 800-m gold medalist in 1960 and 1964 Olympics; held world record for mile, 1962–65.

**SPAHN, WARREN,** Apr. 23, 1921 (Buffalo, N.Y.). U.S. baseball player. Pitcher with the Boston/Milwaukee Braves (1942–64); won NL record 363 games; 20-game winner 13 times; led NL in strikeouts, 1949–52; won Cy Young Award, 1957; inducted into Baseball Hall of Fame, 1972.

**SPEAKER, TRIS**(tram), Apr. 4, 1888 (Hubbard, Tex.)–Dec. 8, 1958. U.S. baseball player. Outfielder with Boston Red Sox (1907–15) and Cleveland Indians (1916–26); had .344 career batting avg.; led AL in batting, 1916; inducted into Baseball Hall of Fame, 1937.

**SPITZ, MARK,** Feb. 10, 1950 (Modesto, Calif.). U.S. swimmer. First athlete to win seven gold medals in a single Olympic games, 1972; won two gold medals in 1968 Olympics; won Sullivan Award, 1971.

**STABLER, KEN,** Dec. 25, 1945 (Foley, Ala.). U.S. football player. Quarterback with the NFL Oakland Raiders in the 1970s; AFC leading passer, 1973, 1976; named NFL MVP, 1974.

**STAGG, AMOS ALONZO,** Aug. 16, 1862 (W. Orange, N.J.)–Mar. 17, 1965. U.S. football coach. Coach of the U. of Chicago football team for 41 years 1892–1932; had five undefeated seasons; introduced huddle, man-in-motion, end-around plays; elected to Football Hall of Fame, 1951.

**STARGELL, WILLIE,** Mar. 6, 1941 (Earlsboro, Okla.). U.S. baseball player. Outfielder/first baseman with Pittsburgh Pirates, led NL in home runs, 1971, 1973; hit 475 career home runs; NL and World Series MVP, 1979.

**STARR, BART,** Jan. 9, 1934 (Montgomery, Ala.). U.S. football player, coach. Quarterback with the NFL Green Bay Packers, 1956–71, head coach, 1975–84. NFL leading passer, 1962, 1964, 1966; named NFL MVP, 1966; named Super Bowl MVP, 1967–8; inducted into Football Hall of Fame, 1977.

**STAUBACH, ROGER,** Feb. 5, 1942 (Cincinnati, Ohio). U.S. football player; won Heisman Trophy at U.S. Naval Academy, 1963; quarterback, with the NFL Dallas Cowboys, 1968–79; NFC leading passer, 1971, 1973, 1977, 1978, 1979.

**STEINBRENNER, GEORGE,** July 4, 1930 (Rocky River, Ohio). U.S. baseball executive, shipbuilder, owner of New York Yankees, 1973– .

**STENGEL, CASEY,** July 30, 1890 (Kansas City, Mo.)–Sept. 29, 1975. U.S. baseball player, manager. A highly colorful former player who managed the New York Yankees to 10 pennants (1949–53, 1955–58, and 1960), winning seven World Series; managed N.Y. Mets during their infancy; known for his "Stengelese" (fractured sentences); elected to Baseball Hall of Fame, 1966.

**STENMARK, INGEMAR,** Mar. 18, 1956 (Tarnaby, Swe.). Swedish skier. Won World Cup championship, 1976–78.

**STEWART, DAVE,** Feb. 19, 1957 (Oakland, Calif.). U.S. baseball player. Pitcher with several major league teams; achieved stardom with Oakland A's, 1986– ; 20-game winner, 1987–89; World Series MVP, 1989.

**STEWART, JACKIE,** June 11, 1939 (Dunbartonshire, Scot.). Scottish auto racer, sportscaster. World Grand Prix champ, 1969, 1971, and 1973; retired with record 27 Grand Prix victories; now a TV commentator on auto racing.

**STOCKTON, JOHN,** Mar. 26, 1962 (Spokane, Wash.). U.S. basketball player. Utah Jazz guard, 1984– ; led NBA in assists, 1988, 1989; led NBA in steals, 1989; set NBA assists record for season, 1988.

**STONES, DWIGHT,** Dec. 6, 1953 (Los Angeles, Calif.). U.S. high jumper. Set indoor and outdoor world records several times in 1970s.

**STRANGE, CURTIS,** Jan. 30, 1955 (Norfolk, Va.). U.S. golfer. PGA leading money winner, 1986, 1987; U.S. Open champ, 1988, 1989.

**STRAWBERRY, DARRYL,** Mar. 12, 1962 (Los Angeles, Calif.). U.S. baseball player. Outfielder with New York Mets, 1983– ; led NL in home runs, 1988.

**SULLIVAN, JOHN L.,** Oct. 15, 1858 (Boston, Mass.)–Feb. 2, 1918. U.S. boxer. Last bareknuckle heavyweight champion, 1882–92; lost to JAMES CORBETT.

**SUTTON, DON,** Apr. 2, 1945 (Clio, Ala.). U.S.

baseball pitcher mostly with Los Angeles Dodgers; won 321 career games.

**SWANN, LYNN,** Mar. 7, 1952 (Alcoa, Tenn.). U.S. football player, sports commentator. Wide receiver with the Pittsburgh Steelers, 1974–83; named Super Bowl MVP, 1975.

**TARKENTON, FRAN(cis),** Feb. 3, 1940 (Richmond, Va.). U.S. football player. Quarterback with the New York Giants (1967–71) and Minnesota Vikings (1961–66 and 1972–79); passed for NFL record 47,003 career yds. (342 TDs); named NFL MVP, 1975.

**TAYLOR, LAWRENCE,** Feb. 4, 1959 (Williamsburg, Va.). U.S. football player. Linebacker for New York Giants, 1981– ; named to Pro Bowl, 1981–89.

**THOENI, GUSTAVO,** Feb. 28, 1951 (Trafoi, It.). Italian skier. Won giant slalom gold medal in 1972 Olympics; World Cup champ, 1971–73 and 1975.

**THOMAS, ISIAH,** Apr. 30, 1962 (Chicago, Ill.). U.S. basketball player. Detroit Pistons guard, 1981– ; All-NBA first team, 1984–86; MVP in all-star game, 1984, 1986; led NBA in assists, 1985.

**THOMPSON, JOHN,** Sept. 2, 1941 (Washington, D.C.). U.S. basketball coach. Player with Boston Celtics, 1964–66; head coach, Georgetown Univ., 1972– ; won NCAA championship, 1984; coach, U.S. Olympic team, 1988.

**THORPE, JAMES** ("Jim"), May 28, 1888 (Prague, Okla.)–Mar. 28, 1953. U.S. athlete, executive. Won pentathlon and decathlon at 1912 Olympics, but was stripped of medals when he was declared not to be amateur (posthumously restored, 1982); football All-American at Carlisle (Pa.) Indian School 1911–12, played baseball with N.Y. Giants and Cincinnati Reds; played pro football with several teams, 1915–26; first pres. of the NFL; elected to Football Hall of Fame, 1963; ranked as outstanding athlete of 20th cent., by AP, 1950.

**TIANT, LUIS,** Nov. 23, 1940 (Havana, Cuba). Cuban-U.S. baseball player. Pitcher with the Cleveland Indians (1964–69), Minnesota Twins (1970), Boston Red Sox (1972–78) and New York Yankees (1979– ); lowest AL ERA, 1968 and 1972; 20-game winner, 1968, 1973, 1974, 1976.

**TILDEN, WILLIAM** ("Big Bill"), Feb. 10, 1893 (Germantown, Pa.)–June 5, 1953. U.S. tennis player. U.S. singles champ, 1920–25 and 1929; Wimbledon champ, 1920, 1921 and 1930; played on 11 Davis Cup teams; voted by AP greatest tennis player of the first half of the 20th cent., 1950.

**TITTLE, Y(elberton) A(braham),** ("The Bald Eagle"), Oct. 24, 1926 (Marshall, Tex.). U.S. football player. Quarterback with NFL Baltimore Colts (1948–50), San Francisco 49ers (1951–60), and New York Giants (1961–64). Named NFL MVP, 1961 and 1963; elected to Football Hall of Fame, 1971.

**TOON, AL,** Apr. 30, 1963 (Newport News, Va.). U.S. football player. Wide receiver for New York Jets, 1985– ; led NFL in passes caught, 1988.

**TORRE, JOE,** July 18, 1940 (Brooklyn, N.Y.).

U.S. baseball player, manager, broadcaster. Played with Milwaukee/Atlanta Braves, St. Louis Cardinals and New York Mets; led NL in batting and named MVP, 1971.

**TRAMMELL, ALAN,** Feb. 21, 1958 (Garden Grove, Calif.). U.S. baseball player. Shortstop for Detroit Tigers, 1977– ; World Series MVP, 1984.

**TREVINO, LEE,** Dec. 1, 1939 (Dallas, Tex.). U.S. golfer. U.S. Open champ, 1968 and 1971; PGA champ, 1974; British Open champ, 1971 and 1972.

**TROTTIER, BRYAN,** July 17, 1956 (Val Marie, Sask.). U.S. hockey player. With the New York Islanders, 1976– ; NHL rookie of the year, 1976; NHL leading scorer, MVP, 1979; Conn Smythe Trophy, 1980.

**TUNNEY, GENE,** May 25, 1898 (New York, N.Y.)–Nov. 7, 1978. U.S. boxer. World heavyweight champion, 1926–28; twice defeated JACK DEMPSEY.

**TURNER, TED,** Nov. 19, 1938 (Cincinnati, Ohio). U.S. broadcasting and sports exec., yachtsman. Won America's Cup in yacht *Courageous,* 1977; Chief executive, Turner Broadcasting System. Owner of NL Atlanta Braves and NBA Atlanta Hawks.

**TYSON, MIKE,** June 30, 1966 (New York, N.Y.). U.S. heavyweight boxer. Youngest heavyweight champion in history; won WBC title, Nov. 1986; WBA title, Mar. 1987; IBF title, Aug. 1987; lost all titles, Feb. 1990.

**TYUS, WYOMIA,** Aug. 29, 1945 (Griffin, Ga.). U.S. sprinter. Won 100-m dash gold medal in 1964 and 1968 Olympics.

**UNITAS, JOHN,** May 7, 1933 (Pittsburgh, Pa.). U.S. football player. Quarterback with Baltimore Colts (1956–72) and San Diego Chargers (1973); passed for TDs in 47 consecutive games, 1957–60; named NFL MVP, 1957 and 1967.

**UNSELD, WES**(tley), Mar. 14, 1946 (Louisville, Ky.). U.S. basketball player, coach. Center with the NBA Baltimore/Capitol/Washington Bullets, 1968–81; named NBA Rookie of the Year, 1969; named NBA MVP, 1969; named MVP in NBA playoffs, 1978; inducted into Hall of Fame, 1987; coach of Bullets, 1987– .

**UNSER, AL,** May 29, 1939 (Albuquerque, N.M.). U.S. auto racer. Won Indianapolis 500 in 1970, 1971, 1978, and 1987. (Brother of B. UNSER.)

**UNSER, BOBBY,** Feb. 20, 1934 (Albuquerque, N.M.). U.S. auto racer. Won Indianapolis 500 in 1968, 1975, and 1981. (Brother of A. UNSER.)

**UPSHAW, GENE,** Aug. 15, 1945 (Robstown, Tex.). U.S. football player. Football Hall of Fame guard played with Oakland Raiders, 1967–81; as head of NFL Players Assn., he lead the 1987 strike of football players.

**VAN BROCKLIN, NORM,** ("The Dutchman"), Mar. 15, 1926 (Eagle Butte, S.D.)–May 2, 1983. U.S. football player, coach. Quarterback with Los Angeles Ramss (1949–57) and Philadelphia Eagles (1958–60); passed for single-game-record 554 yds., 1951; named NFL MVP, 1960; head coach of Minnesota Vikings (1961–67) and Atlanta Falcons (1968–73).

**VALENZUELA, FERNANDO,** Nov. 1, 1960 (Sonora, Mex.). U.S. baseball player. Pitcher for Los Angeles Dodgers, 1980– ; NL Rookie of the Year, Cy Young Award winner, 1981.

**VARE, GLENDA,** June 20, 1903 (New Haven, Conn.)–Feb. 3, 1989. U.S. golfer. Dominated women's golfing in the 1920s; Vare Trophy, named after her, is awarded anually to the woman professional golfer with the best scoring average.

**VIOLA, FRANK,** Apr. 19, 1960 (Hempstead, N.Y.). U.S. baseball player. Pitcher for Minnesota Twins, 1982–89, New York Mets, 1989– ; AL Cy Young Award winner, 1988; World Series MVP, 1987.

**WAGNER, HONUS** ("The Flying Dutchman"), Feb. 24, 1874 (Carnegie, Pa.)–Dec. 6, 1955. U.S. baseball player. Infielder with the Pittsburgh Pirates, 1900–17; led NL in batting, 1900, 1903–04, 1906–09, and 1911; hit career .327; led NL in doubles seven times, RBIs four times; had 3,415 career hits, 722 stolen bases; inducted into Baseball Hall of Fame, 1936.

**WALCOTT, JERSEY JOE,** Jan. 31, 1914 (Merchantville, N.J.). U.S. boxer. World heavyweight champion, 1951–52.

**WALKER, HERSCHEL,** Mar. 3, 1962 (Wrightsville, Ga.). U.S. football player. Running back in USFL, 1983–85; Dallas Cowboys, 1986–89; Minnesota Vikings, 1989– ; won Heisman Trophy, 1982.

**WALSH, BILL,** Nov. 30, 1931 (Los Angeles, Calif.). U.S. football coach. Coach, San Francisco 49ers, 1979–88; led team to Super Bowl championships, 1982, 1985, 1989.

**WALTON, BILL,** Nov. 5, 1952 (La Mesa, Calif.). U.S. basketball player. Center led Portland Trail Blazers to NBA championship, 1977; NBA MVP, 1978.

**WATSON, TOM,** Sept. 4, 1949 (Kansas City, Mo.). U.S. golfer. Won Masters, 1977, 1981; named PGA Player of Year, 1977–80, 1982.

**WEAVER, EARL,** Aug. 14, 1930 (St. Louis, Mo.). U.S. baseball manager. As manager of the Baltimore Orioles, won four pennants (1969–71, 1979) and one World Series (1970).

**WEISSMULLER, JOHNNY,** June 2, 1904 (Windber, Pa.)–Jan. 20, 1984. U.S. swimmer, actor. Won many national championships and set 67 world records; won five gold medals at the 1924 and 1928 Olympics; played Tarzan in 1930s and 1940s films.

**WEST, JERRY,** May 28, 1938 (Chelyan, W. Va.). U.S. basketball player, exec. Guard with the NBA L.A. Lakers, 1960–74, coach 1976–79; NBA leading scorer, 1970; averaged 27 points per game in career; scored 25,192 career points; named first-team All-Star ten times.

**WHITE, RANDY,** Jan. 15, 1953 (Wilmington, Del.). U.S. football player. Defensive lineman with NFL Dallas Cowboys, 1975–88; won Outland Award, 1974.

**WHITWORTH, KATHY,** Sept. 27, 1939 (Monahans, Tex.). U.S. golfer. LPGA leading money-winner, seven times; first to win $1 million on LPGA tour.

WILKINS, (Jacques) DOMINIQUE, Jan. 12, 1960 (Paris, France). U.S. basketball player, Atlanta Hawks, 1982– ; led NBA in scoring, 1986.

WILLIAMS, DOUG, Aug. 9, 1955 (Zachary, La.). U.S. football player. Quarterback for Tampa Bay Buccaneers, 1978–82; USFL, 1984–85; Washington Redskins, 1986–89; Super Bowl MVP, 1988.

WILLIAMS, TED ("The Splendid Splinter"), Aug. 30, 1918 (San Diego, Calif.). U.S. baseball player. Outfielder with Boston Red Sox, 1939–60; last major leaguer to hit .400 (.406 in 1941); .344 career batting avg.; led AL in batting, 1941–42, 1947–48, 1957–58; led AL in homers four times; led AL in RBIs four times; hit 521 career homers; inducted into Baseball Hall of Fame, 1966.

WILLS, HELEN, Oct. 6, 1906 (Centerville, Calif.). U.S. tennis player. U.S. champ, 1923–25, 1927–29, and 1931; Wimbledon champ, 1927–30, 1932–33, 1935, and 1938.

WITT, KATARINA, Dec. 3, 1965 (Karl-Marx Stadt, E. Ger.). East German figure skater. Won world titles, 1984, 1985, 1987, 1988; Olympic gold medalist, 1984, 1988.

WOODEN, JOHN, Oct. 14, 1910 (Martinsville, Ind.). U.S. basketball coach. Coached (1948–75) UCLA to ten NCAA championships, 1964, 1965, 1967–73, and 1975; elected to Basketball Hall of Fame as player (1960) and coach (1970); U.S. Basketball Writers Coach of Year, 1964, 1967, 1969, 1970, 1972, and 1973.

WORTHY, JAMES, Feb. 27, 1961 (Gastonia, N.C.). U.S. basketball player. Forward for the Los Angeles Lakers on 1985, 1986, and 1988 championship teams; NBA playoff MVP, 1988; played for NCAA championship team, tournament MVP, 1982.

WRIGHT, MICKEY, Feb. 14, 1935 (San Diego, Calif.). U.S. golfer. Won Women's Open, 1958–59, 1961, and 1964; LPGA leading money-winner, 1961–64.

WYNN, EARLY, Jan. 6, 1920 (Hartford, Ala.).

U.S. baseball player. Pitcher with the Washington Senators (1939–48), Cleveland Indians (1949–57 and 1963) and Chicago White Sox (1958–62); won 300 major league games; led AL in wins, 1954 and 1959; won Cy Young Award, 1959; 20-game winner five times.

YARBOROUGH, CALE(b), Mar. 27, 1940 (Timmonsville, S.C.). U.S. auto racer. NASCAR champ, 1976–78; won Daytona 500, 1977, 1983–84.

YASTRZEMSKI, CARL ("Yaz"), Aug. 22, 1939 (Southampton, N.Y.). U.S. baseball player. Outfielder/first baseman with Boston Red Sox, 1961–84; won AL Triple Crown, 1967; AL batting champ, 1963, 1967–68; named AL MVP, 1967; first AL player ever to achieve lifetime 400 home runs and 3,000 hits, 1979; played AL record 3,308 games; inducted into Hall of Fame, 1989.

YOUNG, CY, Mar. 29, 1867 (Gilmore, Ohio)–Nov. 4, 1955. U.S. baseball player. Pitcher in NL with Cleveland (1890–98) and St. Louis (1899–1900) and in AL with Boston (1901–08) and Cleveland (1909–11); won record 511 games; pitched perfect game, 1904; 20-game winner 16 times; 30-game winner five times; inducted into Baseball Hall of Fame, 1937; best pitcher of the year award named for him.

YOUNT, ROBIN, Sept. 16, 1955 (Danville, Ill.). U.S. baseball player. Shortstop, outfielder for Milwaukee Brewers, 1974– ; AL MVP, 1982, 1989.

YZERMAN, STEVE, May 9, 1965 (Cranbrook, B.C.). Canadian hockey player. Scoring star for Detroit Red Wings, 1983– ; 50-goal scorer, 1988, 1989, 1990.

ZAHARIAS, BABE, June 26, 1914 (Port Arthur, Tex.)–Sept. 27, 1956. U.S. athlete. All-around athlete who won javelin and 80-m hurdles gold medals at 1932 Olympics; won U.S. Open golf championship, 1948, 1950, and 1954; named AP Woman Athlete of the Century, 1950.

# Entertainers

## U.S. ACTORS

**ABRAHAM, F. MURRAY,** Oct. 24, 1939 (Pittsburgh, Pa.). U.S. actor. Has appeared in numerous roles on stage and in films. Stage: *Uncle Vanya* (Obie Award), 1984. Films: *Serpico*, 1973; *All the President's Men*, 1976; *Amadeus* (Best Actor AA), 1985; *The Name of the Rose*, 1986.
**ADAMS, DON,** Apr. 19, 1927 (New York, N.Y.). U.S. actor, comedian. Best known as inept spy on TV series *Get Smart* (1965–70), for which he won an Emmy in 1967.
**ADAMS, EDIE,** Apr. 16, 1929 (Kingston, Pa.). U.S. actress. Best known for TV work, especially on husband ERNIE KOVACS' TV show (1951-53 and 1956) and cigar commercials.
**ADAMS, MAUDE** (born Maude Kiskadden), Nov. 11, 1872 (Salt Lake City, Utah)–July 17, 1953. U.S. actress. Made stage debut at the age of nine months in *The Lost Child*; first real success in *The Masked Ball*, 1892; most widely known for role as Lady Babbie in *The Little Minister*, 1897-98.
**ADLER, LUTHER** (born Lutha Adler), May 4, 1903 (New York, N.Y.). U.S. character actor. Plays: *Golden Boy*, 1938; *Merchant of Venice*, 1956; *View from the Bridge*, 1957.
**AHERNE, BRIAN,** May 2, 1902 (Worcestershire, Eng.). U.S. actor. "British gentleman" figure of U.S. stage and screen. Films: *Shooting Stars*, 1928; *The Great Garrick*, 1937; *Juarez*, 1939; *Lancelot and Guinevere*, 1963.
**AIELLO, DANNY,** May 20, 1933 (New York, N.Y.). U.S. actor. Went from Broadway to films; best known for roles in Woody Allen movies. Films: *Blood Brothers*, 1979; *Fort Apache, the Bronx*, 1980; *The Purple Rose of Cairo*, 1985; *Radio Days*, 1987; *Do the Right Thing*, 1989.
**AKINS, CLAUDE,** May 25, 1918 (Nelson, Ga.). U.S. actor. Film career as "heavy"; star of TV series *Movin' On*, 1974-75.
**ALBERT, EDDIE** (born Edward Albert Heimberger), April 22, 1908 (Rock Island, Ill.). U.S. actor. Known for "nice guy" film roles; received National Film Critics Award, 1972. Films: *Brother Rat*, 1938;

*Attack!*, 1956; *Heartbreak Kid*, 1972. TV: *Green Acres* (series), 1965-70.
**ALBERTSON, JACK,** June 16, 1910 (Malden, Mass.) –Nov. 25, 1981. U.S. actor. A burlesque straight man and a character actor in films; film career capped by *The Subject Was Roses* (best supporting actor AA), 1968; star of TV series *Chico and the Man* (1974–77), for which he received an Emmy award, 1976.
**ALDA, ALAN,** Jan. 28, 1936 (New York, N.Y.). U.S. actor. Films: *Paper Lion*, 1968; *To Kill a Clown*, 1972; *The Seduction of Joe Tynan*, 1979; *Sweet Liberty*, 1986. TV: *M\*A\*S\*H* (Emmy award, 1974, 1982), 1972-82. (Son of R. ALDA.)
**ALDA, ROBERT** (born Alphonso d'Abruzzo), Feb. 26, 1914 (New York, N.Y.)–May 3, 1986. U.S. actor. Moved from radio and stage to films. Stage: *Guys and Dolls* (Best Actor Tony), 1951. Films: *Rhapsody in Blue*, 1945. (Father of A. ALDA.)
**ALEXANDER, JANE** (born Jane Quigley), Oct. 28, 1939 (Boston, Mass.). U.S. actress. Won 1969 Tony award for *The Great White Hope*. Films: *The Great White Hope*, 1970; *Kramer Vs. Kramer*, 1979; *Brubaker*, 1980.
**ALLEN, DEBBIE,** Jan. 16, 1953 (Houston, Tex.). U.S. actress, dancer, choreographer. First appeared on Broadway in 1970s. Stage: *Purlie*, 1972. TV: *Fame* (series), 1982–83. Films: *Ragtime*, 1981; *Your Life is Calling*, 1986.
**ALLEY, KIRSTIE,** Jan. 12, 1955 (Wichita, Kan.). U.S. actress. TV: *A Bunny's Tale*, 1984; *North and South* (miniseries), 1986; *Cheers* (series), 1987– . Films: *Star Trek 2*, 1982; *Look Who's Talking*, 1989.
**ALLISON, FRAN,** ? (La Porte, Ia.)–June 13, 1989. U.S. actress. Best known for role opposite puppets on TV series *Kukla, Fran and Ollie*, 1948-57.
**ALLYSON, JUNE** (born Ella Geisman), Oct. 7, 1917 (Lucerne, N.Y.). U.S. actress. Played girl-next-door roles in films of the 1940s and 1950s, including *Two Girls and a Sailor* (1944), *High Barbaree* (1947), *Little Women* (1949), *The Glenn Miller Story* (1954). (One-time wife of D. POWELL.)

AMECHE, DON (born Dominic Felix Amici), May 31, 1908 (Kenosha, Wisc.). U.S. actor. Popular leading man in 1930s and 1940s films, including *The Three Musketeers* (1939) and *Heaven Can Wait* (1943); *Cocoon*, 1985 (Supporting Actor AA).

AMES, ED, July 9, 1927 (Boston, Mass.). U.S. singer, actor. Best known as a member of the Ames Brothers; TV: Mingo on *Daniel Boone*, 1964–68.

AMES, LEON (born Leon Wycoff), Jan. 20, 1903 (Portland, Ore.). U.S. character actor. Best known as star of TV series *Life with Father*, 1953–55.

ANDERSON, HARRY, Oct. 14, 1952 (Newport, R.I.). U.S. actor. Has made many appearances on *Saturday Night Live*. TV: *Night Court*, 1984– ; *Tales From the Darkside*, 1984.

ANDERSON, LONI, Aug. 5, 1946 (St. Paul, Minn.). U.S. actress. TV: *WKRP in Cincinnati* (series), 1978–82; *The Jayne Mansfield Story*, 1980. Films: *Stroker Ace*, 1983.

ANDERSON, RICHARD DEAN, Jan. 23, 1953 (Minneapolis, Minn.). U.S. actor. TV: *MacGyver* (series), 1985– .

ANDREWS, DANA (born Carver Daniel Andrews), Jan. 1, 1909 (Collins, Miss.). U.S. actor. A leading man in films of the 1940s and 1950s. Films: *Laura*, 1944; *Best Years of Our Lives*, 1946; *Boomerang*, 1947.

ANN-MARGRET (born Ann Margret Olsson), Apr. 28, 1941 (Stockholm, Swe.). U.S. dancer, singer, actress. Adding to early sex-symbol status, she won reputation as a film actress and nightclub star. Films: *Bye Bye Birdie*, 1962; *Carnal Knowledge*, 1971; *Twice In A Lifetime*, 1985. (Wife of R. SMITH.)

ARCHER, ANNE, Aug. 25, 1950 (Los Angeles, Calif.). U.S. actress. Films: *The All-American Boy*, 1970; *Paradise Alley*, 1978; *Fatal Attraction*, 1987; *Love at Large*, 1990.

ARDEN, EVE (born Eunice Quedens), Apr. 30, 1912 (Mill Valley, Calif.). U.S. comedic actress. Known as wise-cracking second lead. Films: *Stage Door*, 1937; *Mildred Pierce*, 1945. TV: *Our Miss Brooks* (series), 1952–56 (previously on radio, 1948–51).

ARKIN, ALAN, Mar. 26, 1934 (New York, N.Y.). U.S. actor, director. Films: *The Russians Are Coming...*, 1966; *Little Murders* (also directed), 1971; *The In-Laws*, 1979.

ARNAZ, DESI (born Desiderio Alberto Arnaz y de Acha), Mar. 2, 1917 (Santiago, Cuba)–Dec. 2, 1986. Cuban-U.S. singer, bandleader, comic actor. Starred in the TV series *I Love Lucy*, 1951–61. (One-time husband of L. BALL; father of D. ARNAZ, JR., and L. ARNAZ.)

ARNAZ, DESI, JR., Jan. 19, 1953 (Los Angeles, Calif.). U.S. actor. Films: *Red Sky at Morning*, 1971. (Son of L. BALL and D. ARNAZ; brother of L. ARNAZ.)

ARNAZ, LUCIE, July 17, 1951 (Hollywood, Calif.). U.S. actress. Stage: *They're Playing Our Song*, 1979. (Daughter of L. BALL and D. ARNAZ; sister of D. ARNAZ, JR.)

ARNESS, JAMES (born James Aurness), May 26, 1923 (Minneapolis, Minn.). U.S. actor. Played Marshal Dillon in long-running TV series *Gunsmoke*, 1955–75. (Brother of P. GRAVES.)

ARNOLD, EDWARD (born Guenther Schneider), Feb. 18, 1890 (New York, N.Y.)–Apr. 26, 1956. U.S. actor. A lead actor in 1930s films; later did character roles. Films: *Diamond Jim*, 1935; *Mr. Smith Goes to Washington*, 1939; *Dear Ruth*, 1947.

ARQUETTE, ROSANNA, Aug. 10, 1959 (New York, N.Y.). U.S. actress. TV: *Executioner's Song*, 1982. Films: *Baby It's You*, 1983; *Desperately Seeking Susan*, 1985; *Silverado*, 1985; *After Hours*, 1985; *Eight Million Ways to Die*, 1986.

ARTHUR, BEATRICE (born Bernice Frankel), May 13, 1923 (New York, N.Y.). U.S. comedic actress. After Broadway career, starred in the TV series *Maude*, 1972–78 (Emmy award, 1977). *The Golden Girls* (series), 1985– .

ARTHUR, JEAN (born Gladys Greene), Oct. 17, 1905 (New York, N.Y.). U.S. actress. Squeaky-voiced leading lady in 1930s–1950s films, including *Mr. Deeds Goes to Town* (1936), *The Talk of the Town* (1942), *Shane* (1953).

ASHLEY, ELIZABETH (born Elizabeth Cole), Aug. 30, 1939 (Ocala, Fla.). U.S. actress. Films: *The Carpetbaggers*, 1964; *Ship of Fools*, 1965; *Marriage of a Young Stockbroker*, 1971.

ASNER, EDWARD, Nov. 15, 1929 (Kansas City, Mo.). U.S. actor, political, labor activist. TV: *Mary Tyler Moore Show* (series), 1972–77; *Lou Grant* (series), 1977–82; *Roots* (movie), 1977. Pres. Screen Actors Guild, 1981–85.

ASTIN, JOHN, Mar. 30, 1930 (Baltimore, Md.). U.S. actor, director. Starred in the TV series *The Addams Family*, 1964–66. (One-time husband of P. DUKE.)

ASTOR, MARY (born Lucille Langehanke), May 3, 1906 (Quincy, Ill.)–Sept. 24, 1987. U.S. actress. A leading lady in 1920s–40s films, including *Dodsworth* (1936), *The Maltese Falcon* (1941), *Act of Violence* (1949), and *Little Women* (1949).

AUBERJONOIS, RENE, June 1, 1940 (New York, N.Y.). U.S. actor, director. Stage: *Coco* (Tony Award), 1970; *The Good Doctor*, 1974; *Big River*, 1985. TV: *Benson* (series), 1980–86. Films: *Petulia*, 1968; *M*A*S*H*, 1969; *Brewster McCloud*, 1970; *McCabe and Mrs. Miller*, 1970; *The Eyes of Laura Mars*, 1978.

AYRES, LEW, Dec. 28, 1908 (Minneapolis, Minn.). U.S. actor. Leading man in films of the 1930s; made eight "Dr. Kildare" features, 1938–41. Films: *The Kiss*, 1929; *All Quiet on the Western Front*, 1930; *State Fair*, 1933; *Advise and Consent*, 1961. (One-time husband of G. ROGERS.)

AXTON, HOYT, Mar. 25, 1938 (Duncan, Okla.). U.S. singer, actor. Country singer. Films: *Black Stallion*, 1980; *Gremlins*, 1984.

BACALL, LAUREN (born Betty Joan Perske), Sept. 16, 1924 (New York, N.Y.). U.S. actress. Films: *To Have and Have Not*, 1944; *The Big Sleep*, 1946; *Key Largo*, 1948. Plays: *Applause* (Tony award), 1969. (One-time wife of H. BOGART and J. ROBARDS, JR.)

**BACKUS, JIM,** Feb. 25, 1913 (Cleveland, Ohio)–July 3, 1989. U.S. actor. Known for the voice of Mr. Magoo in the 1950s cartoon series; starred in TV series *Gilligan's Island*; 1964–67. Films: *Rebel without a Cause*, 1955; *It's a Mad Mad Mad Mad World*, 1963.

**BAINTER, FAY,** 1892 (Los Angeles, Calif.)–Apr. 16, 1968. U.S. character actress. Films: *Jezebel*, 1937; *Our Town*, 1940; *Children's Hour*, 1962.

**BAIO, SCOTT,** Sept. 22, 1961 (New York, N.Y.). U.S. actor. Has appeared in TV series *Happy Days* (1977–84) and in other juvenile roles. TV: *Joanie Loves Chachi*, 1982–83.

**BAKER, CARROLL,** May 28, 1931 (Johnstown, Pa.). U.S. actress. Sultry leading lady of the 1950s and 1960s. Films: *Baby Doll*, 1956; *The Carpetbaggers*, 1964; *Harlow*, 1965.

**BALL, LUCILLE,** Aug. 6, 1911 (Jamestown, N.Y.)–Apr. 26, 1989. U.S. comedic actress. After prolific film career, largely in B-grade movies, starred in *I Love Lucy* TV series (1950–61); received Emmys in 1952, 1955, 1967, 1968. Films: *Stage Door*, 1937; *Du Barry Was a Lady*, 1943; *Sorrowful Jones*, 1949; *Fancy Pants*, 1950; *Yours, Mine, and Ours*, 1968; *Mame*, 1973. (One-time wife of D. ARNAZ; mother of L. and D. ARNAZ, JR.)

**BALSAM, MARTIN,** Nov. 4, 1919 (New York, N.Y.). U.S. actor. Films: *Twelve Angry Men*, 1957; *Psycho*, 1960; *A Thousand Clowns* (Best Supporting Actor AA), 1965.

**BANCROFT, ANNE** (born Anna Maria Italiano), Sept. 17, 1931 (New York, N.Y.). U.S. actress. After early film roles, won two Tonys, for *Two for the Seesaw* (1958) and *The Miracle Worker* (1959); won best actress AA for lead role in film of *The Miracle Worker*, 1962. Other films: *The Graduate*, 1968; *Young Winston*, 1972; *The Prisoner of Second Avenue*, 1975; *The Turning Point*, 1977; *Agnes of God*, 1985. (Wife of M. BROOKS.)

**BANKHEAD, TALLULAH,** Jan. 31, 1903 (Huntsville, Ala.)–Dec. 12, 1968. U.S. actress. Renowned for gravel voice, wit. Plays: *Little Foxes* (Critics' Circle Award), 1939; *Skin of Our Teeth*, 1944. Films: *Lifeboat*, 1943.

**BARA, THEDA** (born Theodosia Goodman), July 20, 1890 (Cincinnati, Ohio)–Apr. 7, 1955. Silent-screen star in "vamp" (femme fatale) roles in films such as *A Fool There Was* (1916); retired in 1926.

**BARR, ROSEANNE,** Nov. 3, 1952 (Salt Lake City, Ut.). U.S. comedienne, actress. Standup comedienne turned actress. TV: *Roseanne* (series), 1988– . Films: *She-Devil*, 1989. Books: *Roseanne: My Life as a Woman*, 1989.

**BARRIE, BARBARA,** May 23, 1931 (Chicago, Ill.). U.S. actress. Films: *The Caretakers*, 1963; *One Potato, Two Potato*, 1964; *Breaking Away*, 1979; *Private Benjamin*, 1980.

**BARRY, GENE** (born Eugene Klass), June 4, 1922 (New York, N.Y.). U.S. actor. Starred in the TV series *Bat Masterson* (1959–61), *Burke's Law* (1963–66), *Name of the Game* (1968–71).

**BARRYMORE, DREW,** Feb. 22, 1975 (Los Angeles, Calif.). U.S. actress. Films: *E.T.*, 1980; *Firestarter*, 1984; *Irreconcilable Differences*, 1984.

**BARRYMORE, ETHEL** (born Edith Blythe), Aug. 15, 1879 (Philadelphia, Pa.)–June 18, 1959. U.S. actress. Called the "First Lady of American theater," 1900–1940s. Films: *None but the Lonely Heart*, (Best suporting Actress AA), 1944; *The Farmer's Daughter*, 1947. (Sister of J. and L. BARRYMORE.)

**BARRYMORE, JOHN** "The Great Profile" (born John Blythe), Feb. 15, 1882 (Philadelphia, Pa.)–May 29, 1942. U.S. actor. Played Shakespearean stage roles, romantic film leads through the 1930s; later known for dissolute life and film roles. Films: *Dr. Jekyll and Mr. Hyde*, 1920; *Grand Hotel*, 1932; *Dinner at Eight*, 1933. (Brother of E. and L. BARRYMORE.)

**BARRYMORE, LIONEL** (born Lionel Blythe), Apr. 28, 1878 (Philadelphia, Pa.)–Nov. 15, 1954. U.S. actor. Made over 100 films in 30-year career as the leading U.S. character actor, often in sentimental roles; in wheelchair from 1938; played Dr. Gillespie in "Dr. Kildare" film series, 1938–41. Films: *A Free Soul*, (Best Actor AA), 1931; *Grand Hotel*, 1932; *You Can't Take It with You*, 1938; *It's a Wonderful Life*, 1946; *Duel in the Sun*, 1946. (Brother of E. and J. BARRYMORE.)

**BASEHART, RICHARD,** Aug. 31, 1914 (Zanesville, Ohio)–Sept. 17, 1984. U.S. actor. Films: *He Walked by Night*, 1948; *Moby Dick*, 1956. TV: *Voyage to the Bottom of the Sea* (series), 1964–67.

**BASINGER, KIM,** Dec. 8, 1953 (Athens, Ga.). U.S. actress. A Ford model before she broke into films. TV: *Katie: Portrait of a Centerfold*, 1978. Films: *Never Say Never Again*, 1983; *The Natural*, 1984; *9-1/2 Weeks*, 1985; *No Mercy*, 1986; *Blind Date*, 1987; *Batman*, 1989.

**BAXTER, ANNE,** May 7, 1923 (Michigan City, Ind.)–Dec. 12, 1985. U.S. actress. Film leading lady in the 1940s. Films: *The Magnificient Ambersons*, 1942; *The Razor's Edge* (Best Supporting Actress AA), 1946; *All about Eve*, 1950.

**BAXTER-BIRNEY, MEREDITH,** June 21, 1947 (Los Angeles, Calif.). U.S. actress. TV: *Bridget Loves Bernie* (series), 1971–72; *Family* (series), 1976–80; *Family Ties* (series), 1982–88.

**BEATTY, NED,** July 6, 1937 (Louisville, Ky.). U.S. actor. Known for character roles. TV: *The Execution of Pvt. Slovik*, 1974; *Friendly Fire*, 1979. Films: *Deliverance*, 1972; *The Life and Times of Judge Roy Bean*, 1972; *All the President's Men*, 1976; *Nashville*, 1976; *Network*, 1976; *Superman*, 1979; *The Big Easy*, 1987.

**BEATTY, WARREN,** Mar. 30, 1938 (Richmond, Va.). U.S. actor, director, screenwriter. Films: *Splendor in the Grass*, 1961; *Bonnie and Clyde*, 1967; *Shampoo* (also cowrote), 1975; *Heaven Can Wait* (also directed and cowrote), 1978; *Reds*, (Best Director AA), 1982. (Brother of S. MACLAINE.)

**BEDELIA, BONNIE,** Mar. 25, 1948 (New York, N.Y.). U.S. actress. Films: *Lovers and Other Strangers*, 1970; *They Shoot Horses, Don't They?*, 1970; *Heart Like a Wheel*, 1983.

BEERY, NOAH, JR., Aug. 10, 1916 (New York, N.Y.). U.S. actor. Has played character roles in films since childhood. TV: *Rockford Files*, (1974–80).

BEERY, WALLACE, Apr. 1, 1889 (Kansas City, Mo.)–Apr. 15, 1949. U.S. actor. Character actor in films from 1913. Films: *Min and Bill*, 1930; *The Champ* (Best Actor AA), 1931; *Grand Hotel*, 1932; *Dinner at Eight*, 1933; *Tugboat Annie*, 1933; *Viva Villa*, 1934; *Slave Ship*, 1937; *Barbary Coast Gent*, 1944.

BEGLEY, ED, JR., Sept. 16, 1949 (Hollywood, Calif.). U.S. actor. TV: *St. Elsewhere*, 1982–88. Films: *Airport*, 1979; *The In-Laws*, 1979; *The Accidental Tourist*, 1988.

BEL GEDDES, BARBARA, Oct. 31, 1922 (New York, N.Y.). U.S. actress. Plays: *The Moon is Blue*, 1952; *Cat on a Hot Tin Roof*, 1955; *Mary, Mary*, 1961. TV: *Dallas* (series), 1978– .

BELLAMY, RALPH, June 17, 1904 (Chicago, Ill.). U.S. actor. Played in over 100 films, several TV series, and many plays. Films: *The Awful Truth*, 1937; *His Girl Friday*, 1940. Plays: *Sunrise at Campobello* (Tony award), 1958.

BELUSHI, JAMES, June 15, 1954 (Chicago, Ill.). U.S. actor. Films: *About Last Night*, 1986; *Salvador*, 1986; *Red Heat*, 1988; *K-9*, 1989.

BELUSHI, JOHN, Jan. 24, 1949 (Chicago, Ill.) –Mar. 5, 1982. U.S. actor, comedian, writer. First became known through hilarious performances on *Saturday Night Live* (1975–79). Films: *Animal House*, 1978; *The Blues Brothers*, 1980; *Continential Divide*, 1981; *Neighbors*, 1981.

BENJAMIN, RICHARD, May 22, 1938 (New York, N.Y.), U.S. actor, director. Films: *Good-bye Columbus*, 1969; *Diary of a Mad Housewife*, 1970; *Portnoy's Complaint*, 1972. (Husband of P. PRENTISS.)

BENNETT, CONSTANCE, 1904 (New York, N.Y.) –July 24, 1965. U.S. actress. A leading lady of 1930s films, including *Moulin Rouge* (1933) and *Topper* (1937). (Sister of J. BENNETT.)

BENNETT, JOAN, Feb. 27, 1910 (Palisades, N.J.). U.S. actress. A leading lady in many 1930s and 1940s films, including *Private Worlds* (1935) and *The Macomber Affair* (1947); has played in many TV soap operas. (Sister of C. BENNETT.)

BENSON, ROBBY (born Robert Selal), Jan. 21, 1955. (Dallas, Tex.). U.S. actor. Films: *One on One*, 1977; *Harry and Son*, 1985.

BERENGER, TOM, May 31, 1950 (Chicago, Ill.). U.S. actor. Appeared on stage and TV soap opera before film debut. Films: *The Sentinel*, 1977; *Looking for Mr. Goodbar*, 1977; *Butch and Sundance*, 1979; *The Big Chill*, 1984; *Someone to Watch Over Me*, 1987; *Platoon*, 1987; *Betrayed*, 1988; *Love at Large*, 1990.

BERG, GERTRUDE (born Gertrude Edelstein), Oct. 3, 1899 (New York, N.Y.)–Sept. 14, 1966. U.S. comedic actress, writer. Wrote and starred (as Molly Goldberg) in *The Goldbergs* radio and TV series, 1929–54; won 1959 Tony award for her role in *A Majority of One*.

BERGEN, CANDACE, May 9, 1946 (Beverly Hills, Calif.) U.S. actress. Films: *The Group*, 1966; *Carnal Knowledge*, 1971; *The Wind and the Lion*, 1977; *Starting Over*, 1979. (Daughter of E. BERGEN; wife of L. MALLE.)

BERGEN, POLLY (born Nellie Bergin), July 14, 1930 (Knoxville, Tenn.). U.S. actress, beauty executive. Films: *Cape Fear* (1962), *Move Over, Darling* (1963), currently heads own cosmetic firm.

BERGMAN, INGRID, Aug. 29, 1915 (Stockholm, Swe.)–Aug. 29, 1982. Swedish U.S. actress. Had a long and distinguished career as dramatic leading actress. Films: *Casablanca*, 1943; *Gaslight* (Best Actress AA), 1944; *The Bells of St. Mary's*, 1945; *Spellbound*, 1945; *Joan of Arc*, 1948; *Anastasia* (Best Actress AA); 1956; *Murder on the Orient Express* (Best Supporting Actress AA), 1974.

BERNSEN, CORBIN, Sept. 7, 1954 (No. Hollywood, Calif.). U.S. actor. TV: *L. A. Law* (series), 1986– . Films: *Major League*, 1989.

BERRY, KEN, Nov. 13, 1933 (Moline, Ill.). U.S. actor. TV: *F Troop* (series), 1965–67; *Mayberry RFD* (series), 1968–71. Films: *Herbie Rides Again*, 1974.

BERTINELLI, VALERIE, Apr. 23, 1960 (Wilmington, Del.). U.S. actress. TV: *One Day at a Time* (series), 1975–84; *Silent Witness*, 1985; *Rockabye*, 1986; *I'll Take Manhattan* (miniseries) 1987.

BICKFORD, CHARLES, 1889 (Cambridge, Mass.) –Nov. 9, 1967. U.S. actor. Rough-edged character actor. Films: *Of Mice and Men*, 1940; *The Farmer's Daughter*, 1947; *Johnny Belinda*, 1948.

BISSETT, JACQUELINE, Sept. 13, 1946 (Weybridge, Eng.). U.S. actress. Films: *The Grasshopper*, 1970; *Rich and Famous*, 1981.

BIXBY, BILL, Jan. 22, 1934 (San Francisco, Calif.). U.S. actor. TV: *My Favorite Martian* (series), 1963–65; *The Incredible Hulk* (series), 1978–81.

BLACK, KAREN (born Karen Zeigler), July 1, 1942 (Park Ridge, Ill.). U.S. actress. Films: *Easy Rider*, 1969; *Five Easy Pieces*, 1970; *Nashville*, 1975.

BLAKE, AMANDA (born Beverly Neill), Feb. 20, 1929 (Buffalo, N.Y.)–Aug. 16, 1989. U.S. actress. Famed for her portrayal of Kitty in the TV series *Gunsmoke*, 1955–75.

BLAKE, ROBERT (born Michael Gubitosi), Sept. 18, 1933 (Nutley, N.J.). U.S. actor. Began as child actor. Films: *In Cold Blood*, 1968. TV: *Baretta* (series), 1974–78.

BLEDSOE, TEMPESTT, Aug. 1, 1973 (Chicago, Ill.). U.S. actress. TV: *The Cosby Show* (series), 1984– .

BLONDELL, JOAN, Aug. 30, 1909 (New York, N.Y.)–Dec. 26, 1979. U.S. comedic actress. Wise cracking lead or support in 1930s films; later played character roles in movies and TV. Films: *Footlight Parade*, 1933; *A Tree Grows in Brooklyn*, 1945; *The Cincinnati Kid*, 1965.

BLYTH, ANN, Aug. 16, 1928 (Mt. Kisco, N.Y.). U.S. actress. A film singer, then a dramatic lead. Films: *Mildred Pierce*, 1945; *Rose Marie*, 1954; *The Helen Morgan Story*, 1957.

**BOGART, HUMPHREY,** Dec. 25, 1899 (New York, N.Y.)–Jan. 14, 1957. U.S. actor. His 1940s and 1950s screen persona as cynical but good-hearted tough guy had top box-office appeal. Films: *Petrified Forest,* 1936; *Dead End,* 1937; *The Maltese Falcon,* 1941; *Casablanca,* 1943; *To Have and Have Not,* 1943; *The Big Sleep,* 1946; *The Treasure of the Sierra Madre,* 1947; *Key Largo,* 1948; *African Queen* (Best Actor AA), 1952; *The Caine Mutiny,* 1954; *The Barefoot Contessa,* 1954. (Husband of L. BACALL.)

**BOND, WARD,** 1903 (Denver, Col.)–Nov. 5, 1960. U.S. actor. Character actor in many westerns, from 1930; starred in the TV series *Wagon Train,* 1957–60.

**BONET, LISA,** Nov. 16, 1967 (San Francisco, Calif.). U.S. actress. TV: *The Cosby Show* (series), 1984–87; *A Different World* (series), 1987– . Films: *Angel Heart,* 1987.

**BOONE, RICHARD,** June 18, 1917 (Los Angeles, Calif.)–Jan. 11, 1981. U.S. actor. Familiar for rugged face and outlook in dozens of films. TV: *Medic* (series), 1954–56; *Have Gun, Will Travel* (series), 1957–63.

**BOOTH, EDWIN,** Nov. 13, 1833 (Belair, Md.)–June 7, 1893. U.S. actor. One of the greatest 19th-cent. American stage actors, famous for his Hamlet. (Brother of J. W. BOOTH.)

**BOOTH, SHIRLEY** (born Thelma Booth Ford), Aug. 30, 1907 (New York, N.Y.). U.S. actress. Noted for distinguished stage career (won 1953 Tony award for *Time of the Cuckoo*), film appearances (won 1952 Best Actress AA for *Come Back Little Sheba*), and TV roles (won 1963 Emmy for her role in the series *Hazel,* 1961–66).

**BORGNINE, ERNEST** (born Ermes Borgnino), Jan. 24, 1917 (Hamden, Conn.). U.S. actor. Strong character actor in many films, including *From Here to Eternity* (1953), *Marty* (1955; Best Actor AA), and *The Dirty Dozen* (1967); starred in TV sitcom *McHale's Navy,* 1962–65.

**BOSLEY, TOM,** Oct. 1, 1927 (Chicago, Ill.). U.S. actor. Plays: *Fiorello* (Tony award), 1959. TV: *Happy Days* (series), 1974–83.

**BOSTWICK, BARRY,** Feb. 24, 1946 (San Mateo, Calif.). U.S. actor. Many stage, TV, film appearances. Stage: *The Robber Bridegroom* (Tony Award), 1977. TV: *Scruples* (miniseries), 1980; *A Woman of Substance* (miniseries), 1984; *George Washington* (miniseries), 1986; *I'll Take Manhattan* (miniseries), 1987. Films: *The Rocky Horror Picture Show,* 1975.

**BOTTOMS, TIMOTHY,** Aug. 30, 1951 (Santa Barbara, Calif.). U.S. actor. Popular in the 1970s. Films: *Last Picture Show,* 1971; *The Paper Chase,* 1973; *The White Dawn,* 1974.

**BOW, CLARA,** Aug. 6, 1905 (New York, N.Y.)–Sept. 26, 1965. U.S. actress. The "It" girl who personified the flapper in 1920s silents. Films: *Mantrap,* 1926; *It,* 1927.

**BOYD, WILLIAM,** 1895 (Cambridge, Ohio)–Sept. 12, 1972. U.S. actor. Renowned as Hopalong Cassidy in scores of second features and TV episodes.

**BOYLE, PETER,** 1933 (Philadelphia, Pa.). U.S. actor. Films: *Joe,* 1970; *Young Frankenstein,* 1974; *Taxi Driver,* 1976.

**BRACKEN, EDDIE,** Feb. 7, 1920 (New York, N.Y.). U.S. comedic actor. Played many character roles, often as rural type, in films such as *The Miracle of Morgan's Creek* (1943).

**BRANDO, MARLON,** Apr. 3, 1924 (Omaha, Neb.). U.S. actor. "Method actor" in stage dramatic roles such as *A Streetcar Named Desire,* 1947; developed persona of brooding, tough sex symbol. Films: *The Men,* 1950; *A Streetcar Named Desire,* 1951; *Julius Caesar,* 1953; *On the Waterfront* (Best Actor AA), 1954; *Guys and Dolls,* 1955; *Mutiny on the Bounty,* 1962; *The Godfather—Part 1* (Best Actor AA), 1972; *Last Tango in Paris,* 1973; *Apocalypse Now,* 1979.

**BRENNAN, EILEEN,** Sept. 3, 1935 (Los Angeles, Calif.). U.S. character actress. Films: *Divorce, American Style,* 1967; *At Long Last Love,* 1975; *Murder by Death,* 1976; *Private Benjamin,* 1980. TV: *Private Benjamin* (series), 1981–82.

**BRENNAN, WALTER,** July 25, 1894 (Lynn, Mass.)–Sept. 21, 1974. Character actor in over 100 films, including *Come and Get It* (1936; Best Supporting Actor AA), *Kentucky* (1938; Best Supporting Actor AA), *The Westerner* (1940; Best Supporting Actor AA); star of *Real McCoys* TV series, 1957–63.

**BRENT, GEORGE** (born George Brent Nolan), Mar. 15, 1904 (Dublin, Ire.)–May 26, 1979. U.S. actor. Films: *Forty-second Street,* 1933; *Jezebel,* 1938; *The Spiral Staircase,* 1945.

**BRIDGES, BEAU,** Dec. 9, 1941 (Hollywood, Calif.). U.S. actor. Films: *Force of Evil,* 1968; *Gaily Gaily,* 1969; *The Landlord,* 1970; *The Other Side of the Mountain,* 1975; *Norma Rae,* 1979. (Son of L. BRIDGES; brother of J. BRIDGES.)

**BRIDGES, JEFF,** Dec. 4, 1949 (Los Angeles, Calif.). U.S. actor. Made his debut in TV series, *Sea Hunt,* at age eight. Films: *The Last Picture Show,* 1971; *Hearts of the West,* 1975; *Winter Kills,* 1979; *Heaven's Gate,* 1980; *Cutter's Way,* 1981; *Against All Odds,* 1984; *Starman,* 1984; *Jagged Edge,* 1985; *Nadine,* 1987; *Tucker,* 1988. (Son of L. BRIDGES; brother of B. BRIDGES.)

**BRIDGES, LLOYD,** Jan. 15, 1913 (San Leandro, Calif.). U.S. actor. In films from 1941 (*Home of the Brave,* 1949; *The Goddess,* 1958); most famous as star of the TV series *Sea Hunt,* 1957–61. (Father of B. and J. BRIDGES.)

**BRODERICK, MATTHEW,** Mar. 21, 1962 (New York, N.Y.). U.S. actor. Films: *War Games,* 1983; *Ferris Bueller's Day Off,* 1986; *The Freshman,* 1989. Stage: *Torch Song Trilogy,* 1982; *Brighton Beach Memoirs* (Tony Award), 1985; *Biloxi Blues,* 1985; *Glory,* 1990.

**BROLIN, JAMES,** July 18, 1942 (Los Angeles, Calif.). U.S. actor. TV: *Marcus Welby* (series), 1969–76; *Hotel,* 1983–88. Films: *Westworld,* 1973; *Gable and Lombard,* 1976.

**BRONSON, CHARLES** (born Charles Buchinsky), Nov. 3, 1922 (Ehrenfeld, Pa.). U.S. actor. International box-office star in 1970s action films. Films:

*The Magnificient Seven*, 1960; *The Dirty Dozen*, 1967; *Death Wish*, 1974; *Breakheart Pass*, 1976; *Act of Vengeance*, 1986.

BROOKS, ALBERT (born Albert Einstein), July 22, 1947 (Los Angeles, Calif.). U.S. actor, writer, director. Directed "Saturday Night Live." Films: *Taxi Driver*, 1976; *Real Life*, 1979; *Private Benjamin*, 1980; *Modern Romance*, 1982; *Twilight Zone: The Movie*, 1983; *Lost in America* (also writer, director), 1985; *Broadcast News*, 1987.

BROOKS, AVERY, Oct. 2, 19? (Evansville, Ind.). U.S. actor. TV: *Spenser for Hire* (series), 1985–  .

BROWN, BLAIR, 1948 (Washington, D.C.). U.S. actress. TV: *Kennedy*, 1983; *The Days and Nights of Molly Dodd* (series), 1987–  ; *Space* (miniseries), 1985. Films: *Altered States*, 1980; *Continential Divide*, 1981; *A Flash of Green*, 1983.

BRYNNER, YUL (born Youl Bryner), July 11, 1920 (Sakhalin, Jap.)–Oct. 10, 1985. U.S. actor. His bald head and accent led to success in "exotic" roles: starred in stage and film version of *The King and I* (Tony Award) (Best Actor AA, 1956). Other films: *Anastasia*, 1956; *The Magnificient Seven*, 1960.

BUONO, VICTOR, 1938 (Los Angeles, Calif.)– Jan. 1, 1982. U.S. character actor. Films: *Whatever Happened to Baby Jane?*, 1962; *Hush, Hush, Sweet Charlotte*, 1965.

BURGHOFF, GARY, May 24, ? (Bristol, Conn.). U.S. actor. Received 1977 supporting actor Emmy award for his work as Radar O'Reilly in the TV series *M*A*S*H* (1972–79).

BURKE, BILLIE, Aug. 7, 1885 (Wash., D.C.)–May 14, 1970. U.S. stage and film actress. Films: *Dinner at Eight*, 1933; *The Wizard of Oz*, 1939; *The Man Who Came to Dinner*, 1941. (One-time wife of F. ZIEGFELD.)

BURKE, DELTA, July 30, 1956 (Orlando, Fla.). U.S. actress. TV: *Filthy Rich* (series), 1982–83; *Designing Women* (series), 1986–  .

BURSTYN, ELLEN (born Edna Rae Gillooly), Dec. 7, 1932 (Detroit, Mich.). U.S. actress. Films: *The Last Picture Show*, 1971; *The Exorcist*, 1973; *Harry and Tonto*, 1974; *Alice Doesn't Live Here Anymore* (Best Actress AA), 1974; *Same Time, Next Year*, 1978; *Twice in a Lifetime*, 1985.

BUSEY, GARY, June 29, 1944 (Goose Creek, Tex.). U.S. actor, musician. Films: *The Last American Hero*, 1972; *The Buddy Holly Story*, 1978; *Carney*, 1981.

BUSHMAN, FRANCIS X., Jan. 10, 1883 (Baltimore, Md.)–Aug. 23, 1966. U.S. silent-screen actor. Made over 400 films, 1911–18; his fans deserted him after his divorce to marry actress Beverly Bayne in 1918.

BUTTONS, RED (born Aaron Chwatt), Feb. 5, 1919 (New York, N.Y.). U.S. comedian, actor. Films: *Sayonara*, (1957) (supporting actor AA).

BYINGTON, SPRING, Oct. 17, 1893 (Colorado Springs, Col.)–Sept. 7, 1971. U.S. actress. Films: *Little Women*, 1933; *You Can't Take It with You*, 1938. TV: *December Bride* (series), 1954–58.

CAAN, JAMES, Mar. 26, 1939 (New York, N.Y.).

U.S. actor. Films: *Games*, 1967; *The Godfather— Part 1*, 1972; *The Gambler*, 1974; *The Godfather— Part 2*, 1974; *Funny Lady*, 1975; *Rollerball*, 1975; *Gardens of Stone*, 1987. TV: *Brian's Song* (movie), 1971.

CABOT, BRUCE, 1905 (Carlsbad, N.M.)–May 3, 1972. U.S. actor. Played the hero in many 1930s action films; later often played Western film villains. Films: *King Kong*, 1933; *Wild Bill Hickok Rides*, 1942; *The Comancheros*, 1961.

CAGE, NICOLAS (born Nicolas Coppola), 1965 (Long Beach, Calif.). U.S. actor. Films: *Birdy*, 1984; *Peggy Sue Got Married*, 1986; *Raising Arizona* 1987; *Moonstruck*, 1987. (Nephew of F. COPPOLA).

CAGNEY, JAMES, July 17, 1899 (New York, N.Y.)–Mar. 30, 1986. U.S. actor, dancer. Famed for his distinctive mannerisms and staccato delivery. Films: *The Public Enemy*, 1931; *A Midsummer Night's Dream*, 1935; *Yankee Doodle Dandy* (Best Actor AA), 1942; *White Heat*, 1949; *Mister Roberts*, 1955; *Man of a Thousand Faces*, 1957; *Shake Hands with the Devil*, 1959; *One, Two Three*, 1961; *Ragtime*, 1981. Received American Film Inst. Life Achievement Award, 1974.

CALHERN, LOUIS (born Carl Henry Vogt), Feb. 19, 1895 (New York, N.Y.)–May 12, 1956. U.S. stage and film actor who generally played supporting roles in 1940s and 1950s.

CALHOUN, RORY (born Francis Timothy Durgin), Aug. 8, 1923 (Los Angeles, Calif.). U.S. actor. A leading man in 1950s action films.

CAMERON, KIRK, Oct. 12, 1970 (Panorama City, Calif.). U.S. actor. TV: *Growing Pains* (series), 1985–  .

CANDY, JOHN, Oct. 31, 1950 (Toronto, Ont.). Canadian actor. Started with Second City troupes in Chicago and Toronto. Films: *Going Berserk*, 1981; *Stripes*, 1981; *Splash*, 1984; *Brewster's Millions*, 1985; *Summer Rental*, 1985; *Spaceballs*, 1987; *Planes, Trains, and Automobiles*, 1987; *The Great Outdoors*, 1988; *Uncle Buck*, 1989.

CANNON, DYAN (born Samile Diane Friesen), Jan. 4, 1937 (Tacoma, Wash.). U.S. actress. Films: *Bob & Carol & Ted & Alice*, 1969; *Such Good Friends*, 1972; *The Last of Sheila*, 1973; *Deathtrap*, 1982. (One-time wife of C. GRANT.)

CAREY, MACDONALD, Mar. 15, 1913 (Sioux City, Ia.). U.S. actor. Appeared in numerous films, 1940-50s; received two Emmys (1974 and 1975) for best actor in daytime drama, *Days of Our Lives*.

CARIOU, LEN, Sept. 30, 1939 (Winnipeg, Man.). Canadian actor, director. Stage, screen, and TV appearances. Stage: *Damn Yankees*, 1959; *A Little Night Music*, 1973; *Sweeny Todd* (Tony Award), 1979. Films: *A Little Night Music*, 1978; *The Four Seasons*, 1981.

CARNEY, ART(hur), Nov. 4, 1918 (Mt. Vernon, N.Y.). U.S. actor. Featured for many years with Jackie Gleason in TV series *The Honeymooners*; winner of four Emmys. Films: *Harry and Tonto* (Best Actor AA), 1974; *The Late Show*, 1977.

Stage: *The Odd Couple*, 1965; *The Prisoner of Second Avenue*, 1972.

**CARRADINE, DAVID,** Oct. 8, 1936 (Hollywood, Calif.). U.S. actor. Best known as the star of TV series *Kung Fu* 1972–75. (Son of J. CARRADINE; brother of K. CARRADINE.)

**CARRADINE, JOHN** (born Richmond Reed Carradine), Feb. 5, 1906 (New York, N.Y.)–Nov. 27, 1989. U.S. character actor. Films: *Jesse James*, 1939; *Five Came Back*, 1939; *Stagecoach*, 1939; *The Grapes of Wrath*, 1940; *Bluebeard*, 1944. (Father of D. and K. CARRADINE.)

**CARRADINE, KEITH,** Aug. 8, 1949 (San Mateo, Calif.). U.S. actor, songwriter. Films: *Nashville*, 1975. Song: "I'm Easy" (1975 AA). (Son of J. CARRADINE; brother of D. CARRADINE.)

**CARRILLO, LEO,** 1880 (Los Angeles, Calif.)–Sept. 10, 1961. U.S. character actor in numerous films. Films: *The Gay Desperado*, 1936; *History Is Made at Night*, 1937.

**CARTER, DIXIE,** May 5, 1939 (McLemoresville, Tenn.). U.S. actress. TV: *Filthy Rich* (series), 1982–83; *Designing Women* (series), 1986– (Wife of H. HOLBROOK.)

**CARTER, LYNDA,** July 24, 1951 (Phoenix, Ariz.). U.S. actress. Star of TV series *Wonder Woman*, 1977–79.

**CASSAVETES, JOHN,** Dec. 9, 1929 (New York, N.Y.)–Feb. 3, 1989. U.S. actor, director, screenwriter. Films: *Edge of the City*, 1957; *Rosemary's Baby*, 1968; *Husbands*, 1970. Films (dir.): *Shadows*, 1961. Films: (writer/dir.): *Faces*, 1968. Films (writer/dir./producer): *A Woman under the Influence*, 1974; *Gloria*, 1980. (Husband of G. ROWLANDS.)

**CASSIDY, JACK,** Mar. 5, 1927 (New York, N.Y.)–Dec. 12, 1976. U.S. actor, singer. Mostly in the theater. (Father of D. and S. CASSIDY; one-time husband of S. JONES.)

**CHAMBERLAIN, RICHARD,** Mar. 31, 1935 (Beverly Hills, Calif.). U.S. actor. Best known for his starring role in the TV series *Dr. Kildare*, 1961–66. Films: *The Music Lovers*, 1970; *Lady Caroline Lamb*, 1972; *The Last Wave*, 1979; TV mini-series: *Shogun*; *The Thorn Birds*.

**CHANEY, LON,** Apr. 1, 1883 (Colorado Springs, Col.)–Aug. 26, 1930. U.S. silent-screen actor. Known as the "man of a thousand faces." Films: *The Miracle Man*, 1919; *The Hunchback of Notre Dame*, 1923; *The Phantom of the Opera*, 1925.

**CHAPLIN, GERALDINE,** July 31, 1944 (Santa Monica, Calif.). U.S. actress. Films: *Doctor Zhivago*, 1965; *Nashville*, 1975; *Welcome to L.A.*, 1977. (Daughter of C. CHAPLIN; granddaughter of E. O'NEILL.)

**CHER** (born Cherilyn La Pierre), May 20, 1946 (El Centro, Calif.). U.S. actress, singer. Vaulted to prominence in a singing duo with husband SONNY BONO, 1964–74; has turned to acting and received critical acclaim. Films: *Silkwood*, 1983; *Mask*, 1985; *The Witches of Eastwick*, 1987; *Suspect*, 1987; *Moonstruck*, 1988 (best actress AA).

**CLARK, SUSAN** (born Nora Goulding), Mar. 8, 1944 (Sarnia, Ont.). U.S. actress. TV: *Babe* (Emmy Award), 1975. Films: *Coogan's Bluff*, 1968; *Night Moves*, 1975.

**CLAYBURGH, JILL,** Apr. 30, 1944 (New York, N.Y.). U.S. actress. Film actress, with stage experience. Films: *Gable & Lombard*, 1976; *Semi-Tough*, 1977; *An Unmarried Woman*, 1978; *Starting Over*, 1979; *First Monday in October*, 1981; *I'm Dancing As Fast As I Can*, 1982.

**CLIFT, MONTGOMERY,** Oct. 17, 1920 (Omaha, Neb.)–July 23, 1966. U.S. actor. Films: *The Search*, 1948; *Red River*, 1948; *A Place in the Sun*, 1951; *From Here to Eternity*, 1953; *The Young Lions*, 1958; *The Misfits*, 1960; *Freud*, 1963.

**CLOSE, GLENN,** Mar. 19, 1947 (Greenwich, Conn.). U.S. actress. Leading lady on stage and in films. Stage: *Barnum*, 1980; *The Real Thing* (Tony award), 1984. TV: *Something About Amelia*, 1984. Films: *The World According to Garp*, 1982; *The Big Chill*, 1983; *The Natural*, 1984; *Jagged Edge*, 1985; *Fatal Attraction*, 1987; *Dangerous Liaisons*, 1989.

**COBB, LEE J.** (born Lee Jacoby), Dec. 8, 1911 (New York, N.Y.)–Feb. 11, 1976. U.S. actor. The original Willy Loman in the play *Death of a Salesman*, 1949. Films: *Golden Boy*, 1939; *On the Waterfront*, 1954; *Twelve Angry Men*, 1957. TV: *The Virginian* (series), 1962–1966.

**COBURN, CHARLES,** June 19, 1877 (Savannah, Ga.)–Aug. 30, 1961. U.S. character actor. Films: *Bachelor Mother*, 1939; *The Lady Eve*, 1941; *The Devil and Miss Jones*, 1941; *The More the Merrier* (supporting Actor AA), 1943; *The Green Years* (1946).

**COBURN, JAMES,** Aug. 31, 1928 (Laurel, Neb.). U.S. actor. Films: *The Magnificent Seven*, 1960; *The Great Escape*, 1963; *Our Man Flint*, 1966; *The Last of Sheila*, 1973; *Hard Times*, 1975.

**COCO, JAMES,** Mar. 21, 1930 (New York, N.Y.)–Feb. 25, 1987. U.S. actor. Appeared mostly in the theater.

**COLBERT, CLAUDETTE** (born Lily Claudette Chauchoin), Sept. 18, 1905 (Paris, Fr.). U.S. actress. Best known for her role in *It Happened One Night* (Best Actress AA), 1934. Other films: *Imitation of Life*, 1934; *Since You Went Away*, 1944; *The Egg and I*, 1947.

**COLEMAN, DABNEY,** Jan. 3, 1932 (Austin, Tex.). U.S. actor. TV: *Mary Hartman, Mary Hartman* (series), 1976–78; *Buffalo Bill* (series), 1983–84. Films: *Melvin and Howard*, 1980; *9 to 5*, 1980; *On Golden Pond*, 1981; *Tootsie*, 1982; *War Games*, 1983.

**COLEMAN, GARY,** Feb. 8, 1968 (Zion, Ill.). U.S. child actor. Star of the TV series *Diff'rent Strokes*, 1978–86.

**CONNORS, CHUCK,** Apr. 10, 1921 (New York, N.Y.). U.S. actor, athlete. Played with Brooklyn Dodgers (1949), and Chicago Cubs (1951). TV series *The Rifleman*, 1957–62.

**CONRAD, ROBERT** (born Conrad Robert Falk), Mar. 1, 1935 (Chicago, Ill.). U.S. actor. Best known for leading roles in the TV series *Hawaiian Eye*

(1959–63), *Wild, Wild West* (1965–69) and *Baa, Baa Black Sheep* (1976).

**CONRAD, WILLIAM,** Sept. 27, 1920 (Louisville, Ky.). U.S. actor. Radio: *Gunsmoke* (series), 1949–60. TV: *Cannon* (series), 1971–76; *Nero Wolfe*, 1977; *Jake and the Fat Man*, 1987– .

**CONREID, HANS,** Apr. 15, 1915 (Baltimore, Md.) –Jan 5, 1982. U.S. character actor on radio, TV.

**CONSTANTINE, MICHAEL** (born Constantine Efstration), May 22, 1927 (Reading, Pa.). U.S. character actor. TV: *Room 222* (1968–74).

**COOGAN, JACKIE,** Oct. 26, 1914 (Los Angeles, Calif.)–Mar. 1, 1984. U.S. actor. As child actor, appeared in such silent films as *The Kid* (1920) and *Oliver Twist* (1921). TV: (series) *The Addams Family*, 1964–66.

**COOPER, GARY** (born Frank James Cooper), May 7, 1901 (Helena, Mont.)–May 13, 1961. U.S. actor. Best known for his screen portrayals of strong, laconic heroes. Films: *A Farewell to Arms*, 1932; *The Lives of a Bengal Lancer*, 1935; *Mr. Deeds Goes to Town*, 1936; *Beau Geste*, 1939; *Sergeant York* (Best Actor AA), 1941; *Meet John Doe*, 1941; *High Noon* (Best Actor AA), 1952; *Love in the Afternoon*, 1957. Received special AA, 1960.

**COOPER, JACKIE,** Sept. 15, 1921 (Los Angeles, Calif.). U.S. actor, TV director, executive. As child actor, starred in *Our Gang* film shorts (1927–28), *The Champ* (1931), *The Bowery* (1933), and *Treasure Island* (1934). TV: (series) *People's Choice* (1955–58) and *Hennesey* (1959–60).

**CORBY, ELLEN** (born Ellen Hansen), June 3, 1913 (Racine, Wisc.). U.S. character actress. Best known for her role as Grandma in the TV series *The Waltons* (1972–81).

**CORNELL, KATHERINE,** Feb. 16, 1893 (Berlin, Ger.)–June 9, 1974. U.S. stage actress. A celebrated leading lady, 1921–61.

**COSTNER, KEVIN,** Jan. 18, 1955 (Los Angeles, Calif.). U.S. actor. Films: *American Flyers*, 1985; *Silverado*, 1985; *No Way Out*, 1987; *The Untouchables*, 1987; *Bull Durham*, 1989; *Field of Dreams*, 1989; *Revenge*, 1990.

**COTTEN, JOSEPH,** May 15, 1905 (Petersburg, Va.). U.S. actor. Films: *Citizen Kane*, 1941; *The Magnificent Ambersons*, 1942; *Duel in the Sun*, 1946; *The Farmer's Daughter*, 1947; *Portrait of Jenny*, 1948; *The Third Man*, 1949; *Hush, Hush, Sweet Charlotte*, 1964; *Tora! Tora! Tora!*, 1971.

**CRABBE, BUSTER** (born Clarence Linden Crabbe), Feb. 7, 1908 (Oakland, Calif.). U.S. actor, swimmer. Gold medalist in the 400-m freestyle, 1932 Olympics; star of 1930s and 1940s film series as Flash Gordon, Tarzan, Buck Rogers.

**CRAIN, JEANNE,** May 25, 1925 (Barstow, Calif.). U.S. actress. A leading lady of the 1940s. Films: *State Fair*, 1945; *Margie*, 1946; *A Letter to Three Wives*, 1949; *Pinky*, 1949.

**CRAWFORD, BRODERICK,** Dec. 9, 1911 (Philadelphia, Pa.)–Apr. 26, 1986. U.S. actor. Won Best Actor AA for *All the King's Men* (1949); TV (series) *Highway Patrol*, 1955–59.

**CRAWFORD, JOAN** (born Lucille Le Sueur), Mar.

23, 1908 (San Antonio, Tex.)–Feb. 14, 1977. U.S. actress, dancer. Her reputation was tarnished by her daughter's 1978 biography *Mommie Dearest*. Films: *Our Dancing Daughters*, 1928; *Grand Hotel*, 1932; *Rain*, 1932; *A Woman's Face*, 1941; *Mildred Pierce* (Best Actress AA), 1945; *Humoresque*, 1946; *What Ever Happened to Baby Jane?*, 1962.

**CRENNA, RICHARD,** Nov. 30, 1926 (Los Angeles, Calif.). U.S. actor. Star of the TV series *Our Miss Brooks* (1952–55), *The Real McCoys* (1957–63), and *Slattery's People* (1964–65).

**CRUISE, TOM,** July 3, 1962 (Syracuse, N.Y.). U.S. actor. Films: *Endless Love*, 1981; *Taps*, 1981; *Risky Business*, 1983; *The Color of Money*, 1986; *Cocktail*, 1988; *Rainman*, 1988; *Born on the Fourth of July*, 1989.

**CRYSTAL, BILLY,** Mar. 14, 1947 (Long Beach, N.Y.). U.S. comedian, actor. Star of the TV series *Soap* in the 1970s; Films: *Running Scared*, 1986; *Throw Momma From The Train*, 1987.

**CULP, ROBERT,** Aug. 16, 1930 (Oakland, Calif.). U.S. actor. TV: (series) *I Spy*, 1965–67; *The Greatest American Hero*, 1981–82. Films: *Bob & Carol & Ted & Alice*, 1969; *Breaking Point*, 1976.

**CUMMINGS, ROBERT,** June 9, 1910 (Joplin, Mo.). U.S. actor. A leading man in 1940s films. Films: *King's Row*, 1941; *Saboteur*, 1942; *The Bride Wore Boots*, 1946; *Sleep My Love*, 1948; *The Bob Cummings Show*, 1954–61.

**CURTIN, JANE,** Sept. 6, 1947 (Cambridge, Mass.). U.S. actress. TV: *Saturday Night Live*, 1975–79; *Kate and Allie* (series), 1984– (Emmy Award, 1984–85); *Common Ground* (miniseries), 1990.

**CURTIS, JAMIE LEE,** Jan. 22, 1958 (Los Angeles, Calif.). U.S. actress. Films: *Halloween*, 1979; *Halloween 2*, 1981; *Trading Places*, 1983; *Perfect*, 1985; *A Fish Called Wanda*, 1988; *Blue Steel*, 1990. (Daughter of T. CURTIS and J. LEIGH.)

**CURTIS, TONY** (born Bernard Schwartz), June 3, 1925 (New York, N.Y.). U.S. actor. Films: *Houdini*, 1953; *Trapeze*, 1956; *Sweet Smell of Success*, 1957; *The Vikings*, 1958; *Some Like It Hot*, 1959; *Spartacus*, 1960; *The Great Race*, 1965; *The Boston Strangler*, 1968. (One-time husband of J. LEIGH.)

**DAFOE, WILLEM,** July 22, 1955 (Appleton, Wis.). U.S. actor. Films: *To Live and Die in L.A.*, 1985; *Platoon*, 1987; *Mississippi Burning*, 1988; *The Last Temptation of Christ*, 1988; *Triumph of the Spirit*, 1989; *Born on the 4th of July*, 1989.

**DAHL, ARLENE,** Aug. 11, 1928 (Minneapolis, Minn.). U.S. actress, beauty columnist, model. A leading lady in films of the 1950s.

**DAILEY, DAN,** Dec. 12, 1917 (New York, N.Y.)– Oct. 16, 1978. U.S. actor. A song-and-dance man in 1940s and 1950s musicals. Films: *Mother Wore Tights*, 1947; *Give My Regards to Broadway*, 1948; *Chicken Every Sunday*, 1949; *It's Always Fair Weather*, 1955.

**DALY, TYNE,** Feb. 2, 1947 (New York, N.Y.). U.S. actress. Stage: *Gypsy*, 1989– . TV: *Cagney and Lacy* (series), 1982– (Emmy award, 1983, 1984, 1985, 1988).

**DANDRIDGE, DOROTHY,** 1923 (Cleveland, Ohio) –Sept. 8, 1965. U.S. actress. Films: *Carmen Jones*, 1954; *Island in the Sun*, 1957; *Porgy and Bess*, 1959.

**DANIELS, WILLIAM,** Mar. 31, 1927 (Brooklyn, N.Y.). U.S. actor. TV: *St. Elsewhere*, 1982–88 (Emmy 1985, 1986). Films: *A Thousand Clowns*, 1965; *The Graduate*, 1967; *Two For the Road*, 1967; *The Parallax View*, 1974; *Black Sunday*, 1977; *Reds*, 1981.

**DANNER, BLYTHE,** Feb. 3, 1943 (Philadelphia, Pa.). U.S. actress. Won 1971 Tony for *Butterflies Are Free*. Films: *1776*, 1972; *The Great Santini*, 1979; *Brighton Beach Memoirs*, 1987.

**DANSON, TED,** Dec. 29, 1947 (San Diego, Calif.). U.S. actor, producer. TV: *Cheers* (series), 1982– ; *Something About Amelia*, 1984. Films: *The Onion Field*, 1979; *Body Heat*, 1981; *A Fine Mess*, 1986; *Just Between Friends*, 1986; *When the Bough Breaks*, 1986; *Three Men and a Baby*, 1987.

**DANZA, TONY,** Apr. 21, 1951 (Brooklyn, N.Y.). U.S. actor. TV: *Taxi*, 1978–83; *Who's The Boss*, 1984– .

**DARNELL, LINDA** (born Monetta Eloyse Darnell), 1921 (Dallas, Tex.)–Apr. 10, 1965. U.S. actress. Films: *My Darling Clementine*, 1946; *Forever Amber*, 1947; *A Letter to Three Wives*, 1948.

**DA SILVA, HOWARD** (born Howard Silverblatt), May 4, 1909 (Cleveland, Ohio)–Feb. 16, 1986. U.S. actor, theater director. Films: *The Lost Weekend*, 1945; *David and Lisa*, 1962; *1776*, 1972.

**DAVIES, MARION,** Jan. 1, 1900 (New York, N.Y.)–Sept. 1961. U.S. actress. A protégé of WILLIAM RANDOLPH HEARST, who was determined to make her a star; in films, 1917–36.

**DAVIS, BETTE** (born Ruth Elizabeth Davis), Apr. 5, 1908 (Lowell, Mass.)–Oct. 6, 1989. U.S. actress. One of the foremost dramatic actresses in film history. Films: *Of Human Bondage*, 1934; *Dangerous* (Best Actress AA), 1935; *The Petrified Forest*, 1936; *Jezebel* (Best Actress AA), 1938; *A Stolen Life*, 1946; *All about Eve*, 1950; *A Pocketful of Miracles*, 1961; *What Ever Happened to Baby Jane*, 1962; *Hush, Hush, Sweet Charlotte*, 1964; *The Whales of August*, 1987.

**DAVIS, CLIFTON,** Oct. 4, 1945 (Chicago, Ill.). U.S. actor, singer. Star of the TV series *Amen* (1986– ), an ordained minister in real life; began his career on the stage, achieving one of his greatest successes in *Purlie*.

**DAVIS, GEENA,** Jan. 21, 1957 (Ware, Mass.). U.S. actress. Films: *Tootsie*, 1982; *The Fly*, 1986; *The Accidental Tourist*, 1988 (Best Supp. Actress AA). (Wife of J. GOLDBLUM.)

**DAVIS, OSSIE,** Dec. 18, 1917 (Cogdell, Ga.). U.S. actor, director. Mostly in the theater. (Husband of RUBY DEE.)

**DAWBER, PAM,** Oct. 18, 1951 (Farmington Hills, Mich.). U.S. actress. TV: *Mork and Mindy* (series), 1978–82; *My Sister Sam* (series), 1986–88. (Wife of MARK HARMON.)

**DAWSON, RICHARD,** Nov. 20, 1932 (Hampshire, Eng.). British actor, TV game-show host. TV: *Ho-* *gan's Heroes* (series), 1965–71; *Family Feud* (game show), 1976–85.

**DAY, DORIS** (born Doris von Kappelhoff), Apr. 3, 1924 (Cincinnati, Ohio). U.S. singer, dancer, actress. Films: *Young Man with a Horn*, 1950; *Tea for Two*, 1950; *I'll See You in My Dreams*, 1951; *Young at Heart*, 1955; *Love Me or Leave Me*, 1955; *The Pajama Game*, 1957; *Pillow Talk*, 1959; *Midnight Lace*, 1960; *With Six You Get Egg Roll*, 1968. TV: *The Doris Day Show* (series), 1968–72.

**DEAN, JAMES** (born James Byron), Feb. 8, 1931 (Marion, Ind.)–Sept. 20, 1955. U.S. actor. Epitomized restless youth of the early 1950s. Films: *East of Eden*, 1955; *Rebel Without A Cause*, 1955; *Giant*, 1956.

**DEE, RUBY** (born Ruby Ann Wallace), Oct. 27, 1923 (Cleveland, Ohio). U.S. actress. Plays: *Raisin in the Sun*, 1959; *Purlie Victorious*, 1961. Films: *Raisin in the Sun*, 1961. (Wife of O. DAVIS.)

**DEE, SANDRA** (born Alexandra Zuck), Apr. 29, 1942 (Bayonne, N.J.). U.S. actress. Films: *Gidget*, 1959; *Imitation of Life*, 1959; *A Summer Place*, 1959; *Tammy and the Doctor*, 1963; *Take Her, She's Mine*, 1964; *That Funny Feeling*, 1965.

**DE HAVILLAND, OLIVIA,** July 1, 1916 (Tokyo, Jap.). English-U.S. actress. Films: *A Midsummer Night's Dream*, 1935; *Gone with the Wind*, 1939; *To Each His Own* (Best Actress AA), 1946; *The Heiress* (Best Actress AA), 1949; *The Snake Pit*, 1948; *Hush, Hush, Sweet Charlotte*, 1964. (Sister of J. FONTAINE.)

**DEL RIO, DOLORES** (born Dolores Asunsolo), Aug. 3, 1908 (Durango, Mex.)–Apr. 11, 1983. Mexican-U.S. actress. A leading lady of 1920s and 1930s films.

**DEMAREST, WILLIAM,** Feb. 27, 1892 (St. Paul, Minn.)–Dec. 27, 1983. U.S. character actor. Appeared in numerous films, from 1927. TV: *Wells Fargo* (series), 1956–58; *My Three Sons* (series), 1967–71.

**DEMORNAY, RECECCA,** 1962 (Santa Rosa, Calif.). U.S. actress. Films: *Risky Business*, 1983; *Runaway Train*, 1985.

**DE NIRO, ROBERT,** Aug. 17, 1943 (New York, N.Y.). U.S. actor. Films: *Bang the Drum Slowly*, 1973; *The Godfather—Part 2*, (Supporting Actor AA), 1974; *Taxi Driver*, 1976; *New York, New York*, 1977; *The Deer Hunter*, 1978; *Raging Bull* (Best Actor AA), 1980; *True Confessions*, 1981; *The Mission*, 1986; *The Untouchables*, 1987.

**DENNEHY, BRIAN,** July 9, 1940 (Bridgeport, Conn.). U.S. actor. Stage: *Streamers*, 1976. Films: *Semi-Tough*, 1976; *Gorky Park*, 1983; *Silverado*, 1985; *Cocoon*, 1985; *F/X*, 1986.

**DENNIS, SANDY,** Apr. 27, 1937 (Hastings, Neb.). U.S. actress. Films: *Who's Afraid of Virginia Woolf?* (Best Supporting Actress AA), 1966; *Up the Down Staircase*, 1967; *The Out-of-Towners*, 1969. Plays: *A Thousand Clowns* (Tony award), 1963; *Any Wednesday* (Tony award), 1964.

**DENVER, BOB,** Jan. 9, 1935 (New Rochelle, N.Y.). U.S. comedic actor. TV: *Dobie Gillis* (series), 1959–62; *Gilligan's Island* (series), 1964–66.

**DEPP, JOHNNY,** June 6, 1963 (Owensboro, Ky.).

U.S. actor, musician. TV: *21 Jump Street* (series), 1987– . Films: *A Nightmare on Elm Street*, 1984; *Crybaby*, 1990.

**DEREK, JOHN** (born Derek Harris), Aug. 12, 1926 (Hollywood, Calif.). U.S. actor, producer, director. Films: *Knock on Any Door*, 1949; *All the King's Men*, 1949; *Exodus*, 1960.

**DERN, BRUCE,** June 4, 1936 (Chicago, Ill.). U.S. actor. Films: *Silent Running*, 1972; *King of Marvin Gardens*, 1972; *The Great Gatsby*, 1974; *Smile*, 1975; *Black Sunday*, 1977; *Coming Home*, 1978; *That Championship Season*, 1982.

**DEVANE, WILLIAM,** Sept. 5, 1937 (Albany, N.Y.). U.S. actor. Films: *The Marathon Man*, 1977; *Yanks*, 1979. TV: *From Here to Eternity* (movie), 1979; *Knots Landing* (series), 1983– .

**DEVITO, DANNY,** Nov. 17, 1944 (Neptune, N.J.). U.S. actor, director. TV: *Taxi* (series), 1978–83 (Emmy Award, 1981). Films: *One Flew Over the Cuckoo's Nest*, 1975; *Terms of Endearment*, 1983; *Romancing the Stone*, 1984; *The Jewel of the Nile*, 1985; *Ruthless People*, 1986; *Tin Men*, 1987; *Twins*, 1988; *War of the Roses*, 1990 (directing debut).

**DEWHURST, COLLEEN,** June 3, 1926 (Montreal, Que., Can.). U.S. actress. Plays: *All the Way Home* (Tony award), 1961; *A Moon for the Misbegotten* (Tony Award), 1974.

**DEY, SUSAN,** Dec. 12, 1952 (Pekin, Ill.). U.S. actress. TV: *The Partridge Family* (series), 1970–74; *L.A. Law*, 1986– .

**DICKINSON, ANGIE** (born Angeline Brown), Sept. 30, 1931 (Kulm, N.D.). U.S. actress. Films: *Rio Bravo*, 1959; *Point Blank*, 1968; *Dressed to Kill*, 1980. TV: *Police Woman* (series), 1974–78.

**DILLMAN, BRADFORD,** Apr. 14, 1930 (San Francisco, Calif.). U.S. actor. Films: *A Certain Smile*, 1958; *Compulsion*, 1959.

**DILLON, MATT,** Feb. 18, 1964 (New Rochelle, N.Y.). U.S. actor. Films: *Over the Edge*, 1979; *Little Darlings*, 1980; *Tex*, 1982; *The Outsiders*, 1983; *Rumblefish*, 1983; *The Flamingo Kid*, 1984; *Drugstore Cowboy*, 1989.

**DONAHUE, TROY** (born Merle Johnson), Jan. 27, 1936 (New York, N.Y.). U.S. actor. Films: *Parrish*, 1961; *A Summer Place*, 1962. TV: *Surfside Six* (series), 1960–62.

**DOUGLAS, KIRK** (born Issur Danielovitch Demsky), Dec. 9, 1918 (Amsterdam, N.Y.). U.S. actor. Films: *Champion*, 1949; *Young Man with a Horn*, 1950; *The Glass Menagerie*, 1951; *Lust For Life*, 1956; *Gunfight at the OK Corral*, 1957; *Paths of Glory*, 1957; *Spartacus*, 1960; *Lonely Are the Brave*, 1962; *Seven Days in May*, 1964; *Cast a Giant Shadow*, 1966; *Tough Guys*, 1986. (Father of M. DOUGLAS.)

**DOUGLAS, MELVYN** (born Melvyn Hesselberg), Apr. 5, 1901 (Macon, Ga.)–Aug. 4, 1981. U.S. actor. Films: *Captains Courageous*, 1937; *Ninotchka*, 1939; *Hud* (Best Supporting Actor AA), 1963; *Hotel*, 1967; *I Never Sang for My Father*, 1969; *Being There* (Best Supporting Actor AA), 1979.

**DOUGLAS, MICHAEL,** Sept. 25, 1944 (New Brunswick, N.J.). U.S. actor, producer. Films: *Hail Hero*, 1970; *The China Syndrome*, 1979; *Romanc-*

*ing the Stone*, 1984; *The Jewel of the Nile*, 1985; *A Chorus Line*, 1986; *Fatal Attraction*, 1987; *Wall Street*, 1987. TV: *The Streets of San Francisco* (series), 1972–75. (Son of K. DOUGLAS.)

**DOUGLAS, PAUL,** Apr. 11, 1907 (Philadelphia, Pa.)–Sept. 11, 1959. U.S. actor. Character leading man in films. Films: *A Letter to Three Wives*, 1948; *The Solid Gold Cadillac*, 1956.

**DOWNEY, ROBERT, JR.,** Apr. 4, 1965 (Los Angeles, Calif.). U.S. actor. Films: *Back to School*, 1986; *Less Than Zero*, 1987; *True Believer*, 1989; *Chances Are*, 1989.

**DREYFUSS, RICHARD,** Oct. 29, 1947 (New York, N.Y.). U.S. actor. Films: *American Graffiti*, 1972; *The Apprenticeship of Duddy Kravitz*, 1974; *Jaws*, 1975; *Close Encounters of the Third Kind*, 1976; *The Good-Bye Girl*, (Best Actor AA), 1977; *Down and Out in Beverly Hills*, 1986; *Tin Men*, 1987.

**DRYER, FRED,** July 7, 1946 (Hawthorne, Calif.). U.S. actor. Football player turned actor. TV: *Hunter* (series), 1984– .

**DUFFY, JULIA,** June 27, 1951 (St. Paul, Minn.). U.S. actress. TV: *Newhart* (series), 1984–86.

**DUFFY, PATRICK,** May 17, 1949 (Townshead, Mont.). U.S. actor. TV: *Dallas* (series), 1978–85, 1986– .

**DUKAKIS, OLYMPIA,** 1932 (Mass.). U.S. actress. Films: *Moonstruck*, 1987 (Best Supporting Actress AA); *Steel Magnolias*, 1989; *Look Who's Talking*, 1989.

**DUKE, PATTY** (born Anna Marie Duke), Dec. 14, 1946 (New York, N.Y.). U.S. actress. Films: *The Miracle Worker* (Best Supporting Actress AA), 1962; *Valley of the Dolls*, 1967; *My Sweet Charlie*, 1970. TV: *Patty Duke Show* (series), 1963–65. Plays: *The Miracle Worker*, 1959.

**DUNAWAY, FAYE,** Jan. 14, 1941 (Bascom, Fla.). U.S. actress. Films: *Hurry Sundown*, 1967; *Bonnie and Clyde*, 1967; *The Thomas Crown Affair*, 1968; *Oklahoma Crude*, 1973; *Chinatown*, 1974; *The Voyage of the Damned*, 1976; *Network* (Best Actress AA), 1976; *Mommie Dearest*, 1981; *Barfly*, 1987.

**DUNCAN, SANDY,** Feb. 20, 1946 (Henderson, Tex.). U.S. actress, singer, dancer. TV: *Valerie* (series), 1987–88. Stage: *Peter Pan*, 1979.

**DUNNE, IRENE,** Dec. 20, 1901 (Louisville, Ky.). U.S. actress. Films: *Cimarron*, 1931; *Back Street*, 1932; *Show Boat*, 1936; *The Awful Truth*, 1937; *My Favorite Wife*, 1940; *Life with Father*, 1947; *I Remember Mama*, 1948.

**DURBIN, DEANNA** (born Edna Mae Durbin), Dec. 4, 1922 (Winnipeg, Man., Can.). U.S. singer, actress. Popular teenage star in films in 1930s and 1940s; special AA, 1938.

**DURYEA, DAN,** 1907 (White Plains, N.Y.)–June 7, 1968. U.S. character actor. Films: *The Little Foxes*, 1941; *The Woman in the Window*, 1944; *Black Angel*, 1946; *Another Part of the Forest*, 1948; *The Flight of the Phoenix*, 1965.

**DUVALL, ROBERT,** Jan. 5, 1931 (San Diego, Calif.). U.S. actor. Films: *True Grit*, 1969; *The Godfather—Part 1*, 1972; *The Conversation*, 1974; *The Godfather—Part 2*, 1974; *Network*, 1976;

*Apocalypse Now*, 1979; *The Great Santini*, 1979; *True Confessions*, 1981; *Tender Mercies* (Best Actor AA), 1983.

**DUVALL, SHELLEY,** 1949 (Houston, Tex.). U.S. actress. Frequently featured in films by ROBERT ALTMAN. Films: *Thieves Like Us*, 1974; *Nashville*, 1975; *Three Women*, 1977; *Popeye*, 1980.

**DYSART, RICHARD,** Mar. 30, 19? (Augusta, Me.). U.S. actor. Stage: *That Championship Season*, 1972. TV: *L.A. Law*, 1986– .

**EASTWOOD, CLINT,** May 31, 1930 (San Francisco, Calif.). U.S. actor, director. Sprang into prominence as the tight-lipped hero of low-budget "spaghetti" westerns. Films: *A Fistful of Dollars*, 1964; *For a Few Dollars More*, 1965; *The Good, the Bad, and the Ugly*, 1966; *Hang 'Em High*, 1968; *Coogan's Bluff*, 1968; *Play Misty for Me*, 1971; *Dirty Harry*, 1971; *Magnum Force*, 1973; *Every Which Way but Loose*, 1978; *Any Which Way You Can*, 1980; *Sudden Impact*, 1984; *Tightrope*, 1984; *City Heat*, 1984; *Heartbreak Ridge*, 1986. TV: *Rawhide* (series), 1958–65.

**EBSEN, BUDDY** (born Christian Rudolf Ebsen), Apr. 2, 1908 (Belleville, Ill.). U.S. actor, dancer. Originally a song-and-dance man in 1930s films. TV: *The Beverly Hillbillies* (series), 1962–71; *Barnaby Jones* (series), 1973–80.

**EDEN, BARBARA** (born Barbara Huffman), Aug. 23, 1934 (Tucson, Ariz.). U.S. actress. TV: (series) *I Dream of Jeannie*, 1965–69.

**EDWARDS, VINCENT** (born Vincent Edward Zoimo), July 7, 1928 (Brooklyn, N.Y.). U.S. actor. TV: (series) *Ben Casey*, 1960–65.

**EIKENBERRY, JILL,** Jan. 21, 1947 (New Haven, Ct.). U.S. actress. TV: *Uncommon Women and Others*, 1977; *L.A. Law* (series), 1986– . Films: *An Unmarried Woman*, 1977; *Between the Lines*, 1977; *Arthur*, 1981; *The Manhattan Project*, 1986.

**ELLIOTT, SAM,** Aug. 9, 1944 (Sacramento, Calif.). U.S. actor. TV: *The Last Convertible*, 1979; *Murder in Texas*, 1981; *Yellow Rose* (series), 1982–83; *A Death in California*, 1985. Films: *Butch Cassidy and the Sundance Kid* (1969).

**EVANS, DALE** (born Francis Smith), Oct. 31, 1912 (Uvalde, Tex.). U.S. singer, actress. A film star in 1940s westerns, played opposite husband ROY ROGERS in TV series, *The Roy Rogers Show*, 1951–57.

**EVANS, LINDA,** Nov. 18, 1943 (Hartford, Ct.). U.S. actress. TV: *The Big Valley* (series), 1965–69; *Dynasty* (series), 1981–89; *The Gambler, Part 2*, 1983. Films: *Tom Horn*, 1980.

**EVERETT, CHAD** (born Raymond Lee Cramton), June 11, 1937 (South Bend, Ind.). U.S. actor. TV: (series) *Medical Center*, 1969–75.

**EWELL, TOM** (born Yewell Tomkins), Apr. 29, 1909 (Owensboro, Ky.). U.S. comedic actor. Films: *Adam's Rib*, 1949; *The Seven Year Itch*, 1955; *State Fair*, 1962. TV: *Baretta* (series), 1975–78.

**FAIRBANKS, DOUGLAS** (born Douglas Ullman), May 23, 1883 (Denver, Col.)–Dec. 12, 1939. U.S. actor. A silent-screen star, first of great swashbuckling screen heroes; a founder of United Artists

Corp., 1919; honored with posthumous AA for his contribution to motion pictures, 1939. Films: *The Mark of Zorro*, 1920; *The Three Musketeers*, 1921; *Robin Hood*, 1921; *The Thief of Baghdad*, 1923. (One-time husband of M. PICKFORD; father of D. FAIRBANKS, JR.)

**FAIRBANKS, DOUGLAS, JR.,** Dec. 9, 1909 (New York, N.Y.). U.S. actor, TV producer. Films: *Dawn Patrol*, 1930; *Morning Glory*, 1933; *The Prisoner of Zenda*, 1937; *Gunga Din*, 1939; *Sinbad the Sailor*, 1947. (Son of D. FAIRBANKS.)

**FAIRCHILD, MORGAN,** Feb. 3, 1950 (Dallas, Tex.). U.S. actress. TV: *Flamingo Road* (series), 1981–82; *Paper Dolls* (series), 1984; *Falcon Crest* (series), 1985; *North and South* (miniseries, pts. 1 and 2), 1985, 1986. Films: *Pee-Wee's Big Adventure*, 1985.

**FALK, PETER,** Sept. 16, 1927 (New York, N.Y.). U.S. actor. TV: (series) *Columbo* (1971–78). Films: *Murder, Inc.*, 1960; *The Great Race*, 1965; *Luv*, 1967; *Husbands*, 1970; *Murder by Death*, 1976; *The In-Laws*, 1979.

**FARMER, FRANCES,** 1914 (Seattle, Wash.)–Aug. 1, 1970. U.S. actress. Actress of late 1930s-early 1940s; in her autobiography, *Will There Ever Be a Morning*, gave an account of her nearly 30-years battle with mental illness and alcoholism, 1972. Played by JESSICA LANGE in 1983 film, *Frances*.

**FARR, JAMIE,** July 1, 1934 (Toledo, Ohio). U.S. actor. TV: *M\*A\*S\*H* (series), 1973–83.

**FARRELL, MIKE,** Feb. 6, 1939 (St. Paul, Minn.). U.S. actor. TV: *M\*A\*S\*H* (series), 1975–83.

**FARROW, MIA,** Feb. 9, 1945 (Los Angeles, Calif.). U.S. actress. Films: *Rosemary's Baby*, 1968; *The Great Gatsby*, 1973; *Zelig*, 1983; *Broadway Danny Rose*, 1984; *The Purple Rose of Cairo*, 1985; *Hannah and Her Sisters*, 1986; *Radio Days*, 1987; *September*, 1987. TV: *Peyton Place* (series), 1964–67. (Daughter of M. O'SULLIVAN.)

**FAWCETT, FARRAH,** Feb. 2, 1947 (Corpus Christi, Tex.). U.S. actress. TV: *Charlie's Angels* (series), 1976–77. Films: *Sunburn*, 1979; *Extremities*, 1985.

**FAYE, ALICE** (born Ann Leppert), May 5, 1912 (New York, N.Y.). U.S. singer, actress. Films: *In Old Chicago*, 1938; *Alexander's Ragtime Band*, 1938; *Rose of Washington Square*, 1939; *Lillian Russell*, 1940; *State Fair*, 1962. (Wife of PHIL HARRIS.)

**FELDON, BARBARA,** Mar. 12, 1941 (Pittsburgh, Pa.). U.S. actress. Best known for her role in the TV series *Get Smart*, 1965–70.

**FERRER, MEL,** Aug. 25, 1917 (Elberon, N.J.). U.S. actor. Films: *Lost Boundaries*, 1949; *Scaramouche*, 1952; *War and Peace*, 1956.

**FIELD, SALLY,** Nov. 6, 1946 (Pasadena, Calif.). U.S. actress. TV: *Gidget* (series), 1965; *The Flying Nun* (series), 1967–68. Films: *Smokey and the Bandit*, 1977; *Norma Rae*, (Best Actress AA), 1979; *Absence of Malice*, 1981; *Places in the Heart* (Best Actress AA), 1984; *Murphy's Romance*, 1985.

**FISHER, CARRIE,** Oct. 21, 1956 (Beverly Hills, Calif.). U.S. actress. Films: *Star Wars*, 1977. (Daughter of D. REYNOLDS and E. FISHER.)

FLEMING, RHONDA (born Marilyn Louis), Aug. 10, 1923 (Hollywood, Calif.). U.S. actress. A leading lady in 1940s and 1950s films.

FLANDERS, ED, Dec. 29, 1934 (Minneapolis, Calif.). U.S. actor. Noted character actor. TV: *The Legend of Lizzie Borden*, 1975; *Eleanor and Franklin*, 1976; *The Amazing Howard Hughes*, 1977; *St. Elsewhere*, (series), 1982–88.

FLETCHER, LOUISE, 1936 (Birmingham, Ala.). U.S. actress. Films: *One Flew over the Cuckoo's Nest* (Best Actress AA), 1975; *Exorcist II*, 1977.

FLYNN, ERROL, June 20, 1909 (Hobart, Tasmania, Austrl.)–Oct. 14, 1959. U.S. actor. A star of action-adventure films of the 1930s and 1940s. Films: *Captain Blood*, 1935; *The Charge of the Light Brigade*, 1936; *The Adventures of Robin Hood*, 1938; *Elizabeth and Essex*, 1939; *They Died with Their Boots On*, 1941; *Gentleman Jim*, 1942; *The Sun Also Rises*, 1957.

FONDA, HENRY, May 16, 1905 (Grand Island, Neb.)–Aug. 12, 1982. U.S. actor. Best known for his portrayal of upright, reasonable heroes. Films: *Jezebel*, 1938; *Young Mr. Lincoln*, 1939; *The Grapes of Wrath*, 1940; *Chad Hanna*, 1940; *The Lady Eve*, 1941; *The Ox-Bow Incident*, 1942; *My Darling Clementine*, 1946; *Ft. Apache*, 1948; *Mr. Roberts*, 1955; *Twelve Angry Men*, 1957; *Fail Safe*, 1964; *Welcome to Hard Times*, 1967; *On Golden Pond* (Best Actor AA), 1982. (Father of J. and P. FONDA.)

FONDA, JANE, Dec. 21, 1937 (New York, N.Y.). U.S. actress, social activist, author of best-selling exercise books and videos. Films: *Tall Story*, 1960; *Cat Ballou*, 1965; *Barefoot in the Park*, 1967; *Barbarella*, 1968; *They Shoot Horses, Don't They?*, 1969; *Klute* (Best Actress AA), 1971; *A Doll's House*, 1973; *Fun with Dick and Jane*, 1976; *Julia*, 1977; *Coming Home* (Best Actress AA), 1978; *The China Syndrome*, 1979; *9 to 5*, 1980; *On Golden Pond*, 1982; *Agnes of God*, 1985; *The Morning After*, 1987. (Daughter of H. FONDA; sister of P. FONDA.)

FONDA, PETER, Feb. 23, 1939 (New York, N.Y.). U.S. actor. Writer, coproducer, and star of the film *Easy Rider*, 1969. (Son of H. FONDA; brother of J. FONDA.)

FONTAINE, JOAN (born Joan de Havilland), Oct. 22, 1917 (Tokyo, Jap.). English-U.S. actress. Films: *Gunga Din*, 1939; *Rebecca*, 1940; *Suspicion* (Best Actress AA), 1941; *Jane Eyre*, 1943; *Letter from an Unknown Woman*, 1948. (Sister of O. DE HAVILLAND.)

FORD, GLENN (born Gwyllyn Ford), May 1, 1916 (Quebec, Can.). Canadian-U.S. actor. Films: *The Adventures of Martin Eden*, 1942; *Gilda*, 1946; *The Blackboard Jungle*, 1955; *The Sheepman*, 1958. (One-time husband of E. POWELL.)

FORD, HARRISON, July 13, 1942 (Chicago, Ill.). U.S. actor. Films: *American Graffiti*, 1973; *Star Wars*, 1977; *The Empire Strikes Back*, 1980; *Raiders of the Lost Ark*, 1981; *Return of the Jedi*, 1983; *Indiana Jones and the Temple of Doom*, 1984; *Witness*, 1985; *The Mosquito Coast*, 1986.

FORSYTHE, JOHN (born John Freund), Jan. 29, 1918 (Penns Grove, N.J.). U.S. actor. Best known as star of the TV series *Bachelor Father* (1957–62) and *Charlie's Angels* (1976–81); *Dynasty* (1981–   ).

FOSTER, JODIE, Nov. 19, 1962 (New York, N.Y.). U.S. actress. Films: *Alice Doesn't Live Here Anymore*, 1975; *Taxi Driver*, 1976; *Bugsy Malone*, 1976.

FOXWORTH, ROBERT, Nov. 1, 1941 (Houston, Tex.). U.S. actor, director. TV: *Falcon Crest* (series), 1981–87.

FRANCIOSA, ANTHONY (born Anthony Papaleo), Oct. 25, 1928 (New York, N.Y.). U.S. actor. TV: *Valentine's Day* (series), 1964–65; *The Name of the Game* (series), 1968–70; *Search* (series), 1972–73; *Matt Helm* (series), 1975–76; *Finder of Lost Loves*, 1984–85.

FRANCIS, ARLENE (born Arlene Kazanjian), Oct. 20, 1908 (Boston, Mass.). U.S. actress, radio and TV personality. TV: *What's My Line* (game show), 1950–67.

FRANCIS, KAY (born Katherine Gibbs), Jan. 13, 1903 (Oklahoma City, Okla.)–Aug. 26, 1968. U.S. actress. A leading lady in the 1930s "women's" films.

FRANKLIN, BONNIE, Jan. 6, 1944 (Santa Monica, Calif.). U.S. actress, dancer. Play: *Applause*, 1970. TV: *One Day at a Time* (series), 1975–84.

FRAWLEY, WILLIAM, 1887 (Burlington, Ia.)–Mar. 3, 1966. U.S. comedic actor. TV: *I Love Lucy* (series), 1951–60; *My Three Sons* (series), 1960–63.

FREEMAN, MORGAN, 1939 (?). U.S. actor. Stage: *The Gospel at Colonus*, 1987 (Obie Award); *Driving Miss Daisy*, 1987. Films: *Street Smart*, 1987; *Clean and Sober*, 1988; *Lean On Me*, 1989; *Glory*, 1990; *Driving Miss Daisy*, 1989.

FUNICELLO, ANNETTE, Oct. 22, 1942 (Utica, N.Y.). U.S. entertainer. One of Disney Mouseketeers in 1950s, later starred in family and "beach party" films.

GABLE, (William) CLARK, Feb. 1, 1901 (Cadiz, Ohio)–Nov. 16, 1960. U.S. actor. Popular hero of romance-adventure films. Films: *It Happened One Night* (Best Actor AA), 1934; *Mutiny on the Bounty*, 1935; *Call of the Wild*, 1935; *Gone with the Wind*, 1939; *The Hucksters*, 1947; *Command Decision*, 1948; *Teacher's Pet*, 1958; *Run Silent, Run Deep*, 1958; *The Misfits*, 1960.

GABOR, EVA, 1921 (Hungary). Hungarian-U.S. actress. TV: *Green Acres* (series), 1965–71. (Sister of Z. Z. GABOR.)

GABOR, ZSA ZSA (born Sari Gabor), ? (Hungary). Hungarian-U.S. actress. Miss Hungary, 1936. (Sister of E. GABOR.)

GARDNER, AVA, Dec. 24, 1922 (Smithfield, N.C.)–Jan. 25, 1990. U.S. actress. Films: *The Killers*, 1946; *The Hucksters*, 1947; *Show Boat*, 1951; *Mogambo*, 1953; *The Barefoot Contessa*, 1954; *The Sun Also Rises*, 1957; *The Naked Maja*, 1959; *On the Beach*, 1959; *The Night of the Iguana*, 1964.

GARFIELD, JOHN (born Julius Garfinkle), 1913 (New York, N.Y.)–May 21, 1952. U.S. actor. Known for powerful dramatic performances in films. Films: *They Made Me a Criminal*, 1939; *The Sea Wolf*, 1941; *The Fallen Sparrow*, 1943; *Destination Tokyo*, 1944; *Pride of the Marines*, 1945; *The Postman Always Rings Twice*, 1946; *Humoresque*, 1946; *Body and Soul*, 1947; *Gentlemen's Agreement*, 1947; *Force of Evil*, 1949.

**GARNER, JAMES** (born James Baumgarner), Apr. 7, 1928 (Norman, Okla.). U.S. actor. TV: (series) *Maverick*, (1957–62) and *Rockford Files* (1974–79). Films: *Cash McCall*, 1959; *The Thrill of It All*, 1963; *Grand Prix*, 1966; *The Skin Game*, 1971; *Victor/Victoria*, 1982; *Murphy's Romance*, 1986.

**GARR, TERI**, Dec. 11, 1949 (Lakewood, Oh.). U.S. actress. Films: *Conversation*, 1974; *Young Frankenstein*, 1974; *Close Encounters of the Third Kind*, 1977; *One From the Heart*, 1982; *Tootsie*, 1982; *Mr. Mom*, 1983.

**GAYNOR, JANET** (born Laura Gainer), Oct. 6, 1906 (Philadelphia, Pa.).–Sept. 14, 1984. U.S. actress Films: *Seventh Heaven* (Best Actress AA), 1927; *State Fair*, 1933; *A Star Is Born*, 1937.

**GAZZARA, BEN**, Aug. 28, 1930 (New York, N.Y.). U.S. actor. Films: *Anatomy of a Murder*, 1959; *Husbands*, 1969; *Al Capone*, 1974. TV: *Run for Your Life* (series), 1965–68.

**GEER, WILL**, Mar. 9, 1902 (Frankfort, Ind.)–Apr. 22, 1978. U.S. character actor. Best known for the role of the grandfather on the TV series *The Waltons*, 1972–78.

**GERE, RICHARD**, Aug. 31, 1949 (Philadelphia, Pa.). U.S. actor. Films: *Looking for Mr. Goodbar*, 1977; *Days of Heaven*, 1978; *Blood Brothers*, 1978; *Yanks*, 1979; *American Gigolo*, 1979; *An Officer and a Gentleman*, 1983; *Breathless*, 1983; *The Cotton Club*, 1984; *Pretty Woman*, 1990.

**GETTY, ESTELLE**, July 25, 1924 (New York, N.Y.). U.S. actress. TV: *The Golden Girls*, 1985– .

**GIBBS, MARLA**, June 14, 1931 (Chicago, Ill.). U.S. actress. TV: *The Jeffersons* (series), 1974–85; *227* (series), 1985– .

**GIBSON, MEL**, Jan. 3, 1951 (Peekskill, N.Y.). U.S. actor. Films: *Mad Max*, 1980; *Gallipoli*, 1981; *The Year of Living Dangerously*, 1982; *Mad Max 2: The Road Warrior*, 1982; *Mad Max Beyond Thunderdome*, 1985; *Lethal Weapon*, 1987; *Tequila Sunrise*, 1988; *Lethal Weapon 2*, 1989.

**GILBERT, JOHN** (born John Pringle), July 10, 1897 (Logan, Utah)-Jan. 9, 1936. U.S. silent-screen actor whose high-pitched voice brought his career to an end when talkies superseded silent films.

**GILBERT, MELISSA**, May 8, 1964 (Los Angeles, Calif.). U.S. actress. TV: *Little House on the Prairie* (series), 1974–82; *The Diary of Anne Frank*, 1980.

**GILFORD, JACK** (born Jacob Gellman), July 25, 1907 (New York, N.Y.)–June 4, 1990. U.S. comedic actor. Films: *A Funny Thing Happened on the Way to the Forum*, 1966; *Catch-22*, 1971; *Save the Tiger*, 1973; *Cocoon*, 1985.

**GISH, DOROTHY** (born Dorothy de Guiche), Mar. 11, 1898 (Massillon, Ohio)–June 4, 1968. U.S. silent-screen actress. Star of numerous D.W. GRIFFITH films. (Sister of L. GISH.)

**GISH, LILLIAN** (born Lillian de Guiche), Oct. 14, 1896 (Springfield, Ohio). U.S. silent-screen actress. Films: *Birth of a Nation*, 1914; *Intolerance*, 1916; *Way Down East*, 1920; *Orphans of the Storm*, 1927; *Duel in the Sun*, 1946; *Night of the Hunter*, 1958; *The Whales of August*, 1987. (Sister of D. GISH.)

**GLESS, SHARON**, May 31, 1943 (Los Angeles, Calif.). U.S. actress. TV: *Cagney and Lacy* (series), 1982–   (Emmy award, 1986, 1987).

**GLOVER, DANNY**, 1948 (San Francisco, Calif.). U.S. actor. Stage: *Master Harold and the Boys*, 1982. TV: *Chiefs* (miniseries), 1983; *Mandela*, 1987. Films: *Places in the Heart*, 1984; *Silverado*, 1985; *The Color Purple*, 1985; *Lethal Weapon*, 1987; *Lethal Weapon 2*, 1989.

**GODDARD, PAULETTE** (born Marion Levy), June 3, 1915 (Great Neck, N.Y.)–Apr. 23, 1990. U.S. actress. Leading lady in 1940s films, including *The Ghost Breakers* (1940), *The Great Dictator* (1940), *Kitty* (1945), *The Diary of a Chambermaid* (1946).

**GOLDBERG, WHOOPI**, 1949 (New York, N.Y.). U.S. actress. Films: *The Color Purple*, 1985; *Jumpin' Jack Flash*, 1986; *Clara's Heart*, 1988.

**GOLDBLUM, JEFF**, Oct. 22, 1952 (Pittsburgh, Pa.). U.S. actor. TV: *Tenspeed and Brown Shoe* (series), 1980. Films: *Between the Lines*, 1977; *Invasion of the Body Snatchers*, 1978; *The Big Chill*, 1983; *The Right Stuff*, 1983; *Silverado*, 1985; *The Fly*, 1986. (Husband of G. DAVIS.)

**GOODMAN, JOHN**, June 20, 1953 (St. Louis, Mo.). U.S. actor. Stage: *Big River*, 1985. TV: *Roseanne* (series), 1988–  . Films: *True Stories*, 1986; *Raising Arizona*, 1986; *The Big Easy*, 1987; *Punchline*, 1987; *Sea of Love*, 1989; *Stella*, 1990.

**GORDON, GALE**, Feb. 2, 1906 (New York, N.Y.). U.S. actor. TV: *Our Miss Brooks* (series), 1952–56; *Dennis the Menace* (series), 1958–63; *The Lucy Show* (series), 1962–68.

**GORDON, RUTH** (born Ruth Gordon Jones), Oct. 30, 1896 (Wollaston, Mass.)–Aug. 28, 1985. U.S. stage and film actress, screenwriter. Films (actress): *Rosemary's Baby* (Best Supporting Actress AA), 1968; *Where's Poppa?*, 1970; *Harold and Maude*, 1971. Films (writer, with husband GARSON KANIN): *A Double Life* (1948), *Adam's Rib* (1949).

**GOSSETT, LOU, JR.**, May 27, 1936 (Brooklyn, N.Y.). U.S. actor. Noted character actor. TV: *Roots* (Emmy award), 1977; *The Lazarus Syndrome* (TV movie and series), 1979. Films: *A Raisin in the Sun*, 1961; *An Officer and a Gentleman* (supp. actor AA), 1982; *Enemy Mine*, 1984; *A Gathering of Old Men*, 1987.

**GOULD, ELLIOTT** (born Elliot Goldstein), Aug. 29, 1938 (New York, N.Y.). U.S. actor. Films: *Bob & Carol & Ted & Alice*, 1969; *M*A*S*H*, 1970; *Little Murders*, 1971; *The Devil and Max Devlin*, 1981.

**GRABLE, BETTY** (born Elizabeth Grasle) 1916 (St. Louis, Mo.)–July 2, 1973. U.S. actress. Pin-up girl of WW II. Films: *Million Dollar Legs*, 1939; *Moon Over Miami*, 1941; *I Wake up Screaming*,

1941; *Pin Up Girl*, 1944; *Diamond Horseshoe*, 1945; *The Dolly Sisters*, 1945; *Mother Wore Tights*, 1947; *How to Marry a Millionaire*, 1953.

GRAMMER, KELSEY, Feb. 20, 19? (Virgin Islands). U.S. actor. TV: *Cheers* (series), 1984–   .

GRANGER, FARLEY, July 1, 1925 (San Jose, Calif.). U.S. actor. Films: *Rope*, 1948; *Strangers on a Train*, 1951; *The Girl in the Red Velvet Swing*, 1955.

GRANT, LEE (born Loyova Haskell Rosenthal), Oct. 31, 1931 (New York, N.Y.). U.S. actress. Won Supporting Actress AA for *Shampoo* (1975). TV: (series) *Peyton Place*.

GRAVES, PETER (born Peter Aurness), Mar. 18, 1925 (Minneapolis, Minn.). U.S. actor. TV series *Mission Impossible*, 1966–72. (Brother of J. ARNESS.)

GREENE, LORNE, Feb. 12, 1915 (Ottawa, Ont., Can.).–Sept. 11, 1987. Canadian actor. Star of TV series *Bonanza* (1959–71) and *Battlestar Galactica* (1978–79).

GREY, JOEL (born Joel Katz), Apr. 11, 1932 (Cleveland, Ohio). U.S. actor. Strongly identified as host of Kit Kat Club in *Cabaret* (1966 Tony award); Films: *Cabaret* (Best Supporting Actor AA), 1972; *Man on a Swing*, 1974.

GRIFFITH, ANDY, June 1, 1926 (Mt. Airy, N.C.). U.S. actor. Best known as star of the TV series *The Andy Griffith Show*, 1960–69; and *Matlock*, 1986–   . Films: *A Face in the Crowd*, 1957; *No Time for Sergeants*, 1958.

GRIFFITH, MELANIE, Aug. 8, 1957 (New York, N.Y.). U.S. actress. Films: *Body Double*, 1984; *Something Wild*, 1986; *Stormy Monday*, 1988; *Working Girl*, 1989.

GRODIN, CHARLES, Apr. 21, 1935 (Pittsburgh, Pa.). U.S. actor. Films: *The Heartbreak Kid*, 1973; *King Kong*, 1977; *The Lonely Guy*, 1984; *Ishtar*, 1987.

GROSS, MICHAEL, Jun 21, 1947 (Chicago, Ill.). U.S. actor. Stage: *Bent*, 1979. TV: *Family Ties* (series), 1982–89.

GUILLAUME, ROBERT, Nov. 30, 1939 (St. Louis, Mo.). U.S. actor, comedian. Stage: *Guys and Dolls*, 1977; *Purlie*, 1977. TV: *Soap* (series), 1977–81 (Emmy award, 1979); *Benson*, 1979–86.

GUTTENBERG, STEVE, Aug. 24, 1958 (Brooklyn, N.Y.). U.S. actor. TV: *The Day After*, 1984. Films: *Police Academy*, 1984; *Police Academy, Pt. 2*, 1985; *Cocoon*, 1985; *Short Circuit*, 1986; *The Bedroom Window*, 1987; *Three Men and a Baby*, 1987.

HACKMAN, GENE, Jan. 30, 1930 (San Bernardino, Calif.). U.S. actor. Films: *Bonnie and Clyde*, 1967; *I Never Sang for My Father*, 1969; *The French Connection* (Best Actor AA), 1971; *The Poseidon Adventure*, 1972; *The Conversation*, 1974; *Superman*, 1978; *Superman II*, 1980; *Reds*, 1982; *Hoosiers*, 1986; *Twice in a Lifetime*, 1986; *Kid Gloves*, 1987.

HAGMAN, LARRY, Sept. 21, 1931 (Weatherford, Tex.). U.S. actor. Star of the TV series *I Dream of Jeannie* (1965–70) and *Dallas* (1978–   ). (Son of MARY MARTIN.)

HALEY, JACK (born John Joseph Haley), Aug. 10, 1899 (Boston, Mass.).–June 6, 1979. U.S. comedic actor. Best known for role as the Tin Man in the film, *The Wizard of Oz*, 1939.

HALL, ARSENIO, Feb. 12, 1958 (Cleveland, Oh.). U.S. actor, TV talk show host. TV: *The Arsenio Hall Show*, 1988–   . Films: *Coming to America*, 1988.

HAMILL, MARK, Sept. 25, 1951 (Oakland, Calif.). U.S. actor. Stage: *Elephant Man*, 1981; *Amadeus*, 1982. Films: *Star Wars*, 1977; *The Big Red One*, 1979; *The Empire Strikes Back*, 1980; *The Night the Lights Went Out in Georgia*, 1981; *The Return of the Jedi*, 1983.

HAMILTON, GEORGE, Aug. 12, 1939 (Memphis, Tenn.). U.S. actor. Films: *The Light in the Piazza*, 1962; *Act One*, 1963; *Your Cheating Heart*, 1965; *Evel Knievel*, 1972; *Love at First Bite*, 1979.

HARLOW, JEAN (born Harlean Carpenter), Mar. 3, 1911 (Kansas City, Mo.).–June 7, 1937. U.S. actress. Known for her sexy roles in 1930s films. Films:. *Hell's Angels*, 1930; *Public Enemy*, 1931; *Red Dust*, 1932; *Dinner at Eight*, 1933; *China Seas*, 1935.

HAMLIN, HARRY, Oct. 31, 1951 (Pasadena, Calif.). U.S. actor. TV: *Space* (miniseries), 1985; *L.A. Law* (series), 1986–   . Films: *Movie, Movie*, 1978; *Clash of the Titans*, 1981; *Making Love*, 1982; *Laguna Heat*, 1987.

HANKS, TOM, July 9, 1956 (Oakland, Calif.). U.S. actor. TV: *Bosom Buddies* (series), 1980–82. Films: *Splash*, 1984; *Bachelor Party*, 1984; *Volunteers*, 1984; *The Man With One Red Shoe*, 1985; *The Money Pit*, 1986; *Nothing in Common*, 1986; *Everytime We Say Goodbye*, 1986; *Punchline*, 1987; *Joe vs. the Volcano*, 1990.

HANNAH, DARRYL, 1961 (Chicago, Ill.). U.S. actress. Films: *Blade Runner*, 1982; *Splash*, 1984; *Legal Eagles*, 1986; *Roxanne*, 1987; *Wall Street*, 1988.

HARMON, MARK, Sept. 2, 1951 (Burbank, Calif.). U.S. actor. TV: *St. Elsewhere*, (series), 1983–86; *Deliberate Stranger*, 1986. Films: *Comes the Horseman*, 1978; *Let's Get Harry*, 1987; *Presidio*, 1988; *Stealing Home*, 1988.

HARPER, VALERIE, Aug. 22, 1940 (Suffern, N.Y.). U.S. comedic actress. Rose to prominence on the TV series *Mary Tyler Moore Show*, 1970–74; start of the TV series *Rhoda*, 1974–78.

HARRELSON, WOODY, July 23, 19? (Midland, Tex.). U.S. actor. TV: *Cheers* (series), 1985–   .

HARRIS, BARBARA, (born Barbara Markowitz July 25, 1935 (Evanston, Ill.). U.S. actress. Films: *A Thousand Clowns*, 1965; *Who is Harry Kellerman ...?*, 1971; *Nashville*, 1975; *The Seduction of Joe Tynan*, 1979; *Peggy Sue Got Married*.

HARRIS, ED, Nov. 28, 1950 (Englewood, N.J.). U.S. actor. Stage: *Fool For Love* (Obie Award), 1983. Films: *Swing Shift*, 1982; *Under Fire*, 1982; *The Right Stuff*, 1982; *Places in the Heart*, 1983;

*Flash of Green*, 1983; *Alamo Bay*, 1984; *Sweet Dreams*, 1985; *Walker*, 1987.

**HARRIS, JULIE,** Dec. 2, 1925 (Grosse Pointe Park, Mich.). U.S. actress. A Broadway star since 1950. Plays: *The Member of the Wedding*, 1950; *Forty Carats* (Tony Award), 1969; *The Belle of Amherst* (Tony Award), 1976. TV: *Knots Landing* (series), 1979– .

**HART, WILLIAM S.,** Dec. 6, 1870 (Newburgh, N.Y.)–June 23, 1946. U.S. actor. A leading star of silent-screen westerns.

**HAWN, GOLDIE,** Nov. 21, 1945 (Washington, D.C.). U.S. actress, film producer. Rose to prominence on TV's *Laugh-In*, 1968–70. Films: *Cactus Flower* (Best Supporting Actress AA), 1969; *There's a Girl in My Soup*, 1970; *Butterflies Are Free*, 1971; *The Sugarland Express*, 1974; *Shampoo*, 1975; *Foul Play*, 1978; *Private Benjamin*, 1980; *Swing Shift*, 1983; *Protocol*, 1984; *Overboard*, 1987.

**HAYES, GABBY** (born George Hayes), May 7, 1885 (Wellesville, N.Y.)–Feb. 9, 1969. U.S. character actor. Appeared in over 200 westerns, 1929–69.

**HAYES, HELEN** (born Helen Brown), Oct. 10, 1900 (Washington, D.C.). U.S. actress. Considered the first lady of the American stage. Recipient of 1958 Tony award for *Time Remembered*. Films: *The Sin of Madelon Claudet* (Best Actress AA), 1931; *Arrowsmith*, 1931; *A Farewell to Arms*, 1932; *My Son John*, 1951; *Anastasia*, 1956; *Airport* (Best Supporting Actress AA), 1970. (Mother of J. MACARTHUR.)

**HAYS, ROBERT,** Jan. 24, 1947 (Bethesda, Md.). U.S. actor. TV: *Starman* (series), 1986–87. Films: *Airplane*, 1980; *Airplane 2*, 1982.

**HAYWARD, SUSAN** (born Edythe Marrener), June 30, 1917 (Brooklyn, N.Y.)–Mar. 14, 1975. U.S. actress. Films: *Smash-Up*, 1947; *Tap Roots*, 1948; *My Foolish Heart*, 1949; *With a Song in My Heart*, 1952; *I'll Cry Tomorrow*, 1955; *I Want to Live* (Best Actress AA), 1958.

**HAYWORTH, RITA** (born Margarita Carmen Cansino), Oct. 17, 1918 (New York, N.Y.)–May 14, 1987. U.S. actress, dancer. Films: *Only Angels Have Wings*, 1939; *The Strawberry Blonde*, 1941; *My Gal Sal*, 1942; *Cover Girl*, 1944; *Gilda*, 1946; *The Lady from Shanghai*, 1948; *Miss Sadie Thompson*, 1953; *Pal Joey*, 1957; *Separate Tables*, 1958.

**HECKART, EILEEN,** Mar. 29, 1919 (Columbus, Ohio). U.S. character actress. Appears chiefly on the stage. Films: *Butterflies Are Free* (Best Supporting Actress AA), 1972.

**HEFLIN, VAN** (born Emmett Evan Heflin), Dec. 13, 1910 (Walters, Okla.)–July 23, 1971. U.S. actor. Films: *Johnny Eager* (Best Supporting Actor AA), 1941; *Tap Roots*, 1948; *Shane*, 1953; *Patterns*, 1956.

**HELMOND, KATHERINE,** July 5, 1934 (Galveston, Tex.). U.S. actress. TV: *Soap* (series), 1978–81; *Who's the Boss* (series), 1985– . Films: *Brazil*, 1986.

**HELMSLEY, SHERMAN,** Feb. 1, 1938 (Philadelphia, Pa.). U.S. actor, comedian. Stage: *Purlie*, 1970.

TV: *All in the Family* (series), 1973–75; *The Jeffersons* (series), 1975–85; *Amen*, 1986– .

**HEPBURN, AUDREY** (born Audrey Hepburn-Ruston), May 4, 1929 (Brussel, Belg.). U.S. actress. Films: *Roman Holiday* (Best Actress AA), 1953; *Funny Face*, 1957; *Love in the Afternoon*, 1957; *The Nun's Story*, 1959; *Breakfast at Tiffany's*, 1961; *The Children's Hour*, 1962; *Charade*, 1963; *My Fair Lady*, 1964; *Two for the Road*, 1966; *Wait until Dark*, 1967; *Bloodline*, 1979.

**HEPBURN, KATHARINE,** Nov. 8, 1909 (Hartford, Conn.). U.S. actress. Best known for her leading roles opposite SPENCER TRACY in fast-paced film comedies. Films: *A Bill of Divorcement*, 1932; *Morning Glory* (Best Actress AA), 1933; *Stage Door*, 1937; *Bringing Up Baby*, 1938; *The Philadelphia Story*, 1940; *Woman of the Year*, 1942; *Adam's Rib*, 1949; *The African Queen*, 1951; *Pat and Mike*, 1952; *The Rainmaker*, 1956; *Long Day's Journey into Night*, 1962; *Guess Who's Coming to Dinner?* (Best Actress AA), 1967; *The Lion in Winter* (Best Actress AA), 1968; *Rooster Cogburn*, 1975; *On Golden Pond* (Best Actress AA), 1982.

**HERRMANN, ED,** July 21, 1943 (Washington, D.C.). U.S. actor. Noted as a character actor. Stage: *Mrs. Warren's Profssion* (Tony Award best supp. actor), 1976. TV: *Eleanor and Franklin*, 1976. Films: *Reds*, 1981; *Annie*, 1982; *The Purple Rose of Cairo*, 1985.

**HERSHEY, BARBARA,** Feb. 5, 1948 (Hollywood, Calif.). U.S. actress. Films: *With Six You Get Eggroll*, 1968; *Last Summer*, 1970; *The Right Stuff*, 1983; *Hannah and Her Sisters*, 1986; *Shy People*, 1987; *Tin Men*, 1987; *A World Apart*, 1988; *The Last Temptation of Christ*, 1988; *Beaches*, 1988.

**HESSEMAN, HOWARD,** Feb. 27, 1940 (Lebanon, Ore.). U.S. actor. TV: *WKRP in Cincinnati* (series), 1978–82; *Head of the Class*, 1986– .

**HESTON, CHARLTON** (born John Charlton Carter), Oct. 4, 1923 (Evansville, Ill.). U.S. actor. Best known for his leading roles in high-budget film spectaculars; pres., Screen Actors Guild, 1966–71. Films: *The Greatest Show on Earth*, 1952; *The Naked Jungle*, 1954; *The Ten Commandments*, 1956; *Ben Hur* (Best Actor AA), 1959; *Major Dundee*, 1965; *The Agony and the Ecstasy*, 1965; *Khartoum*, 1966; *Planet of the Apes*, 1967; *Two Minute Warning*, 1976.

**HILL, ARTHUR,** Aug. 1, 1922 (Medfort, Sask., Can.). U.S. actor. Stage: *Who's Afraid of Virginia Woolf* (Best Actor Tony), 1962. TV (series): *Owen Marshall, Counselor at Law*, 1971–74.

**HILLERMAN, JOHN,** Dec. 30, 1932 (Dennison, Tex.). U.S. actor. *Magnum P.I.* (series), 1980–88. Films: *Paper Moon*, 1973; *The Day of the Locust*, 1976.

**HINGLE, PAT,** July 19, 1923 (Denver, Col.). U.S. character actor in films, TV, and the theater.

**HIRSCH, JUDD,** Mar. 15, 1935 (New York, N.Y.). U.S. actor. Star of the TV series *Taxi*, 1978–82. Films: *Ordinary People*, 1980; *Without a Trace*, 1983.

**HODIAK, JOHN,** 1914 (Pittsburgh, Pa.)–Oct. 19,

1955. U.S. actor. Films: *Lifeboat*, 1944; *A Bell for Aduno*, 1945.

HOFFMAN, DUSTIN, Aug. 8, 1937 (Los Angeles, Calif.). U.S. actor. Films: *The Graduate*, 1967; *Midnight Cowboy*, 1969; *Little Big Man*, 1971; *Straw Dogs*, 1972; *Papillon*, 1973; *Lenny*, 1974; *All the President's Men*, 1975; *Marathon Man*, 1976; *Straight Time*, 1978; *Kramer vs. Kramer*, 1979; *Tootsie*, 1982; *Rain Man*, 1989.

HOLBROOK, HAL, Feb. 17, 1925 (Cleveland, Ohio). U.S. actor. Received Tony award and N.Y. Drama Critics special citation for one-man play *Mark Twain Tonight*, 1966, which he performed over 2,000 times.

HOLDEN, WILLIAM (born William Beedle), Apr. 17, 1918 (O'Fallon, Ill.)–Nov. 16, 1981. U.S. actor. Films: *Golden Boy*, 1939; *Our Town*, 1940; *Born Yesterday*, 1950; *Stalag 17* (Best Actor AA), 1953; *Executive Suite*, 1954; *The Country Girl*, 1954; *Love Is a Many Splendored Thing*, 1955; *Picnic*, 1955; *The Bridge on the River Kwai*, 1957; *The Counterfeit Traitor*, 1962; *The Wild Bunch*, 1969; *Network*, 1976.

HOLLIDAY, JUDY (born Judith Tuvim), 1922 (New York, N.Y.)–June 7, 1965. U.S. actress. Films: *Born Yesterday* (Best Actress AA), 1950; *The Solid Gold Cadillac*, 1956; *Bells Are Ringing*, 1960.

HOLM, CELESTE, Apr. 29, 1919 (New York, N.Y.). U.S. actress. Films: *Gentlemen's Agreement*, (Best Supporting Actress AA), 1947; *Come to the Stable*, 1949; *All about Eve*, 1950.

HOPKINS, MIRIAM, Oct. 18, 1902 (Savannah, Ga.)–Oct. 9, 1972. U.S. actress. Films: *Becky Sharp*, 1935; *Barbary Coast*, 1935; *Old Acquaintance*, 1943.

HOPKINS, TELMA, Oct. 28, 1948 (Louisville, Ky.). U.S. actress. TV: *Bosom Buddies* (series), 1980–84; *Gimme a Break*, 1984–87; *Family Matters*, 1989– .

HOPPER, DENNIS, May 17, 1936 (Dodge City, Kan.). U.S. actor, director. Films: *Easy Rider*, 1969; *Hoosiers*, 1986; *Blue Velvet*, 1986.

HORSLEY, LEE, May 15, 1955 (Muleshoe, Tex.). U.S. actor. TV: *Matt Houston* (series), 1982–85; *Paradise* (series), 1988– .

HORTON, EDWARD EVERETT, 1886 (Brooklyn, N.Y.)–Sept. 29, 1970. U.S. comedic actor in numerous films since 1922. Films: *Holiday*, 1930; *Trouble in Paradise*, 1932; *The Gay Divorcee*, 1935; *Top Hat*, 1935; *Here Comes Mr. Jordan*, 1941; *Pocketful of Miracles*, 1961.

HOUSEMAN, JOHN (born Jacques Haussman), Sept. 22, 1902 (Bucharest, Rum.). U.S. actor, producer, director. Has produced plays and films since 1934; as actor, starred in the 1973 film *The Paper Chase* (Best Supporting Actor AA), and the TV series of the same name.

HOWARD, KEN, Mar. 28, 1944 (El Centro, Calif.). U.S. actor. Received Tony award for *Child Play*, 1970; star of the TV series *The White Shadow*, 1978–81.

HOWARD, RON, Mar. 1, 1954 (Duncan, Okla.). U.S. actor, director. Began as a child actor in TV series *The Andy Griffith Show*, 1960–68; star of TV series *Happy Days*, 1974–80. Films: (actor) *American Graffiti*, 1974; *The Shootist*, 1976; (dir.) *Splash*, 1984; *Cocoon*, 1985.

HOWELL, C. THOMAS, Dec. 7, 1966 (Los Angeles, Calif.). U.S. actor. Films: *E.T.*, 1982; *The Outsiders*, 1983.

HOWE, SALLY ANN, July 20, 1930 (London, Eng.). U.S. actress. Films: *Thursday's Child*, 1943; *The History of Mr. Polly*, 1948; *Chitty Chitty Bang Bang*, 1968.

HUDSON, ROCK (born Roy Scherer), Nov. 17, 1925 (Winnetka, Ill.)–Oct. 2, 1985. U.S. actor. Films: *Magnificent Obsession*, 1953; *Giant*, 1956; *Written on The Wind*, 1956; *Pillow Talk*, 1959; *Seconds*, 1966. TV: *McMillan and Wife* (series), 1971–76.

HULCE, TOM, 1953 (White Water, Wis.). U.S. actor. TV: *Murder in Missouri*, 1990. Films: *Animal House*, 1978; *Amadeus*, 1984; *Echo Park*, 1986; *Dominick and Eugene*, 1988; *Parenthood*, 1989.

HUNT, LINDA, Apr. 2, 1945 (Morristown, N.J.). U.S. actress. Films: *Popeye*, 1980; *The Year of Living Dangerously* (AA best supp. actress), 1983; *Dune*, 1984; *Silverado*, 1985; *Waiting for the Moon*, 1987.

HUNTER, HOLLY, 1959 (Conyers, Ga.). U.S. actress. TV: *Roe vs. Wade*, 1989 (Emmy award). Films: *Raising Arizona*, 1987; *Broadcast News*, 1988; *Miss Firecracker*, 1989.

HUNTER, KIM (born Janet Cole), Nov. 12, 1922 (Detroit, Mich.). U.S. actress. Films: *A Streetcar Named Desire* (Best Supporting Actress AA), 1951; *Planet of the Apes* series, 1974.

HUNTER, TAB (born Arthur Gelien), July 11, 1931 (New York, N.Y.). U.S. actor. A teenage favorite in 1950s films. Films: *Battle Cry*, 1955; *Damn Yankees*, 1958.

HURT, JOHN, Jan. 22, 1940 (Chesterfield, Eng.). British actor. TV: *The Naked Civil Servant*, 1975; *Crime and Punishment* (Emmy Award), 1979). Films: *A Man for All Seasons*, 1966; *Midnight Express*, 1978; *Alien*, 1978; *The Elephant Man*, 1980; *White Mischief*, 1987.

HURT, MARY BETH (born Mary Supinger), Sept. 26, 1948 (Marshalltown, Ia.). U.S. actress. Stage: *Crimes of the Heart*, 1981 (Obie award). Films: *Interiors*, 1978; *Head Over Heels*, 1979; *The World According to Garp*, 1982.

HURT, WILLIAM, Mar. 20, 1950 (Washington, D.C.). U.S. actor. *Body Heat*, 1978; *Altered States*, 1980; *The Big Chill*, 1983; *The Kiss of the Spiderwoman*, 1985; *Children of a Lesser God*, 1987; *Broadcast News*, 1987; *The Accidental Tourist*, 1988.

HUSTON, ANJELICA, 1952 (Ireland). U.S. actress. Films: *The Last Tycoon*, 1976; *Prizzi's Honor*, 1985 (best supp. actress AA); *The Dead*, 1987; *Gardens of Stone*, 1987; *Enemies: A Love Story*, 1990. (Daughter of JOHN HUSTON.)

HUTTON, BETTY (born Betty Jane Thornburg), Feb. 26, 1921 (Battle Creek, Mich.). U.S. singer, dancer, actress. Films: *Incendiary Blonde*, 1945; *Annie Get Your Gun*, 1950.

**HUTTON, TIMOTHY**, Aug. 16, 1961 (Malibu, Calif.). U.S. actor. Films: *Ordinary People*, 1980 (best supp. actor AA); *Taps*, 1981; *Daniel*, 1983; *The Falcon and the Snowman*, 1985.

**HYMAN, EARLE**, Oct. 11, 1926 (Rocky Mt., Col.). U.S. actor. Primarily on the stage. *Anna Lucasta*, 1943–45; *Othello*, 1957; *The Lady From Dubuque*, 1980; *Long Day's Journey Into Night*, 1981.

**IRONS, JEREMY**, Sept. 19, 1948 (Cowes, Eng.). British actor. Stage: *The Real Thing* (Tony Award), 1984. TV: *Brideshead Revisited* (series), 1980–81. Films: *Nijinsky*, 1980; *The French Lieutenant's Woman*, 1981; *Moonlighting*, 1982; *Betrayal*, 1983; *Swann in Love*, 1984; *The Mission*, 1986.

**IRVING, AMY**, Sept. 10, 1953 (Palo Alto, Calif.). U.S. actress. Stage: *Amadeus*, 1981; *Breakhouse*, 1983. TV: *Anastasia* (miniseries), 1986. Films: *Carrie*, 1978; *Honeysuckle Rose*, 1979; *Yentl*, 1983; *Micki & Maude*, 1984; *Crossing Delancey*, 1988.

**IVES, BURL** (born Burl Icle Ivanhoe), June 14, 1909 (Hunt Township, Ill.). U.S. folk singer, character actor. Films: *Cat on a Hot Tin Roof*, 1957; *The Big Country* (Best Supporting Actor AA), 1958.

**JACKEE** (formerly Jackee Harry), Aug. 14, 19? (Winston-Salem, N.C.). U.S. actress. TV: *227* (series), 1985– .

**JACKSON, ANNE**, Sept. 3, 1925 (Allegheny, Pa.). U.S. actress. Principally a stage actress, often playing opposite husband ELI WALLACH. Plays: *Luv*, 1964; *The Waltz of the Toreadors*, 1973. Films: *The Secret Life of an American Wife*, 1968; *The Shining*, 1980.

**JACKSON, KATE**, Oct. 29, 1948 (Birmingham, Ala.). U.S. actress. TV: *Dark Shadows* (series), 1966–71; *The Rookies* (series), 1972–74; *Charlie's Angels* (series), 1976–80; *Scarecrow and Mrs. King*, 1983–87.

**JACKSON, VICTORIA**, Aug. 2, 1959 (Miami, Fla.). U.S. actress, comedienne. TV: *Saturday Night Live* (series), 1986– . Films: *I Love You to Death*, 1990.

**JAECKEL, RICHARD**, Oct. 10, 1926 (Long Beach, N.Y.). U.S. actor. Specializes in war films. Films: *Guadalcanal Diary*, 1943; *The Sands of Iwo Jima*, 1949; *Come Back Little Sheba*, 1952; *The Dirty Dozen*, 1967; *Sometimes a Great Notion*, 1971; *Starman*, 1984.

**JAFFE, SAM**, Mar. 8, 1891 (New York, N.Y.)– Mar. 24, 1984. U.S. character actor. Stage actor since 1916, in films since 1933. Films: *Lost Horizon*, 1937; *Gunga Din*, 1939. TV: *Ben Casey* (series), 1960–64.

**JAGGER, DEAN** (born Dean Jeffries), Nov. 7, 1903 (Lima, Ohio). U.S. character actor. Films: *Brigham Young*, 1940; *Twelve O'Clock High*, 1949; *Executive Suite*, 1954.

**JANSSEN, DAVID** (born David Meyer), Mar. 27, 1930 (Naponee, Neb.)–Feb. 13, 1980. U.S. actor. TV: *Richard Diamond* (series), 1957–60; *The Fugitive* (series), 1963–67; *Harry-O* (series), 1974–76.

**JEFFREYS, ANNE** (born Anne Carmichael), Jan. 26, 1923 (Goldsboro, N.C.). U.S. actress. A leading lady in 1940s films; star of the TV series *Topper*, 1953–56.

**JEWISON, NORMAN**, July 21, 1926 (Ontario, Can.). Canadian director, producer. Films: *The Cincinnati Kid*, 1965; *The Russians Are Coming, The Russians Are Coming*, 1966; *In the Heat of the Night*, 1967; *The Thomas Crown Affair*, 1968; *Fiddler on the Roof*, 1971; *Jesus Christ Superstar*, 1973; *Agnes of God*, 1985; *Moonstruck*, 1988; *A Soldier's Story*.

**JILLIAN, ANN**, Jan. 29, 1950 (Cambridge, Mass.). U.S. actress, singer. TV: *It's a Living* (series), 1980–86; *Mae West*, 1982; *The Ann Jillian Story*, 1988.

**JOHNSON, BEN**, June 13, 1919 (Foreaker, Okla.). U.S. actor. A fine character actor, mostly in westerns. Films: *The Outlaw*, 1943; *She Wore a Yellow Ribbon*, 1949; *Rio Grande*, 1950; *Shane*, 1953; *The Wild Bunch*, 1969; *The Last Picture Show*, 1971 (best supporting actor AA); *The Sugarland Express*, 1973.

**JOHNSON, DON**, Dec. 15, 1949 (Flat Creek, Mo.). U.S. actor, singer. Stage: *A Boy and His Dog*, 1978. TV: *Miami Vice* (series), 1984–89; *The Long Hot Summer*, 1985. Films: *The Harrad Experiment*, 1973. Album: *Heartbeat*, 1986.

**JOHNSON, VAN**, Aug. 25, 1916 (Newport, R.I.). U.S. actor. Films: *A Guy Named Joe*, 1943; *Thirty Seconds over Tokyo*, 1944; *Weekend at the Waldorf*, 1945; *High Barbaree*, 1946; *In the Good Old Summertime*, 1949; *The Caine Mutiny*, 1954; *The Last Time I Saw Paris*, 1955; *Brigadoon*, 1955.

**JONES, CAROLYN**, Apr. 28, 1933 (Amarillo, Tex.). U.S. actress. Starred in the TV series *The Addams Family*, 1964–66.

**JONES, DEAN**, Jan. 25, 1935 (Morgan City, Ala.). U.S. actor. Films: *The Love Bug*, 1969; *Born Again*, 1978.

**JONES, JAMES EARL**, Jan. 17, 1931 (Tate Co., Miss.). U.S. actor. Tony award for *The Great White Hope*, 1969; *Fences*, 1987. Films: *The Great White Hope*, 1970; *Claudine*, 1973; *Gardens of Stone*, 1987. Voice of Darth Vader in *Star Wars* series.

**JONES, JENNIFER** (born Phyllis Isley), Mar. 2, 1919 (Tulsa, Okla.). U.S. actress. Films: *The Song of Bernadette* (Best Actress AA), 1943; *Duel in the Sun*, 1946; *Portrait of Jennie*, 1948; *Love is a Many Splendored Thing*, 1955; *A Farewell to Arms*, 1958.

**JONES, TOMMY LEE**, Sept. 15, 1946 (San Saba, Tex.). U.S. actor. TV: *The Amazing Howard Hughes*, 1977; *Executioner's Song*, 1982. Films: *The Eyes of Laura Mars*, 1978; *Coal Miner's Daughter*, 1981; *Stormy Monday*, 1988.

**JULIA, RAUL**, Mar. 1, 1944 (San Juan, P.R.). Puerto Rican actor. Many roles both on stage, from Shakespeare to musicals, and films. Stage: *Robber Bridegroom*, 1974; *Threepenny Opera*, 1976; *Nine*, 1982. Films: *Panic in Needle Park*, 1971; *One From the Heart*, 1982; *The Kiss of the*

*Spiderwoman*, 1985; *Compromising Positions*, 1985; *The Morning After*, 1987.
**KAHN, MADELINE,** Sept. 29, 1942 (Boston, Mass.). U.S. comedic actress. Films: *Paper Moon*, 1973; *Blazing Saddles*, 1974; *Young Frankenstein*, 1975; *High Anxiety*, 1977; *Clue*, 1985.
**KANE, CAROL,** June 18, 1952 (Cleveland, Oh.). U.S. actress. TV: *Taxi* (series), 1981–83. Films: *Carnal Knowledge*, 1971; *Hester Street*, 1975; *Dog Day Afternoon*, 1975; *Annie Hall*, 1977.
**KATT, WILLIAM,** Feb. 16, 1951 (Los Angeles, Calif.). U.S. actor. TV: *Greatest American Hero* (series), 1980–82; *Perry Mason*, 1985, 1986. Films: *Carrie*, 1976; *Butch and Sundance*, 1978; *Big Wednesday*, 1978.
**KAVNER, JULIE,** Sept. 7, 1951 (Los Angeles, Calif.). U.S. actress. TV: *Rhoda* (series), 1974–78 (Emmy award 1978); *The Tracey Ullman Show* (series), 1987– ; the voice of Mrs. Simpson of *The Simpsons* (series), 1990– . Films: *Hannah and Her Sisters*, 1985; *Radio Days*, 1987.
**KAYE, DANNY** (born David Daniel Kaminsky), Jan. 18, 1913 (New York, N.Y.)–Mar. 3, 1987. U.S. actor, comedian. Received special AA, for service to the American people, 1954; won Jean Hersholt Humanitarian Award, noted for work with UNICEF. Films: *Up in Arms*, 1944; *The Secret Life of Walter Mitty*, 1947; *Hans Christian Anderson*, 1952; *Knock on Wood*, 1953; *White Christmas*, 1954; *Merry Andrew*, 1958.
**KEACH, STACY,** June 2, 1941 (Savannah, Ga.). U.S. actor. Films: *The Heart Is a Lonely Hunter*, 1968; *That Championship Season*, 1982. Played Mike Hammer in TV series, 1983–87.
**KEATON, DIANE** (born Diane Hall), Jan. 5, 1946 (Santa Ana, Calif.). U.S. actress. Films: *Play It Again Sam*, 1972; *The Godfather*, 1972; *The Godfather—Part 2*, 1974; *Love and Death*, 1975; *Annie Hall* (Best Actress AA), 1977, *Looking for Mr. Goodbar*, 1977; *Interiors*, 1978; *Manhattan*, 1979; *Reds*, 1982; *The Little Drummer Girl*, 1984; *Crimes of the Heart*, 1987; *Baby Boom*, 1987.
**KEATON, MICHAEL,** Sept. 9, 1951 (Pittsburgh, Pa.). U.S. actor, comedian. Films: *Night Shift*, 1982; *Mr. Mom*, 1983; *Dream Team*, 1987; *Beetlejuice*, 1988; *Clean and Sober*, 1988; *Batman*, 1989.
**KEEL, HOWARD** (born Harold Leek), Apr. 13, 1917 (Gillespie, Ill.). U.S. actor. Virile leading man in musical comedy films in the 1950s. Films: *Annie Get Your Gun*, 1950; *Show Boat*, 1951; *Calamity Jane*, 1953; *Kiss Me Kate*, 1953; *Seven Brides for Seven Brothers*, 1954. TV: *Dallas* (series), 1981– .
**KEITEL, HARVEY,** 1947 (New York, N.Y.). U.S. actor. Films: *Alice Doesn't Live Here Anymore*, 1975; *Taxi Driver*, 1976; *Wise Guys*, 1986.
**KEITH, BRIAN** (born Robert Keith, Jr.), Nov. 14, 1921 (Bayonne, N.J.). U.S. actor. Best known as star of the TV series *Family Affair*, 1966–71.
**KEITH, DAVID,** May 8, 1954 (Knoxville, Tenn.). U.S. actor, director. Films: *The Great Santini*, 1979; *Brubaker*, 1980; *An Officer and a Gentleman*, 1982; *The Lords of Discipline*, 1983.
**KELLERMAN, SALLY,** June 2, 1937 (Long Beach,

Calif.). U.S. actress. Films: *M\*A\*S\*H*, 1969; *The Big Bus*, 1976; *That's Life*, 1986.
**KELLEY, DEFOREST,** Jan. 20, 1920 (Atlanta, Ga.). U.S. actor. TV: *Star Trek* (series), 1966–68. Films: *Star Trek*, 1979.
**KELLY, GRACE** (Princess Grace of Monaco), Nov. 12, 1929 (Philadelphia, Pa.)–Sept. 14, 1982. U.S. actress. Retired from career to marry Prince Rainier of Monaco, 1956. Films: *High Noon*, 1952; *Dial M for Murder*, 1954; *Rear Window*, 1954; *The Country Girl* (Best Actress AA), 1954; *To Catch a Thief*, 1955; *High Society*, 1956.
**KENNEDY, ARTHUR,** Feb. 17, 1914 (Worcester, Mass.)–Jan. 5, 1990. U.S. actor. Films: *The Glass Menagerie*, 1950; *Trial*, 1955; *Peyton Place*, 1957; *Lawrence of Arabia*, 1962.
**KENNEDY, GEORGE,** Feb. 18, 1926 (New York, N.Y.). U.S. actor. Films: *The Flight of the Phoenix*, 1965; *The Dirty Dozen*, 1967; *Cool Hand Luke*, 1967 (best supporting actor AA); *Airport*, 1969.
**KERNS, JOANNA,** Feb. 15, 1955 (San Francisco, Calif.). U.S. actress. TV: *Growing Pains* (series), 1985– .
**KILEY, RICHARD,** Mar. 31, 1922 (Chicago, Ill.). U.S. actor, singer. Plays: *Redhead*, (Tony award), 1958; *The Man of La Mancha* (Tony award), 1966. TV (series): *A Year in the Life*, 1987–88.
**KLEMPERER, WERNER,** Mar. 22, 1919 (Cologne, Ger.). U.S. actor. TV: *Hogan's Heroes* (series), 1965–71. (Son of O. KLEMPERER.)
**KLINE, KEVIN,** Oct. 24, 1947 (St. Louis, Mo). U.S. actor. Stage: *On the Twentieth Century* (Tony award), 1978; *The Pirates of Penzance* (Tony and Obie awards), 1983. Films: *Sophie's Choice*, 1982; *The Big Chill*, 1983; *Silverado*, 1985; *A Fish Called Wanda*, 1985 (best supp. actor AA).
**KLUGMAN, JACK,** Apr. 27, 1922 (Philadelphia, Pa.). U.S. actor. Films: *Twelve Angry Men* (1957); starred in the TV series *Harris against the World* (1964–65), *The Odd Couple* (1970–75), and *Quincy* (1976–83), winner of Emmy awards in 1963, 1971, and 1973.
**KNIGHT, TED** (born Tadeus Wladyslaw Konopka), Dec. 7, 1923 (Terryville, Conn.)–Aug. 27, 1986. U.S. comedic actor. TV: *Mary Tyler Moore Show* (series), 1970–77; *Too Close For Comfort* (series), 1980–86.
**KOTTO, YAPHET,** Nov. 15, 1944 (New York, N.Y.) U.S. actor. Films: *Blue Collar*, 1977; *Alien*, 1978.
**KRAMER, STEPFANIE,** Aug. 6, 1956 (Los Angeles, Calif.). U.S. actress. TV: *Hunter* (series), 1984–1990.
**KRISTOFFERSON, KRIS,** June 22, 1936 (Brownsville, Tex.). U.S. actor, singer, songwriter. Films: *Alice Doesn't Live Here Anymore*, 1974; *A Star is Born*, 1976; *Semi-Tough*, 1978. Musical compositions: "Sunday Morning Comin' Down," "Help Me Make It Through the Night," "Me and Bobby McGee," "For the Good Times."
**LADD, ALAN,** Sept. 3, 1913 (Hot Springs, Ark.)–Jan. 29, 1964. U.S. actor. Films: *This Gun for Hire*, 1942; *The Glass Key*, 1942; *Salty O'Rourke*, 1945; *Two Years before the Mast*, 1946; *The*

*Great Gatsby*, 1949; *Shane*, 1953; *The Carpetbaggers*, 1964.

**LADD, CHERYL** (born Cheryl Stoppelmoor), July 12, 1951 (Huron, S.D.). U.S. actress, singer. Best known for role on TV series *Charlie's Angels*, 1977–81.

**LAHTI, CHRISTINE,** Apr. 5, 1950 (Detroit, Mich.). U.S. actress. TV: *Executioner's Song*, 1982; *Amerika*, 1987. Films: *Swing Shift*, 1984; *Stacking*, 1985; *Just Between Friends*, 1986; *Housekeeping*, 1987; *Running on Empty*, 1988.

**LAKE, VERONICA** (born Constance Ockleman), Nov. 14, 1919 (Lake Placid, N.Y.)–July 7, 1973. U.S. actress. A leading lady in 1940s films; her long, straight hairstyle set a national trend. Films: *I Wanted Wings*, 1941; *This Gun for Hire*, 1942; *I Married a Witch*, 1942; *The Blue Dahlia*, 1946.

**LAMARR, HEDY** (born Hedwig Kiesler), Nov. 9, 1913 (Vienna, Austria). Austrian-U.S. actress. A 1930s sex symbol. Films: *Ecstasy*, 1933; *Algiers*, 1938; *Ziegfeld Girl*, 1941; *White Cargo*, 1942; *Samson and Delilah*, 1949; *My Favorite Spy*, 1951.

**LAMAS, LORENZO,** Jan. 2, 1958 (Santa Monica, Calif.). U.S. actor. TV: *Falcon Crest* (series), 1981– . (Son of A. DAHL.)

**LAMOUR, DOROTHY** (born Mary Kaumeyer), Dec. 10, 1914 (New Orleans, La.). U.S. actress. A leading lady in 1930s and 1940s films; known for "Road" films with BING CROSBY and BOB HOPE.

**LANCASTER, BURT,** Nov. 2, 1913 (New York, N.Y.). U.S. actor. Known for lead roles as athletic, tough hero. Films: *The Killers*, 1946; *Sorry Wrong Number*, 1948; *From Here to Eternity*, 1953; *Trapeze*, 1956; *Sweet Smell of Success*, 1957; *Separate Tables*, 1958; *Elmer Gantry* (Best Actor AA), 1960; *Judgment at Nuremberg*, 1961; *Birdman of Alcatraz*, 1962; *Airport*, 1969; *Atlantic City*, 1980; *Local Hero*, 1982; *Tough Guys*, 1986.

**LANDON, MICHAEL** (born Eugene Orowitz), Oct. 21, 1937 (New York, N.Y.). U.S. actor. Star of the TV series *Bonanza* (1959–72) and *Little House on the Prairie* (1974–82); *Highway to Heaven* (1984–89).

**LANGE, HOPE,** Nov. 28, 1931 (Redding Ridge, Conn.). U.S. actress. Films: *Bus Stop*, 1956; *Peyton Place*, 1957; *A Pocketful of Miracles*, 1961; *Blue Velvet*, 1986. TV: *The Ghost and Mrs. Muir* (series), 1968–70; *The New Dick Van Dyke Show* (series), 1971–74.

**LANGE, JESSICA,** Apr. 20, 1949 (Cloquet, Minn.). U.S. actress. Films: *King Kong*, 1976; *All That Jazz*, 1979; *The Postman Always Rings Twice*, 1981; *Frances*, 1982; *Tootsie*, 1982; *Sweet Dreams*, 1985; *Crimes of the Heart*, 1986; *Music Box*, 1989.

**LANGELLA, FRANK,** Jan. 1, 1940 (Bayonne, N.J.). U.S. actor. Films: *Diary of a Mad Housewife*, 1970; *The Twelve Chairs*, 1970; *Dracula*, 1977. Plays: *Seascape* (Tony award), 1975.

**LANSBURY, ANGELA,** Oct. 16, 1925 (London, Eng.). English-U.S. actress. Star of several Broadway musicals including *Dear World* (1969), *Mame* (1972), *Sweeney Todd* (1979); won Tony awards in 1966,

1969, 1974, 1979. TV: (series) *Murder, She Wrote*, 1984– .

**LARROQUETTE, JOHN,** Nov. 25, 1947 (New Orleans, La.). U.S. actor. TV: *Night Court*, 1983– (Emmy awards, 1985–88). Films: *Blind Date*, 1987.

**LASSER, LOUISE,** Apr. 11, 1939 (New York, N.Y.). U.S. actress. Best known as star of TV series *Mary Hartman, Mary Hartman*, 1976. Films: *What's New Pussycat?*, 1965; *Take the Money and Run*, 1969; *Bananas*, 1971.

**LAURIE, PIPER** (born Rosetta Jacobs), Jan. 22, 1932 (Detroit, Mich.). U.S. actress. TV: *The Thorn Birds*, 1983; *Twin Peaks* (series), 1990– . Films: *The Hustler*, 1961; *Carrie*, 1976; *Children of a Lesser God*, 1986.

**LAVIN, LINDA,** Oct. 15, 1937 (Portland, Maine). U.S. actress. Star of the TV series *Alice*, 1976–85.

**LEACHMAN, CLORIS,** Apr. 4, 1926 (Des Moines, Ia.). U.S. actress. Has won four Emmy awards. Films: *The Last Picture Show* (Supporting Actress AA), 1971; *Young Frankenstein*, 1974; *High Anxiety*, 1977. TV: *Mary Tyler Moore Show* (series), 1970–75; *Phyllis* (series), 1975–77; *The Facts of Life* (series), 1987– .

**LEARNED, MICHAEL,** Apr. 9, 1939 (Washington, D.C.). U.S. actress. Star of the TV series *The Waltons* (1972–81).

**LEE, CHRISTOPHER,** May 27, 1922 (London, Eng.). British actor. Has probably played more leading horror roles than anyone else. Films: *The Curse of Frankenstein*, 1956; *The Horror of Dracula*, 1958; *The Mummy*, 1959; *The Face of Fu Manchu*, 1965; *The Howling II*, 1985. Autobiography: *Tall, Dark and Gruesome*, 1977.

**LEIGH, JANET** (born Jeanette Morrison), July 6, 1927 (Merced, Calif.). U.S. actress. Films: *The Romance of Rosy Ridge*, 1947; *Houdini*, 1953; *My Sister Eileen*, 1955; *The Vikings*, 1958; *Psycho*, 1960; *Harper*, 1966. (Mother of J. L. CURTIS.)

**LEMMON, JACK,** Feb. 8, 1925 (Boston, Mass.). U.S. actor. Light-comedy leading actor. Films: *Mister Roberts* (Best Supporting Actor AA), 1955; *Some Like It Hot*, 1959; *The Apartment*, 1960; *Days of Wine and Roses*, 1962; *The Great Race*, 1965; *The Odd Couple*, 1968; *The Out-of-Towners*, 1969; *Save the Tiger* (Best Actor AA), 1973; *The Entertainer*, 1975; *The China Syndrome*, 1979; *Missing*, 1982; *Mass Appeal*, 1984; *That's Life*, 1986.

**LEONTOVICH, EUGENIE,** Mar. 21, 1894 (Moscow, Rus.). Russian-U.S. actress, dramatic coach. Stage career from 1922. Plays: *Grand Hotel*, 1930–32; *Twentieth Century*, 1932; *Tovarich*, 1935, 1937–38; *Anastasia*, 1954. Founder of the Actors' Workshop, Los Angeles (1953) and New York City (1973).

**LESLIE, JOAN** (born Joan Brodell), Jan. 26, 1925 (Detroit, Mich.). U.S. actress. Films: *Sergeant York*, 1941; *Yankee Doodle Dandy*, 1942; *Rhapsody in Blue*, 1945.

**LEVANT, OSCAR,** Dec. 27, 1906 (Pittsburgh, Pa.) –Aug. 14, 1972. U.S. concert pianist, comedic actor. Films: *Rhapsody in Blue*, 1945; *The Barclays*

of Broadway, 1949; *An American in Paris*, 1951; *The Band Wagon*, 1953.

**LIGHT, JUDITH**, Feb. 4, 1949 (Trenton, N.J.). U.S. actress. TV: *One Life to Live* (soap opera, Emmy award, 1979–81); *Who's the Boss* (series), 1984– .

**LINDEN, HAL** (born Harold Lipshitz), Mar. 20, 1931 (New York, N.Y.). U.S. singer, actor. Star of the TV series *Barney Miller*, 1975–82; won 1971 Tony award for *The Rothschilds*.

**LINN-BAKER, MARK**, June 17, 1953 (St. Louis, Mo.). U.S. actor, director. TV: *Perfect Strangers* (series), 1986– . Films: *My Favorite Year*, 1983.

**LITHGOW, JOHN**, Oct. 19, 1945 (Rochester, N.Y.). U.S. actor. A fine character actor, both on stage and in film. Stage: *The Changing Room* (Tony award), 1973; *M. Butterfly*, 1988. Films: *Blowout*, 1973; *All That Jazz*, 1979; *The World According to Garp*, 1982; *Terms of Endearment*, 1983; *Twilight Zone: The Movie*, 1983; *Harry and the Hendersons*, 1987.

**LITTLE, CLEAVON**, June 1, 1939 (Chickasha, Okla.). U.S. actor. Plays: *Purlie* (Tony award), 1970. Films: *Blazing Saddles*, 1974; *Once Bitten*, 1985.

**LLOYD, CHRISTOPHER**, Oct. 22, 1938 (Stamford, Conn.). U.S. actor. TV: *Taxi* (series), 1979–83. Films: *Back to the Future*, 1985; *Back to the Future, Pt. 2*, 1989.

**LLOYD, EMILY**, Sept. 29, 1979 (Eng.). British actress. Films: *Wish You Were Here*, 1987; *Cookie*, 19?; *In Country*; 19?.

**LOCKLEAR, HEATHER**, June 25, 1961 (Los Angeles, Calif.). U.S. actress. TV: *T.J. Hooker* (series), 1982–87; *Dynasty* (series), 1981–89.

**LOGGIA, ROBERT**, Jan. 3, 1930 (Staten Island, N.Y.). U.S. actor. TV: *The Cat* (series), 1968–69; *Mancuso FBI*, 1989– . Films: *An Officer and a Gentleman*, 1982; *Jagged Edge*, 1985; *Prizzi's Honor*, 1985; *Big*, 1988; *Triumph of the Spirit*, 1990.

**LOMBARD, CAROLE** (born Jane Peters), 1909 (Ft. Wayne, Ind.)–Jan. 16, 1942. U.S. actress. Best known for her roles in "screwball" film comedies of the 1930s. Films: *No Man of Her Own*, 1932; *My Man Godfrey*, 1936; *They Knew What They Wanted*, 1940.

**LONDON, JULIE** (born Julie Peck), Sept. 26, 1926 (Santa Rosa, Calif.). U.S. actress, singer. TV: *Emergency* (series), 1972–77. (One-time wife of J. WEBB.)

**LONG, SHELLEY**, Aug. 23, 1949 (Fort Wayne, Ind.). U.S. actress. TV: *Cheers* (series), 1982–87 (Emmy award, 1983). Films: *A Small Circle of Friends*, 1980; *Irreconcilable Differences*, 1984; *The Money Pit*, 1986; *Outrageous Fortune*, 1987.

**LORD, JACK** (born John Joseph Ryan), Dec. 30, 1930 (New York, N.Y.). U.S. actor. Best known as star of the TV series *Stony Burke* (1962–63) and *Hawaii Five-O* (1968–79).

**LOUDON, DOROTHY**, Sept. 17, 1933 (Boston, Mass.). U.S. actress, singer. Principally a stage actress; received Tony award for *Annie*, 1977.

**LOWE, ROB**, Mar. 17, 1964 (Charlottesville, Va.).

U.S. actor. Films: *The Outsiders*, 1983; *St. Elmo's Fire*, 1985; *About Last Night*, 1986; *Bad Influences*, 1990.

**LOY, MYRNA** (born Myrna Williams), Aug. 2, 1905 (Helena, Mont.). U.S. actress. Films: "The Thin Man" series of the 1930s–40s; *The Rains Came*, 1939; *The Best Years of Our Lives*, 1946; *Mr. Blandings Builds His Dream House*, 1948; *Cheaper by the Dozen*, 1950.

**LUCCI, SUSAN**, Dec. 23, 1949 (Westchester Co., N.Y.). U.S. actress. TV: *All My Children* (soap opera), 1970– ; *Mafia Princess*, 1986.

**LUCKINBILL, LAURENCE**, Nov. 21, 1934 (Ft. Smith, Ark.). U.S. actor. Has appeared in numerous Broadway plays and TV dramas. Films: *The Boys in the Band*, 1970. TV: *The Delphi Bureau* (series), 1972–73.

**LUGOSI, BELA** (born B. L. Blasko), Oct. 20, 1882 (Lugos, Hung.)–Aug. 16, 1956. Hungarian-U.S. actor. Best known for horror films, especially *Dracula* (1930). Other films: *Island of Lost Souls*, 1933; *The Black Cat*, 1934; *The Raven*, 1935; *Son of Frankenstein*, 1939; *Frankenstein Meets the Wolf Man*, 1943; *The Body Snatcher*, 1945.

**LUKAS, PAUL**, May 26, 1894 (Budapest, Hung.)–Aug. 15, 1971. Hungarian-U.S. actor. Films: *Dodsworth*, 1936; *The Lady Vanishes*, 1938; *Watch on the Rhine* (Best Actor AA), 1943.

**LUKE, KEYE**, 1904 (Canton, China). Chinese-U.S. actor. Played Charlie Chan's son in 9 1930s films; played Kato in Green Hornet serials. TV: (series), *Kung Fu*, 1972–75.

**LUNT, ALFRED**, Aug. 19, 1893 (Milwaukee, Wisc.)–Aug. 3, 1977. U.S. actor. Known for stage performances for over 40 years; appeared with wife LYNN FONTANNE in numerous Broadway plays.

**LUPONE, PATTI**, Apr. 21, 1949 (Northport, N.Y.). U.S. actress, singer. Achieved fame as the original "Evita" in the Broadway play of the same name. Stage: *Anything Goes*, 1988. TV: *Life Goes On* (series), 1989– . Films: *King of the Gypsies*, 1978; *1941*, 1979; *Driving Miss Daisy*, 1989.

**MACARTHUR, JAMES**, Dec. 8, 1937 (Los Angeles, Calif.). U.S. actor. Appeared in many WALT DISNEY movies; TV: *Hawaii Five-O* (series), 1968–79. (Son of H. HAYES.)

**MACGRAW, ALI**, Apr. 1, 1939 (Pound Ridge, N.Y.). U.S. model, actress. Films: *Goodby Columbus*, 1969; *Love Story*, 1971.

**MACLAINE, SHIRLEY** (born Shirley Beaty), Apr. 24, 1934 (Richmond, Va.). U.S. dancer, actress, author. Films: *Can-Can*, 1959; *The Apartment*, 1959; *Sweet Charity*, 1968; *The Turning Point*, 1977; *Being There*, 1979; *Terms of Endearment* (Best Actress AA), 1983. Books: *Don't Fall off the Mountain*, 1970; *You Can Get There from Here*, 1975. (Sister of W. BEATTY.)

**MACLEOD, GAVIN**, Feb. 28, 1930 (Mt. Kisco, N.Y.). U.S. actor. TV: *McHale's Navy* (series), 1962–64; *The Mary Tyler Moore Show* (series), 1970–77; *The Love Boat* (series), 1977–86.

**MACMURRAY, FRED**, Aug. 30, 1908 (Kankakee, Ill.). U.S. actor. A leading man in films from the late 1930s to the 1960s. Films: *The Trail of the Lonesome Pine*, 1936; *Double Indemnity*, 1944; *The Caine Mutiny*, 1954; *The Shaggy Dog*, 1959; *The Absent-Minded Professor*, 1961. TV: *My Three Sons* (series), 1960–72.

**MACRAE, GORDON**, Mar. 12, 1921 (E. Orange, N.J.)–Jan. 24, 1986. U.S. singer, actor. Films: *The Daughter of Rosie O'Grady*, 1950; *By the Light of the Silvery Moon*, 1953; *Oklahoma*, 1955; *Carousel*, 1956.

**MAIN, MARJORIE** (born Mary Tomlinson), Feb. 24, 1890 (Acton, Ia.)–Apr. 10, 1975. U.S. actress. Films: *Meet Me in St. Louis*, 1944; *The Harvey Girls*, 1945; *The Egg and I*, 1947; "Ma and Pa Kettle" series, 1949–56.

**MAJORS, LEE**, Apr. 23, 1940 (Wyandotte, Mich.). U.S. actor. Starred in the TV series *The Big Valley* (1965–69), and *The Six Million Dollar Man* (1973–78); *The Fall Guy*, 1982–86. (One-time husband of F. FAWCETT.)

**MALDEN, KARL** (born Malden Sekulovich), Mar. 22, 1913 (Chicago, Ill.). U.S. actor. Plays: *Golden Boy*, 1938; *A Streetcar Named Desire*, 1950. Films: *A Streetcar Named Desire* (Best Supporting Actor AA), 1952; *On the Waterfront*, 1954; *Patton*, 1969. TV: *Streets of San Francisco* (series), 1972–77.

**MALKOVICH, JOHN**, Dec. 9, 1953 (Christopher, Ill.). U.S. actor, director. Stage: *Death of a Salesman*, 1984. TV: *Death of a Salesman*, 1985. Films: *Places in the Heart*, 1984; *The Killing Fields*, 1985; *Eleni*, 1985; *Empire of the Sun*, 1987; *Dangerous Liaisons*, 1988.

**MANOFF, DINAH**, Jan. 25, 1958 (New York, N.Y.). U.S. actress. TV: *Soap* (series), 1977–78. Stage: *I Ought To Be in Pictures*, 1980 (Tony award). Films: *Grease*, 1977. (Daughter of L. GRANT.)

**MANSFIELD, JAYNE** (born Vera Jane Palmer), Apr. 19, 1933 (Bryn Mawr, Pa.)–June 29, 1967. U.S. actress. Best known of the Marilyn Monroe imitators.

**MARCH, FREDRIC** (born Ernest Frederic McIntyre Bickel), Aug. 31, 1897 (Racine, Wisc.)–Apr. 14, 1975. U.S. actor. A leading man in stage and film dramas, 1930s–1960s. Plays: *The Royal Family*, 1930; *The Skin of Our Teeth*, 1944; *Long Day's Journey into Night* (Tony award), 1956. Films: *Dr. Jekyll and Mr. Hyde* (Best Actor AA), 1932; *Death Takes a Holiday*, 1934; *Les Miserables*, 1935; *A Star Is Born*, 1937; *The Best Years of Our Lives* (Best Actor AA), 1944; *Inherit the Wind*, 1960; *Seven Days in May*, 1964.

**MARIN, CHEECH**, July 13, 1946 (Los Angeles, Calif.). U.S. actor, writer, comedian. Was part of Cheech and Chong comedy duo. Films: *Up in Smoke*, 1978.

**MARSHALL, E**(verett) **G.**, June 18, 1910 (Owatonna, Minn.). U.S. actor. Plays: *The Iceman Cometh*, 1946; *Waiting for Godot*, 1956; *The Gin Game*, 1978. Films: *12 Angry Men*, 1957; *The Bachelor Party*, 1957. TV: *The Defenders* (series), 1961–65; *The Bold Ones* (series), 1969–72.

**MARSHALL, PENNY**, Oct. 15, 1943 (New York,

N.Y.). U.S. actress. Regular appearances on the TV series *The Odd Couple*, 1972–74; star of the TV series *Laverne and Shirley*, 1976–83.

**MARTIN, DEAN**, June 17, 1917 (Steubenville, Ohio). U.S. actor, singer, entertainer. Comedy act with JERRY LEWIS, 1946–56; TV host for celebrity "roasts," 1970s. Films: *The Young Lions*, 1958; *Bells Are Ringing*, 1960; *Robin and the Seven Hoods*, 1964; *Kiss Me, Stupid*, 1964; *Sons of Katie Elder*, 1965; *The Silencers*, 1966. TV: *The Dean Martin Show*, 1965–74.

**MARTIN, MARY**, Dec. 1, 1913 (Weatherford, Tex.). U.S. actress, singer. Principally a stage actress in musicals, best known for her performance in *Peter Pan*, 1954–56 (on stage and TV). Other plays: *South Pacific*, 1949; *The Skin of Our Teeth*, 1955; *The Sound of Music*, 1959; *I Do, I Do*, 1968. (Mother of L. HAGMAN.)

**MARTIN, STEVE**, 1945 (Waco, Tex.). U.S. actor, comedian, screenwriter. Films: *The Jerk* (also screenwriter), 1979; *Pennies From Heaven*, 1981; *Dead Men Don't Wear Plaid*, 1982; *Man With Two Brains*, 1983; *All of Me*, 1984; *Little Shop of Horrors*, 1987; *Roxanne* (also producer and screenwriter), 1987; *Dirty Rotten Scoundrels*, 1988; *Parenthood*, 1989.

**MARVIN, LEE**, Feb. 19, 1924 (New York, N.Y.)–Aug. 29, 1987. U.S. actor. Involved in landmark "palimony" case, 1979. Films: *Attack*, 1957; *The Man Who Shot Liberty Valance*, 1962; *Cat Ballou* (AA Best Actor), 1965; *The Dirty Dozen*, 1967; *Paint Your Wagon*, 1969; *Emperor of the North Pole*, 1973; *Gorky Park*, 1983. TV: *M Squad* (series), 1958–60.

**MASON, MARSHA**, Apr. 3, 1942 (St. Louis, Mo.). U.S. actress. Films: *Cinderella Liberty*, 1974; *The Goodbye Girl*, 1977; *Chapter Two*, 1979; *Heartbreak Ridge*, 1987.

**MASSEY, RAYMOND**, Aug. 30, 1896 (Toronto, Ont., Can.)–July 29, 1983. Canadian–U.S. actor, director. Films: *The Scarlet Pimpernel*, 1936; *The Prisoner of Zenda*, 1937; *Abe Lincoln in Illinois*, 1940; *Arsenic and Old Lace*, 1944; *Stairway to Heaven*, 1946; *East of Eden*, 1955. TV: *Dr. Kildare* (series), 1961–66.

**MASTRANTONIO, MARY ELIZABETH**, Nov. 17, 1958 (Lombard, Ill.). U.S. actress. Stage: *Amadeus*, 1982; *Sunday in the Park with George*, 1983. Films: *Scarface*, 1983; *The Color of Money*, 1986.

**MATTHAU, WALTER**, Oct. 1, 1920 (New York, N.Y.). U.S. actor. Films: *Charade*, 1963; *The Fortune Cookie*, (Best Supporting Actor AA), 1966; *A Guide for the Married Man*, 1967; *The Odd Couple*, 1968; *Hello Dolly*, 1969; *Pete 'n' Tillie*, 1972; *The Bad News Bears*, 1975; *The Sunshine Boys*, 1975; *House Calls*, 1978; *Hopscotch*, 1980; *I Ought to Be in Pictures*, 1982.

**MATURE, VICTOR**, Jan. 29, 1916 (Louisville, Ky.). U.S. actor. Films: *My Darling Clementine*, 1946; *Kiss of Death*, 1947; *Samson and Delilah*, 1949; *The Robe*, 1953.

**MAY, ELAINE** (born Elaine Berlin), Apr. 21, 1932

(Philadelphia, Pa.). U.S. entertainer, later writer, director. Improvisational comic act with MIKE NICHOLS, 1955–62; The Heartbreak Kid, 1973.

MAYO, VIRGINIA (born Virginia Jones), Nov. 30, 1920 (St. Louis, Mo.). U.S. actress. A leading lady in 1940s and 1950s films, including The Best Years of Our Lives (1946) and The Secret Life of Walter Mitty (1947).

MAZURKI, MIKE, Dec. 25, 1909 (Tarnopol, Aust.). U.S. actor. Films: Black Fury, 1935; Farewell My Lovely, 1944; Blood Alley, 1955; Challenge to be Free, 1976; The Man With Bogart's Face, 1979.

MCCAMBRIDGE, MERCEDES, Mar. 17, 1918 (Joliet, Ill.). U.S. actress. Films: All the King's Men (Best Supporting Actress AA), 1949; Giant, 1956; The Exorcist (as the voice of the devil), 1973.

MCCARTHY, KEVIN, Feb. 15, 1914 (Seattle, Wash.). U.S. actor. Mostly in the theater. Films: Invasion of the Body Snatchers, 1956. (Brother of M. MCCARTHY.)

MCCLANAHAN, RUE, Feb. 21, 1936 (Healdton, Okla.). U.S. actress. TV: Maude (series), 1973–78; Mama's Family (series), 1983–85; The Golden Girls (series), 1985–   (Emmy award, 1987). Stage: Who's Happy Now, 1970 (Obie award), 1970.

MCRANEY, GERALD, Aug. 8, 1947 (Collins, Miss.). U.S. actor. TV: Simon & Simon (series), 1981–?; Major Dad (series), 1989–   . (Husband of DELTA BURKE.)

MCCREA, JOEL, Nov. 5, 1905 (Los Angeles, Calif.). U.S. actor. A leading man in action-adventure films of the 1930s and 1940s. Films: The Most Dangerous Game, 1932; Barbary Coast, 1935; Dead End, 1937; Union Pacific, 1939; Foreign Correspondent, 1940; Sullivan's Travels, 1941.

MCDANIEL, HATTIE, 1895 (Wichita, Kan.)–Oct. 26, 1952. U.S. actress. Won Best Supporting Actress AA for her role in Gone with the Wind, 1939; a former radio singer.

MCGAVIN, DARREN, May 7, 1922 (San Joaquin, Calif.). U.S. actor. Films: The Man with the Golden Arm, 1956. TV: Riverboat (series), 1959–61; The Night Stalker (series), 1974–75.

MCGILLIS, KELLY, 1957 (Newport, Calif.). U.S. actress. Films: Reuben, Reuben, 1983; Witness, 1985; Top Gun, 1986; The Accused, 1988.

MCGOOHAN, PATRICK, Mar. 19, 1928 (New York, N.Y.). U.S. actor. TV: Secret Agent (series), 1959–62; star of British TV series The Prisoner, 1967.

MCGOVERN, ELIZABETH, July 18, 1961 (Evanston, Ill.). U.S. actress. Films: Ordinary People, 1980; Ragtime, 1981; Once Upon a Time in America, 1984; The Bedroom Window, 1987; Handmaid's Tale, 1990.

MCGUIRE, DOROTHY, June 14, 1919 (Omaha, Neb.). U.S. actress. Films: A Tree Grows in Brooklyn, 1944; The Spiral Staircase, 1945; Three Coins in the Fountain, 1954; The Dark at the Top of the Stairs, 1960.

MCQUEEN, BUTTERFLY (born Thelma McQueen), Jan. 7, 1911 (Tampa, Fla.). U.S. actress.

Best known for roles as eccentric servant in films such as Gone with the Wind (1939).

MCQUEEN, STEVE, Mar. 24, 1930 (Indianapolis, Ind.)–Nov. 7, 1980. U.S. actor. Top box-office star of action-adventure films of the 1960s and 1970s. Films: The Magnificent Seven, 1960; The Great Escape, 1963; Love with the Proper Stranger, 1963; The Cincinnati Kid, 1965; Bullitt, 1968; The Reivers, 1970; Papillon, 1973; Towering Inferno, 1974. Starred in TV series, Wanted: Dead or Alive in the 1950s. (One-time husband of A. MACGRAW.)

MEADOWS, AUDREY, Feb. 8, 1924 (Wu Chang, China). U.S. actress. Best known for role of Alice Kramden on The Jackie Gleason Show (1952–55) and the TV series, The Honeymooners, 1955–56. (Sister of J. MEADOWS.)

MEADOWS, JAYNE, Sept. 27, 1920 (Wu Chang, China). U.S. actress. Regular panelist on TV game show I've Got a Secret, 1952–58. (Wife of S. ALLEN; sister of A. MEADOWS.)

MEARA, ANNE, Sept. 20, 1929 (New York, N.Y.). U.S. comedienne, actress. Often appears with husband JERRY STILLER.

MENJOU, ADOLPHE, Feb. 18, 1890 (Pittsburgh, Pa.)–Oct. 29, 1963. U.S. actor. Films: The Front Page, 1931; Little Miss Marker, 1934; A Star Is Born, 1937; Roxie Hart, 1942; State of the Union, 1948; Paths of Glory, 1957.

MERCER, MARIAN, Nov. 26, 1935 (Akron, Oh.). U.S. actress. TV: It's a Living (series), 1980–82. Films: 9 to 5, 1980; Oh God, Book II, 1980.

MEREDITH, BURGESS, Nov. 16, 1908 (Cleveland, Ohio). U.S. actor. Films: Winterset, 1937; Of Mice and Men, 1939; That Uncertain Feeling, 1941; The Story of G.I. Joe, 1945; Advise and Consent, 1962; The Day of the Locust, 1974; Foul Play, 1978; True Confessions, 1982; and the "Rocky" film series.

MERMAN, ETHEL (born Ethel Zimmerman), Jan. 16, 1909 (New York, N.Y.)–Feb. 15, 1984. U.S. singer, actress. Famed for her booming voice in Broadway musicals. Plays: Girl Crazy, 1930; Anything Goes, 1934; Red Hot and Blue, 1936; Dubarry Was a Lady, 1939; Panama Hattie, 1940; Annie Get Your Gun, 1946; Call Me Madam, 1950 (film, 1953); Gypsy, 1959; Tony awards, 1951, 1972. Films: Alexander's Ragtime Band, 1938; Call Me Madam, 1953; There's No Business Like Show Business, 1954; Airplane, 1980.

MERRILL, GARY, Aug. 2, 1915 (Hartford, Conn.)–Mar. 5, 1990. U.S. actor. Films: Twelve O'Clock High, 1949; All About Eve, 1950.

MILLAND, RAY (born Reginald Truscott-Jones), Jan. 3, 1905 (Glamorganshire, Wales)–Mar. 10, 1986. U.S. actor. Films: The Jungle Princess, 1936; Beau Geste, 1939; Lady in the Dark, 1944; Ministry of Fear, 1944; The Lost Weekend (Best Actor AA), 1945; The Big Clock, 1948; Dial M for Murder, 1954; Love Story, 1970; Oliver's Story, 1978.

MILLER, MARILYN (born Mary Ellen Reynolds), Sept. 1, 1898 (Findlay, Ohio)–Apr. 7, 1936. U.S. actress, dancer. Starred on Broadway in the 1920s.

**MILLS, DONNA,** Dec. 11, 1943 (Chicago, Ill.). U.S. actress. TV: *Knot's Landing* (series), 1980– . Films: *Play Misty for Me,* 1971.

**MITCHELL, THOMAS,** July 11, 1892 (Elizabeth, N.J.)–Dec. 17, 1962. U.S. actor. Supporting actor in numerous films: *Stagecoach* (supporting Actor AA); *Gone with the Wind,* 1939; *It's a Wonderful Life,* 1948; *High Noon,* 1952.

**MITCHUM, ROBERT,** Aug. 6, 1917 (Bridgeport, Conn.). U.S. actor. Films: *The Story of G.I. Joe,* 1945; *Night of the Hunter,* 1955; *The Sundowners,* 1960; *Ryan's Daughter,* 1971; *Farewell My Lovely,* 1975; *That Championship Season,* 1982.

**MIX, TOM,** Jan. 6, 1880 (Mix Run, Pa.).–Oct. 12, 1940. U.S. actor. Starred in over 100 film westerns, both silent and sound.

**MONROE, MARILYN** (born Norma Jean Baker), June 1, 1926 (Los Angeles, Calif.)–Aug, 5, 1962. U.S. actress. The sex symbol of the 1950s. Films: *The Asphalt Jungle,* 1950; *All About Eve,* 1950; *Niagara,* 1952; *Gentlemen Prefer Blondes,* 1953; *How to Marry a Millionaire,* 1953; The Seven– Year Itch, 1955; *Bus Stop,* 1956; *Some Like it Hot,* 1959.

**MONTALBAN, RICARDO,** Nov. 25, 1920 (Mexico City, Mex.). U.S. actor. Star of the TV series *Fantasy Island,* 1978–84. Films: *Battleground,* 1950; *Sayonara,* 1957; *Star Trek II: The Wrath of Khan,* 1982.

**MONTGOMERY, ELIZABETH,** Apr. 15, 1933 (Los Angeles, Calif.). U.S. actress. Best known for her TV series *Bewitched,* 1964–72. (Daughter of R. MONTGOMERY.)

**MONTGOMERY, ROBERT,** May 21, 1904 (Beacon, N.Y.)–Sept. 27, 1981. U.S. actor, producer. In films since 1930s, including *Here Comes Mr. Jordan* (1941); *The Lady in the Lake,* 1946; consultant to Pres. D. D. EISENHOWER on TV appearances. (Father of E. MONTGOMERY.)

**MOORE, DEMI,** Nov. 11, 1962 (Rosewell, N. Mex.). U.S. actress. TV: *General Hospital,* 1982–83. Films: *St. Elmo's Fire,* 1985; *About Last Night,* 1986; *Wisdom,* 1988. (Wife of B. WILLIS.)

**MOORE, MARY TYLER,** Dec. 29, 1937 (New York, N.Y.). U.S. actress. Star of the TV series *Dick Van Dyke Show* (1961–66) and *Mary Tyler Moore Show* (1970–77); received Emmy awards in 1964, 1965, 1973, 1974, and 1976. Films: *Thoroughly Modern Millie,* 1967; *Ordinary People* (Best Actress AA), 1980; *Just Between Friends,* 1986.

**MOOREHEAD, AGNES,** Dec. 6, 1906 (Boston, Mass.)–Apr. 30, 1974. U.S. actress. TV: *Bewitched* (series), 1964–72. Films: *Citizen Kane,* 1941; *The Magnificent Ambersons,* 1942; *The Lost Moment,* 1947; *The Woman in White,* 1948; *The Bat,* 1959; *Hush, Hush, Sweet Charlotte,* 1964.

**MORGAN, FRANK** (born Frank Wupperman), June 1, 1890 (New York, N.Y.)–Sept. 18, 1949. U.S. comedic character actor. Best known for the title role in the film *The Wizard of Oz,* 1939. Other films: *The Shop around the Corner,* 1940; *Boom Town,* 1940; *The Human Comedy,* 1943.

**MORGAN, HARRY** (born Harry Bratsburg), Apr. 10, 1915 (Detroit, Mich.). U.S. character actor. Star of the TV series *December Bride* (1954–59), *Dragnet* (1967–70), and "M*A*S*H" (1975–83).

**MORGAN, HELEN** (born Helen Riggins), 1900 (Danville, Ill.)–Oct. 8, 1941. U.S. singer, actress. Originally cafe singer; known for her role in the film *Show Boat,* 1936.

**MORIARTY, MICHAEL,** Apr. 5, 1941 (Detroit, Mich.). U.S. actor. Films: *Bang the Drum Slowly,* 1973; *Pale Rider,* 1985; *The Hanoi Hilton,* 1987. Plays: *Find Your Way Home* (Tony award), 1974.

**MORITA, NORIYUKI "PAT",** June 28, 1930 (Isleton, Calif.). U.S. actor. TV: *Happy Days* (series), 1975–76, 1982–83. Films: *The Karate Kid,* 1984; *The Karate Kid II,* 1986.

**MOSTEL, ZERO** (born Sam Mostel), Feb. 28, 1915 (Brooklyn, N.Y.)–Sept. 8, 1977. U.S. comedic actor. Best known for his portrayal of Tevye in the play, *The Fiddler on the Roof;* received Tony awards in 1961, 1962, and 1964. Other plays: *Rhinoceros,* 1961; *A Funny Thing Happened on the Way to the Forum,* 1962. Films: *The Producers,* 1967.

**MULL, MARTIN,** Aug 18, 1943 (Chicago, Ill.). U.S. actor, singer. TV: *Mary Hartman, Mary Hartman* (series), 1976–77; *Fernwood Tonight* (series), 1977. Screenplays: *The History of White People in American, Vol. 1 and 2,* 1986, 1987.

**MULLIGAN, RICHARD,** Nov. 13, 1932 (Bronx, N.Y.). U.S. actor, playwright. TV: *Soap* (series), 1977–80 (Emmy award, 1980); *Empty Nest* (series), 1988– . Films: *S.O.B.,* 1981.

**MUNI, PAUL** (born Muni Weisenfreund), Sept. 22, 1895 (Lemberg, Poland)–Aug. 25, 1967. U.S. actor. Films: *I Am a Fugitive from a Chain Gang,* 1932; *The Story of Louis Pasteur* (Best Actor AA), 1936; *The Good Earth,* 1937; *The Life of Emile Zola,* 1937; *A Song to Remember,* 1944; *The Last Angry Man,* 1959.

**MURPHY, EDDIE,** Apr. 3, 1961 (Brooklyn, N.Y.). U.S. actor, comedian. First gained wide attention as a regular on *Saturday Night Live.* Films: *Trading Places,* 1983; *Beverly Hills Cop,* 1984; *Beverly Hills Cop II,* 1987; *Coming to America,* 1988.

**MURPHY, GEORGE,** July 4, 1902 (New Haven, Conn.). U.S. actor, politician. Song-and-dance man in films of the 1930s and 1940s. U.S. senator (R. Calif.), 1965–71.

**MURRAY, DON,** July 31, 1929 (Hollywood, Calif.). U.S. actor. Films: *Bus Stop,* 1956; *The Bachelor Party,* 1957; *The Hoodlum Priest* 1961; *Peggy Sue Got Married,* 1986.

**NABORS, JIM,** June 12, 1933 (Sylacauga, Ala.). U.S. actor, singer. Best known for his role in *The Andy Griffith Show* (1963–64) and the TV series *Gomer Pyle, U.S.M.C.,* 1964–70.

**NAGEL, CONRAD,** Mar. 16, 1896 (Keokuk, Ia.). –Feb. 24, 1970. U.S. character actor. Films: *Little Women,* 1919; *Bad Sister,* 1931.

**NAISH, J. CARROLL,** Jan. 21, 1900 (New York, N.Y.)–Jan. 24, 1973. U.S. character actor. Starred as "Luigi" in radio and TV series. Films: *Beau*

Geste, 1939; Blood and Sand, 1941; A Medal for Benny, 1945; Annie Get Your Gun, 1950.

NATWICK, MILDRED, June 19, 1908 (Baltimore, Md.). U.S. character actress. Films: The Trouble with Harry, 1955; Barefoot in the Park, 1967; Kiss Me Goodbye, 1982.

NEAL, PATRICIA, Jan. 20, 1926 (Packard, N.Y.). U.S. actress. Films: The Fountainhead, 1949; The Hasty Heart, 1950; A Face in the Crowd, 1957; Hud (Best Actress AA), 1963; The Subject Was Roses, 1968; The Homecoming, 1971.

NEGRI, POLA (born Appolonia Chalupek), 1899 (Lipno, Pol.)–Aug. 1, 1987. U.S. actress. A silent-screen star.

NELSON, BARRY, Apr. 16, 1920 (San Francisco, Calif.). U.S. actor. Appeared mostly in the theater. Films: Airport, 1970; Pete 'n' Tillie, 1972.

NELSON, CRAIG T., Apr. 4, 1946 (Spokane, Wash.). U.S. actor. TV: Call to Glory, 1984–85; Coach (series), 1989– . Films: Poltergeist, 1983; Silkwood, 1983; The Killing Fields, 1985; Poltergeist II, 1986.

NELSON, HARRIET (born Peggy Snyder), July 18, 1914 (Des Moines, Ia.). U.S. actress. Singer with husband OZZIE NELSON's band; appeared on the TV series, Ozzie and Harriet, 1952–65. (Mother of David and R. NELSON.)

NELSON, OZZIE, Mar. 20, 1907 (Jersey City, N.J.)–June 3, 1975. U.S. bandleader, actor. Appeared in the TV series Ozzie and Harriet, 1952–65. (Husband of H. NELSON, father of David and R. NELSON.)

NELSON, RICK(y), May 8, 1940 (Teaneck, N.J.)–Dec. 31, 1986. U.S. singer, actor, songwriter. Appeared on the TV series Ozzie and Harriet, 1952–65; later a singer and songwriter of pop-rock tunes. (Son of O. and H. NELSON.)

NEWMAN, PAUL, Jan. 26, 1925 (Cleveland, Ohio). U.S. actor. Films: The Long Hot Summer, 1958; Cat on a Hot Tin Roof, 1958; Exodus, 1960; The Hustler, 1961; Sweet Bird of Youth, 1962; Hud, 1963; Cool Hand Luke, 1967; Butch Cassidy and the Sundance Kid, 1969; Judge Roy Bean, 1972; The Sting, 1973; Slap Shot, 1977; Absence of Malice, 1981; The Verdict, 1982; Harry and Son, 1984; The Color of Money (Best Actor AA), 1986. (Husband of J. WOODWARD.)

NICHOLSON, JACK, Apr. 28, 1937 (Neptune, N.J.). U.S. actor. Films: Easy Rider, 1969; Five Easy Pieces, 1970; Carnal Knowledge, 1971; Chinatown, 1974; The Last Detail, 1974; One Flew over the Cuckoo's Nest, (Best Actor AA), 1976; Reds, 1982; Terms of Endearment (Best Supporting Actor AA), 1983; Prizzi's Honor, 1985; The Witches of Eastwick, 1987; Ironweed, 1987.

NIMOY, LEONARD, Mar. 26, 1931 (Boston, Mass.). U.S. actor. Best known as Spock on the TV series Star Trek (1966–69) and the "Star Trek" film series.

NOLAN, LLOYD, Aug. 11, 1902 (San Francisco, Calif.)–Sept. 27, 1985. U.S. character actor. Films: A Tree Grows in Brooklyn, 1944; The House on 92nd Street, 1945; A Hatful of Rain, 1957.

NOLTE, NICK, Feb. 8, 1940 (Omaha, Neb.). U.S. actor. Rose to prominence via starring role in TV miniseries Rich Man, Poor Man, 1976–77. Films: Return to Macon County, 1975; The Deep, 1977; Who'll Stop the Rain, 1978; North Dallas Forty, 1979; 48 Hours, 1982; Down and Out in Beverly Hills, 1985; Extreme Prejudice, 1987.

NORRIS, CHUCK, 1939 (Ryan, Okla.). U.S. actor. A karate champion, plays many martial-arts roles. Films: Enter the Dragon, 1973; Lone Wolf McQuade, 1983; Missing in Action, 1984; The Delta Force, 1986.

NOVAK, KIM, Feb. 18, 1933 (Chicago, Ill.). U.S. actress. Films: Picnic, 1955; The Man with the Golden Arm, 1956; Jeanne Eagels, 1957; Vertigo, 1958; Bell, Book and Candle, 1958; Pal Joey, 1958.

NOVARRO, RAMON, Feb. 6, 1899 (Durango, Mex.)–Oct. 31, 1968. Mexican-U.S. actor. First of Hollywood's Latin lovers. Films: Scaramouche, 1923; The Arabs, 1924; Ben Hur, 1925; The Student Prince, 1928; Mata Hari, 1931.

OAKIE, JACK (born Lewis Offield), Nov. 12, 1903 (Sedalia, Mo.)–Jan. 23, 1978. U.S. comedic actor. Best known for his "double take"; did over 100 films, including The Great Dictator (1940), It Happened Tomorrow (1944), and Around the World in Eighty Days (1956).

O'BRIAN, HUGH (born Hugh Krampe), Apr. 19, 1930 (Rochester, N.Y.). U.S. actor. Best known as star of the TV series Wyatt Earp, 1956–59.

O'BRIEN, EDMOND, Sept. 10, 1915 (New York, N.Y.)–May 9, 1985. U.S. actor. Films: The Killers, 1946; D.O.A., 1949; The Barefoot Contessa, 1954; 1984, 1955; The Third Voice, 1959; Seven Days in May, 1964.

O'BRIEN, MARGARET, Jan. 15, 1937 (San Diego, Calif.). A leading child star of the 1940s. Films: Meet Me in St. Louis, 1944; Our Vines Have Tender Grapes, 1945; Little Women, 1949.

O'BRIEN, PAT, Nov. 11, 1899 (Milwaukee, Wisc.)–Oct. 15, 1983. U.S. actor. Films: The Front Page, 1931; Bombshell, 1933; Angels with Dirty Faces, 1938; Knute Rockne, All American, 1941; The Last Hurrah, 1958; Some Like it Hot, 1959; Ragtime, 1981.

O'CONNOR, CARROLL, Aug. 2, 1924 (New York, N.Y.). U.S. actor. Best known for his role as Archie Bunker on TV series All in the Family, 1971–79; and Archie Bunker's Place, 1979–83. Won Emmy Awards, 1973, 1977, 1978, 1979.

O'CONNOR, DONALD, Aug. 28, 1925 (Chicago, Ill.). U.S. actor, singer, dancer. Films: Mister Big, 1943; Patrick the Great, 1945; Francis, 1949; Singin' in the Rain, 1952; Call Me Madam, 1953; There's No Business like Show Business, 1954; The Buster Keaton Story, 1957.

OLAND, WARNER, Oct. 3, 1880 (Umea, Swe.)–Aug. 6, 1938. U.S. actor. Appeared as Charlie Chan in numerous 1930s films.

OLIVER, EDNA MAY, Nov. 9, 1883 (Boston, Mass.)–Nov. 9, 1942. U.S. character actress. Best known for film roles in David Copperfield (1934),

*Romeo and Juliet* (1936), *Drums Along the Mohawk* (1939), and *Pride and Prejudice* (1940).

**O'NEAL, RYAN,** Apr. 20, 1941 (Los Angeles, Calif.). U.S. actor. TV: *Peyton Place* (series), 1964–69. Films: *Love Story,* 1970; *What's Up Doc?,* 1972; *Paper Moon,* 1973; *Oliver's Story,* 1979; *The Main Event,* 1979; *Tough Guys Don't Dance,* 1987. (Father of T. O'NEAL.)

**O'NEAL, TATUM,** Nov. 5, 1963 (Los Angeles, Calif.). U.S. child actress. Films: *Paper Moon* (Best Supporting Actress AA), 1973; *The Bad News Bears,* 1976. (Daughter of R. O'NEAL; wife of J. MCENROE.)

**ORBACH, JERRY,** Oct. 20, 1935 (New York, N.Y.). U.S. actor. Best known for lead role in the play *The Fantasticks,* 1961; received Tony award for *Promises, Promises,* 1968.

**O'SULLIVAN, MAUREEN,** May 17, 1911 (Boyle, Ire.). U.S. actress. Best known for her role as Jane in the "Tarzan" film series, 1932–42. Other films: *The Barretts of Wimpole Street,* 1934; *Pride and Prejudice,* 1940; *Hannah and Her Sisters,* 1986. (Mother of M. FARROW.)

**O'TOOLE, ANNETTE,** Apr. 1, 1952 (Houston, Tex.). U.S. actress. TV: *The Kennedys of Massachusetts* (miniseries), 1990. Films: *Smile,* 1975; *Cat People,* 1982.

**OUSPENSKAYA, MARIA,** July 29, 1876 (Tula, Rus.)–Dec. 3, 1949. Russian–U.S. actress. As Russian stage actress (1911–23), known for her roles in Chekhov plays. Films: *Love Affair,* 1939; *The Rains Came,* 1939; *The Wolf Man,* 1941; *A Kiss in the Dark,* 1949.

**PACINO, AL**(fred), Apr. 25, 1940 (New York, N.Y.). U.S. actor. Plays: *The Indian Wants the Bronx,* 1968; *Does the Tiger Wear a Necktie?* (Tony award), 1969. Films: *The Godfather—Parts 1 and 2,* 1972, 1974; *Serpico,* 1973; *Dog Day Afternoon,* 1975; *Cruising,* 1980; *Author! Author!,* 1982; *Scarface,* 1983.

**PAGE, GERALDINE,** Nov. 22, 1924 (Kirksville, Mo.)–June 13, 1987. U.S. actress. Films: *Hondo,* 1954; *Sweet Bird of Youth,* 1962; *Pete 'n' Tillie,* 1972; *Interiors,* 1978; *The Trip to Bountiful* (Best Actress AA), 1985.

**PALANCE, JACK** (born Walter Palanuik), Feb. 18, 1920 (Lattimer Mines, Pa.). U.S. actor. Best known as a film "heavy." Films: *Shane,* 1953; *The Big Knife,* 1955.

**PALMER, LILLI** (born Lillie Peiser), May 24, 1914 (Posen, Ger.)–Jan. 27, 1986. U.S. actress, author. Films: *The Rake's Progress,* 1945; *Body and Soul,* 1948; *My Girl Tesa,* 1947; *The Pleasure of His Company,* 1961. Memoirs: *Change Lobsters and Dance,* 1975. (One-time wife of R. HARRISON.)

**PARKER, ELEANOR,** June 26, 1922 (Cedarville, Ohio). U.S. actress. Films: *The Voice of the Turtle,* 1947; *Detective Story,* 1951; *Interrupted Melody,* 1955; *The Sound of Music,* 1965.

**PARKER, FESS,** Aug. 16, 1925 (Fort Worth, Tex.). U.S. actor. Best known for his portrayal of Davy Crockett in film series. TV: *Daniel Boone* (series), 1964–69.

**PARSONS, ESTELLE,** Nov. 20, 1927 (Lynn, Mass.). U.S. actress. Has had great success on the Broadway stage. Films: *Bonnie and Clyde,* 1967 *Rachel, Rachel,* 1968.

**PATINKIN, MANDY,** Nov. 30, 1952 (Chicago, Ill.). U.S. actor, singer. Stage: *Evita,* 1980 (Tony award); *Sunday in the Park with George,* 1984. Films: *Ragtime,* 1981; *Yentl,* 1983; *Daniel,* 1983; *Princess Bride,* 1987; *Alien Nation,* 1988.

**PAYNE, JOHN,** May 23, 1912 (Roanoke, Va.)– Dec. 5, 1989. U.S. actor. Films: *Tin Pan Alley,* 1940; *The Great American Broadway,* 1941; *The Dolly Sisters,* 1945; *Miracle on 34th Street,* 1947; *The Boss,* 1956.

**PECK, GREGORY,** Apr. 5, 1916 (La Jolla, Calif.). U.S. actor. Hollywood leading man for over 30 years; Jean Hersholt Humanitarian Award, 1968. Films: *The Keys of the Kingdom,* 1944; *Spellbound,* 1945; *Duel in the Sun,* 1946; *Gentleman's Agreement,* 1947; *Twelve O'Clock High,* 1949; *The Gunfighter,* 1950; *The Man in the Gray Flannel Suit,* 1956; *Moby Dick,* 1956; *On the Beach,* 1959; *The Guns of Navarone,* 1961; *To Kill a Mockingbird,* (Best Actor AA), 1963; *The Omen,* 1976; *MacArthur,* 1977; *The Boys from Brazil,* 1978.

**PENN, SEAN,** Aug. 17, 1960 (Burbank, Calif.). U.S. actor. Films: *Taps,* 1981; *Fast Times at Ridgemont High,* 1982; *Racing with the Moon,* 1984; *The Falcon and the Snowman,* 1985; *Colors,* 1988; *Casualties of War,* 1989.

**PEPPARD, GEORGE,** Oct. 1, 1928 (Detroit, Mich.). U.S. actor. Films: *Breakfast at Tiffany's,* 1961; *The Blue Max,* 1966; *Rough Night in Jericho,* 1967. TV: *Banacek* (series), 1972–74; *The A-Team,* 1983–87.

**PERKINS, ANTHONY,** Apr. 4, 1932 (New York, N.Y.). U.S. actor. Films: *Desire under the Elms,* 1957; *Psycho,* 1960; *Pretty Poison,* 1968; 2 "Psycho" sequels in the 1980s.

**PERLMAN, RHEA,** Mar. 31, 1948 (Brooklyn, N.Y.). U.S. actress. TV: *Taxi* (series), 1978–82; *Cheers* (series), 1982– (Emmy award, 1984). (Wife of D. DEVITO.)

**PERRINE, VALERIE,** Sept. 3, 1943 (Galveston, Tex.). U.S. actress. Films: *Slaughterhouse Five,* 1972; *Lenny,* 1975; *W.C. Fields and Me,* 1976; *Superman II,* 1980; *The Border,* 1982.

**PERSOFF, NEHEMIAH,** Aug. 14, 1920 (Jerusalem, Palestine [now Israel]). U.S. character actor in films and TV.

**PETERS, BERNADETTE** (born Bernadette Lazzara), Feb. 28, 1948 (New York, N.Y.). U.S. musical– comedy actress. Plays: *George M!,* 1968; *Dames at Sea,* 1968; *Into the Woods,* 1987. Films: *The Jerk,* 1979; *Pennies From Heaven,* 1981; *Heartbeeps,* 1981; *Annie,* 1982. TV: *All's Fair* (series), 1976–77.

**PETERS, BROCK,** July 2, 1927 (New York, N.Y.). U.S. actor, singer. Films: *Porgy and Bess,* 1959; *To Kill a Mockingbird,* 1962; *The Heavens Above,* 1963.

**PFEIFFER, MICHELLE,** Apr. 29, 1957 (Santa Ana, Calif.). U.S. actress. Films: *Grease II,* 1982; *Scarface,*

1983; *Sweet Liberty*, 1986; *The Witches of Eastwick*, 1987; *Tequila Sunrise*, 1988; *Married to the Mob*, 1988; *Dangerous Liaisons*, 1988; *Fabulous Baker Boys*, 1989.

**PHOENIX, RIVER,** Aug. 23, 1970 (Madras, Ore.). U.S. actor. Films: *Stand By Me*, 1986; *Running on Empty*, 1988.

**PICKFORD, MARY** (born Gladys Marie Smith), Apr. 9, 1938 (Toronto, Can.)–May 29, 1979. U.S. actress. A leading lady of the silent screen, then, talkies; in 1919, established United Artists Corp. with (husband) DOUGLAS FAIRBANKS, CHARLIE CHAPLIN, and D. W. GRIFFITH. Films: *Pollyanna*, 1919; *Little Lord Fauntleroy*, 1921; *Tess of the Storm Country*, 1922; *Coquette* (Best Actress AA), 1929.

**PICON, MOLLY,** June 1, 1898 (New York, N.Y.). U.S. actress. Star of Yiddish theater, from 1904 and later, Broadway.

**PINCHOT, BRONSON,** May 2, 1959 (New York, N.Y.). U.S. actor. TV: *Perfect Strangers* (series), 1986– . Films: *Risky Business*, 1983; *Beverly Hills Cop*, 1984.

**PITTS, ZASU,** Jan. 3, 1898 (Parsons, Kan.)–June 7, 1963. U.S. comedic character actress who began in films in 1919.

**PLESHETTE, SUZANNE,** Jan. 31, 1937 (New York, N.Y.). U.S. actress. Films: *The Birds*, 1963; *If It's Tuesday, This Must Be Belgium*, 1969. TV: *The Bob Newhart Show* (series), 1972–78.

**POITIER, SIDNEY,** Feb. 20, 1927 (Miami, Fla.). U.S. actor and director. The first black actor to win Best Actor AA. Films: *The Defiant Ones*, 1958; *A Raisin in the Sun*, 1961; *Lilies of the Field* (Best Actor AA), 1963; *The Bedford Incident*, 1965; *In the Heat of the Night*, 1967; *Guess Who's Coming to Dinner?*, 1967; *To Sir with Love*, 1967; *Buck and the Preacher*, 1972.

**POSTON, TOM,** Oct. 17, 1927 (Columbus, Ohio). U.S. comedic character. TV: *The Steve Allen Show* in the 1950s; *Newhart* (series) in the 1980s.

**POWELL, DICK,** Nov. 14, 1904 (Mt View, Ark.) –Jan. 3, 1963. U.S. actor, producer, director. Films: *42nd Street*, 1933; *Dames*, 1934; *On the Avenue*, 1937; *Christmas in July*, 1940; *Murder My Sweet*, 1944.

**POWELL, JANE** (born Suzanne Burce), Apr. 1, 1929 (Portland, Ore.). U.S. actress, singer. A leading lady in 1940s-1950s films, including *Seven Brides for Seven Brothers* (1954).

**POWELL, WILLIAM,** July 29, 1892 (Pittsburgh, Pa.)–Mar. 5, 1984. U.S. actor. Best known for "The Thin Man" film series, 1934–47. Other films: *The Canary Murder Case*, 1929; *Street of Chance*, 1930; *One-Way Passage*, 1932; *The Great Ziegfeld*, 1936; *My Man Godfrey*, 1936; *Life with Father*, 1947; *Mister Roberts*, 1955. (One-time husband of C. LOMBARD.)

**POWER, TYRONE,** May 5, 1913 (Cincinnati, Ohio) –Nov. 15, 1958. U.S. actor. Handsome leading man of 1940s and 1950s films. Films: *Lloyds of London*, 1937; *In Old Chicago*, 1938; *Alexander's Ragtime Band*, 1938; *Rose of Washington Square*,

1939; *Jesse James*, 1939; *The Mask of Zorro*, 1940; *The Razor's Edge*, 1946; *Witness for the Prosecution*, 1957; *The Sun Also Rises*, 1957.

**POWERS, STEFANIE,** Nov. 2, 1942 (Hollywood, Calif.). U.S. actress. TV: *The Girl From U.N.C.L.E.* (series), 1966; *Hart to Hart* (series), 1979–83; *Mistral's Daughter*, 1984. Films: *Experiment in Terror*, 1962; *The Interns*, 1962; *Stagecoach*, 1964.

**PRENTISS, PAULA** (born Paula Ragusa), Mar. 4, 1939 (San Antonio, Tex.). U.S. actress. Films: *Man's Favorite Sport*, 1964; *What's New, Pussycat?*, 1965; *The Stepford Wives*, 1975. (Wife of R. BENJAMIN.)

**PRESLEY, PRISCILLA,** May 24, 1945 (New York, N.Y.). U.S. actress. TV: *Dallas* (series), 1983– . Films: *The Naked Gun*, 1988. Books: *Elvis and Me*, 1985. (Wife of E. PRESLEY.)

**PRESTON, ROBERT** (born Robert Meservey), June 8, 1918 (Newton, Mass.)–Mar. 21, 1987. U.S. actor. Best known for lead role in *The Music Man* (play, 1957; film, 1962). Plays: *Ben Franklin in Paris*, 1964; *I Do, I Do*, 1966. Films: *Union Pacific*, 1938; *Beau Geste*, 1939; *The Dark at the Top of the Stairs*, 1960; *How the West Was Won*, 1963; *S.O.B.*, 1981; *Victor! Victoria*, 1982.

**PRICE, VINCENT,** May 27, 1911 (St. Louis, Mo.). U.S. stage and screen actor. Best known for his roles in horror movies, particularly those based on Edgar Allan Poe stories. Films: *Tower of London*, 1939; *Laura*, 1944; *House of Wax*, 1953; *The Raven*, 1963; *The Whales of August*, 1987.

**PRINCIPAL, VICTORIA,** Jan. 3, 1945 (Fukuoka, Japan). U.S. actress. Began as a model. TV: *Dallas* (series), 1980–87. Films: *The Life and Times of Judge Roy Bean*, 1972; *The Mistress*, 1987. Books: *The Beauty Principal*, 1984; *The Diet Principal*, 1987.

**PROSKY, ROBERT,** Dec. 13, 1930 (Philadelphia, Pa.). U.S. actor. Stage: *Glengarry Glen Ross*, 1985 (Tony award). TV: *Hill Street Blues* (series), 1984–87. Films: *Lords of Discipline*, 1983; *The Natural*, 1984; *Broadcast News*, 1987; *Things Change*, 1988.

**QUAID, DENNIS,** Apr. 9, 1954 (Houston, Tex.). U.S. actor. Films: *Crazy Mama*, 1975; *Breaking Away*, 1978; *Longriders*, 1979; *The Right Stuff*, 1983; *Innerspace*, 1986; *The Big Easy*, 1986; *Suspect*, 1987; *Great Balls of Fire*, 1989. (Brother of R. QUAID.)

**QUAID, RANDY,** Oct. 1, 1950 (Houston, Tex.). U.S. actor. Stage: *True West*, 1983. TV: *LBJ, The Early Years*, 1986. Films: *The Last Picture Show*, 1971; *The Last Detail*, 1973; *Paper Moon*, 1973; *The Apprenticeship of Duddy Kravitz*, 1975; *Missouri Breaks*, 1976; *Longriders*, 1980; *National Lampoon's Vacation*, 1983. (Brother of D. QUAID.)

**QUINN, ANTHONY,** Apr. 21, 1915 (Chihuahua, Mex.). U.S. actor. Films: *Viva Zapata* (Best Supporting Actor AA), 1952; *La Strada*, 1954; *Lust for Life* (Best Supporting Actor AA), 1956; *The Guns of Navarone*, 1961; *Requiem for a Heavyweight*, 1963; *Zorba the Greek*, 1964; *The Shoes of the Fisherman*, 1968.

**RAFT, GEORGE,** 1895 (New York, N.Y.)–Nov. 24, 1980. U.S. actor. Best known for film roles as gangsters. Films: *Scarface*, 1932; *The Bowery*, 1933; *The Glass Key*, 1935; *Souls at Sea*, 1937; *Each Dawn I Die*, 1939.

RAINER, LUISE, Jan. 12, 1909 (Vienna, Austria). U.S. actress. Retired from film industry after receiving Best Actress AA, for *The Great Ziegfeld* (1936) and *The Good Earth* (1937).

RAINS, CLAUDE, Nov. 10, 1889 (London, Eng.)–May 30, 1967. British-U.S. character actor. Films: *The Invisible Man*, 1933; *Crime without Passion*, 1934; *The Adventures of Robin Hood*, 1938; *Mr. Smith Goes to Washington*, 1939; *King's Row*, 1941; *Casablanca*, 1942; *The Phantom of the Opera*, 1943; *Mr. Skeffington*, 1944; *Notorious*, 1946; *Lawrence of Arabia*, 1962.

RAITT, JOHN, Jan. 19, 1917 (Santa Ana, Calif.). U.S. actor, singer. A leading man in the musical theater.

RANDALL, TONY (born Leonard Rosenberg), Feb. 26, 1920 (Tulsa, Okla.). U.S. actor. Best known for his role as Felix Unger in the TV series *The Odd Couple*, 1970–75. Films: *Will Success Spoil Rock Hunter?*, 1957; *Pillow Talk*, 1959; *Seven Faces of Dr. Lao*, 1964.

RASHAD, PHYLICIA, June 17, 1948 (Houston, Tex.). U.S. actress, singer, dancer. TV: *The Cosby Show* (series), 1984– . (Sister of D. ALLEN.)

RATHBONE, BASIL, June 13, 1892 (Johannesburg, S.A.)–July 21, 1967. English actor. Best known for his role as Sherlock Holmes in a series of 1930s–1940s films. Films: *David Copperfield*, 1935; *Anna Karenina*, 1935; *Captain Blood*, 1935; *The Adventures of Robin Hood*, 1938; *Son of Frankenstein*, 1939; *The Hound of the Baskervilles*, 1939; *The Mark of Zorro*, 1940.

RATZENBERGER, JOHN, Apr. 6, 1947 (Bridgeport, Conn.). U.S. actor. TV: *Cheers* (series), 1982– .

RAY, ALDO (born Aldo de Re), Sept. 25, 1926 (Pen Argul, Pa.). U.S. actor. Beefy character-actor. Films: *The Marrying Kind*, 1951; *Pat and Mike*, 1952; *We're No Angels*, 1955.

RAYE, MARTHA (born Maggie Yvonne O'Reed), Aug. 27, 1916 (Butte, Mont.). U.S. actress. Has played vaudeville, clubs, radio, TV; in films since 1936. Films: *The Boys from Syracuse*, 1940; *Hellzapoppin'*, 1942; *Monsieur Verdoux*, 1947.

RAYMOND, GENE (born Raymond Guion), Aug. 13, 1908 (New York, N.Y.). U.S. actor. A leading man in 1930s second features. (Husband of J. MACDONALD.)

REDFORD, ROBERT, Aug. 18, 1937 (Santa Monica, Calif.). U.S. actor, director. Films: *The Chase*, 1966; *Barefoot in the Park*, 1967; *Butch Cassidy and the Sundance Kid*, 1969; *The Candidate*, 1972; *The Way We Were*, 1973; *The Sting*, 1973; *Three Days of the Condor*, 1975; *All the President's Men*, 1976; *The Electric Horseman*, 1979; *Brubaker*, 1979; *The Natural*, 1984; *Out of Africa*, 1985; *Legal Eagles*, 1986. Won AA as Best Director for *Ordinary People*, 1980.

REED, DONNA (born Donna Mullenger), Jan. 27, 1921 (Denison, Ia.)–Jan. 14, 1986. U.S. actress.

Known for TV series *The Donna Reed Show*, 1958–66. Films: *It's a Wonderful Life*, 1946; *From Here to Eternity* (Best Supporting Actress AA), 1953.

REED, ROBERT, Oct. 19, 1932 (Highland Park, Ill.). U.S. actor. Best known for roles in the TV series *The Defenders* (1961–65) and *The Brady Bunch* (1969–74).

REEVE, CHRISTOPHER, Sept. 25, 1952 (New York, N.Y.). U.S. actor. Stage: *A Matter of Gravity*, 1976; *The Fifth of July*, 1980; *The Marriage of Figaro*, 1985. Films: *Superman: The Movie*, 1978; *Superman II*, 1980; *Deathtrap*, 1982; *Street Smart*, 1987.

REID, TIM, Dec. 19, 1944 (Norfolk, Va.). U.S. actor. TV: *WKRP in Cincinnati* (series), 1978–82; *Simon & Simon* (series), 1983–87; *Frank's Place* (series), 1987–89.

REILLY, CHARLES NELSON, Jan. 13, 1931 (New York, N.Y.). U.S. comedic actor, director. Plays: *How to Succeed in Business without Really Trying* (Tony award), 1962.

REINER, ROB, Mar. 6, 1945 (New York, N.Y.). U.S. actor, director. Best known for role as Mike Stivic in the TV series *All in the Family*, 1971–78. Films: *This is Spinal Tap*, 1984; *Stand By Me*, 1986. (Son of C. REINER.)

REINHOLD, JUDGE, 1956 (Wilmington, Del.). U.S. actor. Films: *Stripes*, 1981; *Fast Times at Ridgemont High*, 1982; *Gremlins*, 1984; *Beverly Hills Cop*, 1984; *Ruthless People*, 1986; *Vice Versa*, 1988.

REMICK, LEE, Dec. 14, 1935 (Quincy, Mass.). U.S. actress. Films: *The Anatomy of a Murder*, 1959; *Days of Wine and Roses*, 1963; *The Omen*, 1976; *Tribute*, 1980. TV: *Jennie* (miniseries), 1975.

REYNOLDS, BURT, Feb. 11, 1936 (Waycross, Ga.). U.S. actor, director. Films: *Deliverance*, 1972; *White Lightning*, 1973; *The Longest Yard*, 1974; *Smokey and the Bandit*, 1977; *Semi-Tough*, 1977; *The End*, 1978; *The Cannonball Run*, 1981; *Best Friends*, 1982; *City Heat*, 1984; *Stick*, 1985. TV: *Gunsmoke* (series), 1965–67; *Dan August* (series), 1970–75.

REYNOLDS, DEBBIE (born Mary Frances Reynolds), Apr. 1, 1932 (El Paso, Tex.). U.S. actress, singer, dancer. Films: *Singin' in the Rain*, 1952; *Tammy and the Bachelor*, 1957; *The Unsinkable Molly Brown*, 1964. (Mother of C. FISHER.)

RICH, IRENE (born Irene Luther), Oct. 13, 1897? (Buffalo, N.Y.). U.S. actress. A silent-film leading lady, later in talkies.

RIEGERT, PETER, 1948 (New York, N.Y.). U.S. actor. Films: *Animal House*, 1978; *Local Hero*, 1983; *Crossing Delancey*, 1988.

RINGWALD, MOLLY, Feb. 14, 1968 (Sacramento, Calif.). U.S. actress. TV: *The Facts of Life* (series), 1979–80. Films: *Tempest*, 1982; *Sixteen Candles*, 1984; *The Breakfast Club*, 1985; *Pretty in Pink*, 1986.

RITTER, JOHN, Sept. 17, 1948 (Burbank, Calif.). U.S. actor. Best known for his lead role in the TV

series *Three's Company*, 1977–84; *Hooperman* (series), 1987– . (Son of country singer T. RITTER.)
**RITTER, THELMA**, Feb. 14, 1905 (New York, N.Y.)–Feb. 5, 1969. U.S. character actress. Films: *Miracle on 34th Street*, 1947; *All about Eve*, 1950; *The Model and the Marriage Broker*, 1951; *Rear Window*, 1954; The Misfits, 1961.
**ROBARDS, JASON, JR.**, July 26, 1922 (Chicago, Ill.). U.S. actor. Best known for his roles in EUGENE O'NEILL's plays. Films: *A Thousand Clowns*, 1966; *All the President's Men* (Best Supporting Actor AA), 1976; *Julia*, 1977; *Melvin and Howard*, 1979; *Max Dugan Returns*, 1983.
**ROBERTS, DORIS**, Nov. 4, 1930 (St. Louis, Mo.). U.S. actress. TV: *Mary Hartman, Mary Hartman* (series); *Remington Steele* (series), 1984– .
**ROBERTS, ERIC**, Apr. 18, 1956 (Biloxi, Miss.). U.S. actor. Films: *King of the Gypsies*, 1978; *The Pope of Greenwich Village*, 1984; *Runaway Train*, 1985.
**ROBERTS, PERNELL**, May 18, 1930 (Waycross, Ga.). U.S. actor. TV: *Bonanza* (series), 1959–65; *Trapper John M.D.* (series), 1979–86.
**ROBERTS, TONY**, Oct. 22, 1939 (New York, N.Y.). U.S. actor. A fixture in many WOODY ALLEN films. Stage: *Barefoot in the Park*, 1964; *How Now Dow Jones*, 1969. Films: *Play It Again, Sam*, 1972; *Annie Hall*, 1977; *Hannah and Her Sisters*, 1986; *Radio Days*, 1987.
**ROBERTSON, CLIFF**, Sept. 9, 1925 (La Jolla, Calif.). U.S. actor, director. Films: *Picnic*, 1955; *P.T. 109*, 1963; *The Best Man*, 1964; *The Honey Pot*, 1967; *Charly* (Best Actor AA), 1968; *Three Days of the Condor*, 1976; *Brainstorm*, 1983.
**ROBERTSON, DALE**, July 14, 1923 (Harrah, Okla.). U.S. actor. In many cowboy films, 1950–60s, starred in the TV series *Tales of Wells Fargo*, 1957–62; *J. J. Starbuck*, 1987.
**ROBINSON, EDWARD G.** (born Emanuel Goldenburg), Dec. 12, 1893 (Bucharest, Hung.)–Jan. 26, 1973, U.S. actor. Rose to prominence in 1930s gangster films, later played a variety of dramatic roles. Films: *Little Caesar*, 1930; *Five Star Final*, 1931; *The Whole Town's Talking*, 1934; *A Slight Case of Murder*, 1938; *Brother Orchid*, 1940; *The Sea Wolf*, 1941; *Double Indemnity*, 1944; *All My Sons*, 1948; *Key Largo*, 1948; *The Cincinnati Kid*, 1965.
**ROBSON, MAY** (born Mary Robison), Apr. 19, 1865 (Melbourne, Austrl.)–Oct. 20, 1942. U.S. character actress. Films: *If I Had a Million*, 1932; *Lady for a Day*, 1933; *Dinner at Eight*, 1933; *A Star Is Born*, 1937; *Bringing Up Baby*, 1938.
**"ROCHESTER"** (born Eddie Anderson), Sept. 18, 1905 (Oakland, Calif.)–Feb. 28, 1977. U.S. character actor best known for his role as Rochester, JACK BENNY's butler, on TV and radio, 1953–65. Films: *Green Pastures*, 1936; *Cabin in the Sky*, 1943.
**ROGERS, CHARLES** ("Buddy"), Aug. 13, 1904 (Olathe, Kan.). U.S. actor. A silent-screen star best known for his performance in *Wings* (1928), the

first film to win an AA. (Husband of M. PICKFORD.)
**ROGERS, ROY** (born Leonard Slye), Nov. 5, 1912 (Cincinnati, Ohio). U.S. actor, singer. Starred in cowboy films 1935–53; costarred with wife DALE EVANS in the TV series *The Roy Rogers Show*, 1951–57.
**ROLAND, GILBERT** (born Luis Damaso de Alonso), Dec. 11, 1905 (Chihuahua, Mex.). Mexican-U.S. actor. A former bullfighter; in U.S. films since the mid-1930s.
**ROLLE, ESTHER**, Nov. 8, 1933 (Pompano Beach, Fla.). U.S. actress. Best known for role as Florida Evans in the *Maude* and *Good Times* TV series in the 1970s.
**ROLLINS, HOWARD, JR.**, Oct. 17, 1950 (Baltimore, Md.). U.S. actor. TV: *In the Heat of the Night* (series), 1988– . Films: *Ragtime*, 1981; *A Soldier's Story*, 1984.
**ROMERO, CESAR**, Feb. 15, 1907 (New York, N.Y.). U.S. actor. In a long film and TV career, best known for his role in the "Cisco Kid" film series of the 1930s and 1940s.
**ROONEY, MICKEY** (born Joe Yule, Jr.), Sept. 23, 1920 (New York, N.Y.). U.S. actor. Began as a child actor in vaudeville, 1922–32. Films: *A Midsummer Night's Dream*, 1935; "Andy Hardy" series, 1937–46; *Ah Wilderness*, 1935; *Boys Town*, 1938; *Babes in Arms*, 1939; *Strike up the Band*, 1940; *The Human Comedy*, 1943; *The Bold and the Brave*, 1956; *Breakfast at Tiffany's*, 1961; *Black Stallion*, 1979. (One-time husband of A. GARDNER.)
**ROSE MARIE**, Aug. 15, 1925 (New York, N.Y.) U.S. actress. Sally Rogers on the TV series *The Dick Van Dyke Show*, 1961–66.
**ROSS, KATHARINE**, Jan. 29, 1943 (Hollywood, Calif.). U.S. actress. Films: *The Graduate*, 1967; *Tell Them Willie Boy Is Here*, 1969; *Butch Cassidy and the Sundance Kid*, 1969; *The Stepford Wives*, 1975.
**ROURKE, MICKEY**, 1956 (Miami, Fla.). U.S. actor. Films: *Body Heat*, 1981; *The Pope of Greenwich Village*, 1984; *9-½ Weeks*, 1986; *Angel Heart*, 1987; *Barfly*, 1987.
**ROWLANDS, GENA**, June 19, 1934 (Cambria, Wisc.). U.S. actress. Films: *Faces*, 1968; *Minnie and Moscowitz*, 1971; *A Woman under the Influence*, 1974; *Gloria*, 1980. (Wife of J. CASSAVETES.)
**RUGGLES, CHARLES**, 1886 (Los Angeles, Calif.)–Dec. 23, 1970. U.S. comedic character actor in over 100 films. Films: *Charley's Aunt*, 1930; *Love Me Tonight*, 1932; *Trouble in Paradise*, 1932; *Ruggles of Red Gap*, 1935; *Bringing Up Baby*, 1938.
**RUSH, BARBARA**, Jan. 4, 1930 (Denver, Colo.). U.S. actress. A leading lady in 1950s and 1960s films; starred in *Flamingo Road* TV series in 1980s.
**RUSSELL, JANE**, June 21, 1921 (Bemidji, Minn.). U.S. actress. A leading lady in 1940s–1950s films. Films: *The Outlaw*, 1940; *Gentlemen Prefer Blondes*, 1953.
**RUSSELL, KURT**, Mar. 7, 1951 (Springfield, Mass.). U.S. actor. Films: *The Absent-Minded Professor*,

1960; *Silkwood*, 1983; *Swing Shift*, 1984; *Tequila Sunrise*, 1988.

**RUSSELL, ROSALIND**, June 4, 1911 (Waterbury, Conn.)–Nov. 28, 1976. U.S. actress. Films: *Night Must Fall*, 1937; *The Citadel*, 1938; *The Women*, 1939; *His Girl Friday*, 1940; *My Sister Eileen*, 1942; *Sister Kenny*, 1946; *Picnic*, 1956; *Auntie Mame*, 1958; *Gypsy*, 1962.

**RUTTAN, SUSAN**, Sept. 16, 1950 (Oregon City, Ore.). U.S. actress. TV: *L.A. Law* (series), 1986– .

**RYAN, IRENE** (born Irene Riordan) 1903–Apr. 26, 1973. U.S. actress. Best known for her role as Granny in the TV series *The Beverly Hillbillies*, 1962–71.

**RYAN, ROBERT**, Nov. 11, 1909 (Chicago, Ill.)–July 11, 1973. U.S. actor. A leading man in films since the mid-1940s. Films: *Crossfire*, 1947; *The Set-Up*, 1949; *Clash By Night*, 1952; *Bad Day at Black Rock*, 1955; *God's Little Acre*, 1958; *Odds Against Tomorrow*, 1959; *Billy Budd*, 1962; *The Dirty Dozen*, 1967.

**SAINT, EVA MARIE**, July 4, 1924 (Newark, N.J.). U.S. actress. Films: *On the Waterfront* (Best Supporting Actress AA), 1954; *A Hatful of Rain*, 1957; *North by Northwest*, 1959; *Exodus*, 1960; *The Russians Are Coming...*, 1966.

**SAINT JAMES, SUSAN** (born Susan Miller), Aug. 14, 1946 (Los Angeles, Calif.). U.S. actress. Best known for TV series *The Name of the Game* (1967–71) and *McMillan and Wife* (1971–77); *Kate and Allie*, (1984– ).

**ST. JOHN, JILL** (born Jill Oppenheim), Aug. 19, 1940 (Los Angeles, Calif.). U.S. actress. Began career at age five, on radio. Starred in several 1960s films.

**SANDERS, GEORGE**, July 3, 1906 (St. Petersburg, Rus. [now Leningrad, USSR])–Apr. 25, 1972. U.S. actor. Films: *Rebecca*, 1940; *The Picture of Dorian Gray*, 1945; *Forever Amber*, 1947; *All about Eve* (Best Supporting Actor AA), 1950; *The Kremlin Letter*, 1970.

**SANFORD, ISABEL**, Aug. 29, 1917 (New York, N.Y.). U.S. actress. Best known for her role as Louise Jefferson on the TV series *The Jeffersons*, 1975–85.

**SARANDON, SUSAN**, Oct. 4, 1946 (New York, N.Y.). U.S. actress. Moved from television soap operas to films. Films: *Joe*, 1970; *The Rocky Horror Picture Show*, 1975; *Atlantic City*, 1981; *Compromising Positions*, 1985; *The Witches of Eastwick*, 1987; *Bull Durham*, 1988.

**SAVALAS, TELLY** (born Aristotle Savalas), Jan. 21, 1924. U.S. actor. Film and TV actor noted for his bald head; star of the TV series *Kojak*, 1973–78. Films: *The Battle of the Bulge*, 1965; *The Dirty Dozen*, 1967.

**SCHEIDER, ROY**, Nov. 10, 1932 (Orange, N.J.). U.S. actor. Films: *The French Connection*, 1971; *Jaws*, 1975; *Marathon Man*, 1976; *All That Jazz*, 1979; *Jaws II*, 1979; *Blue Thunder*, 1983; *2010*, 1984; *The Men's Club*, 1986.

**SCOTT, GEORGE C.**, Oct. 18, 1927 (Wise, Va.). U.S. actor, dir. Films: *Anatomy of a Murder*, 1959;

*The Hustler*, 1961; *The List of Adrian Messenger*, 1963; *Dr. Strangelove*, 1963; *Patton*, (Best Actor AA), 1970; *The Hospital*, 1972; *Hardcore*, 1979; *Taps*, 1982. (One-time husband of C. DEWHURST.)

**SCOTT, MARTHA**, Sept. 22, 1914 (Jamesport, Mo.). U.S. actress. Films: *Our Town*, 1940; *The Desperate Hours*, 1955; *The Ten Commandments*, 1956; *Ben Hur*, 1959; *Airport '75*, 1974.

**SCOTT, RANDOLPH** (born Randolph Crance), Jan. 23, 1898 (Orange County, Va.)–Mar. 2, 1987. U.S. actor. Films: *She*, 1935; *Last of the Mohicans*, 1936; *Virginia City*, 1940; *Western Union*, 1941; *Ride the High Country*, 1962.

**SCOURBY, ALEXANDER**, Nov. 13, 1913 (New York, N.Y.)–Feb. 22, 1985. U.S. stage and film character actor.

**SEGAL, GEORGE**, Feb. 13, 1934 (Great Neck, N.Y.). U.S. actor. Best known for comedy roles. Films: *King Rat*, 1965; *Who's Afraid of Virginia Woolf?*, 1966; *The Owl and the Pussycat*, 1970; *Where's Poppa?*, 1970; *A Touch of Class*, 1973; *Fun with Dick and Jane*, 1977; *Stick*, 1986.

**SELLECCA, CONNIE**, May 25, 1955 (New York, N.Y.). U.S. actress. TV: *The Greatest American Hero* (series), 1981–83; *Hotel* (series), 1983–88.

**SELLECK, TOM**, Jan. 29, 1945 (Detroit, Mich.). U.S. actor. From a successful TV series, *Magnum P.I.* (1980–88), has moved into films. Films: *Three Men and a Baby*, 1989.

**SHACKELFORD, TED**, June 23, 1946 (Oklahoma City, Okla.). U.S. actor. TV: *Knot's Landing*, 1980– .

**SHATNER, WILLIAM**, Mar. 22, 1931 (Montreal, Que., Can.). U.S. actor. Best known for his role as Capt. James Kirk in the TV series *Star Trek*, (1966–69) and the film series; also as star of the *T. J. Hooker* 1980s TV series.

**SHEARER, NORMA**, 1904 (Montreal, Que., Can.)–June 12, 1983. U.S. actress. A leading lady of 1930s films. Films: *The Trial of Mary Dugan*, 1929; *The Divorcee* (Best Actress AA), 1929; *Private Lives*, 1931; *Strange Interlude*, 1931; *The Barretts of Wimpole Street*, 1934; *Romeo and Juliet*, 1936; *The Women*, 1939. (Wife of I. THALBERG.)

**SHEEDY, ALLY**, June 12, 1962 (New York, N.Y.). U.S. actress. Films: *Bad Boys*, 1983; *War Games*, 1984; *St. Elmo's Fire*, 1985; *Maid to Order*, 1987. Books: *She Was Nice to Mice*, 1974.

**SHEEN, CHARLIE** (born Charles Estevez), 1966 (Santa Monica, Calif.). U.S. actor. Films: *Red Dawn*, 1984; *Platoon*, 1986; *Wall Street*, 1987. (Son of M. SHEEN; brother of E. ESTEVEZ.)

**SHEEN, MARTIN** (born Ramon Estevez), Aug. 3, 1940 (Dayton, Ohio). U.S. actor, social activist. Stage, film, TV career. Films: *The Subject Was Roses*, 1968; *Badlands*, 1973; *Apocalypse Now*, 1979; *Gandhi*, 1982; *Loophole*, 1986; *Wall Street*, 1987. (Father of C. SHEEN and E. ESTEVEZ.)

**SHEPHERD, CYBILL**, Feb. 18, 1950 (Memphis, Tenn.). U.S. actress, model. Films: *The Last Picture Show*, 1971; *The Heartbreak Kid*, 1972; *Taxi Driver*, 1976. TV: *Moonlighting* (series), 1985–89.

**SHERIDAN, ANN**. 1915 (Denton, Tex.)–Jan. 21,

1967. U.S. actress. Films: *Angels with Dirty Faces*, 1938; *They Drive By Night*, 1940; *King's Row*, 1941; *The Man Who Came to Dinner*, 1941; *Shine on Harvest Moon*, 1944; *Come Next Spring*, 1956.

**SHIELDS, BROOKE**, May 31, 1965 (New York, N.Y.). U.S. actress. A model, as Ivory Snow baby, at age 11 months. Films: *Pretty Baby*, 1978; *King of the Gypsies*, 1978; *Just You and Me Kid*, 1979; *The Blue Lagoon*, 1980.

**SHIRE, TALIA** (born Talia Coppola), Apr. 25, 1946 (Jamaica, N.Y.). U.S. actress. Best known for her role in *Rocky* film series. Other films: *Godfather—Part 1*, 1972; *Godfather—Part 2*, 1974. (Sister of F. F. COPPOLA.)

**SHORT, MARTIN**, Mar. 26, 1951 (Hamilton, Ont.). U.S. actor, comedian. TV: *SCTV Network 90* (series), 1982–84; *Saturday Night Live* (series), 1985–86. Films: *3 Amigos*, 1986; *Innerspace*, 1987.

**SIDNEY, SYLVIA** (born Sophia Koskow), Aug. 8, 1910 (New York, N.Y.). U.S. actress. Films: *Street Scene*, 1931; *An American Tragedy*, 1931; *You Only Live Once*, 1937; *Summer Wishes, Winter Dreams*, 1973; *I Never Promised You a Rose Garden*, 1978.

**SILVERS, PHIL**, May 11, 1912 (New York, N.Y.)–Nov. 1, 1985. U.S. comedic actor. Best known as star of the TV series *The Phil Silvers Show*, aka *You'll Never Get Rich*, 1955–59. Films: *You're in the Army Now*, 1942; *Cover Girl*, 1944; *It's a Mad, Mad, Mad, Mad World*, 1963; *A Funny Thing Happened on the Way to the Forum*, 1966.

**SKELTON, RED** (born Richard Skelton), July 18, 1910 (Vincennes, Ind.). U.S. comedian, actor. A master of pantomime and slapstick comedy. TV: *The Red Skelton Show*, 1951–71. Films: *Whistling in the Dark*, 1941; *Whistling in Dixie*, 1942; *DuBarry Was a Lady*, 1943; *Three Little Words*, 1950.

**SKERRITT, TOM**, Aug. 25, 1933 (Detroit, Mich.). U.S. actor. TV: *Cheers* (series), 1987–88. Films: *Alien*, 1979; *Top Gun*, 1986.

**SKINNER, CORNELIA OTIS**, May 30, 1901 (Chicago, Ill.)–July 9, 1979. U.S. actress, author. Best known for one-woman shows and monologues, 1925–61; cowrote and starred in the play *The Pleasure of His Company*, 1958. Books: *Our Hearts were Young and Gay*, 1942. (Daughter of O. SKINNER.)

**SKINNER, OTIS**, June 28, 1858 (Cambridge, Mass.)–Jan. 4, 1942. U.S. stage actor, producer, director. Played over 300 roles, directed over 30 plays in 60-year theatrical career. (Father of C. O. SKINNER.)

**SMIRNOFF, YAKOV**, Jan. 24, 1951 (Odessa, USSR). U.S. actor. Films: *Moscow on the Hudson*, 1984; *Brewster's Millions*, 1985; *Heartbeat*, 1986.

**SMITH, ALEXIS**, June 8, 1921 (Penticton, B.C., Can.). U.S. actress. Films: *Gentleman Jim*, 1942; *The Constant Nymph*, 1943; *Of Human Bondage*, 1946; *Any Number Can Play*, 1950; *Once Is Not Enough*, 1975. Plays: *Follies*, 1971.

**SMITH, ALLISON**, Dec. 12, 1969 (New York,

N.Y.). U.S. actress. TV: *Kate & Allie* (series), 1984–89.

**SMITH, JACLYN**, Oct. 26, 1948 (Houston, Tex.). U.S. model, actress. Best known for her role in the TV series *Charlie's Angels*, 1976–80.

**SMITS, JIMMY**, July 9, 1958 (New York, N.Y.). U.S. actor. TV: *L.A. Law* (series), 1986– . Films: *The Believers*, 1987.

**SOMERS, SUZANNE** (born Suzanne Mahoney), Oct. 16, 1946 (San Bruno, Calif.). U.S. actress. Star of the TV series *Three's Company*, 1977–81.

**SOMMER, ELKE** (born Elke Schletz), Nov. 5, 1940 (Berlin, Ger.). U.S. actress. Films: *The Prize*, 1963; *A Shot in the Dark*, 1964; *The Oscar*, 1966.

**SORVINO, PAUL**, 1939 (New York, N.Y.). U.S. actor. Films: *Bloodbrothers*, 1978; *Cruising*, 1980; *Reds*, 1981; *A Fine Mess*, 1986.

**SOTHERN, ANN** (born Harriette Lake), Jan. 22, 1909 (Valley City, N.D.). U.S comedic actress. Films: "Maisie" series, 1939–47; *A Letter to Three Wives*, 1949. TV: *Private Secretary* (series), 1953–57; *The Ann Sothern Show* (series), 1958–61.

**SOUL, DAVID** (born David Solberg), Aug. 28, 1943 (Chicago, Ill.). U.S. actor. Best known as star of the TV series *Starsky and Hutch*, 1975–80.

**SPACEK, SISSY** (born Mary Elizabeth Spacek), Dec. 25, 1949 (Quitman, Tex.). U.S. actress. A leading lady in 1970s films such as *Badlands* (1973), *Carrie* (1976), *Three Women* (1977), and *Welcome to L.A.* (1977); *Coal Miner's Daughter* (Best Actress AA), 1979; *Raggedy Man*, 1981; *Missing*, 1982; *The River*, 1984; *Crimes of the Heart*, 1986; *'Night, Mother*, 1986.

**STACK, ROBERT**, Jan. 13, 1919 (Los Angeles, Calif.). U.S. actor. Films: *Written on the Wind*, 1956; *John Paul Jones*, 1959. TV: *The Untouchables* (series), 1959–63; *The Name of the Game* (series), 1968–71.

**STALLONE, SYLVESTER**, July 6, 1946 (New York, N.Y.). U.S. actor, writer, director. Best known as star and creator of the "Rocky" film series, and as star of "Rambo" film series. Other films: *F.I.S.T.*, 1978; *Paradise Alley*, 1978; *Cobra*, 1986; *Over the Top*, 1987.

**STANLEY, KIM** (born Patricia Reid), Feb. 11, 1925 (Tularosa, N.M.). U.S. actress. Stage and film career. Films: *The Goddess*, 1958; *Seance on a Wet Afternoon*, 1964.

**STANWYCK, BARBARA** (born Ruby Stevens), July 16, 1907 (New York, N.Y.)–Jan. 20, 1990. U.S. actress. A leading lady, usually in dramatic roles, in films of the 1930s and 1940s. Films: *Annie Oakley*, 1935; *Stella Dallas*, 1937; *Golden Boy*, 1939; *The Lady Eve*, 1941; *Meet John Doe*, 1941; *Double Indemnity*, 1944; *The Strange Love of Martha Ivers*, 1946; *Sorry, Wrong Number*, 1948; *Executive Suite*, 1954. TV: *The Big Valley* (series), 1965–69. (One-time wife of ROBERT TAYLOR.)

**STAPLETON, JEAN** (born Jeanne Murray), Jan. 19, 1923 (New York, N.Y.). U.S. actress. After a long stage career, became widely known for her role as Edith Bunker on the TV series *All in the Family*, 1971–79.

**STAPLETON, MAUREEN,** June 21, 1925 (Troy, N.Y.). U.S. character actress. Stage and film career. Plays: *The Rose Tattoo* (Tony Award), 1951; *The Gingerbread Lady* (Tony Award), 1970. Films: *Lonely Hearts*, 1959; *Interiors*, 1978; *Reds* (Supporting Actress AA), 1981; *Cocoon*, 1985; *Sweet Lorraine*, 1987.

**STEENBURGEN, MARY,** 1953 (Little Rock, Ark.). U.S. actress. Films: *Goin' South*, 1978; *Time After Time*, 1979; *Melvin and Howard*, 1980 (best supporting actress AA); *Ragtime*, 1981; *A Midsummer Night's Sex Comedy*, 1982; *Cross Creek*, 1983.

**STEIGER, ROD,** Apr. 14, 1925 (W. Hampton, N.Y.). U.S. actor. Films: *On the Waterfront*, 1954; *The Harder They Fall*, 1956; *Al Capone*, 1958; *The Pawnbroker*, 1965; *In the Heat of the Night* (Best Actor AA), 1967; *The Chosen*, 1982.

**STERLING, JAN** (born Jane Sterling Adriance), Apr. 3, 1923 (New York, N.Y.). U.S. actress. Films: *Johnny Belinda*, 1948; *The High and the Mighty*, 1954.

**STEVENS, CONNIE** (born Concetta Ingolia), Aug. 8, 1938 (New York, N.Y.). U.S. singer, actress. Starred in the series *Hawaiian Eye*, 1959–63.

**STEVENS, STELLA** (born Estelle Egglestone), Oct. 1, 1936 (Yazoo City, Miss.). U.S. actress. Films: *Lil' Abner*, 1959; *The Courtship of Eddie's Father*, 1963.

**STEWART, JAMES,** May 20, 1908 (Indiana, Pa.). U.S. actor. A leading man, usually in comedic roles, in films since the mid 1930s. Films: *Seventh Heaven*, 1937; *You Can't Take It with You*, 1938; *Mr. Smith Goes to Washington*, 1939; *Destry Rides Again*, 1939; *The Shop around the Corner*, 1939; *Philadelphia Story* (Best Actor AA), 1940; *It's a Wonderful Life*, 1946; *Harvey*, 1950; *The Greatest Show on Earth*, 1951; *Rear Window*, 1954; *Vertigo*, 1958; *Anatomy of a Murder*, 1959; *The Man Who Shot Liberty Valance*, 1962; *Shenandoah*, 1965; *Airport '77*, 1977.

**STORM, GALE** (born Josephine Cottle), Apr. 5, 1922 (Bloomington, Tex.). U.S. actress. In films, 1930s–1950s; popular on TV in the 1950s.

**STRAIGHT, BEATRICE** (born Beatrice Whitney Dickerman), Aug. 2, 1918 (Old Westbury, N.Y.). U.S. actress. Distinguished Broadway career; won Best Supporting Actress AA for *Network*, 1976.

**STRASBERG, SUSAN,** May 22, 1938 (New York, N.Y.). U.S. actress. Created the title role in stage production of *The Diary of Anne Frank*, 1955. (Daughter of L. STRASBERG.)

**STRAUSS, PETER,** Feb. 20, 1947 (New York, N.Y.). U.S. actor. Best known for TV miniseries *Rich Man, Poor Man*, 1976. Films: *Soldier Blue*, 1971; *The Last Tycoon*, 1976.

**STREEP, MERYL,** June 22, 1949 (Summit, N.J.). U.S. actress. Much celebrated leading lady of the 1980s. Films: *Julia*, 1977; *The Deer Hunter* (best supp. actress AA), 1978; *Kramer vs. Kramer* (best supp. actress AA), 1979; *The French Lieutenant's*

*Woman*, 1981; *Sophie's Choice* (best actress AA), 1982; *Silkwood*, 1983; *Out of Africa*, 1985; *A Cry in the Dark*, 1988.

**STREISAND, BARBRA,** Apr. 24, 1942 (New York, N.Y.). U.S. actress, singer. Achieved Broadway stardom as Fanny Brice in *Funny Girl*, 1964 (Best Actress AA for film, 1968). Films: *Hello Dolly*, 1969; *The Owl and the Pussycat*, 1970; *What's Up, Doc?*, 1972; *The Way We Were*, 1973; *Funny Lady*, 1975; *A Star is Born*, 1977; *Nuts*, 1987. Record albums: *People*, 1965; *Color Me Barbra*, 1966; *Superman*, 1977; *Wet*, 1979.

**STRITCH, ELAINE,** Feb. 2, 1926 (Detroit, Mich.). U.S. actress, singer. Has had a long musical stage career.

**STRUTHERS, SALLY,** July 28, 1948 (Portland, Ore.). U.S. actress. Best known for her role as Gloria in the TV series *All in the Family*, 1971–78.

**SULLAVAN, MARGARET** (born Margaret Brooke), May 16, 1911 (Norfolk, Va.)–Jan. 1, 1960. U.S. actress. A Broadway star of the 1930s and 1940s. Films: *Only Yesterday*, 1933; *The Shopworm Angel*, 1938; *The Shop around the Corner*, 1940; *Back Street*, 1941. (One-time wife of H. FONDA, W. WYLER, L. HAYWARD.)

**SWANSON, GLORIA,** Mar. 17, 1899 (Chicago, Ill.)–Apr. 4, 1983. U.S. actress. Leading film box office draw, 1918–26. Films: *Male and Female*, 1919; *Sadie Thompson*, 1928; *Sunset Boulevard*, 1950; *The Killer Bees*, 1973; *Airport 1975*, 1974. Known for her interest in fashion and nutrition. (One-time wife of W. BEERY.)

**SWIT, LORETTA,** Nov. 4, 1937 (Passaic, N.J.). U.S. actress. Best known for her role as "Hot Lips" Houlihan in the TV series *M*A*S*H*, 1972–83.

**T, MR.** (born Lawrence Tero), May 21, 1952 (Chicago, Ill.). U.S. actor. TV: *The A-Team* (series), 1983–87.

**TALMADGE, NORMA,** 1893 (Brooklyn, N.Y.)–Dec. 24, 1957. U.S. actress. A silent-film heroine.

**TAMIROFF, AKIM,** 1899 (Russia)–Sept. 17, 1972. Russian-U.S. character actor in some 100 films. Films: *The General Died at Dawn*, 1936; *For Whom the Bell Tolls*, 1943.

**TAYLOR, ELIZABETH,** Feb. 27, 1932 (London, Eng.). English-U.S. actress. Glamorous leading lady of films; began as a child actress. Films: *National Velvet*, 1944; *Life with Father*, 1947; *Little Women*, 1949; *Father of the Bride*, 1950; *A Place in the Sun*, 1951; *Giant*, 1956; *Cat on a Hot Tin Roof*, 1958; *Butterfield 8* (Best Actress AA), 1960; *Cleopatra*, 1962; *Who's Afraid of Virginia Woolf?* (Best Actress AA), 1966; *A Little Night Music*, 1977.

**TAYLOR, ROBERT** (born Spangler Arlington Brugh), Aug. 5, 1911 (Filley, Neb.)–June 8, 1969. U.S. actor. Films: *Magnificent Obsession*, 1935; *Quo Vadis*, 1951; *Knights of the Round Table*, 1953; *The Glass Sphinx*, 1968. TV: *The Detectives* (series), 1959–62. (One-time husband of B. STANWYCK.)

**TAYLOR, ROD,** Jan. 11, 1929 (Sydney, Austrl.). U.S. actor. Films: *The Time Machine*, 1960; *The*

*Birds*, 1964; *V.I.P.'s*, 1964; *Sunday in New York*, 1966; *The Glass Bottom Boat*, 1966; *Hotel*, 1967.

**TEMPLE, SHIRLEY** (Mrs. Charles A. Black), Apr. 23, 1928 (Santa Monica, Calif.). U.S. actress, diplomat. A child film star. Films: *Stand Up and Cheer*, 1934; *Bright Eyes* (awarded special AA), 1934; *Wee Willie Winkie*, 1937; *Heidi*, 1937; *Rebecca of Sunnybrook Farm*, 1938; *Little Miss Broadway*, 1938; *The Blue Bird*, 1940; *Fort Apache*, 1948. TV: *Shirley Temple's Storybook* (series), 1959–61. U.S. rep. to the UN, 1969–70; U.S. amb. to Ghana, 1974–76; White House protocol chief, 1976–77; ambassador to Czechoslovakia, 1989– .

**THOMAS, DANNY** (born Amos Jacobs), Jan. 6, 1914 (Deerfield, Mich.). U.S. actor. Films: *Call Me Mister*, 1948; *Jazz Singer*, 1952. TV: *The Danny Thomas Show* (series), 1953–65, 70–71. Founder of St. Jude's Children's Research Hospital in Memphis, Tenn. (Father of M. THOMAS.)

**THOMAS, MARLO**, Nov. 21, 1943 (Detroit, Mich.). U.S. actress mostly in the theater. TV: *That Girl* (series), 1966–71; *Free to Be... You and Me* (Emmy award), 1974. (Daughter of D. THOMAS; wife of P. DONAHUE.)

**THOMAS, RICHARD**, June 13, 1951 (New York, N.Y.). U.S. actor. Best known for starring role in TV series *The Waltons*, 1972–79. Films: *Winning*, 1969; *Last Summer*, 1969.

**THOMPSON, SADA**, Sept. 27, 1929 (Des Moines, Ia.). U.S. actress mostly in the theater. Films: *Desperate Characters*, 1971. TV: *Family* (series), 1976–79.

**TIERNEY, GENE**, Nov. 20, 1920 (Brooklyn, N.Y.). U.S. actress. Films: *Tobacco Road*, 1941; *Belle Star*, 1941; *Son of Fury*, 1942; *Laura*, 1944; *Leave Her to Heaven*, 1945; *The Razor's Edge*, 1946; *The Ghost and Mrs. Muir*, 1947; *The Left Hand of God*, 1954.

**TOMLIN, LILY**, Sept. 1, 1939 (Detroit, Mich.). U.S. actress, comedienne. Rose to prominence in the TV series *Rowan and Martin's Laugh-In*, 1970–73; starred in several TV specials. Films: *Nashville*, 1975; *The Late Show*, 1977; *9 to 5*, 1980; *The Incredible Shrinking Woman*, 1981; *All of Me*, 1984. Records: *This Is a Recording, And That's the Truth, Modern Scream, On Stage*.

**TONE, FRANCHOT**, Feb. 27, 1905 (Niagara Falls, N.Y.)–Sept. 18, 1968. U.S. actor. Stage and film career. Films: *The Wiser Sex*, 1932; *They Gave Him a Gun*, 1937; *Five Graves to Cairo*, 1943; *Phantom Lady*, 1944; *Advise and Consent*, 1962.

**TORN, RIP** (born Elmore Torn, Jr.), Feb. 6, 1931 (Temple, Tex.). U.S. actor. Films: *The Cincinnati Kid*, 1965; *The Man Who Fell to Earth*, 1976; *City Heat*, 1984; *Extreme Prejudice*, 1987. (Husband of GERALDINE PAGE.)

**TRACY, LEE**, Apr. 14, 1898 (Atlanta, Ga.)–Oct. 18, 1968. U.S. actor. Films: *Dinner at Eight*, 1933; *The Lemon Drop Kid*, 1934; *The Best Man*, 1964.

**TRACY, SPENCER**, Apr. 5, 1900 (Milwaukee, Wisc.)–June 10, 1967. U.S. actor. A leading man in over 80 films, often with KATHARINE HEPBURN. Films: *Captains Courageous* (Best Actor AA), 1937;

*Boys' Town* (Best Actor AA), 1938; *Northwest Passage*, 1940; *Woman of the Year*, 1942; *Adam's Rib*, 1949; *Father of the Bride*, 1950; *Pat and Mike*, 1952; *Bad Day at Black Rock*, 1954; *The Old Man and the Sea*, 1958; *Judgement at Nuremberg*, 1961; *Guess Who's Coming to Dinner*, 1967.

**TRAVANTI, DANIEL J.**, Mar. 7, 1940 (Kenosha, Wisc.). U.S. actor. TV: *Hill Street Blues* (series), 1981–87.

**TRAVOLTA, JOHN**, Feb. 18, 1954 (Englewood, N.J.). U.S. actor. TV: *Welcome Back Kotter* (series), 1975–79. Films: *Carrie*, 1976; *Saturday Night Fever*, 1978; *Grease*, 1978; *Moment by Moment*, 1979; *Urban Cowboy*, 1980; *Blow Out*, 1982; *Staying Alive*, 1983.

**TREVOR, CLAIRE** (born Claire Wemlinger), Mar. 8, 1909 (New York, N.Y.). U.S. actress. Films: *Stagecoach*, 1939; *Murder, My Sweet*, 1944; *Key Largo* (Best Supporting Actress AA), 1948; *The High and the Mighty*, 1954; *How to Murder Your Wife*.

**TUCKER, FORREST**, Feb. 12, 1919 (Plainfield, Ind.)–Oct. 25, 1986. U.S. actor. Star of the TV series *F Troop*, 1965–67. Films: *The Yearling*, 1947; *Sands of Iwo Jima*, 1950; *The Night They Raided Minsky's*, 1968.

**TURNER, LANA**, Feb. 8, 1920 (Wallace, Idaho). U.S. actress. The original "sweater girl." Films: *Love Finds Andy Hardy*, 1938; *Ziegfeld Girl*, 1941; *Somewhere I'll Find You*, 1942; *The Postman Always Rings Twice*, 1945; *Weekend at the Waldorf*, 1947; *Cass Timberland*, 1947; *Peyton Place*, 1957; *Imitation of Life*, 1959.

**TURPIN, BEN**, Sept. 17, 1869 (New Orleans, La.)–July 1, 1940. U.S. comedic actor. Best known for his cross-eyed expression; in films, 1907–40.

**TYSON, CICELY**, Dec. 19, 1933 (New York, N.Y.). U.S. actress. Film and TV career; cofounder of the Dance Theatre of Harlem. Films: *Sounder*, 1972. TV: *The Autobiography of Miss Jane Pitman* (movie, Emmy award), 1973; *Roots* (miniseries), 1977.

**UECKER, BOB**, Jan. 26, 1935 (Milwaukee, Wis.). U.S. actor, baseball player. Played with the St. Louis Cardinals, Philadelphia Phillies, and Atlanta Braves. TV: *Mr. Belvedere* (series), 1985– .

**URICH, ROBERT**, Dec. 19, 1946 (Toronto, Ont.). Canadian actor. TV: *S.W.A.T.* (series), 1975–76; *Vega$* (series), 1978–81; *Spenser for Hire*, 1985– ; *Blind Faith*, 1990.

**VALENTINO, RUDOLPH**, May 6, 1895 (Castellaneta, It.)–Aug. 23, 1926. U.S. actor. Romantic idol of the 1920s. Films: *The Four Horsemen of the Apocalypse*, 1921; *The Sheik*, 1921; *Blood and Sand*, 1922; *Monsieur Beaucaire*, 1924; *The Eagle*, 1925; *The Son of the Sheik*, 1926.

**VAN ARK, JOAN**, June 16, 1943 (New York). U.S. actress. TV: *Dallas* (series), 1978–81; *Knots Landing* (series), 1979– .

**VANCE, VIVIAN**, July 26, 1911 (Cherryvale, Kan.)–Aug. 17, 1979. U.S. actress. Stage and TV career; best known for her role as Ethel Mertz on the TV series *I Love Lucy*, 1951–61.

**VAN CLEEF, LEE,** Jan. 9, 1925 (Somerville, N.J.)– Dec. 16, 1989. U.S. actor. Films: *For a Few Dollars More*, 1965; *The Good, the Bad and the Ugly*, 1966; *The Magnificent Seven Ride*, 1972.

**VAN DOREN, MAMIE** (born Joan Olander), Feb. 6, 1933 (Rowena, S.D.). U.S. actress. Best known for her appearances in "bombshell" roles in films of the 1950s and 1960s.

**VAN DYKE, DICK,** Dec. 13, 1925 (West Plains, Mo.). U.S. actor, singer, dancer. TV: *The Dick Van Dyke Show* (series), 1961–66; *The New Dick Van Dyke Show* (series), 1971–74. Films: *Mary Poppins*, 1964.

**VAN PATTEN, DICK,** Dec. 9, 1928 (New York, N.Y.). U.S. actor. Stage and TV career; best known for his role as Tom Bradford in the TV series *Eight is Enough*, 1977– .

**VAUGHN, ROBERT,** Nov. 22, 1932 (New York, N.Y.). U.S. actor. Best known for role as Napoleon Solo in the TV series *The Man from U.N.C.L.E.*, 1964–68.

**VIGODA, ABE,** Feb. 24, 1921 (New York, N.Y.). U.S. actor. Sad-faced character actor who gained fame as Fish on the *Barney Miller* and *Fish* TV series in the 1970s.

**VINCENT, JAN-MICHAEL,** July 15, 1944 (Denver, Col.). U.S. actor. Films: *The World's Greatest Athlete*, 1973; *Buster and Billie*, 1974; *Bite the Bullet*, 1974; *Baby Blue Marine*, 1976; *Big Wednesday*, 1978.

**VOIGHT, JON,** Dec. 29, 1938 (Yonkers, N.Y.). U.S. actor. Films: *Midnight Cowboy*, 1969; *Catch-22*, 1970; *Deliverance*, 1972; *Conrack*, 1974; *Coming Home* (Best Actor AA), 1978; *Runaway Train*, 1985; *Desert Bloom*, 1986.

**WAGNER, LINDSAY,** June 22, 1949 (Los Angeles, Calif.). U.S. actress. Star of the TV series *The Bionic Woman*, 1976–78. Films: *Two People*, 1972; *The Paper Chase*, 1973.

**WAGNER, ROBERT,** Feb. 10, 1930 (Detroit, Mich.). U.S. actor. TV: *It Takes a Thief* (series), 1968–70; *Switch* (series), 1975–78; *Hart to Hart*, 1979–84. Films: *All the Fine Young Cannibals*, 1959; *The Longest Day*, 1962; *The Towering Inferno*, 1976.

**WAITE, RALPH,** June 22, 1929 (White Plains, N.Y.). U.S. actor. Best known for his role as John Walton in the TV series *The Waltons*, 1972–80.

**WALKEN, CHRISTOPHER,** Mar. 31, 1943 (Astoria, N.Y.). U.S. actor. Films: *Annie Hall*, 1977; *The Deer Hunter*, 1978; *Heaven's Gate*, 1980; *Pennies From Heaven*, 1981; *A View to a Kill*, 1985; *Biloxi Blues*, 1988.

**WALKER, NANCY** (born Ann Myrtle Swoyer Barto), May 10, 1921 (Philadelphia, Pa.). U.S. actress. Plays: *Best Foot Forward*, 1941; *On the Town*, 1944; *Do-Re-Mi*, 1960. TV: *McMillan and Wife* (series), 1971–74; *Rhoda* (series), 1974-78.

**WALKER, ROBERT,** Oct. 13, 1914 (Utah)–Aug. 28, 1951. U.S. actor. Films: "Private Hargrove" series, 1940s; *One Touch of Venus*, 1948; *Strangers on a Train*, 1951.

**WALLACH, ELI,** Dec. 7, 1915 (New York, N.Y.). U.S. actor. Plays: *Rose Tattoo*, (Best Actor Tony), 1950; *Teahouse of the August Moon*, 1954. Films: *Magnificent Seven*, 1960; *The Tiger Makes Out*, 1967; *The Good, the Bad, and the Ugly*, 1967; *Cinderella Liberty*, 1974; *Tough Guys*, 1986. (Husband of A. JACKSON.)

**WALSTON, RAY,** Nov. 2, 1924 (Laurel, Miss.). U.S. actor. TV: *My Favorite Martian* (series), 1963–66. Films: *South Pacific*, 1958; *Damn Yankees*, 1958; *The Sting*, 1973.

**WALTER, JESSICA,** Jan. 31, 1944 (Brooklyn, N.Y.) U.S. actress. TV: *Bare Essence* (miniseries), 1983. Films: *The Group*, 1966; *Play Misty for Me*, 1971; *The Flamingo Kid*, 1984.

**WANAMAKER, SAM,** June 14, 1919 (Chicago, Ill.). U.S. actor. Films: *The Competition*, 1980; *The Aviator*, 1985; *Baby Boom*, 1987.

**WARDEN, JACK,** Sept. 18, 1920 (Newark, N.J.). U.S. actor. Starred in the TV series *N.Y.P.D.*, 1967–69; *Crazy Like a Fox*, 1985–86. Films: *From Here to Eternity*, 1953; *Twelve Angry Men*, 1957; *The Bachelor Party*, 1957; *Shampoo*, 1975; *All the President's Men*, 1976; *Heaven Can Wait*, 1978; *Being There*, 1979; *The Verdict*, 1982.

**WARREN, LESLEY ANN,** Aug. 16, 1946 (New York, N.Y.). U.S. actress. TV: *Family of Spies* (miniseries), 1990. Films: *Victor/Victoria*, 1982; *Clue*, 1985.

**WATERSTON, SAM,** Nov. 15, 1940 (Cambridge, Mass.). U.S. actor. Films: *The Great Gatsby*, 1974; *The Killing Fields*, 1984; *Hannah and Her Sisters*, 1986.

**WAYNE, DAVID** (born Wayne James McMeekan), Jan. 30, 1914 (Traverse City, Mich.). U.S. actor. Plays: *Finian's Rainbow*, 1947; *Mr. Roberts*, 1948; *Teahouse of the August Moon*, 1953. Films: *Adam's Rib*, 1949; *My Blue Heaven*, 1950; *The Last Angry Man*, 1959; *The Apple Dumpling Gang*, 1975.

**WAYNE, JOHN** (born Marion Morrison), May 26, 1907 (Winterset, Iowa)–June 11, 1979. U.S. actor. Known for leading roles in film westerns. Films: *Stagecoach* 1939; *Red River*, 1948; *Fort Apache*, 1948; *Sands of Iwo Jima*, 1949; *The Quiet Man*, 1952; *Rio Bravo*, 1959; *The Longest Day*, 1961; *The Sons of Katie Elder*, 1965; *True Grit* (Best Actor AA), 1968; *Rooster Cogburn*, 1975; *The Shootist*, 1976. Congressional Medal, 1979.

**WEAVER, DENNIS,** June 4, 1924 (Joplin, Mo.). U.S. actor. Best known for roles in the TV series *Gunsmoke* (1955–64) and *McCloud* (1970–77).

**WEAVER, FRITZ,** Jan. 19, 1926 (Pittsburgh, Pa.). U.S. actor mostly in the theater. Plays: *White Devil*, 1955; *A Shot in the Dark*, 1962.

**WEAVER, SIGOURNEY,** Oct. 8, 1949 (New York, N.Y.). U.S. actress. Films: *Alien*, 1979; *The Year of Living Dangerously*, 1983; *Ghostbusters*, 1984; *Gorillas in the Mist*, 1988; *Working Girl*, 1988.

**WEBB, CLIFTON** (born Webb Parmelee Hollenbeck), Nov. 19, 1896 (Indianapolis, Ind.)–Oct. 13, 1966. U.S. character actor. Films: *Laura*, 1944; *The Razor's Edge*, 1946; *Sitting Pretty*, 1947;

*Cheaper by the Dozen*, 1950; *Three Coins in the Fountain*, 1954

**WEBB, JACK,** Apr. 2, 1920 (Santa Monica, Calif.)– Dec. 22, 1982. U.S. actor, producer. Starred as Sgt. Joe Friday in the long-running TV series *Dragnet*; produced the TV series *Adam-12* (1968–75) and *Emergency* (1972–77).

**WELCH, RAQUEL** (born Raquel Tejada), Sept. 5, 1940 (Chicago, Ill). U.S. actress. A sex symbol of the 1960s–70s. Films: *Myra Breckenridge*, 1970; *Kansas City Bomber*, 1972; *The Three Musketeers*, 1974; *Mother, Jugs and Speed*, 1977.

**WELD, TUESDAY** (born Susan Ker Weld), Aug. 27, 1943 (New York, N.Y.). U.S. actress. Films: *The Five Pennies*, 1959; *Return to Peyton Place*, 1961; *Pretty Poison*, 1968; *I Walk the Line*, 1970; *Looking for Mr. Goodbar*, 1977; *Author! Author!*, 1982. (One-time wife of D. MOORE.)

**WEST, MAE,** Aug. 17, 1892 (Brooklyn, N.Y.). U.S. actress. Stage career, from 1897; a sex symbol in films since the early 1930s. Films: *She Done Him Wrong*, 1933; *I'm No Angel*, 1933; *Go West, Young Man*, 1936; *My Little Chickadee*, 1940; *Myra Breckenridge*, 1969.

**WESTON, JACK,** Aug. 21, 1924 (Cleveland, Ohio). U.S. actor. Films: *Please Don't Eat the Daisies*, 1960; *The Four Seasons*, 1981; *Dirty Dancing*, 1987.

**WHITE, BETTY,** Jan. 17, 1924 (Oak Park, Ill.). U.S. actress. Stage, film, TV career. TV: *The Mary Tyler Moore Show* (series), 1973–77; *The Betty White Show* (series), 1977–78; *Golden Girls*, 1985– .

**WHITE, PEARL,** Mar. 4, 1889 (Green Ridge, Mo.) –Aug. 4, 1938. U.S. actress. A silent-film star best known for her role in *The Perils of Pauline*, 1914.

**WHITMORE, JAMES,** Oct. 1, 1921 (White Plains, N.Y.). U.S. actor. Best known for stage impersonations of famous people. Plays: *Command Decision* (Tony award), 1947; *Will Rogers, USA*, 1973. Films: *Black like Me*, 1962; *Give 'em Hell, Harry* (film and play), 1975.

**WIDMARK, RICHARD,** Dec. 26, 1914 (Sunrise, Minn.). U.S. actor. Films: *Kiss of Death*, 1947; *Judgment at Nuremberg*, 1961; *How the West Was Won*, 1962; *Cheyenne Autumn*, 1963; *The Bedford Incident*, 1965; *Madigan*, 1968; *Murder on the Orient Express*, 1974.

**WIEST, DIANE,** Mar. 28, 1948 (Kansas City, Mo.). U.S. actress. Films: *Hannah and Her Sisters*, 1986; *Lost Boys*, 1987; *Parenthood*, 1989.

**WILDE, CORNEL,** Oct. 13, 1915 (New York, N.Y.)–Oct. 16, 1989. U.S. actor. Films: *A Song to Remember*, 1945; *The Bandit of Sherwood Forest*, 1946; *The Greatest Show on Earth*, 1952; *The Naked Prey*, 1966.

**WILDER, GENE** (born Jerry Silberman), June 11, 1935 (Milwaukee, Wisc.). U.S. comedic actor, writer, director. Films: *The Producers*, 1968; *Start the Revolution without Me*, 1969; *Willy Wonka and the Chocolate Factory*, 1971; *Blazing Saddles*, 1974; *Young Frankenstein*, 1974; *Silver Streak*, 1976;

*The Woman in Red*, 1976; *Haunted Honeymoon*, 1986. (Husband of G. RADNER.)

**WILLIAMS, BILLY DEE,** Apr. 6, 1937 (New York, N.Y.). U.S. actor. TV: *Brian's Song*, 1971. Films: *Lady Sings the Blues*, 1972; *The Empire Strikes Back*, 1980; *The Return of the Jedi*, 1983.

**WILLIAMS, CINDY,** Aug. 22, 1947 (Van Nuys, Calif.). U.S. actress. Best known for her role as Shirley in the TV series *Laverne and Shirley*, 1976–82.

**WILLIAMS, ESTHER,** Aug. 8, 1923 (Los Angeles, Calif.). U.S. actress. A former swimming champion. Films: *Bathing Beauty*, 1944; *Take Me Out to the Ball Game*, 1948; *Dangerous When Wet*, 1953.

**WILLIAMS, ROBIN,** July 21, 1952 (Chicago, Ill.). U.S. comedic actor. Star of the TV series *Mork and Mindy*, 1978–82. Films: *Popeye*, 1980; *The World According to Garp*, 1982; *Moscow on the Hudson*, 1984; *Good Morning, Vietnam*, 1988.

**WILLS, CHILL,** July 18, 1902 (Seagoville, Tex.)– Dec. 15, 1978. U.S. character actor. Best known as the voice of Francis the Talking Mule in the film series of the same name, 1940s–50s.

**WINDOM, WILLIAM,** Sept. 28, 1923 (New York, N.Y.). U.S. actor. Film and TV career; played lead roles in the TV series *The Farmer's Daughter* (1963–66) and *My World and Welcome to It* (1969–72).

**WINFIELD, PAUL,** May 22, 1941 (Los Angeles, Calif.). U.S. actor. A leading black film actor. Films: *The Lost Man*, 1969; *Sounder*, 1972; *Conrack*, 1974; *Damnation Alley*, 1977.

**WINGER, DEBRA,** May 16, 1955 (Cleveland, Oh.). U.S. actress. Films: *Urban Cowboy*, 1980; *An Officer and a Gentleman*, 1982; *Terms of Endearment*, 1983; *Legal Eagles*, 1986; *Black Widow*, 1987.

**WINKLER, HENRY,** Oct. 30, 1945 (New York, N.Y.). U.S. actor, producer. Best known for his role as "The Fonz" in the TV series *Happy Days*, 1973–84.

**WINNINGER, CHARLES,** May 26, 1884 (Athens, Wis.)–Jan. 27, 1969. U.S. character actor. Films: *Show Boat*, 1936; *Destry Rides Again*, 1939; *Ziegfeld Girl*, 1941; *State Fair*, 1945; *Give My Regards to Broadway*, 1948; *The Sun Shines Bright*, 1954.

**WINTERS, SHELLEY** (born Shirley Schrift), Aug. 18, 1922 (St. Louis, Mo.). U.S. actress. Films: *The Diary of Anne Frank* (Supporting Actress AA), 1958; *Lolita*, 1962; *Patch of Blue* (Supporting Actress AA), 1965; *Alfie*, 1965; *The Poseidon Adventure*, 1972; *Next Stop Greenwich Village*, 1976.

**WITHERS, JANE,** 1927 (Atlanta, Ga.). U.S. actress. A child star of the 1930s. Films: *Bright Eyes*, 1934; *Ginger*, 1935; *Giant*, 1956. Also known for TV commercials as Josephine the Plumber.

**WONG, ANNA MAY** (born Lu Tsong Wong), Jan. 3, 1907 (Los Angeles, Calif.)–Feb. 3, 1961. U.S. actress. Film career, 1919–60. Films: *Piccadilly*, 1929; *Chu Chin Chow*, 1933; *Java Head*, 1934.

**WOOD, NATALIE** (born Natasha Gurdin), July 20, 1938 (San Francisco, Calif.)–Nov. 29, 1981. U.S. actress. Films: *Miracle on 34th Street*, 1947; *Rebel without a Cause*, 1953; *West Side Story*, 1961; *Bob & Carol & Ted & Alice*, 1969.

WOODS, JAMES, Apr. 18, 1947 (Vernal, Ut.). U.S. actor. TV: *Promise*, 1986 (Emmy award); *My Name is Bill W*, 1989 (Emmy award). Films: *The Gambler*, 1974; *Night Moves*, 1975; *The Onion Field*, 1979; *Against All Odds*, 1984; *Salvador*, 1986; *True Believer*, 1989.

WOODWARD, JOANNE, Feb. 27, 1930 (Thomasville, Ga.). U.S. actress. Films: *Three Faces of Eve* (Best Actress AA), 1957; *Long Hot Summer*, 1958; *Rachel, Rachel*, 1968; *Summer Wishes, Winter Dreams*, 1973. (Wife of P. NEWMAN.)

WORTH, IRENE, June 23, 1916 (Nebraska). U.S. stage actress. Plays: *Toys in the Attic*, 1960; *Sweet Bird of Youth*, 1975; *The Cherry Orchard*, 1977.

WRAY, FAY, Sept. 10, 1907 (Alberta, Can.). U.S. actress. A leading lady in 1930s films; best known for her screams in *King Kong*, 1933.

WRIGHT, TERESA, Oct. 27, 1918 (New York, N.Y.). U.S. actress. Films: *The Little Foxes*, 1941; *Mrs. Miniver* (Best Supporting Actress AA), 1942; *Shadow of a Doubt*, 1943; *The Best Years of Our Lives*, 1946; *The Men*, 1950.

WYATT, JANE, Aug. 10, 1911 (Campgaw, N.J.). U.S. actress. TV: *Father Knows Best* (series), 1954–63. Films: *Lost Horizon*, 1934. Received Emmy awards in 1958, 1959, and 1960.

WYMAN, JANE (born Sarah Jane Fulks), Jan. 4, 1914 (St. Joseph, Mo.). U.S. actress. TV: *Falcon Crest*, 1981– . Films: *My Man Godfrey*, 1936; *The Lost Weekend*, 1945; *Johnny Belinda* (Best Actress AA), 1948; *The Magnificent Obsession*, 1954.

WYNN, ED (born Isaiah Edwin Leopold), 1886 (Philadelphia, Pa.)–June 19, 1966. U.S. comedic

actor. Vaudeville and stage star. Star of the radio show *The Texaco Fire Chief*. Films: *The Great Man*, 1956; *The Diary of Anne Frank*, 1959; *Mary Poppins*, 1964. (Father of K. WYNN.)

WYNN, KEENAN, July 27, 1916 (New York, N.Y.)–Oct. 14, 1986. U.S. actor. Best known for appearances in WALT DISNEY features, 1962–76. (Son of E. WYNN.)

YOUNG, ALAN (born Angus Young), Nov. 19, 1919 (North Shields, Eng.). U.S. actor. Star of the TV series *Mr. Ed*, 1961–65. Films: *Androcles and the Lion*, 1953; *The Time Machine*, 1959.

YOUNG, BURT, Aug. 21, 1927 (Philadelphia, Pa.). U.S. actor. Films: *Cinderella Liberty*, 1973; *Rocky II, III, and IV*, 1972, 1982, 1987.

YOUNG, GIG (born Byron Barr), Nov. 4, 1917 (St. Cloud, Minn.)–Oct. 19, 1978. U.S. actor. Films: *Come Fill the Cup*, 1951; *Teacher's Pet*, 1958; *They Shoot Horses, Don't They?* (Supporting Actor AA), 1969; *Lovers and Other Strangers*, 1970.

YOUNG, LORETTA (born Gretchen Young), Jan. 6, 1913 (Salt Lake City, Utah). U.S. actress. TV: *The Loretta Young Show* (series), 1953–61. Films: *The Story of Alexander Graham Bell*, 1939; *Along Came Jones*, 1946; *The Farmer's Daughter* (Best Actress AA), 1947; *Come to the Stable*, 1949.

YOUNG, ROBERT, Feb. 22, 1907 (Chicago, Ill.). U.S. actor. Starred in the TV series *Father Knows Best* (1954–63) and *Marcus Welby, M.D.* (1969–76).

ZIMBALIST, EFREM, JR., Nov. 30, 1923 (New York, N.Y.). U.S. actor. Starred in the TV series 77 *Sunset Strip* (1958–64) and *The F.B.I.* (1965–74). (Son of E. ZIMBALIST).

## FOREIGN ACTORS

AIMÉE, ANOUK (born Françoise Sorya), Apr. 27, 1932 (Paris, Fr.). French actress. Leading lady in films, *A Man and A Woman* (1966); *Justine* (1969); *A Man and a Woman: 20 Years Later* (1986).

ANDERSON, JUDITH (born Frances Margaret Anderson), Feb. 10, 1898 (Adelaide, Austrl.). Australian actress. Films: *Rebecca*, 1940; *Cat on a Hot Tin Roof*, 1958; *A Man Called Horse*, 1970.

ANDERSSON, BIBI, Nov. 11, 1935 (Stockholm, Swe.). Swedish actress. Success in INGMAR BERGMAN films led to international career. Films: *Wild Strawberries*, 1957; *The Kremlin Letter*, 1970.

ANDRESS, URSULA, 1936 (Switzerland). Swiss actress. Leading film sex symbol of the 1960s. Films: *She*, 1964; *What's New Pussycat?*, 1965; *The Clash of the Titans*, 1981.

ARLISS, GEORGE (born George Andrews), Apr. 10, 1868 (London, Eng.)–Feb. 5, 1946. English actor. After long stage career, became international star of historical films, including *Disraeli* (Best Actor AA), 1929.

ATTENBOROUGH, RICHARD, Aug. 29, 1923 (Cambridge, Eng.). English actor, producer, director. Films, actor: *Sand Pebbles*, 1966; Films, dir.: *Young Winston*, 1972; *A Bridge Too Far*, 1975;

*Gandhi* (Best Director AA), 1982; *A Chorus Line*, 1985; *Cry Freedom*, 1987.

AUMONT, JEAN-PIERRE (born Jean-Pierre Salomons), Jan. 5, 1911 (Paris, Fr.). French actor. Films: *Hotel du Nord*, 1938; *Lili*, 1953; *Day for Night*, 1973.

BAIN, CONRAD, Feb. 4, 1923 (Lethbridge, Alta., Can.). Canadian actor. Played supporting role in the TV series *Maude*, 1971–78; star of the TV series *Diff'rent Strokes*, 1978–86.

BARDOT, BRIGITTE (born Camille Javal) Aug. 28, 1934 (Paris, Fr.). French actress. Billed as "sex kitten." Films: *And God Created Woman*, 1956; *Please, Not Now*, 1961; *Love on a Pillow*, 1962; *Viva Maria*, 1965.

BARTHOLOMEW, FREDDIE (born Frederick Llewellyn), Mar. 28, 1924 (London, Eng.). English actor. Famed as Hollywood child actor. Films: *David Copperfield*, 1935; *Little Lord Fauntleroy*, 1936; *Kidnapped*, 1938; *Tom Brown's Schooldays*, 1940.

BATES, ALAN, Feb. 17, 1934 (Allestree, Eng.). English actor in theater and films. Films: *Zorba the Greek*, 1965; *Women in Love*, 1969; *An Unmarried Woman*, 1977.

BELMONDO, JEAN-PAUL, Apr. 9, 1933 (Neuillysur-Seine, Fr.). French actor. Off-beat French film lead. Films: *Breathless*, 1959; *That Man from Rio*, 1964; *Pierrot le Fou*, 1965; *The Mississippi Mermaid*, 1969; *Borsalino*, 1970; *Stavisky*, 1974.

**BERNHARDT, SARAH**, "The Divine Sarah," (born Henriette Rosine Bernard), Oct. 22/23, 1844 (Paris, Fr.)–Mar. 26, 1923. French actress. Revered stage tragedienne, world-renowned for dramatic life on- and off-stage; made nine U.S. tours.

**BLOOM, CLAIRE** (born Claire Blume), Feb. 15, 1931 (London, Eng.). English actress. Films: *Limelight*, 1952; *The Spy Who Came in from the Cold*, 1966.

**BOGARDE, DIRK** (born Derek van den Bogaerde), Mar. 28, 1920 (London, Eng.). English actor. Successful in comic, dramatic, and character roles. Films: *Quartet*, 1948; *A Tale of Two Cities*, 1958; *The Servant*, 1963; *Darling*, 1965; *The Damned*, 1969; *Death in Venice*, 1970.

**BOYD, STEPHEN** (born William Millar), July 4, 1928 (Belfast, N.Ire.)–June 2, 1977. Irish actor. Films: *Ben Hur* (as Messala), 1959; *The Fall of the Roman Empire*, 1964.

**BOYER, CHARLES**, Aug. 28, 1899 (Figeac, Fr.)–Aug. 26, 1978. French actor. Films: *History Is Made at Night*, 1937; *All This and Heaven Too*, 1940; *Gaslight*, 1944; *The Happy Time*, 1952; *Fanny*, 1962; *Barefoot in the Park*, 1968.

**BRAZZI, ROSSANO**, Sept. 18, 1916 (Bologna, It.). Italian actor. A romantic lead in films such as *Three Coins in the Fountain* (1954), *Summertime* (1955), and *South Pacific* (1958).

**BRUCE, NIGEL**, Feb. 4, 1895 (Mexico)–Oct. 8, 1953. British actor. In numerous films, often playing an amiable upper-class buffoon; played Dr. Watson in "Sherlock Holmes" film series.

**BUCHHOLZ, HORST**, Dec. 4, 1933 (Berlin, Ger.). German actor. Occasionally stars in U.S. films, including *The Magnificent Seven* (1960), *One, Two, Three* (1961), *Fanny* (1961), *The Pilot* (1979), and *Code Name: Emerald* (1985).

**BUJOLD, GENEVIEVE**, July 1, 1942 (Montreal, Que., Can.). French-Canadian actress. Films: *Anne of the Thousand Days*, 1970; *Obsession*, 1976.

**BURR, RAYMOND**, May 21, 1917 (New Westminster, B.C., Can.). Canadian actor. Best known for his starring roles in the TV series *Perry Mason* (1957–66)—TV Films in 1980s, and *Ironside* (1967–75); won Emmy awards in 1961 and 1962.

**BURTON, RICHARD** (born Richard Jenkins), Nov. 10, 1925 (Pontrhydfen, Wales.)–Aug. 5, 1984. Welsh actor. Known for his commanding dramatic presence and stentorian voice; played Hamlet, many other roles, with Old Vic Company, from 1953; greatest fame came with Broadway *Hamlet*, 1961. Musical: *Camelot*, 1960. Films: *The Robe*, 1953; *Look Back in Anger*, 1959; *Becket*, 1964; *Who's Afraid of Virginia Woolf?*, 1966; *Equus*, 1978.

**CAINE, MICHAEL** (born Maurice Micklewhite), Mar. 14, 1933 (London, Eng.). British actor. Films: *The Ipcress File*, 1965; *Alfie*, 1966; *Funeral in Berlin*, 1966; *Sleuth*, 1972; *Educating Rita*, 1983; *Half Moon Street*, 1986; *Hannah and Her Sisters* (Support Actor AA), 1986; *Sherlock and Me*, 1988; *Dirty Rotten Scoundrels*, 1988.

**CAMPBELL, MRS. PATRICK** (born Beatrice Stella Tanner), Feb. 9, 1865 (London, Eng.)–Apr. 9, 1940. British stage actress. G. B. SHAW created the role of Eliza Doolittle in *Pygmalion* for her.

**CARMICHAEL, IAN**, June 18, 1920 (Hull, Eng.). British actor. Leading man in light 1950s and 1960s films, including *I'm All Right, Jack* (1959); featured as Lord Peter Wimsey in the BBC-TV series of DOROTHY SAYERS's mysteries.

**CARON, LESLIE**, July 1, 1931 (Boulogne, Fr.). French actress, dancer. Films: *An American in Paris*, 1951; *Lili*, 1953; *Gigi*, 1958; *Fanny*, 1961; *The L-Shaped Room*, 1962.

**CARROLL, LEO G.**, 1892 (Weedon, Eng.)–Oct. 16, 1972. English character actor. Films: *Rebecca*, 1940; *Spellbound*, 1945; *North by Northwest*, 1959. TV: *Topper* (series), 1953–55; *The Man From U.N.C.L.E.* (series), 1964–67.

**CARSON, JACK**, 1910 (Canada)–Jan. 2, 1963. Canadian comedian, supporting actor. Films: *Stage Door*, 1937; *Mildred Pierce*, 1945; *A Star Is Born*, 1954.

**CHRISTIE, JULIE**, Apr. 14, 1940 (India). British actress. Films: *Billy Liar*, 1963; *Darling* (Best Actress AA), 1965; *Doctor Zhivago*, 1965; *McCabe and Mrs. Miller*, 1971; *Don't Look Now*, 1974; *Shampoo*, 1975.

**COLMAN, RONALD**, Feb. 9, 1891 (Richmond, Eng.)–May 19, 1958. British actor. A leading man in romantic-adventure films of the 1930s. Films: *Beau Geste*, 1926; *Arrowsmith*, 1931; *A Tale of Two Cities*, 1935; *Lost Horizon*, 1937; *The Prisoner of Zenda*, 1937; *A Double Life* (Best Actor AA), 1948.

**CONNERY, SEAN** (born Thomas Connery), Aug. 25, 1930 (Edinburgh, Scot.). Scottish actor. Best known for his role as James Bond in *Dr. No* (1962), *From Russia with Love* (1963), *Goldfinger* (1964), and other spy thrillers. Other films: *The Longest Day*, 1964; *The Anderson Tapes*, 1971; *The Man Who Would Be King*, 1976; *The Great Train Robbery*, 1979; *The Name of the Rose*, 1986; *The Untouchables* (Supporting Actor AA), 1987.

**COURTENAY, TOM**, Feb. 25, 1937 (Hull, Eng.). British actor. London stage career, from 1960. Films: *Billy Liar*, 1963; *The Loneliness of the Long Distance Runner*, 1963; *Doctor Zhivago*, 1965.

**CRISP, DONALD**, 1880 (Aberfeldy, Scotland)–May 26, 1974. British character actor. Films: *Wuthering Heights*, 1939; *How Green Was My Valley* (Supporting Actor AA), 1941; *National Velvet*, 1944.

**CRONYN, HUME** (born Hume Blake), July 18, 1911 (London, Ont., Can.). Canadian character actor. Best known for TV and stage appearances with wife JESSICA TANDY. Films: *Life Boat*, 1944; *Cocoon*, 1985; *Batteries Not Included*, 1987.

**DECARLO, YVONNE** (born Peggy Middleton), Sept. 1, 1922 (Vancouver, B.C., Can.). Canadian actress. Films: *Salome, Where She Danced*, 1945; *Song of Scheherezade*, 1947; *Casbah*, 1948. TV: *The Munsters* (series), 1964–66.

**DELON, ALAIN**, Nov. 8, 1935 (Sceaux, France).

French actor. Films: *Rocco and His Brothers*, 1960; *Is Paris Burning?*, 1966; *The Sicilian Clan*, 1970.

**DENEUVE, CATHERINE** (born Catherine De Dorleac), Oct. 22, 1943 (Paris, Fr.). French actress. Films: *Belle du Jour*, 1967; *April Fools*, 1968; *Hustle*, 1975; *March or Die*, 1977.

**DIETRICH, MARLENE** (born Maria Magdalena von Losch), Dec. 27, 1901 (Berlin, Ger.). German-U.S. actress, singer. Films: *The Blue Angel*, 1930; *Shanghai Express*, 1932; *Destry Rides Again*, 1939; *The Spoilers*, 1942; *A Foreign Affair*, 1948; *Witness for the Prosecution*, 1957; *Judgment at Nuremberg*, 1961. Received special Tony award, 1968.

**DONAT, ROBERT**, Mar. 18, 1905 (Manchester, Eng.)–June 9, 1958. English actor. Films: *The Count of Monte Cristo*, 1934; *The Ghost Goes West*, 1936; *The Citadel*, 1938; *Goodbye Mr. Chips* (Best Actor AA), 1939; *The Young Mr. Pitt*, 1942; *The Winslow Boy*, 1948.

**DONLEVY, BRIAN**, 1903 (Ireland)–Apr. 5, 1972. Irish actor. Films: *Barbary Coast*, 1935; *Beau Geste*, 1939; *Destry Rides Again*, 1939; *The Great McGinty*, 1940; *Two Years before the Mast*, 1944; *The Virginian*, 1945; *Kiss of Death*, 1947.

**DRESSLER, MARIE** (born Leila von Koerber), Nov. 9, 1869 (Coburg, Ont., Can.)–July 28, 1934. Canadian actress. Worked in silent films, then in 1930s comedies. Films: *Tillie's Punctured Romance*, 1915; *Anna Christie*, 1930; *Min and Bill* (Best Actress AA), 1930; *Tugboat Annie*, 1933; *Dinner at Eight*, 1933.

**DUSE, ELEANORA**, Oct. 3, 1858 (nr. Vigevano, It.)–Apr. 21, 1924. Italian stage actress of legendary emotional power. The great rival of SARAH BERNHARDT.

**EGGAR, SAMANTHA**, Mar. 5, 1939 (London, Eng.). British actress. Films: *The Collector*, 1965; *Doctor Doolittle*, 1967.

**EKLAND, BRITT**, Oct. 6, 1942 (Stockholm, Swe.). Swedish actress. Films: *After the Fox*, 1966; *The Night They Raided Minsky's*, 1969.

**EVANS, DAME EDITH**, Feb. 8, 1888 (London, Eng.)–Oct. 14, 1976. English stage and film actress. Known principally for stage appearances, especially Shakespearean roles.

**EVANS, MAURICE**, June 3, 1901 (Dorchester, Eng.). English actor. Distinguished career as producer/actor, Broadway, TV, films.

**FELDMAN, MARTY**, 1933 (London, Eng.)–Dec. 2, 1982. English comedic actor. Films: *Young Frankenstein*, 1974; *The Adventures of Sherlock Holmes' Smarter Brother*, 1976; *Silent Movie*, 1976; *Beau Geste*, 1977.

**FERRER, JOSÉ** (born José Vincente Ferrer y Centron), Jan. 8, 1912 (Santurce, P.R.). Puerto Rican actor, director, producer. Films: *Cyrano de Bergerac* (Best Actor AA), 1950; *Moulin Rouge*, 1952; *Miss Sadie Thompson*, 1953; *The Caine Mutiny*, 1954; *The Shrike*, 1955. Received Tony awards (as actor) in 1947 and 1952. (One-time husband of R. CLOONEY.)

**FINCH, PETER** (born William Mitchell), Sept. 28, 1916 (Kensington, Eng.)–Jan. 14, 1977. English actor. Films: *The Nun's Story*, 1959; *Far from the Madding Crowd*, 1967; *Sunday, Bloody Sunday*, 1971; *Network* (Best Actor AA), 1976.

**FINNEY, ALBERT**, May 8, 1936 (Salford, Eng.). English actor. Films: *Saturday Night and Sunday Morning*, 1960; *Tom Jones*, 1963; *Night Must Fall*, 1963; *Two for the Road*, 1967; *Charlie Bubbles*, 1968; *Murder on the Orient Express*, 1974; *Annie*, 1982.

**FITZGERALD, BARRY** (born William Joseph Shields), Mar. 10, 1888 (Dublin, Ire.)–Jan. 4, 1961. Irish character actor. Films: *The Plough and the Stars*, 1936; *The Long Voyage Home*, 1940; *How Green Was My Valley*, 1941; *Going My Way* (Best Supporting Actor AA), 1944; *And Then There Were None*, 1945; *The Naked City*, 1948; *The Quiet Man*, 1952.

**FITZGERALD, GERALDINE**, Nov. 24, 1913 (Dublin, Ire.). Irish actress. Films: *Dark Victory*, 1939; *Wuthering Heights*, 1939; *Wilson*, 1944; *The Pawnbroker*, 1965.

**FOCH, NINA**, Apr. 20, 1924 (Leyden, Neth.). Dutch actress who appeared in films of the 1940s and 1950s.

**FONTANNE, LYNN**, Dec. 6, 1887 (London, Eng.)–July 30, 1983. English–U.S. actress. Made London debut in 1909, New York debut in 1910. With husband, ALFRED LUNT, most famous couple in American theater. Costarred with husband in numerous plays, including *The Guardsman*, *Design for Living*, *The Taming of the Shrew*, *There Shall Be No Night*, *The Visit*.

**FOX, MICHAEL J.**, June 9, 1961 (Edmonton, Alta.). Canadian actor. TV: *Family Ties*, 1982–89. Films: *Back to the Future*, 1985; *Teen Wolf*, 1985; *Bright Lights, Big City*, 1988; *Back to the Future, Pt. 2*, 1989; *Casualties of War*, 1989.

**GARBO, GRETA** (born Greta Lovisa Gustafsson), Sept. 18, 1905 (Stockholm, Swe.)–Apr. 15, 1990. Swedish actress. Famed for her matchless beauty and reclusive personality. Films: *The Torrent*, 1926; *Flesh and the Devil*, 1927; *Anna Christie*, 1930; *Grand Hotel*, 1932; *Queen Christina*, 1933; *Anna Karenina*, 1935; *Camille*, 1936; *Ninotchka*, 1939; received special AA, for her "unforgettable screen performances," 1954.

**GARSON, GREER**, Sept. 29, 1908 (County Down, Ire.). Irish actress. Films: *Pride and Prejudice*, 1940; *Mrs. Miniver* (Best Actress AA), 1942; *Random Harvest*, 1942; *Madam Curie*, 1943; *Mrs. Parking ton*, 1944; *That Forsyte Woman*, 1949; *Sunrise at Campobello*, 1960.

**GIANNINI, GIANCARLO**, Aug. 1, 1942 (Spezia, It.). Italian actor. Films: *The Seduction of Mimi*, 1972; *Love and Anarchy*, 1973; *Swept Away*, 1975; *Seven Beauties*, 1976.

**GIELGUD, SIR JOHN**, Apr. 14, 1904 (London, Eng.). British actor, director. Long, distinguished career, particularly as Shakespearean actor; gained first fame as Hamlet with Old Vic Co., 1929; greatest early success was in the title role in *Richard II*, which he also directed. Films: *Julius Caesar*,

1953; *Becket*, 1964; *Murder on the Orient Express*, 1974; *The Elephant Man*, 1980; *Arthur* (Supporting Actor AA), 1981; *Gandhi*, 1982; *The Shooting Party*, 1984.

**GINGOLD, HERMIONE**, Dec. 12, 1897 (London, Eng.)–May 24, 1987. English actress. Films: *The Pickwick Papers*, 1952; *Gigi*, 1958; *The Music Man*, 1961.

**GRANGER, STEWART** (born James Stewart), May 6, 1913 (London, Eng.). British actor. Films: *Captain Boycott*, 1947; *King Solomon's Mines*, 1950; *Scaramouche*, 1952; *Beau Brummell*, 1954.

**GRANT, CARY** (born Archibald Leach), Jan. 18, 1904 (Bristol, Eng.)–Nov. 29, 1986. English actor. Peerless light-comedy actor, a film star since the mid-1930s. Films: *The Awful Truth*, 1937; *Bringing Up Baby*, 1938; *Gunga Din*, 1939; *My Favorite Wife*, 1940; *The Philadelphia Story*, 1940; *Suspicion*, 1941; *Arsenic and Old Lace*, 1944; *Night and Day*, 1945; *To Catch a Thief*, 1955; *An Affair to Remember*, 1957; *Houseboat*, 1958; *North by Northwest*, 1959; *Charade*, 1963; *Walk Don't Run*, 1966. Received special AA, 1969.

**GREENSTREET, SYDNEY**, Dec. 27, 1879 (Kent. Eng.)–Jan. 18, 1954. English actor. After a career on stage, became a film star at age 62. Films: *The Maltese Falcon*, 1941; *Across the Pacific*, 1942; *Casablanca*, 1942; *Passage to Marseilles*, 1944; *The Mask of Dimitrios*, 1944; *Three Strangers*, 1946; *The Hucksters*, 1947.

**GRIFFITH, HUGH**, May 30, 1912 (Wales)–May 14, 1980. Welsh actor noted for his flamboyant acting style. Films: *The Titfield Thunderbolt*, 1953; *Lucky Jim*, 1957; *Ben Hur* (Best Supporting Actor AA), 1959; *Tom Jones*, 1963.

**GUINNESS, SIR ALEC**, Apr. 2, 1914 (London, Eng.). English actor. On stage since 1934; knighted, 1959. Films: *Oliver Twist*, 1948; *Kind Hearts and Coronets*, 1949; *The Lavender Hill Mob*, 1951; *The Man in the White Suit*, 1951; *Father Brown*, 1954; *The Bridge on the River Kwai* (Best Actor AA), 1957; *Our Man in Havana*, 1959; *Tunes of Glory*, 1960; *Lawrence of Arabia*, 1962; *Hotel Paradiso*, 1966; *The Comedians*, 1967; *Scrooge*, 1970; *Star Wars*, 1977; *Return of the Jedi*, 1983; *A Passage to India*, 1984; *Little Dorrit*, 1987.

**GUTHRIE, TYRONE**, July 2, 1900 (Tunbridge Wells, Eng.)–May 15, 1971. English theater director. Influenced 20th-cent. revival of interest in traditional theater.

**GWENN, EDMUND**, Sept. 26, 1875 (London, Eng.)–Sept. 6, 1959. English actor. Films: *Pride and Prejudice*, 1940; *Lassie Come Home*, 1943; *Miracle on 34th Street* (Best Supporting Actor AA), 1946; *Pretty Baby*, 1950; *Them!*, 1954; *The Trouble with Harry*, 1955.

**HAGEN, UTA**, June 12, 1919 (Gottingen, Ger.). German actress, teacher. Has had a long and distinguished stage career; received Tony award, for *Who's Afraid of Virginia Woolf?*, 1963.

**HAMPSHIRE, SUSAN**, May 12, 1938 (London, Eng.). English actress. Star of BBC-TV series *The Forsyte Saga* (1967), and *The Pallisers* (1977).

**HARDWICKE, SIR CEDRIC**, Feb. 19, 1893 (Worcestershire, Eng.)–Aug. 6, 1964. British actor. A stage actor, he settled in Hollywood, from 1926. Films: *King Solomon's Mines*, 1937; *On Borrowed Time*, 1939; *Stanley and Livingstone*, 1939; *Tom Brown's Schooldays*, 1940; *Nicolas Nickleby*, 1947; *Richard III*, 1955.

**HARRIS, RICHARD**, Oct. 1, 1933 (County Limerick, Ire.). Irish actor. Films: *Mutiny on the Bounty*, 1962; *This Sporting Life*, 1963; *Camelot*, 1967; *The Molly Maguires*, 1969; *A Man Called Horse*, 1969.

**HARRISON, REX** (born Reginald Carey), Mar. 5, 1908 (Huyton, Eng.)–June 1, 1990. English stage and film actor. Starred on Broadway in *My Fair Lady* (1956). Films: *Major Barbara*, 1940; *Blithe Spirit*, 1945; *Anna and the King of Siam*, 1946; *The Foxes of Harrow*, 1947; *The Reluctant Debutante*, 1958; *Midnight Lace*, 1960; *Cleopatra*, 1962; *My Fair Lady* (Best Actor AA), 1964; *The Agony and the Ecstasy*, 1965; *Dr. Dolittle*, 1967.

**HARVEY, LAURENCE** (born Larushka Mischa Skikne), Oct. 1, 1928 (Joniskis, Lithuania)–Nov. 25, 1973. Lithuanian-British actor. Films: *Room at the Top*, 1959; *Expresso Bongo*, 1959; *Butterfield 8*, 1961; *A Walk on the Wild Side*, 1962; *The Manchurian Candidate*, 1962; *Darling*, 1965; *A Dandy in Aspic*, 1968.

**HAWKINS, JACK**, Sept. 14, 1910 (London, Eng.)–July 18, 1973. English actor. Films: *The Fallen Idol*, 1948; *The Cruel Sea*, 1952; *The Bridge on the River Kwai*, 1957; *Gideon's Day*, 1958; *Lawrence of Arabia*, 1962; *Young Winston*, 1972.

**HAYAKAWA, SESSUE**, 1890 (Chiba, Jap.)–Nov. 23, 1973. Japanese actor. A silent-film star who later played character roles; best known for role in the film *The Bridge on the River Kwai*, 1957.

**HEMMINGS, DAVID**, Nov. 18, 1941 (Guilford, Eng.). English actor. Films: *Blow Up*, 1966; *The Charge of the Light Brigade*, 1968; *Barbarella*, 1968; *The Love Machine*, 1971.

**HENREID, PAUL** (born Paul von Hernried), Jan. 10, 1908 (Trieste, A.-H. [now Italy]). Austrian actor. Films: *Now, Voyager*, 1942; *Casablanca*, 1942; *The Spanish Main*, 1945; *Of Human Bondage*, 1946.

**HILLER, WENDY**, Aug. 15, 1912 (Stockport, Eng.). English actress. Films: *Pygmalion*, 1938; *Major Barbara*, 1940; *Separate Tables*, 1958; *Sons and Lovers*, 1960; *A Man for All Seasons*, 1966; *The Elephant Man*, 1981.

**HOGAN, PAUL**, 1941 (Lightning Ridge, New South Wales, Austrl.). Australian actor. Films: *"Crocodile" Dundee*, 1986; *"Crocodile" Dundee II*, 1988.

**HOMOLKA, OSCAR**, Oct. 12, 1898 (Vienna, Austria)–Jan. 27, 1978. Austrian character actor. Films: *Rhodes of Africa*, 1936; *Sabotage*, 1937; *I Remember Mama*, 1948; *War and Peace*, 1956.

**HOPKINS, ANTHONY**, Dec. 31, 1937 (Port Talbot, Wales). Welsh actor. Films: *Young Winston*, 1972; *Audrey Rose*, 1977; *Magic*, 1978; *The Good Father*, 1987; *84 Charing Cross Road*, 1988. TV:

*War and Peace* (BBC series), 1972; Emmy award for "The Lindbergh Kidnapping Case," 1976.
HOSKINS, BOB, Oct. 26, 1942 (Suffolk, Eng.). British actor. Films: *The Long Good Friday*, 1981; *The Cotton Club*, 1985; *Brazil*, 1985; *Sweet Liberty*, 1986; *Mona Lisa*, 1986; *Who Framed Roger Rabbit?*, 1988.
HOWARD, LESLIE (born Leslie Stainer), Apr. 3, 1893 (London, Eng.)–June 1, 1943. English actor. Films: *Berkeley Square*, 1933; *The Scarlet Pimpernel*, 1935; *The Petrified Forest*, 1936; *Pygmalion*, 1938; *Gone with the Wind*, 1939; *Intermezzo*, 1939.
HOWARD, TREVOR, Aug. 29, 1916 (Kent, Eng.)–Jan. 7, 1988. English actor. Films: *Brief Encounter*, 1946; *The Third Man*, 1949; *The Heart of the Matter*, 1953; *Sons and Lovers*, 1960; *Mutiny on the Bounty*, 1962; *Von Ryan's Express*, 1965; *Ryan's Daughter*, 1970.
HUSTON, WALTER (born Walter Houghston), Apr. 6, 1884 (Toronto, Ont., Can.)–Apr. 7, 1950. Canadian character actor. Introduced "September Song," on stage, 1950. Films: *Rain*, 1932; *Dodsworth*, 1936; *Yankee Doodle Dandy*, 1942; *Mission to Moscow*, 1942; *The Treasure of Sierra Madre* (Best Supporting Actor AA), 1947. (Father of J. HUSTON.)
HYDE-WHITE, WILFRED, May 12, 1903 (Gloucester, Eng.). English character actor in numerous films since 1936.
IRELAND, JILL, Apr. 24, 1936 (London, Eng.)-May 18, 1990. British actress, dancer. Films: *Hard Times*, 1975. Books: *Life Wish*, 1987.
IRELAND, JOHN, Jan 30, 1914 (Vancouver, B.C., Can.). Canadian film actor. Best known for his role in the film *All the King's Men*, 1949.
IRVING, SIR HENRY (born John Henry Brodribb), Feb. 6, 1838 (Somerset, Eng.)–Oct. 13, 1905. English actor. First English actor ever knighted.
JACKSON, GLENDA, May 9, 1938 (Liverpool, Eng.). English actress. Films: *Women in Love* (Best Actress AA), 1970; *Sunday, Bloody Sunday*, 1971; *Mary, Queen of Scots*, 1971; *A Touch of Class* (Best Actress AA), 1973; *Nasty Habits*, 1976; *Stevie*, 1978; *Hopscotch*, 1980; *Turtle Diary*, 1986.
JACOBI, DEREK, Oct. 22, 1938 (London, Eng.). British actor. Stage: *Much Ado About Nothing*, 1985 (Tony award); *Breaking the Code*, 1987. TV: *I Claudius*, ?. Films: *Little Dorrit*, 1987.
JANNINGS, EMIL (born Theodor Emil Janenz), July 23, 1886 (Brooklyn, N.Y.)–Jan. 2, 1950. German-U.S. actor. Films: *The Way of All Flesh* (first Best Actor AA), 1928; *The Blue Angel*, 1930.
JOHNS, GLYNIS, Oct. 5, 1923 (Durban, S. Africa). S. African stage and film actress. Films: *Perfect Strangers*, 1945; *The Court Jester*, 1956; *The Chapman Report*, 1962.
JOURDAN, LOUIS (born Louis Gendre), June 19, 1919 (Marseilles, Fr.). French actor. U.S. and European film career, including *Three Coins in the Fountain* (1954), *Gigi* (1958), and *Can-Can* (1960).
KARLOFF, BORIS (born William Henry Pratt), Nov. 23, 1887 (London, Eng.)–Feb. 3, 1969. English actor. Best known for horror-film roles. Films: *Frankenstein* (as the monster), 1931; *The Mummy*, 1932; *Tower of London*, 1939; *The Body Snatcher*, 1945.
KELLAWAY, CECIL, Aug. 22, 1894 (Capetown, S. Africa)–Feb. 28, 1973. English character actor. Films: *I Married a Witch*, 1942; *Portrait of Jennie*, 1948; *Harvey*, 1950; *Guess Who's Coming to Dinner?*, 1967.
KERR, DEBORAH (born Deborah Kerr-Trimmer), Aug. 30, 1921 (Helensburgh, Scot.). Scottish actress. Films: *The Hucksters*, 1947; *Quo Vadis*, 1951; *From Here to Eternity*, 1953; *The King and I*, 1956; *Tea and Sympathy*, 1956; *An Affair to Remember*, 1957; *Separate Tables*, 1958; *The Sundowners*, 1960; *The Innocents*, 1961; *The Night of the Iguana*, 1964.
KINGSLEY, BEN (born Krishna Banji), Dec. 31, 1943 (Scarborough, Eng.). British actor. Films: *Gandhi*, 1981 (Best Actor AA); *Betrayal*, 1982; *Turtle Diary*, 1985; *Weisenthal, Murderers Among Us*, 1988.
KIDDER, MARGOT, Oct. 17, 1948 (Yellowknife, B.C.). Canadian actress. Films: *Superman*, 1978; *The Amityville Horror*, 1979; *Superman 2*, 1980; *Willie and Phil*, 1980; *Superman 3*, 1983; *Superman 4*, 1985.
KINSKI, KLAUS, Oct. 8, 1926 (Danzig, Pol.). German actor. International character actor. Films: *Dr. Zhivago*, 1965; *Aguirre: Wrath of God*, 1972; *Fitzcarraldo*, 1983; *The Little Drummer Girl*, 1984. (Father of N. KINSKI.)
KINSKI, NASTASSIA, Jan. 24, 1959 (Berlin, Ger.). German actress. Films: *One From the Heart*, 1982; *Cat People*, 1982. (Daughter of K. KINSKI.)
LANCHESTER, ELSA (born Elizabeth Sullivan), Oct. 28, 1902 (London, Eng.)–Dec. 26, 1987. English character actress. Films: *The Bride of Frankenstein*, 1935; *Rembrandt*, 1937; *Witness for the Prosecution*, 1957.
LANGTRY, LILLIE (born Emilie Charlotte Le Breton), Oct. 13, 1853 (Isle of Jersey, G.B.)–Feb. 12, 1929. British actress. First society woman to go on stage, 1881; made U.S. tours.
LAUGHTON, CHARLES, July 1, 1899 (Scarborough, Eng.)–Dec. 15, 1962. English actor. One of the great dramatic actors in film history. Films: *The Sign of the Cross*, 1932; *The Private Life of Henry VIII* (Best Actor AA), 1933; *Les Miserables*, 1935; *Mutiny on the Bounty*, 1935; *The Hunchback of Notre Dame*, 1939; *The Canterville Ghost*, 1944; *The Paradine Case*, 1948; *Witness for the Prosecution*, 1957.
LAWFORD, PETER, Sept. 7, 1923 (London, Eng.)–Dec. 24, 1984. English actor. Films: *Easter Parade*, 1948; *Little Women*, 1949; *Royal Wedding*, 1952. TV: *Dear Phoebe* (series), 1954–56; *The Thin Man* (series), 1957–59.
LAWRENCE, GERTRUDE (born Alexandra Dagmar Lawrence-Klasen), July 4, 1898 (London, Eng.) –Sept. 6, 1952. British actress, revue star. Associated with NOEL COWARD.
LEGALLIENNE, EVA, Jan. 11, 1899 (London,

Eng.). English actress. Founder (1926), director of New York's Civic Repertory Theater; cofounder (1946) of American Repertory Theater; appeared on London and N.Y. stage, from 1915; won a special Tony award, 1964.

LEIGH, VIVIEN (born Vivien Hartley), Nov. 5, 1913 (Darjeeling, India)–July 8, 1967. English film and stage actress. Best known for her AA-winning performance as Scarlett O'Hara in the film *Gone with the Wind* (1939). Films: *A Yank at Oxford*, 1938; *Lady Hamilton*, 1941; *Anna Karenina*, 1948; *A Streetcar Named Desire* (Best Actress AA), 1951; *The Roman Spring of Mrs. Stone*, 1961; *Ship of Fools*, 1965.

LEIGHTON, MARGARET, Feb. 26, 1922 (Barnet Green, Eng.)–Jan. 14, 1976. British actress. Received 2 Tony awards. Films: *The Waltz of the Toreadors*, 1961; *The Go-Between*, 1970; *Lady Caroline Lamb*, 1972.

LEWIS, DANIEL DAY, 1958 (England). British actor. Films: *A Room with a View*, 1985; *My Beautiful Launderette*, 1985; *The Unbearable Lightness of Being*, 1988; *My Left Foot*, 1989 (Best Actor AA).

LOLLOBRIGIDA, GINA, July 4, 1928 (Subiaco, It.). Italian actress. Films: *Bread, Love and Dreams*, 1953; *Trapeze*, 1956; *Solomon and Sheba*, 1959; *Buona Sera, Mrs. Campbell*, 1968.

LOM, HERBERT, Jan. 9, 1917 (Prague, Czech.). Czech-British actor. Portrayed Inspector Dreyfus in *The Pink Panther* film series.

LOREN, SOPHIA (born Sophia Scicoloni), Sept. 20, 1934 (Rome, It.). Italian actress. Known for her beauty and powerful dramatic performances. Films: *Boy on a Dolphin*, 1957; *Houseboat*, 1958; *Two Women* (Best Actress AA), 1961; *Yesterday, Today and Tomorrow*, 1963; *Marriage Italian Style*, 1964; *Lady L.*, 1966; *A Special Day*, 1977. Autobiography: *Sophia*, 1979.

LORRE, PETER (born Laszlo Loewenstein), June 26, 1904 (Rosenberg, Hung.)–Mar. 23, 1964. Hungarian character actor. Films: *M*, 1931; "Mr. Moto" series, 1930s; *The Maltese Falcon*, 1941; *Casablanca*, 1942; *The Mask of Dimitrios*, 1944; *The Beast with Five Fingers*, 1946.

LUPINO, IDA, Feb. 4, 1918 (London, Eng.). British actress, director, producer. Films: *They Drive by Night*, 1940; *High Sierra*, 1941; *Devotion*, 1946; *Roadhouse*, 1948.

MACNEE, PATRICK, Feb. 6, 1922 (London, Eng.). British actor. Films: *The Avengers* (series), 1960–64. Films: *The Howling*, 1980; *A View to a Kill*, 1985.

MAGNANI, ANNA, Mar. 7, 1908 (Alexandria, Egypt)–Sept. 26, 1973. Italian actress. Films: *The Open City*, 1945; *The Rose Tattoo* (Best Actress AA), 1955.

MANDEL, HOWIE, Nov. 29, 19? (Toronto, Ont.). Canadian actor. TV: *St. Elsewhere*, 1982–88.

MARCEAU, MARCEL, Mar. 22, 1923 (Strasbourg, Fr.). French mime. Best known mime of his age; created the character Bip, a white-faced clown.

MARSH, JEAN, July 1, 1934 (London, Eng.). English actress, writer. Best known for creating and starring in BBC and PBS TV series *Upstairs/Downstairs*, 1975–76; received Emmy award, 1975.

MARSHALL, HERBERT, May 23, 1890 (London, Eng.)–Jan. 22, 1966. British actor. Films: *Angel*, 1937; *Foreign Correspondent*, 1940; *The Letter*, 1940; *The Little Foxes*, 1941; *The Moon and Sixpence*, 1942; *Stage Struck*, 1957.

MASON, JAMES, May 15, 1909 (Huddersfield, Eng.)–July 27, 1984. English actor. Films: *The Seventh Veil*, 1945; *The Desert Fox*, 1951; *20,000 Leagues under the Sea*, 1954; *A Star is Born*, 1954; *Journey to the Center of the Earth*, 1959; *Lolita*, 1962; *Heaven Can Wait*, 1978; *The Boys from Brazil*, 1978; *The Verdict*, 1982.

MASTROIANNI, MARCELLO, Sept. 28, 1924 (Fontane Liri, It.). Italian actor. A romantic leading man in Italian films. Films: *White Nights*, 1957; *Days of Love*, 1958; *La Dolce Vita*, 1959; *Bell' Antonio*, 1960; *Divorce Italian Style*, 1962; *Yesterday, Today and Tomorrow*, 1963; *A Place for Lovers*, 1969; *The Priest's Wife*, 1975; *A Special Day*, 1977; *Ginger and Fred*, 1985; *Dark Eyes*, 1987.

MCDOWALL, RODDY, Sept. 17, 1928 (London, Eng.). English actor. Films: *How Green Was My Valley*, 1941; *My Friend Flicka*, 1943; *Lassie Come Home*, 1943; *The Loved One*, 1965; "Planet of the Apes" series, 1967–73.

MCDOWELL, MALCOLM, June 19, 1943 (Leeds, Eng.). English actor. Films: *If* (1969); *A Clockwork Orange* (1971); *Time After Time* (1979).

MCLAGLEN, VICTOR, Dec. 11, 1883 (London, Eng.) Nov. 7, 1959. English-U.S. actor. A former boxer. Films: *What Price Glory?*, 1926; *The Informer* (Best Actor AA), 1935; *Gunga Din*, 1939; *She Wore a Yellow Ribbon*, 1949; *The Quiet Man*, 1952.

MERCOURI, MELINA, Oct. 18, 1925 (Athens, Gr.). Greek actress, political activist. Best known for her role in the film *Never on Sunday*, 1960.

MILES, SARAH, Dec. 31, 1941 (Ingatestone, Eng.). English actress. Films: *Blow Up*, 1966; *Ryan's Daughter*, 1970; *Lady Caroline Lamb*, 1972.

MILLS, HAYLEY, Apr. 18, 1946 (London, Eng.). English actress. Received special AA, 1960. Films: *Tiger Bay*, 1959; *Pollyanna*, 1960; *The Parent Trap*, 1961; *The Chalk Garden*, 1964. (Daughter of JOHN MILLS; sister of JULIET MILLS.)

MILLS, JOHN, Feb. 22, 1908 (Suffolk, Eng.). English actor. Films: *Those Were the Days*, 1934; *Great Expectations*, 1946; *Hobson's Choice*, 1953; *Tiger Bay*, 1959; *The Swiss Family Robinson*, 1961; *The Wrong Box*, 1966; *Ryan's Daughter* (Supporting Actor AA), 1970; *Gandhi*, 1982. (Father of H. and J. MILLS.)

MILLS, JULIET, Nov. 21, 1941 (London, Eng.). British actress. TV: *Nanny and the Professor* (series), 1969–71. Films: *In Which We Serve*, 1942; *Carry On Jack*, 1964; *Oh What a Lovely War*, 1969; *Avanti*, 1972. (Daughter of J. MILLS; sister of H. MILLS.)

MIRANDA, CARMEN, 1913 (nr. Lisbon, Port.)–Aug. 5, 1955. Brazilian singer, actress. Began as cafe entertainer in South America, starred in camp films of the 1940s and 1950s.

**MONTAND, YVES** (born Ivo Levi), Oct. 31, 1921 (Monsummano, It.). French actor. Films: *The Wages of Fear*, 1953; *Let's Make Love*, 1960; *Is Paris Burning?*, 1966; '*Z*', 1968; *On a Clear Day You Can See Forever*, 1969; *State of Siege*, 1973.

**MOORE, DUDLEY**, Apr. 19, 1935 (Essex, Eng.). British actor, musician, composer. Was a member of the famed Beyond the Fringe comedy group. Films: *The Wrong Box*, 1966; *Bedazzled*, 1968; *Foul Play*, 1978; *10*, 1980; *Arthur*, 1982; *Micki & Maude*, 1984.

**MOORE, ROGER**, Oct. 14, 1927 (London, Eng.). English actor. Star of the TV series *The Saint*, 1967–69; best known in films for his role as James Bond in *Live and Let Die* (1973), *The Man with the Golden Gun* (1974), *The Spy Who Loved Me* (1977), *Moonraker* (1978), *For Your Eyes Only* (1981), *Octopussy* (1982).

**MOREAU, JEANNE**, Jan. 23, 1928 (Paris, Fr.). French actress. Films: *The Lovers*, 1959; *Jules et Jim*, 1961; *Diary of a Chambermaid*, 1965; *Viva Maria*, 1965.

**MORENO, RITA** (born Rosita Alverio), Dec. 11, 1931 (Humacao, P.R.). Puerto Rican actress. Best known for roles in the film *West Side Story* (Best Supporting Actress AA; 1961) and the play *The Ritz* (Tony award; 1975).

**MORLEY, ROBERT**, May 26, 1908 (Wiltshire, Eng.). English actor. Films: *Major Barbara*, 1940; *Gilbert and Sullivan*, 1953; *Beat the Devil*, 1953; *Oscar Wilde*, 1960; *Loophole*, 1986.

**MULHARE, EDWARD**, Apr. 8, 1923 (Co. Cork, Ireland). Irish actor. Best known for his role as the ghost in the TV series *The Ghost and Mrs. Muir*, 1968–70.

**NAZIMOVA, ALLA**, June 4, 1879 (Yalta, Rus.) –July 13, 1945. Russian-U.S. actress. Leading dramatic actress on the stage in Russia, from 1904; noted for her IBSEN roles in the U.S. A star in silent films, 1916–23.

**NELLIGAN, KATE**, Mar. 16, 1951 (London, Ont.). Canadian actress. Stage: *London Assurance*, 1974; *Plenty*, 1975. TV: *Therese Raquin*, 1980. Films: *The Romantic Englishwoman*, 1975; *The Eye of the Needle*, 1980; *Eleni*, 1985.

**NEWLEY, ANTHONY**, Sept. 24, 1931 (Hackney, Eng.). English actor, singer, composer. Best known for appearances in stage musicals, notably *Stop the World I Want to Get Off* (1961) and *The Roar of the Greasepaint, the Smell of the Crowd* (cowrote and cocomposed with Leslie Bricusse, 1963). (Onetime husband of JOAN COLLINS.)

**NIVEN, DAVID**, Mar. 1, 1910 (Kirriemuir, Scot.)– July 29, 1983. Scottish-U.S. actor. Debonair leading man. Films: *Dodsworth*, 1936; *The Prisoner of Zenda*, 1937; *Bachelor Mother*, 1939; *Stairway to Heaven*, 1946; *Around the World in Eighty Days*, 1956; *Separate Tables* (Best Actor AA), 1958; *Guns of Navarone*, 1961; *Casino Royale*, 1967; *Murder by Death*, 1976. Memoirs: *The Moon's a Balloon* (1971) and *Bring on the Empty Horses* (1975.)

**OBERON, MERLE** (born Estelle Thompson), Feb. 19, 1911 (Tasmania)–Nov. 23, 1979. British actress. Films: *The Scarlet Pimpernel*, 1934; *The Divorce of Lady X*, 1938; *Wuthering Heights*, 1939; *A Song to Remember*, 1945; *Hotel*, 1967.

**O'HARA, MAUREEN** (born Maureen Fitzsimmons), Aug. 17, 1921 (Dublin, Ire.). Irish-U.S. actress. Stage career with Dublin's Abbey Theatre. Films: *The Hunchback of Notre Dame*, 1939; *The Black Swan*, 1942; *Miracle on 34th Street*, 1947; *Rio Grande*, 1950; *The Quiet Man*, 1952; *The Parent Trap*, 1961.

**O'HERLIHY, DAN**, May 1, 1919 (Wexford, Ire.). Irish actor. Associated with Dublin's Abbey Theatre. Films: *Odd Man Out*, 1946; *The Adventures of Robinson Crusoe*, 1952; *The Dead*, 1987.

**OLIVIER, LAURENCE, LORD**, May 22, 1907 (Dorking, Eng.)–July 11, 1989. English stage and film actor, director, producer. Known for his large repertoire and particularly his Shakespearean heroes; often cited as the best modern actor; received special AA, 1979; knighted, 1947; created a baron, 1970 (the first actor to awarded a life peerage). Films: *The Divorce of Lady X*, 1938; *Wuthering Heights*, 1939; *Rebecca*, 1940; *Pride and Prejudice*, 1940; *Henry V*, 1944; *Hamlet* (Best Actor AA), 1948; *Richard III*, 1956; *The Devil's Disciple*, 1959; *The Entertainer*, 1960; *Marathon Man*, 1976; *The Boys from Brazil*, 1978; *The Jigsaw Man*, 1984.

**O'TOOLE, PETER**, Aug. 2, 1932 (Connemara, Ire.). Irish actor. Films: *Lawrence of Arabia*, 1962; *Becket*, 1964; *Lord Jim*, 1965; *The Lion in Winter*, 1968; *Goodbye, Mr. Chips*, 1969; *The Ruling Class*, 1971; *My Favorite Year*, 1981; *The Last Emperor*, 1987.

**PAPAS, IRENE**, Mar. 9, 1926 (Corinth, Gr.). Greek actress. Known for her interpretations of classical roles. Films: *Electra*, 1962; *Zorba the Greek*, 1964; '*Z*', 1968; *The Trojan Women*, 1971.

**PIDGEON, WALTER**, Sept. 23, 1898 (New Brunswick, Can.)–Sept. 25, 1984. Canadian actor. Films: *Man Hunt*, 1941; *How Green Was My Valley*, 1941; *Mrs. Miniver*, 1942; *Madame Curie*, 1943; *That Forsyte Woman*, 1949; *Executive Suite*, 1954; *Forbidden Planet*, 1956; *Advise and Consent*, 1962; *Funny Girl*, 1968.

**PLEASANCE, DONALD**, Oct. 5, 1919 (Worksop, Eng.). English actor. Best known for his offbeat, sinister roles in films such as *The Caretaker*, 1964.

**PLUMMER, CHRISTOPHER**, Dec. 13, 1929 (Toronto, Ont., Can.). Canadian actor. Films: *The Sound of Music*, 1965; *Waterloo*, 1970; *The Return of the Pink Panther*, 1975; *Murder by Decree*, 1979.

**QUAYLE, (John) ANTHONY**, Sept. 7, 1913 (Lancashire, Eng.)–Oct. 20, 1989. English actor, director. Mostly in the theater.

**REDGRAVE, LYNN**, Mar. 8, 1943 (London, Eng.). English actress. Films: *Tom Jones*, 1963; *Georgy Girl*, 1966; *The Happy Hooker*, 1975. (Daughter of SIR M. REDGRAVE; sister of V. REDGRAVE.)

**REDGRAVE, SIR MICHAEL**, Mar. 20, 1908 (Bristol, Eng.)–Mar 21, 1985, English actor. Films: *The Lady Vanishes*, 1938; *Mourning Becomes Electra*, 1947; *The Importance of Being Earnest*, 1952; *The Quiet American*, 1958; *Oh What a Lovely War*, 1969; *The Go-Between*, 1971. (Father of V. and L. REDGRAVE.)

**REDGRAVE, VANESSA,** Jan. 30, 1937 (London, Eng.). English actress. Also known for her espousal of radical causes. Films: *Morgan*, 1966; *Camelot*, 1967; *Isadora*, 1968; *Mary, Queen of Scots*, 1972; *Murder on the Orient Express*, 1974; *Julia*, 1977; *Agatha*, 1979; *The Bostonians*, 1984; *Steaming*, 1986. (Daughter of SIR M. REDGRAVE; sister of L. REDGRAVE.)

**REED, OLIVER,** Feb. 13, 1938 (London, Eng.). English actor. Films: *The Damned*, 1962; *The Jokers*, 1967; *Oliver!*, 1968; *Women in Love*, 1969; *The Devils*, 1971; *The Three Musketeers*, 1973; *Burnt Offerings*, 1976.

**RENNIE, MICHAEL,** 1909 (Bradford, England) –June 10, 1971. English-U.S. actor. Films: *The Day the Earth Stood Still* (1952); *The Lost World* (1960).

**RICHARDSON, RALPH,** Dec. 19, 1902 (Cheltenham, Eng.)–Oct. 10, 1983. English character actor. Distinguished stage and film career; best known for Shakespearean roles; cordirector of the Old Vic Theatre, 1944–47.

**RIGG, DIANA,** July 20, 1938 (Doncaster, Eng.). English actress. Mostly in the British Theater. Best known for role as Emma Peel in the TV series *The Avengers*, 1966–68.

**RITCHARD, CYRIL,** Dec. 1, 1897 (Sydney, Austrl.) –Dec. 18, 1977. Australian actor, director. Best known for his role as Captain Hook in *Peter Pan*.

**RUTHERFORD, MARGARET,** May 11, 1892 (London, Eng.)–May 22, 1972. English comedic character actress. Long stage and film career; best known for appearances as Miss Marple in films based on AGATHA CHRISTIE books. Films: *Blithe Spirit*, 1945; *The Importance of Being Earnest*, 1952; *The VIPs* (Best Supporting Actress AA), 1963.

**SAMMS, EMMA,** Aug. 28, 1960 (London, Eng.). British actress, dancer. TV: *Dynasty* (series), 1985, 1987– ; *The Colbys* (series), 1985–87.

**SCHELL, MARIA,** Jan. 15, 1926 (Vienna, Austria). Austrian actress. Films: *So Little Time*, 1952; *The Brothers Karamazov*, 1958; *The Odessa File*, 1974. (Sister of M. SCHELL.)

**SCHELL, MAXIMILIAN,** Dec. 8, 1930 (Vienna, Austria). Austrian actor. Films: *Judgment at Nuremberg* (Best Actor AA), 1961; *Five-Finger Exercise*, 1962; *Topkapi*, 1964; *Julia*, 1977. (Brother of M. SCHELL.)

**SCHILDKRAUT, JOSEPH,** Mar. 22, 1896 (Vienna, Austria)–Jan. 21, 1964. Austrian actor. A silent-screen star who also enjoyed an extensive career as a supporting actor in talkies. *King of Kings*, 1927; *The Life of Emile Zola* (Best Supporting Actor AA), 1937; *The Diary of Anne Frank*, 1959.

**SCHWARZENEGGER, ARNOLD,** July 30, 1947 (Graz, Aust.). Austrian actor. Bodybuilder who turned into an actor. Films: *Hercules in New York*,

1970; *Stay Hungry*, 1976; *Pumping Iron*, 1977; *Conan the Barbarian*, 1982; *Conan the Destroyer*, 1984; *Terminator*, 1984; *Red Sonja*, 1985; *Red Heat*, 1988.

**SCOFIELD, PAUL,** Jan. 21, 1922 (Hurst, Eng.). English stage and film actor. Best known for roles in Shakespearean plays. Films: *A Man for All Seasons* (Best Actor AA), 1966.

**SELLERS, PETER,** Sept. 8, 1925 (Southsea, Eng.)– July 24, 1980. English comedic actor. Films: *The Mouse That Roared*, 1959; *I'm All Right, Jack*, 1959; *The Pink Panther*, 1963; *Dr. Strangelove*, 1963; *A Shot in the Dark*, 1964; *What's New Pussycat?*, 1965; *Murder by Death*, 1976; *The Pink Panther Strikes Again*, 1977; *Being There*, 1979.

**SEYMOUR, JANE** (born Jane Frankenberg), Feb. 15, 1951 (Hillingdon, Eng.). British actress. Stage: *Amadeus*, 1980–81. TV: *War and Remembrance* (miniseries), 1985; *The Richest Man in the World* (miniseries, Emmy award), 1985. Films: *Oh, What a Lovely War*, 1970; *Young Winston*, 1972; *The Tunnel*, 1988.

**SHARIF, OMAR** (born Michel Shalhoub), Apr. 10, 1932 (Alexandria, Egypt). Egyptian actor. Films: *Lawrence of Arabia*, 1962; *Dr. Zhivago*, 1965; *Funny Girl*, 1968; *Che!*, 1969; *Juggernaut*, 1974; *Funny Lady*, 1975.

**SHAW, ROBERT,** Aug. 9, 1927 (Westhoughton, Eng.)–Aug. 28, 1978. English actor, playwright. Films: *From Russia with Love*, 1963; *The Luck of Ginger Coffey*, 1964; *A Man for All Seasons*, 1966; *The Sting*, 1973; *Jaws*, 1975, *Black Sunday*, 1977; *Force Ten from Navarone*, 1978. Play (author): *The Man in the Glass Booth*.

**SIDDONS, SARAH** (born Sarah Kemble), July 5, 1756 (Brecknock, Wales)–June 8, 1831. Welsh actress. Best known for tragic-heroine roles as Isabella in *The Fatal Marriage* (1782) and as Lady Macbeth (1785); with the Covent Garden Theatre repertory co., 1803–12.

**SIGNORET, SIMONE** (born Simone-Henriette-Charlotte Kaminker), Mar. 25, 1921 (Weisbaden, Ger.)–Sept. 30, 1985. French actress. Films: *Casque d'Or*, 1951; *Les Diaboliques*, 1954; *Room at the Top* (Best Actress AA), 1959; *Ship of Fools*, 1965; *Le Chat*, 1974; *Madame Rosa*, 1978.

**SIMMONS, JEAN,** Jan. 31, 1929 (London, Eng.). English actress. Films: *Great Expectations*, 1946; *Black Narcissus*, 1946; *Hamlet*, 1948; *The Robe*, 1953; *Guys and Dolls*, 1955; *Elmer Gantry*, 1960; *Spartacus*, 1960; *The Happy Ending*, 1969.

**SMITH, SIR C(harles) AUBREY,** July 21, 1863 (England)–Dec. 20, 1948. English character actor with a long stage and film career.

**SMITH, MAGGIE,** Dec. 28, 1934 (Ilford, Eng.). English actress. Distinguished stage and film career in both Great Britain and U.S. Films: *The VIPs*, 1963; *The Honey Pot*, 1967; *The Prime of Miss Jean Brodie* (Best Actress AA), 1968; *Murder by Death*, 1976; *California Suite* (Best Supporting Actress AA), 1978; *A Room with a View*, 1986; *The Lonely Passion of Judith Hearne*, 1987.

**STAMP, TERENCE,** July 22, 1939 (Stepney, Eng.). English actor. A leading man in 1960s films such as *Billy Budd* (1962), *The Collector* (1965), *Modesty Blaise* (1966) and *Far From the Madding Crowd* (1967).

**STING** (born Gordon Matthew Sumner), Oct. 2, 1951 (Newcastle Upon Tyne, Eng.). British actor, musician. Gained prominence as member of rock group, Police, but turned primarily to acting in 1980s. Films: *Dune,* 1984; *Plenty,* 1984; *Stormy Monday,* 1988.

**SUTHERLAND, DONALD,** July 17, 1934 (St. John, N.B., Can.). Canadian actor. Films: *The Dirty Dozen,* 1967; *M\*A\*S\*H,* 1970; *Little Murders,* 1970; *Klute,* 1971; *Day of the Locust,* 1976; *Invasion of the Body Snatchers,* 1978; *Ordinary People,* 1980; *Eye of the Needle,* 1981.

**SUTHERLAND, KIEFER,** ? (Canada). Canadian actor. Films: *The Lost Boys,* 1987; *Young Guns,* 1988; *Renegades,* 1989. (Son of D. SUTHERLAND.)

**TANDY, JESSICA,** June 7, 1909 (London, Eng.). English actress. Known for long stage career especially with husband, HUME CRONYN. Received best actress Tony (1948) for *A Streetcar Named Desire* (1947). *The Gin Game* (1978), and *Foxfire* (1982). *Driving Miss Daisy* (1989, Academy Award).

**TERRY, ELLEN,** Feb. 27, 1847 (Coventry, Eng.)–July 21, 1928. English stage actress. Especially in Shakespearean roles.

**TERRY-THOMAS** (born Thomas Terry Hoar-Stevens), July 14, 1911 (London, Eng.)–Jan. 8, 1990. English actor. Films: *Private's Progress,* 1956; *Tom Thumb,* 1958; *Carleton Browne of the FO,* 1958; *I'm All Right, Jack,* 1960; *It's a Mad, Mad, Mad, Mad World,* 1963; *Those Magnificent Men in their Flying Machines,* 1965.

**THICKE, ALAN,** Mar. 3, 1947 (Kirkland Lake, Ont.). Canadian actor. TV: *Growing Pains* (series), 1985– .

**THORNDIKE, SYBIL,** Oct. 24, 1882 (Gainsborough, Eng.)–June 9, 1976. English actress. U.S. and British stage career, from 1904; in films; from 1921.

**THULIN, INGRID,** Jan. 27, 1929 (Solleftea, Swe.). Swedish actress. Films: *Wild Strawberries,* 1957; *Winter Light,* 1962; *The Silence,* 1963; *Return from Ashes,* 1965; *The Damned,* 1969; *Cries and Whispers,* 1972.

**TREACHER, ARTHUR,** July 23, 1894 (Brighton, Eng.)–Dec. 14, 1975. English actor. He became Hollywood's favorite butler. Announcer on TV talk show *The Merv Griffin Show,* 1969–72.

**TREE, SIR HERBERT,** Dec. 17, 1853 (London, Eng.)–July, 2, 1917. English actor, producer, playwright. Shakespearean actor on the British stage, 1878–1917; founder of the Royal Acad. of Dramatic Art, London; mgr. and producer of the Haymarket Theatre, London, 1887–96. (Half-brother of SIR MAX BEERBOHM.)

**TUSHINGHAM, RITA,** Mar. 14, 1940 (Liverpool, Eng.). English actress. Films: *A Taste of Honey,* 1961; *The Leather Boys,* 1965; *The Knack,* 1965; *Doctor Zhivago,* 1965.

**ULLMANN, LIV,** Dec. 16, 1938 (Tokyo, Japan). Norwegian actress. A leading lady in INGMAR BERGMAN films. Films: *Persona,* 1966; *The Passion of Anna,* 1970; *Cries and Whispers,* 1972; *Face to Face,* 1976; *Scenes from a Marriage,* 1974; *Autumn Sonata,* 1978. Autobiography: *Changing,* 1977.

**USTINOV, PETER,** Apr. 16, 1921 (London, Eng.). English actor, producer, writer. Films: *Quo Vadis,* 1951; *Spartacus* (Best Supporting Actor AA), 1960; *Romanoff and Juliet,* 1961; *Billy Budd,* 1962; *Topkapi* (Supporting Actor AA), 1964; *Logan's Run,* 1976.

**VIEDT, CONRAD,** Jun 22, 1893 (Potsdam, Ger.)–Apr. 3, 1943. German character actor. U.S. and German film and stage career. Films: *The Cabinet of Dr. Caligari,* 1919; *Dark Journey,* 1937; *Casablanca,* 1942.

**VON SYDOW, MAX,** Apr. 10, 1929 (Lund. Swe.). Swedish actor. Best known for roles in INGMAR BERGMAN films. Films: *The Seventh Seal,* 1956; *The Virgin Spring,* 1959; *The Greatest Story Ever Told,* 1965; *The Passion of Anna,* 1971; *The Emigrants,* 1972; *The Exorcist,* 1973; *Hannah and Her Sisters,* 1986.

**WARNER, H**(erbert) **B**(ryan), Oct. 26, 1876 (London, Eng.)–Dec. 24, 1958. English actor. Stage and film career in U.S. and Great Britain. Films: *King of Kings,* 1927; *Mr. Deeds Goes to Town,* 1936; *Lost Horizon,* 1937; *Victoria the Great,* 1937; *Sunset Boulevard,* 1950.

**WERNER, OSKAR** (born Oscar Schleissmayer), Nov. 13, 1922 (Vienna, Austria)–Oct. 23, 1984. Austrian actor. U.S. film career. Films: *Decision before Dawn,* 1951; *Jules et Jim,* 1961; *Ship of Fools,* 1965; *Fahrenheit 451,* 1966; *Voyage of the Damned,* 1976.

**WHITTY, MAY,** June 19, 1865 (Liverpool, Eng.)–May 29, 1948. British character actress; D.B.E., 1918. Stage career, from 1881; in U.S. films, 1937–48.

**WILDING, MICHAEL,** July 23, 1912 (Essex, Eng.)–July 8, 1979. English actor. Began career as stage actor. Films: *In Which We Serve,* 1942; *Stage Fright,* 1950; *The World of Suzie Wong,* 1960; *Lady Caroline Lamb,* 1972. (One-time husband of E. TAYLOR and M. LEIGHTON.)

**WILLIAMS, EMLYN,** Nov. 26, 1905 (Mostyn, Wales). Welsh actor, playwright. Plays: *Night Must Fall,* 1935; *The Corn is Green,* 1938.

**WILLIAMSON, NICOL,** Sept. 14, 1938 (Hamilton, Scot.). Scottish actor. Best known for his Shakespearean roles, particularly in *Hamlet* (stage and film, 1969–70).

**YORK, MICHAEL** (born Michael York-Johnson), Mar. 27, 1942 (Fulmer, Eng.). English actor. Films: *Romeo and Juliet,* 1967; *Cabaret,* 1972; *Lost Horizon,* 1972; *The Last Remake of Beau Geste,* 1977.

**YORK, SUSANNAH** (born Susannah Fletcher), Jan. 9, 1941 (London, Eng.). English actress. Films: *A Man for All Seasons,* 1966; *The Killing of Sister George,* 1968; *They Shoot Horses, Don't They?* 1969; *Superman,* 1978.

YOUNG, ROLAND, Nov. 11, 1887 (London, Eng.) –June 5, 1953. English character actor. Best known for his role in the "Topper" film series, 1930s–40s.

## DANCERS

ASTAIRE, ADELE (born Adele Austerlitz), Sept. 10, 1898 (Omaha, Neb.)–Jan. 25, 1981. U.S. dancer. Toast of vaudeville in dance team with brother FRED ASTAIRE, 1919–32; appeared with him in musical shows, notably *Lady Be Good* (1926), *The Band Wagon* (1931) and *Funny Face* (1927); retired from show business in 1932.

ASTAIRE, FRED (born Frederick Austerlitz), May 10, 1899 (Omaha, Neb.)–June 22, 1987. U.S. dancer, actor. Leading dance star of his generation on stage (with sister ADELE, 1916–32) and screen (frequently partnered with GINGER ROGERS); in later years, has appeared as character actor in films and on TV. Films: *Gay Divorcee* 1934; *Roberta* 1935; *Top Hat* 1935; *Swing Time* 1936; *Story of Vernon and Irene Castle*, 1939; *Holiday Inn* 1942; *Easter Parade* 1948; *Royal Wedding* 1951; *The Band Wagon* 1953; *Daddy Long Legs* 1955; *Funny Face* 1957; and *Silk Stockings* 1957; *Finian's Rainbow*, 1968; *Ghost Story*, 1981.

BOLGER, RAY, Jan. 10, 1904 (Boston, Mass.) –Jan. 15, 1987. U.S. dancer, actor. Began in vaudeville, 1923; starred in Broadway shows from 1925; moved on to films, in which his best-known role was the Scarecrow in *The Wizard of Oz* (1939). Plays: *Geo. White's Scandals*, 1931; *Life Begins at 8:40*, 1934; *By Jupiter*, 1942; *Where's Charley?*, 1948. Films: *The Harvey Girls*, 1946; *Look for the Silver Lining*, 1949; *Where's Charley?*, 1952; *April in Paris*, 1952.

CASTLE, IRENE, Apr. 7, 1893 (New Rochelle, N.Y.)–Jan. 25, 1969. U.S. dancer. With husband VERNON CASTLE, formed popular dance team, 1912–17; a number of dances are credited to them, including the Turkey Trot, the One-step and the Castle Walk; her appearance popularized bobbed hair and the natural figure.

CASTLE, VERNON (born Vernon Castle Blythe), May 2, 1887 (Norwich, Eng.)–Feb. 15, 1918. U.S. dancer. With wife IRENE CASTLE, the dancing sensation of pre-World War I cabarets; elegance in ballroom dancing their trademark.

CHAMPION, MARGE (born Marjorie Belcher), Sept. 2, 1923 (Los Angeles, Calif.). U.S. dancer, actress. Teamed with her then-husband GOWER CHAMPION in several film musicals including *Show Boat*, 1951. Solo film appearances included *The Story of Vernon and Irene Castle* (1939); later appeared as character actress.

CHARISSE, CYD (born Tula Ellice Finklea), Mar. 8, 1923 (Amarillo, Tex.). U.S. dancer. Stylish, long-legged star of 1950s musicals; occasionally teamed with FRED ASTAIRE. Films: *The Bandwagon*, 1953; *Brigadoon*, 1954; *Silk Stockings*, 1957.

GAYNOR, MITZI (born Francesca Mitzi von Gerber), Sept. 4, 1930 (Chicago, Ill.). U.S. dancer. Best remembered for leading roles in films such as *There's No Business like Show Business* (1954), *Les Girls* (1957), and *South Pacific* (1958); has recently done one-woman concert tours.

GENNARO, PETER, 1924 (Metaire, La.). U.S. dancer, choreographer. Professional since 1949, in Broadway shows; choreographer for many plays, films, and TV shows.

GRAY, GILDA (born Marianna Michalska), 1901 (Pol.)–Dec. 22, 1959. U.S. dancer. Popular dancer of the 1920s; credited with inventing the "shimmy."

HANEY, CAROL, Dec. 24, 1924 (New Bedford, Mass.)–May 10, 1964. U.S. dancer, choreographer. Achieved stardom as dancer in the Broadway show *Pajama Game*, 1954.

HINES, GREGORY, Feb. 14, 1946 (New York, N.Y.). U.S. dancer, actor. Began tap dancing at age three, toured nightclubs with his brother and dad as Hines, Hines and Dad. Stage: *Eubie*, 1978; *Sophisticated Ladies*, 1981. Films: *White Nights*, 1985; *The Cotton Club*, 1985; *Running Scared*, 1986.

KEELER, RUBY, Aug. 25, 1909 (Halifax, N.S., Can.). U.S. dancer, actress. Broadway musical star who gained greatest fame in BUSBY BERKELEY films of 1930s.

KELLY, GENE, Aug. 23, 1912 (Pittsburgh, Pa.). U.S. dancer, choreographer, director. Carefree, athletic dancer of Hollywood musicals of the 1940s and 1950s; turned to direction when musicals went out of style. Films: *For Me and My Gal*, 1942; *Anchors Aweigh*, 1945; *The Pirate*, 1948; *On the Town*, 1949; *An American in Paris*, 1951; *Singin' in the Rain*, 1952; *Brigadoon*, 1954; *Les Girls*, 1957.

KIDD, MICHAEL, Aug. 12, 1919 (Brooklyn, N.Y.). U.S. dancer, choreographer. Appeared with several ballet companies (including Ballet Theatre, 1942–47) before becoming choreographer and dir. for a number of Broadway productions. Plays choreographed: *Finian's Rainbow*, 1947; *Guys and Dolls*, 1950; *Can-Can*, 1953; *Li'l Abner*, 1956; *Destry Rides Again*, 1959 (received Tony Awards for all of these plays).

MCKECHNIE, DONNA, Nov. 16, 1942 (Pontiac, Mich.). U.S. dancer. Won Tony Award for *A Chorus Line*, 1975.

MILLER, ANN (born Lucille Ann Collier), Apr. 12, 1923 (Houston, Tex.). U.S. dancer. Tap Dancer in films and on stage and TV. Films: *You Can't Take It with You*, 1939; *Easter Parade*, 1949; *On the Town*, 1950; *Hit the Deck*, 1952; *Kiss Me Kate*, 1953.

POWELL, ELEANOR, Nov. 21, 1912 (Springfield, Mass.)–Feb. 11, 1982. U.S. dancer. Vivacious, long-legged tap-dancing star of musical films in 1930s and 1940s. Films: *Born to Dance*, 1936; *Rosalie*, 1938.

PROWSE, JULIET, Sept. 25, 1937 (Bombay, India). British dancer. Appeared in movies in the 1950s and 1960s; frequent performer in clubs and on TV in U.S. and Great Britain.

**RIVERA, CHITA,** Jan. 23, 1933 (Washington, D.C.). U.S. dancer, actress. Star of musicals on Broadway, where she created role of Anita in *West Side Story,* (1957). Plays: *Mr. Wonderful,* 1956; *Bye, Bye, Birdie,* 1960; *Chicago,* 1975; *The Rink* (Tony Award), 1984.

**ROBINSON, BILL** "Bojangles" (born Luther Robinson), May 25, 1878 (Richmond, Va.)–Nov. 25, 1949. U.S. dancer. A popular vaudeville tap dancer, best known for his stairway dance and his appearances in several SHIRLEY TEMPLE films.

**ROGERS, GINGER** (born Virginia Katherine McMath), July 16, 1911 (Independence, Mo.). U.S. dancer, actress. Star of movie musicals, many as partner of FRED ASTAIRE. Films: *Flying Down to Rio,* 1933; *The Gay Divorcee,* 1934; *Roberta,* 1934; *Top Hat,* 1935; *Swing Time,* 1936; *Shall We Dance?,* 1937; *Stage Door,* 1938; *The Story of Vernon and Irene Castle,* 1939; Kitty Foyle (Best Actress AA) 1940; *The Barkleys of Broadway,* 1949.

**SWAYZE, PATRICK,** Aug. 18, 1954 (Houston, Tex.). U.S. dancer, actor. Films: *Outsiders,* 1933; *Dirty Dancing,* 1987.

**TUNE, TOMMY,** Feb. 28, 1939 (Wichita Falls, Tex.). U.S. dancer, choreographer, director. Broadway shows: *Seesaw* (Tony Award), 1974; *My One and Only* (Tony Award), 1983. Choreographer-director of the musicals *The Best Little Whorehouse in Texas* (1978); *A Day in Hollywood/A Night in the Ukraine,* 1980; *Nine,* 1982; *Stepping Out,* 1987.

**VERDON, GWEN,** Jan. 13, 1925 (Los Angeles, Calif.). U.S. dancer, actress. Red-haired musical-comedy star on Broadway and in films. Plays: *Can-Can,* 1953; *Damn Yankees,* 1955; *New Girl in Town,* 1957; *Red Head,* 1958; *Sweet Charity,* 1966; *Chicago,* 1975 (won Tony Awards for the first four). (One-time wife of B. FOSSE.)

**VEREEN, BEN,** Oct. 10, 1946 (Miami, Fla.). U.S. dancer, actor. Prominent in Broadway musicals of the 1960s and 1970s; achieved stardom with role on TV miniseries *Roots* (1977) and with dynamic nightclub and TV variety-show act.

## SINGERS

**ABDUL, PAULA,** 1963 (?). U.S. singer. Called the "Madonna of the 1990s"; hits include "Straight Up," "Opposites Attract," "The Way That You Love Me," and "Cold Hearted."

**ANDERSON, IAN,** Aug. 10, 1947 (Blackpool, Eng.). British rock musician. Singer and guitarist; leader of Jethro Tull rock group since 1967.

**ANDREWS, JULIE** (born Julia Wells), Oct. 1, 1935 (Walton, Eng.). British singer, actress. Original Eliza in musical *My Fair Lady* (stage). Films: *Mary Poppins* (Best Actress AA; 1964); *The Sound of Music* 1965; *Star,* 1968; *Darling Lili,* 1970; *Victor/Victoria,* 1982; numerous TV specials.

**THE ANDREWS SISTERS: LAVERNE,** 1915 (Minneapolis, Minn.)–May 8, 1967; **MAXINE,** 1918 (Minneapolis, Minn.); **PATTY,** 1920 (Minneapolis, Minn.). U.S. singers. Formed popular singing group in the 1940s, with several hit records and film appearances. Songs: "Don't Sit Under the Apple Tree with Anyone Else But Me"; "Bei Mir Bist Du Schön"; "Boogie-Woogie Bugle Boy from Company B."

**ANKA, PAUL,** July 30, 1941 (Ottawa, Ont., Can.). Canadian singer, composer. Popular singer from 1956, when he was teen idol. Compositions: "Diana," "Put Your Head on My Shoulder," "My Way," "She's a Lady," "Tonight Show Theme."

**ARNOLD, EDDY,** May 15, 1918 (Henderson, Tex.). U.S. singer. Country-and-western star, with numerous hits since 1944; elected to Country Music Hall of Fame, 1966.

**AUTRY,** (Orvon) **GENE,** Sept. 29, 1907 (Tioga, Tex.). U.S. singer, executive. The "Singing Cowboy," he made over 80 movie Westerns, 1934–54; wrote over 200 songs, including "Here Comes Santa Claus"; owner, Calif. Angels baseball team.

**AVALON, FRANKIE** (born Francis Avallone), Sept.

8, 1940 (Philadelphia, Pa.). U.S. singer. Teen heartthrob of 1960s, made series of "beach party" films, often with ANNETTE FUNICELLO.

**AZNAVOUR, CHARLES** (born Shahnour Aznavourjan), May 22, 1924 (Paris, Fr.). French singer. Singer of romantic ballads and sometime actor. Films: *Shoot the Piano Player,* 1960.

**BAEZ, JOAN,** Jan. 9, 1941 (New York, N.Y.). U.S. singer, political activist. Folksinger active in civil rights and antiwar movements of 1960s; founder of the Resource Center for Non-Violence, 1965.

**BAILEY, PEARL,** Mar. 29, 1918 (Newport News, Va.). U.S. singer. Star of stage, films, TV: won Tony Award for *Hello Dolly* (1967); worked as special U.S. rep. to the UN; played in films *Carmen Jones* (1954), *Porgy & Bess* (1959), *The Landlord* (1969).

**BAKER, ANITA,** Jan. 26, 1958 (Toledo, Oh.). U.S. singer. Singer of pop music whose style has been heavily influenced by SARAH VAUGHN. Albums: *The Songstress,* 1983; *Rapture,* 1986; *Giving You the Best I've Got,* 1989.

**BAKER, JOSEPHINE,** June 3, 1906 (St. Louis, Mo.)–Apr. 10, 1975. U.S.-French singer and dancer. The star of the Folies-Bergère, who made her Parisian debut in 1925 in *La Revue Nègre;* starred in her own Paris revues, from 1930; made triumphal appearances to New York City in the 1970s.

**BASSEY, SHIRLEY,** Jan. 8, 1937 (Cardiff, Wales). English singer. Noted for her dynamic style. Considered one of the best post-WW II female vocalists produced by England. Songs: "As I Love You," 1958; "Kiss Me, Honey, Kiss Me," 1959; "As Long as He Needs Me," 1960; "Something," 1970.

**BEE GEES, THE: BARRY GIBB,** Sept. 1, 1946 (Douglas, Isle of Man., Eng.); **MAURICE GIBB,** Dec. 22, 1949 (Douglas, Isle of Man., Eng.); **ROBIN**

GIBB, Dec. 22, 1949 (Douglas, Isle of Man., Eng.). British singers. Leading 1960s rock group; gained new prominence as disco group in 1970s; wrote and performed score for the film *Saturday Night Fever*, 1977. Songs: "Lonely Days," "How Can You Mend a Broken Heart," "Stayin' Alive," "Jive Talkin'."

BELAFONTE, HARRY, Mar. 1, 1927 (New York, N.Y.). U.S. singer, actor. Noted for calypso songs; his films include *Carmen Jones* (1954), *Island in the Sun* (1957), *Odds against Tomorrow* (1959), and *Uptown Saturday Night* (1974).

BENNETT, TONY (born Anthony Benedetto), Aug. 3, 1926 (New York, N.Y.). U.S. singer. Popular crooner in concert, nightclubs, TV since early 1950s.

BERRY, CHUCK, Oct. 18, 1926 (St. Louis, Mo.). U.S. singer, songwriter. Among first to shape big-beat blues into rock-and-roll; composer of "May-bellene," "Roll over Beethoven," "Johnny B. Goode," "Rock 'n' Roll Music."

BIKEL, THEODORE, May 2, 1924 (Vienna, Austria.). U.S. singer, actor. Popular Yiddish and Hebrew folksinger; was original Capt. Von Trapp in play *Sound of Music*, 1959–61.

BONO, SONNY (born Salvatore Bono), Feb. 16, 1935 (Detroit, Mich.). U.S. singer. Teamed with ex-wife CHER (1964–74) in popular singing duo.

BOONE, PAT (born Charles Eugene Boone), June 1, 1934 (Jacksonville, Fla.). U.S. singer. Top pop singer in 1950s, noted for clean-cut image and white buck shoes. Films: *Bernardine*, 1957; *April Love*, 1957; *State Fair*, 1962. Books: *Twixt Twelve and Twenty*, 1958; *Care and Feeding of Parents*, 1967; *Joy*, 1973.

BOWIE, DAVID (born David Robert Jones), Jan. 8, 1947 (London, Eng.). British musician, actor. Androgynous rock star with many successful albums, including *Hunky Dory*, *Diamond Dogs*, and *Station to Station*. Films: *The Man Who Fell to Earth*, 1976; *Merry Christmas, Mr. Lawrence*, 1983.

BREWER, TERESA, May 7, 1931 (Toledo, Ohio.). U.S. singer. Pop singer of such 1950s song hits as "Music, Music, Music" and "Ricochet Romance."

BROWN, JAMES, June 17, 1928 (Pulaski, Tenn.). U.S. singer. Often called the "King of Soul Music"; records include "Please, Please, Please," "Papa's Got a Brand New Bag," and "Don't Be a Dropout."

BROWNE, JACKSON, Oct. 9, 1948 (Heidelberg, Ger.). U.S. musician. Pop-rock songwriter-singer, his late 1960s songs were sung by many other people; became solo performer, 1971. Songs: "Doctor My Eyes," 1972; "Rock Me on the Water," 1972; "Take It Easy," 1972; "Red Neck Friend," 1974; "Ready or Not."

CAMPBELL, GLEN, Apr. 22, 1936 (Billstown, Ark.). U.S. singer. Country-rock recording star; records include "Gentle on My Mind," "Wichita Lineman," "By the Time I Get to Phoenix," "Rhinestone Cowboy"; star of TV show *Glen Campbell Good Time Hour*, 1969–71; winner of five Grammys, five Country Music Assn. awards.

CARPENTER, KAREN, Mar. 2, 1950 (New Haven, Conn.)–Feb. 4, 1983. U.S. singer with brother,

Richard, produced pop-rock hits such as "Close to You," "Goodbye to Love," "Top of the World," "Only Yesterday," "For All We Know," "Rainy Days and Mondays," "Sing," "Please Mr. Postman."

CARR, VIKKI (born Florencia Bisenta de Casillas Martinez Cardona), July 19, 1941 (El Paso, Tex.). U.S. singer. Pop songstress who frequently sings multilingually; records include "It Must Be Him" and "With Pen in Hand."

CARROLL, DIAHANN (born Carol Diahann Johnson), July 17, 1935 (New York, N.Y.). U.S. singer, actress; won Tony award for Broadway musical *No Strings*, 1962. Films: *Paris Blues* (1961), *Hurry Sundown* (1967), *Claudine* (1972); first black woman to star in a TV series, *Julia*, (1968–69). Appeared in *Dynasty* series, 1984–87. (Wife of V. DAMONE.)

CARTER CASH, JUNE, June 23, 1929 (Maces Spring, Va.). U.S. singer. Member of famed country-and-western Carter Family group. (Wife of J. CASH.)

CASH, JOHNNY, Feb. 26, 1932 (Kingsland, Ark.). U.S. singer. Country-and-western singer, composer, actor. Albums: "I Walk the Line," "At Folsom Prison," "Rockabilly Blues"; starred in own TV series, 1969–71. (Husband of J. CARTER.)

CASH, ROSANNE, May 24, 1955 (Memphis, Tenn.). U.S. singer, songwriter. Known chiefly as a country-western songwriter, achieved her first gold record with crossover hit song: "Seven Year Ache," 1980; other songs include "Blue Moon with Heartache" and "I Don't Know Why You Don't Want Me." (Daughter of J. CASH.)

CASSIDY, DAVID, Apr. 12, 1950 (New York, N.Y.). U.S. singer. Rose to teenybopper idol status through appearances on TV series *The Partridge Family* in early 1970s. (Son of J. CASSIDY; stepson of S. JONES.)

CETERA, PETER, Sept. 13, 1944 (Chicago, Ill.). U.S. singer. Former lead singer for Chicago, left group in 1986 for a highly successful solo career; hits include "The Glory of Love" (#1 song from *The Karate Kid*), "After All" (duet with CHER from *Chances Are*), and "The Next Time I Fall in Love."

CHANNING, CAROL, Jan. 31, 1923 (Seattle, Wash.). U.S. actress, singer. Vivacious blond who created lead in *Hello Dolly* on Broadway, 1964; also starred in *Gentlemen Prefer Blondes* (1949), *Wonderful Town* (1953), *Lorelei* (1974).

CHAPMAN, TRACY, 1965 (Cleveland, Oh.). U.S. singer. Folk/rock singer whose social protest songs catapulted her to fame in late 1980s; hits include "Fast Car," "Talkin' About a Revolution," and "Baby, Can I Hold You?"

CHARLES, RAY (born Ray Charles Robinson), Sept. 23, 1930 (Albany, Ga.). U.S. singer, composer. Blind star of jazz, soul, pop, country-and-western genres; winner of 10 Grammys.

CHECKER, CHUBBY (born Ernest Evans), Oct. 3, 1941 (Philadephia, Pa.). U.S. singer. Helped popularize the Twist dance craze of early 1960s.

CHEVALIER, MAURICE, Sept. 12, 1888 (Paris,

Fr.)–Jan. 1, 1972. French singer, actor. Musical comedy star; starred in many films, including *The Love Parade* (1930), *Folies Bergere* (1935), *Love in the Afternoon* (1957), *Gigi* (1958); known for his straw hat and charming manner.

**CLARK, PETULA,** Nov. 15, 1932. (Ewell, Eng.). English singer. Pop singer, from the early 1960s. Songs: "Downtown," "I Know a Place," "Don't Sleep in the Subway, Darling."

**CLARK, ROY,** Apr. 5, 1933 (Meherrin, Va.). U.S. country-and-western singer, musician. Star of *Hee-Haw* TV show; named Entertainer of the Year by the Country Music Assn., 1973.

**COLE, NATALIE,** Feb. 6, 1950 (Los Angeles, Calif.). U.S. singer. Disco-rock singer; daughter of NAT "KING" COLE; won Grammy awards in 1975, 1976. Songs: "This Will Be," 1975. (Daughter of N. COLE.)

**COLE, NAT "KING",** Mar. 17, 1919 (Montgomery, Ala.)–Feb. 15, 1965. U.S. singer, pianist. Pop singer of numerous hits, including "Straighten Up and Fly Right," "Too Young," "Nature Boy," "Route 66," "Unforgettable," "Ramblin' Rose." (Father of N. COLE.)

**COLLINS, JUDY,** May 1, 1939 (Seattle, Wash.). U.S. folksinger. Has recorded many successful albums, including "Golden Apples in the Sun" (1962), "In My Life" (1966), "Wildflowers" (1967), "Recollections" (1969), and "Living" (1971).

**COMO, PERRY,** May 18, 1912 (Cannonsburg, Pa.). U.S. singer. Easygoing crooner who had a very popular TV show, 1948–63; his hit records include "Prisoner of Love," "If," "It's Impossible."

**COOKE, SAM,** Jan. 22, 1935 (Chicago, Ill.) –Dec. 11, 1964. U.S. singer. Pioneer in soul and rhythm-and-blues movements, began as gospel singer; shot to death in bizarre incident in L.A. Songs: "You Send Me," 1958; "Chain Gang," 1960; "Twistin' the Night Away," 1962; "Shake," 1965.

**COOPER, ALICE** (born Vincent Furnier), Feb. 4, 1948 (Detroit, Mich.). U.S. singer. Bizarre 1970's rock star whose songs often dealt with violent themes and were frequently performed with violent staging.

**CROCE, JIM,** Jan. 10, 1942 (Philadelphia, PA.) –Sept. 20, 1973. U.S musician. Singer, guitarist, songwriter of folk-rock music; was just becoming a star when he died in chartered plane crash. Songs: "You Don't Mess Around with Jim," 1972; "Operator," 1972; "Bad, Bad Leroy Brown," 1973; "I've Got a Name," 1973; "Time in a Bottle," 1973.

**CROSBY, BING** (born Harry Lillis Crosby), May 2, 1903 (Tacoma, Wash.)–Oct. 14, 1977. U.S. singer, actor. Leading crooner of the 1930s and 1940s; radio star, 1931–57; starred in a number of films; including *Anything Goes* (1956), *Pennies From Heaven* (1936), *Going My Way* (Best Actor AA, 1944), *The Bells of St. Mary's* (1945), *White Christmas* (1954), *High Society* (1956) and six "road" pictures with BOB HOPE.

**CROSBY, DAVID,** Aug. 14, 1941 (Los Angeles, Calif.). U.S. singer, musician. A founding member of the Byrds; after leaving Byrds founded another group, Crosby, Stills, Nash, and Young; has continued to play with his partners, STEPHEN STILLS, GRAHAM NASH, and NEAL YOUNG throughout the 1970s and 1980s; best known songs include "Long Time Coming," "Compass," and "Southern Cross."

**DAMONE, VIC** (born Vito Farinola), June 12, 1928 (Brooklyn, N.Y.). U.S. singer. Club and recording star who appeared in some films in 1950s. (Husband of D. CARROLL.)

**DARIN, BOBBY** (born Walden Robert Cassoto), May 14, 1936 (New York, N.Y.)–Dec. 20, 1973. U.S. singer. Major star of rock-and-roll era, with recordings such as "Mack the Knife" and "Splish Splash."

**DAVIDSON, JOHN,** Dec. 13, 1941 (Pittsburgh, Pa.). U.S. singer. Pop star of 1960s; host on TV's *Hollywood Squares.*

**DAVIS, MAC,** Jan. 21, 1942 (Lubbock, Tex.). U.S. country-and-western singer, composer, actor. Songs: "In the Ghetto"; "Friend, Lover, Woman, Wife"; "I Believe in Music".

**DAVIS, SAMMY, JR.,** Dec. 8, 1925 (New York, N.Y.)–May 16, 1990. U.S. singer, actor. In vaudeville, clubs with Will Mastin Trio, 1930–48; star of Broadway shows *Mr. Wonderful* (1956), *Golden Boy* (1964); films include *Porgy and Bess* (1959), *Ocean's 11* (1960), *Sweet Charity* (1968); numerous TV appearances as singer, actor; author of autobiography, *Yes I Can* (1965).

**DEAN, JIMMY,** Aug. 10, 1928 (Plainview, Tex.). U.S. country-and-western singer, businessman. Numerous county-fair and TV appearances, recordings. Best known for "Big Bad John," 1961.

**DENVER, JOHN** (born Henry John Deutschendorf, Jr.), Dec. 31, 1943 (Roswell, N.M.). U.S. singer, composer, actor. Many hit songs, including "Leaving on a Jet Plane," "Rocky Mountain High," "Take Me Home, Country Roads"; made film debut in *Oh God!*, 1977; active in environmental, world hunger movements.

**DIAMOND, NEIL,** Jan. 24, 1941 (Brooklyn, N.Y.). U.S. singer, songwriter. Rock star who wrote and recorded such hits as "Kentucky Woman," "Sweet Caroline," "Young Girl," "Song Sung Blue"; many concert appearances; wrote score for film *Jonathan Livingston Seagull*, 1973.

**DIDDLEY, BO** (born Elias Bates), Dec. 30, 1928 (McComb, Miss.). U.S. musician. Pioneer in rock-and-roll; a singer/songwriter who combined jazz and blues with rock. Songs: "Bo Diddley," 1955; "I'm a Man," 1955; "Say Man," 1959; "Road Runner," 1960; "Ooh Baby," 1967.

**DION** (born Dion Dimucci), July 18, 1939 (New York, N.Y.). U.S. musician. With backup group The Belmonts was popular rock singer of late 1950s. Songs: "A Teenager in Love," 1959; "Where or When," 1960; "Runaround Sue," 1961; "The Wanderer," 1961; "Ruby Baby," 1963; "Drip Drop," 1964; "Abraham, Martin and John," 1968.

**DOMINO, FATS** (born Antoine Domino), Feb. 26, 1928 (New Orleans, La.). U.S. pianist, singer, songwriter. Popular in 1950s boogie-woogie era, with songs such as "Blueberry Hill" and "Ain't That a Shame."

**DONOVAN** (born Donovan Leitch), May 10, 1943 (Glasgow, Scot.). Scottish singer. Leading exponent of "flower power" rock in 1960s, with songs such as "Sunshine Superman" and "Mellow Yellow."

**DYLAN, BOB** (born Robert Zimmerman), May 24, 1941 (Duluth, Minn.). U.S. singer, songwriter. His "Blowin' in the Wind" and "Times They Are A-Changin'" were anthems of the 1960s civil-rights movement; other hits include "Mr. Tambourine Man," "Gates of Eden."

**EDDY, NELSON,** 1901 (Providence, R.I.)–Mar. 6, 1967. U.S. singer, actor. Famed for series of operetta films with JEANETTE MACDONALD, including *Naughty Marietta* (1935), *Rose Marie* (1936), *May Time* (1937), *Sweethearts* (1939), *New Moon* (1940).

**ELLIOTT, CASS**(andra), Sept. 19, 1941 (Baltimore, Md.–July 29, 1974. U.S. singer. Rotund, sweet-voiced pop-rock singer who was part of The Mamas and the Papas, 1963–67; successful solo act, 1967–74. Songs: "Dream a Little Dream of Me."

**ETTING, RUTH,** 1898 (David City, Neb.)–Sept. 24, 1978. U.S. singer. Torch singer popular on radio and in films in the 1930s; subject of film biography *Love Me or Leave Me* (1955).

**THE EVERLY BROTHERS: DON,** Feb. 1, 1937 (Brownie, Ky.): and **PHIL,** Jan. 19, 1938 (Brownie, Ky.). U.S. singers. Popular stars of late 1950s-early 1960s, with hits such as "Bye Bye Love" and "Wake Up, Little Susie."

**FABIAN** (born Fabian Forte), Feb. 6, 1943 (Philadelphia, Pa.). U.S. singer. Teenage idol in the 1950s.

**FABRAY, NANETTE** (born Nanette Fabares), Oct. 27, 1920 (San Diego, Calif.). U.S. singer, actress. In Broadway and film musicals including *High Button Shoes* (1947), *Love Life* (1949), *The Bandwagon* (1953). Many TV appearances.

**FALANA, LOLA,** Sept. 11, 1946 (Philadelphia, Pa.). U.S. singer, actress. One of the highest paid and most popular performers on the Las Vegas casino show circuit.

**FELICIANO, JOSÉ,** Sept. 10, 1945 (Larez, P.R.). Puerto Rican singer, composer, guitarist. Songs: "Light My Fire," 1968; "High Heel Sneakers."

**FIELDS, GRACIE** (born Grace Stansfield), Jan. 9, 1898 (Rochdale, Eng.)–Sept. 27, 1979. English singer, comedienne. Popular music-hall performer.

**FISHER, EDDIE,** Aug. 10, 1928 (Philadelphia, Pa.). U.S. singer. Very popular in 1950s, with many hit records.

**FITZGERALD, ELLA,** Apr. 25, 1918 (Newport News, Va.). U.S. jazz singer. Began with Chick Webb Orchestra, 1934; winner of numerous jazz popularity polls. Best known for record albums of music of IRVING BERLIN, GEORGE GERSHWIN, COLE PORTER, and RODGERS and HART.

**FLACK, ROBERTA,** Feb. 10, 1939 (Black Mountain, N.C.). U.S. singer. Former schoolteacher turned rock performer; hit songs include "The First Time

Ever I Saw Your Face" (1972) and "Killing Me Softly" (1973).

**FOGERTY, JOHN,** May 28, 1945 (Berkeley, Calif.). U.S. singer. Former lead singer with country rock group Creedence Clearwater Revival, his soulful blues-influenced singing gave the group a distinctive sound; now a solo act; hits include "Bad Moon Rising" (with CCR), "Old Man Down the Road" and "Centerfield."

**FOLEY, RED** (born Clyde Julian Foley), June 17, 1910 (Blue Lick, Ky.)–Sept. 19, 1968. U.S. country-and-western singer. Popular radio and recording artist of the 1940s–50s; one of the first to record in Nashville.

**FORD, TENNESSEE ERNIE,** Feb. 13, 1919 (Bristol, Tenn.). U.S. singer. Country singer who had own TV show in the 1960s. "16 Tons" best-known record.

**FRAMPTON, PETER,** Apr. 22, 1950 (Beckenham, Eng.). English rock singer. Teen idol with many hit records; member of the groups Humble Pie (1968–71) and Frampton's Camel (1971–74).

**FRANCIS, CONNIE** (born Constance Franconero), Dec. 12, 1938 (Newark, N.J.). U.S. singer, actress. Popular in late 1950s–early 1960s; film credits include *Where the Boys Are* (1963), *Follow the Boys* (1964).

**FRANKLIN, ARETHA,** Mar. 25, 1942 (Memphis, Tenn.). U.S. singer. Rhythm-and-blues star of records, concerts, TV; winner of Grammys in 1972, 1973.

**GARFUNKEL, ART**(hur), Oct. 13, 1941 (New York, N.Y.). U.S. singer, songwriter. With PAUL SIMON, formed one of the 1960s major folk-rock teams; starred in film *Carnal Knowledge* (1971).

**GARLAND, JUDY** (born Frances Gumm), June 10, 1922 (Grand Rapids, Minn.)–June 22, 1969. U.S. singer, actress. Legendary singer of 1940s–1960s and star of many memorable films; gained fame as Dorothy in *The Wizard of Oz*, 1939; also starred in *Babes in Arms* (1939), *Meet Me in St. Louis* (1944), *The Clock* (1945), *The Harvey Girls* (1946), *Easter Parade* (1948), *In the Good Old Summertime* (1949), *A Star is Born* (1954), *Judgment at Nuremberg* (1960); worldwide concert appearances in 1950s and 1960s. (Mother of L. MINNELLI.)

**GAYE, MARVIN,** Apr. 2, 1939 (Washington, D.C.) –Apr. 1, 1984. U.S. musician. Rhythm-and-blues/soul singer, associated with Motown Records since 1962, credited with doing much to advance popularity of rhythm-and-blues; partnered with Tammi Terrell (1967–70) in many hits. Songs: "How Sweet It Is to Be Loved by You," 1965; "Ain't No Mountain High Enough," 1967; "Ain't Nothing like the Real Thing," 1968; "I Heard It through the Grapevine," 1968; "Mercy Mercy Me," 1971.

**GIBB, ANDY,** Mar. 5, 1958 (Manchester, Eng.)– Mar. 10, 1988. English singer. One of the Gibb Brothers (see BEE GEES); a teen disco idol. Songs: "Shadow Dancing," "I Just Want to Be Your Everything."

**GILLEY, MICKEY LEROY,** Mar. 9, 1936 (Natchez, Miss.). U.S. singer. A country music singer, reached a larger audience through the movie, *Urban Cowboy* (1980), which featured two of his songs.

**GOLDSBORO, BOBBY,** Jan. 11, 1944 (Marianna, Fla.). U.S. singer, songwriter. Country-and-western performer; hits include "Honey," "The Straight Life"

**GORE, LESLEY,** May 2, 1946 (Tenafly, N.J.). U.S. singer. Rock singer of early 1960s. Songs: "It's My Party," 1963; "Judy's Turn to Cry," 1963; "Sunshine, Lollipops and Rainbows," 1965; "That's the Way Boys Are," 1964.

**GORME, EYDIE,** Aug. 16, 1932 (New York, N.Y.). U.S. singer. Often appears with husband STEVE LAWRENCE in clubs and on TV.

**GOULET, ROBERT,** Nov. 26, 1933 (Lawrence, Mass.). U.S. singer, actor. Pop singer and star of several Broadway musicals. (One-time husband of C. LAWRENCE.)

**GRANT, AMY,** 1961 (Augusta, Ga.). U.S. singer. From a top gospel star has moved into mainstream adult contemporary music; biggest hit was "The Next Time I Fall."

**GRAYSON, KATHRYN** (born Zelma Hedrick), Feb. 9, 1922 (Winston-Salem, N.C.). U.S. singer, actress. Leading lady in musical films of 1940s and 1950s, including *Anchors Aweigh* (1945), *Showboat* (1951), *Kiss Me Kate* (1953).

**GUTHRIE, ARLO,** July 10, 1947 (New York, N.Y.). U.S. folk-rock singer. Composed and recorded the hit song "Alice's Restaurant," 1969. (Son of WOODY GUTHRIE.)

**GUTHRIE, WOODY** (born Woodrow Wilson Guthrie), July 14, 1912 (Okemah, Okla.)–Oct. 3, 1967. U.S. folksinger, composer. Folk spokesman for populist and labor movements of the 1930s; his "This Land Is Your Land" was adopted by civil-rights movment of 1960s; other songs include "So Long, It's Been Good to Know You," "Hard Traveling," "Blowing Down This Old Dusty Road."

**HAGGARD, MERLE,** Apr. 6, 1937 (Bakersfield, Calif.). U.S. singer, songwriter. Country-and-western star with numerous number one hits: "Mama Tried," "If We Make It Through December," "Okie From Muskogee."

**HALEY, BILL** (born William John Clifton Haley), July 6, 1925 (Highland Park, Mich.)–Feb. 9, 1981. U.S. musician. Singer/songwriter/guitarist whose The Comets was a pioneering rock-and-roll group of the early 1950s; his musical style paved the way for the combining of country-and-western with rock. Songs: "Shake, Rattle and Roll," 1954; "Rock around the Clock," 1955; "See You Later Alligator," 1956.

**HALL, DARYL,** Oct. 11, 1949 (Pottstown, Pa.). U.S. singer. Lead singer of the soul duo, Hall & Oates, formed 1972, the number one group of the 1980s; hits include "Manhunter," "Kiss on My Lips," "Family Man," "Out of Touch," "Method of Modern Love," and "You Made My Dreams."

**HARRIS, EMMYLOU,** Apr. 2, 1947 (Birmingham, Ala.). U.S. singer, songwriter. Known for country-pop compositions; biggest hit has been the album,

*TRIO*, on which she performs with LINDA RONSTADT and DOLLY PARTON.

**HARRISON, GEORGE,** Feb. 25, 1943 (Liverpool, Eng.). British singer. Member of The Beatles, 1963–70; had some solo success after group split up.

**HARRY, DEBORAH,** July 11, 1945 (Miami, Fla.). U.S. singer. The lead singer for Blondie, one of the first breakthrough "New Wave" bands of the late 1970s and early 1980s; group's biggest hit was "Call Me" from *American Gigolo* (1980), but others included "One Way or Another," "Heart of Glass," and "Rapture"; after retiring for a period in mid-80s, now performs on her own.

**HAYMES, DICK,** Sept. 13, 1918 (Buenos Aires, Arg.)–Mar. 28, 1980. U.S. singer. Popular in the Big Bands of the 1940s. Films: *Irish Eyes Are Smiling* (1944), *State Fair* (1945), and *Up in Central Park* (1948).

**HENDERSON, FLORENCE,** Feb. 14, 1934 (Dale, Ind.). U.S. singer, actress. Stage and TV performer; best known as star of TV sitcom *The Brady Bunch*, 1969–74.

**HENDRIX, JIMI** (born James Marshall Hendricks), Nov. 27, 1942 (Seattle, Wash.)–Sept. 18, 1970. U.S. singer, guitarist. Leading exponent of 1960s "acid rock"; died of drug overdose.

**HOLIDAY, BILLIE** (born Eleanora Holiday), Apr. 7, 1915 (Baltimore, Md.)–July 17, 1959. U.S. singer. Stellar jazz-blues singer of late 1930s and early 1940s; during her last years she struggled with heroin addiction; her autobiography, *Lady Sings the Blues* (1956), inspired 1972 film of same name.

**HOLLY, BUDDY** (born Charles Holley), Sept. 7, 1936 (Lubbock, Tex.)–Feb. 3, 1959. U.S. singer, guitarist. Major influence in early rock-and-roll; leader of The Crickets; hits included "That'll Be the Day," "Maybe Baby," "Peggy Sue," "It Doesn't Matter Anymore."

**HOPKINS, SAM** ("Lightnin'"), Mar. 15, 1912 (Leon County, Tex.)–Jan. 30, 1982. U.S. singer/songwriter. Blues singer, whose style influenced 1970s rock-and-roll.

**HORNE, LENA,** June 30, 1917 (Brooklyn, N.Y.). U.S. singer. Beauteous star of nightclubs, concerts, TV; appeared in 1940s black musicals. Films: *Panama Hattie*, 1942; *Cabin in the Sky*, 1943; *Stormy Weather*, 1943.

**HOUSTON, WHITNEY,** Aug. 9, 1963 (E. Orange, N.J.). U.S. singer. Began career as a model; won grammy awards, 1985–87. Albums: *Whitney Houston*, 1985; *Whitney*, 1986.

**HUMPERDINCK, ENGELBERT** (born Arnold Dorsey), May 3, 1936 (Madras, India). English singer. Many hit records, including "Release Me," "The Last Waltz," "After the Lovin'."

**IAN, JANIS,** Apr. 7, 1950 (New York, N.Y.). U.S. singer/songwriter. Folk-rock star at 16, with her hit "Society's Child" (1966). Songs: "Seventeen," 1977.

**IDOL, BILLY,** Nov. 30, 1955 (London, Eng.). British singer. Began career as front man for British punk band, Generation X; as a solo has met with increasing success in the U.S., with hits such as

"Rebel Yell," "White Wedding," and "Eyes Without a Face."

IGLESIAS, JULIO (born Julio Jose Iglesias de la Cueva), Sept. 23, 1943 (Madrid, Sp.). Spanish singer. When a severe injury ended his soccer career turned to singing and has become an internationally known star; has sold over $100 million of records worldwide; best known songs in U.S. include his duets with WILLIE NELSON ("To All the Girls I've Loved Before") and DIANA ROSS ("All of You").

JACKSON, JANET, 1965 (Gary, Ind.). U.S. singer, actress. Previously known chiefly as MICHAEL JACKSON's baby sister, with album *Control* emerged as a new, fiercely independent voice on the contemporary music scene; hits include "When I Think of You," "Nasty Boys," and "Miss You Much." (Sister of JERMAINE and LA TOYA JACKSON.)

JACKSON, JERMAINE, Sept. 11, 1954 (Gary, Ind.). U.S. singer, musician. The first Jackson to embark on a solo career and the only one to stay with the group's original label, Motown; hits include "Let's Get Serious," "Dynamite," and "Torture" (with the Jacksons). (Brother of MICHAEL, JANET and LA TOYA JACKSON.)

JACKSON, MAHALIA, Oct. 26, 1911 (New Orleans, La.)–Jan. 27, 1972. U.S. singer. Gospel singer, a prime example of link between religious and secular roots of jazz.

JACKSON, MICHAEL, Aug. 29, 1958 (Gary, Ind.). U.S. singer, actor. Started career as member of The Jackson 5, 1969-84, then went on his own and became international superstar. TV. *The Jacksons* (series), 1976–77. Films: *The Wiz*, 1978; *Moonwalker*, 1988. Albums: *Off the Wall*, 1979; *Thriller*, 1982; *Bad*, 1987. (Brother of JANET, JERMAINE, and LA TOYA JACKSON.)

JAGGER, MICK, July 26, 1943 (Dartford, Eng.). English rock singer. Leader of The Rolling Stones group since 1962; wrote many of group's hits, including "Ruby Tuesday," "Brown Sugar," and "Jumpin' Jack Flash"; known for flamboyant onstage mannerisms.

JARREAU, AL, Mar. 12, 1940 (Milwaukee, Wis.). U.S. singer. Often compared to NAT "KING" COLE and SAM COOKE; a favorite with jazz fans, but has sought a wider audience through recordings such as "We Get By," "Breaking Away," and the theme song for the *Moonlighting* TV series.

JEFFERSON, BLIND LEMON, c.1897 (Texas)–1930. U.S. blues singer and guitarist.

JENNINGS, WAYLON, Jun 15, 1937 (Littlefield, Tex.). U.S. singer. Known as "the outlaw," a reference to his wild and sometimes illegal behavior; was a musician with BUDDY HOLLY's Crickets; hits include "Ol' Waylon" and "Waylon and Willie."

JETT, JOAN, Sept. 22, 1960 (Philadelphia, Pa.). U.S. singer. Started at the age of 15 with the all-girl group, The Runaways; after its break-up and a bout with alcohol addiction started her own band, The Blackhearts, to become one of the hottest acts of the 1980s; hits include "I Love to Rock and Roll," "Crimson and Clover" and "Do You Wanna Touch Me (Oh Yeah)."

JOEL, BILLY, May 9, 1949 (Bronx, N.Y.). U.S. singer, songwriter. Exponent of urban rock and roll; writes original, varied ballads. Songs: "Piano Man," "Just The Way You Are," "My Life," "It's Still Rock and Roll To Me."

JOHN, ELTON (born Reginald Dwight), Mar. 25, 1947 (Pinner, Eng.). English rock star. Songs: "Goodbye Yellow Brick Road," "Don't Let the Sun Go Down on Me," "Rocket Man," "Daniel," "Don't Go Breaking My Heart," "Sad Songs."

JOLSON, AL (born Asa Yoelson), May 26, 1886 (Srednick, Rus.)–Oct. 23, 1950. U.S. singer, actor. Musical comedy star (often in blackface); starred in *The Jazz Singer*, the first talking film (1927). (One-time husband of R. KEELER.)

JONES, ALLAN, Oct. 10, 1907 (Scranton, Pa.). U.S. singer. Leading man in films of 1930s, including *A Night at the Opera* (1935), *Show Boat* (1936), and *The Firefly* (1937). (Father of J. JONES.)

JONES, JACK, Jan. 14, 1938 (Hollywood, Calif.). U.S. singer. Popular singer in nightclubs. (Son of A. JONES.)

JONES, SHIRLEY, Mar. 31, 1934 (Smithton, Pa.). U.S. singer, actress. Star of musical comedy films *Oklahoma* (1955), *Carousel* (1956), *The Music Man* (1962); received AA for best supporting actress in *Elmer Gantry* (1960); star of *The Partridge Family* TV series, 1970–74. (One-time wife of J. CASSIDY; mother of Shaun Cassidy; stepmother of D. CASSIDY.)

JONES, TOM (born Thomas Jones Woodward), June 7, 1940 (Pontypridd, Wales). Welsh singer. Sexy, gyrating pop singer. Songs: "It's Not Unusual," "Delilah," "Love Me Tonight," "She's a Lady."

JOPLIN, JANIS, Jan. 19, 1943 (Port Arthur, Tex.)–Oct. 4, 1970. U.S singer. Whiskey-voiced rock superstar; lead vocalist with Big Brother and the Holding Company, 1966–68; Songs: "Me and Bobby McGee," "Try."

KAZAN, LAINIE (born Lainie Levine), May 15, 1942 (Brooklyn, N.Y.). U.S. singer, actress. Frequent performer in clubs and on TV.

KHAN, CHAKA (born Yvette Marie Stevens), Mar. 23, 1953 (Great Lakes, Ill.). U.S. singer. Began career as lead singer for soul/R&B group Rufus; as a solo has collaborated with STEVIE WONDER, PRINCE, MILES DAVIS, QUINCY JONES and many other music legends; hits include "Tell Me Something Good," "I Feel for You," "Ain't Nobody," and "This is My Night."

KING, B.B. (born Riley B. King), Sept. 16, 1925 (Itta Bena, Miss.). U.S. singer, guitarist. Leading exponent of rhythm-and-blues style; many recordings, concert appearances; received Grammy award, 1970.

KING, CAROLE (born Carole Klein), Feb. 9, 1942 (Brooklyn, N.Y.). U.S. singer/songwriter. A popular folk-rock performer of 1970s; with then-husband Gerry Goffin, wrote hit songs in the 1960s recorded by other groups (most notably "The Locomotion" for Little Eva and "Hi-De-Ho" for BLOOD, SWEAT and TEARS). Songs: "So Far Away," "Where You Lead," "Tapestry," "It's Too Late," "You've Got a Friend."

**KITT, EARTHA**, Jan. 26, 1928 (North, S.C.). U.S. singer, actress. Singer in clubs since the 1950s, in U.S. and Europe; featured in the shows *New Faces of 1952* (1952), *Shinbone Alley* (1957) and *Timbuktu!* (1978).

**KNIGHT, GLADYS**, May 28, 1944 (Atlanta, Ga.). U.S. singer. With soul group The Pips, has performed in concerts, and on TV, since 1952. Songs: "Heard It Through the Grapevine," "Midnight Train to Georgia."

**LABELLE, PATTI** (born Patricia Holt), Oct. 4, 1944 (Philadelphia, Pa.). U.S. singer. With her group The Bluebells, an early exponent of the "Philadelphia Sound" in 1960s rock; in the 1970s, led rock-disco singing group LaBelle; solo performer, from 1978. Songs: "Down the Aisle," 1963; "I Sold My Heart to the Junkman," 1964; "You Never Walk Alone," 1964; "All or Nothing," 1966; "Lady Marmalade," 1974.

**LAINE, CLEO** (born Clementina Dinah Duckworth), Oct. 28, 1927 (Middlesex, Eng.). British singer, actress. Won Grammy as best female jazz vocalist, 1986. Stage: *Mystery of Edwin Drood*, 1986.

**LAINE, FRANKIE** (born Frank Lo Vecchio), Mar. 30, 1913 (Chicago, Ill.). U.S. singer. Popular in 1950s. Songs: "That's My Desire," "Mule Train," "The Wild Goose."

**LANG, K.D.**, 1962 (Consort, Alta.). U.S. singer. Country music singer noted for her "torch and twang" style. Albums: *Shadowland*; *Absolute Torch and Twang*.

**LANZA, MARIO** (born Alfredo Cocozza), Jan. 31, 1921 (Philadelphia, Pa.)–Oct. 7, 1959. U.S. singer, actor. Tenor who starred in MGM musicals in 1950s. Films: *The Great Caruso*, 1951; *Because You're Mine*, 1952; *The Student Prince* (voice only), 1954; *Serenade*, 1956.

**LAUPER, CYNDI**, June 20, 1953 (Queens, N.Y.). U.S. singer, songwriter. Breakthrough solo album was *She's Unusual* in 1985 for which she received six Grammy awards, but subsequent albums have been disappointing; hits include "Time After Time," "True Colors," "All Through the Night," and "Girls Just Want to Have Fun."

**LAWRENCE, STEVE** (born Sidney Leibowitz), July 8, 1935 (Brooklyn, N.Y.). U.S. singer, actor. Has appeared in nightclubs, on TV, often with wife EYDIE GORME.

**LEDBETTER, HUDDIE** ("Leadbelly"), c.1888 (Louisiana)–Dec. 6, 1949. U.S. blues singer, guitarist. Composed the song "Good Night, Irene."

**LEE, MICHELE** (born Michele Dusiak), June 24, 1942 (Los Angeles, Calif.). U.S. singer, actress, TV, club, and Broadway career. Films: *How to Succeed in Business...*, 1967. TV (series): *Knots Landing*, 1979.

**LEE, PEGGY** (born Norma Egstrom), May 26, 1920 (Jamestown, S.D.). U.S. singer. Began with BENNY GOODMAN band, 1941–43; appeared in some films; frequent appearances in concerts, clubs.

Records: "Fever," "It's a Good Day," "Manana," "Is that All There Is?"

**LENNON, JOHN**, Oct. 9, 1940 (Liverpool, Eng.)–Dec. 8, 1980. English singer, composer, political activist. Member of The Beatles, 1969–71; wrote (with PAUL MCCARTNEY) many of the group's songs. Films: *A Hard Day's Night*, 1964; *Help!*, 1965.

**LENYA, LOTTE** (born Karoline Blamauer), Oct. 18, 1898 (Vienna, Aus.)–Nov. 27, 1981. Austrian cabaret singer, character actress. The wife of KURT WEILL, known for her interpretations of his songs; fled Germany with Weill (1933) to U.S., where she appeared in plays.

**LEWIS, HUEY** (born Hugh Anthony Craig III), July 5, 1951 (New York, N.Y.). U.S singer, composer. With group, Huey Lewis and the News, 1978– ; hit singles include "Do You Believe in Love." Albums: *Picture This*, 1982; *Sports*, 1983; *Fore!*, 1986.

**LEWIS, JERRY LEE**, Sept. 29, 1935 (Ferriday, La.). U.S. musician. A singer/pianist/songwriter, one of the first rockers to incorporate sexually provocative physical behavior into his act; known for hard-driving style; caused scandal in 1958 by marrying 13-year-old cousin. Songs: "Great Balls of Fire," 1957; "Whole Lotta Shakin' Goin' On," 1958.

**LIGHTFOOT, GORDON**, Nov. 17, 1938 (Orillia, Ont., Can.). Canadian singer/songwriter of folk-rock music in 1960s and 1970s; many of his songs were recorded by other performers; known for haunting lyrics and sad melodies. Songs: "Early Morning Rain"; "If You Could Read My Mind."

**LITTLE RICHARD** (born Richard Penniman), Dec. 25, 1935 (Macon, Ga.). U.S. singer, songwriter. His frenetic style influenced the styles of many rock-and-roll artists; left profession to become a minister. Songs: "Tutti Frutti," "Long Tall Sally," "Good Golly Miss Molly," "Whole Lotta Shakin' Goin' On," "Slippin' and Slidin'."

**LOGGINS, KENNY**, Jan. 7, 1948 (Everett, Wash.). U.S. singer, songwriter. With JIM MESSINA formed country rock duo, 1970–74; solo performer, from 1974.

**LYNN, LORETTA** (born Loretta Webb), Jan. 14, 1935 (Butcher Hollow, Ky.). U.S. singer. Country-and-western singing star; numerous Gold Records; named Country Music Assn. female vocalist of year, 1967, 1972–73. Autobiography: *Coal Miner's Daughter*, 1977.

**MACDONALD, JEANETTE**, June 18, 1903 (Philadelphia, Pa.)–Jan. 14, 1965. U.S. singer, actress. With NELSON EDDY, made a series of films of operettas (1935–42), including *Naughty Marietta* (1935), *Rose Marie* (1936), *Maytime* (1937), *New Moon* (1940). (Wife of G. RAYMOND.)

**MADONNA** (born Madonna Louise Veronica Ciccone), Aug. 16, 1959 (Bay City, Mich.). U.S. singer. Burst onto music scene in 1980s and greatly influenced clothing styles and attitudes; her music is continually changing making it difficult to label; many hit songs include, "Like a Prayer," "Papa

Don't Preach," "Crazy for You'," and "Lucky Star." Films: *Desperately Seeking Susan*, 1985. (Onetime wife of S. PENN.)

MANCHESTER, MELISSA, Feb. 15, 1951 (Bronx, N.Y.). U.S. singer, songwriter. Began her career singing on television commercials; became member of BETTE MIDLER's backup band before striking out on her own; also a gifted pianist and song writer; hits include "Don't Cry Out Loud," "You Should Hear How She Talks About You," and "Come in From the Rain."

MANDRELL, BARBARA, Dec. 25, 1948 (Houston, Tex.). U.S. singer. A country singer, gained recognition in the 1980s after years of struggling; parlayed her popularity into a weekly TV show (1980–82) and parts in various movies; also has performed with her sisters Irlene and Louise as the Mandrell Sisters.

MANILOW, BARRY, June 17, 1946 (New York, N.Y.). U.S. singer, songwriter. Pop-rock singing star who began writing advertising jingles and serving as BETTE MIDLER's accompanist/arranger. Songs: "At the Copa," "Mandy," "I Write the Songs."

MARTIN, TONY, Dec. 25, 1913 (San Francisco, Calif.). U.S. singer. Big Band-era singer who made transition to films. (Husband of C. CHARISSE.)

MATHIS, JOHNNY, Sept. 30, 1935 (San Francisco, Calif.). U.S. singer. Mellow-voiced pop singer of ballads; most popular songs include "Wonderful, Wonderful," "It's Not For Me to Say," "A Certain Smile," "Misty," "Chances Are," and "The Shadow of Your Smile."

MCCARTNEY, PAUL, June 18, 1942 (Liverpool, Eng.). English musician. Lead singer and songwriter for The Beatles, 1962–70; with Wings, 1970–  . Compositions (with J. LENNON): "Yesterday," "Michelle," "Hey Jude," "And I Love Her," "Eleanor Rigby." Compositions (solo): "Wings Wild Life," "My Love," "Band on the Run."

MCENTIRE, REBA, Mar. 28, 1955 (McAlester, Okla.). U.S. singer. A country music superstar, was named best female vocalist of the year for four years in a row by the Country Music Association, 1983–87; won a Grammy and Entertainer of the Year award, 1987.

MCFERRIN, BOBBY, Mar. 11, 1950 (New York, N.Y.). U.S. singer, musician. Jazz singer with the ability to imitate various musical instruments with his voice; hits include "Don't Worry, Be Happy," "Round Midnight," and the theme song for the 4th season of *The Bill Cosby Show*.

MCGOVERN, MAUREEN, July 27, 1949 (Youngstown, Oh.). U.S. singer, composer. Best known for the song "The Morning After" from the soundtrack of *The Poseidon Adventure* (1972).

MCLEAN, DON, Oct. 2, 1945 (New Rochelle, N.Y.). U.S. musician. Singer, songwriter, guitarist; best known for popular 1970s song "American Pie."

MELANIE (born Melanie Safka), Feb. 3, 1947 (New York, N.Y.). U.S. singer, songwriter. Pop-folk-rock singer of the late 1960s and early 1970s. Songs: "Peace Will Come," "Lay Down,"

MELLENCAMP, JOHN COUGAR, Oct. 7, 1951 (Seymour, Ind.). U.S. singer, songwriter. Long known for his songwriting, came to prominence as a singer with his album, *American Fool*, which included the hits, "Jack and Diane" and "Hurts So Good." Albums: *Uh-Huh*, 1983; *Scarecrow*, 1985; *Lonesome Jubilee*, 1988.

MICHAEL, GEORGE, June 25, 1963 (London, Eng.). British singer, musician. Noted for songs and videos that are sometimes explicit; his best-selling debut album *Faith* included hit songs "Faith," "I Want Your Sex," "Kissing a Fool," and "Father Figure."

MIDLER, BETTE ("The Divine Miss M"), Dec. 1, 1945 (Paterson, N.J.). U.S. singer, actress. Started career in gay bathhouse in New York City; first album, "The Divine Miss M," 1972. Films: *The Rose*, 1979; *Down and Out in Beverly Hills*, 1986; *Ruthless People*, 1986; *Outrageous Fortune*, 1987; *Big Business*, 1988; *Beaches*, 1988.

MILLER, ROGER, Jan. 2, 1936 (Ft. Worth, Tex.). U.S. singer, songwriter. Country-western performer, very popular in 1960s; hits include "Dang Me," "England Swings," "King of the Road"; composed Broadway musical "Big River," 1986.

MILSAP, RONNIE, Jan. 16, 1943 (Robinsville, N.C.). U.S. singer. Blind country-and-western singer who has won numerous Grammy awards.

MINNELLI, LIZA, Mar. 12, 1946 (Los Angeles, Calif.). U.S. singer, actress. Daughter of JUDY GARLAND and VINCENTE MINNELLI; successful stage, film and TV career. Stage: *Flora and the Red Menace* (Tony Award), 1967; *The Act* (Tony Award), 1977. Films: *The Sterile Cuckoo*, 1969; *Cabaret* (Best Actress AA), 1972; *New York, New York*, 1977; *Arthur*, 1981.

MITCHELL, JONI (born Roberta Joan Anderson), Nov. 7, 1943 (Macleod, Alta., Can.). Canadian singer, songwriter. Began as folksinger in Toronto coffeehouses, 1964; gained fame with song "Both Sides Now," 1968.

THE MONKEES: Mickey Dolenz, Mar. 8, 1945 (Los Angeles, Calif.); David Jones, Dec. 30, 1945 (Manchester, Eng.); Michael Nesmith, Dec. 30, 1943 (Houston, Tex.); Peter Tork, Feb. 13, 1944 (Washington, D.C.). U.S. musicians, actors. Manufactured TV-rock group, formed 1965 to star in sitcom; group broke up in 1969.

MOORE, MELBA, Oct. 29, 1945 (New York, N.Y.). U.S. singer, actress. Starred on Broadway in *Hair* (1968) and *Purlie* (1970).

MORRISON, JIM, Dec. 8, 1943 (Melbourne, Fla.)–July 3, 1971. U.S. musician. Leading rock vocalist of 1960s, as part of supergroup The Doors 1965–71; victim of drug overdose; one of the first '60s rock sex symbols. Songs: "Light My Fire," 1966; "People are Strange," 1967; "Hello, I Love You," 1968; "Love Her Madly," 1971.

MURRAY, ANNE, June 20, 1945 (Springhill, N.S., Can.). Canadian singer. Songs: "You Needed Me," "Snowbird."

NELSON, WILLIE, Apr. 30, 1933 (Abbott, Tex.). U.S. singer, actor. Country-western musician, a regular with *Grand Ole Opry* since 1964. Films: *The Electric Horseman,* 1979; *Honeysuckle Rose,* 1980; *Songwriter,* 1985.

NEWMAN, RANDY, Nov. 28, 1943 (Los Angeles, Calif.). U.S. singer, songwriter. Pop-rock singer/composer.

NEWTON, WAYNE, Apr. 3, 1942 (Norfolk, Va.). U.S. singer. Extremely popular on Las Vegas show circuit.

NEWTON-JOHN, OLIVIA, Sept. 26, 1948 (Cambridge, Eng.). British-Australian pop singer. Songs: "Let Me Be There," "I Honestly Love You," "Have You Never Been Mellow," "Physical." Films: *Grease,* 1978.

NYRO, LAURA, 1947 (Bronx, N.Y.). U.S. singer, songwriter of the late 1960s and early 1970s, known for her urbanized rock. Compositions: "Stoned Soul Picnic," "Wedding Bell Blues," "And When I Die."

OCEAN, BILLY, Jan. 21, 1952 (Trinidad). Trinidadian singer. A crooner of romantic ballads, attained increased popularity with videos for songs, "Lover Boy," "Caribbean Queen," and the theme song from the film *The Jewel of the Nile:* "When the Going Gets Tough (The Tough Get Going)."

O'CONNELL, HELEN, May 23, 1920 (Lima, Ohio). U.S. singer. Big Band-era singer.

O'DAY, ANITA, Oct. 18, 1919 (Chicago, Ill.). U.S. singer. Best known for stint with GENE KRUPA and STAN KENTON bands in 1940s.

ODETTA (born Odetta Holmes), Dec. 31, 1930 (Birmingham, Ala.). U.S. singer. Leading folksinger of the 1950s and 1960s, known for mellow style and African motifs.

ORBISON, ROY, Apr. 23, 1936 (Vernon, Tex.) –Dec. 6, 1988. U.S. musician. Singer/composer of rock and roll in 1950s, credited with creating mass market for the music; career floundered in middle 1960s. Songs: "Oh, Pretty Woman," "Ooby-Dooby," "Running Scared," "Crying," "Dream Baby," "Blue Bayou."

ORLANDO, TONY (born Michael Anthony Orlando Cassavitis), Apr. 3, 1944 (New York, N.Y.). U.S. singer. Pop singer of "Tie a Yellow Ribbon 'round the Old Oak Tree," "Knock Three Times," "Candida," with Dawn back-up group; had TV variety show in the 1970s.

OSBOURNE, OZZY (born John Osbourne), Dec. 3, 1948 (Birmingham, Eng.). British singer. Known as a wild man, was lead singer for heavy metal band Black Sabbath, 1968–78. Albums: *Bark at the Moon,* 1983; *The Ultimate Sin,* 1986; *Just Say Ozzy,* 1989.

OSMOND, DONNY, Dec. 9, 1957 (Ogden, Utah). U.S. singer. With Osmond Family group since 1961; solo since 1971; with sister MARIE, star of a TV variety show, 1976–79.

OSMOND, MARIE, Oct. 13, 1959 (Ogden, Utah). U.S. singer. With family group since 1966; solo since 1973; starred with brother DONNY on TV variety show, 1976–79.

OWENS, BUCK (born Alvis Edgar Owens, Jr.), Aug. 12, 1929 (Sherman, Tex.). U.S. singer, guitarist. Leader of Buckaroos band, since 1960; star of *Hee-Haw* TV series, 1969–71.

PAGE, PATTI (born Clara Anne Fowler), Nov. 8, 1927 (Claremore, Okla.). U.S. singer. Began on radio, 1946; popular in 1950s and 1960s; hits include "How Much Is That Doggy in the Window?," "In Old Cape Cod," "Hush, Hush, Sweet Charlotte."

PARTON, DOLLY, Jan. 19, 1946 (Seiverville, Tenn.). U.S. singer. Country-and-western singing star who bridged gap into pop; teamed with PORTER WAGONER. Films: *9 to 5,* 1980; *Best Little Whorehouse in Texas,* 1982. Host TV variety show, 1987.

PAYCHECK, JOHNNY, May 31, 1941 (Greenfield, Oh.). U.S. singer. A country music stalwart for nearly three decades; his biggest success was the top 10 crossover hit "Take This Job and Shove It" in the mid-1970s.

PEARL, MINNIE (born Sarah Ophelia Colley Cannon), Oct. 25, 1912 (Centerville, Tenn.). U.S. singer, comedienne. Known for her outlandish clothes and straw hat with price tag hanging on it; a fixture at Nashville's Grand Ole Opry since 1940.

PIAF, EDITH (born Edith Gassion), Dec. 1915 (Paris, Fr.)–Oct. 11, 1963. French singer. Legendary international cabaret star who began as a street singer in Paris, 1930; known for her emotional, powerful voice and delivery, especially in the songs "Milord," "Non, Je Ne Regrette Rien," and "La Vie en Rose."

PICKETT, WILSON, Mar. 18, 1941 (Prattville, Ala.). U.S. singer/songwriter. Rhythm and blues singer, originally with The Falcons. Songs: "If You Need Me," 1963; "Don't Fight It," 1965; "Land of 1,000 Dances," 1966; "Engine Number 9."

PITNEY, GENE, Feb. 17, 1941 (Hartford, Conn.). U.S. musician. Songs: "Town without Pity," "24 Hours from Tulsa," "The Man Who Shot Liberty Valance," "Only Love Can Break a Heart," "Looking through the Eyes of Love."

PRESLEY, ELVIS, Jan. 8, 1935 (Tupelo, Miss.)–Aug. 16, 1977. U.S. singer, actor. Pelvis-grinding king of rock-and-roll in the 1950s and 1960s; in addition to many records, also made musical movies. Songs: "Love Me Tender," "Hound Dog," "Blue Suede Shoes," "Heartbreak Hotel," "Are You Lonesome Tonight," "In the Ghetto," "Don't Be Cruel." Films: *Love Me Tender,* 1956; *Jailhouse Rock,* 1957; *King Creole,* 1958; *Girls, Girls, Girls,* 1962; *Viva Las Vegas,* 1964; many others.

PRICE, (Noble) RAY, Jan. 12, 1926 (Perryville, Tex.). U.S. singer. Country-and-western singer whose greatest hits have been "Crazy Arms," "Release Me," "Danny Boy," "For the Good Times."

PRIDE, CHARLEY, Mar. 18, 1939 (Sledge, Miss.). U.S. singer. One of first blacks in country-and-western field; recorded "Let the Chips Fall," "Kiss an Angel Good Morning," "I'd Rather Love You," "She Made Me Go."

RABBIT, EDDIE, Nov. 27, 1941 (Brooklyn, N.Y.).

U.S. singer. A former truck driver, has written over 300 songs; hits include "I Love a Rainy Night," "Kentucky Rain," "Step by Step," and "Driving My Life Away."

**RAINEY, MA** (born Gertrude Melissa Nix Pridgett), Apr. 26, 1886 (Columbus, Ga.)–Dec. 22, 1939. U.S. musician. Jazz singer, who began in cabarets and then appeared in black vaudeville shows; her blues recordings of 1923–29 are considered major historical items; BESSIE SMITH was her protégé.

**RAWLS, LOU,** Dec. 1, 1936 (Chicago, Ill.). U.S. singer. Started as gospel singer, a leading exponent of rhythm-and-blues. Songs: "A Natural Man," "You'll Never Find Another Love Like Mine."

**RAY, JOHNNIE,** Jan. 10, 1927 (Dallas, Ore.)–Feb. 23, 1990. U.S singer. Pop singer best known for 1950s hits "Cry" and "The Little White Cloud That Cried."

**REDDING, OTIS,** Sept. 9, 1941 (Macon, Ga.)–Dec. 10, 1967. U.S. singer, songwriter. Leading rhythm-and-blues soul singer of 1960s; became a superstar only with posthumous release of his "Dock of the Bay," 1968.

**REDDY, HELEN,** Oct. 25, 1941 (Melbourne, Austrl.). Australian singer, songwriter. Pop star in her native land, came to U.S. (1966). Songs: "I Don't Know How to Love Him," "I Am Woman," "Leave Me Alone," "Ain't No Way to Treat a Lady."

**REED, JERRY,** (born Jerry Hubbard) Mar. 20, 1937 (Atlanta, Ga.) U.S. singer, guitarist. Country-rock performer, known for his slightly offbeat songs (many of which he wrote); hits include "Guitar Man," "U.S. Male," "Amos Moses," "When You're Hot, You're Hot," "Lord, Mr. Ford."

**REED, LOU,** Mar. 20, 1943 (New York, N.Y.). U.S. musician. Bizarre singer/songwriter/guitarist who achieved some fame with group Velvet Underground (1966–71), but had greatest success as solo performer who presaged punk rock with his hard-driving style. Song: "Walk on the Wild Side," 1973.

**REESE, DELLA** (born Delloreese Patricia Early), July 6, 1931 (Detroit, Mich.). U.S. singer who sang with MAHALIA JACKSON, 1945–49; nightclub and concert soloist, 1957– ; appears frequently on TV.

**RICH, CHARLIE** ("The Silver Fox"), Dec. 14, 1932 (Forrest City, Ark.). U.S. singer. Country-and-western singer; best known 1970s hits "Behind Closed Doors," and "The Most Beautiful Girl."

**RICHARDS, KEITH,** Dec. 18, 1943 (Dartford, Eng.). British singer. The heart and soul of The Rolling Stones, one of the group's founding members; has long expressed a love and affinity for American blues. Albums: *Beggars Banquet*; *Let It Bleed*; *Exile on Main Street* (with MICK JAGGER); *Keith Richards* (solo album).

**RICHIE, LIONEL,** June 20, 1949 (Tuskegee, Ala.). U.S. singer, songwriter. A founding member of the Commodores, left due to demands of a solo career; his emotionally resonant songs span a wide range of musical tastes; songs include "Endless Love" (with DIANA ROSS), "Say You, Say Me," "All Night Long," and "Hello."

**RIPERTON, MINNIE,** Nov. 8, 1947 (Chicago, Ill.)–July 12, 1979. U.S. singer. Pop-soul singer of the 1970s, known for her octave range; backup singer, 1963–70; with group Rotary Connection, 1966–70; major hit: "Loving You," 1973.

**RITTER, TEX** (born Woodward Ritter), Jan. 12, 1907 (Murvaul, Tex.)–Jan. 2, 1974. U.S. singer, songwriter. Singing cowboy of stage, screen and broadcasting; starred in 60 films, 1936–45; won AA for singing title song to *High Noon*, 1952; with Grand Ole Opry, 1965–73; elected to Country Music Hall of Fame, 1965. (Father of J. RITTER.)

**RIVERS, JOHNNY** (born John Ramistella), Nov. 7. 1942. (New York, N.Y.). U.S. musician. Singer/guitarist/songwriter who discovered the Fifth Dimension singing group; Alan Freed gave him his name and started his career, 1960; starred at Whiskey-a-Go-Go discotheque in Los Angeles. Songs: "Memphis," "Seventh Son," "Secret Agent Man."

**ROBBINS, MARTY** (born Martin Robinson), Sept. 26, 1925 (Glendale, Ariz.)–Dec. 8, 1982. U.S. country-and-western singer who was a favorite at the Grand Ole Opry. Songs: "El Paso," "My Woman, My Woman, My Wife."

**ROBINSON, WILLIAM "SMOKEY,"** Feb. 10, 1940 (Detroit, Mich.). U.S. singer. A rock music legend, as a singer, songwriter, record producer and v.p. of a record company (Motown) career has spanned an era; started as one of The Miracles with hits such as "Shop Around" and "Tears of a Clown"; has seen a resurgence with hits "Cruising," "Being With You," and "One Heartbeat."

**RODGERS, JIMMIE** ("The Singing Brakeman"), Sept. 8, 1897 (Meridian, Miss.)–May 26, 1933. U.S. singer, songwriter. Former railroadman, first hillbilly-country music star, known for his "blue yodels," 13 songs with distinctive yodel ending.

**ROGERS, KENNY,** Aug. 21, 1938 (Houston, Tex.). U.S. singer. Country-rock singer whose roots were in folk music (was with the New Christy Minstrels, 1965–67); formed The First Edition, 1967. Songs: "Ruby," "Lucille," "The Gambler," "Lady," "I Don't Need You." Has starred in several TV movies.

**RONSTADT, LINDA,** July 15, 1946 (Tucson, Ariz.). U.S. singer. Pop-rock superstar who began as lead singer with Stone Poneys group, 1964–68; starred in the theater and opera in the 1980s. Albums: *Hasten Down the Wind, Simple Dreams, Evergreen, Don't Cry Now; Heart Like a Wheel; Trio* (with DOLLY PARTON and EMMYLOU HARRIS); *Blue Bayou.*

**ROSS, DIANA,** Mar. 26, 1944 (Detroit, Mich.). U.S. singer, actress. With two friends, formed The Supremes (1958), a leading 1960s soul group; solo since 1969; star of films *Lady Sings the Blues* (1972), *Mahogany* (1974) and *The Wiz* (1978).

**ROTH, DAVID LEE,** Oct. 10, 1955 (Bloomington, Ind.). U.S singer. Flamboyant, the model of excess, with the Van Halen brothers and Michael Anthony came to symbolize the "California Sound" of the late 1970s and early 1980s; started as front man for Van Halen, but left group after they hit number one with "Jump," for a solo career; solo hits include "California Girls" and "Just a Gigolo."

**RUNDGREN, TODD,** June 22, 1948 (Upper Darby, Pa.). U.S. singer/guitarist. Rock bandleader of late 1960s (The Nazz, 1968–70) and later a frequent producer of sessions for other rock groups; now a solo act. Songs: "Hello, It's Me," 1969; "We Got to Get You a Woman," 1970; "A Long Way to Go," 1971; "Couldn't I Just Tell You," 1972; "I Saw the Light," 1972.

**RUSHING, JIMMY** ("Mr. Five by Five"), Aug. 26, 1903 (Oklahoma City, Okla.)–June 8, 1972. U.S. musician. Jazz-blues singer with bands in 1920s, but most famous as singer with COUNT BASIE, 1935–50.

**RUSSELL, LILLIAN** (born Helen Leonard), Dec. 4, 1861 (Clinton, Ia.)–June 6, 1922. U.S. singer and actress. Stage beauty of the gaslight era; appeared as a singer with Tony Pastor's shows (from 1880) and with the Weber and Fields Burlesque Co. (1899–1904).

**RYDELL, BOBBY** (born Robert Ridarelli), Apr. 26, 1942 (Philadelphia, Pa.). U.S. singer. Teen idol of the late 1950s–early 1960s; hits include "Kissin' Time," "Wild One," "Volare," "Forget Him."

**SAINTE-MARIE, BUFFY,** Feb. 20, 1941 (Maine), Canadian singer, songwriter. Best known for protest songs, "Universal Soldier."

**SCAGGS, BOZ** (born Wiliam Royce Scaggs), June 8, 1944 (Ohio). U.S. singer. Noted for mixing elements of Soul/R&B with British popular music; hits include "We're All Alone," "Look What You've Done to Me," "Jojo," and "Lowdown."

**SEBASTIAN, JOHN,** Mar. 17, 1944 (New York, N.Y.). U.S. musician. Pop-rock singer/instrumenalist; a major influence in late '60s music for combination of rock, jazz, folk and blues; founded and led Lovin' Spoonful group in the 1960s.

**SEDAKA, NEIL,** Mar. 13, 1939 (New York, N.Y.). U.S. singer, songwriter. Pop-rock star since the 1950s; recorded "Stupid Cupid," "Calendar Girl," "Stairway to Heaven," "Love Will Keep Us Together," "Breaking Up Is Hard to Do," "Laughter in the Rain."

**SEEGER, PETE,** May 3, 1919 (New York, N.Y.). U.S. singer, composer. Dean of American folksingers; collaborator with WOODY GUTHRIE; organizer of The Weavers group, 1949; associated with radical-left politics; sang and composed "Where Have All the Flowers Gone?," "If I Had a Hammer," "Turn, Turn, Turn."

**SHANNON, DEL** (born Charles Westover), Dec. 30, 1939 (Coopersville, Mich.)–Feb. 9, 1990. U.S. musician. Rock singer popular in the 1960s. Songs: "Runaway," "Hats Off to Larry," "Keep Searchin'."

**SHORE, DINAH** (born Frances Shore), Mar. 1, 1917 (Winchester, Tenn.). U.S. singer, talk-show hostess. Pop singer with bands, on radio and TV in the 1940s and 1950s; hostess of TV talk shows *Dinah's Place* (1970–74) and *Dinah!* (1974–79).

**SHORT, BOBBY,** Sept. 15, 1924 (Danville, Ill.).

U.S. singer, pianist. Nightclub and pop singer-pianist. Specializes in interpretations of COLE PORTER songs.

**SIMON, CARLY,** June 25, 1945 (New York, N.Y.). U.S. singer. Rock singer and composer. Songs: *Anticipation, That's The Way I Always Heard It Should Be, You're So Vain.* (One-time wife of J. TAYLOR.)

**SIMON, PAUL,** Nov. 13, 1941 (Newark, N.J.). U.S. singer, composer. Teamed with ART GARFUNKEL in 1960s; solo performer since 1970; hits include "The Dangling Conversation," "Scarborough Fair," "Sounds of Silence," "Bridge over Troubled Water," "The Boxer," "Me and Julio down by the Schoolyard," "Mrs. Robinson," "Slip Slidin' Away."

**SIMONE, NINA** (born Eunice Wayman), Feb. 21, 1933 (Tryon, N.C.). U.S. singer, pianist. Jazz artist, composer since 1954; recorded "The Other Woman," "I Don't Want Him, You Can Have Him," "Black Is the Color," "Children, Go Where I Send You," "Nina's Blues."

**SINATRA, FRANK,** Dec. 12, 1915 (Hoboken, N.J.). U.S. singer, actor. Teen heartthrob of 1940s Big Band era; major pop singer ever since; notable film career. Songs: "Night and Day," "Love and Marriage," "Chicago," "Strangers in the Night," "My Way." Films: *On the Town*, 1949; *From Here to Eternity* (Best Supporting Actor AA), 1953; *High Society*, 1956; *Pal Joey*, 1957; *The Manchurian Candidate*, 1962; *The Detective*, 1968.

**SLICK, GRACE,** Oct. 30, 1939 (Chicago, Ill.). U.S. singer. Rock star as lead vocalist with Jefferson Airplane (1966–72) and Jefferson Starship (1974–  ).

**SMITH, BESSIE,** Apr. 15, 1894 (Chattanooga, Tenn.)–Sept. 26, 1937. U.S. singer. Legendary blues singer of 1920s–1930s who sang in vaudeville and recorded with most major jazz groups of day; after 1930, her career declined because of alcoholism; bled to death in car wreck.

**SMITH, KATE,** May 1, 1909 (Greenville, Va.)–May 17, 1986. U.S. singer. Singer popular in the 1930s, when she had a top-rated weekly radio program; beloved for her rendition of "God Bless America."

**SMITH, KEELY,** Mar. 9, 1935 (Norfolk, Va.). U.S. singer. Jazz-pop singer with LOUIS PRIMA Band since 1948; married Prima, 1953; "That Old Black Magic" her most famous tune.

**SMITH, PATTI,** Dec. 31, 1946 (Chicago, Ill.). U.S. musician. As singer/songwriter, a leading force in the "New Wave" of rock of the late 1970s; one of the first punk stars. Songs: "Piss Factory," 1974; "Hey Joe," 1974.

**THE SMOTHERS BROTHERS: TOM,** Feb. 2, 1937 (New York, N.Y.); and **DICK,** Nov. 20, 1939 (New York, N.Y.). U.S. singers noted as much for their satiric comedy as their singing; their TV show was cancelled in 1968 after a censorship row with CBS; they returned to TV in a comedy-variety show, 1988.

**SNOW, HANK,** May 9, 1914 (Liverpool, N.S., Can.). Canadian singer, guitarist. Country-and-western performer; with Grand Ole Opry since 1950.

**SPRINGFIELD, DUSTY** (born Mary O'Brien), Apr. 16, 1939 (Hampstead, Eng.). English pop singer popular in the 1960s. Songs: "Silver Threads and Golden Needles," "I Only Want to Be with You," "Son of a Preacher Man."

**SPRINGFIELD, RICK,** Aug. 23, 1949 (Sydney, Austrl.). Australian singer, musician. Twice a failed teen idol, hit it big in early 1980s, while also starring on soap opera *General Hospital*; hits include "Jesse's Girl," "Don't Talk to Strangers," and "I've Done Everything for You."

**SPRINGSTEEN, BRUCE,** Sept. 23, 1949 (Freehold, N.J.). U.S. musician. As singer/songwriter/guitarist, a late-1970s leader of the "New Wave" in rock music; known for the insistent images and macho posturings of his music. Albums: *Greetings From Ashbury Park NJ*; *Born to Run*; *Born in the USA*; *Bruce Springsteen and the E Street Band Live.*

**STAFFORD, JO,** Nov. 12, 1918 (Coalinga, Calif.). U.S. singer. Big Band-era singer with the TOMMY DORSEY band, 1941; was featured as soloist and lead singer with the Pied Pipers; known for her pure distinctive tone and timbre. Songs: "Temptation," "Shrimp Boats," "You Belong to Me," "Make Love to Me."

**STARR, RINGO** (born Richard Starkey), July 17, 1940 (Liverpool, Eng.). English musician. Drummer for The Beatles, 1962–70; solo since 1970, branching out into singing and songwriting; acted in some films.

**STEVENS, CAT** (born Steven Georgiou), July 21, 1948 (London, Eng.). English singer, songwriter. Popular in the 1970s.

**STEWART, ROD,** Jan. 10, 1945 (London, Eng.). British rock singer. With Jeff Beck group (1968–69) and Faces (1969–75); came into own as solo performer, 1975; many world tours.

**STONE, SLY** (born Sylvester Stewart), Mar. 15, 1944 (Dallas, Tex.). U.S. musician. Dynamic exponent of psychedelic rock in the late 1960s, with his group Sly and the Family Stone. Songs: "Hot Fun in the Summertime," "Everyday People."

**STOOKEY, (Neal) PAUL,** Dec. 30, 1937 (Baltimore, Md.). U.S. singer. A folksinger, is best known for his composition, "There is Love," often referred to as the "wedding song" because so many couples have it played at their weddings.

**SUMMER, DONNA** (born LaDonna Gaines), Dec. 31, 1948 (Boston, Mass.). U.S. singer. Disco music's leading lady. Songs: "I Feel Love," "Hot Stuff," "Last Girls," "Bad Girls."

**TAYLOR, JAMES,** Mar. 12, 1948 (Boston, Mass.). U.S. singer, guitarist, composer. (One-time husband of CARLY SIMON.)

**THE TEMPTATIONS:** Dennis Edwards, Feb. 3, 1943 (Birmingham, Ala.); Melvin Franklin, Oct. 12, 1942 (Montgomery, Ala.); Eddie Kendricks, Dec. 17, 1939 (Birmingham, Ala.); Otis Williams, Oct. 30, 1941 (Texarkana, Tex.); Paul Williams, July 2, 1939 (Birmingham, Ala.)–Aug, 17, 1973.

U.S. singing group. With DAVID RUFFIN (Edwards joined group in 1965), formed the soul group that was the male equivalent to THE SUPREMES.

**TENNILLE, TONI,** May 8, 1943 (Montgomery, Ala.); and **DARYL DRAGON,** Aug. 27, 1942 (Los Angeles, Calif.). U.S. musicians. Husband and wife pop-rock singing duo, The Captain and Tennille; skyrocketed to fame with 1975 hit "Love Will Keep Us Together"; hosted TV variety show, 1976–78.

**TOWNSHEND, PETER,** May 19, 1945 (London, Eng.). British singer, songwriter. Leader of rock group Who; best known for his rock operas, *Tommy* (1968) and *Quadrophenia* (1973), which redefined and expanded the rock idiom; due to hearing loss no longer performs full-time as a musician. Albums: *All the Best Cowboys Have Chinese Eyes*; *The Who By Numbers*; *The Iron Man*; *Live at Leeds.*

**TORME, MEL,** Sept. 13, 1925 (Chicago, Ill.). U.S. singer, musician. Toured with CHICO MARX band, 1942–43; led Mel-Tones group, 1943–47; solo since 1947; composed among others, "The Christmas Song"; considered one of the leading jazz vocalists of his time.

**TRAVERS, MARY,** Nov. 9, 1936 (Louisville, Ky.). U.S. singer. Best known as a member of the folk music trio, Peter, Paul and Mary.

**TRAVIS, RANDY,** 1959 (Marshville, N.C.). U.S. singer. A rising star in the country music field; hits include "Forever and Ever, Amen" (single) and the albums *Old 8 x 10*, *On the Other Hand*, and *I Won't Need You Anymore.*

**TUCKER, SOPHIE** (born Sophia Abuza), Jan. 13, 1884 (Russia)–Feb. 10, 1966. U.S. singer. Nicknamed "The Last of the Red Hot Mommas," vaudeville star, from 1906; kept active on stage, in clubs, films, and TV until her death. Autobiography: *Some of These Days* (the title of her theme song), 1945.

**TUCKER, TANYA,** Oct. 10, 1958 (Seminole, Tex.). U.S. singer. Country music star who began as a child performer; has appeared in a film (*Jeremiah Johnson*, 1968) and on television shows. Albums: *Delta Dawn*; *TNT*; *Tear Me Apart.*

**TURNER, BIG JOE,** May 18, 1911 (Kansas City, Mo.). U.S. singer. Sang in Kansas City for many years before coming to New York City in 1938; one of great blues "shouters"; "Chains of Love" is his most famous song.

**TURNER, IKE,** Nov. 5, 1931 (Clarksdale, Miss.). U.S. musician. With wife TINA TURNER, had rock-soul group, Ike and Tina Turner Revue.

**TURNER, TINA** (born Annie Mae Bullock), Nov. 26, 1939 (Nutbush, Tenn.). U.S. singer. With husband IKE TURNER, had rock-soul group Ike and Tina Turner Revue; major solo recordings of the 1980s; hit recordings include "What's Love Got to Do With It," "Better Be Good to Me," and "Back When You Started." Has won many Grammy awards.

**TWITTY, CONWAY** (born Harold Jenkins), Sept.

1, 1933 (Friarspoint, Miss.). U.S. singer/composer. Country-and-western composer/entertainer.

**UGGAMS, LESLIE,** May 25, 1943 (New York, N.Y.). U.S. singer, actress. First gained fame as singer on *Sing Along with Mitch* TV show, 1961–64; starred on TV in *Roots* (1977) and *Backstairs at the White House* (1979).

**VALLEE, RUDY** (born Hubert Prior Vallee), July 28, 1901 (Island Pond, Vt.)–July 3, 1986. U.S. singer. Leading crooner of the 1920s, with his band, The Connecticut Yankees; popular on radio and concerts; trademark was a megaphone.

**VALLI, FRANKIE** (born Frank Castelluccio), May 3, 1937 (Newark, N.J.). U.S. singer. With The Four Seasons, later solo; hit recordings include "Sherry," "Big Girls Don't Cry," "Walk Like a Man," "Dawn," "Rag Doll," "My Eyes Adored You," "Grease."

**VAUGHAN, SARAH,** Mar. 27, 1924 (Newark, N.J.)–Apr. 3, 1990. U.S. singer. Jazz vocalist who sang with EARL "FATHA" HINES and Billy Eckstine bands; recorded "Lover Man," "Sometimes I'm Happy," "Broken-Hearted Melody," "A Foggy Day in London Town."

**VINTON, BOBBY,** Apr. 16, 1935 (Canonsburg, Pa.). U.S. singer. Pop-rock singer; star of TV, nightclubs; recorded the hits "Blue on Blue," "Blue Velvet," "Roses are Red," "Mr. Lonely."

**WAGONER, PORTER,** Aug. 12, 1927 (West Plains, Mo.). U.S. singer. With Grand Ole Opry, 1957–  ; formerly teamed with DOLLY PARTON, with whom he won several awards.

**WAITS, TOM,** Dec. 7, 1949 (New York, N.Y.). U.S. singer, songwriter. Raspy voiced musician whose songs show a strong blues influence as well as that of KURT WEILL and FATS WALLER. Songs: *Downtown Train; Jockey Full of Bourbon; Innocent When You Dream.*

**WARFIELD, WILLIAM,** Jan. 22, 1920 (West Helena, Ark.). U.S. singer. Best known for roles in the musicals *Showboat* and *Porgy and Bess.* (One-time husband of L. PRICE.)

**WARWICK, DIONNE,** Dec. 12, 1941 (E. Orange, N.J.). U.S. singer. Pop star known particularly for her renderings of songs by BURT BACHRACH, including "Alfie," "Do You Know the Way to San Jose?," "What the World Needs Now," "I'll Never Love This Way Again."

**WASHINGTON, DINAH** (born Ruth Jones), Aug. 29, 1924 (Tuscaloosa, Ala.)–Dec. 14, 1963. U.S. singer. Rose to fame in LIONEL HAMPTON band (1943–46), then became a solo performer; known for gutsy blues style, like in songs "What a Difference a Day Makes."

**WATERS, ETHEL,** Oct. 31, 1900 (Chester, Pa.)–Sept. 1, 1977. U.S. actress, singer. Stage and film

career. Traveled as a singer on BILLY GRAHAM's crusades. Films: *Cabin in the Sky,* 1943; *Pinky,* 1949; *Member of the Wedding,* 1952. Autobiography: *His Eye Is on the Sparrow,* 1953.

**WHITE, BARRY,** Sept. 12, 1944 (Galveston, Tex.). U.S. musician. Singer/songwriter/orchestra leader of late 1970s pop-soul music; known for his saccharine love songs sung in a deep baritone.

**WHITING, MARGARET** ("Madcap Maggie"), July 22, 1924 (Detroit, Mich). U.S. Singer. Big Band-era singer, best known for her renditions of "Moonlight in Vermont," "A Tree in the Meadow" and "Slippin' Around."

**WILLIAMS, ANDY,** Dec. 3, 1930 (Wall Lake, Ia.). U.S. singer. Began as singer in Williams Bros. Quartet, 1938–52; hits include "Moon River," "Born Free," "The Days of Wine and Roses." TV: *The Andy Williams Show,* 1958–71.

**WILLIAMS, HANK JR.,** May 26, 1949 (Shreveport, La.). U.S. country music singer. Has had 15 gold albums and three platinum. Albums: *Hank Live,* 1987; *Born to Boogie,* 1987. (Son of H. WILLIAMS.)

**WILLIAMS, JOE,** Dec. 12, 1918 (Cordele Ga.). U.S. singer. Specializes in jazz and blues; has appeared with Jimmie Noone, the LIONEL HAMPTON Band, the DUKE ELLINGTON orchestra and COUNT BASIE. TV: *The Bill Cosby Show,* 1987–  .

**WILLIAMS, PAUL,** Sept. 19, 1940 (Omaha, Neb.). U.S. singer, composer. Successful pop-rock performerwriter of songs such as "We've Only Just Begun" and "Rainy Days and Mondays."

**WONDER, STEVIE** (born Stevland Morris), May 13, 1950 (Saginaw, Mich.). U.S. singer, composer. Blind from birth, a child prodigy, now rock-blues singer and songwriter; hits include "I Wish," "You Are the Sunshine of My Life," "Superstition," "My Cherie Amour," "Reggae Woman."

**WYNETTE, TAMMY,** May 5, 1942 (Red Bay, Ala.). U.S. singer. Country-and-western singer; regular on Grand Ole Opry, 1968–  ; Country Music Assn. Female Vocalist of Year, 1968–70; hits include "Stand By Your Man."

**YARROW, PETER,** May 31, 1938 (New York, N.Y.). U.S. singer. Member of Peter, Paul and Mary group.

**YOUNG, Neil,** Nov. 12, 1945 (Toronto, Ont., Can.). Canadian musician. Leader of rock groups Buffalo Springfield and Crosby, Stills, Nash & Young; in the 1980s released a bewildering range of albums from rockabilly to heavy synthesizer sound.

**ZAPPA, FRANK,** Dec. 21, 1940 (Baltimore, Md.). U.S. singer. Founder and leader of the Mothers of Invention rock group.

## COMEDIANS

**ABBOTT, BUD,** Oct. 2, 1895 (Asbury Park, N.J.)–Apr. 24, 1974. U.S. comedian. "Straight man" of comedy team of Abbott and COSTELLO; numerous films in 1940s and 1950s.

**ALLEN, FRED** (born John Sullivan), May 31, 1894 (Cambridge, Mass.)–Mar. 17, 1956. U.S. comedian. Former vaudeville juggler; star of highly rated radio program featuring *Allen's Alley* (1932–49), which had 20 million listeners at its peak; known for his "Down East" humor, zany characters, and his comic "feud" with JACK BENNY.

**ALLEN, GRACIE,** July 26, 1906 (San Francisco, Calif.)–Aug. 27, 1964. U.S. comedienne. With husband GEORGE BURNS, starred for 30 years in radio, in films, and on TV, portraying a lovable scatterbrain.

**ALLEN, STEVE,** Dec. 26, 1921 (New York, N.Y.). U.S. humorist, composer. Originated TV's *Tonight Show*, 1950; host of several talk-variety TV shows; composed some 2,000 songs; starred in the film *The Benny Goodman Story*, 1955.

**ALLEN, WOODY** (born Allen Konigsberg), Dec. 1, 1935 (New York, N.Y.). U.S. comedian, film maker. Began as comedy writer; stand-up comic, 1953–66; writer, producer, dir. of and actor in the films *Bananas* (1971), *Play It Again, Sam* (1972), *Love & Death* (1975), *The Front* (actor only; 1976), *Annie Hall* (Best Picture AA, Best Writer and Director AA 1977), *Manhattan* (1979), *Stardust Memories* (1980), *Zelig* (1983); *Broadway Danny Rose* (1984); *Hannah and Her Sisters* (1986).

**AMSTERDAM, MOREY,** Dec. 14, 1914 (Chicago, Ill.). U.S. comedian. Nightclub and TV comic; regular on TV's *Dick Van Dyke Show,* 1961–66.

**ARBUCKLE, FATTY** (born Roscoe Conkling Arbuckle), Mar. 24, 1887 (Smith Center, Kan.)–June 29, 1933. U.S. comedian. Slapstick star of silent films whose career was ruined in 1921 scandal after death of starlet at a party he gave.

**BENNY, JACK** (born Benjamin Kubelsky), Feb. 14, 1894 (Chicago, Ill.)–Dec. 26, 1974. U.S. comedian. Famed for his reputed stinginess and deadpan delivery; radio show, 1932–55; TV show, 1955–65; played violin with symphony orchestras for charity; made several films.

**BERGEN, EDGAR,** Feb. 16, 1903 (Chicago, Ill.)–Sept. 30, 1978. U.S. ventriloquist. With dummies Charlie McCarthy and Mortimer Snerd, had top-rated radio show, 1937–47; appeared in films with dummies, later as character actor. (Father of C. BERGEN.)

**BERLE, MILTON** (born Milton Berlinger), July 12, 1908 (New York, N.Y.). U.S. comedian. "Uncle Miltie," first TV superstar, 1948–67; came to TV from vaudeville, radio and films.

**BERMAN, SHELLEY,** Feb. 3, 1926 (Chicago, Ill.). U.S. comedian. Stand-up comic and actor who was very popular in nightclubs and on records in 1960s.

**BISHOP, JOEY** (born Joseph Abraham Gottlieb), Feb. 3, 1918 (New York, N.Y.). U.S. comedian. Stand-up comic; some films.

**BLUE, BEN** (born Benjamin Bernstein), Sept. 12, 1901 (Montreal, Que., Can.)–Mar. 7, 1975. U.S. comedian. Rubber-limbed vaudevillian; in films, from 1933.

**BORGE, VICTOR,** Jan. 3, 1909 (Copenhagen, Den.). U.S. comedian. Comedic piano player; has had numerous one-man TV specials and stage shows around the world; guest artist with major symphony orchestras.

**BRENNER, DAVID,** Feb. 4, 1945 (Philadelphia,

Pa.). U.S. comedian. Stand-up comic; frequent *Tonight Show* (TV) guest host.

**BRICE, FANNY** (born Fannie Borach), Oct. 29, 1891 (New York, N.Y.)–May 29, 1951. U.S. singer, comedienne. Long associated with the Ziegfeld Follies; played "Baby Snooks" on radio show 1936–51; play and film *Funny Girl* based on her life.

**BROOKS, MEL,** (born Melvin Kaminsky), June 28, 1926 (New York, N.Y.). U.S. filmmaker, comedian. Writer-dir. of several popular films, including *The Producers* (1968), *The Twelve Chairs* (1971), *Blazing Saddles* (1974), *Young Frankenstein* (1975), *Silent Movie* (1978), *The History of the World—Part I* (1981), *To Be or Not To Be* (1983), *Space Balls* (1987). (Husband of A. BANCROFT.)

**BROWN, JOE E.,** July 28, '1892 (Helgate, Ohio)–July 6, 1973. U.S. comedian. Known for his wide-mouthed appearance, in films such as *You Said a Mouthful* (1932), *Alibi Ike* (1935), *A Midsummer Night's Dream* (1935), and *Show Boat* (1951).

**BRUCE, LENNY,** (born Leonard Schneider), 1926 (Mineola, N.Y.)–Aug. 3, 1966. U.S. comedian, satirist. Known for off-color material; 1974 film *Lenny* based on his career.

**BURNETT, CAROL,** April 26, 1933 (San Antonio, Tex.). U.S. comedienne. Regular on TV's *Garry Moore Show,* 1959–62; star of TV's *Carol Burnett Show,* 1967–78; won five Emmys; in some films.

**BURNS, GEORGE,** (born Nathan Birnbaum) Jan. 20, 1896 (New York, N.Y.). U.S. comedian, actor. With wife GRACIE ALLEN, formed comedy team (1923) that was success in vaudeville, radio, films, TV; best known for TV's *Burns and Allen Show* (1950–58) and movie roles in *The Sunshine Boys* (Best Supporting Actor AA; 1975) and *Oh God!* (1977).

**CAESAR, SID,** Sept. 8, 1922 (Yonkers, N.Y.). U.S. comedian. Mostly on TV, notably *Your Show of Shows* and *Caesar's Hour* in the 1950s.

**CALLAS, CHARLIE,** Dec. 20, ? (New York, N.Y.). U.S. comedian. Stand-up comic in clubs and on TV; turned to acting with regular role on TV's *Switch* (1975–78).

**CAMBRIDGE, GODFREY,** Feb. 26, 1933 (New York, N.Y.)–Nov. 29, 1976. U.S. comedian, actor. Leading black stand-up comic of 1960s; turned actor in the films *Watermelon Man* (1970) and *Cotton Comes to Harlem* (1971).

**CANTOR, EDDIE,** (born Edward Israel Iskowitz), Jan. 31, 1892 (New York, N.Y.)–Oct. 10, 1964. U.S. comedian, song-and-dance man. Appeared in several Ziegfeld Follies; starred in Musicals *Kid Boots* (1923) and *Whoopee* (1928); starred in films and on radio in 1930s; on TV in 1950s; received special AA for film service, 1956.

**CARSON, JOHNNY,** Oct. 23, 1925 (Corning, Ia.). U.S. comedian. Stand-up comic who entered TV as emcee for quiz show *Who Do You Trust?,* 1958–63; host of TV's *Tonight Show,* 1962– .

**CARTER, JACK** (born Jack Chakrin), June 24, 1923 (New York, N.Y.). U.S. comedian, actor. As a comic, played most major nightclubs.

CHAPLIN, CHARLES, Apr. 16, 1889 (London, Eng.)–Dec. 25, 1977. British comedian director, producer. Beloved "Little Tramp" of the silent-film era; made many feature films, including *The Kid* (1920), *The Gold Rush* (1924), *City Lights* (1931), *Modern Times* (1936), *The Great Dictator* (1940) and *Limelight* (1952); received special AA for film achievements, 1972.

CHASE, CHEVY (born Cornelius Crane Chase), Oct. 8, 1943 (New York, N.Y.). U.S. comedian. Regular on NBC-TV's *Saturday Night Live*, 1975–76; particularly noted for his imitation of Pres. GERALD FORD. Films: *Foul Play*, 1978; *Fletch*, 1985; *Spies Like Us*, 1986; *The Three Amigos*, 1986; *Funny Farm*, 1988.

CHEECH & CHONG: Tommy Chong, May 24, 1938 (Edmonton, Alta., Can.); Cheech Marin (born Richard), July 13, 1946 (Los Angeles, Calif.). U.S. comedians. First of the rock-culture comedians, known for their zany routines on long hair, drugs, police, etc., since 1970; made and starred in the highly-successful film *Up In Smoke*, 1978.

CONWAY, TIM, Dec. 15, 1933 (Willoughby, Ohio). U.S. comedian. TV: *McHale's Navy* (series), 1962–66; *The Carol Burnett Show* (variety show), 1975–78. *The Tim Conway Show*, 1980–83.

CORRELL, CHARLES, Feb. 2, 1890 (Peoria, Ill.)–Sept. 26, 1972. U.S. comedic actor. Best known for role as Andy in radio show *Amos 'n' Andy*, in the 1930s.

COSBY, BILL, July 12, 1937 (Philadelphia, Pa.). U.S. comedian, actor, author. Popular stand-up comic of 1960s; first black to star in a TV series (*I Spy*, 1966–68); had own TV show in 1969 and 1972–73; *The Cosby Show*, 1984– .

COSTELLO, LOU (born Louis Cristillo), Mar. 6, 1906 (Paterson, N.J.)–Mar. 3, 1959. U.S. comedian. With partner BUD ABBOTT, made numerous comedy films in 1940s and 1950s.

COX, WALLY, Dec. 6, 1924 (Detroit, Mich.)–Feb. 15, 1973. U.S. comedian. Meek-appearing actor in films, TV and on stage; starred in *Mr. Peepers* TV series, 1952–55; regular on *Hollywood Squares* TV quiz show.

DANGERFIELD, RODNEY (born Jacob Coehn), Nov. 22, 1921 (Babylon, N.Y.). U.S. comedian. Stand-up comic who "gets no respect"; Films: *Caddyshack*, 1980; *Back to School*, 1986.

DE LUISE, DOM, Aug. 1, 1933 (Brooklyn, N.Y.). U.S. comedian. Films: *The Twelve Chairs*, 1971; *Blazing Saddles*, 1974.

DILLER, PHYLLIS, July 17, 1917 (Lima, Ohio). U.S. comedienne. Fright-wigged, gravel-voiced stand-up comic in clubs and TV.

DURANTE, JIMMY ("Schnozzola"), Feb. 10, 1893 (New York, N.Y.)–Jan. 29, 1980. U.S. comedian. Vaudeville performer in partnership with Eddie Jackson, Lou Clayton, 1916–30; numerous film, stage, and TV appearances from 1930s; singer of such memorable songs as "Ink-a-Dink-a-Doo," "You Gotta Start Off Each Day With a Song"; signature was "Good night, Mrs. Calabash..."

ELLIOT, BOB, Mar. 26, 1923 (Boston, Mass.)

U.S. comedian. With partner RAY GOULDING, formed comedy team that played radio, TV, and stage, since 1951.

FIBBER MCGEE AND MOLLY: Jordan, Jim, Nov. 6, 1896 (Peoria, Ill.)–Apr. 1, 1988 and Jordan, Marian, Apr. 15, 1897 (Peoria, Ill.)–Apr. 7, 1961. U.S. entertainers. Husband-and-wife team, formed popular radio comedy duo in the 1930s and 1940s.

FIELDS, W. C. (born William Claude Dukenfield), Jan. 29, 1880 (Philadelphia, Pa.)–Dec. 25, 1946. U.S. comedian. Vaudeville, stage, film and radio performer of considerable eccentricity; noted for red nose, gravel voice, aversion to children and pets, hard drinking; starred in many memorable films, including *David Copperfield* (1934), *Poppy* (1936), *You Can't Cheat an Honest Man* (1939), *My Little Chickadee* (1940), *The Bank Dick* (1941) and *Never Give a Sucker an Even Break* (1941).

FONTAINE, FRANK, 1920 (Cambridge, Mass.)–Aug. 4, 1978. U.S. comedian. Known for his character "Crazy Guggenheim", who appeared on TV shows, most notably *The Jackie Gleason Show*, 1962–66.

FOXX, REDD (born John Elroy Sanford), Dec. 9, 1922 (St. Louis, Mo.). U.S. comedian. In nightclubs since 1941; known for his comedy "party" records; star of TV series *Sanford and Son*, 1972–77.

GLEASON, JACKIE, Feb. 26, 1916 (Brooklyn, N.Y.)–June 24, 1987. U.S. comedian, actor. Starred in the TV series *The Life of Riley* (1949–50), and *The Jackie Gleason Show* (1952–55, 1957–59, and 1966–70), often featuring his character Ralph Kramden. Films: *The Hustler*, 1961; *Gigot*, 1962; *Requiem for a Heavyweight*, 1962; *Papa's Delicate Condition*, 1963; *Smokey and the Bandit*, 1977; *Nothing in Common*, 1986.

GOSDEN, FREEMAN F., May 5, 1899 (Richmond, Va.)–Dec. 10, 1982. U.S. radio comedian. Played Amos in *Amos 'n' Andy* radio show, 1929–60.

GOULDING, RAY, Mar. 20, 1922 (Lowell, Mass.)–Mar. 24, 1990. U.S. comedian. With partner BOB ELLIOTT, formed comedy team that played radio, TV, and stage, since 1951.

GREGORY, DICK, Oct. 12, 1932 (St. Louis, Mo.). U.S. comedian, political activist. Stand-up comic in clubs, on TV, on stage, plus many records; civil-rights leader. Books: *From the Back of the Bus*, 1964; *Up from Nigger*, 1976.

HACKETT, BUDDY (born Leonard Hucker), Aug. 31, 1924 (Brooklyn, N.Y.). U.S. comedian. Rotund comic who appears in clubs, on TV; in a few films.

HARDY, OLIVER, Jan. 18, 1892 (Atlanta, Ga.)–Aug. 7, 1957. U.S. comedian. Joined with STAN LAUREL to form memorable early film team, 1926; in over 200 shorts and features, many of which became classics.

HOPE, BOB (born Leslie Townes Hope), May 29, 1903 (London, Eng.). U.S. comedian, actor. Long stage, radio, TV, and film career; master of quick delivery and one-liners; noted for charitable ventures, especially entertaining servicemen overseas (from 1940); has received numerous awards including Presidential Medal of Freedom, Hersholt

Award, Emmy award, four special AAs; star of many films, including famous "Road" pictures with BING CROSBY; numerous TV specials, from 1950.

**KAPLAN, GABE,** Mar. 31, 1945 (Brooklyn, N.Y.). U.S. comedian, actor. A stand-up comic who created and starred in the TV sit-com *Welcome Back, Kotter,* 1975–1979.

**KEATON, BUSTER** (Joseph), Oct. 4, 1895 (Piqua, Kan.)–Feb. 1, 1966. U.S. comedian, actor. One of leading stars of silent-screen comedy, invariably as a deadpan character, often wearing a porkpie hat; in two-reelers and features from 1917; career declined with advent of talkies.

**KELLY, EMMETT,** Dec. 8, 1898 (Sedan, Kan.) –Mar. 28, 1979. U.S. clown. A fixture of the circus world for generations, beloved for his Willie the Tramp character.

**KING, ALAN,** Dec. 26, 1927 (Brooklyn, N.Y.). U.S. comedian. Stand-up comic in clubs and concerts; has done several TV specials; appeared in a few films; author of *Help! I'm a Prisoner in a Chinese Bakery* (1964) and other books.

**KLEIN, ROBERT,** Feb. 8, 1942 (New York, N.Y.). U.S. comedian, actor. Concert, nightclub, TV, and recording artist.

**KNOTTS, DON,** July 21, 1924 (Morgantown, W. Va.). U.S. actor. Comic character actor, best known as Barney Fife on TV's *Andy Griffith Show,* 1960–68; *Three's Company,* 1979–84; a frequent star in WALT DISNEY films.

**KORMAN, HARVEY,** Feb. 15, 1927 (Chicago, Ill.). U.S. comedian. A popular TV comic on *The Danny Kaye Show* (1963–67) and *The Carol Burnett Show* (1967–78).

**KOVACS, ERNIE,** Jan. 23, 1919 (Trenton, N.J.) –Jan. 13, 1962. U.S. comedian. First major comedy star of TV's "Golden Age," with weekly program for "Muriel Cigars," 1952–53 and 1956. Films: *Operation Mad Ball,* 1957; *Wake Me When It's Over,* 1960. (Husband of E. ADAMS.)

**LAHR, BERT** (born Irving Lahrheim), Aug. 13, 1895 (New York, N.Y.)–Dec. 4, 1967. U.S. comedian. Beloved performer in vaudeville and on radio, he is best remembered as the Cowardly Lion in the film *The Wizard of Oz* (1939); in later years, turned to serious acting in stage productions of *Waiting for Godot.*

**LAUREL, STAN** (born Arthur Stanley Jefferson), June 16, 1890 (Ulverston, Eng.)–Feb. 23, 1965. English comedian. Joined with OLIVER HARDY to form first great film comedy-team, 1926; made over 200 films, many of them classics; received special AA for pioneering work in film comedy, 1960.

**LAWRENCE, VICKI,** Mar. 26, 1949 (Los Angeles, Calif.). U.S. comedienne, singer. TV: *The Carol Burnett Show* (series), 1967–78 (Emmy award, 1976), 1979; *Mama's Family* (series), 1982–84, 1987.

**LENO, JAY,** Apr. 28, 1950 (New Rochelle, N.Y.). U.S. comedian. Appearances on *Late Night with David Letterman* and permanent substitute host for *The Tonight Show.*

**LETTERMAN, DAVID,** Apr. 12, 1947 (Indiana-polis, Ind.). U.S. comedian, TV writer. Has won five Emmy awards. TV: *David Letterman Show,* 1980; *Late Night w/David Letterman,* 1985–  .

**LEWIS, JERRY** (born Joseph Levitch), Mar. 16, 1926 (Newark, N.J.). U.S. comedian, actor. Burst onto comedy scene in zany partnership with DEAN MARTIN, 1946–56; on his own, appeared in a series of nutty movies in 1950s and 1960s; has raised millions with annual telethon for Muscular Dystrophy Assn. Films: *Geisha Boy,* 1958; *The Bellboy,* 1960; *The Nutty Professor,* 1963; *The Patsy,* 1964; *King of Comedy,* 1983.

**LEWIS, JOE E.,** 1902 (New York, N.Y.)–June 4, 1971. U.S. comedian. Fixture in nightclubs with stand-up comedy routine; FRANK SINATRA played him in film bio *The Joker Is Wild,* 1958.

**LILLIE, BEATRICE** (born Constance Sylvia Munston), May 29, 1894 (Toronto, Ont., Can.)–Jan. 20, 1989. English-Can. comedienne, actress. Made her debut in London (1914), where she became popular actress-singer-comedienne in plays and revues—notably those in which she starred with NOEL COWARD, GERTRUDE LAWRENCE; in a few films. Autobiography: *Every Other Inch a Lady,* 1972.

**LITTLE, RICH,** Nov. 26, 1938 (Ottawa, Ont., Can.). Comedian. Impressionist (his RICHARD NIXON is famous) in clubs, on stage and TV.

**LLOYD, HAROLD,** Apr. 20, 1893 (Burchard, Neb.) –Mar. 8, 1971. U.S. comedian, actor. The highest-paid film star of the 1920s, known for his thrill-comedy films, often featuring him in "cliff-hanging" situations, from 1916.

**LOVITZ, JON,** July 21, 1957 (Tarzana, Calif.). U.S. comedian. TV: *Saturday Night Live* (series), 1985–  .

**LYNDE, PAUL,** June 13, 1926 (Mt. Vernon, Ohio) –Jan. 9, 1982. U.S. actor, comedian. Films: *Bye Bye Birdie,* 1963, best known for appearances on TV's *Hollywood Squares.*

**MARTIN, DICK,** Jan. 30, 1923 (Detroit, Mich.). U.S. comedian. Comic partner of DAN ROWAN, from 1952; cohost of TV show *Laugh-In,* 1967–72.

**MARX, ARTHUR** ("Harpo"), Nov. 21, 1888 (New York, N.Y.)–Sept. 28, 1964. U.S. comedian. Silent, harp-playing, blond-chasing member of MARX Bros.; in real life, talkative and intelligent. Autobiography: *Harpo Speaks,* 1961.

**MARX, HERBERT** ("Zeppo"), Feb. 25, 1901 (New York, N.Y.)–Nov. 30, 1979. U.S. comedian. Played romantic relief in early MARX Bros. films; left act to become an agent, 1933.

**MARX, JULIUS** ("Groucho"), Oct. 2, 1890 (New York, N.Y.)–Aug. 19, 1977. U.S. comedian. Mustachioed, cigar-smoking member of the MARX Bros. comedy team; after act broke up (1949) he went on to fame as star of TV quiz show *You Bet Your Life* (1950–61). Films: *Coconuts,* 1929; *Animal Crackers,* 1930; *Monkey Business,* 1931; *Horse Feathers,* 1932; *Duck Soup,* 1935; *A Day at the Races,* 1937. Books: *Groucho and Me,* 1959; *The Groucho Letters,* 1967.

**MARX, LEONARD** ("Chico"), Mar. 26, 1887

(New York, N.Y.)–Oct. 11, 1961. U.S. comedian. The fractured-speaking, piano-playing member of the MARX Bros.; appeared in all the team's films. MARX, MILTON ("Gummo"), 1897 (New York, N.Y.–Apr. 21, 1977. U.S. comedian. Joined with other MARX Bros. and their mother in vaudeville act called The Six Musical Mascots, 1904–18; left act to become their agent and business manager. MASON, JACKIE, June 6, 1931 (Sheboygan, Wis.). U.S. comedian. Standup comedian noted for his ethnic humor. TV: *Chicken Soup* (series), 1989. NEWHART, BOB, Sept. 29, 1929 (Oak Park, Ill.). U.S. comedian, actor. Stand-up comic very popular in 1960s; turned to acting as star of the TV series *The Bob Newhart Show*, 1972–78; *Newhart*, 1982–90. PENNER, JOE (born Joseph Pinter), Nov. 11, 1905 (Budapest, Hung.)–Jan. 10, 1941. U.S. comedian. In vaudeville, on radio, in films; famous catchphrase "Wanna buy a duck?" PRINZE, FREDDIE, June 22, 1954 (New York, N.Y.)–Jan. 29, 1977. U.S. comedian. Standup comic who skyrocketed to fame as star of the TV series *Chico and the Man*, 1974–77; died of self-inflicted gunshot wound. PRYOR, RICHARD, Dec. 1, 1940 (Peoria, Ill.). U.S. comedian/actor. Stand-up comic popular on TV and in concert for his irreverent humor. Films: *Lady Sings the Blues*, 1972; *California Suite*, 1978; *Stir Crazy*, 1980; *Some Kind of Hero*, 1982; *The Toy*, 1984; *Moving*, 1988. RICKLES, DON, May 8, 1926 (New York, N.Y.). U.S. comedian. Stand-up comic known for extremely insulting humor; has appeared in a few films. RIVERS, JOAN, June 8, 1933 (Brooklyn, N.Y.). U.S. comedienne, filmmaker. Stand-up comic from 1960 with Second City (Chicago) improvisation troupe, 1961–62; frequent guest and host of TV's *Tonight Show*, hosted own late-night TV show,

1986–87. Author: *Having a Baby Can Be a Scream*, 1974. ROWAN, DAN, July 2, 1922 (Beggs, Okla.)–Sept. 22, 1987. U.S. comedian. Comic partner of DICK MARTIN, from 1952; cohosted TV series *Laugh-In*, 1968–72. SAHL, MORT, May 11, 1927 (Montreal, Que., Can.). Canadian comedian. Iconoclast whose satires on current events were very popular in 1950s. SALES, SOUPY, Jan. 8, 1926 (Franklinton, N.C.). U.S. comedian. Slapstick comic on TV children's shows; radio host. SHANDLING, GARY, 1950 (Tucson, Ariz.). U.S. comedian. TV: *It's Gary Shandling's Show* (series), 1988– . SHAWN, DICK (born Richard Schulefand), Dec. 1, 1929 (Buffalo, N.Y.)–Apr. 17, 1987. U.S. comedian. Zany film actor in *It's a Mad, Mad, Mad, Mad World* (1963) and *The Producers* (1968), among other films. SHRINER, HERB, May 29, 1918 (Toledo, Ohio) –Apr. 23, 1970. U.S. comedian. Dry wit and Hoosier humor were his trademark in comedy routines; early TV host, from 1948. STILLER, JERRY, June 8, 1929 (New York, N.Y.). U.S. comedian, actor. With wife ANNE MEARA, part of a comedy team, 1961– . WILSON, FLIP, Dec. 8, 1933 (Jersey City, N.J.). U.S. comedian. Stand-up comic, most noted for impersonation of character Geraldine Jones; had own TV variety show, 1970–74. WINTERS, JONATHAN, Nov, 11, 1925 (Dayton, Ohio). U.S. comedian. Numerous TV and film appearances; known for zany characters. YOUNGMAN, HENNY, Jan. 12, 1906 (Liverpool, Eng.). U.S. comedian. TV, radio, and club stand-up comic, noted for his violin playing and equally corny one-liners ("Take my wife—please!")

## U.S. PRODUCERS AND DIRECTORS

ABBOTT, GEORGE, June 25, 1887 (Forestville, N.Y.) U.S. producer/director/playwright. An institution on American stage for over 60 years; still active, he produced his 119th show in 1978; co-wrote many of musical theater's greatest hits. Plays: *The Boys from Syracuse*, 1938; *Where's Charley?*, 1948; *The Pajama Game*, 1954; *Damn Yankees*, 1955; *Fiorello*, 1959 (1960 Pulitzer Prize in drama). ALTMAN, ROBERT, Feb. 20, 1925 (Kansas City, Mo.) U.S. producer/director, writer. Films: *M\*A\*S\*H\**, 1970; *The Long Goodbye*, 1973; *Nashville*, 1975; *Three Women*, 1977; *A Wedding*, 1978; *Quintet*, 1979; *Popeye*, 1980; *Streamers*, 1980. BELASCO, DAVID, July 25, 1853 (San Francisco, Calif.)–May 14, 1931. U.S. producer, playwright. Theatrical giant who made major innovations in techniques and staging; preferred working with little-knowns, whom he developed; produced hundreds of plays. BOGDANOVICH, PETER, July 30, 1939 (Kingston, N.Y.). U.S. film director, producer, screen-

writer. Films: *The Last Picture Show*, 1971; *Nickelodeon*, 1976; *What's Up, Doc?*, 1972; *Paper Moon*, 1973; *Mask*, 1985. BORZAGE, FRANK, Apr. 23, 1895 (Salt Lake City, Utah)–June 19, 1962. U.S. film director. Films: *Seventh Heaven*, 1927; *History Is Made at Night*, 1937; *Stage Door Canteen*, 1943; *The Spanish Main*, 1945; *The Big Fisherman*, 1959. CAPRA, FRANK, May 18, 1897 (Palermo, Italy). U.S. director. Leading film director of 1930s and 1940s, known for his comedies and stories of the common man. Films: *Platinum Blonde*, 1932; *It Happened One Night* (AA), 1934; *Mr. Deeds Goes to Town* (AA), 1936; *Lost Horizon*, 1937; *You Can't Take It with You* (AA), 1938; *Mr. Smith Goes to Washington*, 1939; *Meet John Doe*, 1941; *Arsenic and Old Lace*, 1944; *It's a Wonderful Life*, 1947; *State of the Union*, 1948. CARPENTER, JOHN, Jan. 16, 1948 (Carthage, N.Y.). U.S. director. Films: *Halloween*, 1978; *Starman*, 1984; *They Live*, 1987.

CHAMPION, GOWER, June 22, 1921 (Geneva, Ill.)–Aug. 25, 1980. U.S. director, choreographer, director of stage musicals. *Bye, Bye Birdie, Hello Dolly, The Happy Time, 42nd Street*; won 7 Tony Awards.

CIMINO, MICHAEL, 1948 (New York, N.Y.). U.S. director. Films: *The Deer Hunter*, 1978 (best director and producer AAs); *Heaven's Gate*, 1980; *The Year of the Dragon*, 1985; *The Sicilian*, 1987.

COHEN, ALEXANDER H., July 24, 1920 (New York, N.Y.). U.S. theater and TV producer. Producer of TV's *Tony Awards* shows, 1967–86.

COPPOLA, FRANCIS FORD, Apr. 7, 1939 (Detroit, Mich.). U.S film director, producer, writer. Wrote, produced, and directed films *The Godfather* (AA; 1972); *The Godfather Part II* (3AAs; 1974); *The Conversation* (1974). Other films: *Finian's Rainbow* (writer), 1968; *Patton* (writer), 1970; *The Great Gatsby* (writer), 1974; *Apocalypse Now* (writer/director), 1979. (Brother of T. SHIRE, uncle of N. CAGE.)

CUKOR, GEORGE, July 7, 1899 (New York, N.Y.)–Jan. 24, 1983. U.S. film director. A favorite of the 1930s and 1940s. Films: *Little Women*, 1933; *Dinner at Eight*, 1933; *Camille*, 1936; *The Philadelphia Story*, 1940; *Gaslight*, 1944; *A Double Life*, 1947; *Adam's Rib*, 1949; *Born Yesterday*, 1950; *A Star is Born*, 1954; *My Fair Lady* (AA), 1964.

DEMILLE, CECIL B(lount), Aug. 12, 1881 (Ashfield, Mass.)–Jan. 21, 1959. U.S. director, producer. Hollywood pioneer, most noted for his biblical spectacles. Films: *The Squaw Man*, 1913; *The Ten Commandments*, 1923, 1956; *King of Kings*, 1927; *Sign of the Cross*, 1932; *The Crusades*, 1935; *The Plainsman*, 1936; *Union Pacific*, 1939; *Samson and Delilah*, 1949; *The Greatest Show on Earth* (AA), 1952.

EDWARDS, BLAKE (born William Blake McEdwards), July 26, 1922 (Tulsa, Okla.). U.S. film director. Best known as the writer/director/producer of Pink Panther film series. Films: *Breakfast at Tiffany's*, 1961; *Days of Wine and Roses*, 1962; *Darling Lili*, 1969; *10*, 1979. (Husband of J. ANDREWS.)

FORD, JOHN (born Sean O'Feeney), Feb. 1, 1895 (Cape Elizabeth, Me.)–Aug. 31, 1973. U.S. film director. Directed over 125 films, won 5 AAs; known for action-adventure and Western films. Films: *The Informer* (AA), 1935; *Stagecoach*, 1939; *The Grapes of Wrath* (AA), 1940; *Young Mr. Lincoln; How Green Was My Valley* (AA), 1941; *Fort Apache*, 1948; *She Wore a Yellow Ribbon*, 1949; *Rio Grande*, 1950; *The Quiet Man* (AA), 1952; *Mr. Roberts*, 1955; *The Searchers*, 1956; *The Last Hurrah*, 1958; *The Man Who Shot Liberty Valance*, 1962.

FOSSE, BOB, June 23, 1927 (Chicago, Ill.)–Sept. 23, 1987. U.S. director/choreographer. Directed films, stage and TV. Stage: *Pajama Game*, 1956; *Damn Yankees*, 1957; *Redhead*, 1959; *Sweet Charity*, 1966; *Pippin*, 1972; *Chicago*, 1975; *Dancin'*, 1978. Film: *Cabaret* (AA), 1972.

FRANKENHEIMER, JOHN, Feb. 19, 1930 (Malba, N.Y.). U.S. director. Experienced in stage and TV, best known for his films. Films: *The Manchurian Candidate*, 1962; *The French Connection II*, 1975; *Black Sunday*, 1977. TV: *Studio One, Playhouse 90* programs, 1954–59.

GOLDWYN, SAMUEL (born Samuel Goldfish), Aug. 27, 1882 (Warsaw, Pol.)–Jan. 31, 1974. U.S. film producer. Pioneer in film industry, founded Goldwyn Pictures, 1917; merged to form MGM, 1925; independent after that; known for fractured English. Films: *Arrowsmith*, 1931; *Dodsworth*, 1936; *Stella Dallas*, 1937; *Wuthering Heights*, 1939; *The Little Foxes*, 1941; *The Best Years of Our Lives*, 1946; *Guys and Dolls*, 1955; *Gigi*, 1958; *Porgy and Bess*, 1959.

GRIFFITH, D(avid) W(ark), Jan. 22, 1875 (Floydsfork, Ky.)–July 23, 1948. U.S. film producer, director. Pioneer in industry from 1908, when he joined Biograph Pictures as actor; credited with major innovations, including mobile camera, flashbacks, fades; one of founders of United Artists; made some 200 silent films; never adapted to talkies. Films: *The Birth of a Nation*, 1915; *Intolerance*, 1916; *Way Down East*, 1920; *Orphans of the Storm*, 1922.

HAMMERSTEIN, OSCAR, May 8, 1847 (Stettin, Ger. [now Szczecin, Pol.])–Aug. 1, 1919. U.S. producer. Pioneer opera impresario, with several houses in New York City, including Manhattan Opera House (1906); sold interests in 1910 to Metropolitan Opera Co. (Grandfather of O. HAMMERSTEIN II.)

HAWKS, HOWARD, May 30, 1896 (Goshen, Ind.) –Dec. 26, 1977. U.S. director. Noted equally for his deft film comedies and his action dramas. Films: *Scarface*, 1932; *Twentieth Century*, 1934; *Bringing Up Baby*, 1938; *Saergeant York*, 1941; *To Have and Have Not*, 1944; *The Big Sleep*, 1946; *Red River*, 1948; *Rio Bravo*, 1958.

HAYWARD, LELAND, Sept. 15, 1902 (Nebraska City, Neb.)–Mar. 18, 1971. U.S. producer, agent. Producer of stage plays, notably *Mister Roberts* (1948) and *South Pacific* (1949); agent for many of leading stars of stage and screen in 1930s–1960s.

HILL, GEORGE ROY, Dec. 20, 1922 (Minneapolis, Minn.). U.S. director. Films: *Butch Cassidy and the Sundance Kid*, 1969; *The Sting*, 1973 (best director AA); *The World According to Garp*, 1982; *The Little Drummer Girl*, 1984.

HILLER, ARTHUR, Nov. 22, 1923 (Edmonton, Alta.). Canadian director. Films: *Love Story*, 1970; *The In-Laws*, 1979; *Making Love*, 1982.

HUNTER, ROSS (born Martin Fuss), May 6, 1921 (Cleveland, Ohio). U.S. film producer. Specializes in remakes. Films: *Magnificent Obsession*, 1954; *Pillow Talk*, 1958; *Imitation of Life*, 1959; *Madame X*, 1966; *Thoroughly Modern Millie*, 1967; *Airport*, 1969.

HUROK, SOL, Apr. 9, 1888 (Pogar, Russ.).–Mar. 5, 1974. U.S. impresario. For 65 years, brought to U.S. the greatest stars of performing arts, including

A. SEGOVIA, A. RUBINSTEIN, A. PAVLOVA, R. NUREYEV, the Bolshoi Ballet, etc.

**HUSTON, JOHN,** Aug. 5, 1906 (Nevada, Mo.)– Aug. 28, 1987. U.S. film director, actor. Films as director: *The Maltese Falcon,* 1941; *The Treasure of the Sierra Madre* (AA), 1947; *Key Largo,* 1948; *The African Queen,* 1952; *Moulin Rouge,* 1952; *The Misfits,* 1960; *The Bible,* 1966. Films as actor: *The Cardinal,* 1963; *The Bible,* 1966; *Chinatown,* 1974; *Annie,* 1982; *The Dead,* 1988. (Son of W. HUSTON).

**KANIN, GARSON,** Nov. 24, 1912 (Rochester, N.Y.). U.S. playwright, director, author, screenwriter. With wife RUTH GORDON, wrote screenplays for the films *A Double LIfe* (1948) and *Adam's Rib* (1949); wrote and directed the play *Born Yesterday* (1946); directed the plays *The Diary of Anne Frank* (1955), and *Funny Girl* (1964); author of bestselling books, including *Tracy and Hepburn* (1971).

**KAZAN, ELIA** (born Elia Kazanjoglous), Sept. 7, 1909 (Constantinople [now Istanbul], Turk.). U.S. director, producer, author. A cofounder of the Actor's Studio; directed films and stage productions; author of several popular books. Films: *A Tree Grows in Brooklyn,* 1945; *Gentlemen's Agreement* (AA), 1947; *A Streetcar Named Desire,* 1951; *Viva Zapata,* 1952; *On the Waterfront* (AA), 1954; *East of Eden,* 1955, *America, America,* 1963.

**KRAMER, STANLEY,** Sept. 29, 1913 (New York, N.Y.). U.S. producer, director. Films produced: *Home of the Brave,* 1949; *Champion,* 1949; *Death of a Salesman,* 1951; *High Noon,* 1952; *The Caine Mutiny,* 1954. Films produced and directed: *On the Beach,* 1959; *Inherit the Wind,* 1960; *Judgment at Nuremberg,* 1961; *Ship of Fools,* 1965; *Guess Who's Coming to Dinner?,* 1967.

**KUBRICK, STANLEY,** July 26, 1928 (New York, N.Y.). U.S. filmmaker. Innovative writer, producer, director. Films: *Paths of Glory* (writer-dir.), 1958; *Spartacus* (dir.), 1960; *Lolita* (dir.), 1962; *Dr. Strangelove* (writer-dir.), 1964; *2001* (dir.), 1968; *A Clockwork Orange* (dir.), 1971; *Barry Lyndon* (dir.), 1975, *The Shining* (dir.) 1980; *Full Metal Jacket* (co-writer, dir.), 1987.

**LANDIS, JOHN,** Aug. 3, 1950 (Chicago, Ill.). U.S. director. Films: *National Lampoon's Animal House,* 1978; *The Blues Brothers,* 1980; *An American Werewolf in London,* 1981; *Trading Places,* 1983; *The Twilight Zone,* 1983; *Amigos,* 1986; *Coming to America,* 1988.

**LEAR, NORMAN,** July 27, 1922 (New Haven, Conn.). U.S. producer, director, political activist. His TV shows blazed new trails in comedy and openness; a leader of "People for the American Way." TV series: *All in the Family, Maude, The Jeffersons, Mary Hartman, Mary Hartman, Sanford and Son, Good Times.*

**LEONARD, SHELDON** (born Sheldon Bershad), Feb. 22, 1907 (New York, N.Y.). U.S. TV producer and director, actor. Character actor in numerous films, 1930s–1970s. Producer-dir. of the TV series *The Andy Griffith Show* (1960–68), *The Dick Van*

*Dyke Show* (1961–66), and *I Spy* (1965–68); won Emmy awards for best TV director (1957 and 1961) and for best comedy producer (1970).

**LE ROY, MERVYN,** Oct. 15, 1900 (San Francisco, Calif.)–Sept. 13, 1987. U.S. director. In films since 1924. Films: *Little Caesar,* 1930; *I Am a Fugitive from a Chain Gang,* 1932; *Tugboat Annie,* 1932; *Anthony Adverse,* 1936; *Random Harvest,* 1942; *Quo Vadis,* 1951; *Gypsy,* 1962.

**LESTER, RICHARD,** Jan. 19, 1932 (Philadelphia, Pa.). U.S. film director. Films: *A Hard Day's Night,* 1964; *Petulia,* 1968; *The Three Musketeers,* 1973; *The Four Musketeers,* 1975; *Robin and Marian,* 1976; *The Ritz,* 1976; *Finders Keepers,* 1984.

**LOGAN, JOSHUA,** Oct. 5, 1908 (Texarkana, Tex.) –July 12, 1988. U.S. producer, director. Producer-dir. of many Broadway shows. Coauthor, producer, and dir. of the plays *Mr. Roberts, South Pacific,* and *Fanny;* dir. of the films *Picnic* (1955), *Bus Stop* (1956), *South Pacific* (1958), and *Paint Your Wagon* (1969). Autobiography: *Josh,* 1976.

**LUCAS, GEORGE, JR.,** May 14, 1944 (Modesto, Calif.). U.S. director, producer. Films (as dir.): *American Graffiti,* 1973; *Star Wars,* 1977. Films (as prod.): *The Empire Strikes Back,* 1980; *The Raiders of the Lost Ark,* 1981; *The Return of the Jedi,* 1983; *Indiana Jones and the Temple of Doom,* 1984; *Howard the Duck,* 1986; *Tucker,* 1988.

**LUMET, SIDNEY,** June 25, 1924 (Philadelphia, Pa.). U.S. director. Directed over 200 plays for TV, 1956–61. Films: *Twelve Angry Men,* 1957; *The Pawnbroker,* 1965; *Serpico,* 1974; *Dog Day Afternoon,* 1975; *Network,* 1976; *Equus,* 1978; *Death trap,* 1981; *The Morning After,* 1986; *Running on Empty,* 1988.

**MANKIEWICZ, JOSEPH L**(eo), Feb. 11, 1909 (Wilkes-Barre, Pa.). U.S. writer, director. *Woman of the Year,* 1940; *A Letter for 3 Wives,* 1949; *All about Eve,* 1950; *The Barefoot Contessa,* 1954. Director: *Cleopatra,* 1963; *Sleuth,* 1972.

**MARSHALL, GARRY,** Nov. 13, 1934 (New York, N.Y.). U.S. producer,writer. Was the creator and executive producer for TV series *Happy Days, Laverne and Shirley,* and *Mork and Mindy.* Films: *Flamingo Kid,* 1984; *Beaches,* 1988; *Pretty Woman,* 1990.

**MAYER, LOUIS B.,** July 4, 1885 (Minsk, Russ.) –Oct. 29, 1957. U.S. film producer, executive. Founded Metro Pictures Corp. (1915), parlaying a chain of theaters into a major studio (MGM, 1924); created the star system; led the industry until 1951 retirement.

**MAZURSKY, PAUL,** Apr. 25, 1930 (Brooklyn, N.Y.). U.S. director, writer. Films: *Bob & Carol & Ted & Alice,* 1969; *Harry and Tonto,* 1973; *Next Stop Greenwich Village,* 1976; *An Unmarried Woman,* 1978; *Moscow on the Hudson,* 1984; *Down and Out in Beverly Hills,* 1986; *Moon Over Parador,* 1988.

**MCCAREY,** (Thomas) **LEO,** Oct. 3, 1898 (Los Angeles, Calif.)–July 5, 1969. U.S. producer, director. Producer/director of many popular films of the 1930s and 1940s. Films: *Duck Soup,* 1933; *Ruggles* of Red Gap, 1935; The Awful Truth (AA), 1937; Love Affair (AA), 1939; Going My Way (AA), 1944; The Bells of St. Mary's, 1945.

MERRICK, DAVID (born David Margulies), Nov. 27, 1912 (Hong Kong). U.S. producer. Plays: Fanny, 1954; Gypsy, 1958; Becket, 1960; Stop the World, I Want to Get Off, 1962; Oliver, 1962; Hello Dolly, 1964; Cactus Flower, 1965; Marat/Sade, 1965; I Do, I Do, 1966; Rosencrantz and Guildenstern Are Dead, 1967; Promises, Promises, 1969; Travesties, 1975; 42nd Street, 1985.

MINNELLI, VINCENTE, Feb. 28, 1910 (Chicago, Ill.)–July 25, 1986. U.S. film director. Noted for direction of MGM musicals. Films: Cabin in the Sky, 1943; Meet Me in St. Louis, 1944; The Clock, 1944; Father of the Bride, 1950; An American in Paris, 1951; The Band Wagon, 1953; Brigadoon, 1954; Gigi (AA), 1958; Bells Are Ringing, 1960. (One-time husband of J. GARLAND; father of L. MINNELLI.)

NICHOLS, MIKE (born Michael Igor Peschowsky), Nov. 6, 1931 (Berlin, Ger.). U.S. director. Comedy partner of ELAINE MAY; directs for films and stage. Films: Who's Afraid of Virginia Woolf?, 1966; The Graduate, 1967; Carnal Knowledge, 1971; Silkwood, 1983; Biloxi Blues, 1987; Working Girl, 1988. Plays: Barefoot in the Park, 1963; The Odd Couple, 1965; Plaza Suite, 1968; The Prisoner of Second Avenue, 1971; Streamers, 1976; The Gin Game, 1977; Hurlyburly, 1984.

PAPP, JOSEPH, June 22, 1921 (Brooklyn, N.Y.). U.S. producer/director. Founder (1953) and head of New York Shakespeare Festival; founded the Public Theatre, 1966; credited with producing many of major stage presentations of 1960s and 1970s. Plays: Hair, 1967; Two Gentlemen of Verona, 1971; Sticks and Bones, 1971; That Championship Season 1972; The Cherry Orchard, 1973; A Chorus Line, 1975; Streamers, 1977; The Mystery of Edwin Drood, 1985.

PASTERNAK, JOSEPH, Sept. 19, 1901 (Silagy-Somlyo, Rum. [now Hung.]) U.S. producer. Film producer with Universal Studios since 1923. Films: Destry Rides Again, 1939; The Great Caruso, 1951; Please Don't Eat the Daisies, 1960.

PECKINPAH, (David) SAM(uel), Feb. 21, 1925 (Fresno, Calif.). U.S. film director. Known for violent, beautifully photographed films. Films: Ride the High Country, 1962; The Wild Bunch, 1969; Straw Dogs, 1971; Pat Garrett and Billy the Kid, 1973; The Killer Elite, 1976; Cross of Iron, 1977.

PENN, ARTHUR, Sept. 27, 1922 (Philadelphia, Pa.). U.S. film director. Films: The Miracle Worker, 1962; Bonnie and Clyde, 1967; Alice's Restaurant, 1969; Little Big Man, 1970; Dead of Winter, 1987.

PORTER, EDWIN STANTON, 1870 (Pittsburgh, Pa.)–Apr. 30, 1941. U.S. film pioneer. Associated with T. A. EDISON in the invention and perfection of the motion-picture camera; produced the first "story" film, The Life of an American Fireman (1899); produced The Great Train Robbery (1903), one of the most influential films of all time.

PREMINGER, OTTO, Dec. 5, 1905 (Vienna, Austria)–Apr. 23, 1986. U.S. film director. Films: Laura, 1944; Forever Amber, 1947; The Moon is Blue, 1953; Carmen Jones, 1954; The Man with the Golden Arm, 1955; Anatomy of a Murder, 1959; Exodus, 1960; Advise and Consent, 1961; The Cardinal, 1963.

PRINCE, HAROLD, Jan. 30, 1928 (New York, N.Y.). U.S. producer-director. Responsible for some of Broadway's biggest hits. Plays: Pajama Game, 1954; Damn Yankees, 1955; West Side Story, 1957; Fiorello!, 1959; A Funny Thing Happened on the Way to the Forum, 1962; Fiddler on the Roof, 1964; Cabaret, 1966; Company, 1970; A Little Night Music, 1973; On the 20th Century, 1978; Sweeney Todd, 1978; Phantom of the Opera, 1988.

REINER, CARL, Mar. 20, 1922 (Bronx, N.Y.). U.S. director, writer, actor. Versatile comedian, on stage and in TV; achieved greatest fame as creator/writer/director of TV's Dick Van Dyke Show, 1961–66; formed comedy team with MEL BROOKS, with whom he created famous "2000-year-old-man" character; directs films. (Father of R. REINER.)

ROEG, NICHOLAS, Aug. 15, 1928 (London, Eng.). British director. Films: Walkabout, 1970; Don't Look Now, 1973; The Man Who Fell to Earth, 1976; Track 29, 1987.

ROGERS, FRED, Mar. 20, 1928 (Latrobe, Pa.). U.S. producer, TV show host. Noted as the producer and host for the popular children's show, Mister Rogers Neighborhood, 1965–   , for which he has won two Emmies.

ROSE, BILLY (born William Samuel Rosenberg), Sept. 6, 1899 (New York, N.Y.)–Feb. 10, 1966. U.S. entrepreneur. A shorthand whiz at age 18, taught to take dictation at 350 wpm; songwriter, 1920–30; produced his first play, 1930; owned several theaters and night clubs in New York City. Shows produced: Billy Rose's Crazy Quilt, 1931; Jumbo, 1935; Aquacade, 1939–40; Carmen Jones, 1943; Seven Lively Arts, 1944.

ROSSEN, ROBERT, Mar. 16, 1908 (New York, N.Y.)–Feb. 18, 1966. U.S. screenwriter. After stage experience, came to Hollywood in 1936; films written include The Roaring Twenties (1939), A Walk in the Sun (1945), All the King's Men (also produced and directed; AA, 1949), and The Hustler (also produced and directed; 1961).

SAKS, GENE, Nov. 8, 1921 (New York, N.Y.). U.S. director. Actor turned theater and film director. Plays: Half a Sixpence, 1962; Mame, 1964; Same Time, Next Year, 1975. Films: The Odd Couple, 1967; Barefoot in the Park, 1967; Cactus Flower, 1970; The Prisoner of 2nd Avenue, 1974; Mame, 1974.

SAYLES, JOHN, Sept. 26, 1950 (Schenectady, N.Y.). U.S. director, screenwriter. Films: Return of the Secaucus 7, 1980; The Howling, 1981; Baby, It's You, 1983; Brother From Another Planet, 1984; Matewan, 1987; Eight Men Out, 1988.

SCHARY, DORE, Aug. 31, 1905 (Newark, N.J.)–July 7, 1980. U.S. producer, director, writer. Film producer/director, head of production at RKO

(1945–48) and MGM (1948–56). Films: *Boys' Town* (AA), 1938; *Sunrise at Campobello*, 1958 (play), 1960 (film).

**SCORSESE, MARTIN,** Nov. 17, 1942 (New York, N.Y.). U.S. film director. Films: *Mean Streets*, 1973; *Alice Doesn't Live Here Anymore*, 1974; *Taxi Driver*, 1976; *New York, New York*, 1977; *Raging Bull*, 1980; *The Color of Money*, 1986; *The Last Temptation of Christ*, 1988.

**SELZNICK, DAVID O.,** May 10, 1902 (Pittsburgh, Pa.)–June 22, 1965. U.S. film producer. Associated with Paramount, RKO, MGM, 1926–35. Films: *A Star is Born*, 1937; *Gone with the Wind*, 1939; *Rebecca*, 1940; *Spellbound*, 1945; *Duel in the Sun*, 1946.

**SENNETT, MACK** (born Michael Sinnott), Jan. 17, 1884 (Danville, Que., Can.)–Nov. 5, 1960. U.S. film producer, actor. His name is synonymous with slapstick comedy of silent screen, for the two-reel comedies he produced; formed Keystone Co. studio (1912), created Keystone Kops; gave starts to many famous actors and directors.

**SHUBERT, LEE,** Mar. 15, 1875 (Syracuse, N.Y.)–Dec. 25, 1953. U.S. theatrical producer. With his brothers, Sam and Jacob, built up a theatrical empire that at its peak controlled or owned over 60 theaters; first to stage the modern revues.

**SPELLING, AARON,** Apr. 22, 1928 (Dallas, Tex.). U.S. film producer, writer. Has produced several popular TV series, including *Dynasty, Hotel,* and *The Colbys;* films produced include *Mr. Mom* (1983) and *'Night Mother* (1986).

**SPIELBERG, STEVEN,** Dec. 18, 1947 (Cincinnati, Ohio). U.S. director, producer. Best known for hugely popular block-buster movies. Films (as dir.): *Close Encounters of a Third Kind*, 1977; *Raiders of the Lost Ark*, 1981; *E.T.*, 1982; *Indiana Jones and the Temple of Doom*, 1984. Films (as prod.): *Poltergeist*, 1982; *Gremlins*, 1984; *The Color Purple*, 1985; *Back to the Future*, 1985.

**STEVENS, GEORGE,** Dec. 18, 1904 (Oakland, Calif.)–Mar. 8, 1975. U.S. film director. Films: *Alice Adams*, 1934; *Gunga Din*, 1939; *Woman of the Year*, 1941; *A Place in the Sun* (AA), 1951; *Shane*, 1953; *Giant* (AA), 1956; *The Diary of Anne Frank*, 1959.

**STONE, OLIVER,** Sept. 15, 1946 (New York, N.Y.). U.S. film director. Films: *Salvador*, 1986; *Platoon*, 1987; *Wall Street*, 1987.

**STRASBERG, LEE,** Nov. 17, 1901 (Budzanow, Austria). U.S. theatrical director, teacher, actor. A cofounder of the Group Theatre (1931–37), where he started training in the STANISLAVSKY method; a foremost teacher of acting, has long been associated with the Actor's Studio, as dir. from 1950. (Father of S. STRASBERG.)

**SUSSKIND, DAVID,** Dec. 19, 1920 (New York, N.Y.)–Feb. 22, 1987. U.S. producer, TV host. Producer of many TV shows, movies, and stage shows; hosted syndicated talk show featuring "adult" discussion.

**THALBERG, IRVING,** May 30, 1899 (Brooklyn, N.Y.)–Sept. 14, 1936. U.S. movie executive. As

number-two man under LOUIS B. MAYER (1923–36), controlled the artistic policies of MGM; worked to develop studio contract directors; produced many films, including *Grand Hotel*, 1932; *Mutiny on the Bounty*, 1935; *A Night at the Opera*, 1935; *Naughty Marietta* (1935), *The Good Earth*. (One-time husband of N. SHEARER.)

**TODD, MICHAEL** (born Avron Hirsch Golbogen), June 2, 1909 (Minneapolis, Minn.)–Mar. 22, 1958. U.S. producer. After producing on Broadway (1936–45) entered films; formed company that developed Todd A-O and Cinerama widescreen processes; produced *Around the World in 80 Days* (AA), 1957; killed in plane crash. (Husband of J. BLONDELL and E. TAYLOR.)

**VON STROHEIM, ERICH** (born Erich Oswald Hans Carl Maria von Nordenwall), Sept. 22, 1885 (Vienna, Austria)–May 12, 1957. U.S.-Austrian director, actor. One of silent screen's greatest director/actors, whose career waned with the talkies. Films: *Blind Husbands*, 1919; *Foolish Wives*, 1921; *Greed*, 1923; *The Great Gabbo* (actor only), 1930; *The Grand Illusion* (actor only), 1937; *Sunset Boulevard* (actor only), 1950.

**WALD, JEROME** ("Jerry"), Sept. 16, 1911 (Brooklyn, N.Y.)–July 13, 1962. U.S. film producer. Films: *George Washington Slept Here*, 1942; *Mildred Pierce*, 1945; *Johnny Belinda*, 1948; *Peyton Place*, 1957; *Sons and Lovers*, 1960.

**WALLIS, HAL B**(rent), Sept. 14, 1898 (Chicago, Ill.)–Oct. 5, 1986. U.S. film producer. With Warner Bros., 1923–44; independent since then. Films: *Little Caesar*, 1930; *Casablanca*, 1942; *Gunfight at the OK Corral*, 1957; *Barefoot in the Park*, 1967; *True Grit*, 1969.

**WANGER, WALTER** (born Walter Feuchtwanger), July 11, 1894 (San Francisco, Calif.)–Nov. 18, 1968. U.S. film producer. An independent who worked for many studios. Films: *You Only Live Once*, 1937; *Stagecoach*, 1939; *Foreign Correspondent*, 1940; *Scarlet Street*, 1945; *Invasion of the Body Snatchers*, 1955; *Cleopatra*, 1962.

**WELLES, ORSON,** May 6, 1915 (Kenosha, Wisc.)–Oct. 10, 1985. U.S. actor, director, producer. Founder of Mercury Theater (1937) under whose aegis he directed and acted in plays on stage, radio, film; shocked nation with radio dramatization of H.G. Wells's *War of the Worlds*, Oct. 30, 1938. Best known for directing, starring in and cowriting (AA) *Citizen Kane* (1941). Films: *Jane Eyre*, 1944; *The Magnificent Ambersons*, 1946; *Macbeth*, 1947; *The Lady from Shanghai*, 1948; *The Third Man*, 1949; *A Man for All Seasons*, 1966. (One-time husband of R. HAYWORTH.)

**WELLMAN, WILLIAM,** Feb. 29, 1896 (Brookline, Mass.)–Dec. 9, 1975. U.S. film director. Specialized in action-adventure genre. Films: *Wings*, 1927; *Public Enemy*, 1931; *A Star Is Born* (AA), 1937; *The Ox-Bow Incident*, 1942; *Roxie Hart*, 1942; *The High and the Mighty*, 1954.

**WILDER, BILLY,** June 22, 1906 (Austria). U.S. film director/writer. Awarded Irving Thalberg Award, 1988. Films: *Ninotchka*, 1939; *Double Indemnity*,

1941; *The Lost Weekend* (AA), 1945; *Sunset Boulevard* (AA), 1950; *Stalag 17*, 1953; *Some Like It Hot*, 1959; *The Seven Year Itch*, 1959; *The Apartment* (2 AAs), 1960.

**WINNER, MICHAEL**, Oct. 30, 1935 (London, Eng.). British director. Films: *The Wicked Lady*, 1982; *The Nightcomers*, 1971; *Deathwish*, 1974.

**WISE, ROBERT**, Sept. 10, 1914 (Winchester, Ind.). U.S. director, producer. Films: *Run Silent Run Deep*, 1958; *West Side Story* (AA), 1961; *The Haunting*, 1963; *The Sound of Music* (AA), 1965; *The Sand Pebbles*, 1966; *The Andromeda Strain*, 1970.

**WYLER, WILLIAM**, July 1, 1902 (Mulhouse, Fr.)– July 27, 1981. U.S. film director. Films: *Jezebel*, 1938; *Mrs. Miniver* (AA), 1943; *The Best Years of Our Lives* (AA), 1947; *Roman Holiday*, 1953, *Ben Hur* (AA), 1959 *The Children's Hour*, 1962; *Funny Girl*, 1968.

**YORKIN, BUD** (born Alan Yorkin), Feb. 22, 1926 (Washington, Pa.). U.S. producer, director. Partner with NORMAN LEAR in Tandem Productions, 1959– . Producer of the TV series *All in the Family* (1969–79), *Sanford and Son* (1971–78), *Maude* (1972–78), and *Good Times* (1973–79).

**ZANUCK, DARRYL F**(rancis), Sept. 5, 1902 (Wahoo, Neb.). Dec. 22, 1979. U.S. film producer long associated with 20th Century-Fox. Films: *Grapes of Wrath*, 1940; *Gentlemen's Agreement*, 1947; *The Longest Day*, 1962.

**ZIEGFELD, FLORENZ**, Mar. 21, 1869 (Chicago, Ill.)–July 22, 1932. U.S. producer. His extravagant stage shows, *Ziegfeld Follies*, glorified the American "girl", 1907–30; also produced other stage shows, notably *Show Boat* (1927) and *Bitter Sweet* (1929). (Husband of B. BURKE.)

**ZINNEMANN, FRED**, Apr. 29, 1907 (Vienna, Austria). U.S. film director. Established neorealist movement in U.S. cinema. Films: *The Search*, 1948; *High Noon* (AA), 1951; *From Here to Eternity*, 1953; *Oklahoma*, 1955; *The Nun's Story*, 1958; *A Man for All Seasons* (AA), 1966; *Julia*.

**ZUKOR, ADOLPH**, Jan. 7, 1873 (Ricse, Hung.)– June 10, 1976. U.S. film executive. Helped found Paramount pictures and headed that company from 1935 until shortly before his death.

## FOREIGN PRODUCERS AND DIRECTORS

**ANTONIONI, MICHELANGELO**, Sept. 29, 1912 (Ferrara, It.). Italian film director, scriptwriter. Films: *L'Avventura*, 1959; *The Red Desert*, 1964; *Blow-up*, 1966; *Zabriskie Point*, 1969.

**BERGMAN, INGMAR**, July 14, 1918 (Uppsala, Swe.). Swedish film director, screenwriter. Perhaps the most influential filmmaker of his time, famed for his psychologically penetrating works. Films: *Smiles of a Summer Night*, 1955; *The Seventh Seal*, 1956; *Wild Strawberries*, 1957; *The Virgin Spring*, 1960; *Through a Glass Darkly*, 1961; *Winter Light*, 1962; *The Silence*, 1963; *Persona*, 1966; *Cries and Whispers*, 1972; *Scenes from a Marriage*, 1974; *The Magic Flute*, 1975; *Face to Face*, 1976; *Autumn Sonata*, 1978

**BROOK, PETER**, Mar. 21, 1925 (London, Eng.). English director. Director of stage and film, especially renowned for his interpretations of Shakespeare. Plays: *King Lear*, 1962; *Marat/Sade*, 1964; *Midsummer Night's Dream*, 1970. Films: *Lord of the Flies*, 1969.

**BUÑUEL, LUIS**, Feb. 22, 1900 (Calanda, Spain) –July 29, 1983. Spanish film director. Worked in France in 1920s–30s, then in Mexico (1945–60), before returning to France; known for surreal films that mock hypocrisy and religion. Films: *Un Chien Andalou*, 1928; *L'Age d'Or*, 1930; *Los Olvidados*, 1950; *Robinson Crusoe*, 1952; *Viridiana*, 1961; *The Exterminating Angel*, 1962; *Belle de Jour*, 1966; *The Discreet Charm of the Bourgeoisie*, 1972.

**CHABROL, CLAUDE**, June 24, 1930 (Paris, Fr.). French film director. Credited with starting the "new wave" in French films. Films: *Le Beau Serge*, 1958, *The Beast Must Die*, 1969; *The Butcher*, 1970; *Ophelia*, 1973.

**CLOUZOT, HENRI-GEORGES**, Nov. 20, 1907 (Niort, Fr.)–Jan. 12, 1977. French film director, writer. Noted for his suspense melodramas. Films: *Le Corbeau*, 1943; *Quai des Orfevres*, 1947; *The Wages of Fear*, 1953; *Les Diaboliques*, 1954.

**COSTA-GAVRAS** (born Konstantinos Gavras), 1933 (Athens, Gr.). Greek film director. Films: *The Sleeping Car Murders*, 1966; *'Z'* (AA), 1969; *State of Siege*, 1973; *Missing*, 1982.

**DE BROCA, PHILIPPE**, Mar. 15, 1933 (Paris, Fr.). French film director, producer. Films: *That Man From Rio*, 1963; *King of Hearts*, 1966; *Mademoiselle Mimi*, 1967.

**DE LAURENTIIS, DINO**, Aug. 8, 1919 (Torre Annunziata, It.). Italian film producer. Known for big-budget productions. Films: *Bitter Rice*, 1948; *La Strada*, 1954; *The Bible*, 1966; *Death Wish*, 1974; *King Kong* 1976; *Hurricane*, 1979; *Ragtime*, 1981; *Conan the Barbarian*, 1982.

**DE SICA, VITTORIO**, July 7, 1901 (Sora, It.) –Nov. 13, 1974. Italian film director. Known both for his social realism and his comedies. Films: *Shoeshine*, 1946; *The Bicycle Thief*, 1948; *Umberto D.*, 1952; *Madame De*, 1952; *Two Women*, 1961; *Yesterday, Today and Tomorrow* (AA), 1965; *The Garden of the Finzi-Continis*, 1971; *The Voyage*, 1973.

**EISENSTEIN, SERGEI**, Jan. 23, 1898 (Riga, Latvia [now USSR])–Feb. 11, 1948. Soviet film director. Major influence in world cinema for his theories on film direction. Films: *The Battleship Potemkin*, 1925; *Alexander Nevsky*, 1938; *Ivan the Terrible*, 1944, 1958.

**FELLINI, FEDERICO**, Jan. 20, 1920 (Rimini, It.). Italian film director. Major influence on post-WW II Italian cinema; occasionally appears in his own films. Films: *La Strada*, 1954; *La Dolce Vita*, 1959; *8½*, 1963; *Juliet of the Spirits*, 1965; *Satyricon*,

1969; *The Clowns*, 1970; *Roma*, 1972; *Casanova*, 1977.

**GODARD, JEAN-LUC,** Dec. 3, 1930 (Paris, Fr.). French film director. A leader of the French "new wave" cinema. Films: *Breathless*, 1960; *Les Carbiniers*, 1963; *Alphaville*, 1965; *Pierrot Le Fou*, 1966; *Weekend*, 1967; *Symphony for the Devil*, 1970; *Tout va Bien*, 1972.

**HITCHCOCK, ALFRED,** Aug. 13, 1899 (London, Eng.)–Apr. 29, 1980. English director. Known for suspense/thriller films: Films: *The 39 Steps*, 1935; *The Lady Vanishes*, 1938; *Rebecca*, 1940; *Suspicion*, 1941; *Saboteur*, 1942; *Lifeboat*, 1943; *Spellbound*, 1945; *Notorious*, 1946; *Strangers on a Train*, 1951; *Dial M for Murder*, 1954; *Rear Window*, 1954; *To Catch a Thief*, 1955; *Vertigo*, 1958; *North by Northwest*, 1959; *Psycho*, 1960; *The Birds*, 1963; *Frenzy*, 1972; *Family Plot*, 1976. TV: *Alfred Hitchcock Presents*, 1955–61.

**KORDA, ALEXANDER** (born Sandor Corda), Sept. 16, 1893 (Turkeye, Hung.)–Jan. 23, 1956. Anglo-Hungarian film producer, director. A major figure in the British film industry. Films: *The Private Life of Henry VIII*, 1932; *The Scarlet Pimpernel*, 1934; *The Thief of Baghdad*, 1940; *The Third Man*, 1949.

**LANG, FRITZ,** Dec. 12, 1890 (Vienna, Austria) –Aug. 2, 1976. Austrian director. Leading film dir. in Europe and Hollywood. Films: *M*, 1931; *Western Union*, 1941; *Cloak and Dagger*, 1946; *The Big Heat*, 1953.

**LEAN, DAVID,** Mar. 25, 1908 (Croydon, Eng.). English director. Film dir. in England and Hollywood. Films: *Brief Encounter*, 1946; *Great Expectations*, 1946; *Oliver Twist*, 1948; *The Bridge on the River Kwai* (AA), 1957; *Dr. Zhivago*, 1965; *Lawrence of Arabia* (AA), 1962; *Ryan's Daughter*, 1970; *A Passage to India*, 1984.

**LUBITSCH, ERNST,** Jan. 29, 1892 (Berlin, Ger.) –Nov. 30, 1947. Ger.-U.S. director. Noted for his sophisticated comedy films of the 1930s and 1940s. Films: *Trouble in Paradise*, 1932; *Ninotchka*, 1939; *To Be or Not To Be*, 1942; *Heaven Can Wait*, 1943.

**MALLE, LOUIS,** Oct. 30, 1932 (Thumeries, Fr.). French film director. One of the "new wave" of French film dirs. Films: *The Lovers*, 1958; *Zazie dans le Metro*, 1961; *Le Feu Follet*, 1963; *Souffle au Coeur*, 1971; *Lucien-Lacombe*, 1975. (Husband of C. BERGEN.)

**MILLER, JONATHAN,** July 21, 1934 (London, Eng.). English director, actor, writer, physician. Coauthor of and actor in the play *Beyond the Fringe*, 1961; directed films and TV for the BBC, 1964–67; directed plays, including *Danton's Death*, *The School for Scandal* and *The Merchant of Venice* (all three for the National Theatre, London), 1957–70.

**PARKER, ALAN,** Feb. 14, 1944 (London, Eng.). British director, screenwriter. Films: *Bugsy Malone*, 1977; *Midnight Express*, 1978; *Fame*, 1979; *Shoot the Moon*, 1982; *Birdy*, 1986; *Angel Heart*, 1987; *Mississippi Burning*, 1988.

**POLANSKI, ROMAN,** Aug. 18, 1933 (Paris, Fr.). French film director. Acted in several of his own films; fled U.S. in 1978, to avoid further prosecution on a morals charge. Films: *Knife in the Water*, 1961; *Repulsion*, 1965; *Rosemary's Baby*, 1968; *Chinatown*, 1974; *Tess*, 1980.

**PONTI, CARLO,** Dec. 11, 1913 (Milan, It.). Italian film producer. Credited with discovering SOPHIA LOREN, whom he later married. Films: *War and Peace*, 1956; *Marriage—Italian Style*, 1965; *Operation Crossbow*, 1965.

**PUDOVKIN V(sevolod),** 1893 (Rus.)–July 1, 1953. Soviet director. Films: *Mother*, 1926; *The End of St. Petersburg*, 1927; *Storm over Asia*, 1928.

**REED, CAROL,** Dec. 30, 1906 (London, Eng.)– Apr. 25, 1976. English film director. Active mostly in Britain. Films: *Kipps*, 1941; *Odd Man Out*, 1946; *The Third Man*, 1949; *The Agony and the Ecstasy*, 1965; *Oliver* (AA), 1968.

**RENOIR, JEAN,** Sept. 15, 1894 (Paris, Fr.)–Feb. 12, 1979. French film director. Leading force in world cinema, most remembered for monumental antiwar film *La Grande Illusion* (1937). (Son of P. A. RENOIR.)

**RESNAIS, ALAIN,** June 3, 1922 (Vannes, Fr.). French film director. A founder of the French "new wave" of cinema of the 1950s and 1960s. Films: *Hiroshima Mon Amour*, 1959; *Last Year at Marienbad*, 1961; *La guerre est fini*, 1966; *Je t'aime*, 1969; *Stavisky*, 1974.

**RICHARDSON, TONY,** June 5, 1928 (Shipley, Eng.). English director. Film director, who occasionally directs on the stage. Films: *A Taste of Honey*, 1961; *The Loneliness of the Long Distance Runner*, 1963; *Tom Jones*, 1963; *The Loved One*, 1965; *Joseph Andrews*, 1978.

**ROHMER, ERIC** (born Jean-Marie Maurice Schere), Mar. 21, 1920 (Tulle, Fr.). French director. Disciple of Alfred Hitchcock; former assistant for *Cahiers du Cinema* journal. Films: *My Night at Maud's*, 1969; *Claire's Knee*, 1970; *Chloe in the Afternoon*, 1972; *The Marquis of O*, 1975; *Percival*, 1978.

**ROSSELLINI, ROBERTO,** May 8, 1906 (Rome, It.)–June 3, 1977. Italian film director. Directed *Open City* (1945), *Paisan* (1946). (One-time husband of I. BERGMAN.)

**RUSSELL, KEN,** July 3, 1927 (Southampton, Eng.). English director known for his bizarre, controversial and lavishly produced films, often biographies of famous artists. Films: *Women in Love*, 1969; *The Music Lovers*, 1970; *The Boy Friend*, 1971; *The Devils*, 1971; *Tommy*, 1975; *Lisztomania*, 1975; *Altered States*, 1980.

**STANISLAVSKY, KONSTANTIN,** Jan. 7, 1863 (Moscow, Rus.)–Aug. 7, 1938. Russian actor, director. Noted as the creator of the system or theory of acting called the "method"; cofounder and dir. of Moscow Art Theater, 1898–1938.

**TRUFFAUT, FRANÇOIS,** Feb. 6, 1932 (Paris, Fr.)– Oct. 21, 1984. French filmmaker. Producer, director, writer and actor, from 1957. Films: *The 400 Blows*, 1957; *Shoot the Piano-player*, 1960; *Jules et Jim* 1961; *Fahrenheit 451*, 1966; *The Wild Child*,

1969; *Day for Night*, 1972; *The Story of Adele H.*, 1975; *Small Change*, 1976.

**VISCONTI, LUCHINO**, Nov. 2, 1906 (Milan, It.) –Mar. 17, 1976. Italian film director. Films: *Ossessione*, 1942; *Senso*, 1952, *Rocco and His Brothers*, 1960; *The Leopard*, 1964; *The Damned*, 1970; *Death in Venice*, 1971.

**WERTMULLER, LINA** 1928 (Rome, It.). Italian film director/writer. Began in 1962 as production asst. to FEDERICO FELLINI; wrote and directed popular films Films; *The Seduction of Mimi*, 1974; *Swept Away...*, 1975; *Seven Beauties*, 1976.

**ZEFFIRELLI, FRANCO**, Feb. 12, 1923 (Florence, It.). Italian director, designer. Began as a stage designer in Italy, then moved into designing-directing for opera. Films: *Romeo and Juliet*, 1968; *Brother Sun and Sister Moon*, 1973; *La Traviata*, 1982.

## MUSICIANS

**ADDERLEY, CANNONBALL** (born Julian Edwin Adderley), Sept. 15, 1928 (Tampa, Fla.)–Aug. 8, 1975. U.S. musician. Leading jazz saxophonist.

**ALLEN, RED** (born Henry Allen), Jan. 1, 1900 (Algiers, La.)–Apr. 17, 1967. U.S. musician. Dixieland-jazz trumpet player.

**ALLMAN, DUANE**, Nov. 20, 1946 (Nashville, Tenn.)–Oct. 29, 1971. U.S. guitarist; with brother GREGG, formed Allman Bros. band, a popular 1970s rock group.

**ALLMAN, GREGG**, Dec. 7, 1947 (Nashville, Tenn.). U.S. musician. With brother DUANE, formed Allman Bros. rock band, 1969; organist and lead vocals; after Duane's death, regrouped band; noted for successful kicking of drug habit and brief marriage to CHER. Songs: "Ramblin' Man"; "Blue Skies"; "Midnight Rider."

**ALPERT, HERB**, Mar. 31, 1935 (Los Angeles, Calif.). U.S. musician and record company executive. Trumpeter who founded and leads Tijuana Brass ensemble 1962– ; founder of A&M Records.

**ARMSTRONG, LOUIS** ("Satchmo"), July 4, 1900 (New Orleans, La.)–July 6, 1971. U.S. musician. Leading trumpeter in jazz history; made hundreds of jazz recordings, many classics; originated the "scat" vocal; made numerous film, television, concert appearances.

**ATKINS, CHET**, June 20, 1924 (Luttrell, Tenn.). U.S. musician and record company executive. Country-and-western guitarist; performs with Grand Ole Opry.

**BAKER, GINGER** (born Peter Baker), Aug. 19, 1939 (Lewisham, Eng.). English musician. Drummer for the legendary rock group Cream, 1966–68.

**BASIE, COUNT** (born William Basie), Aug. 21, 1904 (Red Bank, N.J.)–Apr. 26, 1984. U.S. musician. A pianist/composer who has led big jazz bands from 1935. "One'O'Clock Jump"; "Two O'Clock Jump"; "Basie Boogie"; "I Left My Baby."

**THE BEACH BOYS:** Brian Wilson, June 20, 1942 (Hawthorne, Calif.); Alan Jardine, Sept. 3, 1942 (Lima, Oh.); Mike Love, Mar. 15, 1941 (Los Angeles, Calif.); Dennis Wilson, Dec. 4, 1944 (Hawthorne, Calif.); Carl Wilson, Dec. 21, 1946 (Hawthorne, Calif.). U.S. rock group. The epitome of "California-style" rock in the early 1960s, the group foundered in late 1960s, only to resurrect itself into a popular pop-rock group again in late 1970s and 1980s. Songs: "Help Me, Rhonda," 1965; "California Girls," 1965.

**BECHET, SIDNEY,** May 14, 1897 (New Orleans, La.)–May 14, 1959. U.S. musician. Early jazz innovator on the soprano saxophone.

**BEIDERBECKE, BIX** (born Leon Bismarck Beiderbecke), Mar. 10, 1903 (Davenport, Ia.)–Aug. 7, 1931. U.S. musician. Jazz cornetist/composer; first white musician to be considered major innovator in jazz.

**BERIGAN, BUNNY** (born Roland Bernard Berigan), Nov. 2, 1909–June 2, 1942. U.S. trumpet player. Bandleader of 1930s swing era; theme song: "I Can't Get Started with You."

**BLAKEY, ART**, Oct. 11, 1919 (Pittsburgh, Pa.). U.S. jazz drummer. Bandleader, 1940s–70s.

**BLANTON, JIMMY**, c.1921 (Chattanooga, Tenn.) –July 30, 1942. U.S. jazz bass player. Played with DUKE ELLINGTON's band, 1939–42.

**BLOOD, SWEAT & TEARS:** David Clayton-Thomas, Sept. 13, 1941 (Surrey, Eng.); Bobby Colomby, Dec. 20, 1944 (New York, N.Y.); Steve Katz, May 9, 1945 (Brooklyn, N.Y.); Jim Fielder, Oct. 4, 1947 (Denton, Tex.); Dick Halligan, Aug. 29, 1943 (Troy, N.Y.); Fred Lipsius, Nov. 19, 1944 (New York, N.Y.); Lew Soloff, Feb. 20, 1944 (Brooklyn, N.Y.); Chuck Winfield, Feb. 5, 1943 (Monessen, Pa.); and Jerry Hyman, May 19, 1947 (Brooklyn, N.Y.). U.S. jazz-rock group. With AL KOOPER, established the rock instrumental group in 1968 that became one of the most popular of all time and continues successfully today; one of the first rock groups to make use of many instruments other than guitars and drums.

**BOLDEN, BUDDY** (born Charles Bolden), 1868? (New Orleans, La.)–Nov. 4, 1931. U.S. musician. Cornetist who formed first jazz band in the U.S., 1895; his standard numbers included "If You Don't Like My Potatoes, Why Do You Dig So Deep," "Make Me a Pallet on the Floor," and "Bucket's Got a Hole in It."

**BONO** (born Paul Hewson), 1960 (Dublin, Ire.). Irish musician. The lead singer for U2, the internationally famous Irish rock group; distinctive vocals combine American rock and roll, gospel; breakthrough album was *The Joshua Tree;* compositions include "I Still Haven't Found What I'm Looking For," "Bullet the Blue Sky," and "Silver and Gold."

**BROONZY, BIG BILL**, June 26, 1893 (Scott, Miss.)– Aug. 14, 1958. U.S. musician. Blues singer and guitarist.

**BROWN, LES**, Mar. 14, 1912 (Reinerton, Pa.). U.S. musician. Led his Band of Renown since 1938, often appearing with BOB HOPE; wrote the song "Sentimental Journey."

**BRUBECK, DAVE,** Dec. 6, 1920 (Concord, Calif.). U.S. musician. Leading force in contemporary jazz, came to prominence in 1950s as pianist/composer; had own quartet, 1951–67.

**BURDON, ERIC,** May 11, 1941 (Newcastle-on-Tyne, Eng.). English musician. Founder of British rock group The Animals, 1963–68; founded black rock group War (1969) with which he performed until 1971. Songs: "Spill the Wine," 1970.

**BYRD, CHARLIE,** born Charles Lee Byrd, Sept. 16, 1925 (Suffolk, Va.). U.S. guitarist. Jazz guitarist, from 1936–   ; named *Playboy* guitarist of the year, 1964–67.

**THE BYRDS:** Roger McGuinn (born James McGuinn) July 13, 1942 (Chicago, Ill.); Chris Hillman, Dec. 4, 1942 (Los Angeles, Calif.); Gene Clark, Nov. 17, 1941 (Tipton, Mo.); Mike Clarke, June 3, 1943 (New York, N.Y.). U.S. musicians. With David Crosby, (born David Van Cortland), Aug. 14, 1941 (Los Angeles, Calif.), the original members of the popular 1960s band, one of first in the folk-rock genre, 1964–73. Songs: "Mr. Tambourine Man," 1964; "Turn, Turn, Turn," 1965.

**CALLOWAY, CAB**(ell), Dec. 25, 1907 (Rochester, N.Y.). U.S. musician. Has led own band since 1928 in appearances on stage, in films; starred in film *Stormy Weather,* 1943; wrote "Minnie the Moocher"; his autobiography, *Of Minnie the Moocher and Me,* was a best-seller.

**CARTER, BENNY,** Aug. 8, 1907 (New York, N.Y.). U.S. musician. Jazz performer (alto saxophone, clarinet, trumpet), composer, band leader; had his own band, 1932–35 and 1938–46; composed music for films.

**CATLETT, SIDNEY** ("Big Sid"), Jan. 17, 1910 (Evansville, Ind.)–Mar. 25, 1951. U.S. musician. A leading jazz drummer of the 1930s–40s.

**CLAPTON, ERIC,** Mar. 30, 1945 (Surrey, England). English guitarist and vocalist. With GINGER BAKER and Jack Bruce, formed rock trio Cream (1966–68), a major influence in rock music; also founded Derek and The Dominoes, 1970–72; member of Blind Faith band, 1969–70.

**CLARK, DAVE,** Dec. 15, 1942 (Tottenham, Eng.). English musician, lead singer. With four others, formed the Dave Clark Five, a major 1960s rock group, 1964–73. Songs: "Glad All Over," 1964; "Because," 1964.

**COCKER, JOE** (born John Cocker), May 20, 1944 (Sheffield, Eng.). English musician. Singer-drummer of blues-rock in 1960s.

**COLE, COZY** (born William Randolph Cole), Oct. 17, 1909 (E. Orange, N.J.)–Jan. 29, 1981. U.S. jazz drummer. A leading musician of the Big Band era; continued career into the 1970s with own group.

**COLEMAN, ORNETTE,** Mar. 9, 1930 (Ft. Worth, Tex.). U.S. musician. Jazz saxophonist associated with the avant-garde school.

**COLTRANE, JOHN,** Sept. 23, 1926 (Hamlet, N.C.) –July 17, 1967. U.S. musician. Jazz saxophonist who worked with DIZZY GILLESPIE and MILES DAVIS.

**CROSBY, BOB,** Aug. 25, 1913 (Spokane, Wash.). U.S. musician. Bandleader (Bob Crosby and His Bobcats) popular during the 1940s and 1950s; appeared in several films. (Brother of B. CROSBY).

**CUGAT, XAVIER,** Jan. 1, 1900 (Barcelona, Sp.). U.S. musician. Latin bandleader, extremely popular during rhumba, cha-cha, and mambo dance crazes of the 1940s and 1950s.

**DANIELS, CHARLIE,** Oct. 28, 1936 (Wilmington, N.C.). U.S. musician. A fiddle player, with his band performs "good ole boy" music, i.e. country tunes with a passing rock influence; hits include "The Devil Went Down to Georgia," "Still in Saigon," "Powderkeg," and "Uneasy Rider."

**DAVIES, RAY,** June 21, 1944 (London, Eng.). British singer, musician. As leader of the Kinks, wrote many of the British band's songs, including "Lola," "Destroyer," and "Come Dancing."

**DAVIS, MILES,** May 25, 1926 (Alton, Ill.). U.S. musician. Leading figure in jazz since the 1940s; trumpet player and composer who has his own quintet; ushered in the "birth of cool"; albums include *Milestones, Musings of Miles, At Carnegie Hall, Sorcerer,* and *Bitches' Brew..*

**DEFRANCO, BUDDY** (born Boniface Ferdinand Leonard DeFranco), Feb. 17, 1933 (Camden, N.J.). U.S. musician. A clarinetist who performed with GENE KRUPA, TOMMY DORSEY, Charlie Barnet, 1941–46; winner, *Down Beat* poll, 1945–54; featured with GLENN MILLER orchestra, 1966–74.

**DESMOND, PAUL** (born Paul Breitenfeld), Nov. 25, 1924 (San Francisco, Calif.)–May 30, 1977. U.S. jazz alto saxophonist. Associated with DAVE BRUBECK's Quartet, 1951–67.

**DORSEY, JIMMY,** Feb. 29, 1904 (Shenandoah, Pa.)–June 12, 1957. U.S. musician. Important leader of the Big Band era; played clarinet, alto sax; had own band, also played with brother TOMMY DORSEY.

**DORSEY, TOMMY,** Nov. 19, 1905 (Shenandoah, Pa.)–Nov. 26, 1956. U.S. musician. Key figure in Big Band era; played trombone (noted for sweet tone) and trumpet, often with brother JIMMY DORSEY; had own band.

**DUCHIN, EDDY,** 1909 (Cambridge, Mass.)–Feb. 9, 1951. U.S. pianist. Beloved by "high society," played for important balls and social functions; died of leukemia. (Father of P. DUCHIN).

**DUCHIN, PETER,** July 28, 1937 (New York, N.Y.). U.S. musician. Pianist and orchestra leader, popular with "beautiful people" of the 1960s and 1970s. (Son of E. DUCHIN.)

**EDDY, DUANE,** Apr. 26, 1938 (Corning, N.Y.). U.S. musician. Rock-and-roll guitarist/songwriter famed for his "twang" effect; played with backup group The Rebels. Songs: "Rebel Rouser," 1958.

**ELDRIDGE, ROY,** Jan. 30, 1911 (Pittsburgh, Pa). U.S. musician. Jazz trumpeter. Performed with most of the jazz greats.

**FLATT, LESTER,** June 19, 1914 (Overton Co.,

Tenn.)–May 11, 1979. U.S. guitarist. Country-and-western star who for 25 years was partner with EARL SCRUGGS in popular Foggy Mountain Boys band.

**GARCIA, JERRY,** Aug. 1, 1942 (San Francisco, Calif.). U.S. musician. Lead guitarist and a founder (1965) of The Grateful Dead, an acid-rock band of the 1960s.

**GARNER, ERROLL,** May 15, 1921 (Pittsburgh, Pa.)–Jan. 2, 1977. U.S. musician. Jazz pianist; composer of hit tune "Misty."

**GETZ, STAN,** Feb. 2, 1927 (Philadelphia, Pa.). U.S. musician. Jazz saxophonist; won numerous *Metronome* and *Down Beat* awards.

**GILLESPIE, DIZZY** (born John Birks Gillespie), Oct. 21, 1917 (Cheraw, N.C.). U.S. musician. Jazz trumpeter and composer who is credited with developing "bop" style of music.

**GOODMAN, BENNY** ("The King of Swing"), May 30, 1909 (Chicago, Ill.)–June 13, 1986. U.S. musician. Clarinetist who has led his own orchestra since 1933; conducted swing concerts all over the world; appeared on numerous TV and radio programs and in some films; frequent guest-soloist with bands and symphony orchestras.

**HACKETT, BOBBY,** Jan. 31, 1915 (Providence, R.I.)–June 7, 1976. U.S. cornetist. Performed with Big Bands, 1930s–40s; featured soloist on JACKIE GLEASON albums, 1950s.

**HAMPTON, LIONEL,** Apr. 12, 1913 (Birmingham, Ala.). U.S. musician. Jazz vibraphonist and bandleader who performed with Benny Goodman Quartet, 1936–40; has led his own band ever since.

**HANCOCK, HERBIE,** Apr. 20, 1940 (Chicago, Ill.). U.S. musician. A pianist, has worked with everyone from MILES DAVIS (1963–68), during that group's Jazz Fusion period, to Dexter Gordon; on cutting edge of musical forms, his album *Rockit* (1984) stretched parameters of electronic music.

**HARRIS, PHIL,** June 24, 1916 (Linton, Ind.). U.S. bandleader. Had own Big Band; known for long association with JACK BENNY on radio and TV. (Husband of A. FAYE.)

**HAWKINS, COLEMAN,** Nov. 21, 1904 (St. Joseph, Mo.)–May 19, 1969. U.S. musician. Jazz tenor saxophonist; his 1939 recording of "Body and Soul" considered a classic.

**HAYES, ISAAC,** Aug. 20, 1942 (Covington, Ky.). U.S. singer and composer most noted for score to film *Shaft,* 1971. Albums: *Hot Buttered Soul; Soul Man; Juicy Fruit.*

**HENDERSON, (James) FLETCHER,** Dec. 18, 1898 (Cuthbert, Ga.)–Dec. 29, 1952. U.S. musician. First jazzman to use written arrangements, pioneering the regimented jazz bands and dance bands of the 1930s; bandleader and arranger.

**HERMAN, WOODY** (born Woodrow Charles), May 16, 1913 (Milwaukee, Wisc.)–Oct. 29, 1987. U.S. musician. Orchestra leader from 1936.

**HIGGINBOTHAM, JAY C.,** May 11, 1906 (Atlanta, Ga.)–May 26, 1973. U.S. jazz trombonist, singer. Appeared and recorded with such artists as FLETCH-ER HENDERSON, LOUIS ARMSTRONG, and RED ALLEN, from the 1930s.

**HINES, EARL** ("Fatha"), Dec. 28, 1905 (Duquesne, Pa.)–Apr. 22, 1983. U.S. musician. Jazz pianist, bandleader, and composer; leading influence in development of swing.

**HIRT, AL,** Nov. 7, 1922 (New Orleans, La.). U.S. musician. Rotund jazz trumpeter whose career began in 1940; many records, club, concert, TV appearances.

**HODGES, JOHNNY** (born John Cornelius Hodges), July 25, 1906 (Cambridge, Mass.)–May 11, 1970. U.S. jazz alto saxophonist. Popular in 1930s and 1940s; appeared with DUKE ELLINGTON for 40 years.

**JACKSON, MILT,** Jan. 1, 1923 (Detroit, Mich.). U.S. musician. Jazz vibraphonist, pianist and guitarist; with WOODY HERMAN, 1949–50, with Modern Jazz Quartet, 1953–74.

**JAMES, HARRY,** Mar. 15, 1916 (Albany, Ga.)–July 5, 1983. U.S. musician. Trumpeter, bandleader, at peak of his popularity in the 1930s and 1940s. (One-time husband of B. GRABLE.)

**JAN AND DEAN:** Jan Berry, Apr. 3, 1941 (Los Angeles, Calif.); and Dean Torrance, Mar. 10, 1941 (Los Angeles, Calif.). U.S. musicians. The epitome of California surfer-rock of the 1960s, this vocal duo had many hits until 1967 when act disbanded after Jan was seriously injured in auto accident. Songs: "Surf City," 1963; "Dead Man's Curve," 1963; "The Little Old Lady (From Pasadena)," 1964; "Ride the Wild Surf," 1964.

**JOHNSON, BUNK** (born William Geary Johnson), Dec. 27, 1879 (New Orleans, La.)–July 7, 1949. U.S. jazz musician. Cornet and trumpet player of traditional New Orleans jazz style.

**JOHNSON, J. J.,** Jan. 22, 1924 (Indianapolis, Ind.). U.S. musician. Jazz trombonist and composer; with COUNT BASIE, 1945–47; headed own quintet and sextet, 1957–61; with MILES DAVIS group, 1961– .

**JONES, QUINCY,** Mar. 14, 1933 (Chicago, Ill.). U.S. musician. Composer, arranger, conductor; composed film scores, including *Cactus Flower* (1969) and *The Color Purple* (1985); arranged for many singers, including FRANK SINATRA, SARAH VAUGHAN and PEGGY LEE.

**JONES, SPIKE** (born Lindley Armstrong Jones), Dec. 14, 1911 (Long Beach, Calif.)–May 1, 1965. U.S. musician. Bandleader whose forte was zany variations on popular songs, often with odd instruments and sound effects.

**KAYE, SAMMY,** Mar. 13, 1910 (Lakewood, Ohio)–June 2, 1987. U.S. bandleader. Most famous for his "So you want to lead a band?" audience-participation routine and his "swing-and-sway" music.

**KENTON, STAN,** Feb. 19, 1912 (Wichita, Kan.)–Aug. 25, 1979. U.S. musician, arranger. Led own jazz orchestra since 1941; music characterized by the screaming "walls of brass"; worldwide concert appearances; theme songs were "Artistry in Rhythm" and "Eager Beaver."

**KOOPER, AL,** Feb. 5, 1944 (Brooklyn, N.Y.). U.S. musician. Guitarist/singer and record producer who is best known as founder of two important rock groups: The Blues Project, (1965) and BLOOD, SWEAT & TEARS (1967).

**KRUPA, GENE,** Jan. 15, 1909 (Chicago, Ill.) –Oct. 16, 1973. U.S. drummer, bandleader. Played with BENNY GOODMAN, 1935; led own band, 1938–51.

**LADNIER, TOMMY,** May 28, 1900 (Mandeville, La.)–June 4, 1939. U.S. jazz cornetist. Appeared with KING OLIVER, FLETCHER HENDERSON, Noble Sissle.

**LED ZEPPELIN:** John Bonham, May 31, 1947 (Edditch, Eng.); John Paul Jones (born John Baldwin), June 3, 1946 (Sidcup, Eng.); Jimmy Page, Jan. 9, 1944 (Heston, Eng.); Robert Plant, Aug. 20, 1948 (Bromwich, Eng.). English musicians. Formed leading hard-rock group in 1968, which survived through the 1970s; performed at Woodstock, 1969. Songs: "Whole Lotta Love," 1969.

**LEWIS, RAMSEY,** May 27, 1935 (Chicago, Ill.). U.S. musician. Pianist/composer who formed jazz trio (1956) that became very popular after record "The In Crowd," 1965; re-formed trio in 1970.

**LEWIS, TED** (born Theodore Leopold Friedman), June 6, 1892 (Circleville, Ohio)–Aug. 25, 1971. U.S. bandleader. Clarinetist, singer, and band-leader whose trademark was phrase, "Is everybody happy?"; vaudeville, club, and film appearances.

**LOMBARDO, GUY,** June 19, 1902 (London, Ont., Can.)–Nov. 5, 1977. Can.-U.S. bandleader. Led his band, The Royal Canadians, from 1929, into musical history, playing "the sweetest music this side of heaven"; his annual New Year's Eve performance became national event, via radio and TV.

**LUNCEFORD, JIMMIE,** June 6, 1902 (Fulton, Miss.)–July 13, 1947. U.S. musician. Jazz band leader and saxophonist; with FLETCHER HENDERSON orch., 1920; formed own band, 1929.

**MANGIONE, CHUCK,** Nov. 29, 1940 (Rochester, N.Y.). U.S. musician, composer. Discovered "overnight" in late 1970s when his composition "Feels SO Good" became a hit; had played with ART BLAKEY, Kai Winding, and Maynard Ferguson, from 1965; compositions include "Last Dance," "Give It All You've Got" (theme for 1980 Olympics), "Fun and Games," and "The Land of Make-Believe."

**MANN, HERBIE** (born Herbert Jay Solomon), Apr. 16, 1930 (New York, N.Y.). U.S. musician. Jazz flutist, first came to prominence in Matt Mathews Quintet, 1953–54; formed own Afro-jazz sextet, 1959; exponent of the bossa nova; incorporated rhythm-and-blues, disco, reggae into music. "Comin' Home Baby," 1962; "Hi Jack," 1975; "I Got a Woman," 1976.

**MANNE, SHELLY,** June 11, 1920 (New York, N.Y.). U.S. musician. Big Band jazz drummer; since 1939, with several orchestras, including STAN KENTON, WOODY HERMAN; led own band from 1955; owner of the Manne-Hole, a Hollywood jazz club, from 1960.

**MANZAREK, RAY,** Feb. 12, 1935 (Chicago, Ill.). U.S. musician. Member of the Doors (1967-71), played piano with the group; following the breakup of the group became a record producer; in the 1980s has become involved in "new wave," and has produced new acts such as X, a Los Angeles-based band.

**MARLEY, BOB,** Feb. 6, 1945 (St. Ann, Jamaica). –May 11, 1981. W. Indian musician. With his group The Wailers brought *reggae* music to an international audience. Songs: "Rude Boy," 1967; "I Can See Clearly Now," 1973; "I Shot the Sheriff," 1974; "Catch a Fire," 1975; "Natty Dread," 1976.

**MARSALIS, WYNTON,** Oct. 18, 1961 (New Orleans, La.). U.S. musician. A jazz trumpeter, spans jazz and classical music; started as a trumpet soloist with New Orleans Philharmonic; attended Julliard; played with HERBIE HANCOCK and ART BLAKEY (and his Jazz Messengers). Albums: *J-Mood; Carnival; Hothouse Flowers* (Grammy award).

**MCDONALD, "COUNTRY" JOE,** Jan. 1, 1942 (El Monte, Calif.). U.S. singer, bandleader. With his group The Fish, extremely popular protest-rock singer of late 1960s; vaulted to fame with anti-Vietnam War song "I Feel Like I'm Fixin' to Die Rag" (1965); one of performers at Woodstock, 1969.

**MCPARTLAND, JIMMY** (born James Duigald McPartland), Mar. 15, 1907 (Chicago, Ill.). U.S. musician. Leading cornetist in tradition of BIX BEIDERBECKE; often plays with wife MARIAN; one of the "Chicago-style" jazzmen.

**MCPARTLAND, MARIAN,** Mar. 20, 1920 (Slough, Eng.). U.S. musician. Jazz pianist/composer who has had own trio since 1951; known for subtle shadings of music at slow tempos. (Wife of J. MCPARTLAND.)

**MENDES, SERGIO,** Feb. 11, 1941 (Niteroi, Braz.). Brazilian musician. Formed Brasil '66 (later called Brasil '77), Latin pop-rock group that was very popular in late 1960s and 1970s; known for distinctive arrangements of tunes from COLE PORTER, THE BEATLES, others. Songs: "Constant Rain," 1966; "Mas Que Nada," 1967; "Night and Day," 1967; "Fool on the Hill," 1968; "Scarborough Fair," 1969; "Pais Tropical," 1971.

**MESSINA, JIM,** Dec. 5, 1947 (Maywood, Calif.). U.S. musician. With KENNY LOGGINS, formed Loggins and Messina country-rock band, popular in the 1970s; previously with 1960s groups Buffalo Springfield (1967–68) and Poco (1968–70).

**MILLER, GLENN,** Mar. 1, 1904 (Clarinda, Ia.)–Dec. 16, 1944. U.S. bandleader, trombonist. A prime force in the Big Band era of the 1930s and 1940s; noted for producing the "Glenn Miller" sound, a blending of clarinets and saxophones to produce a mellow tone.

**MINGUS, CHARLES,** Apr. 22, 1922 (Nogales, Ariz.)–Jan. 12, 1979. U.S. musician. Jazz bass player and a major figure in jazz of the 1950s and 1960s; renowned as teacher; first to exploit bass as solo instrument; led Jazz Workshop Bands, 1959–1977; semi-retired after 1965 because of ill health. "The Black Saint and the Sinner Lady"; "Thrice Upon a Theme"; "Revelations."

**MONK, THELONIOUS**, Oct. 10, 1917 (Rocky Mount, N.C.)–Feb. 17, 1982. U.S. musician. Pianist/composer and pioneer of "bop"; played with JOHN COLTRANE, DIZZY GILLESPIE, and CHARLIE PARKER, among others.

**MONROE, VAUGHN**, Oct. 7, 1911 (Akron, Ohio)–May 21, 1973. U.S. musician. Bandleader of his own group, from 1940; as singer, known for the "muscular" quality of his voice. Compositions: "Racing with the Moon" (theme song), "Something Sentimental," "Dance, Ballerina, Dance."

**MONTGOMERY, WES** (born John Leslie Montgomery), Mar. 6, 1925 (Indianapolis, Ind.)–June 15, 1968. U.S. musician. Jazz guitarist, first prominent as member of the Mastersounds, 1958; has led own trio since; developed parallel-octaves style of playing that is much imitated.

**MORTON, JELLY ROLL** (born Ferdinand Morton), Sept. 20, 1885 (New Orleans, La.)–July 11, 1941. Considered to be one of the inventors of jazz. Got his start playing piano in the bordellos of New Orleans' notorious Storyville district; traveled U.S., playing and studying ragtime and jazz styles, from 1907; formed and recorded with his own band, The Red Hot Peppers, 1926–30. Compositions: "King Porter Stomp," "Jelly Roll Blues."

**MULLIGAN, GERRY**, Apr. 6, 1927 (New York, N.Y.). U.S. musician. Baritone saxophonist/arranger with a number of jazz groups and bands since 1951.

**NASH, GRAHAM**, 1942 (Lancashire, Eng.). English musician. Guitarist, singer, songwriter, with NEIL YOUNG, David Crosby, and STEPHEN STILLS formed 1960s rock group Crosby, Stills, Nash and Young (1968–70).

**NAVARRO, THEODORE** ("Fats," "Fat Girl"). Sept. 24, 1923 (Key West, Fla.)–July 7, 1950. U.S. musician. Jazz trumpeter of the bop persuasion, noted for clean, pure tone; played with Andy Kirk (1943–44), Billy Eckstine (1944–46), Todd Dameron (1948–49).

**NICHOLS, RED** (born Ernest Loring Nichols), May 8, 1905 (Ogden, Utah)–June 28, 1965. U.S. musician. Cornetist and bandleader known for slick style; his group, The Five Pennies (really 10 people) was very popular in 1930s and 1940s; famous Pennies include JIMMY DORSEY, BENNY GOODMAN, GLENN MILLER.

**NOONE, JIMMIE**, Apr. 23, 1895 (Cut-Off, La.)–Apr. 19, 1944. U.S. musician. Clarinetist who led own group from 1927, when group appeared at Chicago's Apex Club; known for blending of New Orleans and swing. "Sweet Lorraine"; "I Know That You Know"; "Sweet Sue"; "Four or Five Times"; "Apex Blues."

**OATES, JOHN**, Apr. 7, 1948 (New York, N.Y.). U.S. musician. The taciturn half of the 1980s top musical duo (with DARYL HALL), an accomplished songwriter, singer and music producer.

**NORVO, RED**, Mar. 31, 1908 (Beardstown, Ill.). U.S. musician. Pioneer of use of xylophone and vibraphone in jazz; with PAUL WHITEMAN (1924–34), then on own with various-sized groups.

**OLIVER, KING** (born Joseph Oliver), 1885? (Abend, La.)–Apr. 8, 1938. U.S. musician and songwriter. Trumpeter in many New Orleans jazz bands, 1907–19; gave LOUIS ARMSTRONG his start.

**ORY, KID** (born Edward Ory), Dec. 25, 1886 (La Place, La.)–Jan. 23, 1973. U.S. musician. Leading exponent of New Orleans jazz, trombonist known for "tailgate" style; led own band, 1919–24; worked Chicago scene, 1925–29; retired in 1930, but came back in 1942; "Muskrat Ramble" his most famous piece.

**PARKER, CHARLIE** ("Bird," "Yardbird"), Aug. 29, 1920 (Kansas City, Kan.)–Mar. 12, 1955. U.S. musician. Legendary jazz alto saxophonist; co-creator of bebop, 1945; leading force in jazz scene in New York City and a major influence on numerous musicians; arrested and hospitalized for drug abuse, 1946. "Now's the Time"; "Yardbird Suite"; "Confirmation"; "Relaxin' at Camarillo."

**PETERSON, OSCAR**, Aug. 15, 1925 (Montreal, Que., Can.). Pianist. Leading jazz pianist; has led own trio since 1950; *Down Beat* magazine awards, 1950–54, 1960–63, 1965, 1983.

**PETTIFORD, OSCAR**, Sept. 30, 1922 (Okmulgee, Okla.)–Sept. 8, 1960. U.S. musician. Jazz bass player/composer who pioneered use of pizzicato jazz cello. "Singin' til the Girls Come Home"; "Black-Eyed Peas and Collard Greens"; "Tricrotism."

**POWELL, BUD** (Earl), Sept. 27, 1924 (New York, N.Y.)–Aug. 1, 1966. U.S. pianist, composer and modern jazz piano pioneer.

**PRESTON, BILLY**, Sept. 9, 1946 (Houston, Tex.). U.S. musician. Was the keyboardist for JOHN LENNON's Plastic Ono Band and a sideman for LITTLE RICHARD and RAY CHARLES; best known for mid-1970s hit "Nothing From Nothing" and duet with Syreeta Wright, "With You I'm Born Again."

**PRIMA, LOUIS**, Dec. 7, 1912 (New Orleans, La.)–Aug. 24, 1978. U.S. musician. Trumpet-player and singer who led his own band since 1940.

**PRINCE** (born Prince Rogers Nelson), June 7, 1959 (Minneapolis, Minn.). U.S. musician, actor. Rock musician, winner of three Grammy awards. Albums: *For You*, 1978; *1999*, 1983; *Around the World in a Day*, 1983; *Purple Rain*, 1984. Films: *Purple Rain*, 1984; *Sign of the Times*, 1987.

**RICH, BUDDY** (born Bernard Rich), June 30, 1917 (Brooklyn, N.Y.)–Apr. 2, 1987. U.S. musician. Child prodigy on drums, playing in vaudeville at age four; played with many Big Bands and jazz bands, from 1938–74. *Down Beat* awards: 1941–42, 1944, 1947, 1967, and 1970–72.

**RIDDLE, NELSON**, June 1, 1921 (Hackensack, N.J.)–Oct. 5, 1985. U.S. musician. Bandleader and composer of music for TV and films; music dir., Reprise Records, since 1963; guest conductor, Hollywood Bowl, 1954–60.

**ROACH, MAX** (well Lemuel), Jan. 10, 1924 (Elizabeth City, N.C.). U.S. musician. Jazz percussionist who adapted jazz to tympani; winner *Down Beat* poll six times.

**ROGERS, SHORTY** (born Milton M. Rogers), Apr. 14, 1924 (Great Barrington, Mass.). U.S. musician. Trumpeter in several jazz bands in 1940s and 1950s; arranger and composer, chiefly for STAN KENTON; frequent back-up on recordings.

**ROLLINS, SONNY** (born Theodore Rollins), Sept. 7, 1930 (New York, N.Y.). U.S. musician. Tenor saxophonist known for hard bop style; credited by some as first to improvise a complete, overall pattern in solo.

**RUGOLO, PETE**(r), Dec. 25, 1916 (San Piero Patti, Sicily). U.S. musician. Jazz-pop composer who rose to prominence as arranger for STAN KENTON, 1945–49; composed scores for TV series, including *Richard Diamond*, 1958–60; *Thriller*, 1962; *The Fugitive*, 1963–65; *Run for Your Life*, 1965–66.

**RUSSELL, PEE WEE** (born Charles Ellsworth Russell), Mar. 27, 1906 (St. Louis, Mo.)–Feb. 15, 1969. U.S. musician. Jazz clarinetist, part of New York City's 52nd Street jazz scene in the '30s; Dixieland player who branched out into swing and other styles; made comeback in 1951 after near-fatal illness.

**SEVERINSEN, DOC** (born Carl H. Severinsen), July 7, 1927 (Arlington, Ore.). U.S. musician. Trumpeter/bandleader best known as musical director of *Tonight Show* since 1967.

**SHAFFER, PAUL**, Nov. 28, 1949 (Thunder Bay, Ont.). Canadian musician, bandleader. Worked as a music writer and featured performer on *Saturday Night Live* before becoming the bandleader for *Late Night with David Letterman*.

**SHAW, ARTIE** (born Arthur Arshawsky), May 23, 1910 (New York, N.Y.). U.S. musician. Bandleader and clarinetist; formed one of most popular Big Bands, 1936; known for swing and Latin music. "Begin the Beguine" (1940) most popular song. (One-time husband of L. TURNER, A. GARDNER.)

**SHEARING, GEORGE**, Aug. 13, 1919 (London, Eng.). British musician. Blind since birth, a major force in jazz piano since 1950s; became popular in U.S. as pianist at Birdland in New York City.

**SILVER, HORACE**, Sept. 2, 1928 (Norwalk, Conn.). U.S. jazz musician, pianist, composer. Leader of the Horace Silver Quintet, 1955– . Compositions: "Senor Blues," 1956; "Sister Sadie," 1959; "Blowin' the Blues Away," 1959; "Que Pasa?," 1965.

**SINGLETON, ZUTTY** (born Arthur James Singleton), May 14, 1898 (Bunkier, La.)–July 14, 1975. U.S. musician. Pioneer in New Orleans-style jazz drumming; played with most great bands of 1920s–1960s; most famous as member of LOUIS ARMSTRONG's Hot Five.

**SMITH, JOE**, June 1902 (Ohio)–Dec. 2, 1937. U.S. musician. Jazz trumpeter in FLETCHER HENDERSON's Black Swan Jazz Masters group; played for ETHEL WATERS, BESSIE SMITH, many others in 1920s and 1930s.

**SMITH, PINETOP** (born Clarence Smith), June 11, 1904 (Troy, Ala.)–Mar. 14, 1929. U.S. musician. Pioneered the boogie-woogie style of piano playing, developing "8-to-a-bar"; on the MA RAINEY vaudeville circuit; killed in a brawl.

**SMITH, WILLIE** ("The Lion") (born William Henry Joseph Berthel Bonaparte Bertholoff), Nov. 25, 1897 (Goshen, N.Y.)–Apr. 18, 1973. U.S. musician. Major influence in 1920s as ragtime-stride pianist; branched out into jazz, making many recordings.

**SPANIER, MUGGSY** (born Francis Joseph Spanier), Nov. 9, 1906 (Chicago, Ill.)–Feb. 12, 1967. U.S. musician. Cornetist who was central figure in Dixieland jazz scene; with Ted Lewis band, 1929–36; led own band, 1941–43; best known for use of plunger mute.

**STILLS, STEPHEN**, Jan. 3, 1945 (Dallas, Tex.). U.S. musician. Major influence in pop-rock; co-founder of Buffalo Springfield rock group, 1966–7; joined with GRAHAM NASH and DAVID CROSBY to form Crosby, Stills & Nash group, 1968–70; solo performer since 1970. Songs: "Change Partners"; "Blue Bird"; "Suite: Judy Blue Eyes"; "Love the One You're With"; "49 Bye-Byes."

**STITT, SONNY** (born Edward Stitt), Feb. 2, 1924 (Boston, Mass.). U.S. musician. Tenor/alto saxophonist noted for bop work in the 1940s and 1950s; disciple of CHARLIE PARKER; associated with DIZZY GILLESPIE groups, 1945–46 and 1958.

**TATUM, ART**, Oct. 13, 1910 (Toledo, Ohio) –Nov. 5, 1956. U.S. musician. Partially sighted pianist known for highly original technique and harmonic variations; led trio, 1943–55.

**TAYLOR, BILLY**, July 24, 1921 (Greenville, N.C.). U.S. musician. Jazz pianist with orchestras, jazz bands; composer of the musical, *Your Arms Too Short to Box with God*, 1977.

**TEAGARDEN, JACK**, Aug. 20, 1905 (Vernon, Tex.)–Jan. 15, 1964. U.S. trombonist, orchestra leader. Played with Pete Kelly, RED NICHOLS, Ben Pollack (1928–33) and PAUL WHITEMAN (1934–38) bands; had his own orchestra, 1939–46; collaborated with GLENN MILLER on the lyrics for "Basin Street Blues."

**VAN HALEN, EDDIE** (Edward), Jan. 26, 1957 (Nijmegan, Neth.). U.S. musician. Regarded as one of the best guitarists in the world today; began as a drummer with a band formed with his bother Alex, DAVID LEE ROTH, and Michael Anthony, then switched to guitar; today plays with his band, Van Halen, but also on the albums of other superstars, most notably MICHAEL JACKSON's *Thriller*.

**WALLER, FATS** (born Thomas Waller), May 21, 1904 (New York, N.Y.)–Dec. 15, 1943. U.S. musician. Leading jazz pianist; got his start (1919) playing in cabarets; accompanied BESSIE SMITH (and others); began recording, 1934; as stride pianist, refined technique; first to use jazz organ; "Ain't Misbehavin'"; "Honeysuckle Rose"; "Keepin' Out of Mischief Now"; "Squeeze Me."

**WARING, FRED**, June 9, 1900 (Tyrone, Pa.)– July 29, 1984. U.S. orchestra leader, inventor. His band

and choral ensemble, The Pennsylvanians, has sung on numerous tours and radio and TV shows; invented the Waring Blender, 1937.

**WEATHERFORD, TEDDY,** Oct. 11, 1903 (Bluefield, W. Va.)–Apr. 25, 1945. U.S. musician. Pianist and leading exponent of "Chicago-style" jazz in 1920s; went to the Far East (1926), becoming a fixture at the Grand Hotel in Calcutta, India, where he played until his death.

**WEBB, CHICK** (born William Webb), Feb. 10, 1909 (Baltimore, Md.)–June 16, 1939. U.S. musician. Drummer and leader of Harlem Stompers band featured at the Savoy Ballroom in Harlem, 1927–39; introduced ELLA FITZGERALD as vocalist, 1935.

**WELK, LAWRENCE,** Mar. 11, 1903 (Strasburg, N.D.). U.S. musician. An accordionist, he started own band in 1927; his TV show, featuring wholesome soloists, was a big hit on network TV (1955–71) and is still thriving in syndication.

**WHITEMAN, PAUL** ("The King of Jazz"), Mar. 28, 1891 (Denver, Col.)–Dec. 29, 1967. U.S. musician. Jovial, rotund bandleader noted for giving many famous performers their starts; introduced Ferde Grofe's *Grand Canyon Suite* and GEORGE GERSHWIN's *Rhapsody in Blue* in concert.

**WILLIAMS, CHARLES** ("Cootie"), July 24, 1908. U.S. musician. Jazz trumpeter who played with Eagle Eye Shields band (1925–26), DUKE ELLINGTON (1929–40), BENNY GOODMAN, many others.

**WINWOOD, STEVE,** May 12, 1948 (Birmingham, Eng.). British musician. After stints with the Spencer Davis group, Blind Faith, and Traffic retired briefly and returned in early 1980s; hits include "High Life," "The Finer Things," and "Higher Love."

**YANKOVIC, "Weird" AL,** Oct. 10, 1959. U.S. musician, satirist. Well known for his musical parodies, which include "Eat It" (a take-off on MICHAEL JACKSON'S "Beat It") and "Like a Surgeon" (a take-off on MADONNA's "Like a Virgin").

**YARBOROUGH, GLENN,** Jan. 12, 1930 (Milwaukee, Wis.). U.S. musician. Began as folksinger/guitarist in Limeliters group, 1959–63; now a solo performer in country-and-western field; formed Stanyan Music Co. with ROD MCKUEN, 1968.

**YOUNG, LESTER** ("Prez"), Aug. 27, 1909 (Woodville, Miss.)–Mar. 15, 1959. U.S. musician. Jazz saxophonist with the COUNT BASIE, KING OLIVER and Andy Kirk bands; had his own sextette, from 1942; composed several songs, including "Tickle Toe."

## OTHER ENTERTAINERS

**ACUFF, ROY,** Sept. 15, 1903 (Maynardsville, Tenn.). U.S. country-and-western entertainer, record company exec.

**ARLEN, HAROLD** (born Hyman Arluck), Feb. 15, 1905 (Buffalo, N.Y.)–Apr. 23, 1986. U.S. composer. Composed Broadway scores, film musicals (notably, *The Wizard of Oz*, 1939) and many pop standards. Songs: "Get Happy"; "I Love a Parade"; "Stormy Weather"; "Blues in the Night"; "That Old Black Magic"; "It's Only a Paper Moon"; "One for My Baby"; "The Man That Got Away."

**BACHARACH, BURT,** May 12, 1929 (Kansas City, Mo.). U.S. composer, pianist. Wrote many popular songs, composed score for Broadway musical *Promises, Promises* (1969). Songs: "What the World Needs Now"; "I'll Never Fall in Love Again"; "The Look of Love"; "Raindrops Keep Falling on My Head" (AA, 1970); "Close to You"; "One Less Bell to Answer"; "Walk on By"; "Alfie." (One-time husband of A. DICKINSON.)

**BALL, ERNEST,** July 22, 1878 (Cleveland, Ohio) –May 3, 1927. U.S. composer. Wrote many popular turn-of-the-century sentimental songs, including "Mother Machree," "A Little Bit of Heaven," "Let the Rest of the World Go By," and "When Irish Eyes Are Smiling."

**BARNUM, P(hineas) T(aylor),** July 5, 1810 (Bethel, Conn.)–Apr. 7, 1891. U.S. showman. Entrepreneur extraordinaire in entertainment; operated New York City museum (1841–68) featuring freaks, wonders and dwarf Tom Thumb, who attracted millions of visitors; brought JENNY LIND, the "Swedish Nightingale," to U.S. for concert tour; formed Barnum

and Bailey Circus, 1881; reputedly said, "There's a sucker born every minute."

**BERNSTEIN, ELMER,** Apr. 4, 1922 (New York, N.Y.). U.S. composer. Has written scores for numerous films.

**BLANC, MEL,** May 30, 1908 (San Francisco, Calif.) –July 10, 1989. U.S. entertainer. Voice of many cartoon characters, including Bugs Bunny, Porky Pig, Daffy Duck.

**BOCK, JERRY,** Nov. 23, 1928 (New Haven, Conn.). U.S. composer. Composed many Broadway show scores. Plays scored: *Mr. Wonderful,* 1956; *Fiorello!* (Tony), 1959; *She Loves Me,* 1963; *Fiddler on the Roof,* 1964; *The Apple Tree,* 1966; *The Rothschilds,* 1972.

**BOWES, MAJOR EDWARD,** 1874 (San Francisco, Calif.)–June 13, 1946. U.S. radio personality. Originated the *Major Bowes Amateur Hour* (1934), which became (on his death) *Ted Mack's Original Amateur Hour.*

**BREL, JACQUES,** Apr. 8, 1929 (Brussels, Belg.)– Oct. 9, 1978. Belgian composer, singer. Best known in U.S. for musical based on his lyrics, *Jacques Brel Is Alive and Well and Living in Paris,* 1968.

**BURKE, JOHNNY,** Oct. 3, 1908 (Antioch, Calif.)– Feb. 25, 1964. U.S. songwriter. Wrote popular songs such as "Pennies from Heaven," "Moonlight Becomes You," and "Swinging on a Star" (AA, 1944).

**CARMICHAEL, HOAGY** (born Hoagland Carmichael), Nov. 22, 1899 (Bloomington, Ind.)–Dec. 27, 1981. U.S. composer, pianist, singer, actor. Wrote many hits and appeared as actor in some films; regular on the TV series *Laramie,* 1959–63.

Songs: "Georgia on My Mind"; "Rockin' Chair"; "Nearness of You"; "Stardust"; "Two Sleepy People"; "The Nearness of You"; "In the Cool, Cool, Cool of the Evening" (AA, 1951).

**CARTE, (Richard) D'OYLY,** May 3, 1844 (London, Eng.)–Apr. 3, 1901. English impresario. Formed Comedy Opera Company Ltd., which introduced the works of Lecocq and OFFENBACH to England, 1876; founded the Savoy Theatre, home of GILBERT and SULLIVAN productions and London's first theater to use electric lighting, 1881.

**CAVETT, DICK,** Nov. 19, 1936 (Gibbon, Neb.). U.S. entertainer. Comedy writer and performer, later talk-show host.

**COHAN, GEORGE M(ichael),** July 3, 1878 (Providence, R.I.)–Nov. 5, 1942. U.S. entertainer. Best known personality of his day, a versatile actor, singer, dancer, songwriter, and producer; starred in numerous musicals. Songs: "I'm a Yankee Doodle Dandy"; "Give My Regards to Broadway"; "You're a Grand Old Flag"; "Mary's a Grand Old Name"; "Over There."

**COMDEN, BETTY,** May 3, 1919 (New York, N.Y.). U.S. lyricist, singer. Began as performer in Greenwich Village nightclubs; wrote book and lyrics for many Broadway hits, with partner ADOLPH GREEN. Plays: *On the Town*, 1944; *Wonderful Town*, 1953; *Bells Are Ringing*, 1956; *Subways Are For Sleeping*, 1961.

**CROSS, MILTON,** Apr. 16, 1897 (New York, N.Y.)–Jan. 3, 1975. U.S. radio announcer. Best known for his Saturday afternoon broadcasts from the Metropolitan Opera, 1931–74.

**CULLEN, BILL,** Feb. 18, 1920 (Pittsburgh, Pa.)–July 7, 1990. U.S. game show personality. Host and guest on many TV game shows; best known as panelist on *To Tell the Truth* and as a host of *The Price is Right* and *$25,000 Pyramid.*

**DALY, JOHN CHARLES, JR.,** Feb. 20, 1914 (Johannesburg, S.A.). U.S. broadcaster. A radio and TV news correspondent best known as moderator of TV's long-running *What's My Line?*.

**DESYLVA, B(uddy) G(eorge Gard),** Jan. 27, 1895 (New York, N.Y.)–July 11, 1950. U.S. composer, librettist. Wrote, often in partnership with Lew Brown and Ray Henderson, several scores for Broadway and films. Songs: "April Showers"; "California Here I Come"; "If You Knew Susie."

**DIETZ, HOWARD,** Sept. 8, 1896 (New York, N.Y.)–July 30, 1983. U.S. lyricist. In collaboration with ARTHUR SCHWARTZ, wrote scores for Broadway shows and songs. Songs: "I Love Louisa"; "Dancing in the Dark"; "You and the Night and the Music"; "By Myself"; "That's Entertainment."

**DISNEY, WALT(er),** Dec. 5, 1901 (Chicago, Ill.)–Dec. 15, 1966. U.S. film producer. Leader in movie animation; introduced Mickey Mouse in his first cartoon, *Steamboat Willie* (1928); produced first feature-length cartoon, *Snow White and the Seven Dwarfs*, 1937; produced first live-action animated film, *The Reluctant Dragon*, 1941; built Disneyland, 1955; awarded a record 29 Acad. Awards. Movies: *Pinocchio*, 1940; *Fantasia*, 1940;

*Bambi*, 1942; *Lady and the Tramp*, 1956; *The Shaggy Dog*, 1959; *Pollyanna*, 1960; *Mary Poppins*, 1964.

**DONALDSON, WALTER,** Feb. 15, 1893 (Brooklyn, N.Y.)–July 13, 1947. U.S. composer. Wrote music for many Broadway shows and composed songs. Songs: "The Daughter of Rosie O'Grady"; "How Ya Gonna Keep 'em Down on the Farm?"; "Carolina in the Morning"; "Yes Sir, That's My Baby"; "My Blue Heaven"; "Little White Lies."

**DOWNS, HUGH** Feb. 14, 1921 (Akron, Ohio). U.S. TV personality. Announcer of TV's *Jack Paar Show* (later, *Tonight Show*), 1957–62; host of TV's *Today Show*, 1962–72; host of TV game show *Concentration*, 1958–68; host of *Over Easy*, PBS series on aging (1978); co-host *20/20* TV program.

**EDWARDS, CLIFF** ("Ukelele Ike"), 1897 (Hannibal, Mo.)–July 17, 1971. U.S. entertainer. Performed in vaudeville and appeared in some films; was voice of Jiminy Cricket in Disney movie *Pinocchio* (1940) and in subsequent features and shorts.

**EDWARDS, GUS,** Aug. 18, 1879 (Hohensaliza, Ger.)–Nov. 7, 1945. U.S. composer, producer. Vaudeville and stage-show producer who discovered EDDIE CANTOR, GEORGE JESSEL, ELEANOR POWELL, RAY BOLGER, among others; wrote the songs "School Days" and "By the Light of the Silvery Moon."

**EMMETT, DANIEL DECATUR,** Oct. 29, 1815 (Mt. Vernon, Ohio)–June 28, 1904. U.S. minstrel, songwriter. Organized the first "Negro Minstrel show," 1843; composed "Dixie."

**EPSTEIN, BRIAN,** Sept. 19, 1934 (Liverpool, Eng.)–Aug. 27, 1967. English music-group mgr. Managed the Beatles from humble beginnings in 1961 to rock superstardom by the time he died of an overdose of sleeping pills.

**FAIN, SAMMY,** June 17, 1902 (New York, N.Y.)–Dec. 6, 1989. U.S. composer. Wrote Broadway musicals, numerous film scores. Songs: "Secret Love" (AA, 1953); "Love Is a Many-Splendored Thing" (AA, 1955; "Let a Smile Be Your Umbrella"; "When I Take My Sugar to Tea"; "That Old Feeling"; "April Love."

**FIELDS, DOROTHY,** July 15, 1905 (New York, N.Y.)–Mar. 28, 1974. U.S. lyricist. Wrote many Broadway musicals and other songs. Musicals: *Up in Central Park*, 1945; *Annie Get Your Gun*, 1946. Songs: "I Won't Dance"; "Lovely to Look At"; "I Can't Give You Anything But Love"; "The Way You Look Tonight" (AA), 1936.

**FOY, EDDIE** (born Edward Fitzgerald), Mar. 9, 1857 (New York, N.Y.)–Feb. 16, 1928. U.S. entertainer. Appeared in song-and-dance act in vaudeville with "The Seven Little Foys," his children; impersonated in films by his son Eddie, Jr., and BOB HOPE.

**FREED, ALAN,** Dec. 15, 1922 (Johnstown, Pa.)–Jan. 20, 1965. U.S. entertainer. Radio disc jockey of 1940s and 1950s who coined the phrase *rock-and-roll* and was responsible for introducing performers of rhythm-and-blues to general audiences, on long-running WINS (New York City) radio show, 1954–60; emcee of many rock-and-roll concerts nationwide.

**FRIML, (Charles) RUDOLF,** Dec. 7, 1879 (Prague, Czech.)–Nov. 12, 1972. U.S.-Czech. composer. Composed several popular operettas. *The Firefly,* 1912; *Rose Marie,* 1924; *The Vagabond King,* 1925.

**FROST, DAVID,** Apr. 7, 1939 (Tenterden, Eng.). English TV personality. First came to notice in U.S. on satirical prime-time show *That Was the Week That Was* in the 1960s, made news with series of interviews with former Pres. R. M. NIXON, 1977.

**FUNT, ALLEN,** Sept. 16, 1914 (New York, N.Y.). U.S. TV personality. Creator and host of TV's *Candid Camera* program, from early 1950s.

**GARROWAY, DAVE,** July 13, 1913 (Schenectady, N.Y.). U.S. TV personality. Popular in 1950s; host of *Garroway at Large,* 1949–54; frequently appeared on the *Today Show* in the company of a chimpanzee named J. Fred Muggs.

**GERSHWIN, IRA,** Dec. 6, 1896 (New York, N.Y.)–Aug. 17, 1983. U.S. lyricist. Collaborator with brother GEORGE GERSHWIN on Broadway scores; after brother's death, worked with many of the 20th cent.'s most famous composers of theatrical and film music. Musicals: *Lady Be Good,* 1924; *Strike Up the Band,* 1929; *Girl Crazy,* 1930; *Of Thee I Sing* (Pulitzer), 1932; *Porgy and Bess,* 1935.

**GODFREY, ARTHUR,** Aug. 31, 1903 (New York, N.Y.)–Mar. 16, 1983. U.S. broadcaster. Began as newsman; quickly established himself on radio (later on TV) with folksy variety program that was one of the staples of the 1940s and 1950s. Appeared in some films.

**GORDY, BERRY,** Nov. 28, 1929 (Detroit, Mich.). U.S. recording-co. exec. Founder and pres. of Motown records (1959– ), the nation's first successful record co. to feature rhythm-and-blues and soul music; responsible for making famous SMOKEY ROBINSON, THE SUPREMES, THE TEMPTATIONS, MARVIN GAYE, STEVIE WONDER, among others; the music he produced called "Motown Sound."

**GRAHAM, BILL** (born Wolfgang Grajonca), Jan. 8, 1931 (Berlin, Ger.). U.S. entrepreneur. His Fillmore concert halls in San Francisco (opened 1965) and New York City (opened 1968) vaulted rock groups such as Jefferson Airplane, Quicksilver Messenger Service and the Grateful Dead to national prominence.

**GRAZIANO, ROCKY,** June 7, 1922 (New York, N.Y.)–May 22, 1990. U.S. boxer, TV personality. World middle-weight boxing champ, 1947–48; numerous appearances on TV as both guest and pitchman for various products.

**GREEN, ADOLPH,** Dec. 2, 1915 (New York, N.Y.). U.S. actor, playwright, lyricist. Has collaborated on numerous Broadway hit shows with BETTY COMDEN, including *On the Town* (1944), *Wonderful Town* (1953), and *Subways Are For Sleeping* (1962). Awarded Tonys for cowriting music and lyrics for *Hallelujah Baby!* (1967) and

cowriting score for *Applause* (1967). (Husband of P. NEWMAN.)

**GRIFFIN, MERV,** July 6, 1925 (San Mateo, Calif.). U.S. entertainer, talk-show host. Radio show host in San Francisco, Calif., 1945–48; host of TV's *The Merv Griffin Show,* 1962–63, 1965–69, and 1969–72; host of syndicated talk show 1972–87.

**HALL, MONTY,** Aug. 25, 1923 (Winnipeg, Man., Can.). U.S. TV personality. Creator, producer, and host of popular TV game show *Let's Make a Deal,* 1964–86.

**HAMMERSTEIN, OSCAR II,** July 12, 1895 (New York, N.Y.)–Aug. 23, 1960. U.S. lyricist. Chiefly known for collaboration with RICHARD RODGERS on Broadway musicals, although he also worked with RUDOLF FRIML, JEROME KERN and SIGMUND ROMBERG. Musicals: *Rose Marie,* 1924; *Showboat,* 1927; *New Moon,* 1928; *Oklahoma* (Pulitzer), 1943; *Carousel,* 1945; *South Pacific* (Pulitzer), 1949; *The King and I,* 1951; *Flower Drum Song,* 1958; *The Sound of Music,* 1959.

**HARBURG, E(dgar) Y.** ("Yip"), Apr. 8, 1896 (New York, N.Y.)–Mar. 5, 1981. U.S. lyricist, librettist. Wrote lyrics for Broadway musicals and films. Plays: *Ziegfeld Follies,* 1934; *Finian's Rainbow.* Films: *Wizard of Oz,* 1938 (AA for "Over the Rainbow"). Songs: "Brother Can You Spare a Dime?"; "April in Paris"; "Over the Rainbow."

**HART, LORENZ,** May 2, 1895 (New York, N.Y.)–Nov. 22, 1943. U.S. lyricist. Noted for witty, literate, expressive lyrics and his long, successful collaboration with RICHARD RODGERS on musical scores for plays such as *Connecticut Yankee* (1927), *The Boys from Syracuse* (1938), *Pal Joey* (1940), and *By Jupiter* (1942). Songs: "Manhattan," "Blue Moon," "The Lady Is a Tramp," "My Funny Valentine," "Falling in Love with Love," "I Didn't Know What Time It Was."

**HART, MARY,** 1951 (Sioux Falls, S.D.). TV cohost. TV: *Entertainment Tonight* (series), 1982–.

**HARTMAN, DAVID,** May 19, 1935 (Pawtucket, R.I.). U.S. actor, TV host. Acted on several TV series (*The Virginian* [1968–69], *The Bold Ones* [1969–73] and *Lucas Tanner* [1974–75]) before becoming host of ABC's "Good Morning America" show, 1975–86.

**HENSON, JIM,** Sept. 24, 1936 (Greenville, Miss.)–May 16, 1990. U.S. puppeteer, TV producer. Creator of the Muppets, 1954; creator of *Sesame Street* muppets, 1969– ; *Muppet Show,* 1976–81; *Muppet Movie,* 1979; *The Muppets Take Manhattan,* 1984; awarded Emmys for Outstanding Individual Achievement in Children's Programming, 1973–74 and 1975–76.

**HERMAN, JERRY,** July 10, 1932 (New York, N.Y.). U.S. composer, lyricist. Wrote Broadway musicals. Shows: *Milk and Honey,* 1961; *Hello Dolly,* 1964 (Tony award); *Mame,* 1966; *La Cage aux Folles,* 1983 (Tony award).

**HOUDINI, HARRY** (born Ehrich Weiss), Mar. 24, 1874 (Budapest, Hungary)–Oct. 31, 1926. U.S. magician. A superstar of magic and an escape artist, many of whose tricks have not been unraveled to date; noted for escapes from shackles, ropes, handcuffs, and locked containers; campaigned against fake mediums; in some silent films.

**HUTTON, LAUREN,** Nov. 17, 1943 (Charleston, S.C.). U.S. model. Leading cover girl and high-fashion model of the 1970s, noted for her clean, fresh look; closely associated with Revlon, Inc.

**JESSEL, GEORGE,** Apr. 3, 1898 (New York, N.Y.)–May 24, 1981. U.S. entertainer. In vaudeville from childhood; appeared on Broadway first in 1918; called "Toastmaster General of the U.S." for his frequent emcee role at charity affairs.

**JOHNSON, HOWARD E.,** 1888? (Waterbury, Conn.)–May 1, 1941. U.S. songwriter. Wrote lyrics for "When the Moon Comes over the Mountain"; wrote music and lyrics for "M-O-T-H-E-R ("put 'em all together...")," and "There's a Broken Heart for Every Light on Broadway."

**KEESHAN, BOB,** June 27, 1927 (Lynbrook, N.Y.). U.S. TV personality. Appeared as Clarabelle the Clown on TV's *Howdy Doody Show,* 1947–52; best known as creator/producer/star of long-running *Captain Kangaroo* children's show 1955–85.

**KERN, JEROME,** Jan. 27, 1885 (New York, N.Y.)–Nov. 11, 1945. U.S. composer. Composer of over 50 Broadway shows and numerous songs. Shows: *Leave It to Jane,* 1917; *Sally,* 1920; *Showboat,* 1927; *Roberta,* 1933. Songs: "They Didn't Believe Me"; "Look for the Silver Lining"; "Smoke Gets in Your Eyes"; "Ole Man River"; "All the Things Your Are"; "The Last Time I Saw Paris"; "A Fine Romance"; "The Way You Look Tonight."

**KING, LARRY,** Nov. 19, 1933 (Brooklyn, N.Y.). U.S. talk show host. *The Larry King Show* (radio), 1978–  ; *Larry King Live* (CNN), 1985–  .

**LAUDER, HARRY,** Aug. 4, 1870 (Edinburgh, Scot.)–Feb. 26, 1950. Scottish entertainer. A beloved star of British music hall and American vaudeville, known for his recitations while dressed in traditional kilt; appeared in a few films.

**LEE, GYPSY ROSE** (born Rose Louise Hovick), Jan. 9, 1914 (Seattle, Wash.)–Apr. 26, 1970. U.S. entertainer. Queen of U.S. burlesque in the 1930s, famed for her "intellectual" striptease act; musical play and film *Gypsy* based on her life.

**LEGRAND, MICHEL,** Feb. 24, 1932 (Paris, Fr.). French composer, conductor. Writer, arranger, conductor for over 50 film scores.

**LERNER, ALAN JAY,** Aug. 31, 1918 (New York, N.Y.)–June 14, 1986. U.S. playwright, lyricist. Noted for his collaborations with F. LOEWE on Broadway musical comedies. Plays: *Brigadoon,* 1947; *Paint Your Wagon,* 1951; *My Fair Lady* (Tony), 1956; *Camelot,* 1960; *On a Clear Day You Can See Forever,* 1965. Screenplays: *An American in Paris* (AA), 1951; *Gigi* (AA), 1958.

**LEWIS, SHARI** (born Shari Hurwitz), Jan. 17, 1934 (New York, N.Y.). U.S. ventriloquist and puppeteer. She and her famous "Lambchop" entertained children on TV since 1950s; won five Emmys; Peabody Award, 1960.

**LIBERACE,** (Wladziu Valentino), May 16, 1919 (W. Allis, Wisc.)–Feb. 4, 1987. U.S. entertainer. Flamboyant pianist known for glitzy jewelry, sequined costumes, and elaborate candelabra; supreme showman who was a star in concerts and nightclubs for over 25 years.

**LINKLETTER, ART,** July 17, 1912 (Moose Jaw, Can.). Can.-U.S. broadcaster. Popular on radio and TV with several shows (*House Party, People Are Funny,* etc.) in 1950s and 1960s; author of several books, including *Kids Say the Darndest Things.*

**LOESSER, FRANK,** June 29, 1910 (New York, N.Y.)–July 28, 1969. U.S. composer. Composer of Broadway shows and many songs. Musicals scored: *Where's Charley?,* 1948; *Guys and Dolls* (Tony), 1951; *The Most Happy Fella,* 1956; *How to Succeed...* (Pulitzer), 1962. Songs: "Two Sleepy People"; "Thanks for the Memory"; "Baby, It's Cold Outside"; "I Believe in You."

**LOEWE, FREDERICK,** June 10, 1901 (Berlin, Ger.)–Feb. 14, 1988. U.S. composer. Noted for collaboration with A. J. LERNER on Broadway musical comedies. Musicals scored: *Brigadoon,* 1947; *Paint Your Wagon,* 1951; *My Fair Lady* (Tony), 1956; *Camelot,* 1960.

**MANCINI, HENRY,** April 16, 1924 (Cleveland, Ohio). U.S. composer. Pianist/composer of many songs and film scores; frequently collaborated with JOHNNY MERCER. Film scores: *The Glenn Miller Story,* 1953; *Breakfast at Tiffany's,* 1961; *The Pink Panther,* 1963. Songs: "Moon River"; "The Days of Wine and Roses"; "Charade"; "Dear Heart."

**MCBRIDE, MARY MARGARET,** Nov. 16, 1899 (Paris, Mo.)–Apr. 7, 1976. U.S. radio commentator. Conducted a long series of daytime talk shows, featuring her homespun advice and interviews with most of the famous people of her day, 1934–54.

**MCHUGH, JIMMY,** July 10, 1894 (Boston, Mass.)–May 23, 1969. U.S. composer. Wrote scores for musical films and shows, as well as over 500 pop songs. Songs: "I Can't Give You Anything but Love, Baby"; "I Feel a Song Comin' On"; "On The Sunny Side of the Street"; "Lovely to Look At."

**MCMAHON, ED,** Mar. 6, 1923 (Detroit, Mich.). U.S. TV announcer. Best known as the announcer for JOHNNY CARSON, first on the game show *Who Do You Trust?* (from 1958) and then on the *Tonight Show* (1962–  ); co-host *TV's Bloopers and Practical Jokes,* 1984–  .

**MERCER, JOHNNY,** Nov. 18, 1909 (Savannah, Ga.)–June 25, 1976. U.S. lyricist. Wrote many popular songs; an organizer of Capitol Records, 1942. Songs: "Goody-Goody"; "I'm an Old Cowhand"; "Hooray for Hollywood"; "Jeepers Creepers;" "Blues in the Night"; "On the Atchison, Topeka & Santa Fe"; "In the Cool, Cool, Cool of the Evening"; "Moon River"; "Days of Wine and Roses."

**MIELZINER, JO,** Mar. 19, 1901 (Paris, Fr.)–Mar. 15, 1976. U.S. stage designer. Has designed sets for more than 350 stage productions, including *Hamlet, Carousel, Annie Get Your Gun, A Streetcar Named Desire,* and *Death of a Salesman;* introduced the transparent skeletal framework setting to allow separate times and places to be shown simultaneously; with EERO SAARINEN, designed the Vivian Beaumont Theater, New York City.

MILLER, MITCH, July 4, 1911 (Rochester, N.Y.). U.S. music producer. Largely shaped taste in popular music in 1950s; created weekly television program *Sing Along with Mitch* (1961–66), a singalong with superimposed lyrics for the singers at home; discoveries included LESLIE UGGAMS and Diana Trask.

MOORE, GARRY (born Thomas Garrison Morfit), Jan. 31, 1915 (Baltimore, Md.). U.S. TV personality. His show was one of the most popular variety shows in history of the medium, 1950–64; emcee of *I've Got a Secret* (1953–64) and *To Tell the Truth* (1969–77).

MORGAN, HENRY, Mar. 31, 1915 (New York, N.Y.). U.S. entertainer. Known for regular TV appearances on quiz and panel shows, especially *I've Got a Secret,* 1952–76.

MUSBURGER, BRENT, May 26, 1939 (Portland, Ore.). U.S. sportscaster. Started career as an umpire; with CBS Sports, 1974–90; sportscaster of the year, 1971, 1974.

NERO, PETER, May 22, 1934 (New York, N.Y.). U.S. pianist. Pop pianist with wide experience in clubs and on concert stage; many records; began professional career on tour with PAUL WHITEMAN, 1953–57.

OAKLEY, ANNIE (born Phoebe Anne Oakley Mozee), Aug. 13, 1860 (Patterson Twp., Ohio) –Nov. 3, 1926. U.S. entertainer. A markswoman with firearms, she joined BUFFALO BILL's Wild West Show in 1885 and was its star attraction for 17 years.

PAAR, JACK, May 1, 1918 (Canton, Ohio). U.S. TV personality. Former radio announcer; one of the pioneers of the TV talk show as host of the nightly *Tonight Show* (1957–62) and subsequent *Jack Paar Show* (1962–65, 1973).

PARKS, BERT, Dec. 30, 1914 (Atlanta, Ga.). U.S. TV personality. Ubiquitous emcee, best known for his annual hosting of the Miss America Pageant, 1954–79.

PORTER, COLE, June 9, 1893 (Peru, Ind.)–Oct. 15, 1964. U.S. composer, lyricist. Lyricist and composer known for the sophistication of his work. Crippled after a riding accident, 1937. Shows: *50 Million Frenchmen,* 1929; *The Gay Divorce,* 1932; *Anything Goes,* 1934; *DuBarry Was a Lady,* 1939; *Panama Hattie,* 1940; *Kiss Me Kate,* 1948; *Can-Can,* 1953; *Silk Stockings,* 1955. Songs: "Let's Do It"; "Anything Goes"; "You're the Top"; "I Love Paris"; "I Get a Kick Out of You"; "Begin the Beguine"; "I've Got You under My Skin"; "Night and Day."

RINGLING, JOHN N., 1866 (Baraboo, Wisc.)– Dec. 3, 1936. U.S. circus owner. With his brother Charles, founded and operated the Ringling Bros. circus, 1884–1907; merged with Barnum & Bailey to form the "Greatest Show on Earth," 1907.

RODGERS, WILL(iam Penn Adair), Nov. 4, 1879 (Oologah, Indian Terr. [now Okla.])–Aug. 15, 1935. U.S. humorist. Homespun philosopher/humorist of the 1920s and 1930s; a "comedy roper" in Ziegfeld Follies, from 1914; wrote syndicated column, 1926–35; appeared in films, killed with WILEY POST in Alaska plane crash at height of his popularity.

ROME, HAROLD, May 27, 1908 (Hartford, Conn.). U.S. composer. Noted composer and lyricist of the musical theater. Plays scored: *Pins and Needles,* 1937; *Wish You Were Here,* 1952; *Fanny,* 1954; *I Can Get It for You Wholesale,* 1962.

RUBY, HARRY (born Harry Rubinstein), Jan. 27, 1895 (New York, N.Y.)–Feb. 23, 1974. U.S. songwriter. Wrote music and lyrics for Broadway shows and films, many of them associated with the Marx Brothers. Songs: "Who's Sorry Now"; "Three Little Words."

SAJAK, PAT, Oct. 16, 1947 (Chicago, Ill.). U.S. game show host. Host, *The Wheel of Fortune* (1981– ) and *The Pat Sajak Show* (1989–90).

SCHWARTZ, ARTHUR, Nov. 25, 1900 (New York, N.Y.)–Sept. 3, 1984. U.S. composer. Wrote for Broadway, most notably in collaboration with HOWARD DIETZ. Shows scored: *The Band Wagon,* 1931; *Stars in Yours Eyes,* 1939. Songs: "Dancing in the Dark"; "You and the Night and the Music"; "Something to Remember You By."

SMITH, BOB ("Buffalo Bob"), Nov. 27, 1917 (Buffalo, N.Y.). U.S. entertainer. Best known for creating and starring in children's TV series, *The Howdy Doody Show,* in the 1950s.

SONDHEIM, STEPHEN, Mar. 22, 1930 (New York, N.Y.). U.S. composer, lyricist. Leading figure in Broadway musical theater; known for innovative shows on unconventional subjects. Lyrics for shows: *West Side Story,* 1957; *Gypsy,* 1959. Music and lyrics for shows: *A Funny Thing Happened on the Way to the Forum,* 1962; *Anyone Can Whistle,* 1964; *Company,* 1970; *Follies,* 1971; *A Little Night Music,* 1973; *Pacific Overtures,* 1976; *Sweeney Todd,* 1979.

SPECTOR, PHIL, Dec. 26, 1940 (Bronx, N.Y.). U.S. recording exec. Began as songwriter, 1957; formed own record company (Philles Records) in 1962 and served as consultant for a number of 1960s rock stars and their groups, including THE BEATLES, the Righteous Brothers, the Crystals, the Ronettes, etc.

SPIVAK, LAWRENCE, June 11, 1900 (New York, N.Y.). U.S. TV moderator. Cofounder and moderator of long-running news show *Meet the Press.*

STEINER, MAX, May 10, 1888 (Vienna, Austria) –Dec. 28, 1971. U.S.-Austrian composer. One of Hollywood's most important composers. Film scores: *King Kong,* 1933; *Gone With the Wind,* 1939; *The Letter,* 1940; *The Great Lie,* 1941; *Now, Voyager,* 1942; *Casablanca,* 1942; *The Treasure of the Sierra Madre,* 1947; *The Caine Mutiny,* 1954.

STROUSE, CHARLES, June 7, 1928 (New York, N.Y.). U.S. composer. Wrote several popular musical comedies, winning Tony awards for *Bye Bye Birdie* (1959), *Applause* (1970), and *Annie* (1977).

STYNE, JULE, Dec. 31, 1905 (London, Eng.). U.S. composer, producer. An important composer of the

American musical theater. A frequent collaborator with BETTY COMDEN and ADOLPH GREEN. Shows scored: *High Button Shoes*, 1947; *Gentlemen Prefer Blondes*, 1949; *Gypsy*, 1959; *Funny Girl*, 1964; *Hallelujah Baby*, 1967; *Sugar*, 1972.

SULLIVAN, ED, Sept. 28, 1902 (New York, N.Y.)– Oct. 13, 1974. U.S. TV personality, newspaper columnist. Stone-faced emcee of the popular CBS-TV program *The Ed Sullivan Show* (originally *Toast of the Town*), 1948–71; columnist with the *New York Daily News*, 1932–74.

TILLSTROM, BURR, Oct. 13, 1917 (Chicago, Ill). U.S. puppeteer. Creator of Kukla, Ollie, and an assortment of other lovable puppets who have appeared on TV (often with human Fran Allison) since 1947; won Peabody Awards in 1949 and 1964; won Emmy awards in 1953, 1965, and 1971.

VAN HEUSEN, JIMMY (born Edward Chester Babcock), Jan. 26, 1913 (Syracuse, N.Y.)–Feb. 7, 1990. U.S. composer. Author of pop songs and film and stage scores. Scores: "Road" pictures of B. HOPE and B. CROSBY; *Going My Way*, 1944. Songs: "Swinging on a Star"; "High Hopes"; "The Second Time Around"; "Love and Marriage."

VON TILZER, HARRY (born Harry Gumm), July 8, 1872 (Detroit, Mich.)–Jan. 10, 1946. U.S. composer. Music publisher, in partnership with his brothers, 1902–46. Compositions: "A Bird in a Gilded Cage"; "In the Sweet Bye and Bye"; "Wait Till the Sun Shines Nellie"; "I Want a Girl Just Like the Girl Who Married Dear Old Dad"; "When My Baby Smiles at Me."

WILLIAMS, HANK, Sept. 15, 1923 (Georgiana, Ala.)–Jan. 1, 1953. U.S. country-music singer, songwriter. Although he could not read music, com-. posed 125 songs, many of them country-and-western

standards; with the Grand Ole Opry, 1949–53. Songs: "Lovesick Blues"; "I'll Never Get Out of This World Alive"; "Your Cheatin' Heart"; "Wedding Bells"; "Jambalaya"; "Long-gone Lonesome Blues." (Father of H. WILLIAMS JR.)

WILLIAMS, JOHN, Feb. 8, 1932 (New York, N.Y.). U.S. composer, conductor of Boston Pops orchestra 1980– . Films scored: *Valley of the Dolls*, 1967; *The Poseidon Adventure*, 1972; *Jaws*, 1975; *Star Wars*, 1977; *Close Encounters of the Third Kind*, 1977; *Superman*, 1978; *Raiders of the Lost Ark*, 1981; *E.T.*, 1982.

WILLSON, MEREDITH, May 18, 1902 (Mason City, Ia.)–June 15, 1984. U.S. composer, lyricist. Created the musicals *The Music Man* (1957; Tony and Grammy awards), *The Unsinkable Molly Brown* (1960).

WINFREY, OPRAH, Jan. 29, 1954 (Kosciusko, Miss.). U.S. talk show hostess, actress. Became anchor for fading *A.M. Chicago*, 1984; renamed *The Oprah Winfrey Show*, 1985, as it overtook *The Phil Donahue Show* in ratings. Films: *The Color Purple*, 1985.

YELLEN, JACK, July 6, 1892 (Razcki, Pol.). U.S. lyricist, playwright. Lyricist since 1913; wrote lyrics or lyrics and book for several Broadway shows; formed his own music publishing co., 1922. Songs: "Ain't She Sweet?" 1924; "My Yiddishe Mama," 1924; "Happy Days Are Here Again."

YOUMANS, VINCENT, Sept. 27, 1898 (New York, N.Y.)–Apr. 5, 1946. U.S. composer. Collaborated with the greatest names in American musical theater. *Hit the Deck*, 1927; *No, No Nanette*, 1924. Songs: "I Want to Be Happy"; "Tea for Two"; "The Carioca"; "Great Day"; "Without a Song"; "Time on My Hands."

# Other Noted or Notorious Personalities

**ADAMS, ABIGAIL,** Nov. 22, 1744 (Weymouth, Mass.)–Oct. 28, 1818. U.S. First Lady, author of letters. Wife of JOHN ADAMS and mother of JOHN QUINCY ADAMS. *Letters of Mrs. Adams* (2 vols.), 1841; *New Letters of Abigail Adams, 1788–1801,* 1949; *The Adams-Jefferson Letters,* 1959.

**BAILEY, F(rancis) LEE,** June 10, 1933 (Waltham, Mass.). U.S. lawyer. Celebrated criminal lawyer. Won acquittal of Dr. Samuel H. Sheppard at his retrial of conviction in the 1954 murder of his wife; defended Albert DeSalvo, the confessed Boston Strangler; won acquittal of Capt. Ernest L. Medina, accused of killing S. Vietnamese civilians at My Lai; defended PATRICIA HEARST, *The Defense Never Rests* (with Harvey Aronson), 1972; *To Be A Trial Lawyer,* 1983.

**BALENCIAGA, CRISTÓBAL,** Jan. 21, 1895 (Guetaria, Sp.)–Mar. 24, 1972. Spanish fashion designer. First leading couturier in Spain; later designed in Paris; designed elegant gowns, dresses, suits; helped to popularize capes and flowing clothes in 1950s.

**BALMAIN, PIERRE,** May 18, 1914 (Saint-Jean-de-Maurienne, Fr.)–June 29, 1982. French fashion designer. With DIOR and BALENCIAGA, launched the "New Look" of the late 1940s, emphasizing low hemlines, narrow shoulders, and small waists.

**BARBIE, KLAUS,** 1913 (Germany). Nazi war criminal. Known as the "Butcher of Lyons," found guilty of crimes against humanity, 1987.

**BARKER, KATE** ("Ma"), 1872 (nr. Springfield, Mo.)–Jan. 16, 1935. U.S. outlaw. Masterminded robberies, kidnappings, and murders committed by her sons, Lloyd (1896–1949), Arthur (1899–1939), and Fred (1902–1935); the brains of the Barker-Karpis gang, the last of the outlaw bands; accumulated at least $3 million.

**BARNHART, CLARENCE L.,** Dec. 30, 1900 (nr. Plattsburg, Mo.). U.S. lexicographer, editor. Founder and editor of Thorndike-Barnhart dictionaries, 1935– . *U.S. Army Terms,* 1943; *New Century Cyclopedia of Names,* 3 vols., 1954; *New Century Handbook of English Literature,* 1956 and 1967; *The World Book Encyclopedia Dictionary,* 1963.

**BARROW, CLYDE,** Mar. 24, 1909 (Teleco, Tex.)–May 23, 1934. U.S. outlaw. Called "Public Enemy No. 1 of the Southwest"; with companion BONNIE PARKER, accused of 12 murders during a two-year robbery spree in the Southwest; ambushed and shot to death by Texas Rangers and sheriff's deputies.

**BEAN, ROY** ("Judge"), c.1825 (Mason Co., Ky.)–Mar. 16, 1903. U.S. judge, saloonkeeper, teamster, trader. Legendary American frontier judge known as "The Law West of the Pecos"; set up a saloon at a construction camp (now Langtry, Tex.) for the Southern Pacific RR, and became the justice of the peace.

**BEARD, JAMES,** May 5, 1903 (Portland, Ore.)–Jan. 23, 1985. U.S. cookbook author. *James Beard's Treasury of Outdoor Cooking,* 1960; *The James Beard Cookbook,* 1961, *Beard on Bread,* 1973; *The Cook's Catalogue,* 1975; *The New James Beard,* 1981.

**BELLI, MELVIN M.,** July 29, 1907 (Sonora, Calif.). U.S. lawyer. Flamboyant attorney who has defended LENNY BRUCE, Martha Mitchell, and JACK RUBY. *Modern Trials and Modern Damages,* 6 vols., 1954; *Malpractice,* 1955; *The Law Revolt,* 2 vols., 1968; *Melvin Belli: My Life on Trial,* 1976.

**BERKOWITZ, DAVID,** 1953. U.S. serial killer. The notorious "Son of Sam" killer, he is believed to have murdered at least six people and wounded seven others.

**BILLY THE KID** (born William H. Bonney), Nov. 23, 1859 (New York, N.Y.)–July 15, 1881. U.S. outlaw. Gunman in Lincoln Co., Ariz., range war, 1878; rustler, 1878–80; accused of 21 murders; shot by Pat Garrett.

**BLASS, BILL** (born William Blass), June 22, 1922 (Ft. Wayne, Ind.). U.S. fashion designer. Noted for designing feminine clothes for the tailored woman, using clean, classic all-American lines; also designs menswear, furs, luggage, linens, and men's grooming products.

**BLY, NELLIE** (pseud. of Elizabeth Cochrane Seaman), May 5, 1867 (Cochrane's Mills, Pa.)–Jan. 27, 1922. U.S. journalist. As a reporter for the New York *World*, traveled around the world in 72 days, 6 hours, 11 minutes, beating the fictional record set by Phileas Fogg, 1889–90; feigned madness to expose conditions in Blackwell's Is. Asylum.

**BOCUSE, PAUL**, Feb. 11, 1926 (Collonges, Fr.). French chef, restauranteur. Owner of a Michelin "three-star" restaurant in Collonges-au-Mont d'Or, a suburb of Lyon, Fr.; associated with "nouvelle cuisine," which emphasizes freshness and simplicity. *Paul Bocuse's French Cooking*, 1977.

**BOOTH, JOHN WILKES**, May 10, 1838 (nr. Bel Air, Md.)–Apr. 26, 1865. U.S. actor, assassin. Killed Pres. ABRAHAM LINCOLN at the Ford's Theatre in Washington, D.C., on Apr. 14, 1865; shot dead while resisting arrest (Brother of EDWIN BOOTH.)

**BORDEN, LIZZIE**, July 19, 1860 (Fall River, Mass.)–June 1, 1927. U.S. alleged ax murderess. As a 32-year-old spinster, accused of killing her stepmother and father by hacking them with an ax, Aug. 4, 1892; tried and found not guilty, but was popularly believed to be guilty; became the subject of plays, novels, a ballet, an opera, and a musical revue.

**BOYCOTT, CHARLES**, Mar. 12, 1832 (Burgh St. Peter, Norfolk, Eng.)–June 19, 1897. English land-estate manager. A land agent in County Mayo, Ire., became subject (1880) of economic and social isolation when he attempted to collect harsh rents; his name came to be applied to the tactic of isolating one's opponent.

**BRADY, MATHEW B.**, Jan. 15, 1823 (nr. Lake George, N.Y.)–Jan. 15, 1896. U.S. photographer. Photographed every U.S. president from J. Q. ADAMS through WILLIAM MCKINLEY (except W. H. HARRISON); during the Civil War, hired 20 photographers to record the events; himself photographed battlefields at Bull Run, Antietam, and Gettysburg. *Gallery of Illustrious Americans*, 1850.

**BRAILLE, LOUIS**, Jan. 4, 1809 (Coupvray, Fr.)–Jan. 6, 1852. French musician, teacher. Invented the raised-dot system of writing used by the blind, 1829; was blinded himself at age three.

**BRAUN, EVA**, Feb. 6, 1912 (Bavaria)–Apr. 30, 1945. German mistress of ADOLF HITLER. Never seen in public with Hitler, had no political influence on him; married Hitler on the eve of their joint suicide.

**BRINKLEY, JOHN**, July 8, 1885 (Jackson Co., N.C.)–May 26, 1942. U.S. medical quack, radio entrepreneur. Transplanted goat gonads into aging men, from 1917; founded KFKB, the first radio station in Kansas, to push mail-order drugs; revocation (1930) of the KFKB license established the FCC's right to judge program content; established a powerful transmitter (XERA) in Mexico and resumed broadcasting but was silenced by the Mexican government (1937); made millions of dollars.

**BRUCE, AILSA**, June 28, 1901 (Pittsburgh, Pa.)–Aug. 25, 1969. U.S. philanthropist. At the time of her death, considered the richest woman in the U.S.; in 1968 *Fortune* estimated her personal wealth at $500 million; with brother PAUL MELLON, donated $20 million for construction of an annex to the Natl. Gallery of Art, Washington, D.C., 1968; her Avalon Fndn. gave $2.8 million to Lincoln Center for the Performing Arts, 1958. (Daughter of A. W. MELLON; wife of D. K. E. BRUCE).

**BRUMMEL, GEORGE** ("Beau"), June 7, 1778 (London, Eng.)–Mar. 30, 1840. English dandy and wit. An intimate of the Prince of Wales (later George IV); the center of fashionable London society, influenced men toward simplicity and moderation in dress; credited with popularizing trousers to replace breeches.

**BUCHALTER, LOUIS** ("Lepke"), Feb. 1897 (New York, N.Y.)–Mar. 4, 1944. U.S. mobster. Ran Murder, Inc., and New York City garment center rackets, c.1930–1940; executed at Ossining Prison (Sing Sing).

**BULOW, CLAUS VON**, 1926 (Austria). Austrian socialite. Convicted (1982), then acquitted (1985), of the attempted murder of his wife by allegedly administering to her a potentially lethal overdose of insulin.

**BUNDY, TED**, Nov. 24, 1946 (Seattle, Wash.)–Jan. 24, 1989. U.S. mass murderer. Believed to have killed between 18 and 36 women; was the subject of an extensive interstate police and FBI investigation; convicted of two murders which occurred in Florida, and executed.

**BURKE, MARTHA JANE** ("Calamity Jane"), May 1, 1852? (Princeton, Mo.)–Aug. 1, 1903. U.S. frontier adventuress. Noted for dressing, drinking, and cursing like the toughest of men; drifted through construction camps and cow towns from Missouri to Wyoming, working as a dance-hall girl and often involved in prostitution; many legends of her exploits as an Indian fighter and army scout were probably begun in order to promote her as a star in a traveling "dime museum."

**BURNS, WILLIAM J.**, Oct. 19, 1861 (Baltimore, Md.)–Apr. 14, 1932. U.S. detective. Formed his own detective agency in New York City, 1909; established branches all over the U.S.; attracted natl. attention through investigation of sensational murders; dir. of Bureau of Investigation (now FBI), 1921–24.

**BUSH, BARBARA PIERCE**, June 8, 1924 (Rye, N.Y.). U.S. First Lady. Following NANCY REAGAN, has brought a homey touch to the White House, 1989– ; involved in literacy campaign.

**CAGLIOSTRO, COUNT ALESSANDRO**, (orig. Giuseppe Balsamo), June 2, 1743 (Palermo, Sicily)–Aug. 26, 1795. Italian charlatan. With his wife, Lorenza Feliciani, traveled to London, The Hague, Strasbourg, Lyon, Toulouse, Germany, and Russia, posing as an alchemist, medium, soothsayer, necromancer; sold love philters, elixirs of youth; in Paris, imprisoned in Bastille, then released, for implication in the "Affair of the Diamond Necklace," 1785–86; in Rome, condemned to death as a heretic and freemason; sentence commuted to life imprisonment, 1789.

**CAPONE, AL**(phonse) ("Scarface Al"), Jan. 17, 1899 (Naples, It.)–Jan. 25, 1947. U.S. gangster. Dominated organized crime in Chicago and the surrounding area, 1925–31; imprisoned for federal income tax evasion, 1931–39.

**CARDIN, PIERRE,** July 7, 1922 (Venice, It.). French fashion designer. From 1957, creator of elegantly cut clothes for women; introduced first collection for men by a top designer, featuring bias cut, soft semifitted lines, and lavish color, 1960; leader in ready-to-wear for both sexes.

**CARTER, ROSALYNN,** Aug. 18, 1927 (Plains, Ga.). U.S. First Lady. Was one of Pres. JIMMY CARTER's most influential advisors; special interests included mental-health programs and passage of the Equal Rights Amendment; honorary chairperson of President's Com. on Mental Health. *First Lady From Plains,* 1985.

**CAXTON, WILLIAM,** Aug. 13, 1422 (Kent, Eng.)–1491. English printer, translator, publisher. First English printer. Published first book printed in England, *The Recuyell of the Historyes of Troye,* translated from French, 1475; and first illustrated English Book, *The Myrrour of the Worlde,* 1481; printed most of English literature available at the time.

**CAYCE, EDGAR,** Mar. 18, 1877 (Hopkinsville, Ky.)–Jan. 3, 1945. U.S. rural healer, seer. Worked from trances that yielded diagnoses and prescriptions for patients, as well as glimpses into the past and future; reputed to have predicted the 1929 stock market crash and WW II.

**CHANEL, GABRIELLE** ("Coco"), Aug. 19, 1883 (nr. Issoire, Fr.)–Jan. 10, 1971. French fashion designer. One of the most influential couturiers of the 20th cent., she revolutionized women's fashions after WW I with the straight, simple lines of the "Chanel look"; introduced perfume, Chanel #5, 1922.

**CHAPMAN, JOHN** (Johnny Appleseed), Sept. 26, 1774 (Leominster, Mass.)–Mar. 1845. U.S. "patron saint" of orchards and conservation. Planted many apple nurseries from the Alleghenies to central Ohio and beyond, from 1800; sold and gave away thousands of seedlings to pioneers.

**CHAPMAN, MARK DAVID,** 1955 (Honolulu, Hawaii). U.S. assassin. Shot and killed JOHN LENNON in front of his apartment building in New York City, Dec. 8, 1980.

**CHESSMAN, CARYL** ("Red Light Bandit"), born Carol Whittier Chessman, May 27, 1921 (St. Joseph, Mo.)–May 2, 1960. U.S. criminal. Convicted of 17 counts of robbery, kidnapping, sexual abuse, and attempted rape during a three-day crime spree in California, 1948; electrocuted after eight stays of execution during a 12-year fight for his life, during which he wrote four books and smuggled them out of prison; won support from thousands, including ALBERT SCHWEITZER, ALDOUS HUXLEY, BRIGITTE BARDOT; maintained his inno-

cence to the end. *Cell 2455, Death Row,* 1954; *Trial by Ordeal,* 1955; *The Face of Justice,* 1957.

**CHILD, JULIA,** Aug. 15, 1912 (Pasadena, Calif.). U.S. author, TV personality. Noted as the author of several popular cookbooks, beginning with the best-selling *Mastering the Art of French Cooking* (with Louisette Bertholle and Simone Beck, 1961); star of *The French Chef,* a TV show on cooking, begun 1963. *The French Chef Cookbook,* 1968; *From Julia Child's Kitchen,* 1975; *The Way to Cook,* 1989.

**CHIPPENDALE, THOMAS,** baptized June 5, 1718 (Otley, Yorkshire, Eng.)–Nov. 1779. English cabinetmaker, furniture designer. Popularized the Anglicized rococo style in furniture. *The Gentleman and Cabinet-Maker's Director,* 1754.

**CLAIBORNE, CRAIG,** Sept. 4, 1920 (Sunflower, Miss.). U.S. writer. Food editor of *The New York Times,* 1957– . *The New York Times Cook Book,* 1961; *The New York Times International Cookbook,* 1971; *Craig Claiborne's Favorites from the New York Times,* 1975; *Craig Claiborne's Southern Cooking.*

**CROWLEY, ALEISTER** (born Edward Alexander Crowley), 1875 (England)–Dec. 1, 1947. English magician, author, poet. The self-proclaimed "worst man in the world," allegedly practiced black magic and blood sacrifice. *The Diary of a Drug Fiend,* 1970; *Moonchild,* 1970; *The Confessions of Aleister Crowley: An Autobiography,* 1970; *Magick without Tears,* 1973; *Magick in Theory and Practice,* 1974.

**CULBERTSON, ELY,** July 22, 1891 (Poiana de Verbilao, Rum.)–Dec. 17, 1955. U.S. bridge expert. Invented system of contract bridge and, in early 1930s, helped establish it as a leading card game; pres. of The Bridge World, Inc., 1929–55; devoted his later years to working for world peace. *Contract Bridge Complete,* 1936; *Total Peace,* 1943.

**CZOLGOSZ, LEON F.,** 1873 (Detroit, Mich.)–Oct. 29, 1901. U.S. assassin, anarchist. Fatally wounded Pres. WILLIAM MCKINLEY at the Pan-American Exposition in Buffalo, N.Y., Sept. 6, 1901; electrocuted at Auburn, N.Y.

**DARE, VIRGINIA,** Aug. 18, 1587 (Roanoke I., Va. [now in N.C.])–c.1587. American colonial child, the first child born in America of English parents. Granddaughter of Gov. John White, the founder and governor of colony of Roanoke I. (1587); known to have lived at least nine days, until Aug. 27, when White sailed to England for supplies; upon his return (1591), he found no remains of settlers.

**DARROW, CLARENCE,** Apr. 18, 1857 (nr. Kinsman, Ohio)–Mar. 13, 1938. U.S. labor and criminal lawyer. Served as defense counsel in many dramatic criminal trials. Defended EUGENE DEBS, pres. of the American Railway Union, and other union leaders arrested on contempt charges arising from the 1894 Pullman strike; saved RICHARD LOEB and NATHAN LEOPOLD from the death sentence in the sensational Bobby Franks murder case, 1924; defended JOHN SCOPES, 1925. *Crime:*

*Its Cause and Treatment,* 1922; *The Story of My Life,* 1932.

**DAVIS,** (Daisie) **ADELLE,** Feb. 25, 1904 (Lizton, Ind.)–May 31, 1974. U.S. nutritionist, author. Natural-foods crusader and expert on vitamin supplements. *Let's Cook It Right,* 1947; *Let's Have Healthy Children,* 1951; *Let's Eat Right to Keep Fit,* 1954; *Let's Get Well,* 1965.

**DE LA RENTA, OSCAR,** July 22, 1932 (Santo Domingo, D.R.). U.S. fashion designer. Noted for his elegant, sexy clothes for women, especially his lavish, romantic ball gowns for such clients as Mrs. William S. Paley and the DUCHESS OF WINDSOR.

**DIAMOND, JOHN** ("Legs"), c. 1898 (Philadelphia, Pa.)–Dec. 18, 1931. U.S. mobster. Ran some New York City rackets, 1928–31; shot dead in bed, probably on the orders of "DUTCH" SCHULTZ.

**DILLINGER, JOHN,** June 28, 1902 (Mooresville, Ind.)–July 22, 1934. U.S. bank robber. With "PRETTY BOY" FLOYD and "BABY FACE" NELSON, terrorized North-Central states in 1933; gunned down by law officers in front of the Biograph Theater, Chicago, Ill.; gang responsible for 16 murders.

**DIONNE** quintuplets (Marie, Emilie, Yvonne, Annette, and Cécile), May 28, 1934 (Callander, Ont., Can.). Born to Elzire Dionne, a farmer, and his wife Oliva, age 24 and already the mother of six; cared for by Dr. Allan Roy Dafoe, a local gen. practitioner; provided with nursing care by the Canadian Red Cross; made wards of Ontario to avoid exploitation; educated at home until they entered Nicolet C., 1952. Marie died Feb. 27, 1970; Emilie died Aug. 5, 1954.

**DIOR, CHRISTIAN,** Jan. 21, 1905 (Granville, Fr.)–Oct. 24, 1957. French fashion designer. Created the "New Look" popular after WW II; emphasized long hemlines and full skirts; introduced the sack dress, 1950s.

**DOHRN, BERNADINE,** Jan. 12, 1942 (Chicago, Ill.). U.S. radical activist. Leader of the Weathermen, the militant faction of Students for a Democratic Soc.; disappeared late Feb. or Mar. 1970; indicted for unlawful flight to avoid prosecution for mob action, and for conspiracy to violate federal antiriot laws and to bomb buildings, 1970; indictments dismissed, 1973 and 1974.

**DU BARRY, COMTESSE** (born Marie Jeanne Bécu), Aug. 19, 1743 (Valcouleurs, Fr.)–Dec. 8, 1793. French mistress of Louis XV, 1769–74. Of lower-middle-class origins, became mistress of Jean du Barry, a procurer for royalty, 1764–68; to make her suitable as a royal mistress, du Barry married her to his brother Guillaume, Comte du Barry; retired from court following king's death; arrested by ROBESPIERRE, 1793; executed.

**DUVALIER, JEAN-CLAUDE** (known as "Baby Doc"), July 3, 1951 (Port-au-Prince, Haiti). Haitian political leader. Ascended to presidency of Haiti on death of his father, F. DUVALIER, 1971; followed in his father's footsteps and even exceeded him in use of the dreaded "Touton Macoutes," government-

paid assassins used to intimidate opponents; ousted and exiled in popular uprising, 1986, and could find no country that wanted to take him in.

**EARP, WYATT,** Mar. 19, 1848 (Monmouth, Ill.)–Jan. 13, 1929. U.S. law officer, gunfighter. Involved, with his brothers and Doc Holliday, in the controversial shootout at the O.K. Corral, 1881.

**ESCOFFIER, GEORGES AUGUSTE,** Oct. 28, 1846 (Villeneuve-Loubet, Fr.)–Feb. 12, 1935. French chef. Famous Parisian chef known as the "King of Cooks"; served as chef at the Reine Blanche in Paris, the Savoy, Carlton, and Ritz hotels in London, and the Grand Hotel in Monte Carlo.

**FARMER, FANNIE** ("Mother of Level Measurements"), Mar. 23, 1857 (Boston, Mass.)–Jan. 15, 1915. U.S. cookery expert. Established Miss Farmer's School of Cookery, 1902; one of the first to stress the importance of following recipes exactly and using standard, level measurements. *Boston Cooking School Cook Book,* 1896; *A New Book of Cookery,* 1912.

**FAWKES, GUY,** 1570 (York, Eng.)–Jan. 31, 1606. English conspirator. Involved in the unsuccessful Gunpowder Plot (1604–05) to blow up the Parliament building while James I was meeting within with his chief ministers, to avenge the enforcing of penal laws against Catholics; captured and executed; Nov. 5 is celebrated as Guy Fawkes Day in Great Britain.

**FLOYD, CHARLES** (a.k.a. Pretty Boy) c.1901 (nr. Sallisaw, Okla.)–Oct. 22, 1934. U.S. bank robber. Member of the JOHN DILLINGER gang; killed in a gun battle with law officers.

**FORD, ELIZABETH,** Apr. 8, 1918 (Chicago, Ill.). U.S. First Lady. A dancer with the MARTHA GRAHAM Concert Group, 1939–41; as First Lady and later, much admired for her candor, especially about her hospitalization for alcohol and drug abuse (1978).

**FORD, ROBERT,** ?–June 24, 1892. U.S. outlaw. As a new recruit to the James Gang, killed JESSE JAMES, Apr. 3, 1882, earning $10,000 reward; drifted through West; opened saloon in Creede, Col., where he was gunned down.

**FRANK, ANNE,** June 12, 1929 (Frankfurt-am-Main, Ger.)–March 1945. German Jewish girl. A victim of Nazi anti-Semitism; her *The Diary of a Young Girl* (1952), written during two years of hiding, gained wide popularity.

**FROMME, LYNETTE** ("Squeaky"), 1948 (California?). U.S. follower of CHARLES MANSON. Attempted to assassinate Pres. GERALD R. FORD in Sacramento, Calif., 1975; convicted, serving a life sentence at the San Diego Metropolitan Correctional Center.

**GALLUP, GEORGE H.,** Nov. 18, 1901 (Jefferson, Ia.)–July 26, 1984. U.S. public-opinion statistician. Famous as the originator of the Gallup Poll. Founded the American Inst. of Public Opinion (1935) and the Audience Research Inst. (1939); first gained fame with his accurate prediction of the 1936 presidential election. *Guide to Public Opinion Polls,* 1944.

GIVENCHY, HUBERT DE, Feb. 21, 1927 (Beauvais, Fr.). French fashion designer. Parisian designer noted for his separate skirts and tops, unusual printed and embroidered fabrics, tubular evening dresses, sumptuous ball gowns; designer of AUDREY HEPBURN's clothes and film costumes.

GOETZ, BERNHARD, 1947. U.S. vigilante. The so-called "subway vigilante," on a New York City subway shot four youths who were allegedly trying to rob him, 1984; found not guilty of attempted murder and assault, and only convicted of carrying a concealed weapon, 1987.

GONNE, MAUDE (married name: MacBride), Dec. 20, 1866 (London?, Eng.)–Apr. 27, 1953. Irish nationalist. Hailed in her time as the Irish Joan of Arc; a celebrated beauty, she was an impassioned advocate of Irish freedom; pursued unsuccessfully by WILLIAM BUTLER YEATS; term *maudgonning* means agitating for a cause in a reckless, flamboyant fashion. (Mother of S. MACBRIDE.)

GOREN, CHARLES H., Mar. 4, 1901 (Philadelphia, Pa.). U.S. bridge expert, lawyer. Noted bridge player and writer whose point-count bidding system has gained wide popularity; winner of two world bridge championships and 30 U.S. titles; author of "Goren on Bridge," syndicated daily column. *Point Count Bidding*, 1950; *New Contract Bridge in a Nutshell*, 1959; *Goren's Complete Bridge*, 1963.

GREEN, HENRIETTA ("Hetty"), Nov. 21, 1834 (New Bedford, Mass.)–July 3, 1916. U.S. financier. Through shrewd investment in railroads, real estate, and govt. bonds, increased inheritance of $10 million; reputed to have been richest woman in U.S. at her death, with assets estimated at $100 million; her eccentricities (i.e., wearing rags and living in fleabag hotels), earned her the name the Witch of Wall Street.

GUGGENHEIM, PEGGY, Aug. 26, 1898 (New York, N.Y.)–Dec. 23, 1979. U.S. art patron and collector. Noted for having backed some of the most notable modern artists, such as JACKSON POLLOCK; directed her own New York City gallery, Art of This Century, 1943–47; exhibited her private collection all over Europe, from 1951.

GUINAN, TEXAS (born Mary Louise Cecilia), Jan. 12, 1884 (Waco, Tex.)–Nov. 5, 1933. U.S. actress, night club hostess. The quintessence of the 1920s flapper, acted as hostess for several popular speakeasies in New York City, from 1924; greeted patrons from her high stool at the door with the phrase, "Hello, sucker."

GWYN (or Gwynne), NELL (born Eleanor Gwyn), Feb. 2, 1650 (Hereford, Eng.)–Nov. 13, 1687. English actress. Leading comedienne of the King's company, 1664–69; mistress of Charles II, from 1668.

HALSTON (born Roy Halston Frowick), Apr. 23, 1932 (Des Moines, Iowa)–Mar. 26, 1990. U.S. fashion designer. Designer at Bergdorf Goodman, 1959–68; designer at the boutique Halston Ltd., 1968–76; designer and pres., Halston Originals, 1972–75; pres. of Halston Enterprises, 1975–90.

HARRIS, EMILY, Feb. 11, 1947 (Baltimore, Md.); and husband WILLIAM HARRIS, Jan. 22, 1945 (Ft. Sill, Okla.). U.S. revolutionaries. Members of the Symbionese Liberation Army; Held PATRICIA HEARST in hiding after the rest of the SLA was killed in a siege (1974), and eluded capture until 1976; tried, convicted, imprisoned.

HAUPTMANN, BRUNO RICHARD, Nov. 26, 1900 (Kamenz, Germany)–Apr. 3, 1936. U.S. carpenter who was convicted (1935) in a sensational trial of the kidnapping and murder of the son of CHARLES and ANNE MORROW LINDBERGH.

HEAD, EDITH, Oct. 28, 1907 (Los Angeles, Calif.)–Oct. 24, 1981. U.S. fashion designer. Chief designer for Paramount Pictures Corp. since the 1930s; also worked at Universal City Studios; awarded costume-design AA for *The Heiress* (1949), *All About Eve* (1950), *Samson and Delilah* (1950), *A Place in the Sun* (1951), *Roman Holiday* (1953), *Sabrina* (1954), *The Facts of Life* (1960), *The Sting* (1973).

HEARST, PATRICIA (married name: Shaw), Feb. 20, 1954 (San Francisco, Calif.). U.S. kidnap victim, revolutionary. Kidnapped by the Symbionese Liberation Army, a radical terrorist organization, 1974; allegedly joined her abductors in criminal activities as the revolutionary "Tania"; captured by the FBI, 1975; convicted of bank robbery charges, 1976; released after serving 22 months of a seven-year term under an executive clemency order issued by Pres. JIMMY CARTER; married her bodyguard, 1979. (Granddaughter of W. R. HEARST.)

HELOISE, c.1089–May 15, 1164. French abbess. The famous lover of the philosopher PIERRE ABELARD; became his illicit wife and bore his child; outraged relatives had Abelard castrated and placed her in a convent; became abbess at the convent of Paraclete, founded by Abelard.

HEPPLEWHITE, GEORGE, died 1786. English cabinetmaker and furniture designer. Associated with the Neoclassical style; gained fame as the author of *Cabinet-Maker and Upholsterer's Guide* (1788).

HICKOK, JAMES BUTLER ("Wild Bill"), May 27, 1837 (Troy Grove, Ill.)–Aug. 2, 1876. U.S. scout, frontier marshal. Served as a Union scout and spy during the Civil War; dep. U.S. marshal, Fort Riley, Kan., 1866–67; U.S. marshal, Hays City, Kan. (1869–71), and Abilene, Kan. (1871); toured with BUFFALO BILL, 1872–73; shot dead from the rear while playing poker, in Deadwood, Dakota Terr.

HINCKLEY, JOHN, JR., 1956. U.S. would-be assassin. Attempted to killed U.S. Pres. RONALD REAGAN, after a speaking appearance at the Washington Hilton, Mar. 30, 1981; obsessed with actress JODIE FOSTER, he apparently was motivated by his desire to attract her attention.

HINES, DUNCAN, Mar. 26, 1880 (Bowling Green, Ky.)–Mar. 15, 1959. U.S. gourmet. With *Adventures in Good Eating* (1935), a list of 160 superior eating places, plus several other books on restaurants and hotels, built the rating "Recommended by Duncan Hines" to one treasured and displayed by some 10,000 establishments.

**HUTTON, BARBARA** ("The Poor Little Rich Girl"), Nov. 14, 1912 (New York, N.Y.)–May 11, 1979. U.S. heiress. Granddaughter of F. W. WOOLWORTH and heir to family fortune; married seven times, including Prince Alexis Mdivani, CARY GRANT, and Porfirio Rubirosa; a virtual recluse in later years, plagued by ill health and unhappiness.

**JACK THE RIPPER.** Pseudonym of a murderer who terrorized London's East End from Aug. 7–Nov. 10, 1888, killing at least seven women, all of them prostitutes, in the Whitechapel dist.; murders remain one of the greatest unsolved mysteries of all time.

**JAMES, JESSE,** Sept. 5, 1847 (nr. Kearney [then Centerville], Mo.)–Apr. 3, 1882. U.S. outlaw. With his gang executed daring bank and train robberies in the Midwest, from 1866; murdered by one of his gang, ROBERT FORD, in St. Joseph, Mo.

**JOHNSON, CLAUDIA ALTA** ("Ladybird"), Dec. 22, 1912 (Karnack, Tex.). U.S. First Lady. As First Lady, worked for environmental causes and national beautification projects; a successful businesswoman, she built and owned the Texas Broadcasting Corp., Inc., 1943–73.

**JONES, JAMES** ("Jim"), born May 13, 1931 (Lynn, Ind.)–Nov. 18, 1978. U.S. leader of the People's Temple, an agrarian-socialist cult. Ordered the more than 900 members of the People's Temple commune in Guyana to commit suicide by drinking a cyanide-laced concoction, 1979; died of a bullet wound in the head.

**JUDD, WINNIE RUTH,** Jan. 29, 1905 (Oxford, Ind.). U.S. murderer. Killed two people (1932), dismembered the bodies, tried to ship them in a trunk from Arizona to Los Angeles; turned herself in; found guilty and committed to a mental hospital; tried to escape seven times, and was once at large for eight years; declared sane and imprisoned, 1969; paroled, 1971.

**KAEL, PAULINE,** June 19, 1919 (Petaluma, Calif.). U.S. film critic, author. Influential as movie critic for *The New Yorker*, 1968– . *Deeper into Movies*, 1973 (1974 National Book Award); *Reeling*, 1976; *State of the Art*, 1985.

**KAHANE, MEIR,** 1932. U.S.-Israeli political leader. Espouses a program of violence against Palestinians and all other groups in conflict with the aims of the Jewish state; his party, Kach, was banned by the Israeli government due to its extremist views, 1988.

**KARAN, DONNA,** Oct. 2, 1948 (Forest Hills, N.Y.). U.S. fashion designer. Specializes in simple, yet sophisticated clothes for the modern woman; with Anne Klein & Co., 1964–85; owner, designer, Donna Karan, Co., 1984; won Coty awards, 1977, 1981.

**KELLY, GEORGE** ("Machine Gun"), 1897 (Tennessee)–July 18, 1954. U.S. gangster. "Society" bootlegger, kidnapper, robber; best known for his machine-gun marksmanship and for coining the term *G-men* for FBI agents; died of a heart attack

in Alcatraz Prison while serving a life sentence for kidnapping.

**KENNEDY, ROSE FITZGERALD,** July 22, 1890 (Boston, Mass.). U.S. matriarch of a political dynasty. The mother of a president, J. F. KENNEDY, and two senators, R. F. KENNEDY and E. M. KENNEDY; noted for the strength she has shown in the face of multiple tragedies, the loss of her eldest son in WW II, the assassinations of John and Robert, death of a daughter in an air crash, and mental retardation of another daughter.

**KIDD, WILLIAM** ("Captain Kidd"), c. 1645 (Greenock, Renfrewshire, Scot.)–May 23, 1701. Scottish pirate. Commissioned as a privateer to defend English ships against pirates, turned pirate himself because of the threat of mutiny and failure to take prizes; charged with piracy, returned to London to defend himself, convicted and hanged.

**KLEIN, CALVIN,** Nov. 19, 1942 (New York, N.Y.). U.S. fashion designer. Elevated sportswear to the level of haute couture; pres., designer, Calvin Klein, 1969; won Coty awards, 1972, 1974, 1975.

**KUNSTLER, WILLIAM,** July 7, 1919 (New York, N.Y.). U.S lawyer. Radical atty. noted for his defense of political activists, including STOKELY CARMICHAEL, the Chicago 7, and the Catonsville 9, during the 1960s. *The Case for Courage: The Stories of Ten Famous American Attorneys who Risked Their Careers in the Cause of Justice*, 1962; *Deep in My Heart*, 1966.

**LAFFITE** (or Lafitte), **JEAN,** 1780? (Bayonne, France)–1825. U.S. privateer, smuggler. Fought heroically for the U.S. in the War of 1812; rejected British attempts at bribery, warning New Orleans of the impending attack instead.

**LANE, MARK,** Feb. 24, 1927 (New York, N.Y.). U.S. lawyer, author. Controversial attorney who defended Marguerite Oswald, the wife of LEE HARVEY OSWALD, at the Warren Commission hearings, 1964; became an anti-Vietnam War activist; with WILLIAM KUNSTLER, chief defense attorney of militant Indian leaders of the 1973 Wounded Knee, S.D., occupation; as the attorney for People's Temple cult, accompanied by Rep. LEO J. RYAN to Guyana (1978), but escaped the mass suicide. *Rush to Judgement*, 1966; *Conversations with Americans*, 1970.

**LANVIN, JEANNE,** 1867 (Brittany, Fr.)–July 6, 1946. French designer, dressmaker. The founder of La Maison de Couture, a small Paris fashion group that along with a few other designers, set the mode for the world.

**LAROUCHE, LYNDON H.,** Jr., Sept. 8, 1922 (Rochester, N.H.). U.S. political activist. Originally a member of the American Socialist Party, later embraced fascism and is now considered a far right radical "kook"; has expressed anti-semitic views; accused the Queen of England of leading an international Jewish conspiracy, named HENRY KISSINGER as a Soviet spy, etc.

**LAUREN, RALPH** (born Ralph Lifschitz), Oct. 14, 1939 (Bronx, N.Y.). U.S. fashion designer. Noted for his designs that harken back to a more refined

era; head, Polo Fashions, Inc., 1969– ; won Coty awards, 1970, 1973, 1974, 1977, and 1981.
**LEOPOLD, NATHAN, JR.,** Nov. 19, 1904 (Chicago, Ill.)–Aug. 28, 1971; and **LOEB, RICHARD,** c. 1906 (Chicago, Ill.)–Jan. 28, 1936. U.S. criminals. In the "Crime of the Century," kidnapped and murdered 14-year-old Bobby Franks in Chicago, 1924; wealthy and brilliant, the boys became the focus of enormous publicity; their defense attorney, CLARENCE DARROW, saved them from the death penalty; Leopold was released from prison in 1958; Loeb was killed in prison by another inmate. MEYER LEVIN's book *Compulsion* (1956) was based on the case.
**LUCCHESE, GAETANO** (a.k.a. Three-Finger Brown), 1900 (Sicily)–July 13, 1967. U.S. mobster. Reputedly the boss of one of "Five Families" of New York City, 1953–67; "Three-finger" nickname used by police and press only.
**LUCIANO, CHARLES** (a.k.a. Lucky Luciano and Charles Ross, born Salvatore Lucania), Nov. 11, 1896 (nr. Palermo, Sicily)–Jan. 25, 1962. Italian-U.S. mobster. Allegedly the major architect of modern Mafia organization; reputed boss of New York City crime family, 1931–46; imprisoned, 1936; deported, 1946.
**MADISON, DOLLEY,** May 20, 1768 (Guilford Co., N.C.)–July 12, 1849. U.S. First Lady, wife of Pres. JAMES MADISON. Famous as a Washington, D.C., hostess while her husband was U.S. secy. of state (1801–09) and pres. (1809–17).
**MAINBOCHER** (born Main Rousseau Bocher), Oct. 24, 1891 (Chicago, Ill.)–Dec. 26, 1976. U.S. fashion designer. Noted for his expensive, elegant evening clothes; editor of *French Vogue,* 1923–29; founder and pres. of Mainbocher, Paris, 1930–39; founder and pres. of Mainbocher, Inc., New York City, 1940–71; designed uniforms for WAVES (1942), Girl Scouts (1946), Red Cross (1948), and SPARS (1951).
**MALLON, MARY** ("Typhoid Mary"), 1870–Nov. 11, 1938. U.S. cook. A carrier of typhoid fever, she knowingly spread her illness around the New York City area, causing at least 53 cases of typhoid and three deaths, from c.1905 to 1915.
**MANDELBAUM, FREDERICKA** ("Marm"), 1818–1889. U.S. criminal. One of the most successful fences of all time; living quietly in New York City from 1862 sold nearly $4 million in stolen goods and became a millionaire; taught other female criminals how to improve their trade, and youngsters how to pick pockets, burgle, and blackmail.
**MAN O'WAR** ("Big Red"), Mar. 29, 1917–Nov. 1, 1947. U.S. thoroughbred horse. Raced for only two years, winning 20 of 21 races and setting five world records, 1919–20; bred by AUGUST BELMONT near Lexington, Ky.; one of the leading sires of all time.
**MANSON, CHARLES,** Nov. 12, 1934 (Cincinnati, Ohio). U.S. leader of a California "family" of drifters. Convicted, with four young female followers, of murder in the first degree in the 1969 deaths of actress Sharon Tate and six others, 1971 (Charles

"Tex" Watson later also convicted); sentenced to death, but capital punishment voided in California, 1972.
**MATA HARI** (pseud. of Margaretha Geertruida Macleod, née Zelle), Aug. 7, 1876 (Leeuwarden, Neth.)–Oct. 15, 1917. Dutch dancer, courtesan, spy. As a dancer in Paris, joined German Secret Service; betrayed important military secrets she learned from high Allied officers with whom she was intimate; arrested, convicted, and executed by the French, 1917.
**MESTA, PERLE,** Oct. 12, 1889 (Sturgis, Mich.) –Mar. 16, 1975. U.S. diplomat, hostess. The foremost unofficial hostess in Washington, D.C., during the 1940s; U.S. envoy to Luxembourg, 1949–53; the inspiration of IRVING BERLIN's musical *Call Me Madam.*
**MOON, SUN MYUNG** (Reverend), 1920 (N. Kor.). Korean religious leader. Claiming to have had conversations with Jesus Christ, Buddha, and Moses, ordained himself a minister, 1946; founded the Unification Church which claimed to have close to 3 million members worldwide; convicted on income tax fraud charges, 1982.
**MOORE, SARA JANE,** Feb. 15, 1930 (Charleston, W.Va.). U.S. radical. Attempted to assassinate Pres. GERALD R. FORD, 1975; convicted and sentenced to life imprisonment, 1976.
**MULLENS** (Mullins or Mullines), **PRISCILLA.** American pilgrim. Daughter of one of the signers of the Mayflower Compact; married JOHN ALDEN, 1621 or 1623; her role in H.W. LONGFELLOW's poem, *The Courtship of Miles Standish* (1858) is not based on historical fact.
**MUMTAZ MAHAL** (or Mahall), 1592–1631. Favorite wife of Mogul emperor Shah Jahan, who built the famous Taj Mahal at Agra as her mausoleum.
**MUNCHHAUSEN, KARL FRIEDRICH HIERONYMOUS, BARON VON,** May 11, 1720 (Bodenwerder, Ger.)–Feb. 22, 1797. German soldier, huntsman. A great storyteller about his life as a soldier, hunter and sportsman, whose fame was established by Rudolph Raspe's *Adventures of Baron Münchhausen* (1793); his name is now proverbially associated with absurdly exaggerated tales.
**MURRAY, ARTHUR,** Apr. 4, 1895 (New York, N.Y.); and his wife **KATHRYN MURRAY,** Sept. 15, 1906 (Jersey City, N.J.). U.S. dancing teachers. Originated the Arthur Murray School of Dancing, a chain of some 450 dance schools throughout the U.S. Producer and hostess of TV's *Arthur Murray Dance Party,* 1950–60.
**NADER, RALPH,** Feb. 27, 1934 (Winsted, Conn.). U.S. lawyer, consumer advocate, author. A leading advocate of consumer affairs in the U.S. Founded the Center for the Study of Responsive Law, 1969; attained natl. attention for his indictment of the auto industry for its poor safety standards. *Unsafe at Any Speed,* 1965.
**NELSON, GEORGE** ("Baby Face"), Dec. 6, 1908 (Chicago, Ill.)–Nov. 28, 1934. U.S. bank robber.

Member of the JOHN DILLINGER gang; killed in a gun battle with law officers.

NESBIT, EVELYN ("The Girl on the Red Velvet Swing"), 1884 (Pennsylvania)–Jan. 17, 1967. U.S. showgirl. The mistress of millionaire architect STANFORD WHITE, she married multimillionaire HARRY K. THAW; Thaw, tormented by jealousy, murdered White at New York City's Madison Square Garden, 1906.

NESS, ELIOT, Apr. 19, 1903 (Chicago, Ill.)–May 16, 1957. U.S. govt. agent. Best known as the special FBI agent who headed the investigation of AL CAPONE, in Chicago, 1929–32.

NIXON, (Thelma) PATRICIA, Mar. 16, 1912 (Ely, Nev.). U.S. First Lady. Wife of U.S. Pres. R. M. NIXON; decorated with Grand Cross Order of Sun for relief work at the time of Peruvian earthquake, 1971; named in George Gallup polls as among the most admired women, in 1957, 1968, 1969, 1970 and 1971.

NIZER, LOUIS, Feb. 6, 1902 (London, Eng.). U.S. lawyer, author. A founding member (1926) and later senior partner of Phillips, Nizer, Benjamin and Krim, a law firm specializing in cases in the entertainment field. *What to Do with Germany*, 1944; *My Life in Court*, 1962; *The Jury Returns*, 1966.

NORELL, NORMAN, 1900 (Noblesville, Ind.)–Oct. 25, 1972. U.S. designer. One of leading designers in U.S. for over 30 years; began as designer with Hattie Carnegie, 1928; showed first collection, with Anthony Traina as Traina-Norell (New York City), 1941; first independent collection, 1960.

ONASSIS, JACQUELINE BOUVIER KENNEDY, July 28, 1929 (Southampton, N.Y.). U.S. First Lady. As First Lady, planned and conducted the restoration of the White House décor; married Greek shipping magnate ARISTOTLE ONASSIS, 1968; consulting editor at Viking Press, 1975–77; editor at Doubleday & Co., 1977–  .

OSWALD, LEE HARVEY, Oct. 18, 1939 (New Orleans, La.)–Nov. 24, 1963. U.S. assassin. Alleged killer of U.S. Pres. JOHN F. KENNEDY in Dallas, Tex., on Nov. 22, 1963. A former U.S. marine, lived in the USSR (1959–62) and was Cuban communist sympathizer; shot two days after the Kennedy assassination by JACK RUBY.

PARKER, BONNIE, Oct. 1, 1910 (Rowena, Tex.)–May 23, 1934. U.S. outlaw. With CLYDE BARROW, formed the famous duo that robbed and killed on their way across Texas, New Mexico, and Missouri, c.1932; ambushed and shot to death by Texas Rangers and sheriff's deputies.

PARNIS, MOLLIE, Mar. 18, 1905 (New York, N.Y.). U.S. fashion designer. Particularly successful in the 1950s with her simple full-skirted dresses; started, with her husband, Parnis-Livingston, Inc., 1933.

PAYSON, JOAN WHITNEY, Feb. 5, 1903 (New York, N.Y.)–Oct. 4, 1975. U.S. philanthropist, sportswoman. Extended her interests to horse racing, baseball (New York Mets), the arts (a founder of the Museum of Modern Art), and philanthropy

(pres. of Helen Hay Whitney Fndn.); co-owner of Greentree Stud, Inc., (1945–75) and Greentree Stable (1945–75).

PERRY, NANCY LING, 1947 (Santa Rosa, Calif.)–May 24, 1974. U.S. revolutionary. The spiritual and doctrinal leader of the Symbionese Liberation Army. Once a Goldwater supporter, turned to radical politics while at Berkeley U.; lived with Russell Little, a philosophy graduate and prison-reform activist; their home became the first SLA hq.

PINKHAM, LYDIA, Feb. 9, 1819 (nr. Lynn, Mass.)–May 17, 1883. U.S. patent-medicine proprietor. Invented the famous home remedy, "Vegetable Compound," first marketed in 1876; sales peaked at $3.8 million, 1925; compound was a concoction of roots and seeds, plus a generous dose of alcohol as a solvent and preservative.

POCAHONTAS (Ind. name: Matoaka), c.1595 (nr. Jamestown, Virginia)–Mar. 1617. American Indian. Daughter of Powhatan; saved the life of Capt. JOHN SMITH; helped maintain peace between the native Americans and the English colonists at Jamestown, Va.; married John Rolfe, converted to Christianity, and was christened Rebecca.

POLO, MARCO, 1254 (Venice)–1324. Medieval Italian traveler. His account of his journeys to Asia was the chief source of information on the East during the Ren.; traveled to Asia with his father and uncle, 1271; a favorite of KUBLAI KHAN for 16 years; upon his return to Venice (1295), wrote his celebrated account, *Il millione*, in which he described paper currency, asbestos, coal, and other phenomena unknown to Europe.

POT, POL, 1928 (Cambodia). Cambodian communist leader. Led Cambodia during one of that nation's bloodiest periods; his "Year Zero" plan to remove corruption led to the death of 3 million people in the so-called "killing fields" of revolution; ousted from power by Vietnamese invasion, 1979; retreated to the mountains to become a guerilla fighter with the Khmer Rouge forces; reportedly retired from fighting, 1985.

PRINCIP, GAVRILLO, July 25, 1895 (Grahavo Polje, Bosnia)–Apr. 28, 1918. Serbian assassin of Archduke FRANCIS FREDINAND and his wife at Sarajevo, 1914.

PUCCI, EMILIO (Marchese di Barsento), Nov. 20, 1914 (Naples, It.). Italian fashion designer. Noted for his use of brilliant colors in elegant sportswear, silk blouses, scarves, underclothes.

RALEIGH, SIR WALTER, 1554? (Hayes Barton, Devonshire, Eng.)–Oct. 29, 1618. English adventurer, statesman, man of letters. A favorite of ELIZABETH I of England; became captain of the queen's guard, 1587; received grants of monopolies and estates from queen; sent expeditions to Virginia; connected with poetic group known as School of Might; attempted to find the fabled El Dorado, 1595; imprisoned after Elizabeth's death, 1603–16; wrote his *History of the World*, 1614; released, went on ill-fated mission to find gold; eventually beheaded for insubordination. Knighted, 1585.

REAGAN, (Anne Francis) NANCY, July 6, 1921

(New York, N.Y.). U.S. First Lady. A former actress, served as First Lady, 1981–89; years in White House were marked by high spending; involved in anti-drug campaign. *My Turn*, 1989. (Wife of R. REAGAN.)

ROMBAUER, IRMA S., Oct. 30, 1877 (St. Louis, Mo.)–Oct. 14, 1962. U.S. cook-book author. Best known as author of one of the all-time best-selling cookbooks, *The Joy of Cooking*, first published in 1931 at her own expense; *The New Joy of Cooking* (revised ed., 1951) was written with daughter Marion Rombauer Becker.

ROOSEVELT, (Anna) ELEANOR, Oct. 11, 1884 (New York, N.Y.)–Nov. 7, 1962. U.S. First Lady, writer, lecturer. As the wife of Pres. F. D. ROOSEVELT, called "The First Lady of the World." Extremely active in the political affairs of her day; delegate to the U.N., 1945, 1949–52, 1961. *It's Up to the Women*, 1933; *This Is My Story*, 1937; *The Moral Basis of Democracy*, 1940.

ROSENBERG, JULIUS, May 12, 1918 (New York, N.Y.)–June 19, 1953; and his wife ETHEL ROSENBERG, née Greenglass, Sept. 28, 1915 (New York, N.Y.)–June 19, 1953. The first U.S. civilians to be executed for espionage. Dedicated communists who were convicted of turning over to the USSR military secrets that had come into their possession and executed.

ROSS, BETSY, Jan. 1, 1752 (Philadelphia, Pa.)–Jan. 30, 1836. American patriot. According to legend, made the first American flag (1776) at the request of a committee headed by GEORGE WASHINGTON; however, no historical support for this claim exists.

RUBY, JACK (born Jacob Rubenstein), c.1911–Jan. 3, 1967. U.S. nightclub owner (Dallas, Tex.) and slayer of LEE HARVEY OSWALD (1963). Said to have been an ardent supporter of Pres. JOHN F. KENNEDY; convicted of murder, 1964; sentence reversed, 1966; died while awaiting retrial; all charges dismissed, 1967.

SACCO, NICOLA, Apr. 22, 1891 (Apulia, It.)–Aug. 23, 1927. Italian U.S. radical, factory worker. With BARTOLOMEO VANZETTI, tried and convicted of a 1920 robbery and shooting in S. Braintree, Mass.; 1921; doubt as to their guilt led to worldwide support and protest; became martyrs to those who believed in their innocence; vindicated July 19, 1977, by proclamation of Mass. Gov. Dukakis.

ST. LAURENT, YVES, Aug. 1, 1936 (Oran, Algeria). French fashion designer. A protégé of CHRISTIAN DIOR; used leather and fur in introducing the "chic beatnik" look, 1960; introduced the "little boy look" in the mid-60s.

SCHIAPARELLI, ELSA, Sept. 10, 1890 (Rome, It.)–Nov. 13, 1973. Italian-French fashion designer. Noted for her flamboyant, daring innovations; used brilliant colors such as "shocking pink"; introduced the padded shoulder, 1932; by 1935, a leader in *haute couture*. *Shocking Life*, 1954.

SCHULTZ, DUTCH (born Arthur Flegenheimer), Aug. 6, 1902 (New York, N.Y.)–Oct. 24, 1935.

U.S. mobster. Ran bootlegging and other rackets in the Bronx and Harlem, c.1925–34; shot to death, probably on LUCKY LUCIANO's orders.

SHAPIRO, JACOB (a.k.a. Jake Gurrah), May 5, 1897 (Minsk, Rus.)–June 9, 1947. U.S. mobster. Partner of LEPKE BUCHALTER in Murder, Inc.; died of natural causes in Ossining Prison (Sing Sing). (Gurrah is short for *gerarah*, as in New York slang phrase "gerarah here, kid"—i e., "get out of here, kid.")

SHERATON, THOMAS, 1751 (Stockton on Tees, Co. Durham, Eng.)–Oct. 22, 1806. English furniture designer, cabinetmaker. With his *Cabinet-Maker and Upholsterer's Drawing Book* (1791) popularized his emphasis on straight, vertical lines and his delicate, simple style; a leading exponent of neoclassicism.

SIMMONS, RICHARD, July 12, 1948 (New Orleans, La.). U.S. physical fitness specialist. Owner of a nationwide chain of exercise salons; *The Richard Simmons Show*, 1980– . *The Never-Say-Diet Books*, 1980; *Richard Simmons' Better Body Book*, 1983.

SIRHAN, SIRHAN, 1945 (Jerusalem [now in Israel]). Palestinian assassin. Convicted of first-degree murder in the June 1968 killing of Sen. R. F. KENNEDY; sentenced to death, 1969; serving a life sentence; a resident-alien, he objected to Kennedy's pro-Israel stance.

SOBEL, MORTON, Apr. 11, 1917 (New York, N.Y.). U.S. alleged spy. Worked as an engineer for U.S. Navy on top-secret U.S. radar and electronic devices, 1942–47; a codefendant with JULIUS and ETHEL ROSENBERG, convicted of being a member of a spy ring that passed atomic secrets to the USSR, 1951; sentenced to 30 years in prison; released, 1969.

STARR, BELLE (born Myra Belle Shirley), Feb. 5, 1848 (Carthage, Mo.)–Feb. 3, 1889. U.S. outlaw. Hard-living, hard-loving woman who led a band of cattle rustlers and horse thieves that made regular raids on Oklahoma ranches; sheltered JESSE JAMES, 1881.

SURRATT, JOHN H., 1844 (Prince George Co., Md.)–Apr. 21, 1916. U.S. conspirator with J. W. BOOTH in the assassination of Pres. ABRAHAM LINCOLN; arrested (1866), tried (1867), but released (1888) when govt. failed to obtain an indictment. (Son of M.E. SURRATT.)

SURRATT, MARY E., May 1820 (Prince George Co., Md.)–July 7, 1865. U.S. boardinghouse keeper in Washington, D.C. and an alleged conspirator in the assassination of Pres. ABRAHAM LINCOLN; kept the house where J. W. BOOTH lived and met with the other conspirators; hanged for complicity, probably on insufficient evidence. (Mother of J.H. SURRATT.)

THAW, HARRY K., Feb. 1, 1871 (Pittsburgh, Pa.)–Feb. 22, 1947. U.S. murderer. The playboy son of a Pittsburgh railroad and coke magnate; shot and killed architect STANFORD WHITE in Madison Square Garden (1906), apparently motivated by jealousy over his wife, EVELYN NESBIT Thaw, a former chorus girl; judged insane.

TOKYO ROSE (pseud. of Iva Toguri d'Aquino),

July 4, 1916 (Los Angeles, Calif.). U.S. typist, WW II commentator for Radio Tokyo. The only one of the "Tokyo Roses" who broadcast anti-U.S. propaganda during WW II to be imprisoned for treason. Arrested and brought to U.S. from occupied Japan, 1948; charged with eight counts of treason, found guilty on one; sentenced to 10 years in prison, fined $10,000, and deprived of U.S. citizenship; released, 1956; received presidential pardon, 1977.

**TRILLIN, CALVIN,** Dec. 5, 1935 (Kansas City, Mo.). U.S. author. A staff writer for *The New Yorker;* syndicated columnist, 1986– . *American Fired,* 1974; *Alice Let's Eat,* 1978; *If You Can't Say Something Nice,* 1987.

**TSCHIRKY, OSCAR,** Sept. 28, 1866 (Locle, Switz.)– Nov. 6, 1950. U.S. hotelier. Known as "Oscar of the Waldorf," a famous maitre d'hôtel at the Waldorf Hotel, 1893–1943; credited with creation of the Waldorf salad. *Oscar of the Waldorf's Cookbook,* 1903.

**TURNER, NAT,** Oct. 2, 1800 (Southampton Co., Va.)–Nov. 11, 1831. U.S. slave. Leader of the Southampton Insurrection (1831), the only effective slave revolt in U.S. history. Believing he was divinely called to do so, gathered about 60 followers and killed 55 white people; quickly caught and hanged.

**VANZETTI, BARTOLOMEO,** July 11, 1888 (Villafalletto, It.)–Aug. 23, 1927. Italian fish peddler, anarchist. With NICOLA SACCO, convicted and executed for the murders of a factory paymaster and guard during a robbery in South Braintree, Mass., 1920; doubt as to their guilt created a worldwide storm of protest; the controversial trial sparked numerous plays, novels, poems, and radio and TV productions; vindicated July 19, 1977, by proclamation of Mass. Gov. Dukakis.

**WARFIELD, (Bessie) WALLIS, DUCHESS OF**

**WINDSOR,** June 19, 1896 (Blue Ridge Summit, Pa.)–Apr. 24, 1986. U.S. divorcée. The woman for whom EDWARD VIII of England abdicated the throne. *The Heart Has Its Reasons,* 1956.

**WEDGWOOD, JOSIAH,** baptized July 12, 1730 (Burslem, Staffordshire, Eng.)–Jan. 3, 1795. English potter. Known for his jasper ware and queen's ware; a leading scientific thinker; invented pyrometer for measuring temperature. (Grandfather of C. DARWIN)

**WILLIAMS, EDWARD BENNETT,** May 31, 1920 (Hartford, Conn.)–Aug. 13, 1988. U.S. lawyer. Top criminal lawyer who has defended many controversial figures, including ADAM CLAYTON POWELL, JIMMY HOFFA, and SEN. JOSEPH MCCARTHY. *One Man's Freedom,* 1962.

**WILLIAMSONS** ("The Terrible Williamsons"; also eight to ten other pseudonyms, including McDonald and Stewart). Clan of about 2,000 "gyp artists" descended from Robert Logan Williamson, a Scotsman who came to the U.S. around the turn of the century; the police have adopted "Williamsons" as generic name for itinerant hustlers.

**WORTH, CHARLES FREDERICK,** Oct. 13, 1825 (Bourne, Lincolnshire, Eng.)–Mar. 10, 1895. English fashion designer. Left England (1845) for Paris, where he founded (1858) his own ladies' tailor shop, which he developed into a leading fashion house; first to prepare and show a collection in advance; the first prominent man in women's fashions; the founder of Parisian *haute couture.*

**ZANGARA, GIUSEPPE,** Sept. 1900 (Calabria, It.)– Mar. 20, 1933. Italian-U.S. bricklayer. An anarchist (he hated capitalists and kings), attempted to assassinate Pres. FRANKLIN D. ROOSEVELT, in Miami, Fla., on Feb. 15, 1933; Roosevelt escaped, but Chicago Mayor A. J. Cermak was killed and five others were wounded; executed.

# Index